BI 0522008 4
KU-052-527

Investment Analysis and Portfolio Management

Investment Analysis and Portfolio Management

Sid Mittra
Oakland University
with
Chris Gassen
Oakland University

HARCOURT BRACE JOVANOVICH, INC.
New York San Diego Chicago San Francisco Atlanta
London Sidney Toronto

To Our Families

Printed in the United States of America
Library of Congress Catalog Card Number: 80-83976
ISBN: 0-15-546882-0

Preface

Investment analysis and portfolio management is challenging for two reasons. First, the subject embraces many diversified fields, including managerial finance, accounting, economics, statistics, and mathematics. Second, it provides a unique opportunity for students to apply investment theories and concepts to the solution of real-world investment problems.

Our objective throughout this project has been to write an effective and comprehensive textbook for teaching investments. To this end, we have attempted to explain and apply the most important developments in capital market and portfolio theory and the theory of efficient capital markets. We have used a broad theoretical framework to discuss the essentials of investment analysis and portfolio management. We have also ensured that these theories and concepts are applied to the solution of real-world investment problems.

The mathematics and statistics in this book are explained in simple terms and are supplemented by numerical examples. Although a basic background in finance, accounting, economics, statistics, and mathematics is presumed, every effort is made to explain concepts from these disciplines as they arise.

ORGANIZATION

Investment Analysis and Portfolio Management is organized around three major premises. First, the determination of the value of investment instruments is central to decision making. Consequently, we have been particularly careful in our presentation of the basic valuation models so that these models can be used for determining the value of a given security. Second, every informed investor should have a working knowledge of how theories and concepts are applied to the solution of investment problems. We have, therefore, demonstrated the application of the various theories to the valuation of stocks and bonds trading on the market. In addition, we have constructed an actual portfolio so that students can learn the essence of portfolio theory. Third, because, in the final analysis, investment decisions are a personal matter, we have emphasized that in making an appropriate investment decision an investor should determine his or her (1) risk preference, (2) ability and willingness to be an active (rather than a passive) investor, and (3) (if active participation is desired) preference for undertaking fundamental and/or technical analysis.

Against the backdrop of these premises, the book begins with the development of the central theme of risk and return in an efficient market. The discussion then proceeds to the criterion of risk. A discussion of government bonds—the least risky of all securities—is followed by detailed analyses of municipal and corporate bonds, preferred stock, common stock, convertible securities, options, and—finally—such esoteric investments as gold and real estate.

Another important feature is that risk and the Efficient Market Hypothesis (EMH) are discussed in two stages. In Part One only the most essential elements of risk and the EMH are presented so that the student can develop a healthy respect for these topics without getting bogged down in excessive details. Later, these topics are discussed more comprehensively, along with the theoretical topics of the Capital Asset Pricing Model and portfolio theory.

PEDAGOGICAL FEATURES

Real-Life Examples

Throughout the book, examples taken from real-life situations are interspersed to help students understand more clearly the concepts and applications of investment theory. For example, the bond valuation model and the stock valuation model are applied, respectively, to the valuation of a corporate bond and a common stock currently trading on the market. A real-world portfolio is also constructed to demonstrate the use of the portfolio theory.

Gradual Progression

In most chapters, the explication progresses from simple descriptions of basic issues to more complicated and analytical material. Numerical examples are carefully developed to supplement the analytical material in order to make the subject clear and comprehensible.

Questions

At the end of each chapter is a set of questions designed to test the students' capacity to understand, explain, and use the concepts and analyses covered in the chapter. The questions relating to each chapter approximately follow the organization of that chapter.

Problems

An elaborate set of problems of varying difficulty appears at the end of each chapter. Most of these problems are designed to expose the students to the challenge of solving various types of investment problems. Obviously, a thorough understanding of investment theory is required to solve these problems. Some fairly difficult problems are included in a few chapters.

Instructor's Manual

The *Instructor's Manual* comprises an overview of each chapter as well as detailed answers to all the questions and problems included in the text.

Enrichment Pieces

Materials that enhance or extend the topics under discussion are presented as enrichment pieces throughout the text. These pieces have been carefully selected to make the subject matter more interesting or to add a practical note to more theoretical topics.

Figures and Tables

Whenever practical, theoretical concepts are explained in graphic form. A variety of methods is used to make the figures clear and meaningful. A generous use of tables is designed to ensure that the students fully grasp the key concepts. A large number of expository tables provide supplements to the textual matter. In addition, explanatory tables are provided whenever an important concept is discussed.

Outlines, Summary, and A Look Ahead

Each chapter begins with a comprehensive outline designed to enable the student to follow the development of material in each chapter. At the end of each chapter, a summary highlights the important concepts covered in the chapter, and a preview of the next chapter, titled "A Look Ahead," explains how the next chapter is related to the present one.

Footnotes

The footnotes provide additional explanations to topics under discussion, references to supporting and related literature in order to substantiate the views expressed in the text, and mathematical proofs that articulate the main themes presented in the text.

Equations

Algebraic equations are consistently used to explain investment concepts in precise terms. All equations are numbered sequentially for easy reference. Definitions of the variables are also given so that students can study the equations without reference to the textual matter.

Selected Readings

On the assumption that instructors may require students to supplement their study of the text with outside readings, a comprehensive list of selected readings is included at the end of every chapter. The list includes publications in scholarly and specialized journals, books, and reports.

Statistical Data

Every effort is made to provide detailed statistics to supplement the topics under discussion. Wherever possible, use is also made of important empirical findings.

SUGGESTIONS FOR USE

The entire book is designed to be covered in a semester-length course. However, if the book is used in a fast, brief course, the first fourteen chapters will cover the essentials of investment analysis and portfolio management. Moreover, if time is a factor, instructors interested in covering the theory may do so by skipping Chapters 12 (Technical Analysis), 15 (Investment Companies), and 19 (Diversified Investment).

ACKNOWLEDGMENTS

We are indebted to many people who have assisted us in the preparation of this book. We would like to extend special thanks to our colleagues, whose critical comments were invaluable: H. Michael Collins, Executive Vice President, San Diego Securities, Inc.; David Doane, Oakland University; George C. Eshelman, Detroit Bank and Trust Co.; Douglas Gregory, Director, Center for Applied Research, Henry Ford Hospital; Douglas A. Hayes, Professor of Finance, University of Michigan; Young-Ha Hyon, Assistant Professor of Accounting and Finance, School of Business Administration, Temple University; Roland Meulebrouck, Vice President, Merrill Lynch; Donald A. Nast, Florida State University; Kamal Pradhan, Wayne State University; William Sharpe, Timken Professor of Finance, Graduate School of Business, Stanford University; Frederick Shipley, Oakland University; Richard D. Skaggs, Manufacturers National Bank of Detroit; and Theodore Yntema. We appreciate the help of our student assistants, Turgut Guvenli and Mariola Kulikowski, who worked diligently during the final phase of the book. Thanks are also due to Richard Light and Joan Feryus, who assisted us in coordinating the publication task. We are also grateful to Ronald M. Horwitz, Dean of the School of Management, Oakland University, for his understanding and appreciation of this undertaking, as well as for his continued support. Finally, for their editorial and related assistance, we would like to thank the staff at Harcourt Brace Jovanovich: Jack W. Thomas, manuscript editor; Robert Watrous, copyeditor; Geri Davis, designer; Fran Wager, production manager; Sue Lasbury, art editor; and Dianne Malik, proofreader.

Three persons must be singled out for special recognition. The best way we can express our deep gratitude to Professor Richard K. Smith, University of Montana, is to say that he could not have made a more valuable contribution, even if he were a co-author of this book. We are also grateful to Mrs. Rita Edwards, who in various ways contributed to almost every phase of the book. We must also express our sincere thanks to Steven A. Dowling, our sponsoring editor at Harcourt Brace Jovanovich, who steadfastly maintained a deep involvement with our manuscript and a conviction in our ability to produce a readable and useful investments textbook.

Although we have made every effort to ensure that the text is free from errors, we must be realistic in assuming that we have not eliminated all of them. We would be grateful to anyone who would care to point out these errors to us so that they may be corrected in the future.

Oakland University
Rochester, Michigan 48063

Sid Mittra
Chris Gassen

January 1, 1981

Contents

Investment Analysis and Portfolio Management

1 The General Setting

This book deals with investing in common stock, fixed income securities, and alternative investments such as stock options and convertible securities. Primary emphasis has been placed on the determination of investment value and the analysis of equity and fixed income securities. With this objective in mind, we first develop a security valuation model. This is followed by a comprehensive analysis of different types of securities within the framework set by the valuation model.

A prerequisite to a systematic approach to security investment is a thorough understanding of the investment environment. The purpose of Part 1 is to establish the general setting for investment analysis.

Part 1 consists of five chapters. Chapter 1 describes the essential ingredients of investment analysis and serves as an introduction to the book. Chapter 2 discusses the various types of securities available for investment and includes an examination of the types of investors who invest in them. Chapter 3 is a comprehensive review of the purposes and operation of the money and capital markets. A detailed knowledge of these markets is essential for making intelligent investment decisions. Chapter 4 begins with a comprehensive discussion of investment information sources as well as market indicators. Because a fundamental assumption of the functioning of an efficient market is that investors work with detailed information, this chapter supplies investors with information relating to individual securities and guides them to sources where valuable information can be found on a consistent basis.

Although the primary emphasis of this book is on the study of the process of valuation and analysis of individual securities, a theoretical framework is a prerequisite to such a study. Chapter 5 is devoted to a preliminary discussion of risk and return—the two cornerstones of the foundation of investment analysis and management. The issue of market efficiency is also raised in this chapter. The concept of risk and return in an efficient market is the central theme of the book.

Essentials of Investment Analysis

The Concept of Investment
- **An Overview**
- **Definition of Investment**
- **Risk and Uncertainty**
- **Investment Versus Speculation**

The Investment Environment

Risk and Return
- **Concept of Return**
- **Concept of Risk**

The Market Efficiency

Risk, Return, and Security Valuation
- **Bond Valuation**
- **Stock Valuation**
  - Fundamental Analysis
  - Technical Analysis

Portfolio Analysis

Text Organization

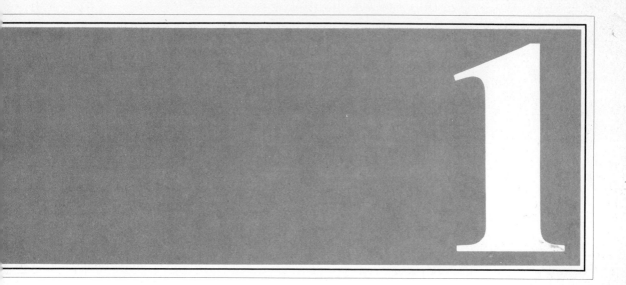

The Concept of Investment

An Overview

Most people would agree that, next to freedom itself, economic affluence is what Americans value most about their country. Even before the turn of the century when the United States became the world's leading industrial power, we boasted about our abundant natural resources and the unlimited opportunities for everyone who lived here. From World War II until the end of the 1970s, notwithstanding stagflation and other economic problems, increasingly exuberant economic growth has accelerated our material progress at an astounding rate.

Interestingly, the success we have achieved during the past three and a half decades has created a challenging problem for us. As our incomes have progressively increased and our current incomes have continually exceeded our current expenditures, we have become increasingly concerned with investing our savings in the most productive manner. However, during the struggle to find productive ways to invest our savings, we have learned that sound investment decisions cannot be made in a vacuum. Both thorough knowledge of what constitutes investment and an understanding of the attendant risks and rewards of different forms of investment are prerequisites to becoming an informed and successful investor.

Definition of Investment

There are many forms of investment. Consider, for example, the case of a person who invests his money in a bank passbook savings account where his money will be perfectly safe. A retired couple invests in public utility stocks.

A successful business executive who expects large investment returns puts her money in commodities, diamonds, and paintings. A conservative investor invests in blue chip stocks which he believes are safe investments. Meanwhile, a risk seeker sells her U.S. government bond and invests her money in gold bullion. All of these are examples of investment. A practical definition of investment is needed, therefore, before we can proceed to a more meaningful discussion of investment analysis.

The *Random House Dictionary* defines investment as "the investing of money or capital in order to secure profitable returns, especially interest or income." For the purposes of this text, we will define investment as the commitment of a given sum of money at the present time in the expectation of receiving a larger sum in the future. This definition underscores two important points. First, the process of investment involves the trading of present income for *future* income. Second, the objective of investment is to receive a *future* flow of funds larger than that originally invested. Thus, we invest to gain a positive return.

Risk and Uncertainty

Clearly, investment decisions are based on the expectation of receiving a positive return *in the future*. Because the future is unknown, uncertainty becomes an integral part of investment.

Consider the following example. A restaurant owner with established clientele has operated from the same location for five years. He now has the option of moving to a new building with larger quarters, which might substantially increase his profits. By moving, however, he risks his current investment, may incur higher operating costs, and cannot be certain whether his steady customers will follow him to the new location four miles away from the old place. In order to decide for or against the move, he must calculate the value of his current location, the flow of traffic to his business by virtue of its location, the certainty of steady, profitable business, and the known costs of his current operation along with a clear profit margin. All of this will be juxtaposed against both the risk of investing additional money in the new location and the uncertainty of his future business.

Note that in this illustration, uncertainty refers to the possibility of realizing a return on the investment *both* below and above the expected return. In a formal sense, risk is defined as the possibility of realizing *less* than the expected return. However, this difference is more theoretical than operational; consequently, in this book no distinction will be made between risk and uncertainty. More precisely, risk will be defined as the uncertainty of receiving the expected rate of return from an investment.

Investment Versus Speculation

Investment and speculation are sometimes used synonymously. However, a distinction needs to be made between the two. According to the *Random House Dictionary*, to speculate is "to buy and sell . . . stocks . . . in the expectation of profit through a change in their market value," whereas investment is defined as "the investing of money or capital in order to secure profitable returns. . . ." At first glance, there appears to be little difference between investment and speculation. However, it is sometimes argued that the time horizon and motivation are the two key factors that differentiate a speculator from an investor. Thus, speculators concentrate on returns expected to be received over relatively short periods of time; in contrast, the objective of an investor is to derive benefits from his investment over a longer horizon. Furthermore, speculators act quickly on the available information which has not yet been analyzed or acted upon by the general public, whereas investors generally base their judgment on investment analysis. In this book, the primary emphasis will be placed on a study of investment.

The Investment Environment

The economic function of all money and capital markets is to serve as intermediaries, channeling savings into productive use. The investment process must be viewed against the backdrop of the market's economic function.

Negotiable financial assets are traded in the money and capital markets. Negotiable securities with a maturity of one year or less are traded in the money market; longer-term securities, including common stocks, are traded in the capital markets. This book discusses in detail the major instruments or vehicles traded in the money and capital markets. These instruments include equities, fixed income securities, and securities of the U.S. government (as well as the lesser-known instruments like options, rights, and warrants).

The structure, operation, and economic function of several types of financial markets are discussed in this text. These include the organized exchanges and the over-the-counter markets where many buyers and sellers trade at competitive prices. We also discuss the National Market System and the role of institutions in the securities markets.

The efficient operation of the securities market depends primarily on the availability and dissemination of a large quantity of information, and many brokerage firms and investment services publish or provide investment information. In addition, up-to-date reports regularly appear in the financial press. This text discusses the major sources of financial information, as well as providing a framework for evaluating them from the standpoint of the investors' needs and objectives.

Risk and Return

Concept of Return

The primary objective of investment, of course, is to realize a satisfactory return on investment. Total nominal return from an investment equals the price change of the security plus income in the form of interest or dividends. In calculating the total real return, however, the loss in the purchasing power of the dollar due to inflation should also be considered.

Concept of Risk

Previously, we have defined investment as the commitment of a given sum of money at the present time in the expectation of receiving a larger sum in the future. This definition emphasizes the fact that investment decisions are based on expected returns on the investment. Basically, the *risk* an investor assumes by investing in a security includes the possibility of his not realizing the *expected* return.

For purposes of investment analysis, it is appropriate to differentiate between the risk associated with fixed income securities which have a limited life and the risk of investing in equities which theoretically have a perpetual life.

Generally speaking, fixed income securities may carry six types of risks: (1) interest rate risk, (2) inflation risk, (3) maturity risk, (4) default risk, (5) callability risk, and (6) liquidity risk. The interest rate risk refers to the possibility of variations in bond prices as a result of fluctuations in market interest rates. A decline in the real value of interest income and principal repayment due to inflation is known as the inflation risk. The maturity risk is based on the theory that because the future is always uncertain, investing in a long-term security always involves the possibility of capital loss. The default risk is based on the possibility that the issuer of the bond will default, either by nonpayment or delayed payment of the interest and/or the face value of the bond. The callability risk refers to the probability of receiving a lower rate of return if the bond is redeemed by the firm before maturity. In general, if a bond is called during a period of falling interest rates, the bondholder would probably be forced to reinvest money at a rate lower than the bond's coupon rate. Finally, the liquidity risk of a bond refers to the cost of trade, search, and information, as well as the price concession an investor must grant in order to quickly convert security holdings into cash. The less liquid a security is, the higher its liquidity risk.

In contrast to bond risks, common stock risks cannot be classified in distinct categories, because neither the dividend stream nor the selling price of a stock is certain. Consequently, a potential stockholder is left with no other alternative than estimating the risk of the common stock on the basis of a measure of the past variability of the price of that stock. However, it is important to point out that the variability of a stock's price is not necessarily a measure of its risk. Variability refers to the *past* record of price fluctuations, whereas risk is a measure of *future* price fluctuations. Nevertheless, for practical purposes, past variability is frequently used as a surrogate for its future risk.

The Market Efficiency

One of the liveliest controversies prevailing in the investment world relates to the efficiency of financial markets. The basis for this controversy is the *Efficient Market Hypothesis* (*EMH*). Proponents of the EMH argue that an efficient market is one in which market prices of securities reflect the impact of all the information publicly available concerning the future prospects of the associated companies. The implication of this argument is that because the current price of a stock impounds all public information and because new information becomes available only at random, all stocks are appropriately valued; consequently, by resorting to investment analysis, an investor cannot "beat the market." This view has been termed the weak form of the EMH. Advocates of the semistrong form of the EMH argue that the current stock price fully reflects even the information which can be uncovered only by a sophisticated analysis of fundamental factors. Finally, proponents of the strong form of the EMH assert that stock prices reflect not only all publicly available information, but the information that is possessed only by super analysts.

Opponents of the EMH concede that the long-term behavior of the capital market shows a fair degree of efficiency. However, they maintain that many studies have demonstrated that in the capital market inefficiency does exist in the short run. Thus, conclude the opponents, with the help of fundamental analysis, it is possible to recognize undervalued stocks and develop strategies for benefiting from investing in them. The market efficiency controversy has not been resolved; its implications will be critically evaluated in subsequent chapters.

Risk, Return, and Security Valuation

Bond Valuation

Investment analysis encompassing the risk–return criterion is first applied to fixed income securities, because these securities have a fixed annual interest and a maturity price. At the heart of bond analysis is the *Bond Valuation Model.* This model is used to calculate the yield to maturity of a bond by discounting the annual interest payments and the maturity price. The yield to maturity is then compared to the appropriate discount rate or the investor's required rate of return; then a determination can be made both as to whether the bond is appropriately priced and as to whether it is an appropriate investment vehicle for that investor.

Stock Valuation

Fundamental Analysis

Next, the discussion moves to a valuation of equity securities—known as fundamental analysis—with the use of the *Common Stock Valuation Model.* The model helps determine the present value of a common stock by discounting the expected dividend stream and the expected future selling price by an appropriate discount rate. Both qualitative and quantitative analyses are used to estimate the values of the three variables cited above. The stock's present value is then compared with its current market price in order to determine whether the stock is over-valued or whether it offers an attractive investment opportunity.

Technical Analysis

In sharp contrast to fundamental analysis, technical analysis refers to the study of equities through use of past data relating to the equities market rather than those fundamental factors reflected in the market and individual stock prices. Technical analysts do not deny the importance of fundamental factors that influence the stock market and individual stock prices. However, they argue that because the market price of a stock reflects all factors affecting it, it is sufficient to study *only* past stock price movements to make intelligent investment decisions. Furthermore, proponents of technical analysis assert that past price patterns repeat themselves in predictable ways. Consequently, a study of these patterns can be used as a tool for predicting future price changes for the stock market in general as well as for individual stocks.

It should be noted that the claims made by technical analysts have little theoretical foundation. Furthermore, several statistical tests conducted in order to test the effectiveness of technical analysis have concluded that the various mechanical trading rules developed by technical analysts do not *consistently* produce superior results.

Portfolio Analysis

As we have mentioned, individual security analysis is one of the main topics of this text. However, the primary objective of many investors—especially institutional investors and portfolio managers—is the construction of an efficient portfolio. An efficient portfolio consists of a group of stocks with diverse characteristics, carefully selected to maximize the expected return in its risk class. Any given portfolio, of course, contains a group of securities. Portfolio theory asserts that, by including a large number of securities with diverse characteristics, the total risk associated with the individual securities can be effectively reduced.

Active portfolio construction and management necessitates a great deal more consideration than that implied by fundamental analysis of individual securities. The variability of a large number of stocks relative to the stock market must be measured. The risk preference of the individual constructing the portfolio must also be taken into account. Given these and other related considerations, a portfolio which maximizes expected return for the specified level of risk can be constructed. This process of security selection is known as diversification through the construction of an efficient portfolio.

Text Organization

This text is devoted to a study of investment analysis and portfolio management. No effort has been made to provide a shortcut for *beating the market.* Instead, the objective of this book is to present a theoretically sound, comprehensive framework for analyzing various investment instruments as well as for constructing an efficient portfolio consistent with investors' individual risk preferences. Implicit in this presentation is the assumption that the investment process is inexact and that a number of important issues, such as market efficiency controversy, are still unsettled. In fact, throughout the book, we endeavor to (1) present the "state of the art," (2) underscore the important investment issues, (3) explain the nature of unsettled controversies, and (4) apply investment theories and concepts to realistic situations.

The chapters of this text have been written to be read consecutively from beginning to end. In most chapters, the explication progresses from simple description of the basic issues to more complicated and analytical materials. This is particularly true of the theory and conceptual chapters. Numerical examples are carefully developed to supplement the analytical materials in order to clarify the subject and make it comprehensible to even the financially uninitiated.

The book is divided into five parts. A premise underlying security analysis is the availability of a reasonable amount of dependable information concerning the economy, the market, and the related securities. Consequently, Part 1 is primarily devoted to a review of financial securities, the money and capital markets, and the major sources of information concerning the securities traded in those markets.

An important feature of the book is the two-stage treatment of risk. In Part 1, the essentials of risk and return are presented so that their role in investment analysis can be understood without the encumbrance of complex details. Later, in Part 4, risk and return are discussed more comprehensively in conjunction with the theoretical topics of the *Capital Asset Pricing Model* and the portfolio theory.

Part 2 begins with the construction of a Bond Valuation Model and continues with an analysis of U.S. government securities and municipal bonds, the least risky of all securities. This is followed by a discussion of corporate bonds and preferred stocks.

Part 3 describes the valuation of equity securities. The Common Stock Valuation Model is presented, then used as a background for a discussion of how fundamental analysis aids in determining the present value of common stock. Finally, for pedagogical reasons, technical analysis is discussed as a technique for making decisions regarding the purchase and sale of common stocks.

Part 4 is devoted to a detailed discussion of portfolio theory and management. The theory and application of portfolio construction and management are followed by an analysis of portfolio management by investment companies. The role of taxes is also considered in the context of making investment decisions.

In Part 5—the final section of the book—we discuss investing in different types of securities as well as such related topics as convertible securities, options, and other esoteric instruments.

Investment Alternatives and the Investors

2

Introduction

This chapter is devoted to a discussion of the investment environment and serves as an introduction to a wide array of investment alternatives. These alternatives can range from simple bank savings accounts to commodity futures or complicated business ventures. However, this chapter focuses on money and capital market securities, including negotiable financial assets such as stocks and bonds. An overview of the various investors operating in the financial markets is also included in this chapter.

Money Market Investments

An Overview

Investments in the money market[1] are debt instruments with maturities of under a year, usually 90 days or less. Because the minimum investment required to purchase money market instruments is generally very large, the market is dominated by commercial banks, state and local governments, financial and nonbank institutions and, more recently, mutual funds. These large investors purchase money market instruments to convert temporary cash surpluses into highly liquid interest-bearing investments.

[1] The functions and purposes of the money, capital, and secondary markets will be discussed in Chapter 3.

Although the various money market instruments have individual differences, because they are all issued by the obligors of the highest credit rating,[2] they are close substitutes for one another in many investment portfolios, and the rates of return on these securities tend to fluctuate closely with short-term interest rates. The principal money market instruments are treasury bills, negotiable certificates of deposit, commercial paper, bankers' acceptances, and repurchase agreements.

Treasury Bills

Treasury bills are the most frequently issued marketable securities of the U.S. government. Normally issued in amounts of $10,000 or more, they are sold weekly or monthly on an auction basis and have a maximum maturity of one year. A treasury bill does not carry an interest coupon; its interest return is the difference between the price paid at auction and that received when sold or received at maturity. Although these securities do not offer the highest yield among short-term debt instruments, they are very "liquid" because they can be quickly converted into cash without undue risk of capital loss.[3] Moreover, treasury bills are absolutely safe because they are fully guaranteed by the U.S. government.

Negotiable Certificates of Deposit

In essence, a negotiable *certificate of deposit* is a receipt issued by a bank or savings and loan association in exchange for a deposit of funds. The bank agrees to pay the amount deposited, plus interest, to the bearer of the receipt on the date specified on the certificate (usually from one month to a year from time of deposit). The minimum deposit for such certificates is $100,000.

Commercial Paper

When a well-known corporation with a good credit rating wishes to borrow money for a short period of time, it issues a promissory note called *commercial paper*. Such notes are usually issued in denominations of $100,000, $250,000, $500,000 or $1,000,000 and reach maturity at a date not exceeding nine months from their time of issuance.

Bankers' Acceptances

Drafts which have been drawn on a bank by a customer and which bear the bank's promise to pay them at maturity are called *bankers' acceptances*. The acceptance reflects the obligation of both the bank and the drawer to pay the

[2] Credit ratings for fixed-income securities will be discussed in Chapters 6, 7, and 8.
[3] Liquidity will be discussed in more detail in Chapter 3.

face amount, usually no less than $100,000. Normally used to finance foreign trade, bankers' acceptances are among the safest of all money market instruments. In the United States, holders of bankers' acceptances have never suffered a loss.

Repurchase Agreements (RPs)

A *repurchase agreement* is a contract in money market instruments. A borrower who needs funds for a few days enters into a contract to sell securities—usually treasury bills—from his inventory and agrees to purchase them back later at a given price. Often the price is stated simply as that amount necessary to provide a certain yield basis to the buyer for the time involved. The normal minimum for RPs is $100,000.

In recent years individual investors have been able to participate in the money market by purchasing shares of money market mutual funds. The investments of many small investors—usually in the range of $1,000–$5,000—are pooled in these funds to purchase the high denomination debt instruments.[4]

Capital Market Investments

An Overview

Money market securities are purchased primarily to earn interest on temporary cash balances. These investments are of short duration and offer a high degree of safety for their principal amount, because the issuers generally have the highest credit ratings. *Capital market investments*, however, include debt instruments with longer maturities as well as equities, which theoretically have no maturity. In the capital market, therefore, investors can commit funds for longer periods of time—and purchase securities with a greater degree of risk—in expectation of higher returns. Capital market investment alternatives include various kinds of bonds and capital stock. These securities will be further analyzed in later chapters.

Bonds

The true nature of a *bond* is best revealed by defining it as a contract to pay money. Under this contract, the issuer agrees to pay the principal sum and a specified rate of interest for the use of "borrowed" money. The payment schedule is stipulated in this contract. There are three major bond issuers: the federal government, state and local municipalities, and corporations.

[4] Mutual funds will be discussed in detail in Chapter 15.

Federal Government Securities

The U.S. government issues a variety of debt instruments in the capital market. Like the issues sold in the money market with maturities of one year or less, because these longer-term securities are also backed by the full faith and credit of the United States, they are regarded as the highest grade issues in existence. Longer-term *government securities* include treasury notes, treasury bonds, and Series EE and HH savings bonds.[5]

It is important to note that, although all the various federal government securities are free from the risk of default, there are fundamental differences between them. These differences include not only the length of maturity, but the minimum denomination needed for purchase, methods for paying interest, procedures for sale by the government, and special tax provisions. Chapter 7 includes a comprehensive discussion of U.S. government securities.

In addition to issues coming *directly* from the government, securities are offered by many government *agencies* established by acts of Congress. Some agency issues are backed by the full faith and credit of the United States; others are guaranteed by the respective issuing agencies.[6] That these issues are virtually free of default risk is borne out by the fact that not one issue has ever defaulted.

Government agency bonds are issued by a number of U.S.-owned and sponsored agencies, including the Tennessee Valley Authority, Federal Home Loan Banks, and the Export–Import Bank. One of the more popular agency issues is from the Government National Mortgage Association (GNMA), which offers investors an opportunity to purchase an interest in a large pool of government approved mortgages.

Municipal Bonds

Municipal bonds are issued by state or political subdivisions, such as counties, cities, towns, and villages. This term also designates bonds issued by state agencies and authorities. In general, interest paid on municipal bonds is exempt from both federal taxes and local income taxes within the state of issue. There are several types of municipal bonds which can be grouped into two broad categories: *general obligation* and *revenue bonds.*[7]

General Obligation Bonds The largest category within the municipal bond section of the bond market is *general obligation bonds.* These bonds are backed by the full faith, credit, and taxing power of the issuing government unit. An investor can buy state issues backed by the state government, school bonds backed by the school district, city bonds backed by the municipality, or various other bonds, generally backed by the county government.

---

[5] Technically, savings bonds can be redeemed by the purchaser after only six months. However, they are generally considered to be a longer-term holding, as will be evident in the discussion in Chapter 7.

[6] Government agencies also issue short-term notes.

[7] Although municipal securities are generally long-term, some short-term obligations are issued. They include tax, revenue, or bond anticipation notes (also known as TANS, RANS, and BANS), and are issued in expectation of tax receipts or the proceeds of a bond issue. These securities are also considered the tax-exempt market's version of commercial paper.

Revenue Bonds *Revenue bonds* are strictly dependent on the income from the issuing governmental unit or project to meet the interest and principal payments. These include both sewer and revenue bonds, as well as bonds used to finance bridges, tunnels, toll roads, airports, hospitals, and even sports stadiums.

In addition to these, investors can consider other types of revenue bonds. For instance, *Special Tax Bonds* are payable from the proceeds of a special tax, such as a tax on gasoline, liquor, or tobacco. Local school bonds are another good example. When these issues are backed by the full faith, credit, and taxing power of the issuing authority, they become general obligation bonds.

A municipality or local authority wishing to attract new industry into the area might issue *Industrial Revenue Bonds.* These bonds are issued to build facilities for corporations whose lease payments cover the interest and principal payments to bondholders.

Housing Finance Authority Bonds are issued by local agencies to build middle-income housing, college dormitories, mental health facilities, or other housing projects, and are usually backed by rental payments. *Public Housing Authority Bonds* are also issued by local authorities to finance low-rent housing projects. These bonds are secured by a pledge of unconditional annual contributions by the Housing Assistance Administration, a U.S. government agency.

Corporate Bonds

A *corporate bond* is a debt instrument or an evidence of an obligation entered into by a company, as opposed to stock which represents ownership. Owners of bonds expect to receive no more than repayment of the bond principal and interest from the issuing firm, because they are creditors rather than owners of the company. However, bondholders must be paid interest on their principal before dividends may be paid to stockholders. Also, in the case of business failure or liquidation, bondholders must be repaid before the equity holders.

There are several types of corporate bonds. Some carry special features and privileges; others are distinguishable by the types of security pledged against bond repayment. Basically, bonds may be *secured* or *unsecured.* With a secured bond, the issuer reinforces its promise to pay the interest and principal by pledging specific property to the bondholders as collateral. In the case of an unsecured bond, the issuer merely promises to pay the stated interest and principal. There are several types of secured and unsecured bonds.

Debentures A *debenture* is a common form of corporate bond. It is backed only by the faith and general credit of the issuing company, rather than secured by a mortgage or lien on any specific property. Although these IOUs have junior claim to all assets relative to all other forms of bonds outstanding, debenture claims equal those of general creditors.

1. A *sinking fund debenture* is the same type of bond as the regular debenture, except that the company is required to set aside funds in anticipation of

repaying the principal, as specified in the bond's indenture.[8] The sinking fund debenture may be *funded* by having cash set aside for its payment in a specific trust account, or it may be *nonfunded* simply by creating a liability for the sinking fund payments in the balance sheet.

2. *Subordinated debentures* are the same as regular debentures, except that in case of liquidation their owners are paid after the regular debenture holders. Thus, subordinated debentures are "junior" to all other bonds.[9]

Guaranteed Bonds A *guaranteed bond* has interest or principal—or both—guaranteed by a company other than the issuer. The railroad industry uses this kind of bond when larger railroads, leasing sections of track owned by small railroads, guarantee the bonds of the smaller railroads.

Mortgage Bonds A *mortgage bond* is a debt obligation secured by a mortgage on property. The value of the property may or may not equal the value of the mortgage bond issued against it. Because these securities are usually issued by giant utility companies, they make up a major segment of the corporate bond market.

Mortgage bonds may be either senior or junior liens, depending on the priority of the claim. Senior liens have the first claim on the property of the company under the mortgage, whereas junior liens have the secondary claim.

Whether the mortgage is *closed end, open end*, or *limited open end* determines the principal amount of bonds outstanding under the mortgage. A closed end issue specifies the principal amount of bonds that can be issued in the indenture; at no time can the company issue additional bonds under the same mortgage and thereby reduce the original bondholders' proportion of interest. An open end issue carries no such restriction; the issuer may sell bonds in any amount and at any time. In such cases, no bond, regardless of when it was issued, has a prior claim to property over another. Limited open end issues are a compromise between the closed and open end varieties. A maximum amount of bonds issuable under a given mortgage is specified, but over time they may be issued in different series.

Collateral Trust Bonds This type of bond is backed by collateral deposited with a trustee. The collateral is often the stocks or bonds of other companies controlled by the issuing company.

Equipment Trust Certificates These bonds represent loans secured by assets other than fixed property—typically by machinery, railroad rolling stock, trucks, and airplanes. Railroads typically issue equipment trust certificates to purchase expensive railroad equipment which they then put up as security for

---

[8] A bond indenture, or contract, specifies various characteristics of the bond: (1) the dates at which interest payments will be made, (2) the maturity date of the bond, (3) the coupon rate, (4) the bond's face value, (5) the name of the bond trustee, and (6) other restrictions to be met by the issuer, such as a set working capital ratio or maximum amount of dividends which may be paid.

[9] Subordinated debentures are most often subordinated to bank credit which is also an unsecured debt.

the loan. Investors purchasing these certificates actually buy ownership in the equipment they finance: A special trust is set up for them to own the equipment and lease it back to the railroad under an elaborate contract.

Convertible Bonds These debt instruments may be exchanged by the owner for common stock or another security—usually of the same company—in accordance with the terms and exchange ratios for the issue. Any of the previously listed types of bonds may be convertible, although most convertible bonds are debentures or subordinated debentures.

Bonds may also be classified according to the way they provide for interest payments.

Income Bonds The issuer of income bonds promises to repay the principal when it becomes due, but to pay interest only when earned. In some cases unpaid interest on an income bond may accumulate as a claim against the corporation when the bond becomes due.

Fixed-charge Bonds This term applies to any bond for which interest payments must be made—whether or not the money is earned—in order for the company to remain technically solvent. Most bonds issued are fixed-charge bonds.

Floating Rate Notes Every six months the interest rate on a floating rate note is adjusted to a fixed percentage above the rate on treasury bills. A few issues can be redeemed at face value at the end of each six-month period; within several years of issuance, most others can be converted to fixed-rate debentures. All floating rate notes have a minimum interest rate payable at the time of conversion, regardless of rate on treasury bills prevailing at that time. These securities were first issued by large commercial banks in 1974, and in recent years they have also been issued by industrial corporations. It is estimated that there are currently over $2 billion of these floating rate notes outstanding.

In addition to the bonds which carry a set maturity date when the principal must be repaid to the bondholder, there are other types of bonds which carry a variable maturity date or no maturity date at all.

Annuity or Maturity Bonds An *annuity bond* bears no maturity date; the interest continues indefinitely. These securities are also called perpetual bonds or perpetuities.

Callable Bonds A *callable bond* has a set maturity date, but it can be redeemed after sufficient notice to the bondholders by the issuer at specified periods.

Corporate and municipal bonds can also be classified according to their risk and return characteristics, but this discussion will be postponed to the chapters on bond analysis.

Stocks

Capital *stock* represents ownership in the issuing company. If you own a percentage of a company's stock, you own that same percentage of the firm's net worth. Your interest would be evidenced by a stock certificate, which states the name of the stockholder, the class of stock, and the number of shares owned.

Types of Capital Stock

A corporation may issue different types of stock according to its charter.[10] Each particular issue carries with it certain rights and restrictions for its shareholders as owners in the corporation. In a corporation there can be both *preferred* and *common* stockholders. Although both are owners in the company, the particular nature of each kind of ownership depends on the type of stock held.[11]

Common Stock Common stockholders simply have an equity in the corporation. Perhaps the most important privilege common stockholders enjoy is that

[10] A company's charter is a document issued by authority of a government. It usually consists of the approved and recorded articles of incorporation, together with the general corporation laws of the government. The articles of incorporation set forth the purpose, duration, principal place of business, and other details of the corporation.

[11] The investment qualities of preferred stock are similar to debt instruments, and will be discussed further in Chapter 8.

Cash Dividends, Stock Dividends, and Stock Splits

As a general rule, a company's board of directors meets every quarter in order to decide how much, if any, earnings will be distributed to stockholders as a *cash dividend*. On common shares, the dividend varies with the performance of the company and the amount of cash on hand. Sometimes a company pays a dividend out of past earnings—called retained earnings—even if it is not currently operating at a profit. At other times, a company declares a dividend payable in additional stock, commonly known as a *stock dividend*. For example, if a company declares a 20 percent stock dividend, a stockholder who owns 100 shares would receive 20 additional shares from the company. However, the stockholder would not own a larger percentage of the firm's net worth as a result of having received the additional shares, because the total number of shares outstanding will also have increased by 20 percent.

A *stock split* is similar to a stock dividend.* For example, if a company has 5 million shares outstanding and declares a three-for-one stock split, after the split there would be 15 million shares outstanding. Simultaneously, the earnings per

* There is a technical difference between a stock dividend and a stock split. A stock dividend is reflected in the company's balance sheet by an increase in the amount of capital stock items and a decrease in the amount of retained earnings. In a stock split, the capital stock account remains the same.

in the event of extraordinary business success they are *usually* the only group to participate in the increased earnings via the increased dividends. They are not personally liable for debts incurred by the corporation, but in the event of business failure or liquidation, common stockholders are the last to be paid. They do, however, retain residual rights to any assets that may remain after all the creditors are paid.

Owners of common stock are entitled to participate in the management of the enterprise to the extent of voting to elect directors and approving specified changes in the company's charter.[12] Generally, common stockholders also have preemptive rights to purchase any new issues of "voting stock" in proportion to their existing percentage of ownership in the company.

Preferred Stock Preferred stock is junior, or subordinate, to all bonds that a company owns. However, owners of preferred stock generally receive a fixed dividend when one is declared by the board of directors of the company. Preferred stock dividends must be paid before any dividends are paid to common stockholders. Furthermore, preferred stockholders have prior claims on the company's assets and, in case of liquidation, are entitled to full payment before

[12] In some cases, a company may issue different classes of common stock, some of which may have limited or no voting rights. For example, Adolph Coors Company subdivides its common stock into Class A voting common stock and Class B nonvoting common stock. These subclasses are technically called *classified stock.*

share and other financial data would be adjusted downward on a per-share basis. Thus, a stockholder holding 100 shares prior to the split would subsequently have 300 shares, but his percentage of ownership in the firm would remain unchanged.

When a company splits its stock or declares a stock dividend while maintaining its current dividend payment *per share*, in effect stockholders receive an increase in dividend payment. However, if the dividend rate is reduced in order to adjust for a split or stock dividend, or if the company does not pay a cash dividend, the stock split or stock dividend is merely reduced to a paper transaction with no real economic meaning.[†]

The immediate effect of a stock dividend or split is to lower the price per share (if the shareholders' dividend income is assumed to remain unchanged). Naturally, a split or a stock dividend results in an increase in the number of outstanding shares, which, in the long run, can produce a wider distribution of the shares at a lower price. Therefore, it is sometimes argued that stock splits or stock dividends make the common stock more attractive and marketable to the investing public.

[†] The effect of a stock split on shareholder wealth is discussed in Chapter 14.

the common stockholders receive anything.[13] Remember, however, that preferred stockholders do not generally participate in company management; they have no voting rights such as the common stockholders possess.

There are different legal issues of preferred stock. If the stock is *cumulative*, the claim to dividends may be carried over from one year to the next; if the company falls behind in dividend payments, it must make up the entire amount before paying dividends to the common stockholders. Another variety, called

[13] Payment is based on the par value or a special liquidating preference value of a preferred stock, not the market value.

Common Stock: Par, Book, and Market Value

Common stock frequently has three values—par value, book value, and market value—and they are usually all different. Common stock is issued with either a par value or a no-par value. The *par value* on the stock is a stated value which appears in the corporate charter, but has no economic significance. (The par value is usually set low for tax and legal considerations.*) When stock is initially issued by a company, the equity section of the balance sheet will carry two accounts. The "capital stock" account records the par value of the stock issued, while the "capital in excess of par" account records the difference between the issue price of the shares minus the par value.

The *book value* of a common stock is a simple accounting concept used by security analysts and others. It is determined by adding all company assets (generally excluding such intangibles as goodwill), then deducting all debts, other liabilities, and the liquidation price of any preferred issues. This total is then divided by the number of common shares outstanding; the result is the book value per common share. Some consider book value to be equivalent to the *liquidating value* of a company, but the liquidation value can be higher or lower. Most steel companies, for example, have large investments in huge plants (listed on their books at cost); however, the resale value of these plants may be far less than their cost, because there is no other use for them except in their own business. On the other hand, some companies hold valuable tracts of land which could easily be sold above cost in case of liquidation. Generally speaking, most assets would be sold at prices below what would be received if the firm were an ongoing entity.†

Finally, the *market price* of a common stock is determined (as discussed in the next chapter) through the interaction of supply and demand via the buy and

* Some states charge excise taxes and franchise fees based on the par value of the stock. Also, in an initial offering, if investors purchase stock at a price below par, they are liable to creditors of the company for the difference between the market value and the par value of the stock.

† Naturally, there are exceptions, such as investment companies—including mutual funds—and other financial corporations, such as insurance companies and banks, which hold most of their assets in securities that can be easily turned into cash.

convertible preferred stock, should be of special interest. Such a stock carries a contractual clause entitling the holder to exchange it for shares of common stock of the same company within a specified period.

Another type of preferred stock is called *participating preferred stock*. As a general rule, preferred stockholders surrender any claim to the residual earnings of their company after the dividends have been distributed. However, the holder of a participating preferred stock not only receives dividends, but shares additional earnings with the common stockholder. Note also that many preferred stocks are *callable*. This means that these shares may be redeemed by the issuing company at a given "call price" within a specified number of years after issuance.

Figure 2–A **Ratio of Market to Book Value, S&P Industrials, 1948–78**

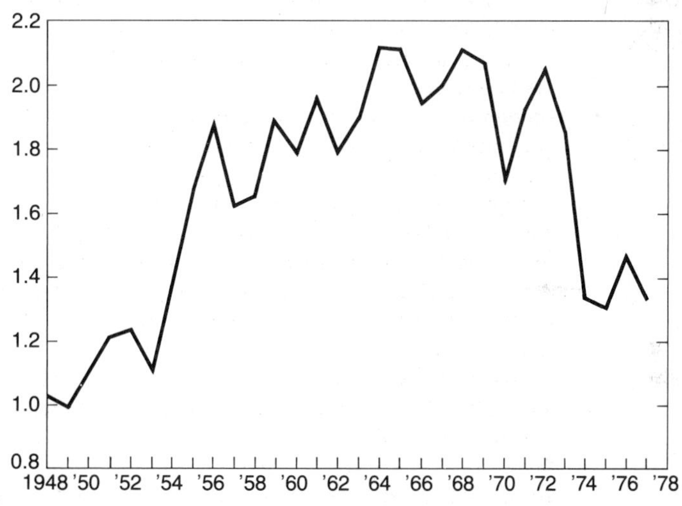

SOURCE: "Common Stocks—A Perspective," Merrill Lynch Pierce Fenner & Smith, Inc., 1978.

sell orders of investors in the marketplace. Although the market value of an individual stock can be above, below, or equal to its book value, Figure 2–A shows that the market value for a broad average of stocks has been consistently above book value. Why the divergence? In fact, for any going concern, the market value of its stock is influenced much more by such factors as earnings, dividends, and prospects for growth, rather than by book value. Book value becomes a much more important figure if a corporation is being liquidated or sold. The valuation of common stock will be discussed in detail in Chapter 8.

Investment Quality

Common stock is also described and analyzed according to its investment qualities—that is, the characteristics it offers in terms of expected return, risk, and other dimensions. Many investors, however, prefer to group stocks according to some of the traditional classifications used on Wall Street—for example, blue chips, growth company stocks, income stocks, and so on. As will become evident, these stock groupings clearly differ in their underlying characteristics of risk and return, because they are based on investors' perceptions of such factors as the firm's size, earnings prospects, and dividend payment policy. In later chapters, beginning with Chapter 5, the techniques that more precisely evaluate and measure the risk and return criteria will be described. At this time, it is sufficient to briefly describe the various traditional investment grades of stock.

Blue Chips *Blue chip stocks* are high-grade investment quality issues from major companies which have long and unbroken records of earnings and dividend payments. They are usually the largest companies in the country, and they hold important, if not leading, positions in their industries. With the advantage of size and market leadership, these corporations can weather economic downturns and post strong earnings gains during upturns, because they have the resources to capitalize on a recovery.

Included in the category of blue chips are stocks of such companies as IBM, Exxon, AT&T, General Motors, General Electric, and DuPont. It should be noted, however, that although there may be approximately two to three hundred issues which are universally accepted as blue chip stocks, possibly an equal number are occasionally included in this category. The reason for this is that because assessments of the quality of a security can vary from one investor to another,[14] stocks may be classified differently by different investors.

Secondary Stocks This broad category includes all stocks which are not classified as blue chips. In some cases, secondary stocks may be issued by established companies with impressive earnings records and excellent future prospects. However, the company may lack the size, corporate resources, or industry position that many consider necessary to qualify as blue chip stocks.

Consider, for instance, the case of Tennant Company. Founded in 1870, Tennant is the world's leading designer and manufacturer of industrial floor maintenance equipment. During the past decade, revenues have expanded at an annual compound growth rate of 17 percent, earnings per share have increased at an uninterrupted rate of 18 percent, and dividends have increased nine times

[14] Some propose, however, that a blue chip stock can be defined as any stock rated A+ or A by Standard & Poor's Earnings and Dividend Rankings for Common Stocks. This ranking system, described in issues of *Standard & Poor's Stock Guide*—not to be confused with Standard & Poor's bond quality ratings—is a computerized scoring system which appraises a company's past performance of earnings and dividends and its relative current standing. These rankings are sometimes used as a general measure of risk for common stocks. However, a more comprehensive risk measure will be developed, beginning in Chapter 5.

in the seven years ending in 1978. But, although Tennant may be rated as highly as blue chip companies in terms of stability of earnings and dividends and may hold a leading position within the industry, it is a relatively small firm (its sales in 1978 were approximately $80 million). Consequently, Tennant stock does not carry blue chip status.

Under these first two general headings that divide the thousands of stocks between "blue chips" and "secondary," stocks can be further categorized according to other important investment features. None of these categories is mutually exclusive; it is possible for some stocks to fall under one or more of the following types.

Growth Company Stocks[15] *Growth company stocks* are shares in companies in which earnings increase at a rate faster than the earnings of the average firm or the growth of the economy. These companies typically pay only a small portion of earnings in dividends, because they can maintain or accelerate their growth by reinvesting earnings in the business. Such firms are also typically aggressive in pursuing profitable ventures; they retain a substantial portion of earnings for research and development.

Growth companies may be further classified as either established or emerging growth companies. Established growth companies have histories of growth in earnings over extended periods and are proven successful performers. Many are also labeled as blue chips, such as Burroughs Corporation, which is considered a classic example of an established growth company. Through the 1960s and the 1970s, Burroughs became a leading producer of business equipment covering major sectors of the data processing market. Its revenue and profits grew during these two decades, at compounded annual rates of, respectively, 15 and 20 percent.

Emerging growth companies are those that have established a record of above average earnings growth, but that have not yet grown sufficiently large or established the extended record of success demonstrated by the established growth companies. Some of the stocks in these companies are called "glamors," because they have become associated with a glamorous new invention or process and as a result have gained widespread popularity. The U.S. Surgical Corporation can be cited as an example of such a firm. Under the name of Auto Suture, the company markets a patented stapling device used in surgical procedures for closing internal or external tissue. From 1970 to 1978, sales of the firm increased from $1.4 million to over $40 million, while over the same period

[15] One can make a distinction between *growth stocks* and stocks of *growth companies*. A growth stock is a security expected to earn an above-average rate of return relative to other stocks in the same risk class; this is sometimes called an "undervalued" stock. As will be discussed in later chapters on common stock valuation, a stock is considered undervalued only when it sells at or below a certain price level. Thus, the stock of a growth company need not necessarily be a growth stock. A growth stock need not necessarily be a stock of a growth company, because any type of stock can be considered undervalued if selling at an appropriate price. For a discussion of the differences between companies and types of stocks, see Frank K. Reilly, "A Differentiation Between Types of Companies and Types of Stock," *Mississippi Valley Journal of Business and Economics*, Vol. 7, No. 1 (Fall 1971), pp. 35–43.

annual earnings advanced rapidly from only $30,000 to over $3.7 million. U.S. Surgical may eventually become an established growth blue chip like IBM or Xerox; alternatively, it could falter from its present enviable position as did, for example, Franklin Mint and Sambo's Restaurants.

Cyclical Company Stocks These are stocks of companies whose earnings fluctuate with the business cycle and are accentuated by it. When patterns in the economy are favorable to their industry, the earnings of cyclical companies peak. When the course of the economy changes direction, they suffer earnings setbacks and adversities. The most common example of a cyclical situation is that of the auto stocks, which rise in price and are a source of increasing dividends during economic booms and recoveries, but which fall during recessions when auto sales ebb.

The stocks of cyclical companies can be contrasted with those that are recession resistant. Such companies sell products and services which enjoy a demand that does not greatly fluctuate with the business cycle. Familiar examples of recession-resistant industries are those involved with health care, food, cosmetics, and computers.

Income Stocks *Income stocks* are characteristic of those firms that pay a high dividend relative to the stock prices. The dividend yields on these securities are above average for stocks and frequently are competitive with the returns on debt instruments. Income stocks are purchased by investors mainly for their current yield, rather than for their potential price appreciation.

The most common examples of income stocks are those issued by public utilities. These stocks sell largely for their dividend yield, because appreciation in stock price due to earnings growth is constrained by government regulation of the utilities' return on investment. The earnings and dividends of these companies are usually secure and stable, even during recessionary periods. For instance, American Telephone and Telegraph has paid a dividend in every year since 1881.[16]

Stocks of many unregulated companies are also bought largely for their dividend yield. Many of these companies do not generate a large return on investment, but frequently pay out a large percentage of their earnings in dividends due to a lack of profitable reinvestment opportunities. Stocks of tire and rubber, textile, and steel companies fit in this category. Naturally, the dividends of these companies are not as secure as those of public utilities.

Combined Return Stocks Stock categories are not necessarily mutually exclusive. Some investors feel that certain stocks possess the characteristics of both income and growth company securities; that is, they offer *combined return* through dividends and price appreciation. Of course, these stocks usually do not have as high a dividend yield as a strict income stock, nor a rate of earnings growth as rapid as the growth company stock. They offer instead a dividend

[16] While preferred stocks may be classified as income stocks, they are analyzed in later chapters in much the same way as debt instruments.

yield generally considered average to above-average and prospects for earnings growth which are substantial, but not spectacular.

Speculative Stocks The term "speculative stock" is usually associated with the class of stock that is frequently traded for short-term profits or one for which the purchaser is assuming an unusually large amount of risk, hoping to earn a very large return. The purchase of any stock can entail speculation; someone could buy the shares of the highest grade blue chip with the intention of selling the shares the next day for a short-term profit. However, speculative stocks usually refer to those stocks that are generally considered to be outright gambles.

Included in this category are a number of "high flying" emerging growth company stocks which have been significantly bid up in price by feverish trading and conjecture over prospects for phenomenal success. Prices of these stocks generally rise to large multiples of their current earnings per share relative to the market average, even though there is little evidence that they can attain the high level of superior performance necessary to support such prices. Many investors purchase these shares not because the price represents a reasonable valuation of the stock's prospects, but because they feel the price will go even higher during the period of speculative trading.

Other speculative stocks include "hot" new issues of companies in glamorous fields, offering plans for the introduction of a new product or service that could fuel rapid earnings growth. These stocks may also rise substantially in price, even though the companies have no record of past performance and have an uncertain future.

Finally, there are stocks in the so-called "penny stock market"—shares of little-known mining or oil companies. Penny stocks are commonly promoted and sold by dealers over the phone or by mail. They pay a few hundred or thousand dollars for a piece of property near a producing mine or oil field and then sell many times the amount of the original purchase in stock to the public for less than $1 a share, usually under the pretext that a rich body of natural resources has been found and that capital is needed for development. Frequently, little of the investors' money is ever used for development, and the stocks eventually become worthless. Nevertheless, investors frequently forgo the safety of their principal in the hope that their speculation in these securities will become profitable.

Other Investment Alternatives

Thus far, we have surveyed various forms of bonds and stocks. We will now briefly survey warrants, rights, and stock options, all of which are considered sophisticated investment instruments. A detailed analysis of these instruments will be undertaken in Chapters 17 and 18.

Warrants and Rights

Broadly speaking, warrants and rights are closely related to stocks and bonds. They neither represent ownership in the issuing company, nor are they a form of debt; they only represent the privilege of purchasing a specified corporate security at a particular price within a specified limit of time. Ownership of these instruments, however, is somewhat episodic rather than of continuous interest.

Warrants

Warrants allow the holder to purchase a corporate security—usually common stock—at a given price within a specified period of time. This time period may be finite or indefinite. A company may issue warrants to shareholders or creditors when a new stock or bond issue is released as an inducement to purchase these securities. Warrants may be traded on the stock exchanges after the security has been issued.[17]

Rights

Rights differ from warrants in one important respect: Unlike warrants, rights have short expiration dates, generally extending between two to ten weeks. Rights to purchase common stock are often given to shareholders when additional stock is issued. Shareholders are then entitled to purchase more stock in proportion to their current holdings in order to maintain their existing percentage equity in the firm. Depending on the particular issue, rights may or may not be traded by the original owner in a secondary market.

Stock Options

Stock options are contracts that can be used to buy or sell stock. There are two types of options: calls and puts. A *call option* allows the holder to purchase 100 shares of stock at a given price within a specified period of time, usually three to nine months. Unlike warrants or rights, call options are not issued by the company, but are written—or sold—by other investors who contract to deliver the shares to the option holders if the options are exercised.

A *put option* allows the holder to sell 100 shares of a stock at a given price within a specified period of time. Whereas a call option is purchased by an investor who expects the stock price to rise before the option expires, a put option is purchased by an investor who foresees a decline in the stock's price.

[17] In some cases, warrants are nondetachable, except upon exercise or possibly the maturity of the bond. In other cases, the warrants are detachable and may be traded separately.

Options are traded for either speculative or conservative purposes; these instruments will be discussed more fully in Chapter 18.

The Investors

An Overview

Investors who deal in the various investment instruments can be conveniently discussed as either individuals or institutions.

The category of individual investors is quite broad; it includes millions of people across the country with a wide range of characteristics. Table 2–1, which summarizes information concerning stock ownership and characteristics of

Table 2–1 **Stock Ownership—Characteristics of Shareowners: 1959 to 1975**

(In thousands of persons. Includes outlying areas, most members of the Armed Forces, citizens living abroad, and minor children. Represents all publicly owned issues of common and preferred stocks. Based on national probability samples; see source for detailed explanation.)

Characteristic	1959	1965	1970	1975	Characteristic	1959	1965	1970	1975
Total*	**12,490**	**20,120**	**30,850**	**25,270**	**Income:**				
					Under $5,000	3,575	3,183	2,577	841
Male	5,740	9,060	15,689	12,698	$5,000–$7,999	3,700	4,479	3,081	1,378
Female	6,347	9,430	15,161	12,508	$8,000–$9,999	2,221	3,113	3,152	1,462
Age:					$10,000–$14,999	1,769	5,199	9,001	4,906
Under 21 years	197	1,280	2,221	1,818	$15,000–$24,999	700	2,649	8,272	9,461
21–34 years	2,444	2,626	4,500	2,838	$25,000 and over	319	1,147	4,437	7,158
35–44 years	2,064	4,216	5,801	3,976					
45–54 years	2,800	4,752	7,556	5,675	**Residence by**				
55–64 years	2,666	3,549	6,084	5,099	**SMSA size:**‡				
65 years and over	2,113	3,347	4,330	5,800	Under 100,000	(NA)	134	175	328
					100,000–249,000	(NA)	1,254	2,245	2,059
Education:					250,000–499,999	(NA)	1,897	2,686	2,691
High school:†									
3 years or less	2,804	3,106	3,566	1,621	500,000–999,999	(NA)	2,156	3,712	3,257
4 years	3,130	5,344	8,697	6,580	1,000,000 and over	(NA)	9,883	14,881	11,893
College:†									
1–3 years	2,587	4,012	5,867	5,301	Nonmetropolitan				
4 years or more	3,566	6,028	9,999	9,886	areas	(NA)	4,639	6,913	4,978
Minors**	197	1,280	2,221	1,818					

NA—Not available.
* Includes small number of shareowners not distributed by breakdown. † Persons 21 years old and over.
** Shareowners whose stockholdings are registered in accordance with the Gifts to Minor Statutes.
‡ SMSA = Standard metropolitan statistical area.

SOURCE: U.S. Bureau of the Census, *Statistical Abstract of the United States, 1978* (99th Edition), Washington, D.C.: GPO, 1978, p. 551. Based on New York Stock Exchange, Inc., "Census of Shareholders."

shareowners, provides an overview of the diversity among investors.[18] In 1975 there were over 25 million stockholders as compared to less than 13 million in 1959. The table reveals that individual investors fall in varied age and income groups, have a wide range of educational background, and reside in cities of different sizes. Not captured by this table are the facts that investors also differ from one another with respect to their individual risk preferences, the amounts they commit, and the types of securities in which they invest.

Unlike that for individual investors, information on institutional investors is more difficult to obtain; therefore, they are less well understood than individual investors. In the aggregate, institutions hold a majority of existing bonds and a large percentage of the outstanding stocks. The larger institutional securities portfolios are worth billions of dollars. This group of investors has clearly become a powerful force in the financial markets.

Today, a variety of institutional investors operates in the market. The primary objective of commercial banks and property liability companies is to earn a return for their shareholders or owners. Other institutions—like trust funds, pension funds, investment companies and life insurance companies—invest and manage the resources of individuals. Acting as intermediaries, these institutions allow more than 100 million Americans to indirectly own securities. It is important to note that many institutional investors, particularly those functioning as intermediaries, operate according to strictly defined objectives; their investment policies are often governed by legal contracts and government regulations.

A Closer Look

A brief examination of bondholders and stockholders will give a better understanding of the investors in the financial markets and a clearer picture of the investment environment.[19]

Bondholders

Table 2–2A presents the ownership of corporate bonds by different sectors of the U.S. economy.[20] The net annual increases in securities holdings are shown for the years 1974 through 1979, with the amounts of securities outstanding for the various investors listed in the last column. Note that individual investors, listed as "Household Direct," own a sizable portion of the total outstanding bonds. However, the market is clearly dominated by institutions, because they

[18] Although the information in this table is dated, it still illustrates the diversity of investor backgrounds. It should also be noted that all individual investors are not included here, only stockholders.

[19] This examination will primarily cover capital market investments. Investors in money market investments were discussed earlier in the chapter.

[20] Table 2–2A also includes foreign bonds, which were not discussed in this chapter. However, because they account for only $44.6 billion of the estimated $475.6 billion total bonds outstanding at the end of 1979, the figures are largely representative of domestic corporate bond ownership.

Table 2–2A **Domestic Corporate & Foreign Bonds Sold in U.S. (billons of dollars)**

	Annual Net Increases in Amounts Outstanding						Amt. Out.
	1974	1975	1976	1977	1978	1979[E]	31 Dec 79
Ownership							
Mutual Savings Banks	0.8	3.5	2.8	1.1	0.1	−0.9	20.7
Life Insurance Companies	4.0	9.1	16.9	18.6	17.0	15.3	173.6
Property Liability Companies	2.0	2.2	3.9	3.6	3.2	3.3	26.1
Private Noninsured Pension Funds	4.7	2.8	1.3	6.5	8.2	6.0	59.8
State & Local Retirement Funds	7.0	4.1	3.3	4.0	5.4	5.8	87.2
Foundations & Endowments	0.7	0.8	0.7	0.6	0.7	0.6	14.1
Taxable Investment Funds	−0.4	1.0	2.2	1.1	−0.9	0.8	6.4
Security Brokers & Dealers	−0.1	0.2	0.5	−0.1	−0.1	0.0	0.4
Total Nonbank Institutions	18.7	23.7	31.6	35.4	33.6	30.9	388.3
Commercial Banks	1.0	1.8	−0.6	−0.3	−0.6	0.5	6.9
Foreign	1.4	1.6	0.8	1.0	0.6	0.8	8.5
Residual: Households Direct	8.0	12.0	7.3	1.3	−0.1	0.6	71.9
Total Ownership	**29.1**	**39.1**	**39.1**	**37.4**	**33.5**	**32.8**	**475.6**

E—Estimate

See source, Table 2–2B.

purchase and hold the majority of securities. Two groups of institutional investors who invest heavily in bonds are life insurance companies and state and local retirement funds. In 1979 their holdings amounted to $173.6 and $87.2 billion, respectively.

Life insurance companies guarantee a fixed rate of return to their policyholders on that portion of their premiums accumulated to build up the cash value of the policies.[21] Life insurance companies frequently invest these premiums, or reserves, in long-term corporate bonds. State regulations limit the investment activities of these institutions in order to protect the funds of the policyholders. By law, life insurance companies are allowed to invest only in better quality fixed income securities and a small amount of common stock.[22]

State and local retirement funds are regulated by state laws in order to protect the pension benefits of state and municipal employees. In the case of such retirement funds, amount of equity investments is usually limited;[23] consequently, a large portion of the retirement funds is invested in corporate bonds.

Table 2–2B presents ownership data for municipal bonds issued by state and local governments. Individuals own a sizable portion of these securities,

[21] This does not apply to term insurance policies, for which there are no investment implications involved.

[22] Insurance companies can also invest heavily in real estate mortgages, which are secured loans similar to the mortgage bonds issued by corporations. A common type of real estate mortgage in the United States is the home mortgage, which is a general obligation of the borrower with the home in question pledged as security.

[23] Regulations vary from state to state. In Michigan, for example, state and local retirement funds cannot hold more than 25 percent of their portfolios in stocks.

Table 2–2B **State & Local Securities (billions of dollars)**

	Annual Net Increases in Amounts Outstanding						Amt. Out.
	1974	**1975**	**1976**	**1977**	**1978**	**1979**[E]	**31 Dec 79**
Ownership							
Mutual Savings Banks	0.0	0.6	0.9	0.4	0.5	−0.2	3.1
Savings & Loan Associations	0.3	0.6	0.1	0.1	0.1	0.1	1.4
Life Insurance Companies	0.2	0.8	1.1	0.5	0.4	−0.2	6.2
Property Liability Companies	2.2	2.6	5.4	10.5	11.7	10.0	70.6
State & Local Retirement Funds	−0.6	2.0	1.4	−0.4	−0.3	−0.5	3.0
Municipal Bond Funds	1.1	2.2	3.1	4.4	2.9	3.3	19.7
Security Brokers & Dealers	−0.4	−0.1	0.3	0.2	−0.4	−0.1	0.9
Total Nonbank Finance	2.8	8.7	12.3	15.7	14.9	12.4	104.9
Commercial Banks	5.7	2.4	2.0	9.6	8.4	9.5	131.5
Business Corporations	0.6	−0.2	−1.1	0.0	0.2	0.3	4.0
Residual: Households Direct	5.4	5.4	3.9	5.8	9.4	−0.2	87.6
Total Ownership	**14.5**	**16.3**	**17.1**	**31.1**	**32.9**	**22.0**	**328.0**

E—Estimate

SOURCE: Salomon Brothers, "1980 Prospects for Financial Markets," Dec. 6, 1979, pp. 22, 26.

although institutions dominate the investment scene. Interestingly, among institutional investors, commercial banks and property liability companies hold the largest amounts of these securities.

Property liability companies, also known as fire and casualty insurance companies, differ from life insurance companies and pension funds in that they invest funds that belong to the owners of the company. Consequently, these companies are subject to federal taxation on investment income, which encourages them to invest a large portion of their portfolios in tax-exempt state and local securities. Although property liability companies are subject to state laws that require them to invest a minimum proportion of their investments in high-quality bonds, most of their funds can be invested at their own discretion. Consequently, they tend to hold a larger proportion of their portfolios in stocks than do life insurance companies and state and local retirement funds.

Commercial banks invest in those securities that help them supplement income from their commercial, consumer, and real estate loans, and that provide the liquidity necessary to meet deposits, withdrawals, or increased demand for loans. By law, securities investments of these banks are limited to high-quality debt instruments;[24] consequently, their securities portfolios are almost entirely

[24] Regulations on commercial bank investments are quite complex. For a more detailed discussion, see Reed, et al., *Commercial Banking* (Englewood Cliffs, New Jersey: Prentice-Hall, 1980), pp. 387–97.

Figure 2–1 **Commercial Banks: Distribution of Securities Held (billions of dollars)**

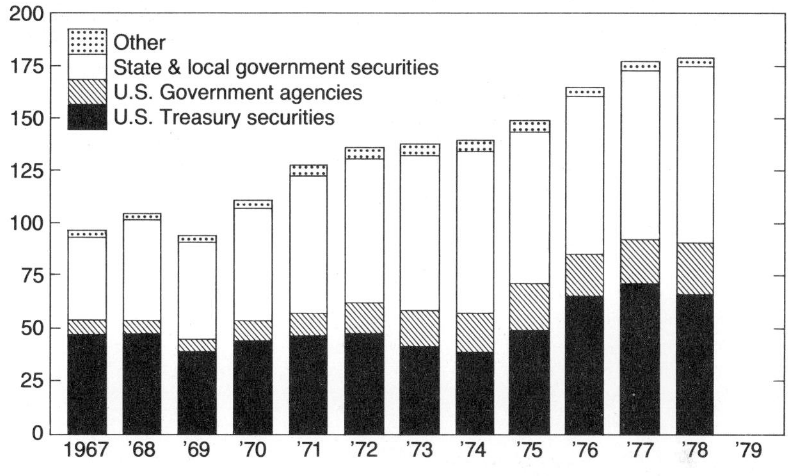

SOURCE: Standard and Poor's *Industry Surveys*, August 23, 1979 (Section 2), p. 825.

comprised of obligations of state and local government, U.S. treasury, and U.S. government agencies, with varying maturities. The distribution of securities held by commercial banks for the years 1967 through 1978 is shown in Figure 2–1. As is the case for property liability companies, the incomes of commercial banks are subject to federal income tax. A large portion of funds invested in state and local government securities, however, earns tax-free income for these banks. Furthermore, because these securities are highly marketable, investments in them remain liquid.

A few conclusions can be made regarding investors in U.S. treasury and U.S. government agency securities. The ownership of U.S. treasury debt, including treasury bills, is spread among almost all types of investors; however, about 85 percent of these holdings are owned, in the order of their importance, by individuals, foreigners, commercial banks, and state and local governments.[25] Furthermore, individuals and commercial banks hold approximately 50 percent of the outstanding U.S. government agency debt. Savings and loan associations, mutual savings banks, and pension funds also have substantial holdings in these instruments.[26]

[25] As described here, ownership does not include holdings of U.S. trust funds, federal agencies, or federal reserve banks.

[26] At the end of 1979 total privately held U.S. treasury debt outstanding was estimated to be over $530 billion; privately held federal agency debt outstanding was estimated at over $220 billion. These estimates and other figures used in this paragraph are taken from the 1980 *Prospects for Financial Markets* (New York: Solomon Brothers, December 6, 1979), pp. 27–28.

Table 2–3 **Market Value of Stockholdings of Institutional Investors and Others (billions of dollars, end of year)**

	1971	1972	1973	1974	1975	1976	1977	1978
1. Private Noninsured Pension Funds	88.7	115.2	90.5	63.3	88.6	109.7	101.9	107.9
2. Open-end Investment Companies	52.6	58.0	43.3	30.3	38.7	43.0	36.2	34.1
3. Other Investment Companies	6.9	7.4	6.6	4.7	5.3	5.9	3.1	2.7
4. Life Insurance Companies	20.6	26.8	25.9	21.9	23.1	34.2	32.9	35.5
5. Property–Liability Insurance Co's	16.6	21.8	19.7	12.8	14.2	16.9	17.1	19.4
6. Personal Trust Funds*	94.1	110.2	94.7	67.7	31.0	93.0	90.5	93.1
7. Common Trust Funds*	5.8	7.4	6.6	4.3	5.9	7.8	N.A.	N.A.
8. Mutual Savings Banks	3.5	4.5	4.2	3.7	4.4	4.4	4.8	4.8
9. State and Local Retirement Funds	15.4	22.2	20.2	20.3	24.3	30.1	30.0	33.3
10. Foundations	25.0	28.5	24.5	18.4	22.7	27.1	26.1	27.0
11. Educational Endowments	9.0	10.7	9.6	6.7	8.8	10.4	9.8	10.2
12. Subtotal	338.2	412.7	345.8	254.1	322.0	382.5	352.4	368.0
13. Less: Institutional Holdings of Investment Company Shares	5.8	6.5	6.7	6.5	8.6	10.0	10.5	10.3
14. *Total Institutional Investors*	332.4	406.2	339.1	247.6	313.4	372.5	341.9	357.7
15. Foreign Investors†	32.9	41.3	37.0	28.4	52.6	63.9	60.1	64.7
16. *Other Domestic Investors***	638.4	690.6	525.3	365.7	483.5	623.3	593.0	618.6
17. *Total Stock Outstanding*‡	1003.7	1138.1	901.4	641.7	849.5	1059.7	995.0	1041.0

* Data for years through 1976 exclude common trust fund holdings which were separately available. Common trust data were not separately available after 1976 and personal trust fund data therefore include assets held in these comingled funds.

† Includes estimate of stock held as direct investment.

** Computed as residual (line 16 = 17 − 14 − 15). Includes both individuals and institutional groups not listed above.

‡ Includes both common and preferred stock. Excludes investment company shares, but includes foreign issues outstanding in the United States.

SOURCE: Securities and Exchange Commission *Statistical Bulletin*, 38 No. 7 (July 1979), p. 16.

Stockholders

Table 2–3 shows the market value of common and preferred stockholdings of institutional and other, primarily individual, investors for the years 1971 through 1978. During this period the market value of individual holdings fluctuated between a high of $690.6 billion in 1972 to a low of $365.7 billion in 1974. Holdings in 1978 were near the high at $620 billion. As a percentage of the total stock outstanding, the holdings of individuals ranged between 57 and 64 percent during the same period. Although individuals hold a majority of stocks in the United States, their percentage of ownership has declined significantly since the 1950s when institutions started to become progressively more dominant in the stock market. This point will be elaborated further in Chapter 3.

The first eleven lines of Table 2–3 show the stockholdings of the eleven major categories of institutional investors. The holdings of this group (line 14) ranged from a high of $406.2 billion in 1972 to a low of $247.6 billion in 1974; group holdings amounted to nearly $360 billion at the end of 1978. Note that there are significant holdings by several institutions, including life insurance companies, property-liability insurance companies, and state and local retirement funds. Investment companies—both open-end (mutual funds) and others—held $36.8 billion in stocks at the end of 1978, of which $26.5 billion was invested with funds provided by individuals who purchased investment company shares.[27] Investment companies also held corporate and municipal bonds, as shown in Table 2–2. The role of investment companies, which act as investment intermediaries, will be discussed in detail in Chapter 15.

A fresh look at Table 2–3 shows that the dominant institutions in stocks are private noninsured pension funds and personal trust funds. At the end of 1978, personal trust funds held over $93 billion in stocks. These funds are administered by trustees, usually bank trust departments, which hold the securities for individuals. The investment policies of trust funds are either specified by the creators of the trusts or are governed by law.

Private noninsured pension funds, holding nearly $108 billion in stock at the end of 1978, have been the driving force behind the institutions emerging as dominant factors in the investment field. These funds are established by American businesses to provide workers with retirement programs in order to safeguard their financial future in their old age.[28] The assets of pension funds have increased dramatically since the 1950s, as both the benefits and the proportion of the labor force eligible for benefits have greatly expanded. Today private noninsured pension funds constitute the largest single source of demand for common stocks.

Business corporations often employ commercial banks or trust companies to manage their pension funds. Generally, these funds formulate less rigid investment policies than those of life insurance companies or state and local retirement funds. As a result, noninsured private pension funds hold a much larger proportion of stocks in their portfolios than those held by insurance companies and retirement funds. In 1974, the Employee Retirement Income Security Act (ERISA) was passed to protect the future pension rights of workers covered by private plans. This act sets forth a prudent-man standard that must be observed in the investment of private retirement fund assets. Basically, the act obligates trustees and administrators to use good judgment and diligence in making investments with regard to the maintenance of the safety of the principal and the generation of income; that is, trustees and administrators formulate investment policies that are neither too conservative nor too risky. Of course, the language of the act is not specific, so the actual requirements of the law are open to individual interpretation.

---

[27] Of the $36.8 billion in stocks held by investment companies, $10.3 billion was invested with funds from other institutional investors; see line 13 in the table.

[28] There are also insured pension funds, which are guaranteed by life insurance companies.

Summary

In the *money market*, investment alternatives consist of debt instruments that have maturities of under one year, with the majority maturing within 90 days. Because they are issued by obligors with highest credit ratings, these instruments are generally close substitutes for one another. Purchasers of money market instruments primarily comprise large investors, because the minimum investment requirements are fairly high. Of course, smaller investors can also participate in this market by purchasing shares of money market funds.

Capital market investment alternatives include debt instruments with maturities of over one year, and equities, which theoretically have no maturity. Capital market securities offer investors the opportunity to commit funds for longer periods and assume greater risks than those offered by money market instruments.

Bonds are one kind of capital market investment. There are three main issuers of bonds—the federal government, state and local municipalities, and corporations. *Federal government securities* are backed by the full faith and credit of the United States and are considered perfectly safe. *Municipal bond* interest payments are exempt from federal taxes, with interest and principal payments secured by either a general obligation of the issuing governmental unit (state, city, county, and so on) or from the income generated by the issuing governmental unit or project. There are several types of *corporate bonds*, distinguishable by special features, privileges, and the types of security pledged against interest and principal payments.

Capital stock represents ownership in the issuing company. Corporations issue two types of capital stock—common and preferred. Owners of *preferred stock* receive a fixed dividend which must be paid before any dividends are paid to common stockholders. The dividend paid on common shares varies with the performance of the company and the amount of cash the company has on hand.

Common stock is described and analyzed according to its investment qualities—that is, the characteristics it offers in terms of expected return, risk, and possibly some other dimensions. Investors make evaluations of these characteristics and group them according to such traditional classifications as *blue chips*, *growth company stocks*, *income stocks*, and so on. A more precise evaluation of risk and returns associated with common stocks is discussed in Chapter 5.

There are several types of investors who participate in the securities markets. Basically, they fall in two broad categories: individuals and institutions. *Individual investors* includes millions of people with a broad range of backgrounds, investment objectives, risk preferences, and amounts to invest.

Institutional investors hold a majority of bonds and a large portion of the outstanding stock in the United States. Larger institutional portfolios are valued at billions of dollars. Some institutions invest primarily to earn income for their shareholders or owners. Others invest and manage the resources of individuals, thus acting as intermediaries. Many institutional investors operate according to strictly defined objectives and government regulations.

A Look Ahead

This chapter introduced the investment environment through a discussion of various investment alternatives and types of investors. The next chapter analyzes the financial markets in which the investors operate to trade these securities.

Concepts for Review

Money market investment
Treasury bills
Certificates of deposit
Commercial paper
Bankers' acceptances
Repurchase agreements
Capital market investments
Bonds
Federal government securities
Municipal bonds
General obligation bonds
Revenue bonds
Corporate bonds
Secured bonds
Unsecured bonds
Debenture
Sinking fund debenture
Subordinated debenture
Guaranteed bonds
Mortgage bonds
Equipment trust certificates
Convertible bonds
Income bonds
Fixed-charge bonds
Floating rate notes
Annuity or maturity bonds
Callable bonds
Common stock
Preferred stock
Cumulative preferred stock
Convertible preferred stock
Participating preferred stock
Blue chips
Secondary stocks
Growth company stocks
Cyclical company stocks
Income stocks
Combined return stocks
Speculative stocks
Warrants
Rights
Stock options
Individual investors
Institutional investors

Questions for Review

1. Discuss the investment features of money market securities. Who invests in them and why?
2. Investor A desires to earn a rate of return substantially higher than the rate on treasury bills. Would you advise him to invest in other money market instruments?

3. In what general ways do capital market securities differ from money market securities?
4. Compare a corporate bond with a preferred stock in terms of their investment characteristics.
5. What are the advantages and disadvantages of fixed-income securities compared with common stock?
6. The common stock of ABC Corporation is selling for $20 per share and paying a $2 annual dividend. The common stock of XYZ Corporation is also selling for $20, but paying only a $1 annual dividend. Would you consider ABC stock to be a better investment based on this information?
7. Other things being equal, would you prefer to purchase a preferred stock or a cumulative preferred stock? Why?
8. Comment on the following statement: "All bonds are safe instruments because interest and principal payments are promised."
9. Can a blue chip stock also be the stock of a cyclical company? Explain.
10. Explain any similarities or dissimilarities between warrants and stock options.
11. The preferred stock of ABC Corporation is selling for $20 per share and paying a $2.25 per share annual dividend. The common stock of ABC Corporation is also selling for $20 per share and currently paying a $2 per share annual dividend. Investor Q is interested in maximizing her dividend income over the next five years. Would you recommend the preferred stock? What considerations would you make?
12. Why do life insurance companies and state and local retirement funds invest heavily in corporate bonds?
13. In what ways might the investment objectives of individuals and institutional investors differ?
14. Commercial banks hold a large portion of the outstanding U.S. treasury and U.S. government agency debt. Why?
15. What governs the investment policies and securities selection of private noninsured pension funds? Why do these funds invest a larger portion of their portfolios in stocks than life insurance companies?

Selected Readings

Ascher, Leonard W. "Selected Bonds for Capital Gains." *Financial Analysts Journal*, March–April 1971.

Atkinson, Thomas R. *Trends in Corporate Bond Quality*. National Bureau of Economic Research. New York: Columbia University Press, 1967.

"Back from the Dead?" *Forbes*, September 17, 1979.

Barker, C. Austin. "Effective Stock Splits." *Harvard Business Review*, January–February 1956.

Barker, C. Austin. "Stock Splits in a Bull Market." *Harvard Business Review*, May–June 1957.

Bildersee, John S. "Some Aspects of the Performance of Non-Convertible Preferred Stocks." *Journal of Finance*, December 1973.

Clendenin, J. C. and George A. Christy. *Introduction to Investments*, 5th ed. New York: McGraw-Hill, 1969.

Cook, Timothy Q., ed. *Instruments of the Money Market*, 4th ed. Richmond: Federal Reserve Bank of Richmond, 1977.

Darst, David M. *The Complete Bond Book*. New York: McGraw-Hill, 1975.

DuBois, Peter C. "Hot-and-Cold Issues." *Barron's*, July 19, 1976.

Ederington, L. H. "The Yield Spread of New Issues of Corporate Bonds." *Journal of Finance*, December 1974.

Fisher, Lawrence and James H. Lorie. "Rates of Return on Investments in Common Stock: The Year-by-Year Record, 1926–1965." *Journal of Business*, July 1968.

Harris, John T. "A Comparison of Long-Term Deep Discount and Current Coupon Bonds." *Financial Analysts Journal*, July–August 1968.

Ibbotson, Roger G. and Rex A. Sinquefield. "Stocks, Bonds, Bills and Inflation: Year-by-Year Historical Returns (1926–1974)." *Journal of Business*, January 1976.

Jen, Frank C. and James E. Wert. "The Effects of Sinking Fund Provisions on Corporate Bond Yields." *Financial Analysts Journal*, March–April 1967.

Jen, Frank C. and James Wert. "The Effects of Call Risk on Corporate Bond Yields." *Journal of Finance*, December 1967.

Reed, Cotter, Gill, and Smith. *Commercial Banking*. Englewood Cliffs, N.J.: Prentice-Hall, 1980.

Reilly, Frank K. "A Differentiation Between Types of Companies and Types of Stock." *Mississippi Valley Journal of Business and Economics*, Fall 1971.

Reilly, Frank K. "Further Evidence on Short-Run Results for New Issue Investors." *Journal of Financial and Quantitative Analysis*, January 1973.

Sharpe, William F. and Guy M. Cooper. "Risk–Return Classes of New York Stock Exchange Common Stocks." *Financial Analysts Journal*, March–April 1972.

Van Horne, J. C. "New Listings and Their Price Behavior." *Journal of Finance*, September 1970.

Weston, J. F. and E. Brigham. *Managerial Finance*, 4th ed. New York: Holt, 1972.

Securities Markets: Purposes and Operation

Introduction

An introduction to the securities markets and investment environment must be based on an understanding of the mechanical process by which an investor's preference for a particular stock or bond is related to competitive bidding and the eventual execution of an order to buy or sell a security as well as an appreciation of the important role that holders of stocks and bonds play in our economy.

To help foster such an understanding, this chapter comprises (1) an overview of financial markets in the United States; (2) an analysis of the functions of primary money and capital markets in general and those of the secondary markets for stocks and bonds in particular; (3) a comprehensive discussion of the trading activity and operations that help establish market prices and execute orders; and (4) an outline of recent trends in security market operations.

Financial Markets

American enterprise has been built at a cost of billions of dollars. Tremendous investments in plants, machines, and tools have enabled the U.S. economy to produce more goods and services than any other nation in the world. The financial markets play a vital role in this capitalistic system, providing both the private and public sectors with a marketplace for securities and thereby facilitating efforts to raise money for operations and expansion. Clearly, if there were no marketplace where the public could easily invest money or sell securities for cash, the financing of economic growth in this country would be severely restricted. In addition, financial markets serve a more important purpose in that they allow public investment funds to flow freely from one enterprise to another, thereby allocating capital to the most efficient producers and, in turn, providing a means through which private individuals can share the risks and rewards of the free enterprise system. A brief review of the *primary* and *secondary* markets will lay the groundwork for a more detailed discussion of the stock and bond markets.

The Primary Markets

The *primary markets* provide users of capital with a *direct* means of obtaining funds. For instance, a corporation might finance a *real* investment (such as the construction of a new plant, the purchase of new equipment or inventory, or the financing of a project that would increase its productivity) by issuing new stock or bonds to investors. The purchasers of the newly issued stocks or bonds make

---

Investment Banking

Investment banking businesses are involved in the distribution of new issues and securities in the capital market. The term "banking" may be misleading in that it suggests the function of deposit. Investment banks are not permitted to engage in deposit banking. In fact, investment banking firms are usually brokerage houses that act alone or as a group called a "syndicate." They function as intermediaries in the capital market by seeking buyers for securities being offered for sale.

Suppose a company decides to sell a large amount of stocks or bonds. An investment bank will be asked to analyze the issue and determine a price for the securities to be paid to the issuing company. An investment bank may also help decide the timing of the sale and the size of the issue, as well as handle other administrative duties associated with the sale. The price is determined by studying potential market demand for the security, the financial condition of the company, and other factors. After a price has been set, the investment bank will market the security by following one of two methods.

In the first method, the bank acts as a *principal* in the transaction. The investment banker underwrites the issue, or guarantees that the issuing company will receive the full agreed-upon price on a given date, even if the issue cannot be sold at that time. In this situation the investment bank, or underwriter, assumes the risk because it actually purchases the security with hopes of reselling the issue to the public at a profit. It is possible that the underwriter will misjudge the market and be forced to sell the securities at a price lower than originally estimated.

The price that the underwriter agrees to pay the issuer can be arrived at in one of two ways. The issuer might consult with one or more underwriters who agree to handle the sale, ultimately arriving at a price through *negotiation*. Alternatively, the

a *financial* investment in expectation of receiving a larger sum in the future. Clearly, these financial investments make it possible for corporations to undertake real investment.

Users of capital obtain cash from investors in two ways. Funds needed only for the short term are acquired in the *money market*, whereas long-term funds are obtained in the *capital market*. Because these markets differ significantly, it is appropriate to discuss them separately.

The Money Market

The *money market* trades in short-term, highly liquid, negotiable debt instruments of one year or less in maturity. Borrowers in the market include corporations, financial institutions, and governments. Money market debt instruments—treasury bills, bankers' acceptances, commercial paper, and certificates of deposit—were introduced and briefly described in Chapter 2.

Suppliers of funds in the money market include almost every type of financial institution in the economy. The major participants are commercial banks, state and local governments, large nonfinancial businesses, and nonbank financial intermediaries, such as insurance companies and pension funds. Foreign banks

issuer might solicit *competitive bidding* by two or more underwriters. In the latter case, the issuer establishes all terms of the issue except price, and announces that bids will be accepted until a given date. The underwriting syndicate offering the best price will be accepted, and he will then resell the issue to the public. Interestingly, although some issuers can frequently secure a better price through competitive bidding, they prefer a negotiated price because the latter process is faster and therefore allows the securities to be sold sooner.

Usually more than one underwriter is involved in an offering. The actual number depends on such factors as the size of the issue, the number of potential purchasers, and the estimated risk associated with the purchase and sale of the issue. The process begins with the formation of an *underwriting syndicate*, which is a temporary joint venture of a number of underwriters, each agreeing to underwrite a specified portion of the total issue. In 1979, over 225 underwriters led by Merrill Lynch and Salomon Brothers participated in the $1 billion public offering of IBM bonds, the largest public borrowing in U.S. corporate history.

After the security has been priced and selling begins, the underwriters may sell the issue themselves, sell some of the securities to other brokers at a wholesale price, or invite additional brokers and dealers to form a *selling syndicate* in order to complete the selling process.

In the second method, investment bankers act solely as *selling agents*, engaging in what is commonly called a "best efforts" offering. In this case, rather than purchasing an issue and reselling it at a profit, investment bankers commit themselves to merely finding prospective buyers for the issue. For this service investment bankers are paid a fee.

and nonbank businesses, however, have become increasingly important suppliers of funds.

Although the money market is centered in New York, it is primarily a "telephone" market, easily accessible from all parts of the nation. This market is composed of numerous "money market banks," including large banks in New York and other important financial centers. There are approximately 34 primary government securities dealers, a dozen odd commercial paper dealers, a few bankers' acceptance dealers, and several money brokers who specialize in locating short-term funds for money market borrowers and placing such funds for money market lenders.[1]

The Capital Market

In contrast to the money market, which brings together borrowers and lenders of short-term funds, the *capital market* facilitates long-term financial arrangements. In this market, there are two broad categories of issuers of new securities —corporations and governments; the different types of stocks and bonds they issue were discussed in Chapter 2. This market also includes the sale of real estate mortgages. Individuals, for instance, raise billions of dollars to finance new home purchases by issuing residential mortgages to banks and other financial institutions.

Corporations, state and local governments, and federal government agencies distribute to investors large amounts of new securities through intermediaries serving as *investment banks.* These banks may sell the securities of a company to the public, or assist in the placing of an issue directly with a large institutional investor (private placement). The federal government usually distributes its securities directly to investors through either the Federal Reserve System or the commercial banks.

Exactly where are these capital markets located? The center for the national capital market is in New York, although other major cities also act as important marketplaces. In fact, the capital markets are multifaceted. They can be national or regional in scope. A large fraction of all financial claims in the United States enjoys a broad market: Securities issued by the best-known corporations, the federal government, certain state governments, and other large investment companies can be sold to investors across the country.

The capital market can be—and frequently is—regional in scope, as is usually the case when a small company or city issues a financial claim. Technically, the capital market may even exist within a small town, as is the case when an individual secures a mortgage loan at a local bank.

The Secondary Markets

After securities are issued and purchased in the primary markets, the *secondary markets* provide a mechanism for their systematic transfer of ownership. The primary function of secondary markets is to facilitate the trading of securities

[1] See James Parthemos, "The Money Market," *Instruments of the Money Market*, ed. Timothy Q. Cook, Federal Reserve Bank of Richmond, 1977, p. 6.

among investors. Because investors would undoubtedly be reluctant to purchase new securities if they could not sell them on short notice, the existence of secondary markets is essential for the successful operation of the primary markets.

There are two broad categories of secondary markets. Large, active, *organized exchanges* provide physical marketplaces for trading in existing securities; *over-the-counter markets* provide a medium for the resale of the financial claims between investors. The remainder of this chapter will be devoted to a discussion of the activities and importance of the stock and bond markets.

Secondary Markets: Stocks

Functions of the Stock Markets

In the United States, the secondary markets for corporate equities perform two important functions. First, because the stock markets in this country are large and well organized, they can absorb and quickly execute a large volume of buying and selling with reasonable price changes. This characteristic provides *liquidity* for corporate equity investments; that is, it enables investors to buy or sell a stock for cash at a price not significantly different from that of the last transaction in that stock. At any given moment a stockholder can decide to buy or sell a security, inform his broker of his decision by phone, and have his order executed within minutes around the current market price. (Contrast this with a decision to sell a house, and you will get a clear picture of the efficiency of the stock market.) Second, the existence of secondary markets encourages potential savers to invest in new and outstanding corporate stock, thereby facilitating the process of real capital investment.

However, the primary economic function of the stock market lies elsewhere. As this secondary market evaluates the issued shares of different firms, it facilitates the flow of capital to those companies with superior performance, and simultaneously disciplines poorly managed firms. The primary function of the stock market is not the creation, but the *allocation* of capital.

Exactly how does the stock market allocate capital? Investors, or stock traders, try to outguess each other about which companies have the most promising prospects—that is, which firms are most likely to produce those goods or services that will earn for them the most profit in the future. Their estimates and projections translate into varying demands for different companies' stocks. The demand for stock can be measured by the ratio of the stock price to earnings—the price/earnings or P/E ratio. A high P/E ratio indicates that investors are optimistic about the future of the company. Consequently, companies with high P/E ratios not only can issue new stock in the primary market more easily, but may even find it easier to borrow money from banks. The stock market's valuation of firms and industries also gives corporate managers an indication of where they might most profitably invest their own retained earnings in order to brighten the future of their own stock.

For example, in 1978 stocks of companies in the gambling industry—such as Resorts International, Caesars World, and Bally Manufacturing—were highly valued by Wall Street. The P/E ratios of gambling company stocks increased dramatically. As a result, these companies found it easier to secure bank debt and issue new stock to finance the construction of casinos in Atlantic City. Other companies, like Ramada Inns and Playboy, were influenced by the stock market's favorable valuation of the gambling industry and decided to invest in this area. Thus, the stock market helped allocate capital to promising new ventures, and undoubtedly took it away from other industries.

At this point, it is apropos to answer two important questions: (1) Is the stock market correct in its appraisal of the prospects for different companies? and (2) Is the P/E ratio of a stock—or an industry—an accurate measure of its intrinsic value? To make the *best* valuation possible, the stock market must be able to process the buy and sell orders of investors efficiently so that the price of a stock at any given time accurately reflects all available information about the company. In other words, it must be what economists call an *efficient market*. This chapter explains *how* the stock market processes the buy and sell orders of investors to determine stock prices. In subsequent chapters, a related question will be raised: Although a stock price may reflect the aggregate information and preferences of investors, is this price a correct valuation of the underlying company? That is, at any given time, does the stock price reflect *all* of the information publicly available about a company?

Stock Market Trading

However preposterous it may appear, trading activities in the securities markets can be profitably compared with the transactions that take place in such primitive goods markets as, say, the Floating Market of Bangkok. The floating market, where all kinds of consumer goods are bought and sold from boats, is one of the most unsophisticated bazaars imaginable. Although this market appears to be a jungle of assorted goods of every conceivable quality, order is maintained and goods are exchanged to the satisfaction of both buyers and sellers.

Imagine that you are in Bangkok and want to buy a commodity, say, coconuts. First, you try to identify and signal to the boat carrying coconuts. When the boat approaches, you evaluate the product and estimate its value. Then you ask the seller his price and, no matter what he demands, you counter with a lower offer. You have laid the foundation for a bargaining process which, as the mutual strengths and weaknesses of both buyer and seller are tested, will eventually lead to an amicable agreement on a fair price for coconuts. Note that the product is not a standard one and that neither you nor the seller is compelled to make this exchange. Yet, when the exchange takes place, both you and the seller are satisfied that a fair bargain has been struck.

The operations in the stock markets are similar to those that take place in the floating market. On the various stock markets are traded thousands of issues, each of them unique because no two companies are alike. Yet, on our nation's stock exchanges and in the over-the-counter market—a sophisticated trading network equipped to handle trading in thousands of stocks—*crude bargaining* is still permitted as a means of determining the trading prices.

Trading activity in the stock markets is handled in one of two ways. A *two-way auction market* system governs activity on the New York, American, and several regional stock exchanges; *negotiated trading* controls trading in the over-the-counter market.

The Stock Market: Two-way Auction

The operation of the two-way auction market is unique. It is not like the conventional auction where there is but one seller and only buyers compete. In the two-way market, bidders compete with each other to purchase at the lowest possible price the shares they want to buy. Simultaneously, those seeking to sell compete with each other to get the highest price for the securities they are offering. When the buyers *bidding the highest price* and the sellers *offering the lowest price* agree on a figure, a transaction is made.

A Transaction

Order to Buy

Assume that Bill Wild of Detroit has studied information about AT&T and has analyzed the prospects for the company. On the basis of his analysis, he decides to buy 100 common shares. Wild calls his broker, Mr. Kay, and puts in an order. At that moment, AT&T is quoted at 50 to $\frac{1}{4}$, last at $50\frac{1}{4}$; in other words, the latest *highest bid to buy* AT&T stock is \$50 a share, the *lowest offer to sell* is $50\frac{1}{4}$ a share, and the last transaction in the stock was at $50\frac{1}{4}$. The difference between the highest bid and lowest offer is called the spread.

Kay writes an order to buy 100 shares of AT&T at the market and has it wired to his New York office, where it is phoned or wired to his firm's partner on the floor of the exchange. Each stock is assigned a specific location at one of the 22 trading posts, and all exchanges in that stock must take place at that location. In this particular case, the floor partner moves over to Post 15, where AT&T is traded.

Order to Sell

At this time, Mr. Stan in Dallas decides to sell 100 shares of AT&T. He calls his broker at Creek & Company, asking her to get a "quote" and sell his stock. That order, too, is wired to the floor. Stan's broker also hurries to the post.

As soon as he enters the AT&T "crowd," he hears Wild's broker yelling, "How's Telephone?" Someone—frequently the specialist—answers, "50 to a quarter."

Competitive Bidding

Wild's broker could without further negotiation buy the 100 shares of AT&T offered at $50\frac{1}{4}$, and Stan's broker could sell his 100 at 50. In that event, had their customers been looking on, they probably would have demanded, "Why weren't you able to get a better price for us?" The customers would be right; that is precisely what the broker is expected to do. When brokers enter the "crowd" of a stock on the floor, they apply their skill and knowledge to get the best possible price for their customers.

Here is how Wild's and Stan's brokers might argue the question of price. Wild's broker: "I can't buy my 100 at 50. Someone has already bid 50 and no one will sell at that price. I think I am going to have to bid up the price to $50\frac{1}{8}$." Stan's broker hears Wild's broker bid $50\frac{1}{8}$ and instantly shouts, "Sold 100 at $50\frac{1}{8}$." These brokers have agreed on a price and a transaction has taken place.

Both the Floating Market of Bangkok and the New York Stock Exchange are instances of the auction market in operation. Thousands of times every day, the same kind of bidding is repeated on the floor of the exchange. Individual decisions, based on people's personal opinions and requirements, are translated into orders to buy and sell. These actions send security prices up and down as transactions are completed.

The two-way auction market operates exclusively in many registered stock exchanges across the country. These are the physical marketplaces alluded to earlier. The most famous of these markets is the New York Stock Exchange, followed by the American Stock Exchange and several regional exchanges.

The New York Stock Exchange

An Overview

The *New York Stock Exchange* (*NYSE*) was established in 1792 as the nation's major stock exchange. It is a rather unusual form of enterprise; its purpose is neither to make a profit nor to act as a charitable organization. Rather, it is an incorporated association of brokers formed to provide facilities and services for the execution of customers' orders. Brokers are provided with a building to house trading activities, a trading floor, communications from the floor to offices of member broker–dealers, a ticker and other communications equipment for reporting trades and prices, and regulations for the trading practices of the Exchange members.

Because only stocks listed on the NYSE may be traded on the Exchange floor, less than 2,000 corporations are listed (less than one percent of the thousands of corporations doing business in the United States and abroad). However, the aggregate value of these listed stocks is greater than half the value of all outstanding corporate stock. A company qualifies for listing on the NYSE when it is judged to be established and has good prospects for continued importance in its field.[2] The sales and prices of a NYSE listed stock are reported promptly over a nationwide network of tickers and displays and are published in newspapers. A NYSE listing is valuable because it provides greater familiarity with and marketability for the company's securities, thus making it easier and less costly for the company to sell new securities when additional financing is needed.

Exchange Members

Trading on the NYSE floor is carried out by members who have purchased a seat[3] on the Exchange. There are 1,366 seats, or memberships, available. About 500 of these are held by brokerage firms, also known as commission houses. Through large nationwide networks of offices, orders from customers are transferred to the brokerage firm representatives on the Exchange floor. These representatives, in turn, act as agents for the firm's customers as they buy and sell shares.

About one quarter of all Exchange members are *specialists* who buy and sell the many securities listed for trading. A specialist's primary function is to see that there is no violent fluctuation in the price of any stock handled by him. The specialist usually attempts to ensure that the price "bid" by the buyer and that "asked" by the seller remain approximately $\frac{1}{4}$ of a point apart.

The auction market on the NYSE takes place on a *continuous* basis; that is, buyers and sellers may enter orders at any time during the trading day. At some point during the day, there may be a temporary imbalance of buy and sell orders. In such a situation, the gap between bid and ask quotations

---

[2] Specific requirements for listing on the New York Stock Exchange are as follows:

a. The firm must have 1,000,000 shares held by the general public.
b. At least 2,000 stockholders must own 100 or more shares.
c. The firm must have pretax income of $2,500,000 for the latest fiscal year and pretax income of $2,000,000 for the preceding two years.
d. The aggregate value of publicly held shares must exceed $16,000,000.
e. The firm must have tangible assets of $16,000,000. The company is also expected to issue quarterly and annual reports and to announce publicly anything that might affect the value of the shares.

Once the firm's securities have been listed for trading on the Exchange, the firm must continue to meet the listing requirements. However, the Exchange gives consideration to delisting when (a) the number of shares in the hands of the general public declines to less than 600,000; (b) when the number of stockholders owning at least 100 shares declines to 1,200; (c) when the market value of the shares publicly held falls below $5,000,000; and (d) when the value of tangible assets falls below $8,000,000. See Herbert B. Mayo, *Basic Finance* (Philadelphia: W. B. Saunders Co., 1978), p. 121.

[3] Actually, members do not purchase a seat in the literal sense. This term has been used since the early years when the brokers remained seated while the president of the Exchange called out the list of securities to be traded.

will widen and price fluctuations will be sharper. The specialist needs to control these imbalances and smooth the price movements in his assigned securities, thereby ensuring a "fair and orderly market."

To perform this function, the specialist is given the sole position of "market maker" on the NYSE. He uses *his own funds* to buy stocks offered for sale when there is no public buyer, and he sells shares from *his own account* when no member of the public is willing to sell a particular security sought by other investors. When a specialist trades for his own account—that is, when he buys or sells stock for himself—he acts as a dealer. He has this priority only if his bid price is higher or his offering price is lower than that of any public order on the Exchange. For instance, suppose that XYZ stock was last sold at $35 a share, and that now the lowest offer to sell is $35 a share and $34 is the highest bid. Depending on prevailing market conditions, the specialist might bid 34\frac{5}{8}$ in order to narrow the temporary spread between supply and demand.

In addition to performing the above function, the specialist must also act as a *broker's broker* by "keeping the book" for the stocks in which he specializes. This means that he acts for other brokers who cannot remain at a trading post until the prices specified by their customers' buy and sell orders are reached. The specialist holds these orders in his book; if the market price reaches the customer's order price, the order is executed and the specialist collects a brokerage commission.

The distinction between a dealer and a broker should now be clear. A broker is an agent who bargains on your behalf. A dealer, on the other hand, bargains with you with the primary objective of making a profit as a principal in the transaction, either by selling you securities that he owns himself or by buying securities from you at an agreed price. Because specialists are so constantly involved with buy and sell orders for their stocks, they are presumably better situated than anyone else to anticipate short-term price fluctuations and therefore be able to trade for abnormally high profits. Although specialists are allowed to trade for profit, the Exchange has established strict rules to control their trading activities.[4]

Besides brokerage firms and specialists, there are other members of the NYSE. *Registered traders* use their membership to buy and sell stocks on the Exchange floor for their own accounts. While they trade for their own profit, they provide the market with added liquidity and expedite the handling of large trades. Like those of the specialist, the transactions of registered traders must meet Exchange requirements. Other members are *floor brokers.* They assist the brokerage firms in executing orders; they also complete transactions for outsiders such as banks, over-the-counter houses, and other institutions.

An *odd-lot dealer* serves investors trading only a few shares at a time rather than the conventional *round lot* of 100 shares. The specialist acts as a dealer on the NYSE and other exchanges for *odd-lot* transactions. On the NYSE these orders are processed by computer and are automatically executed at the next round lot price on the trading post. Periodic reports are then sent to the spe-

[4] Broad guidelines for specialist trading can be found in NYSE Rule 104, "Dealings of Specialists."

Table 3–1 **Market Value and Volume of Sales of Stock on United States Securities Exchanges, August 1979**

Stock Exchange	Value (millions of dollars)	Volume (millions of shares)
New York	25,477	908
American	1,750	110
Midwest	1,375	43
Pacific	859	34
Philadelphia	561	19
Boston	183	6
Cincinnati	87	2
Spokane	1	1
Intermountain	*	*

* Less than 0.5 million

SOURCE: Securities and Exchange Commission, *Statistical Bulletin*, Vol. 38, No. 10 (October 1979).

cialist to inform him how many shares have been added to or subtracted from his account. The specialist charges an additional $\frac{1}{8}$ to $\frac{1}{4}$ point per share for this service, known as the "odd-lot differential." Large brokerage firms—most notably Merrill Lynch Pierce Fenner & Smith—also act as dealers for customers' odd-lot trades, though such firms usually eliminate the differential.[5]

The American Stock Exchange and Regional Exchanges

There are other organized stock exchanges beside the NYSE. Table 3–1 provides a list of the U.S. securities exchanges and their share volume and market value of trades for the month of August 1979. The "Big Board," or NYSE, clearly dominates these categories, followed by the American, Midwest, Pacific, and other smaller exchanges.

The functioning of the *American Stock Exchange* (*AMEX*) resembles that of the NYSE in that trades are made in a similar way on both exchanges. However, there is one important difference: The listing requirements for companies on the AMEX are less stringent than those on the NYSE. Because the companies listed on the AMEX are generally less well established, it serves as a proving ground for new, small, or medium-size companies which meet certain basic standards and expect to grow rapidly. Although the AMEX is a small exchange in comparison to the NYSE, trading activity on the AMEX does accelerate when investor interest, particularly among the larger institutions, is incited by many

[5] Prior to January 1976, odd-lot orders were filled by Carlisle, DeCoppet & Company, the solely franchised odd-lot dealer on the NYSE. The firm withdrew from the business in January, however, when some large brokerage firms began to fill odd-lot orders for their own customers.

Figure 3–1

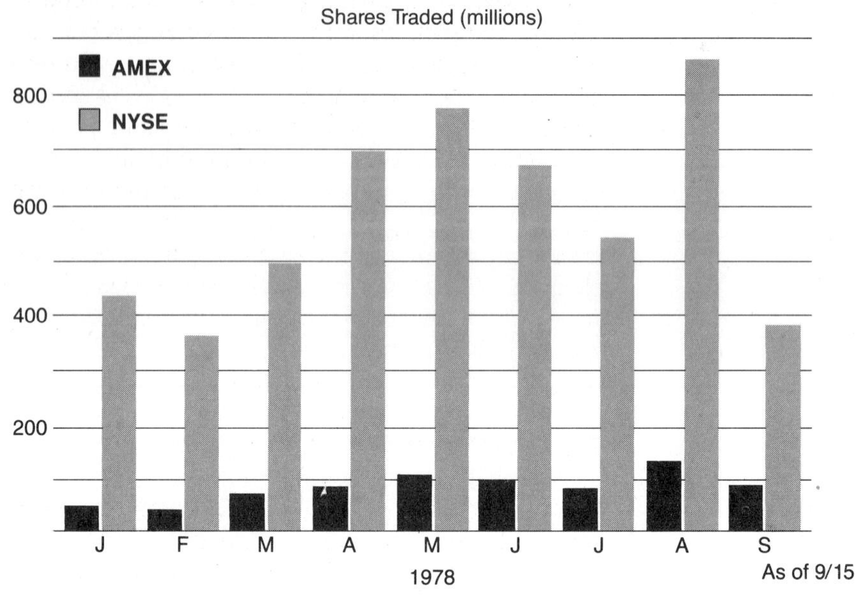

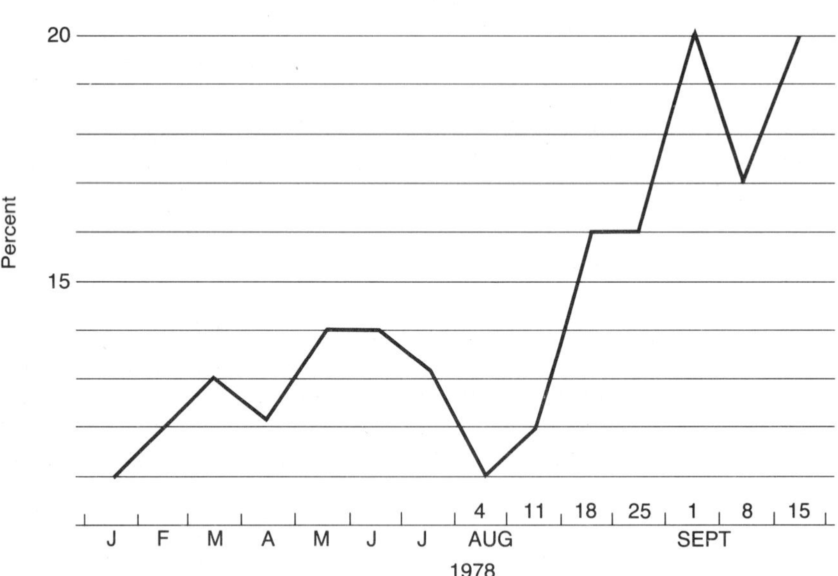

SOURCE: *Forbes*, October 16, 1978, p. 60.

of these smaller companies. During 1978 the ratio of AMEX to NYSE shares traded rose considerably, as depicted in Figure 3–1.

Regional stock exchanges were originally established for the purpose of effecting transactions in local interest stocks, but this is no longer the case. At present, a large majority of the securities traded on regional stock exchanges are also traded on the NYSE. In the early 1970s, institutional trading on regional exchanges in NYSE listed securities became popular as a means of lowering transaction costs on large trades. During this time, the NYSE had a minimum commission rate structure which did not allow institutional investors to receive discounts on many large trades.[6] Moreover, although some of the regional exchanges also had fixed commission rates, these were avoided in many complex ways.[7] However, because the commission rate structure on the NYSE has since been made flexible, much of the comparative advantage of the regional exchanges has now disappeared.[8]

Types of Orders

There are several ways in which an investor can order the purchase or sale of stock in the two-way auction market.

Market Orders

An investor interested in buying or selling a stock immediately orders his broker to buy or sell *at the market*. This is known as a *market order*. The brokerage firm's representative goes to the position on the trading floor where the stock is traded and executes the order at the best obtainable price—either trading with another broker or with the specialist. The investor is certain of execution, but cannot be sure of the price.[9]

Limit Orders

A *limit order* is often placed by investors who wish to buy or sell a stock only if the transaction can be made at a certain price or better. If a *buy-limit order* is entered to buy a stock at $50, it cannot be executed at a price higher than $50. Likewise, a *sell-limit order* cannot be executed below a certain price. In all cases, however, the broker will try to get the best price available on the floor.

---

[6] Steps were taken prior to May 1975 to allow institutional discounts on certain size trades. This will be discussed in later chapters.

[7] These included outright or secret rebates, complicated reciprocal trading arrangements, and even allowing institutional membership on the exchanges.

[8] Regional exchanges still offer some advantages over the NYSE, including lower clearing costs for trades and, in many cases, easier execution of large trades.

[9] Only round-lot orders are handled by this auction market procedure. Odd-lot orders, as explained earlier, are filled by dealers.

For example, suppose a stock is currently quoted at \$25 bid and \$25$\frac{1}{4}$ asked. An investor might place a *limit order to sell* at \$25$\frac{1}{4}$. However, the best price the broker is able to find is a bid of \$25$\frac{1}{8}$. Because the broker cannot execute the order immediately, he may leave it with the specialist who will then enter the limit order in his book. Should market conditions push the price of the security to the desired level, the order to sell would then be executed by the specialist. However, in some instances the stock price could hit \$25$\frac{1}{4}$ and the order might not be executed. Because limit orders are filled in chronological sequence, other orders at the same price on the specialist's book will be filled first and the supply of stock bid at \$25$\frac{1}{4}$ could be exhausted before any given order is executed. Also, the limit order is good only on the exchange where it is placed. If an order is placed on the specialist's book on the NYSE, it would not be executed there merely because the price of the stock had reached the limit order level, known as the trigger price, on a regional exchange.

Stop Orders

There are actually two types of *stop orders*—a stop order to buy and a stop order to sell. Imagine that you bought 100 shares of Ford Motor at \$45 per share. You could then place an order to sell the stock at any price above or below this level.[10] For example, if your stop order to sell were at "40 stop," and Ford Motor declined to \$40 or below, the order would automatically become a market order and would be executed at the best price available on the floor.

Conversely, you might wish to buy Ford Motor stock at a price above its current level of \$45.[11] Should the stock price hit the level of your stop order to buy, your broker would be instructed to make a purchase at the best prevailing market price. In any case, placing a stop order to buy or sell at a given price does not ensure that the order will be executed at this price. Once the stop order becomes a market order, the price of execution may then be made at, above, or below this level.

Other Orders

When using a limit or stop order, a customer can specify that it be good for one day, a week, a month, or *good till cancelled* (*GTC*). A broker might be instructed to cancel a limit order if it cannot be executed immediately. This is known as a "fill-or-kill" order. Sometimes a day limit order may be placed to buy or sell at a specified price, even though the customer still desires to have the order exe-

[10] This might be done to limit the amount of a possible loss if the price declines, or to protect a profit if the price rises.

[11] A buy order above the current price might be used if one desires to wait to buy the stock at a lower price; but, if the stock price rises, the buyer would not want to miss the opportunity to purchase the security before the price gets too high. A "stop buy" order can be used with short selling to avoid a large loss.

cuted that same day whether or not the stock reaches the limit price level. The customer can then have the order marked for execution at the close, regardless of the market level.

Other Types of Trading

Margin Trading

When brokerage house customers purchase securities on margin, they are really buying on credit. Only a percentage of the purchase price of the stock is paid by the customer; the balance is loaned by the brokerage house at a specified rate of interest.

Short Selling

Short selling is the reverse of the usual market transaction. Instead of buying a stock in the hope that it can be sold later at a higher price, a short trader *first sells stock* and later *buys it back* at what he hopes will be a lower price. Short traders borrow stock to sell short from their brokers, who acquire the stock to lend from their margin account customers. However, most short selling is now done not by the public, but by stock exchange members.[12]

The Stock Market: Negotiated Trading

The negotiated market differs from the two-sided auction market in that its operations center heavily on hundreds of securities firms which act as dealers in a few or a large number of securities. No trading takes place on the floor of the stock exchange; instead, securities are bought and sold by dealers who maintain inventories in these various issues. Therefore, the amount an investor pays or receives for securities is arrived at by negotiation rather than an auction system. Negotiations may take place between two dealers or between a dealer and a customer.

Two dealers may negotiate when a customer places a buy or sell order with a securities firm that acts on an *agency basis.*[13] In such cases, the broker checks

[12] For example, a specialist will sell short when he has to sell stock from his own account to maintain an orderly market, but does not have enough shares in his inventory.

[13] Such a firm would usually be a full-service brokerage house such as Merrill Lynch. Of course, there are other securities firms (usually unfamiliar to the general public) which deal exclusively in making markets for over-the-counter securities.

the prices offered by various dealers and negotiates the best price for the customer. To the total cost of the purchase or sale, the broker adds the exact commission (or possibly more) that he would receive on the same number of shares selling at the same price on the NYSE. Interestingly, in the negotiated market as many as 35 dealers may "make a market" in a security as opposed to a single specialist in the auction market.

This trading procedure is significantly altered when the order is placed with a firm acting as *principal* in the trade. In such cases, the firm does not obtain the best price by acting as an agent for its customer; instead, it attempts to make a profit by dealing directly with the customer.

Suppose an order to purchase a stock is placed with a securities firm that "makes a market" in that stock. If the security is not in its inventory, the dealer compares the *asked* prices of other dealers, finds the best available wholesale or dealer price, and finally offers to sell the stock to the customer at a higher price, called the *retail* or *net price*. If the customer finds the price acceptable, the dealer purchases the stock, places it in his inventory, and immediately resells it to the customer. In this type of trade, no commission is charged to the customer, but the net price includes the firm's *markup* or profit for executing the trade.[14]

If the stock ordered for purchase is in the dealer's inventory, the customer is also quoted a net price above the wholesale price the firm offers to other dealers. The customer, however, is free to negotiate for a lower price. As soon as the parties agree to a mutually acceptable price, the transaction is completed.

A Transaction

Assume Bill Wild of Detroit wishes to buy 500 shares of Adolph Coors Company selling on the OTC market. He calls his broker, Mr. Kay, and asks for the market in Adolph Coors. Kay gets in touch with the various dealers making a market for the stock and asks them for bids and offers. For example, if a dealer for Adolph Coors makes a market at "20 bid, offered at 21," he is willing to buy Coors stock from sellers at \$20 a share and sell it at \$21 a share. These are known as wholesale or dealer prices. Interestingly, the quoted bid and asked prices may vary—sometimes significantly—from one dealer to another.

The difference between the bid and ask price—the spread—varies with the type of security traded. For example, on March 30, 1979, *The Wall Street Journal* quoted Anheuser–Busch stock at "$24\frac{1}{2}$ bid, offered at $24\frac{3}{4}$," a spread of only $\frac{1}{4}$ point. However, the quote for the stock of Charles River Breeding Laboratories—a much smaller company with fewer shares outstanding and less active trading—was "24 bid, offered at 25," a spread of a full point. The spread usually widens for inactive securities and tends to increase with the amount of

[14] Similarly, when a customer sells securities, the dealer will check the "bid" prices of other dealers and offer to purchase the stock at a lower price. In such cases, the dealer makes a profit on a markdown.

effort and risk entailed in either finding buyers and sellers, or maintaining an inventory.

After checking the prices of other dealers, Kay informs Wild that the highest bid is $20\frac{1}{8}$ and the lowest offer is 21. Wild feels the offering price is satisfactory and gives the order to buy 500 shares of Adolph Coors at 21. Kay calls the dealer with the lowest offering price and again checks the market, only to discover that the market is still 21. He then checks the "size of the market" to find out the total number of shares available at the offering price. Having discovered that 500 shares are available at 21,[15] Kay submits a bid of $20\frac{1}{2}$ believing that he will succeed in obtaining the stock for Wild at that price. If the dealer is anxious to sell the stock, he may be willing to compromise by lowering his price to, say, $20\frac{3}{4}$. Kay feels that under the prevailing market conditions this is the best obtainable price. He buys the stock at $20\frac{3}{4}$, adds his commission to the purchase price, and submits the total bill to Wild for final payment.

In this case, Wild's broker acted as his agent. Had Kay's firm made a market in Adolph Coors stock and acted as a principal in the deal, Kay would have offered Wild the stock from the firm's inventory at a net price. Wild would not have paid a commission charge in this case, because the net price would have included the firm's markup.[16]

Over-the-Counter Market

Negotiated trading takes place in the *over-the-counter (OTC) market*; the term "over the counter," however, is misleading because there is no counter and no market in the sense of a given place where buyers and sellers meet to trade securities. OTC is a complex national network of trade rooms; these locations are connected by telephones and sophisticated communication facilities. The OTC market, therefore, is actually a *way* of trading in stocks rather than a central marketplace. It is probably the least-known segment of the securities industry.

All transactions that do not occur in an exchange are termed OTC transactions. Of the 30,000 domestic stocks traded over the counter, at least 5,500 to 6,500 are traded fairly actively. Compare this to the approximately 2,200 issues traded on the NYSE (common and preferred) and 1,000 on the AMEX.[17]

OTC stocks include not only most bank and insurance company stocks, but some blue chips that could qualify for trading on major exchanges. Because there are no minimum requirements for a stock to be traded, however, many OTC stocks represent small, often unknown companies. This market expands as more

[15] Whenever a dealer quotes his market, he is obligated to sell at least 100 shares on his offer and buy 100 shares on his bid.

[16] Depending on market conditions and the firm's commission and markup rates, the net price could be higher or lower than the total bill if executed on an agency basis.

[17] Although there are more issues traded over the counter than on the NYSE, the market value of the stocks on the NYSE is greater.

and more companies seek public funds for developing new products and markets. In addition to domestic stocks, most federal, municipal, and corporate bonds, and several foreign stocks[18] are traded on the OTC market.

NASDAQ

In February 1971, in order to facilitate OTC transactions, an automated quotation service called *NASDAQ*—an acronym for National Association of Securities Dealers Automated Quotations—was put into operation. NASDAQ is a computerized communication system that collects, stores, and displays up-to-the-second quotations from a nationwide network of OTC dealers making markets in about 2,500 stocks approved for the system.

[18] American investors can acquire ownership in foreign companies through the purchase of American Depository Receipts (ADRs). An ADR is a document attesting that an American investor owns a specified number of shares being deposited with a foreign bank acting as the agent of an American bank which issues a negotiable receipt. These receipts are traded like other securities and entitle the holder to all privileges accorded a shareholder. ADRs eliminate the necessity of shipping actual stock certificates as well as other problems dealing in foreign securities. The bank issuing the ADR collects the dividends and sends them—along with information about the amount of foreign tax withheld—to U.S. investors. ADRs for some 400 foreign companies are traded in U.S. stock markets, most of which are traded over the counter.

Reading Stock Market Tables

Quotations for NYSE and AMEX listed stocks are reported daily in newspapers across the country. The following is an example:*

52 weeks				Yld.	P/E	Sales				Net
High	Low	Stock	Div.	%	Ratio	100s	High	Low	Close	Chg.
$61\frac{1}{4}$	$48\frac{3}{4}$	Exxon	4.40	8.4	6	4514	$53\frac{1}{8}$	52	$52\frac{1}{2}$	$-1\frac{3}{8}$

Reading from left to right, the stock sold at a high of $61\frac{1}{4}$ and a low of $48\frac{3}{4}$ in the preceding twelve months. The company's name, Exxon, is followed by its current annual dividend rate of $4.40 per share. The rate is based on the last quarterly or semiannual declaration. The yield (Yld.) of 8.4 percent is the return in dividend on the per share investment. P/E ratio means price/earnings, the stock's market price divided by the annual earnings per share; Exxon's price/earnings ratio is 6. Sales 100s signifies the volume of shares traded in hundreds; 4514 means 451,400 shares were traded that day. The high and low figures of $53\frac{1}{8}$ and 52 designate the high and low prices of Exxon stock in that day's trading. The stock closed at $52\frac{1}{2}$, which is the price at which the stock was last traded. Net Chg. shows the change in price of one Exxon share from the last sale in current session from the previous day's closing price.

* *The Detroit News*, January 4, 1980, p. 6C.

The NASDAQ subscriber uses a visual display terminal with a keyboard similar to that of a typewriter; by punching a key, the subscriber can display all the current quotations by market makers in a stock. With this information, a broker can call the dealer offering the best price and complete a transaction. This system eliminates the thousands of telephone calls that were formerly made to determine which dealer was making the best market.[19]

Institutions and the Securities Markets

Growth of Institutional Trading

Since the 1950s, trading activity on the nation's stock exchanges, particularly the NYSE, has become increasingly dominated by such institutional investors as the pension funds, bank trust departments, insurance companies and mutual funds. Table 3–2 provides data on the stockholdings of households, institutions, and

[19] The NASDAQ system also offers other levels of service. One level provides only a median or representative quote of all the firms making a market in a stock. It is used by brokerage house representatives, or account executives, to make tentative judgments about the market. Another level, used by dealers, provides quotations by all market makers in a stock, and also allows the dealer to enter and change his own quotation.

Quotations for stocks traded over the counter are also reported daily. Here is an example:†

Stock & Div.	Sales 100s	Bid	Asked	Net Chg.
La Z Boy Ch .72	25	$9\frac{3}{4}$	$10\frac{1}{2}$	$-\frac{1}{2}$

Reading from left to right, the name of the stock, La-Z-Boy Chair Company, is followed by the annual dividend payment of $.72 per share. On this day 2,500 shares were traded. The stock's Bid and Asked prices of $9\frac{3}{4}$ and $10\frac{1}{2}$ are *representative* quotations by the National Association of Securities Dealers through NASDAQ, the automated system for reporting prices. Because these prices are only representative, La-Z-Boy Chair stock may have been bought or sold that day at a price different from this quote (which, of course, does not include any retail markup, markdown, or commission). The last column indicates the change in price from the previous day; La-Z-Boy Chair stock would have been quoted the previous day at $10\frac{1}{4}$ Bid, 11 Asked. All figures listed include only those transactions affected by NASDAQ market makers.

† *The Wall Street Journal*, January 4, 1980, p. 22.

Table 3–2 **Distribution of Equity Ownership by Sectors (billions of dollars)**

	Total Stock Outstanding*	Institutions		Households†		Rest of World**	
	$	$	%	$	%	$	%
1955	309.5	73.0	23.6	225.2	72.8	11.2	3.6
1960	421.2	112.7	26.8	293.2	69.6	15.3	3.6
1962	461.0	136.5	29.6	308.1	66.8	16.4	3.6
1965	716.7	204.9	28.6	489.0	68.2	22.9	3.2
1968	981.4	272.2	27.7	680.3	69.3	28.8	2.9
1970	859.4	266.8	31.0	563.9	65.6	28.7	3.3
1972	1,138.1	406.2	35.7	690.6	60.7	41.3	3.6
1974	641.7	247.6	38.6	365.7	57.0	28.4	4.4
1976	1,059.7	372.5	35.2	623.3	58.8	63.9	6.0
1978	1,041.0	357.7	34.4	618.6	59.4	64.7	6.2

* Includes market value of both common and preferred stock. Excludes investment company shares, but includes foreign issues outstanding in the United States.

† Computed as a residual. Includes individuals and institutional groups not included in other categories.

** Includes estimate of stock held as direct investment.

SOURCE: Securities and Exchange Commission, *Statistical Bulletin*, Vol. 38, No. 7 (July 1979).

the foreign sector for selected years from 1955 through 1978. Notice the decline in the percentage of shares held by households and the simultaneous increase in that held by institutions. From 1955 to 1978 the percentage of total stock outstanding held by households declined from 72.8 percent to 59.4 percent. During this same period, as a ratio of the total, the holdings of institutions increased from 23.6 percent to 34.4 percent of the total stock outstanding. Since 1972, however, these trends appear to have stabilized.

There are several reasons for the past increase in the share of institutional ownership.[20] In the 1950s, and especially during the 1960s, many investors believed that professional portfolio management of securities could produce returns greater than could be achieved individually. As a result, investors switched from direct investment in equities to the purchase of mutual funds. Another advantage of mutual funds was the enhanced liquidity provided by the right of redemption of mutual fund shares. Investment by individual investors in life insurance and contributions to private pension funds also increased dramatically during this period. The attractiveness of such tax-deferred income sources may well have driven investors away from direct stock investment.

While the institutional share of stock ownership increased during the 1960s and the early 1970s, institutional investors accounted for an even greater per-

[20] See William C. Melton, "Corporate Equities and the National Market System," Federal Reserve Bank of New York, *Quarterly Review*, Winter 1978–79, p. 16.

Table 3–3 **Distribution of Public Volume (Shares Bought and Sold) on the New York Stock Exchange**

	Millions of Shares per Day			Percentage Distribution		Millions of Dollars per Day			Percentage Distribution	
	Total	Ind.	Inst.	Ind.	Inst.	Total	Ind.	Inst.	Ind.	Inst.
1952: Sept.	2.6	1.8	0.8	69.2%	30.8%	NA	NA	NA	NA	NA
1955: June	5.3	4.0	1.3	75.5	24.5	NA	NA	NA	NA	NA
1960: Sept.	5.1	3.5	1.6	68.6	31.4	186	112	74	60.2%	39.8%
1963: Oct.	9.4	6.5	2.9	69.1	30.9	386	250	136	64.8	35.2
1965: March	8.9	5.4	3.5	60.7	39.3	343	182	161	53.1	46.9
1969: I–IV	18.0	7.9	10.1	44.1	55.9	742	283	459	38.1	61.9
1971: I–II	26.6	10.7	15.9	40.3	59.7	940	299	641	31.8	68.2
1974: I	23.2	9.5	13.7	41.1	58.9	708	219	489	31.0	69.0
1976: I	44.1	18.8	25.3	42.7	57.3	1270	377	893	29.7	70.3

Ind. = Individuals not affiliated with NYSE.

Inst. = Investment companies, foundations, personal trusts, insurance companies, pension funds, savings banks, etc.

SOURCE: *Public Transaction Study: 1976*, New York Stock Exchange, p. 10.

centage of the *trading* in the stock market.[21] Table 3–3 details the distribution of total public volume[22] on the NYSE during the period 1952–76. The institutional portion of daily share volume increased from 30.8 percent in 1952 to 57.3 percent in 1976. By 1976, the dollar value of this trading had increased to 70.3 percent of the total. Clearly, since the early 1950s institutions have become the dominating force in the market.

Block Trading

Block trading became increasingly important during the 1960s and early 1970s as institutional investors substantially increased their holdings, purchases, and sales of stocks. Figure 3–2 reveals that NYSE Block Transactions as a percentage of reported volume have increased from about 5 percent in 1967 to over 30 percent in 1980. Because their stockholdings are so large that larger trades are necessary to realign their portfolios over a reasonable period of time, institutions frequently trade in blocks of at least 10,000 shares of stock.

In the normal course of trading, block trades are naturally more difficult to execute than small trades in the Exchange auction market because it is more difficult for the specialists to match a buy or sell order for such a large amount of stock. For example, if a large block of stock is dumped on the market for

[21] In more technical terms, the institutions increased their trading *turnover*—the ratio of the dollar value of trading to the dollar value of holdings.

[22] Public volume does not include trading by member firms for their own accounts.

Figure 3–2 **New York Stock Exchange Block Share Volume as Percent of Reported Volume**

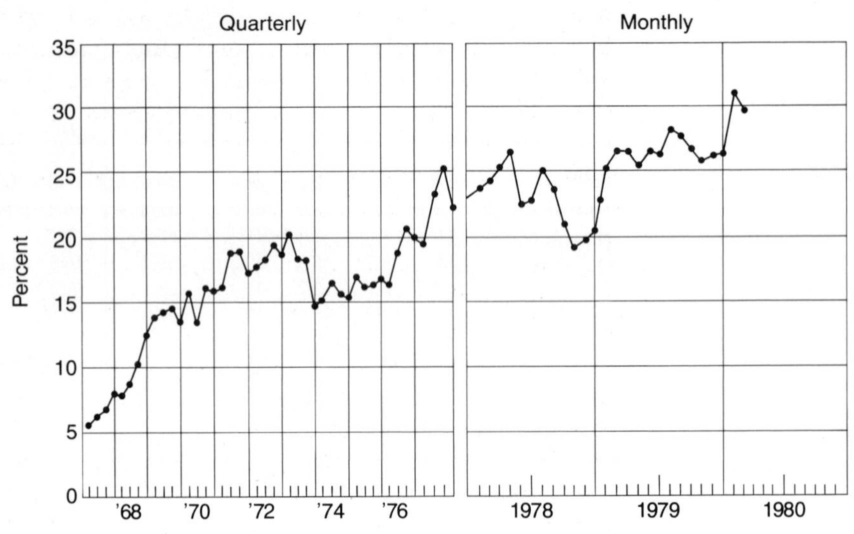

SOURCE: New York Stock Exchange.

sale with no compensating demand, a specialist might attempt to absorb the entire block to keep the market price from dropping violently. This trade, known as a specialist block purchase, is not made public.[23] Specialists, however, frequently do not have sufficient capital—or are unwilling to assume the risk—to execute such transactions on a dealer basis. For this reason, the NYSE has instituted special arrangements for handling these trades, all of which are designed to minimize their price impact and encourage the use of Exchange facilities by institutions.

A brokerage firm acting for a client and wishing to trade a large block of stock[24] frequently locates matching buyers or sellers itself, thereby handling both sides of the transaction by "crossing" the buy and sell orders on the Exchange floor. Because of their size, block trades initiated by sellers are usually negotiated at a price lower than the auction market bid price. However, in order to determine whether any public limit orders have priority to participate in the trade at the negotiated price, the order may not be crossed without first presenting it to both the crowd at the trading post and the specialist.[25]

[23] This arrangement requires approval of a floor governor who must determine that a regular auction market cannot absorb the block within a reasonable period of time without large price changes.

[24] Several broker–dealer firms popularly known as "block houses" specialize in this type of activity.

[25] NYSE Rule 127 requires that public limit orders be allowed to participate in this transaction; they are, however, limited to 1,000 shares or 5 percent of the block, whichever is greater.

Occasionally, a block house will buy a large block of shares for its own account, thereby assuming the risk of reselling them at a later date. Most frequently, however, a block house accumulates a matching order from some of its other clients, or from a registered trader who is interested in handling a large block of stock. One such method for finding a prospective large block buyer or seller involves an automated system for block trading. *Block Automation System (BAS)* is a computer-based information network of brokers and institutional clients designed to facilitate the exchange of information concerning the availability of large blocks of stock. If a subscribing member has a large number of shares to sell, this computer system provides an efficient means of finding a prospective buyer. Besides helping to find the "other side" of a trade preceding the actual execution, BAS also transmits hardcopy confirmations of completed trades from brokers to institutions, regardless of size, within 15 hours of the close of each day's trading.

For very large blocks of stock, the *exchange distribution* or *acquisition* may be employed. This is generally handled by a single brokerage firm that attempts to dispose of or acquire securities through its interested customers. This negotiation is similar to the crossing of orders, but involves more shares and the institution usually pays all brokerage costs. Once the matching orders have been found, the transaction is completed on the floor within the current "bid and asked" range.

Among some of the other techniques used by the NYSE to handle block transactions,[26] secondary distribution deserves mention. When institutions have very large blocks of stock to sell (possibly millions of shares), the stock may be sold to a group of underwriters who assume the risk of selling it to the public. An announcement of the stock offering is made over the Exchange's nationwide ticker system on the day of the sale; the actual offering to the public takes place after the market closes.[27] In order to induce the public to purchase these shares, no commission charge is added to the price of the stock. This cost is absorbed by the selling institution.

Effects of Institutional Trading

One side effect of increased institutional trading has been the fragmentation of the equities market in the United States. As institutional trading increased during the 1960s, institutions began to execute trades for NYSE-listed securities on regional exchanges and in the *third* and *fourth* markets.

The *third market* is essentially an OTC market for NYSE- and AMEX-listed securities. During the 1950s a number of broker–dealer firms which were not

[26] By another technique, known as the special offering, a block of stock is offered for sale or purchase at a price equal to the lower of the last sale or current offer prices. The block must be subject to sale either in whole or in part, and the offering must be open for at least 15 minutes.

[27] The price of the stock in this offering is usually the price at which it sold in the last trade before the market closed. However, it could be higher or lower than this price, depending on the attractiveness of the stock.

members of the NYSE began to make markets in these stocks. (By NYSE Rule 394, later Rule 390, NYSE member firms are not allowed to make a market, or act as dealers in NYSE securities.) Third-market firms act as both dealers and agents. As a dealer, a firm acts as principal to buy stock for its own account when it is offered by an institution, and sells shares when an institution wishes to buy. The dealer's profit comes from the markup or markdown on the trade. Acting as an agent, a third-market firm attempts to match buy and sell orders between institutions in much the same way as do specialists.

The *fourth market* is similar to the third market, except that there is no dealer or market maker. An institution wishing to sell stock, for example, attempts to deal directly with another institution that wishes to buy the stock. Block traders find each other through computerized communications networks run by fourth-market organizations.

Transactions were routed to the regional exchanges and third and fourth markets for a number of reasons. First, until December 1968, the NYSE did not allow brokers to give discounts on commission charges for volume trades. That is, the commission charge per share did not decrease as the number of shares in the order increased (a 40,000 share trade would have a commission charge 400 times that of a 100 share trade), even though the costs per share of executing large transactions are much less than for small transactions. Block traders found that dealer markups or commission charges were lower in the third and fourth markets. Regional exchanges also provided ways for institutions to lower transaction costs.

Investor Protection: An Overview

Following the stock market collapse of 1929–32, the Securities Act of 1933 and the Securities Exchange Act of 1934 were instituted, establishing the Securities and Exchange Commission (SEC) as an independent regulatory agency of the U.S. government to administer and regulate the market. The 1933 Act required the full disclosure of relevant information by companies offering securities to the public; the aim of the act was to prevent the misrepresentations to which investors had previously been subjected. The 1934 Act extended the full disclosure principle to trading in securities already issued. This legislation made it mandatory to disclose information about a listed security and to register with the SEC all securities listed on national securities exchanges as well as certain specified over-the-counter securities. The Act also banned manipulative operations (such as pools and wash sales, false and misleading statements, and deceptive trading practices). Additionally, officers, directors, and owners of 10 percent or more of a company's shares listed on an exchange were required to report any transaction they made in their company's stock within ten days after the month in which it took place.

Besides these powers, the SEC maintains broad controls over the securities markets. It can force the various exchanges to alter certain regulations, if such alterations would enhance public interest. For instance, in 1975, the Securities Acts

Second, many institutional investors were dissatisfied with the service they received on the NYSE. Some block traders felt that the specialist system could not adequately accommodate the quick purchase or sale of a large block of stock. Therefore, institutions moved to the third and fourth markets to receive better prices on the execution.

Third, it became popular to route block trades for NYSE-listed securities to regional exchanges because few limit orders are placed for these stocks on regional exchanges. Block trades could, therefore, be executed at the negotiated price without the participation of public limit orders.

Finally, institutional investors desired to keep their trades secret as long as possible. Third- and fourth-market and regional exchange transactions were not reported over the ticker tape with NYSE and AMEX trades. As a result, institutions could move large blocks of stock without drawing the immediate attention of others who might be encouraged to trade in the same stock. For example, if an institution wished to make a *series* of large volume sales of a given stock on the NYSE, a single trade might trigger other investors to follow the lead. This would tend to exert downward pressure on the market, forcing the institution to make future sales only at lower prices.

What problems ensue with market fragmentation? First, when transactions on the regional exchanges and third and fourth markets are not recorded on the NYSE and AMEX tapes, information is not disseminated equally to all investors. Second, the price of a given stock on the regional exchanges and third and fourth markets can be either higher or lower than that prevailing

---

were amended by Congress, mandating the SEC to facilitate the National Market System.

The Federal Reserve System is empowered to administer that part of the Securities Exchange Act of 1934 which deals with the use of credit for the purchase of securities. The Federal Reserve determines not only how much credit a broker may extend to a customer to purchase listed securities, but the sources from which the broker may borrow money for this purpose. The various security laws are enforced chiefly on the principle of self-regulation under supervision by the SEC. Each securities exchange has primary control over its members and transactions. In the OTC market, almost all reputable dealers are members of the nonprofit, self-regulating organization known as the National Association of Securities Dealers (NASD). Under an Act of Congress passed in 1939, the NASD was authorized to promote high commercial ethics and standardize practices and procedures in the OTC market.

Finally, a brief mention may be made of the *Securities Investor Protection Corporation (SIPC)*. Established as a nonprofit membership corporation by a 1970 Act of Congress, the SIPC provides funds for protecting the deposited cash and securities of customers in the event of a failure of an SIPC member brokerage firm. Protection for securities and cash is limited to $50,000 and $20,000, respectively, per account.

for the same stock traded on the NYSE. Even if the bid and asked prices for a stock are better on other markets than on the NYSE, the investor has no opportunity to take advantage of the more favorable prices. As a result, investors are not always assured of the best available price or execution for their order. With multiple markets for the same securities, institutional investors have access to information and trading on all of them. But too frequently the small investor is limited to only one market—the one to which his broker happens to route small orders.

In a fragmented market, the total volume of trading is spread out, thereby reducing the volume on any given market. Consequently, demand and supply imbalances occur more frequently, leading to increased price fluctuations. A fragmented market is, therefore, less able to absorb a reasonable amount of trading without abrupt price changes than a single, centralized market.

In recent years, action has been taken to reduce the problems of market fragmentation. For instance, in December 1968, to encourage large investors to trade on the NYSE instead of in other markets, the Securities and Exchange Commission ordered the commission rate structure to be changed to allow volume discounts and negotiated commissions for some large trades. There were subsequent changes made before May 1975 when the SEC abolished fixed commissions for all investors.[28] More recently, the SEC has pressured the securities industry to make additional changes including the development of a single national market for stocks.

The National Market System

An Overview

After some comprehensive studies by the SEC in the early 1970s[29] and other extensive Congressional hearings, the Securities Acts Amendment of 1975 was passed; this was the most fundamental and far-reaching securities legislation enacted since the 1930s. Part of this legislation reflected the importance of establishing an effective *National Market System* (*NMS*) to eliminate the existing fragmentation:

> *The linking of all markets for qualified securities through communication and data processing facilities will foster efficiency, enhance competition, increase the information available to brokers, dealers, and investors, facilitate*

[28] On December 5, 1968, the SEC ordered that volume discounts be initiated for commission rates on the portion of orders exceeding 1,000 shares and that negotiations be permitted for the amount of commission in excess of $100,000. On April 5, 1971, negotiated rates were permitted on the portion of orders exceeding $500,000. In April 1972, the breakpoint for negotiated commissions was lowered further to $300,000. In May 1975, fixed commission rates were abolished.

[29] These include the *Institutional Investor Study Report*, submitted to Congress by the SEC in March 1971; the *Statement on the Future Structure of the Securities Markets*, issued on February 2, 1972; and the March 1973 *Policy Statement on the Structure of the Central Market System.*

the offsetting of investors' orders, and contribute to the best execution of such orders.[30]

In addition to solving the problem of fragmentation, the use of electronic communications technology in automating market activity would also be cost effective; the savings potential of such a system has been estimated at more than $100 million a year.

Although the SEC was mandated by Congress to facilitate the implementation of a new market system, the Securities Acts Amendment did not mandate a specific design. Instead, it laid out broad goals for improvement of the industry and left a number of issues to be resolved by the SEC and the securities industry. To develop a nationwide market system that will match purchases and sales at competitive prices, the SEC is looking for three key elements.

The first element, which became fully operational in August 1978, is a *Composite Quotation System* (*CQS*) that electronically displays firms bid and asked prices of all exchange-listed and OTC stocks. This system allows brokers to search for the best prices of stocks throughout the country. Besides the CQS, in June 1975, a *composite tape*, or consolidated stock ticker, was put into operation. This tape reports NYSE- and AMEX-listed stock trades that take place on the two exchanges, on major regional exchanges, as well as those occurring in the third and fourth markets. Both the CQS and composite tape help distribute important information more evenly among all investors.

The second important element is a computerized network which will link securities markets and route the purchase orders placed by brokers or dealers anywhere in the country to the sellers offering the same securities at the best prices. Thus, after the CQS has been queried concerning the best price for a stock, this network would ensure prompt execution of the order in that market.

The third element is a central file where orders from any source could be stored while awaiting execution. Frequently called a *Central Limit Order Book* (*CLOB*), this feature would assure nationwide protection of limit and stop orders. For instance, an investor in Detroit who placed a limit order to purchase 100 shares of XYZ Company at $40 would be assured that the purchase would be made promptly whenever the stock sold at that price on *any* exchange or market.

There are essentially two competing designs for the National Market System. The Intermarket Trading System (ITS), supported by the NYSE, is designed to link existing exchange floors; the Multiple Dealer Trading System (MDTS) is independent of any exchange floor.

Intermarket Trading System

The *Intermarket Trading System* (*ITS*) links the six major stock exchanges—Pacific, Philadelphia, Midwest, Boston, New York, and American—in a single communication vehicle, and retains the specialist as a central figure in the market.

[30] Securities Acts Amendment of 1975, Section 11A.

A modification of the two-way auction market example used earlier in the chapter will help explain how this new market system works. Bill Wild in Detroit decides to buy 100 shares of AT&T. He calls his broker, Mr. Kay, and puts in an order. At that moment, Telephone is quoted in the broker's office as selling at "50 to $\frac{1}{4}$, last at 50$\frac{1}{4}$ on the NYSE."

Kay wires an order to buy 100 shares of AT&T at the market to his New York office, where the order is phoned or wired to his firm's partner on the floor of the NYSE. The floor broker, however, will now use the Composite Quotation System to find the best price available for AT&T stock in different markets throughout the country. Previously, he was forced to execute only on the NYSE floor. The floor broker checks the CQS display screen and finds that the price offered on the NYSE is as good or better than any price offered elsewhere. He moves back to the trading post and executes the purchase order. However, had there been a lower price offered for the shares on, say, the Pacific Stock Exchange, the floor broker could have entered an order through an exchange employee who operates a special ITS terminal. The order could be

The Rule 390 Controversy

In June 1977, the Securities and Exchange Commission released its proposal for abolishing Rule 390 of the New York Stock Exchange. This rule specifies that member firms buying or selling any stock listed on the Exchange must make the trade on the Exchange floor rather than in another market.* The proposed elimination of this rule has generated intense controversy in the investment community.

During the 1950s, many NYSE member firms competed for customer orders under the fixed-commission rate structure by offering special services, which included the privilege of transferring orders to the third market for a lower net execution cost. Subsequently, the NYSE adopted Rule 394 to prohibit this practice. However, according to the SEC,† this rule did not promote the execution of a customer's order at the best possible price. The Commission argued that, when better prices for NYSE-listed securities were available in other markets, member firms were prevented from sending orders off the NYSE to take advantage of them. Therefore, in March 1976, the NYSE modified Rule 394 to facilitate competition for orders by permitting access to the third market. The modification allowed member firms to act as *agents* and orders out of the NYSE to third-market dealers, thereby enabling them to seek the best execution for customer trades. The modified Rule 394 was subsequently renumbered as Rule 390.

In June 1977, a proposal was made to eliminate Rule 390 altogether, thereby allowing NYSE member firms to act as *principals* and make markets in NYSE-listed

* This rule does not apply to odd-lot trades.

† This was emphasized in the SEC's March 29, 1973 *Policy Statement on the Structure of the Central Market System*.

tracked as it was electronically transmitted to the Pacific Stock Exchange for execution.[31]

Although the ITS was initiated on a pilot basis on April 17, 1978, it had not been fully implemented as of 1979 (because the National Association of Securities Dealers, which represents the OTC market, had not yet joined). There are still complex policy and technical problems that must be resolved before OTC market makers are linked to the system.

In addition to the ITS, the SEC has expressed interest in additional marketing system proposals. One is a routing system, or message switch procedure, which would link brokerage houses with all markets. Instead of having to send Bill

[31] The price quoted on the buy order must be the offering price quoted for the destination market on the CQS display, and a sell order must carry the bid quoted for destination market. The floor broker cannot enter a price between the quoted bid and offer. In any case, the specialist at the destination exchange (the Pacific Exchange in our example) has the option of filling the order or cancelling it. He might cancel the order if there has been some sort of malfunction or if he was in the process of changing his quotation.

---

securities off the Exchange floor. The SEC and other proponents of this proposal assert that it will eliminate the monopoly position of NYSE specialists as the sole market makers for stocks, foster more competition in the securities industry, and improve overall efficiency. Such a rule would be *compatible* with a National Market System, in which there is a consolidated limit order book and *all* orders—both dealer and agency—are designed to interact in a common market setting.

Opponents of the proposal, including the president of the NYSE, argue that if Rule 390 is eliminated *before* a central market system is operating, the largest brokerage firms will make more money by trading in securities for their own accounts and siphon off a large volume of trading from the Exchange floor. This would have several adverse consequences. First, if the flow of orders on the Exchange is reduced, there would be wider imbalances between supply and demand, greater price fluctuations, and reduced liquidity in the market. Second, some brokerage firms might execute orders as principals at less favorable terms than could be achieved on the Exchange floor. Finally, because such a move would favor the larger brokerage houses which are better equipped to make markets in securities, it would either force the smaller brokers out of business or speed up the merger movement that has already been strong in this industry since the removal in 1975 of the fixed commissions structure.

Although the SEC is determined that Rule 390 must be rescinded, it has already relented once, allowing the original January 1, 1978 deadline for its removal to pass. The SEC will continue its attempts to help the securities industry develop a trading system consistent with the Congressional mandate for a National Market System within a reasonable period of time, but it is not clear whether the Commission will have Rule 390 abolished before a NMS becomes operational.

Wild's order to the NYSE floor, Kay would be able to learn the best available price and send the order *directly to any market*—even an OTC market—for execution.[32]

Incidentally, the present ITS system does not protect nationwide limit orders. The CQS only displays the best quotations on the various exchanges; the specialists still have exclusive access to the limit orders on their books. It is still possible for a limit order placed on the NYSE to remain unexecuted even though the trigger price has been reached on another exchange. To resolve this problem, the NYSE has informed the SEC that it intends to develop an electronic Market Center Limit Order File (MCLOF) to replace the specialists' limit order books. Brokers would be able to insert limit orders directly into the MCLOF without the intervention of a floor broker or specialist. A computer would accumulate all such orders, rank them according to price, and make the information available through a communications network. With this information, along with details supplied by the limit order file from other exchanges, it would be possible to execute an order against other limit orders on any exchange.

Multiple Dealer Trading System

Another proposal for a National Market System is the *Multiple Dealer Trading System (MDTS)*.[33] The MDTS would establish a central limit order book in which all outstanding limit orders would be inserted, regardless of the market center from which they originated; this system would also establish a facility for automated trading with no dependence on any exchange floor. Information and orders would be processed through a large computer with an extensive electronic communications network instead of through floor brokers and specialists who execute trades. The computer would be instructed to conduct a continuous auction market according to a set of programmed rules. Any broker–dealer with access to the system could enter his own quotations and limit orders, then execute orders for bids and offers that would be displayed almost instantaneously.

In essence, the computer would store all buy and sell quotations in the CQS and all limit orders in the central limit order book; at the same time, it would receive market orders to buy and sell from brokers and dealers. From this information, the computer would complete a transaction according to the demand and supply of the moment, then report the transaction to all investors over a consolidated reporting system. Because there would be only one market center instead of a linkage of several exchanges, the investor would be guaranteed the best execution of his order.

The Cincinnati Stock Exchange is an experimental prototype of this system. It was established by Weeden Holding Company and authorized by the SEC in

[32] In 1979, Merrill Lynch Pierce Fenner & Smith announced that it developed an electronic system that will allow it to find the best market for a customer's trade and send the trade to that securities market in a fraction of a second. The system is called the Merrill Lynch Best Price Selector and will be first used on a pilot basis.

[33] This system is also known as a hard Central Limit Order Book.

April 1978. Two computers in a building in New Jersey handle all trading in forty NYSE-listed stocks. No floor traders or specialists are involved. According to Jack Weeden, who pioneered the system, this type of market can substantially lower costs for the investor and provide a great deal more information about the market than did the traditional system of trading stocks.

There is considerable debate over whether the Intermarket Trading System or the Multiple Dealer Trading System is superior. Some experts feel that the new NMS will evolve from a combination of elements from both systems. In theory, the NMS—in whatever form—should provide greater efficiency, cut costs, and enable individual investors to make decisions based on superior market information; it should also eliminate the trading advantage of the institutions. One trend seems clear: Automating the routine aspects of securities market activities will continue to improve service and reduce costs. In any case, the new type of market will differ significantly from the present one.

Secondary Markets: Bonds

Functions of Bond Markets

The secondary markets for bonds serve several important functions. Their most obvious function is to provide a ready means for bondholders to liquidate their debt claims before maturity. If bonds could not be sold in a secondary market, or could be liquidated only at a substantial expense, investors would not purchase them unless the issuers offered higher yields on their debt instruments.

The amount of outstanding debt claims and transactions in the secondary market is much larger than in the primary market. Consequently, the terms under which new issues can be sold are greatly influenced by the bond prices prevalent in the secondary market. A new bond cannot be sold at a yield significantly below that of the most comparable outstanding issue in the secondary market, because investors buy new or outstanding issues interchangeably.

Although bonds are traded in both auction (such as the bond trading room of the NYSE) and over-the-counter (through a large network of dealers) markets, the market for debt claims exists predominantly in the latter market. There is, of course, a significant volume of trading on the exchanges, particularly on the NYSE. However, the volume of bond trading on the OTC market far exceeds the combined trading volume of all other exchanges.

With the exception of the bond-trading room of the NYSE, the bond market is organized around dealers or market makers and is not an auction market. Investors can buy and sell bonds through their regular brokers who gain access to bond dealers. This is essentially the same process as that for buying stocks through a broker who acts as an investor's agent in the OTC market. Many investors, however, trade directly with the dealers.

Securities of the Federal Government

Securities of the federal government—especially treasury bills, notes, bonds, and various federal agency issues—are purchased by almost every type of investor in the economy. The volume of these transactions in the secondary market is far greater than in any other securities market in the world. These transactions total billions of dollars every month, as commercial banks and other financial institutions buy and sell large volumes of treasury securities to adjust their liquidity positions. The Federal Reserve Bank uses this market to trade in government securities. The purchase and sale of government securities by the Federal Reserve are known as open market operations.

The market is composed of 24 market makers, including specialized departments of commercial banks and nonbank dealers who also handle other securities. These dealers have branches and many correspondent dealers throughout the country. Investors can buy and sell treasury obligations either by dealing with these dealers directly, or through local dealers, banks, and brokers.

Municipal Bonds

Because of their tax advantages, municipal bonds are traded in the secondary market both by individuals in high income tax brackets and by institutions subject to federal income tax. Commercial banks are large holders of municipal bonds and, with broker–dealers, play major roles as dealers in the secondary market for these securities.

Corporate Bonds

The market for corporate bonds centers heavily on dealers who stand ready to buy or sell bonds, frequently in large amounts. Dealers in corporate bonds function much like market makers for stocks. They often deal directly with institutional investors; smaller investors gain access through the large network of brokers available.

As mentioned in Chapter 2, a large fraction of the outstanding corporate bonds are held by financial intermediaries, such as life insurance companies and pension funds. The corporate bond market is, therefore, mainly dominated by institutions that trade in large amounts.

Summary

Stocks and bonds are originally sold by corporations and governments in the *capital market*, where long-term funds needed for real investment are secured from purchasers interested in making a financial investment. The *capital* and *money markets* together comprise the *primary markets*. After securities have been issued in the primary markets, they are traded among investors in the secondary markets.

The *secondary markets* for stocks and bonds serve important functions in the nation's economy. Both markets provide liquidity for these investments; that is, they make it possible for investors to sell their securities quickly without a substantial price concession. The secondary markets for stocks also facilitate the process of real investment by encouraging potential savers to invest in new and outstanding corporate stocks. More importantly, these markets help allocate scarce investment funds to the most efficient and promising businesses and industries. The secondary markets for bonds influence prices for newly issued bonds in the primary markets.

Stocks and bonds can be traded in organized exchanges, such as the *New York Stock Exchange* (*NYSE*), through a *two-way auction market*. Here brokers buy and sell securities for their customers through *competitive bidding* on an exchange floor. The *over-the-counter* (*OTC*) *market*, on the other hand, comprises hundreds of dealers across the country who set prices through negotiation with other dealers or customers. The OTC market is not a physical marketplace like the New York or *American Stock Exchange* (*AMEX*); rather, it is a method of trading securities.

Trading in the stocks of the largest corporations takes place on the NYSE, whereas bond trading takes place principally in the over-the-counter market. In either type of market, the individual preferences for securities are translated into *buy and sell orders* which, through the forces of supply and demand, contribute to an upward or downward adjustment in prices.

A by-product of increased *institutional trading* in recent years has been the fragmentation of the equities market. This has resulted in an unequal dissemination of market information, price discrepancies between exchanges, and trading practices discriminatory toward smaller investors. A fragmented market is also less liquid than a single, centralized market.

The traditional system for trading stocks is currently undergoing changes and is soon expected to evolve into a *National Market System* (*NMS*), which was mandated by Congress in 1975. The objectives of the NMS are to improve disclosure of stock prices in all market centers, improve investor access to these markets, and protect limit orders in all markets. The NMS will also employ several automated features which should reduce the cost of executing orders.

A Look Ahead

This chapter continued the discussion of the investment environment by presenting the purposes and operations of the stock and bond markets. Details have been presented on how the markets process information on securities by executing buy and sell orders, and how this information is reflected in the price of securities. The various sources of information an investor can use to make investment decisions are discussed in Chapter 4.

Concepts for Review

- Primary market
- Real vs. financial investment
- Money market
- Capital market
- Investment banking
- Competitive bidding
- Secondary market
- Over-the-counter (OTC) Market
- Two-way auction market
- Bid and ask prices
- New York Stock Exchange (NYSE)
- Exchange members
- Specialists
- Dealer
- Registered traders
- Floor brokers
- Odd-lot dealer
- Round lot
- Odd lot
- American Stock Exchange (AMEX)
- Regional exchanges
- Market orders
- Limit order
- Buy-limit order
- Sell-limit order
- Stop order
- Good-till-cancelled order
- Margin trading
- Short selling
- Negotiated market trading
- NASDAQ
- Institutional trading
- Block trading
- Block automated system
- Third market
- Fourth market
- Investor protection
- Securities Investor Protection Corporation
- National Market System
- Composite Quotation System
- Central Limit Order Book
- Intermarket Trading System
- Multiple Dealer Trading System
- Rule 390

Questions for Review

1. What are the primary markets for securities? How do they differ from the secondary markets?
2. What are the functions of stock- and bondholders in our economy? What role does the stock market play?
3. Differentiate between the negotiated market and the two-way auction market. Specifically, how are stock prices set in these markets?
4. What are the functions of the stock *exchanges*? Compare the NYSE, the AMEX, and the regional exchanges.
5. What is meant by the term "liquidity"? Why is liquidity important to investors?
6. What are the different types of members of the NYSE? What are their functions?

7. Comment on the following statement: "The over-the-counter market is a *way* of trading securities."
8. How will an OTC order be executed when placed with a securities firm acting on an agency basis? Would there be a difference if the securities firm acted as a principal?
9. A dealer in ABC Company stock, traded over the counter, makes a market at "42 bid, offered at 43." What does this mean?
10. What is NASDAQ? How does it work? What is its function in the over-the-counter market?
11. Why is it sometimes difficult to execute a block trade in an auction market? How can the problem be handled?

    What is meant by the "fragmentation" of the equities market in the United States? What problems stem from market fragmentation?
13. What are the third and fourth markets? Why did it become popular to trade NYSE-listed securities there?
14. "The growth in institutional trading has been disadvantageous to the small investor." Comment on the validity of this statement.
15. Trace the development of the National Market System. Why is it being developed?

Selected Readings

"Are the Institutions Wrecking Wall Street?" *Business Week*, June 2, 1973.

Armour, Lawrence A. "Central Marketplace." *Barron's*, March 1972.

Bagehot, W. "The Only Game in Town." *Financial Analysts Journal*, March–April 1976.

Baker, Guthrie. "Blueprint for Constructive Reform." *Financial Analysts Journal*, November–December 1971.

Barnea, A. "Performance Evaluation of NYSE Specialists." *Journal of Financial and Quantitative Analysis*, September 1974.

Basi, Bart A. "The Responsibility of the Broker–Dealer to the Investing Public." *American Business Law Journal*, Winter 1976.

Baxter, W. F. "NYSE Commission Rates: A Private Cartel Goes Public." *Stanford Law Review*, April 1970.

Black, Fisher. "Toward a Fully Computerized Stock Exchange." *Financial Analysts Journal*, November–December 1971.

Blume, M. E., J. Crockett, and D. Friend. "Stockownership in the United States: Characteristics and Trends." *Survey of Current Business*, November 1974.

Bostian, David B., Jr. "The De-Institutionalization of the Stock Market in American Society." *Financial Analysts Journal*, November–December 1973.

Curran, Ward S. "Some Thoughts on the Stock Exchange Specialist." *Quarterly Review of Economics and Business*, Spring 1965.

Doede, Robert W. "The Monopoly Power of the New York Stock Exchange." Unpublished Ph.D. Dissertation, University of Chicago, 1967.

Farrar, Donald E. "The Coming Reform on Wall Street." *Harvard Business Review*, September–October 1972.

Farrar, Donald E. "Toward a Central Market System: Wall Street's Slow Retreat into the Future." *Journal of Financial and Quantitative Analysis*, November 1974.

Farrar, Donald E. "Wall Street's Proposed 'Great Leap Backward.'" *Financial Analysts Journal*, September–October 1971.

Fenerstein, Donald M. "Toward a National System of Securities Exchanges: The Third and Fourth Markets." *Financial Analysts Journal*, July–August 1972.

Fiske, Heide. "Can the Specialist Cope with the Age of Block Trading?" *Institutional Investor*, August 1969.

Freund, William C. "The Historical Role of the Individual Investor in the Corporate Equity Market." *Journal of Contemporary Business*, Winter 1974.

Freund, William C. "Issues Confronting the Stock Markets in a Period of Rising Institutionalization." *Journal of Financial and Quantitative Analysis*, Supplement, March 1972.

Freund, William C. and David F. Minor. "Institutional Activity on the NYSE: 1975 and 1980." *Perspectives on Planning No. 10*, New York Stock Exchange, Inc., June 1972.

Friend, Irwin. "The Economic Consequences of the Stock Market." *American Economic Review*, May 1972.

Friend, Irwin. "Effect of Institutionalization of Savings on the Long-Term for the Securities Industry." *Journal of Financial and Quantitative Analysis*, Supplement, March 1972.

Friend, Irwin and Marshall Blume. "Competitive Commissions on the NYSE." *Journal of Finance*, September 1973.

Friend, Irwin and Marshall Blume. *The Consequences of Competitive Commissions on the New York Stock Exchange*. Philadelphia: Rodney White Center for Financial Research, Wharton School of Business, University of Pennsylvania, 1972.

Friend, I., J. Longstreet, M. Mendelson, E. Miller, and A. Hess. *Investment Banking and the New Issues Market*. New York: World, 1967.

Furst, Richard W. "Does Listing Increase the Market Price of Common Stocks?" *Journal of Business*, April 1970.

Grier, Paul C. and Peter S. Albin. "Nonrandom Price Changes in Association with Trading in Large Blocks." *Journal of Business*, July 1973.

Ibbotson, Roger G. "Price Performance of New Common Stock Issues." *Journal of Financial Economics*, September 1975.

Institutional Investor Study, Report of the Securities and Exchange Commission, Supplementary Volume 2, 92d Congress, 1st Session. House Document No. 92–64, Part 6, March 10, 1971.

"Individuals and the Corporate Equity Market." Symposium. *Journal of Contemporary Business*, Winter 1974.

James, Ralph and Estelle James. "Disputed Role of the Stock Exchange Specialists." *Harvard Business Review*, May–June 1962.

Jones, L. D. "Some Contributions of the Institutional Investor Study." *Journal of Finance*, May 1972.

Klemkosky, Robert C. "Institutional Dominance of the NYSE." *Financial Executive*, November 1973.

Klemkosky, Robert C. and David F. Scott, Jr. "Withdrawal of the Individual Investor from the Equity Markets." *MSU Business Topics*, Spring 1973.

Kraus, Alan and Hans R. Stoll. "Parallel Trading by Institutional Investors." *Journal of Financial and Quantitative Analysis*, December 1972.

Kraus, Alan and Hans R. Stoll. "Price Impact of Block Trading on the New York Stock Exchange." *Journal of Finance*, June 1972.

Lease, R. C., W. G. Lewellen, and G. C. Schlarbaum. "The Individual Investor: Attributes and Attitudes." *Journal of Finance*, May 1974.

Leuthold, Steven C. "The Causes (and Cures?) of Market Volatility." *Journal of Portfolio Management*, Winter 1976.

Loomis, Carol J. "How the Terrible Two-Tier Market Came to Wall Street." *Fortune*, July 1973.

Lyons, John F. "What Happens When Liquidity Disappears?" *Institutional Investor*, November 1969.

Marcial, Gene G. "Block Traders Capture Bigger Share of Market, But They Pay a Price." *Wall Street Journal*, February 9, 1978.

Martin, W. M., Jr. "The Securities Markets, A Report with Recommendations." Reprinted in Commerce Clearing House, *Federal Security Law Reporter*, August 1971.

Mayo, Herbert B. *Basic Finance*. Philadelphia: W. B. Saunders, 1978.

McDonald, John G. and A. K. Fisher. "New Issue Price Behavior." *Journal of Finance*, March 1972.

Melton, William C. "Corporate Equities and the National Market System." Federal Reserve Bank of New York, *Quarterly Review*, Winter 1978–79.

Mendelson, Morris. *Automated Quotes to Automated Trading: Restructuring the Stock Market in the U.S.* Bulletin of the Institute of Finance, Graduate School of Business Administration, New York University, Nos. 80–82, March 1972.

"Merrill Lynch's Views on the National Market System." Merrill Lynch, Pierce, Fenner, and Smith, Inc., September 1977.

Moore, Thomas G. "Stock Market Margin Requirements." *Journal of Political Economy*, April 1966.

Murray, Roger F. "Indirect Investment in the Securities Market and the Individual Investor." *Journal of Contemporary Business*, Winter 1974.

Murray, Roger F. "Institutionalization of the Stock Market to Be Feared or Favored?" *Financial Analysts Journal*, March–April 1974.

Niederhoffer, V. and M. F. Osborne. "Market Making and Reversal on the Stock Exchange." *Journal of the American Statistical Association*, December 1966.

Nielsen, James F. and Michael D. Joehnk. "Further Evidence on the Effects of Block Transactions on Stock Price Fluctuations." *Mississippi Valley Journal of Business and Economics*, Winter 1973–74.

Officer, Robert R. "The Variability of the Market Factor of the New York Stock Exchange." *Journal of Business*, July 1973.

Parthemos. "The Money Market." *Instruments of the Money Market*. Edited by Timothy Q. Cook. Federal Reserve Bank of Richmond, 1977.

Peake, J. W. "The National Market System." *Financial Analysts Journal*, July–August 1978.

Reilly, Frank K. "A Three Tier Stock Market and Corporate Financing." *Financial Management*, Autumn 1975.

Reilly, Frank K. and Eugene F. Drzycimski. "The Stock Exchange Specialist and the Market Impact of Major World Events." *Financial Analysts Journal*, July–August 1975.

Report of the Special Study of the Securities Markets of the Securities and Exchange Commission. Washington, D.C.: Securities and Exchange Commission, 1962.

Robbins, Sidney. *Securities Industry Study: Report and Hearings*. House Committee on Interstate and Foreign Commerce, Subcommittee on Commerce and Finance, 92d Congress, 1st and 2d sessions, 1972.

Robbins, Sidney. *The Future Structure of the Securities Market*. Washington, D.C.: Securities and Exchange Commission, February 2, 1972.

Robbins, Sidney. *The Security Markets: Operations and Issues*. New York: Free Press, 1966.

Robbins, Sidney. "Some Reflections on the Central Market." Text of the Second Annual Buttonwood Lecture (published under joint sponsorship by Columbia University and the New York Stock Exchange), New York City, December 1972.

Robbins, Sidney. *White Paper on the Structure of a Central Market System*. Washington: The Securities and Exchange Commission, March 30, 1973.

Robertson, Wyndham, "A Big Board Strategy for Staying Alive." *Fortune*, March 1977.

Santomero, A. M. "Economic Effects of the NASDAQ." *Journal of Financial and Quantitative Analysis*, January 1974.

Schaefer, Jeffrey M. and Adolphe J. Warner. "Concentration Trends and Competition in the Securities Industry." *Financial Analysts Journal*, November–December 1977.

Smidt, Seymour. "Which Road to an Efficient Stock Market: Free Competition or a Regulated Monopoly?" *Financial Analysts Journal*, September–October 1971.

Smidt, Seymour. "The Changing Relative Roles of Individuals and Institutions in the Stock Market." *Journal of Contemporary Business*, Winter 1974.

Smith, Clifford W., Jr. "Alternative Methods for Raising Capital." *Journal of Financial Economics*, December 1977.

Stigler, George J. "Public Regulation of the Securities Market." *Journal of Business*, April 1964.

Stoll, Hans R. "Dealer Inventory Behavior: An Empirical Investigation of NASDAQ Stocks." *Journal of Financial and Quantitative Analysis*, September 1976.

Stoll, Hans R. and Anthony J. Curley. "Small Business and the New Issues Market for Equities." *Journal of Financial and Quantitative Analysis*, September 1970.

Tinic, Seha M. and Richard R. West. "Competition and the Pricing of Dealer Service in the Over-the-Counter Market." *Journal of Financial and Quantitative Analysis*, June 1972.

Treasury-Federal Reserve Study of the Government Securities Market. Washington, D.C.: GPO, 1959.

"The Two-Tier Market Lingers on, Sort of." *Fortune, February* 1974.

Weeden, Donald E. "Competition: Key to Market Structure." *Journal of Financial and Quantitative Analysis*, March 1972.

Welles, Chris. "Discounting: Wall Street's Game of Nerves." *Institutional Investor*, November 1976.

Welles, Chris. "The Individual Investor and the Problem of Institutional Power." *Journal of Contemporary Business*, Winter 1974.

Welles, Chris. "The Showdown over Rule 390." *Institutional Investor*, December 1977.

Welles, Chris. "Who Will Prosper? Who Will Fail?" *Institutional Investor*, January 1971.

West, Richard R. "Institutional Trading and the Changing Stock Market." *Financial Analysts Journal*, May–June 1971.

West, Richard R. "On the Difference Between Internal and External Market Efficiency." *Financial Analysts Journal*, November–December 1975.

West, Richard R. "Simulating Securities Markets Operations: Some Examples, Observations, and Comments." *Journal of Financial and Quantitative Analysis*, March 1970.

West, Richard R. and Seha M. Tinic. "Corporate Finance and the Changing Stock Market." *Financial Management*, Autumn 1974.

West, Richard R. and Seha M. Tinic. "Institutionalization: Its Impact on the Provision of Marketability Services and the Individual Investor." *Journal of Contemporary Business*, Winter 1974.

West, Richard R. and Seha M. Tinic. "Minimum Commission Rates on New York Stock Exchange Transactions." *Bell Journal of Economics and Management Science*, Autumn 1971.

White, Shelby. "The New Central Marketplace: The Debate Goes On." *Institutional Investor*, August 1976.

Investment Information Sources and Market Indicators

Introduction

SECTION 1
INVESTMENT INFORMATION SOURCES

An Overview

Sources of Information
- **Raw Data**
  - The Market
  - The Industries
  - The Companies
- **Interpretive Information**
  - The Market
  - The Industries
  - The Companies

Information Selection
- **Category Selection**
- **Specific Source Selection**
  - Raw Data Selection
  - Interpretive Information Selection
- **Cost–Benefit Consideration**
- **Source Selection Summary**

SECTION 2
MARKET INDICATORS

Introduction

Bond Market Indicators
- **Government Securities**
- **Municipal Bonds**
- **Corporate Bonds**

Stock Market Indicators
- **The Dow Averages**
  - The Dow Jones Industrial Average (DJIA)
  - Other Dow Averages
- **Standard & Poor's 500 Index**
- **NYSE Composite Index**
- **ASE Market Value Index**
- **NASDAQ OTC Composite Index**
- **Value Line Composite Average**
- **Other Stock Market Indicators**

Stock Market Indicator Roundup

Summary

A Look Ahead

Introduction

Chapter 2 was devoted to a discussion of investment instruments; in Chapter 3, a survey of the securities markets was undertaken. But markets cannot function efficiently unless detailed information about both the markets and the instruments traded in them is available. Investors need to analyze and interpret this information before making their investment decisions.

This chapter is divided into two sections. Section 1 is a survey and interpretation of investment information sources. Market indicators that measure the activities in the securities markets are discussed in Section 2.

SECTION 1 INVESTMENT INFORMATION SOURCES

An Overview

The price of a stock or bond reflects the interaction of investors' buy and sell orders in the marketplace. These orders, in turn, are based on different types of investment information that enable investors to evaluate various securities and establish their preferences. When evaluating securities, many investors attempt to obtain answers to at least the following three questions:

1. What are the prospects for the economy, general business, and the securities markets?

2. How will the expected behavior of the economy affect specific industries?
3. How will the performance of different industries affect individual companies with which they are associated?

Naturally, to answer these and related questions investors require information. Fortunately, few fields are as abundantly supplied with information sources as the securities business. Although most of the available information sources are useful, each investor is limited to the amount of information he can assimilate and use to evaluate an investment opportunity. In this section, the vast and often confusing array of information sources and types will be organized, and a conceptual groundwork will be laid for approaching and utilizing the investment information necessary to make an informed investment decision.

Sources of Information

Information about investment in stocks and bonds is so plentiful that questions concerning the subject need not go unanswered. However, because the sources of investment information are virtually unlimited, they must be properly classified and organized to allow investors to evaluate the available information in an orderly and efficient manner.

Essentially, sources of investment information can be divided into two broad forms according to their method of reporting. One type simply presents facts or data objectively, leaving interpretation to the investor. The other type presents an analysis and offers the advice, arguments, or conclusions of experts in the field. Investors who feel confident to draw their own conclusions from information will choose the raw, uncolored data. Investors who prefer to rely on the experience and expertise of economists and analysts rather than formulating their own opinions tend to seek information reported in the second manner.

Information sources can be further categorized according to content. The values of stocks or bonds are influenced by the performance of (1) the *market* and general economic conditions, (2) the *industry* in which the company operates, and (3) the *company* itself. It is, therefore, appropriate to distinguish between information sources that provide data and those that report on the securities markets, particular industries, and individual corporations. By utilizing the information in each of these categories, an investor can answer the basic questions listed in the "Overview" and, hopefully, make wise investment choices.

The following is a summary of the simple organizational method just described.

Sources of information
1. Raw data
   a. The market
   b. Industries
   c. Individual companies
2. Interpretive information
   a. The market
   b. Industries
   c. Individual companies

This outline will now be expanded by citing examples and providing descriptions of some of the more popular sources of information included in each of these classifications.

Raw Data

The Market

Broadly speaking, variations in the stock market reflect fluctuations in general business and economic trends. Consequently, it is important to have access to current news in this area, for which there is a veritable mountain of data available. For the skilled analyst or statistician, many U.S. government agencies—Department of Commerce, Federal Reserve System, and the Bureau of the Census—provide virtually any kind of statistics dealing with business, finance, and the economy. *Business Conditions Digest* is one of the most popular sources of information. There are also a number of newspapers and periodicals that follow the economy closely and report valuable up-to-date information, including data on stock and bond market indicators. Many more examples of these sources could be added to those listed in Table 4–1.

Stock and bond market indicators in general, and the Dow Jones Industrial Average and the Standard & Poor's 500 Index in particular, are widely used and closely watched barometers of market performance. The more important market indexes and averages will be discussed in detail in Section 2.

The Industries

Information concerning the general level of business activity and the economy, if examined and applied properly, can also be used to analyze specific industries. For investors who wish to explore the subject in greater depth, many industries supply trade magazines and publications devoted exclusively to developments in their respective fields of business. Data for statistical studies can be found in some U.S. government publications and in selected magazines, trade journals, and advisory service reports. Industry financial ratios used for comparative analysis can be found in sources such as *Key Business Ratios in 125 Lines*, *Quarterly Financial Report for Manufacturing Corporations*, or in

Table 4–1 **The Economy and Market—Raw Data**

U.S. Government Publications

Business Conditions Digest (U.S. Bureau of the Census) Monthly. Contains charts that show lead, coincident, lag, and composite economic indicators. Useful for understanding the current trends in the economy and for forecasting future economic and stock market trends.

Federal Reserve Bulletin (Board of Governors of the Federal Reserve System) Monthly. Articles and statistics on conditions in the money and capital markets as well as business conditions in general.

Statistical Abstract of the United States (U.S. Bureau of the Census) Annually. Includes reference material on many topics compiled as primary data by the other governmental agencies.

Survey of Current Business (U.S. Dept. of Commerce) Monthly. Contains a wealth of business statistics.

U.S. Financial Data; *National Economic Trends*; *Monetary Trends* (Federal Reserve Bank of St. Louis) Free weekly and monthly statistical reports on monetary and economic conditions in the economy.

Newspapers, Periodicals, and Journals

Barron's (Dow Jones & Co., Inc.) Weekly. Essentially has three categories: Leading articles in depth; departments such as "The Trader," "Up & Down Wall Street," and "Capital Markets"; and a substantial statistical section that includes indexes and data on the economy, industry, and individual securities.

Business Week (McGraw-Hill) Weekly. News coverage of fiscal, monetary, government, business, regulatory, and economic developments and of various industries and companies, corporate finance, securities markets, and business conditions.

Forbes (Forbes, Inc.) Biweekly. Articles on economic developments, industries, companies, and special sections giving statistical spotlights and opinions on the stock, bond, and commodity markets.

Wall Street Journal (Dow Jones & Co., Inc.) 5 days a week. Reports on security market conditions, industries, and companies, with investment analysis and opinions, based on speeches by corporate executives, brokerage firm security analysis reports, and experts in the financial community. Market price quotations are also listed.

Other Important Periodicals:

Commercial and Financial Chronicle, Dun's Review, Financial World, Fortune, Money.

Scholarly Journals:

Financial Analysts Journal (Financial Analysts Federation) Bimonthly. Features 7 to 12 articles on varying phases of investment and portfolio management. Reports on current developments in "Securities Law and Regulation," "Accounting for Financial Analysis," and "Corporate Information and Disclosure." Empirical studies emphasized.

Journal of Finance (American Finance Association) Quarterly. More academically and theoretically oriented than the *Financial Analysts Journal.* Written mainly by university professors and security analysts; articles cover not only all phases of finance, but monetary and economic theory as well. Theoretical in nature.

For additional raw data sources see the list of commercial banks in Table 4–4.

the annual *Statement Studies* compiled and published by Robert Morris Associates. Popular business periodicals often include descriptive write-ups on certain industries. However, in these write-ups, the reader must distinguish between unbiased information and personal opinion or forecasting. Examples of raw data sources for industries are listed in Table 4–2.

The Companies

After an investor has discerned a clear picture of the investment climate and evaluated the prospects for specific industries, the same thing can be done for individual companies associated with these industries. To aid the investor, a wealth of information can be obtained from the companies themselves—most popularly in the form of annual reports. A typical annual report contains state-

Table 4–2 **Industries—Raw Data**

Trade Journals

Business Periodical Index and *Science and Technology Index* Major indexes which list articles in all trade journals.

A Guide to Industry Publications for Securities Analysts Published by the New York Society for Security Analysts, an index listing title, source, address, and annual charge for selected publications covering over 40 industries.

A sample of some of the numerous trade journals and papers published:

Chemical Week, Paper Trade Journal, Public Utilities Fortnightly, Ward's Automotive News.

U.S. Government Publications

Current Industrial Reports and *Industry Trend Series* (Dept. of Commerce) A full series of valuable data on industries.

Quarterly Financial Report for Manufacturing Corporations (Federal Trade Commission and SEC) This survey produces, each calendar quarter, a composite income statement and balance sheet for each industry and for several sizes of firms within each industry.

Newspapers and Periodicals

F & S Index of Corporations and Industries (Predicasts, Cleveland) Weekly. Cumulated monthly and annually. An index to articles on industries and companies that appeared in selected business and financial publications and in brokerage firm reports.

Forbes Particularly the "Annual Report on American Industry" issue, published at the beginning of every year.

See specific and selected articles in other newspapers and periodicals listed on Table 4–1.

Advisory and Investment Services

Industry Surveys (Standard & Poor's) Covers over 40 industries. In each case, a *Basic Analysis* is issued which contains statistics and data which would require an extensive expenditure of time for an individual to compile. Data and graphs are provided for forecasting purposes.

Key Business Ratios in 125 Lines (Dun & Bradstreet, Inc.) Provides 14 ratios calculated for a large number of industries. The complete data give the 14 ratios, with interquartile ranges for 125 lines of business activity based on their financial statements.

Statement Studies (Robert Morris Associates) Compiled and published by a national association of bank loan officers, these data consist of representative averages based on financial statements received by banks in connection with loans made. Eleven ratios are computed for 156 lines of business.

ments about achievements of the fiscal period as well as tables showing current financial information relating to net sales, net income, earnings, dividends per share, and so on. The most important aspects of the report are the companies' financial statements—the balance sheet, income statement, statement of changes in financial position, and statement of retained earnings. In addition, many companies now provide a five- or ten-year summary of their financial statements for comparative analysis. Another source of information which contains valuable information on individual corporations is the Form 10-K filed annually by each company with the SEC.[1] Essentials of this form are summarized in Table 4–3. It is important to note that while the annual report and 10-K form are often similar, the annual report is regarded by analysts as being potentially biased. The

[1] Listed and OTC-registered companies are required to file periodic reports in addition to the Form 10-K, Form 10-Q quarterly report which provides summarized financial information. Form 8-K must be filed for each calendar month during which an event occurs requiring reporting (such as a significant acquisition or disposition of assets or a change in control of the registered company).

Table 4–3 **Companies—Raw Data**

From the Company

Annual Report: Contains audited financial statements and highlights of the year's performance. Mailed to shareholders or available on request (described in text).

Direct Request: An investor, particularly a shareholder, should feel free to make direct requests for information to the company, although they may not always be accommodated.

Form 10-K: An annual report which is filed with the SEC, due 90 days after the end of each fiscal year. The financial statements are prepared in compliance with Regulation S-X, which requires that the notes to the statements contain certain details of long-term leases, funded debt, management stock options, classification of inventories, and the basis for computing depreciation. Other information is included which is not required in the annual report, such as supplementary schedules to the statements and sales and earnings for each major line of business. (Available in major business libraries, from the companies themselves, and from the SEC.)

Quarterly Report: Issued by most companies, containing unaudited financial statements released during the fiscal year.

Investment Manuals and Services

Statistics and Fundamental Information:

Bond Record (Moody's, Inc.) Gives interest rates, call prices, yields to maturity, price ranges, ratings, and other data on more than 19,000 bond issues.

Fixed Income Investor (Standard & Poor's); *Bond Survey* (Moody's, Inc.) Weekly. Each issue analyzes new offerings in the corporate and municipal markets, opportunities in convertible bonds, changes in bond ratings, new issue ratings, and bonds called for payment. These services also provide the trends and outlook for interest rates, and other commentary.

Moody's Manuals (Moody's, Inc.) These volumes are published each year and contain reports on thousands of corporations in various fields—industrials, OTC, public utilities, and others. The reports give a financial history and full investment data for a period of years, including the major contractual features of company bonds.

Moody's Handbook of Common Stocks (Moody's, Inc.) Quarterly. Similar in content and form to Standard & Poor's *Stock Reports*, giving statistical information and charts on over 1,000 companies.

Stock Guide; Bond Guide (Standard & Poor's) These are 150- to 200-page books in which all important corporation securities are listed. The stock book shows earnings yield, capital structure, working capital, market price data, earnings per share, and dividends for the last five years, including interim earnings. The bond book contains the most pertinent comparative financial and statistical information on a broad list of bonds.

Stock Reports (Standard & Poor's) Weekly. A looseleaf service of two-page reports on many companies whose stock is traded on the NYSE, AMEX, and OTC. Each report gives the fundamental position, recent developments, earnings,

10-K form is considered more factual, because the SEC requires the disclosure of information that may be generally omitted from the annual report.[2]

Statistical sources concerning the past financial performance and condition of a company can be found in easily readable form from several advisory services, brokerage houses, and investment manuals. A sample page from Standard & Poor's *Stock Reports*, a widely used source of company information, is shown in Figure 4–1. In addition, various sources present raw data about the past price movements of securities in the form of tables and charts. Incidentally, essential data on thousands of bond issues are available from Moody's *Bond Record* and Standard & Poor's *Bond Guide*. Table 4–3 contains several examples of various types of raw data sources mentioned above.

Thus far, we have only mentioned popular sources of unbiased information;

[2] For details of the reporting requirements of the Form 10-K, see Section 12 of the Securities Exchange Act of 1934. Rule 14-C of the Securities Exchange Act discusses the requirements for the annual shareholders' report.

Table 4–3 *(cont.)*

financial statement data, financial position, and other information. Charts on past prices are presented, as well as a short recommendation or appraisal of the security.

Charts and Graphs (Past Price Data) for Technical Analysis:

M. C. Horsey & Co. (New York, N.Y. and Salisbury, Md.) Issues *The Stock Picture,* a book of over 1,700 charts, published every two months. Annually, it also publishes 25-year charts of some 200 leading stocks.)

Trendline (A division of Standard & Poor's) Publishes three chart books. One, called *Daily Basis Stock Charts*, shows the market behavior of about 750 NYSE and ASE stocks plotted on a daily basis and issued every Friday after the close of the market. A second, called *Current Market Perspectives*, is a monthly book of charts on nearly 1,000 listed issues showing weekly, high, low, and closing prices. Each chart covers four years. The third is the *OTC Chart Manual*, covering 840 OTC stocks. (Chartcraft also publishes an *OTC Chartbook*, containing point and figure charts.)

Securities Research Company (Boston, Mass.) Publishes two chart books. One is *3-Trend Security Charts* (monthly), which charts prices, earnings, and dividends on 1,105 leading stocks over the previous 21 months. For a longer view, *3-Trend Cycli-Graphs* (quarterly) charts the same information over the previous 12 years.

Statistical Compilations on Special Securities:

New Issue Outlook (New York, N.Y.) A weekly report on both companies planning to "go public," as well as trading-action reports on over 400 most recently offered new issues.

Over-the-Counter Growth Stock Digest (Greenwich, Conn.) Published quarterly by John S. Herold, Inc. A changing list of the fastest growing OTC companies with relevant facts and figures.

Wiesenberger Services, Inc. (New York, N.Y.) In addition to *Investment Companies*, a basic compendium issued annually, Wiesenberger also issues a companion "Charts & Statistics," a quarterly *Investment Company Management Results*, *Mutual Fund Performance Monthly Service*, *Wiesenberger Facts on Funds*, *Mutual Funds Panorama*, *Wiesenberger Guide to Withdrawal Plans*, and two additional expensive financial advisory services, the *Dealer's Service* and the *Timings Service*.

Others

See Table 4–6 for a list of advisory services. Some, such as *Value Line*, include raw data and statistics in addition to their commentary.

Also see newspapers and periodicals in Table 4–1, especially *The Wall Street Journal,* which is perhaps the best available source of *current*, unbiased corporate information. Brokerage houses, listed in Table 4–6, also provide raw data and statistical compilations of stocks and bonds.

the methods of utilizing them will be discussed in Chapters 6–18. It is, however, important to remember that, without a careful selection and analysis, raw data is of little or no value to the investor.

Interpretive Information

The Market

Some of the best research and commentary available on the economy and business conditions are provided by the economists and research staffs of many of the large U.S. banks in their weekly, biweekly, or monthly reports. Most of these reports are published in the form of concise, easy-to-understand newsletters; subscriptions are available free or for a nominal fee. Some institutions provide specific forecasts on interest rates, the money supply, GNP, and other indicators; others occasionally make projections on the direction of the securities markets.

Figure 4–1

Disney (Walt) Productions 755

NYSE Symbol DIS Options on ASE, CBOE, & Pac

Price	Range	P-E Ratio	Dividend	Yield	S&P Ranking
Nov. 14'79 37	1979 44 1/8–33	11	0.48	1.3%	A+

Summary

This company is generally acknowledged as the leader in the family entertainment field, deriving most of its revenues from its activities as an amusement park operator and producer-distributor of motion pictures. The company should extend its impressive growth record in fiscal 1979–80. In development are additional major projects for the 1980s which would enlarge Disney's scope of operations, including a sizable expansion of the Disney World park.

Current Outlook

Earnings for fiscal 1979–80 should increase moderately from the $3.51 a share (preliminary) of fiscal 1978–9.

The cash dividend, now at $0.12 quarterly, is expected to remain modest.

Although comparisons could be restricted by slower economic activity, and concern over the availability and cost of fuel on theme park operations, revenues and earnings in 1979–80 should continue upward. Increased contributions from consumer products and filmed entertainment should aid comparisons.

Total Revenues (Million $)

Quarter:	1978-9	1977-8	1976-7	1975-6
Dec.	154.7	137.1	119.5	115.7
Mar.	186.7	169.9	140.0	139.5
Jun.	211.8	192.4	165.1	148.7
Sep.	243.6	241.8	205.2	180.0
	796.8	741.2	629.8	583.9

For the fiscal year ended September 30, 1979, revenues rose 7.5% from those of the prior year, as gains from entertainment and recreation, and consumer products and other activities offset lower motion picture receipts. Profitability improved, and net income climbed 15.7% to $3.51 per share, from $3.04.

Common Share Earnings ($)

Quarter:	1978-9	1977-8	1976-7	1975-6
Dec.	0.56	0.41	0.37	0.34
Mar.	0.79	0.71	0.54	0.55
Jun.	0.93	0.76	0.63	0.58
Sep.	1.23	1.16	0.99	0.83
	3.51	3.04	2.53	2.30

TRADING VOLUME THOUSAND SHARES

1974 1975 1976 1977 1978 1979

Important Developments

Nov. '79—Attendance at Disneyland in fiscal 1978-9 was 10,760,000 (virtually unchanged from fiscal 1977-8) and 13,792,000 at Disney World (down 2%).

Oct. '79—Construction began on the new $800 million EPCOT Center, which will be located within the Walt Disney World resort and entertainment complex.

Apr. '79—DIS formalized final agreements with Oriental Land Co. to develop a $300 million Tokyo Disneyland. DIS will be responsible for the design and master planning, and provide guidance on all construction and operational aspects; DIS will receive a royalty percentage of gross revenues from rides, food and merchandise.

Next earnings report due in mid-January.

Per Share Data ($)

Yr. End Sep. 30	1979	1978	1977	1976	1975	1974	[1]1973	1972	1971	1970
Book Value	**NA**	26.71	23.96	21.55	19.31	17.24	15.82	14.40	10.79	8.15
Earnings	**3.51**	3.04	2.53	2.31	1.91	1.51	1.49	[2]1.29	0.91	[2]0.82
Dividends	**0.44**	0.27 7/8	0.14 3/4	0.11 1/2	0.11 1/8	0.10 7/8	0.10 3/4	0.08 [illegible]	0.08 1/4	0.06 1/4
Payout Ratio	**13%**	9%	6%	5%	6%	7%	7%	7%	9%	8%
Prices[3]—High	**44 1/8**	47 1/8	46 7/8	60 [illegible]/4	51 3/4	49 5/8	110 1/4	105 5/8	63 [illegible]/8	33 7/8
Low	**33**	31 1/2	31 5/8	39 3/8	19 3/4	15 1/2	36 1/8	59 1/4	30 1/4	19 1/4
P/E Ratio—	**13–9**	16–10	19–12	26–17	27–10	33–10	74–24	82–46	70–33	41–23

Data as orig. reptd. Adj. for stk. div(s). of 2% Dec. 1977, 3% Dec. 1976, 3% Dec. 1975, 2% Nov. 1974, 2% Nov. 1973, 100% Jan. 1973, 2% Nov. 1971, 100% Mar. 1971, 2% Nov. 1970. 1. Reflects accounting change. 2. Ful. dil. eps: 1.26 in 1972, 0.79 in 1970. 3. Cal. yr. NA-Not Available.

Standard NYSE Stock Reports Vol. 46/No. 227/Sec. 7

November 21, 1979

Standard & Poor's Corp. 25 Broadway, NY, NY 10004

755 Disney (Walt) Productions

Income Data (Million $)

Year Ended Sep. 30	Revs.	Oper. Inc.	% Oper. Inc. of Revs.	Cap. Exp.	Depr.	Int. Exp.	Net Bef. Taxes	Eff. Tax Rate	Net Inc.	% Net Inc. of Revs.
1978	741	216	29.1%	47	39.0	2.02	189	48.1%	98.4	13.3%
1977	630	188	29.9%	45	37.4	NA	157	47.9%	82.0	13.0%
1976	584	172	29.4%	44	35.0	NA	140	46.8%	74.6	12.8%
1975	520	151	29.1%	44	32.8	[2]2.65	[3]116	46.7%	61.7	11.9%
1974	430	126	29.3%	70	29.6	[2]7.71	[3]89	45.4%	48.3	11.2%
1973	385	117	30.3%	87	26.6	[2]4.84	[3]85	43.9%	47.8	12.4%
1972	329	101	30.7%	143	24.7	[2]1.82	[3]74	45.8%	40.3	12.3%
1971	176	56	32.1%	205	7.8	NA	[3]49	44.9%	26.7	15.2%
1970	167	52	30.9%	67	7.9	NA	[3]44	50.2%	21.8	13.0%
1969	148	40	26.9%	31	7.4	NA	33	51.4%	15.8	10.7%

Balance Sheet Data (Million $)

Sep. 30	Cash	Current— Assets	Current— Liab.	Current— Ratio	Total Assets	Ret. on Assets	Long Term Debt	Common Equity	Total Cap.	% LT Debt of Cap.	Ret. on Equity
1978	288	394	114	3.5	1,083	9.6%	NA	861	NA	NA	12.0%
1977	175	290	86	3.4	964	8.9%	8	771	875	0.9%	11.2%
1976	110	196	82	2.4	874	9.0%	7	692	788	0.9%	11.4%
1975	41	125	74	1.7	783	8.1%	6	619	702	0.9%	10.5%
1974	16	91	58	1.6	743	6.8%	61	552	676	9.0%	9.1%
[1]1973	10	69	67	1.0	679	7.4%	44	506	602	7.4%	9.9%
1972	12	75	51	1.5	608	7.0%	53	461	548	9.6%	10.0%
1971	37	87	50	1.7	497	6.7%	102	318	439	23.3%	9.6%
1970	40	93	36	2.6	268	7.6%	1	218	227	0.3%	10.7%
1969	90	126	32	4.0	238	7.8%	51	146	203	25.1%	13.3%

Data as orig. reptd. 1. Reflects accounting change. 2. Net of interest income 3. Incl. equity in earns. of nonconsol. subs. NA-Not Available.

Business Summary

Walt Disney Productions is principally engaged in family-oriented entertainment and recreation operations, including the operation of the Disneyland and Walt Disney World theme park complexes and the production of theatrical and TV films distributed throughout the world. Other activities include the design, production, distribution, and/or licensing of merchandise and publications arising from characters from its movies.

1977-8	Revs.	Profits
Theme parks	63%	50%
Filmed entertainment	21%	28%
Consumer products	16%	22%

Opened in 1955, Disneyland encompasses 230 acres in Anaheim, Calif. Park attendance rose 1.2% in fiscal 1977-8 from that of the prior year, to a record 10,807,000 patrons.

Walt Disney World was opened in 1971, and covers 2,500 acres near Orlando, Fla. It includes three major hotels, a shopping village, campgrounds, golf courses, and other facilities. Park attendance in fiscal 1977-8 advanced 7.8% to 14,071,000. About 69% of theme park division revenues in 1977-8 were derived from operations at Disney World.

The primary audience appeal of Disney motion pictures is to children and families. Successful films are generally re-released once every seven years. Disney has a contract with NBC-TV under which its TV show, The Wonderful World of Disney, is telecast.

The EPCOT (Environmental Prototype Community of Tomorrow) Center at Walt Disney World, incorporating the World Showcase, is scheduled to open October 1, 1982.

Dividend Data

Dividends have been paid since 1957. A dividend reinvestment plan is available.

Amt. of Divd. $	Date Decl.	Ex-divd. Date	Stock of Record	Payment Date
0.12	Nov. 29	Dec. 5	Dec. 11	Jan. 6'79
0.12	Feb. 7	Mar. 12	Mar. 16	Apr. 2'79
0.12	May 30	Jun. 28	Jul. 5	Aug. 4'79
0.12	Sep. 4	Oct. 1	Oct. 5	Nov. 5'79

Next dividend meeting: Nov. 27'79.

Capitalization

Long Term Liabilities: $11,393,000.

Common Stock: 32,257,809 shs. ($1.25 par).
R. E. Disney owns about 5%.
Institutions hold about 34%.
Shareholders: 66,000.

Office—500 South Buena Vista St., Burbank, Calif. 91521. Tel—(213) 845-3141. Pres & CEO—E. C. Walker. Secy—D. A. Smith. Treas & Investor Contact—W. A. Jones. Dirs—D. B. Tatum (Chrmn), C. L. Ahmanson, W. H. Anderson, R. E. Disney, P. M. Hawley, R. W. Miller, R. T. Morrow, E. C. Walker, R. L. Watson. Transfer Agent & Registrar—Bank of America, San Francisco. Incorporated in California in 1938.

SOURCE: Standard & Poor's *Stock Reports*, Standard & Poor's Corp., New York.

Table 4–4 **The Economy and Market—Interpretive Information**

Bulletins from Commercial Banks

Business in Brief (Chase–Manhattan Bank) Bimonthly. Extensive analysis on a variety of topics in each issue.

Economic Comment (Mellon Bank, Pittsburgh, Penn.) Biweekly. Each report features an analysis of a selected economic subject and two pages of economic and financial statistics.

Financial Digest; *Economic Report*; *Business Report* (Manufacturers Hanover Trust) Published weekly, monthly, and quarterly—respectively. All provide analysis. *Financial Digest* lists money market, Federal Reserve, and business indicator data. *Business Report* gives forecasts on GNP.

Monthly Economic Letter (First National City Bank of N.Y.) Currently has a circulation of over 200,000.

Weekly Economic Package and *Monthly Economic Indicators* (Chemical Bank of N.Y.) Provides analysis as well as specific forecasts on interest rates, monetary indicators, and economic indicators. A wealth of graphs and raw data included.

U.S. Government Publications

Economic Report of the President and *Annual Report of the Council of Economic Advisers*. Annually. Discussions of the economic outlook and data on the economic and business situation.

Monthly reviews from each of the twelve Federal Reserve Banks.

Advisory Services

Indicator Digest, Inc. (Palisades Park, N.J.). Publishes a monthly report which concentrates on coverage of stock market indicators with emphasis on market timing and individual stock selections. Also publishes *Technical Stock Reports* on market outlook and selected stock recommendations. *The Directory of Indicators* describes the composition and construction of various technical indicators.

Investment and Barometer Letter (Babson's Reports, Inc., Wellesley Hills, Mass.) Stock market guidance based on fundamentals.

The Outlook (Standard & Poor's) Carries articles on market behavior, the outlook for various industries, important individual issues, purchase or sale recommendations, and sample portfolios.

United Business and Investment Reports (United Business Service Co., Boston, Mass.) A weekly report on general business and stock market trends, including stock selections.

Others

Brokerage houses frequently comment on the economy and prospects for the security markets in widely distributed research letters and reports. See the list of firms in Table 4–6. Information available upon request.

Also see periodicals in Table 4–1 for articles on the economy and market which provide opinions and projections. Regular commentators and columnists usually provide the most straightforward opinionated discussions.

The opinions of economists and other knowledgeable authorities can also be found in newspapers, magazines, and research letters from leading brokerage houses. For the more sophisticated, each of the 12 Federal Reserve Banks publishes a free monthly bulletin containing scholarly articles about banking, economic, and financial topics, sometimes of regional interest.[3]

Many advisory services also make predictions about the future state of the economy and markets as part of their reports and recommendations to subscribers. A summary and specific examples of these sources can be found in Table 4–4.

[3] The twelve Federal Reserve Banks are in Atlanta, Boston, Chicago, Cleveland, Dallas, Kansas City, Minneapolis, New York, Philadelphia, Richmond, St. Louis, and San Francisco.

The Industries

Stock and bond investors need information for evaluating industry conditions that affect the performance of individual companies. Several sources analyze industry data and provide forecasts and outlooks for the performance of individual industries. These include a government publication entitled *U.S. Industrial Outlook*, Standard & Poor's *Industry Surveys*, and research materials from brokerage houses. In addition, many advisory services which comment on market conditions and individual securities also advise on specific industries. The financial pages of newspapers and business-related periodicals often publish news or profiles on various sectors of business with advisory overtones. Table 4–5 is a list of industry interpretive information sources.

The Companies

Any investors unwilling to analyze raw data about individual firms would not be lost, provided they had the tenacity to sift through the avalanche of analysis and advice from numerous sources. There are many advisory services to choose from—large, small, respected, and suspected. They employ different forecasting and analytical techniques to make recommendations about common stocks, fixed income securities, new issues, convertible bonds, mutual funds, over-the-counter securities, and other investment alternatives. Interestingly, their forecasting techniques differ as widely as their prices; some services charge subscribers over $500 a year.

Table 4–5 **Industries—Interpretive Information**

U.S. Government Publications

U.S. Industrial Outlook (U.S. Bureau of Domestic Commerce) Annually. Recent trends for over 100 industries with a ten-year outlook provided.

Advisory Services

Industry Surveys (Standard & Poor's) Besides the *Basic Analysis* published annually (see Table 4–2), a supplementary section entitled *Current Analysis and Outlook* is issued at varying intervals. This report updates the figures in the *Basic Survey*, provides a short-run forecast, and gives brief analyses of representative companies in the industry.

Wall Street Transcript Weekly. Reports on security market conditions, industries, and companies, with investment analyses and opinions, based on speeches by corporate executives, brokerage firm security analysis reports, and experts in the financial community. A specific industry is highlighted each week.

See some of the advisory services listed in Table 4–6 for additional industry recommendations. Industries are ranked each week for probable market performance by *Value Line* and are often evaluated by Standard & Poor's *The Outlook*.

Others

Brokerage houses make frequent industry selections and analyses. See list in Table 4–6.

Also see newspapers and periodicals in Table 4–1.

Investors who are not satisfied with the opinions of advisory services may obtain other opinions from the brokerage industry. By calling ten different stockbrokers on any given day, one could receive analysis and recommendations concerning as many as 100 securities. Incidentally, this advice is not really free; higher trading commissions are usually charged to offset the costs of research.

Finally, a number of columns appearing in newspapers and magazines openly support the purchase or sale of bonds or equities. A sample of these sources is presented in Table 4–6.

Note that although information sources have been classified into specific categories for the purpose of this discussion, such a clear segmentation may not always exist. Some sources do not fit in any single category because they provide information in various areas and use both reporting styles. For instance, some advisory services not only give directions to subscribers by commenting on the market, industries, and companies, but also include a comprehensive amount of

Table 4–6 **Companies—Interpretive Information**

Brokerage Houses

Information in almost every category can be supplied by many of the larger brokerage firms. The following are a few of the major ones:

- Bache Halsey Stuart Shields, Inc., 100 Gold Street, New York
- E. F. Hutton & Co., One Battery Park Plaza, New York
- Loeb Rhoades, Hornblower & Co., 14 Wall Street, New York
- Merrill Lynch, Pierce, Fenner & Smith, One Liberty Plaza, New York
- Paine, Webber, Jackson & Curtis, 140 Broadway, New York

Advisory Services

Edson Gould's Findings & Forecasts (30 Rockefeller Plaza, New York, N.Y. 10017) Provides extensive technical data to back up forecasts of market trends, with emphasis on calling major tops and bottoms. Presents lengthy analyses for individual stock selection.

Investment Bulletin (American Institute Counselors, Inc., Great Barrington, Mass. 01230) Analyzes the economy and individual securities and recommends allocation of investment funds for aims ranging from conservative to speculative.

The Outlook (Standard & Poor's) Each issue contains several stock recommendations selected by a large staff of Standard & Poor's analysts. (See listing in Table 4–5.)

Value Line Investment Survey (Five E. 44th St., New York, N.Y. 10017) Each issue contains three sections: a summary of the *Value Line's* analysis of all the nearly 1,700 stocks it follows, general comments and spotlighted stock selections for the week, and updated analyses of over 100 stocks. Voluminous raw data provided for each stock covered.

Zweig Forecast (747 Third Ave., New York, N.Y. 10017) Major emphasis is market timing based on a number of technical indicators developed by publisher Martin Zweig. A list of "favorable" and "vulnerable" stock issues is maintained.

Also see other advisory service sources in Tables 4–4 and 4–5.

Newspapers and Periodicals

Some magazines and newspapers feature columns written by investment experts who offer recommendations and insights. Examples can be cited from *Forbes* magazine: "Capital Markets," by Ben Weberman; "Stock Comment," by Heinz H. Biel; "Stock Trends," by Ann C. Brown. *The Wall Street Journal* often reports on securities that various market professionals are recommending in the "Heard on the Street" column. See Table 4–1 for a list of newspapers and periodicals.

Figure 4–2 **A Typical Value Line Full-Page Report**

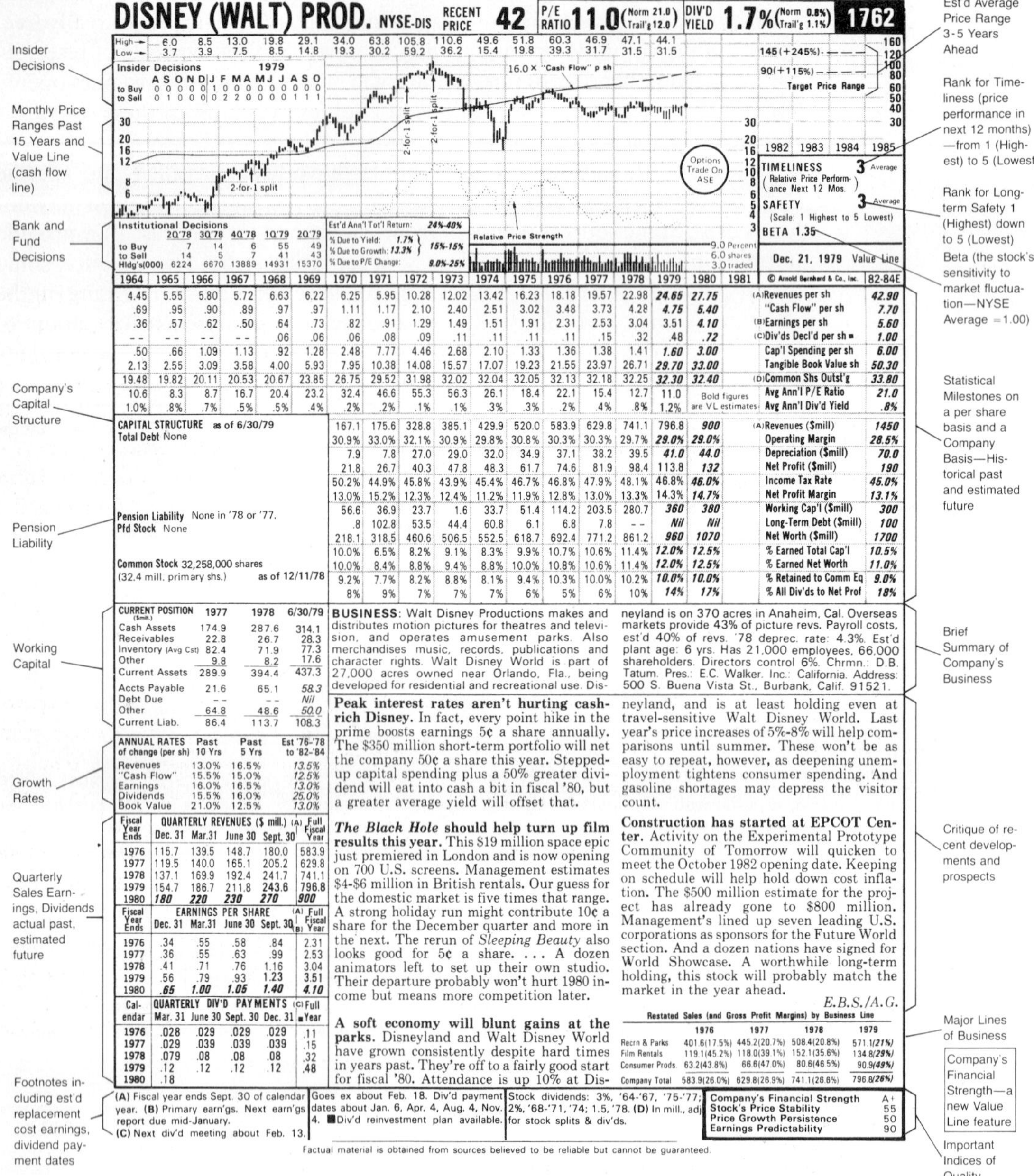

DISNEY (WALT) PROD. NYSE-DIS RECENT PRICE **42** P/E RATIO **11.0** (Norm 21.0 / Trail'g 12.0) DIV'D YIELD **1.7%** (Norm 0.8% / Trail'g 1.1%) **1762**

	1965	1966	1967	1968	1969	1970	1971	1972	1973	1974	1975	1976	1977	1978	1979
High	6.0	8.5	13.0	19.8	29.1	34.0	63.8	105.8	110.6	49.6	51.8	60.3	46.9	47.1	44.1
Low	3.7	3.9	7.5	8.5	14.8	19.3	30.2	59.2	36.2	15.4	19.8	39.3	31.7	31.5	31.5

Insider Decisions 1979

	A	S	O	N	D	J	F	M	A	M	J	J	A	S	O
to Buy	0	0	0	0	0	1	0	0	0	0	0	0	0	0	0
to Sell	0	1	0	0	0	0	2	2	0	0	0	0	1	1	1

Institutional Decisions

	2Q'78	3Q'78	4Q'78	1Q'79	2Q'79
to Buy	7	14	6	55	49
to Sell	14	5	7	41	43
Hldg's(000)	6224	6670	13889	14931	15370

Est'd Ann'l Tot'l Return: *24%-40%*
% Due to Yield: *1.7%*
% Due to Growth: *13.3%* } *15%-15%*
% Due to P/E Change: *9.0%-25%*

TIMELINESS **3** Average (Relative Price Performance Next 12 Mos.)
SAFETY **3** Average (Scale: 1 Highest to 5 Lowest)
BETA 1.35
Dec. 21, 1979 Value Line

1964	1965	1966	1967	1968	1969	1970	1971	1972	1973	1974	1975	1976	1977	1978	1979	1980	1981	© Arnold Bernhard & Co., Inc.	82-84E
4.45	5.55	5.80	5.72	6.63	6.22	6.25	5.95	10.28	12.02	13.42	16.23	18.18	19.57	22.98	**24.65**	**27.75**		(A)Revenues per sh	**42.90**
.69	.95	.90	.89	.97	.97	1.11	1.17	2.10	2.40	2.51	3.02	3.48	3.73	4.28	**4.75**	**5.40**		"Cash Flow" per sh	**7.70**
.36	.57	.62	.50	.64	.73	.82	.91	1.29	1.49	1.51	1.91	2.31	2.53	3.04	3.51	**4.10**		(B)Earnings per sh	**5.60**
--	--	--	--	.06	.06	.06	.08	.09	.11	.11	.11	.11	.15	.32	.48	**.72**		(C)Div'ds Decl'd per sh ■	**1.00**
.50	.66	1.09	1.13	.92	1.28	2.48	7.77	4.46	2.68	2.10	1.33	1.36	1.38	1.41	**1.60**	**3.00**		Cap'l Spending per sh	**6.00**
2.13	2.55	3.09	3.58	4.00	5.93	7.95	10.38	14.08	15.57	17.07	19.23	21.55	23.97	26.71	**29.70**	**33.00**		Tangible Book Value sh	**50.30**
19.48	19.82	20.11	20.53	20.67	23.85	26.75	29.52	31.98	32.02	32.04	32.05	32.13	32.18	32.25	**32.30**	**32.40**		(D)Common Shs Outst'g	**33.80**
10.6	8.3	8.7	16.7	20.4	23.2	32.4	46.6	55.3	56.3	26.1	18.4	22.1	15.4	12.7	11.0	Bold figures		Avg Ann'l P/E Ratio	**21.0**
1.0%	.8%	.7%	.5%	.5%	.4%	.2%	.2%	.1%	.1%	.3%	.3%	.2%	.4%	.8%	1.2%	are VL estimates		Avg Ann'l Div'd Yield	**.8%**
						167.1	175.6	328.8	385.1	429.9	520.0	583.9	629.8	741.1	796.8	**900**		(A)Revenues ($mill)	**1450**
						30.9%	33.0%	32.1%	30.9%	29.8%	30.8%	30.3%	30.3%	29.7%	**29.0%**	**29.0%**		Operating Margin	**28.5%**
						7.9	7.8	27.0	29.0	32.0	34.9	37.1	38.2	39.5	**41.0**	**44.0**		Depreciation ($mill)	**70.0**
						21.8	26.7	40.3	47.8	48.3	61.7	74.6	81.9	98.4	113.8	**132**		Net Profit ($mill)	**190**
						50.2%	44.9%	45.8%	43.9%	45.4%	46.7%	46.8%	47.9%	48.1%	46.8%	**46.0%**		Income Tax Rate	**45.0%**
						13.0%	15.2%	12.3%	12.4%	11.2%	11.9%	12.8%	13.0%	13.3%	14.3%	**14.7%**		Net Profit Margin	**13.1%**
						56.6	36.9	23.7	1.6	33.7	51.4	114.2	203.5	280.7	**360**	**380**		Working Cap'l ($mill)	**300**
						.8	102.8	53.5	44.4	60.8	6.1	6.8	7.8	--	**Nil**	**Nil**		Long-Term Debt ($mill)	**100**
						218.1	318.5	460.6	506.5	552.5	618.7	692.4	771.2	861.2	**960**	**1070**		Net Worth ($mill)	**1700**
						10.0%	6.5%	8.2%	9.1%	8.3%	9.9%	10.7%	10.6%	11.4%	**12.0%**	**12.5%**		% Earned Total Cap'l	**10.5%**
						10.0%	8.4%	8.8%	9.4%	8.8%	10.0%	10.8%	10.6%	11.4%	**12.0%**	**12.5%**		% Earned Net Worth	**11.0%**
						9.2%	7.7%	8.2%	8.8%	8.1%	9.4%	10.3%	10.0%	10.2%	**10.0%**	**10.0%**		% Retained to Comm Eq	**9.0%**
						8%	9%	7%	7%	7%	6%	5%	6%	10%	**14%**	**17%**		% All Div'ds to Net Prof	**18%**

CAPITAL STRUCTURE as of 6/30/79
Total Debt None

Pension Liability None in '78 or '77.
Pfd Stock None

Common Stock 32,258,000 shares (32.4 mill. primary shs.) as of 12/11/78

CURRENT POSITION ($mill.)	1977	1978	6/30/79
Cash Assets	174.9	287.6	314.1
Receivables	22.8	26.7	28.3
Inventory (Avg Cst)	82.4	71.9	77.3
Other	9.8	8.2	17.6
Current Assets	289.9	394.4	437.3
Accts Payable	21.6	65.1	*58.3*
Debt Due	--	--	*Nil*
Other	64.8	48.6	*50.0*
Current Liab.	86.4	113.7	108.3

ANNUAL RATES of change (per sh)	Past 10 Yrs	Past 5 Yrs	Est '76-'78 to '82-'84
Revenues	13.0%	16.5%	*13.5%*
"Cash Flow"	15.5%	15.0%	*12.5%*
Earnings	16.0%	16.5%	*13.0%*
Dividends	15.5%	16.0%	*25.0%*
Book Value	21.0%	12.5%	*13.0%*

Fiscal Year Ends	QUARTERLY REVENUES ($ mill.) (A) Dec. 31	Mar.31	June 30	Sept. 30	Full Fiscal Year
1976	115.7	139.5	148.7	180.0	583.9
1977	119.5	140.0	165.1	205.2	629.8
1978	137.1	169.9	192.4	241.7	741.1
1979	154.7	186.7	211.8	243.6	796.8
1980	**180**	**220**	**230**	**270**	**900**

Fiscal Year Ends	EARNINGS PER SHARE (A) Dec. 31	Mar.31	June 30	Sept. 30	(B) Full Fiscal Year
1976	.34	.55	.58	.84	2.31
1977	.36	.55	.63	.99	2.53
1978	.41	.71	.76	1.16	3.04
1979	.56	.79	.93	1.23	3.51
1980	**.65**	**1.00**	**1.05**	**1.40**	**4.10**

Calendar	QUARTERLY DIV'D PAYMENTS (C) Mar. 31	June 30	Sept. 30	Dec. 31	Full ■Year
1976	.028	.029	.029	.029	.11
1977	.029	.039	.039	.039	.15
1978	.079	.08	.08	.08	.32
1979	.12	.12	.12	.12	.48
1980	.18				

BUSINESS: Walt Disney Productions makes and distributes motion pictures for theatres and television, and operates amusement parks. Also merchandises music, records, publications and character rights. Walt Disney World is part of 27,000 acres owned near Orlando, Fla., being developed for residential and recreational use. Disneyland is on 370 acres in Anaheim, Cal. Overseas markets provide 43% of picture revs. Payroll costs, est'd 40% of revs. '78 deprec. rate: 4.3%. Est'd plant age: 6 yrs. Has 21,000 employees, 66,000 shareholders. Directors control 6%. Chrmn.: D.B. Tatum. Pres.: E.C. Walker. Inc.: California. Address: 500 S. Buena Vista St., Burbank, Calif. 91521.

Peak interest rates aren't hurting cash-rich Disney. In fact, every point hike in the prime boosts earnings 5¢ a share annually. The $350 million short-term portfolio will net the company 50¢ a share this year. Stepped-up capital spending plus a 50% greater dividend will eat into cash a bit in fiscal '80, but a greater average yield will offset that.

***The Black Hole* should help turn up film results this year.** This $19 million space epic just premiered in London and is now opening on 700 U.S. screens. Management estimates $4-$6 million in British rentals. Our guess for the domestic market is five times that range. A strong holiday run might contribute 10¢ a share for the December quarter and more in the next. The rerun of *Sleeping Beauty* also looks good for 5¢ a share. . . . A dozen animators left to set up their own studio. Their departure probably won't hurt 1980 income but means more competition later.

A soft economy will blunt gains at the parks. Disneyland and Walt Disney World have grown consistently despite hard times in years past. They're off to a fairly good start for fiscal '80. Attendance is up 10% at Disneyland, and is at least holding even at travel-sensitive Walt Disney World. Last year's price increases of 5%-8% will help comparisons until summer. These won't be as easy to repeat, however, as deepening unemployment tightens consumer spending. And gasoline shortages may depress the visitor count.

Construction has started at EPCOT Center. Activity on the Experimental Prototype Community of Tomorrow will quicken to meet the October 1982 opening date. Keeping on schedule will help hold down cost inflation. The $500 million estimate for the project has already gone to $800 million. Management's lined up seven leading U.S. corporations as sponsors for the Future World section. And a dozen nations have signed for World Showcase. A worthwhile long-term holding, this stock will probably match the market in the year ahead.

E.B.S./A.G.

Restated Sales (and Gross Profit Margins) by Business Line

	1976	1977	1978	1979
Recrn & Parks	401.6(17.5%)	445.2(20.7%)	508.4(20.8%)	571.1*(21%)*
Film Rentals	119.1(45.2%)	118.0(39.1%)	152.1(35.6%)	134.8*(29%)*
Consumer Prods.	63.2(43.8%)	66.6(47.0%)	80.6(46.5%)	90.9*(49%)*
Company Total	583.9(26.0%)	629.8(26.9%)	741.1(26.6%)	796.8*(26%)*

(A) Fiscal year ends Sept. 30 of calendar year. (B) Primary earn'gs. Next earn'gs report due mid-January. (C) Next div'd meeting about Feb. 13. Goes ex about Feb. 18. Div'd payment dates about Jan. 6, Apr. 4, Aug. 4, Nov. 4. ■Div'd reinvestment plan available. Stock dividends: 3%, '64-'67, '75-'77; 2%, '68-'71, '74; 1.5, '78. (D) In mill., adj for stock splits & div'ds.

Company's Financial Strength	A+
Stock's Price Stability	55
Price Growth Persistence	50
Earnings Predictability	90

Factual material is obtained from sources believed to be reliable but cannot be guaranteed.

SOURCE: *The Value Line Investment Survey*, Arnold Bernhard & Co., New York.

raw data in their reports. An outstanding example of such an advisory service is the *Value Line Investment Survey*. Figure 4–2 is a sample page from this survey. Thanks to the availability of multipurpose sources, an investor can often find a wide spectrum of information within a limited number of sources.

Information Selection

The sample of sources previously listed is indicative of the enormous amount of available information. However, the number of these sources necessitates a certain amount of selectivity on the part of the potential investor. Because all investors do not share the same objectives, strategies, analytical abilities, and financial resources, no single list of sources is suitable for everyone. Nevertheless, a conceptual framework can still be developed for systematically selecting investment information. For convenience, this framework is developed here in three parts—category selection, specific source selection, and cost–benefit consideration.

Category Selection

The initial approach to selecting investment information should be well organized. Blindly choosing from among the huge quantity and variety of available sources is economically wasteful and intellectually sterile. The process of selection should begin with an identification of the investment objectives followed by a critical examination of the various kinds of sources.

Within each category, investors should first assess their own knowledge, then proceed to search for the information that is likely to be most beneficial. For example, a person already conversant with economic and market conditions may decide to concentrate on data relating to industries or companies. Also, based on the depth of their analytical skills and time constraints, investors should decide whether to seek raw data or interpretive information. Such an approach ensures an efficient use of resources and avoids a waste of time and money that might be spent gathering information of dubious value.

Specific Source Selection

Once the appropriate categories and reporting style have been selected, an investor should proceed to locate the specific sources. The techniques for selecting pieces of raw data and interpretive information are discussed below.

Raw Data Selection

Raw data are so abundant in the investment world that, before collecting raw data, an investor should determine the exact nature of the data needed to formulate an investment strategy. More specifically, a model should first be developed which can be used to process raw data and generate the results which can be interpreted and used to formulate investment strategies. *After* a model has been constructed or selected, data are then gathered to fit the specific requirements of the model. Because the quantity and type of raw data are clearly prescribed before the researcher begins the search, the selection process and the use of the time will be orderly and efficient.

Consider the following example. Suppose an investor needs to determine a company's future earnings in the valuation of its common stock, and she assumes that its future earnings will follow the trend established over the past ten years. In order to determine this trend and predict future earnings, the investor would need data on the company's past earnings, which could be obtained from annual reports, investment services, or other sources. The selection of data for this simplified example is straightforward.

As a general rule, investors espouse a common goal of predicting the future course of the market, industries, and companies. However, the approaches used to make such predictions differ—sometimes significantly—from one investor to another. So does the selection of investment information. For example, assume two investors are interested in purchasing the stock of Ford Motor Company. One investor notes that the stock is cyclical—that is, it fluctuates with business cycles. So he selects information about the economy published in *Business Conditions Digest* and attempts to predict economic recessions and booms in order to make his buy-and-sell decisions on Ford Motor stock. The second person—a sound, long-term investor—has little interest in playing the market on a short-term basis. She selects various financial statements and reports, such as those found in the annual report or Form 10-K, carefully analyzes this information, and finally makes her investment decision. The selection of raw data sources primarily depends on the investor's experience, analytical abilities, and method of information analysis.

Interpretive Information Selection

The selection of interpretive or opinionated material involves a different approach. Raw data are selected to fit the requirements of a model or method of analysis, but interpretive information reports the findings and conclusions of research and analyses already completed. Consequently, investors should evaluate these sources and determine whether the recommendations or conclusions offered are suitable for their needs.

Advisory information is not always specific. A commentary on the economy by a large bank, for example, may forecast a recession without specifying how it will affect selected securities. An investor using this information must translate such a commentary into an effective investment strategy. In many cases, interpretive information may be unsuitable for certain investors because it is written to suit the general public rather than individuals. The investor is responsible for determining whether this type of material is compatible with his or her investment knowledge, philosophy, and objectives.

In addition to determining the suitability of interpretive information, an investor should carefully evaluate its sources. Essentially, before one selects and accepts the advice or conclusions of an information source, at least three questions should be asked:

1. What are the background and experience of the researchers? Are they qualified to advise or to make reliable judgments?
2. On what basis are recommendations made? Are legitimate analytical methods used? (Answers to these questions may not be possible to obtain.)
3. What is the track record of the sources? How successful have their predictions been in the past?

These questions are critical when using professional investment advisory services. Although investment advisers are obliged to register with the Securities and Exchange Commission, besides the payment of a registration fee, the only requirement for offering such a service is a record clear of fraud. Although hundreds of registered services publish advisory letters, only a few are inspected each year. It is, therefore, imperative that an investor check the qualifications of the advisers and determine how they formulate their advice. More importantly, the investor should determine not only how well the services select individual investments, but also how well they detect major changes in the direction of the markets.

Finally, investors should be generally critical of advisory service and brokerage house opinions, because such firms tend to follow the trends rather than

Information on Investment Advisers

Investors can obtain valuable information about less well known advisers whose reputation has not been clearly established by asking the Securities and Exchange Commission office for information. Because the SEC maintains a file on all investment advisers registered with the agency, it can furnish investors with the names, educational and business backgrounds, and experience of all principals in the advisory firm. The SEC file also specifically describes the services offered, the fees charged, how each adviser operates, and what limits are put on the advice. There is, however, no data in the SEC files concerning the advisers' performance records.

Files are available from SEC offices in nine regions throughout the country for a fee of 10 cents per page, with a minimum order charge of $3.50. For details write to:

SEC
Washington, DC 20549
ATT: Public Reference

anticipate changes in them. In a bull market, for example, most services become increasingly optimistic and rarely reverse their position until a major reversal is under way. Interestingly, when the average advisory service sentiment becomes overly one-sided, it is viewed by some analysts as a contrary indicator to the market's direction.

Cost–Benefit Consideration

Investors benefit from using information sources when the rate of return on their investments is greater than would have been achieved had no sources been used. Of course, investors would also incur costs in the process of selecting, examining, and utilizing information. Consequently, when selecting and using investment information, investors should carefully weigh the expected benefits against the total cost of obtaining that information.

There are essentially three types of costs associated with the use of information. The first is the *outlay of money* to purchase certain materials. Although some items, such as annual reports of corporations and library materials, can be obtained free of charge, others must be purchased. Newspaper and magazine subscriptions, for example, may cost only a few dollars a year, but advisory service reports can be quite expensive. Second, there is the *opportunity cost* of using one's valuable time to select and analyze information. This cost, however, is not easily quantifiable; the best an investor can do is to estimate the value of the time spent on this activity. Finally, by using information sources, an investor *runs the risk* of following poor advice or making incorrect inferences from data, thereby earning a lower rate of return than would have been the case had the information not been used. Because all of these items either directly or indirectly increase the effective cost of the investment, they should be carefully considered as part of the information cost–benefit analysis.

In practical terms, it is usually difficult to weigh the cost of information against the expected benefits derived from it. Occasionally, however, there are exceptions to this general rule. For example, suppose an investor planning to invest $500 in the stock market can obtain all the relevant investment information for $100. In this case, it would hardly pay to obtain this information, because the investment would have to return 20 percent merely to absorb the information cost. The following illustration demonstrates this point:

	No Information Used	Information Used
Amount invested	$500	$500
Rate of return earned	5%	25%
Amount earned	$ 25	$125
Less cost of information	0	100
Net amount earned	$ 25	$ 25

Note that this example does not consider either the cost of the investor's time to gather and use the information or the risk of using what might turn out to be the wrong information.

In the previous example, it was suggested that information costing $100 would probably be too expensive for an investor with only $500 to invest. However, as revealed by the following illustration, that cost might not be too restrictive for someone with, say, $50,000 worth of investible funds:

	No Information Used	Information Used
Amounted invested	$50,000	$50,000
Rate of return earned	5%	5.2%
Amount earned	$ 2,500	$ 2,600
Less cost of information	0	100
Net amount earned	$ 2,500	$ 2,500

Clearly, in this case, only an increase of 0.2 percent (from 5 to 5.2 percent) in the rate of return would suffice to cover the cost of the information.

Incidentally, the increase in the return on investment that can result from a judicious use of investment information appears to be limited. In most cases, therefore, investment information should be used only when the benefits reasonably expected to be derived from its use would exceed the effective cost of obtaining that information.

Source Selection Summary

Figure 4–3 diagrams the process of information gathering and utilization in four convenient steps.

Step 1: The investor determines the areas for which information will be required—namely, the economy and markets, industries, and/or companies.

Step 2: The investor chooses between the two types of reported information—raw data or interpretive information. The investor must also estimate the cost of gathering and utilizing the information.

Step 3: If raw data for any category are needed, the investor makes a selection based upon the requirements of the model being used. If interpretive information is desired, the investor selects such information after proper application and evaluation.

Step 4: Raw data must be carefully analyzed and studied. Interpretive information provides conclusions or recommendations; however, these recommendations frequently need modification before they can be adapted to satisfy the investment needs of an individual investor.

Figure 4–3

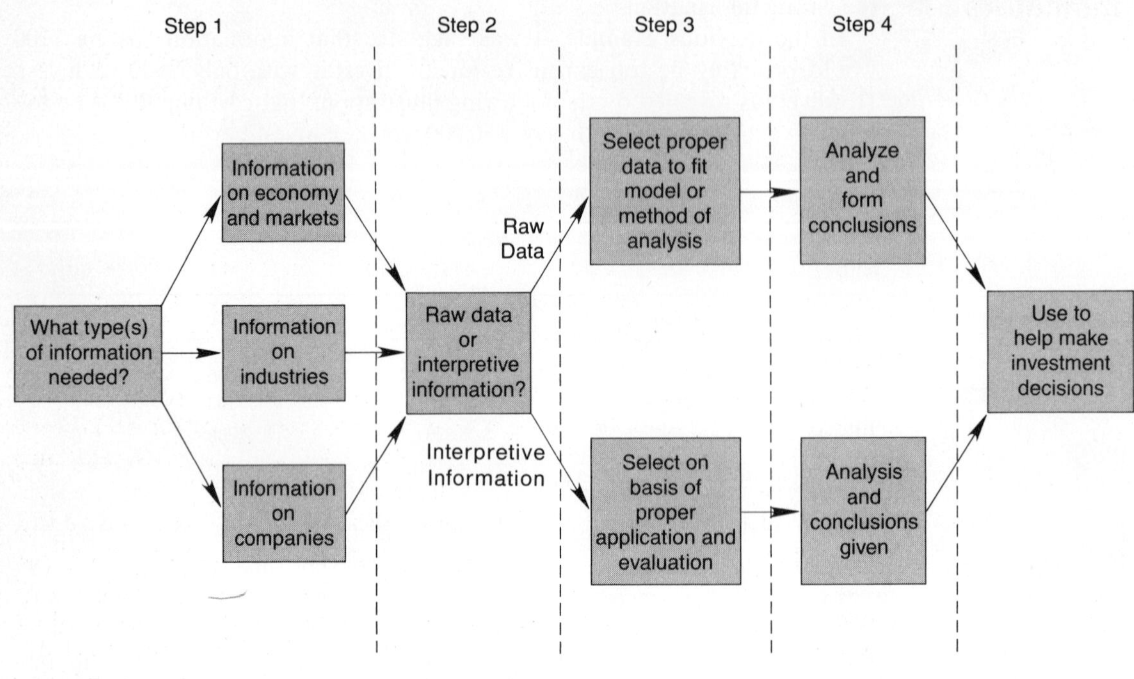

As mentioned, the cost of information is an important consideration in this process. The selection and use of information sources should be limited in order to ensure that the cost does not outweigh a reasonable expectation of the benefits to be derived from the use of this information.

SECTION 2 MARKET INDICATORS

Introduction

Among the principal barometers of conditions in the securities markets are the various market averages and indexes. These figures not only capture the movements in various segments of the market, but quickly reflect the market's reaction to news and information about the economy and business conditions.

This section will present a comprehensive review of market averages and indexes. First, the bond market indicators will be discussed; thereafter, the key stock market indicators will be presented.

Bond Market Indicators

No single average or index represents all types of bonds. It is, therefore, necessary to discuss these indicators under the categories of government, municipal, and corporate bonds.

Government Securities

U.S. treasury securities do not materially differ in quality, because the interest and principal payments for all issues are backed by the United States. Therefore, because all securities with the same maturity rate are expected to provide the same yield, there is no need to construct an average for these bonds. Of course, not all government bonds have the same maturity; and their yields differ primarily on the basis of how long it takes them to mature. Government bond averages are, therefore, constructed to measure the level of yields associated with treasury securities of various maturities.

The left half of Figure 4–4 charts three different averages[4] of yields on U.S. government securities for the years 1946 to 1979. The long-term bond average represents the average yield for a sampling of treasury bonds with maturities of over ten years.[5] The three-to-five year average represents the average yield for government securities of intermediate-term maturity. Finally, the rate on 91-day treasury bills is representative of the short-term yield. Note that the yields on government securities have both increased *and* decreased as the maturity has lengthened. A discussion of these yield structures will be undertaken in later chapters on bond analysis.

Municipal Bonds

Unlike treasury securities, with respect to the principal and interest payments, municipal bonds carry a risk of default. Moreover, the quality of these bonds can vary from one issue to another.[6] Consequently, municipal bond averages are designed to provide a representative yield for various quality issues. The right half of Figure 4–4 shows the average yields for municipal bonds of four quality rating categories from 1945 to 1979. These averages, compiled by Moody's Inc., are constructed solely from a broad sampling of general market names selling in the new issue market. In each rating category, the average yield is formulated from the 20-year yields of representative general obligation issues.

The Moody's averages differentiate between municipal bonds of varying quality; other indexes indicate the total rate of return on sample municipal

[4] These averages were compiled by Moody's, Inc. Other averages are available from Standard & Poor's and the Federal Reserve.

[5] These bonds also have different coupon rates.

[6] The risk of default of municipal bonds, indicated by bond ratings, will be discussed in Chapter 7.

Figure 4–4 (a)

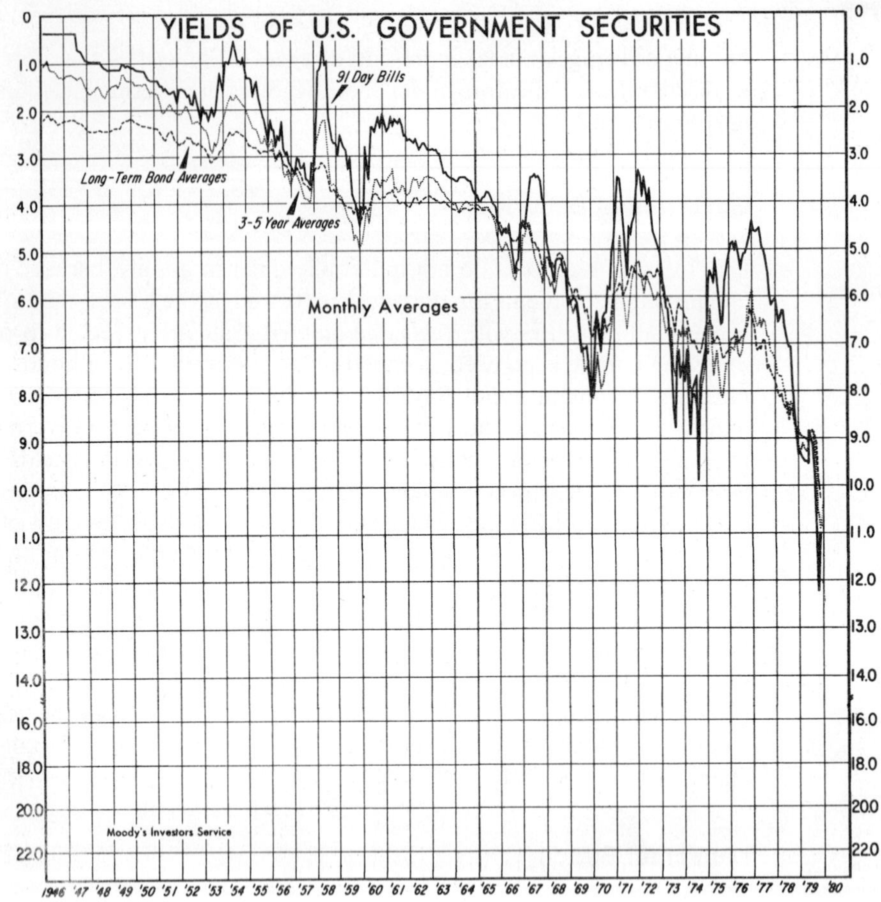

bond portfolios. For instance, the Municipal Bond Buyer Index covers 20 bonds of 20-year maturity; the average quality rating of the portfolio falls midway between Moody's Aa and A.[7] Standard and Poor's also compiles a similar 15-bond municipal index on the basis of 4 percent, 20-year bonds. A comparison of the varying levels of these indexes can provide a measure of the general change in market interest rates.[8]

[7] The bonds evaluated by this index are sometimes replaced in order to keep the same quality mix and to provide continuity as ratings and market standings change.

[8] Changes in Moody's averages can also provide a means for measuring the general change in market interest rates; however, because these averages represent bonds sold during the week, figures can change because bonds of different quality enter the market, rather than because a change has taken place in the level of market interest rates.

Figure 4–4(b) *(continued)*

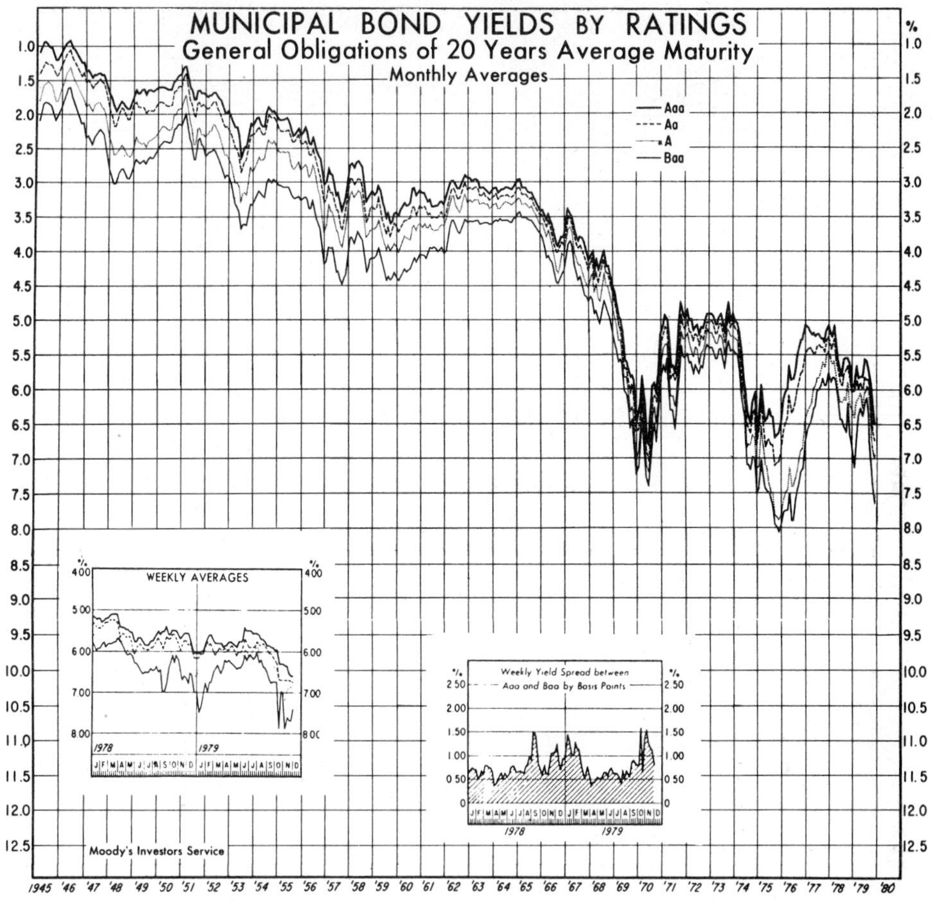

SOURCE: Moody's *Bond Record*, Moody's Investor Service, New York, December 1979, p. 176.

Corporate Bonds

Corporate bond indicators are similar to municipal bond averages in that they formulate representative yields for various quality securities.[9] For example, each week Standard & Poor's compiles representative yields for industrial and utility bonds in four quality rating categories. The yields of the industrial and utility

[9] Some indicators give average bond *prices* rather than yields. However, the representative yield of bonds is generally of greater value to investors.

Figure 4–5

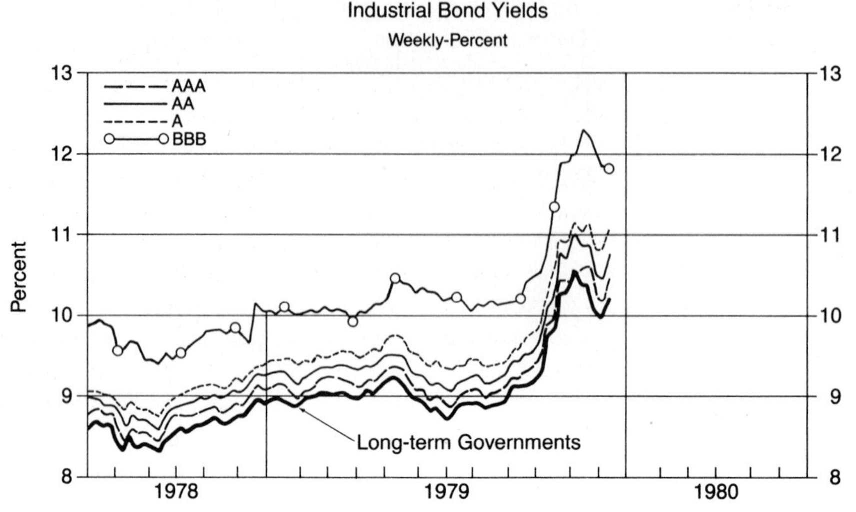

SOURCE: *Standard & Poor's Fixed Income Investor*, Standard & Poor's, Corp., New York, December 22, 1979.

bonds in each category are averaged to form a corporate composite yield. Representative industrial bond yields in four quality rating categories are shown in Figure 4–5.

Moody's also compiles yield averages for industrial, public utility, and railroad bonds in four rating categories. These averages are based on yields to maturity[10] of selected long-term bonds, usually ten in each category. The lists of bonds are adjusted periodically to reflect rating changes or other circumstances and to maintain the comparability of each of the series.

It should be added that bond market indicators are frequently used to *compare* the representative yields of different types of bonds. In Figure 4–5, for instance, the yields on various quality corporate bonds are compared with the yield on long-term government securities. On the basis of this comparison, an investor might switch from government to corporate bonds—that is, if the difference between the yields, or the spread, were sufficiently wide to warrant such a move.[11]

[10] Yield-to-maturity will be defined in Chapter 6. In this chapter, no distinction is made between yield and yield-to-maturity.

[11] The reason for the differences in yields on various types of bonds will be discussed in Part 2 of this book.

Stock Market Indicators

In contrast to bond averages, stock market *averages* and *indexes* are used as more than simply a measure of the price performance of different segments of the market. Movements in stock market indicators are considered benchmarks for measuring the investment results of individual securities and portfolios. Moreover, an effective measurement of fluctuations in individual stock prices relative to fluctuations in the stock market is considered a prerequisite to a successful application of the modern portfolio theory.

One widely held belief among investors is that one unique index or average exists which faithfully represents the state of the market. Actually, no single indicator occupies this venerable position. The basic factors which differentiate the many market indicators are the types and numbers of stocks used in the index or average—the sample—and the importance given to price and number of securities outstanding—the weighting.

The Dow Averages

The Dow Jones averages are the best known and most widely quoted indicators. Although there are only four distinct Dow averages, it is necessary to understand how to interpret and use each of them.

The Dow Jones Industrial Average (DJIA)

This average covers only 30 NYSE stocks—less than 2 percent of the approximately 1,500 common stocks listed on the NYSE, and less than 1 percent of all actively traded U.S. stocks. The DJIA stocks, however, represent well-established companies; they account for approximately 25 percent of the total market value of all NYSE stocks, and approximately 20 percent of all U.S. stock values. A listing of the 30 DJIA stocks and a graph showing the historical movements in the DJIA are in Figure 4–6. Interestingly, in the 1970s, the average reached a high of 1,067 as well as a low of 570.

The DJIA is *price weighted*; that is, it measures changes in the price of its components without regard to the number of shares outstanding for each company. For example, assume the average is derived from only three companies: ABC selling at $50 per share, QRS selling at $30 per share, and XYZ selling at $10 per share. The three-stock average is 30:

ABC	50
QRS	30
XYZ	10
Total	90
Divided by 3 =	30

Figure 4–6

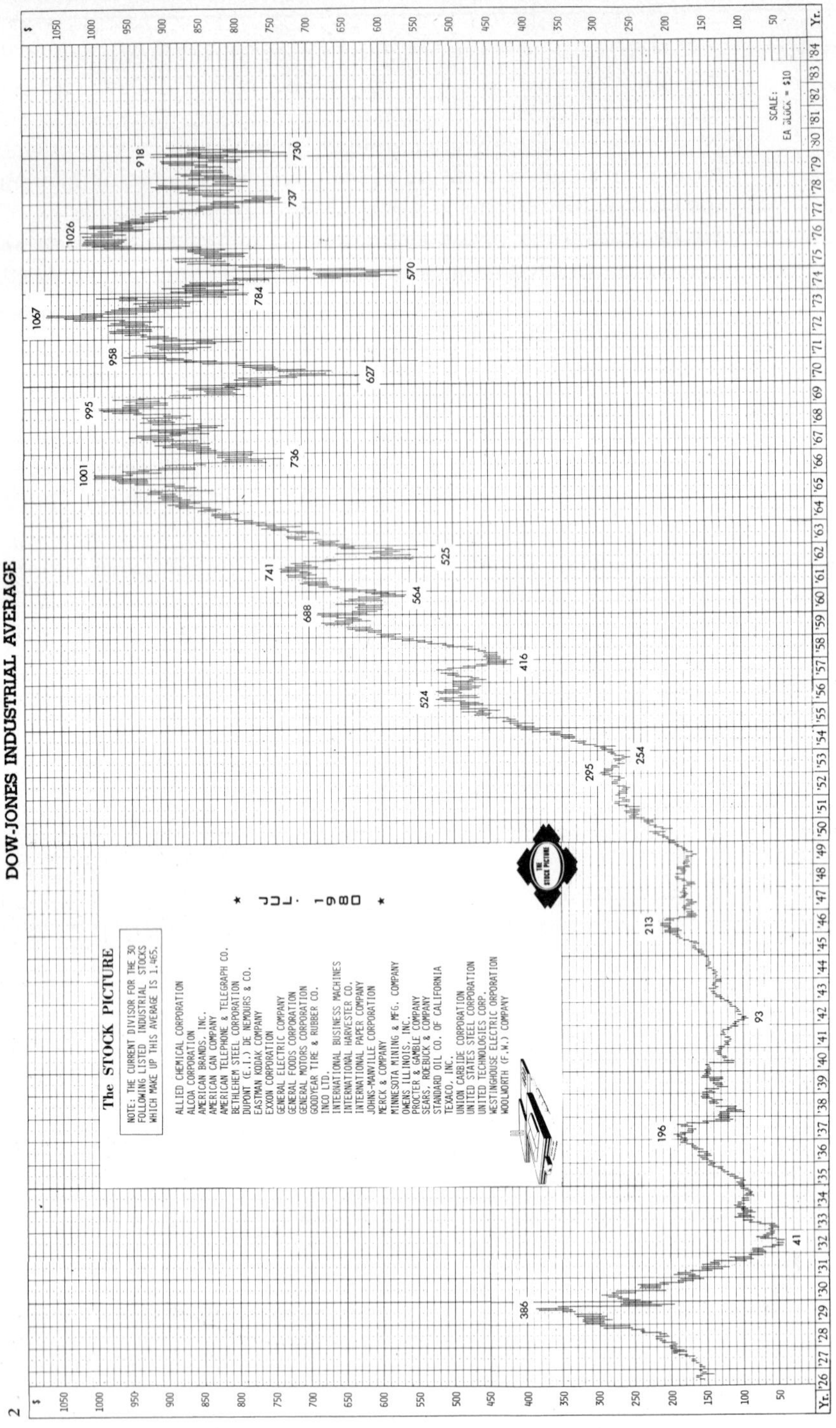

DOW-JONES INDUSTRIAL AVERAGE

The STOCK PICTURE

NOTE: THE CURRENT DIVISOR FOR THE 30 FOLLOWING LISTED INDUSTRIAL STOCKS WHICH MAKE UP THIS AVERAGE IS 1.465.

ALLIED CHEMICAL CORPORATION
ALCOA CORPORATION
AMERICAN BRANDS, INC.
AMERICAN CAN COMPANY
AMERICAN TELEPHONE & TELEGRAPH CO.
BETHLEHEM STEEL CORPORATION
DUPONT (E.I.) DE NEMOURS & CO.
EASTMAN KODAK COMPANY
EXXON CORPORATION
GENERAL ELECTRIC COMPANY
GENERAL FOODS CORPORATION
GENERAL MOTORS CORPORATION
GOODYEAR TIRE & RUBBER CO.
INCO LTD.
INTERNATIONAL BUSINESS MACHINES
INTERNATIONAL HARVESTER CO.
INTERNATIONAL PAPER COMPANY
JOHNS-MANVILLE CORPORATION
MERCK & COMPANY
MINNESOTA MINING & MFG. COMPANY
OWENS ILLINOIS, INC.
PROCTER & GAMBLE COMPANY
SEARS, ROEBUCK & COMPANY
STANDARD OIL CO. OF CALIFORNIA
TEXACO, INC.
UNION CARBIDE CORPORATION
UNITED STATES STEEL CORPORATION
UNITED TECHNOLOGIES CORP.
WESTINGHOUSE ELECTRIC CORPORATION
WOOLWORTH (F.W.) COMPANY

★ JUL. 1980 ★

SCALE: EA BLOCK = $10

SOURCE: M. C. Horsey & Co., *The Stock Picture*, September 1979, p. 2.

Because the DJIA is price weighted and the average has ranged between 570 and 1,067, many investors wonder why the stocks that make up the average are not also priced in the $570 to $1,067 per share range. In fact, all of the DJIA stocks trade below $100 per share. This apparent discrepancy can be explained by referring to the previous example of the three-stock average. Suppose ABC Company split its stock two-for-one. Following the split, there are twice as many shares of ABC stock outstanding, with each new stock valued at half the previous price. ABC stock is, therefore, selling at 25, instead of 50, and the new average is 21.67:

ABC	25
QRS	30
XYZ	10
Total	65
Divided by 3 =	21.67

The new average of 21.67 is 28 percent lower than the previous average of 30, even though no change in the market condition has taken place. To correct this situation, after a stock split the *divisor* is changed so that the average remains unchanged. In this example, if the average is to be left unchanged at 30, the divisor must be lowered from 3 to 2.167 (65/2.167 = 30), as though the number of stocks in the average was reduced from 3 to 2.167.

The method just presented for recalculating the DJIA suggests that each stock split results in a reduction in the divisor. Facts bear this out. By prewar 1939 the divisor was reduced from 30 to 15.1, and by 1950 to 8.92; today the divisor is 1.465.[12] Therefore, if all 30 DJIA stocks sold at $50 per share, the average would be 1,023.89 [(30 × 50)/1.465 = 1,023.89].

The DJIA has been criticized for a number of reasons. First, critics consider that, because the 30 stock sample is representative of only the large, mature blue-chip firms, it is therefore not a reliable indicator of market sentiment or an accurate benchmark for measuring market performance. Second, because the DJIA is price weighted, the higher priced stocks have a greater influence on the average than the lower priced issues. Finally, because the DJIA moves in a high price range, what appear to be large movements in the average are usually small percentage changes. For example, a jump in the DJIA of 5 points from 875 to 880 is an increase of only about $\frac{1}{2}$ of 1 percent. Often such reporting can be confusing.[13]

[12] Prior to the latest revision in June 1979, the divisor was 1.443. When IBM and Merck were brought into the average to replace Chrysler and Esmark, the sum of the constituent stock prices increased. In order to equate the level of the DJIA immediately after the revision with its level immediately before, the divisor was increased to 1.465.

[13] Movements in the DJIA—or, for that matter, movements in any market indicator—only reflect changes in stock prices. Dividend payments are not taken into account in constructing these averages.

Other Dow Averages

Besides the popular Dow Jones Industrial Average, there are three other averages, all of which are computed in a similar manner. The Transportation Average—once comprised of 20 railroad common stocks—still consists of 20 issues, but now represents a broader sample of transportation companies because it includes air transportation and trucking firms. The Public Utility Average represents data for 15 electrical and natural gas utilities. Finally, the Composite Average comprises the 65 stocks included in the Industrial, Transportation, and Utility Averages.

Standard & Poor's 500 Index

The *Standard & Poor's 500 Index* is most widely used by institutional investors; many feel that its broad industry coverage and weighting make it a good substitute for the average common stock portfolio. It covers 88 industry groups and comprises 400 industrial companies, 40 public utilities, 20 transportation companies, and 40 recently added financial corporations. The S&P 500 has recently been updated to include several new component issues now traded over the counter and to reorganize many of the industry groups. The index is *value weighted*; that is, it gives weight to both the *size* and *price* of each stock. Consequently, the highest priced stocks with the largest number of shares outstanding carry the greatest influence in the movement of this indicator. For example, IBM and Exxon, the two companies with the largest capitalization comprise, respectively, about 7 percent and 3.5 percent of the S&P 500.

The S&P 500 is an index. Unlike the Dow Jones averages, it is a statistical yardstick expressed in terms of percentages of a base year. To compute this index, the price of each stock is multiplied by the number of shares in the issue outstanding. This total value is then expressed as a percentage of the average market value during the years 1941–43, and the result is multiplied by 10. Although strictly speaking not a percentage, this index provides a close approximation of percentage variations in stock prices.

The S&P 500 Index is computed in the following manner:

$$\frac{\text{Total Market Value of 500 Stocks}}{\text{Total Market Value in 1941–43}} \times 10$$

The method of constructing this index is explained below by using two stocks:

Stock	Current Price	Number of Shares	Total Value
ABC	$100	1,000	$100,000
QRS	30	2,500	75,000
			$175,000

Assuming that in 1941–43 the market value of the two stocks was \$22,000, the index is 79.55:

$$\frac{\$175{,}000}{\$22{,}000} \times 10 = 79.55$$

Besides the S&P 500, there are separate indexes for the industrial, transportation, utility, and financial companies which are included in this index. Graphs of the Standard & Poor's 500 and 400 Industrials for the years 1962 to 1979 are presented in the top half of Figure 4–7. During this period the S&P 500 fluctuated between the high of 120.24 and the low of 52.32, while the S&P 400 has ranged between 134.54 and 54.80.

NYSE Composite Index

For many years, the Board of Governors of the New York Stock Exchange has been dissatisfied with the DJIA. However, not until July 14, 1966, did it begin to publish new price indexes of common stocks listed on the Exchange. The NYSE Composite Index covers all the common stocks listed on the Big Board. In addition, there are four separate indexes for the industrial, transportation, utility, and financial company stocks included in the composite.

Like the S&P 500, the *NYSE Composite Index* is value weighted; therefore, its major movements are dominated by the issues of larger companies. For example, although the S&P 500 Index represents only about 30 percent of the NYSE listings, that 30 percent represents approximately 75 percent of the market value of all NYSE stocks.

The NYSE Composite Index was assigned a base value of 50 because on the day of its inception this was the approximate average price of NYSE stocks. An index of 55, therefore, indicates that the average market value of NYSE stocks has increased 10 percent above the original level. In recent years the NYSE Composite Index has fluctuated between the low 30s and the mid 60s, as indicated by Figure 4–7.

ASE Market Value Index

The *ASE Market Value Index* covers approximately 1,000 stocks listed on the American Stock Exchange; these account for less than 5 percent of the market value of all U.S. stocks. Unlike those in the NYSE Composite, S&P 500, and the Dow Jones Industrial Average, movements in the ASE Index are heavily influenced by the stocks of smaller companies.

The ASE Index is value weighted. Its method of construction is similar to that of the NYSE Composite Index, except that it uses August 31, 1973 as the base date and 100 as the base value. If on a given day the Index stands at 115, this implies that the value of all American Stock Exchange stocks is

Figure 4–7

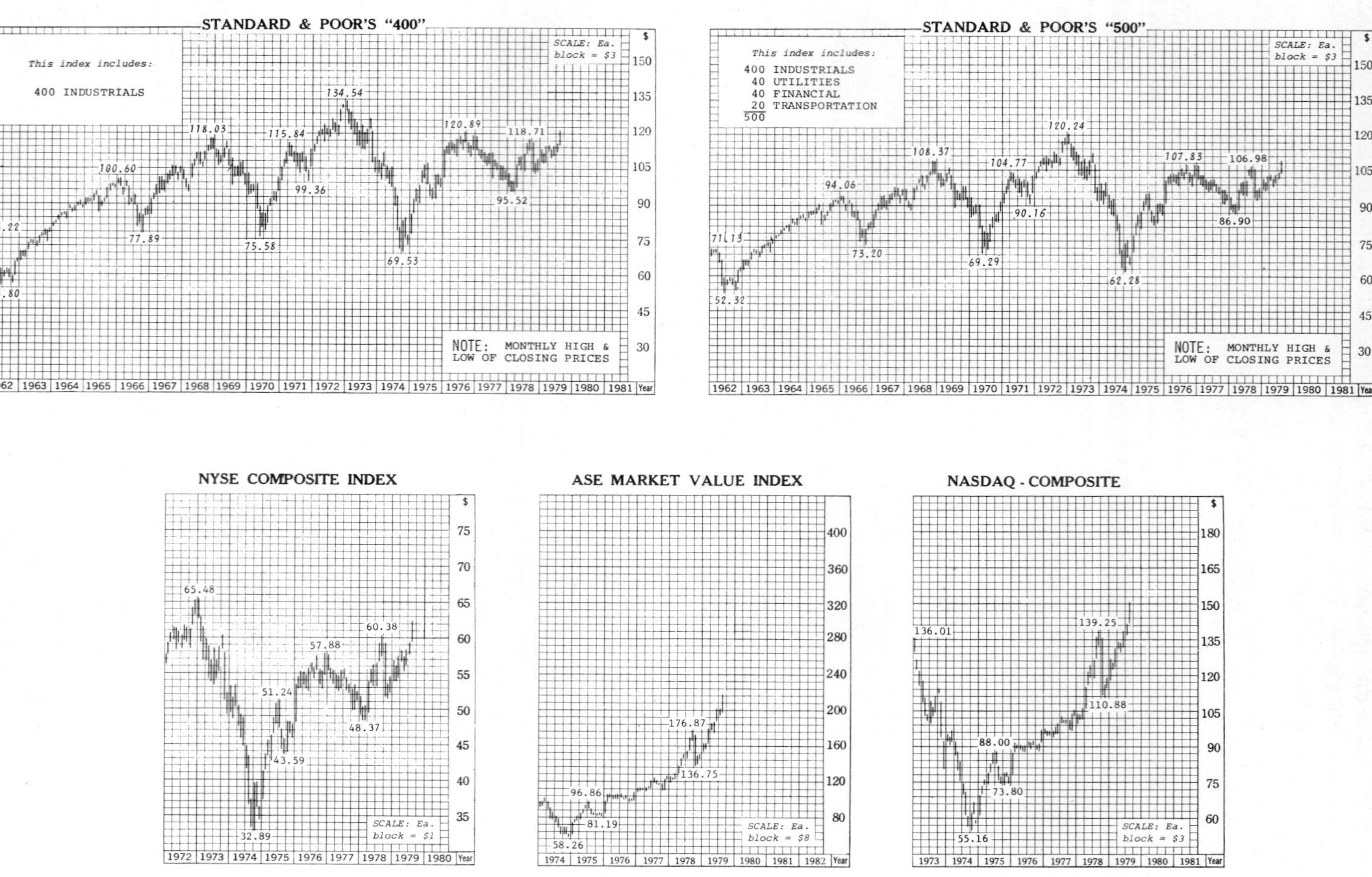

SOURCE: M. C. Horsey & Co., *The Stock Picture*, September 1979, p. 4.

15 percent above its 1973 level. The ASE Market Value Index is graphed in Figure 4–7. In 1974 the Index dropped to the low of 58.26; since then, however, it has risen above the 200 mark.

NASDAQ OTC Composite Index

The *NASDAQ OTC Composite Index* is a value weighted index derived from over-the-counter trading in over 2,000 securities. The Index was started on February 5, 1971 with a base value of 100. Like the ASE Market Value Index, this indicator is also more representative of smaller companies than the NYSE Composite, S&P 500, or the Dow Jones Industrial Average. However, it is heavily influenced by about 100 of the largest stocks on the NASDAQ system, many of which are larger than the largest firms on the American Stock Exchange.

A graph of the NASDAQ OTC Composite Index is included in Figure 4–7. In 1974 the Index dropped to 55.16; in 1979, however, it rose above the 150 level. The NASDAQ OTC Composite is composed of industrial, insurance, and bank stock groups, for which there are also separate indexes.

Value Line Composite Average

The Arnold Bernhard and Company Investment Service, publisher of the *Value Line Investment Survey*, also publishes the *Value Line Composite Average*. This average measures the value of 1,681 common stocks comprising 1,484 industrials, 19 rails, and 178 utilities. Most issues involved in this average are from the NYSE, although a few stocks are also traded on the ASE and the OTC.

The Value Line Composite Average is unique in that it computes a daily net percentage change for the stocks, thereby giving each stock equal weight in the average regardless of its price or size. Put differently, the great bulk of small, lower-priced stocks have just as much influence on this unweighted average as the giants; this measure is, therefore, considered by some analysts to be more representative of trends in the stock market than the weighted indicators. Incidentally, although this indicator is labeled as an average, it is expressed as a percentage of a base value of 100 prevailing on June 30, 1961, and technically can, therefore, be treated as an index.

Other Stock Market Indicators

In addition to the major market indicators, other indexes are available to gauge the performance of the smaller stock groups. *Barron's Group Stock Averages*, for example, is a weekly average based on the Thursday closing prices for stocks in a number of industries. Standard & Poor's also compiles indexes for individual industries, using a representative sample of major companies in each industry. By using these indicators, an investor can compare the price fluctuations of an individual stock to those of its industry average, and rate its relative price performance. The performance of an industry can also be rated by comparing the appropriate average to a broader market measure.

Stock Market Indicator Roundup

The major stock market indicators discussed in this section are summarized in Table 4–7. This table includes the stock sample, representation, weighting, and computation of the indexes and averages. Because the many indicators presented here have different characteristics, they lend themselves to varying uses. For instance, it is often asserted that the broad coverage of the NYSE Composite

Table 4–7

Stock Market Indicator	Sample	Representation	Weighting and Computation
Dow Jones Industrial Average	30 major NYSE industrial companies.	Less than 2% of all NYSE stocks and less than 1% of all actively traded stocks. Accounts for about 25% of market value of NYSE stocks and about 20% of all stock values.	Price weighted arithmetic average with divisor adjusted for stock splits.
S&P 500	400 industrials, 40 utilities, 20 transportation, 40 financial companies (mostly NYSE issues). Separate indexes for each of these groups.	About 75% of NYSE market value and 30% of NYSE issues. Large capitalization companies have heavy influence on index movement.	Value weighted index, as a percentage of the average during 1941–43.
NYSE Composite Index	Approximately 1,550 NYSE listed stocks. Separate indexes for industrial, utility, transportation, and financial stock groups.	Complete coverage of NYSE stocks. Major movements still dominated by stocks of large companies.	Value weighted index, with base of 50.
AMEX Market Value Index	About 1,000 American Stock Exchange stocks.	Complete coverage of smaller companies listed on the American Stock Exchange. Accounts for less than 5% of market value of all stocks.	Value weighted index, with base of 100.
NASDAQ OTC Composite Index	Over 2,000 stocks traded over the counter. Separate indexes for industrial, insurance, and bank stocks.	Covers many small company stocks, but is heavily influenced by about 100 of largest NASDAQ stocks.	Value weighted index, with base of 100.
Value Line Composite Average	1,681 stocks, which include 1,484 industrials, 19 rails, and 178 utilities. Separate averages for each of these groups.	Broad representation of stocks, mostly from the NYSE. All stocks have equal influence on indicator's movement.	Equal weighting, with average expressed as a percentage of a 100 base value.

Index and the Value Line Composite Average makes them the best overall measure of stock prices. However, although the NYSE Composite is more comprehensive than the DJIA and S&P 500, it is not influenced by small companies to the same extent as the NASDAQ or the ASE indicators.

Traditionally, institutional investors have used the Dow Jones Industrial Average for a quick reading of the market trend. However, the S&P 500 is most widely used for evaluating management performance, because it covers the stocks most widely traded by institutions. The Value Line Composite Average, in which all stocks carry equal weight, is considered by some analysts to be the most useful for investors interested in tracking their stocks against the median performance of larger groups.

Recently, the ASE Market Value Index and the NASDAQ OTC Composite Index have become popular, because they concentrate more heavily in stocks of smaller companies. Investor enthusiasm in these issues has moved the ASE and NASDAQ indicators to record highs in 1978, and again in 1979. Figure 4–8

Figure 4–8

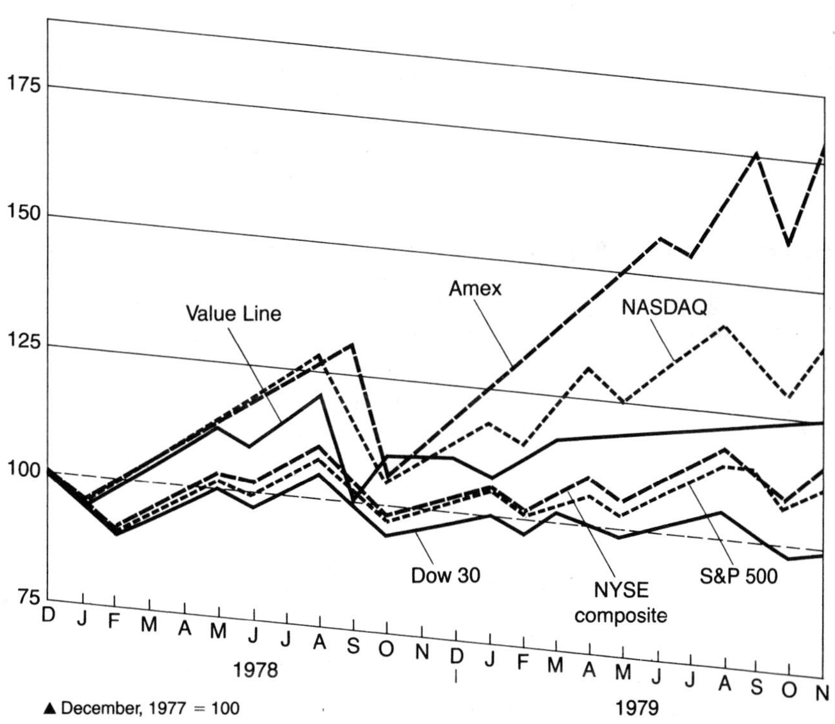

Data: Dow Jones & Co., Standard & Poor's Corp., New York Stock Exchange, American Stock Exchange, NASDAQ, Value Line.

SOURCE: Adapted from *Business Week*, December 31, 1979, p. 147.

reveals that since 1977 these indexes have outperformed the DJIA, S&P 500, and the NYSE Composite, all of which concentrate in larger NYSE issues.

The divergence of the various market averages and indexes illustrates several key points. Investors should not rely on any single average as the sole measure of market performance. Different indexes may show significantly divergent trends during certain periods. Also, when comparing performance of a portfolio of stocks with the market portfolio, the investor should attempt to select an average that is similarly weighted. For instance, a portfolio weighted heavily with blue chips should be compared against the S&P 500 or the DJIA, whereas more diverse portfolios, depending on the types of stocks held, might be compared to other indicators.

Summary

Millions of investors make their buy and sell decisions in the securities markets by using a large number of diversified *information sources*. However, because of resource and time constraints, individual investors are restricted to the amount of information they can employ. Consequently, every investor must approach the problem of selection of investment information in an organized manner.

Information sources can be divided into three categories dealing with (1) the *market* and the *economy*, (2) the *industries*, and (3) individual *companies*. After deciding which of these categories will yield the most useful information, the investor can select *raw data, interpretive information*, or both.

Raw data is selected to fit a model or particular method of analysis. Although interpretive information includes conclusions or recommendations, investors must still evaluate the reliability of the source and modify the information to suit their own investment strategies. The cost of information is an important consideration in the selection process.

A wide variety of *bond* and *stock market indicators* are available to investors. Government bond averages indicate yields on treasury securities of different maturities; municipal and corporate bond averages indicate yields on representative samples of bonds of different quality. Bond market indicators are frequently used to compare the yields on different types of bonds and to measure the general change in market interest rates.

Stock market *averages* and *indexes* are used not only as a measure of the price performance of different segments of the market, but as benchmarks for measuring the investment results of individual securities and portfolios.

Several stock market indicators are published regularly. These include the *Dow Jones Industrial Average*, the *Standard & Poor's 500 Index*, the *NYSE Composite Index*, and other indexes. The basic factors which differentiate them are the stock samples and the weighting methods used. No single indicator lends itself to an all-purpose use, because all have special characteristics.

A Look Ahead

Chapters 2 and 3 introduced the investment environment with a discussion of investment alternatives, the investors, and the purposes and operations of the securities markets. In this chapter, investment information sources have been evaluated, along with the various bond and stock market indicators. However, although understanding how the investment market operates is essential, such knowledge is not a sufficient background for intelligent investors. The two cornerstones of the market are risk and return; understanding them is a prerequisite to an entry into the investment world. Chapter 5 will introduce the essentials of risk and return.

Concepts for Review

Sources of information
Raw data
Interpretive information
Market information
Industry information
Company information
Advisory services
Information selection
Cost–benefit consideration
Bond market indicators
Government security yields
Moody's Municipal Bond Averages
Municipal Bond Buyer Index
S&P Corporate Bond Yields
Stock market indicators
Average
Index
Price weighting
Value weighting
Dow Jones Industrial Average
Standard & Poor's 500 Index
NYSE Composite Index
ASE Market Value Index
NASDAQ OTC Composite Index
Value Line Composite Average
Barron's Group Stock Averages

Questions for Review

1. What are the major risks assumed by an investor who utilizes only interpretive information?
2. Would you prefer to use raw data or interpretive information in making an investment decision? Why?
3. Trace your steps following your decision to use either the raw or the interpretive data.

4. What sources of information would you select if you were considering the purchase of Ford Motor stock?
5. Must the choice between using raw data and interpretive information be absolute, or is a combination of the two possible?
6. Discuss the drawbacks of using only raw data.
7. Where would you go to find authoritative information regarding (a) the economy, (b) the stock market in general, (c) various industries, (d) individual corporations, and (e) the bond market?
8. An advisory service offers buy and sell recommendations on thousands of stocks for a subscription fee of $200 per year. What factors should you consider before subscribing?
9. Comment on the following statement: "It never hurts to acquire additional investment information."
10. What are the shortcomings of the Dow Jones Industrial Average? Are there any other market indicators that provide a better measure of stock market movements?
11. What characteristics differentiate the market indicators? Discuss the differences between the Dow Jones Industrial Average and S&P 500 in your answer.
12. Explain why the performance of the ASE Market Value Index and the S&P 500 can differ significantly over a year's time.
13. Why do institutional investors watch the S&P 500 more than other market indicators?
14. Would a 10-point movement in the NYSE Composite Index, Dow Jones Industrial Average, and NASDAQ OTC Composite Index mean the same thing? Explain.
15. If you were interested in investing in the stock of a small, growth company, how would you obtain the necessary information to help you make an intelligent investment decision?

Selected Readings

"Amex Introduces New Market Value Index System." *American Investor*, September 1973.

Balch, W. F. "Market Guides." *Barron's*, September 19, 1966.

Bildersee, John S. "Some New Bond Indexes." *Journal of Business*, October 1975.

Butler, H. L., Jr., and M. G. Decker. "A Security Check on the Dow-Jones Industrial Average." *Financial Analysts Journal*, February 1953.

Carter, E. E. and K. J. Cohen. "Stock Average, Stock Splits, and Bias." *Financial Analysts Journal*, May–June 1967.

Chandra, G. "Information Needs of Security Analysts." *Journal of Accountancy*, December 1975.

Cohen, Kalman J. and Bruce P. Fitch. "The Average Investment Performance Index." *Management Science*, February 1966.

Cootner, Paul. "Stock Market Indexes—Fallacies and Illusions." *Commercial and Financial Chronicle*, September 29, 1966.

Falk, Haim, Bruce C. Gobdel, and James H. Naus. "Disclosure for Closely Held Corporations." *Journal of Accountancy*, October 1976.

Fama, Eugene F., Lawrence Fisher, and Michael C. Jensen. "The Adjustment of Stock Prices to New Information." *International Economic Review*, February 1969.

Farrell, Maurice L., ed. *Barron's Market Laboratory*. Princeton, N.J.: Dow Jones Books, published annually.

Fisher, Lawrence. "Some New Stock Market Indexes." *Journal of Business*, January 1966 Supplement.

Hershman, A. "Accounting—More Data for Investors." *Dun's Review*, March 1976.

Jaffe, Jeffrey F. "Special Information and Insider Trading." *Journal of Business*, July 1974.

Kaplan, Robert S. and Richard Roll. "Investor Evaluation of Accounting Information: Some Empirical Evidence." *Journal of Business*, April 1972.

Latane, Henry A., Donald L. Tuttle, and William E. Young. "Market Indexes and Their Implications for Portfolio Management." *Financial Analysts Journal*, September–October 1971.

Leuthold, S. C. and K. F. Blaich. "Warped Yardstick." *Barron's*, September 18, 1972.

Leuthold, S. C. and C. E. Gordon, II. "Margin for Error." *Barron's*, March 1, 1971.

"Loomis on Inside Information" (editorial interview). *Financial Analysts Journal*, May–June 1972.

Lorie, James H. and Victor Niederhoffer. "Predictive and Statistical Properties of Insider Trading." *Journal of Law and Economics*, April 1968.

Mechanic, Sylvia. "Key Reference Sources." In *Financial Analyst's Handbook*. Sumner N. Levine, ed. Homewood, Ill.: Dow Jones-Irwin, 1975.

Milne, P. D. "The Dow-Jones Industrial Average Re-examined." *Financial Analysts Journal*, December 1966.

Molodovisky, Nicholas. "Building a Stock Market Measure—A Case Story." *Financial Analysts Journal*, May–June 1967.

Nicholson, John W. "Annual and Interim Reporting under the Securities Exchange Act of 1934." In *The Modern Accountant's Handbook*. James Don Edwards and Homer A. Black, eds. Homewood, Ill.: Dow Jones-Irwin, 1976.

Reilly, Frank K. "Evidence Regarding a Segmented Stock Market." *Journal of Finance*, June 1972.

Reilly, Frank K. "The Original and New American Stock Exchange Price Indicator." University of Wyoming Research Paper No. 68, March 1975.

Reilly, Frank K. "Price Changes in NYSE, AMEX and OTC Stocks Compared." *Financial Analysts Journal*, March–April 1971.

Reilly, Frank K. "A Report on the NASDAQ Over-the-Counter Stock Price Indicators." University of Wyoming Research Paper No. 1, August 1973.

Rudd, Alfred S. "Site Visits." In *Financial Analyst's Handbook*, Vol. II. Sumner N. Levine, ed. Homewood, Ill.: Dow Jones-Irwin, 1975.

Schellbach, Lewis L. "When Did the DJIA Top 1200?" *Financial Analysts Journal*, May–June 1967.

Scholes, Myron S. "The Market for Securities: Substitution Versus Price Pressure and the Effects of Information on Share Prices." *Journal of Business*, April 1972.

Schoomer, B. Alva, Jr. "The American Stock Exchange Index System." *Financial Analysts Journal*, May–June 1967.

Securities Law—Fraud—SEC Rule 10b-5, Vols. 1 & 2. New York: McGraw-Hill, 1971.

Shaw, R. B. "The Dow-Jones Industrials vs. the Dow-Jones Industrial Average." *Financial Analysts Journal*, November 1955.

Sussman, Dorothy Hennessy. "Information Sources: An Overview." In *Financial Analyst's Handbook*, Vol. II. Sumner N. Levine, ed. Homewood, Ill.: Dow Jones-Irwin, 1975.

West, Stan and Norman Miller. "Why the New NYSE Common Stock Indexes?" *Financial Analysts Journal*, May–June 1967.

Risk and Return: An Overview

5

Introduction

In Chapter 2, various types of market instruments, such as common stocks, government and municipal bonds, corporate bonds, and other types of savings instruments were introduced. Although securities and financial markets were discussed in Chapter 3, three important facts have yet to be fully considered. First, some market instruments are riskier than others. Second, the risks associated with individual securities can be reduced by constructing an efficient portfolio of several carefully selected securities. Third, the concept of stock market efficiency involves much more than the efficient processing of buy and sell orders or the availability to investors of up-to-the-minute stock prices. The broad concept of market efficiency—an issue which has yet to be settled—revolves around the premise that the market price and the present value of a security are always equal. Staunch believers in market efficiency assert that because stock prices reflect all the information that is publicly knowable, there is little advantage to analyzing securities. Opponents, however, vehemently argue that the market is never that efficient and that returns can be improved by a careful development of a market strategy designed to exploit the inefficiency of the market.

In this chapter we will (1) define return and risk, (2) analyze various types and sources of risk, and (3) present the techniques for measuring risk. In the discussion of types and sources of risk, a distinction will be made between stocks and bonds on the one hand, and between individual securities and portfolios on the other. The technique of risk measurement will be developed against the backdrop of what is known as the Market Model. The nature of market efficiency will be explored and the controversy surrounding it will be articulated. Finally, risk preferences or the utility function of investors will be examined.

Many Faces of Risk

Most people think of risk as the danger of losing their capital. However, a total loss of capital resulting from bankruptcy is rare in the investment world. Risk is generally associated with more common forms of loss of capital.

Risk and Total Return

Suppose last year you invested \$10,000 in ABC bonds or stock which you sold for \$9,500 this year. You did not necessarily lose \$500. Your loss or gain on the investment really depends on the interest or dividend you collected from your investment. If you had collected \$750 in interest or dividend, you actually realized a *gain* of \$250 before taxes—or 2.5 percent (\$250/\$10,000). A gain or loss, therefore, must be measured against the *total return*—the combination of price change and interest or dividend income.

The total return on an investment can be measured by:

$$\text{Rate of Return} = \frac{\begin{matrix}\text{Terminal}\\ \text{Value}\end{matrix} - \begin{matrix}\text{Initial}\\ \text{Investment}\end{matrix} + \begin{matrix}\text{Additional}\\ \text{Cash Flow}\end{matrix}}{\text{Initial Investment}}$$

Therefore, in this example, your rate of return is 2.5 percent:

$$\text{Rate of Return} = \frac{\$9{,}500 - \$10{,}000 + \$750}{\$10{,}000}$$

$$= .025 \text{ (or } 2.5\%)$$

Change in Price Level

In the illustration just cited, it was tacitly assumed that the general price level remained unchanged, so that both your *real* and money rates of return (as measured by the purchasing power of money) equalled 2.5 percent. Had the inflation rate during the year been more than 2.5 percent, in real terms you would have realized a net *loss* on your investment. If, for instance, your initial \$10,000 investment had been made in 1979 and you sold the bonds or stock in 1980 when the inflation rate had reached 18 percent, although your money rate of return would have remained at 2.5 percent, your *real* rate of return would have been −15.5 percent (2.5 − 18.0 percent) and you would have suffered a \$1,550 loss. Clearly, when estimating returns on investments, investors should consider the possibility of loss in the purchasing power of the total return.

Lost Opportunity

Another form of risk is inherent in the nature of investment. Suppose after a careful investigation of ABC and XYZ stocks, you choose to invest in ABC stock. Subsequently you discover that, while your stock has appreciated 15 percent, the price of XYZ stock has appreciated 25 percent over the same period. Therefore, although you did realize a significant, positive return on your investment, by investing in ABC stock you lost the opportunity to realize a larger return by investing in XYZ stock.

Risk and Uncertainty

The concept of risk relates to *expected*, rather than realized, returns on investment. For instance, in our first example, the 2.5 percent return was unquestionably disappointing, because you could have realized a return twice as large simply by putting your money in a passbook savings account, which would have involved no possibility of capital loss on your part. Therefore, when you purchased the stock, you must have expected a higher return. However, your expectations were not realized, either because the company's performance was disappointing or because the market was generally depressed during this period. In effect, the risk you assumed by investing in the bond or the stock included the possibility of your not realizing the *expected* return. Uncertainty, then, is central to risk-taking. However, in a formal sense, there is a difference between risk and uncertainty which must be spelled out.

The theory of probability provides the necessary tools for dealing with uncertain values. According to this theory, although we cannot be certain how much return we will receive from an investment, we can *predict* with some degree of accuracy how much it is *likely to be*. The probability of an event taking place, or the relative chance of its occurrence, is known as its subjective probability. And therein lies the major difference between risk and uncertainty.

Uncertainty refers to a situation for which at least some of the possible future outcomes and their subjective probabilities are unknown. In contrast, in situations involving *risk*, all the future outcomes together with their associated probabilities of occurrences are assumed to be known. Although situations involving uncertainty are often closer to reality than those involving risk, it is difficult to model uncertainty; risk, however, may be determined with simple statistical tools. Conceptually, risk is often defined as the variability or dispersion in a subjective probability distribution; it is measured by the variance or standard deviation of returns.[1]

[1] Henceforth uncertainty and risk will be used as synonymous terms. In fact, risk is frequently defined as uncertainty regarding the expected rate of return from an investment.

Variance and Standard Deviation

The best estimate of the future return of any investment is the expected value, or mean, of all of the expected returns. It is this mean, or expected return, that an investor attempts to maximize at each level of acceptable risk.

The importance of variance as a measure of risk can be demonstrated by referring to Figure 5–A, which presents the normal distributions of expected annual returns of two stocks. Both stocks have a mean expected return of 10 percent. However, the expected returns of XYZ are much more likely to deviate from the mean than those of ABC. That is, expected returns of XYZ have a higher variance than those of ABC. Consequently, all else being equal, a rational, risk-averse investor will always prefer ABC over XYZ. For this reason, variance, σ^2, of the distribution of expected returns of a stock can be used as a measure of risk.

Although variance is an important measure of risk, it does not have the interpretive properties of the standard deviation, σ (the square root of variance).

The standard deviations for a normal distribution are shown in Figure 5–B. The magnitude of variations from the mean is represented by the standard deviations along the bottom of the curve. The probability of such variations is represented by

Figure 5–A

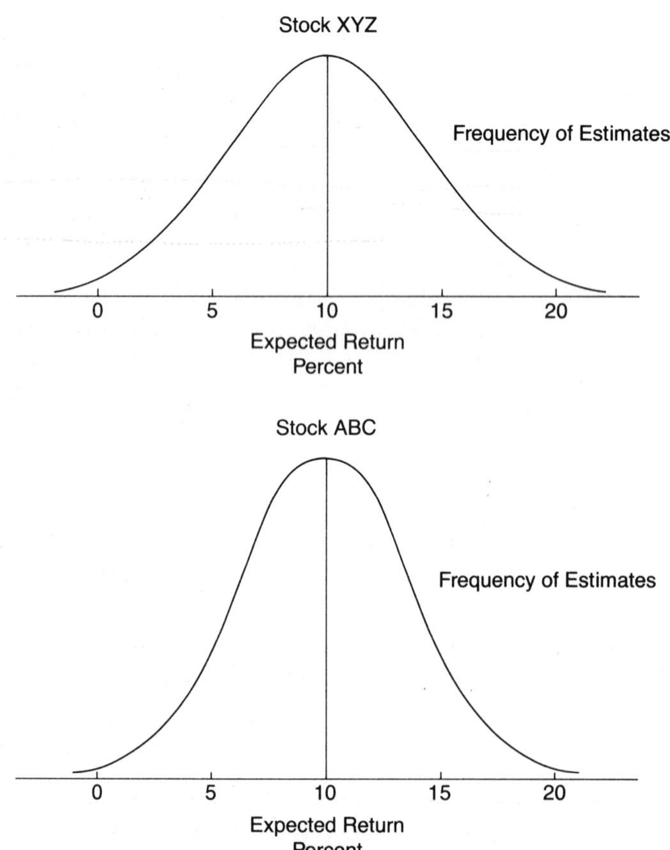

Figure 5–B

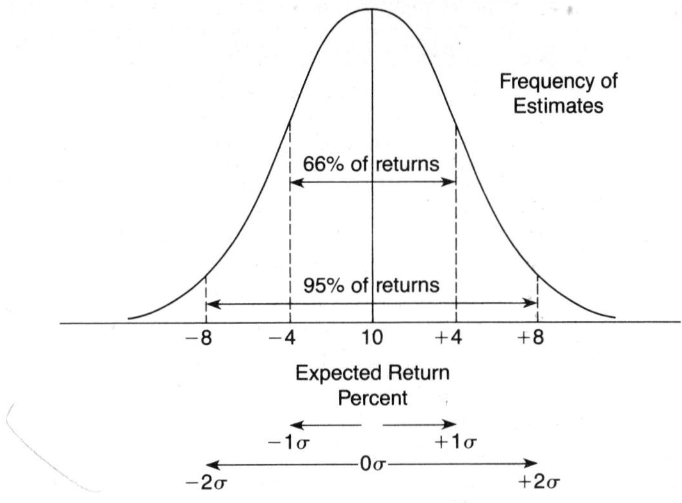

the area under the curve. Therefore, for normally distributed expected returns, 66 percent (roughly two-thirds) of the outcomes will fall within the range of plus, or minus, one standard deviation from the mean (Mean $\pm 1\sigma$), and 95 percent of the returns will fall within the range of plus, or minus, two standard deviations from the mean (Mean $\pm 2\sigma$). In the example presented in Figure 5–B, the mean of expected returns is 10 percent and the standard deviation of the returns is 4 percent. An investor purchasing this stock can conclude that roughly two-thirds of the possible returns will lie between 6 and 14 percent (10 ± 4), and that 95 percent will lie between 2 and 18 percent. Here again it should be noted that, all else being equal, the higher the standard deviation, the higher the risk associated with a given stock.

More specifically, the variance of a distribution is a measure of variability based on squared deviations of (N) individual observations (X_i) from the mean value of the distribution ($\bar{X}$). The formula for the variance is:

$$\sigma^2 = \frac{\sum(X_i - \bar{X})^2}{N}$$

If the distribution has known probabilities, the variance is a weighted average of the squared deviations $[(X_i - \bar{X})^2]$ and the weights are the probabilities of occurrence. That is,

$$\sigma^2 = \sum p_i[X_i - E(X)]^2$$

The standard deviation is the square root of variance, or

$$\sigma = \sqrt{\frac{(X_i - \bar{X})^2}{N}}$$

Details on variance and standard deviation can be found in any standard textbook on statistics. The use of variance in the measurement of risk is discussed later in this chapter.

Risk and Return: A Historical Record

Figure 5–1 is a historical view of the risk factor of returns in the U.S. capital market. The figure charts the growth of investments in common stocks, long-term government bonds, and treasury bills, as well as the increase in the inflation

Figure 5–1 **Wealth Indexes of Investments in the U.S. Capital Markets, 1926–1976**

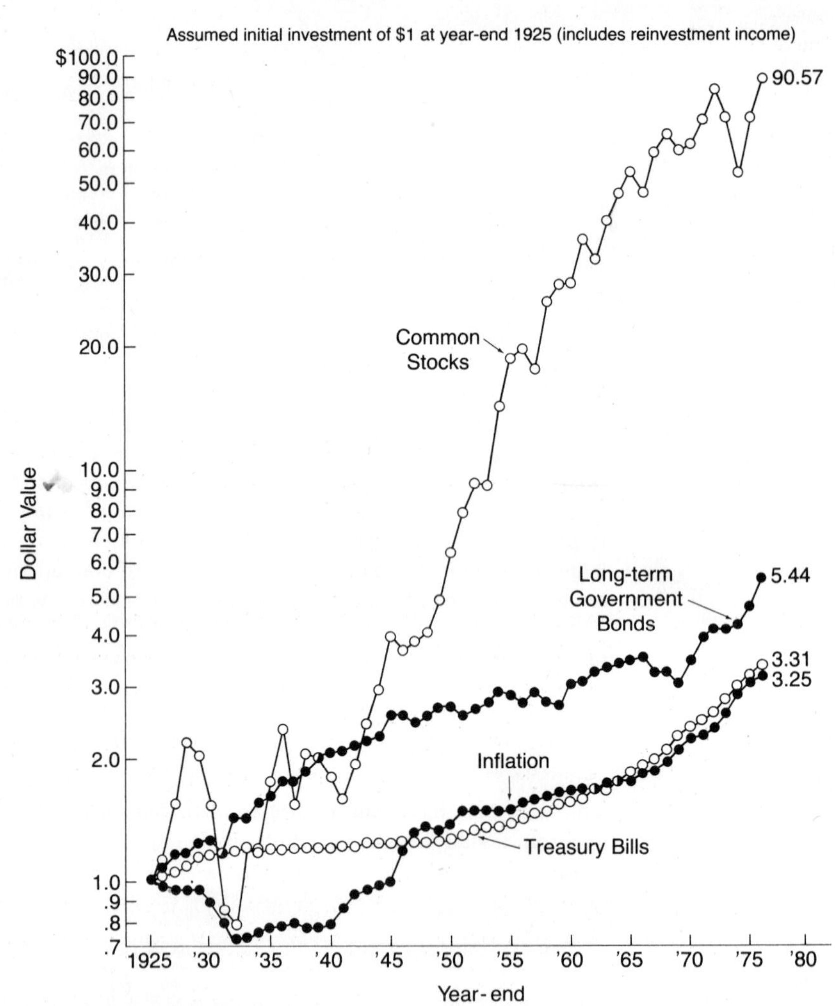

SOURCE: Roger G. Ibbotson and Rex A. Sinquefield, *Stocks, Bonds, Bills and Inflation: The Past (1926–1976) and the Future (1977–2000)* (Charlottesville, Va.: Financial Analysts Research Foundation, 1977), p. 3.

Table 5–1 **Selected Performance Statistics: 1926–76**

Series	Annual (Geometric) Mean Rate of Return	Standard Deviation of Annual Returns	Number of Years Returns Are Positive	Number of Years Returns Are Negative	Highest Annual Return and Year	Lowest Annual Return and Year	Distribution
Common Stocks	9.2%	22.4	34	17	54.0% (1933)	−43.3% (1931)	
Long-term Corporate Bonds	4.1%	5.8	41	10	18.4% (1970)	−8.1% (1969)	
U.S. Treasury Bills	2.4%	2.1	40	1	8.0% (1974)	0.0% (1940)	
Consumer Price Index*	2.3%	4.7	41	10	18.2% (1946)	−10.3% (1932)	−50% 0% +50%

* Data for CPI are inflation rates rather than returns.

SOURCE: Roger G. Ibbotson and Rex A. Sinquefield, *Stocks, Bonds, Bills and Inflation: The Past (1926–1976) and the Future (1977–2000)* Charlottesville, Va.: Financial Analysts Research Foundation, 1977.

index over the 50-year period, 1926–76. Each of the plotted lines assumes an initial investment of $1 at year-end 1925. The vertical scale is logarithmic so that equal distances represent equal percentage changes anywhere along the axis. Of the four items charted, common stocks had the most impressive growth. If $1 were invested at year-end 1925 and all dividends reinvested, the dollar investment would have grown to $90.57 by year-end 1976. In contrast, long-term government bonds with a constant 20-year maturity grew to only $5.44, and treasury bills increased to only $3.31.

The variable long-term growth rates of these investment instruments were associated with varying degrees of risk. Table 5–1 presents a clear view of the risks that were associated with various returns. Over the 1926–76 period, common stocks had an annual (geometric) mean ratio of return of 9.2 percent. However, substantial risks were associated with these returns, as is evident from a large standard deviation (22.4 percent) of returns. The histogram presented in the last column also reveals the wide variations in common stock returns on a year-to-year basis relative to the other types of securities. In contrast, although U.S. treasury bills grew at a compounded annual rate of only 2.4 percent, they also constituted a virtually riskless investment.[2]

Table 5–1 reveals additional measures of risk associated with common stocks relative to corporate bond and treasury bill risks. For instance, during 1926–76, common stocks produced negative returns during 17 years, but treasury bills produced negative returns only once. In fact, from its peak in January 1973 through February 1974, the decline in the market of approximately 40 percent in the Dow Jones Industrial Average and S&P 500 Index was the most dramatic change in stock prices during a brief period since the 1930s. Adjusted for inflation, the record was even more dismal, because the real purchasing power of the dollar suffered a major decline during this period. The historical view of the investment returns on stocks, bonds, and treasury bills (and the risks associated with them) is interesting in that it provides a framework for analyzing risk.

Types of Risk

Fixed Income Security Risk

The risks associated with fixed income securities are significantly different from those affecting a common stock. Unlike that of common stock, a bondholder is promised interest income and the repayment of principal by the issuing company. In this case, the major risks undertaken by bondholders are (1) interest rate risk, (2) inflation risk, (3) maturity risk, (4) default risk, (5) callability risk, and (6) liquidity risk. In Chapter 6 these risks will be discussed in detail; only the essential elements will be presented here.

Interest Rate Risk

In the event of an increase in the market interest rate, the price of an old bond with a lower coupon (interest) rate must fall sufficiently to offer investors yields that compete with new issues with higher coupon rates.[3] In contrast,

[2] An update of these figures shows that during 1926–78 the risks and returns of various instruments were as follows:

Type of Investment	Geometric Mean	Standard Deviation
Common stocks	8.9%	22.2%
Long-term government bonds	4.0%	2.6%
U.S. treasury bills	2.5%	2.2%

[3] For instance, the bond with one year remaining until maturity, a coupon rate of 10 percent, and currently selling at $1,000 will drop to $982.15 if the market interest rate were to increase to 12 percent:

$$\text{Price} = \frac{\$100}{(1+.12)^1} + \frac{\$1{,}000}{(1+.12)^1}$$

$$= \$89.29 + \$892.86$$

$$= \$982.15$$

when the market interest rate declines, prices of bonds outstanding rise, because old bonds with a higher coupon rate will command a premium to make them as attractive as new bonds with a lower coupon rate. A change in the price of a bond due to a change in the market interest rate is known as the *interest rate risk.*

Inflation Risk

When it issues a bond, the corporation promises to pay future interest and principal with current dollars. If a contract is made under which a lender receives a return on a \$1,000 bond of \$100 at the end of one year, the *nominal* return is 10 percent (\$100/\$1,000). However, if during the year the price level is found to have risen by 5 percent, then the *real* return would be only 4.762 percent {[(\$1,100/1.05) – (\$1,000)]/(\$1,000)}. The possibility of receiving a real return lower than the nominal return due to inflation is known as *inflation risk.*

In this context, a distinction should be made between unanticipated and anticipated inflation. If inflation is properly anticipated, no inflation risk occurs—at least in theory—because the interest rate will compensate the bondholder for the loss of purchasing power. Inflation risk is, therefore, associated primarily with unanticipated inflation.

Maturity Risk

Maturity risk refers to the contrasting perceptions of risk by lenders and borrowers. As a general rule, because borrowers fear increases in future interest rates, they prefer to borrow long by offering inducements to the lenders. However, the longer the period for which lenders part with their liquid funds, the more they are *uncertain* about the prospect of realizing a capital loss and the higher the maturity risk.

Default Risk

Uncertainty about the receipt of interest and principal payments is the basis for *default risk.* Although payment of both interest and principal on time is promised by the issuing corporations, due to adverse financial conditions corporations occasionally fail to fulfill their promises. Because this possibility always exists for corporate and municipal bonds, when these types of bonds are purchased investors are subject to default risk.

Callability Risk

Under certain circumstances, the issuer of a bond may force the bondholders to redeem their bonds before they reach maturity. If a bond is called during a period of falling market interest rates, the bondholders will probably be forced to reinvest the proceeds at a lower rate. This is known as the *callability risk.*

Liquidity Risk

A bond may also be subject to the *liquidity risk.* Liquidity refers to the cost of trade, search, and information, as well as the price concession one must grant in order to quickly convert the bond into cash. In general, the less liquid a security, the higher its liquidity risk. Risks associated with fixed income securities are discussed in detail in Chapter 6.

Common Stock Risk

When investing in a stock, an investor assumes the risk of realizing less than the expected return. Closer scrutiny reveals that this risk has two important components—namely, the risk that the variability in return would be caused by factors that affect the prices of all stocks—*market* or *systematic risk*—and factors that are unique to a firm or industry—*nonmarket* or *unsystematic risk.*

The following example contrasts the two types of risk. Suppose you are advised that fluctuations in Digital Equipment stock closely parallel movements in the market (of which the S&P 500 Index, for example, can be used as a measure), and you purchase 100 shares of that stock at $35 per share. One year later, the stock's return is −14 percent and the market return is −10 percent. Because the stock is assumed to be as volatile as the market itself, you might conclude that approximately −10 percent of the stock's return was solely due to the market or systematic risk. But the remaining −4 percent was primarily due to a poor performance by the Digital Equipment Company. Therefore, the −4 percent return represents a nonmarket or unsystematic risk. The two kinds of risk are always present, but the distinction between them is important.

More specifically, systematic or market risk is peculiar to the stock market as a whole. It refers to that portion of the total variability of a stock's return caused by factors which simultaneously affect the average return of *all* marketable securities. The possibility that individual stock returns may fluctuate solely as a result of changes in the overall market is called the systematic risk.

In the previous example, we assumed that the Digital Equipment stock was as volatile as the market (S&P 500 Index). However, not all stocks have this unique relationship with the market. In fact, most stocks are either more or less volatile than the market. While this fact does not change the *nature* of the systematic risk, it does affect the degree of riskiness of a stock. This important concept will be developed later in this chapter.

In contrast to the systematic risk, the unsystematic risk refers to that portion of the variability of a stock's return which is the result of unexpected events or developments within the company or the related industry. Both types of risk are graphed in Figure 5–2, which shows fluctuations in—or variability

Figure 5–2 **Systematic and Unsystematic Risk**

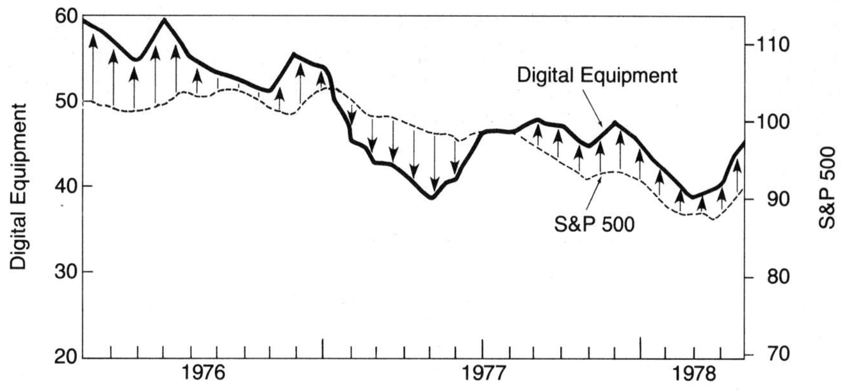

of—the Digital Equipment stock relative to fluctuations in the S&P 500 Index.[4] This figure reveals two important facts. First, *on the average*, the Digital stock fluctuates with the market. That is, part of the stock's fluctuations are due to strengths and weaknesses of the market as a whole. This is the stock's systematic or market risk. Second, sometimes the Digital stock performs better (vertical arrows pointing upward) and at other times it performs worse (vertical arrows pointing downward) than the market. These aberrations from the market trend are examples of unsystematic risk.

An important dimension of the unsystematic risk deserves special mention. Sometimes the tendency exists for homogeneous groups[5] of stocks to move together but in a way that is independent of the market as a whole. Risk arising from comovements of stocks whose movements are independent of those of the market as a whole is known as the *extramarket covariance risk.*

An example of extramarket covariance risk can be found in Table 5–2 which shows varying fluctuations in different industry groups. According to this table, during the quarter ending in November 1978 securities brokerage stocks were the poorest performers. Intense industry competition, shortages of capital, and the stock market decline late in the quarter adversely affected the group. In fact, securities brokerage stocks declined an average of 28.3 percent, whereas the market declined only 11.9 percent. When, say, the Merrill Lynch stock declines simply because it falls in the securities brokerage group, this constitutes an example of Merrill Lynch's extramarket covariance risk.[6]

---

[4] The discussion relates to the volatility of a stock's *return* relative to the market return, whereas Figure 5–2 relates to *price* fluctuations of the stock and the market. It is assumed here that fluctuations in returns and prices are direct and proportional. One study has demonstrated that this assumption is justified. See William F. Sharpe and Guy M. Cooper, "Risk–Return Classes of New York Stock Exchange Common Stocks, 1931–1967," *Financial Analysts Journal* (March–April 1972), pp. 46–54.

[5] The group refers to a certain industry or a certain investment grade.

[6] Here again, it is assumed that price fluctuations faithfully represent fluctuations in returns.

Table 5–2 **Industry Groups: Market Movements**

	Percentage Changes Quarterly Aug. '78 to Nov. '78	Percentage Changes Annual Nov. '77 to Nov. '78	Moody's Index of Market Prices 1957–59 = 100 Nov. '78	Aug. '78	Nov. '77
Aerospace	−22.2	+38.8	235.9	303.2	169.9
Airlines	−25.4	+29.5	296.3	397.3	228.8
Aluminum	−3.3	+9.4	79.4	82.1	72.6
Apparel	−2.6	+19.3	161.9	166.2	135.7
Appliances	−14.0	−12.9	220.4	256.2	253.1
Automobiles	−14.3	−16.5	121.8	142.1	145.9
Automotive Equipment	−13.6	−2.9	236.3	273.6	243.3
Banks	−13.4	−0.9	204.3	236.0	206.1
Building Materials	−20.0	−7.5	192.3	240.3	207.9
Business Equipment	−12.0	+0.8	500.8	568.8	497.0
Cement	−19.6	+1.5	60.7	75.5	59.8
Chemicals	−10.1	−8.1	109.8	122.1	119.5
Cigarettes	−5.4	+10.5	394.5	416.8	357.1
Containers	−14.4	−6.1	141.6	165.5	150.8
Copper	−9.0	+9.6	72.0	79.1	65.7
Cosmetics	−13.1	+9.7	898.3	1,034.2	819.2
Drugs	−14.1	+8.4	461.3	537.0	425.6
Electrical Equipment	−14.6	−6.1	168.3	197.1	179.3
Electric Power	−8.9	−12.8	103.6	113.7	118.8
Electronics	−16.5	0	527.2	631.3	527.2
Farm Equipment	−8.6	+10.2	276.9	302.9	251.3
Finance Companies	−13.7	−7.2	137.1	158.8	147.7
Foods	−10.2	−2.3	266.0	296.2	272.2
Grocery Chains	−12.4	−2.6	129.0	147.2	125.7
Insurance-Life	−15.2	−2.0	204.0	240.5	208.1
Ins.-Property & Casualty	−13.4	−0.4	246.2	284.2	247.3
Liquor	+1.5	+14.8	248.4	244.7	216.3
Machine Tools	−21.1	+18.1	191.4	242.5	162.1
Machinery & Equipment	−13.1	−3.3	351.9	404.8	363.8
Natural Gas	−6.7	−11.4	166.1	178.0	187.4
Nonferrous Metals	−1.2	+0.2	145.0	146.8	144.7
Oil	−1.0	−1.0	201.7	203.7	203.7
Oil Service	−8.2	+9.3	1,549.5	1,688.6	1,418.2
Paper & Products	−14.0	−1.4	125.1	145.5	126.9
Printing & Publishing	−15.3	+6.0	331.9	391.8	313.0
Railroad Equipment	−21.6	+1.3	256.1	326.7	252.7
Railroads	−7.0	−8.2	156.9	168.8	170.9
Retail Stores	−16.9	−24.0	272.6	328.1	358.5
Savings & Loan	−26.1	−2.5	80.5	108.9	82.6
Securities Brokerage	−28.3	−2.5	39.2	54.7	40.2

GROUP MOVEMENTS (August to November)

Best	
Liquor	+1.5%
Oil	−1.0
Nonferrous Metals	−1.2
Apparel	−2.6
Aluminum	−3.3
Worst	
Securities Brokerage	−28.3%
Savings & Loan	−26.1
Airlines	−25.4
Aerospace	−22.2
Railroad Equipment	−21.6

Table 5–2 *(Continued)*

	Percentage Changes Quarterly Aug. '78 to Nov. '78	Annual Nov. '77 to Nov. '78	Nov. '78	Moody's Index of Market Prices 1957–59 = 100 Aug. '78	Nov. '77
Service Companies	−20.6	−3.9	91.9	115.7	95.6
Soap	−5.1	−3.0	434.3	457.8	447.8
Soft Drinks	−12.8	+1.3	770.8	883.8	760.7
Steel	−16.1	−11.9	56.1	66.9	63.7
TV-Radio Broadcasters	−14.5	+7.2	684.1	800.2	638.1
Textiles	−8.7	−12.9	149.6	163.9	171.7
Tire & Rubber	−11.0	−19.7	71.4	80.2	88.9
Market Trend	−11.9	−2.3	51.52	58.48	52.72

SOURCE: *Moody's Handbook*, Winter 1978–79, pp. 12a and 13a.

Sources of Common Stock Risk

Now that the distinction between the systematic and the unsystematic risk is clear, an analysis of the sources of these two types of risk can be undertaken.

Inflation Risk

All investors must learn to live with the inflation risk, because inflation erodes the dollar value of their future returns. For instance, suppose that today you invest \$1,000 in a stock which pays a dividend of 7 percent. Assuming that the general price level remains unchanged during the year, at the end of the year you will receive \$70 in dividend, which represents a 7 percent real rate of return. However, if the economy experienced an unanticipated inflation rate of 10 percent after you invested your money, the real dividend would be only \$63.64. You would receive a real income less than anticipated, as shown below:

$$\text{Real Dividend} = \frac{\text{Current Dividend Amount (\$)}}{\text{Price Index}} \times 100$$

If prices remain unchanged, then

$$\text{Real Dividend} = \frac{\$70}{100} \times 100 = \$70$$

If the price level increases by 10 percent (that is, the price index increases to 110), then

$$\text{Real Dividend} = \frac{\$70}{110} \times 100 = \$63.64$$

Table 5–3

Market Indicators	Nominal Return	Real Return	Net Return or Real Return Minus Alternative Normal Returns (9%) (3%)	(6%)	(9%)
3/31/41 to 6/30/43					
D-J Industrials	12.8	2.7	−0.3	−3.3	−6.3
S&P 425 Industrials	17.6	7.1	4.1	1.1	−1.9
S&P Utilities	6.5	−3.1	−6.1	−9.1	−12.1
S&P Rails	21.3	10.5	7.5	4.5	1.5
S&P 500 Stocks	16.6	6.2	3.2	0.2	−2.8
3/31/46 to 9/30/48					
D-J Industrials	0.2	−11.0	−14.0	−17.0	−20.0
S&P 425 Industrials	−0.7	−11.7	−14.7	−17.7	−20.7
S&P Utilities	−5.8	−16.3	−19.3	−22.3	−25.3
S&P Rails	−6.0	−16.4	−19.4	−22.4	−25.4
S&P 500 Stocks	−1.5	−12.5	−15.5	−18.5	−21.5
3/31/50 to 12/31/51					
D-J Industrials	24.9	16.9	13.9	10.9	7.9
S&P 425 Industrials	31.5	23.1	20.1	17.1	14.1
S&P Utilities	8.5	1.5	−1.5	−4.5	−7.5
S&P Rails	30.1	21.8	18.8	15.8	12.8
S&P 500 Stocks	28.4	20.2	17.2	14.2	11.2
3/31/56 to 3/31/58					
D-J Industrials	−2.1	−5.6	−8.6	−11.6	−14.6
S&P 425 Industrials	−6.2	−9.5	−12.5	−15.5	−18.5
S&P Utilities	7.2	3.4	0.4	−2.6	−5.6
S&P Rails	−16.0	−19.0	−22.0	−25.0	−28.0
S&P 500 Stocks	−3.1	−6.5	−9.5	−12.5	−15.5
12/31/65 to 12/31/73					
D-J Industrials	1.9	−2.8	−5.8	−8.8	−11.8
S&P 425 Industrials	4.4	−0.4	−3.4	−6.4	−9.4
S&P Utilities	−0.8	−5.3	−8.3	−11.3	−14.3
S&P Rails	2.9	−1.8	−4.8	−7.8	−10.8
S&P 500 Stocks	4.0	−0.8	−3.8	−6.8	−9.8
Weighted Average*					
D-J Industrials	5.1	−1.6	−4.6	−7.6	−10.6
S&P 425 Industrials	7.0	0.3	−2.7	−5.7	−8.7
S&P Utilities	1.4	−4.9	−7.9	−10.9	−13.9
S&P Rails	4.7	−1.9	−4.9	−7.9	−10.9
S&P 500 Stocks	6.6	−0.1	−3.1	−6.1	−9.1

* Weights are equal to number of months in each inflationary period.

SOURCE: Updated results as reported in Frank K. Reilly, Glenn L. Johnson, and Ralph E. Smith, "Inflation, Inflation Hedges and Common Stock," *Financial Analysts Journal*, Vol. 26, No. 1 (January–February, 1970), pp. 104–10. Reprinted by permission.

In addition to the partial loss of real dividend income, inflation would also erode the value of your principal. Applying the above formula, duly modified:

$$\text{Real Principal} = \frac{\text{Current Value of Principal (\$)}}{\text{Price Index}} \times 100$$

$$= \frac{\$1{,}000}{110} \times 100$$

$$= \$909.10$$

Losses of real income and principal resulting from unanticipated inflation, known as inflation risk, are distinct possibilities in our inflationary economy.

A controversy surrounds the topic of common stock as an inflation hedge. In order for a common stock to be a perfect inflation hedge, its actual nominal return should equal its noninflationary return plus the amount by which the actual inflation exceeds expected inflation, or, conversely, minus the amount by which the actual inflation falls below expected inflation.

Studies of common stock prices generally do not support the hypothesis that stocks are adequate hedges against inflation on a month-to-month or a year-to-year basis.[7] The results of one such study, which analyzed the behavior of several popular market averages, are presented in Table 5–3. The nominal return is the annual rate of return including dividends for the indicator series during the indicated inflationary period. The real return is the nominal return adjusted for the rate of inflation. The net return is the real return minus an estimate of a "normal" return. If the net return is positive for a given normal return, then it could be interpreted that common stocks were a complete inflation hedge during that period.

The table reveals that during most of the 1941–73 period, with one exception, all the weighted average real returns were negative. This implies that common stocks have not been adequate inflation hedges; it may also justify the conclusion that common stocks are exposed to considerable inflation risk.[8]

Interest Rate Risk

The interest rate risk refers to the risk investors may suffer on their returns from common stocks because of a rise in the market interest rate.

In general, stock returns are inversely related to market interest rates. A rise in the market interest rate exerts a downward pressure on common stock prices, because the return on such alternative investments as bonds becomes more favorable, resulting in a shift of funds from the stock to the bond market. An increase in the market interest rate also raises the cost of borrowing funds for

---

[7] For details, see John Lintner, "Inflation and Security Returns," *Journal of Finance* (May 1975), pp. 259–80.

[8] Inflation will be discussed in greater detail in Appendix 1 to Part 3 "Inflation, Income Taxes, and Stock Prices."

Figure 5–3 **S&P 500 Stock Index**

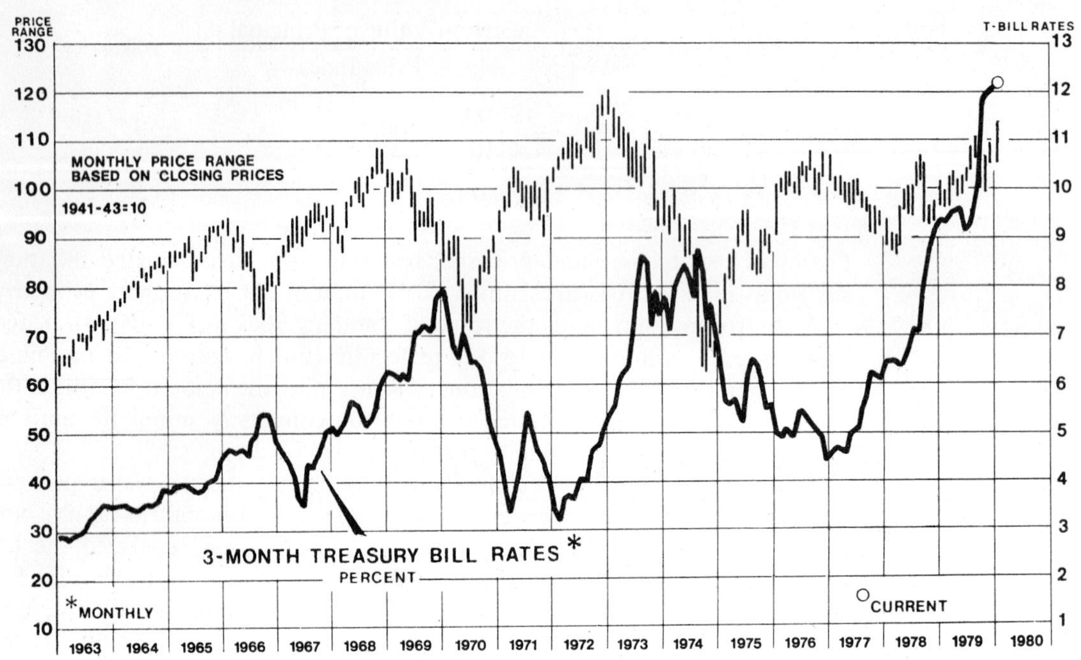

SOURCE: *The Outlook*, Standard & Poor's Corporation. January 28, 1980, front cover.

the purchase of stocks on margin, thereby reducing the prospective demand for stocks. For these reasons, an increase in the market interest rate generally results in a decline in stock prices, whereas the reverse is true when the market interest rate declines.

Figure 5–3 charts the relationship between fluctuations in the stock market (represented by the S&P 500 Index) and the short-term interest rate (represented by the three-month treasury bill rates). The figure reveals the long-term inverse relationship between stocks and the interest rate.

Tangible and Intangible Risks

The third source of risk is known as tangible and intangible risks. *Tangible risks* are associated with market fluctuations caused by variations in the national economic trend. On the average, the market declines during a recession and advances during a period of rapid economic growth. Furthermore, history suggests that the stock market is usually more volatile than the economy. This fact is made evident in Figure 5–4, which shows variations in the S&P 500 Index

Figure 5–4

STOCK MARKET & BUSINESS HISTORY SINCE 1926

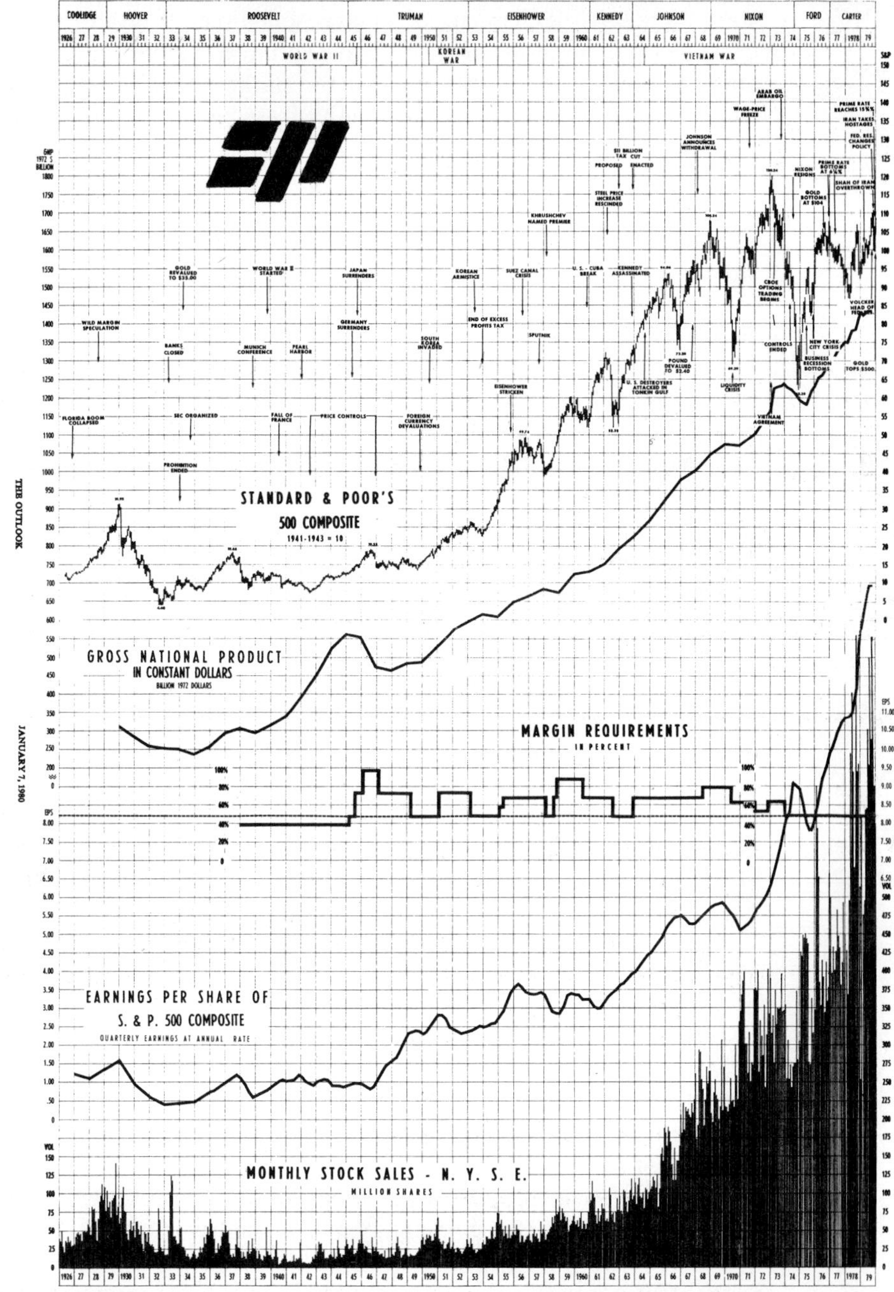

Chart prepared by S&P's TRENDLINE division. Copyright © 1980.

SOURCE: *The Outlook*, Standard & Poor's Corporation, January 7, 1980, pp. 996–97. Chart prepared by Standard & Poor's *Trendline* division.

(1926–79) in relation to changes in the current GNP (during the period 1930–79).

In contrast to tangible risk, *intangible risk* is related to political, social, and psychological factors which cause fluctuations in the stock market. Because the stock market has a character of its own, sometimes its erratic behavior can be explained only in terms of such elusive variables as mass psychology, general uncertainty, and the serious impact on the market of shocking news. Figure 5–4, which also presents stock market and business history since 1926, captures the tangible and intangible risks assumed by common stock investors.

Business Risk

Business risk concerns the probability of incurring a loss or realizing a lower-than-expected profit due to unfavorable operating conditions. Generally, this type of risk can be measured in terms of operating earnings. For instance, the business risk shown in Figure 5–5A is relatively small, because the deviations of operating earnings from the expected levels are relatively small. In contrast, the deviations of operating earnings from the expected earnings shown in Figure 5–5B are large, suggesting a greater probability that the earnings could deviate substantially from the firm's projections.

There are two kinds of business risk – *external* and *internal.* External risk results from operating conditions imposed on the firm by outside forces beyond the control of the firm. An oil embargo imposed on the United States by the Arab countries, an international monetary crisis, a worldwide recession, a failure of economic policy to cure a stubborn stagflation are all examples of external business risks. In addition, each firm faces its own external risks, depending on the specific environment within which the firm operates. Auto companies, for instance, face the risk of stiff pollution, safety, and efficiency controls being imposed by Congress. Similarly, the oil-producing companies must bear the risk of operating within a hostile political climate. Such examples can be easily multiplied.

Internal business risk is associated with the efficiency with which a firm's business is conducted. Risks associated with the operating skills of management, the product diversification obtained, the maturity of the firm, and the efficiency of asset utilization—all are examples of internal business risk.

The heart of corporate success is good management. The development and implementation of corporate strategy is one of the most important functions of management. Effective managers institute appropriate controls over various activities, ensure that operations run efficiently, and build safeguards against the possibility of incurring losses or falling profits. Stockholders of a company always take the risk that a company may be poorly managed.

Diversification is another important dimension of internal risk. Firms that specialize in one product are vulnerable to business cycles and sudden changes in the demand for that product. Diversification is often the answer to reducing

Figure 5–5 **Business Risk. (A) Little business risk; (B) Substantial business risk.**

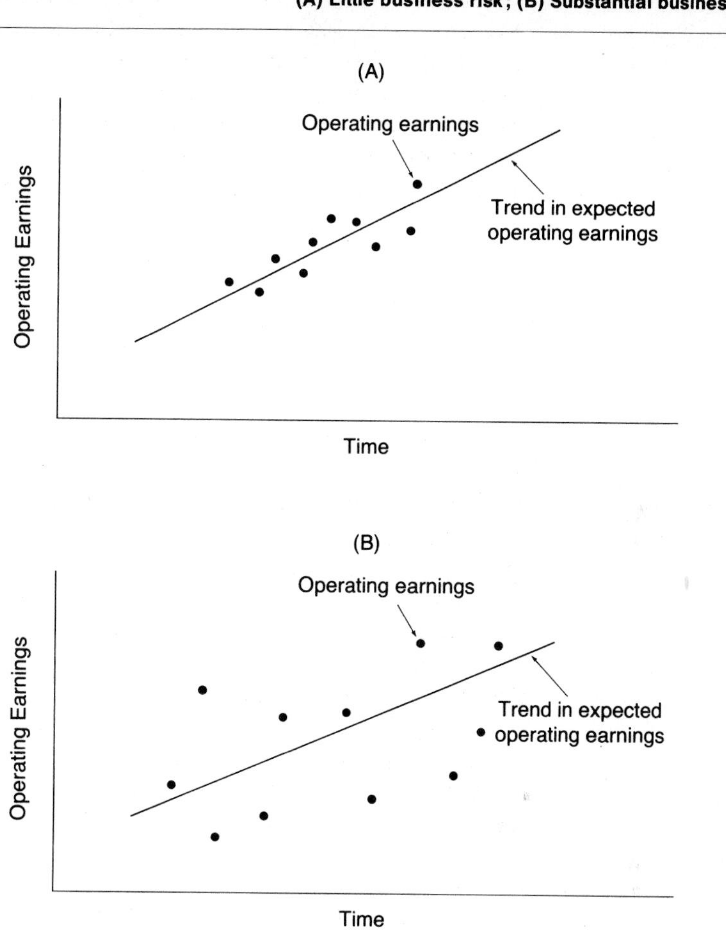

internal risk, because a well-diversified firm can balance falling demand for some of its products against rising demands for others at different stages of the cycle.

Financial Leverage Risk

Financial leverage refers to a firm's use of borrowed funds to increase its earnings. This leverage results because the interest charges on the debt are a fixed expense. That is, these fixed charges do not vary with the firm's earnings before interest and taxes (EBIT); they must be paid regardless of the amount of EBIT available to pay them. *Financial leverage risk* refers to the possibility that the

Figure 5–6

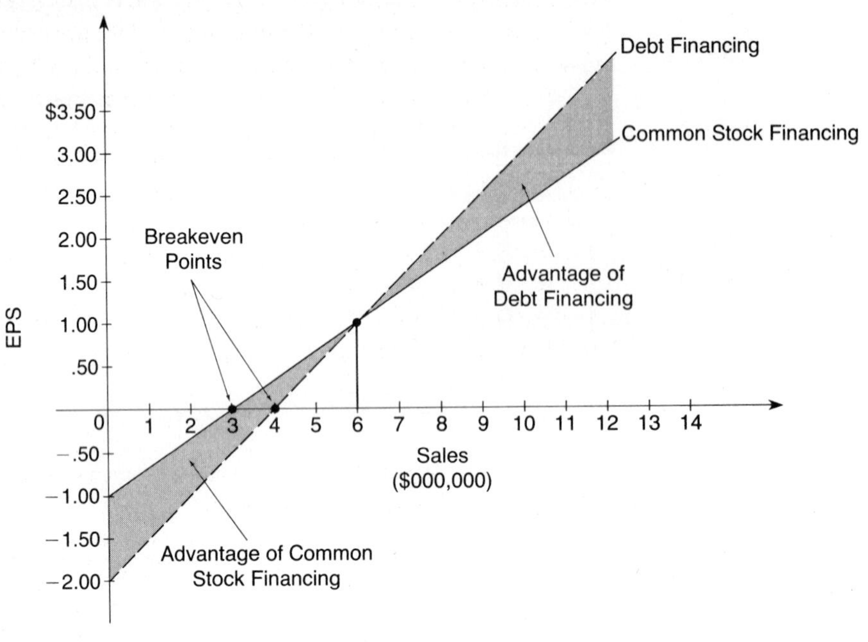

company may not be able to pay the fixed financial charges on borrowed funds because of insufficient EBIT.[9]

Figure 5–6 shows the nature of financial leverage risk. Here, the earnings per share (EPS) of two companies are graphed at various sales levels. The companies are identical except that one uses only common stock financing and the other uses debt financing. If sales are zero, the loss in the case of debt financing is $2

[9] Of course, if the firm successfully uses borrowed funds to magnify its earnings, then it retains the additional earnings after paying the borrowing costs.

The degree of financial leverage (DFL) is defined as the percentage change in earnings per share (EPS) over the percentage change in EBIT; that is

$$\text{DFL} = \frac{\dfrac{\Delta\text{EBIT}}{\text{EBIT} - \text{I}}}{\dfrac{\Delta\text{EBIT}}{\text{EBIT}}} = \frac{\text{EBIT}}{\text{EBIT} - \text{I}}$$

In the situation where EBIT = \$100,000 and I (interest) is \$25,000:

$$\text{DFL} = \frac{\$100{,}000}{\$100{,}000 - \$25{,}000}$$
$$= 1.33 \text{ (or } 133\%)$$

Therefore, a 100 percent increase in EBIT would result in a 133 percent increase in EPS.

per share, as opposed to a loss of $1 per share if common stock financing is used. Note also that the breakeven point with common stock financing is reached when sales are $3 million, whereas the breakeven point with debt financing is $4 million. The higher breakeven point for debt financing is due to a higher level of fixed expenses caused by interest charges on the debt. However, because there are fewer shares with debt financing, any increase in sales (and earnings) will cause earnings per share to rise at a faster rate. As sales volume increases, therefore, the advantage of common stock financing over debt financing grows progressively smaller. In this example, the EPS of the company with debt financing is higher after sales reach $6 million.

A caveat should be added here. Leverage, whether financial or operating (discussion follows), increases both a firm's sensitivity to marketwide economic events, and its risk. Consequently, the degree of financial leverage risk is even greater than that implied in the previous discussion.

Operating Leverage Risk

Operating leverage risk is another dimension of the internal business risk. Operating leverage can be defined in terms of the way a given change in the volume of sales affects operating profits. More precisely, the degree of operating leverage (DOL) is the percentage change in operating profit that results from a percentage change in sales volume.[10] Figure 5–7 demonstrates the concept of operating leverage. Observe that, compared to ABC Company, XYZ Company has a higher degree of operating leverage because, relative to variable costs, the level of its fixed costs is higher; as a result of an increase in sales, its profits rise faster than those of the other firm. However, because XYZ Company has higher fixed costs, it also takes much longer to reach the breakeven point. This suggests that, under unfavorable conditions, XYZ Company is more likely to realize a loss than ABC Company.

---

[10] The degree of operating leverage (DOL) can be calculated by:

$$\text{DOL} = \frac{\dfrac{\Delta \text{EPS}}{\text{EPS}}}{\dfrac{\Delta \text{S}}{\text{S}}}$$

where

$$\text{EPS} = \text{Earnings per share}$$
$$\text{S} = \text{Sales}$$

If, from a sales volume of $50,000 and a profit of $5 per share, as a result of an increase in sales by $10,000, profits increase by $0.25, then the degree of operating leverage is 0.25:

$$\text{DOL} = \frac{\dfrac{\$0.25}{\$5.00}}{\dfrac{\$10{,}000}{\$50{,}000}} = 0.25$$

Figure 5–7

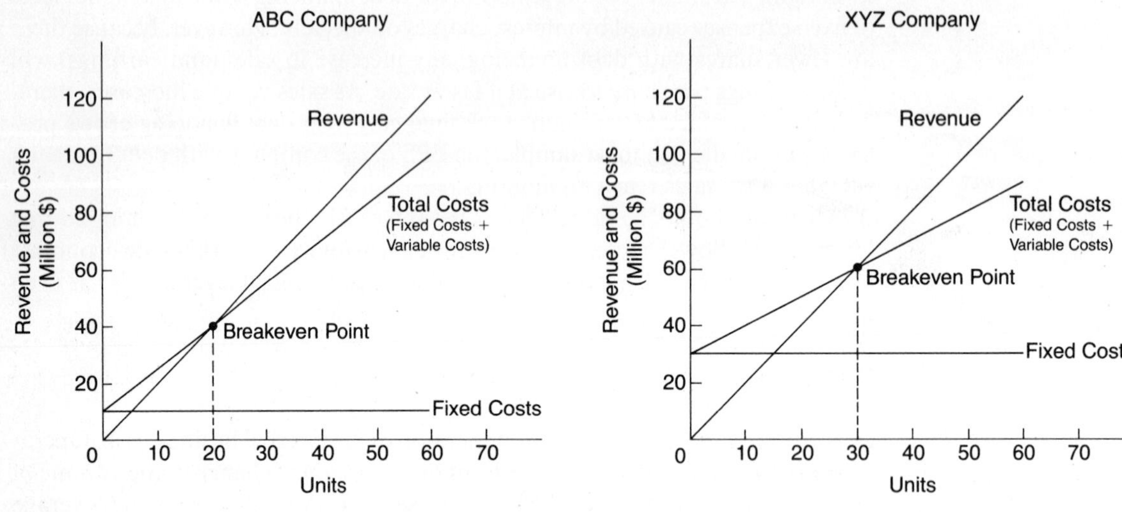

Industry Risk

Finally, the case of industry risk should be mentioned. Strictly speaking, *industry risk* is a combination of external and internal business risk. Sometimes all the firms in a given industry experience variability of return due to some common force which does not significantly affect the majority of firms outside that industry. This is called industry risk. For instance, auto companies are cyclical and suffer from sharply lower profits whenever auto sales hit the bottom of the auto cycle. Similarly, steel companies experience lower profits whenever foreign competition becomes formidable.

Measurement of Risk and Return

Risk—or uncertainty—cannot be dealt with effectively unless it can be statistically measured. Three statistical tools are commonly used to measure risk—beta, alpha and error term, and standard deviation or variance. For convenience, measurement of systematic and unsystematic *returns* will be discussed first. Thereafter, based on the variability of these returns, the method for measuring systematic and unsystematic *risks* will be outlined. For simplicity, the techniques of measurement of risk and return presented in this section are based solely upon the *Market Model*, which asserts that the relationship between returns on individual securities and returns on the market portfolio is linear.[11]

Measurement of Return

The Characteristic Line

Assume that during a two-year period[12] quarterly percentage returns on a given stock, R_s, were related to the market return, R_m, in the following manner:

	Q1	Q2	Q3	Q4	Q5	Q6	Q7	Q8
Market Return (R_m)	0.0	1.0	2.0	3.0	4.0	5.0	6.0	7.0
Stock's Return (R_s)	2.5	6.0	3.0	4.0	1.5	4.0	2.5	10.5

A glance at Figure 5–8 reveals that the changes in this stock's return did not always coincide with those of the market. For instance, the stock's return was only 1.5 percent when the market return was as high as 4.0 percent. However, when the market return was only 2.0 percent, the stock's return was 3.0 percent. In situations like these—where the stock does not move lockstep with the market—it is customary to simplify the representation of the relationship between the two returns by constructing a straight line through the various points plotted on the graph. The statistical method used for this purpose is known as the *least squares regression method.*

---

[11] The Market Model asserts that the relationship between returns on individual securities and returns on the market portfolio is linear and can be expressed by the following regression equation:

$$E(R_s) = \alpha_s + \beta_s E(R_m) + \epsilon_s$$

The Capital Asset Pricing Model (CAPM) states that, in equilibrium, investors will price capital assets so that the expected return on a security is equal to the riskless rate of interest plus a premium that is proportional to the risk measure, beta. In equation form, the CAPM is

$$E(R_s) = R_f + \beta_s[E(R_m) - R_f]$$

Both the Market Model and the CAPM require assumptions not needed by the other; hence acceptance of one model does not imply acceptance of the other. The differences between them and their ramifications for portfolio management will be fully explored in Chapters 13 and 14.

[12] Only eight observations have been selected here solely for illustrative convenience. In the real world, the beta coefficient is derived from a regression analysis between weekly percentage changes in the price of a stock and weekly percentage changes in the S&P 500 Index over a period of, say, five years. Also, because the S&P 500 does not include dividends, to make the comparisons meaningful, dividends paid by the stock, if any, are not taken into account.

Figure 5–8

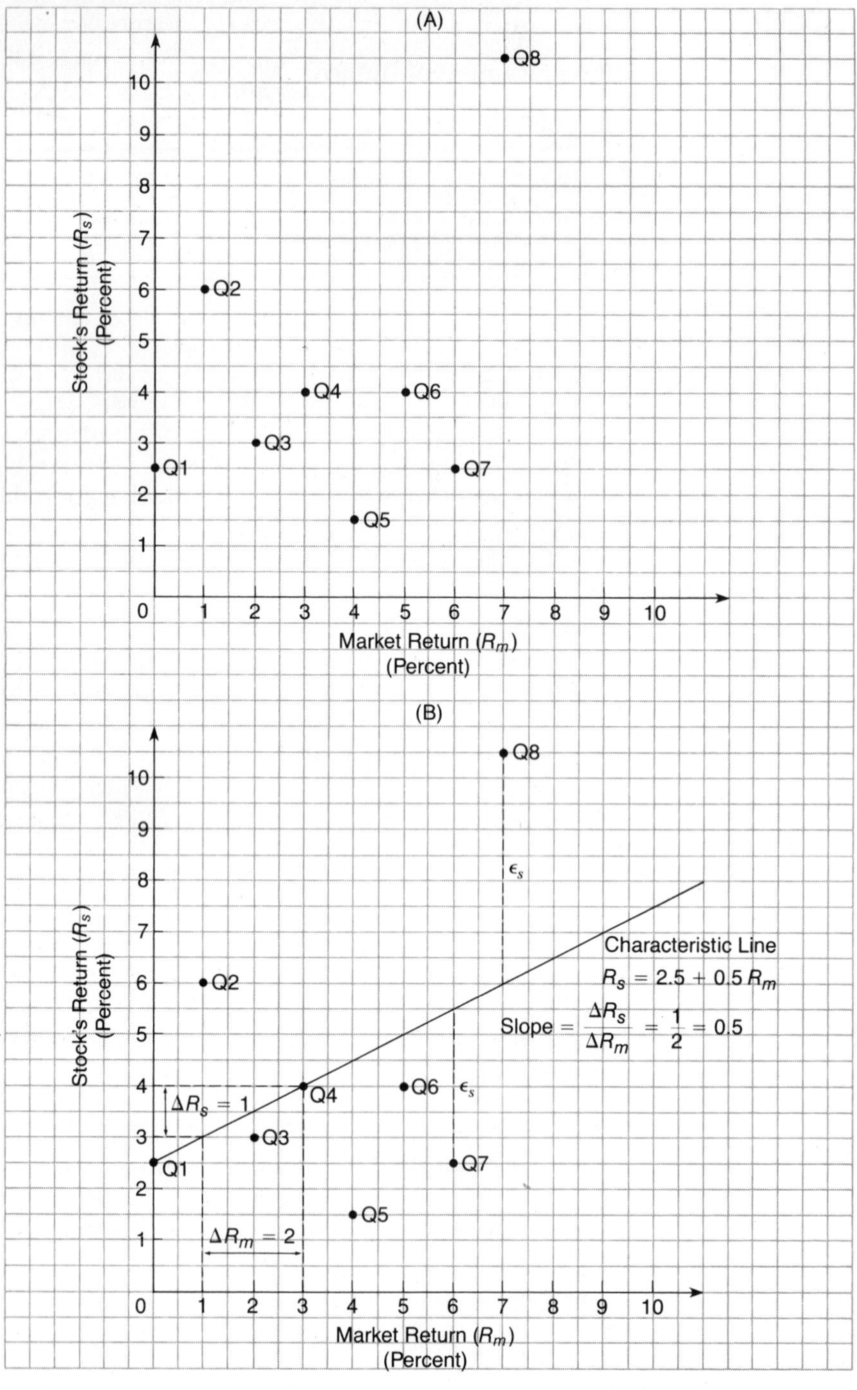
(A)
Stock's Return (R_s) (Percent)
Market Return (R_m) (Percent)
Q1
Q2
Q3
Q4
Q5
Q6
Q7
Q8
(B)
Characteristic Line
$R_s = 2.5 + 0.5 R_m$
Slope = $\frac{\Delta R_s}{\Delta R_m} = \frac{1}{2} = 0.5$
$\Delta R_s = 1$
$\Delta R_m = 2$
ϵ_s

The technique of least squares is widely used for fitting a curve to a set of data and is the most popular method of computing the long-term trend of given data, such as the earnings growth of a firm. The basic task of selecting a method of fitting a trend line is to decide on a criterion for measuring goodness of fit. If the points to which the line is being fitted do not all fall on a straight line, no straight line fits perfectly. Therefore, it becomes a problem of defining what is meant by the line of "best fit." The trend line is not necessarily the one that intersects the most points. The criterion most frequently used is that the *line of best fit* should minimize the sum of the squared deviations of the actual values from the fitted values. The name "least squares" is derived from the use of this criterion. In the investment world, the line of best fit (which approximates the relationship between security and market returns) is commonly called the *characteristic line.*

Note Figure 5–8B. The solid line in the figure is the appropriate characteristic line[13] and the equation for this line is $R_s = 2.5 + 0.5R_m$. The fact that only one return is plotted on this line implies that some of the risks associated with this stock are unsystematic in nature. As will shortly become clear, for single stocks frequently a large percentage of risks is indeed unsystematic, whereas risks of well-diversified portfolios are primarily systematic in nature. Also, the Y-intercept and the slope of this characteristic line are of considerable interest, because they provide the basis for the three statistical measures under discussion.

Beta The characteristic line measures the average variability of the stock's return relative to the market rate of return. For instance, as the market return increases from 1 to 3 percent ($\Delta R_m = 2.0$), the stock's return increases from 3 to 4 percent ($\Delta R_s = 1.0$). This relationship, measured here by $\Delta R_s/\Delta R_m = \frac{1}{2} = 0.5$, is known as the *slope* of the characteristic line; it remains unchanged over the entire range. A slope of 0.5 implies that for every change of, say, 10 percentage points in the market rate of return, the stock's rate of return will change on average by 5 percentage points.

Incidentally, the equation of any straight line takes the general form of $Y = a + bX$, where "b" is the slope of the line. That is why the slope of the characteristic line is called its *beta* and it is measured by the value of the beta. In Figure 5–8B, the equation of the line is $R_s = 2.5 + 0.5R_m$, and the value of b equals 0.5. More importantly, because beta (symbolically written as β_s) measures the average variability of a stock's rate of return relative to the market return, it measures the *systematic return* of a stock.

The stock has a beta of 0.5 ($\beta_s = 0.5$); this means that, as compared to the market, it is a slow-moving stock. It follows, therefore, that a slow-moving stock has a low beta ($\beta_s < 1$), whereas a fast-moving stock has a high beta ($\beta_s > 1$). A stock as volatile as the market itself, of course, has a beta of 1.0 ($\beta_s = 1$). Figure 5–9 shows three lines with varying betas. The line in Figure 5–9A is identical with that of Figure 5–8B. The beta of the stock in Figure 5–9B is 1.5, which means that it is highly volatile. Note that the steeper the line, the higher

[13] See note 13 on page 158.

Figure 5–9

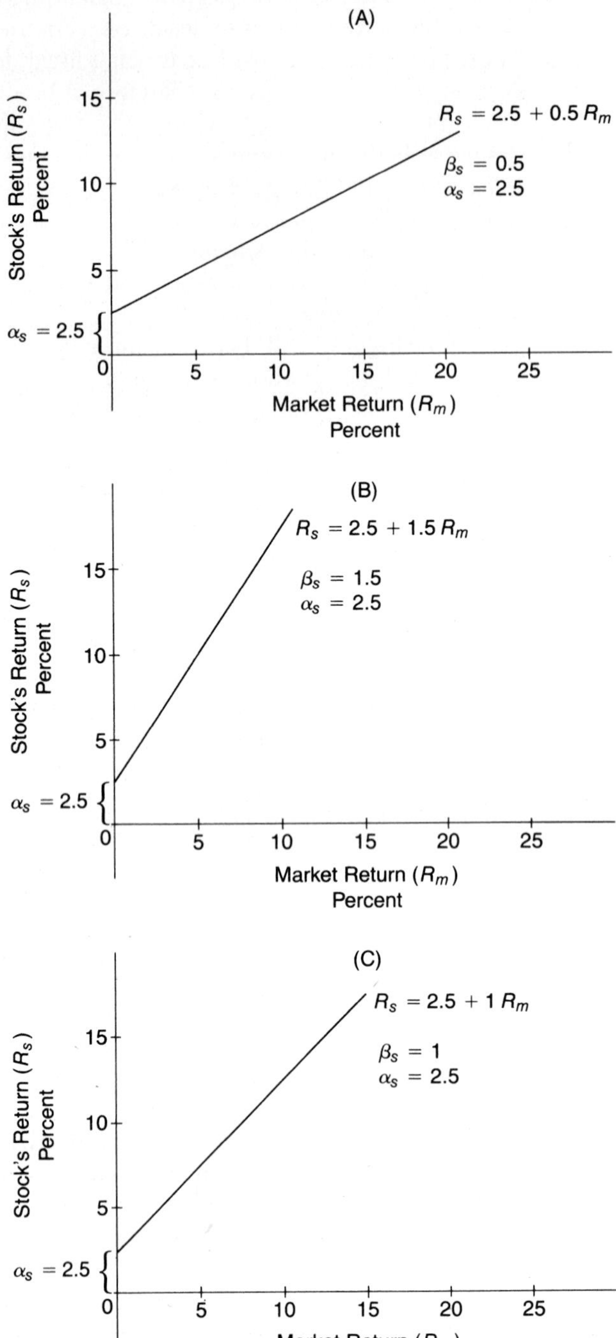
(A)
Stock's Return (R_s) Percent
15
10
5
α_s = 2.5
0
5
10
15
20
25
Market Return (R_m) Percent
$R_s = 2.5 + 0.5\,R_m$
$\beta_s = 0.5$
$\alpha_s = 2.5$
(B)
Stock's Return (R_s) Percent
15
10
5
α_s = 2.5
0
5
10
15
20
25
Market Return (R_m) Percent
$R_s = 2.5 + 1.5\,R_m$
$\beta_s = 1.5$
$\alpha_s = 2.5$
(C)
Stock's Return (R_s) Percent
15
10
5
α_s = 2.5
0
5
10
15
20
25
Market Return (R_m) Percent
$R_s = 2.5 + 1\,R_m$
$\beta_s = 1$
$\alpha_s = 2.5$

the beta of the related stock and the higher its volatility relative to the market. The line in Figure 5–9C has a beta of 1, which implies that this stock is as volatile as the market itself.

Alpha and Error Term It was demonstrated that beta—or beta coefficient—measures how sensitive the stock's return is to changes in the market's return. Changes in a stock's return can also occur due to changes in the industry or in factors unique to the company (such as better-than-expected performance, labor difficulties, unexpected intensification of foreign competition, and so on, all of which are examples of the unsystematic return associated with a stock). A tool must, therefore, be developed for measuring unsystematic return.

The *unsystematic return* of a stock is the sum of two variables—alpha (α_s) and the error term (ϵ_s). The *alpha*, which measures the part of a stock's return not associated with the overall movement of the market, is the so-called *Y*-intercept shown in Figure 5–9C.[14] Given the market return equals to zero, the stock generates a return equals to 2.5 percent; therefore, the value of alpha is 2.5 ($\alpha_s = 2.5$).

Figure 5–10 presents three characteristic lines representing the stock under analysis, all of which have a fixed beta of 0.5, but have different values of α_s at different time periods. This figure suggests that over time alphas can be highly unstable for a given stock. Another point worth emphasizing is that the estimated alpha for one stock may be different from the estimated alpha for another stock with similar characteristics. These points should be remembered when alpha is used as a measure of unsystematic return.

The nature of the residual component of the unsystematic return, known as the *error term*, is best demonstrated by referring to the characteristic line in Figure 5–8B. The figure reveals that the stock's return cannot always be accurately predicted by the equation $R_s = 2.5 + 0.5R_m$. For instance, when the market return was 6 percent, the stock's return was expected to be 5.5 percent:

$$\begin{aligned} R_s &= 2.5 + 0.5R_m \\ &= 2.5 + 0.5(6) \\ &= 5.5\% \end{aligned}$$

Instead, the stock returned only 2.5 percent. Similarly, when the market return was 7 percent, instead of the expected 6 percent, the stock returned 10.5 percent. Each deviation of the actual from the expected return (the vertical distance between the actual return and the characteristic line) is called an error term. The error terms represent the residual portion of a stock's unsystematic return.

[14] In the Market Model, given the value of the stock's beta, alpha simply measures the stock's return when the market return is zero. This is an important difference and it will be explored fully in Chapter 13.

Figure 5–10

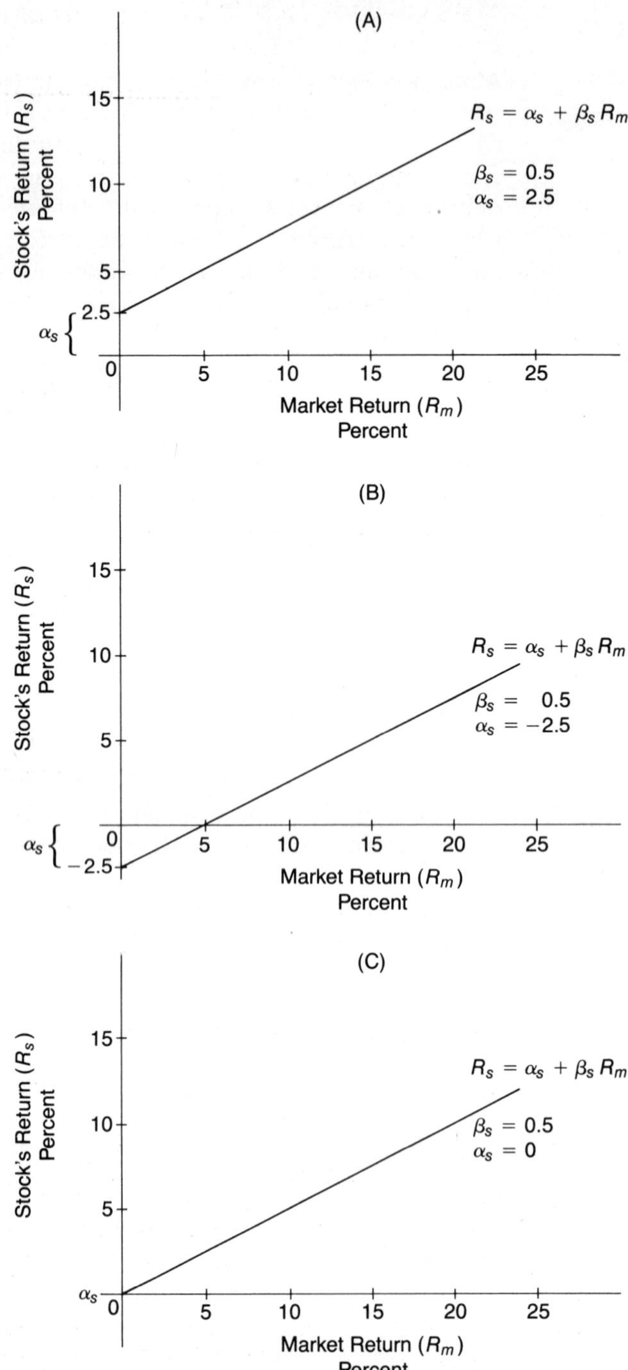
(A)
Stock's Return (R_s) Percent
$R_s = \alpha_s + \beta_s R_m$
$\beta_s = 0.5$
$\alpha_s = 2.5$
15
10
5
2.5
α_s
0
5
10
15
20
25
Market Return (R_m) Percent
(B)
Stock's Return (R_s) Percent
$R_s = \alpha_s + \beta_s R_m$
$\beta_s = 0.5$
$\alpha_s = -2.5$
15
10
5
0
−2.5
α_s
5
10
15
20
25
Market Return (R_m) Percent
(C)
Stock's Return (R_s) Percent
$R_s = \alpha_s + \beta_s R_m$
$\beta_s = 0.5$
$\alpha_s = 0$
15
10
5
α_s
0
5
10
15
20
25
Market Return (R_m) Percent

Security Return: Summing Up

The concept of an individual security return may now be formally stated:

Security Return = Systematic Return + Unsystematic Return

The systematic return of a security is correlated with the market return and is determined by multiplying the stock's beta (β_s) by the market return, R_m. The unsystematic return, which depends on factors unique to the company's industry and to the company itself, is measured by alpha (α_s) and the error term (ϵ_s). The total return on the security, R_s, can be stated as:

$$R_s = \alpha_s + \beta_s R_m + \epsilon_s \tag{5–1a}$$

Equation 5–1a is the general equation for measuring the total return on a stock. When using it for *predicting* future returns on the stock, however, it is customary to modify the equation as follows:[15]

$$E(R_s) = \alpha_s + \beta_s E(R_m) + \epsilon_s \tag{5–1b}$$

where

$$E(R_s) = \text{Expected return on stock}$$
$$E(R_m) = \text{Expected return on market}$$
$$\beta_s E(R_m) = \text{Expected systematic return}$$

As previously mentioned, this model for predicting individual security returns is known as the Market Model.[16]

Measurement of Risk

Expected Return and Variance

Risk—or uncertainty—is the possibility of realizing a return on investment below or above the expected return. More specifically, a security return may fluctuate because of the variability of both the systematic return and the unsystematic return. The statistical tool known as *variance* is used to measure these

[15] In a predictive model (for stock) the error term, ϵ_s, is assumed to be normally distributed and its mean is zero. Consequently, in Equation 5–1b the value of ϵ_s is always zero.

[16] The predictive features of the Market Model will be contrasted with those of the CAPM in Chapter 13.

variations. The following example illustrates the basic relationship between expected return and variance.

Suppose you purchase XYZ stock, expecting it to perform in the following manner:

Conditions Affecting the Stock	Probability of Return (p_i)	Possible Return (R_i)
Highly favorable	25%	50%
Favorable	25	20
Unfavorable	25	0
Highly unfavorable	25	−30

Although no one can accurately forecast conditions affecting the stock, given these figures, you can determine what the *average* expected annual return will be by using the following equation:

$$E(R_s) = \sum_{i=1}^{k} p_i R_i \tag{5–2}$$

where

$$\begin{aligned} E(R_s) &= \text{Expected return on stock} \\ p_i &= \text{Subjective probability that } i^{\text{th}} \text{ rate of return occurs} \\ R_i &= \text{The } i^{\text{th}} \text{ rate of return} \\ k &= \text{Number of possible rates of return} \end{aligned}$$

$$\begin{aligned} E(R_s) &= .25(.50) + .25(.20) + .25(0) + .25(-.30) \\ &= .125 + .05 + 0 - .075 \\ &= .10 \text{ (or } 10\%) \end{aligned}$$

That is, the expected return on a stock is a weighted average of the possible returns, with the probabilities of the possible returns used as the weights.

In the preceding illustration, the expected return is 10 percent. However, according to the probability table presented above, under highly favorable conditions you could earn as much as 50 percent (under deteriorated conditions you could lose 30 percent). Your actual return, obviously, could vary considerably from the expected return. The expected variance, $E(\sigma_s^2)$, is the measure of the variability of returns. It is computed by using the following equation:

$$E(\sigma_s^2) = \sum_{i=1}^{k} p_i[R_i - E(R_s)]^2 \tag{5–3}$$

In our previous example, the expected variance is .085:

$$\begin{aligned} &= .25(.50 - .10)^2 + .25(.20 - .10)^2 + .25(0 - .10)^2 \\ &\quad + .25(-.30 - .10)^2 \\ &= .04 + .0025 + .0025 + .04 \\ &= .085 \end{aligned}$$

Variance, then, is a measure of the variability, or risk, associated with a stock; the larger the variance, the greater the risk of holding the stock.

Probability and Risk: A Formal Approach

Now that the relationship between expected return and risk has been clearly established, we will formally introduce probability distributions in our discussion.

Table 5–4 presents the *subjective probabilities* associated with each of five possible rates of return on Securities A, B, and C. Expected return and variance for each security are also provided in the table.

Table 5–4

SECURITY A			SECURITY B			SECURITY C		
Probability of Return (p_i)	Possible Return (R_i)	Expected Return (p_iR_i)	Probability of Return (p_i)	Possible Return (R_i)	Expected Return (p_iR_i)	Probability of Return (p_i)	Possible Return (R_i)	Expected Return (p_iR_i)
.1	25%	2.5%	.1	50%	5.0%	.1	50%	5.0%
.5	10	5.0	.3	25	7.5	.1	25	2.5
.2	5	1.0	.3	5	1.5	.6	10	6.0
.1	0	0.0	.1	−10	−1.0	.1	−10	−1.0
.1	−10	−1.0	.2	−27.5	−5.5	.1	−27.5	−2.75
1.0			1.0			1.0		
Expected Return, $E(R_s)$:		7.5%	Expected Return, $E(R_s)$:		7.5%	Expected Return, $E(R_s)$:		9.75%
Expected Variance, $E(\sigma_s^2)$:		.0071	Expected Variance, $E(\sigma_s^2)$:		.0550	Expected Variance, $E(\sigma_s^2)$:		.0363

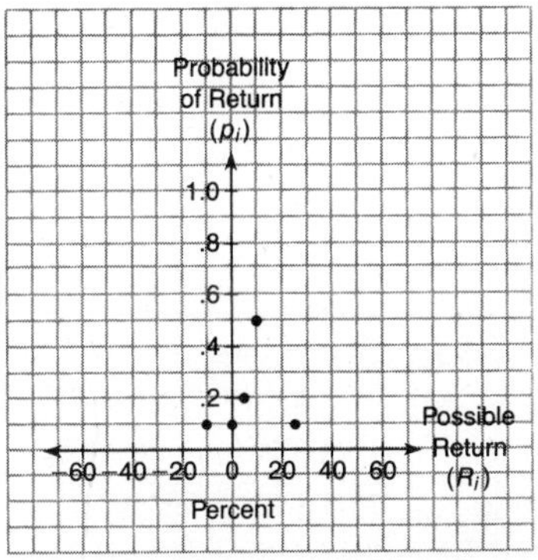

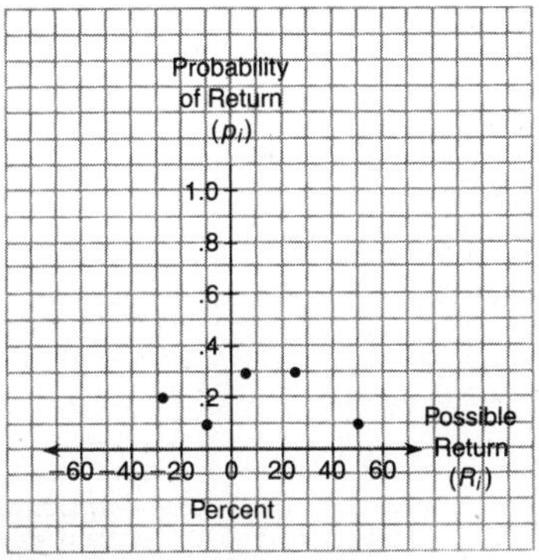

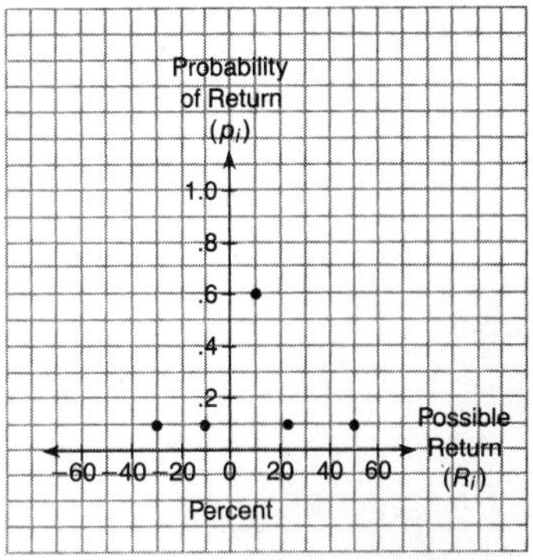

Let us analyze the risk inherent in the three securities. If we ignore risk considerations, then based solely on the criterion of expected returns we should be indifferent between A and B, but should select C because it has a higher expected rate of return than either A or B. However, the nature of the decision changes significantly when variance is introduced as a measure of risk. The graphs at the bottom of Table 5–4 show the distributions of the returns for the three securities. Although both A and B have the same expected return, because B is riskier than A, Security B should be rejected. However, the comparison between A and C is rendered more difficult by the fact that, while C's expected return is more than A's, it is also more risky. Intuitively, a risk-averse investor will choose Security A, whereas a risk seeker might select C if the 2.25 (9.75 − 7.5) percent difference between the two expected returns were sufficient inducement to assume the additional risk. This type of decision is based on the risk preferences of individual investors. Risk preference will be discussed later in the chapter.

Variance and Total Risk

Now that variance has been identified as a key measure of risk, its relationship with systematic and unsystematic risk may be established. Remember that the equation for determining the total return on the security is:

$$R_s = \alpha_s + \beta_s R_m + \epsilon_s \qquad \textbf{(5–1a restated)}$$

The total risk of a security, measured by its variance (σ_s^2), should equal the sum of the variance of alpha [Var (α_s)], the variance of beta multiplied by the market return [Var ($\beta_s R_m$)], and the variance of the error term [Var (ϵ_s)].[17] Symbolically,

$$\text{Var}(R_s) = \text{Var}(\alpha_s) + \text{Var}(\beta_s R_m) + \text{Var}(\epsilon_s)$$

However, because the alpha of a security remains unchanged,[18] its variability is zero. Therefore,

$$\text{Var}(R_s) = 0 + \text{Var}(\beta_s R_m) + \text{Var}(\epsilon_s)$$

[17] This is a simplification of the following equation:

$$\text{Var}(R_s) = \text{Var}(\alpha_s) + \text{Var}(\beta_s R_m) + \text{Var}(\epsilon_s) + 2\,\text{Cov}(\alpha_s, \beta_s R_m) + 2\,\text{Cov}(\alpha_s, \epsilon_s) + 2\,\text{Cov}(\beta_s R_m, \epsilon_s)$$

The above equation will be used in Chapter 13.

[18] The alpha is the *Y*-intercept. It is a constant term for the security; hence, its variability is zero.

Also, since $\mathrm{Var}(\beta_s R_m) = \beta_s^2 \mathrm{Var}(R_m)$,

$$\mathrm{Var}(R_s) = \beta_s^2 \mathrm{Var}(R_m) + \mathrm{Var}(\epsilon_s)$$

Symbolically, the above equation can be rewritten as

$$\underset{\text{Total Risk}}{\sigma_s^2} = \underbrace{\beta_s^2 \sigma_m^2}_{\text{Systematic risk}} + \underbrace{\sigma_{\epsilon_s}^2}_{\text{Unsystematic risk}} \quad \textbf{(5-4)}$$

The topic of total risk will be discussed more fully in Chapter 13.

Portfolio Risk

The risk of an individual security is the sum of the square of the security's beta times the variance of the market's return plus the variance of the error term. That is,

$$\sigma_s^2 = \beta_s^2 \sigma_m^2 + \sigma_{\epsilon_s}^2 \quad \textbf{(5-4 restated)}$$

The portfolio theory asserts that the variance of the error term, $\sigma_{\epsilon_s}^2$, which represents the unsystematic risk of the security, can be eliminated by selecting a large number of securities with diverse characteristics. This process is known as *diversification* through the construction of an efficient portfolio.

Diversification is, of course, statistical in nature. The mean of a standard normal distribution is zero. The error term is assumed to follow a standard normal distribution. Consequently, as the number of securities in a portfolio increases, the mean of the error term approaches zero.[19]

The basic nature of the reduction, and eventual elimination, of unsystematic risk through diversification can be described in simple language. As we have

[19] The mathematical proof is given below:

$$\sum_{i=1}^{k} \frac{\sigma_{\epsilon_i}^2}{K^2}$$

$$\frac{1}{K} \underbrace{\sum_{i=1}^{k} \frac{\sigma_{\epsilon_i}^2}{K}}_{\bar{\sigma}_{\epsilon_i}^2}$$

$$\frac{1}{K} \bar{\sigma}_{\epsilon_i}^2 \to 0 \quad \text{as} \quad k \to \infty$$

seen, individual securities have risk–return characteristics of their own. The objective of constructing an efficient portfolio is to reduce the *portfolio risk* below the aggregate risks of all securities included in it. This is achieved by selecting securities that do not fluctuate in the same way. In a diversified portfolio, the fluctuations of some stocks partly compensate for those of the others, so that the variability of the portfolio's return becomes significantly less than the variability of the individual components of the portfolio.

To see clearly how a portfolio can eliminate unsystematic risk, assume you are interested in the stock of two companies, the Hawk Company and the Dove Company. The Hawk Company manufactures war goods and naturally prospers during a political conflict. In contrast, the Dove Company produces only goods used during peace and enjoys a profitable business when the country is at peace. The following table shows the *expected* return for the two companies during two contrasting political situations:

Political Situation	Hawk Company	Dove Company
Peace	−25%	+50%
War	+50%	−25%

An investor who owns stock in the Dove Company can expect to earn 50 percent if peace prevails, but will lose 25 percent if war breaks out. The reverse will be true if Hawk Company stock has been purchased.

To simplify matters, assume that during any given year there is a 50 percent probability that the country will be at war (and, naturally, a 50 percent probability that the country will be at peace). Under these assumptions, an investor purchasing the stock of either the Hawk Company or the Dove Company will soon discover that half the time the investment earns 50 percent, and half the time it loses 25 percent. That is to say, the *average* expected return on the investment would be 12.5 percent [(50 − 25) ÷ 2]. Note, however, that investing in the stock of either company would be fairly risky, because no one can foretell when the country will be at war or at peace.

Here the pertinent question is: Can this investor reduce the risk without giving up the 12.5 percent expected rate of return? The answer is yes, if the investor *diversifies* the portfolio by investing, say, $1,000 in the following manner. Suppose the investor invests $500 in the stock of the Hawk Company and the other $500 in the stock of the Dove Company. In that case, during the war period the investor will earn 50 percent return ($250) on the investment in the Hawk Company and will lose 25 percent ($125) on the investment in the Dove Company. Thus, the investor will earn $125 ($250 − $125) during war, which is 12.5 percent of his total investment of $1,000. In peacetime, the investor will lose 25 percent ($125) on the investment in the Hawk Company and will gain 50 percent ($250) on the investment in the Dove Company. The net result will be that the investor will earn $125 ($250 − $125) during peace as well, which is also 12.5

percent of the total investment. These details are summarized below:

Political Situation	Return on Hawk Company	Return on Dove Company	Net Return (%) on Total Investment
Peace	−$125	+$250	12.5%
War	+$250	−$125	12.5%

The implications of this example should be clarified. Because no one can accurately predict the political situation for any given period, investment in either of the two companies carries considerable risk; if the prediction is wrong, an investor investing in either company could lose 25 percent of the investment. More specifically, because in neither case can the error term be predicted with any degree of accuracy, investing in either company would entail considerable risk. However, if an investor constructs a portfolio by investing an equal amount in each of two securities, the risk can be completely eliminated without affecting the net return. This is the essence of diversification through portfolio construction.

The preceding example is based on a special condition. It was assumed that the return on the Hawk Company's stock was negatively correlated with the return on the stock of the Dove Company; that is, during any given political situtation these stocks moved in *opposite* directions. In technical jargon, the two companies had a negative *covariance*.[20] Of course, in the real world, stocks with such characteristics are rare. However, that does not negate the benefits of diversification. As long as the correlation[21] between the stocks selected for a portfolio is less than perfect, diversification can reduce risk without simultaneously reducing the portfolio return.

Ostensibly, covariance is the essence of portfolio risk. The expected return of a portfolio is the weighted average of the expected returns of the securities in the portfolio. However, the risk of a fully diversified or efficient portfolio, as measured by its variance, is *smaller* than the weighted average of the variance of individual securities. The reason for this is simple: An efficient portfolio, consisting of securities with less than perfect correlation, actually reduces the inherent risk of the individual securities.

Portfolio risk can also be analyzed in terms of two types of risk. It was observed earlier that risks of individual stocks can be partitioned between systematic risk and unsystematic risk. Enlarging a portfolio by choosing appropriately selected stocks leads to a reduction—and the eventual elimination—of the unsystematic risk. However, diversification cannot eliminate or even reduce the systematic risk. (In theory, under certain special conditions, the systematic risk can be eliminated. This point will be explored in Chapter 13.) Specifically,

[20] See note 20 on page 158.

[21] The statistical measures of correlation and covariance are intimately related. These measures will be formally defined in Chapter 13.

the risk of a *well-diversified portfolio*, which by definition is not affected by unsystematic risk, is simply the beta square of the portfolio, β_p^2, multiplied by the variance of the market return, σ_m^2, or $\beta_p^2\sigma_m^2$. This portfolio, characteristically known as an *efficient portfolio*, commands an intuitive appeal for most investors. Its risk can be expressed as follows:

$$\sigma_p^2 = \beta_p^2\sigma_m^2 \tag{5-5}$$

In this chapter only the rudiments of portfolio risk have been presented. A detailed discussion of the topic will be undertaken in Chapter 13.

Risk in an Efficient Market

By definition, an efficient market is one in which the price of a stock is equal to its present value. Because, as a general rule, the market's efficiency is frequently assumed as given, risk must be discussed in the context of an efficient market.

Individual Security

Equation 5–1b shows that the expected return of a security can be calculated as

$$E(R_s) = \alpha_s + \beta_s E(R_m) + \epsilon_s$$

Given the alpha and beta values of a security, it is possible for investors to develop strategies for outperforming the market. However, that can be done only if the market is inefficient, resulting in the existence of identifiable undervalued stocks. (The conditions necessary for the development of such a strategy will be discussed in Chapter 13.) If the market is efficient, however, all publicly available information is quickly impounded and reflected in security prices in an unbiased fashion. Consequently, investors cannot consistently predict the future price of a stock even if they possess super analytical abilities.

There is little concensus as to what constitutes a successful strategy to outperform the market. In fact, it fuels a lively controversy between financial theorists and financial analysts. This controversy, which revolves around the nature and extent of the market's efficiency, will be discussed in detail in Chapter 14 under the title, Efficient Market Hypothesis. Here we need only survey the essentials of the three forms of the Efficient Market Hypothesis (EMH)—the *weak* form, the *semistrong* form, and the *strong* form.

The weak form of the EMH states that the history of stock-price movements contains no useful information that will enable an investor consistently to outperform a buy-and-hold strategy. This means that because movements in the price of a stock are random in nature, they are not influenced by past prices of that stock. By implication, the weak form of the EMH holds that investors gain nothing by studying past stock prices (technical analysis).

The proponents of the semistrong form of the EMH assert that the current price of a stock reflects all publicly available information possessed by investors and that, because new information becomes available only randomly, there should be no reason to expect systematic movement in stock prices. This assertion implies that there is little point in engaging in an analysis of the financial determinants of a stock's value (fundamental analysis), because the market is so efficient that it reflects all the information that is publicly knowable.

The strong form of the EMH is based on the assumption that the price of a stock reflects not only all publicly available information, but the information that is possessed *only* by corporate insiders, super analysts, and the "pros" as well. The implication of this argument is that even a professional portfolio manager, who supposedly possesses confidential information not publicly available, cannot consistently outperform a simple buy-hold-and-sell strategy.

Numerous statistical tests have been performed to "prove" the validity of the three forms of the EMH just presented. These studies have concluded that each form is valid under varying—and often highly restrictive—assumptions. Although the market is reasonably efficient in the sense of the weak form and the semistrong form, it is not so insofar as the strong form is concerned. That is, by using confidential information, a corporate insider might beat the market in a particular stock. However, SEC rules regulate insider trading to prevent insiders from making abnormal gains in the stock market.

Although the controversy surrounding the EMH is still alive, many analysts believe that the market is sufficiently inefficient to make it possible to predict accurately the future value of a security. That is, superior results can be obtained through an in-depth analysis of individual securities.

Efficient Portfolio

By definition, the error term is zero in an efficient portfolio, and the the risk of a portfolio is given by

$$\sigma_p^2 = \beta_p^2 \sigma_m^2 \qquad \textbf{(5–5 restated)}$$

Here the efficiency issue assumes a different form. An efficient portfolio consists of a combination of securities which will earn the maximum expected return in its risk class (or conversely, the minimum risk at its level of expected return). Anyone holding such a portfolio should not be concerned with unsystematic risk, because there would be no unsystematic risk in that portfolio. Incidentally, it is customary to treat the S&P 500 Index, or some other market index, as an efficient portfolio and refer to it as the *market portfolio.*

The critical question now becomes: How can one successfully beat the market? An investor can consistently beat the market only if he or she can successfully devise a technique that will outperform a market index. As noted, a market index is a surrogate for an efficient portfolio. This important dimension in portfolio construction will be explored more fully in Chapter 13.

Risk and the Risk Taker

Thus far, our discussion of risk has been based on the implicit assumption that all investors are equally risk averse. This, of course, is a gross oversimplification, and possibly a distortion, of actual circumstances. Attitude toward risk depends on the social, economic and psychological outlook of an investor. The amount of risk investors are willing to take in any given instance depends on their attitudes toward risk, or their *risk preference.*

In the economic literature, investor attitude toward the acquisition of an asset, together with the satisfaction or utility derived from it, is discussed in terms of the investor's *utility function* (or indifference curve). Typically, the utility function is expressed in terms of the consumer's wealth—that is, in terms of the successive changes in the consumer's utility as a result of increases in his wealth. Clearly, the utility function can be used to describe an investor's attitudes as well. The basic reason for investment activity is to maximize the investor's personal

Figure 5–11

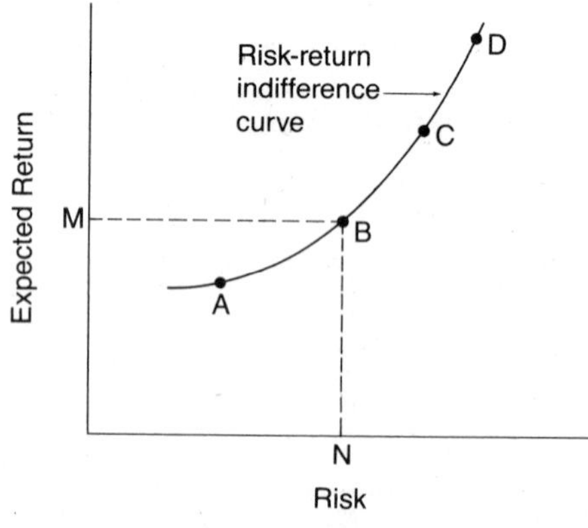

satisfaction, or utility. Investors hope to increase their wealth by investing and thus achieving a higher level of affluence.

The traditional utility function can be adapted to measure an investor's attitude toward risk and return. This is accomplished by labeling the axes with expected return and risk, as shown in Figure 5–11. The level of investor's current risk is designated by N and the expected return is marked as M. The investor's present position, B, is represented as the intersection of this level of risk and expected return. The investor derives the same degree of total satisfaction—and hence is "indifferent"—between points A, B, C, and D, all of which lie on the risk–return indifference curve. As with traditional indifference curves, the choice of any point over point B would depend on the risk–return preference of the investor. For example, an investor who wishes to reduce risk would prefer point A, whereas one anxious to increase the return and willing to assume additional risk might prefer point D.

This risk–return curve is characteristic of the profile of a risk-averse investor. Not all investors fit that category. Investors can also be risk-neutral or risk-seekers, as revealed by Figure 5–12. The profile of a risk-averse investor is given in Figure 5–12A. Risk-averse investors expect progressively higher returns, or demand increasing risk premiums, as they agree to take more risks. Therefore, the expected risk–return curve has an increasing slope.

In contrast to risk-averse investors, risk-seekers actually demand proportionately less premium as they assume greater degrees of risk. That is why the curve in Figure 5–12C increases at a decreasing rate. Risk-neutral investors, of course, demand the same proportionate risk premium regardless of the degree of risk they assume. This is charted in Figure 5–12B.

Figure 5–12

(A) Risk-Averter
(B) Risk-Neutral
(C) Risk-Seeker

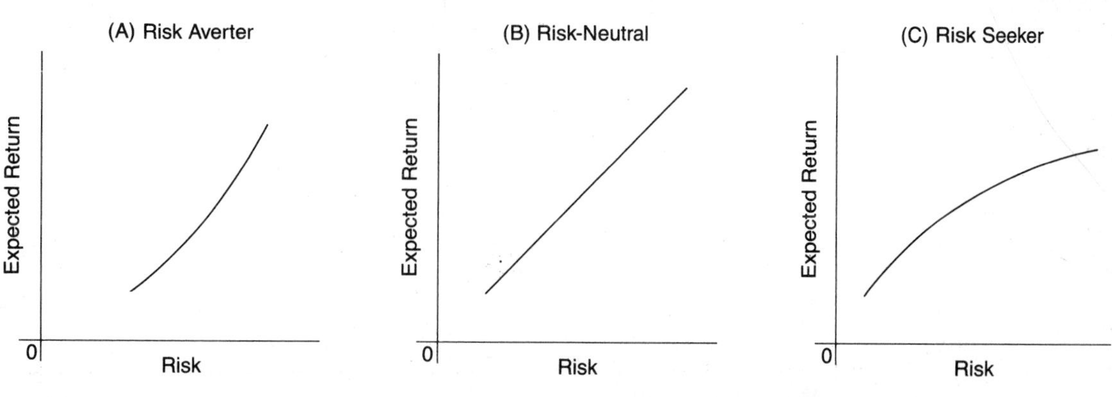

Summary

Risk is associated not only with the possibility of a total loss of capital, but with the possibility of obtaining less return than expected.

Uncertainty refers to a situation for which at least some of the possible future outcomes and their subjective probabilities are unknown. In situations involving risk, all future outcomes and their subjective probabilities are known. In the investment world, risk and uncertainty are used synonymously.

Risks associated with a fixed income security differ significantly from the risk associated with a common stock. Fixed income securities are subject to six types of risk—*interest rate risk*, *inflation risk*, *maturity risk*, *default risk*, *callability risk*, and *liquidity risk*.

There are two types of common stock risk: *systematic risk* and *unsystematic risk*. Systematic risk refers to the variability of a stock's price due to fluctuations in the market as a whole. Unsystematic risk relates to the variability of a stock's price due to factors which are unique to individual firms and to specific industries.

An important dimension of unsystematic risk is the *extramarket covariance risk*. Risk arising from comovements of stocks whose movements are independent of those of the market as a whole is known as the *extramarket covariance risk*.

The direct sources of risk associated with common stock are *inflation risk*, *interest rate risk*, *tangible and intangible risks*, and *business* (*financial leverage*, *operating leverage*, and *industry*) *risks*.

The *Market Model* is constructed by the use of three statistical measures; namely, *beta*, *alpha* and the *error term*. Beta is a measure of the volatility of a stock's return relative to the market return; alpha is the estimated return on the stock when the market return as a whole is zero. The error term represents all of the factors that together with alpha make up unsystematic return.

Total risk, or variability, of a stock can be measured by *variance*. Because the analyst's estimate of alpha for a given stock at a particular time is a fixed amount, its variability is zero. Consequently, the risk of a stock is the square of its beta times the variance of the market return plus the variance of the error term.

While the unsystematic risk of a given stock is always present, it can be largely avoided by selecting a large number of securities with diverse characteristics. This process is known as *diversification* through the construction of an efficient portfolio. Consequently, the total risk of an efficient portfolio is lower than the weighted average risks of individual securities in the portfolio.

Over the years three forms of the *Efficient Market Hypothesis* (*EMH*) have developed. The weak form of the EMH suggests that there is no value to conducting technical analysis. The semistrong form of the EMH maintains that, because the current price of a stock reflects all publicly available information and new information becomes available only randomly, there is no reason to expect systematic movement in stock prices. The strong form of the EMH maintains that even with private information professional investors cannot consistently beat the simple buy, hold, and sell strategy. Although controversy surrounding the EMH is by no means settled, many people believe that in-depth analyses of individual securities as well as portfolios are definitely worthwhile.

A Look Ahead

In this chapter, a risk–return framework has been constructed which will be used as a basis for discussing the determination of the values of individual securities. For simplicity, as well as for reasons of practicality, in Chapter 6 we will begin with a discussion of assets with minimal risk, followed by those bearing higher degrees of risk. More specifically, we will begin with an analysis of government bonds, followed by municipal bonds, corporate bonds, preferred stock, and finally, common stock. Each type of security will first be analyzed as a single unit, and later, in Chapter 13, a discussion of the role of the individual security in a portfolio will be undertaken.

Concepts for Review

Total return
Variability of return
Risk and uncertainty
Types of risk
Fixed income security risk
Interest rate risk
Inflation risk
Maturity risk
Default risk
Callability risk
Liquidity risk
Common stock risk
Systematic risk
Market risk
Unsystematic risk
Extramarket covariance risk
Tangible risk
Intangible risk
Business risk
Financial leverage risk
Operating leverage risk
Industry risk
Risk measurement
Market Model
Least squares regression method
Line of best fit
Characteristic line
Beta
Systematic return
Unsystematic return
Alpha
Error term
Variance
Subjective probability
Diversification
Portfolio risk
Efficient portfolio
Efficient Market Hypothesis (EMH)
Risk preference
Utility function

Questions for Review

1. Explain in general terms the concept of risk. What is the difference between risk and uncertainty?
2. Compare and contrast the nature of fixed income security risk with common stock risk.
3. When considering inflation risk, why is a distinction made between anticipated and unanticipated inflation?
4. Comment on the following statement: "Rising interest rates should not have an adverse effect on the prices of growth company stocks, because these securities generally have low dividend yields."
5. What are systematic and unsystematic risk? What are their sources?
6. What is extramarket covariance risk? How does it differ from the other risks?
7. The debt/equity ratio of ABC Corporation has risen from 25 percent to 45 percent after a recent bond offering. Other things remaining the same, what effect will this have on the variability of net income in future years? Explain.
8. Discuss the concept of return of an individual security in terms of the Market Model. Include an explanation of the alpha and beta coefficients and the error term.
9. What is the characteristic line? How is it constructed?
10. Explain the relationship between the expected return and risk of a security. How can the risk of a security be measured?
11. What are the characteristics of an efficient portfolio. Why would an investor wish to construct such a portfolio?
12. Explain the essentials of the Efficient Market Hypothesis (EMH).
13. Is the risk of a portfolio measured differently than the risk of an individual security? Explain.
14. Why is variance a key measure of risk? What is its relation with unsystematic and systematic risk?
15. Describe the utility functions and risk preferences of investors.

Problems

1. Investor Q purchases 250 shares of ABC Corporation stock at the beginning of the year for $52 per share. After receiving dividend payments of $4.50 per share, she sells the stock at the end of the year for $49.75 per share. What is Investor Q's return on the ABC stock investment?
2. The following information shows the return on XYZ stock and a relevant market index for a five-year period.

Year	RETURNS (%) Market	XYZ Stock
1	7.5	8.0
2	−4.5	−7.0
3	13.2	17.9
4	5.2	6.0
5	−8.0	−7.6

a. Estimate graphically or use the least squares regression method to calculate the characterstic line.
b. What are the alpha and beta coefficients of XYZ stock over this time period?
c. In Year 6 the market is expected to return 8.4 percent. What is the expected return on XYZ stock?
d. Suppose the market returns 8.4 percent in Year 6 and XYZ stock returns 13.9. How would you account for the return on XYZ stock?
e. If XYZ stock returns 13.9 percent in Year 6, what would be the systematic and unsystematic returns?

3. GEH Corporation common stock costs $50 per share and pays no dividend. The table below shows the possible prices that the stock might sell for at the end of the year and the probability of each outcome:

GEH Stock Price at Year-End	Probability
$35	.10
45	.15
50	.20
55	.35
75	.20

a. What is the expected return on GEH stock?
b. What is the variance of the expected return?

4. Listed below are the possible returns an investor might earn on three different stocks, and the associated probabilities:

LMN STOCK		JKL STOCK		NOP STOCK	
Possible Return	Probability	Possible Return	Probability	Possible Return	Probability
−15%	.05	−30%	.10	−25%	.20
−10%	.05	−15%	.20	−15%	.20
0%	.15	15%	.20	15%	.20
5%	.40	20%	.30	25%	.20
15%	.35	25%	.20	30%	.20

Which of the three stocks is the least attractive? Which of the three is the most attractive? Show all computations and state any assumptions necessary to answer these questions.

Footnotes

13. The least squares method is used in the following manner to determine the equation of the least squares line:

	R_m	R_s	R_m^2	$(R_m)(R_s)$	
	0	2.5	0	0.0	
	1	6.0	1	6.0	
	2	3.0	4	6.0	
	3	4.0	9	12.0	Number of observations
	4	1.5	16	6.0	$(n) = 8$
	5	4.0	25	20.0	
	6	2.5	36	15.0	
	7	10.5	49	73.5	
Total ($\sum$)	28	34.0	140	138.5	

$$b = \frac{n(\sum R_m R_s) - (\sum R_m)(\sum R_s)}{n(\sum R_m^2) - (\sum R_m)^2}$$

$$= \frac{8(138.5) - (28)(34)}{8(140) - (28)^2}$$

$$= \frac{1{,}108 - 952}{1{,}120 - 784}$$

$$\approx 0.5$$

$$a = \frac{\sum R_s}{n} - b\frac{\sum R_m}{n}$$

$$= \frac{34}{8} - 0.5\left(\frac{28}{8}\right)$$

$$= 2.5$$

The equation of the least squares line is

$$R_s = 2.5 + 0.5R_m$$

20. In this case, the covariance can be calculated as follows:

$$\text{Cov}_{WP} = p_W[R_H|W - E(R)][R_D|W - E(R)] + p_P[R_H|P - E(R)] \times [R_D|P - E(R)]$$

where

Cov_{WP} = Covariance of war and peace

p_W = Probability of war

p_P = Probability of peace

$R_H|W$ = Actual return from Hawk Company if there is war

$R_D|W$ = Actual return from Dove Company if there is war

$P_H|P$ = Actual return from Hawk Company if there is peace
$R_D|P$ = Actual return from Dove Company if there is peace
$E(R)$ = Average expected return

In the above example, the covariance is $-.141$:

$$\begin{aligned}\text{Cov}_{WP} &= .5(.50-.125)(-.25-.125)+.5(-.25-.125)(.50-.125)\\ &= (.5)(.375)(-.375)+(.5)(-.375)(.375)\\ &= -.141\end{aligned}$$

A *negative* covariance implies that the stocks move in the opposite directions. In contrast, stocks moving in unison in the same direction will have a positive covariance.

Selected Readings

Ambachtsheer, Keith B. "Where Are the Customers' Alphas?" *Journal of Portfolio Management*, Fall 1977.

Arditti, Fred D. "Risk and the Required Return on Equity." *Journal of Finance*, March 1967.

Babcock, Guilford. "A Note on Justifying Beta as a Measure of Risk." *Journal of Finance*, June 1972.

Blume, Marshall E. "Betas and Their Regression Tendencies." *Journal of Finance*, June 1975.

Blume, Marshall E. "On the Assessment of Risk." *Journal of Finance*, March 1971.

Blume, Marshall E. and Irwin Friend. "Risk, Investment Strategy, and Long-run Rates of Return." *Review of Economics and Statistics*, August 1974.

Bower, R. S. and D. H. Bower. "Risk and Valuation of Common Stock." *Journal of Political Economy*, May–June 1969.

Brealey, R. A. *An Introduction to Risk and Return from Common Stocks*. Cambridge, Mass.: MIT Press, 1969.

Cheng, Pao and M. King Deets. "Systematic Risk and the Horizon Problem." *Journal of Financial and Quantitative Analysis*, March 1973.

Cooley, Philip L., Rodney L. Rolnfeldt, and Naval K. Modani. "Interdependence on Market Risk Measures." *Journal of Business*, July 1977.

Cootner, Paul H., ed. *The Random Character of Stock Market Prices*. Cambridge, Mass.: MIT Press, 1964.

Douglas, George W. "Risk in the Equity Market: An Empirical Appraisal of Market Efficiency." Unpublished Ph.D. dissertation, Yale University, 1967.

Fabozzi, Frank J. and Jack C. Francis. "Stability Tests for Alphas and Betas over Bull and Bear Market Conditions." *Journal of Finance*, September 1977.

Fama, Eugene F. "Efficient Capital Markets: A Review of Theory and Empirical Evidence." *Journal of Finance*, May 1970.

Fama, Eugene F. "Random Walks in Stock Market Prices." *Financial Analysts Journal*, September–October 1965.

Fama, Eugene F. "Risk, Return, and Equilibrium." *Journal of Political Economy*, January–February 1971.

Feldstein, M. S. "On the Measurement of Risk Aversion." *Southern Economic Journal*, July 1968.

Fouse, William F., William W. Jahnke, and Barr Rosenberg. "Is Beta Phlogiston?" *Financial Analysts Journal*, January–February 1974.

Frankfurter, George M. and Herbert E. Phillips. "Alpha-Beta Theory: A Word of Caution." *Journal of Portfolio Management*, Summer 1977.

Godfrey, John M. and B. Frank King. "Money Market Certificates: An Innovation in Consumer Deposits." Federal Reserve Bank of Atlanta, *Economic Review*, May–June 1979.

Granger, Clive W. J. "What the Random-Walk Model Does Not Say." *Financial Analysts Journal*, May–June 1970.

Hirshleifer, Jack. "Risk, the Discount Rate, and Investment Decisions." *American Economic Review*, May 1961.

Ibbotson, Roger G. and Rex A. Sinquefield. "Stocks, Bonds, Bills and Inflation: Year-by-Year Historical Returns (1926–1974)." *Journal of Business*, January 1976.

Jacob, Nancy. "The Measurement of Systematic Risk for Securities and Portfolios: Some Empirical Results." *Journal of Financial and Quantitative Analysis*, March 1971.

Jensen, Michael. "Capital Markets: Theory and Evidence." *Bell Journal of Economics and Management Science*, Autumn 1972.

Jensen, Michael C. "Random Walks: Reality or Myth—Comment." *Financial Analysts Journal*, November–December 1967.

Levy, Robert A. "Random Walks: Reality or Myth." *Financial Analysts Journal*, November–December 1967.

Levy, Robert A. "Random Walks: Reality or Myth—Reply." *Financial Analysts Journal*, January–February 1968.

Levy, Robert A. "On the Short-Term Stationarity of Beta Coefficients." *Financial Analysts Journal*, November–December 1971.

Lindahl-Stevens, Mary. "Some Popular Uses and Abuses of Beta." *Journal of Portfolio Management*, Winter 1978.

Logue, Dennis E. "Are Stock Markets Becoming Riskier?" *Journal of Portfolio Management*, Spring 1976.

Lorie, James and Richard Brealey, eds. *Modern Developments in Investment Management: A Book of Readings*, 2d ed. Hinsdale, Il.: Dryden Press, 1978.

Pinches, George. "The Random Walk Hypothesis and Technical Analysis." *Financial Analysts Journal*, March–April 1970.

Pinches, George and William R. Kinney, Jr. "The Measurement of the Volatility of Common Stock Prices." *Journal of Finance*, March 1971.

Robichek, Alexander A. "Risk and the Value of Securities." *Journal of Financial and Quantitative Analysis*, December 1969.

Robichek, Alexander A. and Richard A. Cohn. "The Economic Determinants of Systematic Risk." *Journal of Finance*, May 1974.

Rosenberg, Barr and James Guy. "Prediction of Beta from Investment Fundamentals." Parts One and Two. *Financial Analysts Journal*, May–June 1976 and July–August. 1976.

Rosenberg, Barr and Walt McKibben. "The Prediction of Systematic Risk in Common Stocks." *Journal of Financial and Quantitative Analysis*, March 1973.

Ryan, J. M. and A. O. Gardner. "The Measurement of Dynamic Risk." *Southern Economic Journal*, January 1965.

Samuelson, Paul A. "Proof that Properly Anticipated Prices Fluctuate Randomly." *Industrial Management Review*, Spring 1965.

Sharpe, William F. "Capital Asset Prices: A Theory of Market Equilibrium under Conditions of Risk." *Journal of Finance*, September 1964.

Sharpe, William F. and Guy M. Cooper. "Risk–Return Classes of New York Stock Exchange Common Stocks." *Financial Analysts Journal*, March–April 1972.

Sharpe, William F. and Howard B. Sosin. "Risk, Return and Yield: New York Stock Exchange Common Stocks, 1928–1969." *Financial Analysts Journal*, March–April 1976.

Smidt, Seymour. "A New Look at the Random Walk Hypothesis." *Journal of Financial and Quantitative Analysis*, September 1968.

Telser, L. G. "A Critique of Some Recent Empirical Research on the Explanation of the Term Structure of Interest Rates." *Journal of Political Economy*, August 1967.

Thompson, Donald J., II. "Sources of Systematic Risk in Common Stock." *Journal of Business*, April 1976.

Wallich, Henry C. "What Does the Random-Walk Hypothesis Mean to Security Analysis?" *Financial Analysts Journal*, March–April 1968.

Welles, Chris. "The Beta Revolution: Learning to Live with Risk." *Institutional Investor*, September 1971.

2 Fixed Income Securities: Valuation and Analysis

In Part 2 an in-depth analysis of fixed income securities is undertaken against the backdrop of risk and return. Our basic approach has already been specified: construction of a valuation model, followed by an analysis of securities within the framework established by that model.

Chapter 6 is devoted to the development of a Bond Valuation Model. The model lays the foundation for the determination of present value of different types of bonds and preferred stock. In addition, it provides a basis for an in-depth analysis of fixed income securities through identification of the variables that have a major impact on the value and price of these securities.

The Bond Valuation Model is applied to the valuation of government and municipal bonds in Chapter 7. The analysis is extended to corporate bonds and preferred stock in Chapter 8.

Bond Valuation and Analysis

Introduction

In Chapter 5, a risk–return criterion was developed for analyzing various types of securities. It was also mentioned that the criterion would be initially applied to the least risky government securities, followed by municipal and corporate bonds, preferred stock, and, finally, common stock.

In the course of the discussion on risk, a major theme emerged: The nature of risk associated with fixed income securities differs significantly from that associated with common stocks. It was noted that in the case of a bond the annual interest payments and the payment of the par value at maturity are *promised*, and that the types of risk affecting bonds are interest rate, inflation, maturity, default, callability, and liquidity risks.

The primary objective of this chapter is to develop a Bond Valuation Model within the framework of these six types of bond risks. The valuation model will be the basis for the development of a decision model. We will also demonstrate the use of this model for choosing between bonds with different types of risks and investment features.

Bond Valuation: The Basic Concept

Appropriate Discount Rate and Yield to Maturity

As observed in Chapter 2, a bond is evidence of an indebtedness or IOU entered into by the issuer and is used as a vehicle for borrowing money. Each bond carries the name of the issuer, the serial number, the principal amount, the rate of interest, and the date when the principal is to be paid. Normally, bonds are sold in units of \$1,000. This issue price, known as the *par value* of the bond, is repaid on the maturity date. The interest which the bond issuer is contractually obligated to pay is called the *coupon rate*. For instance, the expression "GM 8s of '99" indicates that GM has issued a bond series that will mature in the year 1999 and the series has a coupon rate of 8 percent. This coupon rate will remain unchanged throughout the life of the bond.

The *present value* of a bond with a given coupon rate and maturity can be calculated by discounting the future interest payments and maturity price by an *appropriate discount rate*, which is frequently referred to as the investor's minimum required rate of return.[1] For example, the present value of a 20-year GM bond with a coupon of 8 percent and a maturity price of \$1,000 is calculated

$$PV = \frac{\$80}{(1+r)^1} + \frac{\$80}{(1+r)^2} + \frac{\$80}{(1+r)^3} + \cdots + \frac{\$80}{(1+r)^{20}} + \frac{\$1{,}000}{(1+r)^{20}}$$

which can be summarized as

$$PV = \sum_{n=1}^{20} \frac{\$80}{(1+r)^n} + \frac{\$1{,}000}{(1+r)^{20}}$$

Finally, introducing C for annual interest payments and P_N for the maturity price, the above equation can be expressed in the form of the Bond Valuation Model:

$$PV = \sum_{n=1}^{N} \frac{C}{(1+r)^n} + \frac{P_N}{(1+r)^N} \tag{6-1}$$

where

PV = Present value of the bond
C = Annual interest payments
P_N = Par value of the bond
N = Maturity of the bond
r = The appropriate discount rate or the investor's minimum required rate of return

For a given bond, the appropriate discount rate or the investor's minimum required rate of return may be less than, equal to, or greater than the bond's *yield to maturity*, which is the rate of return currently offered in the market if the bond is held until maturity.

[1] Henceforth, the appropriate discount rate and the investor's minimum required rate of return will be used synonymously.

When the market price, the coupon rate, the number of years to maturity, and the maturity price of a bond are given, its yield to maturity can be determined by solving for i in the following equation:

$$P_0 = \sum_{n=1}^{N} \frac{C}{(1+i)^n} + \frac{P_N}{(1+i)^N} \tag{6-2}$$

where

P_0 = Market price of the bond
C = Annual interest payments
P_N = Par value of the bond
N = Maturity of the bond
i = Yield to maturity

In the previous example, the GM bond was presumed to have a 20-year maturity, an 8 percent coupon rate, and a maturity price of \$1,000. By applying Equation 6–2 to the GM bond, we obtain:

$$P_0 = \sum_{n=1}^{20} \frac{\$80}{(1+i)^n} + \frac{\$1{,}000}{(1+i)^{20}}$$

Clearly, the yield to maturity, i, can be determined if the current price of the bond, P_0, is known.

The Basic Decision Model

Assuming that an investor wishes to hold the bond until maturity, when a bond is purchased at the current market price, the investor expects to receive the yield to maturity that the market is currently offering on that bond. The function of the *Basic Decision Model* is to enable the investor to determine whether or not the market's yield is sufficiently attractive to warrant the purchase of the bond. This is accomplished by comparing the yield to maturity with the appropriate discount rate, or the investor's minimum required rate of return as follows:

If	Then	Reason
$r = i$	Be indifferent.	The bond is appropriately valued.
$r < i$	Buy the bond.	The bond is undervalued.
$r > i$	Do not buy the bond.	The bond is overvalued.

r = The appropriate discount rate, or the investor's minimum required rate of return
i = The bond's yield to maturity

The Bond Yield

Bond Yield and Present Value Concept

Equation 6–2 uses the present value formula to determine a bond's yield. The equation reveals that the yield to maturity on a bond will be identical to the coupon rate as long as the market price, P_0, equals the par value, P_N, and the bond is held until maturity. However, the yield to maturity would differ from the coupon rate if the market price were to deviate from the par value.

Varying Market Price

According to Equation 6–2, the yield on a ten-year bond carrying a coupon rate of 5 percent, selling at par, \$1,000, and held until maturity, is also 5 percent:[2]

$$\$1{,}000 = \sum_{n=1}^{10} \frac{\$50}{(1+i)^n} + \frac{\$1{,}000}{(1+i)^{10}}$$

$$\$1{,}000 = \sum_{n=1}^{10} \frac{1}{(1+i)^n} \times \$50 + \frac{1}{(1+i)^{10}} \times \$1{,}000$$

Because

$$\sum_{n=1}^{10} \frac{1}{(1+i)^n} = \text{PVAF (present value: annuity factor)}$$

and

$$\frac{1}{(1+i)^{10}} = \text{PVFF (present value: fixed sum factor)}$$

$$\$1{,}000 = (\text{PVAF})(\$50) + (\text{PVFF})(\$1{,}000)$$

At $i = 5\%$, for 10 years (see the Appendix, page 847), PVAF = 7.722 and PVFF = .614. Therefore, at $i = 5\%$,

$$\$1{,}000 = (7.722 \times \$50) + (.614 \times \$1{,}000)$$

$$\$1{,}000 = \$386 + \$614$$

Bonds often sell at prices above or below their par values. For instance, if subsequent to its issue a bond becomes riskier than originally perceived, then its market price will decline, thereby raising its yield. An investor purchasing this bond at a price lower than the par value and holding it until maturity will receive a yield higher than the coupon rate and therefore will be compensated

[2] Some of the examples in this chapter use coupon rates and bond maturities which may not be representative of current market conditions. However, they are still useful for illustrative purposes.

for assuming the higher risk. Similarly, if subsequent to the sale of a bond the market interest rate rises, the price of the bond will decline, thereby making it equally attractive as the new higher coupon bonds. For instance, if the market interest rate rises, say, to 6 percent subsequent to the sale of a 5 percent bond, its market price would drop to \$926 (that is, less than par), thereby increasing its yield to 6 percent:

$$\$926 = \sum_{n=1}^{10} \frac{1}{(1+i)^n} \times \$50 + \frac{1}{(1+i)^{10}} \times \$1{,}000$$

At $i = 6\%$, the PVAF for $n = 10$ years is 7.360 and the PVFF for $N = 10$ years is .558. Therefore, at $i = 6\%$

$$\$926 = (7.360 \times \$50) + (.558 \times \$1{,}000)$$
$$\$926 = \$368 + \$558$$

Similarly, if the market price rises, say, to \$1,170.50 (above par), the yield, i, would be only 3 percent.

Varying Holding Period

It should be obvious that a bond yield varies inversely with price: An increase in the market price of a bond lowers its yield, whereas the reverse is true if the bond price declines. Another variable in the bond yield equation is the *holding period.* The yield on a bond will change if, *ceteris paribus,*[3] the bond is purchased at a price higher or lower than its par value, and if the holding period differs from the total life of the bond. It was observed earlier that the yield is 6 percent on a 5 percent bond maturing in ten years and currently selling at \$926. However, if the investor pays \$926 for a ten-year, 5 percent bond issued seven years ago, the holding period would be only three years and the yield to maturity would be 7.87 percent:

$$\$926 = \sum_{n=1}^{3} \frac{1}{(1+i)^n} \times \$50 + \frac{1}{(1+i)^{3}} \times \$1{,}000$$

At $i = 7\%$, for three years, the PVAF = 2.624 and the PVFF = .816. Therefore, at $i = 7\%$

$$\$947.20 = (2.624 \times \$50) + (.816 \times \$1{,}000)$$

At $i = 8\%$, for three years, the PVAF = 2.577 and the PVFF = .794. Therefore, at $i = 8\%$

$$\$922.85 = (2.577 \times \$50) + (.794 \times \$1{,}000)$$

[3] The term *ceteris paribus* means that, except for the specified variables, all other variables are assumed constant. This term, and an equivalent expression, "all else being equal," will be frequently used to underscore the effect of the change in one independent variable on a dependent variable under study.

Table 6–1

$7\frac{3}{4}\%$				Years and Months				
Yield	18-6	19-0	19-6	20-0	20-6	21-0	21-6	22-0
4.00	148.69	149.58	150.44	151.29	152.12	152.94	153.74	154.52
4.20	145.35	146.15	146.94	147.72	148.47	149.21	149.94	150.65
4.40	142.10	142.84	143.55	144.25	144.94	145.61	146.27	146.91
4.60	138.96	139.62	140.27	140.90	141.52	142.13	142.72	143.30
4.80	135.90	136.50	137.09	137.66	138.22	138.76	139.29	139.81
5.00	132.94	133.48	134.00	134.52	135.02	135.50	135.98	136.44
5.20	130.07	130.55	131.02	131.47	131.92	132.35	132.78	133.19
5.40	127.28	127.71	128.12	128.53	128.92	129.30	129.68	130.04
5.60	124.57	124.95	125.32	125.67	126.02	126.36	126.68	127.00
5.80	121.95	122.28	122.59	122.91	123.21	123.50	123.79	124.06
6.00	119.40	119.68	119.96	120.23	120.49	120.74	120.98	121.22
6.10	118.15	118.41	118.67	118.92	119.16	119.39	119.62	119.84
6.20	116.92	117.16	117.40	117.63	117.85	118.06	118.27	118.48
6.30	115.71	115.93	116.15	116.36	116.56	116.76	116.95	117.14
6.40	114.52	114.72	114.92	115.11	115.30	115.48	115.65	115.82
6.50	113.34	113.53	113.71	113.88	114.05	114.21	114.37	114.52
6.60	112.18	112.35	112.51	112.67	112.82	112.97	113.11	113.25
6.70	111.04	111.19	111.34	111.48	111.61	111.74	111.87	111.99
6.80	109.92	110.05	110.18	110.30	110.42	110.54	110.65	110.76
6.90	108.81	108.92	109.04	109.15	109.25	109.35	109.45	109.55
7.00	107.71	107.82	107.91	108.01	108.10	108.19	108.27	108.36
7.10	106.64	106.72	106.81	106.89	106.96	107.04	107.11	107.18
7.20	105.57	105.65	105.72	105.78	105.85	105.91	105.97	106.03
7.30	104.53	104.59	104.64	104.70	104.75	104.80	104.84	104.89
7.40	103.50	103.54	103.58	103.62	103.66	103.70	103.74	103.77
7.50	102.48	102.51	102.54	102.57	102.60	102.62	102.65	102.67
7.60	101.48	101.50	101.51	101.53	101.55	101.56	101.58	101.59
7.70	100.49	100.49	100.50	100.51	100.51	100.52	100.52	100.53
7.80	99.51	99.51	99.50	99.50	99.49	99.49	99.48	99.48
7.90	98.55	98.54	98.52	98.50	98.49	98.47	98.46	98.45
8.00	97.61	97.58	97.55	97.53	97.50	97.48	97.45	97.43
8.10	96.67	96.63	96.60	96.56	96.53	96.49	96.46	96.43
8.20	95.75	95.70	95.66	95.61	95.57	95.53	95.49	95.45
8.30	94.85	94.79	94.73	94.68	94.62	94.57	94.53	94.48
8.40	93.95	93.88	93.82	93.75	93.69	93.64	93.58	93.53

Interpolating,[4] at $i = 7.87$ percent, the present value of the coupon plus principal payments is equal to the market price of $926. Note that a three-year holding period resulted in a higher yield (7.87 percent) than a ten-year holding period (6 percent). In the first instance, the price appreciation of $74 ($1,000 – $926) occurs in only three years, whereas in the latter case it takes ten years to realize the same price appreciation.

[4] See note 4 on page 200.

Table 6–1 (*cont.*)

$7\frac{3}{4}$%	Years and Months							
Yield	18-6	19-0	19-6	20-0	20-6	21-0	21-6	22-0
8.50	93.07	92.99	92.92	92.85	92.78	92.71	92.65	92.59
8.60	92.20	92.11	92.03	91.95	91.88	91.80	91.73	91.67
8.70	91.34	91.25	91.16	91.07	90.99	90.91	90.83	90.76
8.80	90.49	90.39	90.29	90.20	90.11	90.02	89.94	89.86
8.90	89.66	89.55	89.44	89.34	89.25	89.15	89.07	88.98
9.00	88.84	88.72	88.61	88.50	88.40	88.30	88.20	88.11
9.10	88.02	87.90	87.78	87.67	87.56	87.45	87.35	87.26
9.20	87.22	87.09	86.97	86.85	86.73	86.62	86.52	86.42
9.30	86.43	86.30	86.16	86.04	85.92	85.80	85.69	85.59
9.40	85.66	85.51	85.37	85.24	85.12	85.00	84.88	84.77
9.50	84.89	84.74	84.59	84.46	84.33	84.20	84.08	83.97
9.60	84.13	83.97	83.83	83.68	83.55	83.42	83.30	83.18
9.70	83.38	83.22	83.07	82.92	82.78	82.65	82.52	82.40
9.80	82.64	82.48	82.32	82.17	82.02	81.89	81.76	81.63
9.90	81.92	81.75	81.58	81.43	81.28	81.14	81.00	80.87
10.00	81.20	81.02	80.86	80.70	80.54	80.40	80.26	80.13
10.20	79.79	79.61	79.43	79.26	79.11	78.95	78.81	78.67
10.40	78.42	78.23	78.05	77.87	77.71	77.55	77.40	77.26
10.60	77.09	76.89	76.70	76.52	76.35	76.19	76.03	75.88
10.80	75.79	75.59	75.39	75.20	75.03	74.86	74.70	74.55
11.00	74.53	74.32	74.12	73.93	73.74	73.57	73.41	73.26
11.20	73.30	73.08	72.88	72.68	72.50	72.32	72.15	72.00
11.40	72.10	71.88	71.67	71.47	71.28	71.10	70.93	70.78
11.60	70.93	70.71	70.49	70.29	70.10	69.92	69.75	69.59
11.80	69.79	69.56	69.35	69.14	68.95	68.77	68.60	68.43
12.00	68.68	68.45	68.23	68.03	67.83	67.65	67.47	67.31

SOURCE: Reproduced from *Expanded Bond Value Tables*, Pub. 83, copyright 1970, page 844, Financial Publishing Co., Boston, MA.

Bond Yield Tables

Given the coupon rate, the yield an investor receives from a bond is a function of its purchase price and the holding period. While such a yield can be calculated with the use of the present value tables, there is no need to do so. *Bond tables* of all conceivable yields are readily available, and an investor need only consult such a table to determine the yield. Note that, as a space-saving device, in these tables bond prices are quoted in terms of a par value of $100 instead of the usual par value of $1,000.

Table 6–1 is a typical bond yield table. According to this table, if an investor purchases a bond with a $7\frac{3}{4}$ percent coupon for $80.13 (that is, $801.30) and holds it for 22 years, the yield would be 10 percent. Another way of using this table is to say that an investor willing to hold a $7\frac{3}{4}$ percent bond for 22 years and requiring a minimum yield of 10 percent should pay no more than $801.30 for this bond. Bond tables for different coupon rates and maturities are readily available.

The Appropriate Discount Rate

The Concept

After a bond's yield to maturity has been determined, the appropriate discount rate associated with the bond can be evaluated. The appropriate discount rate is the minimum rate of return which an investor requires to invest in that bond. Intuitively, an investor, who loans funds, expects the borrower to pay for the privilege of using the funds. For simplicity, this return can be called the *risk-free real rate of return*, r_{rf}. In addition, if the investor believes that parting with the funds entails certain risks, he or she would demand an extra return. This can be called a *risk premium*, r_{rp}. The investor's minimum required rate of return, or the appropriate discount rate, then becomes

$$r = r_{rf} + r_{rp} \tag{6-3}$$

As we will observe shortly, the risk-free real rate of return depends on the time preference of consumption and the opportunity cost of parting with liquid funds, whereas the risk premium represents the premiums associated with the six types of risks assumed by a bondholder. These are (1) interest rate risk, (2) inflation risk, (3) maturity risk, (4) default risk, (5) callability risk, and (6) liquidity risk.

Risk-free Real Rate of Interest

For thousands of years people have been lending money to their friends and neighbors, and on occasion they have asked for something extra in return. That something extra is interest—the price of the loan. However, the picture is not complete until interest rates are examined from two points of view—the saver's and the borrower's. To the saver, the interest rate represents the reward for parting with savings. As such, *ceteris paribus*, the higher the interest rate, the greater is the saver's willingness to loan money. To the borrower, interest rate represents the cost of borrowing money. Consequently, the lower the interest rate, the greater is the desire to borrow money. The interest rate that equates the supply of funds to the demand for funds is known as the *equilibrium interest rate.*

Interest rates can be viewed as the price of money. Unlike other prices, they are usually expressed as percentages of the value of the item loaned, rather than as amounts of money. But, like other prices, they are determined by supply and demand. In a monetary economy free of all risks, real rate of interest depends

Figure 6–1 **Estimated Real Long-term Rates of Interest on High Grade Corporate Bonds, 1967–75***

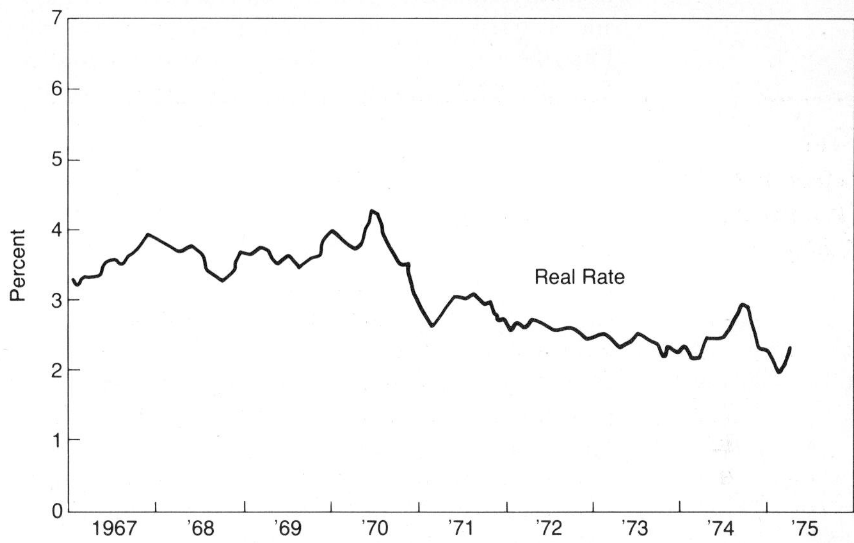

* The Federal Reserve Bank of St. Louis has since discontinued collecting data on this series.

SOURCE: Federal Reserve Bank of St. Louis.

on the supply of, and the demand for, loanable funds,[5] which in turn depend on productivity of capital.

In his celebrated *The Theory of Interest*, published in 1930, Irving Fisher explained the determination of the risk-free real rate even more succinctly. According to Fisher, the risk-free real rate is determined by two factors. One is the so-called "*time preference of consumption*," which implies that savers will postpone present consumption only when adequately compensated to do so. The second factor is the *opportunity cost* of parting with one's money. The higher the investment opportunities measured by the long-run real growth of the economy, the higher the rate savers demand to part with their savings. Therefore, the time preference of consumption, together with the opportunity cost of loaning funds, determines the risk-free real rate of interest. In the United States, this annual real rate has averaged around 3 percent. This is charted in Figure 6–1.

[5] In addition to the loanable funds theory, the determination of the level of interest rates is also explained in terms of the liquidity preference theory. The liquidity preference theoretical structure was developed out of the writings of John Maynard Keynes in the 1930s as an integral part of his macroeconomic model of income determination.

According to the liquidity preference theory, the equilibrium interest rate equates the supply and demand for money. The supply of money is determined by the central bank. The demand for money—the liquidity preference—depends on people's desire to hold money for transaction, precautionary, and speculative purposes.

Risk Premium

The second component of the appropriate discount rate is the *risk premium.* Bond investors assume many different types of risks for which they demand adequate risk premiums. However, risk premiums cannot be demanded at will. First, the *nature* and *extent* of each type of risk must be explored. Only then can the risk premium appropriate for each type of risk be estimated.

Interest Rate Risk

Basic Principles The *interest rate risk* refers to the possibility of variations in bond prices as a result of fluctuations in market interest rates. As a general rule, when market interest rates rise, bond prices decline. For instance, the price of a 20-year ABC bond with a coupon rate of 8 percent is $1,000, if the market interest rate or yield is also 8 percent:

$$P = \sum_{n=1}^{20} \frac{\$80}{(1+i)^n} + \frac{\$1{,}000}{(1+i)^{20}}$$

From the present value tables, at $i = 8\%$, for 20 years, the PVAF = 9.818 and the PVFF = 0.215. Therefore, at $i = 8\%$,

$$\begin{aligned} P_0 &= (9.818)(\$80) + (0.215)(\$1{,}000) \\ &= \$785 + \$215 \\ &= \$1{,}000 \end{aligned}$$

If the market interest rate or the yield on comparable bonds subsequently rises to 10 percent, the price of the ABC bond would decline to $830:

$$\begin{aligned} P_0 &= \sum_{n=1}^{20} \frac{\$80}{(1+.10)^n} + \frac{\$1{,}000}{(1+.10)^{20}} \\ &= (8.514)(\$80) + (0.149)(\$1{,}000) \\ &= \$681 + \$149 \\ &= \$830 \end{aligned}$$

Note that because new bonds of comparable quality and maturity would have a coupon of 10 percent, the demand for the old bonds with an 8 percent coupon rate would continue to drop until the price of these bonds became $830. At that price, the yield on the old bonds would rise to 10 percent:

$$\$830 = \sum_{n=1}^{20} \frac{\$80}{(1+i)^n} + \frac{\$1{,}000}{(1+i)^{20}}$$

At $i = 10\%$,

$$P_0 = (8.514)(\$80) + (0.149)(\$1{,}000)$$
$$= \$830$$

Similarly, if subsequent to the issue of a 20-year, 8 percent ABC bond the market interest rate and yields on comparable bonds drop to 6 percent, the price of the ABC bond would increase to $1,230:

$$P_0 = \sum_{n=1}^{20} \frac{\$80}{(1 + .06)^n} + \frac{\$1{,}000}{(1 + .06)^{20}}$$
$$= (11.470)(\$80) + (0.312)(\$1{,}000)$$
$$= \$918 + \$312$$
$$= \$1{,}230$$

Again, because this increase in the price of the old bonds would make the yield on these bonds identical with those of the new bonds, the prospective investor would have no special preference for either type of bond. This principle is demonstrated in Table 6–2, which shows the impact of changing interest rates on an 8 percent bond.

An important dimension of the interest rate risk should be noted. Sometimes it is argued that if an investor wishes to hold a bond until maturity, then he or she is not exposed to the interest rate risk because a decline in the market price of the bond does not affect the investor in any way. This argument is fallacious because it ignores the opportunity cost of holding a lower-yielding bond.

Table 6–2 **Bond Price Fluctuations for Various Market Interest Rates and Maturities**

Par Value = $1,000
Coupon Rate = 8% = $80

$$P_0 = \sum_{n=1}^{N} \frac{\$80}{(1 + i)^n} + \frac{\$1{,}000}{(1 + i)^N}$$

Years to Maturity N	$i = 8\%$	BOND PRICE (P_0)*: Market Interest Rate Rises: $i = 10\%$	Market Interest Rate Declines: $i = 6\%$
1	$1,000	$982	$1,018
3	1,000	950	1,054
5	1,000	924	1,084
10	1,000	878	1,147
20	1,000	830	1,230

* Rounded to the nearest dollar

Figure 6–2

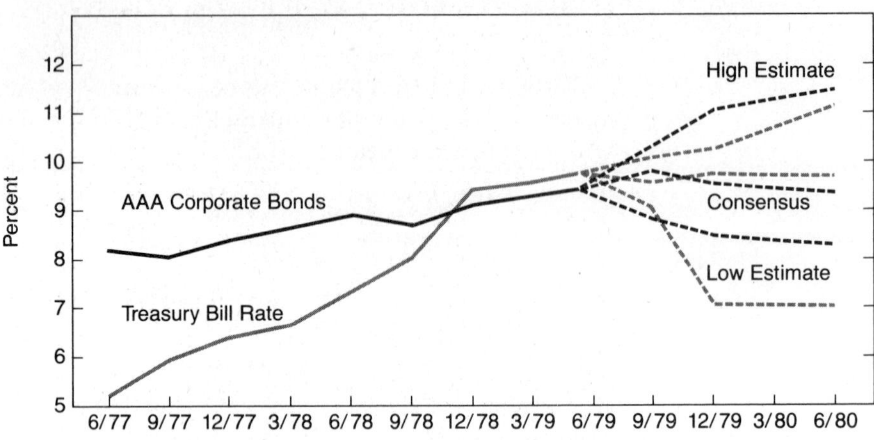

SOURCE: *Financial World*, June 15, 1979, p. 28.

Whether or not the loss is actually realized, an investor holding a lower-yielding bond suffers a loss by losing the opportunity to invest in a higher yielding bond.

Interest Rate Risk Premium The examples presented above reveal that the market interest rate is inversely related to the price of a bond: An increase in market interest rate lowers the price of a bond, whereas the reverse is true when the market interest rate declines.[6] Given this market interest rate–bond price relationship, from an investor's point of view, the key point is how much risk premium to demand for assuming the interest rate risk involved with investing in a bond. Unfortunately, no easy formula can be developed to determine accurately the interest rate risk premium, because the degree of interest rate risk an investor assumes is related primarily to future fluctuations in market interest rates.[7] The better the interest rate prediction, the better is the investor's bond trading strategy, and the less is the interest rate risk assumed. However, this is easier said than done. As Figure 6–2 reveals, even bond market experts differ widely on their interest rate forecasts. So the only possible conclusion is that the more unsure investors are about the future of the interest rates, the higher the interest rate risk premium they are likely to demand in order to protect themselves from the possible losses arising from investment in bonds.

[6] The more advanced relationships between market interest rates and bond prices are discussed later in the chapter.

[7] The coupon rate and the maturity of a bond are two additional variables which influence the degree of risk associated with that bond. This topic will be further explored later in the chapter.

Inflation Risk

Basic Considerations Thus far, no account has been taken of the impact of inflation on bond yields. A dollar loaned today may be worth only ninety cents a year later when it is returned by the borrower. If a contract is made under which a bondholder receives an interest payment of $100 at the end of one year, the *nominal* interest is 10 percent. However, if during the year the price level rises by, say, 6 percent, then the *real* interest would be only 9.4 percent.

$$\text{Real Interest Payment} = \frac{\text{Current Interest Payment (\$)}}{\text{Price Index}} \times 100$$

$$\text{Real Interest Yield} = \frac{\text{Real Interest Payment (\$)}}{\text{Total Investment (\$)}} \times 100$$

If the price level increases by 6 percent—that is, if the price index increases to 106—then

$$\text{Real Interest Payment} = \frac{\$100}{106} \times 100$$

$$= \$94.34$$

$$\text{Real Interest Yield} = \frac{\$94.34}{\$1{,}000.00} \times 100$$

$$= 9.4\%$$

In addition to the partial loss of the real interest, inflation would also erode the value of the principal by approximately 6 percent. Applying the above formula, duly modified, and assuming that the principal is received after one year, the value of $1,000 would drop to $943.40, a loss of 5.66 percent:

$$\text{Real Principal} = \frac{\text{Current Value of Principal (\$)}}{\text{Price Index}} \times 100$$

$$= \frac{\$1{,}000}{106} \times 100$$

$$= \$943.40$$

$$\text{Percentage loss} = \frac{\$1{,}000.00 - \$943.40}{\$1{,}000} \times 100$$

$$= 5.66\%$$

Bondholders recognize the existence of inflation risk and attempt to compensate for assuming this risk by demanding an inflation risk premium approximately

Figure 6–3 **Nominal and Estimated Real Long-term Rates of interest on High Grade Corporate Bonds, 1967–75***

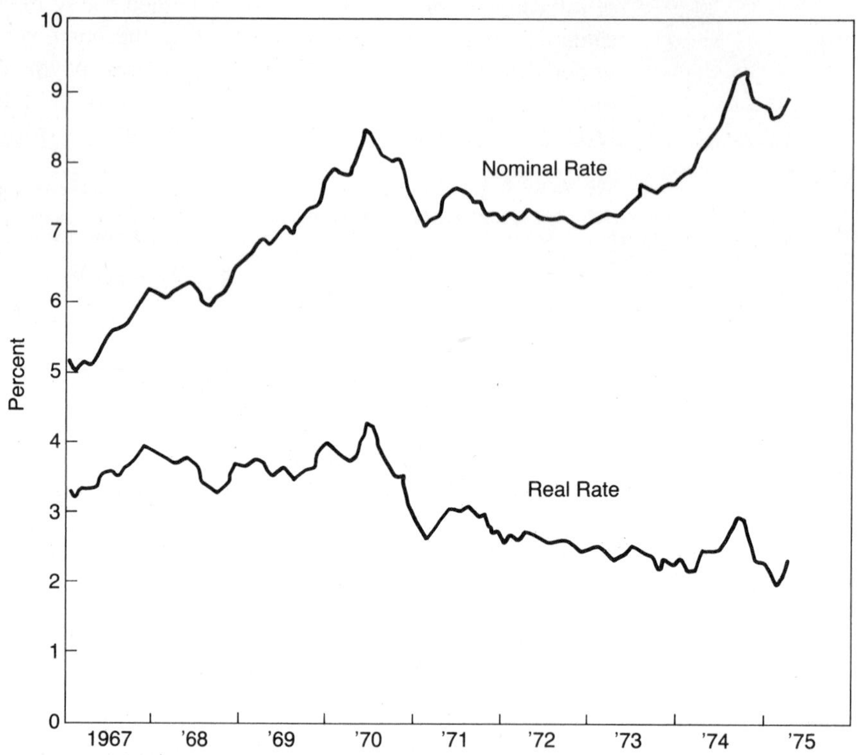

* This series has now been discontinued by the Federal Reserve Bank of St. Louis.

SOURCE: Federal Reserve Bank of St. Louis.

equal to the expected inflation. Figure 6–3 charts the long-term relationship between the nominal and the real interest rate. The difference between the two rates covering the area between the two lines represents the long-term inflation risk premium.[8]

[8] This discussion is based on the assumption that changes in nominal interest rates precede price increases, because lenders demand the inflation premium in expectation of inflation. A study conducted several years ago confirmed the validity of this assumption; it found that there are definite relationships between nominal interest rates and rates of inflation subsequently observed. See E. Fama, "Short-term Interest Rates as Predictors of Inflation," *American Economic Review*, June 1975, pp. 269–82.

Another study showed that for three-month treasury bills, over three-quarters of the changes in interest rates are due to inflationary expectations. This percentage increased to over four-fifths for ten-year treasury bonds. See W. E. Gibson, "Interest Rates and Inflationary Expectations: New Evidence," *American Economic Review*, December 1972, pp. 854–65.

Figure 6–4 **Three-Month Treasury Bill Rate**

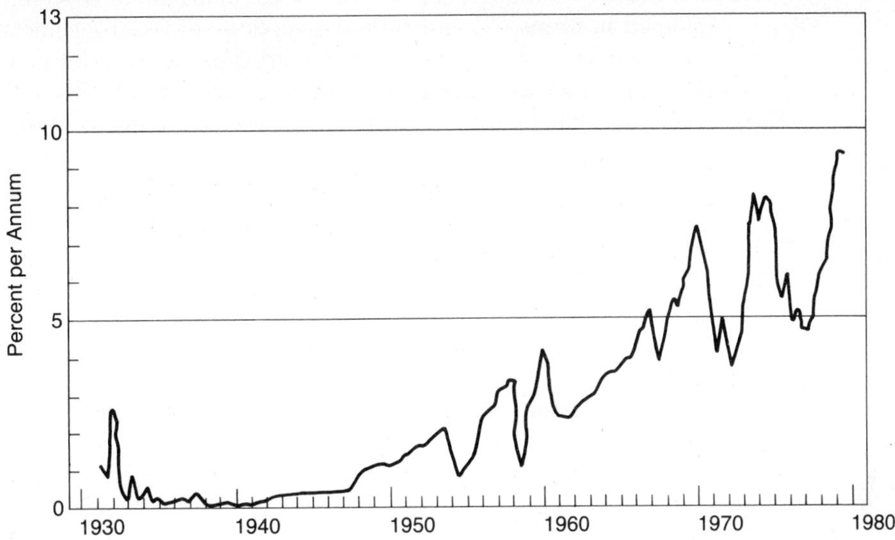

Inflation Risk Premium The preceding discussion has led to the conclusion that the inflation risk approximates the future rate of inflation. The *inflation risk premium* demanded by rational bondholders should, therefore, equal the anticipated rate of inflation. In the real world, however, inflation is not always correctly anticipated. Consequently, a distinction should be made between anticipated and unanticipated inflation. Although bondholders recognize that both types of inflation risk are always present, they generally demand an inflation-risk premium equal to the anticipated inflation only.

An important point should be made concerning treasury bills. Of the many types of risks that can be assumed by a bondholder, because of its safety and short maturity, a three-month treasury bill assumes only the inflation rate risk. Consequently, if the current inflation rate is expected to continue in the long run, the treasury bill rate, which combines the risk-free real rate averaging 3 percent per year and the inflation rate currently anticipated by the market, can be used as a guide for determining the inflation risk premium. For instance, if the three-month treasury bill rate is currently yielding 9 percent, it is reasonable to assume that the market is presently demanding an inflation risk premium of approximately 6 percent.[9] Figure 6–4 presents a long-term picture of the three-month treasury bill rate.

[9] Of course, if the long-run inflation rate is expected to differ significantly from the prevailing rate, the inflation risk premium would have to be adjusted accordingly.

Maturity Risk

Basic Considerations *Maturity risk*, based on the liquidity premium theory, is explained in terms of contrasting perceptions of risk by lenders and borrowers. The theory asserts that although market participants form expectations of future rates, they are uncertain about what actual rates will eventually prevail, believing that future rates actually may turn out to be above or below their current expectations. Because the future is assumed uncertain, investing in a long-term security always involves the risk of capital loss. The theory also asserts that both lenders and borrowers are risk averters—that is, they prefer to minimize risk for a given expected return. These two assumptions of uncertainty and risk imply that lenders of funds will prefer short-term over long-term securities in order to minimize the risk of capital loss.

The essence of the maturity risk may now be presented. Because bondholders, or lenders, prefer short-term investments, they require a liquidity risk premium for investing in long-term securities. Borrowers are willing to pay the premium because they want to avoid the impact of future increases in interest rates.

Maturity Risk Premium Clearly, the *maturity risk premium* demanded by bondholders depends on their perception of the degree of maturity risk they are assuming by investing in it. However, this premium cannot be measured directly. Consequently, the maturity risk premium associated with a bond is estimated by calculating the market's maturity risk premium.

The market's maturity premium, shown in Figure 6–5, has a unique pattern. According to this figure, the maturity risk premium quickly rises to about 1

Figure 6–5

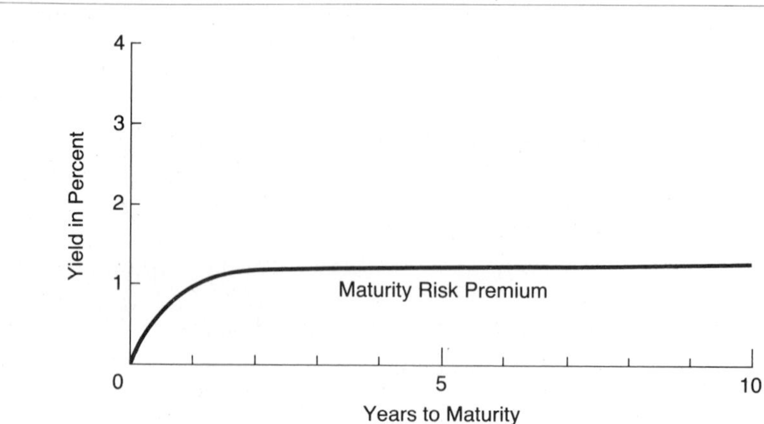

SOURCE: Adapted from Reuben A. Kessel, *The Cyclical Behavior of the Term Structure of Interest Rates*, Occasional Paper 91 (New York: National Bureau of Economic Research, 1965), p. 12.

percent as the maturity approaches one year. Thereafter, the premium rises very slowly, increasing by about 0.25 percent as the maturity approaches ten years. It should be added here that the maturity risk premium prevailing in an economically prosperous market increases dramatically during an economic downturn, because investors become increasingly risk averse under gloomy conditions.[10]

Default Risk

Basic Considerations In the discussion on interest rate risk it was tacitly assumed that the promised returns associated with holding a fixed income security are known with certainty and that there is no risk of delay or failure in receiving those returns. This is not a realistic assumption. In fact, there is a *default risk* associated with bonds; the degree of risk as perceived by investors varies from security to security.

Assume an investor has a choice of investing in either a government bond or a XYZ corporate bond. The government bond is free from default risk, and the return on it can be labeled as the yield on default risk-free bond. The XYZ bond is identical to the government bond in all but one respect. The investor feels that there is a possibility that the issuing corporation will default, either by nonpayment or delayed payment of the interest and/or the face value of the bond. In the case of a possible default, its promised yield to maturity would not be an appropriate measure of its expected yield, because it must reflect the additional default risk assumed by the investor.

The concept of default risk is illustrated in Table 6–3. In Example 1, the investor purchases a five-year, 8 percent government bond for $1,000; the yield to maturity on this default risk-free bond is 8 percent.

In Example 2, the investor purchases the 8 percent, five-year XYZ corporate bond which *promises* to pay the interest and the maturity price on time. The investor believes, however, that the probability is 0.9 that the full $1,000 will be paid at maturity, and the probability is 0.1 that no payment will be paid at maturity. Because the investor is assuming the default risk, he or she is unwilling to pay $1,000 for the XYZ bond.

Table 6–3 shows that, assuming a default risk-free discount rate of 8 percent, the present value of the five-year corporate bond with an expected maturity price of only $900 ($1,000 × 0.9) is only $932. Therefore, if an investor pays $932 for the XYZ bond, the expected yield to maturity would be 8 percent. However, if the company does not default and pays the maturity price of $1,000, the bond's yield to maturity would work out to be 9.78 percent. Put differently, in this case the investor demands a default risk premium of 1.78 percent (9.78 − 8.00 percent) for assuming the default risk inherent in the XYZ corporate bond.

[10] The concept of maturity premium presented here is based on the Liquidity Premium Theory of interest rates, which is not universally accepted. The other two theories, called the Expectations Theory and the Market Segmentation Theory, challenge the conclusions of the Liquidity Premium Theory. Because the empirical evidence suggests that the Liquidity Premium Theory is generally valid for periods of one quarter or longer, it is presented here as part of the discussion on risk premium. A critical evaluation of all the three interest rate theories is undertaken in the appendix to this chapter, "Term Structure of Interest Rates."

Table 6–3 **Default Risk Premium**

Example 1 **Government Bond, Default Risk-free**	*Example 2* **XYZ Corporate Bond, Subject to Default Risk**	
Par Value (P_N) = \$1,000 promised Coupon Rate (C) = 8% = \$80 Years to Maturity (N) = 5 Current Price (P_0) = \$1,000	Par Value (P_N) = \$900 expected*, \$1,000 promised Coupon Rate (C) = 8% = \$80 Years to Maturity (N) = 5	
Find default risk-free yield:	Find *PV* using *expected* maturity price and risk-free discount rate (8%):	Find promised yield using *promised* maturity price and P_0 of \$932:
$P_0 = \sum_{n=1}^{N} \frac{C}{(1+i)^n} + \frac{P_N}{(1+i)^N}$	$PV = \sum_{n=1}^{N} \frac{C}{(1+r)^n} + \frac{P_N}{(1+r)^N}$	$P_0 = \sum_{n=1}^{N} \frac{C}{(1+i)^n} + \frac{P_N}{(1+i)^N}$
$\$1{,}000 = \sum_{n=1}^{5} \frac{\$80}{(1+i)^n} + \frac{\$1{,}000}{(1+i)^5}$	$PV = \sum_{n=1}^{5} \frac{\$80}{(1+.08)^n} + \frac{\$900}{(1+.08)^5}$	$\$932 = \sum_{n=1}^{5} \frac{\$80}{(1+i)^n} + \frac{\$1{,}000}{(1+i)^N}$
Solve for i:	$PV = \$932$	Solve for i:
Promised yield on default risk-free bond: $i = 8\%$		Promised yield on risky bond: $i = 9.78\%$

* Payment Received at Maturity	Probability	Expected Value
\$1,000	.9	\$900
0	.1	0
	1.0	\$900

In this example, the investor was able to predict the degree to which the company would default. This is by no means an easy task, because it requires an investor to have both a technical ability and an analytical skill to make reasonably good default predictions.[11] Fortunately for investors, two bond

[11] The complexity of this task can be judged from a corporate bankruptcy study conducted several years ago. Edward Altman developed the following discriminant function to predict the eventual bankruptcy of corporations with total assets of \$1–\$25 million:

$$Z = 0.012X_1 + 0.014X_2 + 0.033X_3 + 0.006X_4 + 0.999X_5$$

where

X_1 = Working capital/total assets
X_2 = Retained earnings/total assets
X_3 = EBIT/total assets
X_4 = Market value equity/book value of total debt
X_5 = Sales/total assets

X_1 through X_4 are expressed as whole numbers (15 percent = 15), and X_5 is expressed as a decimal (15 percent = .15). Altman concluded that firms with Z values of 3.00 or higher were safe, whereas those with Z values of 2.99 or lower were potentially bankrupt companies with extremely high default risks.

Table 6–4

Factor	Definition	Interpretation
Coverage ratio	Earnings available for payment of bond charges ÷ bond charges	Measures the number of times the company is able to pay off the charges pertaining to the bond issue.
Long-term debt to equity ratio	Long-term debt ÷ total common equity	Measures long-term debt leverage per dollar of common equity. A high ratio could increase the risk of default.
Liquidity (Current) ratio	Current assets ÷ current liabilities	Measures the ability to meet current debts with current assets. The higher the ratio, the lower the probability of default.
Significance of company in industry	Key financial ratios of a given company relative to the industry averages	Indicates the performance of a company relative to other companies within the same industry.
Nature of specific debt issue	If secured, nature of security offered; if unsecured, percentage of unsecured debt to total debt.	The type of debt indicates the commitment a company makes to repay the debt.

investment agencies evaluate the quality of bonds and rank them in categories according to their likelihood of default.

Bond Ratings As a general rule, in rating bonds, the rating agencies take into consideration five major factors. These are (1) the level and trend of fixed charge coverage, (2) the company's long-term debt to equity ratio, (3) the company's liquidity position, (4) the significance of the company in the industry, and (5) the nature (secured versus unsecured, and so on) of the specific debt issue. Table 6–4 summarizes the bond ratings framework.

Two agencies in the United States that rate bonds according to their risks of default are Moody's Investor Service and Standard & Poor's (S&P). The classifications used by the two rating services are presented in Table 6–5. The highest quality bonds are rated AAA while the lowest grade bonds have the rating of C or D. In general, the higher the rating of a bond, the lower is its default risk (and the lower the default risk premium associated with it). For instance, for long-term corporate bonds, the difference between AAA and A can be over 100 basis points (1 percent equals 100 basis points). That is, the default risk premium of an A-rated bond might be more than 1 percentage point, or over 100 basis points higher than a AAA bond.

Three important observations should be made here. First, the difference between an AAA and an A rating—or, for that matter, the difference between an AAA and a B rating—is not a fixed number of basis points, but varies over

Table 6–5 **Investors' Services Rating Classification**

Moody's	General Description	Standard & Poor's
Aaa	Highest Quality	AAA
Aa	High Quality	AA
A	Upper Medium Grade	A
Baa	Medium Grade	BBB
Ba	Lower Medium Grade	BB
B	Speculative	B
Caa	Poor Standing (Perhaps in Default)	CCC–CC
Ca	(Generally) in Default	C for Income Bonds
C	Lowest Grade (in Default)	DDD–D

the business cycle. During a recession, investors become intensely quality conscious and demand a higher yield on lower-rated bonds than they do under favorable economic conditions. Consequently, the spread between AAA- and A-rated long-term corporate bonds can increase to over 1 percent. As economic conditions improve, the spread narrows, eventually reducing to under 50 basis points. Second, bonds with the same rating are not necessarily of exactly the same quality, because ratings of thousands of bonds are compressed into a small number of categories. Third, a bond's rating can change if the financial condition or prospect of the borrowing company changes significantly over time. Consequently, bond ratings should be viewed as reflective of their quality only in general terms.

Default Risk Premium As a general rule, all else being equal, investors prefer default-risk-free bonds to risky bonds, which, in turn, drives up the yield of risky bonds relative to the yield of default-risk-free bonds. At equilibrium, the promised yield to maturity on a default-risk-free bond is lower than the promised yield on a comparable risky bond. The difference between these two yields is called the *default risk premium.* The premium, of course, would vary with the degree of default risk associated with a bond.

Callability Risk

Basic Considerations *Callability risk* refers to the possibility of a bond's being called away before maturity. Call provisions included in a bond's indenture give the issuers the option of prepaying the face value before the maturity date. These provisions specify that a bond is either callable immediately or callable after a deferred period of, say, five years.[12] Typically, if a bond is called, a premium is paid by the issuer to the bondholder; this pre-

[12] Sometimes a bond is "nonrefundable at lower interest cost" during the deferment period. This means that the bond can be called away, but the issuer cannot *reissue* new bonds at a lower interest cost.

mium varies directly with the remaining years to maturity. A common premium for a corporate bond called after five years would be one year's interest.

Although the indenture of a callable bond gives the issuer the option to call the bond, this option is not exercised unless it is in the issuer's self-interest to do so. In general, in a period of falling market interest rates or rising fixed income security prices, higher-coupon securities are likely to be called by the issuer. The reason is obvious: It would be cheaper for the issuer to redeem the high-coupon bonds and sell new bonds at *lower* coupon rates. Conversely, if market interest rates rise, bonds are not likely to be called away, because the issuer *already* will have been paying a low rate of interest vis-a-vis current market rates.

As mentioned, a basic assumption of the call provision is that if interest rates are not expected to drop sufficiently to justify prepaying the face value of the security plus the call penalty and the refinancing costs, the issuer will not be expected to exercise the option to call the security. In that case, investors should value the callable bonds as though they were noncallable, and the yields on these bonds should be calculated by the general bond valuation formula (Equation 6–2). However, if a bond is expected to be called away, its expected holding period yield, i_c, should be calculated[13] by using the following equation:[14]

$$P_0 = \sum_{n=1}^{M} \frac{C}{(1+i_c)^n} + \sum_{n=M+1}^{N} \frac{(i_r)CP}{(1+i_c)^n} + \frac{CP}{(1+i_c)^N} \tag{6-4}$$

where

P_0 = Market price of the bond
C = Annual interest payments
M = Years until bond is called
N = Maturity of the bond
CP = Call price (face value plus the call penalty)
i_r = Interest rate prevailing on the day call option is exercised
i_c = Expected holding period yield on the callable bond

Consider an investor with money to invest for N years. He purchases a bond which will mature in N years and is subject to call. If the bond is called after M years, the investor would reinvest the call price (the face value plus the call penalty), CP, at the prevailing interest rate, i_r, for the period remaining until the original maturity of the bond, $N - M$. The investor's expected holding

[13] The use of this method assumes the reinvestment of the call price and requires forecasting of the future market interest rate.

[14] This approach is developed by Timothy Q. Cook in "Some Factors Affecting Long-term Yield Spreads in Recent Years," Federal Reserve Bank of Richmond, *Monthly Review*, September 1973, p. 9.

period yield, i_c, over the N years equates the price of the bond with the discounted value of the expected future income flows. It is worth emphasizing that because a callable bond is called only when market interest rates drop significantly, the interest rate prevailing on the day the call option is exercised would invariably be lower than the bond's coupon rate.

Callability Risk Premium The nature of the call risk and the call risk premium is demonstrated in Table 6–6. Example 1 shows that the yield to maturity on the DEF bond, which is noncallable, is 10 percent. The GHI bond, analyzed in Example 2, is comparable to the DEF bond in all respects but one: It is callable after five years. Suppose an investor is certain that the GHI bond would be called after five years, and that the market interest rate for the remaining 15 years would be 8 percent. The GHI bond would have a present value of only $958 if the investor required the expected holding period yield, i_c, to equal the 10 percent yield to maturity on the noncallable bond. The right-hand column of Table 6–6 also reveals that if the investor pays $958 for the GHI

Table 6–6 **Callability Risk Premium**

Example 1 **DEF Bond, Noncallable**	*Example 2* **GHI Bond, Callable**	
Par Value (P_N) = $1,000 Coupon Rate ($C$) = 10% = $100 Years to Maturity ($N$) = 20 Current Price ($P_0$) = $1,000	Par Value (P_N) = $1,000 Coupon Rate ($C$) = 10% = $100 Years to Maturity ($N$) = 20	*Call Provision* Callable after 5 years Call Price (CP) = $1,100 (Par value plus one year's coupon) Interest rate expected after 5 years (i_r) = 8%
Find yield to maturity:	Find PV assuming bond is called after 5 years and using an expected holding period yield (i_c) of 10%:	Find yield to maturity using P_0 of $958 and assuming bond is not called:
$P_0 = \sum_{n=1}^{N} \frac{C}{(1+i)^n} + \frac{P_N}{(1+i)^N}$	$PV = \sum_{n=1}^{M} \frac{C}{(1+i_c)^n} + \sum_{n=M+1}^{N} \frac{(i_r)(CP)}{(1+i_c)^n} + \frac{CP}{(1+i_c)^N}$	$P_0 = \sum_{n=1}^{N} \frac{C}{(1+i)^n} + \frac{P_N}{(1+i)^N}$
$\$1{,}000 = \sum_{n=1}^{20} \frac{\$100}{(1+i)^n} + \frac{\$1{,}000}{(1+i)^{20}}$	$PV = \sum_{n=1}^{5} \frac{\$100}{(1+.10)^n} + \sum_{n=6}^{20} \frac{(.08)(\$1{,}100)}{(1+.10)^n} + \frac{\$1{,}100}{(1+.10)^{20}}$	$\$958 = \sum_{n=1}^{20} \frac{\$100}{(1+i)^n} + \frac{\$1{,}000}{(1+i)^{20}}$
Solve for i:	PV = $958	Solve for i:
Yield to maturity on noncallable bond: i = 10%		Yield to maturity if not called: i = 10.50%

bond and it is not called, its yield to maturity would be 10.50 percent—0.5 percent higher than the noncallable DEF bond. In this case, the investor would receive a callability risk premium of 0.5 percent for assuming the callability risk inherent in the GHI bond.

Liquidity Risk

Basic Considerations

The marketability of a fixed income security partly depends on the search and information costs an investor must incur in order to sell it at an acceptable price, and partly on the price concession an investor must grant in order to quickly convert the security into cash. Marketability is made up of two elements—the volume of securities which can be bought or sold at one time without significantly affecting its price, and the amount of time needed to finalize a trade. The less liquid or marketable a security, the higher its *liquidity risk*.

There is considerable evidence to support the view that liquidity risk exists in the bond market in general, and in the privately placed bond market in particular. Private placements are long-term issues sold directly to a small number of institutional investors, usually as investments to be held until maturity. Consequently, secondary market sales of private placements do not occur frequently because there is no established trading market for them. Because of a lack of marketability, private placements frequently carry liquidity risk premiums higher than similar publicly traded securities.

Liquidity Risk Premium

Like the maturity risk, liquidity risk depends on an investor's personal need for marketability as well as the search cost. Consequently, this type of risk does not lend itself to a direct measurement. However, an approximate measure of the *liquidity risk premium* is the spread between the bid and the offered prices that dealers quote when they make a market in a bond. As a general rule, the dealer's spread in a $500,000 to $1 million transaction for a highly marketable corporate bond is typically about $\frac{1}{8}$ point. Spreads for less marketable issues range from about $\frac{1}{4}$ point to $\frac{1}{2}$ point.

This statement concerning bid spread should be duly qualified. The bid-offered spread is influenced by three key factors. The first factor relates to the size of the purchase. Investors purchasing fewer bonds face a larger spread than those who trade in larger quantities. The second factor has to do with the prevailing interest rate outlook. Higher interest rate forecasts encourage bond dealers to widen the spread as a partial hedge against the interest rate risk. Finally, the spread is related to the quality of a bond. Generally, bonds with low ratings are considered less marketable; therefore, their bid-offered spread is wider than that for higher quality bonds. Because of these considerations, the spread for any given bond, or between two comparable bonds, can vary—sometimes widely—between different transactions. Consequently, liquidity risk premium can be estimated only in broad terms. For instance, depending on the circumstances, the same AAA bond might have a spread ranging anywhere between $\frac{1}{4}$ to $1\frac{1}{2}$ points.

A Recapitulation

The investor's required rate of return, or the appropriate discount rate, r, is the sum of two major components: the risk-free real rate and the risk premium. The long-run, risk-free real rate has averaged approximately 3 percent.

The risk premium component represents the premiums associated with six types of risk. Of these, the interest rate, inflation, and maturity risks are broader in scope and affect all bonds in general. In contrast, the default, callability, and liquidity risks are directly related to each bond under consideration. These risks lend themselves to some type of measurement, although the degrees of precision vary greatly between them.

Three caveats should be added here. First, the level of required rates of return for different types of investments changes over time. For instance, the yield on S&P AAA corporate bonds (approximately 3 percent in the 1940s) increased to over 10 percent early in 1980. Second, required rates of return vary significantly for different types of investment. For instance, on December 29, 1979, the yields on alternative investments were as follows: three-month treasury bills, 11.99 percent; five-year treasury bonds, 10.51 percent; Moody's Aaa state and local bonds, 6.50 percent; Baa-rated corporate bonds, 12.22 percent. Third, required rates of return can also vary due to the risk preferences of individual investors.

The Complete Decision Model

The Key Variables

Now that the mechanics for determining the yield to maturity and the appropriate discount rate have been presented, the Basic Decision Model for bond investment may be reproduced:

If	Then	Reason
$r = i$	Be indifferent.	The bond is appropriately valued.
$r < i$	Buy the bond.	The bond is undervalued.
$r > i$	Do not buy the bond.	The bond is overvalued.

r = The appropriate discount rate, or the investor's minimum required rate of return

i = The bond's yield to maturity

If a bond's yield is equal to or more than the minimum return required by the investor ($i \geq r$), clearly it is a good investment. If not ($i < r$), it is overvalued and should be discarded.

An Alternative Approach

Earlier in this chapter, the decision model was constructed around two key variables: the bond's yield to maturity, i, and the appropriate discount rate, r. An alternative approach to bond selection is often preferred by bond investors.

The key variables in the alternative approach are the present value (using the appropriate discount rate) and the current market price of the bond. Suppose an investor has determined that 8 percent is the appropriate rate for discounting the XYZ bond with a coupon of 5 percent and a maturity of three years. This rate represents the risk-free rate plus the total risk premium demanded by the investor for holding this bond. Using this discount rate, the present value of the bond can be calculated:

$$PV = \sum_{n=1}^{3} \frac{\$50}{(1 + .08)^n} + \frac{\$1{,}000}{(1 + .08)^3}$$

At $r = 8\%$, for three years, the PVAF = 2.577 and the PVFF = .794. Therefore,

$$\begin{aligned} PV &= (2.577 \times \$50) + (.794 \times \$1{,}000) \\ &= \$923 \end{aligned}$$

Once the present value of the bond has been calculated, it can be directly compared with the current market price of the bond to complete the selection process. If the market price is higher than the present value, the bond is overvalued and should not be purchased.

The alternative approach to bond selection, which incidentally is equivalent to the method represented by the Basic Decision Model, can be presented in the following form:

If	Then	Reason
$PV = P_0$	Be indifferent.	The bond is appropriately valued.
$PV > P_0$	Buy the bond.	The bond is undervalued.
$PV < P_0$	Do not buy the bond.	The bond is overvalued.

PV = Present value of the bond, determined by using the appropriate discount rate

P_0 = Market price of the bond

The Market Efficiency Issue

In the decision model just presented, the divergence between the bond's yield to maturity and the appropriate discount rate is accepted as a distinct possibility. However, in Chapter 5, in connection with a discussion of the Efficient

Market Hypothesis, it was asserted that the underlying assumption of an efficient market is that the current market price of a security always reflects its present value. Therefore, it follows that, in an efficient market, the appropriate discount rate—which is used to calculate the present value—and the yield to maturity—which is based upon the current market price—must necessarily be identical. How, then, can these two positions be reconciled?

Two plausible explanations can be advanced to support the view that the appropriate discount rate may *not* be identical with the yield to maturity. First, the efficiency of the market cannot always be taken for granted. The process of adjusting a bond's price to all the variables acting on it is complicated, and during this adjustment process the market price may not reflect a bond's present value. Second, the appropriate discount rate of an individual investor interested in a bond may not be the same as the discount rate with which the market discounts that bond. Among the many reasons causing a divergence between the individual and the market discount rates are differences in risk and liquidity preferences of individual investors.

Key Interest Rate–Bond Principles

The necessary and sufficient conditions for a successful operation of the Basic Decision Model are the determination of the appropriate discount rate and the bond's yield to maturity. However, other bond selection strategies can be developed through a more detailed analysis of the relationship between market interest rates and bond price fluctuations. For convenience, we will first present the key interest rate principles.[15]

Principle 1

For a given change in market interest rates, the longer the time remaining to maturity of the bond, the greater will be the price fluctuation from the par value. This is demonstrated in Table 6–7. For instance, if the market interest rate were to increase from 8 to 10 percent, the price of an 8 percent bond with a ten-year maturity would decline from $1,000 to $878, whereas the price of a comparable bond with a 20-year maturity would decline from $1,000 to $830.

According to this principle, the strategy should be to purchase a bond with a long maturity if the market interest rate is expected to decline, and thereby realize the maximum price appreciation resulting from this interest rate decline. However, a bond with a short maturity would be more desirable if the probability of an interest rate rise increases.

[15] Most of these principles are formally derived as bond theorems by B. G. Malkiel, "Expectations, Bond Prices, and the Term Structure of Interest Rates," *Quarterly Journal of Economics*, May 1962, pp. 197–218.

Each of the five interest rate principles presented here can be explained in terms of the basic Bond Valuation Model presented in this chapter.

Table 6–7 **Bond Price Fluctuations from Par Value for Various Maturities**

Par Value = \$1,000
Coupon Rate = 8% = \$80

$$P_0 = \sum_{n=1}^{N} \frac{\$80}{(1+i)^n} + \frac{\$1,000}{(1+i)^N}$$

Years to Maturity N	BOND PRICES (P_0)* $i = 8\%$	Market Interest Rate Rises: $i = 10\%$	Total Price Change
1	\$1,000	\$982	–\$ 18
3	1,000	950	– 50
5	1,000	924	– 76
10	1,000	878	– 122
20	1,000	830	– 170

* Rounded to the nearest dollar

Principle 2

According to the basic interest rate–bond price relationship, an increase in the market interest rate results in a decline in the price of a bond. Additional declines in bond prices, however, diminish progressively as the maturity increases. This principle is demonstrated in Table 6–8. If the market interest rate were to increase from 8 to 10 percent, the price of an 8 percent bond maturing in ten years would decline from \$1,000 to \$878, a decline of \$122. For a similar bond maturing in 15 years, the additional decline in price would be \$31, and the prices of bonds maturing in 20 and 25 years would drop by only an additional \$17 and \$12, respectively. The corollary of this principle is also true:

Table 6–8 **Bond Price Changes for Incremental Years to Maturity**

Par Value = \$1,000
Coupon Rate = 8% = \$80

$$P_0 = \sum_{n=1}^{N} \frac{\$80}{(1+i)^n} + \frac{\$1,000}{(1+i)^N}$$

Years to Maturity N	BOND PRICES (P_0)* $i = 8\%$	Market Interest Rate Rises: $i = 10\%$	Total Price Change	Additional Price Decline for Additional Maturity
1	\$1,000	\$982	–\$ 18	
				\$58
5	1,000	924	– 76	
				46
10	1,000	878	– 122	
				31
15	1,000	847	– 153	
				17
20	1,000	830	– 170	
				12
25	1,000	818	– 182	
				7
30	1,000	811	– 189	

* Rounded to the nearest dollar

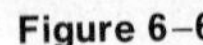

Figure 6–6

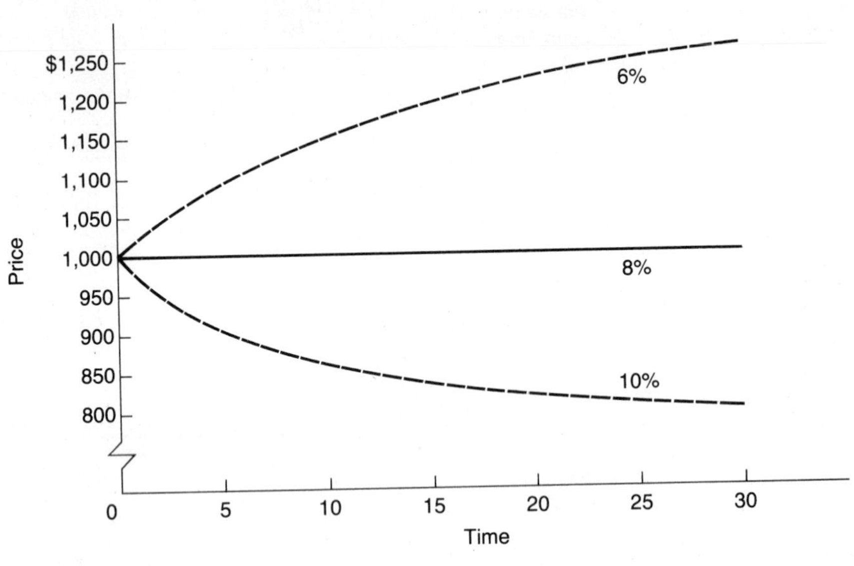

In the event of a decline in the market interest rate, the price of a bond tends to increase; however, prices increase at a diminishing rate as the maturity increases. These relationships are graphed in Figure 6–6 in the form of isoyield curves.

According to Principle 2, in the event of an increase in the market interest rate, one possible strategy might be to hold on to the bond as long as possible so as to minimize the loss. If on the other hand the market interest rate falls, the bondholder might consider unloading the bond quickly because most of the price increase would occur within a short time.

Principle 3

For any given change in the market interest rate, the lower the coupon rate on a bond, the greater will be the fluctuation in its price as a result of a change in the rate. This relationship is shown in Table 6–9. For a 6 percent bond, an increase in the market interest rate from 8 to 10 percent results in a decline in the price of 17.9 percent. For a similar bond with a coupon rate of 10 percent, the decline is only 16.5 percent. Similarly, if the market interest rate drops from 8 to 6 percent, the increase in the price of a 6 percent bond is 24.4 percent, whereas a 10 percent bond registers a price appreciation of only 21.9 percent.

Based on Principle 3, the strategy should be to buy the bond with the highest coupon rate if there is some possibility that the market interest rate might rise. Likewise, a bond with the lowest coupon rate should be purchased if the market interest rate can be expected to decline.

Table 6–9 **Bond Price Fluctuations for Various Coupon Rates**

Par Value = $1,000
Maturity = 20 years

$$P_0 = \sum_{n=1}^{20} \frac{C}{(1+i)^n} + \frac{\$1{,}000}{(1+i)^{20}}$$

BOND PRICES (P_0)*

Coupon Rate C	$i = 8\%$	Market Interest Rate Rises: $i = 10\%$	Percentage Change	Market Interest Rate Declines: $i = 6\%$	Percentage Change
6% = $60	$ 804	$ 660	−17.9%	$1,000	24.4%
7% = $70	902	745	−17.4	1,115	23.6
8% = $80	1,000	830	−17.0	1,230	23.0
9% = $90	1,099	915	−16.7	1,344	22.3
10% = $100	1,197	1,000	−16.5	1,459	21.9

* Rounded to the nearest dollar

Principle 4

The higher the level of the market interest rate from which a certain rate change occurs, the greater is the change in the price of a bond, as revealed by Table 6–10. For instance, an increase in the market interest rate from 4 to 4.8 percent—a rise of 20 percent—leads to a decline in the bond price of 8.9 percent. However, an increase in the market interest rate from 10 to 12 percent—the same 20 percent increase—results in a decline of 15.4 percent in the price of the bond.

According to Principle 4, an investor's strategy should be to invest in a bond when the market interest rate is expected to decline from a high level, because such a decline would result in a sizable appreciation in the bond's price.

Table 6–10 **Bond Price Changes from Various Market Interest Rate Levels**

Par Value = $1,000
Coupon Rate = 8% = $80
Maturity = 20 years

$$P_0 = \sum_{n=1}^{20} \frac{\$80}{(1+i)^n} + \frac{\$1{,}000}{(1+i)^{20}}$$

Bond Price		*Example 1* Falling Securities Prices			*Example 2* Rising Securities Prices		
$i =$	P_0	20% Increase in i $i =$	P_0	Percentage Change in P_0	20% Decline in i $i =$	P_0	Percentage Change in P_0
4%	$1,543	4.8%	$1,406	−8.9%	3.2%	$1,701	10.2%
6%	1,230	7.2	1,083	−11.9	4.8	1,406	14.3
8%	1,000	9.6	860	−14.0	6.4	1,178	17.8
10%	830	12.0	702	−15.4	8.0	1,000	20.5

Table 6–11 **Bond Price Fluctuations**

Par Value = $1,000
Coupon Rate = 8% = $80

$$P_0 = \sum_{n=1}^{N} \frac{\$80}{(1+i)^n} + \frac{\$1{,}000}{(1+i)^N}$$

Years to Maturity N	BOND PRICES (P_0)* $i = 8\%$	Market Interest Rate Rises: $i = 10\%$	Percentage Change	Market Interest Rate Declines: $i = 6\%$	Percentage Change
1	$1,000	$982	−1.8%	$1,018	1.8%
3	1,000	950	−5.0	1,054	5.4
5	1,000	924	−7.6	1,084	8.4
10	1,000	878	−12.2	1,147	14.7
20	1,000	830	−17.0	1,230	23.0

* Rounded to the nearest dollar

Principle 5

For any given maturity, a decline in the market interest rate leads to an increase in the bond's price, whereas the reverse is true when the market interest rate rises. However, the increase in the bond's price due to a given interest rate decline is always larger than the price decline resulting from an equal increase in the market interest rate. Table 6–11 demonstrates this principle. In the case of a 8 percent bond with a 20-year maturity, a rise in the market interest rate from 8 to 10 percent—a 25 percent increase—results in a decline in the price from $1,000 to $830—a decline of only 17.0 percent. A decline in the market interest rate from 8 to 6 percent—the same 25 percent decline—however, increases the price of the bond from $1,000 to $1,230—an increase of 23.0 percent.

Principle 5 does not help in the development of a new bond investment strategy. However, it underscores the idea that the potential for profit on bond investments is greater than the potential for loss, provided the same possibility exists for equal increases and decreases in the market interest rate.

Tax Considerations

The after-tax yield to maturity of a security for a particular investor is the yield, i_t, which equates the price of the security to the discounted (present) value of the future after-tax promised return:[16]

$$P_0 = \left[\sum_{n=1}^{N} \frac{C(1-t_n)}{(1+i_t)^n}\right] + \left[\frac{P_N - (P_N - P_0)cg}{(1+i_t)^N}\right] \tag{6–5}$$

[16] Adapted from Timothy Q. Cook, "Some Factors Affecting Long-term Yield Spreads," p. 5.

where

P_0 = Market price of the bond
C = Annual interest payments
t_n = Marginal income tax bracket of the investor
P_N = Par value of the bond
cg = Tax rate on long-term capital gains
N = Maturity of the bond
i_t = After-tax yield to maturity

Note that the interest income, C, is taxed at the relevant marginal personal income tax rate, while the capital gains $(P_N - P_0)$ are taxed at the capital gains tax rate.[17]

According to Equation 6–5, by specifying the marginal income tax rate, the capital gains tax rate, the maturity date, and a coupon value, it is possible to determine, for any security, the after-tax yield. Table 6–12 demonstrates the use of this equation. In Example 1, assuming no income tax or capital gains tax, under the conditions specified, the yield, i_t, would be 9.62 percent. In Example 2, an imposition of taxes at given rates would result in an after-tax yield, i_t, of 7.14 percent. If these taxes are raised, as is the case in Example 3, the after-tax yield would drop to 4.66 percent.

The Timing Issue

The Basic Decision Model for bond investment helps investors select the bonds that meet their risk–return criteria. However, the model does not identify the *right time* for investing in these bonds.

As a general rule, the best time to buy bonds is when the market interest rates have peaked, because, all else being equal, a decline in the market interest rate tends to increase the value of a bond. At other times, when the interest rates are expected to rise, investment in bonds may still be undertaken successfully if the extent of the rise can be predicted so the appropriate interest rate risk premium can be obtained. Consequently, the success of investors in pinpointing the right time to buy bonds is directly related to their abilities to predict future interest levels and the structure of market interest rates. Unfortunately, this type of prediction is beyond the scope of this book. A very brief review of the monetary and fiscal policies that influence future interest rates must suffice.

Left alone, the market forces tend to set interest rates where they reflect individual propensities to consume and to invest. But in the real world market interest rates *are* affected by governmental attempts to alter the market-determined rate structure.

[17] Issues relating to marginal tax and capital gains tax are discussed more fully in Chapter 16.

Table 6–12 **Tax Effect on Bond Yields**

Market Price of Bond (P_o) = \$900
Years to Maturity (N) = 5
Annual Interest Payments(C) = 7% = \$70
Par Value (P_N) = \$1,000

$$P_0 = \left[\sum_{n=1}^{N} \frac{C(1-t_n)}{(1+i_t)^n}\right] + \left[\frac{P_N - (P_N - P_0)cg}{(1+i_t)^N}\right]$$

Example 1
No Tax

Marginal Tax Rate (t_n) = 0*
Capital Gains Tax Rate (cg) = 0

$$\$900 = \left[\sum_{n=1}^{5} \frac{(\$70)(1-0)}{(1+i_t)^n}\right] + \left[\frac{\$1{,}000}{(1+i_t)^5} - \frac{(\$1{,}000 - \$900)(0)}{(1+i_t)^5}\right]$$

$$= \sum_{n=1}^{5} \frac{\$70}{(1+i_t)^n} + \frac{\$1{,}000}{(1+i_t)^5}$$

Solve for i_t ⓐ

$i_t = 9.62\%$

ⓐ At $i_t = 9\%$

$P_o = (3.890)(\$70) + (.650)(\$1{,}000)$
$= \$922$

At $i_t = 10\%$

$P_o = (3.791)(\$70) + (.621)(\$1{,}000)$
$= \$886$

Interpolating, at $i_t = 9.62\%$†

$P_0 = \$900$

Example 2
Lower Tax Rate

Marginal Tax Rate (t_n) = 30%*
Capital Gains Tax Rate (cg) = 12%

$$\$900 = \left[\sum_{n=1}^{5} \frac{(\$70)(1-.30)}{(1+i_t)^n}\right] + \left[\frac{\$1{,}000}{(1+i_t)^5} - \frac{(\$1{,}000 - \$900)(.12)}{(1+i_t)^5}\right]$$

$$= \sum_{n=1}^{5} \frac{\$49}{(1+i_t)^n} + \frac{\$988}{(1+i_t)^5}$$

Solve for i_t ⓑ

$i_t = 7.14\%$

ⓑ At $i_t = 8\%$

$P_o = (3.993)(\$49) + (.681)(\$988)$
$= \$868$

At $i_t = 7\%$

$P_o = (4.100)(\$49) + (.713)(\$988)$
$= \$905$

Interpolating, at $i_t = 7.14\%$†

$P_0 = \$900$

Example 3
Higher Tax Rate

Marginal Tax Rate (t_n) = 60%*
Capital Gains Tax Rate (cg) = 24%

$$\$900 = \left[\sum_{n=1}^{5} \frac{(\$70)(1-.60)}{(1+i_t)^n}\right] + \left[\frac{\$1{,}000}{(1+i_t)^5} - \frac{(\$1{,}000 - \$900)(.24)}{(1+i_t)^5}\right]$$

$$= \sum_{n=1}^{5} \frac{\$28}{(1+i_t)^n} + \frac{\$976}{(1+i_t)^5}$$

Solve for i_t ⓒ

$i_t = 4.66\%$

ⓒ At $i_t = 5\%$

$P_o = (4.329)(\$28) + (.784)(\$976)$
$= \$886$

At $i_t = 4\%$

$P_o = (4.452)(\$28) + (.822)(\$976)$
$= \$927$

Interpolating, at $i_t = 4.66\%$†

$P_0 = \$900$

* Assume the marginal tax rate remains at the current level through year N.
† The interpolation method is discussed in footnote 4.

The most important institution of the government affecting market interest rates is the Federal Reserve System. Its primary objective is to promote maximum economic growth over the long run, while preserving the domestic purchasing power of the dollar and maintaining its value internationally. In carrying out its policy directives to this objective, the Federal Reserve uses three instruments in a complementary fashion to affect the cost, supply, and availability of credit to commercial banks. These three instruments are rediscount rate,[18] open market operations, and change in reserve requirements.

The mechanism for the transmission of the Federal Reserve's policy actions to the commercial banks in general, and money market conditions in particular, is highly complicated. In simple terms, by affecting the ability of the commercial banking system to advance credit to borrowers, the Federal Reserve System can achieve its aim of accelerating or decelerating the spending and investment in the economy. The immediate impact of a restrictive credit policy by the Federal Reserve is reflected in an upward adjustment in the nominal short-term money market rates. Subsequently, changes in the short-term rates are gradually transmitted to the long-term sectors as investors adjust the maturities of their portfolios. It can be concluded that the monetary policy of the Federal Reserve, along with market forces, determine the level and structure of market interest rates at any given point in time.

The Federal Reserve, however, is not the only agency which influences interest rates. Because of its size and financial needs, the U.S. government also influences the level and structure of interest rates. Part of this influence is simply the result of government's financing of programs that are undertaken throughout the year as a matter of course. Vast sums of money are involved when, for instance, the Treasury enters the market to borrow or engage in refinancing operations. In such instances, the market rates are influenced even if there is no effort on the part of the government to do so. In addition, the government formulates expansionary or contractionary policies, known as fiscal policies, in order to influence the economy. A contractionary fiscal policy generally tends to lower market interest rates, whereas an expansionary policy has the opposite effect on them.

Summary

A bond is evidence of an indebtedness entered into by the issuer and is used as a vehicle for borrowing money. The *present value* of a bond is the sum of the future interest payments plus the maturity price, discounted by a rate that is appropriate for that bond.

The *appropriate discount rate*, or the investor's minimum required rate of return, is the sum of the *risk-free real rate of return* and a *risk premium*. The

[18] The rediscount rate refers to the interest rate charged member banks on loans granted by the Federal Reserve.

risk-free real rate of return is determined by the *time preference of consumption* and the investment opportunities existing in the economy. The long-term risk-free real rate is approximately 3 percent per annum.

The risk premium component of the appropriate discount rate is associated with six types of bond risks; namely, *interest rate, inflation, maturity, default, callability,* and *liquidity* risks. Of these, the first three are associated with all bonds in general; the last three risks are specific in nature and relate to each bond. Techniques are available for estimating risk premiums associated with different types of risk.

The *Basic Decision Model* consists of two key variables: the appropriate discount rate and the bond's yield to maturity. As long as a bond is yielding more than or equal to an investor's appropriate discount rate, it offers an attractive investment opportunity. Alternatively, the present value of a bond, calculated by using the appropriate discount rate, can be compared with the current market price of a bond. If the present value of a bond is higher than or equal to its market price, then the bond should be judged an attractive investment.

Key interest rate–bond principles and taxes are important considerations when investing in fixed income securities. Also, the success of a buy or sell decision depends heavily on carrying out that decision at the most opportune time.

A Look Ahead

In this chapter, a Bond Valuation Model has been constructed which can be used for investing in bonds. Of necessity, this model must be suitably modified to make it applicable to different types of bonds.

In Chapter 7, we will demonstrate the use of the Bond Valuation Model for the valuation of government and municipal bonds which are considered relatively safe. In Chapter 8, we will discuss the valuation of corporate bonds and preferred stock.

Concepts for Review

Bond Valuation Model
Present value
Appropriate discount rate
Basic Decision Model
Bond yield
Holding period
Bond yield table
Risk-free real rate of return
Nominal interest rate
Inflation risk premium
Maturity risk premium
Default risk premium
Bond ratings
Market risk premium
Callability risk premium
Liquidity risk premium

Risk premium
Time preference of consumption
Risk-free real rate of interest
Equilibrium interest rate
Interest rate risk premium
Interest rate principles
Opportunity cost of loaning funds
Tax considerations

Questions for Review

1. Identify the four variables that determine the present value of a bond. Explain how each variable relates to the present value.
2. Explain the relationship between the present value and market price of a bond. When are they equal?
3. What is the difference between a bond's yield and the appropriate discount rate with which the future income stream is discounted?
4. Comment on the following statement: "Every investor must carefully examine the ratings of a bond before investing in it."
5. What comprises the appropriate discount rate for a given bond?
6. Market interest rates and bond prices are inversely related. Explain why.
7. Investor Q purchases bonds that mature in 20 years. Because he intends to hold them until maturity, he claims he is not exposed to interest rate risk. He notes that, even if market interest rates rise and the price of the bonds fall, he will still collect the par value on the maturity date. Is Investor Q's argument valid? Explain.
8. Can the default risk premium demanded by investors for bonds vary over time?
9. Investor X demands a 12 percent return from JKL bond. Investor Y demands a 14 percent return from the same bond. Is this possible? Give reasons for your answer.
10. Investor Q foresees a significant decline in market interest rates and decides to invest in low-coupon, long-term bonds. Comment on this investment strategy.
11. Explain the following statement: "The risk-free real rate of interest is a function of time preference of consumption and the long-run productivity of investment."
12. What is meant by yield to maturity?
13. Explain the difference between the nominal and real interest rate.
14. ABC bond is rated AA by Standard & Poor's; DEF bond is rated A by the same agency. Investor Q states that ABC bond is less risky. What is your response?
15. How do call features affect bond yields?

Problems

1. XYZ Corporation bonds are selling for $930 in 1980. They mature in 1990 and have a 10 percent coupon rate. If your appropriate discount rate for these bonds is 12 percent, would you consider them to be an attractive investment?

2. ABC bonds have a coupon rate of 9 percent, mature in 20 years, and are selling at par ($1,000).
   a. Find the yield to maturity.
   b. Find the yield to maturity, assuming the bonds are selling for $800 instead of at par.
   c. Find the market price of the bonds, assuming the market interest rate on similar bonds drops to 8 percent.
   d. Find the market price of the bonds, assuming the market interest rate on similar bonds drops to 8 percent and there are only 15 years remaining until maturity.
3. On January 1, 1980, a bond with a 9 percent coupon which matures on December 31, 1980 sold for par to yield 9 percent. A relevant price index was 100.0 on January 1, 1980, and 108.7 on December 31, 1980. Assuming the interest was paid at the end of the year, what are the nominal and real interest yields? What is the effect of inflation on the principal received at year-end?
4. An investor in the 35 percent tax bracket wishes to purchase a 10 percent coupon bond to mature in ten years and selling for $900. What is the after-tax yield to maturity? Assume a long-term capital gains tax rate of 14 percent.
5. ABC bond has a 10 percent coupon, matures in 20 years, and has a yield to maturity of 9 percent. XYZ bond is similar to ABC bond in all respects except that it carries a 7 percent coupon.
   a. Find the market price of each bond.
   b. Compute the percentage change in the market price of each bond, assuming the market interest rate on these securities declines 1 percent.
   c. Compute the same as in (b) above, but assume a 1 percent *increase* in the market interest rate.

Footnote

4. The value of i can be interpolated in the following manner:

$$\frac{8-i}{8-7} = \frac{\$922.85 - \$926.00}{\$922.85 - \$947.20}$$

$$-194.8 + 24.35i = -3.15$$

$$24.35i = 191.65$$

$$i = 7.87$$

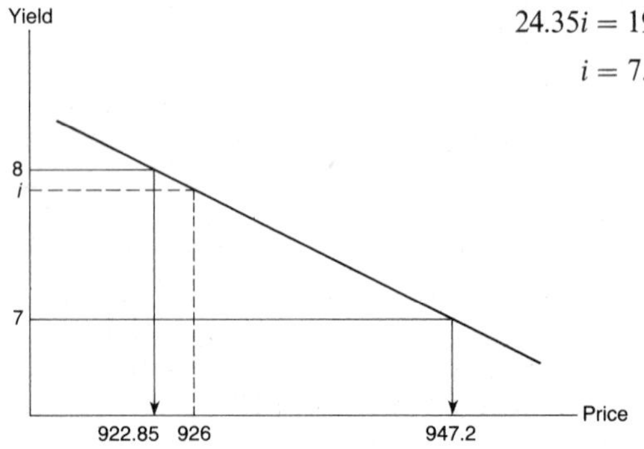

Yield

8

i

7

922.85 926

947.2

Price

Selected Readings

Ahearn, Daniel S. "The Strategic Role of Fixed Income Securities." *Journal of Portfolio Management*, Spring 1975.

Ang, James S. and K. A. Patel. "Bond Rating Methods: Comparison and Validation." *Journal of Finance*, May 1975.

Axilrod, Stephen A. and Ralph A. Young. "Interest Rates and Monetary Policy." *Federal Reserve Bulletin*, September 1962.

Baskin, Elba F. and Gary M. Crooch. "Historical Rates of Return on Investments in Flat Bonds." *Financial Analysts Journal*, November–December 1968.

Bierman, Harold and Jerome Hass. "An Analytical Model of Bond Risk Differentials." *Journal of Financial and Quantitative Analysis*, December 1975.

Bowlin, Oswald D. and John D. Martin. "Extrapolations of Yields Over the Short Run; Forecast or Folly?" *Journal of Monetary Economics*, 1975.

Brimmer, Andrew F. "Credit Conditions and Price Determination in the Corporate Bond Market." *Journal of Finance*, September 1960.

Bullington, Robert A. "How Corporate Debt Issues are Rated." *Financial Executive*, September 1974.

Carter, Andrew M. "Value Judgements in Bond Management." *Bond Analysis and Selection*, Financial Analysts Research Foundation, 1977.

"Classes of Long-term Securities, 1950–1966." *Journal of Finance*, June 1969.

Cohen, Kalman J., Robert L. Kramer, and W. Howard Waugh. "Regression Yield Curves for U.S. Government Securities." *Management Science*, December 1966.

Conard, Joseph W. and Mark W. Frankena. "The Yield Spread Between New and Seasoned Corporate Bonds." *Essays on Interest Rates*, Vol. 1, 1969.

Cook, Timothy Q. "Some Factors Affecting Long-term Yield Spreads in Recent Years." Federal Reserve Bank of Richmond, *Monthly Review*, September 1973.

Culbertson, J. A. "The Term Structure of Interest Rates." *Quarterly Journal of Economics*, November 1957. Also, Michaelson. "Comment." QJE, February 1963. And J. A. Culbertson. "Reply." QJE, November 1963.

Ederington, Louis H. "The Yield Spread on New Issues of Corporate Bonds." *Journal of Finance*, December 1974.

Fama, Eugene F. "Inflation Uncertainty and Expected Returns on Treasury Bills." *Journal of Political Economy*, June 1976.

Fama, Eugene F. "Short-term Interest Rates as Predictors of Inflation." *American Economic Review*, June 1975.

Fisher, Lawrence. "Determinants of Risk Premiums on Corporate Bonds." *Journal of Political Economy*, June 1959.

Fisher, Lawrence and Romand L. Weil. "Coping with the Risk of Interest-Rate Fluctuations: Returns to Bondholders from Naive and Optimal Strategies." *Journal of Business*, October 1971.

Gibson, W. E. "Interest Rates and Inflationary Expectations; New Evidence." *American Economic Review*, December 1972.

Grier, P. and S. Katz. "The Differential Effects of Bond Rating Changes Among Industrial and Public Utility Bonds by Maturity." *Journal of Business*, April 1976.

Hickman, W. B. *Corporate Bond Quality and Investor Experience.* Princeton: Princeton University Press, 1958.

Hopewell, M. H. and G. G. Kaufman. "Bond Price Volatility and Term to Maturity: A Generalized Respecification." *American Economic Review*, September 1973.

Homer, Sidney. "Distortions Within Bond and Money Markets." *Financial Analysts Journal*, July–August 1968.

Homer, Sidney. "The Historical Evolution of Today's Bond Market." *Journal of Portfolio Management*, Spring 1975.

Jen, Frank C. and James E. West. "The Deferred Call Provision and Corporate Bond Yields." *Journal of Financial and Quantitative Analysis*, June 1968.

Jen, Frank C. and James E. West. "The Effect of Call Risk on Corporate Bond Yields." *Journal of Finance*, December 1967.

Joehnk, Michael D. and James F. Nielsen. "Return and Risk Characteristics of Speculative Grade Bonds." *Quarterly Review of Economics and Business*, Spring 1975.

Johannesen, Richard I., Jr. "The Effect of Coupon on Bond Price Fluctuations." *Financial Analysts Journal*, September–October 1968.

Johnson, Ramon E. "Term Structure of Corporate Bond Yields as a Function of Risk of Default." *Journal of Finance*, May 1967.

Kaplan, Mortimer. "Yields on Recently Issued Corporate Bonds: A New Index." *Journal of Finance*, March 1962.

Katz, Steven. "The Price Adjustment Process of Bonds to Rating Reclassifications: A Test of Bond Market Efficiency." *Journal of Finance*, May 1974.

Leibowitz, Martin L. "How Swaps Can Pay Off." *Institutional Investor*, August 1973.

Lindvall, John R. "New Issue Corporate Bonds, Seasoned Market Efficiency and Yield Spreads." *Journal of Finance*, September 1977.

Malkiel, Burton G. "Expectations, Bond Prices, and the Term Structure of Interest Rates." *Quarterly Journal of Economics*, May 1962.

Malkiel, Burton G. *The Term Structure of Interest Rates: Theory, Empirical Evidence, and Applications.* New York: McCaleb-Seiler, 1970.

Meiselman, D. *The Term Structure of Interest Rates.* Englewood Cliffs, N.J.: Prentice-Hall, 1962.

Modigliani, F. J. and R. J. Shiller. "Inflation, Rational Expectations and the Term Structure of Interest Rates." *Economica*, 1973.

Modigliani, F. J. and R. C. Sutch. "Innovation in Interest Rate Policy." *American Economic Review*, Papers and Proceedings, 1966.

Percival, John. "Corporate Bonds in a Market Model Context." *Journal of Business Research*, October 1974.

Pinches, George and J. C. Singleton. "The Adjustment of Stock Prices to Bond Rating Changes." *Journal of Finance*, March 1978.

Pogue, Thomas F. and Robert M. Soldofsky. "What's in a Bond Rating." *Journal of Financial and Quantitative Analysis*, June 1969.

Pye, G. "The Value of Call Deferment on a Bond: Some Empirical Results." *Journal of Finance*, December 1967.

Rea, John D. "The Yield Spread Between Newly Issued and Seasoned Corporate Bonds." Federal Reserve Bank of Kansas City, *Monthly Review*, June 1974.

Reilly, Frank K. and Michael D. Joehnk. "The Association Between Market-Determined Risk Measures for Bonds and Bond Ratings." *Journal of Finance*, December 1976.

Roll, Richard. "Investment Diversification and Bond Maturity." *Journal of Finance*, March 1971.

Ross, Irwin. "Higher Stakes in the Bond-Rating Game." *Fortune*, April 1976.

Shakin, Bernard. "Swinging in Bonds." *Barron's*, October 11, 1976.

Sharpe, William F. "Bonds Versus Stocks: Some Lessons from Capital Market Theory." *Financial Analysts Journal*, November–December 1973.

Walker, C. "Federal Reserve Policy and the Structure of Interest Rates on Government Securities." *Quarterly Journal of Economics*, February 1954.

Weil, Roman. "Realized Interest Rates and Bondholder's Returns." *American Economic Review*, June 1970.

White, Shelby. "Unwelcome Call: It's On the Way to Holders of High-Coupon Bonds." *Barron's*, October 4, 1976.

Williamson, J. Peter. "Computerized Approaches to Bond Switching." *Financial Analysts Journal*, July–August 1970.

Yohe, W. P. and D. S. Karnosky. "Interest Rates and Price Level Changes, 1952–69." *Review*, St. Louis Federal Reserve Bank, December 1969.

Appendix 6-A: Term Structure of Interest Rates

Simply stated, the term structure theory concentrates on why securities which are alike in all respects except their term to maturity should provide different market yields.

As a general rule, interest rates on securities with different maturities vary. In Figure 6–A, interest rates for treasury securities on May 31, 1978 are plotted according to the maturity of the securities. Market interest rates are plotted on the vertical axis and year of maturity along the horizontal axis. The solid line drawn through these points is called the *yield curve* or *term pattern.* This figure reveals that in the spring of 1978, interest rates on short-term securities were lower than those on long-term securities, and the yield curve for treasury securities was upward sloping.

History suggests that all yield curves are *not* upward sloping. In fact, yields often exhibit variable trends. This can be seen from Figure 6–B. Three alternative theories explain both the structure of the curve at any given time and the changes in the curve through time. These are the *expectations theory*, the *liquidity premium theory*, and the *market segmentation theory*.[1]

[1] The term structure theory described here is the Preferred-Habitat Model first proposed by Modigliani and Sutch in 1966. See F. J. Modigliani and R. C. Sutch, "Innovation in Interest Rate Policy," *American Economic Review*, Papers and Proceedings, 1966, pp. 179–97. Subsequently, Modigliani and Shiller have shown that the measurement of the term structure, based on this theory, can be significantly improved when explicit allowance is made in the original Modigliani–Sutch model for two additional factors, designed to measure the expected value of future inflation

Figure 6–A

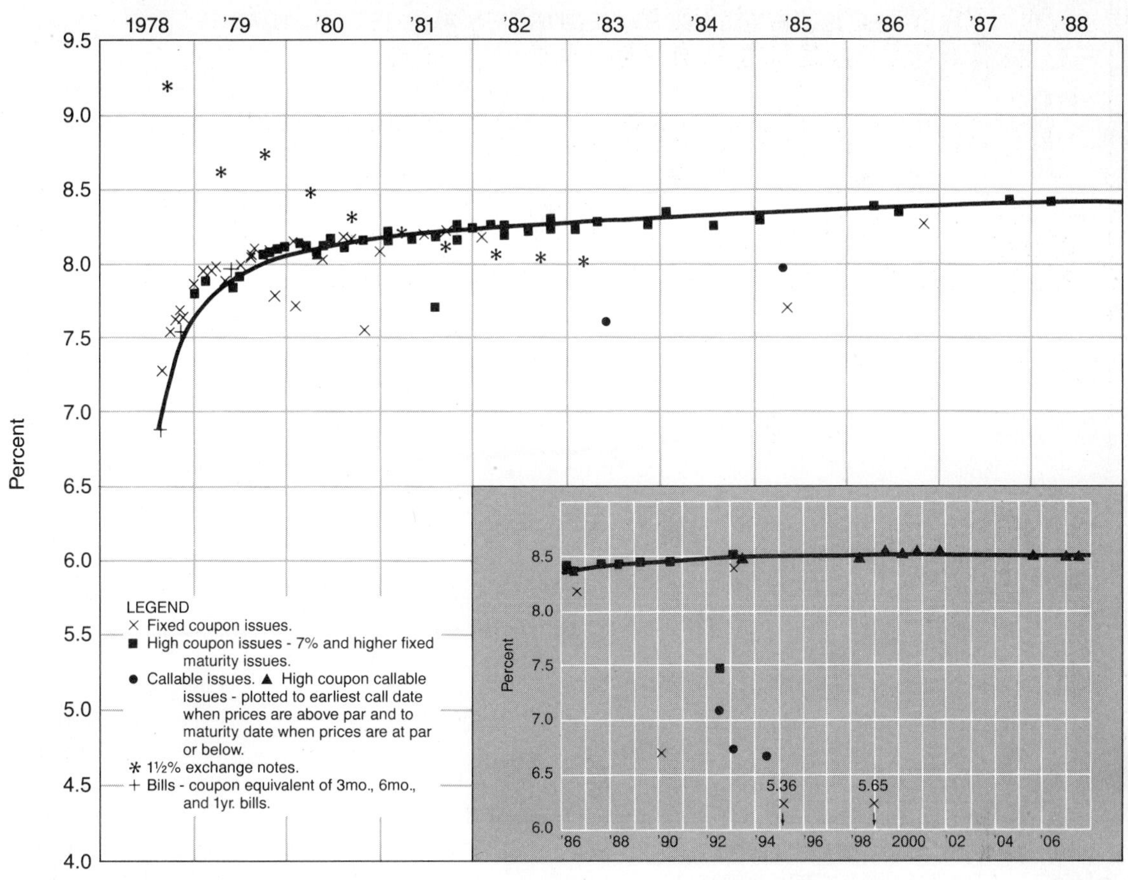

SOURCE: *Treasury Bulletin*, June 1978, p. 70.

The Expectations Theory

The expectations theory assumes the operation of a free market in securities where there are no default risks, no transaction costs, and no other special features such as tax and call features, different coupons, or marketability. In such a market, all securities are alike in all particulars except in their maturity dates, and investors are motivated solely by the desire to maximize profits.

and the market's uncertainty about the future course of interest rates. See F. J. Modigliani and R. J. Shiller, "Inflation, Rational Expectations and the Term Structure of Interest Rates," *Economica*, Vol. 40, 1973, pp. 12–43.

Figure 6–B

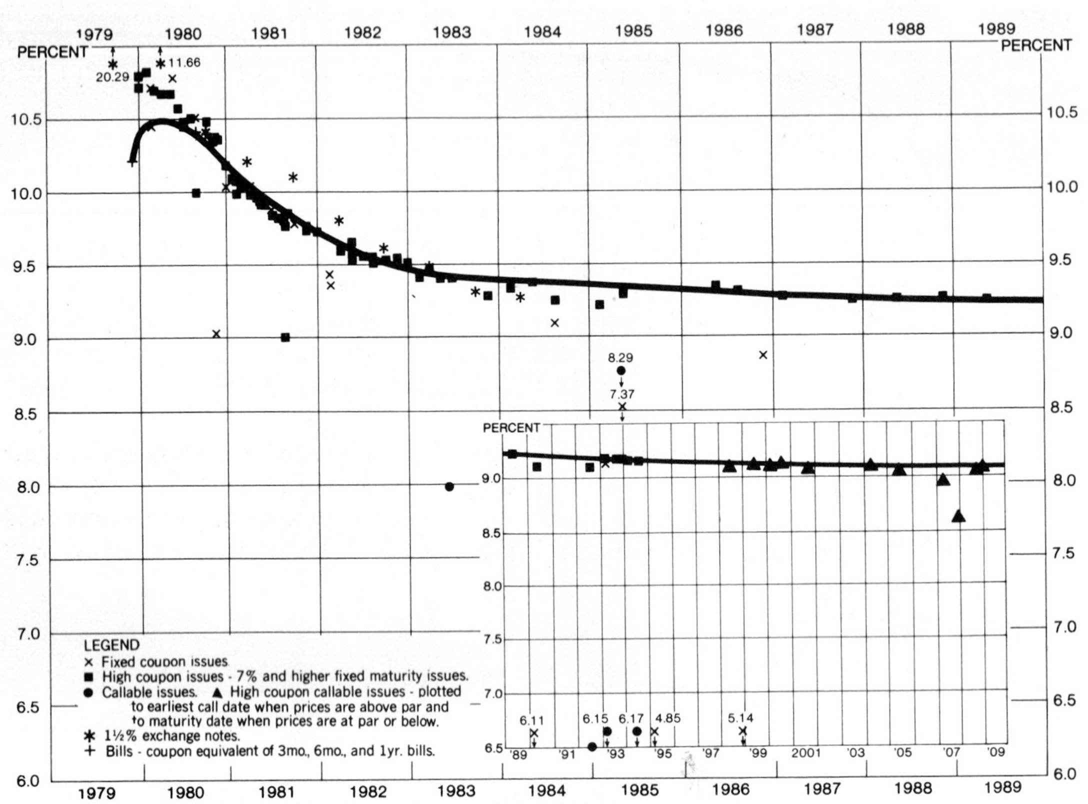

SOURCE: *Treasury Bulletin*, September 1979, p. 84.

The expectations theory asserts that, although market participants do not know what actual interest rates will prevail in the future, they do form expectations about future short-term interest rates, and that investors who want to hold bonds over a particular period of time can choose between two strategies. First, they can simply buy an issue that matures at the end of the holding period. Second, they can buy a succession of short-term issues, reinvesting the interest and principal until the end of the holding period.[2] Using either strategy, the total yield over the period should be the same.

Suppose an investor wants to hold bonds over a two-year period. He discovers that two-year bonds offer 7.5 percent and one-year bonds 6.8 percent. If the investor put \$10,000 into the two-year bond, he would have a total of \$11,556 at the end of the period:

$$\text{Ending value} = \$10{,}000(1.075)(1.075) = \$11{,}556$$

Alternatively, if he bought the one-year bond, he would have \$10,680 at the end of the first year:

$$\text{Ending value} = \$10{,}000(1.068) = \$10{,}680$$

The question, then, is: What yield would he need on an investment of \$10,680 during the second year in order to give him a total of \$11,556 at the end of the second year? Because the answer to this question depends solely on the yield prevailing during the second year, this problem can be solved by the following method:

$$\begin{matrix}\text{Ending Value of}\\ \text{Strategy 1}\end{matrix} \times (1 + \text{Yield During Year 2}) = \begin{matrix}\text{Ending Value of}\\ \text{Strategy 2}\end{matrix}$$

$$\begin{aligned} \$10{,}680(1 + r_{m_2}) &= \$11{,}556 \\ \$10{,}680 r_{m_2} &= \$11{,}556 - \$10{,}680 \\ r_{m_2} &= .082 \text{ (or } 8.2\%) \end{aligned}$$

Clearly, then, the market expects the rate on one-year issues to be 1.4 percentage points (8.2 − 6.8 percent) higher in a year.

This illustration, which is fairly simple, can now be formally stated:

$$(1 + {}_nR_{m_2}) = [(1 + {}_nr_{m_1})(1 + {}_{n+1}r_{m_1})]^{1/2} \qquad \text{(6A–1)}$$

[2] Holding period in this discussion refers to the length of time between purchase and sale of a security by an investor, regardless of the maturity. However, in the discussion of the callability risk premium, the years to maturity is assumed to be the investor's holding period.

where

R_{m_2} = Current market long-term interest rate on a two-year security
r_{m_1} = Current market short-term interest rate on a one-year security
Prescript n = The year in which the interest rate holds ($n + 1$ represents the interest rate expected a year from today)

In our previous example,

$$(1 + .075) = [(1 + .068)(1 + {}_2r_{m_1})]^{1/2}$$

Solving the above equation for ${}_2r_{m_1}$ we get ${}_2r_{m_1} = 8.2\%$. That is, the market expects the rate on one-year issues to be 8.2 percent in a year.

Figure 6–C

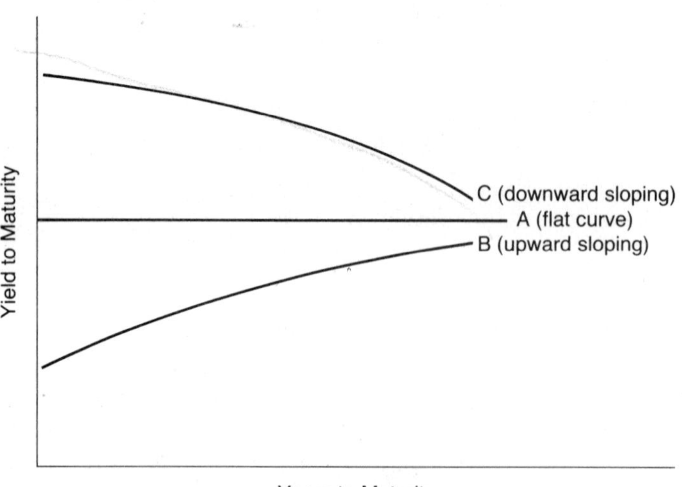

A = Short-term interest rates in the future are expected to be at the *same level* as at present.
B = Short-term interest rates in the future are expected to be *higher* than at present.
C = Short-term interest rates in the future are expected to be *lower* than at present.

Equation 6A–1 pertained to a two-year holding period. It can now be stated in its general form:

$$(1 + {}_nR_{m_N}) = (1 + {}_nr_{m_1})(1 + {}_{n+1}r_{m_1})(1 + {}_{n+2}r_{m_1}) \cdots (1 + {}_{n+N-1}r_{m_1})^{1/N} \tag{6A–2}$$

Equation 6A–2 reveals that if the market expects the future short-term rates to rise above the short-term rates currently prevailing in the market, the current long-term rates (${}_nR_{m_N}$) will be higher than the current short-term rates. In contrast, if future short-term rates are expected to decline, then the current long-term rate will be lower than the current short-term rate. Finally, if the market expects the future short-term rate to remain unchanged, the current long-term rate will be equal to the current short-term rate. These relationships are shown in Figure 6–C.

To recapitulate, according to the expectations theory, an investor is able to obtain the same yield for a given holding period, regardless of whether he purchases a security with a maturity date equal to the desired holding period, or any combination of maturities which he may hold over the same period. It follows that, under such circumstances, the structure of yield on different securities can be explained by a very simple relationship—the current yield on a long-term bond of a given maturity is a geometric average of the current short-term rate and all future expected rates over the term to maturity.

The Liquidity Premium Theory

The liquidity premium theory differs from the expectations theory in one important respect: It modifies the assumption of complete confidence in investors' forecasts of future rates. This theory asserts that market participants form expectations of future rates, but are uncertain about what rates will *actually* prevail, believing that future rates may turn out to be above or below their current expectations of these rates. The uncertainty is interpreted by two groups of participants in the opposing manner, as explained below.

The liquidity premium theory argues that savers and borrowers do not have firm interest rate expectations. Rather, they operate in a world of uncertainty and are averse to bearing risk. Consequently, the higher the risk, the higher will be the premium savers demand and the lower will be the premium the borrowers are willing to pay. This is the basis for the existence of the liquidity premium.

The theory goes further than merely recognizing the existence of liquidity premium. It asserts that because short-term securities are more liquid than long-term securities, lenders bid more strongly for the former, driving their prices up and their yields down. Therefore, yield curves are positively sloped,

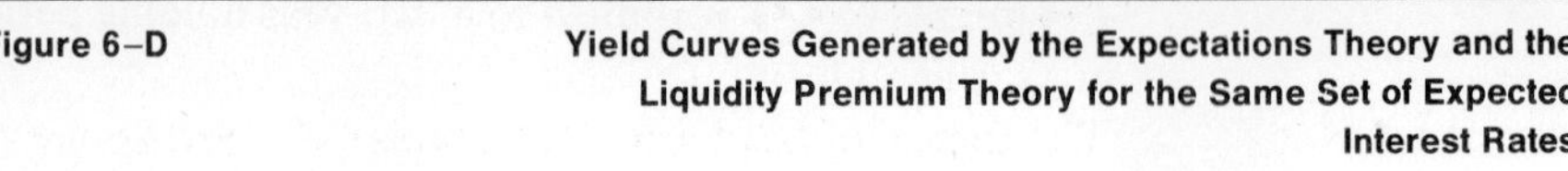

Figure 6–D **Yield Curves Generated by the Expectations Theory and the Liquidity Premium Theory for the Same Set of Expected Interest Rates**

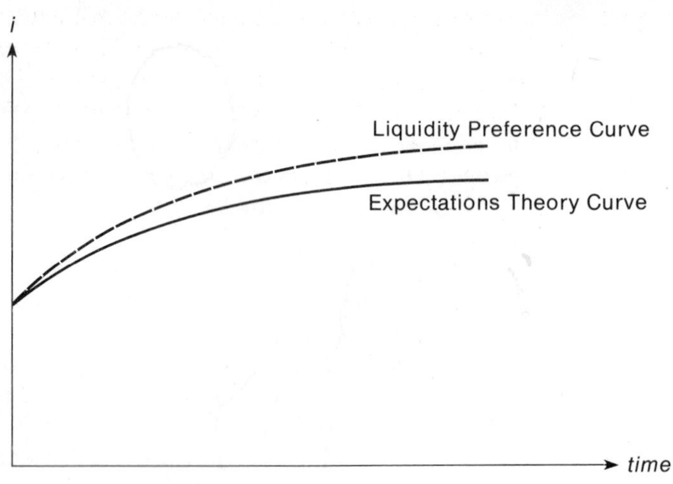

indicating that short-term yields are lower than intermediate-term and longer-term yields. This is shown in Figure 6–D. The top curve, showing the actual market yield, is the result of the addition of the liquidity premium to the expected yield.

The Market Segmentation Theory

The market segmentation theory differs significantly from the expectations theory (which assumes that investors are indifferent to maturity) and from the liquidity premium theory (which postulates that the longer the maturity, the higher the premium over rates on shorter-term securities). The segmentation theory emphasizes that investors have different maturity preferences, that some lenders prefer long-term rather than short-term investments, whereas others prefer only short-term investments. Investors such as life insurance companies or pension funds are concerned with guaranteed certainty of income over the long run, and risk aversion on their part would lead to a preference for long-term securities. In contrast, because of their nature of business, banks and savings and loan associations concentrate on short-term maturities. This theory asserts that, regardless of the structure of interest rates, investors will not change their preferred markets. Accordingly, the yield structure is determined by the relative forces of supply and demand within each of the segmented markets, because securities of different maturities constitute noncompeting groups.

Empirical Evidence

The theory of the term structure is not a settled matter, as can be seen from the three principal theories advanced to explain the relationship. A large number of empirical studies have been conducted to date, but they have not been able to prove fully or disprove the validity of these three theories. The only general conclusion that can be reached is that short-run changes in the term structure reveal patterns more consistent with the market segmentation theory, whereas changes over periods of one quarter or longer are more consistent with both the expectations theory and the liquidity premium theory.

Government Bonds: Treasury, Federal Agencies, Municipals

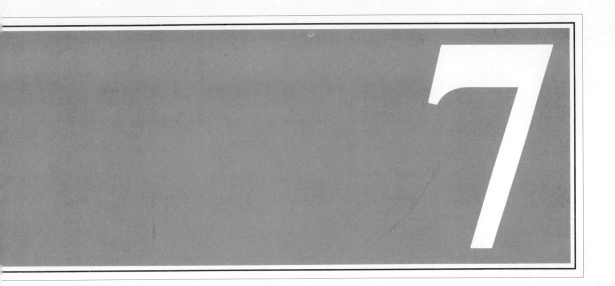

Introduction

In Chapter 6, a Basic Decision Model was developed for the evaluation and selection of different types of bonds. The model specified that the two key decision variables are the yield to maturity of a bond and the appropriate discount rate with which an investor wishes to discount the future income stream generated by that bond. As long as the yield is higher than this discount rate, the bond may be treated as *undervalued*, and will therefore offer an attractive investment opportunity. Conversely, a bond is *overvalued* if its yield to maturity is lower than the investor's appropriate discount rate. Finally, if the yield is identical to this discount rate, the bond is considered as fully priced.

The appropriate discount rate, or the required rate of return, it may be recalled, comprises the risk-free real rate plus a risk premium. The risk premium, in turn, is associated with six types of risks—interest rate risk, inflation risk, maturity risk, default risk, callability risk, and liquidity risk. Although the risk-free real rate can be assumed to be relatively fixed, risk premiums vary—sometimes widely—between different types of bonds.

Thousands of bonds are traded on the market. However, as revealed by Table 7–1, conceptually they can be divided into five broad categories—treasury bills, treasury notes and bonds, government agency issues, municipal bonds, and corporate bonds. Each group of bonds carries a different set of risks and is associated with varying tax features.

This chapter is divided into two sections. In Section 1, a detailed analysis of treasury bills, treasury bonds and agency issues is undertaken. In Section 2,

Table 7–1 **Selected Investment Features of Fixed Income Securities**

	Features	Treasury Bills	Treasury Notes and Bonds	Agency Issues	Municipal Bonds	Corporate Bonds	Preferred Stocks
Risk features	Interest rate risk		Present	Present	Present	Present	Present
	Inflation risk	Present	Present	Present	Present	Present	Present
	Maturity risk		Present	Present	Present	Present	Present
	Default risk			Present (theoretically)	Present	Present	Present
	Callability risk		*		*	Present	Present
	Liquidity risk				Present	Present	Present
Tax features	Federal tax exemption				Present		Present (for corporations)
	State/Local tax exemption	Present	Present	Present	Present		

* Some treasury bonds and municipal bonds are callable.

municipal bonds, which differ significantly from government bonds, are evaluated. For practical reasons, corporate bonds and preferred stock are analyzed in Chapter 8.

SECTION 1 TREASURY SECURITIES AND AGENCY ISSUES

An Overview

Government Bonds

Federal government bonds are issued to allow the government to borrow large sums of money. In fact, the federal debt has increased from $270.8 billion in 1954 to a staggering $789 billion in 1978. And this upward trend in federal debt continues unabated.

When viewed against the backdrop of the growth in the other types of debt in the economy, shown in Figure 7–1, the federal debt provides a new perspective. In the three years ending in 1978, corporate debt rose 36 percent to slightly more than $1 trillion, and state and local government debt increased just 33 percent to $295 billion, whereas total debt in the economy increased 42 percent to $3.9 trillion. Even more rapid growth rates were registered by consumer installment debt which increased by 49 percent to $300 billion, by residential mortgage debt which rose by 54 percent to $750 billion, and by the U.S. government debt which increased by 47 percent to $789 billion.

Although treasury borrowing is the government's most visible presence in the credit market, the debts of federal agencies grow faster and with the more

Figure 7–1

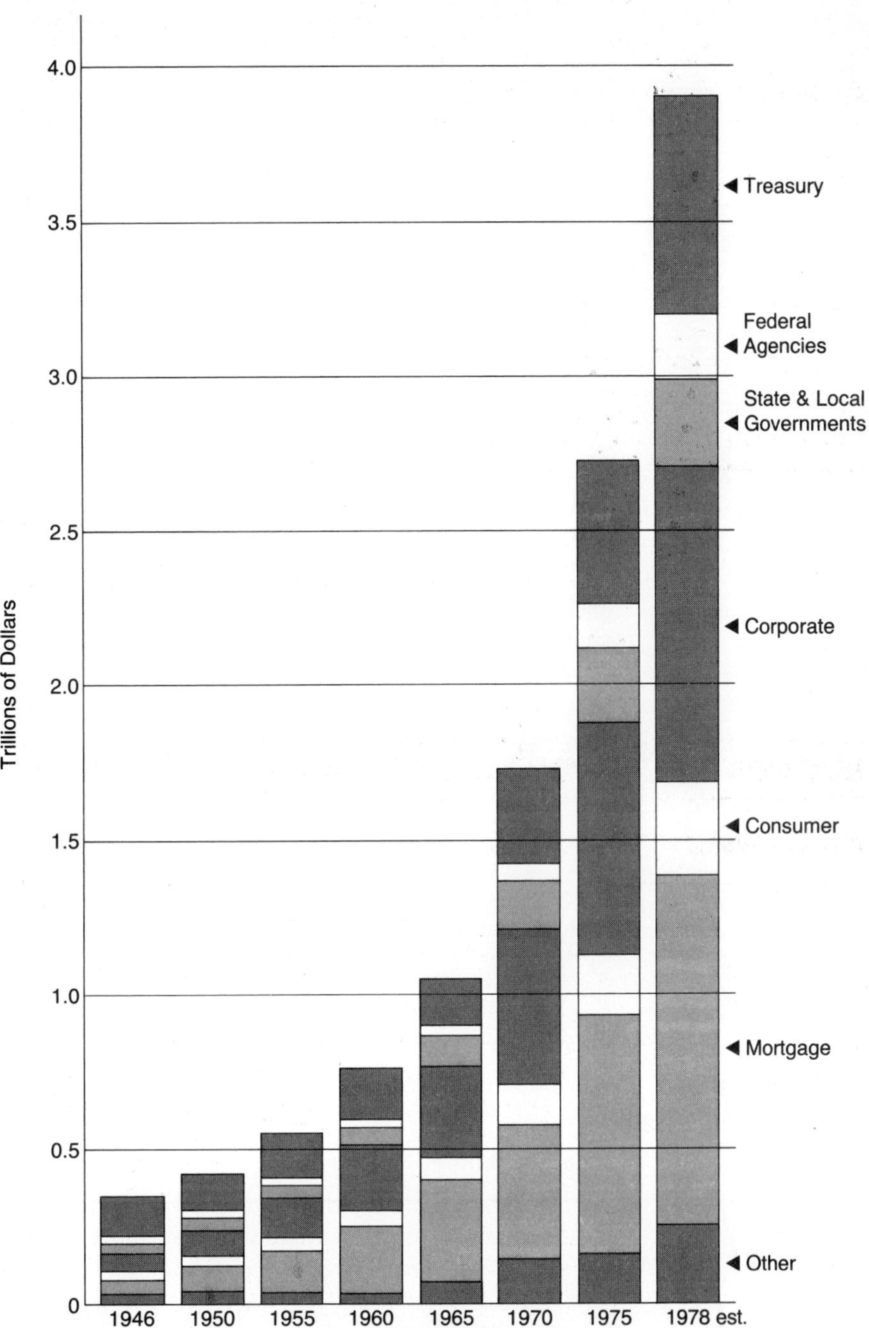

SOURCE: *Business Week*, October 16, 1978, p. 76.

direct impact on the key sectors of the economy. In 1978, federally guaranteed lending increased by 20 percent, and the guaranteed loans outstanding reached the all-time high of $240 billion.

Agency Issues

Agency issues represent the bonds issued by two types of agencies. The first group, called *federal agencies*, includes a large number of agencies, all of which are fully owned by the U.S. government. This group includes, among others, the Export–Import Bank, Federal Housing Administration, Government National Mortgage Association (GNMA), and the Tennessee Valley Authority (TVA). Federal agencies are authorized to issue debt securities on their own behalf. Some agency issues are backed by the full faith and credit of the United States, whereas others are guaranteed by the respective issuing agencies. However, because none has ever defaulted, these securities are assumed to carry only a small degree of default risk. These agencies cover a wide spectrum of activities, ranging from financing agricultural industry to providing the funds necessary to satisfy America's need for homes.

The second group, called *government-guaranteed agencies*, comprises agencies whose capital stock was originally owned by the U.S. Treasury, but has since been transferred to the general public and to organizations served by a small number of agencies. Debt securities issued by these agencies, which include Banks for Cooperatives and Federal Home Loan Banks, are not guaranteed by the U.S. government, although they raise money under the Treasury's supervision. Most of the activities of these agencies are concentrated in the area of farm credit and housing.

The phenomenal growth in the federal debt has other implications for the bondholder. Higher levels of federal debt increase not only the supply, but the variety of government bonds. A wider variety of bonds increases the choices of prospective bondholders both in terms of maturities and the different types of bonds they can buy.

Investment Characteristics

Treasury Issues

The Treasury currently issues three types of marketable securities—*bills*, *notes*, and *bonds*. The Treasury places new securities directly with investors, rather than using dealers to underwrite new issues as is done in the corporate and municipal bond markets.

Treasury securities are available in registered, bearer, or book-entry form. Registered securities are inscribed with the owner's name and held by the owner. Ownership is recorded on the books of the Treasury department and interest is paid by check to the owner of record; coupons are not attached. The security is payable at maturity to the owner. Registered securities may be transferred by assignment by the registered owner or the owner's authorized representative.

Bearer securities are payable to the holder of the securities and ownership is not recorded. Title is passed by delivery without endorsement and without notice to the Treasury. A "coupon" security is a bearer security with interest coupons attached. The coupons must be detached and presented at a Federal Reserve Bank or the Treasury for payment when interest is due.

Book-entry securities are not issued in the form of engraved certificates, but are held as entries in accounts at Federal Reserve Banks in the names of member banks of the Federal Reserve System. Member banks in turn keep accounts of their own security holdings and those they hold for their customers and for financial institutions for which they act as correspondents.

The three types of treasury securities outstanding—bills, notes, and bonds—are distinguished primarily by the period to maturity at the time of their issuance. They also differ in the methods and terms under which they are sold and in the way interest payments are computed.

Treasury bills are the shortest-term marketable U.S. obligations offered and, by law, cannot exceed one year to maturity. In fiscal year 1976, the U.S. government sold $367 billion worth of treasury bills, and redeemed $334 billion worth of bills, raising a net of $33 billion. This is shown in Table 7–2. Total treasury bills outstanding at the end of 1976 amounted to $164 billion. The amount was virtually unchanged over the next three years.

Since fiscal year 1970, treasury bills have accounted for 85 percent of all marketable offerings and 46 percent of net funds raised. Bills are sold on a discount basis; that is, the investor pays a price lower than the face value and on maturity receives the face—or par—value.

Notes are U.S. government coupon obligations with an original maturity of one to five years. Notes bear interest at a fixed rate payable semiannually. Bonds are long-term issues with an original maturity of more than five years from the date of issue until the principal amount becomes payable. Bonds may be issued with a call option, meaning that on four months' notice the Treasury can request their redemption on or after specified dates before maturity. Bonds bear interest at a fixed rate, payable semiannually. Interest ceases when the principal amount becomes payable, whether at maturity or at an earlier call date. Bonds are generally subject to an interest rate ceiling, although Congress has allowed exemptions from this limitation.[1] Notes and bonds are issued in bearer, registered, or book-entry form in denominations of $1,000, $5,000, $10,000, $100,000, and $1 million.

[1] The U.S. Treasury is currently authorized to issue up to $10 million of bonds with no ceiling on the interest rate.

Table 7–2 (Billions of dollars)

FISCAL YEARS	1970	1971	1972	1973	1974	1975	1976	T.Q.* 1976	Oct.–Mar. 1977
				Gross Amounts Issued (Par Value)					
Total marketable securities	226.1	252.2	278.2	277.3	285.2	356.4	447.7	119.5	221.0
Treasury bills	191.4	209.2	243.6	244.2	262.9	295.2	367.0	91.7	176.7
Regular weekly (3- and 6-month)	155.3	172.4	211.3	218.4	224.7	253.4	317.9	82.9	152.4
Regular monthly (52-week)†	19.4	20.4	20.4	21.2	23.4	26.5	38.8	8.8	22.3
All other	16.7	16.4	11.9	4.5	14.8	15.7	10.3	—	2.0
Cash management	—	—	—	—	—	—	8.3	—	—
Notes and bonds	34.7	42.9	34.6	33.2	22.3	61.1	80.7	27.8	44.3
Yield auctions	—	—	—	—	—	43.9	64.9	18.3	43.3
Price auctions‡	—	4.3	16.2	17.4	22.3	17.3	2.6	—	1.0
Subscription offerings	10.7	3.4	—	—	—	—	13.2	9.5	—
Exchange offerings	24.0	35.2	18.4	15.7	—	—	—	—	—
				Net Funds Raised					
Total marketable securities	6.4	12.8	11.8	5.8	3.6	49.0	77.0	15.1	27.7
Treasury bills	7.8	10.4	8.0	5.4	5.0	23.6	32.6	0.3	2.8
Regular weekly (3- and 6-month)	5.2	7.4	11.6	3.1	2.2	19.8	21.6	−0.5	0
Regular monthly (52-week)†	0.8	1.0	0	2.5	0.2	4.9	12.3	0.7	0.7
All other	1.8	2.0	−3.6	−0.2	2.6	−0.9	−1.6	—	2.0
Notes and bonds	−1.3	2.4	3.8	0.4	−1.4	25.5	44.3	14.8	25.0
Yield auctions	—	—	—	—	—	22.2	38.2	11.8	24.0
Price auctions‡	—	4.3	7.2	3.5	−0.4	4.0	1.6	—	1.0
Subscription offerings	2.2	2.3	—	—	—	—	5.5	4.4	—
Cash redemptions	−3.6	−4.3	−3.5	−3.2	−1.0	−0.8	−0.9	−1.4	—

* Transition quarter between fiscal years 1976 and 1977.
† Prior to August 1973, regular monthly bills include 9-month and 1-year issues.
‡ Price auctions include conventional price auctions and uniform price auctions.

SOURCES: *Treasury Bulletin* and *Annual Report of the Secretary of the Treasury on the State of the Finances.*

Special Government Bonds

Among the long-term bonds issued by the Treasury department, Series EE and Series HH bonds require special consideration. These are *not* marketable bonds. Frequently referred to as "savings bonds," they are more like time certificates in a savings bank and are redeemable directly from the U.S. Treasury. Furthermore, the Treasury guarantees that these bonds will not be called away before maturity. These bonds can be purchased, free of commission, at any bank, post office, or from the Treasury itself.

Series EE Bonds

Table 7–3 presents the essential characteristics of EE and HH bonds which have replaced the old E and H bonds. Series EE bonds are sold in denominations of $50 to $10,000. The initial purchase price for any denomination is 50

Table 7–3 **Comparison of Series EE and Series HH Bonds**

Characteristics	Series EE	Series HH
Denominations	$50, 75, 100, 200, 500, 1,000, 5,000, 10,000	$500, 1,000, 5,000, 10,000
Purchase price	50% of denomination	Denomination value
Interest rate	6.5% to maturity 4% the first six months, with gradually increasing rate to maturity	6.5% to maturity, length of bond
Maturity	11 years	10 years
Payment of interest	Increase in the redemption value	By semiannual check to the bondholder
Tax status	Taxed as current income or may be deferred until redemption; interest exempt from state and local taxes	Taxed as current income; interest exempt from state and local taxes
Redemption	Any time after six months from issue date	Any time after six months from issue date
Exchange provision	May be exchanged for Series HH bond; $500 minimum	None

percent of its final maturity value. The maturity of these bonds is 11 years, and they have an annual purchase limitation of $15,000. Series EE bonds use the discount method to pay interest; that is, the investor pays an amount less than the face value at the time of purchase, but receives the face value when the bond matures. The price the Treasury will pay if it is turned in for cash by the investor is incremented every six months.

Series EE bonds cannot be redeemed until six months after they were originally issued. Furthermore, if these bonds are redeemed before maturity, the effective rate is less than the 6.5 percent it would have been if held until maturity. They are registered in the name of the owner, and a beneficiary can be named to whom ownership can be transferred automatically at the death of the original owner.

Interest on Series EE bonds is taxable as ordinary income. However, if these bonds are held for their entire life, bondholders may elect to postpone federal income taxes on the gain in principal amounts until maturity. Bondholders have the additional option of switching from Series EE to Series HH bonds in multiples of $500 without paying taxes on the accumulated interest value. The owner would then pay taxes on the interest checks he or she receives twice a year on the HH bonds, but would not pay tax on the total interest accumulated until the HH bonds themselves are redeemed.

Series HH Bonds

Unlike Series EE bonds, which are bought at a discount and pay face value at maturity, Series HH bonds are bought at face value and pay interest semiannually. These bonds are issued in face amounts of $500, $1,000, $5,000, and $10,000, and the annual limitation of purchase is placed at $20,000. The maturity of HH bonds is ten years; when purchased for cash rather than in exchange for other bonds, they are subject to an interest penalty if redeemed before maturity. HH bonds carry an interest rate of 6.5 percent, and the interest payments are taxed as ordinary income.

Flower Bonds

One type of U.S. government bond, known as "flower" bonds, deserves special mention. Deep discount treasury bonds—that is, bonds selling well below their par value—that are redeemable at par when used to pay federal estate taxes are called "flower" bonds. The name is derived from the assumption that the sale of these bonds generally provides just enough money to pay for estate taxes and purchase flowers for the funeral. Prior to the passage of the 1976 Tax Reform Act, beneficiaries computed the gain or loss on inherited property on the basis of the fair market value of the property at the date of the decedent's death. In the case of flower bonds, the IRS permitted the value of the inheritance to be determined according to the par value of the bond rather than its fair market value. Consequently, no capital gains tax had to be paid on the difference between the purchase price and the par value of the bond. Under the 1976 Tax Reform Act, however, the difference between the par value of the flower bonds used for estate tax purposes and the original cost or market value at the end of 1976, whichever is greater, is subject to capital gains taxation. The new provision, therefore, significantly reduces the tax advantage of flower bonds.[2]

Agency Issues

The investment characteristics of agency issues are different from those of Treasury issues. The size of the denominations varies considerably from one agency to another. For the Federal Intermediate Credit Banks and the Banks for Cooperatives, for example, the minimum purchase is $5,000. The Federal Land Banks issue securities in $1,000 denominations, whereas the Federal Home Loan Banks issue in $10,000 denominations. The investment characteristics of the debt securities also vary widely, as shown in Table 7–4. In general, agency issues vary widely in terms of their investment characteristics and the minimum amount necessary to invest in them. Understandably, the agency issues are far fewer and are traded less actively than the treasury issues.

[2] Interestingly, the 1978 Revenue Act retroactively restored the full benefits of flower bonds until 1980. The result was a sharply rising demand for these bonds.

Table 7–4 **Government Agency Security Investment Characteristics**

	Purpose	Guarantying Agency of U.S. Government	Security Denominations	Minimum Purchase Requirements	Tax Exempt Status
GOVERNMENT–SPONSORED ENTERPRISES					
Banks for Cooperatives (Co-ops)	Make loans to farmers' cooperative associations	All Co-op banks	$5,000, $10,000, $50,000, $100,000	$5,000	No state & local taxes
Federal Intermediate Credit Banks (FICBs)	Provide money to various specialized banks and financial institutions	12 FICBs	$5,000, $10,000, $50,000, $100,000, $500,000	$5,000	No state & local taxes
Federal Home Loan Banks (FHLBs)	Advance funds to savings-related institutions facing large deposit outflows	12 FHLBs	$10,000, $50,000, $100,000, $1,000,000	$10,000 ($100,000 for short-term notes)	No state & local taxes
Federal Home Loan Mortgage Corporation (FHLMC)	Buys residential mortgages from federally insured savings institutions during periods of tight money	FHLMC which, in turn, is backed by the full faith and credit of U.S. government	$25,000, $100,000, $500,000, $1,000,000	$25,000	No exemption
Federal Land Banks (FLBs)	Provide local Federal Land Bank Associations with funds for long-term loans to farmers	12 FLBs	$1,000, $5,000, $10,000, $50,000, $100,000, $500,000	$1,000	No state & local taxes
Federal National Mortgage Association (FNMA)	Purchases residential mortgages (primarily those insured by FHA, V.A. or Farmers Home Administration) to provide mortgage liquidity during periods of tight credit	Authority to borrow $2.25 billion from the U.S. Treasury	$10,000, $25,000, $50,000, $100,000, $500,000	$10,000	No exemption
FEDERAL AGENCIES					
Export–Import Bank (Exim Bank)	Raises money to provide loans, credit insurance, and other guarantees in order to facilitate U.S. international trade	Full faith and credit of U.S. government	$5,000, $10,000, $25,000, $100,000, $500,000, $1,000,000	$5,000 ($100,000 for short-term certificates)	No exemption

Table 7–4 *(Continued)* **Government Agency Security Investment Characteristics**

	Purpose	Guarantying Agency of U.S. Government	Security Denominations	Minimum Purchase Requirements	Tax Exempt Status
Farmers Home Administration (FHDA)	Raises money to extend housing and real estate loans to farmers and other rural citizens	U.S. government guaranteed	None	None	No exemption
Federal Housing Administration (FHA)	Makes payments to holders of FHA-insured mortgages which have gone into default	U.S. government	\$50, \$100, \$500, \$1,000, \$5,000, \$10,000	\$50	No exemption
Government National Mortgage Association (GNMA)	Provides funds for financing residential housing programs where home financing facilities are inadequate	Full faith and credit of U.S. government	\$5,000, \$10,000, \$25,000, \$100,000, \$500,000, \$1,000,000	\$5,000	No exemption
Tennessee Valley Authority (TVA)	Raises money to help develop the industrial and agricultural resources of the Tennessee Valley and surrounding areas	Authority to borrow up to \$150 million from U.S. government	\$1,000, \$5,000, \$10,000, \$100,000, \$1,000,000	\$1,000	No state & local taxes
U.S. Postal Service	Raises funds to upgrade the mail system	Not guaranteed by U.S. government, but could be if requested by postal service	\$10,000; \$25,000, \$100,000, \$500,000	\$10,000	No state & local taxes
Other Federal Agency Securities	Fund various agencies and programs: SBA, student loans, Washington Transit, HUD, and so on	Partial, if not total, government backing	Varies	Varies	Varies

The issues of the Government National Mortgage Association ("Ginnie Mae") deserve special mention. This agency provides money for financing residential housing programs in areas where established home financing facilities are inadequate. Three types of such securities are available. Mortgage-backed bonds issued by the Federal Home Loan Corporation, but guaranteed by Ginnie Mae are known as *Ginnie Mae bonds*. The maturity for these securities ranges from one to 25 years; they are available in denominations of $25,000 and over. Also available are *GNMA participation certificates*, which are conventional securities backed by mortgages. These securities mature within four years and are sold in denominations of $5,000 and up. The third type of GNMA issue, called *Ginnie Mae pass-through securities*, represents interest in pools of government-backed mortgages. They are called pass-throughs because the monthly payment of principal and interest by the mortgagors are passed directly through the investor. The minimum denomination of these securities is $25,000.

Investors might also consider Jeeps, another relatively new mortgage-based investment. Jeeps, or GPMs (pools of graduated payment mortgages), are similar to Ginnie Mae pass-through securities in that they represent an interest in a pool of mortgages. However, for these mortgages, the total payments in the early years are kept low to enable people to afford more expensive homes. In later years the payments increase. Although the GPM mortgage pays less in the first few years of the mortgage, Jeep investors also receive less interest during the early years, with the payments and interest income rising as time passes. Therefore, Jeeps yield more than Ginnie Maes. Jeeps can be particularly attractive for investors nearing retirement, because the higher amounts of interest income from the security will be received after retirement (when the investor will probably be in a lower tax bracket).

Financing Techniques

Treasury Bills[3]

Regular Offerings of Three- and Six-Month Bills

The most frequent and most popular treasury bill issues are the three-month and six-month maturities which are offered on a weekly basis. Bids (tenders) for both issues are usually invited approximately a week prior to the auction. At that time, the amount offered and the terms of offering are announced, with the terms for the two issues being similar. Both the three- and six-month bills are sold on a discount basis under competitive and noncompetitive bidding. Bill auction results are reported in the newspapers on the day after the auction. The Treasury announces the lowest bid price accepted (which is the highest discount from par value). If the investor bids *competitively*, he will know from his own bid whether it was accepted or not. The competitive bidding method usually involves large investors—groups or financial institutions submitting sealed bids by the specified time to the Treasury. If the investor bid *noncompetitively*—that is, offering to purchase the bond at the offered price—the amount of his or her discount is

[3] With suitable modifications, this section reproduces Margaret E. Bedford, "Recent Developments in Treasury Financing Techniques," *Monthly Review*, Federal Reserve Bank of Kansas City, July–August 1977, pp. 15–21.

the *average* discount rate accepted in that auction. Understandably, small investors who have an inadequate knowledge of the bills market typically submit noncompetitive bids.

Tenders must be for a minimum of $10,000 and in multiples of $5,000 beyond the minimum. Bills are issued in par value denominations of $10,000, $15,000, $50,000, $100,000, $500,000, and $1 million. The three- and six-month bills are issued only in book-entry form.

Regular Offerings of 52-Week Bills

One-year bills (52-week bills) are offered every four weeks at a discount by the auction method under terms similar to those for the regular weekly bill sales. Tenders for the 52-week bills are usually invited on Thursday prior to the auction. The auction is held on the following Wednesday, and allotments are made at that time by the same procedures used for the regular weekly bills. Payment for the bills must be completed on the date of issue. Despite the longer period to maturity, the rate is still computed on a bank discount basis of 360 days, as it is for other treasury bill issues.

Special Bill Issues

In addition to regular bill offerings, the Treasury has found it necessary from time to time to meet short-term financing needs through the sale of special issues of treasury bills. In August 1975, the Treasury introduced cash management bills, also known as federal funds bills or short-dated bills. These bills are designed to raise funds quickly and for only a brief period.

A cash management bill offering is announced one to ten days prior to the auction. Only competitive tenders are invited. The offering usually represents an additional amount of an outstanding issue with an original maturity of six months, although additional amounts have been issued for original 52-week maturity bills. The minimum acceptable bid is $10 million with increments of $1 million over that amount. Denominations issued, calculation of interest, determination of acceptable competitive bids, and other features of a cash management bill sale are similar to those for regular bills.

In addition to cash management bills, the Treasury has issued some special bills of longer maturities when additional funds were needed for less than one year. Federal Financing Bank bills are also special issues that have all the characteristics of treasury bills.

Treasury Notes and Bonds

The sale of notes and bonds is more involved than the sale of treasury bills. Each time the Treasury needs to raise funds in the coupon market or sell new securities to refund maturing securities, it must choose the maturities to be offered, the size of individual issues, and the method of sale. The type of security sold and the method of sale may in turn lead to decisions about price, interest rate, payment term, call features, and other terms of financing. In recent years, however, the more routine scheduling of coupon offerings has somewhat limited the decisions on maturity of securities to be offered.

Offering Schedules for Notes and Bonds

Tenders for the two-year notes are invited approximately six days prior to the sale. Delivery and payment follow about ten days to two weeks after the deadline for receipt of tenders. Unlike other note issues, the two-year notes are offered in minimum denominations of $5,000.

The Treasury also makes offerings of four- and five-year notes. For these notes, sales are announced approximately a week in advance. Payments must be completed on the issue date, which falls approximately two weeks after the sale.

In addition to the regular note cycles, a major refunding operation occurs near the middle of each quarter. This happens when a large volume of securities is about to mature and must be rolled over[4] or paid off. In periods of rising cash needs, the Treasury can use the quarterly refunding operation to raise new cash as well as to refinance maturing debts by issuing new securities.

Methods of Sale

A number of marketing techniques have been used to sell notes and bonds. The method used depends in part on the volume to be financed—which fluctuates throughout the year as cash needs vary—and other objectives the Treasury wishes to achieve, such as broadening investor interest or minimizing interest costs.

Auction Sales Under all auction methods, competitive and noncompetitive tenders are invited. Tenders must be accompanied by a deposit of predetermined amount.

The Treasury announces that if noncompetitive tenders absorb all or most of the offering, competitive tenders will be accepted to the extent necessary to provide a fair determination of yield or price. Competitive bidders are notified of the acceptance or rejection of their bids. Noncompetitive bidders are notified only when the tender is not accepted in full or when the price is over par, that is, above the face value.

Subscription Offerings In a subscription offering, the Treasury announces the amount to be sold, the interest coupon on the issue, the price of the issue, the deposit requirements, and the method of alloting the tenders.

Investors enter subscriptions for the amount of securities they wish to purchase at the Treasury's given price and yield. Because investors may enter subscriptions totaling more than the amount offered by the Treasury, the allotment

[4] The expression "roll over" refers to the process of offering new bonds in exchange for bonds which are about to mature. Under this method, the investor can exchange the old securities for the same face amount of the new securities.

procedure becomes important for limiting the size of the issue. Allotments can be made by awarding a percentage of the amount subscribed by each tender or by setting a maximum dollar amount to be accepted for each tender.

Exchange Sales Exchange sales offer holders of selected outstanding issues the right to turn in their securities for the same face amount of a new issue on which an interest rate is set prior to the sale. Holders of eligible securities who do not wish to invest in the new issue may sell their "right" to the new issue to other investors or redeem maturing securities for cash. Because exchange sales merely refund outstanding securities but do not provide new funds (and in the case of cash redemptions result in a net paydown), the Treasury began to use alternative sales techniques when cash needs rose in the 1970s, and exchange offerings were discontinued with the February 1973 refunding.

Agency Issues

Agency issues are a heterogeneous group of bonds available in a variety of amounts and maturity periods. Unlike those for treasury bonds, methods and terms of financing agency issues vary so much from one agency to another that there is no consistent method of financing them.

Direct Purchase of New Government Issues

Generally, commercial banks and brokerage houses charge a commission of approximately $30 for handling each sale of new government issues. Investors can avoid this commission charge by purchasing the issues directly from a Federal Reserve Bank or from the Treasury. Direct bids on government bonds are noncompetitive; the investor must commit himself to purchasing these securities at the average rate set by bids on all the securities sold on that day.

Applications for purchasing new government securities can be made either in person or by mail. If an application is mailed, the maturity date of the desired issues should be clearly specified, and the order must be postmarked by midnight of the day prior to the auction. All bids require a deposit of at least 5 percent of the intended purchase.

Although the direct purchase of government securities is cheaper, it can nevertheless be cumbersome. Because treasury bills are auctioned every week, it is difficult to purchase them by mail, and investors frequently have to purchase them in person. Although notes and bonds can be purchased by mail, they cannot be sold in that manner. Investors intending to sell government securities must request the Federal Reserve to transfer the securities to a broker for resale; the broker, in turn, completes the transaction in the secondary market for a small fee.

Further details concerning the purchase of government securities can be obtained by calling the Treasury (202-376-0271) or by sending for the publication, "U.S. Securities Available to Investors" (PD 800-A) from the Bureau of the Public Debt, Securities Transaction Branch, Room 2134, U.S. Treasury Building, Washington, D.C., 20226.

An agency issue may be created when a federal agency enters the market to borrow long-term funds. Some agencies—like the Government National Mortgage Association (Ginnie Mae)—enter the capital market quite frequently, whereas the capital needs of others—like the Export–Import Bank—are limited.

Investors are lured to agency issues rather than treasury securities because the perceived small degree of default risk associated with the agency issues is compensated for by their higher yield. For instance, if a particular treasury note yields 8.8 percent, a comparable agency issue may return as much as, say, 9.6 percent.

An investor can buy an agency issue from any stockbroker or through a bank. Investors pay a fee of about $18.75 for a $5,000 buy; this fee may rise to $31.25 for a $50,000 purchase. However, in selling an agency issue, an investor would do better at a firm that makes a secondary market in government bonds than at a neighborhood broker or bank.

Although the liquidity of agency issues is not as high as that of treasury bonds, it is fairly good. However, in selling an agency issue, an investor may suffer a price differential,[5] although the loss is usually limited to no more than $60 on a $25,000 sale.

Bond Valuation Model

Alternative Decision Model

Now that the investment characteristics and techniques of financing of government bonds and agency issues have been discussed, it is appropriate to ask: How should an investor select between the different types of treasury and agency securities being traded on the market? Normally, this question can be answered by using the Basic Decision Model presented in Chapter 6. However, for reasons that will follow, that model is not directly applicable in this case. Therefore, an alternative selection process needs to be developed.

Selected Investment Features

The selected investment features of bonds were presented in Table 7–1. Treasury bills are backed by the full faith and credit, including the ability to tax, of the United States. Consequently, for these securities there is no risk of default, because the federal government is not expected to renege on its promise to meet its debt obligations. The liquidity risk is also barely present,[6] because the daily volume and variety of transactions in treasury bills are so large that an investor is assured of being able to complete a trade almost instantaneously. Because

[5] A price differential refers to a price concession that an investor must make in order to liquidate a security.

[6] In the case of treasury bills, the bid–ask spread does exist; however, it is only about $\frac{1}{32}$ of a point and does not represent a significant liquidity risk.

treasury bills are not subject to call provisions, the callability risk is also non-existent. In addition, because treasury bills are short-term in nature, their interest rate risk is almost negligible, and they carry no maturity risk. For these reasons, treasury bills are called "safe" investments.

Occupying the second position on the list of safe investments are treasury notes and bonds. Like treasury bills, these issues do not carry default or significant liquidity risks. They are, however, subject to inflation risk, and, because all notes and bonds are issued on a long-term basis, are subject to both interest rate and maturity risks. Also, some treasury bonds carry callability risk.[7]

Agency issues are a close third on the safe investment list. Basically, they carry the same risks as treasury notes and bonds. However, because they are backed by the credit of the U.S. government only *indirectly*, agency issues are theoretically assumed to carry a small degree of default risk.

These facts overlook one important aspect of government bonds which should be carefully spelled out. Treasury bills are generally considered as perfectly safe, *short-term* savings instruments; whereas treasury notes, bonds and agency issues are treated as safe, *long-term* savings instruments. Furthermore, the government bond market is assumed to be the most efficient segment of the capital market. This implies that the present discounted values of government bonds are identical with, or at least close to, their market prices. For these reasons, investors in government bonds do not apply the Basic Decision Model to identify the undervalued and overvalued bonds. Instead, investors assume that these bonds are *appropriately valued* and make their investment decisions by treating these bonds as safe, short- or long-term investments.[8]

Determination of Yield

Although the yield for corporate bonds is calculated by using the present value formula, the market yields for various types of government securities must be obtained by different means.

Yield Without Tax Considerations

Treasury Bills Because treasury bills are discount issues[9] and typically mature in less than one year, their yields are not *directly* comparable with other bonds.

[7] Some treasury bonds are callable during a specified period, usually five to ten years prior to maturity. For example, the $8\frac{1}{2}$ percent bonds of 1994–99 mature in 1999, but can be called at par value on any scheduled interest date beginning in 1994. The primary purpose of the call feature is to give the Treasury more flexibility in new financing near the maturity date. If an investor believes a callable issue will be redeemed before maturity, an expected holding period yield can be computed in place of the yield to maturity, as discussed in Chapter 6.

[8] Government bond yields will be compared with yields on riskier bonds in Chapter 8.

[9] A discount issue is a security that does not pay interest on a regular basis. Instead, the investor purchases the security at a price below the face value and receives the face value on maturity. The difference between the face value and the purchase price is the interest. For example, if an investor pays $9,700 for a treasury bill today and receives $10,000 on maturity three months later. the interest over the three-month period is $300. All treasury bills are issued on a discount basis.

Consequently, a method must be found to calculate the treasury bill yield comparable to the yield of other bonds.

Treasury bill prices are stated on the basis of 100, with no more than three decimals (for example, 97.472). The annual rate of return associated with the price is calculated on the *bank discount* basis as follows:

$$\frac{\text{Par} - \text{Price}}{\text{Par}} \times \frac{360}{\text{Days to Maturity}}$$

For example, a 182-day bill priced at 97.472 would yield an annual rate of 5.00 percent:

$$\frac{100 - 97.472}{100} \times \frac{360}{182} = .0500 \text{ (or } 5.00\%)$$

The bank discount yield is not strictly comparable to other bond yields because it is calculated on a 360-day basis. The formula for converting the bank discount rate to the equivalent coupon rate is:

$$\frac{\text{Bank Discount Rate} \times 365}{360 - \left(\begin{matrix}\text{Bank Discount} \\ \text{Rate}\end{matrix} \times \begin{matrix}\text{Days to} \\ \text{Maturity}\end{matrix}\right)}$$

Therefore, for this example, the equivalent coupon rate is 5.2 percent:

$$\frac{.05 \times 365}{360 - (.05 \times 182)} = \frac{18.25}{350.9} = .0520 \text{ (or } 5.2\%)$$

The same result could be obtained from an appropriate conversion table. For instance, Table 7–5 confirms that, for a 182-day treasury bill with a bank discount rate of 5 percent, the equivalent coupon rate is 5.2 percent.

This discussion on the bank discount yield and the equivalent coupon rate on a treasury bill has been presented purely for illustrative purposes. In both initial offerings and in secondary-market trading, treasury bill yields are quoted on a true bill annualized yield basis. For instance, on June 11, 1979, the following quotation appeared in the newspaper:

Nov 19 . . . . . 8.16 7.94 +2 8.35

The date, November 19, indicates the maturity of the bill. The 8.16 indicates the discount rate which results from the prices dealers will pay to buy these bills (called the bid price) from investors, and the 7.94 represents the discount rate which results from the prices at which dealers will sell these bills (called the ask price) to investors. The difference between the bid and ask prices is the dealer's compensation for trading in treasury bills.

Table 7–5 **Discount Yields Converted into Bond Equivalent Yields**

Discount Yield, %	Bond equivalent yields for maturity, %			
	30 Days	91 Days	182 Days	364 Days
2.00	2.03	2.04	2.05	2.07
2.50	2.54	2.55	2.57	2.60
3.00	3.05	3.07	3.09	3.11
3.50	3.56	3.58	3.61	3.65
4.00	4.07	4.10	4.14	4.18
4.50	4.58	4.61	4.67	4.73
5.00	5.09	5.13	5.20	5.27
5.50	5.60	5.65	5.74	5.82
6.00	6.11	6.18	6.27	6.38
6.50	6.63	6.70	6.81	6.94
7.00	7.14	7.22	7.36	7.50
7.50	7.65	7.75	7.90	8.07
8.00	8.17	8.28	8.45	8.82
8.50	8.68	8.81	9.01	9.43
9.00	9.19	9.34	9.56	10.04

The +2 in the quotation implies that the bid price of the November 19 treasury bills changed by 2 basis points (100 basis points = 1 percent) from the bid price of the previous day, or from an 8.14 percent bid discount rate to 8.16 percent bid discount rate.

The last number in the quotation, 8.35, is the most important from an investor's point of view. It is the equivalent coupon rate, annualized on a 365-day yearly basis. Put differently, had an investor received a discount rate of 7.94 percent for the November 19 bills, the annual yield from this investment would have been 8.35 percent.

Treasury Notes and Bonds Treasury notes and bonds are not discount issues. Their prices are quoted in percentages of $1,000 par value, and fluctuations in their prices are expressed in $\frac{1}{32}$nds of a point. A typical price quotation for a treasury bond follows:

Feb '87, 9s . . . . . 91.30 92.7 +.1 10.59

This quotation represents a treasury note with a 9 percent coupon, maturing in February of 1987. The dealer's bid quotation was 91.30, or $91\frac{30}{32}$, equal to $919.38 per $1,000 par value, and the offered quotation was 92.70, or $92\frac{7}{32}$, equal to $922.19 per $1,000 par value. The +.1 shows that the bid price increased by $\frac{1}{32}$ of a point over the bid price prevailing at the close of the previous day. The last number, 10.59, reveals that had an investor purchased the note at the offered price of $922.19, he would have received a yield to maturity of 10.59 percent, which would have been higher than the coupon rate (9.00 percent) because the market price of the bond was lower than its par value.

Agency Issues The quotation of agency issues is similar to that of treasury notes and bonds. For example, the *Wall Street Journal* published the following quotation for one of the securities listed under the Federal Home Loan Bank category:

May '87 7.60 5–87 83.20 84.8 10.77

This issue, carrying a coupon of 7.60 percent, was due to mature in May 1987, or 5–87. The bid price was 83.20, or $83\frac{20}{32}$, which equaled $836.25 per $1,000 par value. The ask price was 84.8, or $84\frac{8}{32}$, which equaled $842.50 per $1,000 par value. The 10.77, or 10.77 percent, represented an investor's yield to maturity if she had purchased this agency issue at the ask price and held the issue until maturity.

Yield with Tax Considerations

All U.S. government securities, whether bills, notes, or bonds, and most agency issues, are subject to federal income taxes; however, the interest income from these securities is exempt from state and local taxes. Consequently, a way must be found to make returns on government securities comparable to those on fully taxable bonds.

The relationship between fully taxable securities and state and local tax-exempt government securities can be expressed in terms of the following formula:

$$\begin{matrix}\text{Equivalent Fully}\\ \text{Taxable Yield}\end{matrix} = \frac{\text{Government Security Yield}}{1 - \begin{bmatrix}\text{Marginal} & & \text{Marginal}\\ \text{State Tax} & + & \text{Local Tax}\\ \text{Rate} & & \text{Rate}\end{bmatrix}} \qquad (7\text{–}1)$$

Assume a married couple is interested in purchasing treasury bonds selling at par with a 7 percent coupon. Their total taxable income puts them into the (1) 42 percent marginal federal tax bracket, (2) 6 percent state tax bracket, and (3) 3.5 percent marginal city tax bracket.[10] The interest on the treasury bills would be subject only to the marginal federal tax rate of 42 percent, giving them an after-federal tax return of 4.06 percent [.07 × (1 − .42)]. If they wish to receive the same after-tax return from a fully taxable security selling at par, the security would have to have a 7.73 percent coupon:

$$\begin{matrix}\text{Equivalent Fully}\\ \text{Taxable Yield}\end{matrix} = \frac{.07}{1 - (.06 + .035)} = \frac{.07}{.905} = 7.73\%$$

[10] See Chapter 16 (pp. 689–92) for a discussion of marginal tax brackets.

There is, however, an important limitation to Equation 7–1. The tax-exempt feature of government securities applies only to interest income, not to capital gains. Consequently, the equation expresses the relationship between the yields to maturity on government and fully taxable securities when they are selling at, or very near, their par value. If securities were trading at prices significantly different from their par values, the tax effect on the capital gains and losses that will be realized at maturity would have to be taken into account. In such cases, the returns from these securities can be compared on an after-tax basis by using Equation 6–5 (p. 194).

Treasury Bill Versus Other Short-term Investments

Investor H, who lives in New York State, is considering investing $10,000 in one of three short-term instruments—a six-month treasury bill, a six-month money market certificate from a bank, or shares in a money market fund. In early 1979, the following yields were quoted:

1. Six-month treasury bills (discount basis): 9.457%;
2. Money market certificate: 9.457%;
3. Money market fund (approximate): 10.10%

The methods for calculating Investor H's before- and after-tax yields are explained below.

Before-tax Yield

The before-tax yield on the money market certificate and the money market fund are as stated above. However, the six-month treasury bill is quoted on a discount basis: Because the 182-day bill will sell at the discounted price of $9,521.90, it will have a bank discount yield of 9.457 percent:

$$\frac{100 - 95.219}{100} \times \frac{360}{182} = .09457 \text{ (or } 9.457\%)$$

On maturity, the investor will receive $10,000, of which $478.10 will be interest income. The 9.457 percent bank discount rate is not strictly comparable to the other yields because it is calculated on a 360-day basis. Converting the discount rate to a 365-day basis, the before-tax yield is 10.07 percent:

$$\frac{(.09457)(365)}{360 - (.09457)(182)} = .1007 \text{ (or } 10.07\%)$$

After-tax Yield

For Investor H, of course, the after-tax yield is most important. The tax features are specified in Table 7–A. Note that while all three instruments are subject to federal income tax, only treasury bills are exempt from state and local taxes. Assuming

SECTION 2 MUNICIPAL BONDS

An Overview

General Remarks

In Section 1, federal government securities and agency issues were analyzed. Section 2 is devoted to municipal bonds. These differ from government bonds in at least two important respects. First, unlike government bonds, municipal bonds carry varying degrees of default and liquidity risks. Second, the interest from municipal bonds is always exempt from federal income taxes, and can be

Table 7–A **Investment Alternatives**

Investment Instrument	Comparable Before-tax Yield	Applicable Rate	After-tax Yield
Treasury Bill	10.07%	Federal 30%	7.049%
Money Market Certificate	9.457%	Federal 30% State 15%	5.626%*
Money Market Fund	10.10%	Federal 30% State 15%	6.009%*

* It is assumed that Investor H itemizes his deductions for federal tax calculations, and deducts the state income tax from taxable income. Under this assumption the after-tax yield for the money market certificate would be computed as: (.09457)(1 − .30)(1 − .15) = 5.626%. For the money market fund the computation would be (.1010)(1 − .30)(1 − .15) = 6.009%.

Investor H is in the 30 percent marginal federal tax bracket, by investing in this treasury bill he would earn an after-tax yield of 7.049 [10.07% × (1 − .30)] percent.

Interest income from money market certificates and money market funds are taxable by New York State, where the state income tax rate can go as high as 15 percent, and even higher for residents of New York City. If Investor H is in the 15 percent marginal state tax bracket, he would receive an after-tax yield of, respectively, 5.63 percent and 6.01 percent from the six-month certificate and money market fund. Clearly, the treasury bill provides Investor H with the highest after-tax return.

Investor H also notes that, because he is in the 15 percent marginal state tax bracket, the money market certificate or money market fund would have to yield 11.85 percent to provide the same after-tax return.

$$\text{Equivalent Fully Taxable Yield} = \frac{.1007}{(1 - .15)} = \frac{.1007}{.85} = 11.85\%$$

Figure 7–2 **State and Local Governments**
Amount Outstanding; End of Year, 1946–51; End of Quarter, 1952–79

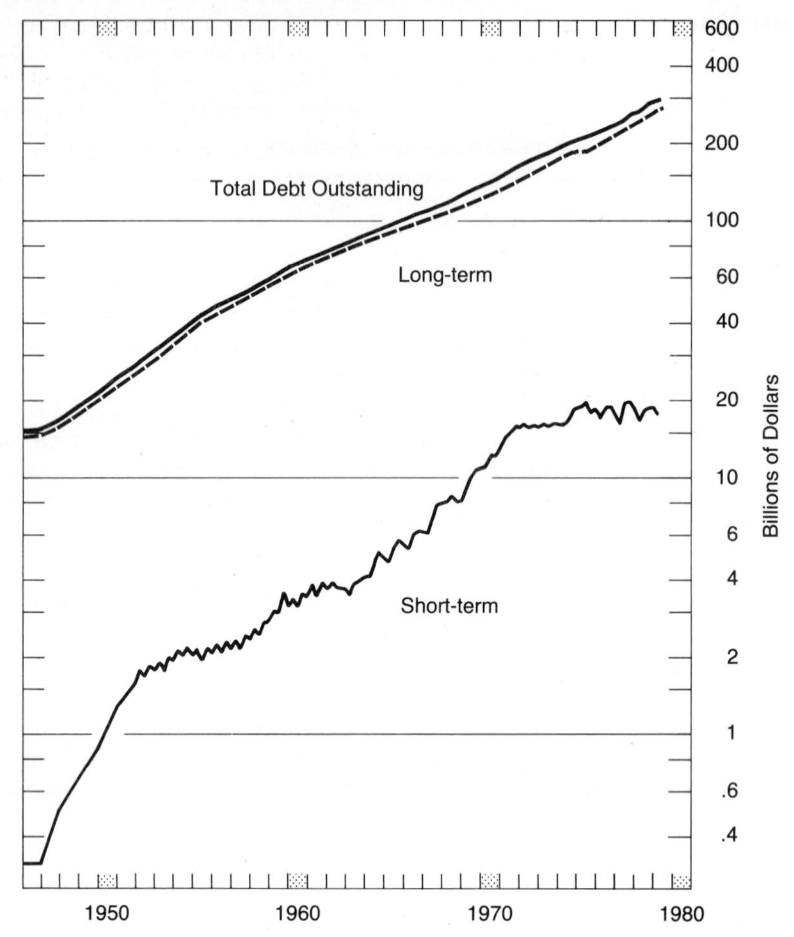

SOURCE: *1979 Historical Chart Book,* Board of Governors of the Federal Reserve System, p. 57.

exempt from state and local taxes as well.[11] This second feature makes them an attractive investment for many investors, especially those in high income tax brackets.

Municipal bonds are created when state and local governments must borrow funds. Figure 7–2 presents the growth in state and local debt during 1945–79.

[11] The exemption of municipal bonds from state taxes applies only to the taxes of the state issuing the bonds, or, in the case of municipals issued by local governments and state and local agencies, to the taxes of the state in which the local government or agency is located.

Two recent developments have had opposite effects on state and local debt and, therefore, on the growth of municipal bonds. First, the Tax Reform Act of 1976 made tax-exempt investments more attractive. It raised the maximum tax rate on income from savings, corporate bonds, stocks, and so on, to 70 percent. In addition, Congress removed many of the traditional tax shelters, such as movie and cattle deals. These changes made municipal bonds relatively more attractive.

The tax revolt in the wake of California's Proposition 13 had a negative impact on the municipal bond market. Although the full impact of the revolt will not be known for several years, bond analysts believe that such limitations on property taxes as those imposed by Proposition 13 will act as a strong constraint on state and local debt. Nevertheless, because an increasing number of cities and states are facing potential financial strains, it is reasonable to assume that the municipal bond market will continue to be active.

Over 20,000 separate governmental bodies have issued more than 50,000 separate municipal bond issues. Each serial bond issue may be viewed as perhaps 20 or more separate bond issues, each maturing in a different year. So, in effect, at any one time there are probably more than a million different issues of municipal bonds outstanding. The city of Truth or Consequences, New Mexico, for instance, has about 40 issues by itself. By far, the largest dollar amounts of municipal bonds stem from the obligations of municipalities. Smaller issuers include counties, school districts, townships, and special bodies such as park districts and sewer agencies. Municipal bonds are also issued to finance long-term projects such as bridges and highways.

Types of Municipal Bonds

Table 7–6 presents a summary of the various types of municipal bonds. These bonds were introduced in Chapter 2. A brief review of each type follows.

General Obligation Bonds

Known as GOs, general obligation bonds are generally considered the best credit risks because they are secured by the unlimited authority to tax held by cities and states. A prospective investor in GOs can find municipal bonds backed by state governments, school districts, municipalities, and county governments.

A variation of GOs is the group of bonds issued by agencies of the state or municipality. Although these bonds are not general obligations of the state or municipality, they carry the *implied* backing of those units of government. If an agency of the state issues a general obligation bond, investors generally assume that the state will not allow one of its agencies to default on payment of interest or principal, even though the state has no legal mandate to support the bonds.

But how strong is this implied backing? Actually, the implied backing has no legal precedent and has never been tested in the courts. During the first

Table 7–6

Type of Bond	Description	Sampling of Recent Issues: Security	S&P Rating	Recent Price	Yield to Maturity Percent
General obligation	Known as GOs, these bonds were long considered the best credit risks because they are secured by the cities' and the states' unlimited authority to tax. But since New York City's near-default, many GOs, especially in the Northeast, have lost their allure. Investors fear that community debt loads are becoming too huge, and there are practical limits to taxing powers. Also, information about municipal finances has often proved both scanty and unreliable.	Illinois 5s due 1997	AAA	99	5.1%
		New York State $5\frac{1}{2}$s due 1997	AA	97	5.75
Revenue	These bonds are secured by particular sources of income, from cigarette taxes to rental payments. "Revs" have become popular with investors because yields are usually fatter than on the GOs and because financial statements are more complete. But investors must worry about what could go awry with the flow of income available to pay interest and principal. Some examples:				
Water and power	These are usually backed by long-term leases or contracts with utility companies. Revenues could suffer if a utility cannot get rate increases from its power commission.	Washington Public Power Supply System Nuclear Project No. 2 5.70s due 2012	AAA	Par	5.7
Turnpike, bridge, and tunnel	These are secured by tolls. Two roads, the West Virginia Turnpike and Chicago's Calumet Skyway, have been in default because of insufficient traffic. Toll-related bonds suffered when investors feared that rising gasoline prices would restrict auto travel.	New Jersey Turnpike Authority 6s due 2014	A	Par	6.0
Hospital	These are popular with many investors because more than 90% of the revenues usually comes from Medicare and Medicaid payments. Other investors worry about hospital management and about malpractice suits. Thus, hospital bonds have a slightly higher yield.	Tulsa Industrial Authority First Mortgage Hospital $6\frac{1}{2}$s due 2007	A	Par	6.5
Housing Finance Authority	These are issued by local agencies, principally to build middle-income housing but sometimes college dormitories, mental health facilities, and nursing homes as well. Security is usually rental payments, but deals can vary widely. HFA bonds are not to be confused with public housing authority bonds, which are all rated AAA because they are federally guaranteed.	Minnesota Housing Finance Authority $6\frac{1}{4}$s due 2020	AA	Par	6.25

Table 7–6 *(cont.)*

Type of Bond	Description	Sampling of Recent Issues: Security	S&P Rating	Recent Price	Yield to Maturity Percent
Airport	These are secured largely by leases to airlines. As with toll road bonds, these dropped during the energy crisis, when investors feared that fuel costs would jeopardize the airlines' ability to meet lease payments.	Atlanta Airport Series 1977 6.3s due 2007	BBB+	Par	6.3
Sports complex	These are secured largely by income from athletic teams and other sports events, but ticket sales might decline dramatically in poor seasons.	New Jersey Sports & Exposition Authority $7\frac{1}{2}$s due 2009	BBB	108	6.88
Industrial revenue	A hybrid of corporate and municipal bonds, these bonds are issued by a municipality or authority to build facilities for a company whose lease payments cover payments of interest and principal. In effect, the corporation puts its credit behind the deal and gets financing at tax-exempt rates, which are lower than taxable corporate rates. A few years ago Congress limited such issues to $5 million, except in the case of port facilities and pollution control facilities, which now account for the bulk of the new issues. Highly popular with investors who find corporations easier to analyze than municipalities.	Valdez (Alaska) Marine Terminal (Sohio and British Petroleum 6s due 2007	AA	Par	6.0
		River Rouge (Mich.) Pollution Control (Detroit Edison) $6\frac{5}{8}$s due 1997	BBB	$101\frac{1}{2}$	6.4
Tax, revenue, or bond anticipation notes	Known as TANs, RANs, and BANs, these are the tax-exempt market's version of commercial paper. They are issued in expectation of monies coming in, mature in 30 days to a year, and are low-yielding. Usually they are grabbed up by commercial banks, but some trade publicly.	Oneida County (N.Y.) TAN 3.09s due 12/30/77	—	100.18	2.7

SOURCE: *Business Week*, July 25, 1977, p. 128.

quarter of 1975, the New York Urban Development Corporation, an agency of New York State, defaulted on some of its notes. Investors were anxious to discover whether the implied backing of New York State had any basis in fact, or whether it was just a myth perpetuated by the issuing authority to make the bonds more saleable as general obligation bonds than as revenue bonds. However, the corporation subsequently honored its obligation, and the issue of implied state backing was never clarified.

Revenue Bonds

Revenue bonds are secured by particular sources of income, such as cigarette taxes or rental payments. As described in Table 7–6, revenue bonds include industrial revenue bonds, Housing Finance Authority bonds, hospital bonds, and so on. "REVs" have become popular with investors because yields on them are usually higher than on the GOs. Investors in revenue bonds, however, often worry about the possible interruption of the flow of income available to pay interest and principal.

Tax, Revenue, and Bond Anticipation Notes

Known as TANs, RANs, and BANs, these notes are the tax-exempt market's version of commercial paper. They are issued in expectation of an inflow of money, mature in 30 days to a year, and have a low yield. They are usually held by commercial banks, although some are traded publicly as well.

Investment Characteristics

Tax Exemption

As previously mentioned, municipal obligations have special exemptions from federal income taxes and quite often from state and local income taxes as well. Interest on the obligations of states, cities, and their political subdivisions is free from federal income taxes. In addition, most states do not tax interest on their own obligations or on those of subdivisions within the state. For example, in 1979 a ten-year Baa-rated municipal bond had a yield of around 6.5 percent, as compared with 5.5 percent for AAA issues. The equivalent taxable yields (assuming the bonds were selling at par) were 12.8 and 10.8 percent, respectively, for people in the 49 percent income tax bracket, and 10.3 and 8.7 percent in the 37 percent tax bracket. Because tax exemption is one of the main features of municipal bonds, it will be discussed in detail later in the chapter.

Safety

The expectation that principal and interest payments will be made is one of the key investment characteristics of municipal bonds. As previously observed, because general obligation bonds are backed by the full faith, credit, and taxing power of the issuing authorities, they are as safe as the issuing authorities themselves. Revenue bonds issued to finance projects designed to provide essential services are also considered relatively safe investments. Historically, with the exception of industrial revenue bonds, the risk associated with municipal bonds has been microscopic. In investment terminology, delaying an interest payment is called a technical default, whereas skipping the payment altogether is called a substantive default. Over the 21 years from 1954 to 1975, only 18 new bankruptcy cases were filed, and most ended with little or no permanent loss to creditors. In fact, default created permanent capital losses of only $10 million—only .001 percent of the outstanding amount. It should be mentioned, however, that the undeniable safety of municipal bonds has been challenged in recent years.

Diversity and Flexibility

In addition to their tax-exempt feature, two of the major attractions of municipal bonds are their diversity and flexibility. There are more municipal bonds than all the other types of bonds combined. As previously observed, over 20,000 separate government bodies have more than 50,000 separate issues, an aggregate of over a million different serial bonds outstanding.

Municipal bonds also offer investors a wide variety of choices with respect to geographical location, types of communities, and economic situations. Most municipal bonds are issued with *serial* maturities. This means that a portion of the total bonds issued matures each year until the entire issue is retired. For example, buyers of a certain issue can choose from bonds maturing every year of the issue's life, which might range anywhere from one to 50 years. Coupon rates on the bonds would of course vary, depending on the different maturities.

Financing Techniques

Municipal bonds are sold to the public by underwriting syndicates consisting of municipal dealer firms, brokerage firms, investment banking firms, and commercial banks. Bonds are sold by two methods: competitive bidding and negotiation. Under the competitive bidding method, the municipality invites bids and accepts the highest bid from among those submitted. Under the negotiated method, underwriting syndicates negotiate a coupon rate for the bonds.

There are two forms of municipal bonds—coupon and registered. A coupon bond is transferable by delivery to bearer; a registered bond is registered on the books of the municipality and title can only be transferred by endorsement. For coupon bonds, the coupon rate is shown on the attached coupon, which the holder detaches and presents for payment of the interest. For registered bonds, the coupon rate is shown on the bond itself, and the interest payment is sent directly to the registered holder by the paying agent.

Table 7–7 **Sample Page from a Basis Book 6% Coupon**

Yield	Months to Maturity 34-6	35-0	35-6	36-0	36-6	37-0
4.00	137.25	137.50	137.74	137.98	138.22	138.65
4.20	132.64	132.85	133.06	133.26	133.46	133.65
4.40	128.26	128.44	128.61	128.77	128.94	129.10
4.60	124.10	124.24	124.38	124.51	124.65	124.78
4.80	120.13	120.25	120.36	120.47	120.57	120.68
5.00	116.36	116.45	116.54	116.62	116.70	116.78
5.20	112.77	112.83	112.90	112.96	113.02	113.08
5.40	109.34	109.39	109.44	109.48	109.52	109.56
5.60	106.08	106.11	106.14	106.16	106.19	106.22
5.80	102.97	102.98	103.00	103.01	103.02	103.03
6.00	100.00	100.00	100.00	100.00	100.00	100.00
6.10	98.57	98.56	98.55	98.55	98.54	98.54
6.20	97.17	97.15	97.14	97.13	97.12	97.11
6.30	95.80	95.78	95.76	95.75	95.73	95.72
6.40	94.46	94.44	94.42	94.40	94.38	94.36
6.50	93.15	93.13	93.10	93.08	93.05	93.03
6.60	91.88	91.85	91.82	91.79	91.76	91.73
6.70	90.63	90.59	90.56	90.53	90.49	90.46
6.80	89.41	89.37	89.33	89.29	89.26	89.23
6.90	88.21	88.17	88.13	88.09	88.05	88.02
7.00	87.04	87.00	86.96	86.91	86.87	86.83
7.10	85.90	85.85	85.81	85.76	85.72	85.68
7.20	84.79	84.74	84.69	84.64	84.59	84.55
7.30	83.69	83.64	83.59	83.54	83.49	83.45
7.40	82.62	82.57	82.52	82.46	82.41	82.37
7.50	81.58	81.52	81.47	81.41	81.36	81.31
7.60	80.55	80.49	80.44	80.38	80.33	80.28
7.70	79.55	79.49	79.43	79.38	79.32	79.27
7.80	78.57	78.51	78.45	78.39	78.34	78.28
7.90	77.61	77.55	77.49	77.43	77.37	77.32
8.00	76.67	76.61	76.54	76.48	76.43	76.37
8.10	75.75	75.68	75.62	75.56	75.50	75.45
8.20	74.85	74.78	74.72	74.66	74.60	74.54
8.30	73.96	73.90	73.83	73.77	73.71	73.66
8.40	73.10	73.03	72.97	72.91	72.85	72.79
8.50	72.25	72.18	72.12	72.06	72.00	71.94
8.60	71.42	71.35	71.29	71.23	71.17	71.11
8.70	70.61	70.54	70.48	70.41	70.35	70.29
8.80	69.81	69.74	69.68	69.61	69.55	69.50
8.90	69.03	68.96	68.90	68.83	68.77	68.72
9.00	68.27	68.20	68.13	68.07	68.01	67.95
9.10	67.52	67.45	67.38	67.32	67.26	67.20
9.20	66.78	66.71	66.65	66.58	66.52	66.46
9.30	66.06	65.99	65.92	65.86	65.80	65.74
9.40	65.35	65.28	65.22	65.15	65.10	65.04

Table 7–7 (*cont.*) **Sample Page from a Basis Book 6% Coupon**

Yield	34-6	35-0	35-6	36-0	36-6	37-0
			Months to Maturity			
9.50	64.66	64.59	64.52	64.46	64.40	64.35
9.60	63.98	63.91	63.84	63.78	63.72	63.67
9.70	63.31	63.24	63.18	63.12	63.06	63.00
9.80	62.65	62.59	62.52	62.46	62.40	62.35
9.90	62.01	61.94	61.88	61.82	61.76	61.71
10.00	61.38	61.31	61.25	61.19	61.14	61.08
10.20	60.15	60.09	60.03	59.97	59.91	59.86
10.40	58.97	58.91	58.85	58.79	58.74	58.69
10.60	57.83	57.77	57.71	57.66	57.60	57.55
10.80	56.74	56.67	56.62	56.56	56.51	56.46
11.00	55.68	55.62	55.56	55.51	55.46	55.41
11.20	54.65	54.60	54.54	54.49	54.44	54.39
11.40	53.67	53.61	53.56	53.51	53.46	53.41
11.60	52.71	52.66	52.61	52.56	52.51	52.47
11.80	51.79	51.74	51.69	51.64	51.60	51.55
12.00	50.90	50.85	50.80	50.75	50.71	50.67

Basic Decision Model in Action

The Key Variables

The two key variables in the Basic Decision Model for municipal bonds are the yield and the appropriate discount rate, or the investor's minimum required rate of return. Once the values of the two variables have been determined, the model can be used to select municipal bonds.

Determination of Yield

Most municipal bonds are quoted on a yield-to-maturity basis, rather than a percentage-of-par basis. Instead of being quoted as 99½, as might be the case with corporate, federal agency, or U.S. government bonds, the investor might see 5 percent coupon municipal bonds with 12 years to maturity quoted at 5.05 percent. The yield to maturity of this bond can be calculated by using the Bond Valuation Model. However, for this purpose, it is more convenient to use a set of tables, popularly known as a *basis book*, available in most brokerage houses, banks, and libraries. Tables in a basis book combine four factors: time, coupon rate, price, and yield. Given any three of these factors, the fourth can be easily determined.

Table 7–7 reproduces a sample page from a basis book relating to a municipal bond which carries a coupon rate of 6 percent. This table reveals that if a 6 percent bond is due to mature in 36 months and is selling for 55.51 or $555.10, it has a yield to maturity of 11.00 percent. Similarly, if an investor wishes to obtain a yield of 7.00 percent from a municipal bond which has a 6 percent coupon and is due to mature in 35 months, the bond must be purchased for 87.00 or $870.00.

After-tax Yield

A typical quotation of a bond price is "City of Detroit, Michigan, 6 of '95 at 6.05%." This means that bonds issued by the City of Detroit, Michigan, carrying a 6.0 percent coupon and maturing in 1995, are offering a yield to maturity of 6.05 percent. The interest income from the bond is exempt from federal income taxes, and because the bond is selling very near its par value,[12] there will be no significant capital gain realized at maturity. Consequently, the 6.05 percent yield to maturity will also be the approximate yield to maturity of the bond after federal taxes (and possibly state and local taxes, depending on the state of residence of the investor).

However, if a municipal bond is selling at a significant discount from par value, at maturity a capital gain will be realized. Because the capital gain is not exempt from tax, the after-tax yield to maturity will not equal the quoted yield to maturity. In such cases, Equation 6–5 (p. 194) can be used to account for the capital gains tax and derive an after-tax return for the bond.

Equivalent Fully Taxable Yield

Many investors find that a municipal bond's equivalent fully taxable yield is a useful measure of the bond's relative attractiveness. For example, in the case of the Detroit, Michigan bond, it was not obvious from the quotation that the yield of 6.05 percent is not directly comparable to the taxable yields of other securities. Simple formulas can be used to determine the rate of return that must be earned on a fully taxable issue, such as a corporate bond, so that its after-tax yield equals the yield of a municipal bond.

The following equations express the relationship between the yield to maturity on tax-exempt and taxable securities, but *only* when they are selling at or near par value.

Federal Tax Exemption Because the interest paid on municipal bonds is always exempt from federal income taxes, the following equation can be used to calculate the equivalent fully taxable yield:

$$\begin{array}{c}\text{Equivalent}\\ \text{Fully Taxable Yield}\end{array} = \frac{\text{Tax-exempt Yield}}{1 - \begin{array}{c}\text{Marginal Federal}\\ \text{Tax Rate}\end{array}} \qquad (7\text{–}2)$$

[12] Remember that when a bond sells at par value, its coupon rate will equal its yield to maturity.

For example, if an investor's marginal tax bracket is 43 percent, the equivalent fully taxable yield of a 6 percent tax-free bond is 10.53 percent:

$$\text{Equivalent Fully Taxable Yield} = \frac{.06}{1 - .43} = 10.53\%$$

Fortunately, there are convenient tables that convert tax-free yields into taxable yields for investors in varying marginal federal income tax brackets. Table 7–8 confirms that the equivalent fully taxable yield for a 6 percent tax-free bond is 10.53 percent.

Thus far, the investor's current marginal tax rate has been used as the basis for calculating equivalent fully taxable yields. However, it is important to realize that often an investor's income and marginal tax rate will change over the life of the bond. If changes in the investor's marginal tax rate are taken into account, equivalent fully taxable yields may be higher than those indicated by Table 7–8.

Suppose that in 1979 an investor filing a single return had an income of $33,000, which put her in the 44 percent marginal federal income tax bracket (assume no state or local taxes). According to Table 7–8, for a 6 percent municipal bond, her equivalent fully taxable yield was 10.71 percent.

Table 7–8 **The Tax-free Edge of Municipal Bonds**

(Taxable income in thousands of dollars.) Based on tax tables effective beginning January 1, 1979.

Single Return		$15–18		$18–23		$23–28		$28–34	$34–41		$41–55	
Joint Return	$20–24		$24–29		$29–35		$35–45		$45–60	$60–85		$85–109
% Tax Bracket	**28**	**30**	**32**	**34**	**37**	**39**	**43**	**44**	**49**	**54**	**55**	**59**
Tax-exempt Yields												
4.00	5.56	5.71	5.88	6.06	6.35	6.56	7.02	7.14	7.84	8.70	8.89	9.76
4.50	6.25	6.43	6.62	6.82	7.14	7.38	7.89	8.04	8.82	9.78	10.00	10.98
5.00	6.94	7.14	7.35	7.58	7.94	8.20	8.77	8.93	9.80	10.87	11.11	12.20
5.50	7.64	7.86	8.09	8.33	8.73	9.02	9.65	9.82	10.78	11.96	12.22	13.41
6.00	8.33	8.57	8.82	9.09	9.52	9.84	10.53	10.71	11.76	13.04	13.33	14.63
6.50	9.03	9.29	9.56	9.85	10.32	10.66	11.40	11.61	12.75	14.13	14.44	15.85
7.00	9.72	10.00	10.29	10.61	11.11	11.48	12.28	12.50	13.73	15.22	15.56	17.07
7.50	10.42	10.71	11.03	11.36	11.90	12.30	13.16	13.39	14.71	16.30	16.67	18.29
8.00	11.11	11.43	11.76	12.12	12.70	13.11	14.04	14.29	15.68	17.39	17.78	19.51
8.50	11.81	12.14	12.50	12.88	13.49	13.93	14.91	15.18	16.67	18.48	18.89	20.73
9.00	12.50	12.88	13.24	13.64	14.29	14.75	15.79	16.07	17.65	19.57	20.00	21.95

SOURCE: "Investments for a Changing Economy," Merrill Lynch Pierce Fenner and Smith, Spring 1979, p. 15.

Now suppose that the rate of inflation was 8 percent and the investor received an increment in her salary which matched the inflation rate. Her 1980 taxable income of $35,640 would put her in the 49 percent tax bracket,[13] where the equivalent fully taxable yield on a 6 percent municipal bond would be 11.76 percent. If inflation persists and her taxable income continues to rise in future years, she will be subject to even higher tax rates. As a result, the equivalent fully taxable yield on the municipal bond will also continue to increase with each tax bracket jump (until her income reaches the highest bracket), making the municipal bond increasingly more attractive relative to bonds without the tax exemption.

State and Local Tax Exemptions The equivalent fully taxable yield of a municipal bond exempt from federal, state, and local taxes can be calculated by modifying Equation 7–2 in the following manner:

$$\begin{matrix}\text{Equivalent} \\ \text{Fully Taxable Yield}\end{matrix} = \frac{\text{Tax-exempt Yield}}{1 - \begin{bmatrix}\text{Marginal} & & \text{Marginal} & & \text{Marginal} \\ \text{Federal} & + & \text{State} & + & \text{Local} \\ \text{Tax Rate} & & \text{Tax Rate} & & \text{Tax Rate}\end{bmatrix}} \qquad (7\text{–}3)$$

If an investor's marginal tax rates are 42 percent, 5 percent, and 3 percent, respectively, for federal, state, and local levels, his equivalent fully taxable yield for a 6 percent municipal bond is 12 percent:

$$\begin{aligned}\begin{matrix}\text{Equivalent} \\ \text{Fully Taxable Yield}\end{matrix} &= \frac{.06}{1 - (.42 + .05 + .03)} \\ &= \frac{.06}{.50} \\ &= .120 \text{ (or } 12.0\%)\end{aligned}$$

Note that Table 7–8 has only a limited use. It can be used to find the equivalent taxable yield for fully tax-exempt bonds (as well as for bonds that are exempt from federal taxes only), but only if the sum of the marginal federal, state, and local tax rates is equal to the rate shown at the head of any of the columns in the table. In other cases, an investor must use Equation 7–3 for calculating the appropriate yield.

Determination of Appropriate Discount Rate

As previously mentioned, the appropriate discount rate is the sum of the risk-free real rate plus a risk premium representing the required compensation for the risk the investor is willing to assume by investing in a municipal bond.

[13] It is assumed that the tax rates in 1980 would remain unchanged.

The five types of risk associated with a municipal bond are interest rate, inflation, maturity, default, and liquidity risks.[14] Of these, the first three relate to all bonds, and have already been discussed in Chapter 6. The last two risks—the default risk and the liquidity risk—however, deserve special mention.

Default Risk

Basic Issues Because municipal bonds are not backed by the federal government, their safety is not as good as that of securities of the federal government. However, general obligation bonds are backed by the full faith, credit, and taxing power of the state or the local government. These bonds have an excellent record of paying interest and principal, even during the Depression. However, in recent years financial experts began to doubt whether some of the larger cities in the United States can continue to meet their debt obligations. Although this "crisis in confidence" is the result of a host of factors, it was precipitated in August 1975 by New York City's inability to float new bonds in order to redeem its maturing notes. The city's de facto default sent shock waves through the municipal bond market. In fact, this crisis, characteristically called "the New York effect," forced municipalities to issue new bonds at higher coupon rates.[15]

The current lack of confidence in general obligation bonds was not precipitated merely by New York City's default. At the heart of this turbulence are the serious fiscal problems of large cities in the United States. The rising costs of providing services, together with a contracting revenue base during recessionary periods, have created chronic budget deficits and resulted in borrowing on a massive scale. The progressively heavier debt burden, the ever-increasing cost of servicing the debt, and the regressive tax structure of the cities, have caused great concern over the safety of municipal bonds among financial analysts. In 1978, only two of the country's 25 leading cities—Houston and Dallas—had their bond ratings raised. Five cities—Cleveland, Detroit, New Orleans, Pittsburgh and St. Louis—had their ratings lowered, and Boston and Philadelphia were publicly ranked on the critical list. The city of Cleveland has already defaulted, and analysts speculate that at some future date other large cities will declare bankruptcy.

Revenue bonds issued to finance public works designed to provide essential services possess a high degree of safety. In contrast, bonds financed by revenues derived from such projects as toll bridges, toll roads, sporting complexes, and industrial works are often high risk investments. In fact, experience has shown that, whenever revenues from these types of projects have fallen short of their

---

[14] Some municipal bonds are callable at specified dates and prices, and occasionally the issuing authority must make payments into a sinking fund to periodically redeem bonds. In such cases the investor may demand a callability risk premium, as discussed in Chapter 6. Further analysis of callability risk and sinking funds is provided in Chapter 8; although that discussion deals with corporate bonds, the principles may be applied to municipal securities as well.

[15] "The New York effect" raised the Bond Buyer Index by 50 basis points (0.5 percent) and added as many as 67 basis points (0.67 percent) to several bonds issued in 1976.

projected targets, the related bond prices have quickly dropped to a fraction of their base values.

Although the attractiveness of the revenue bonds relating to nonessential services has been limited at best, their future could be even less bright. First, the energy crisis resulting from the shortage of gasoline and increasing gasoline prices should have a negative impact on people's overall travel plans. This trend could reduce the attractiveness of revenue bonds associated with toll bridges and toll roads. Second, despite the rapid rise in sports revenues in the past, the current trend appears to be toward an increasing consumer resistance to ever higher ticket prices, to say nothing of a growing reluctance to support the tremendous proliferation of new sports and new teams competing for sports dollars. This trend could have an adverse effect on revenue bonds that are supported by sporting events. Third, the many-faceted economic problems, which in the past have plagued our economy in general and private corporations in particular, could worsen; that would make industrial revenue bonds progressively more vulnerable. The safety of industrial revenue bonds depends on the stability of the corporations backing them—not on the standing of the governmental unit that officially issues them. Therefore, if the financial problems of private corporations increase, industrial revenue bonds will lose part of their attractiveness.

Bond Ratings To some degree the safety of a municipal bond can be judged by the way it is rated by a rating agency. Rating agencies rate municipal bonds on the basis of (1) the federal income tax exemption status of the bond, (2) state and local tax structure, (3) the size and future growth prospects of the community issuing the bonds, (4) the stability and diversity of the population as well as of the business community, (5) the debt structure of the state or locality issuing the bond, and (6) the existing debt limits of the community.

Municipal bonds are rated by Standard & Poor's and Moody's. Normally, bonds rated A or better are considered safe investments, although Baa-rated municipal bonds are also considered safe. In fact, banks and other institutions regulated by federal and state agencies are not permitted to invest in bonds with lower than Baa ratings.

It is important to note that in recent years the inadequacy of municipal bond ratings as an *exclusive* measure of default risk has become obvious. For example, New York's financial woes had been growing for some years, but the rating did not reflect the changing financial conditions. New York City's bonds carried a Moody's A rating long after the city's problems made the news; then, suddenly, the rating was lowered to Ba and subsequently to Ca. In another instance, during the third quarter of 1975, Standard & Poor's gave New York's Battery Park Authority bonds an A rating, even though dealers were bidding less than 40 percent of par for $6\frac{3}{8}$ percent bonds maturing in the year 2014. This practice reflected a yield of approximately 17 percent at a time when the average yield on A-rated municipals was about 7.5 percent. The rating services are generally reluctant to lower municipal bond ratings below the Baa level, because they believe that such an action would seriously endanger the financial stability of the relevant cities. Because banks and other institutions regulated by state and federal agencies are not allowed to buy bonds with ratings lower than Baa, the rating of municipal bonds lower than Baa would invariably impede the ability of the cities to service their debts through refinancing of the maturing bond issues. In view of these considerations, investors should probably take a very conservative attitude when estimating the default risk of a bond based on its rating.

Liquidity Risk

Two types of secondary markets exist for trading in outstanding municipal bonds. The *auction market* deals with bonds listed on national exchanges. In this market a broker competes with other brokers in open auction for the best possible trade. However, only a fraction of all outstanding municipal bonds are traded this way. The bulk of municipal bond trading is handled in *over-the-counter markets* consisting of about 500 dealers and several hundred commercial banks located throughout the country. Here individuals may act on their own behalf or arrange for a recognized dealer to act for them in obtaining the best bid for the securities. Some dealers specialize in certain types of municipal bonds, but most trade in a wide range of issues. The most active dealers advertise in a publication called *The Blue List*, which frequently lists bond offerings totaling $1 billion or more. Normal round-lot trades of municipal bonds are made in amounts of $100,000 par value.

Naturally, the more well-known the issuer and the better its credit standing, the more bids a dealer can secure—and, consequently, the lower will be the bid–ask spread of that issue. Only under rare circumstances are investors unable to secure any bids for their bonds; municipal bonds are generally marketable and enjoy a high degree of liquidity.

However, individual investors are penalized for being unable to trade municipal bonds in large quantities. Municipal bonds are normally issued in denominations of $5,000. Because institutions normally buy bonds in blocks of $100,000 or more, an investor attempting to sell a $5,000 bond on the open market is not as likely to find an eager buyer. Because the small size of the bond makes it unattractive for institutional buyers, the investor will probably be forced to offer a broker a liberal commission to sell the bond. Because they increase the liquidity risk of the securities, these limitations should be carefully evaluated when estimating the liquidity risk premium of municipal bonds.

Although in theory an investor can buy a municipal bond of any maturity, in practice such a free choice is limited because the municipal bond market is dominated by large financial institutions. Consequently, when municipal bonds are first offered to the public, large institutions quickly acquire the best bonds and individual investors must be content with the "leftovers." Because financial institutions generally must keep their assets highly liquid, they frequently purchase municipal bonds that will mature within five years. This

State of California Bond: A Short Analysis

Pertinent Details

In early 1979, a broker phoned Investor Q and suggested that he purchase a recently issued general obligation bond from the State of California. This was a $100 million issue in serial form, with portions of the total issue maturing annually from 1979 to 1998. The broker gave him the following quote on a recommended bond: "State of California, 5.30 of '90 at 5.32%."* Investor Q also had the option of purchasing a U.S. treasury bond maturing in 1990; this bond was selling near par with a coupon rate and yield to maturity of 8.90 percent. Although the investor felt that the return on the treasury bond provided an adequate compensation for the inflation, interest rate, and maturity risks associated with the government security, he wondered if the State of California bond might not be a better alternative.

Determination of Yield

The yield to maturity of the State of California bond was quoted at 5.32 percent. The bond was selling very near its par value, because the yield to maturity was almost equal to the 5.30 coupon. As a result, the return on the bond would be earned almost entirely in interest income, which is exempt from federal tax. Therefore, the after-tax yield to maturity would be approximately 5.32 percent. Investor Q pays no state or local income tax, so this is not a consideration.

Equivalent Fully Taxable Yield

To make the after-tax return on the municipal bond comparable to other securities, the equivalent fully taxable yield is calculated. Because Investor Q is in the 42 percent marginal federal tax bracket, a security subject to federal tax and selling at par would have to yield 9.17 percent to earn the same after-tax return:

$$\begin{array}{c}\text{Equivalent Fully}\\ \text{Taxable Yield}\end{array} = \frac{\text{Tax-exempt Yield}}{1 - \begin{bmatrix}\text{Marginal Federal}\\ \text{Tax Rate}\end{bmatrix}} = \frac{.0532}{1 - .42} = 9.17\%$$

Investor Q compares this return to the 8.90 percent yield on the treasury bond, selling at par, and finds it to be slightly higher.†

* Bonds are callable after November 1, 1993. However, because this bond matures in 1990, it does not carry a callability risk.

† The treasury bond is not fully taxable since it is not subject to state or local tax. However, since the investor in this example does not pay state or local income tax, the treasury bond yield can be compared to the municipal bond's equivalent fully taxable yield.

Changing Tax Rate

Investor Q is not completely satisfied with the comparison of the municipal and treasury yields, because the equivalent taxable yield assumes that his marginal federal tax rate would remain constant for the life of the bond. Investor Q assumes that his taxable income will increase by an average of 7 percent each year, which will progressively push him into higher marginal tax brackets.

Table 7–B lists Investor Q's estimated marginal federal tax bracket for the years 1980 through 1990. It also shows the annual interest income (per each $1,000 invested) from the State of California bond, which is adjusted in the third column to indicate the equivalent fully taxable interest for each year. For example, in 1986 Investor Q expects to be in the 54 percent marginal federal tax bracket. In that year he would have to receive $115.20 in interest from a bond subject to federal tax in order to provide the same after-tax interest he would earn from the municipal bond. The last column shows the interest income received from the treasury bond, which is of course subject to federal tax.

A comparison of the two investments shows that in the future the advantage of investing in the municipal bond is expected to widen significantly. As Investor Q moves into higher tax brackets, the equivalent taxable interest from the State of

Table 7–B **State of California Bond—5.30% Coupon**

Year	Estimated Marginal Federal Tax Rate*	Interest (Per each $1,000 Invested†)	Equivalent Fully Taxable Interest‡	Treasury Bond Interest—8.90% Coupon (Per each $1,000 Invested)
1980	42%	$53	$ 91.40	$89
1981	42	53	91.40	89
1982	46	53	98.10	89
1983	46	53	98.10	89
1984	46	53	98.10	89
1985	46	53	98.10	89
1986	54	53	115.20	89
1987	54	53	115.20	89
1988	54	53	115.20	89
1989	54	53	115.20	89
1990	54	53	115.20	89

* 1979 tax rates for head of household.

† Interest income is expressed this way for simplicity. Municipal bonds are generally sold in $5,000 denominations.

‡ Computed with the following formula:

$$\text{Equivalent Fully Taxable Interest} = \frac{\text{Municipal Bond Interest}}{1 - \left[\text{Marginal Federal Tax Rate}\right]}$$

California bond increases from $91.40 in 1980–81 to $98.10 in 1982–85, and finally to $115.20 in 1986–90, becoming increasingly greater than the $89.00 interest from the treasury bond. While the equivalent fully taxable yield to maturity was 9.17 percent in the previous computation, it would be about 10 percent after considering the changing tax rates.[‡]

The Selection Process

By investing in the State of California general obligation bond, Investor Q would receive a higher after-tax yield than from the government bond; however, this benefit would not be without cost. Investor Q could safely assume that in both cases the inflation, maturity, and interest rate risks would be *roughly* the same. However, the municipal bond did carry liquidity risk and also some degree of default risk.

The State of California bond was certainly not as marketable as the government bond. Because the size of his trade would be small relative to institutional transactions in $100,000 round lots, the spread between the dealer's bid and offer prices for this particular security could be as high as $1\frac{1}{2}$ points. For a $10,000 investment, for example, Investor Q might have to pay nearly $150 if he wanted to sell the bond before maturity. But because Investor Q was interested in a long-term investment, he felt that there was only about a 20 percent probability that he would sell the bond before 1990. Consequently, Investor Q figured that his expected financial sacrifice was about $30 (.20 × $150 = $30), which he did not consider to be significant for a $10,000 investment.**

Investor Q then examined the default risk of the municipal bond. In June 1978 S&P suspended its ratings on State of California securities because of the enactment of Proposition 13 which severely limited the taxing powers of the State. Subsequently, however, S&P analyzed the situation and gave the bond a AAA rating, thereby implying that the bond's default risk was very small. Investor Q felt confident that he would receive prompt and full payments until 1990. However, because the California bond was not totally free of default risk, he felt that its fully taxable yield should exceed the treasury bond yield by about 30 to 40 basis points (0.30 to 0.40 percent), which was the approximate default risk premium offered in the market for AAA corporate bonds at the time.

After a careful consideration of all the facts, Investor Q compared the 8.90 percent treasury bond yield with the equivalent fully taxable yield of approximately 10 percent from the State of California bond and concluded that the extra return he expected from the California bond would more than compensate for the additional risks he would assume by investing in it. In other words, the yield to maturity on the municipal bond was higher than his required rate of return. So, Investor Q finally invested in the State of California bond.

---

‡ A precise yield to maturity is difficult to compute because the stream of interest payments is uneven.

** Assuming a $30 expected cost of selling the bonds after five years and no change in the bid and offered prices, the five-year expected return would only be about 0.06 percent lower than the yield to maturity.

makes it difficult for small investors to locate good quality municipal bonds with maturities of up to five years. In fact, small investors are occasionally given the option of buying only those short-term municipal bonds that the institutional investment community considers overpriced.

The Selection Process

The process of selecting municipal bonds involves the Basic Decision Model presented in Chapter 6:

If	Then	Reason
$r = i$	Be indifferent.	The bond is appropriately valued.
$r < i$	Buy the bond.	The bond is undervalued.
$r > i$	Do not buy the bond.	The bond is overvalued.

r = The appropriate discount rate, or the investor's minimum required rate of return
i = The bond's yield to maturity

Summary

Three types of marketable treasury securities are bills, notes, and bonds. *Treasury bills* are sold at auction on a discount basis and have a maximum maturity of one year. *Treasury notes* are coupon obligations with an original maturity of one to five years. *Treasury bonds* have a maturity of more than five years. A variety of securities are also issued by federal and government-guaranteed agencies.

Treasury bills are subject only to inflation risk. Notes and bonds, like treasury bills, do not carry default or significant liquidity risks; however, they are subject to inflation risk, and because all notes and bonds are issued on a long-term basis, are subject to both interest rate and maturity risk. *Agency issues* basically carry the same risk as treasury notes and bonds, but are also assumed to carry a small degree of default risk because they are backed by the credit of the U.S. government only *indirectly*. Therefore, agency issues have higher yields than comparable treasury securities.

Because the government bond market is considered efficient and these bonds are treated primarily as short- or long-term savings instruments, the Basic Decision Model presented in Chapter 6 is not directly applicable. Instead, government bonds are assumed to be appropriately valued and investors make their decisions by treating these bonds as safe, short- or long-term investments.

All U.S. government securities, whether bills, notes, or bonds, and most agency issues, are subject to federal income taxes; however, the interest income from these securities is exempt from state and local taxes.

Two major types of municipal bonds are general obligation and revenue bonds. *General obligation bonds* are secured by the unlimited authority to tax held by cities and states; *revenue bonds* are secured by particular sources of income, such as cigarette taxes or rental payments. The yield on revenue bonds is usually higher than on general obligation bonds, because the flow of income available to pay interest and principal on the former is generally not as secure.

Municipal obligations have special exemptions from federal taxes and quite often from state and local income taxes as well. Many investors compute a municipal bond's equivalent fully taxable yield to measure its relative attractiveness.

In addition to interest rate, maturity, and inflation risks, municipal bonds also carry default and liquidity risks. Overall, municipal bonds have an excellent record of paying interest and principal; however, the degree of default risk of individual securities can vary considerably. Concerning liquidity risk, municipal bonds in general are marketable and enjoy a high degree of liquidity, but individual investors are penalized for being unable to trade these bonds in large quantities.

A Look Ahead

For practical reasons, the discussion in this chapter has been limited to government and municipal bonds. We can now apply the Basic Decision Model to corporate bonds.

Concepts for Review

Treasury bills
Treasury notes
Treasury bonds
Agency issues
Municipal bonds
Federal agencies
Government-guaranteed agencies
Series EE bonds
Series HH bonds
Treasury bill yield
Equivalent fully taxable yield
General obligation bonds
Revenue bonds
Municipal bond ratings

Questions for Review

1. Summarize the important investment characteristics of U.S. treasury bills, notes, and bonds.
2. Discuss the advantages and disadvantages of investing in federal agency issues instead of in U.S. Treasury securities.
3. What method do you use for making comparable quotations on treasury bills and treasury bonds?
4. What are the advantages and disadvantages of treasury bills as an investment for the individual investor?
5. What types of investors can benefit most from investing in savings bonds?
6. Compare the characteristics of EE and HH bonds.
7. Investor W mentions that he recently purchased a risk-free U.S. Treasury note. Comment on his statement.
8. Income from municipal bonds is taxed differently than income from government bonds. Explain this statement.
9. Explain the alternative decision model applicable to treasury bills, notes and bonds. Why is the Basic Decision Model not applicable in these cases?
10. Discuss the safety of municipal bonds. Are there any municipal bonds that would not require a default risk premium?
11. Distinguish between revenue bonds and general obligation bonds. Why might revenue bonds be more attractive to certain investors than general obligation bonds?
12. What types of investors are interested in municipal bonds in general?
13. What is meant by the "liquidity risk of a municipal bond"? How do you estimate the risk premium associated with it?
14. Under what circumstances will the after-tax income from a municipal bond vary from investor to investor?
15. An investor is considering either an 8 percent U.S. Treasury bond or a 5 percent municipal obligation. Both securities are selling at par and both mature in 15 years. The investor asks your advice about which to purchase. What factors would you have to consider to advise the investor properly?

Problems

1. A 182-day treasury bill is priced at 93.991. What is the bank discount yield? What is the equivalent coupon rate?
2. An investor whose marginal federal and state tax brackets are 45 percent and 8 percent, respectively, is considering two bonds. One is a fully taxable corporate bond carrying a $9\frac{1}{2}$ percent coupon and selling at par. The other is a municipal bond with a $5\frac{1}{2}$ percent coupon, also selling at par. The investor's interest income from the municipal bond would

be exempt from state taxation. Assuming all other relevant factors are equal, which bond should the investor select?

3. An investor is considering either a $10\frac{1}{4}$ percent fully taxable bond or a $6\frac{3}{4}$ percent municipal obligation. How high would the investor's marginal federal tax bracket have to be before the municpal bond would offer greater after-tax interest income? Show the appropriate computations. Assume the interest income is not exempt from state and local taxes.
4. For an investor whose marginal federal and state tax brackets are 50 percent and 7 percent, respectively, determine which of the following securities offers the highest after-tax yield to maturity:
   a. A municipal bond with a 7 percent coupon and issued by the investor's state of residence.
   b. A municipal bond issued by another state with an $8\frac{1}{4}$ percent coupon.
   c. A fully taxable corporate bond with a $12\frac{1}{2}$ percent coupon.

   (Assume each security sells at par and the investor's federal and state tax brackets will remain the same.)

Selected Readings

Ayres, Herbert F. and John Y. Barry. "The Equilibrium Yield Curve for Government Securities." *Financial Analysts Journal*, May–June 1979.

Bedford, Margaret E. "The Federal Reserve and the Government Securities Market." *Economic Review*, April 1978.

Bedford, Margaret E. "Recent Developments in Treasury Financing Techniques." Federal Reserve Bank of Kansas City, *Monthly Review*, July–August 1977.

Browne, Lynn E. and Richard F. Syron. "The Municipal Market since the New York City Crisis." Federal Reserve Bank of Boston, *New England Economic Review*, July–August 1979.

Davis, E. H. *Of the People, By the People, For the People—An Informal Analysis of Tax-Free Public Bonds*. New York: John Nuveen Co., 1958.

Donlan, Thomas G. "Mini-Municipals." *Barron's*, August 6, 1979.

The Federal Budget: Its Impact on the Economy. New York: National Industrial Conference Board, 1968.

Handbook of Securities of the United States Government and Federal Agencies. New York: The First Boston Corporation, biennial editions, even years.

Hastie, K. Larry. "Determinants of Municipal Bond Yields." *Journal of Financial and Quantitative Analysis*, June 1972.

Hemple, George H. *Postwar Quality of State and Local Debt*. NBER General Series, No. 94. New York: Columbia University Press, 1971.

Hoffland, David L. "The 'New York City Effect' in the Municipal Bond Market." *Financial Analysts Journal*, March–April 1977.

Industrial Aid Financing. New York: Goodbody & Co., 1965.

Rosenbloom, Richard H. "A Review of the Municipal Bond Market." Federal Reserve Bank of Richmond, *Economic Review*, March–April 1976.

"Savings Bonds—Do They Make Sense Now?" *Changing Times*, April 1980.

Smith, Warren L. "The Competitive Position of Government Securities." *Debt Management in the United States*, Study Paper No. 19. Joint Economic Committee, 86th Congress, 2d Session, January 28, 1960.

The Story of Municipal Bonds. New York: Merrill Lynch Pierce Fenner & Smith, 1972.

Treasury–Federal Reserve Study of the Government Securities Market, 1959. Washington, D.C. : U.S. Government Printing Office, 1959 and 1960, Parts 1–3.

U.S. Treasury Department. *Treasury Bulletin* (monthly).

Corporate Bonds and Preferred Stock

Introduction

Chapter 7 was devoted to a discussion of government securities and municipal bonds, the two *safest* groups of fixed income securities. In this chapter, we will discuss two additional types of securities—corporate bonds and preferred stocks. Corporate bonds are subject to all the six types of risk that affect fixed income securities. Preferred stocks have features of both corporate bonds and common stocks. However, preferred stocks can be analyzed more conveniently as bonds than as stocks.

The first part of this chapter will be devoted to corporate bonds. An overview of corporate bonds, including financing techniques will be presented. Thereafter, corporate bonds will be examined in terms of financial analysis and risk. Next, some of the more sophisticated bond strategies will be discussed. Finally, the topic of corporate bonds and taxation will be covered.

The second part will begin with an overview of preferred stocks in the real world. Next, the Preferred Stock Valuation Model will be presented. Thereafter, preferred stocks will be analyzed in terms of risk. The section will conclude with a discussion of tax considerations of investing in preferred stock.

SECTION 1 CORPORATE BONDS

An Overview

The Purchasers and the Issuers

The major purchasers of corporate bonds are life insurance companies, households, private and public pension funds, and mutual savings banks. Historically, the largest and steadiest buyers of corporate bonds have been life insurance companies; however, the amount they hold relative to the total outstanding fell from 53 percent in 1960—$48 billion out of a total of $90 billion—to approximately 35 percent in 1979. In contrast, between 1960 and 1979, the percentage of total corporate bonds outstanding held by households increased from 11 percent to over 15 percent. Another development of major import is that the corporate bond holdings of private and public pension funds have increased dramatically since the 1960s, almost reaching the level of life insurance company holdings. These developments indicate a growing interest in a variety of corporate bonds on the part of individuals and pension fund managers, and a continued attempt on the part of the corporations to satisfy these diverse interests.

On the issuers' side of the market, corporations have made large adjustments in their approach to financing. From 1960 through the early 1970s, corporations increased the debt portion of their capital structures. Financial leverage—or the ratio of debt to total financing—of nonfinancial corporations rose by about 20 percent, and the ratio of bonds to total financing recorded a somewhat lower increase. A lower level of uncertainty or expected variability of corporate income before interest and taxes may have encouraged corporations to increase debt financing during the early and mid-1960s. From 1968 through 1974, a new influence was felt. As the inflation-adjusted cost of debt financing declined due to an acceleration in the rate of inflation, firms issued larger amounts of debt capital, which led to an increase in their financial leverage. In 1975, however, financial leverage declined for the first time in 15 years. The decline occurred in part because of the reduction of short-term debt as inventories were liquidated; it might also have reflected the response of corporations to greater economic uncertainty. Subsequently, this declining trend was arrested, and by 1978 the level of financial leverage appeared to have reached an equilibrium.

Major Changes in Corporate Bond Markets

Enormous growth, particularly in the recent past, is the most noticeable characteristic of the corporate bond market.[1] The amount of corporate bonds outstanding increased from $75.6 billion in 1967 to $235.3 billion in 1977—an increase of 311 percent over a ten-year period.

The industry distribution of corporate bonds has undergone some modification in recent years, primarily as a result of relatively heavy industrial and finance issuance. Utilities, which constituted 59 percent of the total dollar volume of all public straight corporate bonds outstanding in 1972, dropped to 52 percent in 1977. Industrials still ranked second with 28 percent of the totals, and finance issues rose from 11 percent to 15 percent.

In 1977, three-quarters of the dollar volume of corporate bonds outstanding had a current maturity in excess of ten years. Utilities had longer maturities than other industry groups. They constituted 64 percent of all issues in excess of 20 years, as opposed to only 41 percent of those with shorter maturities. Almost

[1] This section borrows heavily from *The Anatomy of the Secondary Market in Corporate Bonds: Year-end, 1977 Update*. New York: Salomon Brothers. 1978, pp. 1–6.

all of the bonds with maturities of over 30 years were utilities. On the other hand, industrials had proportionately more issues maturing between five and 20 years. Finance issues seemed to have the shortest average maturity, with a median maturity of less than ten years.

Because the public market usually prefers relatively safe investments, it discriminates against lower rated offerings. Evidence of this preference for quality can be seen in the fact that over half of the total volume of all publicly offered straight corporate bonds outstanding in 1977 had credit ratings of AAA or AA (over four-fifths were rated better than BBB). Utilities and finance issues were apparently somewhat more heavily concentrated in high investment quality issues, with nearly seven-eighths of the total volume of these industry groups rated A or better.

Perhaps the most interesting development concerning corporate bonds is the significant increase in coupon rates. In 1972, 56 percent of the total amount outstanding bore coupon rates lower than 7 percent. But by 1977, 53 percent of the total amount outstanding had a coupon ranging from 7 to 8.9 percent; 19 percent of the bonds had even higher coupon rates. This general increase in coupon rates indicates that the market's perception of the risks associated with bonds has dramatically increased in recent years.

Financing Techniques[2]

New corporate bonds are either sold in the public market or placed directly with particular lenders. Private placements are often made by less highly regarded or less widely known companies. The ratio of publicly offered to total corporate bond borrowing fluctuates with the business cycle. Public utilities are better able to pass on higher borrowing costs to their customers than are industrial firms. Consequently, during periods of high, rising interest rates, the volume of publicly offered utility issues remains fairly high, whereas the volume of industrial issues—particularly those of weaker firms that are generally placed privately—is reduced because of the increase in borrowing costs.

Because investment banking firms—the major underwriters—either purchase an issue themselves or guarantee the issuer a specific price for the bonds, they bear the risk of gain or loss when the bonds are sold in the open market. In some cases, bonds are sold through competitive bidding to the underwriter that offers the highest price for the bonds; this provides the lowest interest cost to the issuer. The winning underwriter then attempts to sell the bonds to the public at a price that will cover the capital funds tied up in the transaction and yield some profit.

On many high-quality industrial issues, the flotation cost—the difference between the price the underwriter pays for the bonds and the price paid by the

[2] This section is based on Burton Zwick, "The Market for Corporate Bonds," Federal Reserve Bank of New York, *Quarterly Review*, Autumn 1977, pp. 29, 31. The information presented here is an elaboration of the data about investment bankers presented in Chapter 3.

public—is $\frac{7}{8}$ percent. An underwriting commission of 0.2 percent is shared on a pro rata basis by all members of the underwriting syndicate, and the managers receive an additional fee of 0.175 percent. The remaining $\frac{1}{2}$ percent, or $5 per $1,000 bond, is typically paid out as a selling "concession" to salesmen. On utility issues, the total spread is usually between 0.45 percent and 0.75 percent. The lower underwriting spread on utility issues is due to their greater marketability. For both industrial and utility issues, the total underwriting spread does not include other flotation costs, such as legal, printing, and other costs necessary to satisfy the registration requirement of the SEC. These can run from about 1 percent of total proceeds for issues of under $10 million to about $\frac{1}{4}$ percent for issues over $100 million.[3]

Corporate Bond Quotations

At the end of 1978, nearly 2,000 bonds were listed for trading on the NYSE and about 200 on the AMEX. However, the total volume of bonds traded on the over-the-counter market far exceeded the combined volume of bonds traded on these two exchanges.

On December 20, 1978, in the *Wall Street Journal*, under the New York Exchange Bonds the following quotation appeared:

Bonds	Cur Yld	Vol	High	Low	Close	Net Chg
ATO $10\frac{3}{4}$s 98	11	17	$97\frac{7}{8}$	97	97	-1

The column labeled "Bonds" lists the abbreviated name of the issuer, the coupon rate, and the maturity date. "ATO" stands for ATO, Incorporated—a conglomerate specializing in fire protection, industrial equipments, instruments, and recreational facilities. The ATO bonds are referred to as the ten-and-three-quarters ($10\frac{3}{4}$s) of 1998 (98), meaning they carry a coupon rate of $10\frac{3}{4}$ percent and mature in 1998.

The volume column (Vol) tells the reader that on this day 17 ATO bonds were traded. The next three columns indicate the high, low, and closing prices for the day. Bonds are always quoted in terms of a par value of $100 instead of the usual par value of $1,000, so the closing price (Close 97) is $970.

The last column, "Net Chg," shows how much the closing price differs from the previous day's closing price. In this case the net change equals 1 percent of the face value of $1,000, or $10. Because the bond price dropped from $980 to $970 from the close of the previous trading day, the change is -1.

[3] Of course, for issues as small as $500,000 or $1,000,000, these "other flotation costs" are likely to be several percent of the total proceeds.

Finally, notice the second term in the quotation, "Cur Yld, 11." Expressed as a percentage, the *current yield* of a bond is the ratio of its coupon rate to its current market price. The current yield of ATO is 11 percent:

$$\text{Current Yield} = \frac{\text{Coupon}}{\text{Market Price}}$$

$$= \frac{\$107.50}{\$970}$$

$$= .11 \text{ (or } 11\%)$$

Note that because the ATO's current market price of \$970 is lower than its maturity price of \$1,000, the current yield of 11 percent is higher than the coupon rate of $10\frac{3}{4}$ percent.

The current yield of the bond may differ, sometimes significantly, from its yield to maturity. In this case, the ATO bond has a maturity of 20 years (1978–98), and its yield to maturity is 11.13 percent:[4]

$$P_0 = \sum_{n=1}^{20} \frac{\$107.50}{(1+i)^n} + \frac{\$1,000}{(1+i)^{20}}$$

At $i = 11.13\%$, for 20 years,

$$P_0 = \$970$$

In this example, the yield to maturity was calculated on the assumption that the interest was compounded on an annual basis. If compounding is done on a semiannual basis to reflect the payment of semiannual interest, the yield would be slightly higher than 11.13 percent.

It is not always necessary to use the long formula to calculate the yield to maturity. Appropriate bond tables can provide the yield to maturity of any given bond. If such a table is not readily available, however, the following simplified equation can be used to approximate the yield to maturity:

$$i = \frac{C + (P_N - P_0)/N}{(P_N + P_0)/2} \qquad \textbf{(8–1)}$$

where

i = Yield to maturity
C = Annual interest payments
P_N = Par value of the bond
P_0 = Market price of the bond
N = Maturity of the bond

[4] See note 4 on page 297.

Using Equation 8–1, the yield to maturity of ATO is 11.07 percent:

$$i = \frac{\$107.50 + (\$1{,}000 - \$970)/20}{(\$1{,}000 + \$970)/2}$$

$$= \frac{109}{985}$$

$$= .1107 \text{ (or } 11.07\%)$$

Note that Equation 8–1 *approximates* the ATO's yield to maturity at 11.07 percent (compared to its yield to maturity of 11.13 percent calculated by the general bond valuation equation).

In this illustration, the current yield was close to the yield to maturity. However, current yield and yield to maturity will not always be so similar. For example, consider the ABC bond which has a coupon rate of 6 percent and a maturity of five years. If ABC is selling for $900, its current yield is 6.67 percent:

$$\text{Current Yield} = \frac{\$60}{\$900}$$

$$= .0667 \text{ (or } 6.67\%)$$

If the simplified equation is used, the yield to maturity of ABC bond works out to 8.42 percent:

$$i = \frac{C + (P_N - P_0)/N}{(P_N + P_0)/2}$$

$$= \frac{\$60 + (\$1{,}000 - \$900)/5}{(\$1{,}000 + \$900)/2}$$

$$= \frac{80}{950}$$

$$= .0842 \text{ (or } 8.42\%)$$

Furthermore, if the long equation is used, the yield to maturity of the ABC bond is 8.55 percent.

Risk Considerations

Corporate bonds carry all six types of risk associated with fixed income securities. Of these, the interest rate, inflation, and maturity risks affect corporate bonds in the same manner in which they affect other long-term bonds. Because these risks have been covered in Chapter 6 in detail, they will not be discussed here. However, default risk, callability risk, and liquidity risk deserve special attention here.

Default Risk

Issuers of corporate bonds are committed to making interest and principal payments. However, no corporate issuer is considered as safe as the U.S. Treasury, and all corporate bonds are assumed to carry some degree of default risk. A default occurs when a corporation delays a payment or altogether skips it when it becomes due.

As a general rule, when evaluating the default risk of a bond, most investors rely heavily on the judgment of the rating agencies.

Agency Ratings

Method of Evaluation As might be expected, the two rating agencies—S&P and Moody's—generally begin with a thorough financial analysis of the respective companies. Financial analysis involves examination of a corporation's income statements and balance sheets. The purpose of analyzing an income statement is to determine sources of revenue, categories of expenses, and net revenues available for meeting obligations relating to debt service, capital expansion, taxes, and dividends. An analysis of the past trends of these and related variables helps a rating agency determine the financial health of the firm under investigation.

One of the most useful approaches to income statement analysis is through the derivation of ratios. By examining various ratios, analysts can evaluate a firm's level of performance. In order to assess the extent of a company's future profits, it is useful to compare the company's recent ratios with those of the past and those of the industry in general. Some of the more commonly used ratios are presented in Table 8–1.

Rating agencies also examine the balance sheets of the respective corporations. The balance sheet indicates the company's standing at a particular point in time and provides a measure of its capitalization, plant account, fund balances, and current accounts. Ratios relating different categories of balance sheet items provide the most useful measure of the firm's condition, particularly when compared with industry ratios and previous ratios for the same firm to indicate trends. Some of the useful ratios in balance sheets are indicated in Table 8–2.

Besides analyzing a company's income statement and balance sheet, ratings agencies examine other financial data as well. For example, consider the S&P analytical framework of Caesars World Senior Subordinated Sinking Fund Debentures.

A Case Study[5] On February 21, 1979, Caesars World offered $15 million worth of 12 percent senior subordinated sinking fund debentures at a price of

[5] For details see *Fixed Income Investor*, February 24, 1979, pp. 725–26.

Table 8–1 **Examples of Financial Ratios**

Description	How Determined	Use	Illustration
Operating ratio (related to capital turnover ratio: low capital turnover ratio = low operating ratio)	(Operating & Maintenance Expense + Depreciation + Taxes) / Gross operating revenue	Measure of gross revenues expended for expenses (may express maintenance only, if useful). The cost of doing business before compensation of capital; complement is "return margin."	90 percent indicates proportions of annual revenues devoted to cost of doing business; 10 percent is return margin. Company will probably have high capital turnover ratio, indicating relatively low capital requirements.
Interest coverage or debt service coverage ratios	(Net revenues or Income available for interest) / Total interest due (Net revenues or Income available for debt service) / Total debt service due	Measure of revenue available for coverage of interest or debt service.	5.5 times indicates relation of annual income available to interest required; total debt service, including principal, will be lower
Interest or debt service safety margin	Net available after interest / Gross revenues Net available after debt service / Gross revenues	Amount that gross revenues could decline and still cover interest or debt service (assuming operating and maintenance to be constant).	

SOURCE: Jackson Phillips, "Analysis and Rating of Corporate Bonds," in Sumner Levine, Ed., *Financial Analyst's Handbook*, Vol. 1 (Homewood, Ill.: Dow Jones-Irwin, 1975), p. 222–23. ©1975 by Dow Jones-Irwin, Inc.

$915. The company owned and operated Caesars Palace in Las Vegas and was planning to construct an Atlantic City hotel–casino in summer 1979. Reflecting problems extraneous to its gaming activities, the company's erratic operating record had resulted in an inconsistent level of fixed charge coverage. Although the January 1979 sale of 500,000 shares of common stock added much needed equity to the capital structure, leverage and debt/capital ratios remained near historically high levels with thin cash flow and asset protection.

The capitalization of the company on October 31, 1978, adjusted to reflect the bond offering and the stock sales, was as follows:

Figure 8–1 **Industrial Bond Yields**

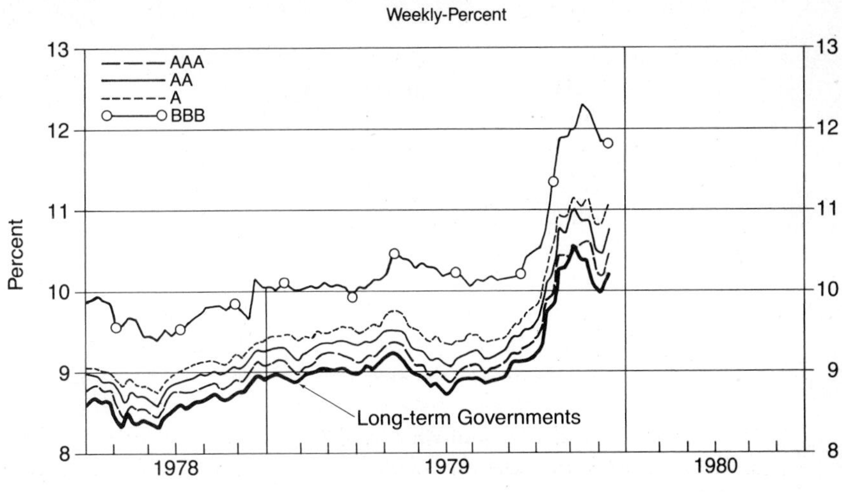

SOURCE: Standard & Poor's *Fixed Income Investor*, December 22, 1979.

to its financial condition, as revealed in Table 8–3. Of course the rating of issues is also influenced by other, qualitative considerations.

In general, the better a company's credit rating, the higher the quality of its bonds. The highest quality bonds tend to sell at higher prices with correspondingly lower yields, as first presented in Chapter 4 and reproduced in Figure 8–1.

Default Risk Premium

Differences in the yields on bonds with different degrees of default risk reflect an implicit default risk premium in the market. For example, suppose a government bond and the XYZ corporate bond are identical in all respects except that only the latter is subject to default risk. The difference in their yields would obviously represent the default risk premium that the market associates with the corporate bond:[7]

[7] Note that the market's default risk premium associated with a bond can be isolated in this manner only if the bonds are identical in all other respects. However, there are usually other differences between a corporate and government bond such as callability and liquidity risks and possibly tax considerations, which will also be reflected in the yield spread between the two securities.

Bond	Par Value	Market Value	Years to Maturity	Coupon	Yield to Maturity	Market's Default Risk Premium
Government	$1,000	$1,000	5	8.00%	8.00%	None
XYZ	1,000	932	5	8.00%	9.78%	1.78%

However, an investor might feel that the market's yield does not adequately reflect the default risk associated with a bond. In that case, a better alternative would be to calculate the *expected yield* of the bond based on the probability of default. Assume an investor is analyzing the XYZ corporate bond. If the XYZ and government bonds are identical in all respects except that only XYZ carries a risk of default, the investor would find the default risk premium on the XYZ bond adequate only if its *expected* yield to maturity is at least 8.0 percent.

Suppose the investor believed that there is a 0.9 probability that the $1,000 principal will be repaid at maturity, and a 0.1 probability that no such payment will be made. As revealed by Table 6–3 (p. 182), under the specified default assumptions, the promised yield on the XYZ bond is 9.78 percent, while the *expected* yield on the XYZ bond is 8.0 percent. Therefore, the market's 1.78 percent default risk premium would represent an adequate compensation for the perceived default risk of the corporate bond.

Let us modify the default risk assumptions. Suppose the investor believes there is a 0.95 probability of full payment at maturity and only a 0.05 probability of default on the maturity date. Under these assumptions, the *expected* yield on the XYZ bond would be 8.9 percent,[8] or 0.9 percent higher than the government bond yield. Obviously, in that case, the investor would find the market's default risk premium to be more than adequate compensation for the default risk assumed by investing in the XYZ bond.

Although many investors associate default risk with the probability that the bond under consideration would become worthless, that is frequently not the case. Even when an issuer declares bankruptcy, bondholders may still receive a partial payment of principal and interest according to a variety of arrangements worked out under the bankruptcy rules. Naturally, these considerations add complexity to default risk analysis.

One important note should be added to the preceding discussion: Even if the expected yield on a corporate bond equals the promised yield on a government bond, an investor may not necessarily be indifferent between the two securities. Although discussed previously in Chapter 5, the reason for this may be repeated here. Although the expected returns from the two securities are the same, the variability of their expected returns is not. The expected variance of the return on a government bond held until maturity should be zero, because the coupon and principal payments on it are virtually assured. In contrast, the yield actually received from a corporate bond can vary from as high as the promised yield (if full and timely payments are made) to a negative return (in cases of default).

[8] See note 8 on page 298.

Therefore, as a compensation for this added variability of return, an investor may well demand a higher expected return from the corporate bond, the amount of which would of course depend on the investor's utility function.

Callability Risk

Basic Considerations

Bonds subject to call by the issuing companies are known as *callable bonds*. Not all callable bonds are necessarily called away, but a substantial drop in interest rates, causing bond prices to advance, would surely encourage the issuer to call an issue. The logic for this is obvious. A significant drop in the interest rate makes it possible for a company to call away the old bonds carrying the higher coupon rates and reissue new bonds with lower coupon rates, thereby reducing the firm's overall debt cost. As demonstrated in Table 6–6 (p. 186), if market interest rates fall and a bond is called, bondholders will earn a lower return when their money is reinvested at a lower interest rate for the remainder of the holding period. For this reason, they will demand a callability risk premium to ensure that their expected holding period yield, i_c—which accounts for the reinvestment of call proceeds—will at least equal the yield to maturity, i, of a comparable noncallable security.

There is, however, an exception. In Chapter 6, we stated that callable bonds need not necessarily carry callability risk premiums. If market interest rates are *not* expected to drop significantly to make it worthwhile for the issuer to call the security (given the fact that the issuer pays a call penalty and incurs refinancing costs), the bond should not be expected to be called. In that case, investors will not demand a yield higher than that on a security with more call protection.

First Call[9]

An alternative way of illustrating the effect of the call feature on yields is to compute the *yield to first call* (by assuming that the call price is paid at the end of the period of call protection) and compare it to the yield to maturity for a given security. If future interest rates are expected to be lower than current interest rates, this will lead to higher coupon rates on new securities with a call provision, so that the higher yields realized during the call protection period will compensate for the subsequent lower yields expected on the call proceeds. Figure 8–2 shows the spread between the yield to call and yield to maturity of $8\frac{1}{2}$–$9\frac{1}{8}$ percent coupon Aa utility bonds with a five-year call protection period issued in 1970, when long-term interest rates were at a record high. The figure indicates that when interest rates are high, investors in securities

[9] Timothy Q. Cook, "Some Factors Affecting Long-term Yield Spreads in Recent Years," Federal Reserve Bank of Richmond, *Monthly Review*, September 1973, pp. 10–11.

Figure 8–2 **Yield to Maturity on $8\frac{1}{2}$–$9\frac{1}{8}$ Coupon Bond and Spread Between Yield to Call and Yield to Maturity***

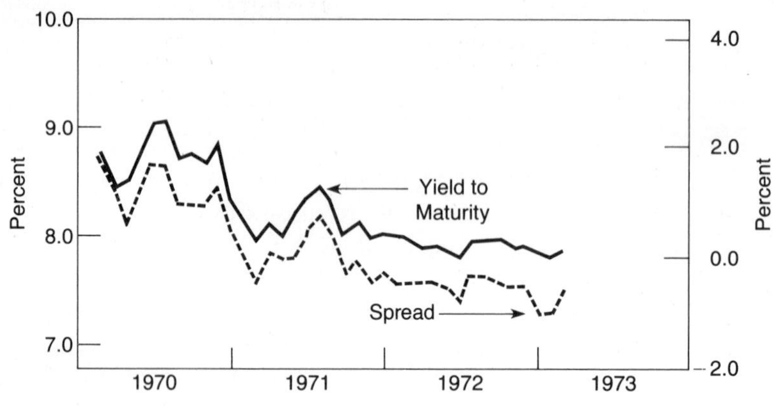

* Yield series are for Aa seasoned utility bonds.

SOURCE: Timothy Q. Cook, "Some Factors Affecting Long-term Yield Spreads in Recent Years," Federal Reserve Bank of Richmond, *Monthly Review*, September 1973, p. 11.

with call provisions demand an adequate compensation for the expected lower yield following the end of the call protection period. Note, however, that in this case the differential in the two yields was wiped out before the end of the call protection period when long-term rates declined at the end of 1970 and the beginning of 1971.[10]

Average Life

In our discussion of callability risk, it was assumed that callable bonds would be retired by the issuer at the first opportunity. However, the most common method of repayment for corporate bonds is through a *sinking fund.* Under this arrangement, the company makes payments into a fund in order to redeem a certain percentage of outstanding bonds at predetermined regular intervals during the life of the issue. For example, the indenture of a 20-year bond might specify that no sinking fund payments will be made for the first ten years, and that 10 percent of the issue will be retired in each of the next ten years.

[10] Because of the call penalty, a yield to call greater than yield to maturity *does not* necessarily imply an expectation of falling interest rates. However, given an expectation of no change in interest rates, a fall in interest rates from a level at which a deferred callable security has a higher yield to maturity than a noncallable security will decrease the spread between the yield to call and yield to maturity of the deferred callable security.

Table 8–4 **ABC Bond Average Life**

Years to Maturity: 20
Sinking fund provisions: No redemptions for the first 10 years; 10% of issue redeemed in each of the next 10 years

(1) Life of Bonds (years)	(2) Probability	(3) (1) × (2)
1–10	0	0
11	.1	1.1
12	.1	1.2
13	.1	1.3
14	.1	1.4
15	.1	1.5
16	.1	1.6
17	.1	1.7
18	.1	1.8
19	.1	1.9
20	.1	2.0
	1.0	15.5 = Average Life

The bonds to be retired under sinking fund arrangements can be called at a specified price, although in many cases they can be purchased in the secondary market. The latter method of retirement would be preferable to the issuer when the bonds are trading at a discount from their par value. When bonds are called at a specified price, the securities to be retired are selected on a random basis in a lot-drawing.

Consider the case of ABC bonds. If an investor expects these bonds to be called and the redemption process is random, he cannot know the precise life of his bonds. Therefore, the investor should determine the *average life* of the bonds. The average life of ABC bonds, calculated in Table 8–4, is 15.5 years.[11] A sinking fund provides some benefits to the investor. A sinking fund reduces default risk by providing an orderly reduction of the outstanding principal. Also, if the company makes retirements through secondary market purchases, additional liquidity is added to the market. However, a sinking fund also adds callability risk to a bond. If the bonds are called before maturity, the investor will face the problem of reinvesting the funds at a lower interest rate. In the case of the ABC bonds, the bondholder, assuming the average life to be 15.5 years, might have a lower expected holding period yield, i_c, than the yield to maturity, i, if the reinvestment rate for the remaining 4.5 years of the 20-year holding period is lower than the coupon rate.[12]

[11] Of course, if the investor expects the company to make some (or all) retirements through purchases in the secondary market, the average life of his bonds would be different from that specified here.

[12] If there is a call penalty associated with the bond redemption, the expected holding period yield might be greater than the yield to maturity even if the reinvestment rate is lower than the coupon rate.

Deep Discount Bonds

Deep discount bonds frequently offer greater appreciation potential and call protection than bonds selling near par with the same yield to maturity. A *deep discount bond* is one selling at a price of, say, 15 or 20 percent or more below its par or maturity price. In terms of market prices, bonds that sell for $850 or less and return $1,000 to the holder on maturity generally qualify as deep discount bonds. Deep discount bonds have a greater appreciation potential than bonds trading at par with the same yield to maturity, because of the lower probability that they will be called away in the event of a decline in the market interest rates.

Table 8–5 demonstrates the effect of an interest rate drop on two corporate bonds. The ABC is an A-rated bond, with 20 years to maturity. It is selling at par and carries a coupon rate and yield to maturity of 10 percent. The XYZ bond is similar to the ABC bond in all respects but one: Its coupon rate is only 7 percent, and is therefore currently selling for only $745.

Suppose that the market interest rate drops to 8 percent. Because this constitutes a substantial drop in the interest rate, the ABC bond will surely be called away. The bondholders will receive the call price of $1,100 and conse-

Table 8–5

	ABC	XYZ
Market price	$1,000.00	$745.00
Years to maturity	20 years	20 years
Coupon rate	10%	7%
Type of bond	Par bond, A-rated	Deep discount bond, A-rated
Call provision	Immediately callable	Immediately callable
Yield to maturity	10%	10%
Call price	$1,100.00 (Par + 1 year's coupon)	$1,070.00 (Par + 1 year's coupon)
Market interest rate drops to	8%	8%
Investor receives	$1,100.00 (call price)	$902.26†
Percentage gain	$\frac{\$1,100 - \$1,000}{\$1,000} = 10\%$	$\frac{\$902.26 - \$745}{\$745} = 21.1\%$

Note: XYZ bond will not be called away until the interest rate drops substantially below its coupon rate of 7%. Tax considerations are ignored in these examples.

$$^{\dagger} P_0 = \sum_{n=1}^{N} \frac{C}{(1+i)^n} + \frac{P_N}{(1+i)^N}$$

$$= \sum_{n=1}^{20} \frac{\$70}{(1+.08)^n} + \frac{\$1,000}{(1+.08)^{20}}$$

$$= (\$70)(9.818) + (\$1,000)(.215)$$

$$= \$902.26$$

quently realize a capital gain of 10 percent, and will be forced to reinvest the call proceeds at a lower interest rate.

The interest rate decline will have a totally different impact on the XYZ bond. Because its coupon rate is 7 percent, the bond will not be called until the interest rate drops to, say, 6 percent. As demonstrated in Table 8–5, a drop in the interest rate to 8 percent will increase the price of XYZ to $902.26. Investors will therefore realize a capital gain of 21.1 percent,[13] and they will not face the problem of reinvesting the call proceeds at a lower interest rate.

Liquidity Risk

The *liquidity risk* of a corporate bond refers to the possibility that a holder wishing to sell that bond may have difficulty locating a buyer and could conceivably take a loss for reasons unrelated to any deterioration in the corporation's financial position. Bond liquidity depends on both its breadth of ownership and its volume of activity. The lower the liquidity of a bond, the higher its liquidity risk will be (and, consequently, the higher its liquidity risk premium).

A surrogate for the liquidity risk premium is the spread between the bid and the offered prices that dealers quote when they make a market in a bond. The dealer's spread in a $500,000 to $1 million transaction for a highly marketable corporate bond is typically about $\frac{1}{8}$ point. Spreads for less marketable issues range from about $\frac{1}{4}$ point to $\frac{1}{2}$ point. The following example clarifies this idea:

Bond	Bid	Ask	Spread
Duquesne Light	$99\frac{1}{4}$	$99\frac{3}{4}$	$\frac{1}{2}$
Beneficial	99	$99\frac{1}{8}$	$\frac{1}{8}$

In this example, assuming that the differences in spread are due entirely to liquidity risks, Beneficial is a highly marketable bond, but Duquesne Light is not. Implicitly, because the difference between the spreads of the two bonds is $\frac{3}{8}$ point ($\frac{1}{2} - \frac{1}{8}$), the market imposes an additional liquidity risk premium of $\frac{3}{8}$ point on Duquesne Light. Of course, as mentioned in Chapter 6, the spread for any given bond can substantially increase when smaller trades are made as well as when higher market interest rates are forecast.

[13] In Chapter 6 it was explained (see Interest Rate Principle No. 3) that for any given change in the interest rate, the lower the coupon rate on a bond, the greater will be the fluctuation in its price as a result of a change in the interest rate. This principle applies to deep discount bonds as well. That is, deep discount bonds have a trading advantage even when they do not have a call protection, when interest rates decline.

The Decision Model

The decision to invest or not to invest in a corporate bond depends primarily on an investor's minimum required rate of return for investing in that bond and its yield. The required rate of return is the sum of the risk-free real rate plus a premium associated with different risks carried by the bond. The corporate Bond Decision Model follows:

If	Then	Reason
$r = i$	Be indifferent.	The bond is appropriately valued.
$r < i$	Buy the bond.	The bond is undervalued.
$r > i$	Do not buy the bond.	The bond is overvalued.

r = The appropriate discount rate, or the investor's minimum required rate of return

i = The bond's yield to maturity

A real-world example demonstrating the use of this model can be found in the Appendix to this chapter.

Sophisticated Strategies

Variable Reinvestment Rate

In all previous discussions on bonds, it has been assumed that coupon payments received until maturity are reinvested at the rate with which these payments are discounted. This is an oversimplified assumption, because the reinvestment rate can vary from zero percent (if the investor spends the coupon payments) to almost any other amount, depending on the interest rate prevailing in the market when the coupon payments are received. Table 8–6 demonstrates that the yield realized on a bond is a function of this reinvestment rate. An investor developing a bond strategy should use this *effective rate*, i_e, as well as the yield to maturity, i, which is based on the simplified assumption of a reinvestment rate equivalent to the coupon rate.

Assume an investor purchases a 5 percent bond for $1,000, due to mature in five years. The investor would receive annual interest payments of $50 for five years in addition to the principal of $1,000 at the end of the fifth year. The $50 interest received at the end of the first year would be invested for four years, interest received at the end of the second year would be invested for three years, and so on. Interest received at the end of the fifth year would not be reinvested at all. This process of investing the coupon payments for de-

Table 8–6

\$1,000 Face Value Bond
Market Interest Rate = 5%
Maturity = 5 years

Year 1 Coupon Payments	Year 2	Year 3	Year 4	Year 5	Year 6	Value of Coupon Payments Reinvested at c_r = 3%	Value of Coupon Payments Reinvested at c_r = 5%	Value of Coupon Payments Reinvested at c_r = 7%
	\$50	\$50	\$50	\$50	\$50			
	$50 \times (1.0 + C_{r_1})^4$					\$ 56.28	\$ 60.78	\$ 65.54
		$50 \times (1.0 + C_{r_2})^3$				54.64	57.88	61.25
			$50 \times (1.0 + C_{r_3})^2$			53.05	55.13	57.25
				$50 \times (1.0 + C_{r_4})^1$		51.50	52.50	53.50
					$50 \times (1.0 + C_{r_5})^0$	50.00	50.00	50.00
Total value of coupon payments after reinvestment						\$ 265.47	\$ 276.29	\$ 287.54
Add the principal paid back at end of 5th year						\$1,000.00	\$1,000.00	\$1,000.00
Total amount received after 5 years						\$1,265.47	\$1,276.29	\$1,287.54
Annual yield on \$1,000 investment						4.82%	5.00%	5.18%

Note: \$1,000 is invested at beginning of year 1. Coupon payments (at 5%) = \$50 per year. It is assumed that the bond is purchased at par value. c_r = Reinvestment rate.

clining time periods can be articulated as follows:

$50 Interest Received at the End of Year	Would Grow for	And the Total Investment Value Would Equal
1	4 years	$50 \times (1.0 + c_{r_1})^4$
2	3 years	$50 \times (1.0 + c_{r_2})^3$
3	2 years	$50 \times (1.0 + c_{r_3})^2$
4	1 year	$50 \times (1.0 + c_{r_4})^1$
5	0 year	$50 \times (1.0 + c_{r_5})^0$

When the bond matures at the end of Year 5, the total compounded value of all interest payments received during the five-year period would depend on c_r (the rates at which interest payments are reinvested). If interest payments are reinvested at a rate equivalent to the coupon rate on the bond, the effective rate, i_e, and the coupon rate will be identical. For example, as revealed by Table 8–6, if a bond is originally purchased at par and interest payments are reinvested at 5 percent, the effective rate is 5 percent. However, if the reinvestment rate is 3 percent, the effective rate is only 4.82 percent; for a reinvestment rate of 7 percent, the effective rate is 5.18 percent. If the bond is purchased at par value, the following relationship will hold:

If	Then
$c_r < C$	$i_e < C$
$c_r = C$	$i_e = C$
$c_r > C$	$i_e > C$

where

c_r = Reinvestment rate

C = Annual interest payments (coupon rate)

i_e = Effective rate

An understanding of the effective rate concept should help investors improve their bond trading strategies. It has been established that, subsequent to the issue of a bond, an increase in the market interest rate lowers its price and thereby imposes an opportunity cost on the bondholder. The variable reinvestment rate demonstrates that the opportunity cost is not as large as it first appears, because following an interest rate rise the bondholder is able to reinvest the coupon payments at a higher rate.

Swapping Techniques[14]

Swapping—switching between various fixed income securities—is a useful device for increasing the amount of current income, the yield to maturity, or both. However, many sophisticated swapping operations demand technical

[14] For an excellent discussion of swapping techniques, see David M. Darst, *The Complete Bond Book* (New York: McGraw-Hill, 1975), pp. 299–313.

Table 8–7

	Buy/ Sell	Company	Maturity (years)	S & P Rating	Coupon %	Price $	Yield to Maturity (%)	Type of Swap	Purpose of Swap
Example 1	Sell	ABC	10	A	7.0	1,000.00	7.00	Equivalent securities	Take advantage of
	Buy	XYZ	10	A	7.0	990.00	7.14	with different prices	short-term market imperfection
Example 2	Sell	ABC	10	A	3.5	753.75	7.00	Different coupons	Earn additional
	Buy	XYZ	10	A	6.0	929.50	7.00		interest income
Example 3	Sell	ABC	10	AAA	7.0	1,000.00	7.00	Different quality	Increase return
	Buy	XYZ	10	BB	7.0	816.25	10.00	ratings	by assuming higher risk
Example 4	Sell	ABC	10	A	7.0	1,000.00	7.00	Different categories	Take advantage of
	Buy	XYZ	10	A	4.0 (tax free)	1,000.00	4.00	with contrasting tax features	a favorable tax situation

Note: In these examples transaction costs are ignored.

competence, investment sophistication, and large investible funds rarely achieved by average investors. Consequently, complicated swapping should be avoided by all but the most sophisticated investors.

Our discussion will demonstrate the nature of several simple swapping operations by means of simplified examples, given in Table 8–7. All transaction costs are ignored in these examples, and, for simplicity, the inherent risks associated with these cases are not thoroughly explored.

In each of the four examples shown in Table 8–7, the investor switches from ABC to XYZ bond, but the reason for the swap differs in each case. In Example 1, an ABC bondholder feels that ABC and XYZ are identical bonds, but notices that the market favors the XYZ over the ABC bond.[15] This is evidenced by the fact that the XYZ bond offers a higher yield to maturity than that offered by ABC. The investor therefore swaps ABC for XYZ to capitalize on what she feels is the prevailing yield differential. In Example 2, the purpose of the switch is the earning of additional interest income (at 6 percent instead of 3.5 percent), although additional money is needed to purchase the XYZ bond. Presumably, in this case the investor predicts that the future reinvestment rate will increase substantially to make this swap worthwhile.

In Example 3, the investor is agressive and switches to XYZ to improve his yield. He realizes, of course, that the rating of XYZ is much lower than that of ABC, but is willing to assume the extra risk for an additional yield of

[15] It should be reiterated that, even though both bonds are rated A by S&P, their default risks may not be identical.

3 percent (10 percent versus 7 percent). Finally, in Example 4, the investor switches from ABC corporate bond yielding 7 percent to the XYZ tax-exempt municipal bond which has a tax-free yield of 4 percent. Apparently, this investor is in a sufficiently high income tax bracket—say 50 percent—so she finds the swap attractive.

These four examples are presented purely for illustrative purposes and are by no means complete. In fact, they do not even suggest a possibility of a "reverse swap"—the return to the original investment position—which is sometimes available.[16]

Investment in Junk Bonds

In Wall Street terminology, corporate bonds rated BB+ or lower by S&P are characterized as *junk bonds*. The connotation is that the investment community believes that, under unfavorable economic conditions, market prices of junk bonds will significantly drop, producing at least a paper loss.[17]

Table 8–8 presents a list of junk bonds. Clearly, the table indicates that most junk bonds offer high yields, reflecting the substantial default risks they carry. For instance, in January 1978 Diversified Industries had a yield to maturity of 14.33 percent[18] and Rapid-American had a yield to maturity of 12.34 percent.[19] The comparable yield on an AA corporate bond was around 8.6 percent.

The strategy of dealing in junk bonds is based on a clear understanding of the psychological dimension of the default risk premium. During periods of economic recession or high inflation, investors become increasingly concerned about the future of the economy and consequently become increasingly quality conscious. As investors become progressively conservative, they demand higher default risk premiums as a compensation for assuming higher default risk. More importantly, the prices of junk bonds can possibly decline far below their present or intrinsic value, thereby laying the foundation for the development of a junk bond strategy. Sophisticated investors who are able to spot *undervalued* junk bonds can capitalize on the high yields they offer.

[16] The advantages of a swap are reduced—sometimes significantly—when trading costs are taken into consideration. This factor is ignored in these discussions.

[17] Deep discount bonds should not be confused with junk bonds. Deep discount bonds sell at discount prices primarily because they carry a low coupon rate; junk bonds sell well below par because they carry substantial default risk.

[18]
$$i = \frac{\$98.75 + (\$1{,}000 - \$700)/13}{(\$1{,}000 + \$700)/2} = \frac{121.83}{850} = 14.33\%$$

[19]
$$i = \frac{\$70 + (\$1{,}000 - \$570)/16}{(\$1{,}000 + \$570)/2} = \frac{96.875}{785} = 12.34\%$$

Table 8–8

Company	Coupon %	Maturity	S&P Rating	Interest Coverage	Recent Price	1977 Price Range	Type
Altec	6¾	1988	CCC	1.35	59¼	64–55½	Debentures
Avco	7½	1993	B	2.92	79¾	80⅞–76	Subordinated Debs.#
Budget Capital	6	2010	B	1.69	59½	62–55	Income Debs.§
CNA Financial	8½	1995	BB	2.40	89⅝	93–88	Debentures
Chase Manhattan Mtge.	7½	1983	C*	0.16	68½	71¾–52¼	Subordinated Notes#
City Investing	8	1991	B	3.32	81⅞	86–78	Subordinated Debs.
Diversified Industries	9⅞	1991	CCC	0.15	70	78–61¼	Senior Debs.§
Fedders	8⅞	1994	B	1.19	81¾	90–76	Subordinated Debs.
Fuqua Industries	7	1988	B	2.11	78¾	81⅝–73¼	Subordinated Debs.#
General Host	7	1994	CCC	−0.55	68½	71⅜–64	Subordinated Debs.#
Gulf & Western—A	7	2003	NR	2.23	68	78–67¼	Subordinated Debs.#
Jones & Laughlin Ind.	6¾	1994	B	1.38	62¼	69¼–55	Subordinated Debs.
Keystone Steel & Wire	7¼	1993	BB	2.16	75	84⅝–75	Debentures
LTV	9¼	1997	B	1.32	79¾	87–74¼	Debentures
Lykes	7½	1994	CCC	1.43	62⅜	77–49⅝	Subordinated Debs.#
McCrory	7½	1994	CCC	1.13†	59½	67½–47⅜	Subordinated Debs.
Missouri Pacific RR	5	2045	B	3.26	56½	56½–49½	Income Bond‡#
NVF	5	1994	B	1.83	51	55–45	Subordinated Debs.
Rapid-American	7	1994	CCC	1.13	57	63⅞–46¼	Subordinated Debs.#
Standard Packaging	6	1990	B	1.33	62	65–60	Subordinated Debs.#
Telex	9	1996	CCC	1.62	78¾	85–67	Subordinated Debs.
White Motor	7¼	1993	B	1.29	70¾	73–65	Debentures
Wilson Foods	7⅞	1997	BB	1.26	80⅛	88¾–79¾	Debentures
Wisconsin Central RR	4½	2029	BB	4.38†	46¼	51¼–43¾	General Income
Zayre	8	1996	BB	1.11	88	91⅜–85	Debentures
INTEREST IN DEFAULT							
Chicago Milwaukee††	4	1994	D	−0.21	38⅜	39½–35½	First Mortgage
Guardian Mtge.	7½	1979	NR	−1.47	37	47–37	Senior Notes§#
Reading Co.	3⅛	1995	D	NA	36	36–17½	First Mortgage
Tri-South Mtge.	7¾	1980	NR	0.17	43	56–39	Senior Debs.§#

* Fitch Investors Service. † Coverage of parent company. ‡ Interest payable in April. †† Company will not be making next interest payment. # No sinking fund provision. § Subordinated. NR—Not Rated.

SOURCE: Adapted from "Is It Time for 'Junk'?" *Forbes*, January 23, 1978, p. 67.

Table 8–9

Particulars	ABC Bond	DEF Bond
Market Price of the bond (P_0):	\$1,000.00	\$693.00
Maturity of the bond (N):	10 years	10 years
Annual Interest Payments (C):	10% = \$100	5% = \$50
Description:	Par bond, A-rated	Deep discount bond, A-rated
Yield to Maturity:	10%	10%
Marginal tax rate (t_n)*:	50%	50%
Tax rate on long-term capital gains (40% of t_n)(cg):	20%	20%

ABC Bond

$$P_0 = \left[\sum_{n=1}^{N} \frac{C(1-t_n)}{(1+i_t)^n}\right] + \left[\frac{P_N - (P_N - P_0)(cg)}{(1+i_t)^N}\right]$$

$$\$1{,}000 = \left[\sum_{n=1}^{10} \frac{\$100(1-.5)}{(1+i_t)^n}\right] + \left[\frac{\$1{,}000 - (\$1{,}000 - \$1{,}000)(.20)}{(1+i_t)^{10}}\right]$$

$$\$1{,}000 = \sum_{n=1}^{10} \frac{\$50}{(1+i_t)^n} + \frac{\$1{,}000}{(1+i_t)^{10}}$$

Solve for i_t:

$$i_t = 5\%$$

DEF Bond

$$P_0 = \left[\sum_{n=1}^{N} \frac{C(1-t_n)}{(1+i_t)^n}\right] + \left[\frac{P_N - (P_N - P_0)(cg)}{(1+i_t)^N}\right]$$

$$\$693 = \left[\sum_{n=1}^{10} \frac{\$50(1-.5)}{(1+i_t)^n}\right] + \left[\frac{\$1{,}000 - (\$1{,}000 - \$693)(.20)}{(1+i_t)^{10}}\right]$$

$$\$693 = \sum_{n=1}^{10} \frac{\$25}{(1+i_t)^n} + \frac{\$939}{(1+i_t)^{10}}$$

Solve for i_t†:

$$i_t = 6.28\%$$

* Assume the tax bracket remains constant through year N.

† Solve through interpolation. See Chapter 6, footnote 4.

The Tax Issue

With the exception of discount bonds, corporate bonds offer no special tax advantages. A *discount bond* is one that sells at less than its par value. There is, of course, no tax advantage to discount bond insofar as the interest income is concerned. However, because discount bonds are sold at less than par value, investors holding discount bonds until maturity *automatically* realize a capital gain equal to the difference between the purchase price and the par value, thereby receiving the more favorable capital gains treatment.

For example, assume an ABC bond, due to mature in ten years, is selling at par with a coupon of 10 percent and its yield to maturity also equals 10 percent. Investors also have the choice of buying DEF, a deep discount bond. DEF is of the same quality and maturity and has the same yield to maturity as ABC, but has a coupon of only 5 percent, and is therefore currently selling for $693. At first glance, it might seem that investors should be indifferent in choosing between these two bonds, because both offer the same before-tax yield of 10 percent. However, as revealed in Table 8–9, an investor in the 50 percent tax bracket would realize an after-tax yield, i_t, of 6.28 percent from the DEF bond; the after-tax return from the ABC bond would be only 5 percent. The investor gains more from investing in the DEF bond by realizing a long-term capital gain, of which only 40 percent is subject to tax.

SECTION 2 PREFERRED STOCKS

An Overview

Basic Characteristics

A corporation may raise cash in the capital market by issuing three kinds of securities: common stock, corporate bonds, or preferred stock. *Preferred stock* is a kind of hybrid security characterized by features of both common stocks and bonds. It is similar to a bond in that preferred stock dividends are fixed. It is similar to a common stock in that preferred and common stocks together represent the equity or ownership of the corporation. However, preferred stock has several unique characteristics.

First, preferred stock dividends—which are frequently stated as a fixed percentage of the par value—must be paid before any distribution can be made to common stockholders.[20] Second, in the case of preferred stock with cumulative dividend features, if the company decides to skip payments for a year or more, the arrearages must be paid in full before any distribution can be made to common stockholders.[21] Third, after the preferred dividend has

[20] Note that in the case of a bond, a failure to pay interest or principal on specific dates constitutes a default; however, a failure to pay a dividend on preferred stock does not.

[21] In the case of a noncumulative dividend, once the dividend is skipped, it is gone forever.

been paid, a participating preferred stockholder participates along with common stockholders in the distribution of earnings. Finally, in the event of liquidation, preferred stockholders must be satisfied as to par or liquidation value, dividends, and premiums, if any, before any distribution can be made to common or junior security holders.

As mentioned in Chapter 2, an important type of preferred stock that has become increasingly popular in recent years is the convertible preferred. This type of stock carries a provision permitting the owner to convert it into a specified number of shares of common stock. For example, when selling a convertible preferred, a company might specify that every share of the new $100 preferred can be exchanged for, say, five shares of the company's common stock. If the common stock is currently selling at, say, $15 per share, this convertible feature has no value at this time. Nevertheless, the fact that the common stock has the *potential* for future price increases generally makes the convertible preferred stock more valuable than a nonconvertible, all else being equal. Therefore, a corporation can initially finance an operation by issuing convertible preferred stock which carries a smaller fixed dividend payment than that on a nonconvertible preferred stock. Analysis of convertible preferred stock parallels the analysis of convertible bonds (discussed in Chapter 17), although there are some differences between them. This section examines only nonconvertible preferred stock.

The Purchasers and the Issuers

The Purchasers

Until the early 1970s, preferred stock came to market in multimillion dollar issues with units almost always priced at $100 par value. The most important buyers of preferred stocks were insurance companies; they found preferred stock an attractive investment for at least one important reason: 85 percent of the preferred stock dividends received by these companies were tax exempt.[22]

However, in the 1970s the market for preferred stock shifted somewhat from its traditional domination by insurance companies and other large institutions toward more active participation by small investors. There were several reasons for this shift. For one thing, utility companies experienced a spectacular increase in demand for liquid funds which prompted them to offer new issues of preferred stock. For another, large institutions themselves experienced acute shortages of funds, and entered the preferred market as sellers rather than buyers. Utility companies attempted to offset declining institutional demand for their preferred stock by offering shares at $50, $25, even $10 per share to attract small investors.[23] To further attract individual investors, utilities began in the early 1970s to make sinking fund arrangements, which, as will be discussed later, made the preferred shares more attractive.

[22] The special tax feature of preferred stocks is discussed on pages 293–94.

[23] Small investors would presumably find lower priced shares more appealing because they can purchase a larger number of shares with a given amount of money.

The Issuers

Traditionally, nearly 90 percent of all preferred stock has been issued by utility companies. Utility companies generally maintain a balance between debt on the one hand and equity (common and preferred stock) on the other. The massive need for heavy investment triggered by explosive growth in the demand for energy, coupled with the sky-rocketing construction costs, have made it almost impossible for these companies to maintain the balance. Consequently, utility companies have needed equity to balance their debt-laden capitalizations and to lay the foundation for leveraging for future growth. However, in recent years their efforts to issue common stock have been frustrated because their stock prices have been depressed, and any increase in the number of outstanding common shares has become painfully dilutive. Issuing preferred stock was their next best choice.

Utilities are not the only institutions with financing problems. An increasing number of industrial firms have also needed additional funds to finance capital intensive projects—and have entered the preferred stock market as their next best alternative, despite its biggest drawback, the cost of preferred stock over debt. The interest on debt is tax deductible. But dividends on preferred stock, like those on common stock, are paid from after-tax income, which makes their cost to corporations roughly twice that of debt (assuming a 46 percent corporate tax rate).[24]

The Valuation Model[25]

The Basic Model

The Bond Valuation Model can be adapted for valuing preferred stock. The Bond Valuation Model is:

$$PV = \sum_{n=1}^{N} \frac{C}{(1+r)^n} + \frac{P_N}{(1+r)^N} \qquad \textbf{(6–1 restated)}$$

where

PV = Present value of the bond

C = Annual interest payments

P_N = Par value of the bond

N = Maturity of the bond

r = The appropriate discount rate or the investor's minimum required rate of return

[24] This tax aspect also helps explain why the most important issuers of preferred stock are utility companies. Utilities can declare taxes as an expense when filing with regulatory authorities for rate increases, and can thereby pass on taxes to customers in the form of higher prices. As a result, tax deductibility is not as important a consideration for utilities as it is to industrial firms.

[25] This model applies only to nonconvertible, nonparticipating preferred stock.

Because preferred stocks (1) pay dividends, D (rather than interest), (2) do not have a maturity price,[26] and (3) pay dividends forever, Eq. 6–1 can be rewritten as:

$$PV = \sum_{n=1}^{\infty} \frac{D}{(1+r)^n} \tag{8–2}$$

Finally, because dividend payments, D, are fixed, and if the appropriate discount rate, r, is assumed constant, Eq. 8–2 can be simplified[27] to what is known as the *Capitalization Formula*:

$$PV = \frac{D}{r} \tag{8–3}$$

Therefore, assuming an appropriate discount rate of 10 percent, the present value of a preferred stock paying an annual dividend of \$8 is \$80:

$$PV = \frac{\$8}{.10}$$
$$= \$80$$

Clearly, the present value of the preferred stock is inversely related to the discount rate. For example, an increase in the discount rate to 12 percent would lower the present value to \$66.67 (\$8/.12), whereas a decline in the discount rate to 6 percent would increase it to \$133.33 (\$8/.06).

The Current Yield

The Capitalization Formula can be further modified by substituting the market price, P_0, for the present value, PV, and the yield, i, for the appropriate discount rate, as follows:

$$P_0 = \frac{D}{i} \tag{8–4}$$

---

[26] However, if the issue has a sinking fund, this effectively creates a maturity date. Sinking funds are discussed on pages 289–90.

[27] Under continuous compounding conditions, Equation 8–2 is rewritten as:

$$PV = \int_0^{\infty} D(n)e^{-rn}\,dn$$

If $D(n)$ and r are constant, then:

$$PV = D\left[-\frac{1}{r}e^{-rn}\right]_{n=\infty} - D\left[-\frac{1}{r}e^{-rn}\right]_{n=0}$$
$$= \frac{D}{r}$$

With a slight modification, the equation can be used to determine the yield on a preferred stock:

$$i = \frac{D}{P_0} \tag{8-5}$$

where

P_0 = Current market price of preferred stock
D = Annual dividend payment
i = Yield on preferred stock

Note that because there is no maturity date on the preferred stock, the yield is expressed as the ratio of the dividend payment to the current market price, which is simply the current yield. Suppose the market price and dividend on a preferred stock are \$50 and \$5, respectively. The yield, reflecting a constant annual income return, would be 10 percent:[28]

$$\begin{aligned} i &= \frac{\$5}{\$50} \\ &= 10\% \end{aligned}$$

Risk Considerations

As with bonds, an investor's required rate of return on a preferred stock should equal a risk-free real rate of return plus a premium for the risk assumed with the investment:

$$r = r_{rf} + r_{rp} \qquad \text{(6-3 restated)}$$

where

r = The appropriate discount rate or the investor's minimum required rate of return
r_{rf} = Risk-free real rate of return
r_{rp} = Total risk premium

[28] However, it is assumed that the investor will hold a preferred stock for a finite period at the end of which it will be either sold or redeemed. Consequently, the return earned on the stock over the holding period will not necessarily be the same as the current yield, because the sale or redemption price can be different from the purchase price, in which case the investor will realize a capital gain or loss as well. This point will be evident as the discussion proceeds.

The total risk premium reflects the six types of risk—interest rate, inflation, maturity, default, callability, and liquidity risks.[29] Of these, interest rate, callability, and default risks are somewhat unique in the case of preferred stock and will be discussed here.

Interest Rate Risk

Like all fixed income securities, preferred stocks are subject to interest rate risk; an increase in the market interest rate tends to lower the market price of a preferred stock, whereas the reverse is true when the market interest rate declines. Because preferred stocks have no maturity dates, prices of these securities will advance and decline with the long-term market rate of interest for a given risk level. However, as demonstrated in Table 6–7 (p. 191), price fluctuations for fixed income securities will be greater (for a given market interest rate change) as the term to maturity increases. Consequently, for a given market interest rate change, the price changes in preferred stock with no maturity will be greater than price changes in fixed income securities that have a maturity date.

This last point is demonstrated in Table 8–10 in which Table 6–7 is modified to include the price change of a preferred stock as the market interest rate rises from 8 percent to 10 percent. Note that if the market interest rate is 8 percent, and the stock pays an $8 annual dividend, the price of the stock will be $100;

$$P_0 = \frac{\$8}{.08}$$

$$= \$100$$

If the market interest rate advances to 10 percent, the price of a preferred stock will fall to $80:

$$P_0 = \frac{\$8}{.10}$$

$$= \$80$$

Likewise, a $1,000 investment in the preferred stock would decline to $800, as indicated in Table 8–10.

Note, however, that the price of a 20-year bond with an 8 percent coupon declines from $1,000 to only $830 for the same market interest rate change. In this example, the preferred stock is clearly more volatile. Of course, a decline in market interest rates would also produce a greater price advance for the preferred stock investment.

[29] This is not entirely accurate. Because preferred stocks represent equity, they bear elements of systematic and unsystematic risks as well. In fact, Bildersic has demonstrated that realized returns on lower quality preferred stocks behave more like common stocks with low systematic risks. See J. Bildersic, "Some Aspects of the Performance of Nonconvertible Preferred Stocks," *Journal of Finance*, December 1973, pp. 1187–1201. However, because preferred stocks *generally* behave like bonds, they are discussed within the bond risk framework.

Table 8–10 **Bond and Preferred Stock Price Fluctuations for Various Maturities**

Valuation Models

Bond (with maturity date)	Preferred Stock (no maturity date)
Par value = $1,000	Par value = $100
Coupon rate = 8% = $80	Dividend rate = 8% = $8
$P_0 = \sum_{n=1}^{N} \frac{\$80}{(1+i)^n} + \frac{\$1,000}{(1+i)^N}$	$P_0 = \frac{\$8}{i}$

	Years to Maturity N =	**Prices (P_0)*** i **= 8%**	**Market Interest Rate Rises: i = 10%**	**Total Price Change**
Bond	1	$1,000	$982	−$ 18
	3	1,000	950	− 50
	5	1,000	924	− 76
	10	1,000	878	− 122
	20	1,000	830	− 170
Preferred Stock	No Maturity	1,000†	800	− 200

* Rounded to the nearest dollar.
† 10 shares purchased at $100 par value per share, for a $1,000 investment.

Callability Risk

Standard Call

In order to protect the interest of the issuer of preferred stock, most company charters include call provisions. These provisions basically state at what time and price, and on how much notice, an issuer may force the redemption of any given issue. A call provision protects the welfare of the issuer; that is, the issuer is allowed to retire an issue after a drop in market interest rates, and subsequently secure new capital at a lower cost.

The most common type of call provision is known as a *standard call.*[30] This generally provides that a company may not redeem an issue for a specified period

[30] Another type of call provision is known as the *conventional call.* This type of provision does not restrict the issuer as to when the stock may be redeemed. It merely states that redemption may be forced by the company through any means at specific prices plus accrued dividends on 30–60 days' notice. Although the issuer is not restricted as to means of redemption, the premium which must be paid tends to be considerably higher than the standard call premiums. For details, see Dennis A. Kraebel, "Analysis of Preferred Stock," in *Financial Analyst's Handbook,* ed. Sumner N. Levine (Homewood, Ill.: Dow Jones-Irwin, 1975), pp. 210–11.

(usually five years) except through the issuance of common stock at a premium to issue price. After the end of this call protection period, no restriction is placed on the means of redemption; however, some premium redemption price usually remains in effect for approximately 20 years.

Because the call price is above the par value or issue price, a preferred stockholder is afforded *some* protection if the issue is called. For example, suppose an investor purchases preferred stock with an \$8 annual dividend for \$100 per share. The current yield would be 8 percent. However, assume the issue is callable after five years at \$108 per share and that at the end of the call protection period the market interest rate declines significantly, prompting the company to call the issue. In this instance the investor's *yield to call* (covering the five-year period) would be 9.23 percent, which is higher than the 8 percent current yield. The yield to call can be approximated by using the following equation:

$$i_{cl} = \frac{D + (P_c - P_0)/M}{(P_c + P_0)/2} \tag{8-6}$$

where

i_{cl} = Yield to call on preferred stock
D = Annual dividend payment
P_c = Call price of stock
P_0 = Current market price (or purchase price) of stock
M = Years until stock is called

In this example

$$i_{cl} = \frac{\$8 + (\$108 - \$100)/5}{(\$108 + \$100)/2}$$

$$= \frac{9.6}{104} = 9.23\%$$

Although it might appear from this example that a call feature is beneficial to the investor, that is really not the case. The capital gain received from the forced redemption would be less than could be realized if the same stock is noncallable. Suppose, for example, that the market interest rate declines from 8 to 7 percent for a *noncallable* preferred stock. The stock price would rise from \$100 to \$114.29

$$P_0 = \frac{\$8}{.07}$$

$$= \$114.29$$

However, if the market interest rate drops to 7 percent and the preferred stock is not protected from call, an investor will not realize the same gain, because the company can redeem the issue at the \$108 call price. Therefore, an investor's potential capital gain from a preferred stock is limited by a call feature.

The impact of callability risk can also be examined from another standpoint. If the market interest rate on a preferred stock declines from 8 to 7 percent, and the investor is able to sell his stock for \$114.29, he could reinvest the \$114.29 in preferred stock with a current yield of 7 percent (the new market interest rate) and still earn the same \$8 annual dividend:

$$i = \frac{D}{P_0}$$

$$.07 = \frac{D}{\$114.29}$$

$$D = (.07)\$114.29$$

$$D = \$8$$

However, if the investor reinvests the \$108 proceeds from the call in preferred stock with a 7 percent yield, his annual dividend income will drop from \$8 to \$7.56:

$$i = \frac{D}{P_0}$$

$$.07 = \frac{D}{\$108}$$

$$D = (.07)(\$108)$$

$$D = \$7.56$$

Note also that if an investor purchases a preferred stock at a price higher than the call price *during* the period of call protection (as in the previous example, during the first five years), he could incur a capital loss if the company calls the stock *after* the call protection period is over.

Sinking Funds

A preferred stock sinking fund *obligates* a company issuing the stock to annually retire a certain number of preferred shares over a certain number of years at a set price until the *entire issue* has been retired. The company can either buy those shares on the open market, or it can call them at the previously announced set price (frequently without a premium over par).

A sinking fund provision is attractive to preferred stock investors because it provides the issue with more price stability than nonsinking fund preferred stock.[31] Even if market interest rates rise and the preferred stock price falls below par, the investor knows that eventually the par value will be returned.[32] In this regard, a preferred stock with a sinking fund begins to resemble a bond, because such a provision provides it with a maturity date and price.[33] As previously discussed, a change in market interest rates has a less pronounced effect on the price of a fixed income security with a maturity date than on the price of a preferred stock with no maturity.

Of course, investors should also be aware of the fact that sinking funds act as a price ceiling, because the issuing companies can always be expected to call the outstanding preferred stock if the call price is lower than the prevailing market price. Consequently, investors are hesitant to purchase a sinking fund preferred at a premium over the call price, because they will suffer a capital loss if the stock is called.

Investors generally find sinking preferred stocks more attractive than nonsinking fund preferred stocks, other things being equal. This is usually reflected in the relative market prices and yields of these securities. For example, in 1979, average yields on A-rated utility sinking fund preferred stocks were approximately .60 to .85 percent below those on A-rated utility nonsinking fund preferred stocks. That is, investors were willing to accept a lower yield in exchange for the sinking fund provision.

Default Risk

A preferred stock carries the risk that the company will not meet the timely payment of preferred stock dividends.[34] Technically, a company does not default for nonpayment of dividends, because holders of preferred stock have no legally enforceable right to dividends. However, the risk associated with these fixed income securities is effectively the same as the default risk on bonds. Preferred stockholders would, of course, assume a greater default risk than bondholders of the same company, because any interest payments must be made before dividends are paid. Also, in the event of liquidation or reorganization, the claims of preferred stockholders must be met after the claims of bondholders.

[31] Sinking fund preferreds are also attractive to many institutional investors because in certain situations the accounting treatment of these investments is more favorable than the accounting treatment of nonsinking fund preferreds.

[32] If the price of the preferred stock falls below par, the company can use the sinking fund to buy stock on the open market rather than call the stock at par (or at par plus a premium). However, if the investor does not sell on the open market, eventually the stock would have to be redeemed through a call. Incidentally, open market purchases by the issuer would create a demand for the issue and provide a price support, although this would not necessarily create a price floor.

[33] Actually, although a sinking fund provision specifies that the preferred stock will be redeemed, an investor cannot predict with certainty the year in which the stock will be redeemed. Consequently, investors buying sinking fund preferred stocks often calculate the *average life* (demonstrated for bonds earlier in the chapter) and use this as the maturity date. The yield-to-average life can be used as a measure of a stock's return over this period.

[34] In the case of sinking fund preferred issues, there is no guarantee that the sinking fund obligations will be met.

Table 8–11 **Standard & Poor's Preferred Stock Rating Definitions**

"AAA" This is the highest rating that may be assigned by Standard & Poor's to a preferred stock issue and indicates an extremely strong capacity to pay the preferred stock obligations.

"AA" A preferred stock issue rated "AA" also qualifies as a high-quality fixed income security. The capacity to pay preferred stock obligations is very strong, although not as overwhelming as for issues rated "AAA."

"A" An issue rated "A" is backed by a sound capacity to pay the preferred stock obligations, although it is somewhat more susceptible to the adverse effects of changes in circumstances and economic conditions.

"BBB" An issue rated "BBB" is regarded as backed by an adequate capacity to pay the preferred stock obligations. Whereas it normally exhibits adequate protection parameters, adverse economic conditions or changing circumstances are more likely to lead to a weakened capacity to make payments for a preferred stock in this category than for issues in the "A" category.

"BB," "B," "CCC" Preferred stock rated "BB," "B," and "CCC" are regarded, on balance, as predominately speculative with respect to the issuer's capacity to pay preferred stock obligations. "BB" indicates the lowest degree of speculation and "CCC" the highest degree of speculation. While such issues will likely have some quality and protective characteristics, these are outweighed by large uncertainties or major risk exposures to adverse conditions.

"CC" The rating "CC" is reserved for a preferred stock issue in arrears on dividends or sinking fund payments but that is currently paying.

"C" A preferred stock rated "C" is a non-paying issue.

"D" A preferred stock rated "D" is a non-paying issue with the issuer in default on debt instruments.

NR indicates that no rating has been requested, that there is insufficient information on which to base a rating, or that S&P does not rate a particular type of obligation as a matter of policy.

Plus (+) or Minus (−) To provide more detailed indications of preferred stock quality, the ratings from "AA" to "BB" may be modified by the addition of a plus or minus sign to show relative standing within the major rating categories.

SOURCE: Standard & Poor's *Stock Guide*, August 1979, p. 5.

Clearly, the higher the firm's financial leverage, the lower will be the protection afforded preferred stockholders.

An effective way to gauge the default risk associated with a preferred stock is to examine its rating by either of two major rating agencies, Standard & Poor's or Moody's. S&P's rating definitions are listed in Table 8–11. They are an assessment of a capacity and willingness of the issuing company to pay dividends on the stock and any applicable sinking fund obligations. In addition to considering the likelihood of these payments, the ratings are also based on the nature and provisions of the issue, as well as the relative position of the issue in the event of bankruptcy, reorganization, or other arrangements affecting creditors' rights. Because preferred stock is subordinate to debt within a particular capital structure, the preferred stock rating will generally not be higher than the bond rating of the senior debt of the same issuer.[35]

[35] A more detailed discussion of preferred stock analysis, including analysis of key financial ratios, can be found in *Standard & Poor's Ratings Guide* (New York: McGraw-Hill, 1979), pp. 57–64.

Figure 8–3 **Preferred Stock Yields**

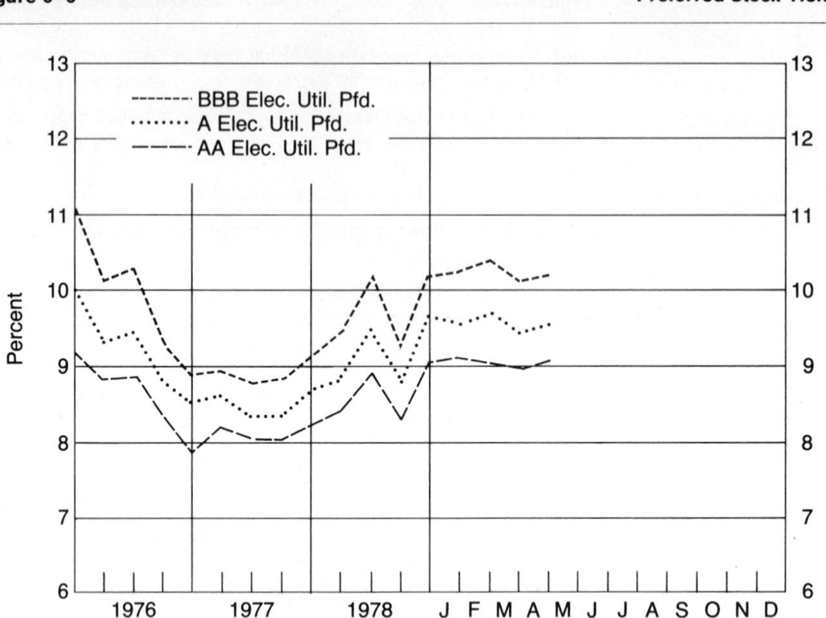

SOURCE: Dillon, Read & Co., Inc., "Preferred Stock Review and Outlook," Vol. 2, No. 4 (May 18, 1979), p. 9.

Naturally, preferred stocks with higher ratings will have lower current yields, and vice versa, reflecting the differences in the risk.[36] Figure 8–3 is a graph of representative yields on AA-, A-, and BBB-rated nonsinking fund electric utility preferred stock. As is the case with bonds, the spreads between the yields on preferred stock will vary over time.

Preferred Stock Investing

The Decision Model

As it does for bonds, the decision to buy or not to buy preferred stock depends on an investor's required rate of return and the stock's yield. If the yield is higher than the required rate of return, the stock is considered an attractive investment.

When comparing investments in a preferred stock and a corporate bond (assumed to be of the same company to make the comparison easier), an investor

[36] Of course, as it does with bonds, the default risk of preferred stocks within the same rating category will vary. Therefore, one could expect the yield on preferred stock in the same rating category to vary as well.

Table 8–12 Yields on High Quality Corporate Bonds and Preferred Stocks

	Aaa Corporate Bonds*	Preferred Stocks†
1970	8.04	7.22
1971	7.39	6.75
1972	7.21	7.27
1973	7.44	7.23
1974	8.57	8.23
1975	8.83	8.38
1976	8.43	7.97
1977	8.02	7.60
1978	8.73	8.25
1979	9.63	9.07

* Averages of daily figures from Moody's Investors Service.
† Standard & Poor's corporate series. Rate based on a sample of ten issues: four public utilities, four industrials, one financial, and one transportation.

SOURCE: Data from *Federal Reserve Bulletin.*

would generally require a higher rate of return from the preferred stock, because a preferred stock would have greater interest rate and default risks than a comparable bond. However, there are times when the yield on a preferred stock is less than or equal to the yield on the bonds of the same corporation.

This apparent phenomenon can be seen in Table 8–12, which shows representative yields, over time, on Moody's highest rated (Aaa) corporate bonds, and on preferred stocks in Standard & Poor's Preferred Stock Price Index. Although the stocks in S&P's Index are ten high grade issues, only two issues carry S&P's highest preferred rating (AAA); the majority carry an A− to A+ rating.[37] An individual investor, therefore, would generally expect the average yield on these preferred stocks to be *at least* as high as the average yield on the Aaa corporate bonds, and probably higher. Table 8–12 clearly indicates, however, that over the years the yield on preferred stocks has actually been *lower.* These low yields are the result of special tax features of these stocks.

Tax Features

In order to prevent triple taxation, the law permits corporations to deduct 85 percent of dividend income from investment in taxable corporations, which includes investment in preferred stocks.[38] *No such exemption is allowed individual investors.* Consequently, this tax provision has produced a market for

[37] Two issues are rated AAA, one issue is rated AA, six are rated A− to A+, and another is not rated.

[38] Suppose Corporation A owns stock in Corporation B, and Corporation B pays a dividend out of its after-tax earnings. First, Corporation B would pay its regular taxes. Corporation A would then pay a tax on the dividend received from Corporation B. Finally, the stockholders in Corporation A would be subject to tax on dividends they receive. This would constitute triple taxation. To alleviate this problem, federal tax law allows intercorporate dividends (for example, dividends paid by Corporation B to Corporation A) to be taxed at very low rates.

preferred stocks which favors the institution; individual investors are effectively priced out of the market.

To better understand this point, consider the 1979 yields for the preferred stocks and high quality corporate bonds in Table 8–12. A corporation holding a corporate bond with a 9.63 percent yield (assume it is selling at par), and in the 46 percent marginal tax bracket (corporate tax rate) would receive an after-tax return of 5.2 percent $[9.63\% - (9.63\%)(46\%)]$. The preferred stock yield is only 9.07 percent; however, a corporation's *after-tax* return, taking into account the 85 percent dividend excluded, is 8.44 percent:

$$(9.07\%) - [(9.07\%)(46\%)(15\%)] = 8.44\%$$

For corporations, the preferred stock clearly provides a higher *after-tax* return than the corporate bond. This higher return can adequately compensate them for the perceived risk differential between these securities. Consequently, institutions are willing to purchase preferred stocks at pretax current yields which individual investors, without the tax exclusion, often find unattractive.

Summary

Newly issued corporate bonds are sold either through a public offering or through private placement with institutional investors. Major purchasers of corporate bonds include insurance companies, households, and pension funds. The bond market has experienced enormous growth in recent years. There has also been a general increase in the level of coupon rates.

According to the Bond Decision Model, an investor should consider a corporate bond suitable for purchase if its yield is higher than the appropriate discount rate, also known as the investor's minimum required rate of return for the bond. The required rate of return, of course, equals a risk-free real rate plus a premium for the risks associated with the bond.

Corporate bonds are subject to the interest rate, inflation, and maturity risks that affect all types of bonds; in addition, they are subject to default, callability, and liquidity risks.

Sophisticated strategies relating to corporate bonds include various *swapping techniques* as well as investing in *deep discount* and *junk bonds.*

Because the annual dividends on preferred stocks are fixed and these stocks have no maturity date, they can be valued by the *Capitalization Formula.* Accordingly, the yield on a preferred stock is expressed as the ratio of the dividend payment to the current market price, which is simply the current yield.

As with bonds, an investor's required rate of return on a preferred stock equals a risk-free real rate of return plus a premium for the risks assumed with the investment. This chapter focused in particular on three important risks of preferred stocks: interest rate risk, callability risk, and default risk.

Present tax laws permit corporations, but not individual investors, to deduct 85 percent of dividend income from investment in taxable corporations, which includes investment in preferred stocks. As a result, even when the *pretax* yield on a preferred stock is below that on a comparable corporate bond, the stock can provide a corporation with a higher *after-tax* return (and adequate compensation for the perceived additional risk) than the bond. However, the pretax preferred stock yields which corporations are willing to accept are often unattractive to individual investors (who do not receive the tax exclusion).

A Look Ahead

In Part 2, consisting of Chapters 6 through 8, we have discussed investments in fixed income securities. In Chapter 6, a theory of bond analysis was developed which provided a framework for analyzing government and municipal bonds, corporate bonds, and preferred stocks.

In Part 3, we will discuss investments in common stock. In Chapter 9, a theory of common stock analysis will be developed. This will be followed in later chapters by fundamental and technical analysis of common stock.

Concepts for Review

Financing techniques of corporate bonds
Bond quotations
Yield to maturity
Current yield
Corporate bond ratings
Default risk
Expected yield
Callability risk
Callable bond
First call
Sinking fund
Average life
Deep discount bonds
Liquidity risk
Bid–ask spread
Effective rate
Variable reinvestment rate
Swapping techniques
Junk bonds
Preferred stock
Capitalization Formula
Standard call
Preferred stock ratings
Corporate dividend exclusion

Questions for Review

1. Explain some of the factors that Standard & Poor's uses to rate corporate bonds.
2. Explain the relationship between a bond's rating and its default risk.
3. If the yields to maturity on callable and noncallable bonds (similar in all other respects) are the same, what should this indicate to an investor?

4. How is the average life of a bond determined?
5. Explain why you as a prospective bond buyer would prefer to invest in a bond with a generous call protection.
6. Explain the concept of variable reinvestment rate. Why is it important to bond investors?
7. Why do corporate bonds have higher liquidity risk than government bonds?
8. What is the difference between a discount bond and a junk bond?
9. Distinguish between current yield, yield to maturity, and coupon rate. Discuss the concepts involved.
10. Other things being equal, why might an investor prefer a discount bond over a bond selling above par?
11. How does the valuation model for preferred stocks differ from the valuation model for corporate bonds?
12. XYZ Company $8\frac{1}{2}$s of 2000 are rated AA by Standard & Poor's and are selling at par. ABC Corporation $8\frac{1}{2}$s of 2000 are also rated AA by Standard & Poor's, but are selling at $98\frac{1}{4}$. In general terms, discuss the possible reasons for the difference in price.
13. Explain interest rate and default risk as they apply to preferred stock.
14. Can a preferred stockholder ever benefit from a call?
15. Contrast the before-tax and after-tax yield on a preferred stock for both individuals and corporations. How do taxes affect the attractiveness of preferred stock to both types of investors?

Problems

1. Determine the yield to maturity on the following bonds using the approximation method. Use 1980 as the current year.

Bond	Market Price	Coupon Rate	Year of Maturity
XYZ	97	10.0%	2000
ABC	$95\frac{1}{4}$	7.5	1998
QRS	106	12.25	2005
DEF	$102\frac{3}{4}$	9.75	1990

2. ABC Corporation has outstanding an 8 percent coupon bond selling at 98, with ten years remaining to maturity.
   a. What is the promised yield to maturity?
   b. What is the expected yield to maturity?

   Assume all interest payments will be made on schedule, and that the following probabilities will apply with regard to the principal repayment at maturity.

Payment	Probability
$1,000	.85
500	.10
0	.05

c. Suppose a U.S. treasury bond with ten years to maturity is presently yielding 7.75 percent. How will this information influence your decision to purchase the ABC bond?

3. LTL Company preferred stock is selling at $100 per share and paying a $9.75 per share annual dividend.
   a. What is the current yield?
   b. At what price would you expect LTL preferred stock to sell if the market interest rate for this security were 8 percent? 11 percent?
   c. Suppose the LTL preferred stock is callable at 109.75 at the end of a five-year call protection period, and at the end of this period the market interest rate is 8 percent. What would you expect to be an investor's return on this stock for the five-year holding period? What if the market interest rate is 11 percent?
   d. Suppose LTL Company has outstanding a 20-year bond selling at par and yielding 10 percent. Compare the after-tax yields on the bond and preferred stock for a corporation and individual investor. Assume both investors are in the 46 percent tax bracket. [Ignore the assumptions made in (c) of this exercise.]

4. The following two bonds are currently traded:

	ABC	XYZ
Coupon:	$6\frac{3}{4}$%	10%
Maturity:	20 years	20 years
Current Price:	$72\frac{1}{2}$	100
Call Feature:	Callable after 5 years	Callable after 5 years
Call Price:	106.75	110
Rating:	A	A

Based on this information, and assuming the market interest rate for both securities will be 8 percent after five years, which bond would you find more attractive? Specify any other assumptions you make in answering this question.

5. Analyze a corporate bond of your choice, considering all the applicable risk premiums. Do you find it suitable for purchase? Show all your work and assumptions. (Note: You can consult *Moody's Bond Record* or *Standard & Poor's Bond Guide* for current bond data. The major contractual features of a company's bonds can be found in a recent edition of one of *Moody's Manuals*.) Hint: Study the Caesars World Bond Analysis in the Appendix before attempting this question.

Footnotes

4. The yield to maturity is derived in the following manner:

$$\$970 = \sum_{n=1}^{20} \frac{\$107.50}{(1+i)^n} + \frac{\$1{,}000}{(1+i)^{20}}$$

At $i = 12\%$, and $N = 20$ years, PVAF = 7.469, and PVFF = .104,

$$P_0 = (\$107.50)(7.469) + (\$1{,}000)(.104)$$
$$= \$802.92 + \$104$$
$$= \$906.92$$

At $i = 11\%$ and $n = 20$ years, PVAF = 7.96, and PVFF = 0.124

$$\begin{aligned} P_0 &= (\$107.50)(7.96) + (\$1{,}000)(0.124) \\ &= \$855.7 + \$124 \\ &= \$979.70 \end{aligned}$$

Interpolating:

$$\frac{12 - 11}{12 - i} = \frac{\$906.92 - \$979.70}{\$906.92 - \$970.00}$$

$$-873.36 + 72.78i = -63.08$$

$$72.78i = 810.28$$

$$i = 11.13$$

Therefore, at $i = 11.13\%$

$$P_0 = \$970$$

8. $$\$932 = \sum_{n=1}^{5} \frac{\$80}{(1+i)^n} + \frac{\$950}{(1+i)^5}$$

At $i = 9\%$

$$P_0 = \$928.60$$

At $i = 8\%$

$$P_0 = \$965.97$$

Interpolating:

At $i = 8.9\%$

$$P_0 = \$932$$

Selected Readings

Altman, Edward I. "Financial Ratios, Discriminant Analysis and Prediction of Corporate Bankruptcy." *Journal of Finance*, September 1968.

The Anatomy of the Secondary Market in Corporate Bonds: Year-end, 1977 Update. New York: Salomon Brothers, 1978.

Atkinson, Thomas R. *Trends in Corporate Bond Quality*. National Bureau of Economic Research. New York: Columbia University Press, 1967.

Bildersec, John. "Some Aspects of Performance of Nonconvertible Preferred Stocks." *Journal of Finance*, December 1973.

Cook, Timothy Q. "Some Factors Affecting Long-term Yield Spreads in Recent Years." Federal Reserve Bank of Richmond, *Monthly Review*, September 1973.

Darst, David M. *The Complete Bond Book*. New York: McGraw-Hill, 1975.

Donaldson, Gordon. *Corporate Debt Capacity*, Part 2. Boston, Mass.: Harvard University, Graduate School of Business Administration, 1961.

Donaldson, Gordon. "In Defense of Preferred Stocks." *Harvard Business Review*, July–August 1962.

Edmister, Robert O. "An Empirical Test of Financial Ratio Analysis for Small Business Failure Prediction." *Journal of Financial and Quantitative Analysis*, March 1972.

Ehrbar, A. F. "Unraveling the Mysteries of Corporate Profits." *Fortune*, August 27, 1979.

Hickman, W. Braddock. *Corporate Bond Quality and Investor Experience*. New York: National Bureau of Economic Research, 1958.

Kaufman, Henry. *The Anatomy of the Secondary Market in Corporate Bonds*. New York: Salomon Brothers, 1973.

Kraebel, Dennis A. "Analysis of Preferred Stock." In *Financial Analyst's Handbook*. Sumner N. Levine, ed. Homewood, Ill.: Dow Jones-Irwin, 1975.

Pinches, George E. "The Role of Subordination and Industrial Bond Ratings." *Journal of Finance*, March 1975.

Pinches, George E. and Kent A. Mingo. "A Multivariate Analysis of Industrial Bond Ratings." *Journal of Finance*, March 1973.

Standard & Poor's Ratings Guide. New York: McGraw-Hill, 1979.

West, Richard R. "An Alternative Approach to Predicting Bond Ratings." *Journal of Accounting Research*, Spring 1970.

Zwick, Burton. "The Market for Corporate Bonds." Federal Reserve Bank of New York, *Quarterly Review*, Autumn 1977.

Appendix 8-A: Caesars World Bond: A Short Analysis

In early 1979 Investor A considers the purchase of Caesars World Senior Subordinated Sinking Fund debentures. The bond has a 12.0 percent coupon, matures in 15 years (1994), and has a market price (ask price) of 96.25. These securities carry Standard & Poor's B rating.

Bond Yield

Using Equation 8–1, the bond's yield to maturity works out to 12.48 percent:[1]

$$i = \frac{\$120 + (\$1{,}000 - \$962.50)/15}{(\$1{,}000 + \$962.50)/2}$$

$$= 12.48\%$$

[1] Using Equation 6–2 (p. 167):

$$\$962.50 = \sum_{n=1}^{15} \frac{\$120}{(1+i)^n} + \frac{\$1{,}000}{(1+i)^{15}}$$

and interpolating, the yield to maturity, i, is slightly higher than 12.48 percent.

The current yield of 12.47 percent ($120/$962.50) is slightly lower than the yield to maturity because the bond is selling at a small discount from par value.

Appropriate Discount Rate

After determining that the market is offering a 12.48 percent yield to maturity on the bond, given her risk preference, Investor A proceeds to determine whether or not this return is adequate; that is, if the yield is greater than the appropriate discount rate, or her minimum required rate of return (which is, of course, comprised of a risk-free real rate plus a risk premium that reflects the various types of risks associated with the bond).

Next, Investor A proceeds to analyze the various types of risk associated with the Caesars World debentures. Naturally, the perception and analysis of these bond risks can vary between individuals; consequently, this particular evaluation may not be universally acceptable.

A Reference Point

In her analysis, as a reference point, Investor A uses the yield on government bonds with approximately the same maturity as the Caesars World debentures. She notes that the yield on treasury bonds maturing in 1994 is 8.9 percent, and assumes that it comprises a 3.0 percent risk-free real rate of return and a 5.90 percent premium for inflation, maturity, and interest rate risks. Investor A notes that these bonds carry no default and callability risks, and negligible liquidity risk.

Investor A expects the Caesars World bonds to yield approximately 8.9 percent to provide the same risk-free real return plus compensation for inflation, maturity, and interest rate risks.[2] However, in this case she expects a higher return because these bonds *also* carry default, callability, and liquidity risks.

The Caesars World bonds, of course, have a promised yield of 12.48 percent. Investor A attempts to determine if the 3.58 percent spread between the two yields is sufficient for the extra risks she would assume by purchasing the

[2] Of course, the degree of risk discussed here would not be exactly the same for both bonds. For example, the prices of higher quality bonds are more responsive to market interest rate fluctuations than lower rated bonds, because the proportion of the total yield representing interest rate, maturity, and inflation risk premiums is greater for higher quality bonds than lower quality bonds. As a result, an upward shift in market interest rates, due to higher anticipated inflation, for example, would produce a greater proportional change in the yield of the higher quality issues. However, in this analysis it is assumed that Investor A is willing to accept the 8.9 percent government bond yield as adequate for the risk-free real return and inflation, maturity, and interest rate risk premiums associated with the Caesars World issue.

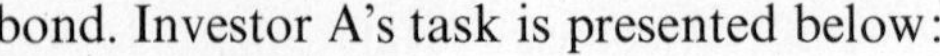

bond. Investor A's task is presented below:

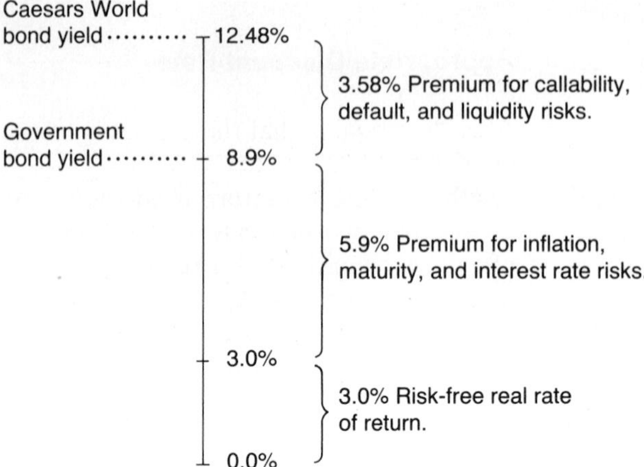

Is the premium offered for the extra risk of the Caesars World bond sufficient for Investor A? If the yield spread is considered acceptable, this would imply that the bond's yield meets Investor A's minimum required rate of return.

One way to determine if the extra yield is adequate to compensate for the additional risk is to adjust the 12.48 percent promised yield for the possibility that Investor A would actually receive a lower rate of return. If the adjusted or expected yield is greater than 8.9 percent, Investor A will conclude that the yield spread is acceptable.

Callability Risk

Until 1984[3] Caesars World debentures carry a call protection. From 1985 through 1993, the company will make mandatory annual payments of $1,125,000 (7.5 percent of the original $15 million issue) into a sinking fund. Each year, the fund will be used to retire bonds—a total of 67.5 percent of the issue prior to maturity. Depending on the level of market interest rates, Caesars World may retire the bonds at the call price of 100 or buy the bonds in the open market if the market price is below 100. Although Investor A does not feel that she can accurately predict the future market interest rates for this analysis, she assumes that 7.5 percent of the issue will be called each year after 1984, leaving a 32.5 percent or .325 probability that her bonds would be retired on the maturity date.[4] These features are presented in Table 8–A. The average life is computed to be about 12 years.

[3] These bonds may be called prior to 1984 at a premium, but are not refundable at lower interest cost. Investor A does not expect a call during this period.

[4] This assumption not only facilitates Investor A's analysis, but is also reasonable, because the bonds are selling close to par. A small decline in the market interest rate would push the market price over 100 and make a call advantageous to Caesars World. If the bonds were selling at a large discount, however, the above assumption might not be reasonable.

Table 8–A

(1) Year	(2) Probability of Call	(3) Life of Debenture (Years)	(4) Col (2) × (3)
1985	.075	6	.450
1986	.075	7	.525
1987	.075	8	.600
1988	.075	9	.675
1989	.075	10	.750
1990	.075	11	.825
1991	.075	12	.900
1992	.075	13	.975
1993	.075	14	1.050
1994	.325	15	4.875
	1.000		Average Life = 11.625

The callability risk premium is calculated by using Equation 6–4 (p. 185):

$$P_0 = \sum_{n=1}^{M} \frac{C}{(1 + i_c)^n} + \sum_{n=M+1}^{N} \frac{(i_r)(CP)}{(1 + i_c)^n} + \frac{CP}{(1 + i_c)^N}$$

Investor A uses the average life of 12 years as the period to call, M, and assumes that, for the remaining three years, she can reinvest the proceeds received from the forced redemption, or $CP = \$1{,}000$ per bond, at 9.0 percent. Incroporating this information in Equation 6–4, we obtain:

$$\$962.50 = \sum_{n=1}^{12} \frac{\$120}{(1 + i_c)} + \sum_{n=13}^{15} \frac{(.09)(\$1{,}000)}{(1 + i_c)^n} + \frac{(\$1{,}000)}{(1 + i_c)^{15}}$$

To solve this equation, the value of the *expected holding period yield*, i_c, is calculated at 12.30 percent.[5] Investor A notes that, although this 12.30 percent yield is smaller than the 12.48 percent yield to maturity, it is nevertheless higher than the 8.9 percent government bond yield. Of course, Investor A realizes that she has yet to consider the additional risks carried by the Caesars World bond.

---

[5] For any i_c

P_0 = (\$120)(PVAF for 12 years) + (\$90)(PVAF for 15 years − PVAF for 12 years) + (\$1,000)(PVFF for 15 years)

At $i_c = 12\%$

$$P_0 = (\$120)(6.194) + (\$90)(6.811 - 6.194) + (\$1{,}000)(.183) = \$982$$

At $i_c = 14\%$

$$P_0 = (\$120)(5.660) + (\$90)(6.142 - 5.660) + (\$1{,}000)(.140) = \$863$$

Interpolating, at $i_c = 12.30\%$, $P_0 = \$962.50$. To simplify the calculations, the average life of 11.625 years computed in Table 8-A was rounded to 12 years.

Default Risk

Initial and Comparative Analysis

Investor A considers the default risk of the Caesars World debentures. As previously mentioned, these bonds carry Standard & Poor's B rating, which is assigned to speculative grade bonds which carry substantial default risk. A substantial default risk premium largely reflects the yield spread between this bond and similar maturity government bonds.[6]

However, Investor A is confident about the prospects for the gambling industry in general and Caesars World in particular. She thinks that the company's erratic operating record should stabilize once its Atlantic City casino is opened, which in turn will result in a more consistent level of fixed charge coverage. Therefore, even though the company's current financial condition is very weak, and the default risk is significant, Investor A is more confident about the ability of Caesars World to make full and timely interest and sinking fund payments than other companies which have about the same capitalization and fixed charge coverage ratios, and B-rated bonds with roughly equivalent maturities and yields. Furthermore, she also sees the distinct possibility that the bond's rating will be upgraded in the near future, in which case, *ceteris paribus*, the yield spread between the Caesars World and government bond would narrow considerably. Based on this initial analysis and comparison, Investor A believes that the market does not share her optimistic forecast about these bonds, and that the default risk premium included in the yield spread should be an adequate compensation for the risk of default she would assume by investing in the bond.

Probability of Default

For many investors, the initial and comparative analysis might be sufficient to determine whether a bond offers adequate compensation for default risk. However, Investor A will attempt to undertake a more sophisticated analysis of the bond's default risk. Consequently, in order to calculate the expected yield, she has assigned statistical probabilities to the chance that Caesars World might not make the scheduled interest and principal payments.[7]

---

[6] Of course, callability and liquidity risk premiums would also be included in this spread.

[7] The total probability of default assigned by Investor A in this section to the Caesars World bond is consistent with the *default rate* experience for bonds rated BB and less for the period 1900–44. See Walter Braddock Hickman, *Corporate Bond Quality and Investor Experience* (New York: National Bureau of Economic Research, 1958), p. 10. However, to assign such a probability would normally require a complete analysis of the present and future financial position of the company, as well as certain subjective considerations. Also, although determining the probability of default is obviously a difficult task, estimating the time of default as well as the amount and time of payment makes the task even more onerous.

Investor A's most pessimistic forecast is that there is a 20 percent probability that (1) Caesars World will default before the end of the 12-year average life, (2) it will pay interest only for the first ten years, and (3) it will make no interest or principal payments thereafter. Under these assumptions the return on the bond would be only 4.23 percent:[8]

$$\$962.50 = \sum_{n=1}^{10} \frac{\$120}{(1+i)^{10}} + \sum_{n=11}^{15} \frac{\$0}{(1+i)^n} + \frac{\$0}{(1+i)^{15}}$$

$$i = 4.23\%$$

She also assigns a 20 percent probability that the company will default after paying interest for ten years, pay no interest thereafter, and make a \$500 liquiditing payment in the fifteenth or last year. The yield would then be 8.0 percent:

$$\$962.50 = \sum_{n=1}^{10} \frac{\$120}{(1+i)^{10}} + \sum_{n=11}^{15} \frac{\$0}{(1+i)^n} + \frac{\$500}{(1+i)^{15}}$$

$$i = 8.0\%$$

After assigning a 40 percent *total* probability of default to the bond, Investor A assigns a 60 percent probability that she will receive the 12.30 percent expected holding period yield estimated in the previous section. The various probabilities are summarized as follows:

Yield (1)	Probability (2)	Col (1) × (2)
12.30%	.60	7.38%
8.00	.20	1.60
4.23	.20	.85
	1.00	9.83%

After adjusting the original 12.48 percent yield to maturity for the callability and default risks, the expected yield on the Caesars World debentures is only 9.83 percent, or 2.65 percent lower than the 12.48 percent promised yield to maturity. However, the expected yield is still greater than the 8.9 percent government bond yield. At this point the Caesars World debentures still appear to be an attractive investment, which is consistent with her earlier evaluation.

Liquidity Risk Considered

If Investor A wishes to sell her Caesars World bonds prior to maturity, she will have to pay a substantial cost for the following reasons. Because her trade would be relatively small in comparison to trades in multiples of 100 bonds

[8] Actually, the bond could have a selling price even after default, if payments from the company were still expected. In that case, the yield would be higher.

by large investors, and because this issue is of lower quality and not actively traded, Investor A estimates that the bid–ask spread could easily range from one to two points.[9]

The liquidity risk of this bond could be significant if Investor A's expected holding period is short. For example, if she intends to sell the bond after one year in the secondary market, her return over this period could be reduced by 1 to 2 percent.[10] However, Investor A has been analyzing the bonds under the assumption that she intends to hold them until they mature or are called.[11] Consequently, she does not consider the liquidity risk to be a significant factor.

The Decision

After analyzing the callability, default, and liquidity risks associated with the Caesars World debentures, Investor A concludes that the yield spread provides sufficient compensation for the additional risks she would assume by investing in them. Specifically, she notes that, after adjusting for callability and default risks, the expected yield of the debentures is 9.83 percent, which is higher than the 8.9 percent yield she would accept for the risk-free real return and a premium for inflation, maturity, and interest rate risks. Consequently, she concludes that the 12.48 percent yield to maturity provided by the Caesars World bonds exceeds her minimum required rate of return.

Investor A, of course, realizes that although this bond may constitute a sound investment, other securities—especially deep discount bonds—might offer more attractive investment opportunities. Furthermore, she also recognizes that no sound investment strategy can be developed without considering the tax consequences of such investment.

[9] For a discussion of bid–ask spreads on bonds carrying varying degrees of liquidity risk, see Chapter 6, page 187.

[10] Note, however, that when bonds are held for a longer period, the impact of a secondary market sale diminishes. Suppose, for example, the Caesars World bonds are sold in the fifteenth year in the secondary market. If they were sold at the bid price of $985, the yield to maturity (for the 15-year holding period) would be only slightly lower than the yield to maturity if the $1,000 maturity price were received.

[11] Of course, if the bonds are called, she might have to pay dealer fees when reinvesting her money for the remainder of the holding period. Also, in the case of default, it is assumed that she would hold the bonds until the final liquidating payments were made.

3 Common Stock: Valuation and Analysis

In Part 3, we begin the process of analyzing equity securities. In keeping with our original approach, we first build a valuation model; subsequently, this model is used as a basis for analyzing individual securities.

In Chapter 9, we construct a model for calculating the present value of a common stock. The model identifies dividends, price changes, and the appropriate discount rate as the independent variables for determining the present value.

Chapters 10 and 11 are devoted to a detailed discussion of the techniques for estimating the values of the three independent variables. Chapter 10 begins with a discussion of general economic conditions which affect the value of a common stock. This is followed by an analysis of industry conditions which also influence common stocks. Finally, a detailed analysis of company earnings is undertaken on the premise that earnings are the basic component of a stock's present value. Chapter 11 deals with the valuation model and extends the discussion of common stock valuation through a demonstration of the technique for estimating each of the three key variables of the Common Stock Valuation Model

Finally, Chapter 12 deals with technical analysis and various techniques for forecasting future market prices of stocks on the basis of past price changes.

Common Stock Valuation and Analysis

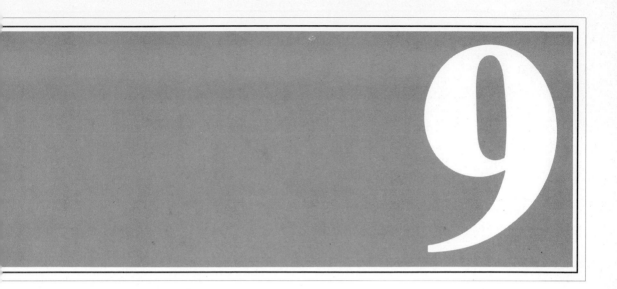

Introduction

In Chapter 6, a Bond Valuation Model was constructed which was subsequently used for the valuation and analysis of government and corporate bonds. In this chapter, a Common Stock Valuation Model will be constructed, to be used for the analysis of common stock.

More specifically, a Perpetual Dividend Model will be introduced to underscore the point that common stocks have a perpetual life and that, therefore, dividends might be paid forever. However, because this model is difficult to use, a more practical model—the Holding Period Dividend Model—will be presented and the key variables of this model will be identified. Next, the techniques for estimating the values of each of these variables will be discussed. Finally, the Decision Model will be presented, along with a demonstration of its use to identify undervalued and overvalued stocks.

Common Stock Valuation Model

Perpetual Dividend Model

In Chapter 6, it was emphasized that the present value of a bond is the stream of future interest payments plus the maturity price, discounted by the interest rate appropriate for the risk associated with the bond. The construction of the Bond Valuation Model is simplified by the fact that (1) throughout the life of a bond the annual interest payments remain fixed, and (2) every bond has a maturity date and a maturity price.[1]

But the Bond Valuation Model cannot be used directly for the valuation of common stocks for two reasons. First, unlike fixed coupon payments on a bond, dividend payments on a common stock fluctuate—sometimes widely—and therefore they cannot be treated as fixed. Second, because common stocks have a perpetual life, they do not have a maturity date or a maturity price. Therefore, a new model must be developed for the valuation of common stocks.

Because common stocks do not have a maturity price, dividends on common stocks may theoretically be received forever. Consequently, the present value of a common stock may be expressed as a stream of future dividend payments, discounted to perpetuity by an interest rate appropriate for the relevant risk involved. Symbolically, the *Perpetual Dividend Model* can be represented as

$$PV = \frac{D_1}{(1+r)^1} + \frac{D_2}{(1+r)^2} + \frac{D_3}{(1+r)^3} + \frac{D_4}{(1+r)^4} + \frac{D_5}{(1+r)^5} + \cdots + \frac{D_\infty}{(1+r)^\infty} \tag{9-1}$$

where

PV = Present value of the common stock
$D_1, D_2, \ldots, D_\infty$ = Annual dividend payments from Period 1 to infinity
r = The appropriate discount rate or the investor's minimum required rate of return

Equation 9–1 can be used to determine the present value of a stream of variable dividend payments, discounted by a fixed discount rate.[2] In this case, because the appropriate discount rate is assumed to remain fixed, Equation 9–1 can be reduced to the following convenient form:[3]

$$PV = \sum_{n=1}^{\infty} \frac{D_n}{(1+r)^n} \tag{9-2}$$

[1] Perpetual bonds do not have a maturity date. However, in this country this type of bond has never been issued.

[2] Most common stock valuation models assume that the discount rate remains fixed. Cases involving variable dividend and discount rates can be handled by using the following modified equation:

$$PV = \frac{D_1}{(1+r_1)} + \frac{D_2}{(1+r_1)(1+r_2)} + \frac{D_3}{(1+r_1)(1+r_2)(1+r_3)} + \cdots + \frac{D_\infty}{(1+r_1)(1+r_2)(1+r_3)\cdots(1+r_\infty)}$$

Note that if $r_1 = r_2 = r_3 = r_\infty$, this equation reverts to Equation 9–1.

[3] If, in addition to the assumption of fixed discount rate, the dividend payment is also assumed constant, then under conditions of continuous compounding Equation 9–2 becomes:

Holding Period Dividend Model

Basic Concept

The Perpetual Dividend Model can be used only if the annual dividend payments expected to be received *forever* can be accurately predicted. In the real world, forecasting of annual dividends into infinity is a statistical nightmare if not a virtual impossibility. Fortunately, the Perpetual Dividend Model can be converted into a *Holding Period Dividend Model.*

A convenient starting point is to modify the Bond Valuation Model by (1) substituting variable stock dividend payments for annual bond interest payments, and (2) substituting the sale price at the end of the holding period for the maturity price of the bond. Even though a common stock does not have a maturity date, in view of the fact that most investors invest in common stocks with the objective of selling them sometime in the foreseeable future, it is reasonable to assume that it has a finite holding period. Therefore, the modified Bond Valuation Model can be expressed as:

$$PV = \sum_{n=1}^{N} \frac{D_n}{(1+r)^n} + \frac{P_N}{(1+r)^N} \tag{9-3}$$

where

PV = Present value of the common stock

D_n = Annual dividend payments

P_N = Price at which the stock is expected to be sold at the end of period N

N = Number of years the stock is expected to be held

r = The appropriate discount rate or the investor's minimum required rate of return

---

$$\begin{aligned} PV &= \int_0^{\infty} D(n)e^{-rn}dn \\ &= D\left[-\frac{1}{r}e^{-rn}\right]_{n=\infty} - D\left[-\frac{1}{r}e^{-rn}\right]_{n=0} \\ &= \frac{D}{r} \end{aligned}$$

Note that this is the Preferred Stock Valuation Model. This model suggests that the value of a stock paying a fixed dividend forever and discounted by a constant discount rate is determined by dividing the annual dividend payment by the discount rate. Therefore, the present value of a stock paying an annual dividend of \$5 and discounted by a rate of 8 percent is \$62.50:

$$\begin{aligned} PV &= \frac{\$5}{.08} \\ &= \$62.50 \end{aligned}$$

Figure 9–1 **What is the Present Value (*PV*) of a Stock That Will Be Sold at the End of Three Years?**

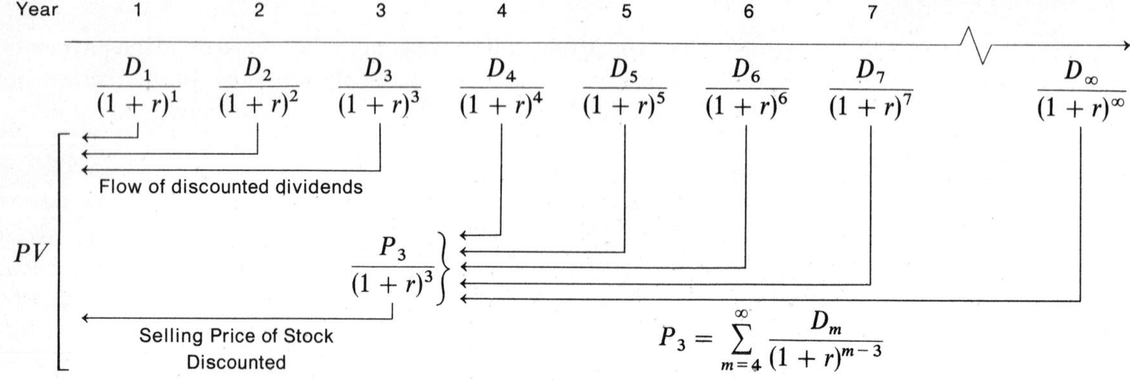

General Formula

$$PV = \sum_{n=1}^{N} \frac{D_n}{(1+r)^n} + \frac{P_N}{(1+r)^N} \tag{9–3}$$

According to Equation 9–3, the present value of a common stock can be determined by discounting both the expected dividend stream during the holding period and the price at which it is expected to be sold at the end of that period. If the holding period is assumed to be, say, three years, then Equation 9–3 can be rewritten as

$$\begin{aligned} PV &= \frac{D_1}{(1+r)^1} + \frac{D_2}{(1+r)^2} + \frac{D_3}{(1+r)^3} + \frac{P_3}{(1+r)^3} \\ &= \sum_{n=1}^{3} \frac{D_n}{(1+r)^n} + \frac{P_3}{(1+r)^3} \end{aligned} \tag{9–4}$$

Interestingly, Equation 9–4 and Equation 9–1 are equivalent, as will shortly become clear.

It was stated earlier that the present value of the common stock is the stream of future dividends, discounted to perpetuity. The same logic can be applied to the present value of a common stock at the end of a finite period, say, three years. Specifically, the present value of a stock at the end of the third year can be assumed to be the sum of the discounted values of all dividend payments from the beginning of Year 4 until infinity.[4] This is demonstrated in Figure 9–1.

Symbolically,

$$P_3 = \frac{D_4}{(1+r)^{4-3}} + \frac{D_5}{(1+r)^{5-3}} + \cdots + \frac{D_\infty}{(1+r)^{\infty-3}} \tag{9–5a}$$

[4] It is assumed that the present value of a stock at the end of period N is equal to the stock's price prevailing at N (that is, $PV_N = P_N$).

Discounting P_3 (the price expected to be received three years from today) to the present, we obtain the present value (PV) of P_3:

$$PV = P_3 \times \frac{1}{(1+r)^3}$$

$$= \left[\frac{D_4}{(1+r)^{4-3}} \times \frac{1}{(1+r)^3}\right] + \left[\frac{D_5}{(1+r)^{5-3}} \times \frac{1}{(1+r)^3}\right] + \cdots$$

$$+ \left[\frac{D_\infty}{(1+r)^{\infty-3}} \times \frac{1}{(1+r)^3}\right]$$

$$= \frac{D_4}{(1+r)^4} + \frac{D_5}{(1+r)^5} + \cdots + \frac{D_\infty}{(1+r)^\infty} \tag{9–5b}$$

Substituting Equation 9–5a into Equation 9–4 produces:

$$PV = \frac{D_1}{(1+r)^1} + \frac{D_2}{(1+r)^2} + \frac{D_3}{(1+r)^3} + \frac{D_4}{(1+r)^4} + \frac{D_5}{(1+r)^5} + \cdots + \frac{D_\infty}{(1+r)^\infty}$$

which is the same as Equation 9–1.

Because Equations 9–1 and 9–4 are equivalent, the Holding Period Dividend Model can be expressed in the following general terms:

$$PV = \sum_{n=1}^{N} \frac{D_n}{(1+r)^n} + \frac{P_N}{(1+r)^N} \tag{9–3 restated}$$

where

$$P_N = \sum_{m=N+1}^{\infty} \frac{D_m}{(1+r)^{m-N}} \tag{9–6}$$

The use of the Holding Period Dividend Model for common stock valuation can be demonstrated best by means of two illustrations.

One Year Holding Period

Let us start with a simple example in which the holding period is one year. The expected dividend is \$5, the price at which the stock is expected to be sold is \$60, and the appropriate discount rate is 12 percent. The present value of the stock is \$58.03:

$$PV = \frac{\$5}{(1+.12)} + \frac{\$60}{(1+.12)}$$

$$= \$4.46 + \$53.57$$

$$= \$58.03$$

If the appropriate discount rate were to drop to 10 percent, the present value would rise to \$59.08; an increase in the appropriate discount rate to, say, 14 percent would lower the present value to \$57.01.

Multiple Year Holding Period

The holding period, of course, need not be limited to one year. A similar process can be used to show that, no matter how long the desired holding period, Equation 9–3 can be used. For instance, assume that in the above example all factors remain the same (that is, $D_n = \$5$, $P_N = \$60$, $r = 12$ percent) except that the holding period is changed to five years. The present value of the stock is \$52.05:

$$PV = \frac{\$5}{(1+.12)^1} + \frac{\$5}{(1+.12)^2} + \frac{\$5}{(1+.12)^3} + \frac{\$5}{(1+.12)^4} + \frac{\$5}{(1+.12)^5} + \frac{\$60}{(1+.12)^5}$$

$$= \sum_{n=1}^{5} \frac{\$5}{(1+.12)^n} + \frac{\$60}{(1+.12)^5}$$

If $r = 12\%$ and $N = 5$, the $PVAF = 3.605$, and the $PVFF = .567$, then

$$\begin{aligned} PV &= (PVAF)(\$5) + (PVFF)(\$60) \\ &= (3.605)(\$5) + (.567)(\$60) \\ &= \$18.03 + \$34.02 \\ &= \$52.05 \end{aligned}$$

Note that, given a finite holding period, the present value of a stock is directly related to the expected dividends and the expected selling price and inversely related to the discount rate.

The Decision Model: A Preview

Now that the key variables of the Common Stock Valuation Model have been identified, the basic element of the decision model should be more readily understandable. First, for a given stock the values of the future dividend stream, the expected selling price, and the appropriate discount rate should be estimated. Next, the present value of the stock should be calculated using these values. Finally, the present value of the stock should be compared with its current market price. As long as the present value exceeds the current price, the stock can be treated as undervalued; if the current price exceeds the present value, it should be treated as an overvalued stock. If the present value is equal to the current price, the stock is said to be appropriately priced. Obviously, this decision model assumes that an investor is able to estimate the values of the three key variables of the Common Stock Valuation Model.

The Dividend Stream, D_n

Dividends are paid from the earnings of a company.[5] The proportion of the earnings distributed as dividends is defined as the *payout ratio.* Any attempt to estimate a company's future annual dividend payments must, therefore, begin with an estimation of its future earnings.

Earnings

Earnings change over time. The forecasting of annual earnings is a complicated task because a host of economic and noneconomic factors can affect a company's future earnings. Consequently, as a first approximation, earnings may be assumed to grow at a fixed percentage rate.[6]

Assume that the current earnings per share, E_0, of ABC Company are \$5 and that they are expected to grow at an annual rate of 10 percent. Earnings per share over the next five years would grow in the following manner:

Year	Earnings Growth	Growth Pattern	Annual Earnings per Share
Current	—	E_0	$E_0 = \$5.00$
First	$\$5(1 + .10)$	$E_0(1 + g)$	$E_1 = \$5.50$
Second	$\$5.50(1 + .10) = \$5(1 + .10)^2$	$E_1(1 + g) = E_0(1 + g)^2$	$E_2 = \$6.05$
Third	$\$6.05(1 + .10) = \$5(1 + .10)^3$	$E_2(1 + g) = E_0(1 + g)^3$	$E_3 = \$6.66$
Fourth	$\$6.66(1 + .10) = \$5(1 + .10)^4$	$E_3(1 + g) = E_0(1 + g)^4$	$E_4 = \$7.33$
Fifth	$\$7.33(1 + .10) = \$5(1 + .10)^5$	$E_4(1 + g) = E_0(1 + g)^5$	$E_5 = \$8.06$

Note: $E_1, E_2, E_3, \ldots$ = Annual earnings for Years 1, 2, 3, . . .
g = Expected constant growth rate of earnings

Clearly, if earnings per share are assumed to grow at a fixed annual rate, for any given year they can be easily estimated. For instance, earnings for Year 3 equal either $E_2(1 + g)$ or $E_0(1 + g)^3$; similarly, earnings for Year 5 equal either

[5] Of course, dividends are paid out of after-tax earnings or net income. In this discussion the terms "earnings" and "net income" are used synonymously.

[6] More advanced methods of earnings estimation will be discussed in Chapters 10 and 11.

$E_4(1 + g)$ or $E_0(1 + g)^5$. Therefore, earnings growth can be expressed in the following general form:

$$E_n = E_{n-1}(1 + g)$$
$$= E_0(1 + g)^n \quad \text{(9–7)}$$

In this example, the earnings per share of ABC Company at the end of the fifteenth year can be directly estimated to be \$20.89:

$$E_{15} = \$5(1 + .10)^{15}$$

From the compound value table given in the Appendix (page 841), we find

$$(1 + .10)^{15} = 4.177$$

Therefore,

$$E_{15} = \$5(4.177)$$
$$= \$20.89$$

Fixed Payout Ratio

If we make an additional assumption that a fixed proportion of annual earnings is distributed as dividends—that is, that the payout ratio remains fixed—then dividends for any given year can also be easily estimated.

Assume the payout ratio for ABC Company is 50 percent. If the earnings for Year 5 and Year 15 are \$8.06 and \$20.89, then the dividends for these years, respectively, are \$4.03 (50 percent of \$8.06) and \$10.45 (50 percent of \$20.89). Symbolically,

$$D_n = (1 - s)E_n$$

where

D_n = Annual dividend payments
s = Retention ratio (percentage of earnings retained by the company)
$1 - s$ = Payout ratio
E_n = Earnings per share for year n

Let us refer to our basic stock valuation equation:

$$PV = \frac{D_1}{(1 + r)^1} + \frac{D_2}{(1 + r)^2} + \frac{D_3}{(1 + r)^3} + \cdots + \frac{D_\infty}{(1 + r)^\infty}$$

Because $D_1 = (1 - s)E_1, D_2 = (1 - s)E_2, \ldots$, Equation 9–1 can be presented as:

$$PV = \frac{(1 - s)E_1}{(1 + r)^1} + \frac{(1 - s)E_2}{(1 + r)^2} + \frac{(1 - s)E_3}{(1 + r)^3} + \cdots + \frac{(1 - s)E_\infty}{(1 + r)^\infty} \quad \text{(9–8)}$$

However, because earnings are assumed to grow at a constant rate, E_1 can be expressed as $E_0(1 + g)^1$, E_2 as $E_0(1 + g)^2$, and so on. Therefore, Equation 9–8 can be expressed in the following convenient form:

$$PV = \frac{(1 - s)(E_0)(1 + g)^1}{(1 + r)^1} + \frac{(1 - s)(E_0)(1 + g)^2}{(1 + r)^2} + \frac{(1 - s)(E_0)(1 + g)^3}{(1 + r)^3} + \cdots + \frac{(1 - s)(E_0)(1 + g)^\infty}{(1 + r)^\infty} \quad \text{(9–9)}$$

Equation 9–9 can now be understood in terms of a dividend stream, because the dividend payout ratio, $1 - s$, is constant, and the current dividend can be expressed as the payout ratio multiplied by current earnings, or, $D_0 = (1 - s)E_0$. Under this assumption, Equation 9–9 becomes

$$PV = \frac{D_0(1 + g)^1}{(1 + r)^1} + \frac{D_0(1 + g)^2}{(1 + r)^2} + \frac{D_0(1 + g)^3}{(1 + r)^3} + \cdots + \frac{D_0(1 + g)^\infty}{(1 + r)^\infty} \quad \text{(9–10)}$$

By using Equation 9–10, an investor can calculate the present value of a stock, provided that the current dividend, the expected constant growth rate of the earnings, and the appropriate discount rate are known. Equation 9–10 becomes more functional when we realistically assume that most investors have a finite holding period, N, and that they expect to sell their stock at a price, P_N, at the end of the holding period. Under the finite holding period assumption, Equation 9 – 10 becomes:

$$PV = \left[\frac{D_0(1 + g)^1}{(1 + r)^1} + \frac{D_0(1 + g)^2}{(1 + r)^2} + \frac{D_0(1 + g)^3}{(1 + r)^3} + \cdots + \frac{D_0(1 + g)^N}{(1 + r)^N}\right] + \frac{P_N}{(1 + r)^N} \quad \text{(9–11)}$$

Finally, Equation 9–11 can be presented in the following convenient form:

$$PV = \sum_{n=1}^{N} \frac{D_0(1 + g)^n}{(1 + r)^n} + \frac{P_N}{(1 + r)^N} \quad \text{(9–12)}$$

Equation 9–12 states that the present value of the stock is the sum of the discounted values of a stream of dividend payments received during the holding period plus the discounted value of the sale price of the stock received at the end of the holding period. It also assumes that, during the holding period,

Table 9–1 **Common Stock Valuation Model**

Pertinent Details:

$E_0 = \$2$	$1 - s = 80\%$
$g = 5\%$	$P_N = \$51$
$N = 5$ years	$r = 12\%$

The present value of this stock is \$35.53, as shown below:

$$\begin{aligned} D_0 &= (1 - s)E_0 \\ &= (.8)(\$2) \\ &= \$1.60 \end{aligned}$$

$$\begin{aligned} PV &= \sum_{n=1}^{5} \frac{\$1.60(1 + .05)^n}{(1 + .12)^n} + \frac{\$51}{(1 + .12)^5} \\ &= \left[\frac{\$1.68}{(1 + .12)^1} + \frac{\$1.76}{(1 + .12)^2} + \frac{\$1.85}{(1 + .12)^3} + \frac{\$1.94}{(1 + .12)^4} + \frac{\$2.04}{(1 + .12)^5}\right] + \frac{\$51}{(1 + .12)^5} \\ &= [\$1.50 + \$1.40 + \$1.32 + \$1.23 + \$1.16] + \$28.92 \\ &= \$6.61 + \$28.92 \\ &= \$35.53 \end{aligned}$$

earnings grew at a constant rate and the payout ratio remained fixed.[7] A fixed payout ratio implies that the expected constant growth rate of earnings, g, is identical to the expected constant growth rate of dividends.

Table 9–1 illustrates the use of the Common Stock Valuation Model. Note that, under appropriate assumptions, the present value of the stock may be calculated by estimating the future dividend payments. For example, assume that a company's current earnings are \$2 per share, the expected future selling price of its stock is \$51, and the appropriate discount rate and the holding period are, respectively, 12 percent and five years. If the company's payout ratio and earnings growth rate are expected to remain at 80 percent and 5 percent, respectively, over the holding period, then the present value of the stock would be \$35.53.

The form in which Equation 9–12 is presented assumes that the investor has a finite holding period and that the common stock has a terminal value, P_N. A more general form of the model assumes that the firm and its stream of earnings are perpetual:

$$PV = \frac{(1 - s)(E_0)(1 + g)^1}{(1 + r)^1} + \frac{(1 - s)(E_0)(1 + g)^2}{(1 + r)^2} + \frac{(1 - s)(E_0)(1 + g)^3}{(1 + r)^3} + \cdots + \frac{(1 - s)(E_0)(1 + g)^\infty}{(1 + r)^\infty}$$

[7] Implications of a variable payout ratio will be discussed in Chapters 10 and 11.

or

$$PV = \sum_{n=1}^{\infty} \frac{(1 - s)(E_0)(1 + g)^n}{(1 + r)^n} \tag{9-13}$$

For events in which n continues to infinity, and the payout ratio, $1 - s$, the expected growth rate of earnings, g, and the appropriate discount rate, r, remain constant, Equation 9–13 reduces to

$$PV = \frac{(1 - s)(E_1)}{r - g} \tag{9-14}$$

Also, because $D_1 = (1 - s)(E_1)$, Equation 9–14 can be rewritten as[8]

$$PV = \frac{D_1}{r - g} \tag{9-15}$$

Equations 9–9, 9–13, 9–14, and 9–15 are merely different forms of the dividend model. These forms clearly demonstrate the relationship between current earnings, current dividend, the growth rate of earnings and dividends, the payout ratio, and the appropriate discount rate, often called the investor's minimum required rate of return.

A comment should be made here about an assumption implicit in Equation 9–15, which was derived from Equation 9–13. If the expected constant growth rate of earnings, g, exceeds the appropriate discount rate or the required rate of return, r, in Equation 9–13, then the present value of this infinite series becomes infinite. In the real world, however, there are many firms whose current or short-term earnings growth rates exceed the appropriate discount rate applicable to their earnings; however, their stocks do not sell at infinite prices. This apparent contradiction is best explained in terms of the Petersburg Paradox.[9] Although the current or short-term earnings growth rate of a firm might exceed the appropriate discount rate or the required rate of return, it is generally believed that its earnings growth rate cannot *indefinitely* exceed the appropriate discount rate.[10] Thus, if g is defined in Equation 9–15 as the expected constant growth rate of earnings and dividends, then the assumption that g is less than r ($g < r$) over the long run can be routinely made.

Variable Dividend Growth Rate

There is, of course, no reason to believe that the dividend growth rate will always remain fixed. In fact, for many stocks, like the cyclical stocks, the growth rates of dividends may vary from year to year.

[8] See note 8 on pages 339–40.

[9] David Durand argued that the best explanation for this contradiction was the expectation that the reinvestment rate would decline or that the investment opportunities would not be available for an infinite time period. That is, in the long run, $g < r$. See David Durand, "Growth Stocks and the Petersburg Paradox," *Journal of Finance*, September 1957, pp. 348–63.

[10] Generally, growth rates are assumed to regress toward some mean rate. Also, many investors correctly believe that r does not remain constant, but increases through time to allow for the increased uncertainty of more distant earnings.

For the sake of simplicity, we will assume that the dividend growth rate will remain at an abnormally high or low level until the end of the holding period.[11] This will be called the *abnormal* growth rate of dividends, or g_a. The dividend growth rate beyond the holding period will be allowed to vary upward or downward from the abnormal level. This will be called the *normal* growth rate of dividends, or g. These variables can be incorporated into the original model. The starting point is the Holding Period Dividend Model:

$$PV = \sum_{n=1}^{N} \frac{D_0(1+g)^n}{(1+r)^n} + \frac{P_N}{(1+r)^N}$$

However,

$$P_N = \sum_{m=N+1}^{\infty} \frac{D_m}{(1+r)^{m-N}} \qquad \textbf{(9–6 restated)}$$

Therefore, we can say that

$$PV = \sum_{n=1}^{N} \frac{D_0(1+g)^n}{(1+r)^n} + \sum_{m=N+1}^{\infty} \frac{D_m}{(1+r)^{m-N}} \times \frac{1}{(1+r)^N}$$

However, because it is assumed that the dividend grows at the abnormal rate, or g_a, until the end of the holding period, and at a normal rate, g, thereafter, the above equation becomes

$$PV = \sum_{n=1}^{N} \frac{D_0(1+g_a)^n}{(1+r)^n} + \sum_{m=N+1}^{\infty} \frac{D_N(1+g)^{m-N}}{(1+r)^{m-N}} \times \frac{1}{(1+r)^N} \qquad \textbf{(9–16)}$$

Now, if the normal growth rate, g, and the appropriate discount rate, r, are assumed constant, since m in the second term in Equation 9–16 goes to infinity, the second term can be treated as an infinite series and expressed as

$$\sum_{m=N+1}^{\infty} \frac{D_N(1+g)^{m-N}}{(1+r)^{m-N}} \times \frac{1}{(1+r)^N}$$

$$= \frac{D_{N+1}}{r-g} \times \frac{1}{(1+r)^N} \qquad \textbf{(9–17)}$$

Incorporating Equation 9–17 into Equation 9–16, we obtain

$$PV = \sum_{n=1}^{N} \frac{D_0(1+g_a)^n}{(1+r)^n} + \left(\frac{D_{N+1}}{r-g}\right) \times \left(\frac{1}{(1+r)^N}\right) \qquad \textbf{(9–18)}$$

[11] Of course, we need not assume that the growth rate will remain fixed until the end of the holding period. Investors may choose any period in which they believe the growth rate will be abnormally high or low. Also, the following method can be adapted to account for more frequent variations in the growth rate.

where

PV = Present value of the common stock
D_0 = Dividend payment in the current period
D_{N+1} = Annual dividend payment following period N
g = Normal growth rate
g_a = Abnormal growth rate
N = Number of years the stock is expected to be held
r = The appropriate discount rate or the investor's minimum required rate of return

Consider the following example. The ABC Company is currently paying an annual dividend of \$2 per share. Dividends are expected to grow at an abnormal rate of 14 percent during the next five years, and thereafter at a normal rate of 3 percent a year. The appropriate discount rate, or the investor's required rate of return, is 12 percent. The present value of the stock is \$35.52, as shown in Table 9–2.

Dividend and Present Value: Further Consideration

The Concept

In the preceding section, we demonstrated that the present value of a stock is positively related to dividends distributed by the firm. But the effects of dividend policy on the present value of a stock are currently quite controversial. In order to appreciate fully the essence of this controversy, it is necessary to recast the dividend model by introducing the variable known as the internal rate of return, i_{rr}. The *internal rate of return* is the return earned on earnings that are reinvested in the company.[12] As will shortly become clear, the dividend model predicts that, under a set of simplified assumptions, the dividend policy does not affect the present value of a stock, provided that the internal rate of return, i_{rr}, equals the appropriate discount rate, r. Additionally, if $i_{rr} > r$, the present value of the stock decreases with an increase in the payout ratio. The reverse is true when the internal rate of return is less than the appropriate discount rate, or $i_{rr} < r$.

[12] In theory, the present value of a stock remains unchanged if the internal rate of return equals the discount rate. However, the stock's value declines if the internal rate of return is less than the appropriate discount rate. In the latter case, the stock's value would decline even further if the payout ratio were increased.

Table 9–2 **Present Value of Stock: Variable Dividend Growth Rate**

Pertinent Data:

$D_0 = \$2.00$ $N = 5$ years

$g_a = 14\%$ $g = 3\%$

$r = 12\%$ $D_{N+1} =$ Dividend during 6th year

Formulas:

Holding Period Dividend Model:

$$PV = \sum_{n=1}^{N} \frac{D_0(1+g)^n}{(1+r)^n} + \frac{P_N}{(1+r)^N} \quad \textbf{(9–12)}$$

For varying dividend growth rates it becomes:

$$PV = \sum_{n=1}^{N} \frac{D_0(1+g_a)^n}{(1+r)^n} + \left(\frac{D_{N+1}}{r-g}\right)\left(\frac{1}{(1+r)^N}\right) \quad \textbf{(9–18)}$$

Step 1: *PV* of dividends during the abnormal growth period.

End of year: *n*	Dividend: $\$2(1.14)^n$	PV factor $(1.12)^{-n}$	*PV*
1	\$2.28	.893	\$ 2.04
2	2.60	.797	2.07
3	2.96	.712	2.11
4	3.37	.636	2.14
5	3.85	.567	2.18

$$\sum_{n=1}^{5} \frac{\$2(1+.14)^n}{(1+.12)^n} = \$10.54$$

Step 2: *PV* of Stock Price at end of 5th year.

$$\frac{P_5}{(1+r)^5} = \left(\frac{D_{5+1}{}^*}{(r-g)}\right)\left(\frac{1}{(1+r)^5}\right)$$

$$= \left(\frac{(\$3.85)(1.03)}{(.12-.03)}\right)\left(\frac{1}{(1+.12)^5}\right)$$

$$= (\$44.06)(.567)$$

$$= \$24.98$$

$$PV = \$10.54 + \$24.98$$

$$= \$35.52$$

* The dividend for the 6th year will equal the 5th year dividend (\$3.85) multiplied by the new growth pattern, (1.03).

Basic Assumptions

The basic assumptions of the dividend model are

1. There is no external financing, that is, no external debt or allowance for new shares to be issued. Therefore, dividends must be paid out of retained earnings.
2. The appropriate discount rate, r, remains fixed.
3. The internal rate of return, i_{rr}, remains constant.
4. The retention ratio, s, and equivalently the payout ratio, $1 - s$, remain fixed.
5. The growth rate of earnings, g, is assumed constant. Also, because all retained earnings are reinvested at i_{rr}, over time, earnings are assumed to grow at the rate of $g = (s)(i_{rr})$.
6. The growth rate of earnings, g, is smaller than the appropriate discount rate, r; that is, $g < r$.
7. Taxes are assumed to be nonexistent.
8. The firm's stream of earnings is assumed to be perpetual; that is, there is no finite holding period.

The Model in Action

Based on these simplified assumptions, the present value of a stock is determined as

$$PV = \frac{D_1}{r - g} \quad \textbf{(9–15 restated)}$$

Equation 9–15 can be rewritten to incorporate earnings, the payout ratio, and the internal rate of return into the dividend model. Because D_1 equals $E_1(1 - s)$ and g equals $(s)(i_{rr})$, Equation 9–15 becomes

$$PV = \frac{E_1(1 - s)}{r - (s)(i_{rr})} \quad \textbf{(9–19)}$$

Conclusions of the Model

The dividend model, represented by Equation 9–19, underscores an important point. On a new investment, if the internal rate of return is equal to the appropriate discount rate (that is, $i_{rr} = r$), then the present value of the stock remains unchanged regardless of the payout ratio or the dividend policy. For instance, if $i_{rr} = r$, Equation 9–19 becomes

$$PV = \frac{E_1(1 - s)}{r - sr}$$

$$= \frac{E_1(1 - s)}{r(1 - s)}$$

$$= \frac{E_1}{r}$$

Because the payout ratio is not included in this equation, when $i_{rr} = r$, the dividend policy is irrelevant. If, on the other hand, $i_{rr} > r$ (that is, retained earnings grow at a rate higher than the appropriate discount rate), then the present value increases as the payout ratio, $1 - s$, decreases: The higher the amount of earnings retained, the higher the present value of the stock. The reverse is true if $i_{rr} < r$ (that is, if the internal rate of return is lower than the appropriate discount rate). These relationships are presented in Table 9–3. Note that when the internal rate of return, i_{rr}, and the appropriate discount rate, r, equal 12 percent, the present value of the stock remains unchanged at $41.67 (Case 2) regardless of the payout ratio. However, the present value declines from $46.88 to $43.48 (Case 1) as the payout ratio increases when the internal rate of return exceeds the appropriate discount rate. The reverse is true when the internal rate of return is lower than the appropriate discount rate.

Table 9–3 **Stock Valuations for Various Payout Ratios and Internal Rates of Return**

Pertinent Details: $E_1 = \$5$, $r = 12\%$ Valuation Model: $PV = \dfrac{E_1(1-s)}{r-(s)(i_{rr})}$

Payout Ratios	Internal Rates of Return		
	Case 1	Case 2	Case 3
	$i_{rr} = 14\%$	$i_{rr} = 12\%$	$i_{rr} = 10\%$
$(1-s) = 60\%$	$PV = \dfrac{\$5(1-.4)}{.12-(.4)(.14)}$	$PV = \dfrac{\$5(1-.4)}{.12-(.4)(.12)}$	$PV = \dfrac{\$5(1-.4)}{.12-(.4)(.10)}$
	$= \$46.88$	$= \$41.67$	$= \$37.50$
$(1-s) = 70\%$	$PV = \dfrac{\$5(1-.3)}{.12-(.3)(.14)}$	$PV = \dfrac{\$5(1-.3)}{.12-(.3)(.12)}$	$PV = \dfrac{\$5(1-.3)}{.12-(.3)(.10)}$
	$= \$44.87$	$= \$41.67$	$= \$38.89$
$(1-s) = 80\%$	$PV = \dfrac{\$5(1-.2)}{.12-(.2)(.14)}$	$PV = \dfrac{\$5(1-.2)}{.12-(.2)(.12)}$	$PV = \dfrac{\$5(1-.2)}{.12-(.2)(.10)}$
	$= \$43.48$	$= \$41.67$	$= \$40.00$

Nature of the Controversy

Myron Gordon has demonstrated that, under the simplifying assumptions of the dividend model just presented, the dividend policy is indeed irrelevant when the internal rate of return equals the appropriate discount rate. However, when some of these assumptions are relaxed to make the model more realistic, the dividend irrelevance argument falls through. That is, in the real world, for various reasons, dividends do matter even when $i_{rr} = r$.[13]

One of the basic assumptions of the simplified dividend model is that the appropriate discount rate, r, remains fixed. However, Gordon argues that, because risk increases with time, a realistic model should assume that r will increase over time. Therefore, Gordon concludes, if the *current* internal rate of return equals the appropriate discount rate,[14] that is $i_{rr} = r$, the present value of the stock will eventually decline as risk increases with futurity, and r exceeds i_{rr}, or $i_{rr} < r$.

Franco Modigliani and Merton Miller have disagreed with Gordon. By making the dividend model more general to allow for external financing, they

[13] Myron Gordon, *The Investment, Financing and Valuation of the Corporation* (Homewood, Ill.: Richard D. Irwin, 1962), pp. 6–14. © 1962 by Richard D. Irwin, Inc.

[14] This implies that earnings are currently retained and reinvested to earn a constant internal rate of return equal to the appropriate discount rate.

have demonstrated that the dividend policy is indeed irrelevant, because variations in the retention or the payout ratio do not affect the present value of a stock.[15] However, the Modigliani-Miller study has not resolved the controversy regarding the dividend policy, because it has not accounted for such critical variables as tax considerations and capital gains resulting from the sale of stock. Consequently it is generally believed that although the average investor favors larger cash dividends, because of tax considerations, wealthier investors prefer higher growth in stock prices to higher cash dividends.

The Selling Price, P_N

An Overview

Equation 9–3 defined the Holding Period Dividend Model as

$$PV = \sum_{n=1}^{N} \frac{D_n}{(1+r)^n} + \frac{P_N}{(1+r)^N}$$

We will now discuss the method of estimating the expected sale price at the end of the holding period, or P_N.

The Holding Period Dividend Model underscored an important point: The selling price of a stock at the end of the holding period, P_N, is assumed equal to the present value of the dividend stream expected to be received from the year following the end of the holding period until infinity. Symbolically,

$$P_N = \sum_{m=N+1}^{\infty} \frac{D_m}{(1+r)^{m-N}} \qquad \textbf{(9–6 restated)}$$

Although this view of a stock's selling price is theoretically sound, it has at best a limited application, because the task of estimating dividend payments for each year beyond the holding period is almost an impossibility. A practical alternative must therefore be developed to effectively estimate the expected selling price of a stock at the end of the holding period.

Earnings Multiple Approach

Basic Form

The present value of a stock is the discounted value of the future dividend stream. Because earnings are the primary source of funds to a firm for the payment of dividends over the long run, investors and security analysts frequently express

[15] M. H. Miller and F. Modigliani, "Dividend Policy, Growth and the Valuation of Shares," *Journal of Business*, October 1961, pp. 411–33.

the current stock price (P_0) in relation to the earnings per share (EPS). For example, if P_0 is \$50 and the EPS is \$5, then the stock is selling at 10 times its earnings, or at a P/E (price–earnings) ratio of 10. This can be stated in following the general form:

$$P_0 = (P/E)_0 \times E_0 \tag{9–20}$$

Investors and analysts can also estimate the *future* price of a common stock in relation to EPS. For example, if at some future date the EPS is expected to be \$7 and the stock is expected to sell at 10 times its earnings on this date, then the stock would sell for \$70 (\$7 × 10).

Earnings Multiple and P/E Ratio

Investors relate a firm's current earnings to its current price by using the P/E ratio. However, when they are able to estimate earnings for some *future* time period, they apply an *earnings multiple* (*EM*) to this figure to arrive at an *expected* price for the stock. Although EM and P/E ratio are equivalent and therefore interchangeable concepts, for illustrative purposes we will make the following distinction between them: The *current* earnings are multiplied by the P/E ratio to arrive at the current price; the expected *future* earnings are multiplied by the *EM* to arrive at the expected future price of a stock. More specifically,

$$P_N = (EM)_N \times E_N \tag{9–21}$$

$$P_0 = (P/E)_0 \times E_0 \tag*{(9–20 restated)}$$

The Key Variables

When the payout ratio, $1 - s$, is fixed and the earnings growth rate, g, is assumed to remain constant, the present value of a common stock is

$$PV = \frac{(1-s)(E_0)(1+g)^1}{(1+r)^1} + \frac{(1-s)(E_0)(1+g)^2}{(1+r)^2} + \frac{(1-s)(E_0)(1+g)^3}{(1+r)^3} + \cdots + \frac{(1-s)(E_0)(1+g)^\infty}{(1+r)^\infty} \tag*{(9–9 restated)}$$

When the market for a stock is in equilibrium, the stock sells for its present value, and $PV = P_0$. Making this substitution, and dividing both sides of the equation by the current earnings, E_0, we obtain

$$\frac{P_0}{E_0} = \frac{(1-s)(1+g)^1}{(1+r)^1} + \frac{(1-s)(1+g)^2}{(1+r)^2} + \frac{(1-s)(1+g)^3}{(1+r)^3} + \cdots + \frac{(1-s)(1+g)^\infty}{(1+r)^\infty} \tag{9–22}$$

Because the time in Equation 9–22 continues to infinity, and P_0/E_0 is the P/E ratio for the current year, the equation can be reduced to[16]

$$P/E = \frac{1 - s}{r - g} \tag{9–23}$$

Equation 9–23 suggests[17] that if the values of $1 - s$, r, and g can be estimated for the period beyond the holding period, then the EM can be calculated for the end of any given holding period, N. Symbolically,[18]

$$(EM)_N = \frac{(1 - s)_N}{r_N - g_N} \tag{9–24}$$

where

$(EM)_N$ = Earnings multiple at the end of period N
$(1 - s)_N$ = Payout ratio beyond period N
r_N = Appropriate discount rate beyond period N
g_N = Growth rate of earnings beyond period N

Equation 9–24 reveals three important facts. First, the factors that influence the EM are the payout ratio, the earnings growth rate, and the appropriate discount rate. Second, the EM is positively related to both the growth rate of earnings and the payout ratio—the higher the expected payout ratio and growth rate, the higher the earnings multiple. Third, the EM is negatively correlated with the appropriate discount rate—the greater the riskiness of the stock, the lower the earnings multiple.

Measurement of Earnings Multiple

An Overview The earnings multiple is a function of three rates: the growth rate of earnings, the payout ratio, and the appropriate discount rate. In this model, these rates may be assumed to be fixed, in which case the EM can be easily calculated.

For example, if the payout ratio, the appropriate discount rate, and the growth rate for the years beyond the holding period are expected to be, respectively, 80 percent, 12 percent, and 10 percent, then the EM at the end of the

[16] Note that the factor, $r - g$, is the dividend yield or the dividend capitalization rate.

[17] Technically, the formula for the value of an infinite series of this variety, where $g < r$, should be written as follows:

$$\frac{P_0}{E_1} = \frac{1 - s}{r - g}$$

Note that this constant growth valuation formula uses E_1 instead of E_0. However, it can be shown that the use of E_0 is correct, provided that earnings and dividends grow continuously at the rate g, and that dividends are paid out and discounted continuously at the rate r.

[18] Technically the equation should read as follows:

$$(EM)_N = \frac{(1 - s)_{N+1}}{r_N - g_N}$$

However, for reasons already explained, the use of $(1 - s)_N$ is permissible.

Table 9–4

$$(EM)_N = \frac{(1-s)_N}{r_N - g_N}$$

	Growth Rate, g_N	Appropriate Discount Rate, r_N	Payout Ratio, $(1-s)_N$	Earnings Multiple, $(EM)_N$
Section 1	4%	10%	50%	8.33
Growth Rate	6%	10%	50%	12.50
Varies	8%	10%	50%	25.00
Section 2	6%	10%	50%	12.50
Discount Rate	6%	12%	50%	8.33
Varies	6%	14%	50%	6.25
Section 3	6%	10%	40%	10.00
Payout Ratio	6%	10%	50%	12.50
Varies	6%	10%	60%	15.00

holding period will be 40:

$$(EM)_N = \frac{(1-s)_N}{r_N - g_N}$$

$$(EM)_N = \frac{.80}{.12 - .10}$$

$$= 40$$

Of course, different estimates will produce different values for EM. If the expected appropriate discount rate were to increase to, say, 13 percent while the expected growth rate of earnings were reduced to 5 percent, the $(EM)_N$ would be only 10:

$$(EM)_N = \frac{.80}{.13 - .05}$$

$$= 10$$

Table 9–4 presents $(EM)_N$ values under different values of g_N, $(1-s)_N$, and r_N. Section 1 presents changes in the EM when only the growth rate varies. In Section 2 only the appropriate discount rate is allowed to change. Finally, in Section 3 both the growth rate and the appropriate discount rate remain fixed, but the payout ratio is changed. Note that, as expected, the EM increases as the growth rate and the payout ratio increase, but declines as the appropriate discount rate increases.

Growth Rate of Earnings, g_N The variable g_N represents the expected long-term average annual normalized growth rate in future earnings.[19] The term *normalized* represents an important statistical concept; it refers to a readjustment

[19] If the payout ratio is fixed, the growth rates of earnings and dividends are identical.

of reported earnings by filtering out the effects of temporary fluctuations due to random factors. Normalized earnings reflect only a long-term, constant trend in earnings.

As mentioned earlier, forecasting earnings on a *year-to-year basis* beyond the holding period is almost an impossibility. However, the Earnings Multiple Approach requires the use of a constant expected growth rate of earnings for the determination of the holding period price. No one, of course, expects the earnings to grow at the same rate each year. However, the assumption of a constant long-term growth rate is justifiable on the ground that in most instances that is what investors expect will be approximately true.

The Payout Ratio, $(1 - s)_N$ Empirical analyses of financial data indicate that the payout ratio (the ratio of dividends to earnings) is not a fixed number, but varies from year to year. The reason for this variation is not difficult to understand. For most firms, earnings fluctuate over time. However, because corporate executives generally like to attain a target dividend payment, they frequently have to adjust their payout ratios to reach their targeted dividends.

The task of making a realistic prediction of a firm's future payout ratio will be undertaken in Chapter 11. At this time, we will make the simplified assumption that the payout ratio remains fixed.

The Appropriate Discount Rate, r_N Issues relating to the determination of the appropriate discount rate will be discussed later in this chapter. For now, the appropriate discount rate beyond the holding period will be treated as given.

Determination of Selling Price, P_N

The Mechanics

The equation for determining the expected sale price of a stock at the end of the holding period, P_N, is

$$P_N = (EM)_N \times E_N \qquad \textbf{(9–21 restated)}$$

Assuming that the values for g_N, $(1 - s)_N$, and r_N at the end of the holding period are 7, 45, and 11 percent, respectively, and if the earnings are expected to be \$5, the price of the stock, P_N, would be \$56.25:

$$(EM)_N = \frac{(1 - s)_N}{r_N - g_N} \qquad \textbf{(9–24 restated)}$$

$$= \frac{.45}{.11 - .07}$$

$$= 11.25$$

$$P_N = 11.25 \times \$5$$

$$= \$56.25$$

Methods for determining the values of g_N and $(1 - s)_N$ will be undertaken in Chapter 11; these will lead to the determination of a more realistic value for holding period price, P_N.

Low Dividend, High Price Puzzle

Equation 9–23 indicates that the P/E ratio is positively related to the payout ratio; that is, *given* the values of r and g, the higher the payout ratio, the higher the P/E ratio. We have also seen that the price of a stock is the product of the current earnings and the earnings multiple $[P_0 = (P/E)_0 \times E_0]$.

In this context, firms that do not pay dividends present an interesting case. According to the framework just developed, since the payout ratio, and hence the P/E ratio, is zero, their stock price also will be zero. However, in the real world such a case does not exist.

The seeming contradiction can be explained in the following manner. Even if a firm does not pay dividends for years as its earnings grow, the fact that it *could* pay dividends now, and the *expectation* that it *will* pay dividends in the future, produces the share price appreciation. More specifically, for the equation

$$PV = \sum_{n=1}^{N} \frac{D_n}{(1+r)^n} + \frac{P_N}{(1+r)^n} \qquad \textbf{(9–3 restated)}$$

we would expect $P_N/(1 + r)^n$ to be large and $D_n/(1 + r)^n$ to be small. P_N would have to be very large because, by definition

$$P_N = \sum_{m=N+1}^{\infty} \frac{D_m}{(1+r)^{m-N}}$$

That is, the price of a stock currently paying little or no dividend will appreciate only if investors expect the company to pay larger dividends after the holding period has ended.[20]

The Appropriate Discount Rate, *r*

An Overview

The process of determining a present capital value to discount a stream of future returns is called *capitalization*. The rate of interest used for capitalization is called the appropriate discount rate. For a finite holding period, the appropriate discount rate is the required rate of return during that period. The

[20] It would be more realistic to assume that dividends will be paid at some future date, not necessarily after the holding period.

higher the appropriate discount rate, the lower the present value of a stock. The appropriate discount rate is defined as the minimum rate of return required by the investor for a particular common stock determined by the investor's perception of risk inherent in that stock. This perception of risk is central to the determination of the appropriate discount rate.

The nature of the relationship between risk and return for common stock was fully discussed in Chapter 5 and needs only to be summarized here.

The variability of a stock's rate of return relative to the market return, known as the systematic risk, is measured by the line of least squares, otherwise known as the characteristic line. The slope of the characteristic line, called beta (β_s), multiplied by the market return R_m measures the systematic return of a stock. The unsystematic return of a stock is measured by two variables—alpha (α_s) and the error term (ϵ_s). Therefore the total return of a stock, R_s, can be stated as

$$R_s = \alpha_s + \beta_s R_m + \epsilon_s \qquad \textbf{(5–1a restated)}$$

where

R_s = Total return of the stock

α_s, ϵ_s = Alpha and error term, representing the unsystematic return of the stock

$\beta_s R_m$ = Systematic return of the stock

The return of a security may fluctuate because of the *variability* of both the systematic and the unsystematic return. The statistical tool known as variance is the measure of the total variation. Symbolically,

$$\text{Var}(R_s) = \text{Var}(\alpha_s) + \text{Var}(\beta_s R_m) + \text{Var}(\epsilon_s)$$

Also, because $\text{Var}(\beta_s R_m) = \beta_s^2 \text{Var}(R_m)$, and $\text{Var}(\alpha_s) = 0$,

$$\text{Var}(R_s) = 0 + \beta_s^2 \text{Var}(R_m) + \text{Var}(\epsilon_s)$$

Symbolically, it can be written as

$$\underbrace{\sigma_s^2}_{\text{Total Risk}} = \underbrace{\beta_s^2 \sigma_m^2}_{\text{Systematic risk}} + \underbrace{\sigma_{\epsilon_s}^2}_{\text{Unsystematic risk}} \qquad \textbf{(5–4 restated)}$$

This equation underscores an important point: The product of the variance of the market return and the square of a stock's beta measures its systematic risk, and the variance of the error term measures its unsystematic risk. Equation 5–4 also indicates that the beta of a stock is the basis for measuring both its systematic return and systematic risk.

Having summarized the theoretical relationship between risk and return of a common stock, we will now develop two methods for estimating the appropriate discount rate. The first method, called the *Historic Approach*, implicitly recognizes the risk–return relationship; the *Risk–Return Approach* explicitly uses the relationship as a basis for estimating the appropriate discount rate.

Method 1: The Historic Approach

The simplest, yet understandably the least desirable, method for estimating the appropriate discount rate is the Historic Approach to risk premium calculation. The Ibbotson and Sinquefield data indicate that common stocks and treasury bills have generated average annual returns of 11.2 percent and 2.5 percent, respectively, from 1926 through 1978. Because treasury bills can be treated as a surrogate for risk-free assets, the difference—8.7 percent—can be assumed to be the risk premium for holding common stocks over treasury bills. Using this Historic Approach, during a given period, the risk premium for a stock can be estimated to be approximately 8.7 percent. Therefore, if the prevailing treasury bill rate is, say, 9.0 percent, the total return on common stock will approximate 17.7 (9.0 + 8.7) percent. The study also indicates that the average annual return on long-term corporate bonds has been approximately 4.1 percent, and that the risk premium for holding common stocks as opposed to good quality long-term corporate bonds is 7.1 percent (11.2 – 4.1 percent). Investors can use this relationship between common stocks and bonds for cross checking their stocks–treasury bills estimates of the common stock risk premium.

Like all long-term averages, the Historic Approach ignores both short-term variations in risk premium and the risks of individual stocks. For instance, although the implicit risk premium has averaged 8.7 percent between 1926 and 1978, there have been wide variations on both sides of the figure (the premium was much higher in the early 1950s and much lower in the late 1960s).

There are other compelling reasons for developing a better technique than the Historic Approach. For instance, since the 1960s, other changes in the marketplace have significantly impacted the common stock risk premium. The structure of expected returns from common stocks, for example, has changed a great deal during the past 30 years. Before the 1960s, dividend income accounted for the largest part of total stock return. With the bull market of the 1950s and early 1960s, dividend yields gradually diminished to around 3 percent per annum, while annual earnings growth rose to a fairly consistent 5 percent. Dividends have become the smallest component of expected returns and have continued so until the present time, with the adjustments to inflation having produced dividend yields averaging around 5 percent and dividend growth rates ranging between 8 and 10 percent. Because the uncertainty of return from capital appreciation is greater than the uncertainty of return from dividend income, this shift in the structure of expected returns would justify some enlargement of the implicit risk premium. On the other side of the spectrum, however, in recent years risk premiums have tended to decline as a result of the increase in common stocks held by institutions. During the past 30 years, institutions have assumed ownership of an increasingly high percentage of common stocks—more than 40 percent at the present time. The accumulation of larger pools of equity capital have permitted greater diversity in individual holdings, and many institutional entities have a clear fiduciary responsibility to diversify. The result has been significantly diminished exposure to risks unique to particular companies and industries.

Significant changes have recently occurred in the stock market which have tended to both increase and decrease the risk premiums associated with common stocks. Although it is difficult to pinpoint the net impact of these changes on the implicit risk premium, a range of 6–9 percent over treasury bills seems to be a reasonable approximation for the implicit common stock risk premium.

Method 2: Risk–Return Approach

The more sophisticated, and unquestionably superior, approach to estimating the risk premium is the Risk–Return Approach. The broad parameters of this approach can be briefly stated.

The appropriate discount rate is the rate of return sufficient to induce an investor to assume the risk inherent in a common stock. As noted earlier, the risk of a single stock comprises both systematic and unsystematic risk; however, unsystematic risk tends to disappear when an efficient portfolio is constructed. Assuming an investor chooses to construct an efficient portfolio, the riskiness of a single stock should be evaluated in terms of its effect on the riskiness of the portfolio, which is equivalent to the stock's sensitivity to overall market movements. Consequently, the appropriate discount rate, or minimum required rate of return, for a stock should be higher than the expected market return if the stock is more volatile than the market, and vice versa. A simple way to estimate the appropriate discount is to calculate the product of the stock's beta and the expected market return—the expected systematic return. This Risk–Return Approach and its practical application will be discussed in relation to the fundamental analysis of stocks in Chapter 11. Later, when portfolio analysis is discussed in Chapter 13, a more advanced model will be introduced which will relate the return on a security to both the market return and the return on risk-free assets.

The Decision Model

Under the assumption that an investor has a finite holding period, the techniques for estimating the following variables have been presented:

1. The appropriate discount rate, r.
2. The expected earnings at the end of the holding period, E_N.

3. The earnings multiple at the end of the holding period, $(EM)_N$.
4. The future annual dividend stream, D_n.

We are now in a position to present two different methods of evaluating a common stock.

Method 1: Present Value vs. Price

The starting point is the Holding Period Dividend Model:

$$PV = \sum_{n=1}^{N} \frac{D_n}{(1+r)^n} + \frac{P_N}{(1+r)^N} \qquad \textbf{(9–3 restated)}$$

Because $P_N = (EM)_N \times E_N$, the above equation can be modified as:

$$PV = \sum_{n=1}^{N} \frac{D_n}{(1+r)^n} + \frac{(EM)_N \times E_N}{(1+r)^N} \qquad \textbf{(9–25)}$$

where

PV = Present value of the common stock
D_n = Annual dividend payments
$(EM)_N$ = Earnings multiple at the end of period N
E_N = Earnings per share at the end of period N
N = Number of years the stock is expected to be held
r = The appropriate discount rate or the investor's minimum required rate of return

Assuming that the values of D_n, $(EM)_N$, E_N and r are determined by using the techniques already presented and that the holding period, N, is specified, the present value of the stock can be determined by solving for PV.

The Decision Model may now be presented in general terms. As long as the present value of a stock is higher than its current market price, it is an undervalued stock and constitutes an attractive investment. If, on the other hand, the present value is lower than the market price, the stock can be characterized as an overvalued stock and should not be purchased, or should be sold if already owned. Finally, if the present value and the current market price are equal, the stock might be considered appropriately priced.

Method 2: Appropriate Discount Rate vs. Yield

Method 2—another way of using the same model—requires the investor to compare the stock's holding period yield with the appropriate discount rate. The method of estimating the appropriate discount rate has already been discussed. The holding period yield can be calculated by substituting the current price, P_0, for the present value, PV, and the yield or expected return, i, for the appropriate discount rate, r:

$$P_0 = \sum_{n=1}^{N} \frac{D_n}{(1+i)^n} + \frac{P_N}{(1+i)^N} \tag{9-26}$$

In this equation, P_0, D_n, and P_N are known, but the yield, i, is unknown. The equation should be solved for i, the stock's yield.

Method 2 can now be presented. As long as the yield or the expected return of a stock, i, is higher than the appropriate discount rate, or the required rate of return, r, it is an undervalued stock and constitutes an attractive investment. The reverse is true if the yield is lower than the appropriate discount rate.

Figure 9–2 **(A) Method 1: Calculation of Stock's Present Value (*PV*)**

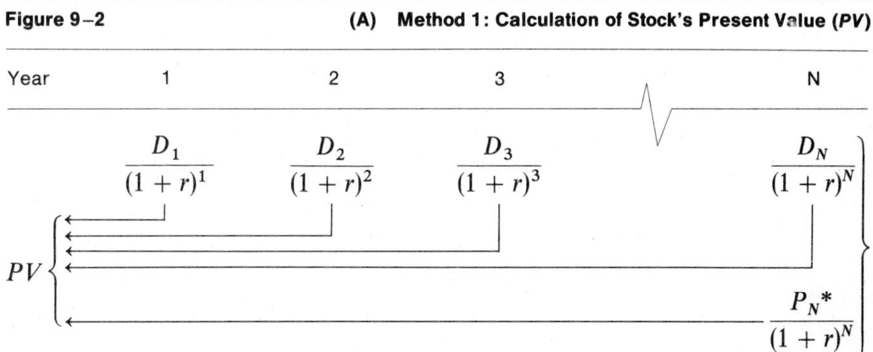

Given values for D_1 through D_N, r, and P_N, calculate the PV and compare with current price (P_0) to determine if stock is undervalued or overvalued.

(B) Method 2: Calculation of Stock's Yield (*i*)

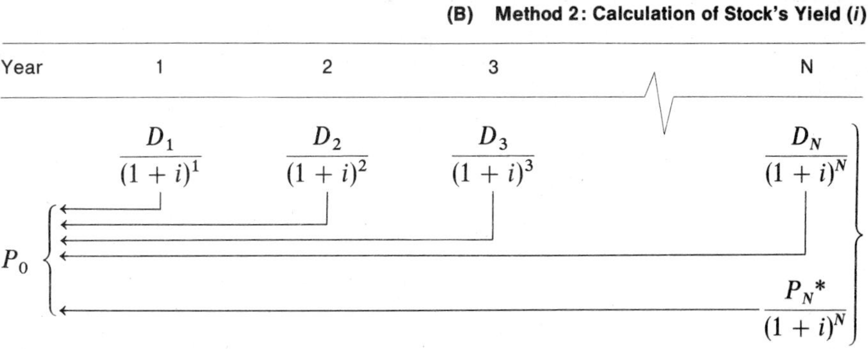

Given values for D_1 through D_N, P_0, and P_N, calculate the yield (i) and compare with the appropriate discount rate (r). If $i > r$, the stock is undervalued.

$* \; P_N = (EM)_N \times E_N$

The conceptual framework of the two methods just described is presented in Figure 9–2. A summary of the decision process of the Model follows:

If		Then	Reason
Method 1	Method 2		
$PV = P_0$	$r = i$	Be indifferent.	The stock is appropriately valued.
$PV > P_0$	$r < i$	Buy the stock.	The stock is undervalued.
$PV < P_0$	$r > i$	Do not buy the stock.	The stock is overvalued.

PV = Present value of the stock, determined by using the investor's appropriate discount rate

P_0 = Current market price of the stock

r = The appropriate discount rate or the investor's minimum required rate of return

i = Holding period yield or expected return

Summary

The Bond Valuation Model cannot be directly used for the valuation of common stocks, because stocks have no maturity price or fixed dividend payments.

Although the *Perpetual Dividend Model* is conceptually sound, it is of little practical value because of the difficulty of estimating dividend payments to infinity.

Under the assumption that every investor has a finite holding period for a stock, the *Holding Period Dividend Model* is developed. According to this model, the present value of a common stock can be determined by discounting both the expected future dividend stream and the price at which the stock is expected to be sold at the end of the holding period. The three key variables of the model are the expected *dividend stream*, D_n, the *future selling price*, P_N, and the *appropriate discount rate*, r.

There are simple techniques for estimating the key variables of the model and demonstrating its use. Earnings growth and the dividend payout ratio are assumed to remain constant over the holding period. The stock's future selling price is estimated by multiplying future expected earnings per share by an *earnings multiple* (*EM*). The appropriate discount rate is estimated by using either the Historic or the Risk–Return Approach. A more detailed discussion of the techniques for estimating the key variables of the model will be undertaken in Chapters 10 and 11.

A *Decision Model* is presented to identify undervalued and overvalued stocks. As long as the present value of a stock is higher than its current market price, it can be treated as an undervalued stock. If, however, the present value is lower than the current market price, the stock is overvalued. Another way of using the Decision Model is to compare the stock's holding period yield with the appropriate discount rate. A stock is considered undervalued if the holding period yield exceeds the appropriate discount rate.

A Look Ahead

In this chapter, a Common Stock Valuation Model has been developed. The use of this model for the identification of undervalued and overvalued stocks has also been demonstrated.

It has been clearly demonstrated that the effectiveness of the model is basically dependent on the investor's ability to (1) analyze the fundamental strength or weakness of a firm and its industry, and (2) use this analysis to predict the firm's future earnings, dividends, and the earnings multiple. Fundamental analysis of common stock will therefore be the subject of our study in the next chapter.

Concepts for Review

Perpetual Dividend Model
Holding Period Dividend Model
Dividend stream
Fixed payout ratio
Future selling price
Dividend: Normal growth
Dividend: Abnormal growth
Dividend Model
Internal rate of return
P/E ratio
Earnings multiple
Growth rate of earnings
Appropriate discount rate
Historic approach
Risk–Return approach
Decision Model

Questions for Review

1. Contrast the Bond Valuation Model with the Common Stock Valuation Model. Why is it more difficult to determine the value of a common stock than the value of a bond?
2. Discuss the significance of earnings and dividends as sources of common stock values.
3. How would you interpret the investment potential of a stock whose current price is \$40 and whose present value is \$45?
4. Investor R mentions that ABC stock is a better investment than XYZ stock because the present value of the former security is greater. What is your reply?

5. Explain the process of capitalizing an expected income stream.
6. Investor Q states that the value of a common stock is based on future cash dividend payments. Investor Y states that the value of a common stock is based on future cash dividend payments and the future selling price. Which statement is correct? Can they be reconciled?
7. The authors suggest that the Perpetual Dividend Model is impractical. Do you agree or disagree? Give reasons for your answer.
8. Critically evaluate the following statement: "Dividend policy is irrelevant."
9. Explain the Holding Period Dividend Model. What are the key variables of this model?
10. Explain how an investor's appropriate discount rate for a given stock can be estimated. What considerations are important?
11. What is the Earnings Multiple Approach to forecasting the selling price of a stock? What are the limitations of this method?
12. QRS stock has a P/E ratio of 8; GHI stock has a P/E ratio of 15. What are the possible reasons for this difference?
13. Under what conditions would you use the formula $PV = D_1/(r - g)$ for calculating the present value of a stock?
14. Explain the difference between a normal and an abnormal growth rate. How do you account for differences in dividend growth in evaluating a common stock?
15. An investor can compare the expected return of a stock to the appropriate discount rate in order to determine if the security is undervalued. Can you think of any difficulties one might encounter in implementing this approach?

Problems

1. ABC stock currently sells for $50 per share. You expect the company to pay an annual dividend of $2 per share for the next five years, and estimate that the stock will sell for $65 at the end of the fifth year.
   a. If your holding period is five years and your appropriate discount rate is 12 percent, would you purchase ABC stock?
   b. What is the lowest return you would accept from this stock to make it suitable for purchase at the current price?
   c. Suppose conditions change so that you are willing to accept a 10 percent return from this stock. What is the highest price you would then pay for the security?
2. QRS Company stock currently sells for $33.75 per share and pays an annual dividend of $1.65 per share. Over the next six years, dividends are expected to grow at an annual rate of 10 percent, and thereafter to stabilize at 4 percent per year. Assuming an appropriate discount rate of 14 percent, would you be willing to buy this at the current price?
3. STE Corporation earned $3.12 per share in the last year and paid out $1.62 per share in dividends. Find the present value of STE common stock assuming (a) a continuation of the current payout ratio, (b) an appropriate discount rate of 12 percent, and (c) an estimated earnings per share growth at a constant rate of 8 percent.

4. Which of the following two stocks would you consider the more attractive investment? Base your decision only on an analysis of present values. Assume the dividend payout ratio will remain constant and your holding period is four years.

	LMN Stock	QTE Stock
Market price	\$35.00	\$108.75
Current EPS	\$ 6.50	\$ 8.05
Current dividend rate	\$ 3.10	\$ 1.13
Expected EPS growth for the next four years	4%	22%
Estimated Earnings Multiple at end of fourth year	5	11
Appropriate discount rate	12%	15%

5. Suppose you received the following report from a brokerage house: "Floating Terminal Systems is a leading manufacturer of specialized scientific computers. Earnings are expected to advance from this year's \$1 per share by 15 percent annually over the next five years. Over the longer-term, earnings growth should continue at a 10 percent annual rate. Currently paying a \$0.40 annual dividend and selling at only 14 times earnings, Floating Terminal Systems shares appear to be undervalued and an attractive investment opportunity."

Based on this appraisal and assuming (a) the payout ratio remains constant, (b) an appropriate discount rate of 14 percent, and (c) a five-year holding period, would you purchase this stock?

Footnote

8. Equation 9–15 can be derived in the following manner:

$$PV = \frac{D_1}{(1+r)^1} + \frac{D_2}{(1+r)^2} + \frac{D_3}{(1+r)^3} + \frac{D_4}{(1+r)^4} + \frac{D_5}{(1+r)^5} + \cdots + \frac{D_\infty}{(1+r)^\infty} \quad \textbf{(9–1)}$$

If the time period is n, Equation 9–1 can be rewritten as:

$$PV = \frac{D_1}{(1+r)^1} + \frac{D_2}{(1+r)^2} + \frac{D_3}{(1+r)^3} + \cdots + \frac{D_n}{(1+r)^n} \quad \textbf{(9–a)}$$

If the growth rate, g, of dividend is assumed constant, Equation 9–a becomes:

$$PV = \frac{D_0(1+g)^1}{(1+r)^1} + \frac{D_0(1+g)^2}{(1+r)^2} + \cdots + \frac{D_0(1+g)^n}{(1+r)^n} \quad \textbf{(9–b)}$$

Equation 9–b can be rearranged in the following manner:

$$PV = D_0\left[\frac{(1+g)^1}{(1+r)^1} + \frac{(1+g)^2}{(1+r)^2} + \cdots + \frac{(1+g)^n}{(1+r)^n}\right] \quad \textbf{(9–c)}$$

Multiplying both sides by $\frac{(1+r)^1}{(1+g)^1}$, Equation 9–c becomes:

$$PV\left[\frac{(1+r)^1}{(1+g)^1}\right] = D_0\left[1 + \frac{(1+g)^1}{(1+r)^1} + \frac{(1+g)^2}{(1+r)^2} + \cdots + \frac{(1+g)^{n-1}}{(1+r)^{n-1}}\right] \quad \textbf{(9–d)}$$

Subtracting Equation 9–c from Equation 9–d, we have:

$$\left[\frac{(1+r)^1}{(1+g)^1} - 1\right] PV = D_0\left[1 - \frac{(1+g)^n}{(1+r)^n}\right] \tag{9–e}$$

Rearranging Equation 9–e we get:

$$\left[\frac{(1+r)-(1+g)}{(1+g)}\right] PV = D_0\left[1 - \frac{(1+g)^n}{(1+r)^n}\right] \tag{9–f}$$

Assuming $r > g$, as $n \to \infty$, the term in brackets on the right hand side of Equation 9–f goes to 1. Therefore, Equation 9–f becomes:

$$\left[\frac{(1+r)-(1+g)}{(1+g)}\right] PV = D_0 \tag{9–g}$$

Rearranging Equation 9–g we have:

$$\left[\frac{r-g}{(1+g)}\right] PV = D_0 \tag{9–h}$$

or

$$PV = \frac{D_0(1+g)}{r-g} \tag{9–i}$$

But $D_1 = D_0(1+g)$. Therefore Equation 9–i becomes:

$$PV = \frac{D_1}{r-g} \tag{9–j}$$

Equation 9–15 can also be derived from the Common Stock Valuation Model. Under conditions of continuous compounding, assuming g and r are constant and $r > g$, we have

$$\begin{aligned}PV &= \int_1^\infty D_1 e^{gn} e^{-rn}\, dn \\ &= \int_1^\infty D_1 e^{-n(r-g)}\, dn \\ &= D_1\left[-\frac{1}{r-g} e^{-n(r-g)}\right]_{n=\infty} - D_1\left[-\frac{1}{r-g} e^{-n(r-g)}\right]_{n=0} \\ &= D_1\left[-\frac{1}{r-g} e^{-\infty}\right] - D_1\left[-\frac{1}{r-g} e^{-0}\right] \\ &= \frac{D_1}{r-g}\end{aligned}$$

Selected Readings

Ahlers, David M. "SEM: A Security Analysis Model." In *Analytical Methods in Banking.* ed. Kalman J. Cohen and Frederick S. Hammer. Homewood, Ill.: Richard Irwin, 1966.

Babcock, Guilford C. "The Concept of Sustainable Growth." *Financial Analysts Journal,* May–June 1970.

Baker, H. K., M. B. Hargrove, and J. A. Harlem. "An Empirical Analysis of the Risk–

Return Preferences of Individual Investors." *Journal of Financial and Quantitative Analysis*, September 1977.

Ben-Sharar, Haim and Marshall Sarnat. "Reinvestment and the Rate of Return on Common Stocks." *Journal of Finance*, December 1966.

Black, Fischer. "The Dividend Puzzle." *Journal of Portfolio Management*, Winter 1976.

Black, Fischer. "Yes, Virginia, There Is Hope: Tests of the Value Line Ranking System," *Financial Analysts Journal*, September–October 1973.

Black, Fischer and Myron Scholes. "The Effects of Dividend Yield and Dividend Policy on Common Stock Prices and Returns." *Journal of Financial Economics*, May 1974.

Bower, Dorothy H. and Richard S. Bower. "Test of a Stock Valuation Model." *Journal of Finance*, May 1970.

Bower, Richard S. and Dorothy H. Bower. "Risk and the Valuation of Common Stock." *Journal of Political Economy*, June 1969.

Brealey, Richard A. *An Introduction to Risk and Return from Common Stock Prices.* Cambridge, Mass.: MIT Press, 1969.

Brealey, Richard A. *Security Prices in a Competitive Market.* Cambridge, Mass.: MIT Press, 1971.

Brigham, Eugene F. and Myron J. Gordon. "Leverage, Dividend Policy, and the Cost of Capital." *Journal of Finance*, March 1968.

Brigham, Eugene F. and James L. Pappas. "Rates of Return on Common Stock." *Journal of Business*, July 1969.

Cowles, Alfred and Herbert F. Jones. "Some A Posteriori Probabilities in Stock Market Action." *Econometrica*, July 1937.

Cragg, John G. and Burton G. Malkiel. "The Consensus and Accuracy of Some Predictions of the Growth of Corporate Earnings." *Journal of Finance*, March 1968.

Dudley, Carlton L., Jr. "A Note on the Reinvestment Assumptions in Choosing Between Net Present Value and Internal Rate of Return." *Journal of Finance*, September 1972.

Durand, David. "Growth Stocks and the Petersburg Paradox." *Journal of Finance*, September 1957.

Eiteman, David K. "A Computer Program for Common Stock Valuation." *Financial Analysts Journal*, July–August 1968.

Fama, Eugene F. "The Behavior of Stock Market Prices." *Journal of Business*, January 1965.

Fama, Eugene F. and H. Babiak. "Dividend Policy: An Empirical Analysis." *Journal of the American Statistical Association*, December 1968.

Fisher, Lawrence and James H. Lorie. "Rates of Return on Investments in Common Stocks." *Journal of Business*, January 1964.

Fisher, Lawrence and James H. Lorie. "Rates of Return on Investments in Common Stocks: The Year-by-Year Record, 1926–1965." *Journal of Business*, July 1968.

Fisher, Lawrence and James H. Lorie. "Some Studies of Variability of Returns on Investment in Common Stocks." *Journal of Business*, April 1970.

Fisher, Lawrence and James H. Lorie. *A Half Century of Returns on Stocks and Bonds.* Chicago: University of Chicago, Graduate School of Business, 1977.

Foster, Earl M. "The Price-Earnings Ratio and Growth." *Financial Analysts Journal*, January–February 1970.

Francis, Jack Clark. "Do Some Stocks Consistently Lead or Lag the Market?" Working Paper No. 5–12, Rodney L. White Center for Financial Research, University of Pennsylvania, n.d.

Friend, Irwin and Marshall Blume. "Risk and the Long-Run Rate of Return on NYSE Common Stocks." Working Paper No. 18–72, The Wharton School of Finance and Commerce, Rodney L. White Center for Financial Research, 1972.

Friend, Irwin and Marshall Puckett. "Dividends and Stock Prices." *American Economic Review*, September 1964.

Gordon, M. J. *The Investment, Financing and Valuation of the Corporation*. Homewood, Ill.: Richard Irwin, 1962.

Hagin, Robert L. "An Empirical Evaluation of Selected Hypotheses Related to Price Changes in the Stock Market." Unpublished Ph.D. dissertation, University of California, Los Angeles, 1966.

Hagin, Robert L. (with Chris Mader). *The New Science of Investing*. Homewood, Ill.: Dow Jones-Irwin, 1973.

Hirshleifer, Jack. "Investment Decisions Under Uncertainty: Applications of the State-Preference Approach. *Quarterly Journal of Economics*, May 1966.

Ibbotson, Roger G. "Price Performance of Common Stock New Issues." *Journal of Financial Economics*, September 1975.

Jaffe, D. M., B. G. Malkiel and R. E. Quandt. "Predicting Common Stock Prices: Payoffs and Pitfalls." *Journal of Business Research*, January 1974.

Joy, O. Maurice, Robert H. Litzenberger, and Richard W. McEnally. "The Adjustment of Stock Prices to Announcements of Unanticipated Changes in Quarterly Earnings." *Journal of Accounting Research*, Autumn 1977.

Levy, Robert A. "On the Short-term Stationarity of Beta Coefficients." *Financial Analysts Journal*, November–December 1971.

Lorie, James and Richard Brealey, eds. *The Stock Market: Theories and Evidence*. Homewood, Ill.: Richard D. Irwin, 1974.

Malkiel, Burton G. "Equity Yields, Growth, and the Structure of Share Prices." *American Economic Review*, December 1963.

Malkiel, Burton G. and John G. Cragg. "Expectations and the Structure of Share Prices." *American Economic Review*, September 1970.

Mandelbrot, Benoit. "The Variation of Certain Speculative Prices." *Journal of Business*, October 1962.

Mandelbrot, Benoit. "The Variation of Some Other Speculative Prices." *Journal of Business*, October 1967.

Mao, James C. T. "The Valuation of Growth Stocks: The Investment Opportunities Approach." *Journal of Finance*, March 1966.

Miller, Merton and Franco Modigliani. "Dividend Policy, Growth, and the Valuation of Shares." *Journal of Business*, October 1961.

Modigliani, Franco and Merton Miller. "The Cost of Capital, Corporation Finance, and the Theory of Investment." *American Economic Review*, June 1958.

Molodovsky, Nicholas. *Investment Values in a Dynamic World: Collected Papers of Nicholas Molodovsky*. Homewood, Ill.: Richard D. Irwin, 1974.

Moore, Arnold B. "A Statistical Analysis of Common Stock Prices." Unpublished Ph.D. dissertation, University of Chicago, 1962.

Nerlove, Marc. "Factors Affecting Differences Among Rates of Return on Individual Common Stocks." *Review of Economics and Statistics*, August 1968.

Nicholson, S. F. "Price-Earnings Ratios." *Financial Analysts Journal*, July–August 1970.

Niederhoffer, Victor. "Clustering of Stock Prices." *Operational Research*, March–April 1965.

Niederhoffer, Victor. "The Predictive Content of First Quarter Earnings Reports." *Journal of Business*, January 1970.

Niederhoffer, Victor and M. F. M. Osborne. "Market Making and Reversal on the Stock Exchange." *Journal of the American Statistical Association*, December 1966.

Press, S. James. "A Compound Events Model for Security Prices." *Journal of Business*, July 1967.

Reilly, Frank K. "The Misdirected Emphasis in Security Valuation." *Financial Analysts Journal*, January–February 1973.

Roberts, Harry V. "Stock Market 'Patterns' and Financial Analysis." *Journal of Finance*, March 1959.

Robichek, A. A. and Stewart C. Myers. "Conceptual Problems in the Use of Risk-adjusted Discount Rates." *Journal of Finance*, December 1966.

Robichek, A. A., and Stewart C. Myers. "Risk and the Value of Securities." *Journal of Financial and Quantitative Analysis*, December 1969.

Rose, Stanford. "The Stock Market Should Be Twice as High as It Is." *Fortune*, March 12, 1979.

Rosenberg, Barr and Vinay Marathe. "Common Factors in Security Returns: Microeconomic Determinants and Macroeconomic Correlates." *Proceedings of the Seminar on the Analysis of Security Prices*, University of Chicago, May 1976.

Tobias, Andrew. *The Only Investment Guide You'll Ever Need*. New York: Harcourt Brace Jovanovich, 1978.

Sharpe, William F. "Bonds Versus Stocks: Some Lessons from Capital Market Theory." *Financial Analysts Journal*, November–December 1973.

Staubus, George J. "Earnings Periods for Common Share Analysis." *Journal of Business*, October 1968.

Stekler, H. O. *Profitability and Size of Firm*. Berkeley: University of California Institute of Business and Economic Research, 1963.

Williams, John Burr. *The Theory of Investment Value*. Cambridge, Mass.: Harvard University Press, 1938.

Williamson, J. Peter. *Investments: New Analytic Techniques*. New York: Praeger, 1970.

Working, Holbrook. "New Ideas and Methods for Price Research." *Journal of Farm Economics*, December 1956.

Fundamental Analysis: Determination of Earning Power

10

Introduction

In Chapter 9, it was explained that, for an investor with a finite holding period, the present value of common stock can be calculated by discounting future dividends and the expected selling price at the end of the holding period (holding period price) by the investor's appropriate discount rate. Symbolically,

$$PV = \sum_{n=1}^{N} \frac{D_n}{(1+r)^n} + \frac{P_N}{(1+r)^N} \qquad \textbf{(9–3 restated)}$$

where

PV = Present value of the common stock

D_n = Annual dividend payments

P_N = Price at which the stock is expected to be sold at the end of period N

N = Number of years the stock is expected to be held

r = Appropriate discount rate, or the investor's minimum required rate of return

According to this equation, the present value of a stock is a function of the future dividend stream, the holding period price, and the appropriate discount rate. Dividends, of course, are paid out of the earnings of the firms. Also, the holding period price is the product of earnings and the earnings multiple at the

Table 10–1

	Benjamin King Study	Richard Brealey Study
Number of stocks analyzed	63	217
Period covered	June 1927–December 1960	1948–1966
Variance of individual stock prices attributable to:		
Market	52	21
Industry	10	21
Company	38	58
Total	100	100

SOURCE: Reprinted from "Market and Industry Factors in Stock Price Behavior," by Benjamin King, *Journal of Business*, January 1960, pp. 139–90 by permission of the University of Chicago Press. © 1960 by the University of Chicago. Reprinted by permission of MIT Press from Richard Brealey, *An Introduction to Risk and Return from Common Stocks* (Cambridge, Mass.: MIT Press, 1969), pp. 47–54. © 1969 by the Massachusetts Institute of Technology.

end of the holding period. The earnings multiple, in turn, is partly influenced by the expected growth rate of the company's earnings beyond the holding period. It is, therefore, necessary to predict the company's future earnings growth. Future earnings growth depends not only on the performance of the company, but also on the future success of the industry of which it is a part. Generally, when an industry prospers, most firms within that industry stand to benefit as well. Conversely, when an industry experiences adverse economic conditions, the earnings of related firms tend to fall.

The future prospects of an industry, in turn, are closely tied to the general economic conditions prevailing in the country. During periods of economic boom, industry earnings tend to increase, whereas during an economic recession, industry earnings decline. Clearly, a growing economy and growing industry earnings are positively related.

The appropriate discount rate with which a stock's future dividend stream and holding period price are discounted is also affected by the prevailing economic conditions. Because a deterioration of economic conditions increases the investor's perception of market risk, it leads to an increase in the appropriate discount rate. The reverse is true when the economy experiences healthy growth.[1]

Studies have shown that security price changes are related to concurrent changes in the market; the market acts as a surrogate for the economy as well as for the various groups of industries. Table 10–1 presents the results of two representative studies. Although these studies reveal that the degree of relationship between changes in security prices and factors influencing them varies widely, the fact that they are interrelated is clearly established. Furthermore, in view of the fact that the present value of a stock is directly related to earnings

[1] The discount rate can also be influenced by the outlook for interest rates, which in turn depends upon the economic outlook of the company. If interest rates are rising, investors will demand a higher rate of return, and vice versa.

growth, the influence of national economic and industry conditions on the earnings growth of a company is evident.

This chapter is organized along the following lines. First, the topic of forecasting the *gross national product* (*GNP*) and its components is discussed. Being able to determine the overall picture—that is, accurately evaluating the probable outlook for the American economy and the market in general—helps an investor predict the future earnings of individual companies. Second, particular industries are analyzed against the backdrop of national economic trends. This is an important step because, as previously stated, studies have shown that a significant portion of variations in particular security prices are due to industry performance. Third, we focus on individual companies. A critical examination of a firm's *earning power* can help an investor estimate the present value of its common stock, because the present value is positively related to the expected earnings growth of the company.

General Economic Conditions

The Basic Framework

Analysis of the nation's economic conditions is not an end in itself. It is important to analyze and forecast general economic conditions because there is a direct relationship between the economy and the performance of an individual firm, of which earning power is a key measure. The reasons for this relationship are obvious. In times of economic recession[2] unemployment is high and production is depressed. When the growth of the real GNP slows down, the sales and earnings of most firms decline below their normal levels. In times of an economic boom these relationships are reversed. As the GNP grows at a higher than normal rate, sales, earnings, and eventually dividends grow at a rapid rate as well. In general, the growth in the real GNP, reflecting the nation's economic health, and changes in earning power, representing the performance of individual firms, are positively related.

Once the positive relationship between the GNP and earnings power is understood, the problems associated with forecasting economic conditions can be discussed. George Bernard Shaw once said, "To every question there is a simple answer. Unfortunately, it is always wrong." There is nothing simple about forecasting economic conditions.

Our economic system, in the words of Joseph Schumpeter, "not only never is but never can be stationary." There are, of course, long-term or *secular* trends of

[2] The National Bureau of Economic Research has developed an elaborate system for identifying the turning points of overall economic activity, commonly known as business cycles. The upward turning point signals the beginning of an economic boom, whereas the downward turning point marks the starting of an economic recession.

Table 10–2 **(A) GNP & Key Components (1978–1984E) (billions of dollars)**

	1978	1979E	1980E	1981E	1982E	1983E	1984E
Consumption	1340	1492	1636	1832	2021	2270	2505
Investment	346	377	413	462	528	599	640
Nonresidential	223	252	276	307	353	409	447
Residential	107	110	120	135	150	165	170
Inventory	16	15	17	20	25	25	23
Net Exports	−12	−5	−3	−6	−3	Nil	Nil
Government	434	478	530	597	657	718	800
Federal	154	169	185	200	218	239	260
State & Local	280	309	345	397	439	479	540
Gross National Product	2108	2342	2576	2885	3203	3587	3945
Real GNP ($1972 bill.)	1386	1414	1435	1492	1537	1583	1615
% Change, GNP	11.7%	11.1%	10.0%	12.0%	11.0%	12.0%	10.0%
% Change, Real GNP	4.0%	2.0%	1.5%	4.0%	3.0%	3.0%	2.0%
Inflation Rate*	7.4%	9.0%	8.0%	7.5%	8.0%	8.5%	8.0%
Consumption/GNP	63.6%	63.7%	63.5%	63.5%	63.1%	63.3%	63.5%
Investment/GNP	16.4%	16.1%	16.0%	16.0%	16.5%	16.7%	16.2%
Net Exports/GNP	−0.6%	−0.2%	−0.1%	−0.2%	−0.1%	Nil	Nil
Government/GNP	20.6%	20.4%	20.6%	20.7%	20.5%	20.0%	20.3%
Total	100%	100%	100%	100%	100%	100%	100%
Corporate Profits	130.5	147	155	177	200	222	245

(B) GNP & Key Component Rates of Change (1978–1984E)

	1978	1979E	1980E	1981E	1982E	1983E	1984E
Consumption	11.0%	11.3%	9.7%	12.0%	10.3%	12.3%	10.4%
Investment	17.7%	9.0%	9.5%	11.9%	14.3%	13.4%	6.8%
Government	9.9%	10.1%	10.9%	12.6%	10.0%	9.3%	11.4%
GNP	11.7%	11.1%	10.0%	12.0%	11.0%	12.0%	10.0%
Real GNP	4.0%	2.0%	1.5%	4.0%	3.0%	3.0%	2.0%
Inflation Rate	7.4%	9.0%	8.0%	7.5%	8.0%	8.5%	8.0%
Corporate Profits	15.6%	12.6%	5.5%	14.2%	13.0%	11.0%	10.4%

* The inflation rate is measured by changes in the GNP Deflator, a broad measure of inflation throughout the economy. Changes in the Consumer Price Index, a poor inflation measure, can be a full percentage point greater in any one year.

SOURCE: *The Value Line Investment Survey*, July 6, 1979, p. 661.

growth or decline in population and national output, as well as in individual industries. These secular trends must be differentiated from *random* movements that result from wars, political developments, transitory factors, even weather conditions. In addition to secular trends and random movements, *seasonal* and *cyclical* fluctuations occur in such economic series as department store sales, automobile output, housing starts, and so on.

It is not surprising that many investors find the task of economic forecasting formidable. Future economic conditions depend on many highly unpredictable noneconomic (political, social, and so on) variables, and investors are seldom sufficiently versed in the techniques of forecasting to predict accurately future economic conditions. An average investor might therefore be well advised to refrain from making economic forecasts and accept the economic forecasts made by the *National Bureau of Economic Research* (*NBER*), professional forecasting institutions, or other sources.[3] Informed investors may, however, wish to *modify* the forecasts made by the government or professional institutions according to their own independent analysis of general economic conditions.

Thus far, no distinction has been made between *long-range* and *short-range forecasting*. Long-range forecasting is infinitely more difficult than short-range forecasting. Generally, forecasts for ten years or more—which are seldom undertaken—are not very accurate.[4] In fact, even a five-year forecast of the GNP and its components is difficult to find. One such forecast, made by Value Line, is reproduced in Table 10–2 to illustrate this point. Primarily because of the difficulties inherent in long-term forecasting, and also because many professional common stock valuations are based on national economic projections of five years or less,[5] the discussion that follows will center on short-term economic forecasting.

For convenience, the discussion on economic forecasting will be undertaken in three stages. First, the forecasting method used by the venerable NBER and a refinement over the NBER method used by the government will be presented. Second, the economic forecasts made by several advisory services will be summarized. Finally, more sophisticated forecasting methods undertaken by astute investors will be reviewed.

National Bureau of Economic Research

Economic Indicators[6]

The NBER is famous for its pioneering and comprehensive statistical studies of over 100 economic indicators. These indicators, as demonstrated in Table 10–3,

---

[3] Other sources of general economic forecasts include, for example, the President's Economic Report and *Fortune*.

[4] See John W. Kendrick, "Investment Implications of Long-Run Economic Trends," *Financial Analysts Journal*, September–October 1961, pp. 229–34. Kendrick made a ten-year projection of the economy. Unfortunately, his projections were not very satisfactory.

[5] Even for the investor with a long-time horizon, it is practical to break this long-term period into several short-term periods; that is, the investor's long-term forecasts can be divided into a series of short-term forecasts. A five-year period can be accepted as convenient for short-term forecasts.

[6] For details see Leonard H. Lempert, "Leading Indicators," in *How Business Economists Forecast*, ed. William F. Butler and Robert A. Kavesh (Englewood Cliffs, N.J.: Prentice-Hall, 1966).

Table 10–3 **Cross-Classification of Cyclical Indicators, by Economic Process and Cyclical Timing**

Economic Process \ Cyclical Timing	Leading Indicators	Roughly Coincident Indicators	Lagging Indicators
1. Employment and Unemployment	Marginal employment adjustments	Job vacancies Comprehensive employment Comprehensive unemployment	Long-duration unemployment
2. Production, Income, Consumption, and Trade		Comprehensive production Comprehensive income Comprehensive consumption and trade	
3. Fixed Capital Investment	Formation of business enterprises New investment commitments	Backlog of investment commitments	Investment expenditures
4. Inventories and Inventory Investment	Inventory investment and purchasing		Inventories
5. Prices, Costs, and Profits	Sensitive commodity prices Stock prices Profits and profit margins Cash flows	Comprehensive wholesale prices	Unit labor costs
6. Money and Credit	Flows of money and credit Credit difficulties	Bank reserves Interest rates	Outstanding debt Interest rates

SOURCE: Bureau of the Census, Department of Commerce, *Business Conditions Digest*, June 1975, p. 2.

are classified according to economic process and cyclical timing. Note that the cyclical timing classification has three broad categories for leading, coincident, and lagging indicators.

The *leading indicators* are a selection of statistical data that typically indicates peaks or troughs in the business cycles *ahead* of the overall economy. These include series on unemployment, new investment, profits, and inventory investments. The *coincident indicators* are those series whose peaks and troughs

Table 10–4 **Short List of NBER Cyclical Indicators, by Timing**

Leading	Lagging	Roughly Coincidental
1. Average work week for production workers in manufacturing (hours)	1. Unemployment rate, persons unemployed 15 weeks or more	1. Personal income
2. Average weekly initial claims for state unemployment insurance	2. Business expenditures for new plant and equipment	2. GNP in current dollars
3. New business formation	3. Book value of manufacturing and trade inventories	3. GNP in constant dollars
4. New orders in durable goods industries	4. Labor cost per unit of output in manufacturing	4. Industrial production
5. Contracts and orders for plant and equipment	5. Commercial and industrial loans outstanding as reported weekly by large commercial banks	5. Manufacturing and trade sales
6. New building permits for private housing units	6. Bank rates on short-term business loans	6. Sales of retail stores
7. Change in book value of manufacturing and trade inventories		7. Employees on nonagricultural payrolls
8. Industrial materials prices		8. Unemployment rate, total
9. Stock prices of 500 leading common stocks		
10. Corporate profits after taxes		
11. Ratio of price to unit labor cost in manufacturing		
12. Change in consumer installment debt		

SOURCE: National Bureau of Economic Research.

roughly coincide *with* those of general business. These include the GNP, industrial production, wholesale prices, and retail sales. Finally, the *lagging indicators follow* the swings of general business. These include series of plant and equipment expenditures, consumer installment debts, and bank rates on short-term business loans. Table 10–4 is a "short list" of 26 series. Of these, twelve are leading indicators, eight are coincident indicators, and six are lagging indicators. The short list of indicators is graphically presented in Figure 10–1. Each shaded portion on the graph represents a recession as defined by the NBER. Note, for instance, that the index of leading indicators declined nine months prior to the 1974–75 recession and eleven months prior to the 1960–61 recession. In contrast, the index of lagging indicators declined ten months *after* the beginning of the 1974–75 recession and two months after the 1960–61 recession.[7]

[7] The index of leading indicators and the index of lagging indicators are diffusion indexes. Diffusion indexes are explained on pages 354–55.

Figure 10–1 **Cylical Indicators: Composite Indexes and Their Components***

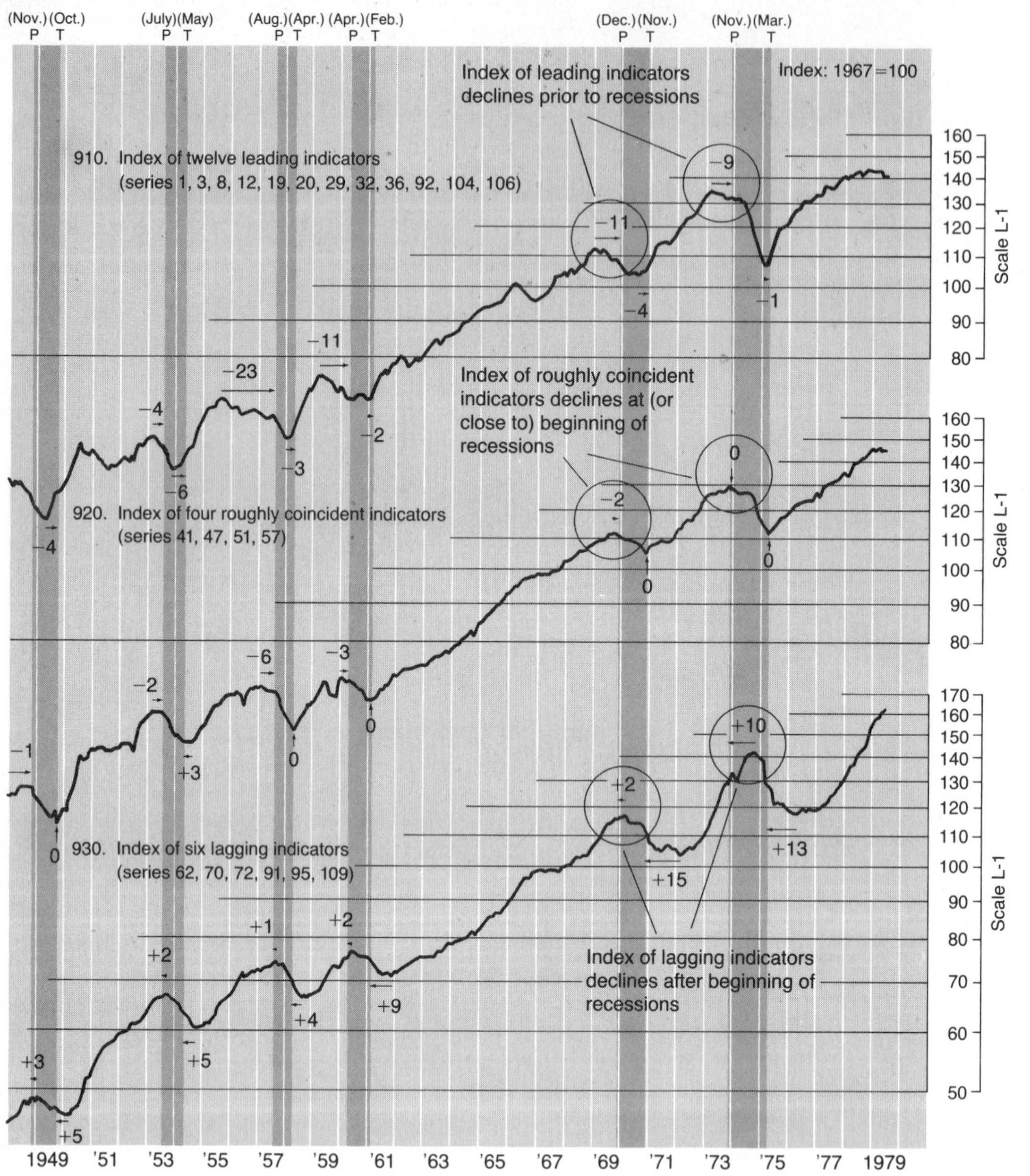

*Numbers entered on the chart indicate length of leads (−) and lags (+) in months from reference turning dates. Current data for these series are shown on page 60.

SOURCE: Bureau of the Census, Department of Commerce, *Business Conditions Digest*, June 1979, p. 10.

The NBER numerically rates each of the items on the short list. The system of numerical ratings is designed to help investors evaluate the current behavior of each indicator. The rating system evaluates each indicator from 0 to 100 in accordance with six major criteria:

1. Economic significance of the indicator in business cycle analysis.
2. Statistical adequacy of this series in terms of reporting systems.
3. Historical conformity of the indicator to business cycles.
4. Cyclical timing records of the indicator in relation to cyclical turning points.
5. Smoothness of the series.
6. Promptness of the data.

The higher the rating, the greater the weight of the indicator. In general, a rating of over 85 is considered excellent, 70–85 good, 60–70 fair, and below 60 less than fair.

Figure 10–2 **Rate of Change in U.S. Leading Index During Preceding Six Months***

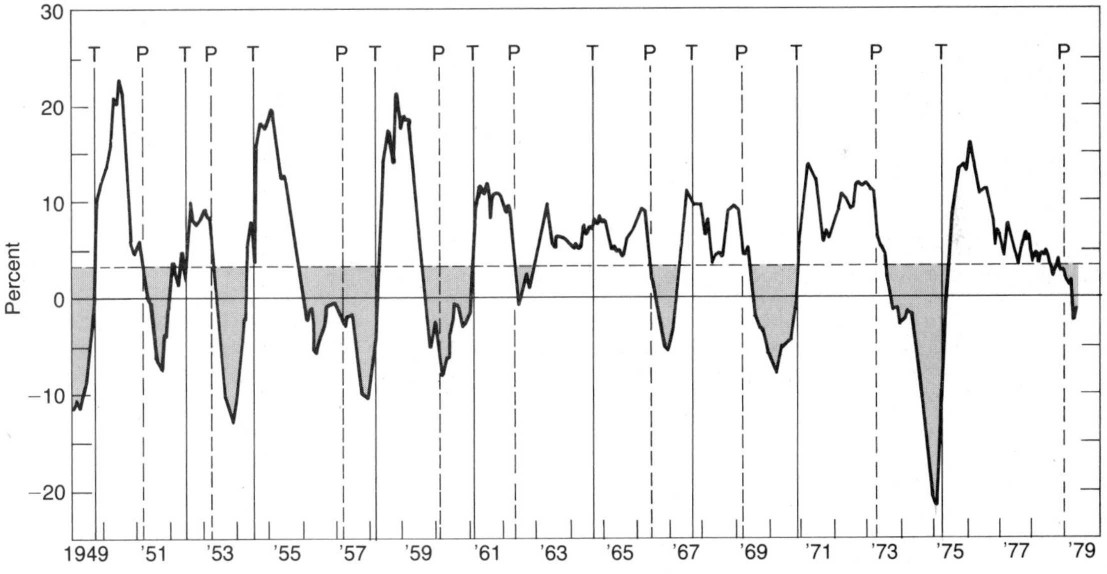

*Vertical lines mark the peaks (P) and troughs (T) in the growth cycle (National Bureau of Economic Research). The December 1978 peak is tentative. The rate of change in the leading index (U.S. Department of Commerce) is equal to the current month's index divided by the average of the twelve preceding months, expressed at an annual rate. The horizontal broken line is the long-term growth rate in the index, 3.3 percent, 1948–78.

SOURCE: Geoffrey H. Moore, "Growth Cycles: A New: Old Concept," *The Morgan Guaranty Survey*, August 1979, p. 14.

Figure 10–3

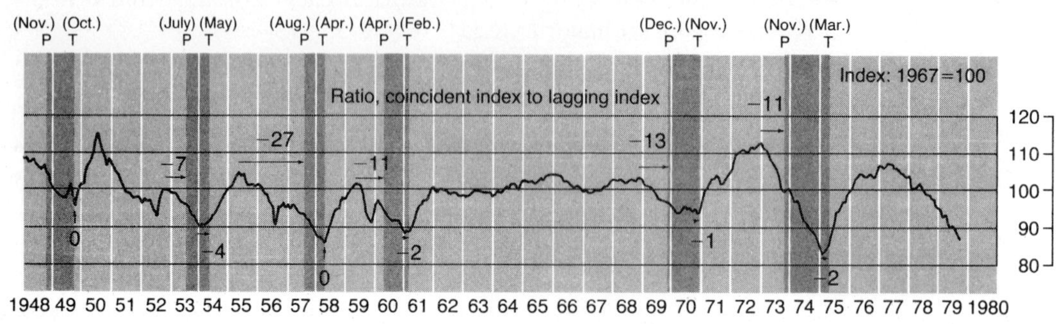

SOURCE: Bureau of the Census, Department of Commerce, *Business Conditions Digest*, September 1979, p. 11.

Another, more direct, use of the leading indicators should be mentioned. It has been a rule of thumb among many analysts that when the index of leading indicators declines for six months, recession is fairly imminent. Figure 10–2 shows the rate of change in the leading indicator index during six-month periods prior to recessions. Every time the growth of the leading index fell below its long-term rate of 3.3 percent per year, a peak in the growth in GNP was reached.

Another index used by government to signal a recession is shown in Figure 10–3. This is a ratio of the index of four coincident indicators of the economy divided by the index of six lagging indicators. This ratio, sometimes called the *leading-leading index*, tends to signal turning points in the economy in *advance* of the 12-component index of leading indicators.

Diffusion Indexes[8]

The NBER indicators chart the overall behavior of the series, but they do not indicate the behavior within the series. *Diffusion indexes* specify the proportion of reporting units in a series that show a given result. For instance, if 500 firms report their investment spending, the diffusion index will reveal what proportion of these firms reported lower investment spending during a recession.

There are two types of diffusion indexes available to economic forecasters. The first type of index, which can be called the comprehensive diffusion index, measures the strength in the movements of individual indicators in a group. It

[8] For details, see Albert T. Sommers, "Diffusion Indexes," in *How Business Economists Forecast*, ed. Butler and Kavesh.

is expressed as a ratio of rising indicators to total indicators. For example, if 10 out of 12 leading indicators advanced during a given month, the comprehensive diffusion index would be expressed as $10 \div 12 = 0.833$. In the next month the index would change to 0.5 if only six of the 12 indicators registered an increase. A rise in the comprehensive diffusion index would indicate a bright future; the reverse would be true if the index declined.

The other type of diffusion index is constructed to measure the breadth of movements in overall economic activity. This index tells forecasters how many industries within the indicator experienced upturns, how many registered downturns, and how many remained unchanged.

Forecasters using the diffusion indexes generally construct a weighted average known as the *duration of run index*. This index is constructed by weighting each series by the number of months it has risen. The weights of all the component series are first added; this sum is then divided by the number of the component series to provide the duration of run index. This index can be used as the basis for making short-term economic forecasts.

Professional Forecasts

Data published by the NBER require careful interpretation, because they are not presented as cogently and clearly as the economic forecasts by professional institutions. Professional forecasts not only include short-term forecasts of the GNP and its components, but also frequently evaluate the effects of government policies on the economic outlook of the nation. Reproduced below are summaries of several professional forecasts.

Moody's Forecasts[9]

Table 10–5 reveals Moody's analysis of preliminary economic data published by the Department of Commerce and its economic forecast for the last three quarters of 1979 and the first quarter of 1980. Moody's forecast is indeed comprehensive. In the text that accompanied this forecast, Moody's analyzed not only the near-term effects of monetary and fiscal policies on the economy, but also the outlook for retail sales of key industries, shifts in capital markets, prediction of consumer demand, and developments in the foreign sector. Moody's predicted the rate of inflation through 1980, and estimated the growth in GNP in current and constant dollars.

[9] "Inflation Trend Holds Key to Near-Term Prospects," in Moody's *Industry Surveys*, 1979, pp. 10a, 11a.

Table 10–5 **Economic Expectations: Looking Ahead Four Quarters***
(billions of dollars, annual rate)

	Reported	Estimated			
	IQ	IIQ	IIIQ	IVQ	IQ
Gross National Product	2,264.8	2,322.7	2,378.7	2,433.2	2,486.0
Personal Consumption Expenditures	1,440.4	1,484.4	1,521.8	1,558.5	1,594.2
Durable Goods	211.4	215.9	219.7	223.4	228.5
Non-Durable Goods	567.9	586.0	600.1	614.6	627.9
Services	661.0	682.5	702.0	720.5	737.8
Gross Private Domestic Investment	371.1	383.8	384.9	390.2	400.8
Producers' Durable Equipment	158.9	166.8	163.4	169.2	174.8
Non-Residential Structures	85.2	88.0	90.0	90.5	91.0
Residential Investment	107.2	116.0	117.0	118.5	118.0
Change in Business Inventories	16.6	13.0	14.5	12.0	17.0
Net Export of Goods and Services	−5.3	−10.5	−10.0	−9.5	−9.0
Gov't. Purchase of Goods and Services	458.5	465.0	482.0	494.0	500.0
Federal	164.5	167.0	175.0	180.0	186.0
National Defense	103.9	105.5	108.0	110.0	112.5
Nondefense	60.6	61.5	67.0	70.0	73.5
State and Local	294.0	298.0	307.0	314.0	314.0
Personal Disposable Income	1,563.2	1,615.4	1,661.8	1,701.8	1,734.8
Personal Savings	84.9	87.2	99.7	115.7	112.8
Savings as % of Disposable Income	5.4%	5.4%	6.0%	6.8%	6.5%
Gross National Product (1972 dollars)	1,416.3	1,424.2	1,429.3	1,431.6	1,433.2
Implicit Price Deflator (1972 = 100)	159.91	163.51	167.06	170.60	174.10

* Department of Commerce and Moody's Estimates. Totals may not add because of rounding.

SOURCE: "Inflation Trend Holds Key to Near-term Prospects," in Moody's *Handbook*, Summer, 1979, p. 10a–11a

Value Line Forecasts[10]

As demonstrated in Figure 10–4, in early 1979 the *Value Line Investment Survey* made a short-run forecast of the real GNP. The Survey forecast that the real GNP would register losses in 1979 and in early 1980. However, the Survey predicted that if the country could survive energy price increases, business expansion would begin in the second quarter of 1980 and last until 1984.

Other Forecasts[11]

Table 10–6 reproduces the forecasts of two other well-known institutions—Harris Trust and Savings Bank and the Conference Board. Similar forecasts are

[10] "Prospects for the Value Line Composite of Industrial Companies," *Value Line Investment Survey*, July 6, 1979, pp. 650–52.

[11] For details, see *Business Forecasts 1979*, Federal Reserve Bank of Richmond, February 1979.

Figure 10–4 **The Business Prospect: A Perspective on Recession***

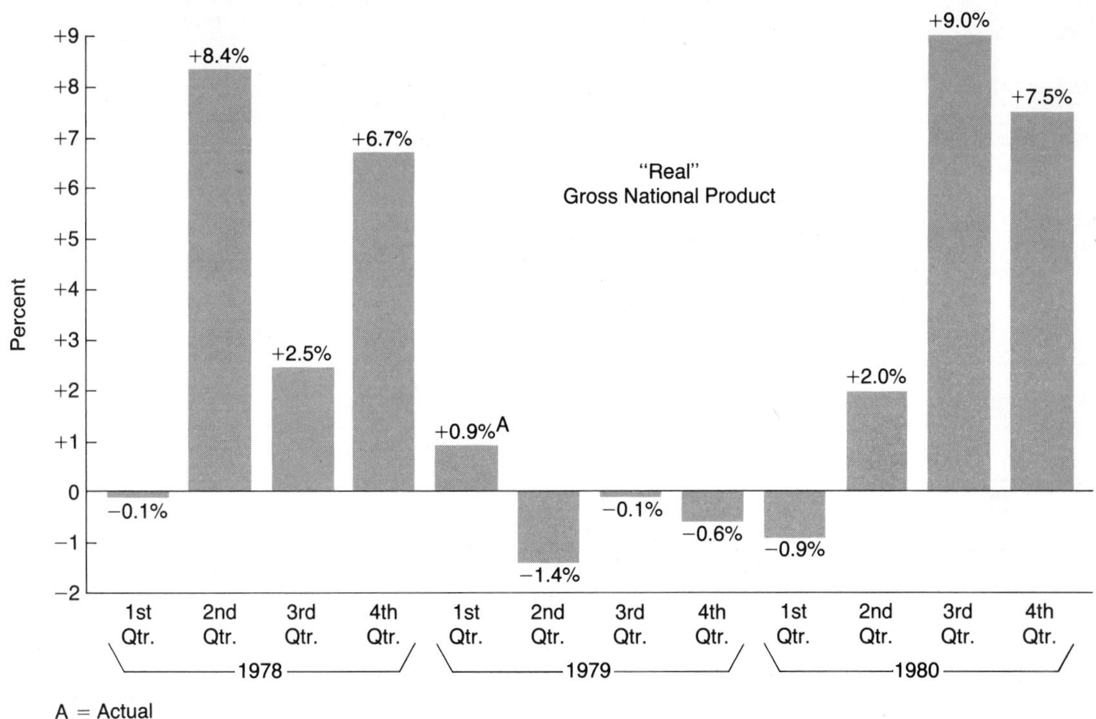

*This chart demonstrates fluctuations in the current business cycle. Percent figures are annualized quarterly rates of change for GNP in constant dollars. Note the trough in the 1st quarter of 1980 and the subsequent sharp recovery in the 3rd quarter.

SOURCE: "Prospects for the Value Line Composite of Industrial Companies," *Value Line Investment Survey*, July 6, 1979, p. 650.

regularly published by such institutions as Gulf Oil Corporation, Metropolitan Life, National Securities and Research Corporation, and United Business Services.

All of these short-term GNP forecasts predicted a recession in 1979 and part of 1980. A consensus on short-term economic forecasts can help investors formulate a better earnings forecast of the industries and companies in which they are interested.

Independent Forecasting

Astute investors often make independent analyses of the national economy in order to *modify* the forecasts of government and professional services. Several

Table 10–6 **(billions of dollars, annual rate)**

Forecaster and Date	Summary	Gross National Product	Personal Consumption Expenditures	Gross Private Domestic Investment
Herbert E. Neil, Jr. Harris Trust and Savings Bank "Business and Money: Review and Outlook 1979" November 29, 1978	"The American economy, on an expanding course since early 1975, will be heading into rough weather next year. . . . business will continue to expand in the early part of next year but at a moderate pace. Highly expansive Government policies . . . have set the stage for substantial inflation in 1979 . . . close to an 8% annual rate. . . . As the Federal Reserve hopefully moves to slow the rate of monetary expansion, interest rates will rise further and available credit will tighten with little immediate slowing of inflation. Financial stringency, necessary to slow inflation in the 1980s, is likely to bring about at least a moderate recession by late 1979."	$2300.0 (Estimated 1978 GNP: $2105.0)	Total: $1460.0 Durables: $200.0 Nondurables: $570.0 Services: $690.0	Total: $360.0 New construction: $190.0 Producers' durable equipment: $160.0 Change in business inventories: $10.0
Albert T. Sommers The Conference Board "Summary of the Annual Outlook Meeting of The Conference Board Economic Forum" December 1978	"The results of our pre-meeting poll for 1979 call for a real growth rate of 2.4 percent for the year as a whole, and an inflation rate of 7.4 percent. . . .With regard to real performance in 1979, we have described a slack year, falling somewhere between a growth recession and a general, albeit mild, genuine recession. . . . With respect to unemployment, our annual average of 6.5 percent reflects a range of estimates running from 6.1 percent to 7 percent."	$2305* $2313.4† (Estimated 1978 GNP: $2105.1) 1972 dollars: $1417.3†	Total: $1473* Durables: $213* Nondurables: $570* Services: $690*	Total: $356* Residential structures: $99* Nonresidential structures: $86* Producers' durable equipment: $160* Change in business inventories: $11*

* Projections by Forum participants, with some Conference Board interpolations.
† Results of pre-meeting poll, incorporating submissions by Forum participants.

Table 10–6 (*continued*)

Net Exports	Government Purchases	Housing and Construction	Index of Industrial Production	Employment and Unemployment	Price Indexes
$0	Total: $480.0 Federal: $170.0 State and local: $310.0	Housing starts: "... approximately $1\frac{3}{4}$ million units next year...."	148.0	Rate of unemployment: 7.0%	Consumer: 210.0 Producer finished goods: 210.0
−$1*	Total: $477* Federal: $170* State and local: $307*		148.8†	Rate of unemployment: 6.5%†	Consumer: 210.5† Producer: 208.8† GNP deflator: 163.22†

SOURCE: *Business Forecasts, 1979*, Federal Reserve Bank of Richmond, February 1979, pp. 8–9.

types of analysis of the national economy are used by sophisticated investors.[12]

National Income and Product Accounts

The most widely used, as well as the most complicated, method of short-term forecasting used by independent analysts involves analysis of national income and product accounts to forecast the GNP. The GNP is the aggregate money value in current prices of the goods and services produced in a given period. Through standard statistical analysis, valuable historical relationships can be found among the different components and subcomponents of GNP. In addition, the current data relating to each component and subcomponent of GNP can be used to make important forecasts.[13] There are many ways to subdivide the GNP, but it is commonly divided according to the familiar accounting identity:

$$Y = C + I + G + X - M$$

where

Y = Gross National Product

C = Personal consumption expenditure

I = Private investment (nonresidential fixed investment in plant and equipment + residential construction + inventory investment)

G = Government expenditure (federal government expenditure + expenditures by state and local government)

$X - M$ = Net exports (exports minus imports)

Most *econometric models* are ultimately designed to describe and/or forecast one or more of these major components of the GNP. Obviously, a task of such magnitude and complexity requires large-scale econometric models and the extensive use of giant computers. That these models are formidable and beyond the reach of all but the sophisticated econometricians and model builders is evident from Figure 10–5, which presents a highly *simplified* flow chart of a famous econometric model.

---

[12] This discussion on National Income and Product Accounts and Input–Output Analysis is both general and superficial. A more complete discussion of these topics can be found in a macroeconomics text. This discussion is included here merely to point out the existence of these forecasting techniques.

[13] For a fuller treatment, see F. Gerard Adams and Peter E. deJanosi, "Statistics and Econometrics of Forecasting," In *How Business Economists Forecast*, ed. Butler and Kavesh; Daniel B. Suits, "Forecasting and Analysis with an Econometric Model," *American Economic Review*, March 1962; William F. Butler and Robert A. Kavesh, "Short-term Forecasting of the Gross National Product," in *How Business Economists Forecast*; John P. Lewis and Robert C. Turner, *Business Conditions Analysis* (New York: McGraw-Hill, 1967), Chapters 17–24.

Figure 10–5 **Simplified Flow Chart of the Wharton Mark III Quarterly Econometric Model**

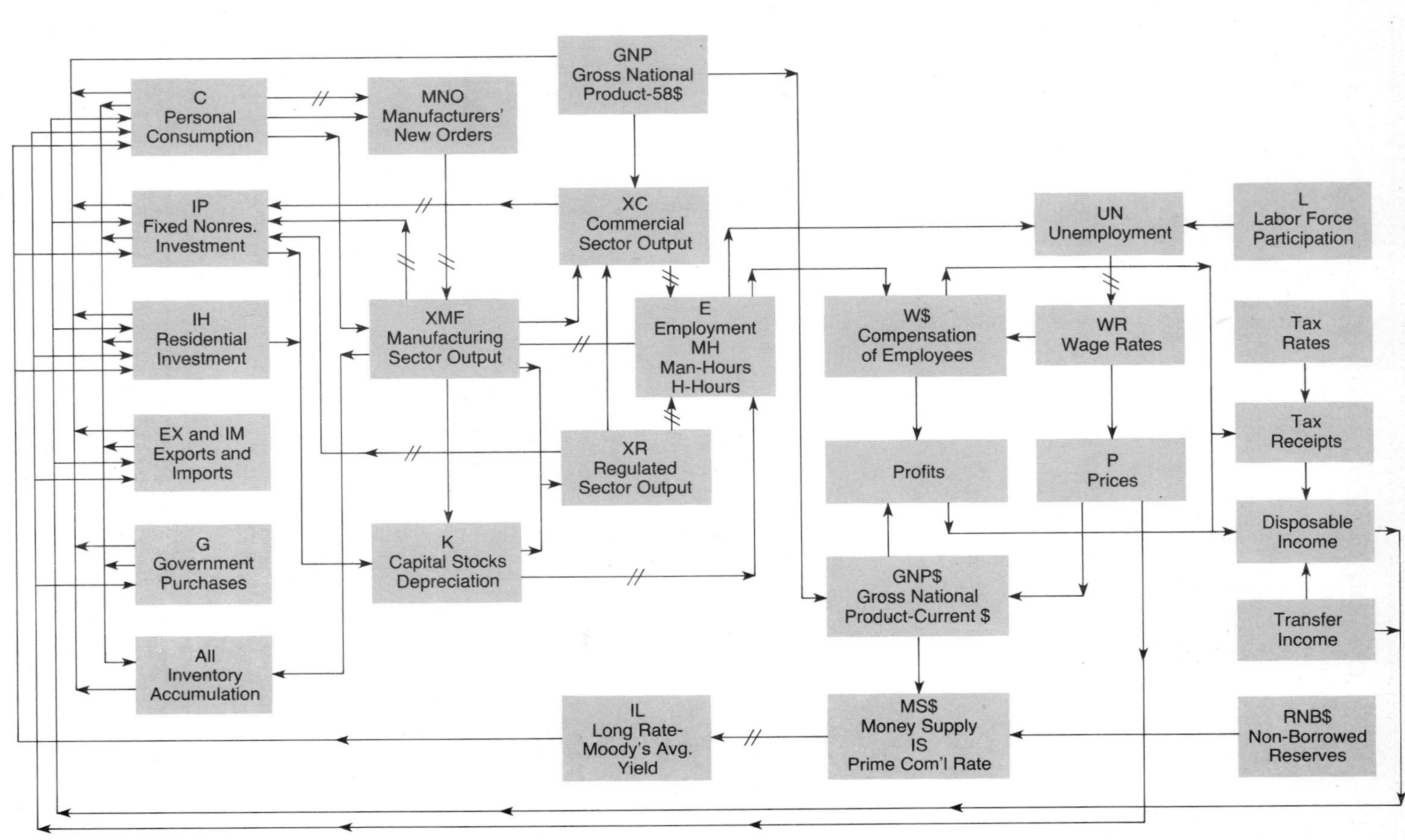

SOURCE: Michael D. McCarthy, *The Wharton Quarterly Econometric Forecasting Model Mark III,* Economics Research Unit, Department of Economics. Wharton School of Finance and Commerce, University of Pennsylvania, 1972.

Obviously, a detailed study of a large-scale econometric model is beyond the scope of this book. Instead, we will briefly describe the essential elements of the Brookings–S.S.R.C. Quarterly Econometric Model of the United States—the largest econometric model existing for the U.S. economy (over 300 equations).[14]

The model is primarily based on the following equation:

$$I_t = -0.86 + 0.0868X_{t-1} + 0.104X_{t-5} - 0.145K_{t-1} - 1.116R_{t-5}$$

where

I = Gross nonresidential fixed business investment in the manufacturing sector

K = Stock of capital goods in the manufacturing sector

R = Average corporate bond yield, percent

t = Subscript representing time: t = current quarter, $t - 1$ = previous quarter, $t - 5$ = five quarters in the past

X = Gross national product

The coefficients in the equation (for example, 0.104, + 0.0868) that measure the relationship between business investment (I) and the explanatory variables (X, K, and R) were estimated by the well-known technique of regression analysis. The equation includes variables influencing nonresidential fixed investments. Capacity utilization is represented by the variables X and K. As GNP (X) rises and the stock of capital goods (K) remains constant, the rate of capacity utilization increases and investment expenditures tend to rise. Similarly, if GNP remains constant while the stock of capital rises, the rate of capacity utilization decreases—hence the negative sign on the coefficient of K. As Kavesh and Platt have noted, "The rate of interest is the cost of external financing, and its coefficient has the expected negative sign. Missing from the equation . . . is a variable measuring the availability of internally generated funds. Notice that the estimated equation indicates that it takes six quarters for the maximum impact of interest rates and output to be exerted on actual investments pending."[15]

Input–Output Tables

Although the econometric models are valuable tools in the armory of economic forecasters, they ignore interindustry relationships. Consequently, they forecast inconsistent changes within individual industries. This problem is partly obviated by the use of *input–output table* analysis, which explicitly considers interindustry relationships. By noting these relationships, an analyst can more easily obtain consistent estimates of the sales of different industries, given predicted changes in the aggregate variables. Table 10–7 presents a *simplified* hypothetical

[14] See G. Froman and L. R. Klein, "The Brookings–S.S.R.C. Quarterly Econometric Model of the United States: Model Properties," *American Economic Review*, May 1965, pp. 348–61.

[15] Robert A. Kavesh and Robert B. Platt, "Economic Forecasting," in Sumner Levine, Ed., *Financial Analyst's Handbook* (Homewood, Ill.: Dow Jones-Irwin, 1975), p. 933. © 1975 by Dow Jones-Irwin, Inc.

Table 10–7 **Hypothetical Transactions Table: Industry Purchasing**

		Processing Sector						Final Demand					
	Outputs* → / ↓ Inputs†	(1) A	(2) B	(3) C	(4) D	(5) E	(6) F	(7) Gross Inventory Accumulation (+)	(8) Exports to Foreign Countries	(9) Government Purchases	(10) Gross Private Capital Formation	(11) Households	(12) Total Gross Output
Payments Sector	(1) Industry A	10	15	1	2	5	6	2	5	1	3	14	64
	(2) Industry B	5	4	7	1	3	8	1	6	3	4	17	59
	(3) Industry C	7	2	8	1	5	3	2	3	1	3	5	40
	(4) Industry D	11	1	2	8	6	4	0	0	1	2	4	39
	(5) Industry E	4	0	1	14	3	2	1	2	1	3	9	40
	(6) Industry F	2	6	7	6	2	6	2	4	2	1	8	46
Processing Sector Industry Producing	(7) Gross inventory depletion (−)	1	2	1	0	2	1	0	1	0	0	0	8
	(8) Imports	2	1	3	0	3	2	0	0	0	0	2	13
	(9) Payments to government	2	3	2	2	1	2	3	2	1	2	12	32
	(10) Depreciation allowances	1	2	1	0	1	0	0	0	0	0	0	5
	(11) Households	19	23	7	5	9	12	1	0	8	0	1	85
	(12) Total gross outlays	64	59	40	39	40	46	12	23	18	18	72	431

* Sales to industries and sectors along the top of the table from the industry listed in each row at the left of the table.

† Purchases from industries and sectors at the left of the table by the industry listed at the top of each column.

SOURCE: William H. Miernyk, *The Elements of Input–Output Analysis* (New York: Random House, 1965), p. 9.

Table 10–8 **List of Key Indicators**

Employment	Personal Income
Industrial Production	Wholesale Prices
Durable Goods Orders	Retail Sales
Consumer Price Index	Savings Rate
Monetary Base	Leading Indicators
Savings Rate	

input–output table. The processing sector of the economy is divided into six basic industries labeled A–F. In addition, a payments sector is composed of inventory changes, exports, government purchases, private capital formations, and households. Each horizontal row of figures shows the distribution of the output of one sector among other sectors of the economy (including itself). The vertical columns show how each sector obtains its input from the other sectors. Together they measure the interindustry relationships.

Interpretation of Business Indicators

In addition to the types of analyses previously discussed, sophisticated investors also use a number of important business indicators as a basis for making a judgment on the future of the economy. Most investors consider the data produced by the U.S. government by far the best in terms of their accuracy and timeliness. However, several problems are associated with government data. First, the amount of data available is so overwhelming that most investors find it difficult to handle. Second, frequently the government revises the data on key variables like money supply and unemployment, thereby making previous predictions based on them vulnerable. Third, not all indicators move in the same direction, making the task of forecasting difficult.

Table 10–8 provides a simplified list of key indicators. The indicators consist of consumer price index, employment, industrial production, savings rate, personal income, and so on. Each indicator performs a valuable function. By analyzing these indicators, a person can make judgments about the state of the economy.[16]

Fluctuations in some of the indicators included in Table 10–8, along with others, are presented in Figure 10–6. Because not all indicators move simultaneously in the same direction, a careful analysis is needed to develop an informed opinion of the direction in which the economy is likely to move.

[16] *Business Week* grades many of these indicators in terms of stability and accuracy. See *Business Week*, December 31, 1979, p. 101.

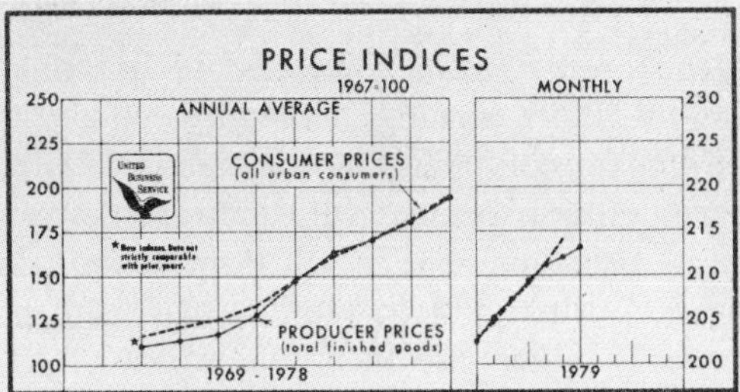

The rapid rise in consumer and producer prices continued during the second quarter, with the climb most evident in the cost of food and fuel. However, some moderation is expected by late this year.

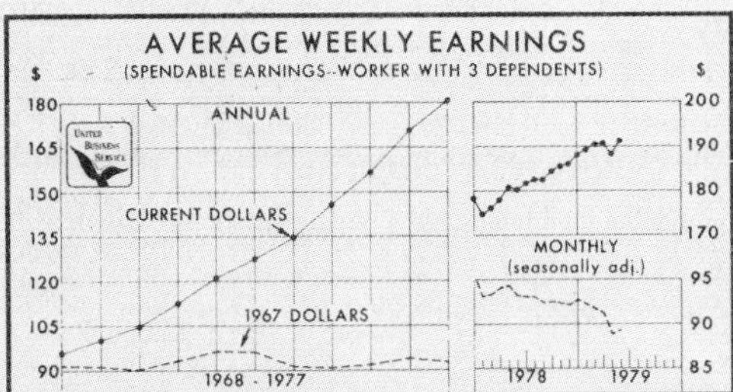

Average wages have been inching higher in current dollars, but inflation has exacted a heavy toll in real (1967) dollars. A weak economy and still-rising consumer prices appear to rule out near term relief.

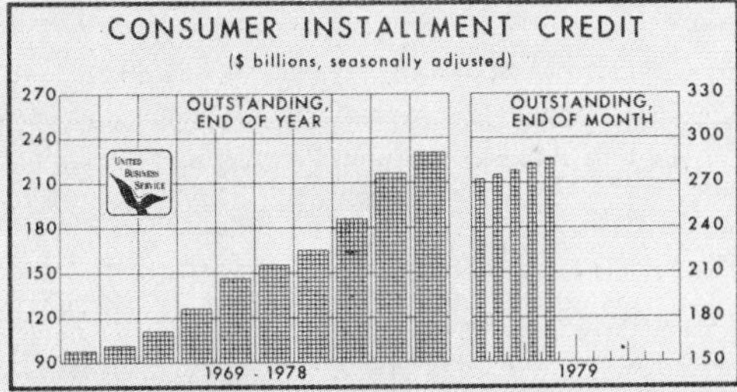

Outstanding consumer installment credit has been moving higher month by month. However, a more restrained spending pattern — already apparent in auto and general retail sales — should whittle away at these statistics.

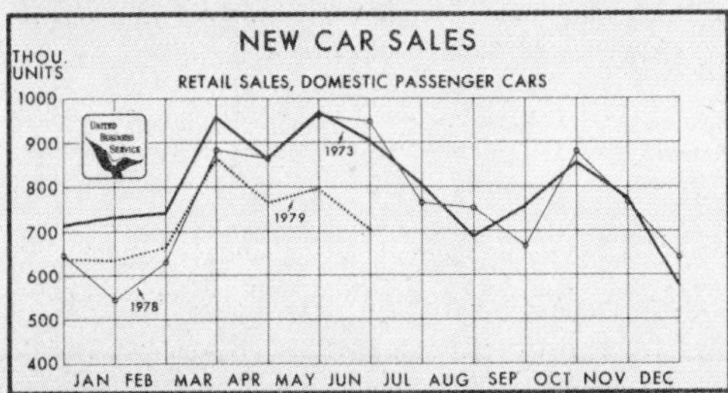

Domestic auto sales fell sharply in the last three months despite strength in small models. Soaring gasoline prices, supply shortages, and recession fears hurt volume. Sales will probably remain soft through the rest of '79.

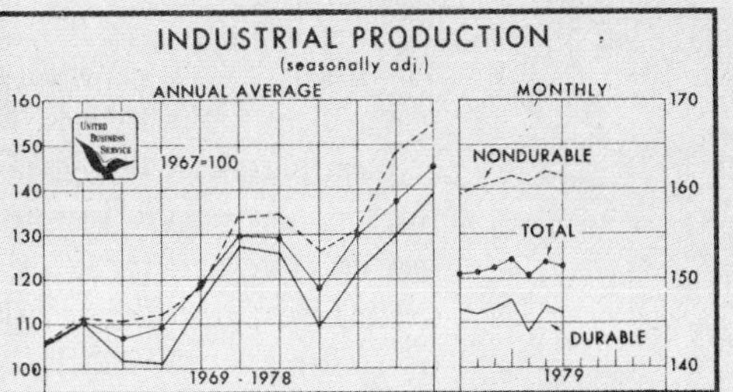

Industrial output fell in the April-June period, the first quarterly decline since early 1975. Durable goods were hardest hit, but nondurables were also affected. The downtrend will likely persist during the second half.

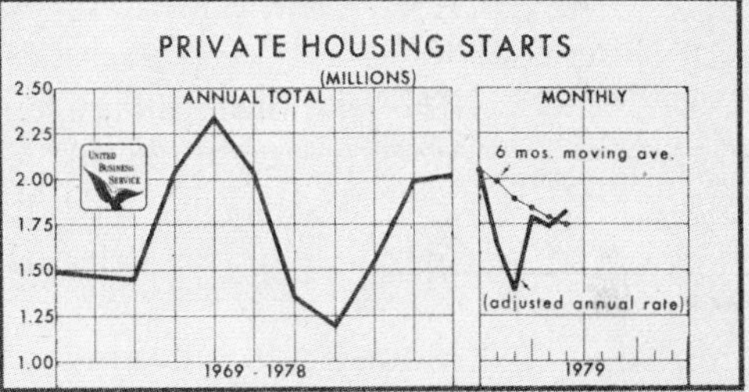

Housing starts have fluctuated during recent months, but the trend appears to be definitely downward. Nevertheless, substantial underlying demand should brake the rate of descent and fuel a rebound early next year.

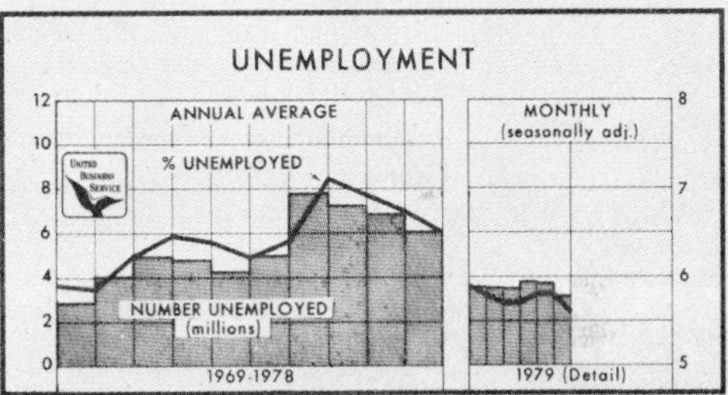

The jobless rate dipped to 5.6% in June. However, this reading is deceptive. The recession is expected to increase layoffs, thereby exerting upward pressure on unemployment over the next several months.

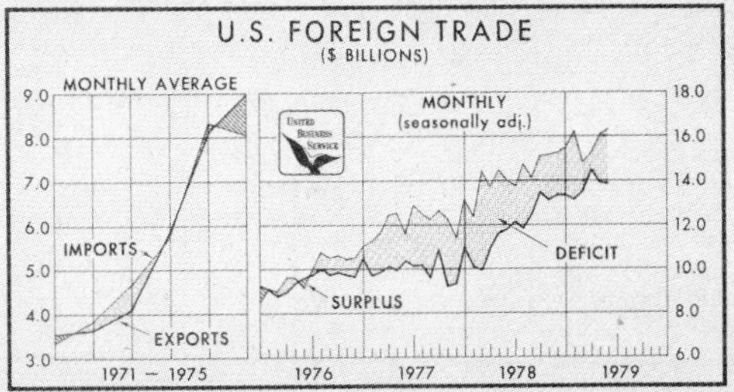

Higher-priced OPEC oil will swell import costs this year. However, exports should benefit from relative economic strength abroad. This favorable development should hold down the full year merchandise trade deficit.

SOURCE: *United Business and Investment Report*, United Business Service, July 23, 1979, p. 296.

Conclusions

The main objective for studying the forecasts of the GNP and its components is to develop a basis for forecasting the future earnings of a company. During an economic recession, the earnings of many companies show a predictable decline, whereas economic booms are generally associated with increases in earning power. Investors can study the forecasts done by the NBER, professional forecasting institutions or other sources. Alternatively, they may, if so disposed, try to forecast the GNP themselves. In either case, their goal is to use the GNP forecasts to predict the future earnings of industries and individual companies.

Forecasting Monetary Policy

The relationships between money and GNP on the one hand and money and stock prices on the other are supposedly both direct and intimate. Therefore, investors may find it desirable to study the forecasts of monetary policies as well to reinforce their forecasts of the GNP.

Money and Income

It is a fairly well established economic proposition that money supply and income are related. However, a great deal of controversy still surrounds the

Figure 10–7 **Levels of Gross National Product and Money 1953–73**

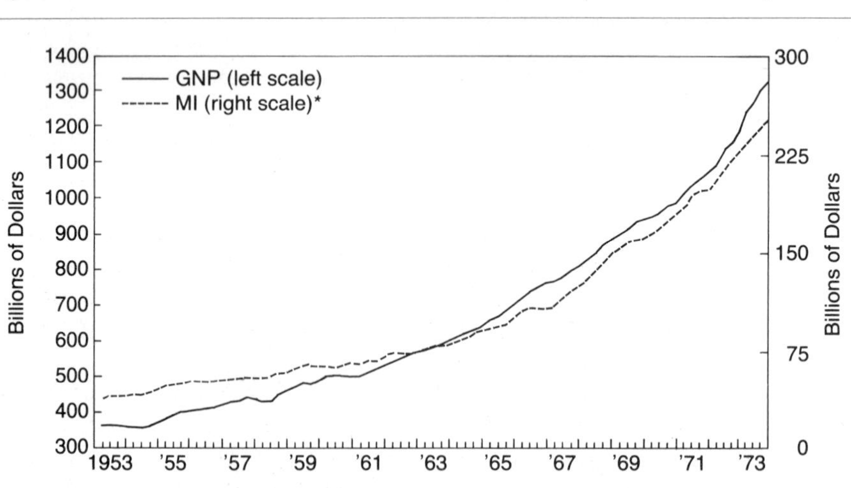

* Cash plus demand deposits at commercial banks.

SOURCE: Robert D. Auerbach and Jack L. Rutner, "Money and Income: Is There a Simple Relationship?" *Monthly Review*, Federal Reserve Bank of Kansas City, May 1975, p. 16.

Figure 10–8 **Determined Values of Gross National Product and Money, 1953–73**

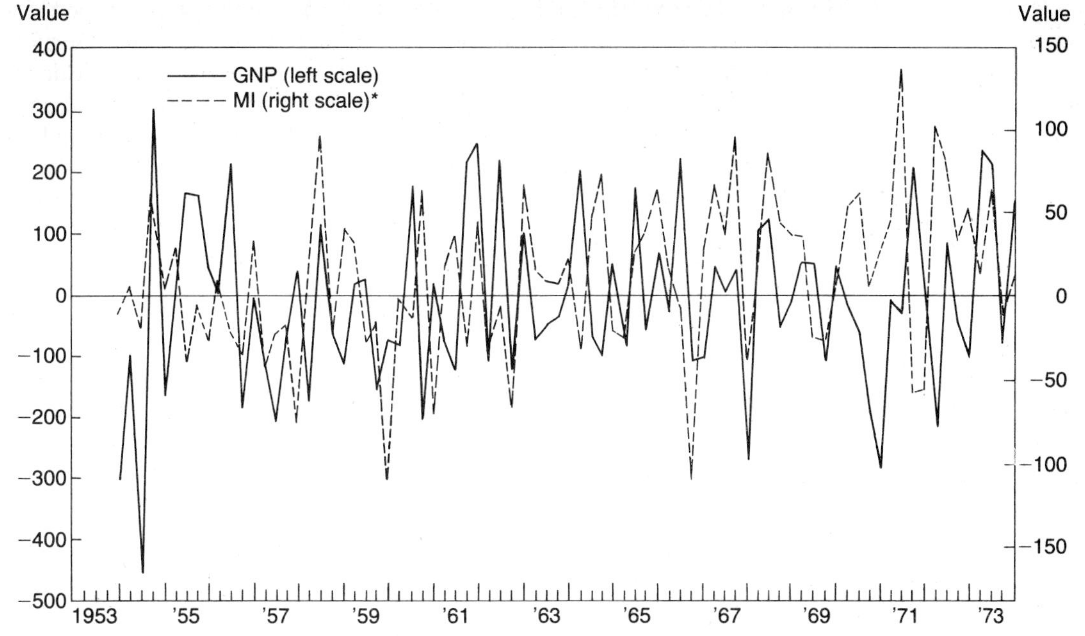

* Cash plus demand deposits at commercial banks.

SOURCE: Robert D. Auerbach and Jack L. Rutner, "Money and Income: Is There a Simple Relationship?" *Monthly Review*, Federal Reserve Bank of Kansas City, May 1975, p. 17.

nature of this relationship. For instance, if it could be established that changes in monetary policy affect the GNP in a certain way, then predicting future monetary policy would be equivalent to predicting future GNP. If, on the other hand, it is discovered that GNP affects monetary policy, then the predictive power of monetary policy would be minimal.

As charted in Figure 10–7, during the 20-year period ending in 1973, both the GNP and money supply maintained a strong upward trend. A study[17] removed the trend from the data, producing the detrended values shown in Figure 10–8, and analyzed the influence of money over GNP. The study did not show that fluctuations in GNP were primarily caused by changes in money. However, the study did point out that a strong and significant association between money and income were found when the effects of feedback from past income to money were

[17] Robert D. Auerbach and Jack L. Rutner, "Money and Income: Is There a Simple Relationship?" *Monthly Review*, Federal Reserve Bank of Kansas City, May 1975, pp. 13–19.

taken into account. Because this causality between money and income, with money as the independent variable, is not clearly established, great care should be taken when using monetary policy as a tool for predicting income.

Money and Stock Prices

The theory linking money supply to stock prices is fairly straightforward. Investors tend to have strong preferences about the amount of cash they wish to hold relative to other assets. When the Federal Reserve increases the money supply *unexpectedly*, the cost arising from holding additional amounts of money exceeds the benefits. Individuals then attempt to reduce their money balances by acquiring goods and financial assets, including common stocks. Consequently, an expansionary monetary policy, represented by an increase in the rate of growth of money supply, should lead to a rise in stock prices, whereas a contractionary monetary policy should have a dampening effect on stock prices.

Figure 10–9 presents the relationship between growth in money supply and stock market returns during 1965–75. The figure suggests that these two variables are closely related. However, a closer examination of the figure reveals, as

Figure 10–9

* The money supply is defined here as cash plus demand deposits at commercial banks, MI.

SOURCE: A. H. Ehrbar, "How Money Supply Drives the Stock Market," *Fortune*, October 1975, p. 108.

other studies confirm,[18] that money supply lags behind, rather than leads, changes in the stock market. Consequently, investors must conclude that although money supply is related to stock prices, consistent gains in the stock market cannot be realized simply by predicting the future direction of monetary policy.

Industry Analysis

The Basic Framework

We have previously analyzed the nation's economic conditions under the assumption that the real GNP and the earning power of individual companies are positively related. However, for several reasons, *industry analysis* is also a prerequisite to a comprehensive analysis of individual companies.

First, variations in earnings of individual companies are closely related to variations in earnings of the related industries. This can be inferred from the fact that an important part of the price variations of an individual stock is the result of average price variations of all companies within the related industry. According to the study by Benjamin King, 10 percent of the total variation in the market price of the average common stock analyzed was influenced by its industry factor. Another study conducted by Richard Brealey found that 21 percent of the change in annual earnings for the average firm was due to changes in the aggregate earnings of all companies within the related industry. These and other studies on this subject support the view that an industry analysis is essential for a comprehensive approach to investment in common stock. Second, not all industries are affected in the same manner by a recession or an economic boom. During a recession, for example, the poorest performers are typically the so-called cyclical industries, whereas industries providing vital products and services are among the better performers. Industry analysis helps an investor identify stocks that are expected to perform well during recessions and economic booms. Third, an investor can learn a great deal about specific companies by comparing their performance against industry norms. This may help to identify stocks with abnormally high or low growth potential.

Industry analysis also helps an investor develop a longer-term view of the companies associated with an industry. As will shortly become clear, each industry passes through an industrial life cycle, in which it goes through different stages of growth. In addition, a closer examination of an industry can uncover the underlying long-term trends in such key variables as product demand and capacity utilization. These long-term trends have important long-range implications concerning the earning power of the related firms.

[18] See Michael S. Rozeff, "The Money Supply and the Stock Market," *Financial Analysts Journal*, September–October, 1975, pp. 18–26; and "Money and Stock Prices: Market Efficiency and the Lag in Effect of Monetary Policy," *Journal of Financial Economics*, September 1974, pp. 1–57.

Having established the importance of short- and long-term industry analysis, it is appropriate to discuss evaluation of industry returns as a filtering process for selecting individual stocks. The key industry fundamentals that contribute to superior industry performance can then be gainfully analyzed.

Prediction of Industry Risk and Return

Industry Risk

Before undertaking an analysis of industry returns, let us briefly review the risk associated with individual industries. Table 10–9 shows the results of a study which calculated beta values for a large number of industries.[19] The study found that intraindustry risks as represented by the industry beta values vary considerably. During the period 1958 through 1970, for example, the range was from 1.426 for air transportation to −.002 for gold mining. However, the study also found that the beta values for individual industries were reasonably stable for alternate periods. Based on these observations, the long-term beta of an industry can be safely used as a measure of risk associated with that industry. In general, the higher the risk of an industry, the higher its beta, and the higher its expected return.

Industry Returns

Because a significant portion of the total variations in the earnings of the average firm is influenced by its industry factor, it is important to evaluate the growth potential of individual industries before estimating the future earnings of individual firms within those industries. This can be done by using regression and correlation analysis as well as other more sophisticated statistical procedures. However, a more generalized analysis will be undertaken here. More specifically, the key industry fundamentals will first be presented. Thereafter, advisory service analysis of industry data will be carefully integrated with industry fundamentals, leading ultimately to a presentation of a comprehensive industry analysis. The automobile industry will be used as a basis for this presentation.

Key Industry Fundamentals

Most industries have important individual characteristics that affect the values of their securities. Analysis of these fundamentals can help an investor identify those industries that are likely to record superior performance. Some of the more important industry characteristics are historical performance, economic structure, capital investment, government regulations, and labor conditions.

[19] Frank K. Reilly and Eugene Drzycimski, "Alternative Industry Performance and Risk," *Journal of Financial and Quantitative Analysis*, June 1974, p. 442.

Table 10–9 **Industry Beta Values for All Periods Examined**

Number of Weeks	1958 to 1970 679	1958 to 1964	1965 to 1970	1/2/58 to 5/28/59 (R) 74	5/28/59 to 10/27/60 (F) 74	10/27/60 to 12/14/61 (R) 59	12/14/61 to 6/28/62 (F) 28	6/28/62 to 2/10/66 (R) 189	2/10/66 to 10/6/66 (F) 34	10/6/66 to 12/5/68 (R) 113	12/5/68 to 5/28/70 (F) 77	5/28/70 to 12/30/70 (R) 31
Aircraft Mfg.	1.192	.754	1.557	.472	.717	1.227	.719	.761	2.273	1.232	1.147	2.141
Air Transp.	1.426	1.149	1.657	1.095	1.014	1.181	.838	1.385	2.368	1.776	1.257	1.803
Autos	1.259	1.164	1.330	1.134	1.238	1.053	1.004	1.340	1.113	1.553	1.301	1.296
Auto Equipment	.922	.921	.924	1.042	1.071	.632	.827	.961	.847	1.110	.737	.928
Banks	.751	.624	.858	.548	.304	.397	.833	.758	.865	.676	1.063	.715
Bldg. Materials	.983	.850	1.017	.720	.793	1.032	.815	.911	.815	1.041	1.101	.883
Chemicals	1.085	1.134	1.040	1.358	1.332	1.084	.910	1.069	.722	1.379	.977	.904
Drugs	1.103	1.156	1.059	.985	1.006	1.387	1.335	1.203	.787	1.092	1.187	.942
Electrical Equip.	1.037	1.174	.923	1.046	1.262	1.163	1.165	1.240	1.127	1.079	.819	.437
Farm Equipment	.970	.948	.978	.893	.883	.648	.872	1.106	1.144	.951	.863	.994
Food & Beverages	.756	.742	.767	.579	.674	.505	.842	.780	.417	1.033	.866	.559
Gold Mining	−.002	.363	−.304	.714	.452	.911	.144	−.089	.022	−.874	−.138	−.634
Grocery Chains	.662	.751	.585	.719	.616	.617	.699	.827	.524	.340	.954	.140
Installment Fin.	.799	.748	.845	.434	.340	.802	1.340	.654	.396	.920	.928	.981
Insurance	.887	.672	1.061	.591	.441	.299	.885	.825	.899	.773	1.361	1.139
Liquor	.633	.637	.626	.626	.648	.674	.647	.650	.666	.728	.569	.380
Machine Tools	.861	.814	.904	.280	.663	1.487	.952	.849	.933	1.143	.569	.968
Heavy Machinery	1.101	1.026	1.167	.886	1.053	1.103	1.082	.942	.837	1.182	1.256	1.319
Motion Pictures	1.161	1.024	1.285	.500	.765	1.169	.936	1.304	1.353	1.175	1.266	1.522
Office Equipment	1.266	1.321	1.225	1.099	.956	.801	1.635	1.512	1.183	1.190	1.145	1.552
Oil	.949	1.005	.902	1.227	1.279	1.127	.911	.839	.813	.813	.965	.971
Packing	.988	1.219	.808	1.127	1.339	.855	1.324	1.246	.723	.813	.616	.639
Paper	.863	.707	1.007	.648	.678	.719	.705	.732	.824	1.104	1.190	.854
Railroad Equip.	1.040	.977	1.092	.816	1.003	.784	1.148	1.039	1.264	1.064	1.051	.868
Retail Merch.	.867	.863	.867	.609	.751	.554	.984	1.016	.485	.963	1.020	.763
Rubber	1.156	1.269	1.068	1.124	1.133	1.520	1.035	1.446	1.022	1.193	1.151	.732
Steel and Iron	1.038	1.163	.935	1.423	1.253	1.298	1.014	1.012	.727	1.199	.904	.792
Television	1.422	1.343	1.484	.673	.950	1.248	1.786	1.616	1.853	1.521	1.144	1.512
Textiles	1.066	1.080	1.047	.742	1.322	.881	1.023	1.218	1.090	1.016	.860	.980
Tobacco	.707	.806	.625	.268	.628	.593	1.137	.956	.342	.572	.681	.718

SOURCE: Frank K. Reilly and Eugene Drzycimski, "Alternative Industry Performance and Risk," *Journal of Financial and Quantitative Analysis*, Vol. 9, No. 3 (June, 1974), p. 442. Reprinted by permission. © June 1974.

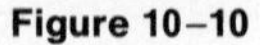

Figure 10–10 **Industrial Life Cycle**

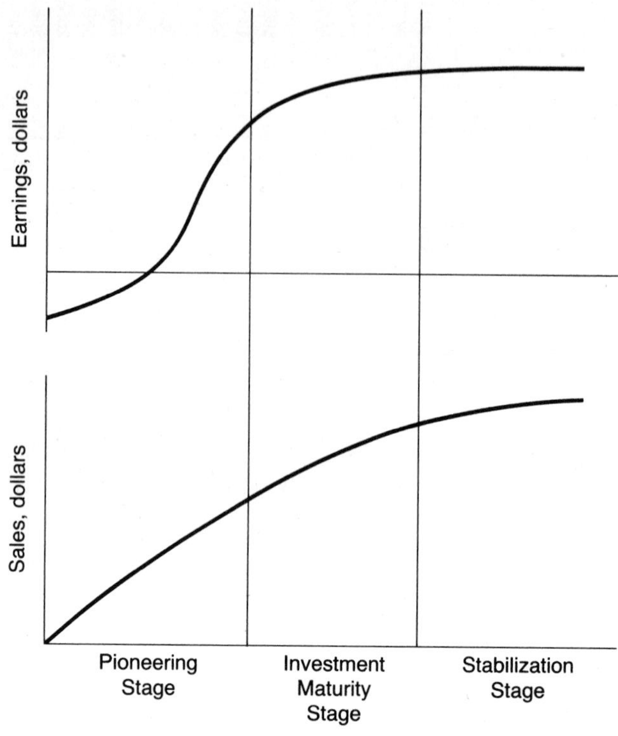

Historical Performance

There are two ways of analyzing historical performance. One way is to examine the position of an industry within the industrial life cycle; the other is to analyze its performance during business cycles.

Industrial Life Cycle As shown in Figure 10–10, the *industrial life cycle* goes through three distinct stages of growth: the pioneering stage, the investment maturity stage, and the stabilization stage.[20] During the pioneering stage, all industries are tested for their viability. Although the mortality rate is highest during this stage, industries with a high potential for survival experience rapid growth in sales and an impressive growth in earnings. The competition is usually not severe at this stage, and most successful industries are able to develop pro-

[20] Julius Grodinsky, *Investments* (New York: The Ronald Press, 1953) pp. 64–77.

duction techniques, marketing channels, and product differentiation. In addition, these industries are able to develop a sound financial basis for future expansion and growth.

After an industry has successfully completed the pioneering stage, it enters the investment maturity stage. Having proven to the investment community that they are viable, a handful of the most efficient, well-managed and financially mature companies usually consolidate their market positions and begin to encroach on their competitors' market shares. This is accomplished by broadening the capital base as well as establishing sound earnings and dividend policy.

After a period of time, the high rate of growth begins to slow down as these industries enter the stabilization stage. In this stage the "going gets rough" as innovations slow down, products become standardized, unit costs become stable, and the market itself becomes saturated. Although these industries do not fade away, they stop growing; during the stabilization stage, companies within these industries generate earnings barely sufficient to stay in business.

The automobile industry provides a classic example of the three stages of industrial life cycle.[21] Between 1900 and 1908, more than 500 automobile companies were organized. Of these, about 300 went bankrupt. By 1917, 76 companies were active in the industry, but ten produced over 75 percent of the total output. At the present time, the auto industry is in the stabilization stage—only three companies dominate the U.S. auto industry.

The industrial life cycle portrays the lifetime profile of an industry and all the companies associated with it. An analyst can make some judgments about the attractiveness of a company on the basis of the stage its industry has reached in the industrial life cycle.

Although understanding the concept of industrial life cycle is useful in evaluating the growth potential of different companies, several criticisms have been leveled against it. First, it has been asserted that a new industry is not always started by a large number of small companies which engage in a fierce battle of survival. Second, not all companies stagnate after reaching the stabilization stage; some companies in the third stage oscillate between prosperity and depression. Third, in associating each stage with a different degree of investment characteristics, the concept ignores the factors of stock prices and values. These limitations should be remembered when the concept of industrial life cycle is used as an investment tool.

Performance During a Business Cycle Performance during a business cycle is another important aspect of historical performance. The performance of cyclical industries, such as autos and capital goods, fluctuates with changes in the business cycle, whereas the performance of defensive industries remains relatively stable during economic downturns.[22] Examples of defensive industries include

[21] *Automobile Facts and Figures.* (Detroit: Automobile Manufacturers Association, 1979).

[22] Cyclical industries generally have high betas, whereas low betas are associated with more stable industries.

supermarkets and public utilities, whose products are basic consumer necessities and enjoy stable demand. Interestingly, the performance of some defensive industries is actually countercyclical. Gold mining is an excellent example of such an industry. Growth industries are generally characterized by expectations of above average earnings growth, often without variation in response to general economic conditions.[23] Over the past several years the office equipment manufacturers (computers and photocopiers) have exhibited this type of earnings pattern. Certain other industries are adversely affected whenever the country is faced with special economic problems. For instance, airlines and certain recreation-related industries are most vulnerable in the wake of an energy crisis. Table 10–10 presents the stock price fluctuations of groups associated with several industries during past recessions. A large percentage of these fluctuations, of course, is due to fluctuations in earnings of these groups.

Economic Structure

Another important industry fundamental is the degree of competition which prevails within the industry. Some industries, such as retailing, are highly competitive; others lack effective competition. Although there are important exceptions, many competitive industries are quite stable, because they bring together well-managed companies that maintain a stable earning power in the long run.

Capital Investment

Industries can be generally classified as more or less capital intensive. Highly capital intensive industries usually make effective long-term plans for capital investment and are generally technologically more advanced than less capital intensive industries. They sustain increases in sales by undertaking heavy investment in expensive, long-lived plants and equipment.

As a general rule, capital intensive industries have a much larger growth potential than labor intensive industries. The reasons for this are simple. Capital is the life blood of a capitalistic system and most increases in productivity stem from the ability of the labor force to use more technologically advanced equipment. Also, historically wage rates have risen faster than productivity, thereby slowing down the real growth of corporations.

However, the negative impact of continuing high rates of inflation on these companies should not be overlooked. During an inflationary period, for example, the replacement cost of plant and equipment may rise significantly. How-

[23] Growth industries and growth companies generally share the same characteristics. However, there is an important distinction between growth industries, growth companies, and *growth stocks*. A growth stock is basically considered an undervalued security. However, because any security might be considered undervalued at any point in time, a growth stock need not necessarily be a stock of a growth company, or the stock of a company in a growth industry.

Table 10–10 **Performance of Stock Groups in Recessions**

Stock Group	Average Change During Past 6 Recessions	Number of Recessions in which Group Gained	*Biggest Recession Loss (%)	*Biggest Recession Gain (%)
Gold Mining	+26.5%	5	57.6 (1973)	0.7 (1957)
Entertainment	+18.1	4	83.8 (1973)	38.1 (1969)
Tobacco	+15.0	5	43.3 (1960)	17.0 (1953)
High-grade Stocks	+14.6	5	34.8 (1960)	5.9 (1969)
Foods	+12.2	4	42.3 (1960)	6.2 (1969)
Aerospace	+11.4	4	67.6 (1953)	32.5 (1969)
Coal	+10.5	3	56.5 (1969)	21.6 (1957)
Office Equipment	+9.8	4	45.5 (1953)	27.6 (1973)
Paper	+6.4	3	49.8 (1953)	18.4 (1969)
Drugs	+6.2	4	16.3 (1957)	13.7 (1973)
Utilities	+4.2	3	22.2 (1960)	18.1 (1973)
Chemicals	+3.4	3	24.5 (1953)	11.7 (1957)
Oil	+3.1	4	23.8 (1953)	19.2 (1973)
Steel	+2.9	3	38.8 (1973)	18.1 (1957)
Building Materials	+2.4	4	23.0 (1953)	10.6 (1973)
Retail Stores	+2.2	5	9.3 (1948)	18.5 (1973)
Brewers	+0.9	2	54.0 (1948)	53.9 (1973)
S&P 500	+0.1	3	18.3 (1953)	17.9 (1973)
Banks N.Y.C.	−0.1	4	12.3 (1960)	24.5 (1973)
S&P 400	−0.3	3	19.7 (1953)	18.1 (1973)
Consumer Goods	−0.9	3	10.1 (1953)	17.1 (1973)
Machine Tools	−1.2	2	48.9 (1953)	38.4 (1973)
Capital Goods	−1.7	3	26.9 (1953)	19.7 (1973)
Textiles	−1.9	3	7.5 (1948)	16.4 (1973)
Autos	−3.7	3	13.9 (1953)	24.7 (1973)
Low-priced Stocks	−5.8	1	3.3 (1973)	23.3 (1969)
Copper	−7.3	2	21.8 (1953)	22.4 (1969)
Railroads	−7.9	1	5.2 (1960)	21.4 (1957)
Home Furnishings	−12.1	0	—	19.3 (1953)

* Year in parenthesis is year in which the recession started.

SOURCE: *The Outlook,* Standard & Poor's July 23, 1979, p. 653.

ever, depreciation allowances are based on the purchase price of these assets and can therefore be significantly understated. In this situation, profits will be overstated, and income tax liabilities will increase relative to actual earnings.[24]

[24] This is only a limited discussion of the impact of inflation on a firm. A more detailed coverage of this topic will appear in an appendix to the stock valuation chapters (pp. 505–11).

Government Regulations

The regulation of business by government agencies is an important consideration for investors forecasting the future performance of an industry. Some industries, such as utilities and manufacturers of war goods, are subject to continual government intervention, and should be analyzed with care. When other industries threaten to become monopoly powers, they are in danger of antitrust suits by the government and may ultimately be subjected to unfavorable publicity by the investment community. Still other industries may, by virtue of their products, invite attacks from environmentalist groups.

Labor Conditions

An analysis of industry labor conditions, which includes consideration of labor costs and the possibility of a strike, is an important element in any industry forecast. This is especially true when analyzing industries dominated by strong labor unions (such as the auto and airline industries), because in such industries labor costs generally rise faster and the possibility of a strike is greater than in industries where union power is weak or nonexistent. The history of labor negotiations and the impact of previous strikes can be of some help in determining the risks associated with these industries.

Miscellaneous Factors

In addition to the industry factors already mentioned, several other factors may influence investors' evaluation of the industry. These include the price and income elasticities of demand for products, changes in consumer tastes, foreign competition, and the availability and cost of raw materials. For instance, if the product of an industry is income elastic, then a deep recession would have a profound effect on the industry's profits. Similarly, industries vulnerable to foreign competition—such as steel and automobile industries—would be adversely affected by increased foreign competition.

Analysis of the Automobile Industry[25]

A case study of the auto industry will (1) demonstrate the nature of a fairly sophisticated industry analysis, (2) explain how national and industry-wide data can be integrated for making industry forecasts, and (3) demonstrate the use of industry fundamentals to modify industry forecasts.

[25] This discussion is based upon the following sources: *The Value Line Investment Survey*, July 6, 1979, Auto & Truck Industry, pp. 129–30; S&P's *Industry Surveys*, March 8, 1979 (Section 3), "Auto-Auto Parts, Current Analysis," pp. A127–A132; S&P's *Industry Surveys*, October 12, 1978 (Section 2), "Auto-Auto Parts, Basic Analysis," pp A137–A148, A155–A166.

State of the Industry

As a general rule, increases in population and average income combined with representation in the rapidly growing foreign market should lead to increased earnings in the automobile industry. However, the industry lacks outstanding growth characteristics, competition is keen, and government regulation of the industry has become increasingly tight.

Demand for new cars is influenced not only by general business conditions, but by trends in population; the number of multicar families; auto prices in relation to all consumer prices; the average age at which cars are scrapped; the availability, cost, and average maturity of credit; and style, engineering, safety, and antipollution changes that may hasten the obsolescence of existing vehicles. As will be observed shortly, many of these factors contribute to the development of a less than optimistic long-term forecast for the automobile industry.

Industry Fundamentals

Industrial Life Cycle The automobile industry provides a classic example of the three stages of the industrial life cycle discussed earlier. During the early part of this century—when the auto industry passed through the pioneering stage—hundreds of auto companies were established. Within a few years the majority of these companies went bankrupt. By 1920, less than a dozen companies produced over three-quarters of the total industry output; the industry had reached the investment maturity stage. Today, the industry is clearly in the stabilization stage; only three large companies dominate the U.S. auto industry.

Business Cycle Performance Table 10–11 presents a historical view of the auto industry from 1947 to 1977. Long-term fluctuations in the key variables—earnings per share, profit margin, dividends, P/E ratio and stock price—all point to an unequivocal fact: This is a cyclical industry. For example, earnings per share dropped from $11.60 in 1973 to a little over $4 during the 1974–75 recession years, but rebounded dramatically to $16.69 in 1977. The P/E ratio recorded a high of 33.29 in 1970, moved down to a 1973 low of 4.99, then climbed back to 17.42 in 1975. Similar fluctuations can be observed in the dividend yield and profit margin.

Over major market swings, the movement of stock prices within the auto group usually conforms to that of the industrial average, because the auto industry plays a key role in the nation's economy. Figure 10–11 charts fluctuations in the S&P auto stock index relative to fluctuations in the S&P 400 Industrial Index for the period 1951–78. The figure reveals that after outperforming the market in 1975 and 1976, the auto industry underperformed the general market in 1977 and 1978, reflecting investors' expectations of a cyclical downturn in profits.

Table 10–11

Automobiles
Per Share Data—Adjusted to Stock Price Index Level.
Average of Stock Price Indexes, 1941–1943 Equals 10.

						Earnings		Dividends		Price 1941–43 = 10		Price/Earn. Ratio		Div. Yields %		Book Value			
	Sales	Oper. Profit	Profit Margin %	Depr.	Income Taxes	Per Share	% of Sales	Per Share	% of Earn.	High	Low	High	Low	High	Low	Per Share	% Return	Working Capital	Capital Expenditures
1947	26.75	3.68	13.76	0.42	1.51	1.68	6.28	0.74	44.05	16.00	13.07	9.52	7.78	5.66	4.63	7.97	21.08	5.69	1.16
1948	33.17	5.15	15.53	0.58	2.03	2.57	7.75	1.10	42.80	16.19	12.89	6.30	5.02	8.53	6.79	9.46	27.17	6.78	1.05
1949	40.18	6.84	17.02	0.64	2.61	3.70	9.21	1.84	49.73	17.12	12.85	4.63	3.47	14.32	10.75	11.31	32.71	8.15	0.91
1950	48.88	10.04	20.54	0.69	5.06	4.46	9.12	2.78	62.33	24.88	17.33	5.58	3.89	16.04	11.17	12.86	34.68	9.22	1.29
1951	50.00	8.02	16.04	0.73	4.80	2.63	5.26	1.93	73.38	25.12	21.67	9.55	8.24	8.91	7.68	13.70	19.20	8.73	1.93
1952	50.97	8.56	16.79	0.84	5.11	2.94	5.77	1.86	63.27	31.56	23.09	10.73	7.85	8.06	5.89	14.60	20.14	7.19	2.34
1953	65.85	8.98	13.64	1.12	5.28	2.96	4.50	1.86	62.84	31.80	24.47	10.74	8.27	7.60	5.85	15.66	18.90	7.16	3.07
1954	54.33	8.17	15.04	1.30	3.68	3.49	6.42	2.14	61.32	41.30	26.62	11.83	7.63	8.04	5.18	16.54	21.10	7.31	4.15
1955	71.80	12.82	17.86	1.55	6.28	5.29	7.37	2.71	51.23	64.58	39.84	12.21	7.53	6.80	4.20	20.31	26.05	10.59	3.70
1956	62.01	8.81	14.21	1.86	3.94	3.37	5.43	2.46	73.00	60.04	51.15	17.82	15.18	4.81	4.10	21.69	15.54	8.59	5.32
1957	66.66	9.89	14.84	2.24	4.05	3.99	5.99	2.50	62.66	58.07	41.50	14.55	10.40	6.02	4.31	23.36	17.08	9.99	2.91
1958	53.97	6.36	11.78	2.23	1.88	2.52	4.67	2.40	95.24	61.75	42.29	24.50	16.78	5.68	3.89	23.90	10.54	10.89	1.87
1959	65.73	10.08	15.34	2.15	4.21	4.13	6.28	2.44	59.08	71.99	56.56	17.43	13.69	4.31	3.39	25.55	16.16	12.75	2.45
1960	74.14	11.13	15.01	2.08	5.04	4.49	6.06	2.52	56.12	72.10	51.42	16.06	11.45	4.90	3.50	28.02	16.02	14.16	3.08
1961	64.34	9.80	15.23	2.15	4.01	4.01	6.23	3.06	76.31	73.90	53.60	18.43	13.37	5.71	4.14	28.83	13.91	15.48	2.71
1962	80.77	14.69	18.19	2.27	6.66	6.50	8.05	3.58	55.08	74.39	57.69	11.44	8.88	6.21	4.81	31.98	20.33	17.69	3.40
1963	93.37	17.36	18.59	2.44	8.10	7.30	7.82	4.67	63.97	109.46	73.28	14.99	10.04	6.37	4.27	34.39	21.23	18.31	3.32
1964	98.31	17.29	17.59	2.56	7.27	8.08	8.22	5.27	65.22	128.15	98.13	15.86	12.14	5.37	4.11	37.49	21.55	17.19	5.43
1965	116.84	20.98	17.96	2.90	8.94	9.74	8.34	6.15	63.14	138.54	115.54	14.22	11.86	5.32	4.44	41.64	23.39	17.68	7.06
1966	119.94	18.09	15.08	3.47	6.89	8.24	6.87	5.51	66.87	131.88	81.27	16.00	9.86	6.78	4.18	45.20	18.23	17.55	6.92

1967	117.83	15.59	13.23	3.84	5.63	6.36	5.40	4.74	74.53	114.45	85.11	18.00	13.38	5.57	4.14	46.98	13.54	18.10	5.43
1968	138.94	20.75	14.93	3.97	8.86	8.44	6.07	5.24	62.09	115.50	95.74	13.68	11.34	5.47	4.54	50.61	16.68	20.35	4.67
1969	145.05	18.87	13.01	4.17	7.64	7.51	5.18	5.24	69.77	106.02	82.15	14.12	10.94	6.38	4.94	53.82	13.95	19.97	6.31
1970	127.19	8.95	7.04	4.45	1.59	3.02	2.37	4.09	135.43	100.54	74.21	33.29	24.57	5.51	4.07	52.80	5.72	15.36	5.97
1971	169.85	21.24	12.51	4.72	7.92	8.55	5.03	4.11	48.07	112.08	95.76	13.11	11.20	4.29	3.67	57.48	14.87	21.91	6.54
1972	195.21	24.68	12.64	4.96	9.77	10.45	5.35	5.23	50.05	110.62	94.69	10.59	9.06	5.52	4.73	62.90	16.61	27.24	6.93
1973	229.41	25.58	11.15	5.04	9.87	11.60	5.06	6.23	53.71	110.32	57.85	9.51	4.99	10.77	5.65	68.49	16.94	30.13	7.56
1974	221.65	12.22	5.51	5.16	2.81	4.17	1.88	4.42	106.00	70.72	38.68	16.96	9.28	11.43	6.25	68.89	6.05	26.64	8.35
1975	239.09	14.37	6.01	5.32	4.20	4.02	1.68	3.03	75.37	70.03	46.00	17.42	11.44	6.59	4.33	70.07	5.74	28.77	6.72
1976	305.33	29.04	9.51	5.53	11.47	13.52	4.43	6.10	45.12	96.39	72.00	7.13	5.33	8.47	6.33	78.03	17.33	35.52	5.96
1977	363.78	35.34	9.71	5.85	14.19	16.69	4.59	7.68	46.02	93.37	77.96	5.59	4.67	9.85	8.23	87.38	19.10	38.36	13.18

Stock Price Indexes for this group extend back to 1918.
* American Motors (5-5-54)
* Chrysler (1-2-18)
* Ford Motor (8-29-56)
* General Motors (1-2-18)

Hudson Motor Car (12-31-25 to 4-28-54)
Mack Trucks (1-7-20 to 1-9-52)
Nash-Kelvinator Corp. (12-31-25 to 4-28-54)
Packard Motor Car (1-7-20 to 9-29-54)
Studebaker Corp. (10-6-54 to 4-22-64)

SOURCE: Standard & Poor's Corp.

Figure 10–11

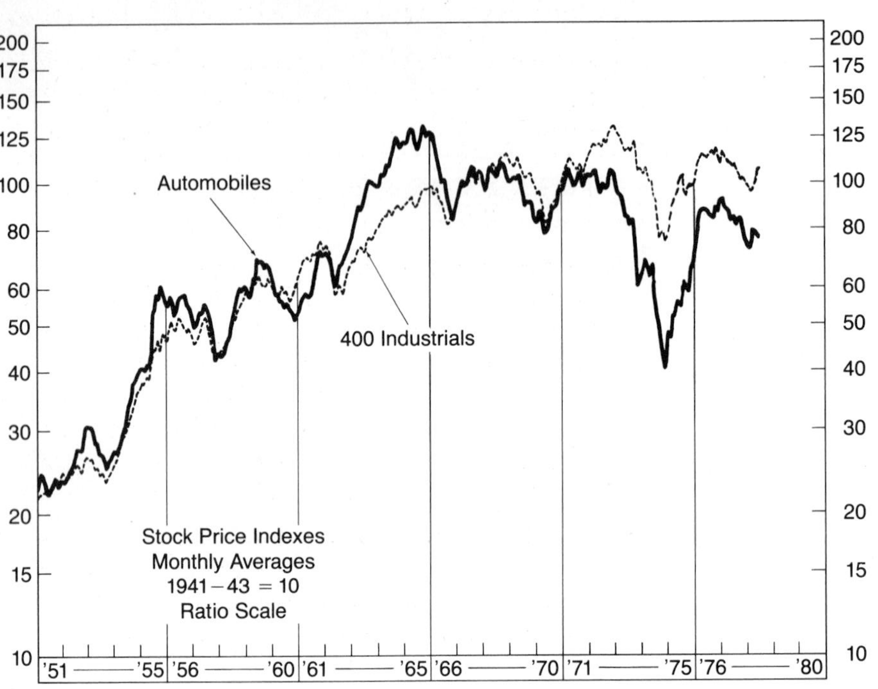

SOURCE: Standard & Poor's Corp.

Economic Structure The U.S. auto industry is an oligopoly. General Motors (58 percent of 1978 U.S. output) dominates three other U.S. competitors—Ford Motor (28 percent of U.S. total), Chrysler (10 percent), and American Motors (2 percent). Although competition within the industry is considered keen, in 1979 the Federal Trade Commission was engaged in a broad antitrust investigation, probing industry pricing policies, economies resulting from large-scale operations, vertical integration, and distribution practices. Auto industry leaders, however, argued the existence of new competition in the field and pointed to the fact that auto prices have risen less rapidly than prices of consumer goods as a whole.

Competition in the U.S. market from foreign automakers will undoubtedly affect the performance of the U.S. automakers. Recently, the imports' share of the market has set new records. Although the latest gasoline shortage has increased the demand for smaller cars, the Big Three were not prepared to meet this demand. Over the longer-term, however, a number of factors may stem the flow of imported cars into the market. These factors include the fall of the

U.S. dollar relative to the key foreign currencies, the imposition of trade restrictions on overseas shipments of autos by foreign makers, and the U.S. automakers' push to reduce auto sizes and gain fuel economy.

Capital Investment The amount of invested capital in the auto industry is enormous. In 1978, GM had nearly $30 billion in assets; Ford Motor's assets were over $20 billion. Heavy investments in plants and machines have enabled the auto manufacturers to enjoy considerable cost efficiencies; however, they also impose a tremendous fixed cost burden. As a result, profits diminish significantly during periods of declining unit sales.

Government Regulations The industry is faced with the difficult problem of appreciably increasing the gasoline mileage in order to satisfy conservation requirements, while at the same time reducing exhaust emissions to meet government standards. It is estimated that between 1978 and 1985 the industry could make capital investments, totaling as much as $70–$80 billion, primarily on projects to meet the more stringent gas mileage and exhaust emission standards. All of this would undoubtedly add to the cost of the average car and have an adverse effect on the industry's earnings and dividends.

Labor Conditions The wages and benefits of auto workers have traditionally risen more rapidly than the selling prices of automobiles. This forces the auto companies to pursue greater unit volume and increased efficiency in order to realize a growth in earnings. The possibility of a strike against either GM or Ford after the labor contract was due to expire in the second half of 1979 injected an element of uncertainty into any industry forecast. However, over the longer term, it can be assumed that the new labor contract with the United Auto Workers will contribute significantly to the higher cost of production.

Short-term Forecast

Sales Past experience with the industry suggests that actual auto sales (in units) exceed the general trend for about two years before one or two years of sales below trend. This is shown in Figure 10–12. Partly based on this

Figure 10–12

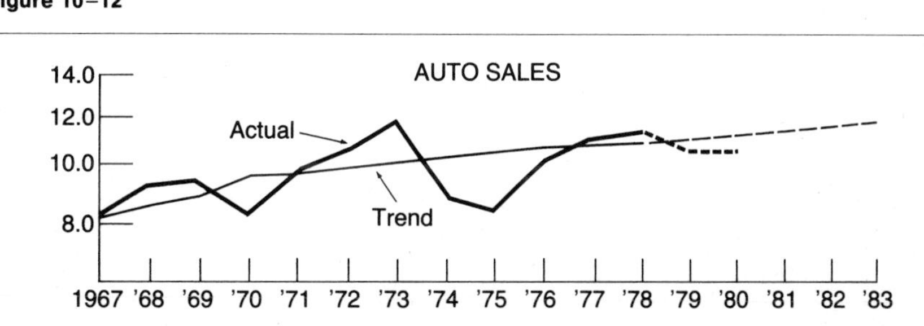

SOURCE: *The Value Line Investment Survey*, July 6, 1979, p. 129.

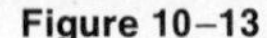

Figure 10–13 **Confidence Index**

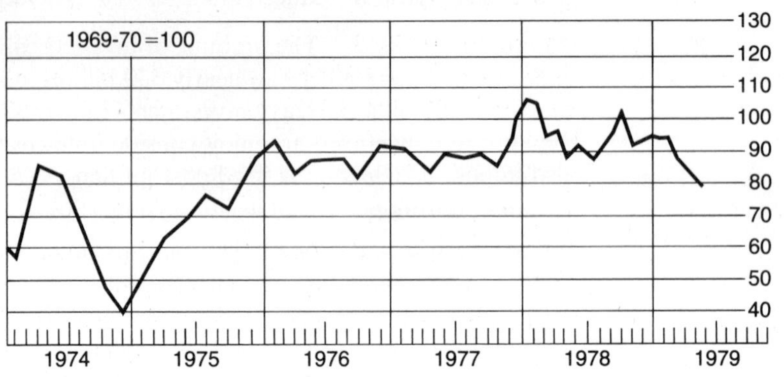

SOURCE: *The Value Line Investment Survey*, July 6, 1979, p. 129.

Figure 10–14 **Unit Sales of Autos**

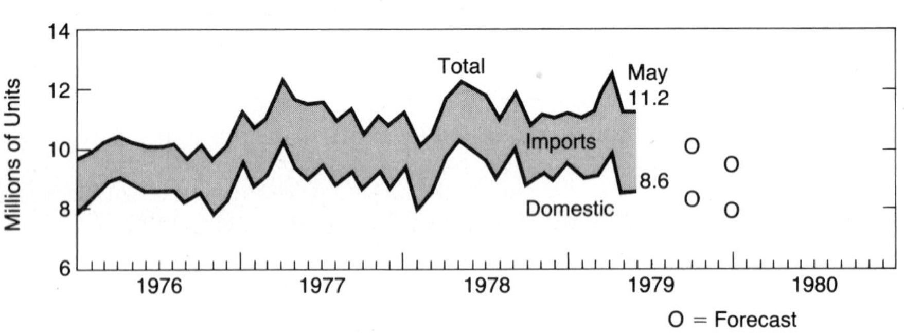

SOURCE: Chemical Bank, "Monthly Economic Indicators," June 28, 1979, Chart 9.

observation, and partly for reasons which will follow, a slowdown in sales was expected through 1980, and possibly through 1981.

First, an increased share of the U.S. market was taken by imports. Second, the public's real income had been declining, thereby reducing people's capacity to pay for the ever-increasing cost of owning new cars. Third, according to Figure 10–13, the consumer confidence index[26] had been declining. Generally,

[26] This index measures consumer optimism about the economic future.

a decline in this index is followed by a drop in auto sales, because consumers who are unsure of the future refrain from purchasing expensive items like automobiles. Forecasts by the Chemical Bank of New York, presented in Figure 10–14, predicted falling unit sales of domestic autos through 1979; the Value Line Investment Survey predicted a drop from 9.31 million car sales in 1978 to 8.7 million in 1981. Dollar sales could easily rise, however, with rising prices.

Earnings and Dividends There were several reasons for forecasting a decline in earnings and dividends for the industry. First, given the industry's heavy fixed cost burden, the expected decline in sales would tend to lower industry earnings. Second, because the profit margin for small cars is considerably lower than that for big cars, the unit profit would also decline in response to the popularity of small cars among an increasingly energy-conscious public. Third, the President's *voluntary* price guidelines limited the ability of the industry to pass along rising costs to consumers. Fourth, costs were expected to rise even higher following the new United Auto Workers contract negotiated in the fall of 1979. Finally, government-mandated capital investment for improving fuel economy would continue to put upward pressure on production costs. The predicted lower sales, higher costs, and lower earnings suggested that dividend increases over the short term were not likely. In fact, cutbacks seemed a strong possibility.

Longer-term Forecast

The slowdown in the auto industry that started in 1979 was predicted to continue through 1980 and perhaps through 1981. However, during the next upturn in the auto cycle, expected around 1982–84, *unit auto sales* could easily exceed the last sales peak by over 10 percent.

The Value Line industry forecast[27] presented in Table 10–12 estimated that auto *dollar sales* in 1982–84 will be up over 61 percent from the reported 1978 level, with net profits up about 48 percent for the same industry cycle. These figures represent annual growth rates over five years of about 11 percent for sales and 8 percent for profits. However, because of the negative industry fundamentals described earlier, the industry operating margin was expected to fall from 9.6 percent in 1977 to 7.7 percent in 1980, but to recover only to 8.5 percent in 1982–84. A similar pattern was expected for the net profit margin and return on total capital and equity. Even with a slightly lower tax rate, these measures of profitability were expected to be lower in 1982–84 than in the previous peak years of 1977–78. As a result, profit growth over the long run may be more difficult to achieve.

---

[27] Although this forecast also includes truck companies, it is still representative of conditions existing in the auto industry.

Table 10–12

Consolidated Financial Report & Forecast of Eight Auto & Truck Companies

1975	1976	1977	1978	1979	1980	© Arnold Bernhard & Co., Inc.	82–84E
78769	100028	119182	130672	***148000***	***163000***	Sales ($mill)	***211000***
5.9%	9.4%	9.6%	9.0%	***8.0%***	***7.7%***	Operating Margin	***8.5%***
1741.4	1814.7	1915.5	2231.4	***2650***	***3050***	Depreciation ($mill)	***3950***
1186.8	4349.4	5386.8	5240.8	***4900***	***5250***	Net Profit ($mill)	***7750***
51.1%	45.6%	46.0%	46.0%	***47.5%***	***46.5%***	Income Tax Rate	***45.5%***
1.5%	4.4%	4.5%	4.0%	***3.3%***	***3.2%***	Net Profit Margin	***3.7%***
9942.7	12141	13224	13764	***14100***	***14900***	Working Cap'l ($mill)	***22200***
4748.0	4483.5	4721.9	4395.9	***4350***	***5800***	Long-term Debt ($mill)	***6800***
23496	26149	29137	32418	***35400***	***38000***	Net Worth ($mill)	***51500***
4.8%	14.8%	16.5%	14.7%	***12.8%***	***12.5%***	% Earned Total Cap'l	***14.0%***
5.1%	16.6%	18.5%	16.2%	***13.8%***	***13.8%***	% Earned Net Worth	***15.0%***
.8%	9.3%	10.2%	9.3%	***8.0%***	***8.1%***	% Retained to Comm Eq	***8.6%***
84%	45%	45%	44%	***42%***	***42%***	% All Div'ds to Net Prof	***42%***
16.0	6.3	5.1	4.8	Bold figures		Avg Ann'l P/E Ratio	***10.5***
5.2%	7.0%	8.9%	9.0%	are VL estimates		Avg Ann'l Div'd Yield	***4.0%***

SOURCE: *The Value Line Investment Survey*, July 6, 1979, p. 129.

When assessing the future prospects of the industry, it is important to recognize that the automobile is such an integral part of the American lifestyle that only a gasoline shortage could alter the dependence on it. Due to the increasing use of small cars which get better gas mileage, even the energy shortage might not materially reduce the heavy reliance on cars.

The fact that autos are a basic necessity does not necessarily mean that the demand for cars is totally inelastic with respect to price. Due to the higher cost of automobile ownership and operation, both the expansion and replacement segments of demand will probably grow at a more *moderate pace in the future.* In addition, for cost reasons, the number of cars per household may not expand as it had in the 1960s and early 1970s. The smaller number of persons reaching driving age—a reflection of the decline in birth rates since the early 1960s—could be another limiting factor. These prospects could explain why Ford Motor predicted in December 1977 that in the 1977–85 period annual passenger car sales in the United States would grow at an *average* rate of 2.3 percent. The Department of Transportation forecast that the number of automobiles on the road would increase from 110 million at the end of 1976 to over 130 million in 1990—an annual growth rate of only a little above 1 percent.

A Summary View

This analysis leads to two important conclusions about the future of the auto industry. First, during the years 1979–84, the industry could be expected to follow the normal auto cycle of a slowdown in the 1979–81 period, followed by a healthy recovery in 1982–84. Second, because of significant changes in income patterns, a slowdown in population growth, stringent government regulations, and the actions of a powerful labor union, the long-run profit outlook for the automobile industry is not as bright as might otherwise be expected. However, although the outlook for the auto *industry* might lack outstanding growth characteristics, an *individual* auto company over any given time period may outperform the industry forecast.

The foregoing analysis has not only identified the factors that contribute to the overall growth of the auto industry, but has demonstrated that, for a host of reasons, the past may not be the best predictor of the future. The discussion has also underscored the fact that the longer-term outlook of an industry may differ significantly from the short-term prospects. Finally, it has pointed out that, although all auto companies are affected by the same forces which affect the entire automobile industry, any given auto company may do better or worse than the industry. Clearly, an industry analysis of the type just presented should help investors form better judgments about the earning power of any company within the industry.

Company Analysis

The Basic Framework

Thus far, the central theme of this chapter has been that the present value of a company's common stock depends on the company's ability to generate earnings—its *earning power*. Earning power, in turn, depends on such factors as the company's production and operating efficiency, profitability, and capital structure. Although earning power is influenced by national economic and industry conditions, it is also determined to a great degree by the company itself, as evidenced by the King and Brealey studies already cited.

The model that relates earnings to stock price is known as the *Earnings Capitalization Model*. This model states simply that the share price is the product of earnings per share (EPS) and the stock's P/E ratio. EPS is a quantitative measure of the value produced by the firm for its shareholders; the P/E ratio reflects to some extent the expected growth pattern of the company's earnings, as well as the risk associated with the investment.

The major thrust of Chapter 9, which presented the Common Stock Valuation Model, was the determination of the present value of a stock and its relation to the current market price. At the beginning of this chapter, it was

Figure 10–15 **Determinants of EPS**

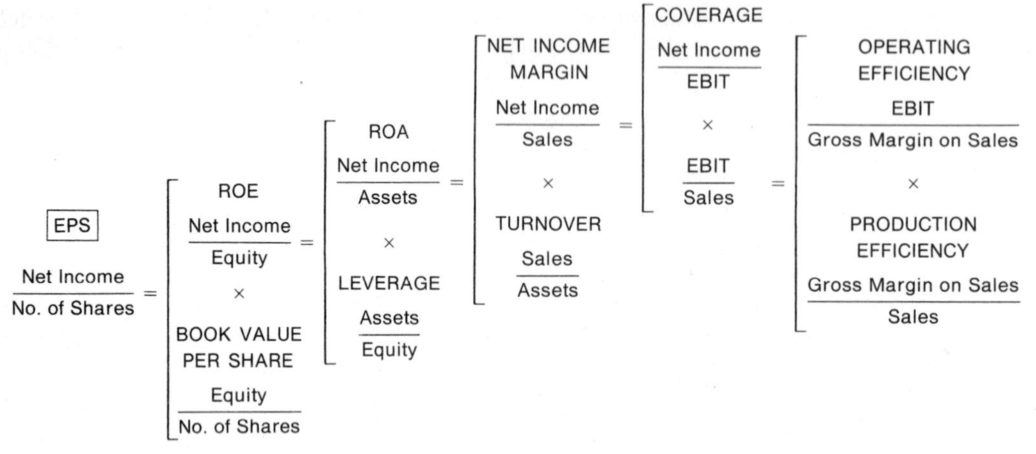

SOURCE: Adapted from Samuel S. Stewart, "Corporate Forecasting," in Sumner N. Levine, Ed. *Financial Analyst's Handbook* (Homewood, Ill.: Dow Jones-Irwin, 1975), p.912. © 1975 by Dow Jones-Irwin, Inc.

clearly stated that the expected earnings growth of the related firm is central to the present value calculation of a stock. We have already discussed how national economic and industry conditions can affect the earnings growth of a company. We will now analyze how earnings growth is related to the company's performance.

Analysis of a company can be divided into five stages. First, the determinants of earnings of a company can be studied. Second, factors affecting earnings growth can be identified. Third, techniques for forecasting future earnings can be presented. Fourth, the techniques for estimating the future dividend stream and the holding period price can be established. Finally, the use of key variables to determine the present value of a stock can be demonstrated.

Obviously, a comprehensive company analysis is both complicated and challenging. In order to keep the task within manageable limits, in this chapter only the first two stages of the analysis will be discussed. The last three stages will be covered in Chapter 11.

Determinants of Earnings

Figure 10–15 summarizes the determinants of EPS. The figure reveals that EPS can be determined by multiplying several financial ratios which are calculated from accounting data. A closer examination of these ratios and the interrelationship between them will underscore the complexity of evaluating a company's earning power and its earnings growth potential.

Earnings per Share

As revealed by Figure 10–15, EPS is net income divided by the number of shares of common stock.[28] It can be calculated by multiplying a firm's *return on equity* (*ROE*) by its *book value* (or stockholders' equity) *per share*:[29]

$$\text{EPS} = \text{ROE} \times \begin{matrix}\text{Book Value}\\ \text{per Share}\end{matrix}$$

$$\frac{\text{Net Income}}{\text{No. of Shares}} = \frac{\text{Net Income}}{\text{Equity}} \times \frac{\text{Equity}}{\text{No. of Shares}}$$

Companies obtain their capital from two external sources—stockholders and creditors. Return on equity is the percentage return on the stockholders' portion of the capital. The importance to the firm of attaining a high net income return on the stockholders' investment cannot be overemphasized. Not only does the ROE directly determine the EPS, but an adequate ROE justifies a reinvestment of earnings in the firm, thereby ensuring the possibility of an increase in the firm's book value for future EPS growth. In recent years, the ROE for major companies in the United States, as measured by the average of S&P 400 Industrials, has been approximately 14 percent. However, the ROE of some industries has averaged over 20 percent, whereas the ROE of a small number of companies has passed the 30 percent mark.

Return on Equity

Although the ROE is an important measure of a company's earning power, it is in fact merely a summary of the company's profitability and financing decisions. In an accounting sense, the ROE is a product of the *return on assets* (*ROA*) and the financial *leverage*:

$$\text{ROE} = \text{ROA} \times \text{Leverage}$$

$$\frac{\text{Net Income}}{\text{Equity}} = \frac{\text{Net Income}}{\text{Total Assets}} \times \frac{\text{Total Assets}}{\text{Equity}}$$

---

[28] For simplicity, this definition of EPS is used. Earnings per share is actually reported in two ways on a company's income statement: primary and fully diluted. Primary EPS is computed by dividing the net income available to common shareholders (net income less dividends paid on preferred stock) by the *average* number of common shares outstanding during the period. The calculation of fully diluted EPS takes into account the number of common shares that would be outstanding if all the convertible securities or warrants were exchanged or exercised. For companies that have not issued convertible stocks or bonds or warrants, primary EPS equals fully diluted EPS.

[29] Stockholders' equity for these calculations should only include that of the common shareholders. Also, many analysts prefer to use the *average* equity and average number of common shares outstanding during the year.

The ROA is considered a basic measure of a firm's profitability; that is, it reflects management's ability to utilize effectively the company's resources for generating profit. For companies that derive all their capital from common equity, the ROE equals ROA.

The leverage factor measures the amount of funds borrowed by the firm. A company that employs debt wisely can boost its ROE well above its ROA. Notice that when a company increases leverage by borrowing additional capital, it increases its total assets but not its common equity. If the company succeeds in using the additional borrowed capital to earn a rate of return higher than the cost of the debt, its net income will increase, leading ultimately to an increase in the ROE.

Financial leverage which increases the earnings and the ROE is called a *favorable leverage*, whereas the leverage that leads to a decline in earnings and the ROE is called an unfavorable leverage. It is important to recognize that beyond a certain point a favorable leverage eventually turns into an unfavorable leverage. Put differently, when the leverage factor is low, the cost of debt is generally lower than the return the company can earn on the borrowed funds. As the leverage ratio increases, however, the marginal cost of debt tends to rise progressively. If this rising trend continues, eventually the cost of additional debt will exceed the additional return it can generate, leading to an eventual decline in net income and the ROE.

Return on Assets

The ROA is both a basic measure of a firm's profitability and a key determinant of the ROE. It is a function of the *net income margin* multiplied by the *turnover ratio*:

$$\text{ROA} = \text{Net Income Margin} \times \text{Turnover Ratio}$$

$$\frac{\text{Net Income}}{\text{Total Assets}} = \frac{\text{Net Income}}{\text{Sales}} \times \frac{\text{Sales}}{\text{Total Assets}}$$

The turnover ratio measures the sales generated by the firm's assets, including cash, accounts receivables, inventories, fixed assets (plant and machinery), and intangible assets (goodwill and patents).[30] Several factors can influence the size of this ratio, including the proportion of total assets held in each of these categories, production efficiency and capacity, the inventory levels maintained, and the demand for the firm's products and services. If a firm holds a large amount of unsalable inventories or other nonproducing assets, or if a significant portion of its plant capacity is not utilized, turnover ratio is likely to be low.

[30] Many analysts consider only tangible assets when evaluating a firm's earning power.

The net income margin measures the ability of the firm to earn profits from the sales generated by the asset base. Because the ROA is a product of the firm's turnover ratio and the net income margin, a decline in either ratio has a negative impact on the ROA.

Net Income Margin

Figure 10–15 reveals that a firm's ability to generate net income from sales is the product of the firm's *coverage ratio* and the ratio of *earnings before interest and taxes (EBIT) to sales:*

$$\text{Net Income Margin} = \text{Coverage} \times [\text{EBIT/Sales}]$$

$$\frac{\text{Net Income}}{\text{Sales}} = \frac{\text{Net Income}}{\text{EBIT}} \times \frac{\text{EBIT}}{\text{Sales}}$$

The coverage ratio is a measure of a company's tax rates and interest expense;[31] it increases when the interest expense and tax rates decline, making net income higher relative to EBIT. Generally, a company's tax rate falls in the 44–50 percent range. However, a firm can lower its tax rate if it can take advantage of various tax credits or if it has foreign operations which are taxed at lower rates. The interest expense, of course, is determined by the firm's financing decisions and market interest rates. If a company has boosted its ROE by leveraging on low-interest debt, investors will want to know how long the favorable leverage will continue. When the low-interest debt matures, it may have to be refinanced at a higher interest rate which could exceed the firm's ROA.

The EBIT/Sales ratio is a measure of a company's *operating and production efficiency*:

$$\frac{\text{EBIT}}{\text{Sales}} = \text{Production Efficiency} \times \text{Operating Efficiency}$$

$$= \frac{\text{Gross Margin on Sales}}{\text{Sales}} \times \frac{\text{EBIT}}{\text{Gross Margin on Sales}}$$

The gross margin on sales refers to the difference between sales revenue, adjusted for returns and allowances, and the total cost of the goods or services produced. The production efficiency ratio indicates how well the company's products can be manufactured and sold, and is determined by the pricing policies and cost efficiencies of the enterprise. In contrast, the operating efficiency ratio measures the firm's effectiveness at controlling various sales, general, and administrative expenses relative to its gross margin on sales. The

[31] Some analysts consider the *net* interest expense for the year—interest expense less interest income.

product of the production and operating efficiency ratios is the EBIT/Sales ratio, which is an indicator of the overall profitability of the company's business activity.

Conclusions

A firm's ability to realize earnings for its shareholders is a function of a heterogeneous set of variables. At a basic level, the EPS can be defined as the ROE multiplied by the book value per share. However, the ROE can be linked to a network of other variables that measure a firm's profitability.[32]

The derivation of earnings per share is demonstrated in Table 10–13. The upper half of the table shows the various financial ratios leading to the 1978 EPS for Ford Motor Company; the lower half shows the same for General Motors.

In 1978, Ford earned $13.35 per share, GM earned $12.24. However, GM had a considerably higher ROA than Ford (11.4 percent vs. 7.2 percent), a result of both a higher turnover and a net income margin. Note that GM's net income margin was higher because its larger EBIT/Sales ratio (11.0 percent vs. 6.95 percent) made up for its lower coverage (50.3 percent vs. 53.4 percent). Both higher production and operating efficiency contributed to the superior EBIT/Sales measure. Even though GM's leverage was lower than Ford's, its ROE was still 20.2 percent (compared to Ford's 16.4 percent). However, because Ford had a higher book value per share, its EPS was larger than GM's. Obviously, because GM has *less* equity per share than Ford, GM must earn a *higher* return on the equity to make a comparable amount of profit *per share* of stock.

The objective of this example has been to illustrate how various factors interrelate in the process of the derivation of the EPS rather than to make a judgment about the performance of the individual companies. Investors frequently make such judgments by comparing a firm's profitability measures with those of its industry or a broader company average.[33] A comparison of a company's most recent financial ratios with those of prior years can also be a gauge of its overall progress.

The foregoing analysis has underscored an important point: In addition to its own performance, the earnings of a firm can be influenced by national economic conditions as well as by industry conditions. For instance, in the auto industry analysis presented earlier, the industry was faced with rising labor costs,

[32] The approach used in this section to analyze a firm's earning power covered basic elements of ratio analysis. A more comprehensive discussion of ratio analysis, as well as other techniques to analyze a company, can be found in several good managerial finance texts. The topic of company analysis will be discussed further in Chapter 11.

[33] Comparing a firm's financial ratios with an industry or broad company average can be difficult for several reasons. First, a company may extend its business into more than one industry, in which case no single industry average may be comparable. Also, because accounting policies frequently differ between companies and industries, reported income statement and balance sheet numbers are often difficult to compare. This will be discussed further in Chapter 11.

Table 10–13 **Derivation of EPS**

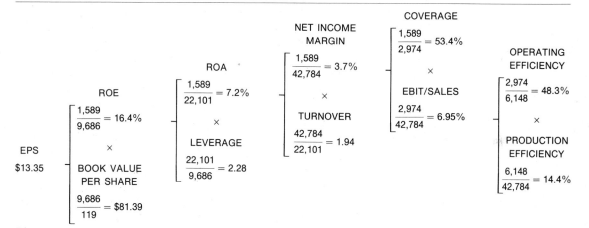

FORD MOTOR
1978

Financial Data
($000,000)

Sales:	**42,784**	**Equity:**	**9,686**
Net Income:	**1,589**	**Gross Margin**	
EBIT:	**2,974**	**on Sales:**	**6,148**
Assets:	**22,101**	**No. of Shares: 119 million**	

EPS $13.35

- ROE: $\frac{1,589}{9,686} = 16.4\%$
  - ROA: $\frac{1,589}{22,101} = 7.2\%$
    - NET INCOME MARGIN: $\frac{1,589}{42,784} = 3.7\%$
      - COVERAGE: $\frac{1,589}{2,974} = 53.4\%$
      - ×
      - EBIT/SALES: $\frac{2,974}{42,784} = 6.95\%$
        - OPERATING EFFICIENCY: $\frac{2,974}{6,148} = 48.3\%$
        - ×
        - PRODUCTION EFFICIENCY: $\frac{6,148}{42,784} = 14.4\%$
    - ×
    - TURNOVER: $\frac{42,784}{22,101} = 1.94$
  - ×
  - LEVERAGE: $\frac{22,101}{9,686} = 2.28$
- ×
- BOOK VALUE PER SHARE: $\frac{9,686}{119} = \$81.39$

GENERAL MOTORS
1978

Financial Data
($000,000)

Sales:	**63,221**	**Equity:**	**17,286**
Net Income:	**3,495**	**Gross Margin**	
EBIT:	**6,952**	**on Sales:**	**11,946**
Assets:	**30,598**	**No. of Shares: 285.5 million**	

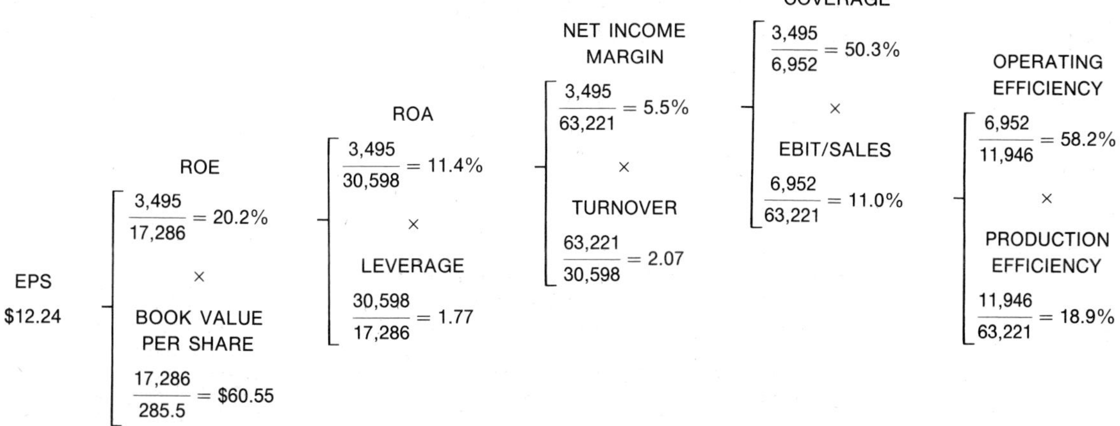

government regulations, and the increasing popularity of smaller cars—all of which led to a lower gross margin on sales. Such problems will tend to lower the auto companies' production efficiency, which will have an adverse effect on the EBIT/Sales ratio, ROA, ROE, and EPS. A drop in car sales, caused by an economic downturn, will hurt the auto manufacturers' turnover. The EBIT/Sales ratio will also be negatively affected because there will be less revenue to cover the firms' high fixed costs. Of course, the impact of national and industry conditions on individual auto companies does not tell the complete story; each company maintains some control over its earning performance as well. It sets the capital structure, controls certain costs, sets marketing strategies for its products, makes investment decisions, and performs many other management functions, all of which affect its earning power. For these reasons, a comprehensive fundamental analysis must consider the impact of national economic and industry conditions as well as the performance of the company on the earning power of that company.

Determination of Earnings Growth

We have already examined the key determinants of the EPS. However, to evaluate the present value of a stock, investors must consider the future earnings *growth* of a company. The ROE multiplied by the book value per share of a firm equals the EPS. However, it is the ROE and the *earnings retention ratio*—often called the plowback ratio—that determine the growth rate of earnings. More specifically, for any given year, the earnings retention ratio multiplied by the ROE equals the ratio of retained earnings to common equity, known as the *reinvestment rate*:

$$\text{Reinvestment Rate} = \text{ROE} \times \begin{matrix}\text{Earnings}\\ \text{Retention Ratio}\end{matrix}$$

$$\frac{\text{Retained Earnings}}{\text{Equity}} = \frac{\text{Net Income}}{\text{Equity}} \times \frac{\text{Retained Earnings}}{\text{Net Income}}$$

If a company maintains a *constant* ROE and earnings retention ratio, the reinvestment rate will equal the *future* growth rate of its earnings.

During a given year the amount of retained earnings, or the net income minus dividends, represents the dollar amount by which book value is increased during the year. The reinvestment rate—the ratio of retained earnings to equity—indicates the *growth rate* in equity. If the return earned on the common equity and the earnings retention ratio remain constant, the growth rate of net income will equal the growth rate of equity.

Consider, for instance, the example presented in Table 10–14. Assuming the ROE is 10 percent and the earnings retention ratio is 50 percent, the future growth rate in earnings equals 5 percent (.10 × .50) if these two variables remain constant.

Table 10–14

Pertinent Details:

Return on Equity (ROE) = 10% (to remain constant)

Earnings Retention Ratio = 50% (to remain constant)

(1) Year	(2) ROE	(3) Book Value per Share	(4) EPS (2) × (3)	(5) Earnings Retention Ratio	(6) Amount of EPS Retained (4) × (5)
1	10%	$20.00	$2.00	50%	$1.00
2	10	21.00	2.10	50	1.05
3	10	22.05	2.21	50	1.11
4	10	23.16	2.32	50	1.16
5	10	24.32	2.43		
			↓ EPS growth = 5%		

Table 10–15

EXAMPLE 1
Constant Return on Equity (ROE)
Rising Earnings Retention Ratio

(1) Year	(2) ROE	(3) Book Value per Share	(4) EPS (2) × (3)	(5) Earnings Retention Ratio	(6) Amount of EPS Retained (4) × (5)
1	10%	$20.00	$2.00	50%	$1.00
2	10	21.00	2.10	60	1.26
3	10	22.26	2.23	70	1.56
4	10	23.82	2.38	80	1.90
5	10	25.72	2.57		

EXAMPLE 2
Rising Return on Equity (ROE)
Constant Earnings Retention Ratio

Year	ROE	Book Value per Share	EPS	Earnings Retention Ratio	Amount of EPS Retained
1	10.0%	$20.00	$2.00	50%	$1.00
2	10.5	21.00	2.21	50	1.11
3	11.0	22.11	2.43	50	1.22
4	11.5	23.33	2.68	50	1.34
5	12.0	24.67	2.96		

In Year 1, with the book value or common equity per share assumed to be \$20, a ROE of 10 percent earns \$2 (.10 × \$20) per share. Because the retention ratio is 50 percent, the company retains \$1 of the \$2 EPS, thus increasing its \$20 per share book value by \$1.[34] In Year 2, the 10 percent ROE on the new book value produces earnings of \$2.10 (.10 × \$21) per share, a 5 percent increase over the previous year. When 50 percent of the second year's EPS is retained and added to equity, the constant ROE produces an additional 5 percent increase in earnings for Year 3 of \$2.21. This earnings growth continues indefinitely as long as the ROE and earnings retention ratio remain constant. Of course, there is no reason to believe that the ROE and earnings retention ratio will remain unchanged. A change in these variables will naturally alter the earnings growth rate.

Table 10–15 presents two hypothetical examples to demonstrate this last point. As in the previous example (Table 10–14), the ROE and earnings retention ratio in Year 1 are 10 percent and 50 percent, respectively. In the first example, however, the earnings retention ratio increases from 50 percent in Year 1 to 80 percent in Year 4. Because more earnings are reinvested into the business, the EPS growth over the five-year period is over 6 percent, as compared to the 5 percent growth rate under the assumption of a constant 50 percent earnings retention ratio.

In the second example in Table 10–15, the earnings retention ratio is assumed constant, but the ROE continues to improve from 10 percent in Year 1 to 12 percent in Year 5. Here again the 10 percent growth in the EPS is well above the previous rate of 5 percent.

Our discussion on earnings growth can be briefly restated as follows: A company's earnings growth rate is a function of its ROE multiplied by the earnings retention ratio, known as the reinvestment rate. This rate equals the future earnings growth provided that the ROE and the earnings retention ratio remain constant. If the company desires higher earnings growth, it will have to improve its ROE or declare dividends to stockholders at a lower rate.[35] More specifically, to increase its ROE a company must take appropriate steps to bring about one or more of the following improvements: (1) increase the operating and/or production efficiency to improve the EBIT/Sales ratio, (2) increase the coverage ratio through a lower tax rate or lower cost of debt, (3) increase the turnover ratio, or (4) increase the use of the favorable leverage.

---

[34] Technically, if on January 1 of Year 1 the book value is \$20, the EPS is \$2, and the earnings retained at the end of the year is \$1, then the book value at the end of Year 1 is \$21 (\$20 + \$1). In that case, the EPS of \$2 would *not* be 10 percent of the book value per share of \$21, as might be implied by the ROE of 10 percent. However, for simplicity, the illustration on Table 10–14 is used to explain the reinvestment rate concept.

[35] Earnings *per share* can also be increased by selling additional common stock at prices *above* book value (thereby increasing book value *per share*), or by purchasing the firm's shares for the treasury at prices below book value, other things being the same. Although the infusion of additional common equity into a firm will reduce the leverage ratio and ROE, all else being being equal, a lower ROE times a higher book value per share can produce higher EPS. Companies can also increase their capital by issuing preferred stock. If they take that step and maintain the return on net worth at a level higher than the return paid to the preferred shareholders, the return on common equity will increase.

Summary

The present value of a common stock is a function of the future dividend stream, the holding period price of the stock, and the investor's appropriate discount rate. The first two variables are directly related to the future earnings growth of a company. It is, therefore, necessary to predict this future earnings growth.

Future earnings growth depends not only on the performance of the company, but on the future success of the industry of which it is a part. The future prospects of an industry, in turn, are closely tied to the *general economic conditions* prevailing in the country.

An investor can accept forecasts of general economic conditions made by the *National Bureau of Economic Research* or by various professional forecasting institutions such as the *Value Line* or the *Moody's*. These forecasts may also be modified on the basis of the investor's independent forecast of the *GNP*.

It is frequently argued that because money supply and GNP are directly related, an independent forecast of GNP is facilitated by a forecast of monetary policy. However, studies have shown that a direct causal relationship does not exist between monetary policy and GNP on any consistent basis.

Industry returns are affected by such fundamental factors as patterns of performance, economic structure, capital investment, government regulations, and labor conditions.

An important aspect of company analysis is an examination of various financial ratios. Such an analysis identifies the main determinants of earnings as *operating* and *production efficiency*, *coverage* and *turnover ratios*, and *financial leverage*.

A company's earnings growth rate is a function of its ROE multiplied by the earnings retention ratio, known as the reinvestment rate. The *reinvestment rate* equals the future earnings growth, provided that the ROE and the earnings retention ratio remain constant. If the company desires higher earnings growth, it must increase its ROE or the earnings retention ratio. The ROE can be increased by increasing operating and production efficiency, the coverage ratio, the turnover ratio, or the use of the favorable leverage.

A Look Ahead

In this chapter the general economic conditions and industry conditions that affect the earning power of a company have been analyzed. Determinants of earnings and variables of earnings growth have also been presented as an introduction to company analysis.

The discussion of company analysis will continue in Chapter 11 as the techniques for estimating future earnings and dividends are presented. The determination of the future stock price at the end of the holding period will also be discussed. Finally, the use of the key variables in determining the present value of a stock will be demonstrated.

Concepts for Review

GNP
General economic conditions
Earning power
National Bureau of Economic Research (NBER)
Long-range forecasting
Short-range forecasting
Leading, lagging, coincident indicators
Numerical rating of short list
Diffusion indexes
Duration of run index
Moody's survey
Value Line survey
National Income and Product Accounts
Econometric model
Input–output table
Money and GNP
Money and stock prices
Industry analysis
Industry risk
Industry returns
Key industry fundamentals
Industrial life cycle
Company analysis
Determinants of earnings
Earnings per share
Return on equity (ROE)
Book value per share
Return on assets (ROA)
Leverage
Favorable leverage
Net income margin
Turnover
Coverage
EBIT/Sales
Operating efficiency
Production efficiency
Earnings retention ratio
Reinvestment rate

Questions for Review

1. Why would you expect a relationship to exist between general economic conditions and stock price movements?
2. What are leading, lagging, and coincident indicators? How are they used to forecast economic conditions?
3. What approaches would you consider if you were required to forecast the GNP for the next year?
4. Explain the relationship between monetary policy, GNP, and stock prices.
5. How do general economic conditions influence the earnings performance of individual companies? Be specific.
6. How would you use key industry fundamentals to evaluate the industry impact on a firm's earning power?
7. Explain in general terms the value of industry analysis.
8. When considering potential stock investments, Investor W states that he only looks at companies in industries with prospects for above-average earnings growth. Comment on this approach.

9. Explain the industrial life cycle. What factors influence the growth rate of an industry during each stage?
10. Investor Q mentions that because the performance of different firms within an industry can vary greatly, there is little value in undertaking industry analysis. What is your response?
11. Why is return on equity an important consideration in company analysis?
12. What is return on assets? Why do some analysts consider a company's return on assets to be a better actual measure of performance than return on equity?
13. What is the reinvestment rate? Explain the relationship between the reinvestment rate and earnings growth.
14. Describe ways in which a company can *improve* its earnings growth.
15. Comment on the following statement: "When a company increases leverage, it increases total assets but not common equity. As a result, an increase in leverage leads to a higher return on equity and greater earnings growth."

Problems

1. Write an analysis of an industry of your choice, focusing on key industry fundamentals. What are the industry's short-term and long-term earnings growth prospects?
2. Assume that sales of NPC Company for the next year are forecast to be $220 million. The coverage and EBIT/Sales ratios are expected to be 56 percent and 11 percent, respectively. Assets are expected to be $100 million. If NPC is financed with 55 percent equity and 45 percent debt and has 5 million common shares outstanding, forecast the following:
   a. Net income.
   b. Return on assets.
   c. Return on equity.
   d. Earnings per share.
3. The following are financial data for MJC, Inc. for the years 1977 and 1978:

	(in millions)	
	1978	1977
Sales	$229.3	$186.8
Gross Margin on Sales	127.6	94.0
EBIT	19.3	20.5
Net Income	8.7	10.3
Assets	150.2	121.1
Equity	70.3	61.9
Number of Common Shares	4.3	4.3

   a. Compute the 1977 and 1978 EPS.
   b. Analyze the data and account for the change in EPS from 1977 to 1978. Base your analysis on a comparison of the financial ratios which determine EPS.

4. The following are financial data for three companies for the most recent year:

	Company N	Company Q	Company Z
Earnings per share	$ 2.95	$5.10	$ 1.12
Dividend rate	$ 1.28	$3.20	$ 0.24
Return on assets	10.5%	6.5%	13.7%
Capital structure			
Debt (million)	$2,200	$2,400	$ 0
Equity (million)	7,580	2,700	79.6
Current stock price	19	47	15

Based on this data, answer the following questions. State all the necessary assumptions.

a. What is the expected EPS growth of each company?

b. What is the present value of each stock? Assume the appropriate discount rates for Companies N, Q and Z are 13 percent, 12 percent, and 14 percent, respectively. Which stock(s) are suitable for purchase?

Selected Readings

Adams, F. Gerard and Peter E. deJanosi. "Statistics and Econometrics of Forecasting." In *How Business Economists Forecast*. William F. Butler and Robert A. Kavesh, eds. Englewood Cliffs, N.J.: Prentice-Hall, 1966.

Ahlers, David M. "SEM: A Security Evaluation Model." In *Analytical Methods in Banking*. Kalman J. Cohen and Frederick S. Hammer, eds. Homewood, Ill.: Richard D. Irwin, 1966.

Andersen, Theodore A. "Trends in Profit Sensitivity." *Journal of Finance*, December 1963.

Andrews, John R., Jr. "The Fundamental Case for Investing in Growth." *Financial Analysts Journal*, November–December 1970.

Auerbach, Robert D. "Money and Stock Prices." Federal Reserve Bank of Kansas City, *Monthly Review*, September–October 1976.

Auerbach, Robert D. and Jack L. Rutner. "Money and Income: Is There a Simple Relationship?" Federal Reserve Bank of Kansas City, *Monthly Review*, May 1975.

Babcock, Guilford C. "The Concept of Sustainable Growth." *Financial Analysts Journal*, May–June 1970.

Babcock, Guilford C. "The Trend and Stability of Earnings per Share." *Proceedings of the Seminar on the Analysis of Security Prices*, University of Chicago, November 1970.

Ball, Ray and Philip Brown. "An Empirical Evaluation of Accounting Income Numbers." *Journal of Accounting Research*, Autumn 1968.

Ball, Ray and Ross Watts. "Some Time Properties of Accounting Incomes." *Journal of Finance*, June 1972.

Barnes, D. P. "Materiality—An Illusive Concept." *Management Accounting*, October 1976.

Basi, Bart, Kenneth Carey and Richard Twark. "Accuracy of Corporate and Security Analysts' Forecasts." *Accounting Review*, April 1976.

Basu, Sanjoy. "The Information Content of Price–Earnings Ratios." *Financial Management*, Summer 1975.

Basu, Sanjoy. "Investment Performance of Common Stocks in Relation to Their Price–Earnings Ratios: A Test of the Efficient Market Hypothesis." *Journal of Finance*, June 1977.

Beaver, William H. "Financial Ratios as Predictors of Failure." *Journal of Accounting Research*, Autumn 1966, Supplement.

Beaver, William H. "Market Prices, Financial Ratios and the Prediction of Failure." *Journal of Accounting Research*, Autumn 1968.

Beaver, William H. and Dale Morse. "What Determines Price–Earnings Ratios?" *Financial Analysts Journal*, July–August 1978.

Benishay, Haskell. "Market Preferences for Characteristics of Common Stocks." *Economic Journal*, March 1973.

Benishay, Haskell. "Variability in Earnings–Price Ratios of Corporate Equities." *American Economic Review*, March 1961.

Bernstein, Leopold A. "Extraordinary Gains and Losses—Their Significance to the Financial Analyst." *Financial Analysts Journal*, November–December 1972.

Bernstein, Leopold A. and Joel G. Siegel. "The Concept of Earnings Quality." *Financial Analysts Journal*, July–August 1979.

Bodie, Z. "Common Stocks as a Hedge Against Inflation." *Journal of Finance*, May 1976.

Bower, Richard S. and Dorothy H. Bower. "Risk and the Valuation of Common Stock." *Journal of Political Economy*, May–June 1969.

Breen, William. "Low Price–Earnings Ratios and Industry Relatives." *Financial Analysts Journal*, July–August 1969.

Brigham, Eugene F. and James L. Pappas. "Duration of Growth, Change in Growth Rates, and Corporate Share Prices." *Financial Analysts Journal*, May–June 1966.

Brigham, Eugene F. and James L. Pappas. "Rates of Return on Common Stock." *Journal of Business*, July 1969.

Brown, Philip and John W. Kennelly. "The Informational Content of Quarterly Earnings: An Extension and Some Further Evidence." *Journal of Business*, July 1972.

Brown, Philip and Victor Niederhoffer. "The Predictive Content of Quarterly Earnings." *Journal of Business*, October 1968.

Burton, John C. "The Changing Face of Financial Reporting." *Journal of Accountancy*, February 1976.

Business Forecasts 1979. Richmond: Federal Reserve Bank of Richmond, February 1979.

Butler, William F. and Robert A. Kavesh. "Short-term Forecasting of the Gross National Product." In *How Business Economists Forecast*. Ed. William F. Bulter and Robert A. Kavesh. Englewood Cliffs, N.J.: Prentice-Hall, 1966.

Cairncross, Alec. "Economic Forecasting." *Economic Journal*, December 1969.

"Consolidated Return Earnings and Profits Regulations." *CPA Journal*, November 1976.

Copeland, R. M. and R. J. Marioni. "Executives' Forecasts of Earnings per Share Versus Forecasts of Naive Models." *Journal of Business*, October 1972.

Cowles, Alfred. "Can Stock Market Forecasters Forecast?" *Econometrica*, July 1933.

Cowles, Alfred. "A Revision of Previous Conclusions Regarding Stock Price Behavior." *Econometrica*, October 1960.

Cragg, J. G. and Burton G. Malkiel. "The Consensus and Accuracy of Some Predictions of the Growth of Corporate Earnings." *Journal of Finance*, March 1968.

Crowell, Richard. "Earnings Expectations, Security Valuation and the Cost of Equity Capital." Unpublished Ph.D. dissertation, Massachusetts Institute of Technology, 1967.

Curley, Anthony J. "Conglomerate Earnings Per Share." *Accounting Review*, July 1971.

Cushing, Barry. "The Effects of Accounting Policy Decision on Trends in Reported Corporate Earnings Per Share." Ph.D. dissertation, Michigan State University, 1969.

Dale, Edwin L., Jr. "Statistics Watching for Fun and Prophecy." *Money*, July 1976.

Darling, P. G. "The Influence of Expectations and Liquidity on Dividend Policy." *Journal of Political Economy*, June 1957.

Davidson, Sidney and T. Carter Hagaman. "Should Companies Be Required to Publish Their Earnings Forecasts?—A Debate." *The Institutional Investor*, April 1972.

Dew, Kurt. "Practical Monetarism and the Stock Market." Federal Reserve Bank of San Francisco, Spring 1978.

Ellis, Charles D. "The Loser's Game." Reprinted from *Financial Analysts Journal*, July–August 1975.

Fama, Eugene F. "Behavior of Stock Market Prices." *Journal of Business*, January 1965.

Fama, Eugene F. "Efficient Capital Markets: A Review of the Theory and Empirical Work." *Journal of Finance*, May 1970.

Fama, Eugene F. "The Empirical Relationship Between the Dividend and Investment Decisions of Firms." *American Economic Review*, June 1974.

Fama, Eugene F., et al. "The Adjustment of Stock Prices to New Information." *International Economic Review*, February 1969.

Fisher, L. and J. H. Lorie. "Rates of Return on Investments in Common Stock: The Year-by-Year Record, 1926–1965." *Journal of Business*, January 1968.

Fluegel, Frederick K. "The Rate of Return on High and Low P/E Ratio Stocks." *Financial Analysts Journal*, November–December 1968.

Friedman, Milton and Anna J. Schwartz. *Monetary History of the United States, 1867–1960.* Princeton, N.J.: Princeton University Press, 1963.

Friend, Irwin. "Equity Yields, Growth, and the Structure of Share Prices: Comment." *American Economic Review*, December 1964.

Friend, Irwin and Marshall Puckett. "Dividends and Stock Prices." *American Economic Review*, September 1964.

Froman, G. and L. R. Klein. "The Brookings–S.S.R.C. Quarterly Econometric Model of the United States: Model Properties." *American Economic Review*, May 1965.

Getschow, George. "Paper Profits." *Wall Street Journal*, June 20, 1980.

Granger, C. W. and D. Morgenstern. "The Special Analysis of New York Stock Market Prices." *Kyklos*, 1963.

Gray, William S., III. "Developing a Long-term Outlook for the U.S. Economy and Stock Market." *Financial Analysts Journal*, July–August 1979.

Green, David., Jr. and Joel Segall. "The Predictive Power of First Quarter Earnings Reports." *Journal of Business*, January 1967.

Grodinsky, Julius. *Investments.* New York: The Ronald Press, 1953.

Gupta, Manak C. "Money Supply and Stock Prices: A Probabilistic Approach." *Journal of Financial and Quantitative Analysis*, January 1974.

Hagaman, T. Carter and Arnold E. Jensen. "Investment Value and Security Analysis." *Financial Analysts Journal*, March–April 1977.

Halpern, Paul J. "Empirical Estimates of the Amount and Distribution of Gains to Companies in Mergers." *Journal of Business*, October 1973.

Harris, Maury and Deborah Jamroz. "Evaluating the Leading Indicators." Federal Reserve Bank of New York *Monthly Review*, June 1976, pp. 165–72.

Haugen, Robert A. "Do Common Stock Quality Ratings Predict Risk?" *Financial Analysts Journal*. March–April 1979.

Hershman, A. "Accounting—More Data for Investors." *Dun's Review*, March 1976.

Homa, Kenneth E. and Dwight M. Jaffee. "The Supply of Money and Common Stock Prices." *Journal of Finance*, December 1971.

Horrigan, James. "The Determination of Long-term Credit Standing with Financial Ratios." *Journal of Accounting Research*, Supplement, Autumn 1966.

Ibbotson, R. G. and R. A. Sinquefield. "Stock, Bonds, Bills and Inflation: Simulations of the Future (1976–2000)." *Journal of Business*, July 1976.

"Inflation Trend Holds Key to Near-Term Prospects." In Moody's *Industry Surveys*, 1979.

Johnson, Keith B. "Stock Splits and Price Change." *Journal of Finance*, December 1966.

Karnosky, Denis S. "The Link Between Money and Prices—1971–1976." Federal Reserve Bank of St. Louis, June 1976.

Kavesh, Robert A. and Robert B. Platt. "Economic Forecasting." In *Financial Analyst's Handbook*. Ed. Sumner N. Levine. Homewood, Ill.: Dow Jones-Irwin, 1975.

Kendall, Maurice G. "The Analysis of Economic Time Series—Part I: Prices." *Journal of the Royal Statistical Society*, Series A (General), 1953.

Kendrick, John W. "Investment Implications of Long-Run Economic Trends." *Financial Analysts Journal*, September–October 1961.

King, A. M. "Current Value Accounting Comes of Age." *Financial Executive*, January 1976.

King, Benjamin F. "Market and Industry Factors in Stock Price Behavior." *Journal of Business*, January 1966.

Kisor, Manown, Jr. and Van A. Messner. "The Filter Approach and Earnings Forecasts." *Financial Analysts Journal*, January 1969.

Kopcke, Richard W. "The Decline in Corporate Profitability." *New England Economic Review*, May–June 1978.

Kutscher, Ronald E. "Revised BLS Projections to 1980 and 1985: An Overview." *Monthly Labor Review*, March 1976.

Latane, Henry Allen and Donald L. Tuttle. "An Analysis of Common Stock Price Ratios." *Southern Economic Journal*, January 1967.

Lempert, Leonard H. "Leading Indicators." In *How Business Economists Forecast*. Ed. William F. Butler and Robert A. Kavesh. Englewood Cliffs, N.J.: Prentice-Hall, 1966.

Levy, Robert A. "A Note on the Safety of Low P/E Stocks." *Financial Analysts Journal*, January–February 1973.

Lewis, John P. "Short-Term General Business Conditions Forecasting: Some Comments on Method." *Journal of Business*, October 1962.

Lewis, John P. and Robert C. Turner. *Business Conditions Analysis*. New York: McGraw-Hill, 1967.

Lintner, John and Robert Glauber. "Higgledy Piggledy Growth in America." Unpublished paper prepared for the Seminar on the Analysis of Security Prices, University of Chicago, May 1967.

Mabert, Vincent A. and Robert C. Radcliffe. "Forecasting—A Systematic Modeling Methodology." *Financial Management*, Autumn 1974.

Malkiel, Burton. "Equity Yields, Growth, and the Structure of Share Prices." *American Economic Review*, December 1963.

Malkiel, Burton G. and Cragg, John G. "Expectations and the Structure of Share Prices." *American Economic Review*, September 1970.

Mao, James C. T. "The Valuation of Growth Stocks: The Investments Opportunity Approach." *Journal of Finance*, March 1966.

McElhattan, Rose. "Has the Money–GNP Relationship Fallen Apart?" Federal Reserve Bank of San Francisco, Summer 1976.

Miller, Merton and Franco Modigliani. "Dividend Policy, Growth, and the Valuation of Shares." *Journal of Business*, October 1966.

Modigliani, Franco and Merton Miller. "The Cost of Capital, Corporate Finance and the Theory of Investment." *American Economic Review*, June 1958.

Molodovsky, Nicholas, C. May, and S. Chottiner. "Common Stock Valuation: Theory and Tables." *Financial Analysts Journal*, March–April 1962.

Moore, Geoffrey H. and Philip A. Klein. "Recovery and Then? New Techniques Are Being Developed to Track the Business Cycle with Precision." *Across the Board*, October 1976.

Murphy, Joseph E., Jr. "Relative Growth of Earnings Per Share—Past and Future." *Financial Analysts Journal*, November–December 1966.

Murphy, Joseph E., Jr. "Return, Payout and Growth." *Financial Analysts Journal*, May–June 1967.

National Planning Association. *National Economic Projection Series*, Report 75 N-2: "Investment in the Eighties" by Robert Dennis. Washington, D.C.: National Planning Association, April 1976.

Nelson, C. "The Analysis of World Events and Stock Prices." *Journal of Business*, April 1971.

Nelson, Charles R. "Rational Expectations and the Predictive Efficiency of Economic Models." *Journal of Business*, July 1975.

Nerlove, Marc. "Factors Affecting Differences Among Rates of Return on Investments in Individual Common Stocks." *Review of Economics and Statistics*, August 1968.

Newell, Gale E. "Revisions of Reported Quarterly Earnings." *Journal of Business*, July 1971.

Nicholson, S. Francis. "Price Ratios in Relation to Investment Results." *Financial Analysts Journal*, January–February 1968.

Niederhoffer, Victor and Patrick J. Regan. "Earnings Changes, Analysts Forecasts, and Stock Prices." *Financial Analysts Journal*, May–June 1972.

Partee, J. Charles. "The State of Economic Forecasting." *Business Horizons*, October 1976.

Pettit, R. "Dividend Announcements, Security Performance, and Capital Market Efficiency." *Journal of Finance*, December 1972.

"Prospects for the Value Line Composite of Industrial Companies." *Value Line Investment Survey*, July 6, 1979.

Reilly, Frank K. and K. Hatfield. "Investors Experience with New Stock Issues." *Financial Analysts Journal*, September–October 1969.

Reilly, Frank K., G. L. Johnson and R. E. Smith. "Inflation, Inflation Hedges, and Common Stocks." *Financial Analysts Journal*, January–February 1970.

Roberts, Harry V. "Stock Market 'Patterns' and Financial Analysis: Methodological Suggestions." *Journal of Finance*, March 1959.

Robichek, Alexander A. and Marcus C. Bogue. "A Note on the Behavior of Expected Price/Earnings Ratios Over Time." *Journal of Finance*, June 1971.

Rogalski, R. and J. Vinso. "Stock Returns, Money Supply, and the Direction of Causality." *Journal of Finance*, September 1977.

Rozeff, Michael S. "Money and Stock Prices." *Journal of Financial Economics*, September 1974.

Rozeff, Michael S. "The Money Supply and the Stock Market." *Financial Analysts Journal*, September–October 1975.

Scholes, Myron. "The Market for Securities: Substitution Versus Price Pressure and the Effects of Information on Share Prices." *Journal of Business*, April 1972.

Snavely, H. J. "Financial Statement Restatement." *Journal of Accountancy*, October 1976.

Sommers, Albert T. "Diffusion Indexes." In *How Business Economists Forecast*. Ed. William F. Butler and Robert A. Kavesh. Englewood Cliffs, N.J.: Prentice-Hall, 1966.

Suits, Daniel B. "Forecasting and Analysis with an Econometric Model." *American Economic Review*, March 1962.

Treynor, Jack L. "The Trouble With Earnings." *Financial Analysts Journal*, September–October 1972.

Umstead, David A. "Forecasting Stock Market Prices." *Journal of Finance*, May 1977.

Walter, James. "Dividend Policies and Common Stock Prices." *Journal of Finance*, March 1956.

Watts, Ross. "The Information Content of Dividends." *Journal of Business*, April 1973.

Waud, R. N. "Public Interpretation of Discount Rate Changes: Evidence on the 'Announcement Effect.'" *Econometrica*, 1971.

Wendt, Paul F. "Current Growth Stock Valuation Methods." *Financial Analysts Journal*, March–April 1965.

Whitbeck, V. and M. Kisor. "A New Tool in Investment Decision Making." *Financial Analysts Journal*, May–June 1963.

Wippern, Ronald F. "Financial Structure and the Value of the Firm." *Journal of Finance*, December 1966.

Appendix 10-A: Determinants of Earnings Growth: Further Consideration[1]

A firm's rate of earnings growth depends on two basic factors—the firm's rate of return on assets and the percentage of earnings retained by the firm. Symbolically,

$$g = (a)[(s)(1 - t)] \tag{A–1}$$

where

g = Growth rate of earnings

s = Earnings retention ratio

a = Rate of return on assets, or EBIT/Total Assets

t = Corporate tax rate

A third factor which will also influence the growth rate is the firm's use of financial leverage, which can be measured by the ratio of the firm's debt to shareholders' equity (the debt/equity ratio). We will demonstrate the effect of these factors on the earnings growth, first by assuming that there is no external financing, and later by relaxing that assumption.

[1] Some ratios and definitions used here may slightly differ from those used in the chapter. Also, in this discussion, taxes are explicitly taken into account.

Table A–1 **ICA Corporation**

Balance Sheet
Beginning of Year 1

		Total Debt (7% interest cost)	$1,000,000
		Shareholders' Equity (common stock plus retained earnings)	1,000,000
Total Assets	$2,000,000	Total Liabilities and Shareholders' Equity	$2,000,000

Income Statement
for Year 1

Revenues	$3,000,000
Cost and expenses	2,755,000
EBIT	245,000
Less: Interest expense (7% × $1,000,000)	70,000
Net income before taxes	175,000
Less: Income taxes (40%)	70,000
Net income	$ 105,000

No External Financing

Let us begin with an analysis of ICA Corporation. We assume that the firm will not resort to external financing and that it will attempt to maintain its present EBIT/Total Assets ratio.

An income statement and balance sheet of ICA Corporation are presented in Table A–1. Currently, ICA's EBIT/Total Assets ratio is 0.1225 ($245,000/ $2,000,000)[2], and its net income is $105,000.

The ICA Corporation now has three choices. It can (1) pay out the entire earnings as dividends, (2) reinvest all the earnings, or (3) retain part of the earnings and pay out the rest as dividends. If the firm opts for the first choice and decides against external financing, ICA will reach a stationary state and no growth in earnings or assets would be possible in the next year.

The second choice, however, would result in earnings growth. If the entire net income of $105,000 were reinvested in the firm, total assets would increase to $2,105,000. Assuming ICA Corporation maintains the existing EBIT/Total

[2] Analysts generally use either total assets at the end of the year or average assets during the year to measure a company's return on assets. However, to simplify this example, the EBIT/Total Assets ratio is computed using total assets at the beginning of the year.

Assets ratio, net income would increase in the following manner:

Assets: \$2,000,000 + \$105,000	= \$2,105,000
EBIT (.1225 × \$2,105,000)	257,862
Less: Interest expense	70,000
Net income before taxes	187,862
Less: Income taxes (40%)	75,145
Net income	\$112,717

This example reveals that the policy of retaining all earnings would result in an improvement in earnings in the following year.

From this, we can infer that the third choice would also result in improved earnings, although not as much as would result from selecting the second alternative. For instance, if ICA Corporation decided on a 40 percent earnings retention ratio, that would lead to a dividend payment of \$63,000 (60 percent of \$105,000) with \$42,000 (40 percent of \$105,000) to be retained by the firm. The final result of this policy would be as follows:

Assets: \$2,000,000 + \$42,000	= \$2,042,000
EBIT (.1225 × \$2,042,000)	250,145
Less: Interest expense	70,000
Net income before taxes	180,145
Less: Income taxes (40%)	72,058
Net income	\$ 108,087

All three cases may be summarized as follows:

	Net Income Year 1	Net Income Year 2	Percentage Growth in Net Income	Dividend Policy	Earnings Retention Ratio
Case 1	\$105,000	\$105,000	0%	Pay out all earnings as dividends	0%
Case 2	\$105,000	\$112,717	7.35%	Retain all earnings; no dividends	100%
Case 3	\$105,000	\$108,087	2.94%	Pay out part of earnings as dividends	40%

Dividend Policy and Earnings Growth

The earnings growth resulting from any of the three dividend policies can be determined by using Equation A–1:

$$g = (a)[(s)(1 - t)]$$

For the ICA Corporation, if in Year 1 the company distributed its entire earnings as dividends, in Year 2 its growth rate would be nil:

$$\begin{aligned} g &= (.1225)[(0)(1 - .4)] \\ &= 0 \end{aligned}$$

If, however, only 60 percent of the earnings were paid out as dividends and 40 percent were retained, the growth rate in net income would be 2.94 percent:

$$\begin{aligned} g &= (.1225)[(.4)(1 - .4)] \\ &= (.1225) \times (.24) \\ &= .0294 \text{ (or } 2.94\%) \end{aligned}$$

Equation A–1 can be used to estimate the growth rate of net income under any dividend policy, provided of course the rate of return on assets and the tax rate are known. For instance, if the ICA Corporation wished to retain only 25 percent of its earnings for reinvestment, the growth in income would be 1.8 percent:

$$\begin{aligned} g &= (.1225)[(.25)(1 - .4)] \\ &= (.1225) \times (.15) \\ &= .018 \text{ (or } 1.8\%) \end{aligned}$$

External Financing

The growth rate of earnings can be affected by a firm's policy to *maintain* a predetermined debt/equity ratio. This point can be demonstrated only if allowance is made for external financing.

According to the balance sheet in Table A–1, ICA Corporation is a leveraged firm. The company pays 7 percent interest on its debt and its debt/equity ratio is 1.0 ($1,000,000/$1,000,000). Intuitively, one can see that the ICA Corporation must earn a rate of return of more than 7 percent on the borrowed funds in order to make such borrowing worthwhile. In technical jargon, an instance in which the rate of return on borrowed funds is higher than the borrowing cost is referred to as favorable leverage; the reverse instance is known as unfavorable leverage.

In order to measure the effect of leverage policy on the earnings growth of a leveraged firm, Equation A–1 must be modified as follows:

$$g = [a + d(a - c)][s(1 - t)] \tag{A–2}$$

where

$$\begin{aligned} d &= \text{Debt/equity ratio} \\ c &= \text{Interest cost on debt} \end{aligned}$$

Table A–2 **ICA Corporation**

Balance Sheet Beginning of Year 1				Income Statement for Year 1		
		Total Debt		EBIT (.1225 × $2,000,000)		$245,000
		(7% interest cost)	$1,000,000	Less: Interest expense		
		Shareholders' Equity		(7% × $1,000,000)		70,000
		(Common stock plus retained earnings)	1,000,000	Net income before income taxes		$175,000
Total Assets	$2,000,000	Total Liabilities and Shareholders' Equity	$2,000,000	Less: Income taxes (40%)		70,000
				Net income		$105,000
				Earnings reinvested:	40% × $105,000 =	$ 42,000
				Dividends paid:	60% × 105,000 =	63,000
						$105,000

Balance Sheet Beginning of Year 2				Income Statement for Year 2	
		Total Debt		EBIT (.1225 × $2,084,000)	$255,290
		(7% interest cost)	$1,042,000	Less: Interest expense	
		Shareholders' Equity		(7% × $1,042,000)	72,940
		(Common stock plus retained earnings)	1,042,000	Net income before income taxes	$182,350
Total Assets	$2,084,000	Total Liabilities and Shareholders' Equity	$2,084,000	Less: Income taxes (40%)	72,940
				Net income	$109,410

Earnings growth in Year 2:

$$\frac{\$109,410 - \$105,000}{\$105,000} = 4.2\%$$

In the previous example (which assumed no external financing), the earnings growth was calculated as 2.94 percent when the earnings retention rate was 40 percent. However, if the firm wishes to maintain its debt/equity ratio at 1.0, given the 7 percent interest cost on debt, the earnings growth would be 4.2 percent:

$$\begin{aligned} g &= [.1225 + 1.0(.1225 - .07)][.4(1 - .4)] \\ &= (.1225 + .0525)(.24) \\ &= (.175) \times (.24) \\ &= .042 \text{ (or } 4.2\%) \end{aligned}$$

This 4.2 percent earnings growth can also be demonstrated with the following illustration. Table A–2 presents the income statements and balance sheets of ICA Corporation for two successive years. Note that the first year's retained earnings of $42,000 increase the next year's shareholders' equity by $42,000 to $1,042,000. However, in order to maintain a debt/equity ratio of 1.0, ICA must also increase its debt by $42,000. This provides the company with $84,000 ($42,000 + $42,000) of additional assets. As a result of this larger asset base, ICA's net income in the second year increases to $109,410—a 4.2 percent increase over the previous year's net income.

The earnings growth rate of ICA Corporation was larger (4.2 percent) than the growth rate (2.94 percent) expected when external financing was not taken into account because the leverage was favorable—or, more precisely, because the 12.25 percent return on assets, a, was greater than the 7 percent interest cost, c. More generally, Equation A–2 reveals that if *a equals c*, then this equation is reduced to Equation A–1 which is applicable to situations with no external funding:

$$g = [a + d(a - c)][s(1 - t)] \qquad \textbf{(A–2 restated)}$$

if $a = c$, then

$$g = [a + d(0)][s(1 - t)]$$
$$g = (a)[(s)(1 - t)] \qquad \textbf{(A–1 restated)}$$

In contrast, if the return on assets is *less* than the interest cost, the leverage would have a negative effect on the company's earnings growth:

$$g = [a + d(a - c)][s(1 - t)]$$

if $a < c$, then

$$g = [a - d(c - a)][s(1 - t)]$$

The subtraction of the term $d(c - a)$ from the rate of return implies that the growth rate would be lower than if the term were added to the return.

We may conclude, therefore, that the earnings retention ratio, return on assets, and the use of financial leverage are the major determinants of the future earnings growth rate of a company.

Fundamental Analysis: The Valuation Model

Introduction

In Chapter 9 the Common Stock Valuation Model was constructed on the foundation of three variables—the future dividend stream, D_n, the selling price at the end of the holding period, P_N, and the appropriate discount rate, r. Figure 11–1, which reproduces the model, reveals that the future dividend stream and selling price are directly related to a firm's future earnings growth. Therefore, for reasons of practicality, this chapter will be divided into two sections. Section 1 will be devoted exclusively to the various issues relating to the forecasting of a firm's earnings growth. In Section 2, techniques for estimating all three key variables of the Common Stock Valuation Model will be presented. The importance of undertaking national, industry, and company analysis as an integral part of the operation of the model will be emphasized in both sections.

SECTION 1 THE EARNINGS GROWTH

Forecasting Earnings Growth

The Basic Framework

In Chapter 9, the Common Stock Valuation Model was analyzed on the basis of the simplified assumption that the earnings of a firm would grow at a constant rate. In Chapter 10, the key variables affecting a firm's earnings growth

Figure 11–1 **Common Stock Valuation Model**

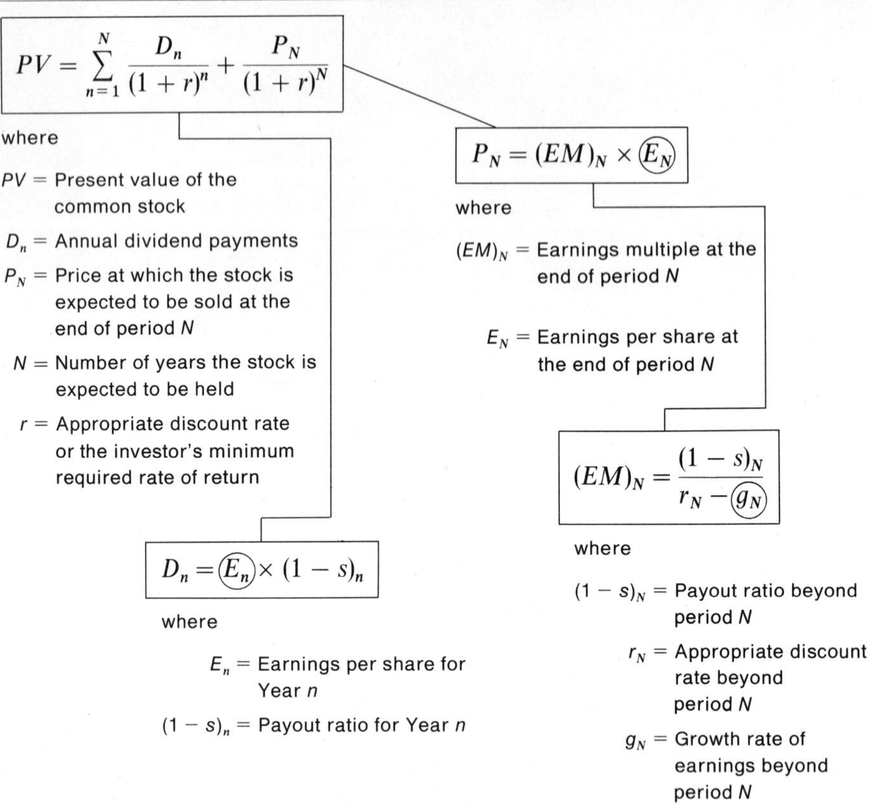

$PV = \sum_{n=1}^{N} \frac{D_n}{(1+r)^n} + \frac{P_N}{(1+r)^N}$
where
PV = Present value of the common stock
D_n = Annual dividend payments
P_N = Price at which the stock is expected to be sold at the end of period N
N = Number of years the stock is expected to be held
r = Appropriate discount rate or the investor's minimum required rate of return
$P_N = (EM)_N \times E_N$
where
$(EM)_N$ = Earnings multiple at the end of period N
E_N = Earnings per share at the end of period N
$(EM)_N = \frac{(1-s)_N}{r_N - g_N}$
where
$(1-s)_N$ = Payout ratio beyond period N
r_N = Appropriate discount rate beyond period N
g_N = Growth rate of earnings beyond period N
$D_n = E_n \times (1-s)_n$
where
E_n = Earnings per share for Year n
$(1-s)_n$ = Payout ratio for Year n

were identified. We are now in a position to discuss other important issues relating to earnings growth.

Application of the Common Stock Valuation Model requires two *earnings growth* forecasts. First, earnings must be forecast for each year of the investor's holding period in order to estimate the future dividend stream. In addition, as discussed in Chapter 9, a long-term average annual growth rate forecast for the years beyond the holding period is needed to estimate the stock's future earnings multiple and selling price.

The forecasting techniques explained in this section (beginning with issues relating to the measurement of a company's past earnings growth rate) are generally used to project earnings for a period of approximately five years. Consequently, they are more appropriate to forecasting earnings for the holding period years. Forecasting the long-term average annual growth rate beyond the holding period will be discussed in Section 2 in connection with estimating the future selling price of the stock.

Measurement of Past Growth Rate

Collection of Earnings Data

Analysts examine the past earnings growth rate for some indication as to what the expected future growth rate may be. The first step toward determining the past growth rate of earnings is to collect the earnings data from published sources. Because the long-term or secular growth rate of past earnings must be determined, it is imperative that data for a fairly long period be collected. Although quarterly earnings data might be preferred in some cases, in most instances annual earnings data are preferable. During certain periods of the year, a firm's sales and earnings might show above or below average activity. For example, although earnings of most department stores are above average immediately preceding Christmas, earnings of summer recreational equipment manufacturers drop in winter. In measuring the past growth of earnings, these seasonal fluctuations should be eliminated from the data. Annual earnings data are already adjusted for seasonal variation and need no further modification.

Trend Analysis of Past Data[1]

Before annual earnings data can be subjected to *trend analysis*, the data should be normalized by eliminating random disturbances. Periodically, random events such as wars, an oil embargo, or an overall social upheaval temporarily affect a firm's earnings. Because these variations in earnings are probably transitory, they should be eliminated by normalizing earnings. A standard normalization procedure is to substitute "averages" for data influenced by random events.

The Growth Rate

Normalized earnings data contain a component known as the *trend*. Because we are dealing with long-term data, this component may be called the secular trend. This trend, which may be linear or nonlinear, is in fact the past growth rate of earnings.

Statistical measures available for determining the past growth rate range from simple to highly complicated procedures. For example, a straight line can be fitted by using the freehand method, by the semiaverage method, and by the well-known least squares method. The last method deserves a closer examination.

In simple models, it is customary to assume that past earnings have grown at a constant rate. Under that assumption, the past growth rate can be cal-

[1] The technique of trend analysis is an established statistical technique, a discussion of which can be found in any standard statistics text.

culated by using the following compound value equation:

$$E_n = E_0(1 + g)^n \quad \textbf{(9–7 restated)}$$

where

E_n = Earnings per share for Year n
E_0 = Earnings per share at the beginning of the time period
g = Growth rate of earnings

Table 11–1 **Calculation of Stanley Works EPS Trend Line**

Exponential Model

The exponential equation form: $Y_c = (a)(b)^X$

The log-linear form: $\log Y_c = \log a + (\log b)X$

Least Squares Method

Calculate constants log *a* and log *b*:

Year	EPS Y	log Y	X	X^2	X(log Y)
1969	$1.12	.0492	1	1	.0492
1970	1.15	.0607	2	4	.1214
1971	1.36	.1335	3	9	.4005
1972	1.71	.2330	4	16	.9320
1973	1.97	.2945	5	25	1.4725
1074	1.71	.2330	6	36	1.3980
1975	1.62	.2095	7	49	1.4665
1976	2.29	.3598	8	64	2.8784
1977	2.75	.4393	9	81	3.9537
1978	3.50	.5441	10	100	5.4410
	Σ = $19.18	2.5566	55	385	18.1132

$$\log b = \frac{(N)\sum X(\log Y) - (\sum \log Y)(\sum X)}{(N)\sum X^2 - (\sum X)^2} = \frac{(10)(18.1132) - (2.5566)(55)}{(10)(385) - (55)^2}$$

$$= .049114$$

$$\log a = \frac{\sum \log Y}{N} - (b)\left[\frac{\sum X}{N}\right] = \frac{2.5566}{10} - (.049114)\left[\frac{55}{10}\right]$$

$$= -.014467$$

Log-linear trend: $\log Y_c = -.014467 + (.049114)X$

*Expressed in the exponential form:**

$$Y_c = (.9673)(1.1197)^X$$

* Using logs in base 10:

$10^{-.014467} = .9673$

$10^{.049114} = 1.1197$

Assuming $E_n = Y_c$; $E_0 = a$; $(1 + g) = b$; and $n = X$, Equation 9–7 can be rewritten as:

$$Y_c = ab^X$$

Using the *least squares method*, an exponential trend line can be estimated to describe the past data. However, it is difficult to estimate the constants a and b in this *exponential form*. Therefore, we take the logarithm of both sides of the equation to obtain the *log-linear form*:

$$\log Y_c = \log a + (\log b)X$$

Calculations in Table 11–1 show how a trend line is computed for the 1969–78 EPS of Stanley Works. The trend line is first calculated by computing the values of the constants $\log a$ and $\log b$; thereafter, the above equation is reexpressed in the original form:

$$Y_c = ab^X$$

Note that in this equation, b is the underlying growth factor $(1 + g)$ in the EPS (earnings per share) of Stanley Works. The actual EPS for the company and the trend line are graphed in Figure 11–2.

Earnings Growth Rate: Naive Forecasting

Expected Holding Period

Forecasting of the earnings growth rate is intimately related to the issue of an investor's holding period[2]. It is generally assumed that forecasting earnings on a year-to-year basis for more than five years or so is all but impossible. Consequently, as a practical matter, investors with holding periods of over five years generally make the simplified assumption that the earnings growth rate forecast for five years would continue until the end of the holding period. Of course, more conservative investors with longer holding periods may wish to make a downward adjustment to the projected five-year earnings growth rate on the grounds that uncertainty—or risk—dramatically increases as one ventures into the distant future. As a practical matter, however, this objective is accomplished by leaving the predicted earnings unchanged and making an upward adjustment in the appropriate discount rate.

[2] The "holding period issue" refers to the process involved in the determination of an investor's planning horizon. The holding period return must account for both the uncertainty surrounding the dividend payments during the holding period and the price expected to be received at the end of the holding period. Clearly, total holding period returns would probably reflect changes in the expected holding period. Ideally, then, the expected holding period return should be determined by calculating the weighted average of possible holding period returns, using the probabilities of obtaining these returns as weights. The following discussion does not address the holding period issue. For simplicity, in this and all future discussions, the holding period is assumed as given.

Figure 11–2 **The Stanley Works—EPS Trend**

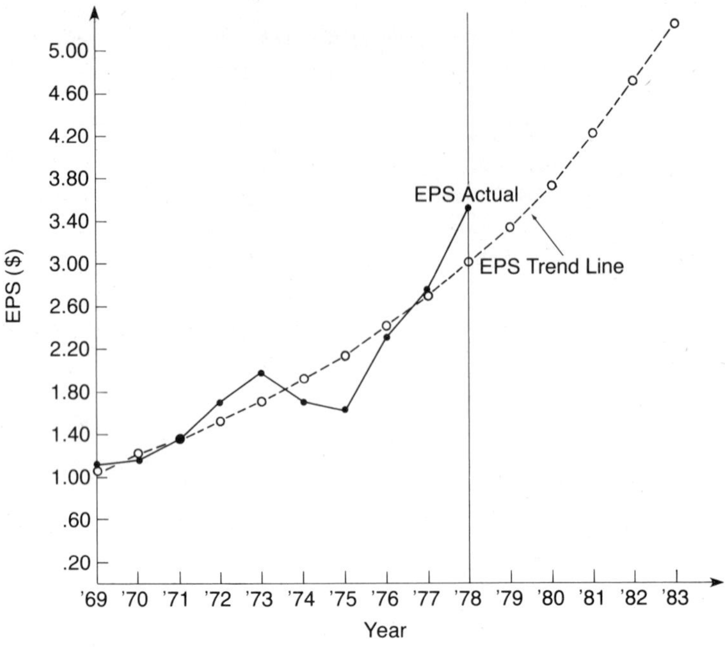

Year	X	EPS per trend: $Y_c = (.9673)(1.1197)^X$	Actual EPS
1969	1	$1.08	$1.12
1970	2	1.21	1.15
1971	3	1.36	1.36
1972	4	1.52	1.71
1973	5	1.70	1.97
1974	6	1.91	1.71
1975	7	2.13	1.62
1976	8	2.39	2.29
1977	9	2.68	2.75
1978	10	3.00	3.50

NOTE: The trend line equation will produce a straight line when the points are plotted on a semilogarithmic chart.

Naive Forecasting

Various techniques are used to forecast earnings growth for periods covering up to five years. In naive models, it is assumed that the past trend will continue in the future. Based on that assumption, future earnings can be forecast merely by extending the least squares trend line previously discussed. Consider, for instance, the example with Stanley Works. From Table 11–1, the trend in EPS was estimated using the exponential equation:

$$Y_c = ab^X$$
$$= (.9673)(1.1197)^X$$

By merely extending the trend line, the earnings per share for the 1979–83 period can be forecast as follows:

Year	Stanley EPS Forecast (per trend)
1979	$3.36
1980	3.76
1981	4.21
1982	4.71
1983	5.28

Note that EPS is forecast to grow continually at the estimated 11.97 percent annual rate.[3]

Problems with Naive Forecasting

Naive forecasting of earnings growth is simple to use because this method assumes that the future is an extension of the past. Frequently, however, the past is not a good predictor of the future, and a technique must be developed for forecasting a *modified* growth rate. Before discussing the development of such a technique, let us briefly review some of the problems associated with using past growth rate to predict the future earnings growth rate.

The technique of naive forecasting is valid under two key assumptions. First, it is assumed that the factors determining the past earnings growth rate will not materially change in the future; that is, the future national, industry, and company conditions will be similar to those prevailing in the past. This simplistic assumption is usually not valid. The second assumption is that the reported earnings data *truly* reflect the earning power of the firm. This, too, may not always be a valid assumption, as will become clear from the following discussion.

The methods used by companies to derive their EPS vary widely. Management has a good deal of latitude in estimating the useful life of depreciable assets, in timing asset write-offs, and in selecting an inventory accounting method. Note, for instance, the effects of applying various generally accepted accounting principles given in Table 11–2. Company Y could state earnings

[3] In this example, the underlying growth factor in the exponential form, b, equals $(1 + g)$ or 1.1197. Therefore, the growth rate of earnings, g, equals 11.97 percent.

Table 11–2 **Effect of Applying Alternative Generally Accepted Accounting Principles**

	Company X as Reported	Company Y Reported Higher Income as a Result of: FIFO Pricing of Inventory Alternative 1	Use of Straight-Line Depreciation Alternative 2	Investment Credit Flow-through Alternative 3	Deferred Research Costs Alternative 4	Minimum Pension Funding Alternative 5	Stock Options in Lieu of Cash Bonuses Alternative 6	Company Y as Reported
Sales in units	100,000 units							100,000 units
Unit sale price	$ 100							$ 100
Sales in dollars	$10,000,000							$10,000,000
Costs and expenses—								
Cost of goods sold	$ 6,000,000							$ 6,000,000
Selling and administrative expenses	1,500,000							1,500,000
LIFO inventory reserve	400,000	(400,000)						—
Depreciation	400,000		(100,000)					300,000
Investment credit	(15,000)			(135,000)				(150,000)
Research and development costs	100,000				(80,000)			20,000
Pension costs	200,000					(100,000)		100,000
Officers' compensation:								
Base salaries	200,000							200,000
Bonuses	200,000						(200,000)	—
Total Costs and Expenses	$ 8,985,000	$(400,000)	$(100,000)	$(135,000)	$(80,000)	$(100,000)	$(200,000)	$ 7,970,000
Income before income taxes	$ 1,015,000	$ 400,000	$ 100,000	$ 135,000	$ 80,000	$ 100,000	$ 200,000	$ 2,030,000
Income taxes	487,000	192,000	48,000	65,000	38,000	48,000	96,000	974,000
Net income as reported	$ 528,000	$ 208,000	$ 52,000	$ 70,000	$ 42,000	$ 52,000	$ 104,000	$ 1,056,000
Earnings per share on 600,000 shares	$ 0.88	$0.35	$0.09	$0.11	$0.07	$0.09	$0.17	$ 1.76
Market value at:								
10 times earnings	$ 8.80	$3.50	$0.90	$1.10	$0.70	$0.90	$1.70	$17.60
15 times earnings	13.20	5.25	1.35	1.65	1.05	1.35	2.55	26.40
20 times earnings	17.60	7.00	1.80	2.20	1.40	1.80	3.40	35.20
25 times earnings	22.00	8.75	2.25	2.75	1.75	2.25	4.25	44.00

( ) Denotes deduction.

Alternative 1: Company X prices its ending inventories on the LIFO (last-in, first-out) method. Company Y prices its ending inventories on the FIFO (first-in, first-out) method. **Alternative 2**: Company X records accelerated depreciation for both book and tax purposes. Company Y uses straight-line depreciation for book purposes and accelerated depreciation for tax purposes with appropriate deferred income tax accounting. **Alternative 3**: Company X amortizes the investment credit over the lives of the related property. Company Y takes the entire investment credit into income in the year the related property is purchased. **Alternative 4**: Company X expenses all research and development costs as incurred. Company Y defers its research and development costs, and amortizes the deferred amount over a five-year period. **Alternative 5**: Company X provides for pension costs on the maximum permitted basis including amortization of past-service costs over a ten-year period. Company Y provides for pension costs on a minimum basis with past-service cost being amortized over a forty-year period. **Alternative 6**: Company X pays its officers a cash bonus. Company Y grants its officers stock options in lieu of cash bonuses.

SOURCE: Alfred P. Haake, Jr., "Fundamental Research," in *The Stock Market Handbook*, ed. Frank Zarb and Gabriel T. Kerekes (Homewood, Ill.: Dow Jones-Irwin, 1970), pp. 463–64.

as low as $0.88 or as high as $1.76 from the same financial data, remaining well within the legal and ethical framework for generally accepted accounting principles.[4]

Another potential problem with using past earnings data is that management can successfully manipulate earnings so the EPS shows a consistent pattern of growth when earnings growth did not take place. Management can do this by merely replacing equity with debt financing, thereby reducing the number of outstanding shares. Consider, for example, the following data:

Year	Earnings	Shares Outstanding	EPS	Growth in EPS
1	$1,000,000	1,000,000	$1.00	
2	$800,000	700,000	$1.14	+14%

Even though the earnings in Year 2 were 20 percent below the previous year's level, EPS grew by 14 percent solely because of a reduction in the number of outstanding shares. This was accomplished by raising debt capital and using it to purchase outstanding stock in the open market.

The limitations of the use of past earnings data without modification are articulated in the following passage:

> *The professional investor knows that reported earnings numbers are often the product of deliberate choices between various accounting treatments and business options. In order to assess true earning power, the analyst must make some determination of the quality of earnings.*
>
> *The quality of a reported earnings figure can be lowered if management recognizes revenues or expenditures either prematurely or belatedly, or chooses a liberal accounting treatment over a more conservative one. The analyst should be particularly wary of changes in accounting policy.*[5]

The previous discussion suggested that in forecasting earnings growth an investor should take into account both the quality of reported earnings as well as possible changes in the factors that affect earnings growth. However, the discussion also leads to the inevitable conclusion that investors should rely heavily on past earnings data for forecasting future growth. This conclusion of course is based on the assumption that the relationship between the past and future earnings is both direct and close. Unfortunately, studies have shown that this may not always be a valid assumption.

[4] Some of the accounting practices used to construct Table 11–2 may have subsequently changed. However, this would not change the fact that the management can manipulate reported earnings.

[5] Leopold A. Bernstein and Joel G. Siegel, "The Concept of Earnings Quality," *Financial Analysts Journal*, July–August 1979, p. 72.

Figure 11–3 **Percent Change in EPS**

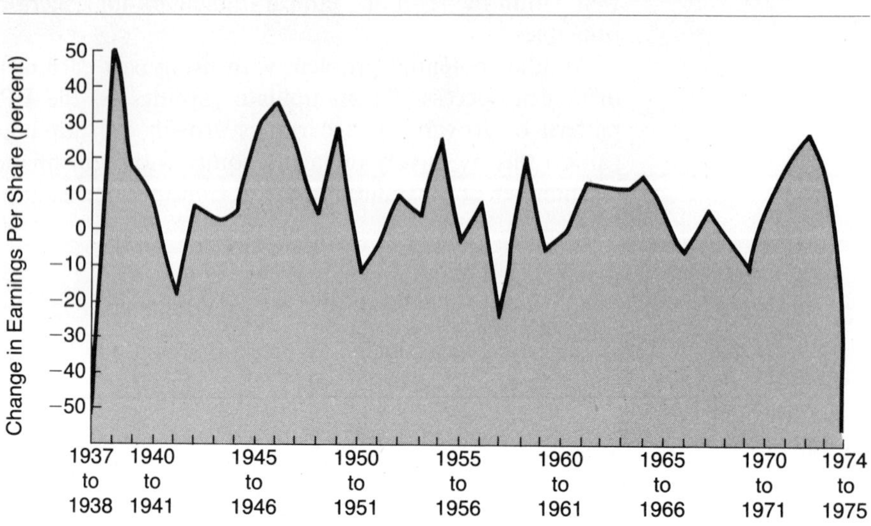

> *Financial analysts have routinely studied historical changes in earnings in order to guide them in formulating views about earnings in future years. It was with great shock, therefore, that I.M.D. Little's original work, "Higgledy Piggledy Growth,"[6] was received in both the academic and national communities. Little reported on his study of earnings for British firms and found that changes in earnings, like prices, followed a random walk. This meant that successive changes in earnings per share were statistically independent and that the study of the sequence of historical changes in earnings per share was useless as an aid to predicting future changes. In other terms, historical rates of growth in earnings provide no clue to future rates of growth.*[7]

An investor exposed to this passage might conclude that the use of reported earnings data for predicting future earnings growth is worthless because future corporate earnings are unrelated to past experience; that is, they follow a random walk.[8] Figure 11–3, recording the short-term percentage changes in EPS

[6] Ian M. D. Little, "Higgledy Piggledy Growth," *Institute of Statistics*, Vol. 24, No. 4, November 1962.

[7] J. Lorie and M. Hamilton, *The Stock Market: Theories and Evidence.* (Homewood, Ill.: Richard D. Irwin, 1973), p. 158. © 1973 by Richard D. Irwin, Inc.

[8] This matter is further complicated by the argument that EPS do not count. In a study, Stern writes: "That EPS is easy to understand and simple to calculate is an insufficient excuse for employing it as an analytical device. An EPS criterion for corporate policy can result in costly decisions that severely misallocate a company's resources and shortchange the firm's common shareholders. Sophisticated investors, who dominate the market, focus their attention on FCF [Free Cash Flow]. EPS doesn't count." See Joel M. Stern, "Earnings Per Share Don't Count," *Financial Analysts Journal*, July–August 1974, p. 15.

Table 11–3 **Length and Number of Runs of Better-than-Average and Worse-than-Average Earnings Growth, 610 Firms, 1950–1964**

Length of Run	Actual Number of Runs of Good Years	Actual Number of Runs of Bad Years	Number of Runs of Good or Bad Years Expected if the Odds Each Year Were 50-50, Regardless of Past Performance
1	1,152	1,102	1,068
2	562	590	534
3	266	300	267
4	114	120	133
5	55	63	67
6	24	20	33
7	23	12	17
8	5	6	8
9	3	3	4
10	6	0	2
11	2	0	1
12	1	0	1
13	0	0	0
14	0	1	0

SOURCE: Reprinted from *An Introduction to Risk and Return from Common Stocks* by Richard Brealey by permission of the MIT Press, Cambridge, Massachusetts. Copyright © 1969.

of Dow Jones Industrial companies, underscores the short-term instability of earnings, suggesting that fluctuations in earnings follow a random walk.[9]

Several studies have tested the hypothesis that past earnings are a good predictor of future growth in earnings. Table 11–3 presents the results of one such study. This study[10] examined the earnings of 610 industrial companies during the period 1950 through 1964, and interpreted each year's earnings as follows. Each year, the percentage change in earnings over the previous year was classified as "good" if the change was in the top half of all recorded changes. Similarly, all percentage changes in earnings that were included in the bottom half were recorded as "bad." In columns 2 and 3 of the table, an actual number of runs of good and bad years are recorded, while in column 4 the unbiased estimates of good or bad years not based on the past performance are recorded. This table demonstrates that past earnings are *not* a good predictor of future earnings; that is, investors may not assume that companies with an impressive earnings growth in the past will necessarily continue their superior perfor-

[9] This would also suggest that fluctuations in earnings are consistent with the Random Walk Hypothesis, which is characterized as similar to the weak form of the Efficient Market Hypothesis that was discussed in Chapter 5 (pp. 150–51). A detailed discussion of the Random Walk Hypothesis and issues relating to market efficiency is in Chapter 14.

[10] Richard Brealey, *An Introduction to Risk and Return from Common Stocks* (Cambridge, Mass.: MIT Press, 1969).

mance in the future. Other studies, covering longer periods and using different companies have reached similar conclusions.[11]

Interestingly, the Brealey study went further than merely claiming that past earnings are not a good predictor of future earnings. The study examined the relationship between changes in earnings of 217 corporations between 1948 and 1966 and changes in economy-wide earnings represented by the S&P 425 Stock Index. Earnings changes of these corporations were also compared with changes in industry earnings. The study revealed that 21 percent of variations in the earnings of a typical corporation could be attributed to changes in the economy-wide earnings another 21 percent to and those in the earnings of all corporations belonging to that industry.

Implicit in the foregoing discussion is the suggestion that, because factors influencing the past growth rate of earnings often change significantly, a modified growth rate of future expected earnings should be calculated. Consequently, we will now focus on the technique for *modifying* the past growth rate; this modification will permit a more realistic forecast of earnings growth.

Forecasting Modified Growth Rate: Basic Technique

Modifying the past growth rate based on the outlook for national economic, industry, and company conditions is more realistic than the naive technique. This technique assumes that conditions relating to the economy, the industry, and the company influence one or more of the factors that affect the earnings growth. More specifically, it assumes that the earnings growth of a company is influenced by two key variables—the earnings retention ratio and the return on equity (ROE). The ROE, in turn, is a function of several variables, such as taxes and interest expense, the leverage factor, the turnover ratio, and the EBIT/Sales ratio. As will be observed shortly, changes in national, industry, or company conditions invariably affect one or more of these variables. Consequently, a study of these conditions not only establishes a connection between these conditions and the financial variables but provides the basis for modifying the naive forecast of the future earnings growth rate. It should be remembered, however, that the purpose of such a study is to indicate the *direction* and *general magnitude of change* rather than to calculate the exact percentage by which the naive forecast of the growth rate should be changed.

General Economic Conditions

In Chapter 10, the relationship between general economic conditions and a firm's performance was explored in detail. Only the highlights of that discussion will be summarized here. With the general exception of companies in growth and defensive industries which have a tendency to buck the trend,

[11] See, for instance, John Lintner and Robert Glauber, "Higgledy Piggledy Growth in America," in *Modern Developments in Investment Management*, ed. James Lorie and Richard Brealey (New York: Praeger 1972).

most companies are directly influenced by changes in general economic conditions. During a recession, sales of a typical company drop—sometimes significantly—thereby adversely affecting its performance and financial condition, which is in turn reflected in several key financial ratios. For example, if a recession is predicted, it would be safe to assume that the firm's sales would decline during the recessionary period. A drop in sales would probably lower production efficiency, asset turnover, and profitability, which would inevitably result in a lower EPS. The performance of an auto company like GM provides an excellent example of how variations in the general economic outlook can influence the EPS forecast.

Industry Conditions

Changes in industry conditions also have a significant impact on the EPS. For example, as a successful firm moves from the pioneering stage to the stabilization stage of an industrial life cycle, its high rate of growth reaches a plateau and then slows down, eventually approaching an average rate of 5 percent or less. Consider, for instance, firms in the computer industry. In the 1960s and 1970s, when the computer industry was presumably in a pioneering stage, earnings of many computer firms like IBM and Burroughs Corporation recorded an impressive growth. However, after the industry reaches the stabilization stage, the high growth rates of the related firms will probably slow down. Forecasting earnings growth rates for firms expected to move from the pioneering to the stabilization stage, therefore, should be done conservatively.

Another example of a change in industry conditions is provided by Resorts International, Inc. The company was the sole owner and operator of a casino–hotel in Atlantic City. Because of massive expansion and skillful promotional activities, Resorts' EPS, which fluctuated between 1–25 cents during the 1964–77 period, jumped to $4.57 in 1978 and to around $6.75 in 1979. However, because of increased competition from other firms entering the casino business in Atlantic City, the nature of the business, and legal complexities, slower earnings growth could be predicted beyond 1979.

As expected, changes in industry conditions affect the key financial ratios and EPS growth. For example, in the case of Resorts International, increased competition could lower the net income margin and turnover, which would have a negative impact on the ROE and EPS growth. Consequently, as in the case of general economic conditions, any anticipated change in the industrial life cycle, labor conditions, government regulations, and so on, which would affect the various key financial ratios, should provide a basis for modifying the naive forecast of the future earnings growth rate.

Company Factors

Of the three levels of influence on the earnings growth, the one associated with company factors assumes special importance. Consequently, these factors will be discussed in greater detail. Here again, it is worth repeating that these factors affect one or more of the key financial ratios and EPS growth.

Production and Marketing Methods One of the most important company factors which could influence the future earnings growth relates to an improvement in production and marketing methods. Good production methods may include an assessment of geographical location, the process by which the product is manufactured, and the steps being taken to improve the product. Often, this is where intelligent and active management can truly contribute to a company's future.

An interesting example of the institution of a new production method can be found in Goodyear's plan to revolutionize its production capability by introducing Goodyear-designed, highly automated machinery. Until 1978, because of a lack of complete automation, labor had accounted for one-third of a tire's cost. The automation plan would not only reduce labor costs, but would improve product uniformity as well.

Many successful corporations develop a well-balanced, diversified line of products. This often contributes not only to a sustainable growth, but to stability in earnings, because a slack in the sales of one product is often balanced by an increase in sales of another product. In addition, in order to maintain their market leadership, successful corporations devote considerable attention to creating and developing various products and establishing patents and goodwill.

Development of a well-balanced line of products is only a means to an end. A successful marketing strategy must be developed to maintain an effective earnings growth. An example of an effective marketing strategy can be found in the cosmetic industry. Avon Products has been able to successfully market its numerous products through its "Avon lady" sales force. Another company, McDonald's Corporation, has achieved superior performance in the fast-food industry by providing excellent service to customers and through a highly effective advertising campaign.

New Strategies To improve future earnings many companies adopt new and innovative strategies. These strategies can take many forms. For example, after being a slow-moving, nickel and dime store chain for many years, Kresge was transformed into the famous K-Mart discount stores. The company's sales and earnings grew dramatically thereafter.

The strategy of merger and acquisition is another means of diversifying and revitalizing a company. Some companies diversify by merging with firms that produce different products; others grow stronger by merging with companies that produce similar products. An example of the former type can be found in Philip Morris, a cigarette manufacturing company. After many years of EPS growth exceeding 20 percent, the company realized that past sales growth could probably not be sustained due to widespread adverse publicity against the product. Consequently, the company acquired Miller Brewing in 1969 and Seven-Up in the late 1970s, thereby diversifying its business and building a base for a healthy growth in the future. Heileman Brewing provides an interesting example of the second type of merger. Originally the company was an insignificant regional brewer operating in Wisconsin and a few nearby states. However, after making several acquisitions of other regional breweries, Heileman's business currently stretches from coast to coast. In 1979, Heileman's ROE had reached over 23 percent, the highest in the brewing industry, with a high EPS growth of over 20 percent. Acquisitions of this type, when executed and managed properly, can improve the production and operating efficiency as well as the turnover ratio, thereby positively affecting ROA, ROE, and EPS growth.

Accounting Practice Certain accounting practices can significantly affect the quality of reported earnings, which would have an impact on future earnings. The accounting policies of Franklin Mint Corporation provide an example.

Franklin Mint is probably the largest private mint in the world. Its business is to create and produce limited edition collectors' items, such as commemorative medals, art medals, collectors' plates, miniature ingots, metallic jewelry, and coin of the realm for foreign governments. In 1976, Franklin Mint completed its tenth successive year of increased sales and earnings. Sales had risen from $2.7 million in 1967 to $306.9 million in 1976; EPS climbed from $0.34 in 1970 to $2.92 in 1976—an annual growth rate of almost 40 percent.

Although an investor analyzing Franklin Mint in 1976 would have been impressed by its consistently high rate of growth, he or she would have also discovered an accounting practice that would probably have a negative impact on future earnings.[12]

Somewhat unconventionally but legally, the company decided to defer its promotional expenses and charge them off in *future* years, a practice which could lead to a dramatic decline in the future profit margin. In fact, a closer examination of the financial statement revealed that in two quarters of 1976 the increase in deferred promotional expenses exceeded the increase in earnings.[13] Clearly, in the case of Franklin Mint, in 1976 an uncritical projection of the past earnings growth rate into the future would have been unwarranted.

The accounting policy regarding deferred expenses is only one item an investor should examine when evaluating the earnings quality of a company. A list of some of the other important accounting alternatives a company could choose to either minimize or telescope reported earnings is outlined in Table 11–2. Generally speaking, the more conservative a company's reporting methods, the higher will be the quality of earnings, and the less the likelihood that the company will borrow from future earnings to increase its current reported profits.

Quality of Management Good management is the backbone of success of every company. A corporation must know how to develop its marketing and financial plans, organize its production, and develop good public relations strategy. Good management is necessary to accomplish all of these requirements.

An effective management is responsible for developing and instituting criteria for operating efficiency and production efficiency. The effectiveness of management is assessed through the evaluation of past performance, creativity, aggres-

[12] For details, see "The Costly Troubles at Franklin Mint," *Business Week*, May 30, 1977, pp. 28–29.

[13] Franklin Mint's EPS dropped sharply from $2.92 in 1976 to only $0.85 in 1977. The EPS in the following year increased to $1.40; however, it was still far below the 1976 level.

siveness, and certain character impressions obtained in personal interviews with management. Indications of good management, which scrutinizing investors seek, include the soundness of the corporate strategy, the efficiency of plant operations, labor relations, control of personnel, and corporate structuring policy.

A good measure of management quality is the deep management commitment to the results of corporate endeavors. A good example of this commitment can be found in Lee Iacocca's move from Ford to Chrysler against the backdrop of Chrysler's serious financial problems. Iacocca reportedly made a firm commitment to "turn the company around."

Advanced Forecasting Technique

The Basic Framework

Clearly, a naive forecast of earnings growth should be duly modified by analyzing the impact of national, industry, and company conditions on such variables as leverage, turnover, net income margin, and production and operating efficiency. However, a precise quantitative forecast of these variables is difficult to make. Such a forecast requires a careful analysis of various types of developments both within the industry and nationally, changes in production methods and operations, new financial strategies, and a host of other related factors. Therefore, in the following section, a case study of General Motors will be presented in a *descriptive* mode, primarily to demonstrate the complex nature of the task on hand. In this study, projected financial statements will be constructed and the influence of both macro and micro variables on earnings growth will be evaluated.

Most investors undertaking a fundamental analysis of a company do so in order to make a *rough* modification of the earnings growth trend. Only the professionals and sophisticated investors with quantitative skills and resources and great knowledge of the market, the industry, and the company have the courage to venture into the esoteric world in which earnings are forecast with precision.

General Motors: A Case Study[14]

An in-depth analysis of General Motors should appropriately begin with an examination of the firm's income statement for the preceding dozen or more years. For example, Table 11–4 presents an analyst's worksheet with income statement data from 1962 to 1974 that was used to make estimates from 1975 through 1978–80. The worksheet contains such important ratios as operating profit margin, pretax profit margin, and income tax rate. This information was supplemented by a series of charts, presented in Figure 11–4, which graphically

[14] This analysis is based upon Arnold Bernhard, *Investing in Common Stocks* (New York: The Value Line Investment Survey, 1975), pp. 41–43.

Table 11-4

Analyst's Income Statement Worksheet (for General Motors—reduced in size)

	1962	1963	1964	1965	1966	1967	1968	1969	1970	1971	1972	1973	1974	1975	1976	1977	1978	1978-80
Sales	14640.2	16494.8	16997.0	20734.0	20208.5	20026.3	22755.4	24295.1	18752.4	28263.9	30435.2	35798.3	31549.6	35500	43000			55000
Profit Margin	21.7%	22.4%	21.3%	21.6%	18.7%	18.0%	18.1%	16.7%	7.9%	16.3%	16.3%	14.4%	7.6%	7.0%	8.8%			11.1%
Cost of Sales	10645.1	11913.7	12454.9	15250.2	15404.1	15401.0	17492.2	18998.0	16273.0	22538.4	24312.5	29195.1	27783.0					
Selling, Gen. Exp.	718.6	770.5	810.8	871.2	919.9	905.6	1028.0	1120.1	1007.6	1106.8	1162.5	1440.9	1363.9					
Empl. Bonus	105.0	112.0	116.0	130.0	114.0	107.0	111.0	110.0	—	90.0	101.4	112.8	5.9					
Operating Profit	3171.6	3698.6	3615.3	4482.5	3770.5	3613.5	4123.7	4066.8	1472.5	4618.7	4960.2	5162.3	2402.7	2474	3805			6119
Depreciation	444.6	475.2	494.8	556.7	654.1	712.6	729.1	765.8	821.5	873.1	912.4	902.9	846.6	935	965			1150
Other Inc., less ded.	60.1	84.4	119.6	112.2 dr	11.6	56.3	78.3	102.4	57.1	(36.4)	71.0	150.7	6.7					
Eq. Earns. Unc. Subs	50.6	47.5	45.0	54.9	50.3	57.0	51.9	50.6	70.4	100.6	103.7	103.0	114.4					
Interest	4.7	1.5	1.5	1.3	.7	.8												
Pretax Income	2934.5	3353.9	3283.7	4091.6	3270.8	3013.4	3524.8	3454.0	778.5	3719.7	4222.6	4513.1	1677.2	1689	3004			5060
%	20.0%	20.3%	19.3%	19.7%	16.2%	15.0%	15.5%	14.2%	4.2%	13.2%	13.9%	12.6%	5.3%	4.8%	7.0%			9.2%
Income Taxes	1475.4	1762.1	1548.9	1966.0	1477.4	1386.1	1792.9	1743.3	169.4	1784.1	2059.8	2115.0	727.1					
%	50.3%	52.5%	47.2%	48.0%	45.2%	46.5%	50.9%	50.5%	21.8%	48.0%	48.8%	46.9%	43.4%	44%	47%			47%
Net Income	1459.1	1591.8	1734.8	2125.6	1793.4	1627.3	1731.9	1710.7	609.1	1935.6	2162.8	2398.1	950.1	946	1592			2683
Preferred Dividend	12.9	12.9	12.9	12.9	12.9	12.9	12.9	12.9	12.9	12.9	12.9	12.9	12.9	13	13			13
Available/Common	1446.1	1578.9	1721.9	2112.7	1780.5	1614.4	1719.0	1697.8	596.2	1922.8	2149.9	2382.2	937.1	933	1579			2670
Common Dividends	850.5	1135.8	1266.3	1496.8	1298.1	1084.4	1227.4	1227.4	971.0	972.4	1273.1	1501.3	973.3	689	689			1660
Number of Shares	283,968,396	284,652,505	285,184,960	285,577,691	285,678,101	285,703,248	285,794,937	285,762,541	286,037,134	286,225,1[illegible]	286,342,18[illegible]	285,730,153	286,992,876	287,000,000	287,500,000			289,000,000
Earnings Per Share	5.09	5.55	6.04	7.40	6.23	5.65	6.02	5.94	2.08	6.72	7.52	8.35	3.27	3.25	5.50			9.25
Dividends Per Share	3.00	4.00	4.45	5.25	4.55	3.80	4.30	4.30	3.40	3.40	4.45	5.25	3.40	2.40	2.40			5.50
Cash Earn'gs Per Sh.				9.35	8.52	8.14	8.61	8.67	4.95	9.77	10.71	11.51	6.23	6.50	8.85			13.20
Cash Earnings	1903.7	2067.0	2229.5	2682.3	2447.5	2339.9	2461.0	2476.5	1430.6	2808.8	3075.2	3301.0	1796.6	1881	2557	3000	3450	3833
Work.Cap'l-1st of Yr.	3058.6	3528.0	3727.4	3651.0	3684.9	3606.0	4006.4	4230.2	4352.0	3010.5	45304	5564.8	6196.9	5542	5921	6526	7201	8251
Sale of Properties	17.5	29.8	31.8	33.5	50.7	46.4	42.1	42.7	32.9	57.4	57.2	67.8	67.0					
New Financing	29.1	23.0	DC 11.7 DEF 17.8	36.2 17.2	31.25 5.5	66.4	3.7	36.5	0.7	336.8	176.0	0	120.1	600			500	500
Other	70.4	75.8	4.5	89.4 dr	4.7	21.6		4.8	-95.3	92.5	-98.4	-149.3	106.4					
Tooling Amort.	526.9	605.4	591.3	744.7	860.8	839.6	853.1	891.7	677.3	917.6	874.2	1081.0	858.4					
Total Funds IN	5606.2	6329.0	6614.0	7244.3	7116.8	6919.9	7366.3	7682.4	3398.2	7223.6	8614.6	9865.3	9145.4					
Total Dividends Paid	863.4	1148.7	1279.2	1509.7	1311.0	1097.3	1240.3	1240.4	984.0	985.4	1286.0	1514.2	986.3	702	702	988	1313	1673
Plant & Equipment	645.1	647.2	929.6	1322.0	1188.1	912.6	860.2	1043.8	1134.2	1013.0	940.0	1163.4	1458.5	1300	1400	1400	1600	1600
Other Investment	18.4	130.1	cr. 37.9	cr. 28.6	cr. 12.7	17.5	109.0	180.2	86.9	cr. 9.2	cr. 74.7	158.4	13.6					
Capital Retired	21.1	69.8	40.2	26.5	16.3	4.9	60.5	3.0	34.0	0	0	34.4	0					
Other												-143.0	49.5					
Tooling Exp.	530.2	591.9	751.9	729.8	890.8	881.3	865.8	863.1	1148.6	630.7	898.5	941.0	1095.6					
Total Funds OUT	2078.2	2601.6	2963.0	3559.4	3510.8	2913.5	3135.8	3330.5	3387.7	2693.2	3049.8	3688.4	3603.5					
Work Cap'l-Year end	3528.0	3727.4	3651.0	3684.9	3606.0	4006.4	4230.2	4352.0	3010.5	4530.4	5564.8	6196.9	5541.9	5921	6526	7201	8251	9224
Net Worth																		
Payout Ratio	45.4%	55.6%	57.4%	56.3%	53.6%	46.9%	50.4%	50.0%	68.8%	35.1%	41.8%	45.9%	54.9%	37.3%	27.5%			43.6%
Work. Cap'l Sales	24.1%	22.6%	21.5%	17.8%	17.8%	20.0%	18.6%	17.9%	16.1%	16.0%	18.3%	17.3%	17.6%	16.7%	15.2%			16.8%

SOURCE: Arnold Bernhard, *Investing in Common Stocks* (New York: The Value Line Investment Survey, 1975), p. 41.

Figure 11–4

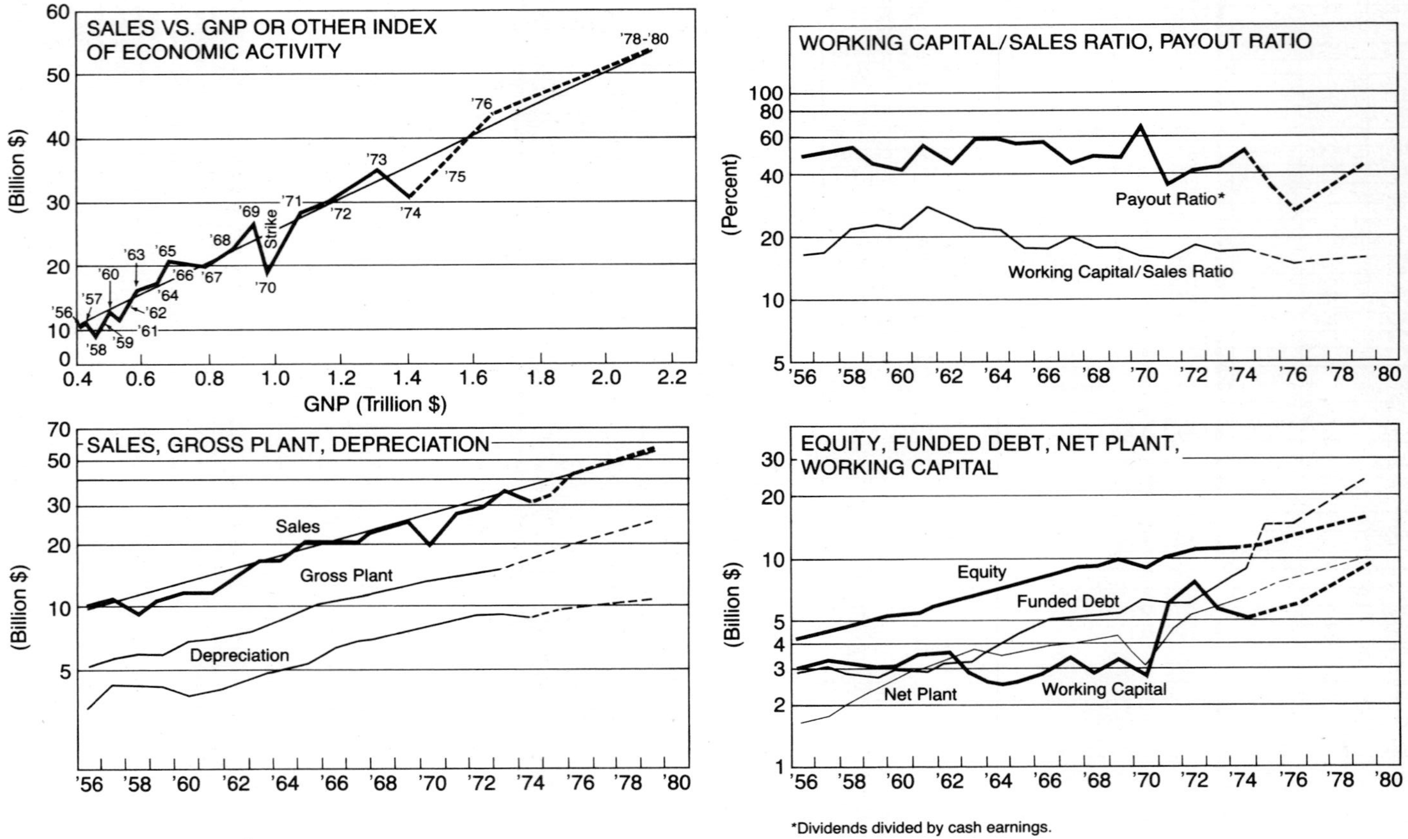
SALES VS. GNP OR OTHER INDEX OF ECONOMIC ACTIVITY
(Billion $)
GNP (Trillion $)
Strike
'78-'80
WORKING CAPITAL/SALES RATIO, PAYOUT RATIO
(Percent)
Payout Ratio*
Working Capital/Sales Ratio
SALES, GROSS PLANT, DEPRECIATION
Sales
Gross Plant
Depreciation
EQUITY, FUNDED DEBT, NET PLANT, WORKING CAPITAL
Equity
Funded Debt
Net Plant
Working Capital

*Dividends divided by cash earnings.

SOURCE: Arnold Bernhard, *Investing in Common Stocks* (New York: The Value Line Investment Survey, 1975), p. 42.

depict key past relationships between (1) GM and the general economic environment, and (2) the income statement and the balance sheet. Statements and graphs such as these are analyzed against the backdrop of a forecast of the probable trend of the economy by quarters through the coming year and a forecast of the economic environment three to five years in the future. This analysis comprises a four-step operation.

Step 1: Sales Forecast As might be expected, the first estimate made for GM is that of sales. Fluctuations in the sales volume from year to year correlate to variations in one of the key national income series, such as GNP, Disposable Income, Personal Income, Consumption Expenditures, or Investment in Producers' Goods and Equipment.

After studying the relationship in the past, a preliminary judgment is made as to what sales would be in the year ahead if the past relationships continue. This figure is then modified on the basis of the expected introductions of major new products, acquisitions, divestments, changes in the competitive climate, government regulations, labor union contracts, and any other factor that is likely to affect the level of sales in coming years. When developing the sales estimate, one must not only consider the demand for GM's products and their probable selling prices, but judge whether plant capacity is adequate for the projected sales volume. If it is not, one must calculate how much investment in new plants will be required and how it will be financed; otherwise, the sales estimate must be limited to existing capacity.

Step 2: Operating Profit Forecast Next, the probable profitability of the volume should be analyzed. To arrive at an operating profit estimate, the following factors must be considered: (1) rate of change of sales; (2) cost of raw materials and fuel; (3) cost of labor, including fringe benefits; (4) prospective sales mix; (5) special advertising or promotion expense; and (6) start-up costs. After considering these and other related factors that may potentially affect operating costs and expenses, a decision should be made concerning the amounts of operating costs and operating profit relative to the forecast volume of sales.

Step 3: Earnings and Dividend Forecast Once the sales and operating profit estimates have been made, the income statement should be carefully examined to estimate (1) depreciation, (2) interest paid, (3) other income, (4) pretax income, (5) income tax rate, (6) net income, and (7) the dividend. In making the earnings forecast, one must consider the factors—such as capital spending budget—that will affect depreciation, the leverage policy which will have an impact on interest paid, and the availability of tax shelters that will change the effective tax rate.

Step 4: Cross Checking of Forecasts Because forecasts of earnings are based on a host of predictions about other variables, the final step inevitably should consist of a check of the reasonableness of the net income estimate. This check is based on computations of the indicated percent return on the total capital being employed by GM and of the return on net worth that the net income estimate implies. If these returns are not consistent with GM's past experience, a rational explanation should be provided for the expected changes.

Forecasting Earnings Growth: Concluding Remarks

In this section several variables have been presented that should be carefully examined as a basis for forecasting earnings growth. There are, of course, more sophisticated forecasting techniques such as probabilistic forecasting, conditional forecasting, and computer models for forecasting earnings.[15] Probabilistic forecasting is the technique of recognizing the important variables and measuring their impact on earnings to forecast a range of expected earnings with an appropriate probability of occurrence associated with each earnings forecast. Conditional forecasts of earnings are based on related data that have already been forecast by different groups of forecasters. For example, earnings forecasts may be based on estimates of, say, GNP, rates of inflation, and inventory build-up which are estimated by the U.S. Department of Commerce. An advantage of this type of forecasting is that different analysts can forecast different parts of the total prediction and thereby maximize gains associated with the division of labor.

Finally, the computer models for forecasting earnings should be mentioned. Considerable literature is currently available that explains computerized earnings forecasting models.[16] Although computer models vary greatly in size, complexity and sophistication, all of them test the relationship between earnings as the dependent variable and several independent variables that are assumed to affect earnings. On the basis of computer tests, investors attempt to predict future earnings with various degrees of certainty.

SECTION 2 FORECASTING KEY VARIABLES OF THE MODEL

Methods of forecasting earnings have been elaborated earlier in this chapter. We will proceed to issues related to estimating the three key variables of the Common Stock Valuation Model—the future dividend stream, the holding period price, and the appropriate discount rate.

[15] For a detailed discussion of the techniques, see J. Peter Williamson, *Investments: New Analytic Techniques* (New York: Praeger 1970). See especially Chapter V on "Security Analysis," and Chapter VI on "Stock-Selection Techniques."

[16] See, for example, Dorothy Bower and Richard S. Bower, "Test of the Stock Evaluation Model," *Journal of Finance*, May 1970; Richard H. Chase, Jr., et al, *Computer Applications in Investment Analysis* (Hanover, N.H.: Dartmouth College, 1966); Heich A. Fiske, "The Computer: How It Is Changing the Money Manager," *Institutional Investor*, April 1968; J. Peter Williamson and David H. Downes, *Manual for Computer Programs in Finance and Investments* (Hanover, N.H.: The Amos Tuck School of Business Administration, Dartmouth College, 1971).

The Dividend Stream, D_n

Estimating the future dividends on a stock not only requires forecasting EPS for each year of the investor's holding period, but estimating the portion of earnings the firm will pay as dividends in each of these years. Therefore, an analysis of a company's dividend payment policy is essential to forecasting the future dividend stream. The following are four major types of dividend *payout ratios* that companies maintain:

1. No dividend payment, or *zero payout ratio.*
2. Fixed or *stable payout ratio.*
3. *Variable payout ratio* with a steady dividend growth.
4. *Variable payout ratio* with variable dividend growth.

No Dividend Payment

Growth-oriented companies often pay no dividends because their main objective is to reinvest all of their earnings in order to maximize their growth. Table 11–5 presents a sample of two such companies and their earnings data. Tandy Corporation is the largest domestic retailer of consumer electronic products through its Radio Shack store network. Even though its earnings increased steadily from $0.25 in 1969 to $2.75 in 1978, it did not declare any dividends. Similarly, Prime Computer, which produces small computers, continued to maintain its zero payout ratio policy. Interestingly, Toys "R" Us, which operates a growing chain of retail toy supermarts, currently pays no dividend. The reason

Table 11–5

TANDY CORPORATION				PRIME COMPUTER*			
Year	EPS	Dividend	Payout Ratio	Year	EPS	Dividend	Payout Ratio
1978	$2.75	Nil	Nil	1978	$1.46	Nil	Nil
1977	2.09	Nil	Nil	1977	.70	Nil	Nil
1976	1.87	Nil	Nil	1976	.26	Nil	Nil
1975	.95	Nil	Nil	1975	.08	Nil	Nil
1974	.48	Nil	Nil	1974	(.13)	Nil	Nil
1973	.44	Nil	Nil				
1972	.35	Nil	Nil				
1971	.31	Nil	Nil				
1970	.28	Nil	Nil				
1969	.25	Nil	Nil				

* Went public in 1974

Table 11–6

	PROCTER & GAMBLE			AT & T			STANDARD BRANDS		
Year	EPS	Dividend	Payout Ratio	EPS	Dividend	Payout Ratio	EPS	Dividend	Payout Ratio
1978	$6.19	$2.70	44%	$7.74	$4.50	58%	$2.68	$1.34	50%
1977	5.59	2.40	43	6.97	4.10	59	2.44	1.28	52
1976	4.86	2.05	42	6.05	3.70	61	2.42	1.21	50
1975	4.05	1.90	47	5.13	3.40	66	2.40	1.07	45
1974	3.85	1.80	47	5.27	3.16	60	2.02	.93$\frac{5}{8}$	47
1973	3.68	1.56	42	4.98	2.80	56	1.77	.87$\frac{7}{8}$	50
1972	3.38	1.50	44	4.34	2.60	60	1.60	.83$\frac{1}{4}$	52
1971	2.91	1.40	48	3.92	2.60	66	1.48	.80	54
1970	2.60	1.32$\frac{1}{2}$	51	3.99	2.60	65	1.40	.78$\frac{3}{4}$	57
1969	2.25	1.25	54	4.00	2.40	60	1.32	.75	57

is that, until 1992, it is prohibited from paying cash dividends on the common stock.[17]

In the case of companies with a history of a zero payout ratio, forecasting the dividend stream may be unnecessary because in the past no dividend payments were made.[18] Because there is no track record to gauge the size of the payout ratio, and because the initial dividend payments are likely to be small, for these companies an assumption of no dividend payment in the foreseeable future appears reasonable. But even these companies can be expected to pay dividends sometime in the future, as did, for example, McDonald's and Xerox.

Stable Payout Ratio

Companies that pay no dividends are relatively few. Among those that have a positive payout ratio, a large number attempt to maintain a constant, or at least a relatively stable, payout ratio. Standard Brands, Inc., is one such company. It is a major producer of branded, packaged consumer foods, confectionery products, and distilled spirits and wines. Another company, Procter & Gamble, is a leading domestic merchandiser of numerous household products. A third company, American Telephone & Telegraph, is the leader in telecommunications. All three companies have one common feature—a stable payout ratio policy, which can be seen in Table 11–6. A fixed or stable payout ratio implies a growth rate of dividends roughly equal to the growth rate of earnings.[19]

[17] Terms of the agreement covering the 8 percent senior notes due in 1992 prohibit the payment of cash dividends on the common stock.

[18] Persons investing in these companies expect the stock price to record a significant increase as a compensation for the lack of dividend payments.

[19] Of course, a company might not maintain a fixed or stable payout policy if its earnings do not continue to increase at a steady rate.

Table 11–7

	SOUTHWESTERN PUBLIC SERVICE			PHILLIPS-VAN HEUSEN		
Year	**EPS**	**Dividend**	**Payout Ratio**	**EPS**	**Dividend**	**Payout Ratio**
1978	$1.64	$1.20	73%	$2.74	$.60	22%
1977	1.87	1.10	59	(1.13)	.60	NM
1976	1.54	.98	64	1.50	.55	35
1975	1.16	.90	78	1.05	.40	37
1974	1.22	.82	67	(.33)	.43	NM
1973	1.08	.79	77	1.31	.43	33
1972	.97	.75	77	2.05	.40	19

NM—not meaningful

Variable Payout Ratio with Stable Dividend Payment

One group of companies has a history of fluctuating payout ratio. Companies included in this group—typically utility companies—generally maintain a record of stable dividend payment regardless of fluctuations in their earnings. Phillips-Van Heusen is one such company; it paid a dividend of $0.43 in 1973 and 1974; its earnings in 1973 were $1.31, but it had a loss of $0.33 in 1974. Southwestern Public Service is an electric utility which falls in this category. The dividend records of these companies are shown in Table 11–7.

Because the earnings and the payout ratio of companies included in this group fluctuate even though dividends show a consistent growth, it is more practical to forecast the dividend growth of these companies through trend analysis of dividends. The technique to be used here is similar to the technique used for making a trend analysis of earnings.

Variable Payout Ratio with Variable Dividend Growth

Finally, for some companies, fluctuations occur in earnings, the payout ratio, and dividends. These are primarily cyclical companies, of which the auto companies are the best examples. Table 11–8 presents the earnings and dividend records of Ford Motor and General Motors.

Accurately predicting dividend growth for cyclical companies is a complicated task, requiring the application of sophisticated analytical techniques and superior economic knowledge. Because this type of analysis is beyond the scope of this book, it may be assumed that the future dividend growth rate of companies with variable payout ratio and dividend is approximately equal to their modified forecast of earnings growth rate.

Table 11–8

	GENERAL MOTORS			FORD MOTOR		
Year	**EPS**	**Dividend**	**Payout Ratio**	**EPS**	**Dividend**	**Payout Ratio**
1978	$12.24	$6.00	49%	$13.35	$3.50	26%
1977	11.62	6.80	58	14.16	3.04	22
1976	10.08	5.55	55	8.36	2.24	27
1975	4.32	2.40	55	1.95	2.08	107
1974	3.27	3.40	104	3.09	2.56	83
1973	8.34	5.25	63	7.30	2.56	35
1972	7.51	4.45	59	6.82	2.14	31
1971	6.72	3.40	51	4.94	2.00	39
1970	2.09	3.40	163	3.82	1.92	50
1969	5.95	4.30	72	4.02	1.92	48

The Selling Price, P_N

In Chapter 9, we demonstrated that the selling price at the end of the holding period, P_N, can be estimated by:

$$P_N = (EM)_N \times E_N \qquad \textbf{(9–21 restated)}$$

where

P_N = Price at which the stock is expected to be sold at the end of period N

$(EM)_N$ = Earnings multiple at the end of period N

E_N = Earnings per share at the end of period N

N = Number of years the stock is expected to be held

The techniques for forecasting earnings have already been presented in Section 1. Methods for forecasting the earnings multiple[20] follow.

[20] As mentioned in Chapter 9 (p. 326), EM and P/E ratio are equivalent and interchangeable concepts. However, for illustrative purposes, we multiply the *future* expected earnings by the EM to arrive at the expected future price of a stock, whereas we multiply *current* earnings by the P/E ratio to arrive at the current price.

Forecasting Earnings Multiple

The Basic Approach

The earnings multiple of a common stock at the end of the holding period can be calculated as:[21]

$$(EM)_N = \frac{(1 - s)_N}{r_N - g_N} \quad \textbf{(9–24 restated)}$$

where

$(EM)_N$ = Earnings multiple at the end of period N
$(1 - s)_N$ = Payout ratio beyond period N
r_N = Appropriate discount rate beyond period N
g_N = Growth rate of earnings beyond period N
N = Number of years the stock is expected to be held

For instance, if the payout ratio, the appropriate discount rate, and the earnings growth rate for the years after the holding period are expected to be .75, .14, and .09, respectively, then the EM at the end of the holding period, N, would be 15:

$$(EM)_N = \frac{.75}{.14 - .09}$$
$$= 15$$

Therefore, the value of the EM can be predicted for any given year if the values of the three related variables can be forecast.

It was mentioned earlier that dividend payment policies vary widely among companies, with payout ratios ranging from zero to 100 percent. However, experience suggests that most firms have a *target* payout ratio that remains fairly stable over time. Consequently, it is reasonable to assume that, in the absence of additional information, the past *average* payout ratio is the best predictor of the future ratio. The past average ratio should, however, be adjusted

[21] Because the equation is based on the constant growth valuation model, it should be written as:

$$(EM)_N = \frac{(1 - s)_{N+1}}{r_N - g_N}$$

However, under the assumptions that earnings and dividends grow continuously at the rate g_N, and that dividends are paid out and discounted continuously at rate r_N, the error resulting from substituting $(1 - s)_{N+1}$ by $(1 - s)_N$ is negligible.

upward or downward if it is warranted by a predicted change in the relevant factors.

Techniques were presented earlier in the chapter for forecasting earnings growth for approximately five years in order to estimate the future dividend stream. Investors with holding periods longer than five years frequently assume that this five-year growth rate will remain constant until the end of the holding period; more conservative investors might lower their prediction of the growth rate between, say, Year 6 and the end of the holding period. The estimation of the earnings multiple, however, requires that a long-term average annual earnings growth rate be forecast from the end of the holding period to infinity.[22] Here, again, an extrapolation of the five-year earnings growth rate is permissible. But because we are dealing with a distant future, it would be realistic to adjust the growth rate upward or downward if there were a valid reason to believe that the short-run forecast growth rate is not likely to prevail in the long run. There is, of course, no established means for making this adjustment. However, one method that appears to be functional is to predict a long-term, average return on equity (ROE) and an average retention ratio. The product of the two predicted ratios is an approximation of the average annual long-term earnings growth rate beyond the holding period.[23]

The last step toward the calculation of the EM is the calculation of the appropriate discount rate. A technique for calculating the rate was described in Chapter 9.[24] A standard assumption is that the current appropriate discount rate will remain constant throughout the valuation period. However, if the riskiness of the stock is predicted to change in the future, the appropriate discount rate should be modified accordingly. After the dividend payout ratio, the earnings growth rate, and the appropriate discount rate have been forecast, the value of the EM can be calculated by using Equation 9–24.

The P/E Ratio Approach

A more pragmatic approach to forecasting the EM is to make the prediction on the basis of a study of the past P/E ratios of the firm. Simplicity is one of its main virtues, but several problems are inherent in this approach, two of which are described below.

P/E ratios fluctuate not only according to changes in the prospects of companies, but in response to psychological factors affecting the market as a whole. Table 11–9 presents the P/E ratios of the S&P 400 Industrials for the period 1948 through 1978. During this period the P/Es ranged from the low of 5.52 to the high of 22.76. Underlying these wide swings, of course, is the changed mood of investors over this period, part of which is assumed to be psychological.

---

[22] This was demonstrated in Chapter 9, using Equations 9–22, 9–23, and 9–24.
[23] This concept was discussed in detail in Chapter 10.
[24] A step-by-step method for calculating the appropriate discount rate will be presented beginning on page 439.

Table 11–9

400 Industrials*
Per Share Data—Adjusted to Stock Price Index Level.
Average of Stock Price Indexes, 1941–43 = 10

	Price/Earnings Ratio High	Low
1948	6.88	5.52
1949	7.76	6.21
1950	7.46	5.92
1951	9.65	8.27
1952	10.99	9.51
1953	10.50	8.83
1954	13.84	9.23
1955	13.84	9.96
1956	15.22	13.06
1957	15.08	11.89
1958	19.99	14.64
1959	18.82	16.43
1960	19.12	16.28
1961	22.76	18.06
1962	19.64	14.31
1963	18.69	15.44
1964	18.82	16.44
1965	17.92	15.71
1966	17.14	13.27
1967	18.89	15.18
1968	19.16	15.43
1969	18.96	15.95
1970	19.01	13.97
1971	19.40	16.64
1972	19.47	16.43
1973	15.13	11.63
1974	11.62	7.24
1975	12.52	9.06
1976	11.31	9.51
R1977	10.31	8.66
1978	9.06	7.29

* Based on 74 individual groups.
Stock Price Indexes for this group extend back to 1918.
R—revision

SOURCE: Standard & Poor's *Analysts Handbook*, 1979.

The task of forecasting the EM on the basis of the past P/E ratios is further complicated by variations in the distribution of these ratios at different time periods. Table 11–10 shows the breakdowns of the P/E of all stocks listed on the New York Stock Exchange during January 1973 and May 1977. The table reveals that in May 1977, when the P/E median was 8, 63 percent of the P/E ratios of all stocks were within the 7–12 multiple range. In early 1973, when the median P/E was 14, only 43 percent of the P/Es fell within that range. The table also

Table 11–10 **P/E Distribution of All Listed Stocks***

P/E Range	Jan. 1973	May 1977
1–3	Nil	1%
4–6	1%	19
7–9	14	43
10–12	29	20
13–15	17	9
16–18	9	3
19 & over	30	5
Total	100%	100%
Median P/E	*14*	*8*

* On trailing 12 months' earnings

reveals that in January 1973, 55 percent of all the P/Es were within the 10–18 range, whereas the figure for May 1977 was only 32 percent. This compression and spreading out of P/E ratios make the task of forecasting burdensome.

Despite the difficulties inherent in the study of the past P/E ratios, several attempts have been made to forecast the EM on the basis of past P/E ratios. One such study was conducted in 1963 by Whitbeck and Kisor.[25] Using the cross-section multiple regression techniques, they analyzed June 8, 1962 data relating to 135 firms, and developed the following equation:

$$\text{P/E} = 8.2 + 1.5G + 6.7D - 0.2\sigma$$

where

P/E = Earnings multiple, or theoretical P/E ratio
G = Growth in earnings
D = The payout ratio
σ = Earnings instability, measured by percentage deviation from trend in earnings

According to this model, differences in P/Es between stocks could be explained by projected (1) earnings growth, (2) dividend payout, and (3) variations in the rate of earnings growth. Using this model, the authors calculated a theoretical P/E ratio for each of the 135 stocks and compared it with the prevailing P/E ratio. Stocks that had the actual P/E ratios 15 percent below their theoretical P/E ratios were classified as undervalued; those with P/E ratios 15 percent over their theoretical ratios were considered overvalued. The authors discovered

[25] Volkert S. Whitbeck and Manown Kisor, "A New Tool in Investment Decision Making," *Financial Analysts Journal*, May–June 1963, pp. 55–62.

that, on the basis of rate of return, the undervalued group consistently outperformed (and the overvalued group underperformed) the S&P 500 Index.

The conclusions derived from the operation of the Whitbeck–Kisor model were quite impressive; however, doubts were soon raised about its predictive power. In constructing this model, the authors had used price over "normalized" earnings; in addition, they had adjusted historical data on the basis of current and projected events. Consequently, the study failed to offer much hope for those whose objective was to use the past P/E ratios as the data base for forecasting EM.[26]

Another model, constructed by Malkiel and Cragg,[27] was tested for its ability to select securities by comparing the actual P/E ratios with the "theoretical" or "normal" P/E ratios. The authors used past financial ratios and expected values of such variables as payout ratio, beta, a risk variable, and the variance of earnings. This model, too, provided disappointing results in that it was largely unsuccessful in *predicting* the future earnings multiple. Therefore, it is appropriate to conclude that until a better predictive model is developed, it would be unwise to use the P/E Ratio Approach for forecasting the earnings multiple.

The Holding Period Price

The holding period price, P_N, is the product of the earnings per share and the earnings multiple prevailing at the end of the holding period. Now that the methods of forecasting these variables have been presented, the holding period price can be easily calculated. For example, if the holding period is five years and the earnings per share and earnings multiple are expected to be \$5 and 20, respectively, then the expected price of the stock at the end of Year 5 would be \$100 (\$5 × 20).

Appropriate Discount Rate

In Chapter 9 we stated that the appropriate discount rate of a stock, which is included in an efficient portfolio, can be estimated by multiplying the stock's beta, β_s, by the expected market return, $E(R_m)$, or $\beta_s E(R_m)$. We will use this approach for the estimation of the appropriate discount rate.

[26] Following the Whitbeck–Kisor study, other studies on the same topic were undertaken. However, the results of none of these studies were conclusive. See R. S. Bower and D. H. Bower, "Risk and the Valuation of Common Stock," *Journal of Political Economy*, May–June 1969, pp. 349–62; Burton G. Malkiel and John G. Cragg, "Expectations and the Structure of Share Prices," *American Economic Review*, September 1970, pp. 601–17.

[27] Burton G. Malkiel and John G. Cragg, "Expectations and the Structure of Share Prices," *American Economic Review*, September 1970, pp. 601–17.

Determination of Current Discount Rate

Expected Market Return

The first step is to estimate the expected market return. Of the several methods that can be used for this purpose, the one that utilizes the dividend model applicable to a single stock can be conveniently adapted for this purpose.

The dividend model used to determine the present value of a stock is:

$$PV = \frac{D_1}{r - g} \tag{9–15 restated}$$

At equilibrium, the current price of a stock, P_0, is likely to equal its present value, PV; therefore, PV may be replaced by P_0. Replacing PV with P_0 and rearranging it, Equation 9–15 becomes:

$$r = \frac{D_1}{P_0} + g \tag{11–1}$$

Finally, under certain simplified assumptions, D_0 can be substituted for D_1,[28] thereby replacing Equation 11–1 with:

$$r = \frac{D_0}{P_0} + g \tag{11–2a}$$

Two observations are apropos here. First, because the stock market can be considered as a portfolio of all stocks trading on the market, Equation 11–2a can be applied to the market as well. Second, at equilibrium all stocks in the market are appropriately valued. Consequently, in such a market, the expected market return, $E(R_m)$, will also equal the appropriate discount rate [that is, $E(R_m) = r$]. Consequently, Equation 11–2a can be replaced by:

$$E(R_m) = \frac{D_0}{P_0} + g \tag{11–2b}$$

where

$$E(R_m) = \text{Expected market return}$$

Let us demonstrate the use of Equation 11–2b for estimating the expected market return. Many investors use the S&P 400 Industrials as a surrogate for the market, although the S&P 500, New York Stock Exchange Composite Index, or the Dow Jones Industrial Average could also serve the purpose. For convenience, we will use the S&P 400 for our calculation.

Historical data on dividend yield and dividend per share are regularly published by S&P. Assume that the current dividend yield, D_0/P_0, is 6 percent. Also, using the compound value model, we find that over the past ten-year period, the dividends have been growing at an average annual rate of 5 percent. Because the past growth rate of dividends is assumed to remain constant in the future, the

[28] It can be demonstrated that E_0 and D_0 can be substituted for E_1 and D_1 in a constant growth valuation model, provided the following assumptions are made: (1) Earnings and dividends grow continuously at the rate g, and (2) dividends are paid out and discounted continuously at the discount rate r.

expected market return can be estimated at approximately 11 percent:

$$E(R_m) = \frac{D_0}{P_0} + g$$
$$= 6\% + 5\%$$
$$= 11\%$$

In this simple technique, the expected market return was estimated on the basis of *past* dividends data. Although for most investors this technique is satisfactory, some analysts claim that computerized models can forecast the expected market return more accurately.[29]

Expected Systematic Return

The next step involves the calculation of expected systematic return of the stock (the expected market return multiplied by the beta of the stock). Because the expected market return has already been calculated, we will determine a stock's beta.

The *beta* of a stock can be obtained from one of several beta services available on the market, which include Wilshire Associates, Merrill Lynch, the Value Line Investment Survey, and Rosenberg Beta Service. For example, according to one of the beta services, in 1979 the beta of Corning Glass was 1.19. Therefore, the expected systematic return of Corning Glass was 13.09:

$$\text{Expected Systematic Return} = \beta_s \times E(R_m)$$
$$= 1.19 \times 11\%$$
$$= 13.09\%$$

Final Considerations

As a general rule, the expected systematic return just calculated can be used as the appropriate discount rate associated with the stock under investigation. However, it is possible to add some important caveats concerning the expected systematic return. We have learned that the expected systematic return of a stock is a product of its beta and the expected market return. As the following discussion will show, both variables can change over time.

Although it is not evident from the previous discussion, for the reasons specified below, the beta of a single security is not always a reliable measure of its volatility, at least in the short run. First, beta does not perform well in the short run. Empirical studies show that on several occasions in the past stocks with

[29] Note, for example, the following forecast made by the Chemical Bank: "Corporate bonds are currently yielding $9\frac{1}{2}\%$ (new issue, Aaa Telephone), as against an 'implied rate of return' of $13\frac{5}{8}\%$ available from equities. (Implied rate of return is that discount rate which is needed to make the current price of equities equal to the expected stream of future dividends.) The 4 percentage point spread is sufficiently large by historical standards to compensate for the extra risk of investing in equities. The current level of yields on bonds and stocks indicates that the financial markets are expecting a long-run rate of inflation of around 7 percent per year, which is in line with our own five-year forecast." See James Winder, "Yield Spread Outlook," *Weekly Economic Package*, Chemical Bank, July 24, 1979, p. 3c.

lower betas have fluctuated more than stocks with higher betas. Second, there have been serious questions raised regarding how to measure beta—that is, which market index to use to measure the volatility of a given security. Third, it is sometimes asserted that beta estimates for individual stocks are not very accurate.

Despite these limitations, however, beta is not altogether a useless measure of risk. For one thing, although individual security betas are not very reliable, beta is considered an accurate measure of the risk of a portfolio; that is, the average beta in an efficient portfolio is a good predictor of performance. For another, beta is a reliable predictor of long-term relationships.

An equally important observation is that the market return (as reflected in the prevailing discount rate) can vary over time. Figure 11–5 shows one set of estimates of the discount rates for stocks with different betas at selected time periods. Each stock is assigned to a risk class, based on its expected sensitivity to market fluctuations. After a rate of return and risk class have been estimated for each stock, the information is plotted on a graph. The rate of return is read on the vertical axis, and the average beta level of each class on the horizontal axis. A line is then fitted to the points; this line underscores the relationship

Figure 11–5

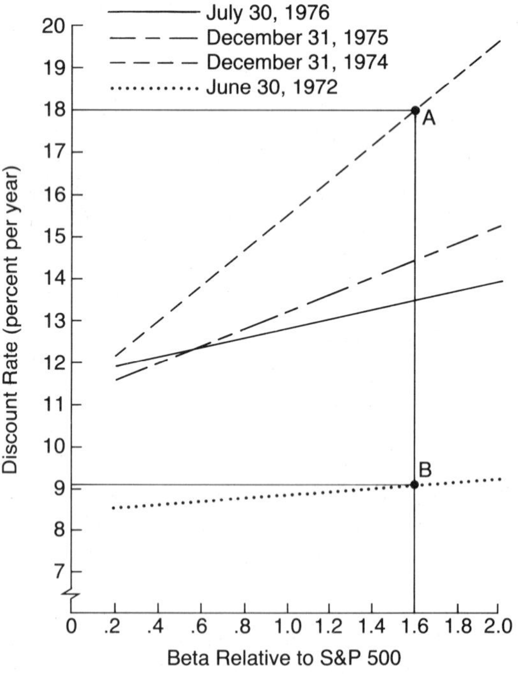

SOURCE: Wells Fargo Bank, *Security Market Line Report*, August 2, 1976.

between return and risk in the market on a given date. The returns are the implicit discount rates, because they are the returns expected by investors; risk is measured by beta. For example, a beta of 1.6 was associated with an 18 percent discount rate (point A) on December 31, 1974, whereas the discount rate for the same beta on June 30, 1972 was 9 percent (point B).[30]

Forecasting Discount Rate

To use the Common Stock Valuation Model, we must forecast the appropriate discount rate that is likely to prevail in the future. Having determined the current appropriate discount rate, we need a technique for forecasting it. However, as mentioned earlier, a standard assumption is that the appropriate discount rate remains constant throughout the valuation period. The reason for this is obvious. The discount rate represents an investor's perception of risk associated with a given stock. Although no one ever expects the riskiness of a stock to remain unchanged over time, there is no way to forecast accurately this riskiness on a year-to-year basis. Therefore, we assume that the currently prevailing appropriate discount rate will remain unchanged.

The Model in Action

Now that we have discussed in detail the techniques for estimating the future dividend stream, the holding period price, and the appropriate discount rate, the Common Stock Valuation Model can be put into action. We will demonstrate the use of the Model as a tool for making stock selection by applying it to the Stanley Works. To make the discussion interesting, the Model will be used by Investor W, who is interested in determining whether or not the common stock of Stanley Works is undervalued. In order to keep the discussion simple, Investor W will analyze the company by making a set of simplified assumptions. He will also make a number of value judgments based on his utility function; these judgments are not universally applicable.

The Basic Framework

In early 1979, Investor W is advised by his stockbroker to purchase the common stock of Stanley Works at the market price of $29.50 per share. The broker is enthusiastic about Stanley Works because the company sells products in the growing home improvement do-it-yourself market. Influenced by his broker's advice, Investor W decides to undertake a brief analysis of the proposed investment. He will compare the current price of the stock with its present value to

[30] Figure 11–5 reveals that the line—called the Security Market Line (SML)—can shift over time. An upward shift in the SML (with no change in the slope) implies that investors are demanding a higher risk-free rate. Conversely, a rise in the SML's slope occurs when investors perceive the market as being more risky (and consequently demand a higher risk premium per unit of risk). The use of SML in investment analysis will be fully explored in Chapters 13 and 14.

determine whether the stock is undervalued. After reviewing the company's background and past financial data, Investor W will forecast Stanley's earnings growth and derive values for the future dividend stream, D_n, the appropriate discount rate, r, and the future selling price, P_N. These values will then be used in the following Common Stock Valuation Model in order to determine the present value of the stock:

$$PV = \sum_{n=1}^{N} \frac{D_n}{(1+r)^n} + \frac{P_N}{(1+r)^N} \qquad \text{(9–3 restated)}$$

Company Background

The Stanley Works is the world's largest manufacturer of *hand tools* for the construction, industrial, and consumer markets. It is one of the oldest companies listed on the New York Stock Exchange, having been incorporated in 1852. Besides hand tools, Stanley Works also produces *household products* (hinges, decorative hardware, shelves, drapery hardware); *builders' products* (hinges, doors, door openers); and *industrial products* (strapping, cabinets, heavy-duty power tools, cold rolled steel). In 1978, the firm's net income was $41.6 million based on a revenue of $754 million. Contributions in 1978 from the four basic product lines were as follows:

	Sales %	Profits %
Tools	45	50
Builders' Products	25	22
Industrial Products	19	17
Household Products	11	11
	100	100

Sales outside the United States and Canada accounted for 33 percent of total sales and 25 percent of net income.

Consumer hand tools and household products are sold in the do-it-yourself market for home improvement and other projects. However, as is evident from the data pertinent to its sales and profit, a good portion of Stanley's business is still tied to the construction and industrial markets.

Financial Data

A summary of the company's important financial data from 1969 through 1978 is presented in Table 11–11. Investor W feels that an analysis of ten years of data should be sufficient, because the time period will encompass various phases of the business cycle, including the two recessionary periods which occurred in 1970 and 1974–75.

A review of Stanley's sales and earnings data reveals that it has been both a growth and a cyclical firm. Sales and earnings of the firm have grown steadily over the past ten years; however, there were interruptions in the growth trend

Table 11–11 **The Stanley Works Financial Data***

Year	Sales	EBIT†	Assets	Equity	Net Income	EPS	Book Value Per Share
	(millions of dollars)						
1978	754	90.1	495	275	41.6	$3.50	$22.75
1977	640	75.5	428	244	32.9	2.75	20.26
1976	562	66.4	402	224	27.4	2.29	18.22
1975	464	43.1	374	203	19.1	1.62	16.75
1974	487	43.8	370	190	19.9	1.71	15.73
1973	434	46.5	341	176	22.8	1.97	14.59
1972	399	41.4	278	162	19.9	1.71	13.35
1971	304	32.2	231	145	15.3	1.36	12.44
1970	258	25.5	199	135	12.5	1.15	11.89
1969	258	25.8	185	128	12.3	1.12	11.21

* Data from Standard & Poor's *Stock Reports*; *The Value Line Investment Survey* published by Arnold Bernhard & Co., Inc.

† Derived by adding interest expense to pretax income.

during national economic downturns. The EPS dropped from $1.97 in 1973 to $1.71 in 1974 and to $1.62 in 1975, but rebounded to show strong gains through 1978. The pattern of sales roughly paralleled earnings: In 1975 sales dropped 5 percent from the previous year, but increased by 21.1 percent in 1976, 13.9 percent in 1977, and 17.8 percent in 1978. The cyclical pattern during the earlier recession of 1970 showed similar characteristics.

Earnings Forecast

Investor W makes a rough earnings projection. First he will make a simple naive forecast. Then, after considering the future trend of Stanley's ROE and earnings retention ratio, he will make a modified projection. Somewhat arbitrarily, Investor W decides on an initial holding period of five years. He realizes that later he might decide to hold the stock longer than five years, depending partly upon his liquidity requirements. Investor W recognizes, of course, that he will need the EPS forecast for the period 1979–83 in order to estimate the future dividend stream. Additionally, he will require a long-term growth rate for the years after 1983 in order to estimate the price at which the stock is expected to sell in 1983, the terminal year of the holding period.

Naive Forecast

From the EPS data found in Table 11–11, Investor W calculates a trend line using the least squares method. Because Stanley's EPS have shown growth characteristics from 1969 to 1978, he uses the exponential model. The exponential trend equation which best fits the data is $Y_c = (.9673)(1.1197)^X$. (The actual calculations were presented in Table 11–1 and the trend line was graphed in Figure 11–2).

Figure 11–6 **The Stanley Works 1978 EPS**

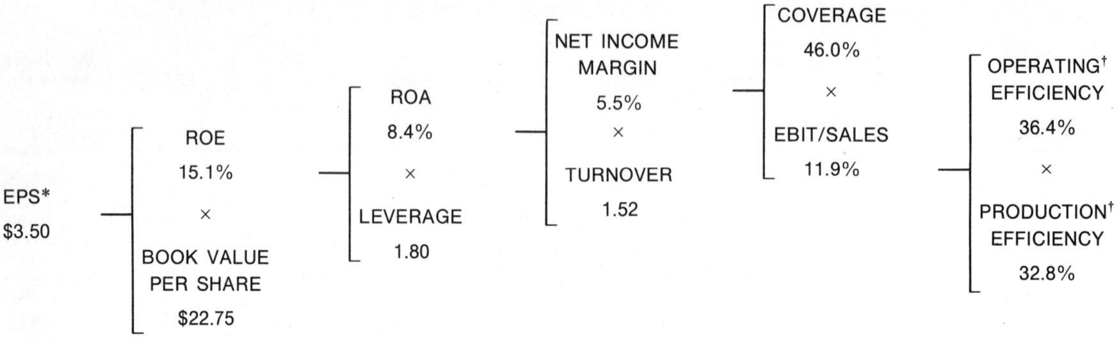

EPS* $3.50
- ROE 15.1%
  - ROA 8.4%
    - NET INCOME MARGIN 5.5%
      - COVERAGE 46.0%
      - ×
      - EBIT/SALES 11.9%
        - OPERATING† EFFICIENCY 36.4%
        - ×
        - PRODUCTION† EFFICIENCY 32.8%
    - ×
    - TURNOVER 1.52
  - ×
  - LEVERAGE 1.80
- ×
- BOOK VALUE PER SHARE $22.75

* Book value per share × ROE only approximates the EPS in this example, because the former includes only tangible assets.

† Gross margin on sales in 1978 was $247 million.

Investor W discovers that the underlying growth rate of Stanley's past earnings approximates 12 percent. One of Investor W's options is to make the simple assumption that the future growth in the EPS will follow the past trend, in which case he can make the following naive forecast:

Year	EPS Naive Forecast
1979	$3.36
1980	3.76
1981	4.21
1982	4.71
1983	5.28

However, a more sophisticated, and certainly more realistic option is to assume that the past trend will change as a result of significant influences in the national economic, industry, and company factors that affect Stanley's ROE. Investor W carefully considers both options and finally prefers the latter.

Modification of Naive Forecast

Investor W has learned that the process of modifying the naive forecast of earnings growth must begin with an analysis of Stanley's return on equity (ROE) and earnings retention. Figure 11–6 outlines the financial ratios which are used to calculate Stanley's $3.50 EPS figure for 1978. Investor W notes that the company earned 15.1 percent on its shareholders' invested capital.[31] This ROE is a product of a ROA of 8.4 percent and a leverage ratio of 1.80. If Stanley's latest 15.1 percent ROE and 71 percent earnings retention ratio remain constant,

[31] For simplicity, in this calculation, the ROE is based on Stanley Works' year-end equity rather than the average shareholders' equity for the year.

its 1978 EPS of $3.50 will continue to grow at the reinvestment rate of 10.72 percent (.151 × .71). Using this reinvestment rate, Investor W estimates Stanley's EPS from 1979 to 1983:

Year	EPS	Annual Increase of
1978	$3.50	
1979	3.88	
1980	4.29	10.72%
1981	4.75	
1982	5.26	
1983	5.82	

Investor W recognizes that the use of the modified forecasting technique produces an EPS forecast which is higher than that produced by the naive forecast. The naive forecast extends the past *average* annual growth rate of 11.97 percent into the future. The reinvestment rate forecast of 10.72 percent, however, assumes a constant *marginal* growth rate based on Stanley's 1978 earnings performance. Because Stanley's 1978 EPS of $3.50 were higher than the 1978 trend line estimate of $3.00, the 10.72 percent annual growth rate starting from 1978 projects a higher five-year EPS than the 11.97 percent annual growth in the trend. However, in the long run the earnings forecast by the naive method will exceed the earnings forecast by the constant reinvestment rate, because the latter method assumes a *constant* ROE and earnings retention ratio, whereas the naive method reflects an *improvement* in ROE over the 1969–78 period and projects it into the future.

The obvious problem with the modified EPS forecast using the 1978 reinvestment rate is that it is based on the assumption that the 1978 ROE and earnings retention ratio will remain unchanged. For Investor W, this is a difficult assumption to accept because he notices that Stanley's ROE has fluctuated considerably over the past ten years, as revealed by Table 11–12A. From 1969 to 1978, the pattern of fluctuations in the ROE matched that of the EPS; both dropped during economic downturns, but maintained an overall uptrend. A closer examination revealed that the rise in the ROE from 1969 to 1973 was largely due to an increase in leverage; the leverage ratio rose from 1.45 to 1.94 during this period. Furthermore, since 1973, despite a decline in the leverage ratio to the 1.75–1.85 level, the ROE still increased beyond its cyclical peak of 13 percent in 1973 to 15.1 percent in 1978 due primarily to a significant improvement in the ROA.

Investor W discovered that Stanley's ROE dropped in 1970, 1974, and 1975 when its ROA was depressed. As evidenced in Table 11–12B, fluctuations in the ROA were accompanied by similar movements in the turnover and net income margin. For example, in 1975 there was a sharp drop in the ROA to 5.1 percent due primarily to the lowest net income margin and turnover in the entire ten-year period under study.

Table 11–12C gives the breakdown of net income margin between EBIT/Sales and the coverage ratio. Since 1976, Stanley's net income margin increased from

Table 11–12

	A RETURN ON EQUITY (ROE)			B RETURN ON ASSETS (ROA)			C NET INCOME MARGIN		
Year	ROA ×	Leverage =	ROE	Net Income Margin	× Turnover =	ROA	Coverage ×	EBIT/Sales =	Net Income Margin
1978	8.4%	1.80	15.1%	5.5%	1.52	8.4%	46.2%	11.9%	5.5%
1977	7.7	1.75	13.5	5.1	1.50	7.7	43.6	11.7	5.1
1976	6.9	1.79	12.4	4.9	1.40	6.9	41.3	11.8	4.9
1975	5.1	1.84	9.4	4.1	1.24	5.1	44.3	9.3	4.1
1974	5.4	1.95	10.5	4.1	1.32	5.4	45.4	9.0	4.1
1973	6.7	1.94	13.0	5.3	1.27	6.7	49.0	10.7	5.3
1972	7.2	1.72	12.4	5.0	1.44	7.2	48.1	10.4	5.0
1971	6.6	1.59	10.5	5.0	1.32	6.6	47.5	10.6	5.0
1970	6.2	1.47	9.1	4.8	1.30	6.2	49.0	9.9	4.8
1969	6.7	1.45	9.7	4.8	1.39	6.7	47.7	10.0	4.8

4.9 to 5.5 percent despite a stable EBIT/Sales ratio. The improvement was due largely to increased coverage ratio, brought about by lower tax rates.

The improvement in the ROE from 9.4 percent in 1975 to 15.1 percent in 1978 resulted in a significant increase in the EPS. For example, increases in the EPS in 1976, 1977, and 1978 were 41 percent, 20 percent, and 27 percent, respectively. This strong uptrend helped boost the ten-year EPS growth trend to the 12 percent level. Investor W notes that his analysis of the future prospects for Stanley's ROE will help him further modify his EPS forecast. This analysis will involve an overview of general economic, industry, and company fundamentals.

General Economic Conditions Information published by the National Bureau of Economic Research and other professional advisory services[32] indicates to Investor W that there will be an economic slowdown in the latter part of 1979, 1980, and possibly in 1981. This will have an adverse impact on Stanley's sales, particularly in its building and industrial product groups. In the past, a slowdown in sales has been accompanied by a drop in ROA because of the negative impact on the firm's EBIT/Sales and turnover ratios. If industry and company factors remain unchanged, the anticipated downturn in the economy could easily have the same effect on Stanley's profitability over the next two to three years.

Industry Factors The various markets in which Stanley operates are highly competitive; it encounters active competition from both larger and smaller companies producing similar as well as different products appropriate for the same use. In the hand tool market, for example, competing firms include Easco, Cooper Industries, Triangle, and McDonough Company.

[32] See Chapter 10 for a detailed discussion of this topic.

Investor W notes with interest that in recent years there has been a resurgence of growth in hand tools, probably because their sales have been tied to the fast growing do-it-yourself market. Since 1967, outlays in the home improvement market have increased at an average rate of 11 percent. The fastest growing segment of this market is do-it-yourself work, because homeowners are now trying to avoid the high cost of professional labor. Even more importantly, the do-it-yourself segment appears to be recession resistant; sales growth continued even through the 1970 and 1974–75 recessions. Investor W feels that the expanding sales of consumer hand tools and household products in this market should ease the traditional cyclical pressure on Stanley's ROA.

Company Factors

1. *Production and Marketing Methods* For years Stanley has been viewed as just a manufacturing firm; however, recent advertising and promotional programs have also expanded its influence on the consumer marketing area. Since 1976, Stanley's surge in sales was due in part to an innovative national TV advertising program which tied the use of Stanley products to various do-it-yourself activities. Despite stiff competition, Stanley's strong advertising program is helping to increase its share of the tool market.

2. *New Strategies* Recently, Stanley Works has undergone an evolutionary change. In order to improve its net income margin and ROA, the company has placed greater emphasis on those business segments for which a position of market leadership can be obtained. Stanley has succeeded in acquiring a dominant position not only in the hand tools business, but in various household products, pneumatic tools for the auto industry, and insulated doors for the new house market. Furthermore, Stanley has consolidated its position by withdrawing from those markets for which leadership is more difficult to obtain and for which the growth potential is limited.

3. *Accounting Practice* Because Investor W finds that Stanley's accounting practices are conservative, he therefore concludes that the earnings quality of the company is good. Specifically, after reviewing a statement of Stanley's accounting policies in a recent annual report, he finds that the company uses LIFO accounting on a substantial portion of its inventories and writes off goodwill rapidly, amortizing it over 15 years or less. In addition, unfunded prior service pension costs are written off in 25 years rather than over the normal 40-year period. Stanley's depreciation policy also appears to be conservative; for book purposes, the accelerated method is used to depreciate over 60 percent of assets. Because the company has not used accounting practices to magnify current earnings at the expense of future profits, Investor W feels that no significant modifications are required in this area.

4. *Quality of Management* Stanley's management continues to increase the sales capacity of its asset base. Capital expenditures have increased from $11 million in 1974 to a record $37.5 million in 1978. Approximately one-third of the 1978 expenditure was for increased production capacity; the rest was for cost reductions and scheduled replacement. Projected expenditures for 1979

are $49 million, with about half of that amount budgeted for the hand tool division. Because hand tool sales are expected to continue at more or less the same rate during the upcoming recession, the risk that the additional plant capacity will become idle and hurt Stanley's turnover is limited.

Although capital expenditures of the company have increased, since 1975 its leverage ratio has remained fairly stable. Investor W believes that the present leverage ratio will continue to be maintained, because part of the capital expenditure program will probably be financed with debt. However, Stanley's financing decisions since 1974 do not indicate that the leverage ratio will soon be significantly increased.

5. *Other Factors* Stanley's tax rate recently dropped because of foreign currency translation effects. Although this benefit may not reoccur, the coverage ratio could still benefit from lower tax rates in the future. Investor W learns that, effective 1979, the federal corporate tax rate will be lowered from 48 percent to 46 percent.

The Forecast

On the basis of the foregoing fundamental analysis, Investor W formulates an EPS projection for the next five years, and a long-term growth rate for the period thereafter.

Five-Year Projection

Investor W believes that, because of improved performance, in 1979 Stanley will meet its goal of a ROE of 16–17 percent. If the leverage ratio remains constant at 1.80, the ROE will increase to 16 percent, with an improvement in the ROA to 8.9 percent. Investor W recalls that in 1978, the ROA, turnover ratio, and net income margin were, respectively, 8.4 percent, 1.52, and 5.5 percent. An 8.9 percent ROA is attainable, for example, with a turnover of 1.56 times and a net income margin of 5.7 percent. Investor W believes this can be accomplished with a sales growth of 16–20 percent and a lower tax rate. In making this observation, Investor W takes into account the fact that, although an economic downturn is expected in the latter half of 1979, its impact is not likely to be felt by the firm until 1980.

Investor W feels that due to the expected economic slowdown in 1980 and 1981, the firm's ROE will decline. However, he predicts that the drop in sales will not be as severe as it was during the 1974–75 recession because of the improvements in Stanley's market share and sales in the do-it-yourself market. Assuming a drop in turnover to the 1.4–1.5 level and a lower net income margin, Investor W predicts that in 1980 and 1981 the ROE will fall to the 13–14 percent level.

Finally, Investor W predicts that by 1983 the ROE should rebound to at least the 1979 peak level. This prediction assumes that the current leverage ratio is maintained. Additional favorable leverage, of course, would further improve the ROE.

How does this estimated ROE trend translate into future EPS growth? In Table 11–13A, Investor W uses estimated ROE values and a constant earnings

Table 11–13

A
THE STANLEY WORKS
FIVE-YEAR EPS FORECAST

Year	EPS	EPS Retained $	EPS Retained % of EPS	Book Value Per Share	ROE (EPS ÷ Book Value) per Share
1979	$4.09	$2.86	70%	$25.61*	16.0%
1980	4.13	2.89	70	28.50	14.5
1981	4.24	2.97	70	31.47	13.5
1982	5.48	3.84	70	35.31	15.5
1983	6.44	4.51	70	39.82	16.2

* The 1979 year-end book value per share was derived as follows:

1978 year-end book value per share (Table 11–11)	:	$22.75
Plus: EPS retained in 1979	:	2.86
Equals: 1979 year-end book value per share	:	$25.61

Likewise, the 1979 year-end book value per share of $25.61 plus the $2.89 EPS retained in 1980 equals the 1980 year-end book value per share of $28.50. Year-end book value is used in calculating ROE, which differs from the approach used in the illustrative example in Chapter 10 (Table 10–14).

B
EPS FORECASTS

Year	Naive Forecast	Constant Reinvestment Rate	Modified Forecast
1979	$3.36	$3.88	$4.09
1980	3.76	4.29	4.13
1981	4.21	4.75	4.24
1982	4.71	5.26	5.48
1983	5.28	5.82	6.44

retention ratio in order to develop a "rough" earnings forecast. This modified forecast varies markedly from the forecast developed by the exponential trend line and the EPS values derived from the constant reinvestment rate (Table 11–13B). The annual growth rate implicit in these figures from the 1978 EPS of $3.50 is about 13 percent. The earnings pattern, which reflects the recent changes in industry and company factors, is somewhat different from the past in that the EPS is not as cyclically volatile.

Long-term Growth Rate

For the period beyond 1983, Investor W recognizes that he needs to forecast only a constant EPS growth rate. The average annual growth rate expected to prevail after 1983 is obtained by multiplying the expected average ROE by the

Table 11–14 The Stanley Works Dividend Payments

Year	EPS	Dividend	Payout Ratio	Earnings Retention Ratio
1978	$3.50	$1.02	29%	71%
1977	2.75	.81	29	71
1976	2.29	.75	33	67
1975	1.62	.65	40	60
1974	1.71	.64	37	63
1973	1.97	.60	30	70
1972	1.71	.53	31	69
1971	1.36	.52	38	62
1970	1.15	.47	41	59
1969	1.12	.45	40	60

expected average earnings retention ratio. A 70 percent earnings retention ratio (explained later) and the average ROE forecast for the 1979–83 period are used as the basis for calculating the expected growth rate.[33] Stanley's performance during 1979–83, predicted to be less cyclical than in the past, is felt to be most representative of Stanley's future long-term record. Consequently, the average ROE of 15.14 percent over this period is used in the long-term growth rate projection. On the basis of the several predictions just made, Investor W finally arrives at the forecast for the long-term EPS growth rate, g_n, as shown below:

$$\begin{aligned}\text{EPS growth rate} &= .1514 \times .70 \\ &= 10.598\% \approx 10.6\%\end{aligned}$$

Determination of Present Value

Having completed the earnings forecast, Investor W turns to the task of estimating the values for the future dividend stream, the appropriate discount rate, and the future selling price.

Dividend Stream

An examination of Stanley's dividend record, presented in Table 11–14, shows that the company's policy has been to increase dividend payments each year regardless of declines in the EPS. To maintain a record of increasing dividends, at times Stanley has had to adjust its payout ratio upward. For example, the company's EPS fell from $1.97 in 1973 to $1.71 in the following year, and Stanley raised its payout ratio from 30 percent to 37 percent in order to raise

[33] In many cases, the *past* average ROE may not be an acceptable estimate of the *future* average ROE. For example, a number of companies have averaged a ROE from 20–30 percent for the past five years. However, it may be unrealistic to expect this performance to be maintained over the long term.

the dividend from \$0.60 to \$0.64 per share. Investor W notes, however, that although dividends have increased every year since 1969, the percentage increase has been smaller during those years when the EPS have either dropped or showed small gains.

Stanley's average payout ratio from 1969 to 1978 was about 35 percent. However, since 1976 the ratio has dropped to the 30 percent level. Investor W feels that a 30 percent payout ratio will prevail in the future, because he foresees a more stable EPS pattern with no significant downward fluctuation such as occurred in 1974–75.

Using the EPS forecast developed earlier, and assuming a 30 percent payout ratio, Investor W estimates the dividend stream as follows:

Year	EPS	Payout Ratio	Dividend
1979	\$4.09	30%	\$1.23
1980	4.13	30	1.24
1981	4.24	30	1.27
1982	5.48	30	1.64
1983	6.44	30	1.93

Appropriate Discount Rate

Investor W uses the Risk–Return Approach to find an appropriate discount rate. This approach utilizes the Market Model to estimate the *expected systematic return* from Stanley Works stock, which will equal the expected market return multiplied by the stock's beta coefficient.

Expected Market Return The current *expected* market return is represented by the sum of the current market dividend yield plus the current consensus of the future dividend growth rate. Using the S&P 400 Industrials in place of the market, Investor W finds the current dividend yield to be 5.0 percent. The consensus of the future growth rate, estimated by taking the average annual growth in dividends over the past five years, is approximately 9.5 percent. The discount rate for the market therefore works out to be approximately 14.5 percent:

$$E(R_m) = \frac{D_0}{P_0} + g \qquad \textbf{(11–2b restated)}$$

$$= .05 + .095$$

$$= 14.5\%$$

Expected Systematic Return Stanley's beta coefficient of 1.0, multiplied by the expected market return of 14.5 percent, equals an expected systematic return of 14.5 percent for the stock. The appropriate discount rate for Stanley Works is equal to the expected systematic return of 14.5 percent. Although this discount rate could easily fluctuate in the future, Investor W assumes for his present value calculation that it will remain constant.

Future Selling Price

Next, Investor W estimates the future selling price of Stanley Works' stock at the end of the five-year holding period in 1983. Using the Earnings Multiple Approach (Equation 9–21), he determines that the selling price in 1983 will equal the Earnings Multiple (EM) multiplied by the EPS in 1983. Assuming a payout ratio of 30 percent, a discount rate of 14.5 percent, and a long-term average annual earnings growth rate of 10.6 percent for the period after 1983, the EM in 1983[34] is estimated to be 7.7[35]:

$$(EM)_N = \frac{(1-s)_N}{r_N - g_N} \qquad \textbf{(9–24 restated)}$$

$$= \frac{.30}{.145 - .106}$$

$$= 7.7$$

With the 1983 EPS estimated at \$6.44 and with a value of EM equal to 7.7 for that year,[36] the future selling price is estimated to be \$49.59:

$$P_N = (EM)_N \times E_N \qquad \textbf{(9–21 restated)}$$

$$= 7.7 \times \$6.44$$

$$= \$49.59$$

Stanley Works' Present Value

Using the Common Stock Valuation Model, the estimated future dividend stream and selling price are discounted by the appropriate discount rate to determine the present value as:

$$PV = \frac{D_1}{(1+r)^1} + \frac{D_2}{(1+r)^2} + \frac{D_3}{(1+r)^3} + \frac{D_4}{(1+r)^4} + \frac{D_5}{(1+r)^5} + \frac{P_5}{(1+r)^5}$$

$$= \frac{\$1.23}{(1.145)^1} + \frac{\$1.24}{(1.145)^2} + \frac{\$1.27}{(1.145)^3} + \frac{\$1.64}{(1.145)^4} + \frac{\$1.93}{(1.145)^5} + \frac{\$49.59}{(1.145)^5}$$

$$= \$1.07 + \$0.95 + \$0.85 + \$0.95 + \$0.98 + \$25.20$$

$$= \$30.00$$

[34] For the year 1978, the P/E ratio was around 8 (\$29.50/\$3.50). Consequently, the EM for 1983 was expected to be approximately equal to the 1978 figure.

[35] Many growth companies have never paid a dividend and have a very high past earnings growth rate. Nevertheless, the Earnings Multiple Approach assumes the projection of a payout ratio that is greater than zero and a long-term earnings growth rate that is less than the discount rate.

[36] Note the importance of the EM in the valuation model. A minor readjustment in the value of EM can have a significant impact on the present value of the stock.

The Final Decision

Investor W compares Stanley's current market price of $29.50 with its present value of $30.00 and concludes that the stock is appropriately valued.[37] Although Stanley Works stock would be suitable for purchase, Investor W realizes that there is little margin for error in his valuation projections. Recognizing that his analysis of Stanley Works is based on a number of simplified assumptions and a series of approximations, Investor W decides to analyze other stocks using the same procedure with hopes of finding one that is a better buy. His decision is based on his belief that the market is not efficient in processing all available information and that some stocks are undervalued and others are overvalued.

Summary

The Common Stock Valuation Model is constructed on the basis of three key variables—the future dividend stream, the selling price of the stock at the end of the holding period, and the the appropriate discount rate. The future dividend stream and selling price are directly related to the company's future earnings growth.

Two methods of forecasting a firm's future earnings growth rate are the *naive forecasting* method and the *modified growth rate* technique. Naive forecasting is simple in that it assumes that the past growth rate (which can be measured by applying trend analysis to past earnings data) will remain constant in the future. However, it is often unreliable because it is based upon oversimplified assumptions.

The basic technique for forecasting modified growth rate requires an analysis of general economic conditions, industry conditions, and company factors which have an impact on the future growth rate of a firm's earnings. Professionals and sophisticated investors often use more advanced techniques to forecast earnings with greater precision.

Forecasting future dividend stream requires assumptions about a firm's future *payout ratio*. Past dividend policies provide a firm basis for predicting these ratios.

The *holding period price* can be estimated by predicting a firm's earnings and the *earnings multiple* (EM). The EM can be predicted after estimating the firm's future payout ratio, expected growth rate of earnings and the appropriate discount rate.

[37] The decision model presented here is equivalent to the model that compares the expected rate of return with the required rate of return. In this example, if the current market price, P_0, of $29.50 is substituted for *PV*, the expected rate of return will approximate 14.5 percent. As expected, that return is roughly equal to the required rate of return.

The appropriate discount rate can be estimated by calculating the *expected systematic return* of the stock. It is calculated by multiplying the expected market return by the stock's beta.

A Look Ahead

This chapter has laid the foundation for identifying undervalued and overvalued stocks with the help of fundamental analysis and the Common Stock Valuation Model developed in Chapter 9. There is, however, a different type of analysis used by many investors which does not consider fundamental factors that determine present value, but which endeavors to predict future stock prices based on past price behavior. This method of analysis, known as technical analysis, will be the subject of Chapter 12.

Concepts for Review

Earnings growth
Measurement of past growth rate
Trend analysis
Normalized earnings
Least squares method
  Exponential form
  Log-linear form
Naive forecasting
Forecasting modified growth rate
Advanced forecasting technique
Forecasting dividend stream
Payout ratio
  Zero ratio
  Stable ratio
  Variable ratio
Earnings multiple
P/E ratio
Forecasting holding period price
Forecasting appropriate discount rate
Expected market return
Expected systematic return
Beta

Questions for Review

1. Describe naive forecasting as a method of estimating future earnings growth. What assumptions must be made to use this method?
2. What problems ensue in using past earnings to predict future earnings?
3. What are the major factors one must take into account when modifying a naive earnings growth forecast?

4. Comment on the following statement: "Qualitative considerations are of little importance in estimating the future earnings growth of a company."
5. What is meant by the quality of reported earnings? How might the accounting policies of a company influence your estimate of its future earnings growth?
6. Describe the process of making a detailed quantitative earnings and dividends forecast of a company. What are the major steps in this type of analysis?
7. How would a forecast of general economic conditions and economic series be used in forecasting a company's earnings growth? What other key factors would an analyst consider?
8. In determining the present value of a stock, could future earnings per share be discounted just as easily as future dividends per share? Explain your answer.
9. Describe different types of dividend payout policies which companies use. Explain how each type would affect your estimation of the future dividend stream.
10. Describe two methods for forecasting the earnings multiple of a stock at the end of the holding period.
11. What problems ensue from using the past P/E ratio of a stock as a basis for predicting its future earnings multiple?
12. How is the appropriate discount rate of a stock determined? Could two investors determine two different appropriate discount rates for the same stock?
13. Why should a stock with a higher beta be associated with a higher appropriate discount rate than a stock with a lower beta?
14. Investor B estimates the present value of QBE stock is $62, while the current market price is $59. Would you recommend that she purchase the stock immediately? Explain.
15. Investor B determines the present value of QBE stock is $62. Investor H, on the other hand, determines the present value of QBE stock to be $49. Can QBE stock have more than one present value? Explain.

Problems

1. The following are past earnings per share data for KDB Corporation:

	EPS
1978	$3.02
1977	2.62
1976	2.39
1975	1.65
1974	1.62
1973	2.16
1972	1.97
1971	1.78
1970	1.51
1969	1.44

Forecast EPS for the years 1979 through 1983 using the naive forecasting method. Show all work.

2. Per share earnings and dividend data for three companies follow:

	Company A		Company B		Company C	
	EPS	Div.	EPS	Div.	EPS	Div.
1978	$4.92	$2.41	$3.87	$2.04	$10.12	$2.75
1977	4.55	2.28	3.41	1.89	8.60	2.25
1976	4.29	2.17	3.06	1.73	5.49	1.35
1975	3.91	1.89	2.19	1.60	4.69	1.15
1974	3.52	1.69	2.85	1.50	7.22	2.00
1973	3.06	1.53	2.92	1.40	5.85	1.50
1972	2.73	1.37	2.38	1.27	4.95	1.35
1971	2.46	1.28	1.49	1.17	3.60	.75
1970	2.20	1.08	1.17	1.08	3.12	.75
1969	2.00	1.00	2.00	1.00	4.00	1.00

Analyze the dividend payout policy of each company over the 1969–78 period. Based on this above data, what type of dividend payment policy would you expect over the next three to five years?

3. Refer to Problem 1 relating to the KDB Corporation. You forecast that KDB's earnings growth will continue *after* 1983 at a rate of 6.1 percent, and expect the dividend payout ratio to remain constant at 47 percent.
   a. Assume an appropriate discount rate of 12.0 percent. What is your estimate of the earnings multiple of KDB stock at the end of 1983?
   b. Estimate the present value of the KDB stock. Use the EPS forecast developed in Problem 1 to make your estimate. Assume that a constant appropriate discount rate of 12.0 percent is applicable and that the stock will be sold at the end of 1983. Would you buy KDB at $36 per share?

4. Select a common stock of your choice and estimate its present value. Show all your work and state all important assumptions. Do you find the stock suitable for purchase?

Selected Readings

Ball, Philip and John W. Kennelly. "The Informational Content of Quarterly Earnings: An Extension and Some Further Evidence." *Journal of Business*, July 1972.

Bernhard, Arnold. *Investing in Common Stocks.* New York: The Value Line Investment Survey, 1975.

Bernstein, Leopold A., and Joel G. Siegel. "The Concept of Earnings Quality." *Financial Analysts Journal*, July–August 1979.

Bower, Dorothy, and Richard S. Bower. "Test of the Stock Evaluation Model." *Journal of Finance*, May 1970.

Bower, Richard S., and Dorothy Bower. "Risk and the Valuation of Common Stock." *Journal of Political Economy*, May–June 1969.

Brealey, Richard. *An Introduction to Risk and Return from Common Stocks.* Cambridge, Mass.: MIT Press, 1969.

Buffett, Warren E. "How Inflation Swindles the Equity Investor." *Fortune*, May 1977.

Cagan, Phillip. "Common Stock Values and Inflation—The Historical Record of Many Countries." National Bureau of Economic Research, Report No. 13, March 1974.

Chase, Richard H., Jr. et al. *Computer Applications in Investment Analysis.* Hanover, N.H.: Dartmouth College, 1966.

"The Costly Troubles at Franklin Mint." *Business Week*, May 30, 1977.

Eisemann, Peter C. and Edward A. Moses. "Stock Dividends: Management's View." *Financial Analysts Journal*, July–August 1978.

Elton, Edwin J. and Martin J. Gruber. "Improving Forecasting Through the Design of Homogeneous Groups." *Journal of Business*, October 1971.

Fiske, Heich A. "The Computer: How It Is Changing the Money Manager." *Institutional Investor*, April 1968.

Graber, Dean E. and Bill D. Jarnagin. "The FASB—Eliminator of 'Managed Earnings'?" *Financial Analysts Journal*, March–April 1979.

Lintner, John. "Distribution of Incomes of Corporations among Dividends, Retained Earnings and Taxes," *American Economic Review*, May 1956, pp. 97–113.

Lintner, John. "Dividends, Earnings, Leverage, Stock Prices and the Supply of Capital to Corporations." *Review of Economics and Statistics*, August 1962.

Lintner, John. "Inflation and Common Stock Prices in a Cyclical Context." National Bureau of Economic Research, 53rd Annual Report, September 1973.

Lintner, John. "Inflation and Security Returns." *Journal of Finance*, May 1975.

Lintner, John and Robert Glauber. "Higgledy Piggledy Growth in America." In *Modern Developments in Investment Management.* Ed. James Lorie and Richard Brealey. New York: Praeger Publishers, 1972.

Little, Ian M. D. "Higgledy Piggledy Growth." *Institute of Statistics*, November 1961.

Lorie, James and M. Hamilton. *The Stock Market: Theories and Evidence.* Homewood, Ill.: Dow Jones-Irwin, 1973.

Malkiel, Burton G. "An Atheist Glimpses Heaven." *Forbes*, February 18, 1980.

Malkiel, Burton G. and John G. Cragg. "Expectations and the Structure of Share Prices." *American Economic Review*, September 1970.

McKibben, Walt. "Econometric Forecasting of Common Stock Investment Returns: A New Methodology Using Fundamental Operating Data." *Journal of Finance*, May 1972.

Miller, Merton H. and Franco Modigliani. "Dividend Policy, Growth, and the Valuation of Shares." *Journal of Business*, October 1961.

Modigliani, Franco and Richard A. Cohn. "Inflation, Rational Valuation and the Market." *Financial Analysts Journal*, March–April 1979.

Praetz, Peter D. "The Distribution of Share Price Changes." *Journal of Business*, January 1972.

Stern, Joel M. "Earnings Per Share Don't Count." *Financial Analysts Journal*, July–August 1974.

Whitbeck, Volkert S. and Manown Kisor. "A New Tool in Investment Decision Making." *Financial Analysts Journal*, May–June 1963.

Williamson, J. Peter. *Investments: New Analytic Techniques.* New York: Praeger Publishers, 1970.

Williamson, J. Peter and David H. Downes. *Manual for Computer Programs in Finance and Investments.* Hanover, N.H.: The Amos Tuck School of Business Administration, Dartmouth College, 1971.

Winder, James. "Yield Spread Outlook." *Weekly Economic Package*, Chemical Bank, July 24, 1979.

Working, Holbrook. "A Random–Difference Series for Use in the Analysis of Time Series." *Journal of the American Statistical Association*, March 1934.

Zacks, Leonard. "EPS Forecasts—Accuracy Is Not Enough." *Financial Analysts Journal*, March–April 1979.

Technical Analysis

Introduction

To this point, much of this book has been concerned with the determination of present value of individual securities, because such analysis is essential if capital markets are to be efficient. Chapters 6 through 8 were devoted to a discussion of the valuation of fixed income securities. Subsequently, in Chapters 9 through 11, attention was focused on the calculation of present value of common stock through the application of fundamental analysis.

Proponents of fundamental analysis believe that the present value of a common stock is a function of a set of variables relating to the economy, the industry to which the company belongs, and the related company. Consequently, they argue that the present value of a stock can be determined by analyzing these *fundamental factors* or variables.

The relationship between efficient markets and fundamental analysis is both direct and intimate. According to the semistrong (and strong) form of the Efficient Market Hypothesis (EMH), in an efficient market, stocks tend to sell at their present values. Fundamental analysts argue, however, that there can be a temporary imbalance between a stock's price and its present value.[1] Consequently by making a careful and sophisticated forecast of future dividend payments, the expected selling price at the end of the holding period and the appropriate discount rate an investor can identify undervalued securities and obtain above average returns by investing in them.

[1] The three forms of the EMH were introduced in Chapter 5 and they will be discussed more fully in Chapter 14.

The theories and techniques of *technical analysis* are at complete odds with the EMH. Proponents of technical analysis do not concern themselves with fundamental factors because the relationship between present value and market price is of little interest to them. Technical analysts believe that the future expected price of a stock—the only variable that matters—can be predicted by carefully analyzing its past price behavior, because movements in past prices create discernible patterns that tend to repeat themselves in predictable ways. Consequently, technicians concern themselves with predictions of short-term price movements in an effort to determine the best *timing* for purchases and sales of common stocks. For these reasons, it is sometimes claimed that the fundamental technique is generally best for selecting *what* to buy or sell, whereas technical analysis primarily helps one decide *when* to trade in stocks.

As previously mentioned, this book emphasizes fundamental analysis in an efficient market. For various reasons, little attention is given to technical analysis. For example, much of the "proof" offered to support technical theories is inconclusive, and many theories have never been rigorously tested. Also, the basis for technical analysis is essentially a *non sequitur*: In order to reject the EMH, technical analysts must demonstrate that by using their techniques and theories, one can consistently outperform the market. Unfortunately, such evidence has never been presented in a generally acceptable form.

Despite the limitations alluded to in the foregoing discussion, studying technical analysis can be valuable. For one thing, in one form or another, many investors and security analysts continue to use technical analysis. For another, for pedagogical reasons it is appropriate to learn about the philosophy, the tools, and the techniques of technical analysis.

In this chapter, we will present the basic theories of technical analysis and discuss the important tools used in this type of analysis. For reasons already specified, we will not attempt to evaluate critically the theories and techniques of technical analysis. Furthermore, we will not challenge the claims made by technical analysts that by resorting to their techniques investors can consistently outperform the market. Simply stated, in this chapter our objective is to present an *uncritical* yet comprehensive view of the essentials of technical analysis.

Theory of Technical Analysis

An Overview

Technical analysts endeavor to predict future price levels of stocks by analyzing past data from the market itself. *Technical analysis* is

> *the study of the internal stock exchange information as such . . . . The current market price is assumed to represent the total knowledge of the investment community about any given security at a particular moment; that price discounts all the good news and all the bad. The sum of the knowledge*

which has led to the determination of price is greater than that available to any individual investor or to any group of investors.[2]

Clearly, technical analysis is *internally* oriented. That is, technicians "believe that the value of the stock depends primarily on supply and demand and may have little relationship to any intrinsic value."[3]

Technical analysts do not deny the fact that fundamental factors influence the supply and demand conditions. However, they argue that because the market price of a stock reflects *all* factors affecting it, a study involving only stock price movements is necessary.

Technical analysis is not concerned with such fundamental factors as future dividends, holding period selling price, and the appropriate discount rate reflecting the risk of a stock. The theory of technical analysis "rests upon the assumption that history tends to repeat itself in the stock exchange. If a certain pattern of activity has in the past produced certain results nine times out of ten, one can assume a strong likelihood of the same outcome whenever this pattern appears in the future."[4] Based on the available evidence, it appears that a large part of the theory of technical analysis lacks a solid foundation.[5]

The Terminology

In order to appreciate fully the theory of technical analysis, it is necessary to understand the basic terminology. In every transaction involving stocks, there are always a buyer and a seller. However, nearly always, one of the two parties is *more eager* than the other to complete the transaction. When the seller is the more anxious, he or she will agree to sell at a price lower than the price of the last sale. The transaction then takes place on a *downtick.* It is obvious that transactions can take place consistently on a downtick only when sellers are willing to make a major concession in price. Such a development in the marketplace is evidence of a movement of stocks from strong to weak hands; that is, from those who had a strong interest in holding them to those whose primary inducement to buy is lower stock prices. Movement of stocks from strong to weak hands is called a *distribution.*

In a bull market, the reverse trend is recorded. In that market, buoyed by the optimistic economic and financial forecasts, buyers become willing to offer progressively higher prices for stocks they are anxious to own. Consequently, trade takes place on an *uptick.* More specifically, major advances in stock prices on a large block trade are viewed as evidence of *accumulation,* because stocks move from weak to strong hands.

[2] Felix Rosenfeld, ed., *The Evaluation of Ordinary Shares,* Summary of the Proceedings of the 8th Congress of the European Federation of Financial Analysts Societies (Paris: Dunod, 1975), p. 297.

[3] George E. Pinches, "The Random Walk Hypothesis and Technical Analysis," *Financial Analysts Journal,* March–April 1970, pp. 104–10.

[4] Rosenfeld, *The Evaluation of Ordinary Shares,* pp. 297–98.

[5] The theory of technical analysis does not specify the relative importance that should be attached to various technical factors. More specifically, each analyst must personally decide (1) which of

Trend is another popular term of technical analysts who examine both short and long views of stock price fluctuations to distinguish a minor or a major uptrend or downtrend in the market. These trends then form the basis for technical forecasting of the stock market in general, or of any given stock in particular.

Frequently the market pauses and moves sideways; that is, stock prices fluctuate slightly for some time, before the market reverses its trend. This period, which is not part of either an upturn or a downturn, is known as the period of *consolidation*.

Finally, the use of several additional terms frequently employed by technical analysts may be summarized:

> *The market is made up of investors (shareholders interested in price trends) and traders (shareholders interested in near-term price changes); of bulls (those hoping for rises) and bears (those hoping for declines); of longs (those who own the shares they hold) and shorts (those who sold shares they borrowed); of the floating supply (shares that can be purchased at prices slightly higher than current quotations) and investment holdings (shares that can be purchased only at prices much higher than current quotations).*[6]

Basic Assumptions

The theory of technical analysis is based on several assumptions; three of the key assumptions are described below.[7]

Assumption 1

The stock market, or an individual stock, acts like a *barometer* rather than a thermometer; that is, it predicts a future condition rather than measuring an existing condition. It is this predictive power that prompts the technical analysts to study the behavior of the market or a given stock.

Assumption 2

Every major downturn in a stock is preceded by a period of distribution. Conversely, before a stock experiences a major advance, a period of accumulation takes place.

---

the many technical factors *must* be analyzed in any given situation, and (2) how much weight should be put on the results associated with each factor analyzed before making a final judgment. Although such a state of affairs leaves considerable room for differences of opinion regarding the prevailing technical strength or weakness of the market or the stock, it does underscore the fact that technical analysis must be viewed more as an art than a science.

[6] From *The Stock Market* by Wilford Eiteman, et al. (New York: McGraw-Hill, 1966), p. 403. Copyright © 1966 McGraw-Hill. Used with the permission of McGraw-Hill Book Company.

[7] Alan R. Shaw, "Technical Analysis," in *Financial Analyst's Handbook*, ed. Sumner N. Levine (Homewood, Ill.: Dow Jones–Irwin, 1975), p. 945. © 1975 by Dow Jones–Irwin, Inc.

Figure 12–1

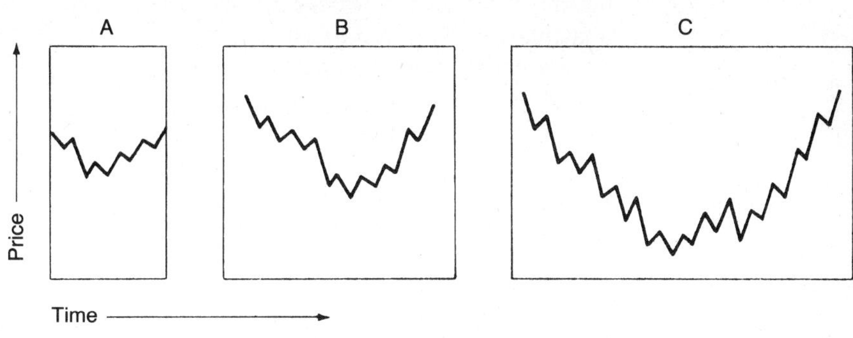

SOURCE: Alan R. Shaw, "Technical Analysis," in *Financial Analyst's Handbook*, ed. Sumner N. Levine (Homewood, Ill.; Dow Jones-Irwin, 1975), p. 947.

Assumption 3

Movements in the market are usually related. The relationship between movements that are an integral part of either an upturn or a downturn is easily recognized. However, even when the market is undergoing a phase of short- or long-term consolidation, movements in the market have a relationship, because they are generally part of a longer downward or upward movement. This is clearly shown in Figure 12–1. In Figure 12–1A, the minor downward movement in price was followed by a short-term consolidation phase before the stock began to move up once again. In Figure 12–1B, however, because the downside adjustment was somewhat more severe, the consolidation pattern was slightly longer in perspective. Finally, Figure 12–1C is an extreme case, because it reflects both a major downtrend and an uptrend.

The Dow Theory

An Overview

For many investors, the theory of technical analysis and the *Dow Theory* are synonymous expressions. It is widely held that there is a unique, magic formula, or average, by which everyone can judge the state of the market. Actually there is no single formula or average that can be described as the market average. Several averages are used, of which the Dow Jones Averages are the most popular. The behavior of these averages is explained by the Dow Theory.

In the latter part of the nineteenth century, Charles H. Dow of New York City evolved a stock market theory that was unique at the time, but is still accepted today by some technical analysts. He recognized that astute investors operated not according to the fluctuations of individual stocks, but according to the basic trend of the market as a whole. This was possible because most stocks tended to move up and down together. There were exceptions, of course, but most well-known stocks advanced in a strong market and declined in a weak market. If this is basically true, Dow argued, it should be possible to judge the market trend by computing an average for a carefully selected sample of stocks. This marked the beginning of what are popularly known as the Dow Jones (Industrial, Transportation, and Utility) Averages. The first Dow Jones Industrial Average started on May 26, 1896, was an average of the prices of 12 major stocks of that period. In 1916, in order to make the average more representative, the list of stocks was broadened to 20; in 1928, the number was increased to 30, a figure that has since remained unchanged.

Charles Dow, who was also the founder–editor of the celebrated *Wall Street Journal*, died in 1902. William P. Hamilton succeeded Dow as editor of the journal and, a staunch supporter of the Dow theory, went further than Dow in analyzing the relationships between stock market movements and general business. It was Hamilton who associated the Dow theory with the technical approach and pointed out the distinction between that approach and the fundamental approach.

Dow and Hamilton argued that at any given moment the stock market reflects three movements: a major trend (like the ocean's tide) either upward or downward; an intermediate trend (the wave); and the day-to-day fluctuations (the ripple). If this is true, they argued, then one must have a satisfactory way of identifying the major (tides), intermediate (waves), and minor (ripples) trends. After all, a price fluctuation lasting a few hours—in which the price of a stock goes from 90 to $90\frac{1}{2}$, falls back to $90\frac{1}{4}$, and then rises to $90\frac{3}{4}$—is of little consequence. However, a six-month increase in the Dow Jones Industrial Average (DJIA) from 631 to 775 must be recognized as a major uptrend. Consequently, Dow and Hamilton explained their formula for identifying the three trends as follows: The market always has three movements, or trends, all going on at the same time. The first is the narrow movement, from day to day, which may be called a minor trend. The second is the short swing, running from two weeks to a month or more, which is probably a secondary trend. The third movement—of at least four years' duration—may be called a major trend.

Dow's original theory was made more sophisticated by Hamilton in at least two ways. Hamilton maintained that a major uptrend in the market is confirmed when either the industrial or the transportation average advances beyond the previous high, followed by similar advances in the other average. Similarly, when both averages dip below a previous low, such an event should be regarded as a signal for a decline in the market.

Another dimension added to the Dow theory is the *equilibrium* concept. Movement of stock prices within a narrow range for several weeks—that is, a sideways movement of the market—indicates a period of accumulation and distribution. During this period, buyers and sellers reach a state of equilibrium, and the upper and the lower market levels are established. When the Dow Jones Industrial and Transportation Averages rise above the upper level, the market is probably ready for a major upward move. Conversely, a decline in these averages below their previous levels establishes a basis for a major downtrend in the market.

Surprisingly, even though it was formulated several decades ago, the Dow Theory still reigns all-important in the minds of its proponents. However, over the years it has undergone one important modification: It is now believed that a major movement can last from less than one year to as many as six years.

Basic Assumptions

Charles Dow, the founder of the Dow Theory, did not clearly state his assumptions. However, the following three assumptions are implicit in his Theory.[8]

Assumption 1

Stock market profits are made largely by following the primary trend in the market. The primary trend continues anywhere from one to four years and provides an investor with ample opportunities to make profits.

Assumption 2

During a primary uptrend phase, each secondary trend is associated with a peak higher than the previous peak, and a trough higher than the previous trough. Conversely, when the market is in a downward primary trend, each secondary peak and trough is lower than the preceding ones.

Assumption 3

The primary trend is generally confirmed by a movement of different stock averages in the same direction. For example, when the primary trend is up, both the industrial average and the transportation average will show an uptrend.

The Record

Technical analysts claim that the record of the Dow Theory as a predictive tool has been impressive.[9] It is asserted that between 1920 and 1975 the Dow Theory signals registered 68 percent of the moves of the industrial and transportation averages, and 67 percent of the moves of the S&P 500 Index. On the basis of this record, a supporter of technical analysis concludes that "Dow Theory confirmations by their nature—relying on penetration of significant lows or highs by both averages—cannot get a trader out at the top or in at the bottom. What the theory can do—and has done with only one notable miss in the 79

---

[8] See W. P. Hamilton, *The Stock Market Barometer* (Princeton: Dow Jones, 1922); Robert Rhea, *The Dow Theory* (Princeton: Dow Jones, 1932); G. W. Bishop, Jr., ed., *Charles H. Dow, Economist* (Princeton: Dow Jones, no date.)

[9] These claims have never been adequately supported, and few fundamentalists accept the conclusions presented here.

Figure 12–2

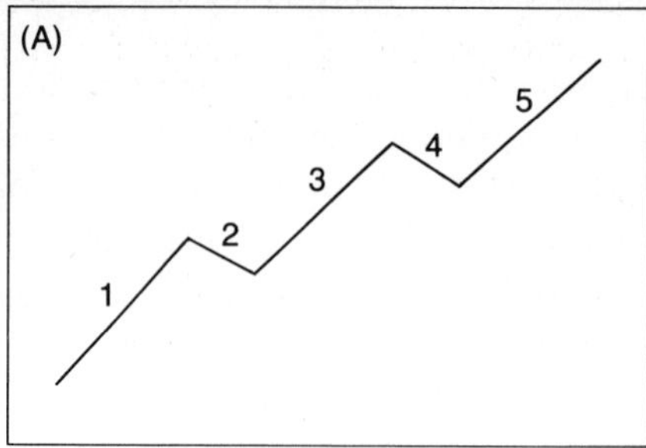

A. Graph Showing a Major Move in Five Successive Steps

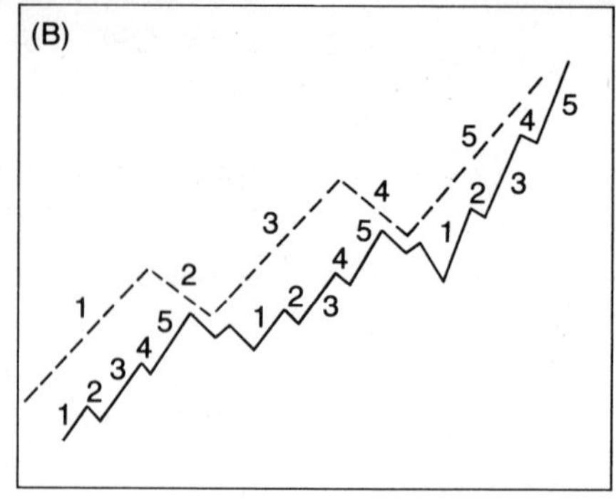

B. A Close-Up of the Five-Step Market Moves

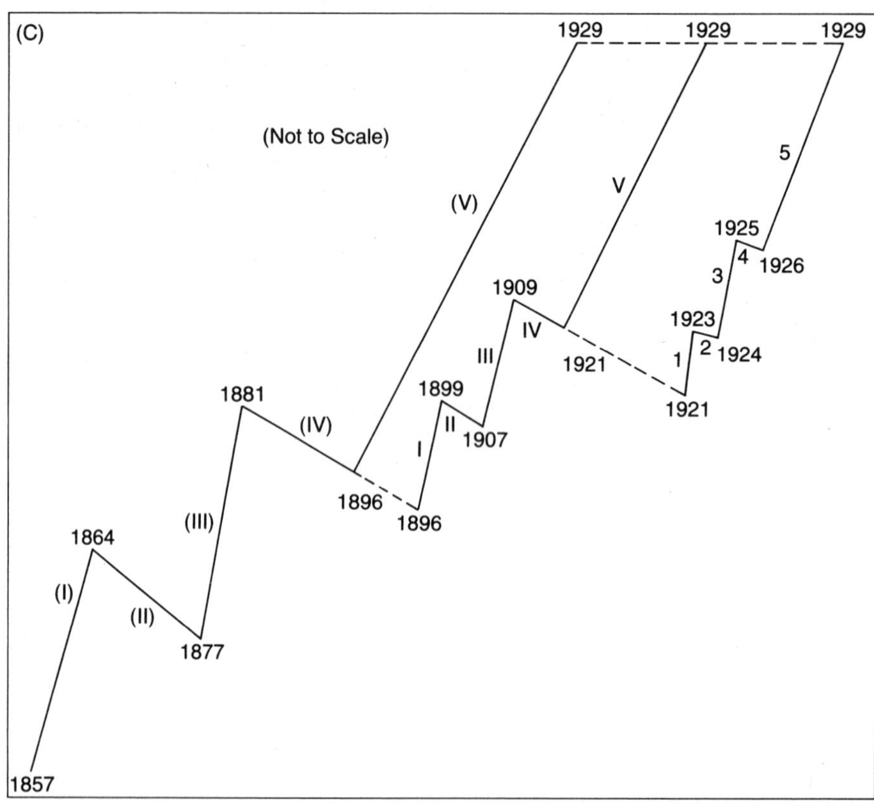

C. Waves, Subwaves, and the DJIA

NOTE: Each of waves (I) (III) (V) breaks down into five subwaves, as do waves I, III, V, and waves 1, 3, 5. Corrective waves (II) (IV), II, IV, and 2, 4 break down into three subwaves.

SOURCE: Edmund W. Tabell and Anthony W. Tabell, "The Case for Technical Analysis," *Financial Analysts Journal,* March–April 1964, pp. 68–69.

years since Charles H. Dow began writing his *Wall Street Journal* editorials on the market—is keep the investor on the right side of the biggest part of extended moves."[10]

Elliott Wave Principle

The Dow Theory provides the basic framework for technical analysts; however, it has several limitations. The Dow Theory might work only when a long, wide, upward or downward movement is registered in the market. It is mostly unsuitable as a market predictor when the market trend frequently reverses itself in the short or the intermediate term. Another major drawback is that the theory does not attempt to explain a consistent pattern of the stock price movements.

One theory that attempts to develop a rationale for a long-term pattern in the stock price movements is the *Elliott Wave Principle* (EWP), established in the 1930s by R. N. Elliott and later popularized by Hamilton Bolton. The EWP states that major moves take place in five successive steps resembling tidal waves. In a major bull market, the first move is upward, the second downward, the third upward, the fourth downward, and the fifth and final phase upward. The waves have a reverse flow in a bear market. The EWP, claimed to be a valuable tool for market prediction, is demonstrated in Figure 12–2.

Figure 12–2A is a simple demonstration of the EWP when the stock market advance goes through five clearly marked stages. In Figure 12–2B, we see that a major five-stage advance, indicated by broken lines, may run concurrently with several mini five-stage advances (indicated by a solid line). The EWP is applied to an actual situation in Figure 12–2C, where it is demonstrated that past movements in the DJIA have followed the five-stage advance principle. For example, the major advance in the DJIA between 1896 and 1929 can be viewed as two minor five-stage advances, one covering the period 1896 to 1909, and the other covering the years 1921 through 1929.

Proponents of the EWP claim that it offers investors a basis for developing important market strategies. However, even they do not deny the fact that the EWP has two major limitations. First, it is difficult to identify the turning point of each stage. Second, investors frequently cannot distinguish between a major and a minor five-stage movement.

The Role of Technical Factors

Technical analysts apply their theories to the development of investment strategies through the use of several techniques. For the most part, interpretation of a set of technical factors by technicians constitutes the use of their techniques.

[10] John C. Boland, "How Now, Dow Theory?" *Barron's*, September 5, 1977, p. 5. However, Boland does not provide proof for such a strong assertion.

Table 12–1

Activity Factors	Directional Factors
High–Low Index	Daily Trading Barometer
Advances–Declines Index	Directional Moves
Most Active Stocks	
Lo/Price Activity Ratio	Contrary Opinion Factors
Dow Jones Momentum Ratio	Short Interest
	Odd-Lot Index and Odd-Lot Index Sales
Market Strength Factors	NYSE Specialists' Short Sales Ratio
Breadth Index	Advisory Service Sentiment
Relative Strength Index	Credit Balances
Volume of Trading	
Large Block Transactions	Confidence Factor
	Barron's Confidence Index

Also, most technical analysts rely heavily on charts of prices and volumes for their analysis.

Several technical factors are outlined in Table 12–1.[11] As we describe each factor, we will specify the claims made by technical analysts, but will make no attempt to present the arguments or evidence that dispute these claims. As previously mentioned, most claims of technical analysis are based on inconclusive studies.

Activity Factors

The first set of factors grouped under this heading deals with the level of activities registered in the market.

High–Low Index

The *high–low index* is an indicator of the technical strength of the market. It is an average of the number of NYSE stocks making new highs (that is, surpassing their previously established highest price levels for the preceding 52 weeks) minus the number making new lows. New highs and new lows during a given week are listed in Table 12–2; similar information is presented in graphic form in Figure 12–3.

The high–low index measures the strength of the market leaders and the ability of the market to advance to a higher ground, or its inability to resist sinking to a lower ground. It is asserted that during a rising market an increasing number of stocks reach new highs and a decreasing number of stocks reach new lows. The reverse is true in a declining market. Consequently, an increase in the high–low index indicates the market's technical strength; conversely, a decline in the index reflects a technical weakness in the market.

[11] Several techniques discussed in this section are included in Robert J. Nurock, "Wall Street Week: Technical Market Index," Merrill Lynch Pierce Fenner & Smith, October 22, 1976.

Table 12–2

New Highs & Lows

Week Ended October 5, 1979

NYSE—COMPOSITE

New Highs 283

ACF Ind	Buff Forge	EmpirGas	Hecla Mng	La Pacif	PioneerCp wi	StdOilOh
ASA	Bunk Ramo	Enserch	HelmPayn	Lynch CSys	Pneumo Cp	Standex
Acme Clev	BunkRm pf	Esmark	HelmPayn wi	Macmilln pf	PogoProd	StanleyWk
Adams Exp	Buttes Gas	ExCellO	Hemisp Cap	Madisn Fd	Pope Talb	Sunsh Mng
Alaska Int	CBI Ind s	Fairchild s	Hershy Fds	MaratOil s	Premier Ind	Superior Oil
AlbanyInt s	CIT Financl	FedExpress	HewlettPk s	Marriott	QuakStOil wi	TRW Inc
Albertsons	Callah Mng	FedPapBd	High Volt	Marsh McL	Rdg Bates	TRW 4.40pf
AlcanAlum	CampRLk g s	FePa 1.20pf	Homestke	Martin M	Reich Chem	TRW 4.50pf
Alco Stand	CdnPac g	FstMiss Cp	HudsBMn g	Maytag	RepFnSvc s	Talcott Nat
Allied Chem	CarpTech	FstNatBos	IUInt Cp	McMoranOil	Republic Stl	Tappan Co
AmaxInc s	CarsPir	Fisher Sci	IUInt A	Metromed	Reynold Ind	Teradyne In
Amerace Cp	Cascde NGs	Flintkote	IUInt pf	MirroCorp	Reynln 2.25pf	Texaco Inc
Amerace pf	Ceco Corp	Flintkt pfB	IUInt 1.36pf	Monsanto	Richardsn	TexEastn
Am Distill	Centex Corp	FluorCp s	Incom Cap	MorKnud	Rockwel Int	TexGasT pf
AGenConv	CentLaEn	Fluor pfB	Indiana Gas	Motorola	RockwInt pf	Texas Inst
AmGen Ins	CessnaAir	FooteConB	IntMin Chm	Murphy Oil	RockInt pfB	TexOil Gas
Am Hoist	Cities Svc	For McKess	Int Rectif	NL Ind	Rollins Inc	TexPac Ld
Am Hospit	Colum Pict	FoMcK pfA	IowaBeef s	Nat Gypsm	Rosario Res	Texasgulf
AmNat Res	ComPsyc	Franklin Mt	Itek Corp	NatLibty n	Rowan	Texglf 3pf
AmerStores	Comptrvsn s	Fuqua Ind	Jewelcor	NatMedEnt s	Safegrd Ind	Times Mirr
Ampex Cp	ConocoInc	GATX Cp	KaisrAlum	Nat Semicn	StJoe Min	Toys R Us n
AnalogDv s	Con Foods	GATX Cp pf	KaisrAl 57pf	Natomas	StRegis Pap	Tri Cont
ApacheCp s	Cooper Ind	GCA Corp	KanebSvc	NevadPow	Sanders	UGI Corp
ArmcoInc pf	CoopIn cvpf	GK Tech	Kennecott	Newhall Ld	SantaFe Ind	Unarco Ind
Arrow Elect	CoreInd s	GK Tec 1.94pr	KerrGls 1.70pf	NewprkRes	SanFeInd pf	Un Carbide
AtlRichfl	CorroonB	Gannett Co	KerrMcG	Niagra Shre	Schlumbrg s	Union Corp
AtlRh 2.80pf	Crane Co	Gemini Cap	Kidde Co	NorNat Gas	ScieAtlnta s	UnEnRes
Auto Data	CrumFor	GenAm Inv	Kidde prA	NwstEnrgy s	Scot LFd	UtdRefg s
Avery Inter	Dan River	GenDynam s	Kidde prB	PPGInd	Scottys	Unitrode Cp
BakerInt	Dart Ind	GnDyn 4.25pf	Kidde pfC	PSA Inc	Seagram g	Varian Asso
BauschLb s	DeereCo	Geosrce	Kidde 1.64pr	Pac Lghtg	SealdPow	VeecoInst
Baxt Travnl	DigitalEq	GettyOil	LFE Corp	Pac Tin	SEDCO Inc	WarnrCom s
Beker Ind	Divers Ind	GiffdHill s	LFECp pfA	ParkerDrl s	Signode Cp	WeisMkts s
BelcoPet s	DowJones	Global Mar	LanierBP	Patrick Petl	Smith Int	WnCo NAm
Beth Steel	Dresser Ind	Goodrich	Lehman Cp	PaylsDg	Smithkline s	Westvaco
BigThree	Dun Bradst	Grace Co	Lennar s	PengoInd	SoNatRes	Weyerhsr
BlairJohn s	DynaCp Am	Grummn Cp	Lilly Eli	Pennzoil Co	SouUnCo	Weyerhsr pf
Boise Cascd	EG&G Inc	Gulf Resrc	Lionel Corp	Petrolane s	SpectraPhys	WoodsPetl
Borg Warn	E Systm s	GlfRes pfA	Litton pfA	PhillpsPet	StaleyMfg	YatesInd s
Brit Pet	EatonCp s	GlfRes pfB	LouLd Exp	Pioneer Cp	StdOil Ind	Zapata Cp
BrushWell s	Elixir Ind	GlfRs pfC				

New Lows 164

AVX Cp s	CinG 9.28pf	duPnt 3.50pf	IndiM 2.15pf	NevP 1.95pf	PaPL 8.40pf	SchrPlo 5.70pf
AlaPw dep pf	CinG 9.52pf	duPnt 4.50pf	IndiM 2.25pf	NEngPw pf	PPL 9.24pf	SingerCo pf
AlaP 8.16pf	CocaCola	DukeP pfH	Itel Corp	NYS 3.75pf	PaPL 8.70pf	SCarEG pf
AlaP 8.28pf	ColdwlBnkr s	DukeP pfN	Itel 1.44pf	NiM 4.10pf	PhEl 4.30pf	SouNET pfA
AlgLud 2.19pf	CwE 2pf	DukeP pfM	JerCenP 8pf	NiM 4.85pf	PhEl 4.68pf	SoRy 2.60pf
AmAir 2.18pf	CwE 8.38pf	DukeP pfK	JhnMnv 5.40pf	NiM 10.60pf	PhilaEl 7pf	Swest PSvc
AmBrd 2.75pf	CwE 2.37pf	DuqLt 2.10prK	KLM Airl	NSPw 4.16pf	PhEl 7.80pf	StdBrand pf
AmCan pf	CwE 8.40pf	East Kodak	KCPL 2.20pf	NSPw 6.80pf	PotEl 4.04pf	Tex Util
AmEl Pw	CwE 7.24pf	Fst Penna	KCPL 2.33pf	NSPw 7.84pf	PubSvc Col	Texfi Ind
AmStr 5.51pf	ConNGas pf	FlexiV 1.61pf	KC Sthn pf	NSPw 8.80pf	PSInd 8.96pf	TolEd 2.36pf
AmTT pfA	CnPw 7.45pf	FtDearbn S	KanGasEl	NwtPip 2.36pf	PSNH 2.81pf	TolEd 8.84pf
AmTT pfB	CnPw 7.76pf	Garfnkl Brk	KansPL 2.32pf	OhE 3.90pf	PSEG 1.40pf	TWC 1.90pf
ApPw 2.35pf	CnPw 2.23pr	GMtr 3.75pf	KerrGls 1.70pf	OhE 4.40pf	PSEG 5.28pf	UGICp pf
ArizPSv pf	DaytPL pfF	GenMot 5pf	Kuhlman	OhEd 9.12pf	PSEG 2.17pf	UnEl 2.72pf
BaltGE pfB	DaytPL pfG	GnTIEI pf2.48	LamsnSesn s	OhE 10.48pf	PSEG 6.80pf	UnEl 7.44pf
BkTr 4.22pf	DetE 7.68pf	GTFI 8.16pf	LiggGrp 7pf	OhPow pfG	PSEG 2.43pf	UtPL 2.04pf
BosE 8.88pf	DetE 7.45pf	GaPw 2.52pf	LongIL pfP	OhPw 14pfA	PSEG 7.70pf	Vestaur Sec
BurlNor pf	DetE 7.36pf	GaPw 7.80pf	LongILt pfO	OhPow 14pf	PSEG 7.80pf	VaEP 8.84pf
CentSo West	DetE 2.75pf	GaPw 7.72pf	Memorex	OhPw 8.48pf	PSEG 7.52pf	VaEP 8.60pf
CIIILt 2.87pf	DetE 2.75pfB	Goodyear	MinnMM	Okla GE	PSEG 7.40pf	WabRR pf
ChasMnh 6.75pf	DetE 2.28pr	Hayes Alb	Mutl Omah	OklaGE pf	PSEG 9.62pf	WaynGos pf
ChasMnh 7.60pf	DiGior pfB	IIIPw 4.42pf	NDist 4.50pf	Pac TelTel	QuakStOil wi	WeanU pfA
ChespkVa s	DillonCos s	IIIPw 7.56pf	NatFuelG pf	PaPL 8.60pf	StPaul Sec	WisEl 8.90pf
CinG 9.30pf	DrPepper	IIIPw 8.94pf				

AMEX—COMPOSITE

New Highs 138

AZL Res	CdnHomstd g	Day Mines	GtBas Pet	Interplast	PennRl Est	SundanceO
AZL Res pf	CdnMerrill g	DelhiOil	GREIT Rlty	Israel Devel	Penob Shoe	SunshJr Str
Aberdn Mf	CdnSupOil g	Designc Jwl	Gross Tlcst	JeteroCp	PetroLew	SupronEnr s
AirExpress n	CenSec pfC	DevCp Am	Guards Ch	Juniper Pet	PlacerDev g	Tech Sym
Alpha Ind	CenvillC	DevonGp s	GulfCan g	KenaiCp	PrestonMin g	Tejon Rnch
Altermn Fd	ChiefDev g s	DorchstrGas n	HallsMot T	KinArk Cp	PrimeMot s	Tidwell Ind
AmBus Pds	CityGas Fla	Driver Harr	Heinicke	KirbyExp	PropCap T	TransctlOil
Andrea Rad	Claremont	EAC Ind	HiShear	Landmk Ld	Ranchr Ex	Transtech
AngloCo Ltd	Colwell Co	EECO Inc	HighInd Cap	ManorCr	RangerOil g	TritonOG n
AsameraO g	Com Allian	Earth Rsrcs	Hipotronic	Marshall In	Rem Arms	UnitAircPd
AugatInc s	Coml Metal	Electrogr	Howell Ind	Masters In	RepNY Cp	Univ Cigar
Aydin Cp	CommdreInt s	EmrsRad	HubellA	MatrlRsh s	RialOil n	Univ Resrcs
BanistrCtl g	Conrock Co	EnergyRes	HubellB	Mich Sugar	Roblin Ind	Wainoc Oil
Baruch Fost	ConOil Gas	Felmnt Oil	Huck Mfg	NFC n	SGL Ind	Wang B s
Bolt Berank	CoreLabs	FlaRock In	IFS Inds	NatHlthEnt	Sorg Paper	Wang C s
Bowmar Ins	CrossAT	Forest Labs	IRT Prop	NewMexAr	Std Metals	Weathrfrd n
Brad Natl	Crutchr Res	GTI Corp	ImperInd s	NoCdnOil g	StarSupmk s	Westbrne g s
BristlBras	CrystalOil s	GatesLrjet	ImperOil A	Park Elect	Stepan Chm	Wichita Ind
BrooksPrk s	DCL Inc	GerberScie	Integrt Res	ParsonsCp s	Struth Well	WrightHar g
CampbChib g	Damson Oil	GntYellow g	IntrCtyGs g	Pat Fashion		

New Lows 44

Alcoa pf	Courtaulds	KanGE pf	PGE 2.57pfW	PGE 2.40pfK	SDie 9.84pf	SCE 3.96pf
Amdahl	DowneySL s	Leisur Tec	PGE 2.32pfV	PGE 2.32pfJ	SDie 7.80pf	TenneyEng s
Am Seating	ExecutvInd	Money Mgt	PGE 2.54pfT	PLtg 4.50pf	SDie 2.68pf	TolEd 4.25pf
ApldDevcs	G Housewar	PGE 1.50pf	PGE 2.62pfS	PLtg 7.64pf	SCE 2.21pf	TownerPet n
Capitol Fd	Hannafrd	PGE 1.37pfB	PGE 2.37pfR	ParsonsCp s	SCE 7.58pf	Walbar n
CmlAlln 1.60pf	Hofm Ind	PGE 1.25pfE	PGE 2pfO	Robintech	SCE 8.70pf	WynnsInt s
ContlTel wt	InplsPL pf					

s-Stock split or dividend amounting to 25% or more paid since January 1. n-New issue since January 1. The 52-week range begins with the start of trading in the split or new issue and doesn't cover the entire 52-week period.

SOURCE: *Barron's*, **October 8, 1979**, p. 81.

Figure 12–3 **High–Low Index**

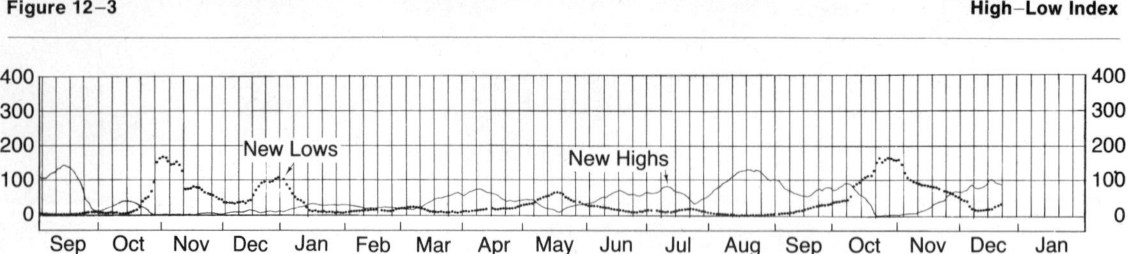

SOURCE: *3-Trend Security Charts* (Boston, Mass.: Securities Research Company, January 1980), p. 3.

Advances–Declines Index

A somewhat different view of the technical performance of the market is taken by use of the *advances–declines index*. This index represents a ratio of the number of issues that advanced to the number that declined, relative to the total number of stocks that changed in price. The S&P advances–declines index is presented in Figure 12–4.

The calculation of the advances–declines index starts with an arbitrary number, say, 100. Assume on a given day 700 issues advance, 300 decline, and 600 remain unchanged. The change in the index is $+0.40$ $[(700 - 300)/1{,}000]$ and the new index is $100 + 0.40 = 100.40$. If on a succeeding day the situation is reversed (that is, 700 issues decline and 300 advance), the index will revert to 100 (that is, $100.40 - 0.40 = 100$).

The traditional belief is that, given the behavior of the advances–declines index and the behavior of the DJIA, the short-term market trend can be predicted. The nature of these predictions is summarized as follows:

Advances–Declines Indicator	DJIA	Future Market Trend: Same as DJIA	Future Market Trend: Opposite to DJIA
Rise	Rise	X	
Rise	Fall		X
Fall	Rise		X
Fall	Fall	X	

The logic for the predictive power of the index is simple. The DJIA is constructed on the basis of only a few stocks, whereas *the market* embraces all stocks traded in it. Consequently, it is believed, for a few days the DJIA may move counter to the all-inclusive market trend; but eventually the DJIA must move in the same direction in which the majority of the stock prices are moving.

More technical-minded analysts construct a biweekly advances–declines moving average based on daily figures of the total number of stocks advancing

Figure 12–4

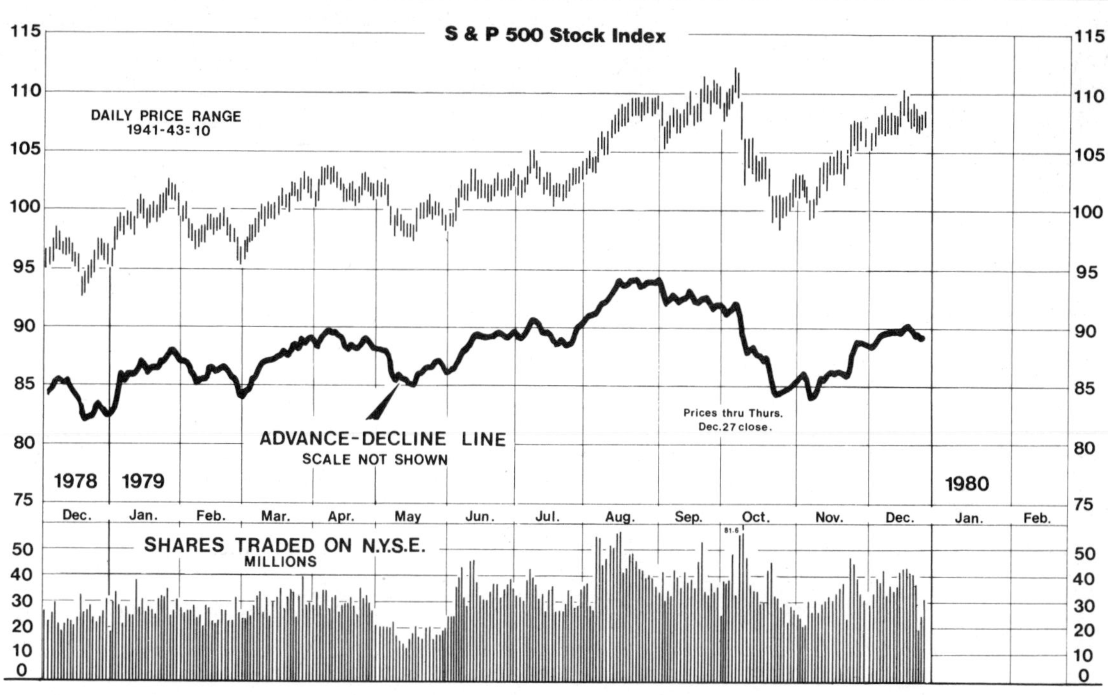

SOURCE: *The Outlook*, Standard & Poor's Corporation, December 31, 1979, Front Cover.

plus half of the number of stocks remaining unchanged, divided by the total number of issues traded. The index then measures the upward or downward momentum, and the underlying trend of the general market, as well as the degree of overbought or oversold conditions at turning points.

Most Active Stocks

A technical factor of major import is the nature of the stocks which are *popular* among investors and traders. Every day the *Wall Street Journal* publishes lists of the most active stocks and their high, low, and closing prices on the New York and American stock exchanges. Samples of these listings are shown in Table 12–3.

Variations in the active stock list occur with changes in the *quality* of market leadership, because, as a general rule, high-quality stocks command relatively higher prices than low-quality issues. Therefore, on any given day, the majority of the most active stocks may represent the blue chips or high-quality stocks, in which case the average price will be relatively high; on another day, the active list may consist of highly speculative, low-quality, low-priced stocks, in which

Table 12–3 **Most Active Stocks**

NEW YORK STOCK EXCHANGE

	Open	High	Low	Close Chg.	Volume
Texas Intl	$18\frac{3}{8}$	$18\frac{3}{8}$	$17\frac{3}{4}$	$18\frac{3}{8} + 1$	679,400
Am Cyan	$31\frac{1}{2}$	$33\frac{1}{4}$	$31\frac{1}{4}$	$32\frac{3}{8} + 1\frac{1}{4}$	416,400
K mart	24	$24\frac{1}{4}$	$23\frac{7}{8}$	24	394,100
SearsRoeb	$18\frac{3}{8}$	$18\frac{1}{2}$	$18\frac{1}{4}$	$18\frac{3}{8} - \frac{1}{8}$	379,800
IBM s	$65\frac{1}{8}$	$65\frac{1}{4}$	$64\frac{5}{8}$	$65 - \frac{1}{4}$	329,700
Colum Pict	$33\frac{3}{4}$	$36\frac{1}{4}$	$33\frac{3}{4}$	$35\frac{5}{8} + 2\frac{1}{8}$	283,200
Exxon	56	$56\frac{5}{8}$	$55\frac{7}{8}$	$56\frac{1}{2} + \frac{1}{4}$	274,500
Amer T&T	53	$53\frac{1}{8}$	$52\frac{7}{8}$	$53 - \frac{1}{8}$	272,000
Arlen Rlty	$3\frac{1}{2}$	4	$3\frac{1}{2}$	$3\frac{7}{8} + \frac{1}{2}$	250,600
Tenneco	$38\frac{3}{8}$	$39\frac{1}{8}$	$38\frac{1}{4}$	$39 + \frac{3}{8}$	247,600
Pennzoil Co	53	$56\frac{1}{8}$	53	$56\frac{1}{8} + 3\frac{1}{8}$	236,200
StdOil Cal	$56\frac{3}{4}$	$56\frac{7}{8}$	$56\frac{3}{8}$	$56\frac{7}{8} - \frac{3}{8}$	234,100
Wllms Cos	$26\frac{1}{4}$	$27\frac{3}{4}$	$26\frac{1}{4}$	$27\frac{1}{2} + 1\frac{1}{4}$	228,100
Gen Motors	$51\frac{1}{2}$	$52\frac{1}{8}$	$50\frac{3}{4}$	$51\frac{7}{8} + \frac{3}{8}$	223,000
GenDynam s	57	$59\frac{1}{4}$	$56\frac{5}{8}$	$59\frac{1}{8} + 2\frac{3}{4}$	212,000

AMERICAN STOCK EXCHANGE

	Volume	Close Chg.
HouOilM	274,900	$22\frac{3}{4} + 1\frac{1}{2}$
Instrum Sys	213,000	$1\frac{1}{8} + \frac{1}{8}$
IntrCtyGs g	177,800	$18\frac{1}{2} + 1$
AsameraO g	144,600	$19\frac{1}{2} + 2$
Champ Ho	140,900	$1\frac{1}{4} + \frac{1}{8}$
BowValley g	128,600	$35 + \frac{7}{8}$
GulfCan g	126,400	$93\frac{1}{4} + 1\frac{3}{4}$
AmIsraeli s	125,600	$2\frac{1}{4} + \frac{1}{2}$
DomePetr g s	107,300	$41\frac{1}{4} - 1\frac{1}{2}$
Earth Rsrcs	103,100	$31\frac{3}{8} + 1\frac{3}{8}$

SOURCE: Reprinted by permission of *The Wall Street Journal*, December 14, 1979, pp. 35, 38.

case the average price would be lower than that of the blue-chip average. Because of the degree of risk involved in holding them, the market is generally more vulnerable when low-quality stocks become popular.

Lo/Price Activity Ratio

The *Lo/Price Activity Ratio* compares activity in speculative stocks to that in quality issues. It represents the weekly ratio of volumes in Barron's Lo/Price Stock Index to volume in the DJIA. The assumption is that high speculative activity usually occurs at the top of the market; whereas low speculative activity occurs at the bottom.

Dow Jones Momentum Ratio

The Dow Jones Momentum Ratio measures the spread between the DJIA and its 30-day moving average, and is assumed to pinpoint turning points in the market. It is claimed that, in a bull market, a differential of between 30 to 40 points indicates that the market has reached the top, and a spread of −30 to 50 suggests that the market has reached the bottom. Similarly, in a bear market, a spread of 20 to 30 points signals a market top, whereas a spread of −50 to 70 signals a market bottom.

Market Strength Factors

The second group of factors measures the overall strength or weakness of the market.

Breadth Index

An important variant of the advances–declines indicator is the *breadth index.* This index is computed by subtracting the number of advances from the number of declines every week and dividing the result by the number of stocks that remained unchanged during that week. If during a certain week 1,000 stocks advance, 500 decline, and 500 remain unchanged, the breadth index would be 1 [(1,000 − 500)/500]. Each week the index figure for that week is added to, or substracted from, the previous week's figure. These data are then plotted on a graph, and the trend in the market is determined from the direction of the movement in the breadth index.

There are many ways of measuring the breadth of the market. A popular method is to subtract the declines from the advances, thereby arriving at the net positive or negative figure representing the breadth index. Figure 12–5 is an example of a breadth index chart.

Relative Strength Index

The *relative strength index* is the ratio of the price of a stock to the DJIA; it measures the performance of a given stock relative to the market. As long as this ratio continues to rise, that stock price is rising at a faster rate than the market, and vice versa.

Suppose on a trading day the price of the ABC stock is $78 per share and the DJIA is 780. The ratio of the two, or the relative strength factor, is 78/780 = 0.10. The next day the price of the stock rises to $90, whereas the DJIA increases to 785. The factor then becomes 90/785 = 0.12. This advance in the index indicates that the ABC stock is acting stronger than the Dow Average. Incidentally, relative strength proponents believe that those stocks that display the greatest relative strength in a bull market also show the greatest weakness in a bear market.[12]

[12] The belief of the relative strength proponents (that stocks which display the greatest relative strength in a bull market also show the greatest weakness in a bear market) is consistent with the notion that a stock has the same beta in a bull market as in a bear market.

Figure 12–5 **The Breadth Index**

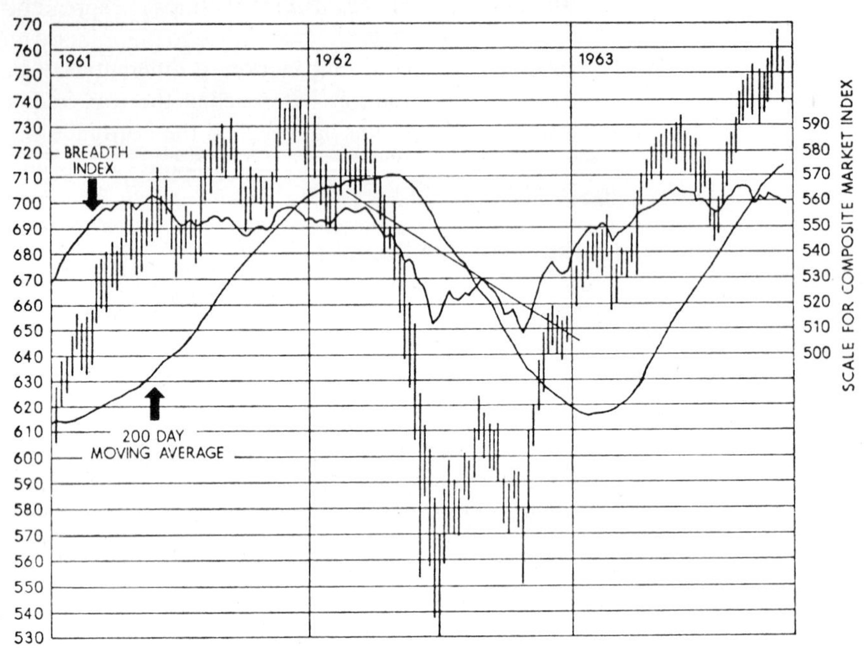

SOURCE: Edmund W. Tabell and Anthony W. Tabell, "The Case for Technical Analysis," *Financial Analysts Journal*, March–April 1964, p. 71.

Volume of Trading

In the stock market the barometer of excitement is the *volume of trading*—that is, the number of issues changing hands. A high trading volume shows interest on the part of investors, either in the form of buying or selling of stocks; a low volume suggests a lack of interest in the market. Figure 12–6 gives the volume of shares traded in the NYSE over a four-month period in 1979.

Some analysts believe that a rise or decline in stock prices on high volume signals a continuation of the existing price trend, whereas a low volume points to an impending reversal of the price trend. It is also asserted that volume tends to be high after a long advance and low after a long decline, because most investors feel comfortable about purchasing stocks after a long bull market but hesitate to take losses at the end of a bear market. In addition, bull markets are associated with spectacular stories about fortunes made overnight. Such stories inevitably attract small investors into a rising market. After entering the market, many small investors continue to operate there, even during a long declining market.

Figure 12–6

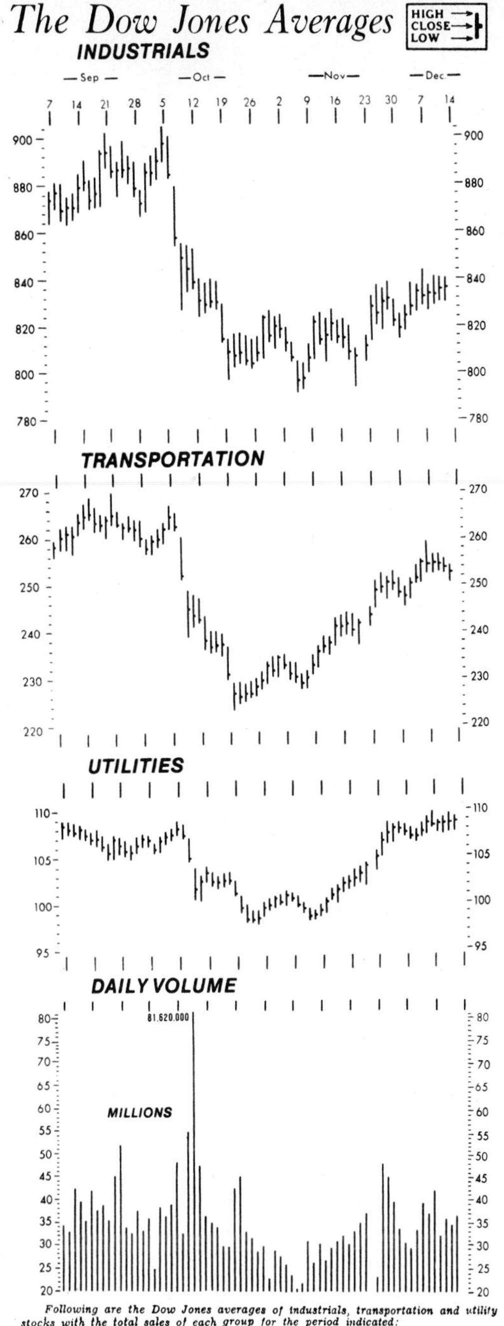

SOURCE: *The Wall Street Journal*, December 14, 1979, p. 39.

Table 12–4 **Large Block Transactions New York Stock Exchange (25,000 Shares and Over)**

OCT. 29	Price	Volume	Prev Sale	OCT. 30	Price	Volume	Prev Sale	OCT. 31	Price	Volume	Prev Sale
Beckman Instru	27	90,000	27	Stanley Works	30¾	34,300	O.T.	LI Lighting (RtWi)	6/64	35,000	O.T.
Joy Mfg	26½	31,900	O.T.	Con Ed NY	22¼	30,000	O.T.	Sterling Drug	18¾	41,000	O.T.
Bally Mfg	27⅞	35,000	O.T.	Pan Am Air	5⅞	55,000	O.T.	Texaco	28	49,400	O.T.
Caesars World	16⅞	28,000	O.T.	Bally Mfg	29¾	40,000	O.T.	CIT Fin'l	57	91,000	O.T.
La Land & Explor	52¾	30,000	52¾	ITT	25	35,000	O.T.	Pan Am Air	6⅜	55,000	O.T.
La Land & Explor	52¾	30,000	52¾	Pittston	20⅞	57,000	21	Cluett Peabody	9	43,400	9
Exxon	57	29,900	O.T.	Pan Am Air	6	64,200	6	Gen'l Motors	56¼	25,000	O.T.
Panhandle East Pipe	52	25,000	O.T.	Detroit Edison	13	65,000	13	Texaco Inc	28	30,000	28
Petrie Stores	30	28,600	30¼	Massey-Ferguson	8½	100,000	8⅞	IBM	64	37,500	O.T.
Ohio Edison	14¼	53,600	14¼	Florida P&L	25	110,300	25	Caesars World	18	50,000	O.T.
Ralston Purina	10⅝	25,000	10½	Exxon	56½	50,000	56¾	Data Gen'l	51¾	157,000	O.T.
Natl Airlines	47½	25,000	47½	Burroughs	69¾	25,000	69¾	Burlington Ind	15¾	25,000	15⅝
Household Finance	17⅜	31,300	17¾	Kennecott Copper	23⅞	180,400	23⅞	Sambo's Restaurants	6⅞	27,000	O.T.
Square D	22¼	37,900	22¼	McDonnell Douglas	26¼	30,000	26⅛	Great Western Fin'l	21½	50,000	O.T.
PepsiCo	24	25,000	24⅛	Reliance Elec	69	181,400	69	Charter Co	43¼	32,000	O.T.
PS New Hampshire	16½	39,900	16⅛	Western Airlines	8	50,000	8⅛	US Steel	21	107,000	21¼
Xerox	58¼	61,200	58⅜	Std Oil Indiana	76	37,500	76	Middle South Utils	13⅜	100,000	13¼
Georgia Pacific	25	51,600	24⅞	Transamerica	16⅝	25,000	16½	Williams Cos	22⅛	25,000	22⅛
Gould Inc	23¾	62,300	23¾	Singer Co	8	100,000	8	LI Lighting(RtWi)	6/64	80,500	6/64
Transco Cos	35	42,600	34½	DuPont	38½	25,000	38¾	Polaroid	24½	42,700	O.T.
Texas Oil & Gas	48½	25,000	48⅜	Masco	22¼	50,000	22⅜	Cummins Engine	29	56,000	O.T.
Pennzoil	46	49,200	46¼	Humana	28½	26,500	29⅛	Central & S West	13½	100,000	13½
Adams Millis	5¼	25,000	5¼	Dow Chemical	29½	25,000	29¾	PS Electric & Gas	19⅜	100,000	19⅜
Pacific G&E	22	75,700	22⅛	Detroit Edison	13	31,000	13	Jefferson Pilot	30½	82,700	30¼
PepsiCo	24⅛	25,000	24⅛	Wal Mart Stores	29	51,600	29	Whittaker Corp	15½	50,000	15½
Gulf Oil	32¾	78,200	32¾	Best Products	23⅜	33,600	23½	Cont'l Illinois	25	26,000	24¾
Mesa Petroleum	67⅜	34,200	67¾	Bemis Co	28	25,600	O.T.	Massey Ferguson Ltd	8¾	25,200	8⅞
Northwest Airlines	26	47,400	26	Greyhound	12½	50,000	12¼	San Juan Racing	16¼	25,000	16¼
Genl Motors	55⅜	33,000	55⅜	NCR Corp	63	117,000	63⅛	ITT	25½	35,000	25⅜
Gen Electric	48⅛	29,000	48⅛	Massey Ferguson	8½	287,700	8¾	Duke Power	17⅞	60,000	18
Middle South Utils	13⅛	80,200	13¼	Standard Oil Calif	53⅜	50,000	53⅜	Bally Mfg	31⅞	95,000	O.T.
Eastman Kodak	49⅜	35,000	49⅝	Dow Chemical	29¾	25,000	29⅞	Pacific G&E	22½	100,000	22¼
EMI Ltd	3	50,000	2⅞	Standard Oil Calif	53⅝	30,000	53½	Amer Elec Power	18⅞	45,000	19
Mesa Royalty Tr (wi)	28	26,000	28	Champion Intl	24	59,500	24	Union Camp	44¼	50,000	44¾
Seagrams Ltd	34	35,000	34	LI Light (Rt wi)	⅛	150,000	O.T.	Pertec Computer	15⅝	50,000	15⅝
Potomac El Pwr	12	28,000	12¼	EMI Ltd	2⅞	44,300	2⅞	McLean Trucking	12¾	30,000	13
Northern Ind PS	13⅜	70,000	13½	Intl Flavors & Frag	19	100,000	19	LI Lighting (RtWi)	5/64	25,000	6/64

Braniff Intl	7½	40,000	7½	Reliance Elec	69	60,000	69⅛	Bemis Co	27½	117,100	27⅝
Du Pont	37½	25,000	37⅞	Storage Technology	14¾	106,000	14⅝	Wisconsin Elec Power	23¼	46,000	23⅜
Southern Co	12⅛	28,400	12¼	Sears Roebuck	18⅛	75,000	18¼	CBS Inc	46½	30,000	46⅞
PS Elec & Gas	18⅝	50,000	18½	Phillips Petroleum	42¾	30,000	42	Schering Plough	29½	150,000	29¾
Champion Intl	24	25,000	24⅛	Pan Am World Air	6⅛	36,800	6⅛	SoCal Edison	24	80,000	24
Va El & Pwr	11⅜	28,700	11¼	US Ind	9	30,000	9	EMI Ltd	3	80,000	3
Southern Co	12¼	53,400	12⅛	PepsiCo	24⅜	27,000	24⅜	EMI Ltd	3	35,000	3
Armstrong Cork	16	48,200	16	Dow Chemical	29⅞	25,000	29⅞	Mobil	49⅜	25,000	49¼
				Niagara Mohawk Pwr	12⅛	44,300	12¼	Pacific G&E	22⅜	100,000	22½
				Time Inc (pfd B)	30⅞	97,200	30⅝	Modern Merch	14⅜	25,000	14⅝
				Time Inc	42½	70,000	42½	Penn Central	16⅝	38,700	16¾
				Boise Cascade	33	25,000	32⅞	US Tobacco	30⅜	48,800	30⅞
				Peabody Intl	20¾	25,900	21	Great Western Fin'l	20¾	40,000	21
				Comwlth Edison	21¼	64,100	21¼	IBM	63½	43,100	63⅜
				Phelps Dodge	23⅝	39,800	23⅝	Snap-On Tools	23	31,500	23¼
				Delta Air Lines	36¼	26,000	36¼	Champion Int'l	24⅜	50,000	24⅝
				Stauffer Chemical	19½	100,100	19⅜	First Chicago	15	70,000	15⅛
				Amer Brands (pfd B)	29¼	32,000	O.T.	PepsiCo	24	75,000	24
				UAL Inc	21⅛	30,000	21	PepsiCo	24	38,700	24
				McDonnell Douglas	26¼	28,400	26⅜	Houston Ind	27⅜	25,000	27⅜
				Advanced Micro Devices	33	25,000	33	Edison Bros	24	67,000	24¼
				ARA Services	35	30,000	35⅝	Magic Chef	7½	100,000	7½
				American Standard	48¾	25,000	48¾	Storage Technology	15⅛	50,000	15⅜
				Deere & Co	36¼	37,700	36⅜	Martin Marietta	35¾	28,400	35⅞
				Delta Air	36½	50,000	36½	Champion Int'l	24⅜	50,000	24⅜
				Best Products	23⅜	53,800	23¼	Best Products	24⅝	25,000	24⅝
				Panhandle East Pipe	52¼	50,000	51¾	RCA Corp	22	30,000	22⅛
				Louisville G&E	17⅝	42,400	18	LI Lighting	5/64	35,000	5/64
				Munsingwear	12½	26,000	12½	Champion Int'l	24⅜	60,000	24⅜
				Signals Cos	32¾	27,700	32⅝	Amer Express	30	33,600	30¼
				Dow Chemical	30⅛	25,000	30⅛	Ford Motor	37	25,000	37⅛
				Gulf Oil	33	36,000	33	City Investing	17¾	100,000	17¾
				Contl Telephone	15	25,500	15	Braniff Int'l	7½	40,000	7⅝
				Magic Chef	7½	60,000	7⅜	Arcata	22⅝	25,000	22⅜
				Texaco	27⅞	33,000	27⅞	Central & SW	13¼	29,100	13¼
				Georgia Pacific	25	50,000	25	Mesa Petroleum (wi dis)	36½	29,200	37
				Brunswick	12¼	30,000	12	Teleprompter	17	25,000	17
				Allis Chalmers	34	29,000	34	McDonnell Douglas	25	97.000	25
				Delta Air Lines	36¾	25,000	36¾	Best Products	24½	25,000	24½
				Con Ed NY	22¼	60,300	22¼	Modern Merch	14⅛	25,000	14¼
				Baltimore G&E	21½	73,100	21⅞				

O.T. — Opening Trade

SOURCE: *Barron's*, November 5, 1979, p. 110.

Large Block Transactions

Another indicator, which is related to the one just mentioned, is large block transactions. Financial journals regularly publish data concerning large transactions (say, 25,000 shares and over) in specified stocks and the prices at which these transactions were made. A sample list of these transactions is presented in Table 12–4. Large blocks of shares traded on downticks (that is, at prices lower than the previously quoted prices) indicate a weak market. Conversely, large transactions traded on upticks suggest a strong bull market.

Directional Factors

The third group of factors measures the direction of change in the market.

Daily Trading Barometer

Frequently, in periods of advance, some groups of stocks advance significantly, while others perform poorly. Likewise, in periods of decline, some stocks register precipitous declines while others hold up fairly well. In order to identify these intermediate-term points of reversal, Barron's has developed the *Daily Trading Barometer* (*DTB*), a weighted composite of three oscillating factors. One oscillator is based on a last seven days of advances and declines on the NYSE. The second is the algebraic sum of the last 20 days of plus and minus volumes on the NYSE. The third oscillator is simply the ratio of the closing value of the DJIA to the average closing price for the last 28 days.

The DTB is an oscillator. It moves up and down coincident with market price movements and fluctuates within well-defined limits. Proponents of the DTB argue that it is a reliable indicator of overbought and oversold market conditions. The DTB is shown graphically in Figure 12–7.

Directional Moves

A loosely defined technical indicator of the market is the directional move of the Dow Jones Averages. On any typical day these averages move independently of one another. For example, on any given day the industrial average may rise 10 points, while the other two averages may decline. On another day, all three averages may decline or rise in any combination. Such divergent movements are not unusual; what gives the market its characteristic predictive power, however, is the belief that this divergence in averages is not likely to persist for long. Consequently, some technical analysts assume that if Dow Jones Averages move in different directions, the future of the market can be predicted with a relatively high degree of accuracy. More specifically, it is asserted that movements in the weaker segment of the market precede movements in their stronger counterparts. Because, in terms of quality, transportation companies are considered a poorer investment than industrial companies, during a strong market the transportation average reaches its peak and turns downward before a decline in the

Figure 12–7

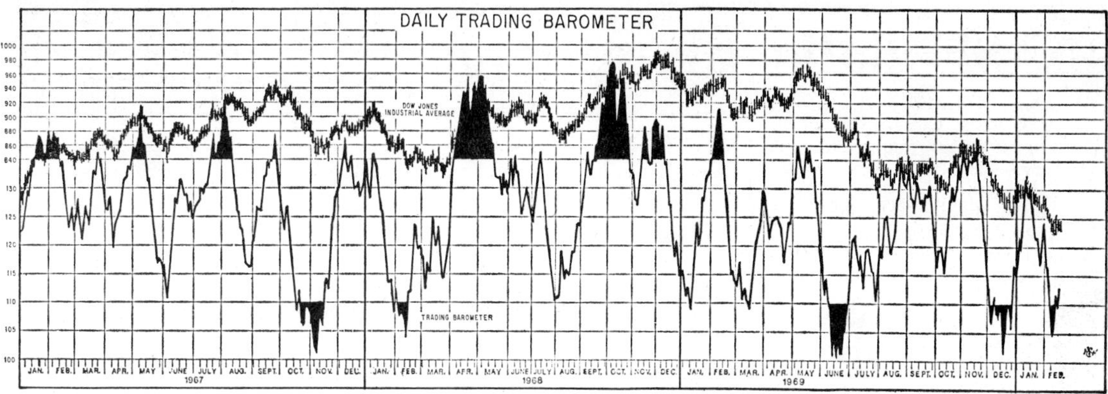

Source: Edson Gould, "Daily Trading Barometer: It Signals a Market Rally," *Barron's*, February 16, 1970, p. 26.

SOURCE: Edson Gould, "Daily Trading Barometer: It Signals a Market Rally," *Barron's*, February 16, 1970, p. 26.

industrial average. This relationship between the two averages is reversed in a bear market. A recognition of this relationship may help an analyst predict the future trend in the market.

Contrary Opinion Factors

The fourth group of factors consists of indicators that signal an imminent reversal of the prevailing market trend.

Short Interest

Short interest is a measure of short sales. An investor is said to be selling short when, without first owning a stock, he or she sells it at a certain price in the hope of later being able to buy it at a lower price, thereby realizing a profit. Table 12–5 presents a sample of short interest prevailing on a typical day.

The size of the short interest outstanding in the NYSE, as reported by the exchange every month, is subject to two contradictory interpretations. A trader who has a short interest in the market is naturally bearish and expects prices to go down in the near future. Consequently, a large short interest indicates widespread expectation of a price decline and is therefore bearish. On the other hand, a trader who is short must purchase stocks sometime in the future to cover his or her obligations. Consequently, because a large short interest also indicates a strong potential demand for stocks, it also suggests a possible advance in stock prices.

Table 12–5

Short Interest

NYSE Ratio Rises to 1.59

SHORT INTEREST on the New York Stock Exchange as of the Dec. 14 settlement date increased to 53,845,625 shares from Nov. 15's 49-,641,533 shares.

The short interest ratio rose to 1.59 from 1.44. With calculations based on the trading dates from Nov. 7 through Dec. 7, the average daily trading volume fell to 33,934,048 shares from the 34-,521,391 shares reported in the comparable month-earlier period.

As of Dec. 14 there were 2,184 stocks and 11 warrants listed on the Exchange. Of those, 961 issues had either a short position of 5,000 or more shares, or a change of 2,000 shares since the previous monthly report. The following table lists such issues, showing their current short position and average daily trading volume for the preceding month.

—*Philip E. Natoli*

	12/14/79	11/15/79	Avg. Daily Volume
ASA Ltd	77,980	44,555	59,833
Abbott Labs	50,600	66,964	60,647
Advanced Micro Dev	55,750	15,950	32,233
†Aetna Life Casualty	129,467	106,426	68,471
†Ahmanson (H.F.) & Co	112,300	111,667	6,528
Air Products & Chem	57,504	44,429	49,728
Alaska Interstate	47,238	51,033	42,171
Alco Standard	40,500	20,900	4,819
Allegheny Ludlum Ind	23,357	22,707	14,333
Allen Group	59,468	51,438	6,152
Allied Chemical	56,138	34,019	70,809
Allis-Chalmers	74,277	79,462	10,404
AM International	47,393	28,780	24,861
Amax	28,646	12,267	40,723
†Amerada Hess	113,153	86,141	90,152
Amer Airlines	41,270	52,570	45,404
Amer Airlines Wts	72,700	85,400	17,328
American Brands	31,573	27,842	18,100
Amer Brands$2.75 Pr	84,124	98,281	3,347
†Amer Broadcasting	147,203	200,627	91,414
Amer Cyanamid	21,591	5,452	95,690
Amer Electric Power	6,959	102,330	81,166
American Express	26,543	27,007	91,809
Amer General Ins	24,308	30,708	15,504
Amer Hoist & Derrick	35,346	41,826	44,128
Amer Home Products	27,955	22,756	84,871
Amer Hospital Supply	32,862	69,397	41,195
Amer Medical Int	84,419	46,657	31,704
†Amer Motors	262,195	178,600	56,714
American Standard	36,934	35,785	11,409
Amer Tel&Tel 3.74 Pr	32,038	11,804	12,547
†Amer Tele&Tel	121,331	74,852	156,533
Amfac	28,900	6,300	6,919
AMP Inc	56,320	38,490	44,695
Ampex	25,900	17,900	24,666
Apache	71,105	68,971	31,176
Applied Dig Data	42,425	43,425	23,519
†ARA Services	119,131	91,687	19,285
Arcata National	21,500	16,700	4,104
Archer-Daniels-Midld	2,595	19,726	61,814
Arctic Enter	21,700	30,800	3,357
Arizona PS	99,788	None	40,033
Armco	31,970	38,791	18,638
Arrow Electronics	27,026	23,420	3,333
Asarco	157,185	83,784	63,690
Ashland Oil	69,018	23,693	45,819
Athlone Ind	54,166	34,566	6,200
†Atlantic Richfield	241,509	240,430	107,123
Auto Data Processing	59,323	84,923	20,357
†Avco	104,338	75,867	119,047
Avnet	34,085	58,835	17,566
†Avon Products	258,108	292,509	92,157
AVX Corp	32,400	30,000	19,652
†Baker Intl	139,962	91,620	45,642
†Bally Mfg	987,480	884,766	256,071
BankAmerica	32,436	21,525	86,142
Bausch Lomb	57,070	41,947	56,523
Baxter Travenol Lab	49,199	51,842	43,685
†City Investing	257,026	204,948	43,185
Clark Oil & Refining	23,100	22,200	12,028
CNA Financial	68,895	61,331	11,238
†Coastal States Gas	168,486	20,971	103,914
Coastal St Gal $1.83 PrB	22,535	300	8,085
Coca-Cola	80,695	79,315	82,980
Colgate-Palmolive	24,050	33,079	95,938
Columbia Picture Ind	57,943	43,036	34,314
Comb Equip Asso	45,276	49,053	15,033
Combustion Engneerng	71,929	25,700	19,457
Commonwealth Edison	37,940	13,881	67,080
†Compugraphic	111,755	110,853	20,866
Computer Sciences	50,964	42,170	40,080
Computervision	59,644	53,945	26,095
†Conoco	129,958	65,458	103,285
Cons Edison of NY	11,609	100,867	28,390
†Consumers Power	111,674	1,395	42,600
Continental Air	20,254	29,354	62,300
Contl Group	41,435	940	35,471
†Control Data	270,089	203,544	73,128
Cooper Ind	53,588	54,138	13,414
†Cooper Labs	145,883	170,198	8,333
Corning Glass	113,521	163,326	21,461
Cummins Engine	68,305	47,917	14,828
Curtiss-Wright	34,600	34,512	10,761
Dana	87,394	95,815	32,066
Data General	118,952	68,418	52,871
Data Terminal Sys	182,069	175,436	32,357
Datapoint	95,692	100,445	17,690
Dayco	88,626	87,039	3,652
Dayton-Hudson	20,917	16,085	11,404
Deere & Co	56,145	60,150	55,600
Delta Air	43,482	39,417	31,609
Deltona	34,400	43,757	5,404
Denny's Inc	20,320	34,220	16,328
Diamond Shamrock	205,111	186,046	102,147
†Digital Equip	382,705	316,171	74,823
Disney Productions	87,056	118,884	54,333
Diversified Ind	21,500	20,500	19,704
Diversified Mtg Inv	23,000	23,000	9,152
Dome Mines	22,614	14,056	13,880
Donnelley (RR) & Sons	22,394	22,744	16,695
Dow Chemical	257,180	118,207	123,028
Dr Pepper	26,350	8,050	56,757
Dresser Ind	38,899	23,099	46,300
Dun & Bradstreet	59,281	71,392	25,214
DuPont	275,207	179,440	87,585
Duquesne Light	355	165,310	36,285
E F Johnson Co	30,800	32,700	5,152
EMI Ltd Am Sh	50,550	18,350	79,223
E-Systems	8,751	26,746	13,523
Eastern Air	38,150	7,750	89,257
†Eastman Kodak	216,457	210,732	129,952
Eastn Gas&Fuel	28,200	15,100	63,733
EG & G Inc	41,915	21,631	10,000
El Paso Co	8,245	30,964	40,309
Electro Memo & Mag	5,300	17,300	7,404
Electronic Data Sys	22,691	20,341	4,152
Emery Air Freight	70,665	78,075	68,728
Engelhard Min & Chem	23,869	63,030	63,023
Enserch	34,329	18,769	34,119
Esmark	60,966	143,802	21,533
Evans Products	42,298	44,775	7,966
†Exxon	135,145	119,874	180,995
Far West Financial	22,400	23,000	1,390
Federal Express	36,378	19,900	41,376
Federal Mogul	15,400	3,610	6,276
Federal Paper Board	20,611	1,220	17,152
Federated Dept Stores	27,682	48,323	35,961
Filmways	11,845	27,857	19,895
Firestone	79,698	45,667	47,790
First Charter Fin	146,617	135,850	28,661
First Intl Bankshare	32,387	32,472	17,466
First Miss	57,850	33,500	36,780
First Penn	6,000	22,200	61,404
Fleetwood Enterprise	23,770	16,335	28,690
Flexi-Van	32,387	34,225	15,423
Flintkote	82,043	17,886	38,471
Florida P&L	1,000	22,943	61,566
Fluor	121,387	51,181	57,342
Ford Motor	70,829	107,275	192,123
Foster Wheeler	21,333	9,276	51,533
Four-Phase Sys	28,150	30,800	22,423
Fred S James & Co	81,025	1,232	13,409
Freeport Minerals	108,572	51,907	46,071
Frigitronics	48,400	51,561	5,547
GAF Corp	30,800	29,200	18,380
Gannett	54,100	60,160	28,233
GATX Corp	66,100	53,840	24,280
GCA Corp	86,423	33,618	27,109
GDV Inc	17,650	2,950	26,042
Gearhart Owen Ind	36,264	50,114	10,261
Gelco	20,660	12,060	5,509
†Gen Tel & Elect	185,276	51,477	86,780
General Care	19,121	8,800	23,957
†General Dynamics	237,934	135,072	83,133
General Electric	113,192	36,874	110,409
General Foods	20,875	38,787	40,114
General Host	21,266	23,198	5,771
Indianapolis P&L	17,500	500	10,833
Inexco Oil	50,085	77,095	58,671
Ingersoll-Rand	22,430	44,030	17,476
Inland Steel	13,946	971	22,266
Insilco	21,392	31,881	7,685
Int Flavor & Frag	42,308	45,803	28,553
Int Tel&Tel PrK	25,428	928	15,061
Inter Business Mach	639,720	436,380	331,552
Inter Harvester	21,589	18,247	27,128
Inter Minerals & Chem	86,156	32,791	20,733
†Inter Tel & Tel	142,145	167,589	129,095
Inter Paper	34,178	20,108	52,323
Iowa Electric L&P	38,863	670	7,114
Itek	60,425	56,225	35,104
Itel	602,247	471,204	118,019
Jantzen	11,650	200	25,542
Jewel Cos	34,096	341	13,980
Jim Walter Corp	22,950	23,469	11,057
Johns Manville	42,568	27,329	16,776
Johnson & Johnson	91,316	65,015	55,409
Johnson Control	48,654	56,454	13,942
K mart	81,407	84,866	118,557
Kaiser Steel	99,905	100,275	44,871
Kaneb Services	104,100	26,922	48,080
†Katy Ind	179,963	187,558	12,352
Kaufman & Broad	78,397	81,597	26,228
Kellogg	25,247	17,167	15,338
Kenilworth Rlty	21,540	17,666	1,952
Kennecott Copper	58,550	36,250	39,719
Kentucky Util	16,500	None	13,880
Kerr-McGee	24,600	11,500	37,090
La Quinta Motors	39,738	42,890	5,609
Lanier Bus Prod	r96,150	s64,941	9,095
Lennar	36,299	21,500	13,376
Levi Strauss & Co	194,014	171,510	28,352
LFE Corp	17,659	2,115	8,085
Liggett Group	21,648	5,942	56,014
Lilly (Eli) & Co	70,673	59,589	41,680
†Litton Ind	226,444	78,236	117,652
Lockheed	92,860	32,260	61,052
†Loews	154,231	309,145	9,085
Lomas & Nettleton	24,350	7,495	4,423
Long Island Light Pr O	800	27,100	1,619
Long Island Light	27,000	275,848	77,852
Longs Drug Stores	480	11,480	5,109
Loral	26,669	13,974	9,971
Louisiana Land	58,307	94,601	142,823
Louisiana Pacific	24,520	34,850	26,090
Louisville G&E	22,100	None	11,566
†LTV Corp	706,736	721,701	41,366
Lubrizol	4,183	14,235	27,171
M/A Com Inc	62,345	59,301	10,676
Macy (R H) & Co	93,250	7,300	14,257
Mapco	41,474	9,547	44,647
Marley	22,000	19,800	8,338
Marriott	77,641	227,748	26,923
†Masco	156,250	153,950	14,714
Masonite	14,800	71,000	15,676
Massey-Ferguson	64,721	64,900	20,828
Mattel	36,448	35,514	27,709
May Dept Stores	309,606	648,405	28,033
McDonald's	146,001	141,815	67,504
†McDonnell Douglas	241,482	261,160	91,671
MCA Inc	30,060	9,560	28,395
†McDermott (J Ray) & Co	114,063	151,373	87,395
McDermott $2.60 Pr	23,400	None	3,823
McMoran Oil & Gas	52,480	44,560	43,642
Mead	16,550	62,144	16,828
Measurex	26,450	29,150	18,104
Melville	66,945	3,845	20,152
Memorex	35,244	39,878	30,647
Mercantile Texas	22,033	24,434	4,404
Merck & Co	126,462	111,209	52,238
Merrill Lynch & Co	150,517	163,529	54,566
Mesa Petroleum	300,415	398,948	103,957
MGIC Inv	110,600	105,150	68,285
Mgmt Assistance	34,835	21,190	13,800
Mich Wis P&L 2.67 Pr	11,439	22,993	1,190
Middle So Util	409,300	1,100	161,495
Minnesota Min & Mfg	40,550	48,508	77,342
Missouri Pac	12,542	25,395	11,247
Mobil	30,638	292,158	173,442
Modern Merchandising	39,660	38,590	14,861
Mohawk Data Sciences	71,150	41,255	58,923
Monsanto	43,658	44,363	33,014
Morgan (JP) & Co.	5,200	42,218	35,028
Morris, Philip	106,585	45,482	86,142
Motorola	81,320	90,018	49,242
Murphy Oil	21,103	15,369	15,923
NL Ind	104,849	80,210	87,228
†Nat Dist & Chem	181,599	254,734	63,566
Nat Service Ind	23,800	8,500	3,628
National Can	11,472	49,670	7,257
National Detroit	194	34,108	6,276
Nat Med Enter	35,930	21,567	34,966
Nat Presto Ind	62,350	62,550	4,442
†Nat Semiconductor	285,326	340,932	84,323
Natomas	47,474	44,436	74,366
†NCR Corp	130,398	114,219	63,338
†Newmont Mining	150,362	199,631	28,190
Newpark Resources	21,015	8,300	19,609
Niagara Mohawk Power	133,460	183,990	19,028
Norfolk & Western Ry	2,716	16,133	32,219
Northeast Util	200	15,600	25,523
Northern Telecom	47,568	40,461	30,066
Northrop	24,055	5,563	45,890
Northwest Air	43,915	86,096	29,985
Northwest Ind	242,646	74,136	23,542
Norton Simon Inc	4,548	15,582	40,900
NVF Co	38,953	36,134	17,580

SOURCE: *Barron's*, December 24, 1979, p. 69.

Figure 12–8

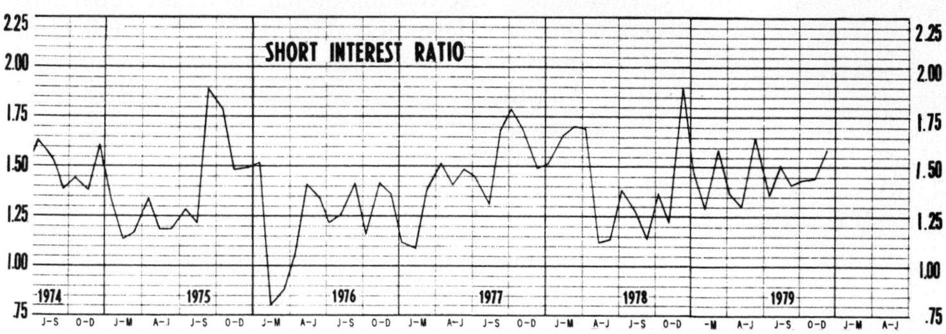

SOURCE: *Trendline's Current Market Prospects*, January 1980, p. 9.

It is interesting to note that many technical analysts calculate the ratio of total short interest to the average daily volume for the period for which the short interest has been tallied. These analysts generally consider a ratio of below 1.00 bearish, a ratio of above 1.00 bullish, and a ratio of above 2.00 extremely bullish. Figure 12–8 is a chart of the NYSE Short Interest Ratio from 1974 through 1979.

Odd-Lot Index and Odd-Lot Sales Index

The *odd-lot index*, shown in Figure 12–9, is the ratio of odd-lot sales to odd-lot purchases. An odd lot is an amount of stock less than the established 100-share unit. Trades of less than 100 shares are handled by specialists and some brokerage firms who accept the responsibility for buying and selling odd lots for their own accounts, the prices of which are geared to the auction market.

Figure 12–9

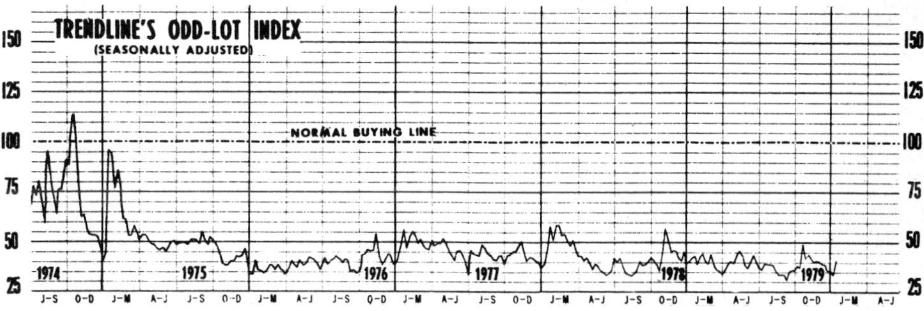

SOURCE: *Trendline's Current Market Prospects*, January 1980, p. 9.

Odd-lot statistics derive their importance as a technical indicator from a concept, popularized by Garfield Drew. According to Drew, changes in odd-lot transactions portend significant market trends. A basic assumption of the concept is that small investors, who typically buy and sell less than 100 shares, are ill informed and can be counted on to make the wrong moves at critical moments. This implies that if odd-lotters are net buyers (that is, buying more than they are selling), then small investors are entering the market and are "providing the opportunity" for "smart money" to get out. Many technical analysts believe that, in general, a small investor can be expected to sell when the market is about to resume its upward trend and buy when a downswing is in the offing.

It is generally believed that the strongest bull signal occurs when odd-lotters become both net sellers and short sellers. The odd-lot short sale index is calculated by dividing odd-lot short sales by total odd-lot sales. This ratio measures the extremes of sentiment of small investors who, at important turning points, are regarded as usually emotional and likely to make unwise moves.

NYSE Specialists' Short Sales Ratio

The *NYSE Specialists' Short Sales Ratio* is a ratio of specialists' short sales to total NYSE short sales. It measures extremes of sentiment of NYSE specialists who, in the process of maintaining an orderly market, tend to sell short most heavily at market tops when nonmember enthusiasm for buying is greatest and less heavily at bottoms when selling by the general public is accelerated.

Advisory Service Sentiment

The strength of the stock market can be judged by constructing a weekly index of the percentage of leading bearish advisory services. When the advisory service sentiment becomes overly one-sided, technical analysts view it as a contrary indicator, because most services tend to follow trends rather than anticipate changes in them. For example, Figure 12–10 reveals that frequently the advisory sentiment trails the stock market.

Credit Balances

Customers' net credit balances are the aggregate amount of cash carried by investors in cash and margin accounts with brokerage firms. These balances constitute a measure of sentiments of unsophisticated investors; professionals are unlikely to keep their cash balances at brokerage firms which do not earn interest. Consequently, it is argued that when cash balances increase, small and uninformed investors are bearish and stock prices are likely to rise.

Confidence Factor

The fifth and last group consists of one indicator that measures investor confidence in the market.

Figure 12–10

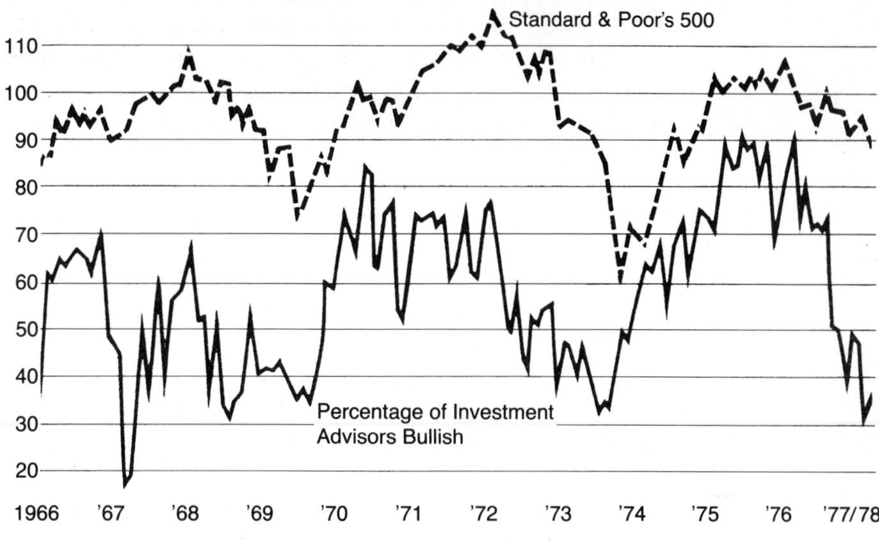

SOURCE: David Dreman, "Don't Go with the Pros," *Barron's*, May 8, 1978, p. 11.

Barron's Confidence Index

Barron's Confidence Index (*CI*) is a ratio of high-grade to low-grade bond yields. The specific series used are *Barron's* average yield on the ten highest-grade corporate bonds, and Dow Jones' average yield on 40 bonds of a lower average quality. An example of the CI is given in Figure 12–11.

The value of the CI as a technical tool, as proposed by technical analysts, may be explicitly stated. High-quality bond yields are always *lower* than low-quality

Figure 12–11

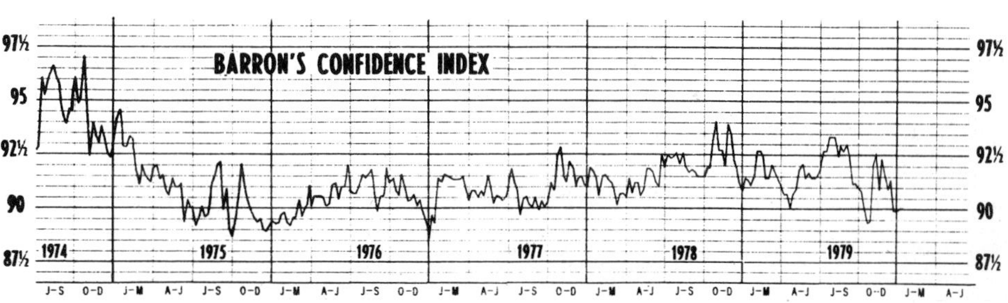

SOURCE: *Trendline's Current Market Prospects*, January 1980, p. 9.

bond yields, because investors have more confidence in them. During periods of economic recession, investors attach more importance to safety; during prosperity they are more willing to undertake risks at the cost of safety. It is claimed that in a rising market the CI rises, indicating investors' preference for lower-quality, high-yielding bonds. In contrast, when the CI slides downwards, the market is believed to be getting ready for a downturn, because investors are presumably reluctant to place confidence in lower-quality bonds.

Charting as a Technical Tool

An Overview

Most technicians rely heavily on charts of prices and trading volume for their analysis of the market and individual stocks. Because of its relative importance, a comprehensive discussion of chart reading and analysis is necessary.

Technical analysts claim that stock price fluctuations generally form characteristic patterns which have important predictive value.

> *No one of experience doubts that prices move in trends and trends tend to continue until something happens to change the supply–demand balance. Such changes are usually detectable in the action of the market itself. Certain patterns of formation, levels or areas, appear on the chart which have a meaning that can be interpreted in terms of probable future trend development. They are not infallible, it must be noted, but the odds are definitely in their favor.*[13]

A noted chartist explains the value of chart reading even more succinctly:

> *The purpose of "chart reading" or "chart analysis" is to determine the probable strength of demand versus pressure of supply at various price levels, and thus to predict the probable direction in which a stock will move, and where it will probably stop.*
>
> *The clues are provided by the history of a stock's price movements, as recorded on a chart. In the market, history does repeat itself—often. On the charts, price fluctuations tend, with remarkable consistency, to fall into a number of patterns, each of which signifies a relationship between buying and selling pressures. Some patterns, or "formations," indicate that demand is greater than supply, others suggest that supply is greater than demand, and still others imply that they are likely to remain in balance for some time.*[14]

[13] Robert D. Edwards and John Magee, *Technical Analysis of Stock Trends* (Springfield, Mass.; John Magee, 1958), p. 6. Note, however, that these views are completely at odds with the weak form of the EMH.

[14] William L. Jiler, "How Charts Can Help You in the Stock Market," *Trendline*, Standard & Poor's Corporation, 1962.

Types of Charts

The three basic types of charts are line, bar, and point-and-figure. In each case, the type of chart chosen to record price activity is determined by the amount of information available.

Line Chart

On a *line chart*, the closing prices of successive time periods are connected by straight lines, with no notice taken of the highs and lows of stock prices for each period. Figure 12–12 is a line chart of Walt Disney Productions.

Bar Chart

Most investors interested in charting use *bar charts*—primarily because they have meanings familiar to a technical analyst, but also because these charts are easy to draw.

The procedure for preparing a vertical line or bar chart is simple. Suppose you were to draw on graph or logarithmic paper a series of vertical lines, each line representing the price movements for a time period—a day, a week, or even a year. The vertical dimensions of the line represent price; the horizontal dimension indicates the time involved by the chart as a whole. In a daily chart, for example, each vertical line represents the range of each day's price activity, and the chart as a whole may extend for a month. You extend the line on the graph paper from the highest transaction of each day down to the lowest and make a cross mark to indicate the closing price.

Figure 12–12 **Walt Disney Productions**

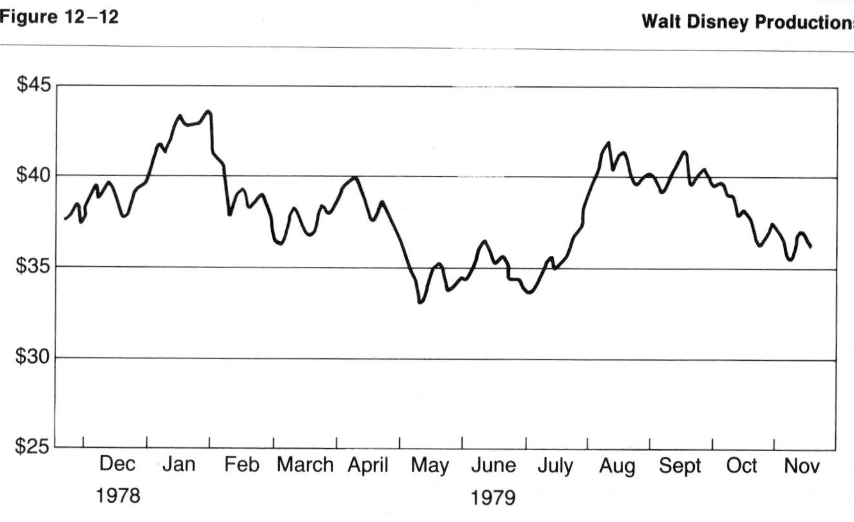

Figure 12–13 **ABC Corporation**

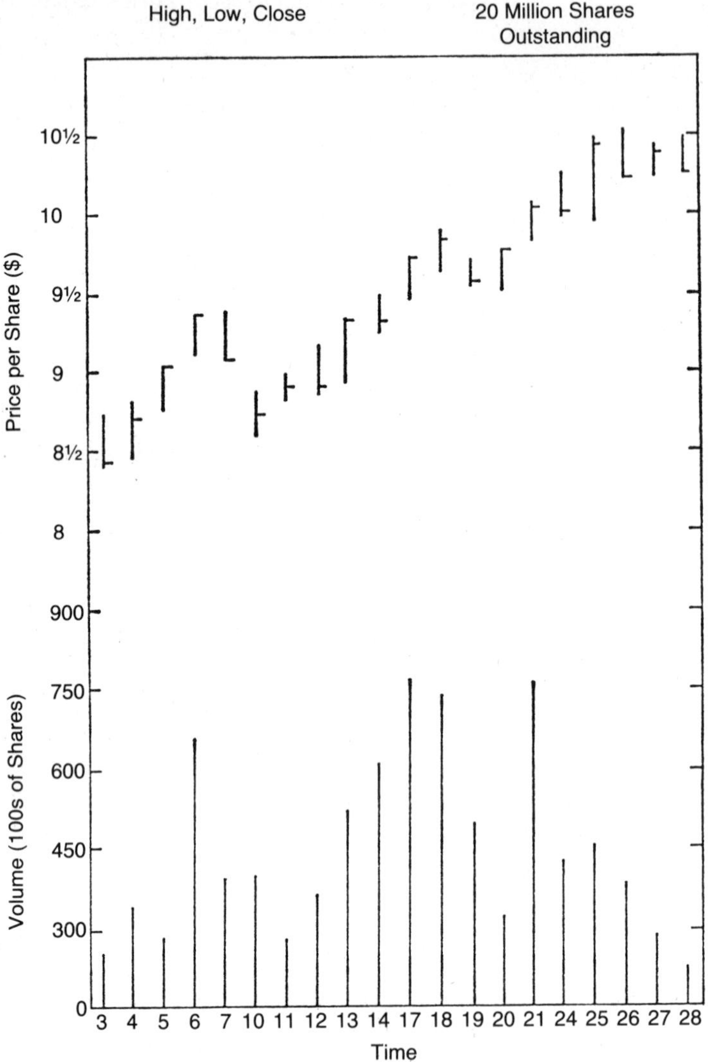

Another feature of the bar chart is that volume can also be shown on it by adding a second set of vertical lines at the bottom of the chart. Each line is proportional in height to the total number of shares traded during each time period shown in the upper part of the chart. In Figure 12–13, a vertical line chart for movements in the stock of the ABC Corporation is shown. The chart covers a month's activities and each vertical line represents one day's action. Bar charts

Figure 12–14

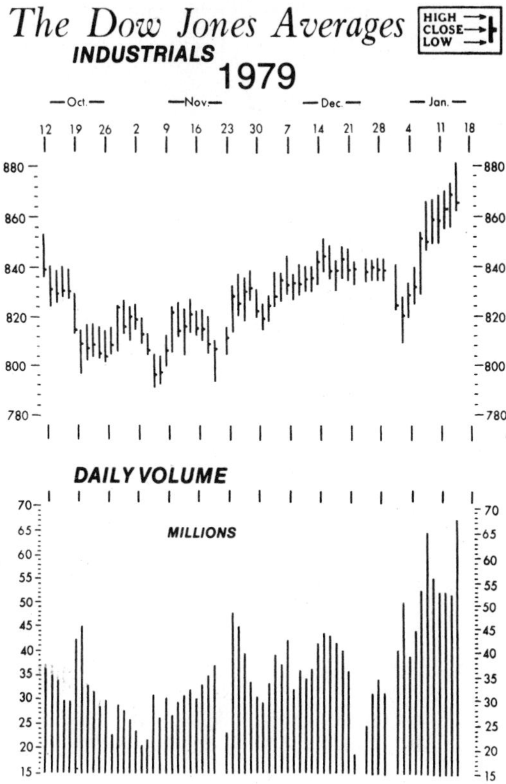

SOURCE: *The Wall Street Journal*, January 17, 1980, p. 37.

are also used for charting movements in the market. A bar chart for the Dow Jones Industrial Average is presented in Figure 12–14. The volume of the NYSE is also shown at the bottom of the figure.

Point-and-Figure Chart

Bar chartists count on discovering certain buying and selling forces in the market, on the basis of which they predict future price trends. These forces consist of three factors—time, volume, and price. Members of another school, known as the point-and-figure chartists, question the usefulness of the first two factors. They argue that the way to predict future price fluctuations is to analyze *price changes only*. Consequently, they assert, no volume action need be recorded, and the time dimension (day, week, or month) should also be ignored. If only significant price changes are important, then one need only capture the significant

Figure 12–15 **The Point-and-Figure Chart and Its Construction**

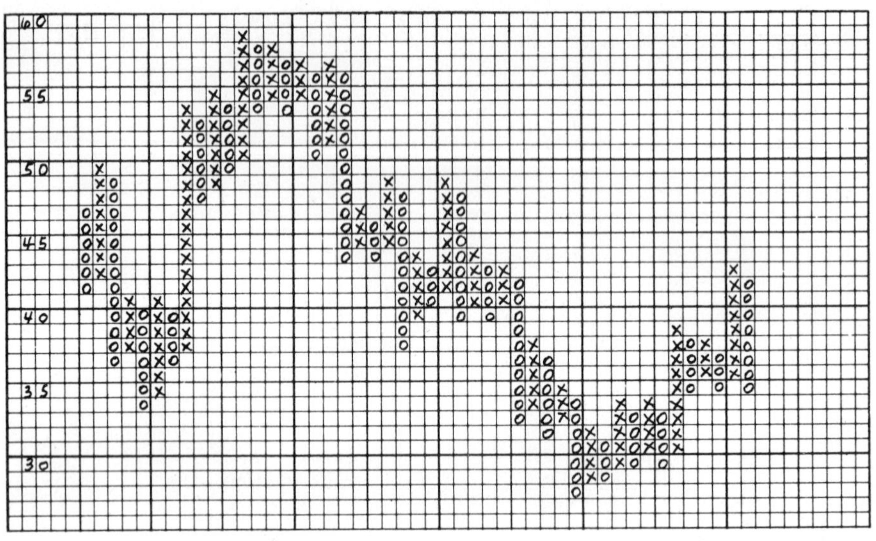

(say, one point or more, ignoring all fractions) price changes in a stock, no matter how long it takes for the stock to register this change.

The first step in drawing a *point-and-figure chart* is to put an X in the appropriate price column of a graph. Then you enter successive price increases (of one point or more, ignoring fractions) in an upward column as long as the uptrend continues. If the price drops by one point or more, the figures move to another column and the O's are entered in a downward progression until the downtrend is reversed. When you use such a chart over a reasonable period of time, you have a "king-size tic-tac-toe game" which can be used for prediction. Note, however, that you should cover a fairly long period so that definite shapes can be observed on the graph paper. Figure 12–15 is a sample point-and-figure chart for ABC Company.

Important Chart Patterns

Charts are a means to an end. They help a technical analyst not only to identify stocks which are technically strong or weak but to decide *when* to buy or sell a stock. Figure 12–16 shows illustrative bar charts of stock prices. Analysts, of course, use several techniques to examine various chart patterns.[15]

[15] The following discussion is primarily based on Alan R. Shaw, "Technical Analysis," pp. 955–75. © 1975 by Dow Jones-Irwin.

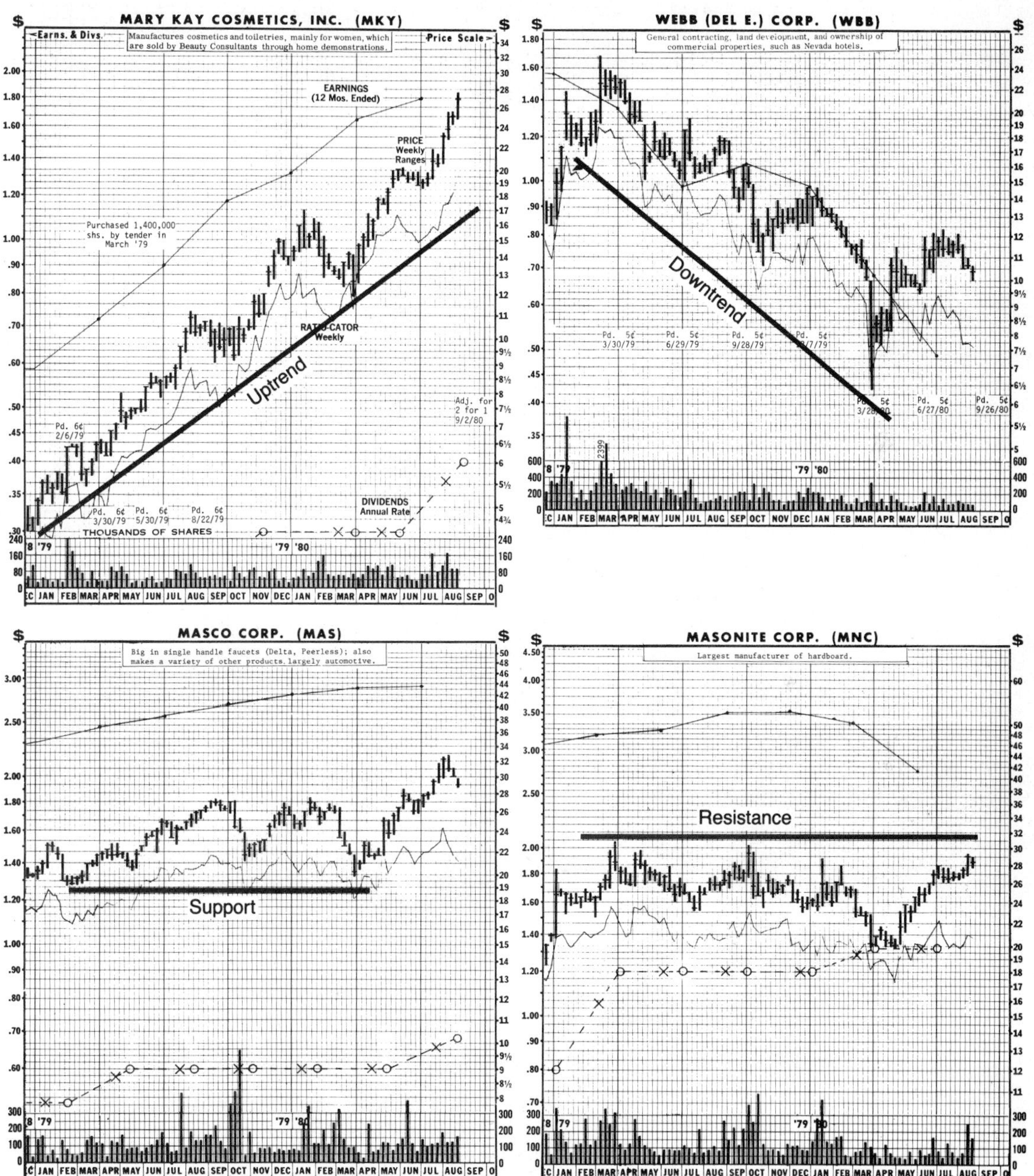

SOURCE: *3-Trend Security Charts*, January 1980, pp. 25, 39, 148, 192.

Figure 12–17

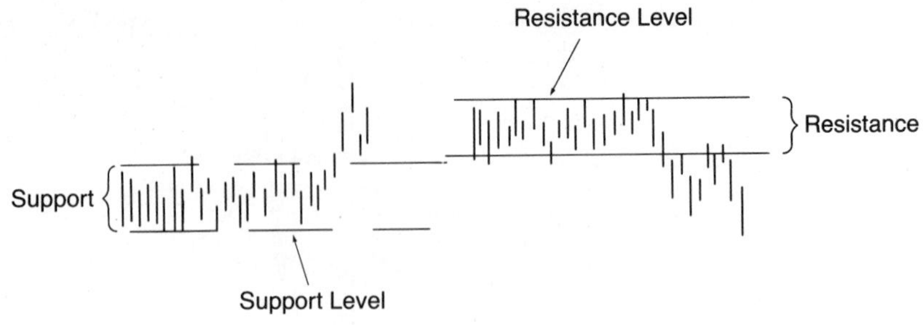

SOURCE: Alan R. Shaw, "Technical Analysis," in *Financial Analyst's Handbook*, ed. Sumner N. Levine (Homewood, Ill.: Dow Jones-Irwin, 1975), p. 958.

Support and Resistance Levels

One of the most important aspects of chart analysis is the identification of support and resistance levels, as shown in Figure 12–17. A support level is a barrier to price decline; a resistance level is a barrier to price advancement. Although the barrier is an obstruction, it is by no means impassable; stock prices do break support and resistance barriers.

Assume ABC stock is currently trading at 35. In the recent past, it has been as low as 30 and as high as 43. When the stock approaches 30, it becomes an attractive investment. A flurry of buying activity follows, and the stock begins to advance in price. Should the stock cross its previous high of 40, however, investors will probably view it as overpriced and begin to liquidate their investment in the stock. Based on these observations, the ABC stock has a support level at 30, with a potential resistance level at 40.[16] The predictive value of these levels should be noted: A stock breaking its support level is technically weak; conversely, a stock breaking the resistance level is technically strong.

Head and Shoulders Configurations

Basic reversal patterns help analysts identify the turning points so that they can decide when to buy or sell stock. The key reversal pattern is popularly known as the head and shoulders configuration. This configuration, shown in Figure 12–18, is merely another name for an uptrend or a downtrend in a stock; the "neckline" is the familiar resistance or support level.

Head and shoulders formation should be analyzed against the background of volume trend. As the head and shoulders top is formed, resistance to further

[16] Support and resistance levels are not such precise numbers. In this situation, the support level would be expressed at 30–32, whereas the resistance level would be specified as 40–42.

Figure 12–18

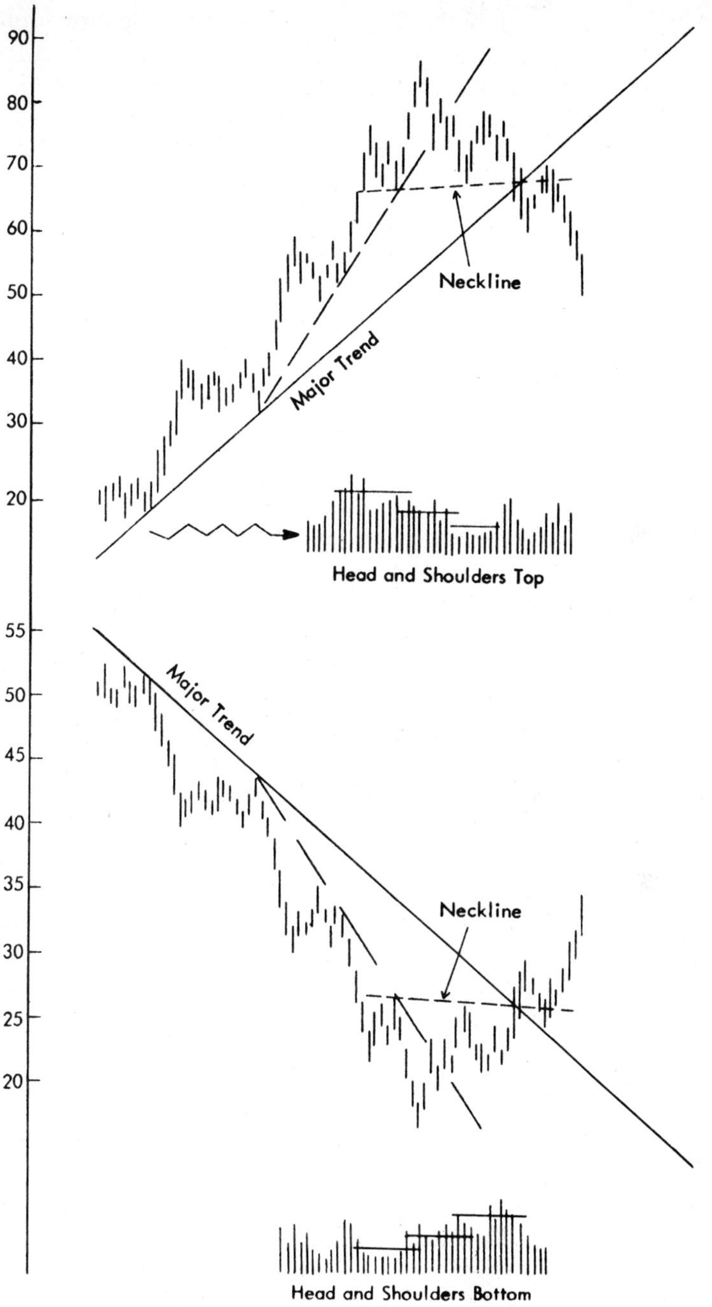

SOURCE: Alan R. Shaw, "Technical Analysis," in *Financial Analyst's Handbook*, ed. Sumner N. Levine (Homewood, Ill.: Dow Jones-Irwin, 1975), p. 963.

price increases dampens investor enthusiasm; therefore the volume decreases on each of the rally phases within the top formation. The reverse is true when the head and shoulders bottom is under formation. It should be emphasized that the completion of a head and shoulders top or bottom is not considered final until the penetration of the neckline is apparent.

There are many variations of such reversal formations. Of these, the so-called double and triple tops and bottoms, shown in Figure 12–19, are particularly interesting.

Figure 12–19

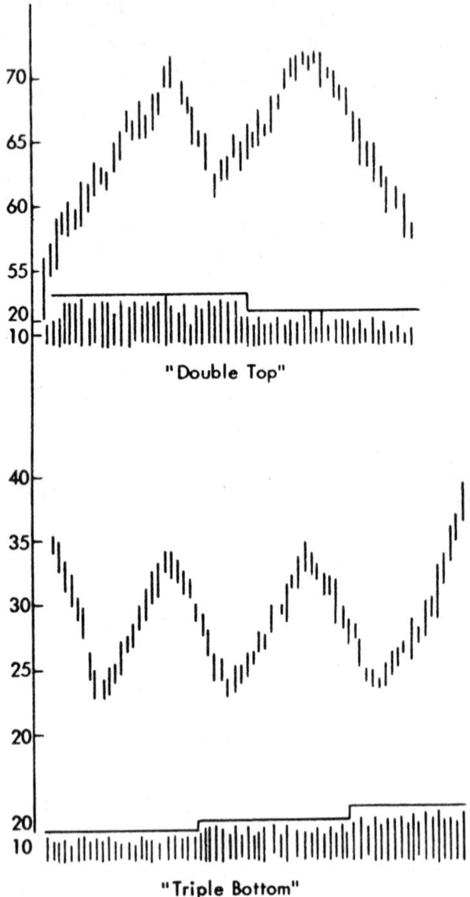

SOURCE: Alan R. Shaw, "Technical Analysis," in *Financial Analyst's Handbook*, ed. Sumner N. Levine (Homewood, Ill.: Dow Jones-Irwin, 1975), p. 964.

Trend Analysis

Establishing a major trend is one of the most vexing problems encountered by a technical analyst. Alan Shaw has devised seven questions which are helpful in analyzing the major trend of a stock.[17]

Question 1 Does the stock have a move of substance to reverse? The major reversal formation certainly would not be looked for in a stock that has only moved from 20 to 26, but if a move from 20 to 45 had been experienced, any reversal in trend could be major.

Question 2 Has the stock fulfilled readable price objectives? A major trend is usually preceded by notable advancement in price.

Question 3 Has the stock violated its trends? If a trend violation does occur, it could be the forerunner or an early warning of a reversal in the major direction of the stock's price movement.

Question 4 Are signs of distribution or accumulation evident? A major uptrend is preceded by accumulation, whereas distribution is generally followed by a downturn.

Question 5 If distribution or accumulation is evident, is it significant enough to imply that more than a minor movement in price could be in the offing?

Question 6 Has the stock violated a readable support or resistance level?

Question 7 Has the stock initiated a downward or an upward trend?

A "floater" question can be inserted between any of the above seven questions: Is there any evidence of unusual price and/or volume action?

Figure 12–20 demonstrates the relevance of these questions to the analysis of a major uptrend and a downtrend in the price of the stock. Note, for example, the reversal of a major uptrend at point A; this suggests that the stock has violated its trend (Question 3). Furthermore, point B is the beginning of a significant distribution which, according to Question 5, signals a significant decline in the stock's price. Similarly, at point C the stock penetrates its support level (Question 6) and therefore becomes technically weak.

[17] Alan R. Shaw, "Technical Analysis," pp. 964–65. © 1975 by Dow Jones-Irwin.

Figure 12–20 **The 7 Questions (with a "Floater")**

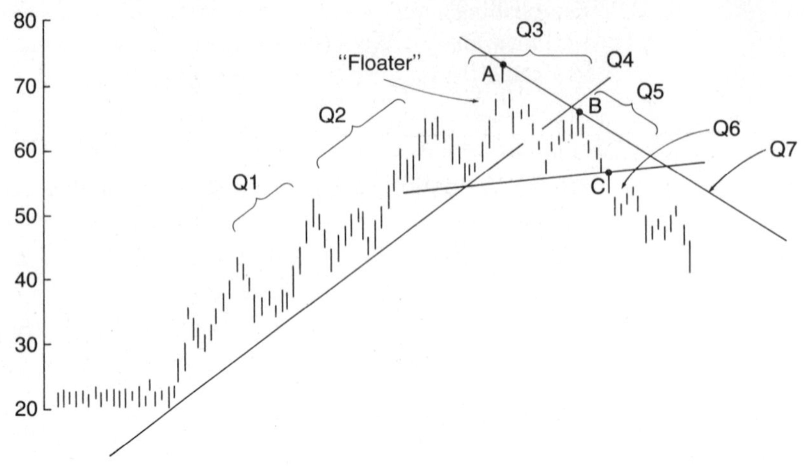

SOURCE: Alan R. Shaw, "Technical Analysis," in *Financial Analyst's Handbook*, ed. Sumner N. Levine (Homewood, Ill.: Dow Jones-Irwin, 1975), p. 966.

Triangles, Pennants, Wedges, and Flags

Certain price configurations are more easily identified than head and shoulders configurations. These configurations, known as triangles, are shown in Figure 12–21. In addition, a number of other technical configurations qualify as consolidation patterns. These patterns, known as wedge, flag, and pennant, are

Figure 12–21 **Triangles**

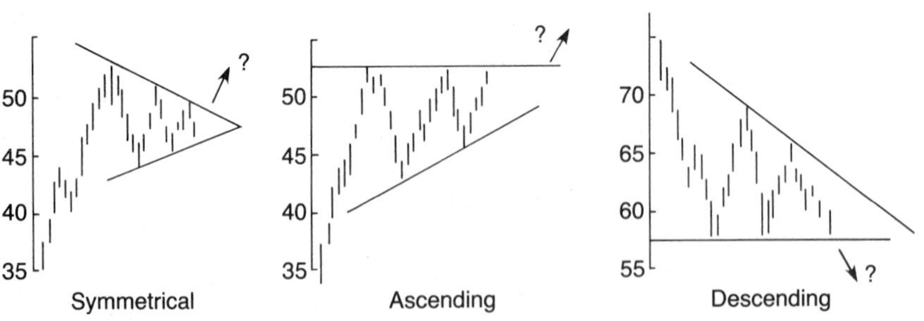

SOURCE: Alan R. Shaw, "Technical Analysis," in *Financial Analyst's Handbook*, ed. Sumner N. Levine (Homewood, Ill.: Dow Jones-Irwin, 1975), p. 966.

Figure 12–22

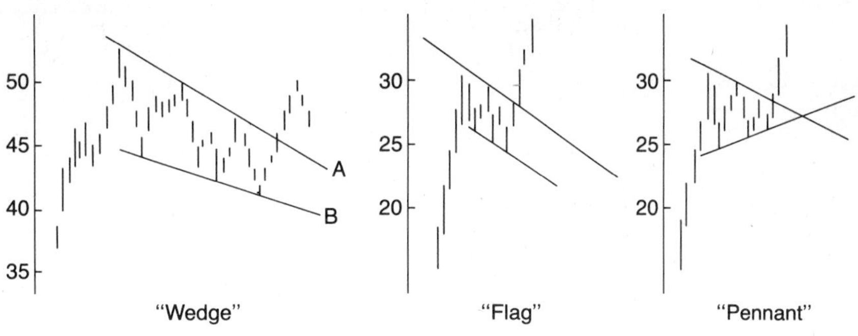

SOURCE: Alan R. Shaw, "Technical Analysis," in *Financial Analyst's Handbook*, ed. Sumner N. Levine (Homewood, Ill.: Dow Jones-Irwin, 1975), p. 967.

shown in Figure 12–22. For example, a *falling* wedge of the type shown here usually occurs in a major uptrend pattern for the following reason. Sellers in this case are aggressive, as is evident from the steep decline of line A. In contrast, buyers are not quite as discouraged as sellers, as revealed by the relative flatness of the declining line B. Incidentally, all three types of formations shown here are short-term in nature and occur early in an upward or a downward trend phase.

Point-and-Figure Configurations

Point-and-figure configurations differ markedly from bar chart configurations in that they recognize only the price movement of a certain magnitude and ignore both the volume and time dimensions. In Figure 12–23 point-and-figure charts for two companies are shown. Notice that in both instances the chartist has marked the patterns which appear on the charts in order to tell with reasonable accuracy how stocks are likely to behave in the future. A closer look at these charts also reveals that, like bar charts, these charts show trends, support and resistance levels, head and shoulders, and rounding top or bottom. More importantly, like the bar chart, point-and-figure charts have their peculiar patterns, designated by such esoteric names as "inverse fulcrum," "duplex horizontal," and "inverse saucer." Some of these special patterns are shown in Figure 12–24.

It is worth noting that of all the many chart patterns and techniques discussed above, five broadly classified patterns are claimed to best describe the price behavior of most stocks. As shown in Figure 12–25, these patterns should be self-explanatory.

Figure 12–23

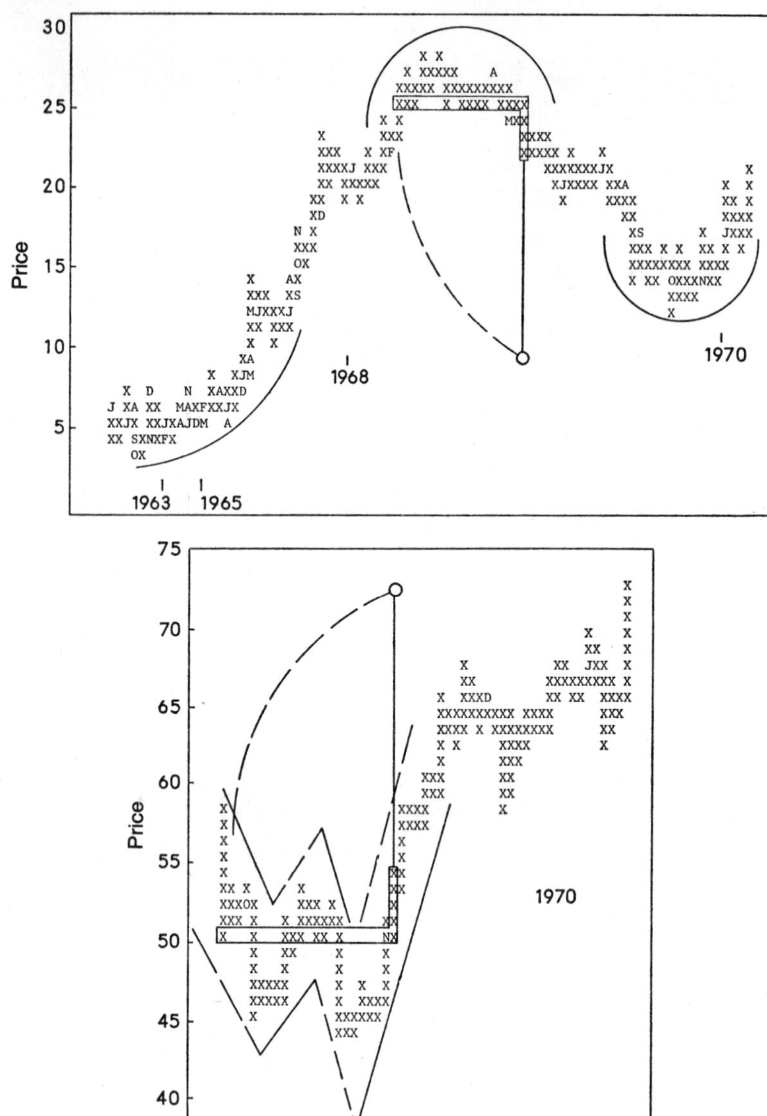

SOURCE: Adapted from Lerro and Swayne, *Selection of Securities* (Braintree, Mass.: D. H. Mark, 1970), p. 10.

Figure 12–24

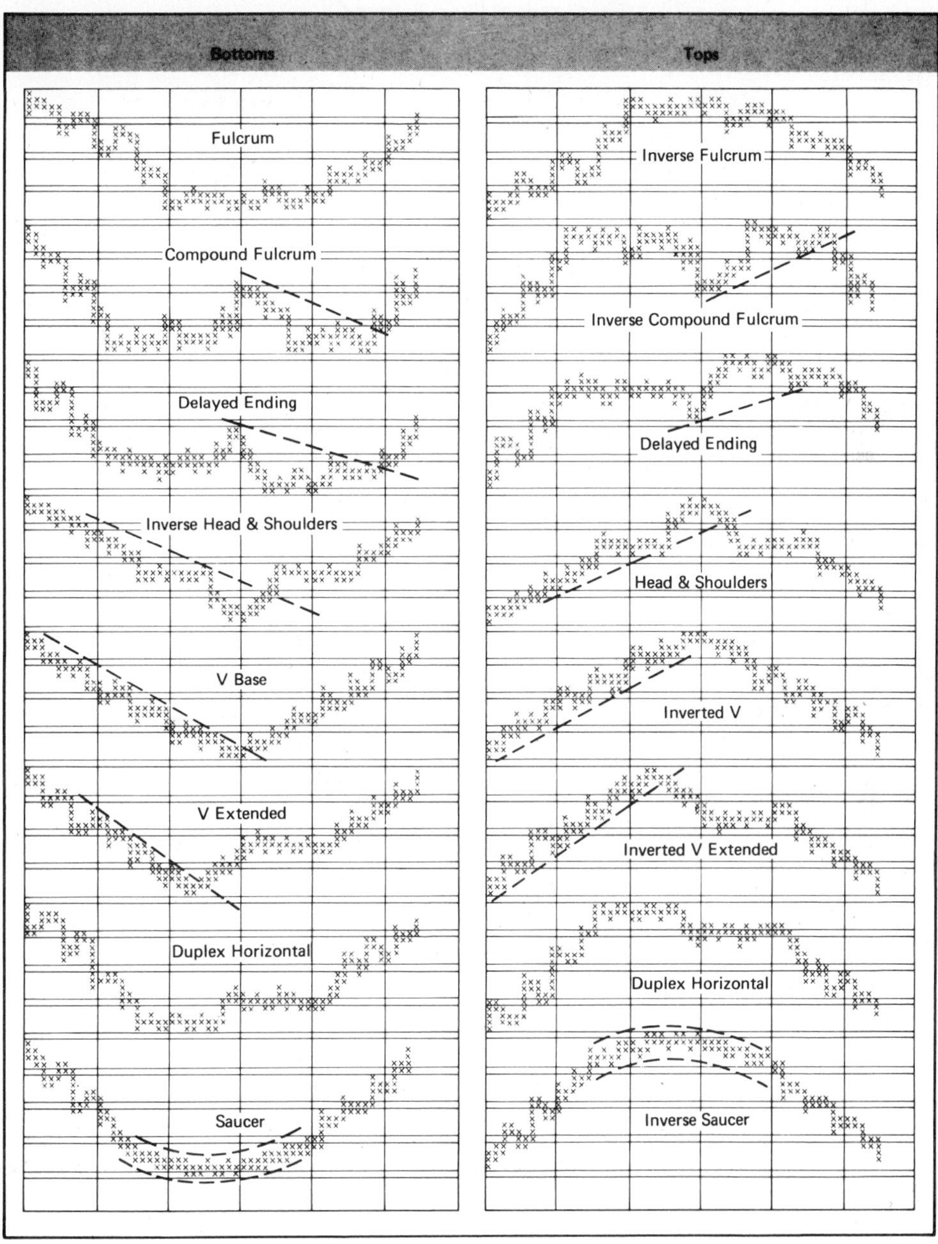

SOURCE: Morgan, Rogers, & Roberts, 150 Broadway, New York. Reprinted in Alan R. Shaw, "Technical Analysis," in Sumner N. Levine, ed., *Financial Analyst's Handbook* (Homewood, Ill.: Dow Jones—Irwin, Inc., 1975) I, 971.

Figure 12–25

Five Standard Chart Patterns

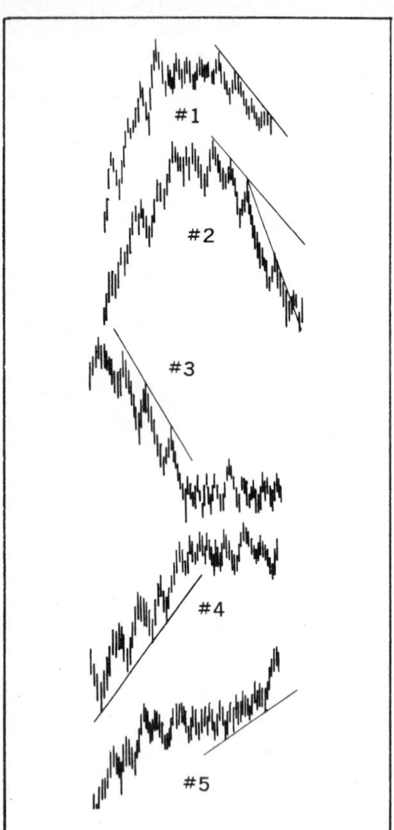

Chart Pattern #1

Stocks with vulnerable trends and/or possible downside potential.

Chart Pattern #2

Stocks with less vulnerability that appear to have reached possible lows, but need consolidation.

Chart Pattern #3

Stocks that have declined and experienced consolidation, and could do well in a favorable market.

Chart Pattern #4

Stocks that have performed relatively well but are currently in "neutral" trends.

Chart Pattern #5

Stocks in established uptrends and/or with possible upside potential.

SOURCE: Yale Hirsch, *The 1971 Stock Trader's Almanac* (Old Tappan, N.J.: The Hirsch Organization, 1970), p.37.

Summary

Technical analysis endeavors to predict future price levels of stocks by analyzing past data from the market itself. This analysis is based on the belief that the price of the stock depends primarily on supply and demand and may have little relationship to any intrinsic value.

Technical analysts make three basic assumptions: (1) The price patterns and trading volumes of the stock market and individual stocks predict a future condition rather than an existing condition. (2) Every major downturn in a stock is preceded by a period of *distribution*. Conversely, before a stock experiences a major advance, a period of *accumulation* takes place. (3) Most movements in the market have a relationship to each other.

One of the most widely held, and the oldest, technical theories is known as the *Dow theory*. This theory is based on three postulates: (1) The primary trend continues anywhere from one to four years. (2) During a primary uptrend phase, each secondary trend is associated with a peak higher than the previous peak, and a trough higher than the previous trough. Conversely, when the market is in a downward trend, each secondary peak or trough is lower than the preceding peak or trough. (3) The primary trend is confirmed by a co-movement of stock averages.

Technical analysts make judgments about the market by analyzing such technical factors as *activity factors*, *market strength factors*, *directional factors*, *contrary opinion factors*, and *confidence factors*. However, not all factors move in the same direction at any given time and technical analysis does not specify the relative importance that should be attached to each of them.

Technical analysis of individual stocks involves the interpretation of important chart patterns known by such esoteric names as *head and shoulders*, *triangles*, *pennants*, *wedges*, *flags*, and *saucers*. Each pattern signals to technical analysts a major or minor upward or downward movement in the stock.

Many of the proofs offered in support of technical theories have never been tested with rigor. Also, technical analysis primarily rests on a *non sequitur*; its supporters have failed to demonstrate that by using technical theories and techniques one can consistently outperform the market.

A Look Ahead

Chapters 9 through 11 were devoted to a discussion of the fundamental factors that determine the present or intrinsic value of a stock. In this chapter we have surveyed the technical factors that are concerned with the study of supply and demand or the price movements of common stocks within the general stock market framework.

In Chapter 5 we presented the essentials of the concept and measurement of risk and return. In Chapter 13, within the risk–return framework, we will discuss the modern portfolio theory.

Concepts for Review

Technical Analysis
Distribution and Accumulation
Trend Analysis
Large block transactions
Directional factors
Daily Trading Barometer

- Assumptions of technical analysis
- Dow Theory
- Elliot Wave Principle
- Activity Factors
- High–low Index
- Advances–declines Index
- Lo/Price Activity Ratio
- Dow Jones Momentum Ratio
- Market strength factors
- Breadth Index
- Relative Strength Index
- Volume of trading
- Directional moves
- Barron's Confidence Index
- Confidence factor
- Advisory service sentiment
- Odd-lot Index
- Short interest
- Contrary opinion factors
- NYSE Specialists' Short Sales Ratio
- Line chart
- Bar chart
- Point-and-figure chart
- Support and resistance levels
- Head and Shoulders configurations

Questions for Review

1. Briefly describe the essence of fundamental and technical analysis.
2. Would you advise an investor to use technical analysis as the only basis for investment decisions? Explain.
3. A technical analyst explains that the stock market acts like a barometer rather than a thermometer. What does this mean?
4. Would a technical analyst subscribe to the Efficient Market Hypothesis?
5. Why do technical analysts consider the volume of trading to be important?
6. Describe at least three ways a technical analyst might use information on any of the Dow Jones Averages.
7. What is the Relative Strength Index? Is it possible for a stock's relative price index to increase during a bear market? Explain.
8. Explain the relationship between technical analysis and the old cliche, "Buy low and sell high."
9. What is the theory behind the advisory service sentiment? How does a technical analyst use it as a decision tool?
10. What is Barron's Confidence Index? What is the theory behind it?
11. When an investor sells a stock short, he expects the price of the security to decline. However, a technical analyst can become optimistic as the short interest *goes up*. Why?
12. What value do technical analysts find in chart reading?
13. What are support and resistance levels? Why are they expected to occur?
14. Explain the nature and methodology of trend analysis.
15. What is the primary difference between bar charting and point-and-figure charting?

Selected Readings

Bishop, G. W., Jr., ed. *Charles H. Dow, Economist*. Princeton: Dow Jones, n.d.

Boland, John C. "How Now, Dow Theory?" *Barron's*, September 5, 1977.

Branch, Ben. "The Predictive Power of Stock Market Indicators." *Journal of Financial and Quantitative Analysis*, June 1976.

Cohen, A.W. *The Chartcraft Method of Point and Figure Trading*. Larchmont, N.Y.: Chartcraft, 1963.

Cohen, A. W. *Technical Indicator Analysis by Point and Figure Technique*. Larchmont, N.Y.: Chartcraft, 1963.

Crouch, Robert L. "Market Volume and Price Changes." *Financial Analysts Journal*, July–August 1970.

Dines, James. *How the Average Investor Can Use Technical Analysis for Stock Profits*. New York: Dines Chart Corporation, 1974.

Drew, Garfield A. "A Clarification of the Odd Lot Theory." *Financial Analysts Journal*, September–October 1967.

Drew, Garfield A. *New Methods for Profit in the Stock Market*, 4th ed. Wells, Vermont: Fraser Publishing Co., 1966.

Edwards, Robert D. and John Magee. *Technical Analysis of Stock Trends*. Springfield, Mass.: John Magee, 1958.

Ehrbar, A. F. "Technical Analysts Refuse to Die." *Fortune*, August 1975.

Eiteman, Wilford, et al. *The Stock Market*. New York: McGraw-Hill 1966.

Fama, Eugene F. and Marshall E. Blume. "Filter Rules and Stock Market Trading." *Journal of Business*, January 1966.

Gould, Alex and Maurice Buchsbaum. "A Filter Approach to Stock Selection." *Financial Analysts Journal*, November–December 1969.

Hamilton, W. P. *The Stock Market Barometer*. Princeton: Dow Jones, 1922.

Hanna, M. "Short Interest: Bullish or Bearish?—Comment," *Journal of Finance*, June 1968.

Jiler, William L. *How Charts Can Help You in the Stock Market*. New York: Commodity Research Publication Corp., 1962.

Kewley, T. J. and R. A. Stevenson. "The Odd-Lot Theory as Revealed by Purchase and Sales Statistics for Individual Stocks." *Financial Analysts Journal*, September–October 1967.

Kisor, Manown, Jr. and Victor Niederhoffer. "Odd-Lot Short Sales Ratio: It Signals a Market Rise." *Barron's*, September 1, 1969.

Klein, D. J. "The Odd-Lot Stock Trading Theory," Ph.D. dissertation, Michigan State University, 1964.

Levy, Robert A. "Conceptual Foundations of Technical Analysis." *Financial Analysts Journal*, July–August 1966.

Levy, Robert A. "An Evaluation of Selected Applications of Stock Market Timing Techniques, Trading Tactics and Trend Analysis," Unpublished Ph.D. dissertation, The American University, Washington, D.C., 1966.

Levy, Robert A. *The Relative Strength Concept of Common Stock Forecasting*. Larchmont, N.Y.: Investors Intelligence, 1968.

Levy, Robert A. "Relative Strength as a Criterion for Investment Selection." *Journal of Finance*, December 1967.

Levy, Robert A. and Spero L. Kripotos. "Sources of Relative Price Strength." *Financial Analysts Journal*, November–December 1969.

May, A. Wilfred. "On Stock Market Forecasting and Timing." *The Commercial and Financial Chronicle*, November 14, 1957.

Mayor, T. H. "Short Trading Activities and the Price of Equities: Some Simulation and Regression Results." *Journal of Financial and Quantitative Analysis*, September 1968.

Nurock, Robert J. "Wall Street Week: Technical Market Index." Merrill Lynch Pierce Fenner & Smith, Inc., October 22, 1976.

Pinches, George E. "The Random Walk Hypothesis and Technical Analysis." *Financial Analysts Journal*, March–April 1970.

Rhea, Robert. *The Dow Theory*. Princeton: Dow Jones, 1932.

Rosenfeld, Felix, ed. *The Evaluation of Ordinary Shares*. Summary of the Proceedings of the 8th Congress of the European Federation of Financial Analysts Societies. Paris: Dunod, 1975.

Seligman, Daniel. "The Mystique of Point-and-Figure." *Fortune*, March 1962.

Seneca, Joseph J. "Short Interest: Bearish or Bullish?" *Journal of Finance*, March 1967.

Seneca, Joseph J. "Short Interest: Bullish or Bearish?—Reply." *Journal of Finance*, March 1967.

Sharpe, William F. "Likely Gains from Market Timing." *Financial Analysts Journal*, March–April 1975.

Shaw, Alan R. "Technical Analysis." In *Financial Analyst's Handbook*. Ed. Sumner N. Levine. Homewood, Ill.: Dow Jones-Irwin, 1975.

Smith, Randall D. "Short Interest and Stock Market Prices." *Financial Analysts Journal*, November–December 1968.

Tabell, Edmund W. and Anthony W. Tabell. "The Case for Technical Analysis." *Financial Analysts Journal*, March–April 1964.

Van Horne, James C. and George G. C. Parker. "Technical Trading Rules: A Comment." *Financial Analysts Journal*, July–August 1968.

Wu, Hsiu-Kwant, and Alan Z. Zakon. *Elements of Investments: Selected Readings*. New York: Holt, 1965.

Ying, Charles C. "Stock Market Prices and Volume of Sales." *Econometrica*, July 1966.

Appendix 1 to Part 3: Inflation, Income Taxes, and Stock Prices*

An Overview

The recent performance of equity values certainly seems perverse to investors who purchased common stock believing that earnings, dividends, prices of business products, and therefore share values generally would rise together over the years. As shown in Figure 12–A and Table 12–A, equity values have fallen well behind reported corporate earnings, the prices of business products, and the prices of other assets since the late 1960s. Consequently, stock price–earnings ratios and the purchasing power of equity have fallen by half during the past decade.

This recent performance is especially disturbing in view of the rather steady increase in the purchasing power of equity before the late 1960s. Share values generally increased faster than the prices of goods and services as stockholders benefited from the persistent gains in corporate earnings. Just as the attractive performance of stocks during the first two decades after World War II supported the conventional belief that equity was a good hedge against inflation, providing investors growth in real purchasing power, the dismal performance of the last decade has severely challenged this belief. From 1968 to 1972 real stock prices

* With suitable modifications, this appendix reproduces parts of an article by Richard Kopcke, "Are Stocks a Bargain?" *New England Economic Review*, May–June 1979, pp. 5–11, 18.

Figure 12–A **Equity Values and Corporate Earnings**

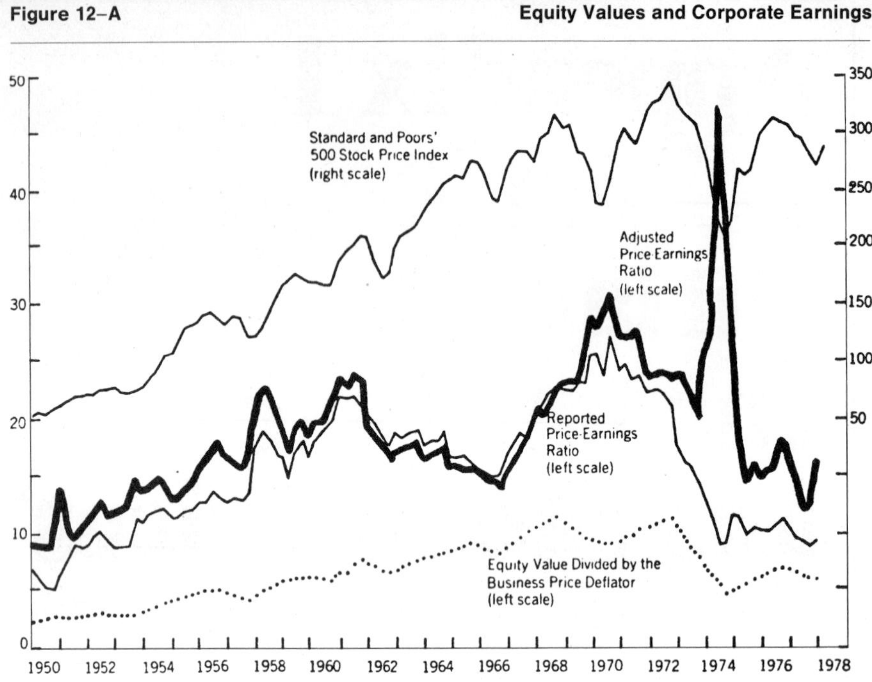

NOTE: Equity value divided by the Business Price Deflator equals the Standard & Poor's 500 stock price index divided by the implicit price deflator for business output (Table 7.5, National Income and Product Accounts, U.S. Department of Commerce, *Survey of Current Business*).

Reported Price–Earnings Ratios equal the product of the reciprocal of the Standard & Poor's 500 dividend–price ratio and dividends of nonfinancial corporations divided by profits after tax of nonfinancial corporations (Table 1.15, *SCB*).

Adjusted Price–Earnings Ratios are identical to the Reported Price–Earning Ratios except that corporate profits with inventory valuation and capital consumption adjustments less profits tax liabilities replaces profits after tax (Table 1.15, *SCB*).

Table 12–A **Average Annual Growth on Investment (1968–78)**

Chinese Ceramics	19.2%	Farmland	10.6%
Gold	16.3	Housing	9.2
Stamps	15.4	Silver	9.1
Old Masters	13.0	Foreign Exchange	6.2
Coins	13.0	Consumer Price Index	6.1
Diamonds	12.6	Bonds	6.1
Oil	11.5	Stock	2.8

SOURCE: Salomon Brothers, Stock Research Department, July 1978.

Figure 12–B **Stock Prices, Dividends, and the Rate of Return on Nonfinancial Corporate Capital**

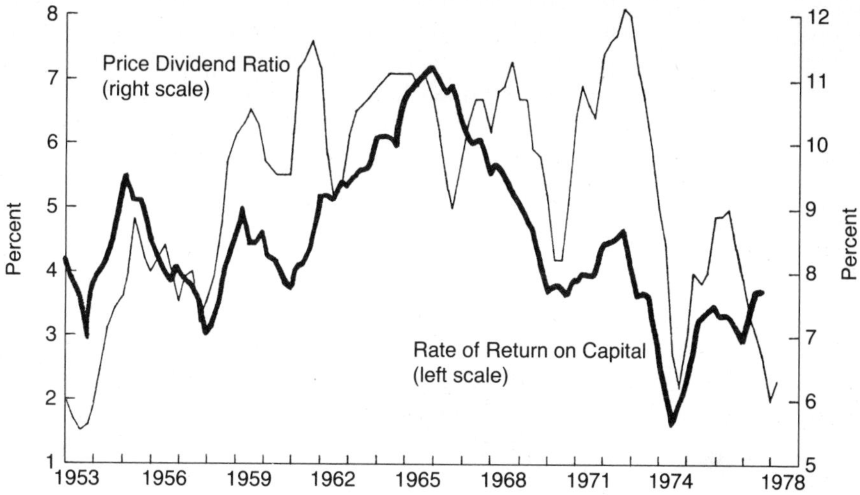

NOTE: The Price–Dividend Ratio is the reciprocal of the Standard & Poor's 500 Dividend–Price Ratio.
The rate of return equals nonfinancial corporate profits with inventory valuation and capital consumption adjustments less profits tax liability plus net interest divided by the current replacement value of nonfinancial assets. (See R. W. Kopcke, "The Decline in Corporate Profitability," *New England Economic Review*, May–June 1978, pp. 36–40, 57.)

failed to surpass previous peaks, and since 1972, the purchasing power of equity has declined sharply.

While stock prices appear unusually low relative to historic norms, an analysis of Figures 12–A and 12–B suggests that this conclusion is premature. The heavy line in Figure 12–A describes an alternative price–earnings ratio for corporate equity: Earnings have been adjusted so that depreciation allowances more accurately measure business capital consumption expenses and "inventory profits" are excluded. These adjustments have lowered substantially the measured operating income of corporate enterprise since the late 1960s. According to this more accurate measure of earnings, stock prices are not so dramatically low—recent price–earnings ratios are comparable to those of the mid-1960s.

Note that the thin line in Figure 12–B that plots the postwar profile of the value of equity divided by corporation dividends. This line generally rises from the early 1950s to the mid-1960s. Throughout most of the 1960s and early 1970s, the price–dividend ratio only occasionally attains new peaks; after 1973, it declines. Stock values at first outpaced dividend growth only to fall behind in the last ten years.

The heavy line in Figure 12–B indicates the total *after-tax* rate of return on tangible capital assets for nonfinancial corporations. From the early 1950s to the mid-1960s the rate of return to capital increased approximately 50 percent, and these increasing returns meant that the value of stock could rise even faster than earnings, dividends or the prices of business products. Since this period, however, the rate of return has fallen more than 40 percent, leading to a decline in the real "earning power" of corporate capital which has been reflected in stock prices.[1] Matching the drop in the total rate of return, the market value of corporate capital assets relative to the replacement cost of these assets has fallen approximately 40 percent since the late 1960s. This lower market valuation has been achieved through depressed real equity values.

Of the several possible explanations for declining rates of return—such as relatively high materials costs, capital goods prices, and labor expenses—one is particularly important for public policy: Corporate income tax liabilities relative to operating profits have been rising since 1965. Although evidence suggests that the prevalent rates of return during the mid-1960s were especially generous and were bound to be reduced by competition, the added burden of higher taxation may have been responsible for much of the total decline in after-tax rates of return.[2] By implication, then, these same tax burdens may have contributed substantially to the languid behavior of share values.

The Impact of Inflation and Income Taxes

Because common stock represents an ownership claim on a share of the nation's productive assets, the value of equity reflects the prospective after-tax earnings commanded by these assets. Even though the prices of goods and services generally have risen during the past ten years—suggesting that corporate earnings and equity values might have risen as well—inflation also effectively increased business and personal income tax rates. These rising tax rates have reduced stockholders' prospective "take-home pay," thereby deflating equity values.

---

[1] Although this broad concept of "Profitability" embraces the returns earned by stockholders and debtholders alike, the total rate of return to capital is one of the primary determinants of stockholders' earnings. Because the proportion of corporate capital financed by debt has not fallen during the past decade, (the ratio of credit market debt to the replacement cost of fixed capital for nonfinancial corporations is now roughly equal to its value of the late 1960s), both rising interest rates and declining total returns to capital have squeezed stockholders' earnings, implying that the falling rate of return shown in Figure 12–B understates the drop in stockholders' rates of return.

Contrary to some popular arguments, stockholders have not received substantial capital gains on existing capital assets to compensate for the higher nominal cost of debt. The declining total return to capital has depressed the real value of the corporate capital stock.

[2] For more discussion of postwar trends in corporate profitability see Richard W. Kopcke, "The Decline in Corporate Profitability," *New England Economic Review*, May–June 1978. If the effective corporate income tax rate had not risen with the inflation rate, the after-tax return to corporate capital would have been approximately 20 percent higher in recent years. Although stockholders' income tax liabilities relative to total pretax returns to capital have been falling recently, the decline reflects the greater share of total pretax income earned by bondholders, not a decline in effective income tax rates.

Reported profits rest on historical cost accounting principles that presume prices are reasonably stable from year to year. For example, depreciation allowances are tied to the original acquisition prices of plant and equipment. Accordingly, capital consumption allowances reflect asset prices that may be significantly out of date after a period of rising prices. The cost of doing business is therefore understated, profits are overstated, and business income tax liabilities increase relative to actual earnings. The cost of production is also linked to the purchase prices of raw materials and intermediate products. Due to the lags between product acquisition, production, and sales, products are held in process or inventory for lengthy periods before being sold. Consequently, the cost of materials behind current sales also may be understated during periods of inflation, creating "inventory holding gains." These "inventory profits" are included in reported income, and they are taxed accordingly. Therefore, the effective corporate income tax rate on operating income, which excludes "inventory" and "depreciation profits," rises with the inflation rate.[3]

Not only does the effective corporate income tax rate rise with inflation, but the effective personal income tax rate on corporate earnings rises as well. Because a portion of corporate earnings are reinvested in the firm, stockholders receive these retained earnings not as dividends but as capital gains on existing equity. When the accumulated capital gains are redeemed by stockholders selling equity, this deferred income is taxed according to personal capital gains income tax rates. Investors may also expect equity values to rise with the prices of goods and services; but, in this case, the increasing stock prices, which only maintain stockholders' purchasing power, are also subject to capital gains taxes even though these capital gains do not represent deferred income. Equity values must fall relative to dividends and corporate earnings with the first signs of higher inflation to raise the nominal yield on stocks enough to compensate new investors for the higher real tax burden due to this taxation of capital gains caused by inflation. Consequently, stock prices are lower than they otherwise would have been if the inflation-induced capital gains on equity had not been taxed. The higher the expected rate of inflation, the lower stock price–earnings ratios must fall to sustain stockholders' real "take-home" compensation.[4]

An unexpected increase in the rate of inflation, however, does provide stockholders with one benefit which may offset temporarily some of the burden of

[3] For further discussion of this point, see T. N. Tideman and D. P. Tucker, "The Tax Treatment of Business Profits under Inflationary Conditions," and S. Davidson and R. L. Weill, "Inflation Accounting: Implications of the FASB Proposal," both in *Inflation and the Income Tax*, ed. H. J. Aaron (Washington, D.C.: Brookings Institution, 1976). Also see the article cited in footnote 2, and R. W. Kopcke, "Current Accounting Practices and Proposals for Reform," *New England Economic Review*, September–October, 1976.

[4] Inflation increases real personal income tax burdens through the well-known "bracket effects" as well as the taxation of nominal capital gains. This article treats only capital gains. For a more general discussion of inflation and personal income taxes see R. E. Brinner, "Inflation and the Definition of Taxable Personal Income," and E. M. Sunley, Jr., and J. A. Pechman, "Inflation Adjustments for the Individual Income Tax," both in *Inflation and the Income Tax*, ed. H. J. Aaron.

higher tax rates. The unexpectedly high inflation rate may cause a widespread revision of inflation forecasts that in turn may produce higher interest rates. Businesses having previously secured long-term debt or lease contracts at fixed yields may temporarily avoid paying prevailing rates for borrowed funds.[5]

As after-tax corporate earnings or dividends payments fall, so must the value of common stock. In other words, the flow of investment funds into the stock market responds to changes in returns. Lower yields on equity may induce investors to seek other assets or perhaps reduce overall saving.[6] Accordingly, the price of equity tends to fall until the prospective after-tax yield rises enough to reward investors adequately.

Anticipated and Unanticipated Inflation

Higher inflation will not always depress stock values. If investors and business managers correctly anticipate variations in the inflation rate over the lifespan of capital investments at the time these projects are undertaken, real equity values may neither rise nor fall in response to the inflation rate. For example, if management correctly anticipates higher inflation rates ten years hence, it also will foresee that the income from long-lived investment projects undertaken today will be taxed at higher rates a decade from now. The accurate expectation of higher inflation permits businesses to prepare for the concomitant reduction in after-tax returns in their capital budgeting strategies: Projects which provide unacceptably low after-tax earnings ordinarily will be rejected. In other words, when businesses correctly expect higher inflation to raise "inventory" and "depreciation profits," thereby raising a project's tax burden too severely, the project will be abandoned. In this event, fully anticipated increases in the inflation rate need not lower the after-tax rate of return to capital investments.

When management expects higher inflation rates to increase the effective corporate income tax rate, business investment spending will probably decline. Although real equity values then will increase more slowly (because the stock of plant, equipment, and business inventories will increase more slowly), real

[5] However, the holding gains on debt are offset by the holding losses of corporate pension fund assets (both debt and stock). Considering pension plans and long-term debt positions together, the rise in the expected inflation rate since the late 1960s has conferred on equity no profit from lower real debt burden—on average, net holding gains cannot have provided for any improvement in real equity values. Some estimates of unfunded pension liabilities are large enough to suggest that pension fund losses exceed the gains on debt, depressing equity values still further. Of course, firms carrying heavier than average debt loads and modest pension obligations, such as some utilities, will benefit by inflation; whereas some manufacturing businesses with relatively light debt loads and substantial pension commitments will suffer when inflation rates unexpectedly rise.

[6] Not only may the personal saving rate respond to rates of return on investments but households can divert flows of funds from assets yielding unattractive rates of return, and from financial institutions acquiring those assets, to alternative investments—including real assets such as housing or land.

stock prices need not decline when inflation rates rise. In fact, the stock of real nonfinancial corporate tangible assets increased approximately 40 percent during the 1970s. Because today's ratio of debt to the replacement cost of these assets roughly equals its value ten years ago, real equity values would also have increased considerably since the late 1960s if the return on investment has been as high as planned. The decline in real stock prices indicates that after-tax operating returns on many investments must have fallen well short of expectations during the past decade.

Unlike fully anticipated inflation, unexpected changes in the inflation rate or revisions of price forecasts, like any new information, must always disturb real equity values, because previous capital purchases were justified by now-obsolete information.[7] It is presumed that the high inflation of the mid-1970s and the current forecasts of continuing high inflation for the coming decade were not anticipated by investors during the mid-1960s. Therefore, much of today's capital stock was purchased when investors did not accurately foresee today's high inflation rate.[8]

[7] For a more complete discussion of information and stock prices, see N. G. Berkman, "A Primer on Random Walks in the Stock Market," *New England Economic Review*, September–October 1978, pp.32–50.

[8] What little evidence there is does not contradict the assumption that the inflation of the 1970s was not anticipated in the 1960s. To the extent businesses cannot avoid the burden of higher taxation, even if it is fully anticipated, the assumption may be relaxed.

Appendix 2 to Part 3: Margin Trading

An Overview

Investors use two major types of brokerage house accounts to purchase securities. The first type is a *cash account*, in which an investor pays the total cost of securities purchased within five business days of the trade date. The second type is a *margin account*, in which the investor puts up only a portion of the total purchase cost, borrowing the balance from the brokerage house. The main reason for purchasing stocks on margin is to *leverage* the amount of money invested in them. That is, for a given cash outlay, investors can control more shares of stock purchased on margin than if they had made a purchase of stocks with cash. However, margin trading also increases an investor's risk, as will shortly become clear.

The Power of Leverage

Margin trading magnifies the results of investment in securities. For example, if an investor purchases a stock on margin and subsequently sells it at a profit, the rate of return on his investment will be greater than if he had purchased the stock in a cash account.[1] Similarly, if the stock is sold at a loss, the margin

[1] This may not be the case when the interest expense on the margin loan is considered. Interest expense will be discussed later.

Table 12–B

	The Profit Picture* Market Value of Stock Increases 20 Percent		The Loss Picture* Market Value of Stock Declines 20 Percent	
	Cash Account	**Margin Account**	**Cash Account**	**Margin Account**
ABC Stock Purchased:				
Investor's cash	$15,000	$15,000	$15,000	$15,000
Borrowed from broker		5,000		5,000
Total Cost	$15,000	$20,000	$15,000	$20,000
ABC Stock Sold:	18,000	24,000	12,000	16,000
Profit (Loss)	$ 3,000	$ 4,000	($ 3,000)	($ 4,000)
Profit (Loss) as a % of investor's cash investment:	$ 3,000 / $15,000 = 20%	$ 4,000 / $15,000 = 26.67%	($ 3,000) / $15,000 = (20%)	($ 4,000) / $15,000 = (26.67%)

* Interest expense, commissions, and taxes ignored. No dividends paid on ABC stock.

trader will lose a greater percentage of his capital.[2] This is known as the power of leverage.

The power of leverage can be demonstrated with a simple example. Table 12–B presents the results of trading in ABC stock under different circumstances. First examine the columns under the heading "The Profit Picture." Suppose an investor purchases $15,000 worth of ABC stock in a cash account, and subsequently sells it after the market value rises 20 percent to $18,000. He would make a $3,000 profit, which is a 20 percent return on his $15,000 cash investment. However, the investor could have increased his return by purchasing the same security on margin. For example, as shown under the "Margin Account" column, the investor leverages his $15,000 investment by purchasing an additional $5,000 worth of ABC stock with a margin loan. If the market value of the stock rises 20 percent, the resulting profit will be $4,000 ($20,000 × 20%), which is a 26.67 percent return on the investor's $15,000 cash investment. Note that even though the investor puts up only 75 percent of the total cost of the stock purchase ($15,000/$20,000), he receives all of the profit. Consequently, in this example, the return from margin trading is higher than the cash account transaction, both in dollars and as a percent of the investor's cash investment.

The columns under the heading "The Loss Picture" are equally revealing. Here it is assumed that the market value of ABC stock *declines* 20 percent. For a $15,000 cash account transaction, the investor loses $3,000, or 20 percent of his investment. However, when additional stock is bought with a $5,000 margin loan, a 20 percent decline in the market value of the stock results in a $4,000

[2] The margin trader can also increase his return in terms of dollars, as will be demonstrated shortly.

loss—26.67 percent of the investor's cash investment. In this case, the investor puts up only 75 percent of the total purchase cost, but must assume the entire loss. Again, it can be seen that margin trading magnifies investment results, and hence increases the investor's risk.

The example presented in Table 12–B illustrated a case in which securities were purchased on 75 percent margin; that is, the investor put up three quarters of the total purchase cost. However, if the investor had bought the ABC stock by putting up less of his capital, the percentage gain or loss on the same transaction would have been greater. For example, if he purchased the same $20,000 worth of stock by putting up only $10,000 (50 percent margin), a $4,000 profit or loss would be 40 percent of the investor's cash investment.[3]

Interest Expense

The previous example demonstrated the power of leverage, but was simplified by ignoring the interest expense on the margin loan.[4] However, interest expense is an important consideration for the margin trader.

When a brokerage firm finances part of an investor's purchase, it either uses its own capital or borrows the money from a bank, using the securities as collateral. The rate charged to brokerage houses on such loans, or *call money*[5] is approximately 1 percent higher than the rate on treasury bills. The broker charges the investor a rate that will generally vary with the amount of money borrowed. A large investor borrowing over $50,000, for example, might be charged about $\frac{1}{2}$ to 1 percent above the call money rate. A small investor borrowing less than $15,000 might be charged a rate 2 to $2\frac{1}{2}$ percent higher than the call money rate. Of course, as the call money rate fluctuates, so will the rate on margin loans.

The impact of interest expense on margin trading is demonstrated in Table 12–C. Here, the example given in Table 12–B is extended by assuming that the investor pays 12 percent interest on the $5,000 margin loan. If the stock is held one year, a $600 interest expense is incurred. As a result, the return on the margin trader's cash investment after a 20 percent increase in the stock's market value is only 22.67 percent. When the market value of ABC stock declines 20 percent, as a percentage of his cash investment the loss is over 30 percent. Interest expense is clearly a drawback to margin trading. Of course, the impact may be more or less severe than shown in this example, depending on the level of the interest rate and the amount of money borrowed.

---

[3] Of course, the investor could also purchase the stock on 50 percent margin by putting up $15,000 and borrowing $15,000 to make a $30,000 purchase. In this case, a 20 percent increase in the stock's market value will result in a $6,000 profit ($30,000 × 20%). However, the percentage return on the investor's cash investment will still be 40 percent ($6,000/$15,000).

[4] For simplicity, taxes and commissions were also ignored.

[5] Because brokerage firms promise to repay these loans "on call" at any time the bank requests the money, the name "call money" is used.

Table 12–C

	The Profit Picture* Market Value of Stock Increases 20 Percent		The Loss Picture* Market Value of Stock Declines 20 Percent	
	Cash Account	Margin Account	Cash Account	Margin Account
ABC Stock Purchased:				
Investor's cash	$15,000	$15,000	$15,000	$15,000
Borrowed from broker	—	5,000		5,000
Total Cost	$15,000	$20,000	$15,000	$20,000
ABC Stock Sold	18,000	24,000	12,000	16,000
Profit (Loss) before interest expense	$ 3,000	$ 4,000	($ 3,000)	($ 4,000)
Interest Expense ($5,000 × 12% for one year):	—	(600)	—	(600)
Profit (Loss) after interest expense	$ 3,000	$ 3,400	($ 3,000)	($ 4,600)
Profit (Loss) after interest expense as a % of investor's cash investment	$\frac{\$ 3,000}{\$15,000} = 20\%$	$\frac{\$ 3,400}{\$15,000} = 22.67\%$	$\frac{(\$ 3,000)}{\$15,000} = (20\%)$	$\frac{(\$ 4,600)}{\$ 15,000} = (30.67\%)$

* Commissions and taxes ignored. No dividends paid on ABC stock.

Margin Trading Rules

Although the idea of margin trading is simple, the process of borrowing money to buy securities can be complicated, because it is regulated by the government, the New York Stock Exchange, and various brokerage houses.

General Requirements

As a general rule, all securities purchased on margin must be left with the broker and registered in the name of the brokerage house, or in "street name."[6] The investor must also sign a hypothecation agreement whereby he authorizes the broker to pledge the margined securities as collateral to finance the extension of credit. In addition, most brokerage firms assume that investors grant them a blanket permission to lend their securities to other investors who want to sell short.

Purchase Requirements

In 1934, under a little known rule called Regulation T, the Board of Governors of the Federal Reserve System (FRS) started exercising its authority in establishing *initial margin requirements*—the percentage of the total purchase the

[6] When stocks are held in the name of the brokerage house, the broker receives any dividends and credits them to the customer's account.

investor is required to put up as a downpayment.[7] As shown in Table 12–D, the initial margin requirements have ranged from as low as 40 percent to as high as 100 percent; since 1974, the rate has been 50 percent. Interestingly, the initial margin requirement set by Regulation T takes into account not only the securities being purchased by an investor, but the market value of securities the investor may already have in his margin account.

The following example should help explain the requirements of Regulation T. An investor currently owns no securities, has borrowed no money from his broker, and has decided to purchase $20,000 worth of ABC stock on margin. He will receive a Regulation T call which requires that he put up at least $10,000, or 50 percent of the total cost.

Let us now consider a different example in which the investor previously purchased securities which are currently in his margin account and have a market value of $10,000. After he buys the ABC stock worth $20,000 his total portfolio will have a $30,000 market value. Therefore, the investor can borrow as much as $15,000 to finance the $20,000 stock purchase, because his total borrowings as a result of the purchase will not exceed 50 percent of the $30,000 market value of the portfolio.

[7] Another margin requirement must be met. It is commonly referred to as the New York Stock Exchange minimum initial requirement. Under this requirement, investors must establish an equity to at least $2,000 every time they enter into a new commitment in a General Margin Account.

Reasons for Changes in Margin Requirements by Federal Reserve Board*

Statements by the Board of Governors of the Federal Reserve System as shown in excerpts of its Annual Reports, in addition to shedding light on the philosophy of margin, could also serve as an outline of American economic history since 1934.

For example, when the requirements were raised to 100% (from 75%) on January 21, 1946, for the only time in history, the Governors reasoned:

> *During the period of reconversion from a wartime to a peacetime economy, the country was being exposed to powerful inflationary pressures . . . This period had also been characterized by public pressure for premature removal of governmental wartime controls, with the consequent effect of promoting speculative activity.*
>
> *Restriction of the use of credit in the securities market would tend to discourage speculative activity which was both a characteristic and a feeder of inflation. In these circumstances, any expansion in the use of credit for the purpose of buying or trading in registered securities was, in the judgment of the Board, an excessive use of credit and consequently should be prevented under the legislative mandate to the Board.*

* The New York Stock Exchange, "Margin," November 24, 1972, p. 7. Reprinted with the permission of the New York Stock Exchange, Inc.

Table 12–D

	Initial Margin Requirements
Oct. 29, 1929	No Govt.-Regulated Margin
Oct. 15, 1934, to Jan. 31, 1936	45%
Feb. 1, 1936, to Oct. 31, 1937	55
Nov. 1, 1937, to Feb. 4, 1945	40
Feb. 5, 1945, to July 4, 1945	50
July 5, 1945, to Jan. 20, 1946	75
Jan. 21, 1946, to Jan. 31, 1947	100
Feb. 1, 1947, to Mar. 29, 1949	75
Mar. 30, 1949, to Jan. 16, 1951	50
Jan. 17, 1951, to Feb. 19, 1953	75
Feb. 20, 1953, to Jan. 3, 1955	50
Jan. 4, 1955, to Apr. 22, 1955	60
Apr. 23, 1955, to Jan. 15, 1958	70
Jan. 16, 1958, to Aug. 4, 1958	50
Aug. 5, 1958, to Oct. 15, 1958	70
Oct. 16, 1958, to July 27, 1960	90
July 28, 1960, to July 9, 1962	70
July 10, 1962, to Nov. 5, 1963	50
Nov. 6, 1963, to June 7, 1968	70
June 8, 1968, to May 5, 1970	80
May 6, 1970, to Dec. 5, 1971	65
Dec. 6, 1971, to Nov. 23, 1972	55
Nov. 24, 1972, to Jan. 2, 1974	65
Jan. 3, 1974, to ______	50

On February 1, 1947, when the Board reduced the requirements from 100% to 75%:

In contrast with the behavior of most prices, stock prices, which had risen sharply for several months prior to January 1946 and continued to rise somewhat further after that time, subsequently declined materially . . . At the same time, the volume of credit in the stock market had been substantially reduced until that used for carrying listed securities was at about the lowest level in the last 30 years.

A further reduction—to 50%—went into effect on March 30, 1949, about which the Board stated:

There were increasing evidences that inflationary pressures were subsiding and that a readjustment from a highly inflationary situation was taking place. It was the view of the Board that, in these conditions, the time had arrived when action to reduce margin requirements should be taken.

Taking the example a step further, assume the investor already has $10,000 worth of securities in his account, but that he also owes his broker $3,000. In this case, the investor could borrow as much as $12,000 to make the $20,000 stock purchase. After the purchase, his total margin debt would be $15,000—exactly 50 percent of the $30,000 market value of the portfolio.

It should be evident that if the market value of the investor's portfolio increases, he will have additional buying power. Consider an investor with securities in his margin account worth $30,000 and debt to his broker of $15,000. If the market value of his portfolio increases from $30,000 to, say, $40,000, he could purchase an *additional* $10,000 worth of stock without putting up any money. After the purchase, the market value of his portfolio would be $50,000 ($40,000 plus the $10,000 purchase). Consequently he would be allowed to borrow an additional $10,000, and his total debt would not exceed the $25,000 (50 percent) limit.

Maintenance Requirements

The FRB regulates only margin purchases. Once the purchase is made, Regulation T no longer applies, even if the initial margin requirement is subsequently raised. However, an investor's margin account is still regulated thereafter by the NYSE's Rule 431, which currently requires investors to maintain in their accounts a 25 percent equity of the market value of all their securities. Many brokerage firms, however, usually follow a more restrictive policy; currently, most firms require their customers to maintain a 30 percent equity.

Consider again the example in which the investor put up $10,000 to purchase $20,000 worth of ABC stock. His equity, which is the market value of the securities in his account less any debt to his broker, is $10,000. Because his $10,000 equity is 50 percent of the $20,000 market value of the securities, he meets the broker's 30 percent *minimum maintenance requirement.*

But suppose the market value of his securities drops from $20,000 to $14,000. The investor's equity will decline to $4,000 ($14,000 market value less $10,000 debt), which is only 28.6 percent of the market value. Because the brokerage house requires the investor's equity to be at least 30 percent, or $4,200 ($14,000 × 30%), the investor will receive a *margin call* for an additional $200. The brokerage firm might give him as long as a week to put up the money. If the investor fails to comply, the brokerage firm will sell securities from his account to reduce his debt and raise his equity to the required maintenance level.

Like Regulation T, the minimum maintenance requirement applies to the market value of *all* the securities in the investor's account,[8] not just the last securities purchased. This is important because most margin investors have more than one stock in their accounts. Even if the price of one stock falls rapidly, a margin call may not necessarily result, because the market value of the margin

[8] Technically, all NYSE stocks and some ASE and OTC stocks are included in this category.

portfolio may not decline to the point where the investor's equity falls below minimum maintenance requirement.

Sometimes an investor's equity as a percent of his portfolio's market value might fall below the FRB's initial margin requirements, but it may still remain above the minimum maintenance requirement. In such a case the investor will not be given a margin call, but his account will be *restricted.* In a restricted account, the investor cannot withdraw more than 30 percent of the proceeds from any sale; the remaining 70 percent would be retained to reduce the investor's debt.

Types of Margin Accounts

The preceding discussion focused on margin trading in the *General Margin Account*—the most common of the various types of margin accounts. It is used for trading listed stocks and warrants, and certain over-the-counter stocks approved for margin trading by the FRB. There are, however, other types of margin accounts for purchasing convertible and nonconvertible corporate bonds, as well as U.S. treasury and government agency securities. These accounts operate in essentially the same manner as the General Margin Account, except that margin requirements often vary for the different types of securities.

Would Hamlet Have Invested on Margin?*

The investor who is resolute, organized, objective, and financially and temperamentally in such shape that he can bear the risks of substantial losses with reasonable equanimity is an excellent candidate for a margin account's opportunities for increasing his purchasing power through leverage.

Hamlet would never have made the grade.

He has been described by some as a scrupulous person—a good quality for any investor—but he was too introspective, irresolute, dilatory, and disorganized to work with even the most patient broker in the margin investment area. And his deep spells of melancholy would never have been soothed by a margin call.

The awareness of Hamlet's unstable temperament may well have been Polonius's reason for cautioning the rest of the world, through his son, Laertes: "Neither a borrower nor lender be!"—a dictum which, if followed at all would have eliminated any possibility of an Industrial Revolution because there would have been no way to finance it.

Perhaps Artemus Ward, in his "Natural History," offered the best basic philosophy for the margin investor: "Let us be happy and live within our means, even if we have to borrow money to do it."

* The New York Stock Exchange, "Margin," November 24, 1972, p. 11. Reprinted with the permission of the New York Stock Exchange, Inc.

4 Portfolio Analysis and Management

During the last 30 years or so, a clear division has existed between security analysis and portfolio management. The security analyst attempts to distinguish between stocks which are undervalued, overvalued, or appropriately valued. The portfolio manager's task is to manage a pool of investible funds in order to maximize the return, given the level of risk which the investor is willing to assume.

In Chapter 5, the risk-return criterion was first applied to the modern portfolio theory. It was learned that an efficient, well-diversified portfolio eliminates unsystematic risk and carries only systematic risk. In Chapter 13, we extend this discussion and examine the topic of portfolio analysis as it applies to Markowitz diversification and the Capital Asset Pricing Model.

Chapter 14 is devoted exclusively to portfolio management in an efficient market. First, the efficiency of the market issue is examined in detail; its implications for portfolio management are articulated. Then the technique of portfolio management is applied to the construction of a "real world" portfolio. This not only demonstrates the use of the technique, but also underscores the complexity of the problem.

The best evidence of portfolio management can be found in the records of investment companies. Chapter 15 is devoted to a detailed discussion of the types and selection of mutual funds. The historical record of mutual funds is also reviewed in this chapter.

No discussion of portfolio construction or management can be complete without an active consideration of the tax strategy and the cost of investing. In Chapter 16 we analyze various tax strategies available to investors and discuss the ways in which transaction costs can affect investment performance.

Portfolio Analysis

Introduction

In Chapter 5, the topic of risk and return of a single security and a portfolio was presented. It was pointed out that the total risk of a group of securities can be reduced by constructing a diversified portfolio.

Beginning with Chapter 6, the discussion focused on the analysis of a single bond or a single stock. Because most investors hold more than one stock or one bond at any given time, they should be appropriately concerned with the building of a well-diversified, efficient portfolio. However, prerequisite to the construction of such a portfolio is a complete understanding of the theory of portfolio management

This chapter is divided into three sections. In Section 1, we discuss the Markowitz Portfolio Model, which led to the development of the Efficient Frontier. Measurement of risk and return as well as different forms of diversification are also discussed.

In Section 2, the model implied by portfolio theory, known as the Capital Asset Pricing Model, is presented. This model is also contrasted with the Market Model. In Section 3, the discussion moves to the construction of the Capital Market Line and the Security Market Line. The chapter concludes with a brief review of the technique of selecting the optimum portfolio against the backdrop of risk preferences of individual investors.

Table 13–1

Year	Quarter I	Quarter II	Quarter III	Quarter IV
1	−2.17	10.51	8.39	−0.75
2	−3.32	14.06	9.23	17.40
3	4.23	−5.10	8.81	14.48
4	7.00	6.22	3.45	−3.07
5	3.83	13.50	0.21	10.03
6	16.03	18.32	3.11	−2.79
7	−8.19	0.33	3.76	16.80
8	5.67	−3.32	2.46	2.83
9	−8.52	1.72	−3.77	7.55
10	−10.73	−13.73	13.82	−7.05

Mean Return = 3.78

Variance = 68.48

Standard Deviation = 8.28

SOURCE: Jerome L. Valentine, *Investment Analysis and Capital Market Theory*, Occasional Paper No. 1 (Charlottesville, Va.: The Financial Analysts Research Foundation, 1975), p. 20.

SECTION 1 MARKOWITZ MODEL AND THE EFFICIENT FRONTIER

Portfolio Theory: A Historical Overview

In 1952, Harry Markowitz developed a novel approach to stock investment. It virtually revolutionized the thinking of the academic community. In fact, the basic elements of modern portfolio theory are based on a series of propositions concerning rational investor behavior that were first developed by Markowitz in 1952.[1]

The basis of Markowitz's approach was the use of fluctuations or variability of investment returns as an approximation of the risk of investment. If Stock A is expected to yield 8 percent $\pm$ 2 percent (that is, between 6 and 10 percent) and Stock B is expected to yield 8 percent $\pm$4 percent (that is, between 4 and 12 percent), then both stocks have the same expected return (8 percent). But because the return on Stock B can go much lower (4 percent) than on Stock A (6 percent), Stock B is considered more risky and therefore, *ceteris paribus*, less desirable than Stock A. First, Markowitz sought to formalize this concept of risk by using the statistical concept of variance. Then he developed the portfolio

[1] Harry M. Markowitz, *Portfolio Selection—Efficient Diversification of Investments* (New Haven, Conn.: Yale University Press, 1959).

Figure 13–1

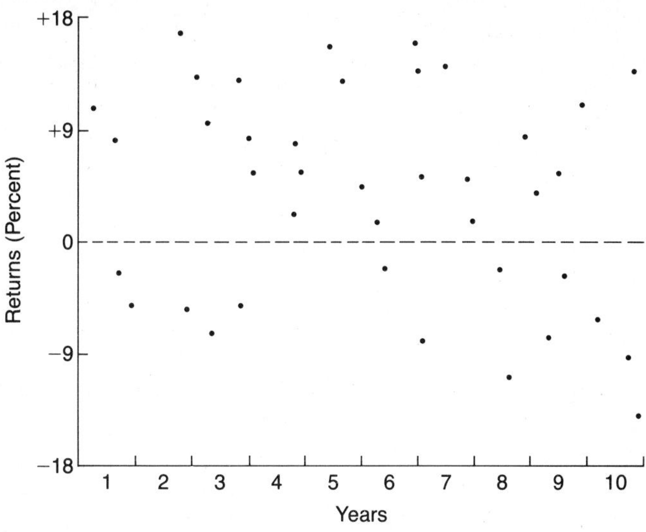

SOURCE: Jerome L. Valentine, *Investment Analysis and Capital Market Theory*, Occasional Paper No. 1 (Charlottesville, Va.: The Financial Analysts Research Foundation, 1975), p. 21.

theory by demonstrating that once the level of risk the investor is willing to assume is established, a computerized theoretical model can be used as a basis for the systematic selection of the optimum portfolio that would maximize the rate of return.

Markowitz used the statistical concept of variance to describe the variability of returns on investments. Assume that the quarterly returns on a stock are computed over a ten-year period.[2] These returns are given in Table 13–1 and graphed in Figure 13–1. The table and figure show no obvious pattern, presumably because the successive rates of return are independent of each other. However, close scrutiny of the figure shows that the returns cluster around the mean value of the set of returns. This can be observed clearly in Figure 13–2, which is a histogram[3] constructed from Table 13–1. This histogram, then, provides a visible basis for the measurement of *risk*. Markowitz argued that, given the mean of all rates of return, a single number can be calculated to measure, on

[2] Jerome L. Valentine, *Investment Analysis and Capital Market Theory*, Occasional Paper No. 1 (Charlottesville, Va.: The Financial Analysts Research Foundation, 1975), pp. 20–22.

[3] It is often desirable to graph a frequency distribution in order to gain the attention of the casual reader to the statistical data being presented. One type of chart, which uncovers important characteristics and relationships not easily discernible from a perusal of a frequency table, is called a histogram. Specifically, a histogram is a bar chart of continuous data, so the class limits have no gaps between them.

Figure 13–2

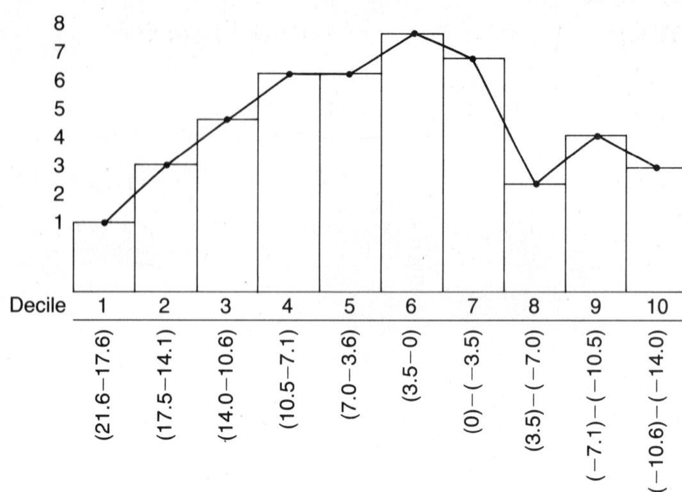

SOURCE: Jerome L. Valentine, *Investment Analysis and Capital Market Theory*, Occasional Paper No. 1 (Charlottesville, Va.: The Financial Analysts Research Foundation, 1975), p. 22.

the average, the *spread* or deviations of individual returns from the mean return. This single number—known as the *variance*, or the square root of variance called *standard deviation*—*is* the risk of the investment in that stock. Even more important, this risk can be measured precisely and expressed quantitatively. For example, in this case, the mean is 3.78, the variance is 68.48, and the standard deviation is 8.28. Assuming that the above returns were normally distributed, about two-thirds of the quarterly returns can be expected to fall within one standard deviation of the mean or, more precisely, between -4.50 and 12.06 (3.78 ± 8.28). It follows that another stock with an identical mean return, 3.78, but with larger variance would entail greater risk. It should be added here that in Figure 13–2 risk is represented only by the *righthand* tail of the return distribution, because the area to the right of the mean return refers to the possibility of receiving lower than the mean return. However, as long as the distribution of returns is symmetric—or largely symmetric—a variance or standard deviation measure can be used as a proxy for risk.

Once variance was established as a measure of risk, Markowitz applied the complicated mathematics of quadratic programming to show how to diversify portfolio holdings—that is, how best to reduce the risk by selecting from a list of hundreds of individual securities those that possess unique characteristics. This concept of risk reduction through diversification is fundamental to modern portfolio theory, and will be fully explored in the following pages.

Measurement of Risk and Return

Single Security Risk and Return

Security Return

The nature of *risk* and *return* of a single security was presented in detail in Chapter 5 and will only be summarized here. Assume the rates of return and the associated subjective probabilities of ABC stock are as follows:

1 Probability of Return (p_i)	2 Possible Return (R_i)
.05	30%
.70	15
.15	0
.10	−20
1.00	

The *expected return* on the stock, $E(R_s)$, is

$$E(R_s) = \sum_{i=1}^{k} p_i R_i \qquad \text{(5–2 restated)}$$

where

$$\begin{aligned} E(R_s) &= \text{Expected return on stock} \\ p_i &= \text{Subjective probability that } i^{\text{th}} \text{ rate of return occurs} \\ R_i &= \text{The } i^{\text{th}} \text{ rate of return} \\ k &= \text{Number of possible rates of return} \end{aligned}$$

In this example, the $E(R_s)$ equals 10 percent:

$$\begin{aligned} E(R_s) &= (.05)(.30) + (.70)(.15) + (.15)(0) + (.10)(-.20) \\ &= .10 \text{ (or } 10\%) \end{aligned}$$

Note that none of the returns given in column 2 of the table matches the expected return. The reason is that the $E(R_s)$ is the weighted *average* of the returns, the subjective probabilities being the relative weights of the returns.

Security Risk

The risk of the security is the dispersion of its returns around the expected return, and it is measured by expected variance of the distribution:

$$E(\sigma_s^2) = \sum_{i=1}^{k} p_i[R_i - E(R_s)]^2 \qquad \textbf{(5–3 restated)}$$

where

$$E(\sigma_s^2) = \text{Expected variance}$$

In this example, the expected variance is .014:

$$\begin{aligned} E(\sigma_s^2) &= (.05)(.30 - .10)^2 + (.70)(.15 - .10)^2 + (.15)(0 - .10)^2 \\ &\quad + (.10)(-.20 - .10)^2 \\ &= .014 \end{aligned}$$

The standard deviation of the distribution, which is merely the square root of variance, is 11.8 percent. If the returns of the security were normally distributed, then 95 percent of all returns will fall within two standard deviations of the mean. As will be observed later, returns of a diversified portfolio tend to be normally distributed. Also, because standard deviation lends itself to the above convenient interpretation whereas variance does not, it is customary to express *portfolio risks* in terms of standard deviation.

Portfolio Risk and Return

Portfolio Return

Assume the following ABC portfolio returns are given:

Security (i)	Weight (w_i)	Expected Returns [$E(R_i)$]	$w_iE(R_i)$
1	.3	.15	.045
2	.7	.05	.035
	1.0		.080

The expected return of the portfolio is 8 percent:

$$\begin{aligned} E(R_p) &= w_1E(R_1) + w_2E(R_2) \qquad \textbf{(13–1)} \\ &= (.30)(.15) + (.70)(.05) \\ &= .080 \text{ (or 8\%)} \end{aligned}$$

For k securities, Equation 13–1 can be rewritten as

$$E(R_p) = \sum_{i=1}^{k} w_i E(R_i) \tag{13–2}$$

where

$E(R_p)$ = Expected return of a portfolio
w_i = Weight of the ith security in the portfolio
$E(R_i)$ = Expected return from the ith security in the portfolio
k = Number of securities in the portfolio

Note that the expected return of a portfolio is the weighted average of the expected returns of the individual securities in the portfolio, the weights being the proportions invested in individual securities. The implications of this relationship can be comprehended by means of the following example.

Table 13–2 presents expected returns of two securities as well as five two-asset portfolios with different combinations of security weights. The table suggests that, given the expected returns on individual stocks, and *with relative risks unspecified*, in constructing a portfolio an investor should put more weight in the stocks with higher expected returns. For instance, Portfolio 1 has a higher expected return, 13.5 percent, than, say, Portfolio 3, which has an expected return of 11.1 percent, because in Portfolio 1 more emphasis was put on the security with higher expected return than was done in Portfolio 3.

Portfolio Risk

The measurement of *portfolio risk* is complicated by the fact that the interrelationship between the returns of individual securities must also be taken into account. This relationship, known as *covariance*, measures the direction and magnitude of change in one random variable as other associated variables change. A positive covariance between two assets indicates that both tend to

Table 13–2

Portfolio No.	First Stock		Second Stock		Portfolio Return $E(R_p) = w_1E(R_1) + w_2E(R_2)$
	Weight (w_1)	Expected Return $E(R_1)$	Weight (w_2)	Expected Return $E(R_2)$	
1	$\frac{1}{8}$	10%	$\frac{7}{8}$	14%	13.5%
2	$\frac{3}{9}$	10	$\frac{6}{9}$	14	12.7
3	$\frac{5}{7}$	10	$\frac{2}{7}$	14	11.1
4	$\frac{11}{13}$	10	$\frac{2}{13}$	14	10.6
5	$\frac{15}{16}$	10	$\frac{1}{16}$	14	10.3

Table 13–3

	Security 1	Security 2
Relative Weights (w_i)	.30	.70
Expected Return [$E(R_i)$]	.15	.05
Variance (σ_i^2)	.20	.15
Standard Deviation (σ_i)	.4472	.3873
Covariance (cov_{12}) = .07		

$$\text{Correlation Coefficient } (\rho_{12}) = \frac{\text{cov}_{12}}{\sigma_1\sigma_2} = \frac{.07}{(.4472)(.3873)}$$
$$= .40$$

$$\begin{aligned} E(R_p) &= w_1E(R_1) + w_2E(R_2) \\ &= (.30)(.15) + (.70)(.05) \\ &= .080 \text{ (or } 8\%) \end{aligned}$$

$$\begin{aligned} E(\sigma_p^2) &= w_1^2\sigma_1^2 + w_2^2\sigma_2^2 + 2w_1w_2 \text{ cov}_{12} \\ &= (.3)^2(.2) + (.7)^2(.15) + 2(.3)(.7)(.07) \\ &= .018 + .0735 + .0294 \\ &= .1209 \end{aligned}$$

change in the same direction; a negative covariance suggests that they change in the opposite direction.[4]

Table 13–3 presents data relating to Portfolio ABC. The expected variance of a two-security portfolio can be calculated:

$$E(\sigma_p^2) = w_1^2\sigma_1^2 + w_2^2\sigma_2^2 + 2w_1w_2 \text{ cov}_{12} \qquad \textbf{(13–3)}$$

where

$E(\sigma_p^2)$ = Expected variance of the portfolio
$w_1; w_2$ = Weights of Securities 1 and 2 in the portfolio
$\sigma_1^2; \sigma_2^2$ = Variances of Securities 1 and 2 in the portfolio
cov_{12} = Covariance between Securities 1 and 2 in the portfolio

Table 13–3 reveals that the risk of the portfolio, measured by its expected variance, $E(\sigma_p^2)$, is .1209. Note that the risk of the portfolio is *smaller* than the risk or variance of Security 1, .20, and Security 2, .15. This is an important point: The risk of any given two-stock portfolio is *not* necessarily the weighted average of individual security risks. In general, the risk or variance of a two-security portfolio will be lower than the risk or variance of either security, so long as the

[4] See note 4 on pages 577–78.

correlation coefficient (p) between the securities (discussed shortly) is less than the ratio of the smaller standard deviation to the larger standard deviation. Symbolically,

$$\rho_{12} < \frac{\sigma_1}{\sigma_2}, \qquad \text{if} \quad \sigma_1 < \sigma_2$$

$$\text{or,} \qquad \rho_{12} < \frac{\sigma_2}{\sigma_1}, \qquad \text{if} \quad \sigma_2 < \sigma_1$$

In the example given in Table 13–3,

$$\rho_{12} < \frac{\sigma_2}{\sigma_1}$$

$$.40 < \frac{.3873}{.4472}$$

$$\text{or,} \qquad .40 < .87$$

This confirms our assertion of the nature of risk reduction of a portfolio.

It should be emphasized here that when the portfolio is expanded to include, say, k securities, the risk of such a portfolio is measured by:

$$E(\sigma_p^2) = \sum_{i=1}^{k} \sum_{j=1}^{k} w_i w_j \operatorname{cov}_{ij} \qquad \textbf{(13–4)}$$

where cov_{ij}, the covariance of a security with itself ($i = i, j = j$), or with identical securities ($i = j$), is equal to variance. Clearly, if $k = 2$, Equation 13–4 reverts to Equation 13–3, which specifies a two-security portfolio.[5]

The ABC portfolio had a unique characteristic—Securities 1 and 2 did not closely covary or move together, therefore the value of cov_{12} was small. Not all portfolios have a small covariance. The relationship between the movements in any two stocks can range from perfectly positive to perfectly negative. Because the comovements between portfolio securities is a critical variable in portfolio risk measurement, it is customary to use the *correlation coefficient* as an alternative to covariance, because the correlation coefficient has unique interpretive properties not associated with covariance. The two statistical measures, of course, are closely related; the covariance between the returns on two assets can

[5] The expected return and expected variance of a three-asset portfolio are given by the following equations:

$$E(R_p) = w_1 E(R_1) + w_2 E(R_2) + w_3 E(R_3)$$

$$E(\sigma_p^2) = w_1^2\sigma_1^2 + w_2^2\sigma_2^2 + w_3^2\sigma_3^2 + 2w_1w_2 \operatorname{cov}_{12} + 2w_1w_3 \operatorname{cov}_{13} + 2w_2w_3 \operatorname{cov}_{23}$$

Obviously, the equations for multi-asset portfolios become quite cumbersome.

be represented by the correlation coefficient in the following manner:

$$\rho_{12}\sigma_1\sigma_2 = \text{cov}_{12} \tag{13–5a}$$

or

$$\rho_{12} = \frac{\text{cov}_{12}}{\sigma_1\sigma_2} \tag{13–5b}$$

where

ρ_{12} = Correlation coefficient between Securities 1 and 2 in the portfolio

$\sigma_1\sigma_2$ = Standard deviation of Security 1 times the standard deviation of Security 2 in the portfolio

cov_{12} = Covariance between Securities 1 and 2 in the portfolio

The correlation coefficient, ρ_{12}, can vary between $+1$, signaling perfect positive correlation, and -1, reflecting perfect negative correlation. A correlation coefficient of zero indicates no relationship between the two variables. Implications of different values of correlation coefficient will be explored later in this chapter.

The relationship between the risk of a portfolio of two securities and the relevant variables including the correlation coefficient can be demonstrated by incorporating Equation 13–5a into Equation 13–3:

$$E(\sigma_p^2) = w_1^2\sigma_1^2 + w_2^2\sigma_2^2 + 2w_1w_2\rho_{12}\sigma_1\sigma_2 \tag{13–6}$$

Similarly, Equation 13–4 can be expressed as

$$E(\sigma_p^2) = \sum_{i=1}^{k}\sum_{j=1}^{k} w_iw_j\rho_{ij}\sigma_i\sigma_j \tag{13–7}$$

where

$E(\sigma_p^2)$ = Expected variance of the portfolio

w_i, w_j = Weights of ith and j^{th} securities in the portfolio

ρ_{ij} = Correlation coefficient between i^{th} and j^{th} securities in the portfolio

$\sigma_i\sigma_j$ = Standard deviation of ith times j^{th} securities in the portfolio

k = Number of securities in the portfolio

Referring to Table 13–3, the risk of the ABC portfolio can be expressed in terms of the correlation coefficient:

$$\begin{aligned} E(\sigma_p^2) &= w_1^2\sigma_1^2 + w_2^2\sigma_2^2 + 2w_1w_2\rho_{12}\sigma_1\sigma_2 \\ &= (.3)^2(.4472)^2 + (.7)^2(.3873)^2 + 2(.3)(.7)(.4)(.4472)(.3873) \\ &= 0.1206 \end{aligned}$$

Note that the expected variance of the portfolio using the coefficient correlation measure is identical to the variance calculated by using the measure of covariance.[6]

Forms of Diversification

In Chapter 5, we pointed out that the risk of an individual security is given by:

$$\sigma_s^2 = \beta_s^2\sigma_m^2 + \sigma_{\epsilon_s}^2 \qquad \textbf{(5–4 restated)}$$

In this equation, $\beta_s^2\sigma_m^2$ represents the systematic risk, whereas the unsystematic risk of the security is measured by $\sigma_{\epsilon_s}^2$. The systematic risk is inherent in the market and therefore cannot be diversified away. Consequently, the objective of *diversification* is to reduce and eventually eliminate the unsystematic risk.

Thus far, the discussion has implicitly assumed that portfolio construction can reduce the risk below that of investing in a single security. Although that is generally the case, two major exceptions need recognition. First, under certain conditions, portfolio construction merely averages, rather than reduces, individual security risks. Second, it is *conceptually* possible to reduce—and even eliminate—both unsystematic and systematic risks.

Perfect Positive Correlation

It is appropriate to begin with a two-asset portfolio construction in which the securities have *perfect positive correlation*—that is, $\rho_{12} = +1$. In this case, the expected variance of the portfolio is

$$E(\sigma_p^2) = w_1^2\sigma_1^2 + w_2^2\sigma_2^2 + 2w_1w_2\rho_{12}\sigma_1\sigma_2 \qquad \textbf{(13–6 restated)}$$

When perfect positive correlation exists, $\rho_{12} = +1$, Equation 13–6 becomes

$$E(\sigma_p^2) = w_1^2\sigma_1^2 + w_2^2\sigma_2^2 + 2w_1w_2\sigma_1\sigma_2$$

or

$$E(\sigma_p^2) = (w_1\sigma_1 + w_2\sigma_2)^2 \qquad \textbf{(13–8a)}$$

or

$$E(\sigma_p) = w_1\sigma_1 + w_2\sigma_2 \qquad \textbf{(13–8b)}$$

Equation 13–8b reveals that when $\rho_{12} = +1$, the risk of a portfolio is simply the weighted average of the risks of individual securities, and no reduction in risk is achieved by constructing such a portfolio.

[6] Variance of the portfolio using covariance can be found in Table 13–3. The insignificant difference between .1209 and .1206 is purely due to rounding.

Perfect Negative Correlation

In the case of *perfect negative correlation*, it is possible to develop a strategy to eliminate the total portfolio risk. If $\rho_{12} = -1$, Equation 13–6 becomes

$$E(\sigma_p^2) = w_1^2\sigma_1^2 + w_2^2\sigma_2^2 - 2w_1w_2\sigma_1\sigma_2$$
$$E(\sigma_p^2) = (w_1\sigma_1 - w_2\sigma_2)^2 \quad \text{(13–9)}$$

Intuitively, if it could be so arranged that $w_1\sigma_1$ would be equal to $w_2\sigma_2$, then the risk of the portfolio would be nil. For example, suppose a portfolio is constructed in which w_1/w_2 was equal to σ_2/σ_1. That is,

$$\frac{w_1}{w_2} = \frac{\sigma_2}{\sigma_1}$$

or

$$w_1\sigma_1 = w_2\sigma_2$$

Substituting this equation into Equation 13–9, we have

$$E(\sigma_p^2) = (w_1\sigma_1 - w_1\sigma_1)^2$$
$$= 0$$

This implies that, if $\rho_{12} = -1$, an investor can construct a portfolio such that the ratio of the relative weights equals the ratio of the standard deviation of the two securities in the reverse order, thereby totally eliminating the portfolio risk.[7]

Zero Correlation

If $\rho_{12} = 0$, Equation 13–6 becomes

$$E(\sigma_p^2) = w_1^2\sigma_1^2 + w_2^2\sigma_2^2 \quad \text{(13–10)}$$

This equation suggests that, if properly constructed,[8] the risk of a portfolio consisting of Securities 1 and 2 would be *less* than the risk associated with either security. For example, assume a given sum is equally invested in two securities and each had a variance of .10 ($\sigma_1^2 = \sigma_2^2 = .10$). The portfolio risk would be only .05:

$$E(\sigma_p^2) = (.5)^2(.1) + (.5)^2(.1)$$
$$= .025 + .025$$
$$= .05$$

[7] The Hawk and Dove Portfolio presented in Chapter 5 had a perfect negative correlation. That is why the total risk of the portfolio, which included both systematic and unsystematic risks, was eliminated.

[8] See note 8 on page 578.

Figure 13–3

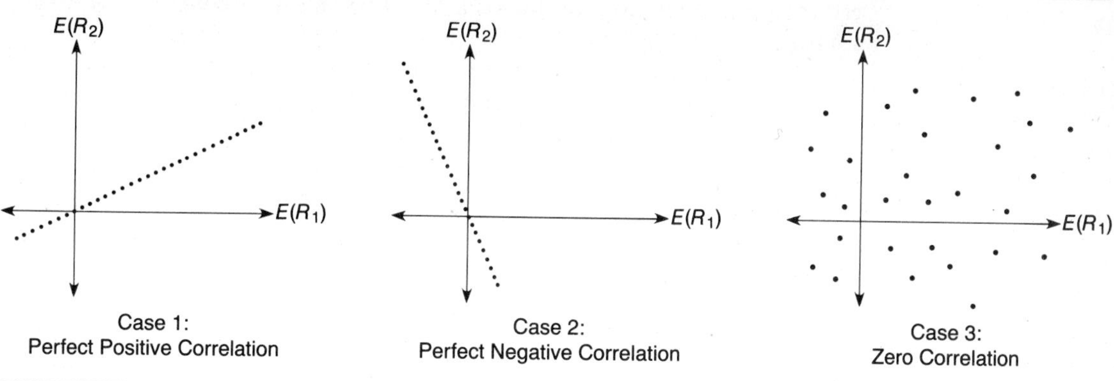

Case 1: Perfect Positive Correlation

Case 2: Perfect Negative Correlation

Case 3: Zero Correlation

Figure 13–3 shows three possible results of diversification—perfect positive correlation, perfect negative correlation, and zero correlation. From our discussion of them, we may draw three conclusions. First, construction of portfolios consisting of stocks with perfect positive correlation is meaningless; it does not reduce risk, and therefore should receive no further consideration. Second, stocks whose returns have perfect negative correlation are ideal candidates for a portfolio, because such a portfolio can completely eliminate the individual security risks. However, in the real world, stocks with negatively correlated returns are rare. Third, portfolios consisting of stocks whose returns have a zero correlation generally reduce risk. Incidentally, in the real world the correlation coefficient of most stocks falls between 0 and +1, and risk reduction through diversification can be achieved if portfolios are constructed in which stocks have low positive correlation. This is an important point which will be elaborated further in a later section.

Markowitz Diversification

Basic Assumptions

Diversification through choice of stocks with zero correlation was the basis for the development of the *Markowitz Portfolio Model.* This Model was based on four specific assertions:

First, the two relevant characteristics of a portfolio are its expected return and its riskiness.

Second, rational investors will choose to hold efficient portfolios which maximize expected returns for a given degree of risk or, alternatively and equivalently, minimize risk for a given expected return.

Third, it is theoretically possible to identify efficient portfolios by properly analyzing each security according to its expected return, the variance of that return, and the relationship between its return and the returns of every other security in the portfolio.

Fourth, a specified, manageable computer program that utilizes the three kinds of necessary information about each security can identify a set of efficient portfolios. The program indicates the proportion of an investor's fund which should be allocated to each security in order to achieve efficiency—that is, the maximization of return for a given degree of risk or the minimization of risk for a given expected return.[9] Successful application of the Markowitz Model depends on the ability of an investor to identify a set of *efficient portfolios* with a specified risk associated with each portfolio. Articulation of a set of efficient portfolios has come to be known as the *Efficient Frontier.*

The Efficient Frontier

In order to delineate the *Efficient Frontier*, one must first measure portfolio risk and return. The expected return of a portfolio is calculated

$$E(R_p) = \sum_{i=1}^{k} w_i E(R_i) \qquad \textbf{(13–2 restated)}$$

Note that the $E(R_p)$ is not influenced by the stocks' correlation coefficient. In other words, given the relative weights and expected returns of individual securities, the expected return of a portfolio will remain fixed regardless of what value the correlation coefficient assumes. In contrast, given the relative weights and standard deviations of individual securities, the risk of a portfolio varies *directly* with the correlation coefficient. This can be clearly seen from the following example. Suppose an investor divides his funds equally between two stocks ($w_1 = w_2 = .5$), whose standard deviations are 0.2 and 0.4, respectively. The risk of the portfolio is given by:

$$\begin{aligned} E(\sigma_p^2) &= w_1^2\sigma_1^2 + w_2^2\sigma_2^2 + 2w_1w_2\rho_{12}\sigma_1\sigma_2 \qquad \textbf{(13–6 restated)} \\ &= (.5)^2(.2)^2 + (.5)^2(.4)^2 + (2)(.5)(.5)\rho_{12}(.2)(.4) \\ &= .01 + .04 + .04\rho_{12} \\ &= .05 + .04\rho_{12} \end{aligned}$$

Note that the expected variance, or risk, of the portfolio, $E(\sigma_p^2)$, increases with the value of the correlation coefficient, ρ_{12}. Because ρ can vary between -1 to $+1$, it should be interesting to see how the risk of a portfolio changes as the correlation coefficient varies from -1 to $+1$.

Table 13–4 presents the changes in the expected returns and standard deviations of a two-security portfolio as a result of changes in the relative weights of securities and the correlation coefficients. For example, for Item 1 the standard

[9] Quoted from James H. Lorie and Mary T. Hamilton, *The Stock Market: Theories and Evidence* (Homewood, Ill.: Richard D. Irwin, 1973), pp. 172–73. © 1973 by Richard D. Irwin, Inc.

Table 13–4

Pertinent Data

Security 1: $E(R_1) = 5\%;\ \sigma_1 = .2$

Security 2: $E(R_2) = 10\%;\ \sigma_2 = .4$

Relative Weights (w_i)	Portfolio Return [$E(R_p)$] $E(R_p) = w_1E(R_1) + w_2E(R_2)$ $= w_1(.05) + w_2(.10)$	Portfolio Risk [$E(\sigma_p)$] $E(\sigma_p)^* = \sqrt{w_1^2\sigma_1^2 + w_2^2\sigma_2^2 + 2w_1w_2\rho_{12}\sigma_1\sigma_2}$ $= \sqrt{w_1^2(.04) + w_2^2(.16) + 2w_1w_2\rho_{12}(.2)(.4)}$ where ρ_{12} = correlation coefficient				
		$\rho_{12} = -1.0$	$\rho_{12} = -.5$	$\rho_{12} = 0$	$\rho_{12} = .5$	$\rho_{12} = 1.0$
1. $w_1 = .5$ $w_2 = .5$	7.5%	10%	17.3%	22.4%	26.5%	30.0%
2. $w_1 = .25$ $w_2 = .75$	8.8%	25%	27.8%	30.4%	32.8%	35.0%
3. $w_1 = .667$ $w_2 = .333$	6.7%	0%	13.3%	18.7%	23.1%	26.4%

* $E(\sigma_p^2) = w_1^2\sigma_1^2 + w_2^2\sigma_2^2 + 2w_1w_2\rho_{12}\sigma_1\sigma_2$

deviation of the portfolio increases from 10 percent to 22.4 percent, and finally to 30 percent as the ρ_{12} increases from -1.0 to zero, and finally to $+1$. The table also reveals that the $E(R_p)$ changes as the relative weights of Securities 1 and 2 are changed.

Figure 13–4, which presents different values of $E(\sigma_p)$ and ρ_{12}, is also quite revealing. Figure 13–4A, B, and C show the risk–return relationships at values of ρ_{12} equal to -1.0, $+1.0$, and 0, respectively; Figure 13–4D presents the overall relationship. These figures reveal three important facts.

First, given the correlation coefficient, the expected return of the portfolio increases with an increase in the risk; that is, risk and return are positively related. This is demonstrated by Points Y and Q in Figure 13–4D.[10]

Second, *ceteris paribus*, starting with $\rho_{12} = +1$, as the value of coefficient correlation moves toward -1, the portfolio risk progressively declines. Note that in Figure 13–4D, as ρ_{12} declines from $+1$ to zero, the portfolio risk declines from Point Z to Point Y without a corresponding decline in the expected return.

Third, if efficiently constructed with stocks of perfectly negative correlation, portfolio risk can be completely eliminated (Point F). This implies that *Markowitz diversification can lower not only unsystematic but systematic risk as well,* provided that an investor succeeds in locating securities with perfect, or at least very high, negative correlations.

[10] See note 10 on page 578.

Figure 13–4

$\rho_{12} = -1.0$

$E(R_p)$	$E(\sigma_p)$
6.7%	0.0%
7.5%	10.0%
8.8%	25.0%

(A)

$\rho_{12} = +1.0$

$E(R_p)$	$E(\sigma_p)$
6.7%	26.4%
7.5%	30.0%
8.8%	35.0%

(B)

$\rho_{12} = 0$

$E(R_p)$	$E(\sigma_p)$
6.7%	18.7%
7.5%	22.4%
8.8%	30.4%

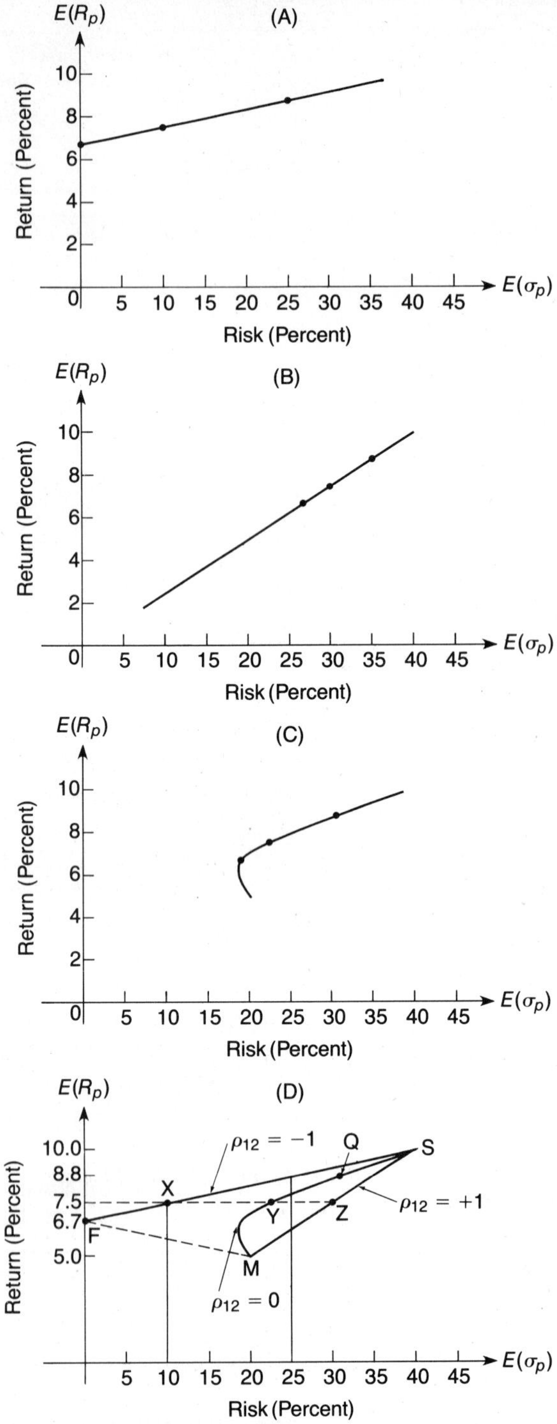

(C)

(D)

Figure 13–5

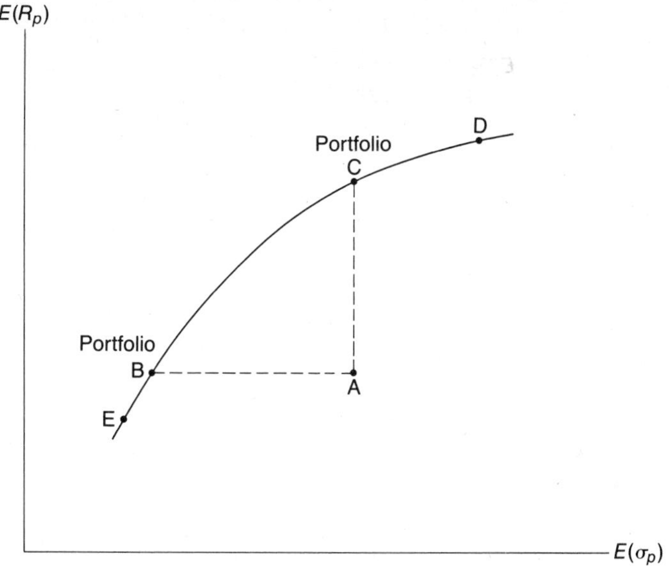

This third observation is extremely important, for it provides an insight into the strategy of "beating the market." Unfortunately, real world considerations suggest that no significance should be attached to this strategy, for stocks with high negative correlations are either nonexistent or practically untraceable.[11] Instead, it is generally assumed that, in the real world, correlation coefficients of most stocks fall somewhere between zero and +1. Consequently, the loci of expected returns of all portfolios are expected to be clustered around a curve which has the shape of curve MYQS in Figure 13–4D. Such a curve, which is convex to the vertical axis, has come to be known as the *Efficient Frontier*.

The logic behind calling the MYQS-type curve the Efficient Frontier is straightforward. The Markowitz Model can be used to construct numerous portfolios with different combinations of stocks. These portfolios will differ from each other not only with regard to the individual securities they contain, but with regard to the relative weights of individual securities. Assume that the Model has identified portfolios A, B, and C in Figure 13–5. Clearly, B is preferable to A; both offer the same expected return, but B is less risky than the latter. Similarly, C is preferable to A, because it offers higher expected return, even though it is in the same risk class as A. However, portfolio B is *not* clearly preferable to portfolio C, because it offers lower expected return but also has smaller risk. An aggressive investor might prefer C, but a conservative investor would probably choose B.

[11] Gold mining stocks provide an interesting exception to this general case. Usually these stocks are negatively correlated with the market.

From the foregoing discussion, a clear theme emerges. All portfolios *below* the EBCD curve are inefficient portfolios because, compared to the portfolios on the curve, they either offer lower returns or assume higher risks. Furthermore, all portfolios *on* the curve are efficient in that each portfolio offers the highest expected return for its risk class. For these reasons, the EBCD curve is known as the Efficient Frontier.

Limitations of Markowitz Model

The Markowitz Model in general, and the Efficient Frontier in particular, are major landmarks in the investment world. Markowitz's approach to portfolio construction not only revolutionized the thinking of the academic world, but forced the investment community to think seriously in terms of patterning its investment decision after his portfolio theory. However, one major practical difficulty with the Markowitz Model has become apparent. In order to identify Markowitz's efficient set of portfolios, it is necessary to know the expected return for each security, its variance, and its covariance or correlation coefficient with each of the other securities. An investor dealing with, say, 1,000 securities would have to calculate 1,000 expected returns, 1,000 variances, and 499,000 covariances. More importantly, any attempt to alter the composition of the portfolios would require similar formidable computations. Clearly, the computational cost would be prohibitive, not to mention the huge transaction and other related costs. For these reasons, the Markowitz Model virtually remained a mystery to the investment community until 1963, when William Sharpe suggested a simplification of that model.[12] Sharpe argued that because all stocks are correlated with the market, the relationship of each security to the market could act as a surrogate for the covariances for each security relative to other securities. Sharpe's simplification reduces the number of estimates that the analyst must produce from 501,000 to 3,002 for a list of 1,000 securities. Although the simplification suggested by Sharpe made the Markowitz Model more palatable, Sharpe continued his work in this area and soon developed a theoretical framework that is known as the *Capital Asset Pricing Model.*

SECTION 2 THE MARKET MODEL VERSUS THE CAPITAL ASSET PRICING MODEL

The Market Model

The Markowitz Model was theoretically elegant and conceptually sound. However, its serious limitation was that it related each security to every other security in the portfolio, demanding the sophistication and volume of work well beyond

[12] William A. Sharpe, "A Simplified Model for Portfolio Analysis," *Management Science*, Vol. 9, No. 1, 1963, pp. 277–93; "Capital Asset Prices: A Theory of Market Equilibrium under Conditions of Risk," *Journal of Finance*, September 1964, pp. 425–42.

the capacity of all but a few analysts. Consequently, its application remained severely limited until William Sharpe published a model simplifying the mathematical calculations required by the Markowitz Model.

Sharpe assumed that, for the sake of simplicity, the return on a security could be regarded as being linearly related to a single index like the market index. Theoretically, the market index should consist of *all* the securities trading on the market. However, a popular average, like the S&P 500 Index, can be treated as a surrogate for the market index. Acceptance of the idea of a market index, Sharpe argued, would obviate the need for calculating thousands of covariances between individual securities, because any movements in stocks could be attributed to movements in the single underlying factor being measured by the market index. The simplification of the Markowitz Model has come to be known as the *Market Model.*

The Market Model was presented in Chapter 5 and may be briefly reviewed here. This model generates a characteristic line by specifying the relationship between returns on individual securities and return on the market portfolio in the following manner:

$$R_s = \alpha_s + \beta_s R_m + \epsilon_s \qquad \textbf{(5–1a restated)}$$

where

R_s = Total return of the stock

α_s, ϵ_s = Alpha and error term, representing the unsystematic return of the stock

$\beta_s R_m$ = Systematic return of the stock

It was also explained that α_s, the *alpha* of the security, represents the return on the stock when the market return is zero, whereas β_s is the ratio of a change in the stock's return to a change in the market return. Equation 5–1a generates a straight line with alpha being its Y-intercept and *beta* being its slope. Figure 13–6 is a graph of the Equation 5–1a for a security with an alpha of 3 percent (that is, the security returns 3 percent when the market return is zero) and a beta of 2. The regression on the characteristic line represents what the returns on the security are for different levels of market return. For example, a 2 percent market return is associated with a 7 percent security return.

In Chapter 5 it was also pointed out that a security's future return (assuming that the mean of the distribution of the error term is zero, and therefore $\epsilon_s = 0$) can be predicted by:

$$E(R_s) = \alpha_s + \beta_s E(R_m)$$

where

$E(R_s)$ = Expected return on stock

$E(R_m)$ = Expected return on market

$\beta_s E(R_m)$ = Expected systematic return

Figure 13–6 **The Market Model**

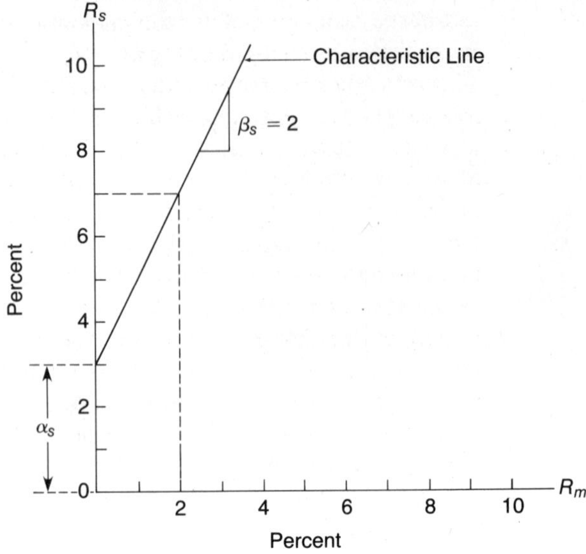

Note the simplifying quality of the Market Model. The assumption of the relationship of individual securities to a single market index $E(R_m)$ makes it possible to compute all of the expected values, variances, and covariances needed to construct a set of portfolios by using relatively simple statistical procedures.

The model in Equations 5–1a and 5–1b involves only one security; however, it can be applied to portfolios as well. Specifically, the Market Model holds that returns on an individual security or a portfolio are linearly related to an index of market returns. This relationship can be specified for either a security or a portfolio with a characteristic line.

Capital Asset Pricing Model

Basic Framework

The *Capital Asset Pricing Model* (*CAPM*), also known as the Sharpe–Lintner model, is a *pricing model*. It represents the price of immediate consumption and the price of risk.

The Market Model provided the conceptual foundation for the CAPM in that it shifted the attention from variance, which measures total risk, to beta, which measures systematic or nondiversifiable risk. In fact, this shift in risk consideration was characterized as the *beta revolution*. It eventually led to the development of the celebrated CAPM.

Once beta was accepted as a measure of the sensitivity of a stock to changes in the market, or, more appropriately, as the measure of systematic risk, the next development introduced risk-free return into the general discussion. The relationship between risky and risk-free returns was carefully established around beta as the key variable of the model.

It is universally assumed that in an efficient market assets with the same risk should have the same expected rate of return. Based on this assumption, an investor holding a risky portfolio with the same risk as that implicit in the market portfolio ($\beta = 1$) should receive the same return as that of the market portfolio. For this purpose, the market portfolio is broadly defined as one that contains all the securities trading on the market; but it is measured by a suitable market index such as the S&P 500 Index.[13] Similarly, an investor holding a riskless portfolio should earn the return on a riskless asset. For a 90-day holding period, a treasury bill can be treated as a riskless asset. A more aggressive investor who invests half of her money in a risky portfolio and the other half in a riskless portfolio should receive an average of the returns of the market portfolio and of riskless assets. It is the general form of this third alternative which forms the basis for the development of the modern portfolio theory.[14]

Assume an investor invests a proportion (w) of his money in the risky portfolio (the market portfolio), and ($1 - w$) in the riskless asset. The beta of this portfolio, which measures its risk, is the weighted average of the betas of individual stocks, where the weights are the proportions of individual stocks in the portfolio. Consequently, the risk of the composite portfolio, measured by the portfolio beta, β_p, is a weighted average of the beta of the risky or market portfolio and the risk-free asset. However, by definition, the market beta is 1.0[15] and the beta of a risk-free asset is zero.[16] Therefore, symbolically,

$$\beta_p = (1 - w)(0) + (w)(1) \qquad \textbf{(13–11)}$$

$$\beta_p = w$$

Equation 13–11 is most revealing: The risk of the portfolio, β_p, is equal to the fraction of money invested in the risky portfolio. More specifically, (1) if 100 percent of the total investible funds is invested in the market portfolio, β_p will be 1.0; (2) if the investor invests all of his money in a riskless portfolio, β_p will be

[13] Specifically, the portfolio which includes all assets in proportion to their market values, is known as the *market portfolio.*

[14] Franco Modigliani and Gerald A. Pogue, "An Introduction to Risk and Return: Concepts and Evidence," in *Financial Analyst's Handbook I*, ed. Sumner N. Levine (Homewood, Ill.: Dow Jones-Irwin, 1975), pp. 1315–17. © 1975 by Dow Jones-Irwin.

[15] This can be seen from the following example. The equation of the characteristic line is

$$R_s = \alpha_s + \beta_s R_m + \epsilon_s \quad \text{and} \quad \beta_s = \frac{\text{cov}_{s}, R_m}{\sigma_m^2}$$

Using this equation, the beta of the market is calculated:

$$\beta_m = \frac{\text{cov}_{Rm}, R_m}{\sigma_m^2} = \frac{\sigma_m^2}{\sigma_m^2} = 1$$

[16] Because the risk-free rate is assumed to remain fixed, its variability with the market return is zero.

zero; and (3) if the investor invests in both the risky and the riskless portfolios, the beta of the composite portfolio will be between 0 and 1 ($0 < \beta_p < 1$), the exact values reflecting the proportion in which the funds are divided between the risky and the riskless portfolios.

What should be the expected return on a portfolio consisting of both risk-free and risky assets? Intuitively, an investor holding such a portfolio would expect a return *greater* than the return on risk-free assets. Symbolically,

$$E(R_p) = (1 - w)R_f + wE(R_m) \tag{13–12}$$

where

$E(R_p)$ = Expected return on a portfolio
R_f = Rate of return on a risk-free asset
$E(R_m)$ = Expected return on market
w = Proportion of money invested in the risky portfolio
$1 - w$ = Proportion of money invested in risk-free asset

Figure 13–7

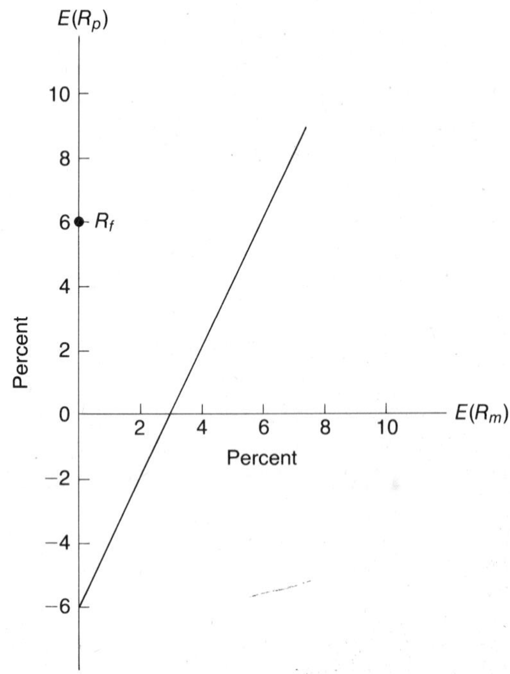

Incorporating Equation 13–11, according to which $\beta_p = w$, into Equation 13–12, we obtain:

$$\begin{aligned} E(R_p) &= (1 - \beta_p)R_f + \beta_p E(R_m) \\ &= R_f - (\beta_p R_f) + \beta_p E(R_m) \\ &= R_f + \beta_p[E(R_m) - R_f] \end{aligned} \quad \text{(13–13)}$$

Equation 13–13 represents the CAPM. It says that, in equilibrium,[17] investors will price capital assets so that the expected return on a portfolio is equal to the risk-free rate plus a risk premium that is proportional to the risk measure, beta. Figure 13–7 is a graph of Equation 13–13 for a portfolio with a beta of 2 and an assumed risk-free rate of 6 percent. Note that the Y-intercept is −6; that is, the expected portfolio return is −6 percent when the expected market return is zero:

$$\begin{aligned} E(R_p) &= R_f + \beta_p[E(R_m) - R_f] \\ &= 6 + 2(0 - 6) \\ &= -6\% \end{aligned}$$

Assumptions of CAPM

The implications of Equation 13–13 have already been presented. However, seven assumptions are implicit in the effective operation of the CAPM:

1. All investors choose portfolios on the basis of their single period mean and variance of return.
2. All investors can borrow or lend at a given riskless rate of interest and there are no restrictions on short sales of any asset.
3. All investors have identical subjective estimates of the joint probability distribution on the returns of all assets.
4. All assets are perfectly liquid and divisible.
5. There are no taxes and transaction costs.
6. The quantities of all assets are given and all investors are price takers.
7. The markets are in equilibrium; that is, all securities are perfectly priced.

Under these assumptions, asserts the CAPM, because the risk of a portfolio is proportional to the money invested in risky securities, the expected return on such a portfolio should exceed the risk-free rate by an amount proportional to the portfolio beta.

[17] Equilibrium refers to a market condition in which there is no pressure for change. In the context of the CAPM, it refers to the condition where the risk-adjusted excess return of each security in the portfolio is zero. This will become evident later in the discussion.

CAPM Versus Market Model

Risk–Premium Form

For a meaningful comparison of the two models just presented, it is desirable to recast each of them in a *risk–premium form.*

CAPM

According to the CAPM, in equilibrium, the expected return of a portfolio is equal to the risk-free rate plus a risk premium that is proportional to its beta. Because at any given time the risk-free rate can be assumed to be given and can be treated as a constant, investors frequently are interested in calculating the *risk premium* that is included in the expected return of the portfolio. The risk premium can be obtained by subtracting the risk-free rate from the expected rate of return. That is, the expected portfolio risk premium is determined:

$$E(R_p) = R_f + \beta_p[E(R_m) - R_f] \qquad \textbf{(13–13 restated)}$$

Subtracting R_f from both sides, we obtain

$$\begin{aligned} E(R_p) - R_f &= R_f - R_f + \beta_p[E(R_m) - R_f] \\ &= \beta_p[E(R_m) - R_f] \qquad \textbf{(13–14)} \end{aligned}$$

where

R_f = Risk-free rate of return

$E(R_p) - R_f$ = Expected portfolio risk premium or excess return (over the risk-free rate)

$E(R_m) - R_f$ = Expected market (systematic) risk premium or excess return (over the risk-free rate)

Figure 13–8 presents the CAPM both in its general form and the risk–premium form. Note that the risk–premium form of CAPM, given in Figure 13–8B, relabels both axes so as to measure the expected market and portfolio *risk premiums.* In this form, the origin is defined as the point where the expected excess return (over the risk-free rate) is zero for both the portfolio and the market. The result is that the characteristic line, which still has the same slope ($\beta_p = 2$), now passes through the origin.

Market Model

Recasting of the Market Model into the risk–premium form involves a different operation. We begin with the Market Model for a portfolio in the form presented

Figure 13–8

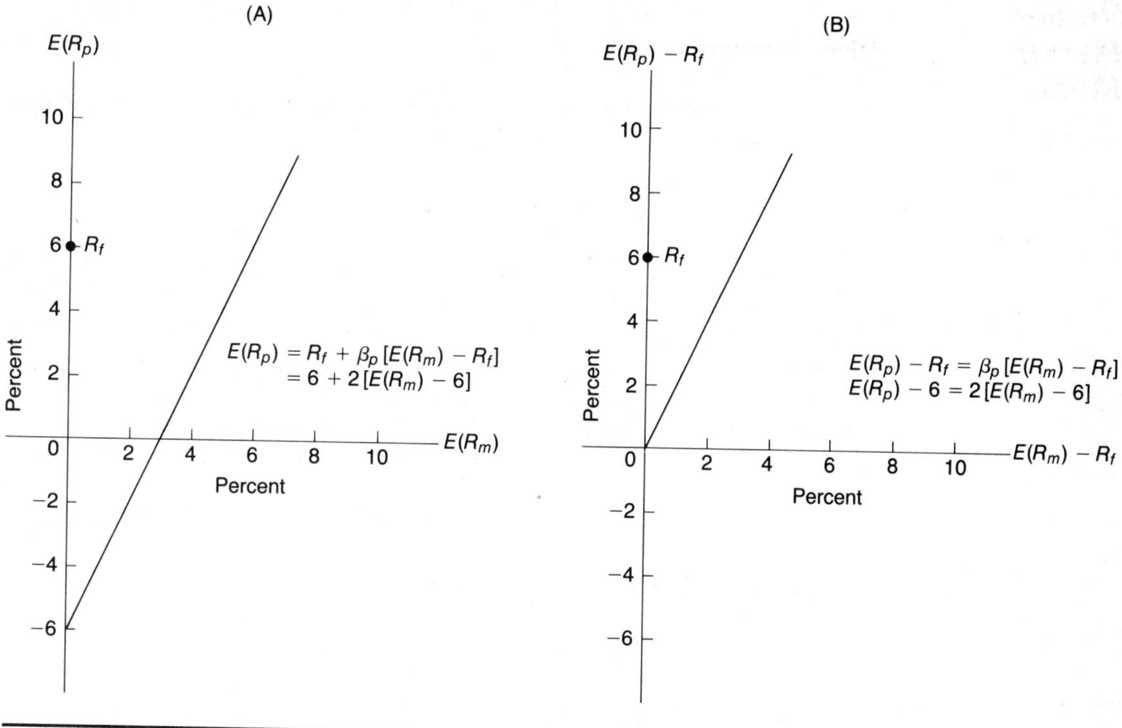

earlier in Equation 5–1a:

$$R_p = \alpha_p + \beta_p R_m + \epsilon_p \quad \textbf{(5–1a restated)}$$

When the model is presented in the risk–premium form, the equation becomes:

$$R_p - R_f = \alpha_p - R_f(1 - \beta_p) + \beta_p(R_m - R_f) + \epsilon_p \quad \textbf{(13–15)}$$

The derivation of this new form deserves a more elaborate explanation.

The Market Model is essentially a regression model. When a regression or characteristic line is developed with R_m on the X-axis and R_p on the Y-axis (such as Equation 5–1a), the β_p is determined by the sensitivity of the portfolio's return to the market return, and the Y-intercept of the characteristic line is called the alpha (α_p) of the portfolio. When the axes are changed to $R_m - R_f$ and $R_p - R_f$ to present the model in a risk–premium form, however, a new regression or characteristic line is developed. Because the risk of the portfolio remains unaffected, the β_p of the new characteristic line remains unchanged, but the α_p, or the Y-intercept, changes to α_p^* as follows:

$$\alpha_p^* = \alpha_p - R_f(1 - \beta_p)$$

where

α_p^* = Risk-adjusted excess return

α_p = Return on the portfolio when the market return is zero

Specifically, α_p^* represents the excess return that the portfolio earns when the market return equals the risk-free rate—that is, when the *excess* market return is zero. Figure 13–9 presents three positions of α_p^*. Note that the α_p^* can be positive (Figure 13–9A), negative (Figure 13–9B), or zero (Figure 13–9C). It should also be noted that α_p^* can be lower, higher, or identical with α_p.[18]

An important observation is apropos here. If a portfolio has a positive risk-adjusted excess return [$\alpha_p^* > 0$, or equivalently $\alpha_p > R_f(1 - \beta_p)$], then it will yield a return *greater* than its expected return consisting of the risk-free rate plus a risk premium proportional to its beta. This can be clearly seen from the following:

$$R_p - R_f = \alpha_p - R_f(1 - \beta_p) + \beta_p(R_m - R_f) + \epsilon_p \qquad \textbf{(13–15 restated)}$$

Because $\alpha_p^* = \alpha_p - R_f(1 - \beta_p)$, the equation becomes:

$$R_p - R_f = \alpha_p^* + \beta_p(R_m - R_f) + \epsilon_p \qquad \textbf{(13–16)}$$

Rearranging, and assuming that the mean of the distribution of ϵ_p (the error term) equals zero, we have:[19]

$$R_p = \underbrace{\alpha_p^*}_{\substack{\text{Risk-adjusted}\\ \text{excess return}}} + \underbrace{R_f}_{\substack{\text{Risk-free}\\ \text{rate}}} + \underbrace{\beta_p(R_m - R_f)}_{\substack{\text{Market or systematic}\\ \text{risk premium}}}$$

This is an extremely important result affecting portfolio management. It states that if the risk-adjusted excess return of a portfolio is positive ($\alpha_p^* > 0$), then the portfolio return will be greater than normally expected; that is, an investor holding a portfolio with a positive α_p^* has succeeded in *beating the market.* Likewise, a portfolio with a negative α_p^* has underperformed the market.

---

[18] The relationship of α_p and α_p^* can be categorically stated as

$\alpha_p^* < \alpha_p$ when $\beta_p < 1$

$\alpha_p^* > \alpha_p$ when $\beta_p > 1$

$\alpha_p^* = \alpha_p$ when $\beta_p = 1$

[19] Note that $\beta_p(R_m - R_f)$ is the market or systematic component of the portfolio's excess return or risk premium, while α_p^* is the nonmarket or unsystematic component.

Figure 13–9

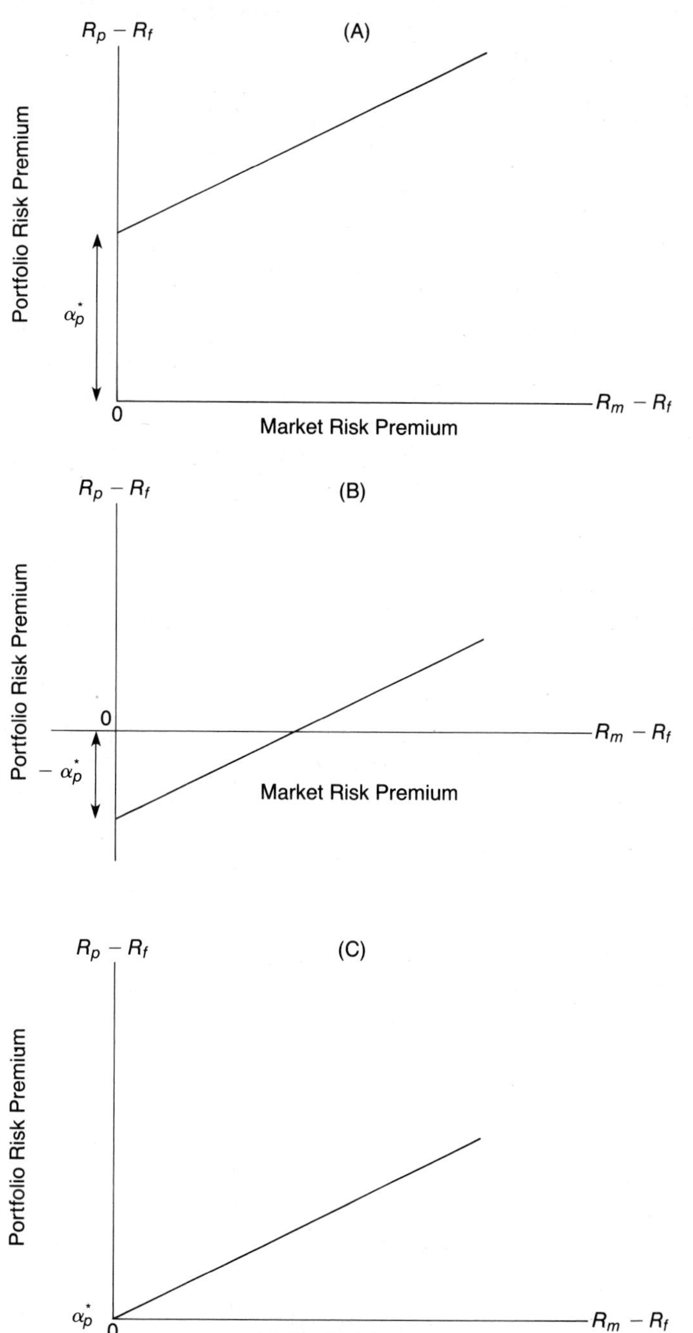

(A)
$R_p - R_f$
Portfolio Risk Premium
α_p^*
0
$R_m - R_f$
Market Risk Premium
(B)
$R_p - R_f$
Portfolio Risk Premium
0
$-\alpha_p^*$
$R_m - R_f$
Market Risk Premium
(C)
$R_p - R_f$
Portfolio Risk Premium
α_p^*
0
$R_m - R_f$
Market Risk Premium

It is common to express Equation 13–16 as an expectational model so that a portfolio's expected excess return or risk premium $[E(R_p) - R_f]$ can be predicted:

$$E(R_p) - R_f = \alpha_p^* + \beta_p[E(R_m) - R_f] \quad \textbf{(13–17)}$$

In this form of the Market Model, α_p^* represents the *expected* risk-adjusted excess return.[20]

Security in Equilibrium

A closer examination of the Market Model and the CAPM reveals that, except when the portfolio is in equilibrium, the expected excess returns or risk premiums on a portfolio are different under the two models. Assume the alpha is 3 percent ($\alpha_p = 3$), the risk-free rate is 6 percent ($R_f = 6$), the beta is 2 ($\beta_p = 2$), and the expected market return is 10 percent $[E(R_m) = 10]$. The expected risk premiums on the portfolio under the two models in their risk–premium forms are as follows:

Market Model

$$\begin{aligned} E(R_p) - R_f &= \alpha_p^* + \beta_p[E(R_m) - R_f] \quad \textbf{(13–17 restated)} \\ &= \alpha_p - R_f(1 - \beta_p) + \beta_p[E(R_m) - R_f] \\ &= 3 - 6(1 - 2) + 2(10 - 6) \\ &= 3 + 6 + 8 \\ &= 17\% \end{aligned}$$

CAPM

$$\begin{aligned} E(R_p) - R_f &= \beta_p[E(R_m) - R_f] \quad \textbf{(13–14 restated)} \\ &= 2(10 - 6) \\ &= 20 - 12 \\ &= 8\% \end{aligned}$$

The only time the expected risk premium of a portfolio under both models is identical is when the portfolio is in equilibrium. That happens when the risk-adjusted excess return is expected to be zero ($\alpha_p^* = 0$), or when the alpha (α_p) is expected to equal the risk-free rate multiplied by the quantity of one minus beta $\alpha_p = R_f(1 - \beta_p)$.[21] In this example, when $\alpha_p = 6(1 - 2)$ or -6, or equivalently

[20] In this equation for the expected value of a portfolio's (or security's) excess return, α_p^* is not designated as an expected value in the form $E(\alpha_p^*)$, because α_p^* by definition is already an expected value. That is, α_p^* is an expected value of a probability distribution of excess returns.

[21] See note 21 on page 579.

$\alpha_p^* = 0$, then the expected risk premiums under both models are identical:

Market Model

$$\begin{aligned} E(R_p) - R_f &= -6 - 6(1 - 2) + 2(10 - 6) \\ &= -6 + 6 + 8 \\ &= 8\% \end{aligned}$$

CAPM

$$\begin{aligned} E(R_p) - R_f &= 2(10 - 6) \\ &= 8\% \end{aligned}$$

Change in Market Return

Although the two models generate the same expected portfolio risk premiums only when the portfolio is in equilibrium, or when $\alpha_p^* = 0$, the relationship between changes in a portfolio risk premium and changes in the market return is *always* identical. Assume that the expected market return increases to 12 percent. The *changes* in the expected portfolio premium under the two models are:

Market Model

$$\begin{aligned} E(R_p) - R_f &= 3 - 6(1 - 2) + 2(12 - 6) \\ &= 3 + 6 + 12 \\ &= 21 \\ \Delta[E(R_p) - R_f] &= 21 - 17 \\ &= 4\% \end{aligned}$$

CAPM

$$\begin{aligned} E(R_p) - R_f &= 2(12 - 6) \\ &= 12 \\ \Delta[E(R_p) - R_f] &= 12 - 8 \\ &= 4\% \end{aligned}$$

Risk-Adjusted Excess Return

A comparison of the two models reveals that, with the Market Model, the value of *risk-adjusted excess return* (α_p^*) can be positive, zero, or negative. However, the CAPM asserts that the value of α_p^* is zero. Reasons for this assertion can be discussed in terms of the risk–premium forms of both models.[22]

[22] William F. Sharpe, "Efficient Capital Markets: A Review of the Theory," *Is Financial Analysis Useless*? (Charlottesville, Va.: The Financial Analysts Research Foundation, 1975), pp. 8–10.

A comment must be made about the use of the word "alpha." In the real world, alpha is used to denote both the security or portfolio return when the market return is zero (Y-intercept in the Market Model, or α_p) *and* the portfolio risk premium when the market risk premium is zero (risk-adjusted excess return, or α_p^*). However, in order to add clarity, in our discussion we have used the word alpha only to refer to the Y-intercept in the Market Model, and will only use α_p^* to refer to the risk-adjusted excess return.

The Market Model asserts that any given portfolio, or security, can generate a positive, zero, or negative risk-adjusted excess return when the risk-adjusted excess return on the market is zero. That is, the α_p^* can be positive, negative, or zero. The CAPM, however, maintains that the risk-adjusted excess return, α_p^*, is zero.

Figure 13–10 presents the profile of a risky security relative to the market portfolio and a portfolio consisting of a risk-free security (treasury bill) and a risky security. Note that the figure is presented in the risk–premium form; therefore, the origin measures a zero expected excess return (over the risk-free rate).

Let us begin with the characteristic line of the *market portfolio*. By definition, the expected excess return on the market portfolio (vertical axis) must always be equal to the expected excess return on the market portfolio (horizontal axis). Consequently, the value of α_p^* of this portfolio must be zero and the value of the beta must be one. The characteristic line of the market portfolio is therefore a 45-degree line passing through the origin.

Next we turn to a security which is less volatile than the market ($\beta_s = .8$), but which also has unsystematic risk because its α_s^* is -2 percent. In this case, it is not clear if this security is preferable to the market portfolio.

Finally, let us consider the third alternative. An investor could split funds between the market portfolio and treasury bills in a manner designed to give the same level of systematic risk as that associated with the security. In this case, the appropriate division would result in 80 percent invested in the market portfolio and 20 percent in treasury bills. This strategy would have a characteristic line passing through the origin (that is, an α_p^* of zero) with a beta of .8 and it would clearly be a better investment than the single security. The reason should be obvious. Because the beta of the treasury bill is zero, the mixed portfolio would have the same level of systematic risk, would have no unsystematic risk, and would offer an expected advantage of 2 percent, because the α_p^* is zero as compared to the security α_s^* of -2 percent, regardless of how the market performs. The result is predictable. Investors will begin to switch from the single security to a mixed portfolio. The security would be subjected to heavy selling pressure. Its price would fall, causing its characteristic line to rise until α_s^* becomes zero.

In this example, the beta of the single security was assumed to be less than one. The result will be the same if a security has a beta greater than one. In such a case, however, the appropriate strategy for purposes of comparison would require margined purchase of the market portfolio, the drawing down of an investor's

Figure 13–10

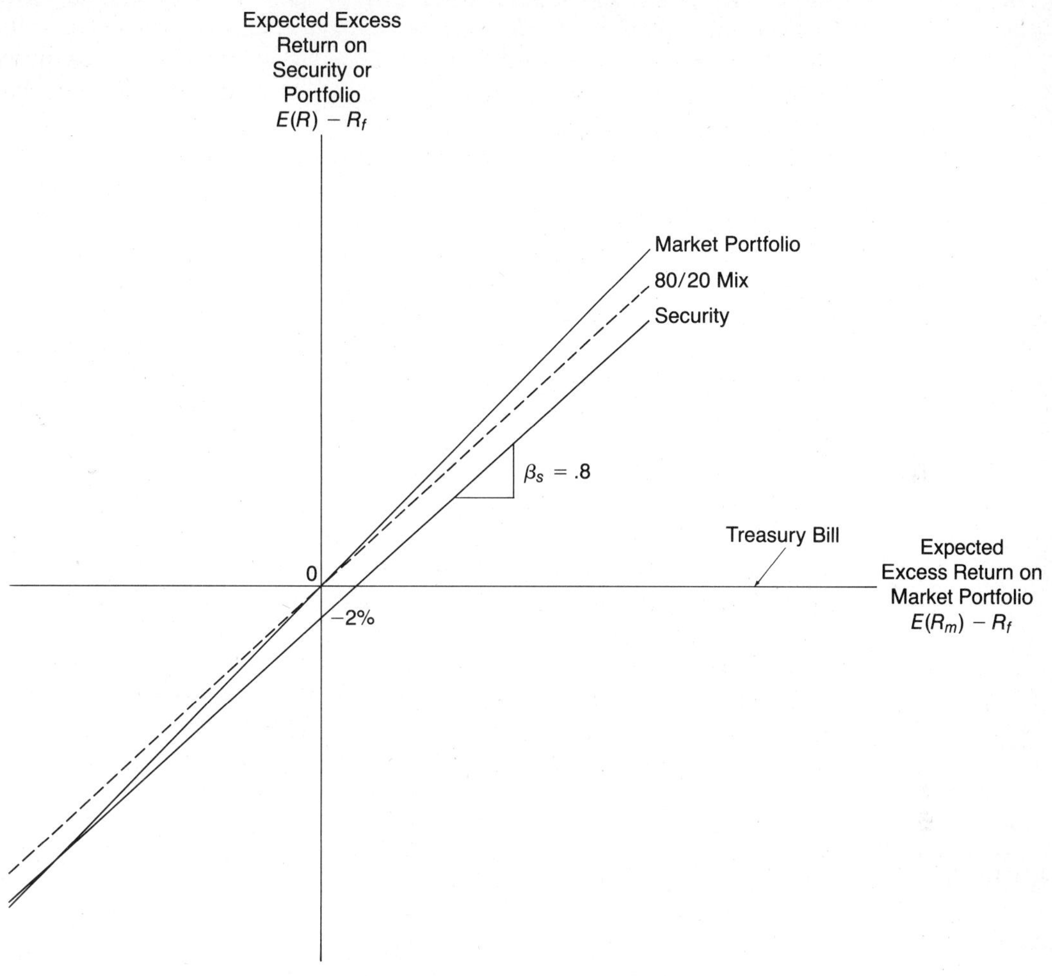

SOURCE: William F. Sharpe, "Efficient Capital Markets: A Review of the Theory," in *Is Financial Analysis Useless?* (Charlottesville, Va.: The Financial Analysts Research Foundation, 1975), p. 10.

savings account, or some other action of this type. To keep the analysis simple, it is assumed that this can be accomplished at a cost equal to the risk-free rate.

The conclusion of this discussion can be directly stated. Regardless of the beta of a security, if the market is efficient, no security will be priced to have a negative risk-adjusted excess return, or $-\alpha_s^*$. Furthermore, because the α_p^* of the market portfolio is simply the weighted average of the α_s^* values of the component securities, and because by definition the α_p^* of the market portfolio is zero,

Figure 13–11

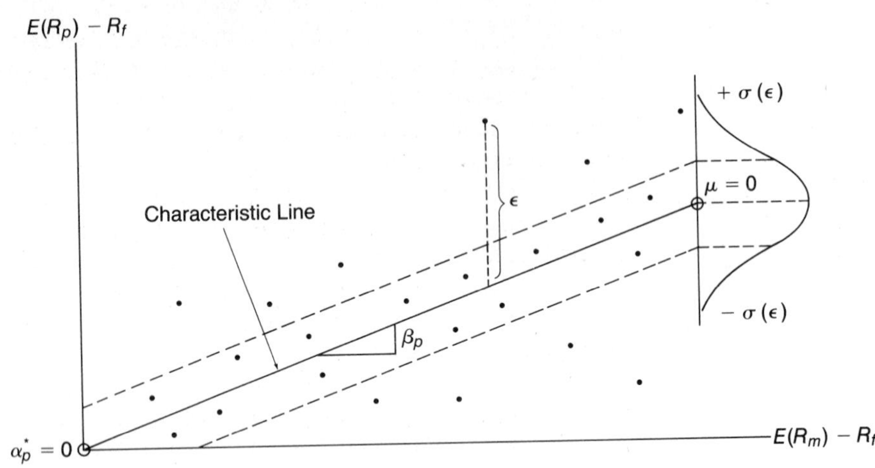

no security can have a positive α_s^*. That is, in an efficient market, the α_s^* of every security and thus the α_p^* of any given portfolio must be zero.[23]

Figure 13–11 presents the profile of a perfectly diversified portfolio in the CAPM. The right-hand corner of the figure shows that the error term is normally distributed and its mean is zero. It also shows that the expected risk-adjusted excess return, α_p^*, of the portfolio is zero and that the slope of the characteristic line is the beta of the portfolio.

SECTION 3 THE CAPITAL MARKET LINE AND THE SECURITY MARKET LINE

Capital Market Line and the Efficient Frontier

In Section 1, the Efficient Frontier (Figure 13–5) was developed based on the Markowitz Model. In a world where borrowing and lending opportunities do not exist, the Efficient Frontier is a locus of all efficient portfolios; that is, each efficient portfolio offers the highest expected return for its risk (both systematic and unsystematic) class. The Efficient Frontier is plotted on a graph with expected portfolio return, $E(R_p)$, on the Y-axis, and the expected standard deviation of the portfolio, $E(\sigma_p)$, measuring total portfolio risk, on the X-axis.

[23] When the market is not in equilibrium, investors can beat the market by investing in stocks with positive risk-adjusted excess returns ($\alpha_s^* > 0$).

In Section 2, the discussion concentrated on the Capital Asset Pricing Model (CAPM). It was stated that because an efficient portfolio carries only systematic risk (unsystematic risk is eliminated through diversification), the expected return of an efficient portfolio equals the risk-free rate plus a risk premium proportional to its risk measure, beta. The CAPM was presented in Figure 13–7, which was based on a linear relationship between expected portfolio return [$E(R_p)$ measured on the Y-axis] and the expected market return [$E(R_m)$ measured on the X-axis].

It was previously mentioned that the Markowitz Model, which recognized the existence of both systematic and unsystematic risk, did not allow for borrowing and lending opportunities. We are now in a position to demonstrate that when borrowing and lending opportunities are included in the analysis, a linear set of investment opportunities called the *Capital Market Line* (*CML*) emerges. However, in order to derive the CML, the $E(R_m)$ on the X-axis of the CAPM must be replaced by $E(\sigma_p)$, because the discussion concentrates on the relationship between expected portfolio return and the total portfolio risk, measured by the expected standard deviation of the portfolio.

Derivation of the Capital Market Line

Figure 13–12 presents the CML, which represents a linear relationship between expected portfolio return [$E(R_p)$ on the Y-axis] and expected standard deviation of the portfolio [$E(\sigma_p)$ on the X-axis]. In this figure, R_f is the risk-free rate, $E(R_m)$ is the expected return on the market portfolio (the Market Index),

Figure 13–12

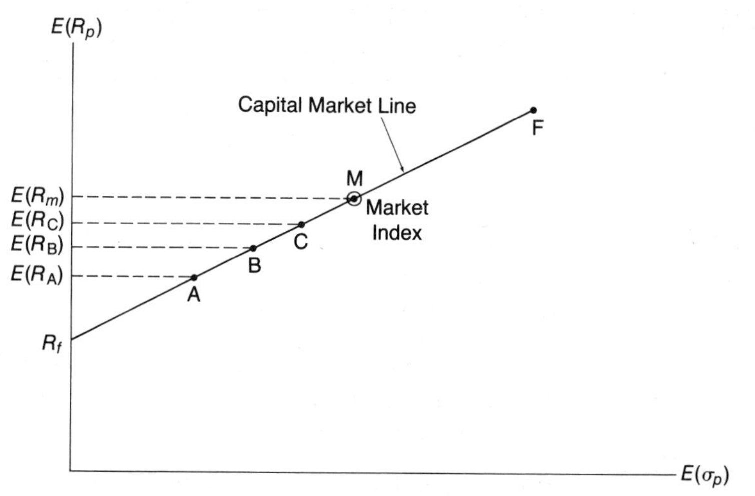

and $E(R_A)$, $E(R_B)$, $E(R_C)$ and so on are the expected returns on Portfolios A, B, and C, which consist of both the risky and risk-free assets. As expected, the expected return on, say, Portfolio A, $E(R_A)$, is greater than the risk-free rate, R_f, by an amount which is proportional to its total risk. By assuming that both lending and borrowing opportunities exist (explained in detail in the following section), it is possible to select a combination of risk-free and risky assets which will lie on the R_fMF line. Because this line is the locus of all efficient portfolios,[24] it has come to be known as the *Capital Market Line.*

Note that the CML, on which all efficient portfolios must lie, is a straight line. The slope of the line is the price of risk; that is, it measures the expected return per unit of total risk associated with any efficient portfolio.

The fact that the CML must be a straight line can be demonstrated by means of the return and risk relationships developed earlier. Remember that the return of a portfolio consisting of a risk-free asset, R_1, and a risky asset, R_2, is calculated

$$E(R_p) = w_1 E(R_1) + w_2 E(R_2) \tag{13–1 restated}$$

The risk of the portfolio is calculated

$$E(\sigma_p^2) = w_1^2\sigma_1^2 + w_2^2\sigma_2^2 + 2w_1w_2\rho_{12}\sigma_1\sigma_2 \tag{13–6 restated}$$

However, because the variance of the risk-free asset is zero, Equation 13–6 is reduced to

$$E(\sigma_p^2) = w_2^2\sigma_2^2$$

or,

$$E(\sigma_p) = w_2\sigma_2 \tag{13–6a}$$

Because Equations 13–1 and 13–6a are both linear, the CML must be a straight line, starting with the risk-free portfolio and connecting numerous other efficient portfolios combining a risk-free asset with risky assets.

CML and Efficient Frontier

An important conclusion of the Markowitz Model was that all efficient portfolios must lie on the Efficient Frontier (EF). However, we have just demonstrated that, under specified assumptions, all efficient portfolios must lie on the Capital Market Line (CML). It is now possible to synthesize the two positions.

Figure 13–13 presents the EF and the CML. In the absence of a risk-free asset and the CML, each portfolio lying on the EF offers the highest return

[24] The word "efficient" means providing the highest return for a given level of risk. Therefore, by definition, there is only one efficient portfolio for each risk level.

Figure 13–13

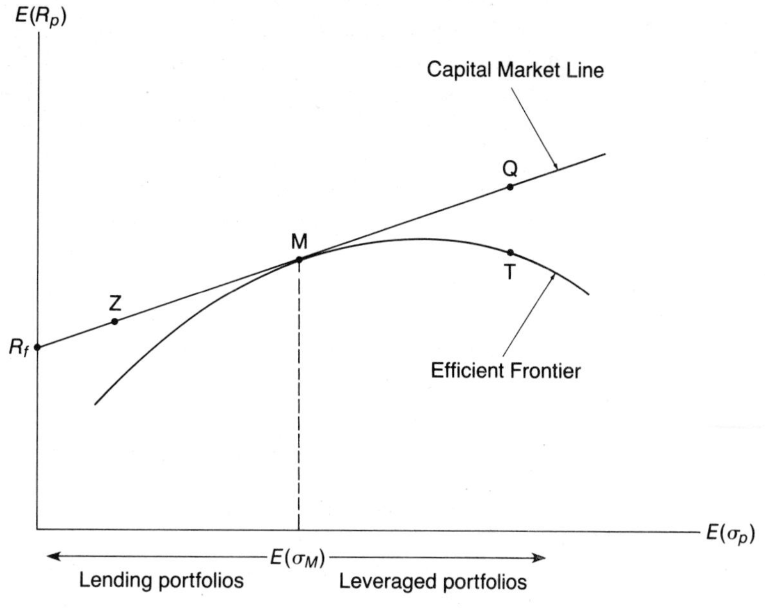

in its risk class. However, with the introduction of the CML, the situation significantly changes. With the exception of Portfolio M, which lies on both the CML and the EF, all portfolios lying on the CML offer higher returns than those on the EF.

Portfolio M, which is the point of tangency between the CML and the EF, assumes special significance. One assumption of the CAPM is that the market is in equilibrium; this implies that the supply of all market securities is also equal to the demand for them. Consequently, when the market is in equilibrium and lending and leveraged portfolios are nonexistent,[25] the *market portfolio*, M, which includes all assets in proportion to their market values,[26] becomes the only portfolio that satisfies the market equilibrium condition. The reason for this is obvious. Because the supply of securities in the market must be assumed as given, the market will be in equilibrium only when all the securities are demanded and included in a portfolio. That, by definition, is the market portfolio. Therefore, at equilibrium the market portfolio is the optimum portfolio.

[25] Leveraged and lending portfolios are discussed later in the chapter.

[26] The market portfolio includes stocks and bonds, as well as other risky assets. Because it is assumed to be a completely diversified portfolio, it does not contain unsystematic risk.

Leveraged Portfolio

Basic Elements

In the foregoing analysis it was tacitly assumed that investors holding Portfolio M did so entirely with their own funds. This is not a realistic assumption. In the real world, investors often purchase securities with borrowed funds. The implications of buying securities on margin may now be explored.

Assume an investor holds the market portfolio and wishes to increase his return above the market. That is, in Figure 13–13, he wishes to move from Point M to, say, Point Q. He can only do so if he borrows at the risk-free rate and invests in a high-risk portfolio.[27] Herein lies the advantage of buying on margin or owning what is known as a *leveraged portfolio*. An aggressive investor can improve his portfolio return over the market portfolio by borrowing at the risk-free rate and investing it in risky assets. However, leveraging also involves a trade-off—the risk of a leveraged portfolio is always higher than that of the market portfolio.

A Numerical Illustration

The process of leveraging can be illustrated by means of a numerical example. In this example, we will assume that (1) the investor wishes to move from Portfolio M to Portfolio Q, and (2) the market portfolio, M, is a composite of all securities. For *simplicity* it can be treated as a single security.

Assume one unit of Portfolio M costs $100. There is an equal chance, $p = .5$, that the portfolio would return either -2 percent $(-.02)$ or 30 percent (.30). The expected return on such a portfolio is 14 percent:

$$\begin{aligned} E(R_M) &= \sum_{i=1}^{2} p_i R_i \\ &= (.5)(-.02) + .5(.30) \\ &= -.01 + .15 \\ &= .14 \text{ (or } 14\%) \end{aligned}$$

Assuming the likelihood of the outcomes being -2 percent and 30 percent, the expected variance of the portfolio, calculated as a single security, is .0256:

$$\begin{aligned} E(\sigma_M^2) &= \sum_{i=1}^{2} p_i[R_i - E(R_M)]^2 \\ &= (.5)(-.02 - .14)^2 + (.5)(.3 - .14)^2 \\ &= .0128 + .0128 \\ &= .0256 \end{aligned}$$

[27] This discussion assumes the ability of the investor to borrow at the risk-free rate. The possibility of borrowing at a higher rate will be discussed later.

Table 13–5

	Alternative 1: Portfolio M returns −2%. Probability = .5	**Alternative 2: Portfolio M returns 30%. Probability = .5**
Investment		
Original Investment in one unit of Portfolio M:	$100	$100
Extra unit of Portfolio M purchased with money borrowed at 6%:	$100	$100
Total Investment: 2 units of Portfolio M = Portfolio Q:	$200	$200
Return on Investment		
Return on Portfolio Q (either −2% or 30% on $200):	($ 4)	$60
Less: Interest paid on $100 at 6%:	($ 6)	($ 6)
Total Return:	($10)	$54
Total Return on *Original Investment** of $100:	($10)/$100 = −10%	$54/$100 = 54%

* The return on the $200 *total* investment is not computed here because $100 must be repaid; thus the $100 original investment is used.

Now suppose that this investor prefers to take a higher risk. He borrows money at, say, a 6 percent risk-free rate and buys an additional unit of M, thereby creating the leveraged Portfolio Q.[28] His expected return on Portfolio Q will be either −10 percent or 54 percent, as shown in Table 13–5. Assuming that there is an equal probability of either outcome, the expected return of Portfolio Q is 22 percent:

$$
\begin{aligned}
E(R_Q) &= [(.5)(-.10)] + [(.5)(.54)] \\
&= -.05 + .27 \\
&= .22 \text{ (or } 22\%)
\end{aligned}
$$

The risk of Portfolio Q is .102:

$$
\begin{aligned}
E(\sigma_Q^2) &= [(.5)(-.10 - .22)^2] + [(.5)(.54 - .22)^2] \\
&= .051 + .051 \\
&= .102
\end{aligned}
$$

[28] Note that in deciding to leverage his portfolio the investor did not change the composition of the portfolio. His decision to leverage was purely financial in that he purchased an additional unit of the market portfolio with borrowed funds.

That is, the leveraged portfolio promises a much higher return (22 percent as compared to 14 percent), but it also carries a higher expected variance (.102 as compared to .0256).

Lending Portfolio

Basic Elements

In the previous discussion it was assumed that for obtaining better returns the investor was willing to assume a higher degree of risk than that implied in the market portfolio. However, not all investors fall in this category. Many persons are conservative investors; they prefer to invest in portfolios less risky than the market portfolio. These investors prefer portfolios that lie on the CML between R_f and M in Figure 13–13. Any portfolio lying in this range can be created in three stages. First, an amount equal to the market value of one or more units of the market portfolio is saved. Second, part of the savings is invested in a fraction of the market portfolio. Third, the balance of the savings is loaned to the government through the purchase of treasury bills. It is this third step that is the basis for referring to these as *lending portfolios.*

A Numerical Illustration

Just as leveraged portfolios result in an increase in both risks and returns, lending portfolios *reduce* risks and returns below the levels associated with the market portfolio. This is demonstrated in Table 13–6. Assume a conservative investor first discovers that the expected return and risk of the market portfolio, M, are 14 percent and .0256, respectively.[29] On the assumption that this portfolio has more risk than she is willing to assume, this investor buys a half unit of the market portfolio for $50 and buys treasury bills with an equivalent amount, thereby constructing Portfolio Z (Figure 13–13). Assuming that there is an equal chance that she will earn either 2 or 18 percent on her investment, the expected return on Portfolio Z is 10 percent:

$$\begin{aligned} E(R_Z) &= (.5)(.02) + (.5)(.18) \\ &= .01 + .09 \\ &= .10 \text{ (or } 10\%) \end{aligned}$$

The risk of Portfolio Z is .0064:

$$\begin{aligned} E(\sigma_Z^2) &= [(.5)(.02 - .10)^2] + [(.5)(.18 - .10)^2] \\ &= .0032 + .0032 \\ &= .0064 \end{aligned}$$

[29] The market's risk and return are assumed to be the same as those used in the preceding example.

Table 13–6

	Alternative 1: Portfolio M returns −2%. Probability = .5	Alternative 2: Portfolio M returns 30%. Probability = .5
Investment		
½ unit of Portfolio M:	\$ 50	\$ 50
Treasury bills:	\$ 50	\$ 50
Total Investment:	\$100	\$100
Return on Investment		
Return on Portfolio M (either −2% or 30% on \$50):	(\$1)	\$15
Return on treasury bills (6% on \$50):	\$3	\$ 3
Total Return:	\$2	\$18
Total Return on \$100 Investment:	\$2/\$100 = 2%	\$18/\$100 = 18%

As expected, Portfolio Z has lower risk than Portfolio M, but its return is lower than the market portfolio as well. This is the essence of investing in a lending portfolio.

Separation Theorem

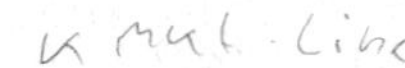

The initial discussion of the CML underscored an important point: The market portfolio is the universally desired portfolio of risky assets; in fact, it is frequently characterized as the *optimal combination of risky securities*. Subsequent discussion of the importance of the CML revealed that, starting from the market portfolio, investors may choose to adopt a leveraged or a lending portfolio, depending on their individual risk preferences. This point requires elaboration.

The existence of an optimal combination of risky securities together with the opportunity accorded an investor to construct a leveraged or a lending portfolio has led to the development of the *Separation Theorem*. This theorem derives its name from the fact that the issue of what constitutes an efficient portfolio is separate from identifying the best portfolio for an investor, given his or her risk preferences or utility function.[30]

Specifically, the Separation Theorem has two distinct components. First, the theory asserts that the market portfolio has the optimal combination of risky assets. Consequently, in choosing an efficient portfolio, the starting point

[30] William Sharpe, *Portfolio Theory and Capital Markets* (New York: McGraw-Hill, 1970), p. 70. The Separation Theorem was developed by Tobin. See James Tobin, "Liquidity Preference as Behavior Towards Risk," *Review of Economic Studies*, February 1958, pp. 65–85.

for *all investors* is the market portfolio; and no other investment considerations can direct them to a more efficient portfolio. Second, the market portfolio is associated with a level of risk which may be too low or too high for investors with varying risk preferences. Therefore, according to the separation theorem, aggressive investors may prefer a leveraged portfolio which would have a higher risk and return than the market. In contrast, a conservative investor might prefer a lending portfolio which would have lower risk and return than the market. However, the decision to hold a leveraged or lending portfolio is purely a *financial decision* based on an investor's risk preference; it has nothing to do with the *investment decision* to construct an efficient portfolio. In the final analysis, the market portfolio is the only efficient portfolio, although any portfolio—including the market portfolio—that lies on the CML and also satisfies the risk preference for an investor is the best portfolio for that investor.[31]

CAPM: Further Consideration

The Diversification Issue

One of the key elements of the CAPM is that the market portfolio is the optimum portfolio. However, the market portfolio consists of hundreds of securities—which makes it virtually impossible for anyone to invest in it. This difficulty must be viewed against the twin facts that diversification reduces unsystematic risk and *only* the fully diversified market portfolio succeeds in completely eliminating unsystematic risk. The question therefore becomes: What is the minimum number of securities an investor must buy in order to reduce *most* of the unsystematic risk?

In an earlier discussion of diversification, we pointed out that when perfect positive correlation exists between individual securities, no reduction in risk is achieved by including these securities in a portfolio. We also argued that although in the case of perfect negative correlation the portfolio risk can be totally eliminated, such a situation is rarely found in the real world. We will therefore concentrate on two cases—zero correlation and less than perfect positive correlation.

Zero Correlation

The risk equation associated with a two-asset portfolio is:

$$E(\sigma_p^2) = w_1^2\sigma_1^2 + w_2^2\sigma_2^2 + 2w_1w_2\rho_{12}\sigma_1\sigma_2 \qquad \textbf{(13–6 restated)}$$

[31] Investor's risk preference is discussed later in the chapter.

If there is zero correlation between the two securities, that is, $\rho_{12} = 0$, then the third term in the above equation drops out and Equation 13–6 becomes:

$$E(\sigma_p^2) = w_1^2\sigma_1^2 + w_2^2\sigma_2^2 \qquad \text{(13–10 restated)}$$

If an investor puts an equal amount of money in the two securities, and if the standard deviation of the return of each security is, say, 20 percent, then the risk of the portfolio is:

$$\begin{aligned} E(\sigma_p^2) &= (1/2)^2(20)^2 + (1/2)^2(20)^2 \\ &= 2[(1/2)^2(20)^2] \end{aligned}$$

It is possible to generalize from this result: If the total number of securities in a portfolio is measured by N, and the standard deviation of the return of each security is 20 percent, then,

$$\begin{aligned} E(\sigma_p^2) &= N(1/N)^2(20)^2 \\ &= \frac{N}{N^2} \times (20)^2 \\ &= \frac{20^2}{N} \end{aligned}$$

So,

$$\begin{aligned} E(\sigma_p) &= \sqrt{\frac{20^2}{N}} \\ &= \frac{20}{\sqrt{N}} \end{aligned}$$

This is an interesting result. It shows that the portfolio risk is the average standard deviation of individual returns divided by the square root of the number of securities in the portfolio.

Data presented in Figure 13–14 illustrate the nature of risk reduction through the pooling of securities with zero correlation. Note that initially the portfolio risk drops significantly; however, as more securities are added to the portfolio, the decline in risk gets progressively smaller.

Positive Correlation

The real world is characterized by securities which are positively correlated. What is the nature of risk reduction in the case of a portfolio consisting of positively correlated stocks? The answer to this question is found in a study conducted several years ago, results of which are presented in Figure 13–15. It can be observed that the risk of the market portfolio was 11.91 percent. The

Figure 13–14

Standard Deviation of Individual Returns	N	$E(\sigma_p)$	Change in $E(\sigma_p)$
20%	1	20.00%	
			−5.86%
	2	14.14	
			−5.20
	5	8.94	
			−2.62
	10	6.32	
			−1.85
	20	4.47	
			−1.65
	50	2.82	

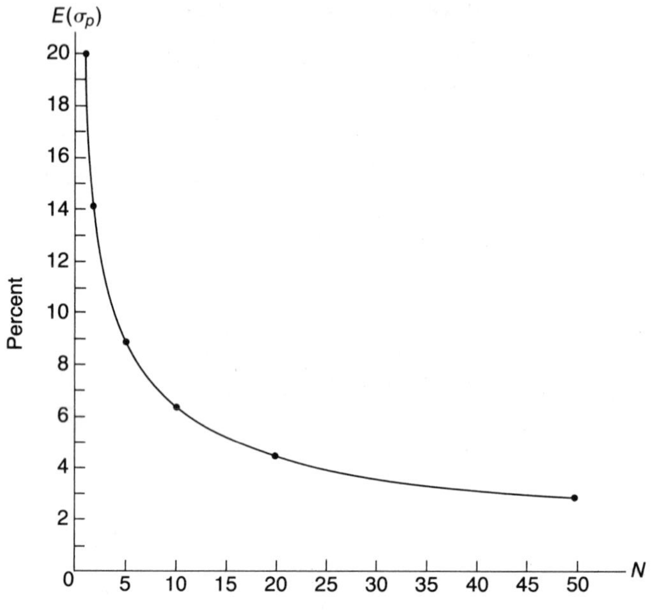

total risk of a one-stock portfolio was 20.54 percent and that of a two-stock portfolio was 16.22 percent. That is, a decrease of slightly more than 21 percent [(16.22 − 20.54)/20.54] in the portfolio's total risk resulted from adding just one more security to it. However, when 50 stocks were included in the portfolio, the risk was reduced to 12.08 percent, which represented only a 3.3 percent [(12.08 − 12.49)/12.49] reduction from the risk of the 15-stock portfolio.

The table reveals another interesting fact: The risk of a 15-stock portfolio is 12.49 percent as compared to the risk of 11.91 percent associated with the

Figure 13–15 **Reduction of Portfolio Risk as the Number of Assets in the Portfolio Increases**

Number of Stocks	Total Risk (%)	Percentage of Portfolio Risk: Systematic Risk	Percentage of Portfolio Risk: Residual Risk
1	20.54	57.98	42.02
2	16.22	73.43	26.57
3	14.79	80.53	19.47
4	14.07	84.65	15.35
5	13.64	87.32	12.68
6	13.35	89.21	10.79
7	13.14	90.64	9.36
8	13.00	91.62	8.38
10	12.63	94.30	5.70
15	12.49	95.36	4.64
20	12.34	96.52	3.48
50	12.08	98.59	1.41
100	11.9963	99.29	0.71
1,000	11.91863	99.93	0.07
Market Portfolio	11.91	100.00	0.0

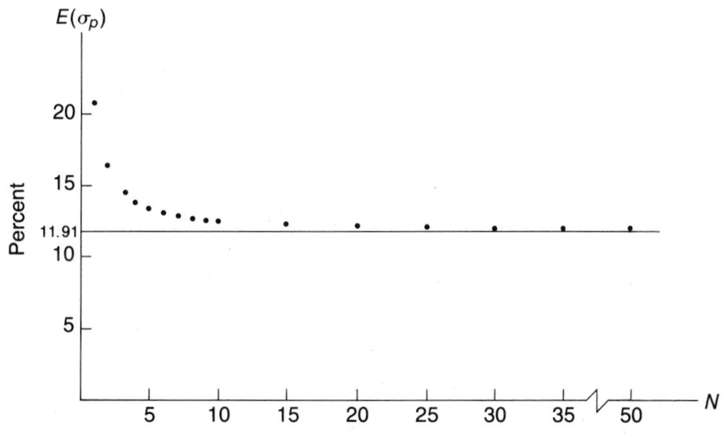

SOURCE: John Leslie Evans, "Diversification and the Reduction of Dispersion: An Empirical Analysis," Ph.D. dissertation, Graduate School of Business Administration, University of Washington, 1968.

market portfolio. At the 15-stock level, approximately 95 percent of the portfolio's total risk was systematic and only 5 percent was unsystematic. In general terms, a 15-stock portfolio diversifies away most of the unsystematic risk and its total risk approaches the risk of the market portfolio which by definition contains only systematic risk. This phenomenon is clearly reflected in the chart at the bottom of Figure 13–15.

Figure 13–16

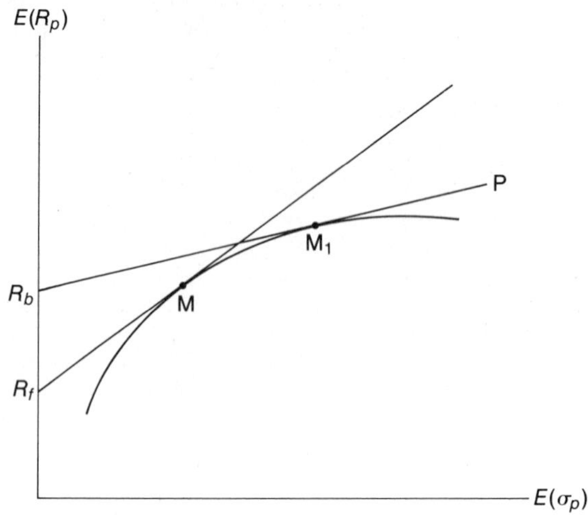

Borrowing Versus Lending Rate

Another comment on the CAPM relates to the assumption that only one risk-free rate exists in the market at any given time and that investors willing to assume higher risk are able to leverage their portfolios by borrowing at that rate. This is not a realistic assumption, because the market's borrowing rate is generally higher than the lending rate.

The implication of the dual-level borrowing–lending rate can be seen from Figure 13–16. If R_f is the risk-free lending (savings) rate and R_b is the rate at which margin loans can be obtained, the optimal portfolio is the *range* designated by MM_1. Furthermore, in that world, the CML is no longer a straight line but a curve such as the one identified by $R_f MM_1 P$.

Empirical Tests

According to the probability theory, there are three possible shapes for probability distribution—symmetric, skewed to left, and skewed to right. Of these, the type of the first distribution, known as the normal curve, is of considerable interest because of its interpretive properties.

Considerable statistical work has been done to test whether or not portfolio returns are normally distributed. Figure 13–17 presents the results of one such study in the form of a distribution of monthly returns for a 100-security diversified

Figure 13–17 **Rate of Return Distribution for a Portfolio of 100 Securities (equally weighted) January 1945–June 1970**

	Range		Freq.	1 . . . 5 . . . 10 . . . 15 . . . 20 . . . 25 . . . 30 . . . 35 . . . 40 . . . 45 . . . 50
1	−13.6210	−12.2685	1	*
2	−12.2685	−10.9160	2	**
3	−10.9160	−9.5635	2	**
4	−9.5635	−8.2110	3	***
5	−8.2110	−6.8585	8	********
6	−6.8585	−5.5060	9	*********
7	−5.5060	−4.1535	17	*****************
8	−4.1535	−2.8010	18	******************
9	−2.8010	−1.4485	27	***************************
10	−1.4485	−0.0960	28	****************************
11	−0.0960	1.2565	30	******************************
12	1.2565	2.6090	50	**
13	2.6090	3.9615	35	***********************************
14	3.9615	5.3140	33	*********************************
15	5.3140	6.6665	18	******************
16	6.6665	8.0190	14	**************
17	8.0190	9.3715	4	****
18	9.3715	10.7240	2	**
19	10.7240	12.0765	2	**
20	12.0765	13.4290	3	***

Average return = 0.91 percent per month.
Standard deviation = 4.46 percent per month.
Number of observations = 306.

SOURCE: Franco Modigliani and Gerald Pogue, "An Introduction to Risk and Return: Concepts and Evidence," *Financial Analysts Journal*, March–April, 1974.

portfolio covering the period January 1945–June 1970. It was constructed by dividing the range of returns into equal intervals, then recording the frequency with which returns fell within each interval. The figure reveals that portfolio returns *approximately* followed a normal distribution.[32]

The average return of the selected diversified portfolio was 0.91 percent per month and the standard deviation was 4.46 percent per month. As a rule of thumb for normal distributions, it is suggested that roughly two-thirds of the possible returns will lie within one standard deviation to either side of the expected value, and that 95 percent will be within two standard deviations. Applying this rule to the portfolio returns given in Figure 13–18, we discover that roughly two-thirds of the possible returns will lie between −3.55 and +5.37

[32] Franco Modigliani and Gerald Pogue, "An Introduction to Risk and Return: Concepts and Evidence," *Financial Analysts Journal*, March–April 1974.

Figure 13–18

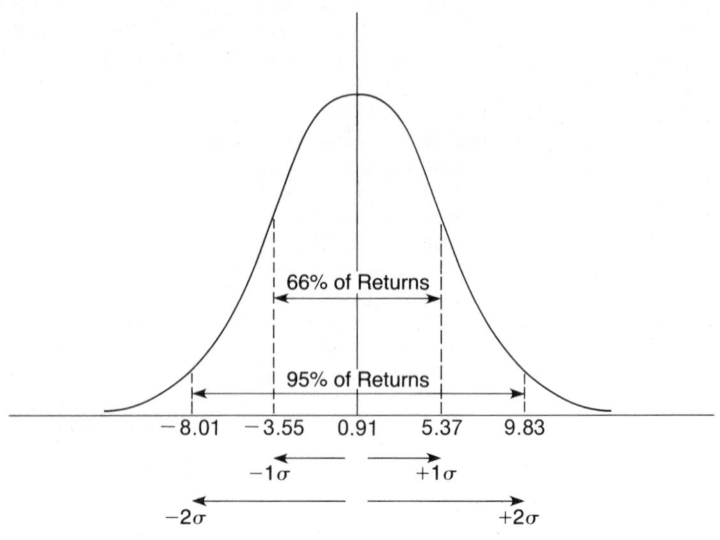

percent, and that 95 percent will be within −8.01 and +9.83 percent. This is an important discovery: If the returns of a diversified portfolio are in fact normally distributed, then, given its mean and standard deviation, predictions of its expected returns can be made in more precise terms.

Empirical tests of a different sort have been conducted to test the validity of the assumption that the expected return on an asset will equal the rate of return from a riskless security, R_f, plus additional return to compensate for systematic (beta) risk. One study [33] conducted by Black, Jensen, and Scholes (BJS) divided all NYSE stocks among ten portfolios in each year from 1931 to 1965. The BJS study, presented in Figure 13–19, discovered that higher returns were obtained from more risky portfolios. However, they also found that low risk stocks seemed underpriced, whereas high risk stocks seemed overpriced. According to these results, an investor could have beaten the market by borrowing at the risk-free rate and investing in low risk stocks, thereby capitalizing on the spread between the two rates. Although additional empirical tests are still being conducted, it appears that the simplest form of the CAPM is somewhat inadequate for explaining common stock returns.[34]

[33] Fischer Black, Michael C. Jensen, and Myron Scholes, "The Capital Asset Pricing Model: Some Empirical Tests," in *Studies in the Theory of Capital Markets*, ed. M. C. Jensen (New York: Praeger Publishing Co., 1972), pp. 79–121.

[34] For example, a detailed analysis of post-World War II capital market line relationships is provided in Marshall Blume and Irwin Friend, "A New Look at the Capital Asset Pricing Model," *Journal of Finance*, March 1973, pp. 1–33.

Figure 13–19 **Black–Jensen–Scholes Results (Average Monthly Returns Versus Systematic Risk)**

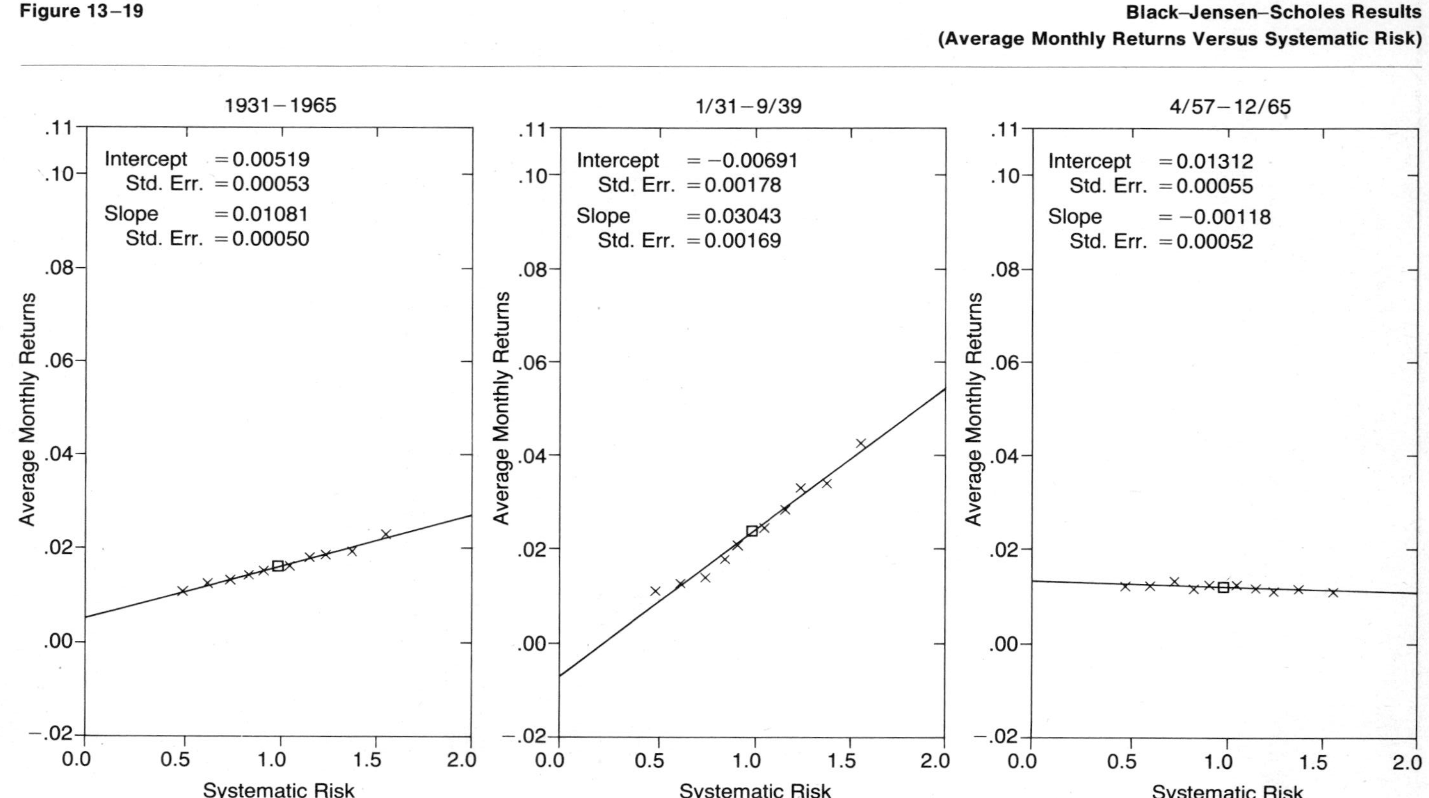

SOURCE: Fischer Black, Michael C. Jensen, and Myron Scholes, "The Capital Asset Pricing Model: Some Empirical Tests," in *Studies in the Theory of Capital Markets*, ed. M.C. Jensen (New York: Praeger, 1972), pp. 79–121, Figure 7, 8, 11.

Security Market Line

Under the assumption that the market is at equilibrium, the CAPM asserts that (1) the expected value of the error term and the value of the risk-adjusted excess return are zero, and (2) the expected return of a portfolio is related to the market return by the beta (or systematic risk) of the portfolio. With these considerations in mind, and by introducing the risk-free asset and total risk into the discussion, the Capital Market Line was developed. The CML, presented in Figure 13–12, relates total expected portfolio risk to the expected portfolio return. Note that this line measures the total (systematic and unsystematic) risk and is one on which only portfolios may lie.

Our discussion of individual securities relative to the market portfolio has led to two important conclusions. First, beta relates individual security risks to the market risk. Second, beta measures only the systematic risk of a security. Because the unsystematic risk tends to be diversified away by the construction of an efficient portfolio, it is desirable to develop an alternative to the CML which will use beta as the independent variable and will accommodate both portfolios and individual assets. Such a line is called the *Security Market Line* (*SML*). The difference between the two lines should be noted. The CML is a linear relationship between the expected return of a portfolio and the *total* risk associated with it; it generates a line on which only efficient portfolios can lie. The SML is a linear relationship between expected return and beta or systematic risk on which both portfolios and individual securities can lie.

Figure 13–20 presents a SML which has beta as the independent variable[35] and the expected return of portfolios and individual securities as the dependent variable. The SML has a positive slope, indicating that the expected return increases with risk (beta). By definition, the risk of a risk-free asset, R_f, is zero; therefore, R_f is the point at which the SML crosses the vertical axis, the Y-intercept point. The beta of the market portfolio, which measures the systematic risk of the market relative to itself, is 1. Therefore, the point where beta equals 1 is associated with the expected market return. This is an important point, because all securities and portfolios with a beta of less than 1 lie to the left of M on the SML and are called defensive securities. Likewise, securities with a beta of more than 1 are riskier than the market and are called aggressive securities.

[35] The risk of a portfolio, of course, is its covariance with the market portfolio. The relationship between beta and $\text{cov}_{p,m}$ can be seen from the following derivation:

$$E(R_p) = R_f + \beta_p(E(R_m) - R_f)$$

But $\beta_p = \text{cov}_{p,m}/\sigma_m^2$. Therefore

$$E(R_p) = R_f + \frac{\text{cov}_{p,m}}{\sigma_m^2}(E(R_m) - R_f)$$

Rearranging we have

$$E(R_p) = R_f + \left[\frac{E(R_m) - R_f}{\sigma_m^2}\right](\text{cov}_{p,m})$$

Figure 13–20 **Security Market Line**

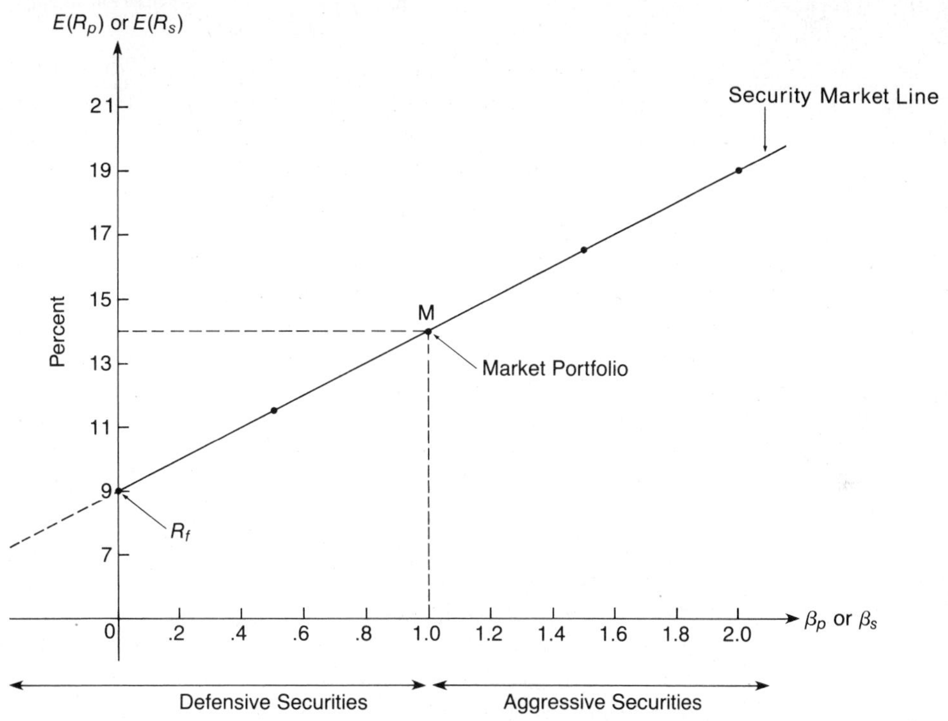

In addition, the expected return of a security on the SML is determined by the risk-free rate plus a systematic risk premium which is proportional to its beta.[36] Symbolically,

$$E(R_s) = R_f + \beta_s[E(R_m) - R_f] \tag{13–18}$$

The use of the SML as a decision tool can be illustrated with a numerical illustration. Suppose the short-term, risk-free interest rate, R_f, equals 9 percent, and the expected return on the market, $E(R_m)$, is 14 percent. The expected risk premium for holding the market portfolio is 5 percent (the difference between 14 percent and the risk-free rate of 9 percent). Investors holding the market portfolio should expect a return of 14 percent, or 5 percent higher than they

[36] The expected return of a security on the SML is also an investor's minimum required rate of return for that security, or its appropriate discount rate. Remember that in Chapters 9 and 11 we defined a stock's appropriate discount rate as its expected systematic return, which is equal to its beta (or systematic risk) multiplied by the expected market return. Although this relationship is not entirely accurate, it was presented in this simple form purely for pedagogical reasons. Now that the risk-free rate and the CAPM have been introduced, it can be seen that, except for portfolios with a beta of 1, the expected systematic return of a portfolio always differs from its expected return as determined by the SML.

Table 13–7 **Expected Return for Different Levels of Portfolio Beta**

Portfolio	Beta (β_p)	Expected Return $E(R_p)$
A	0.0	9.0%
B	0.5	11.5
C	1.0	14.0
D	1.5	16.5
E	2.0	19.0

Pertinent details

$$R_f = \text{Risk-free rate of return} = 9\%$$

$$E(R_m) = \text{Expected market portfolio rate of return} = 14\%$$

$$E(R_m) - R_f = 5\%$$

$$\begin{aligned} E(R_p) &= R_f + \beta_p[E(R_m) - R_f] \\ &= 9\% + \beta_p[14\% - 9\%] \\ &= 9\% + \beta_p[5\%] \end{aligned}$$

would if they invested in, say, treasury bills. Likewise, the expected returns on portfolios with different levels of risk can be determined in the manner shown in Table 13–7. According to this table, Portfolio D, which has a beta of 1.5, should have an expected return of 16.5 percent, whereas Portfolio B, with a beta of .5, should have an expected return of 11.5 percent.

The implications of the SML are enormous. If individual assets and portfolios are priced correctly—a realistic assumption in an efficient market—then all correctly priced assets and portfolios must lie on the SML, because the beta value of a security or a portfolio represents its contribution to the risk of the market portfolio. It follows, therefore, that an asset lying above the SML is undervalued, because it offers a return higher than what is consistent with the systematic risk it carries. Similarly, assets lying below the SML are overvalued, because they offer returns lower than what investors should expect from investing in them. Therefore, the SML can become the cornerstone for developing effective portfolio strategies. This important point will be developed further in Chapter 14.

Investor Preference and Portfolio Selection

In previous discussions it was frequently suggested that, in the final analysis, selection of the *best* portfolio depends on the utility function (the risk preference) of an investor. It is customary to discuss the topic of investor preference by means of indifference curves of individual risk preference.

In the context of portfolio selection, an investor's indifference curve shows all combinations of risks and returns that yield the same satisfaction to the investor. An investor is *indifferent* between the combinations indicated by any

Figure 13–21

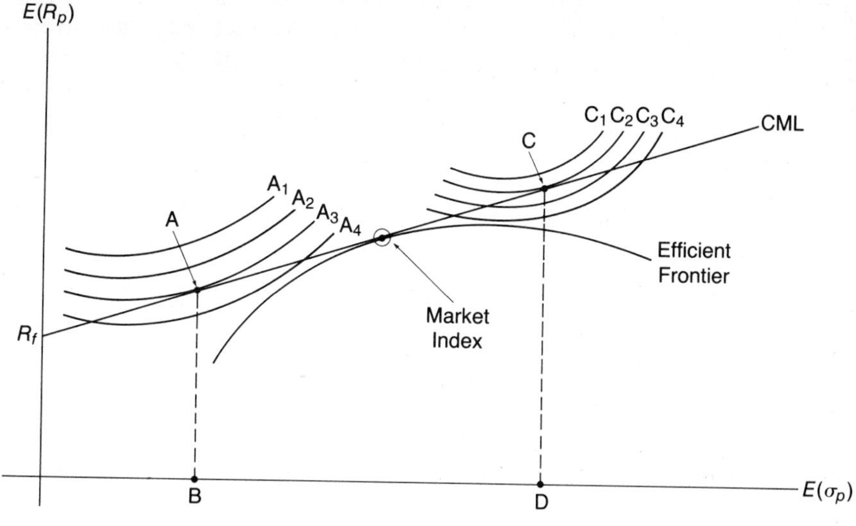

two points on an indifference curve. Furthermore, any points above the indifference curve which lie on a higher indifference curve show combinations of risk and return that the investor would prefer to combinations of points on the curve. It follows, therefore, that every investor would prefer to be on the *highest possible indifference curve.*

Figure 13–21 presents the CML developed earlier with a set of indifference curves or utility functions superimposed on it. A conservative or defensive investor, one who prefers to assume a level of risk lower than the market risk, will have to choose a lending portfolio lying to the left of point M on the CML. If he decides to assume a risk level designated by B, he will then examine indifference curves A_1, A_2, A_3, A_4, and so on, all of which are associated with that risk class. However, the investor will recognize that, although he prefers A_1 over others, because he must choose a portfolio which lies on the CML, his highest indifference curve can only be A_3 and his best choice is Portfolio A, the point of tangency between the highest possible indifference curve and the CML. Similarly, an agressive investor, one who chooses the risk class designated by D, would select Portfolio C which lies both on the CML *and* the highest indifference curve, C_2, in that risk class.

Summary

In the 1950s, Harry Markowitz used fluctuations or variance of investment returns as an approximation of the risk of investment. He then developed the portfolio theory by demonstrating that once the level of risk the investor is willing to assume is established, a computerized theoretical model can be used as a basis for selecting the optimum portfolio that would maximize the rate of return.

In constructing a portfolio three forms of diversification are possible. If there is *perfect positive correlation* between securities, diversification merely averages individual security risks and no risk reduction takes place. In contrast, if the securities have *perfect negative correlation*, then it is possible to construct a portfolio such that both systematic and unsystematic risks are completely eliminated. However, in the real world, such relationships are not likely to be found. In the event that there is low or zero *positive correlation*, diversification will reduce risks associated with individual securities.

In a world where no lending and borrowing of funds are possible and where stocks have either zero or positive correlation, efficient portfolios offering the highest returns for each risk class will lie on the *Efficient Frontier*.

According to the Market Model, the systematic return of a stock or a portfolio is proportional to the market return, and it can be expressed as a factor, β, multiplied by the market return, R_m. The unsystematic return, which is independent of market returns, is the sum of the average of the residual returns, α, and the residual returns, ϵ.

The CAPM states that, in equilibrium, investors will price capital assets so that the expected return on a portfolio is equal to the risk-free rate plus a risk premium that is proportional to the risk measure, beta.

According to the Market Model, the risk-adjusted excess return of a portfolio, α_p^*, can be positive, negative, or zero. The CAPM asserts that the value of α_p^* is zero.

When borrowing and lending are permitted at the risk-free rate, then efficient portfolios are assumed to lie on the *Capital Market Line*, (*CML*). If, however, the borrowing rate is higher than the risk-free rate, the CML is no longer a straight line, but takes the shape of a curve.

The market portfolio has the optimum mix of all risky assets. An aggressive investor can increase his or her expected return by leveraging the portfolio—borrowing at the risk-free rate and investing the borrowed funds in the market portfolio. Leveraged portfolios fall on the CML to the right of the market portfolio, and they increase both expected risk and return. Likewise, a conservative or defensive investor can reduce his or her expected risk and return by moving leftward from the market portfolio, but staying on the CML by investing part of his or her funds in the market portfolio and putting the rest into risk-free assets. This is the essence of the *Capital Asset Pricing Model.*

The *Separation Theorem* implies that the market portfolio satisfies the investment mix requirements of all investors regardless of their individual risk preferences. Depending on their personal risk preferences, however, investors can reduce or increase their risk by constructing a lending or a leveraged portfolio while staying on the CML.

The *Security Market Line* (*SML*) is a linear relationship between the expected return and systematic risk. It is a straight line on which both individual securities and portfolios can lie. Furthermore, the SML clearly segregates defensive from aggressive securities.

A Look Ahead

This chapter was devoted to a detailed discussion of portfolio theory. In Chapter 14, we will demonstrate the practical application of the portfolio theory to the construction and management of diversified portfolios.

Concepts for Review

Markowitz Portfolio Model
Variance and standard deviation
Risk and return
Probability of return
Expected return
Security risk
Security return
Portfolio return
Portfolio risk
Covariance
Correlation coefficient
Diversification
Perfect positive correlation
Perfect negative correlation
Zero correlation
Markowitz diversification
Efficient Frontier
Unsystematic, systematic and total risk
Market portfolio
Market Model
Alpha
Beta
Risk–premium form
Risk-adjusted excess return
Capital Asset Pricing Model (CAPM)
Capital Market Line (CML)
Leveraged portfolio
Lending portfolio
Separation Theorem
Borrowing and lending rates
Security Market Line (SML)
Investor risk preference

Questions for Review

1. What is the difference between security risk and portfolio risk?
2. What is covariance? Why is it important in portfolio theory?
3. Explain the concept of diversification. Will all forms of diversification reduce total risk? Unsystematic risk? Systematic risk?
4. Describe the Efficient Frontier in detail.

5. What are the characteristics of an efficient portfolio? Distinguish between a feasible and an efficient portfolio in the Markowitz sense.
6. Why did Sharpe develop the CAPM? What were the problems with the Markowitz Model?
7. Explain the relationship between the Market Model and the CAPM. Does acceptance of one imply the acceptance of the other?
8. How is the Capital Market Line derived? What does it represent? Why does it have a positive slope?
9. The Capital Market Line is often called the "new" Efficient Frontier. Why?
10. Describe portfolio diversification in terms of modern portfolio theory.
11. Explain the Separation Theorem.
12. Contrast the Security Market Line with the Capital Market Line.
13. The horizontal axis of the Capital Market Line is the standard deviation, whereas the Security Market Line measures beta on the horizontal axis. Is there a connection between the two?
14. What are the implications of the Security Market Line?
15. What are the generally accepted ranges for defensive and aggressive betas?

Problems

1. Securities Q and K display the following parameters:

	Expected Return $E(R_s)$	Expected Variance $E(\sigma^2)$	Covariance cov_{QR}
Security Q	.16	.09	.06
Security K	.22	.16	

Find the expected return and standard deviation for each of the portfolios having the following weights:

Portfolio	Security Q	Security K
1	1.00	0
2	.75	.25
3	.50	.50
4	.25	.75
5	0	1.00

Interpret your results. Is there any advantage to holding some of Q and some of K? Explain.

2. Repeat the previous problem assuming correlation coefficients between securities Q and K of 1.0, 0, and −1.0. Under what conditions could the portfolio risk be reduced to zero?
3. Repeat the first problem, assuming Security K is a riskless security with an expected return of 10 percent. Interpret your results.

4. Assume that the Market Model Y-intercept for a portfolio (α_p) is −2.9 percent, the beta coefficient (β_p) is 1.6.
   a. Find the expected return on the portfolio, assuming that the expected return on the market is 12 percent.
   b. Assuming the risk-free rate is 5.5 percent, what is the expected risk-adjusted excess return (α_p^*) on the portfolio? What do your results indicate?
   c. Repeat part (b), but assume the beta is 0.7 and the Market Model Y-intercept is 1.50. Is this a more favorable situation?
   d. Given the information in (a) and (b), what is the portfolio's expected return according to the CAPM?
   e. When would the Market Model and CAPM give the same expected return?
5. Consider the following data:

Risk-free rate:	10.9%
Expected return on market portfolio:	14.7%

Security	Beta
A	.60
B	.98
C	1.13
D	1.82

   a. Using this data, draw a graph of the SML.
   b. What return would you expect from each of the above securities?
   c. Given the information below, what return would you expect from each portfolio?

	Portfolio Weights			
Securities	**A**	**B**	**C**	**D**
Portfolio 1	25%	25%	25%	25%
Portfolio 2	10	10	10	70
Portfolio 3	40	15	45	0

Footnotes

4. Covariance of a two-security portfolio can be measured by:

$$\text{cov}_{\text{AB}} = E(\text{AB}) - [E(\text{A})E(\text{B})]$$

Assume Stocks A and B vary in the following manner:

Condition	Probability of Return	Expected Return of A	Expected Return of B
Favorable	.5	$100	$10
Unfavorable	.5	−$ 50	−$ 5

The expected return and variance of Stock A would be 25 and 5,625, respectively:

$$\begin{aligned} E(R_A) &= (.5)(100) + (.5)(-50) \\ &= 25 \\ \sigma_A^2 &= (.5)(100 - 25)^2 + (.5)(-50 - 25)^2 \\ &= 5{,}625 \end{aligned}$$

The expected return and variance of Stock B would be 2.5 and 56.25, respectively:

$$\begin{aligned} E(R_B) &= (.5)(10) + (.5)(-5) \\ &= 2.5 \\ \sigma_B^2 &= (.5)(10 - 2.5)^2 + (.5)(-5 - 2.5)^2 \\ &= 56.25 \end{aligned}$$

The covariance between Stocks A and B would be 562.5:

$$\begin{aligned} \text{cov}_{AB} &= E(AB) - [E(A)E(B)] \\ &= [(.5)(100)(10)] + [(.5)(-50)(-5)] - [(25)(2.5)] \\ &= 625 - 62.5 \\ &= 562.5 \end{aligned}$$

A positive covariance confirms that both stocks move in the same direction.

8. An improper construction refers to the case where diversification does not reduce portfolio risk, despite the fact that $\rho_{12} = 0$. Assume the following particulars:

Stock	Weight	σ^2
A	.1	.9
B	.9	.1

$$\begin{aligned} E(\sigma_p^2) &= (.1)^2(.9) + (.9)^2(.1) \\ &= .009 + .081 \\ &= .09 \end{aligned}$$

Note that, in this case, diversification did not reduce individual security risk.

10. If that were not the case—that is, if less return were expected for taking higher risks—the graph on a risk–return space would look quite different. For example, suppose we have the following implausible situation:

Assets	$E(R)$	σ	W (1)	W (2)	W (3)
A	9%	30%	$\frac{1}{3}$	$\frac{1}{2}$	$\frac{3}{4}$
B	12%	20%	$\frac{2}{3}$	$\frac{1}{2}$	$\frac{1}{4}$

Because A has a lower expected return even though it is more risky, regardless of the relative weights of A and B, the graph will appear inverted, as can be observed from the following figure:

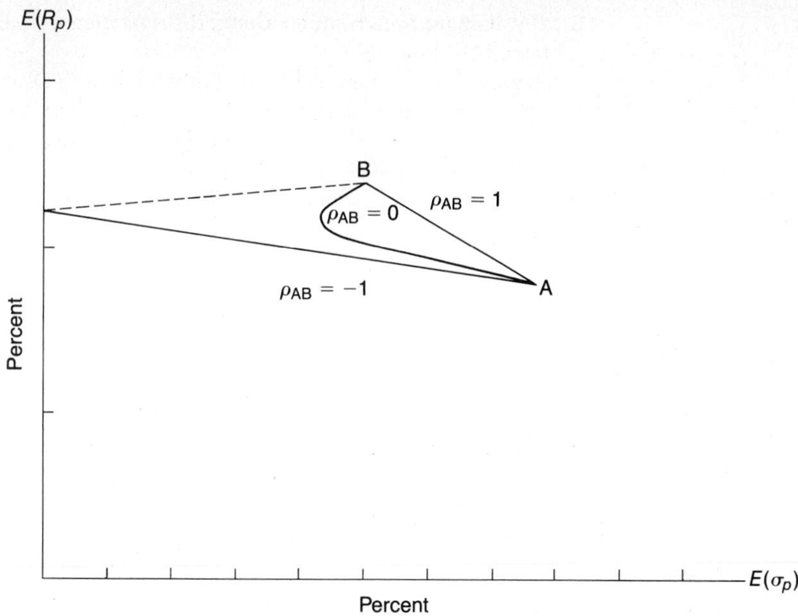

21. This relationship can be clearly seen from the following derivation. For a portfolio, assuming $\epsilon_p = 0$, the two models are

$$E(R_p) = \alpha_p + \beta_p E(R_m) \qquad \text{Market Model}$$
$$E(R_p) = R_f + \beta_p[E(R_m) - R_f] \qquad \text{CAPM}$$

Assuming the $E(R_p)$ in both models is the same, we have:

$$\begin{aligned}\alpha_p + \beta_p[E(R_m)] &= R_f + \beta_p[E(R_m) - R_f] \\ \alpha_p &= R_f + \beta_p[E(R_m) - R_f] - \beta_p[E(R_m)] \\ &= R_f + \beta_p E(R_m) - \beta_p R_f - \beta_p E(R_m) \\ &= R_f - \beta_p R_f \\ &= R_f(1 - \beta_p)\end{aligned}$$

Selected Readings

Arditti, Fred D. "Risk and the Required Return on Equity." *Journal of Finance*, March 1967.

Black, Fischer, Michael C. Jensen, and Myron Scholes. "The Capital Asset Pricing Model: Some Empirical Tests." In *Studies in the Theory of Capital Markets*. Ed. Michael C. Jensen. New York: Praeger Publishers, 1972.

Black, Frank E. "Elements of Portfolio Construction." *Financial Analysts Journal*, May–June 1969.

Blume, Marshall E. "On the Assessment of Risk." *Journal of Finance*, March 1971.

Blume, Marshall E. "Portfolio Theory: A Step Towards Its Practical Application." *Journal of Business*, April 1970.

Brealey, Richard A. *An Introduction to Risk and Return from Common Stocks.* Cambridge, Mass.: MIT Press, 1969.

Brennan, Michael J. "Capital Market Equilibrium with Divergent Borrowing and Lending Rates." *Journal of Financial and Quantitative Analysis*, December 1971.

Cohen, K. J. and J. A. Pogue. "An Empirical Evaluation of Alternative Portfolio Selection Models." *Journal of Business*, April 1967.

Evans, John L. "An Examination of the Principle of Diversification." *Journal of Business Finance and Accounting*, Summer 1975.

Evans, John and S. H. Archer. "Diversification and the Reduction of Dispersion: An Empirical Analysis." *Journal of Finance*, December 1968.

Fama, Eugene F. "Efficient Capital Markets: A Review of Theory and Empirical Work." *Journal of Finance*, May 1970.

Fama, Eugene F. "Risk, Return and Equilibrium: Some Clarifying Comments." *Journal of Finance*, March 1968.

Fama, Eugene F. and James D. MacBeth. "Risk, Return, and Equilibrium: Empirical Tests." *Journal of Political Economy*, May–June 1973.

Fisher, Lawrence. "Using Modern Portfolio Theory to Maintain an Efficiently Diversified Portfolio." *Financial Analysts Journal*, May–June 1972.

Frankfurter, George M., Herbert E. Phillips and John P. Seagle. "Performance of the Sharpe Portfolio Selection Model: A Comparison." *Journal of Financial and Quantitative Analysis*, June 1976.

Gaumnitz, Jack E. "Maximal Gains from Diversification and Implications for Portfolio Management." *Mississippi Valley Journal of Business and Economics*, Spring 1971.

Gaviria, Nestor G. "Inflation and Capital Asset Market Prices: Theory and Tests." Unpublished Ph.D. dissertation, Graduate School of Business, Stanford University, 1973.

Hirshleifer, Jack. "Efficient Allocation of Capital in an Uncertain World." *American Economic Review*, May 1964.

Jensen, Michael C. "Capital Markets: Theory and Evidence." *The Bell Journal of Economics and Management Science*, Autumn 1972.

Jensen, Michael C. "Risk, the Pricing of Capital Assets, and the Evaluation of Investment Portfolios." *Journal of Business*, April 1969.

Jensen, Michael C. "Tests of Capital Market Theory and Implications of the Evidence." Research Paper No. 1, Financial Analysts Research Foundation, 1975.

Johnson, K. H. and D. S. Shannon." "A Note on Diversification and the Reduction of Dispersion." *Journal of Financial Economics*, December 1974.

Lintner, John. "The Valuation of Risk Assets and the Selection of Risky Investments in Stock Portfolios and Capital Budgets." *Review of Economics and Statistics*, February 1965.

Lintner, John. "Security Prices, Risk, and the Maximal Gains from Diversification." *Journal of Finance*, December 1965.

Lorie, James H. "Diversification: Old and New." *The Journal of Portfolio Management*, Winter 1975.

Lorie, James H. and Mary T. Hamilton. *The Stock Market: Theories and Evidence.* Homewood, Ill. Richard D. Irwin, 1973.

Mao, James. "Essentials of Portfolio Diversification Strategy." *Journal of Finance*, December 1970.

Markowitz, Harry. "Markowitz Revisited." *Financial Analysts Journal*, September–October 1976.

Markowitz, Harry. "Portfolio Selection." *Journal of Finance*, March 1952.

Markowitz, Harry. *Portfolio Selection—Efficient Diversification of Investments.* New Haven, Conn.: Yale University Press, 1959.

Martin, A. D., Jr. "Mathematical Programming of Portfolio Selections." *Management Science*, January 1955.

Modigliani, F. and Gerald A. Pogue. "An Introduction to Risk and Return: Concepts and Evidence." In *Financial Analyst's Handbook.* Ed. Sumner N. Levine. Homewood, Ill.: Dow Jones-Irwin, 1975.

Mossin, Jan. "Equilibrium in a Capital Asset Market." *Econometrica*, October 1966.

Mossin, Jan. "Security Pricing and Investment Criteria in Competitive Markets." *American Economic Review*, December 1969.

Pogue, Gerald A. "An Extension of the Markowitz Portfolio Selection Model to Include Variable Transaction Costs, Leverage, Policies, and Short Sales." *Journal of Finance*, December 1970.

Phillips, Herbert E. "Capital Asset Pricing Model and Traditional Risk for Capital Budgeting: A Comment." *Financial Review*, Fall 1977.

Roll, Richard. "A Critique of the Asset Pricing Theory's Test. Part I: On Past and Potential Testability of the Theory." *Journal of Financial Economics*, March 1977.

Samuelson, Paul A. "General Proof that Diversification Pays." *Journal of Financial and Quantitative Analysis*, June 1967.

Samuelson, Paul A. "Proof That Properly Anticipated Prices Fluctuate Randomly." *Industrial Management Review*, Spring 1965.

Sharpe, William. "Adjusting for Risk in Portfolio Performance Measurement." *Journal of Portfolio Management*, Winter 1975.

Sharpe, William. "Bonds Vs. Stocks: Some Lessons from Capital Market Theory." *Financial Analysts Journal*, November–December 1973.

Sharpe, William. "Capital Asset Prices: A Theory of Market Equilibrium Under Conditions of Risk." *Journal of Finance*, September 1964.

Sharpe, William. *Portfolio Theory and Capital Markets.* New York: McGraw-Hill, 1970.

Sharpe, William. "Risk Aversion in the Stock Market." *Journal of Finance*, September 1965.

Sharpe, William. "Risk Market Sensitivity and Diversification." *Financial Analysts Journal*, January–February 1972.

Sharpe, William. "A Simplified Model for Portfolio Analysis." *Management Science*, January 1964.

Tobin, James. "Liquidity Preference as Behavior Towards Risk," *Review of Economic Studies*, February 1958.

Tobin, James. "The Theory of Portfolio Selection." In *The Theory of Interest Rates.* Ed. F. H. Hahn and F.P.R. Brechling. London: Macmillan, 1965.

Treynor, Jack L. "Toward a Theory of Market Value of Risky Assets." Unpublished manuscript, 1961.

Upson, Roger, Paul Jessup, and Keishiro Matsumoto. "Portfolio Diversification Strategies." *Financial Analysts Journal*, May–June 1975.

Valentine, Jerome L. *Investment Analysis and Capital Market Theory*, Occasional Paper No. 1. Charlottesville, Va. The Financial Analysts Research Foundation, 1975.

Wagner, W. H. and S. C. Lau. "The Effect of Diversification on Risk." *Financial Analysts Journal*, November–December 1971.

Wallingford, B. A. "A Survey and Comparison of Portfolio Selection Models." *Journal of Financial and Quantitative Analysis*, June 1967.

Portfolio Management in an Efficient Market

Introduction

In Chapter 13, the essentials of the modern portfolio theory were presented and the theoretical foundations for portfolio construction and management were established. No effort, however, was made either to construct an efficient portfolio or to discuss the implications of building such a portfolio in an efficient market. These topics form the basis of discussion in the present chapter.

More specifically, Section 1 is devoted to a detailed discussion of the Efficient Market Hypothesis and its implications for portfolio construction and management. In Section 2, passive and active portfolio management are presented, along with plans for constructing, monitoring, and updating each type of portfolio. In this section, a portfolio is also constructed with real world data, partly to demonstrate the complex nature of portfolio management.

SECTION 1 EFFICIENT MARKET HYPOTHESIS: CONCEPT AND EVIDENCE

An Overview

The Inefficiency Issue

Paradoxical though it may seem, historically the capital market has been considered both efficient and inefficient. The market is thought to be efficient if it quickly and accurately executes buy and sell orders.[1] In this sense, the

[1] The operational efficiency of the market also includes broadcasting up-to-the-minute data on stock prices and sales volume. The market's operational efficiency was discussed in Chapter 3.

market is generally considered efficient. In a totally different context, however, at least until the 1950s, the market has been assumed to be inefficient. More precisely, many persons have believed that the market is so inefficient at processing new information that current stock prices do not always reflect the intrinsic or present value of the respective stocks. This divergence between the value of a stock and its market price provides unique investment opportunities which can be capitalized on by investors who take the actions suggested later in this chapter.

In Chapter 9, a framework for fundamental analysis of common stocks was presented: By estimating the future dividend payments, the expected selling price at the end of the investor's holding period, and the appropriate discount rate, the present value of a stock can be calculated.[2] Stocks with present values higher than their respective market prices are undervalued, whereas those selling at market prices higher than their present values are overvalued. Recognition of the existence of market disequilibria, where there is assumed to be a temporary divergence between present value and price, leads to the emergence of a unique market strategy: Buying undervalued stocks[3] when the market is in disequilibrium, and reversing the process when the equilibrium is restored, will always yield trading profits for the investor.[4] Furthermore, as explained in Chapter 12, if by undertaking technical analysis investors can improve their market timing for the purchase and sale of securities, they will increase their trading profits. Historically, this view of an inefficient capital market has been universally accepted.

In the late 1950s and the early 1960s, an important controversy developed concerning the process by which the prices of common stock are determined. Initially, a handful of academicians challenged the hypothesis that the market was inefficient—that is, that disequilibrium conditions could exist in the market and that successive changes in the prices of common stocks were dependent on each other and could be accurately predicted. Later, a great deal of statistical work was done on the subject, the outcome of which was the establishment of the *Efficient Market Hypothesis* (*EMH*).

Historical Development

The roots of the EMH date back to 1905.[5] However, the concept of efficiency was not systematically applied to the stock market until 1959,[6] when Roberts and Osborne published research suggesting that changes in stock prices were

[2] Because the interest payments and the maturity price are fixed, the present value of a bond can be calculated by estimating the appropriate discount rate. In the discussion that follows, the market strategy for dealing with stocks is assumed to be similar to that for dealing with bonds.

[3] Selling overvalued securities short will achieve similar results. However, short selling constitutes a somewhat complex process and is omitted from this discussion.

[4] The investor's profits would include dividends as well. However, for simplicity, dividends are excluded from this discussion.

[5] Karl Pearson and the Right Honorable Lord Rayleigh, "The Problem of the Random Walk," *Nature*, Vol. 72, No. 1865, pp. 294, 318, 342. In 1905, it was demonstrated that the most efficient

Figure 14–1

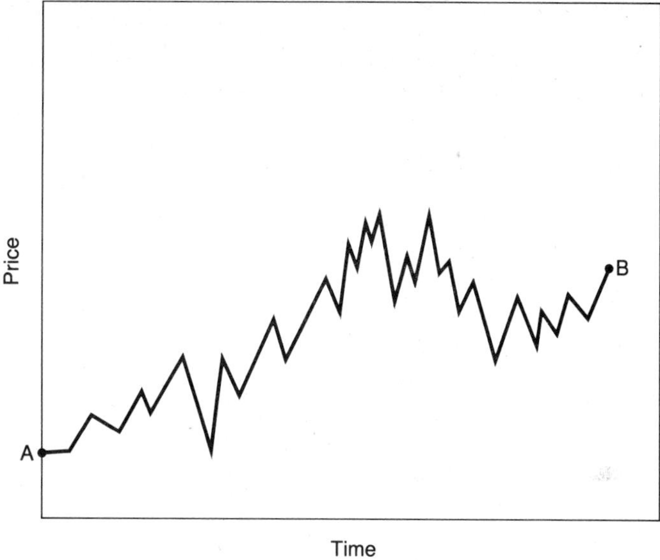

SOURCE: Adapted from Jerome L. Valentine, *Investment Analysis and Capital Market Theory* (Charlottesville, Va.: The Financial Analysts Research Foundation), 1975, p. 2.

random.[7] The work of Roberts and Osborne had major spin-offs in the academic world. Tests of the randomness of stock price changes by Moore (1962), Granger and Morgenstern (1963), Fama (1965), and others, supported Roberts and Osborne.

The way the concept of market efficiency was initially applied to the stock market is quite interesting. Assume a drunk is standing in a desert at point A and his objective is to move eastward. Because he is drunk, he takes short steps northeast or southeast, in a random fashion. After a while, when the drunk has reached point B, the pattern of his footprints in the sand might resemble the pattern in Figure 14–1. Now suppose that Figure 14–1 presents movements in the price of a stock. Because stock prices normally fluctuate within a narrow range and follow a long-term trend, this figure, which in fact represents the random walk of a drunk, also creates the appearance of a *rational* pattern of stock price behavior.

way to find a drunk in a vacant field after a lapse of time is to start the search at the point at which he was left. However, the idea of market efficiency differs significantly from that contained in the 1905 study.

[6] Harry V. Roberts, "Stock Market 'Patterns' and Financial Analysis: Methodological Suggestions," *Journal of Finance*, March 1959, pp. 1–10; M. F. M. Osborne, "Brownian Motion in the Stock Market," *Operations Research*, March–April 1959, pp. 145–73.

[7] The realization that stock prices might be randomly distributed was the basis for the development of the Random Walk Theory. This theory is discussed in the next section.

Figure 14–2

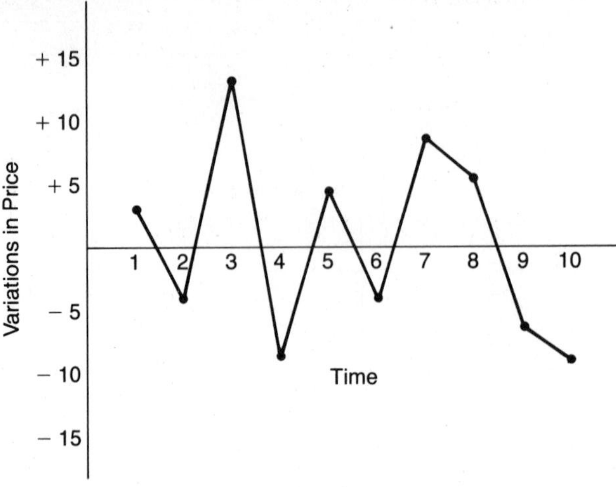

SOURCE: Adapted from Jerome L. Valentine, *Investment Analysis and Capital Market Theory* (Charlottesville, Va.: The Financial Analysts Research Foundation), 1975, p. 3.

Figure 14–3 **Levels of Stock Market Prices for 52 Weeks***

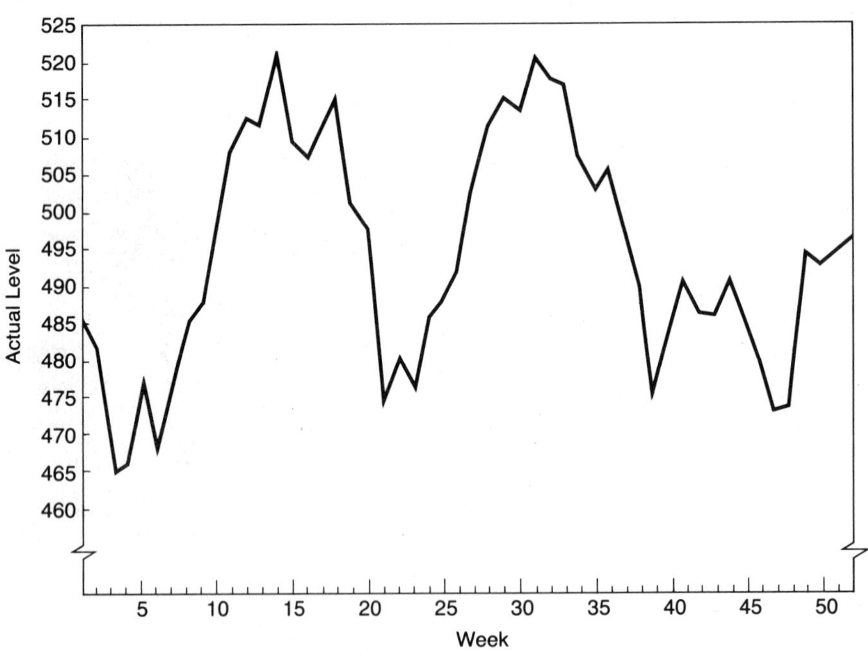

* Friday closing levels, December 30, 1955–December 28, 1956, Dow Jones Industrial Average

SOURCE: Harry V. Roberts, "Stock Market 'Patterns' and Financial Analysis: Methodological Suggestions," *Journal of Finance*, March 1959, pp. 5–6.

Figure 14–4 **Changes in Weekly Stock Prices for 52 Weeks***

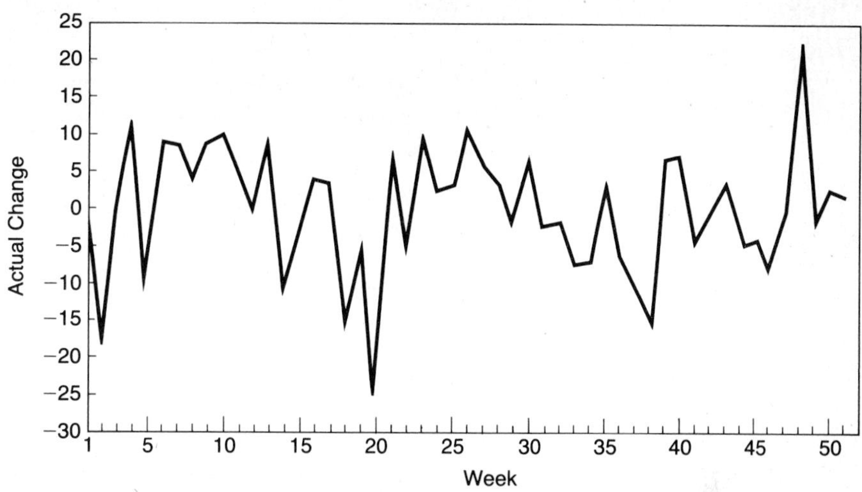

*Changes from Friday to Friday (closing) January 6, 1956–December 28, 1956, Dow Jones Industrial Average

SOURCE: Harry V. Roberts, "Stock Market 'Patterns' and Financial Analysis: Methodological Suggestions," *Journal of Finance*, March 1959, pp. 5–6.

After the first connection between a random walk and stock price movement was made, statistical tests were performed to determine the possibility of randomness of stock prices by examining the historical *changes* in, rather than the historical price *levels* of, stock prices.[8] Figure 14–2 presents the *changes* in the level of stock prices presented in Figure 14–1. Once again, the randomness in the changes in stock prices is evident.

Although the two figures presented above are hypothetical, the discussion need not be confined to the hypothetical world. Figure 14–3 presents actual *levels* of the DJIA during the period December 30, 1955 through December 28, 1956; Figure 14–4 presents *changes* in the DJIA during January 6, 1956 through December 6, 1956. These figures suggest that, to a large extent, stock prices fluctuate in a random fashion. It is not surprising, then, that the efficiency of the capital market has been consistently tested[9] and the results of such tests have been extensively analyzed in order to better understand the market efficiency issue.

[8] Investors are, of course, primarily interested in the rate of return from investing in a common stock, of which the percentage change in the stock price is a component.

[9] For a recent comprehensive statistical study, see Robert A. Schwartz and David K. Whitcomb, "Evidence on the Presence and Causes of Serial Correlation in Market Model Residuals," *Journal of Financial and Quantitative Analysis*, June 1977, pp. 291–313.

Tests of Market Efficiency

The controversy surrounding the market efficiency issue cannot be comprehended without a clear definition of an efficient market. The market is said to be efficient if it satisfies the following five conditions.[10]

1. Because transaction costs and taxes are negligible, the outcomes do not materially differ from the outcomes resulting from decisions made in a world with no taxes and transaction costs.
2. Investors who desire to buy or sell stocks are able to do so immediately without significantly affecting the prices of these stocks.
3. Investors behave in a rational manner by investing their money in securities yielding highest returns for a given stock.
4. There is an effective information flow—that is, new information spreads quickly among investors.
5. Stock prices change quickly in response to changes in new information—that is, the market price of a stock reflects all that is knowable about the related company.

Most of these conditions refer to the operational efficiency of the market. As mentioned in Chapter 3, the market is generally assumed to be operationally efficient. Consequently, tests of market efficiency have concentrated on the last category. More specifically, these tests have been conducted on three broad forms—the weak form, the semistrong form, and the strong form.

The weak form states that movements in stock prices are random in nature; consequently, investors do not stand to gain by studying the behavior of past stock prices. The semistrong form asserts that the current stock prices reflect all publicly available information possessed by investors. Furthermore, because new information becomes available only randomly, a systematic movement in stock prices should not be expected. The strong form is based on the assumption that the price of a stock not only reflects all publicly available information, but reflects the information that is possessed only by corporate insiders and by super analysts.

The Weak Form

Basic Characteristics

The weak form of the EMH has also been characterized as similar to the *Random Walk Hypothesis* (*RWH*). The weak form implies that knowledge of the past fluctuations in stock prices does not help investors to improve their

[10] Charles D. Kuehner, "Efficient Markets and Random Walk," in Sumner N. Levine, Ed., *Financial Analyst's Handbook* (Homewood, Ill.: Dow Jones–Irwin, 1975), pp. 1227–28. © 1975 by Dow Jones–Irwin, Inc.

performance. The RWH suggests that stock prices move randomly around a trend line based on anticipated earnings power.[11] That is, the proponents of the RWH contend that (1) analyzing past data does not enable the analyst to forecast the movement of stock prices around the trend line, and (2) new information affecting stock prices enters the market in a random fashion and therefore cannot be consistently predicted.

In essence, then, the RWH says that the market is both an information network and an institution for buying and selling securities. Because an investor has almost no chance of acquiring information that is not already known to the market, the RWH asserts that the prices of stocks already reflect everything that can be known about these stocks. An investor can still buy "risky" or "safe" stocks, but there is little reason to believe that he or she can buy them more intelligently than the remainder of the public. These views are articulated in the following precise definition: "The [Random Walk] Hypothesis holds that all price changes are serially independent; that trends are spurious or imaginary manifestations; and that tools of technical analysis such as charts or the Dow Theory are without investment value."[12]

Let there be no misunderstanding, however. RWH does *not* deny the possibility of predicting long-term upward trends in stock prices. However, it requires that short-term fluctuations in stock prices be random. Therefore, the RWH is of special interest to technical analysts who attempt to profit by devising methods of predicting future prices in the short run on the basis of the "signals" discernible in market movements.

Survey of Evidence[13]

As will shortly become evident, of the three forms of the EMH, the weak form has been subjected to the most intensive scrutiny. The reason for this is fairly obvious. The validity of the weak form only suggests that technical analysis is without value; it leaves open the possibility for realizing gains in the stock market by undertaking fundamental investment strategies. In contrast, the validity of the other two forms implies that no such gains can be realized even when fundamental analysis is used. The academic community has been much more willing to test the weak form than the other two forms, because it is acceptable to security analysts (and perhaps because it is easier to test).

Empirical analysis of the weak form has been concerned with both testing for independence in stock price changes and determining whether the past history of prices provides information that can be used to predict their future movements and thus provide the basis for a profitable trading rule. These

[11] Sidney Robbins, *The Securities Markets* (New York: Free Press, 1966), pp. 44–47.

[12] F. E. James, "Moving Monthly Averages—an Effective Investment Tool?" *Journal of Financial and Quantitative Analysis*, September 1968, p. 315.

[13] After suitable editing, this section, and the two surveys of evidence relating to semistrong and strong forms, are reproduced from Neil G. Beckerman, "A Primer on Random Walks in the Stock Market," *New England Economic Review*, Federal Reserve Bank of Boston, September–October, 1978, pp. 39–45.

issues are closely related, of course; if price changes are random, it will be impossible to predict future changes from past changes. Nevertheless, it is worth considering the tests separately, because the basic technique applied in trading rule tests is also widely used in tests of market efficiency generally.

The most straightforward test for independence has been the "runs" test,[14] which measured the stock price changes during the 1928–64 period in terms of the last day of the month closing values of the S&P Composite Index. The observed probabilities were 0.59 for a price increase and 0.41 for a price decrease.[15] Under the assumptions that these probabilities hold for the period

[14] A run is defined as a sequence of one or more price changes of the same sign. For example, replacing the numerical value of price changes with a "+" when the change is positive and with a "−" when the change is negative, the sequence "− − − + − + + −" consists of five runs. For given probabilities of a stock price increase or decrease, if positive changes tend to be followed by positive changes and negative changes by further negative changes, then the number of runs in a particular price series will be less than if the changes are independent. Similarly, if there is a tendency for positive changes to be followed by negative changes, then the number of runs will be greater than if the changes are independent.

[15] Of the 442 price changes observed during this period, 259 were increases and 183 were decreases. Therefore, an estimate of the probability of a price increase is 259/442 = .59 and of a price decrease is 183/442 = .41.

The Concept of Efficient Markets[†]

One form of an efficient market, the so-called "weak form," in which the "information" is only the history of the price itself, can be stated quite simply as:

$$E(P_{t+j} | P_t, P_{t-1}, P_{t-2}, \ldots) = E(P_{t+j} | P_t) \qquad \textbf{(14–A)}$$

Equation 14–A states that the mathematical expectations, E, of the Price, P, to prevail j periods hence (P_{t+j}), given our knowledge of the current price and the previous history of this price, is precisely equal to the expected value of the price j periods hence given only the knowledge of the current price. In other words, knowledge of past prices is irrelevant. Alternative definitions of market efficiency differ primarily by extending the range of information upon which the expectations of the future price in Equation 14–A is made conditional. In addition, a more concrete notion of market efficiency would suggest that, the probability density function of the future security price, given the market's set of information, is equal to the true density function of the future price, given the available information.

The efficient market theory, however, says more than Equation 14–A. Let us define the information available to the market at time t as Z_t. Then, if the market is efficient,

$$E(P^*_{t+j} | Z_t) = P_t \qquad \textbf{(14–B)}$$

[†] Joseph Bisignano, "Inflation and the Efficiency of Capital Markets," Federal Reserve Bank of San Francisco, Summer 1976.

1965–77 and that price changes are random, the expected number of runs in the latter period is 76.5.[16] The actual number of runs was 73, well within the expected range for standard levels of statistical significance. Therefore, the result of this runs test suggests that one should accept the hypothesis that the sequence of monthly price changes between 1965 and 1977 is random.

Another popular method of analyzing stock prices is to estimate the correlation coefficient between successive price changes over a long period of time. The Random Walk Model argues that because the sign and the magnitude of

[16] The expected number of runs was calculated as follows: There were 156 months in the 1965–77 period. Assuming the probabilities of an increase and a decrease of .59 and .41, respectively, 92 price increases and 64 price decreases are expected. Under the null hypothesis that the changes are random, the expected number of runs is then computed as:

$$\frac{2(92)(64)}{(92 + 64)} + 1 = 76.5$$

with a standard deviation of 6.02:

$$\sqrt{\frac{2(92)(64)[2(92)(64) - 92 - 64]}{(156)^2(155)}} = 6.02$$

---

where the * denotes that the future price is a random variable; that is, not known with certainty. If we define the change in the future price from time t, we have

$$\Delta P^*_{t+j} = PU_{t+j} - P_t \quad \textbf{(14–C)}$$

From Equation 14–B and Equation 14–C it is clear that the expected price change, given the information available, Z_t, is equal to zero,

$$E(\Delta PU_{t+j} | Z_t) = 0 \quad \textbf{(14–D)}$$

While the above concepts of market efficiency may appear somewhat esoteric, they are important concepts for enhancing our general understanding of financial markets. Equation 14–B, for example, states that in an efficient market the current price is an unbiased estimate of the future price. It also implies that successive changes in the price of the security ought to be uncorrelated, that is, statistically unrelated. Indeed, a wealth of information on stock market prices indicates that the equity market is efficient under these definitions. In recent years, a number of nontechnical publications have stressed this notion that prices in the stock market follow a "random walk"; that is, successive price changes are independent. Although this concept is not formally equivalent to the statement that the stock market is an efficient market, it says something very similar. The general point is the same—the market incorporates price information in such a manner that one cannot exploit this information in a systematic fashion to make a profit.

price changes from period to period are unrelated, the correlation between them should be zero. The estimated correlation coefficients between successive monthly, quarterly, and yearly changes in the S&P Composite Index for the 1928–77 period are all quite small in absolute value, and none is different from zero in the statistical sense. Furthermore, the percentage of the variability of current price change explained by its correlation with the previous change is virtually zero. The correlation between successive price changes in this Index, therefore, provides no information useful for prediction. Consequently, the results of the test also support the Random Walk Model.

The goal of a trading rule test is to determine whether information on past stock prices and trading volumes can be used to earn profits greater than could be earned without the information. In other words, can information about the past history of a stock's price be used to earn profits greater than would be earned if one just bought the stock and held it? An archetypal chartist trading scheme that has been tested in this way is the *filter rule*.[17] Under this rule, if its price increases by x percent, a stock is purchased and held until its price declines by x percent from a subsequent high, at which time the trader simultaneously sells and goes short, covering his or her position when the price increases by x percent from a subsequent low. Price movements of less than x percent are ignored. For filters ranging in size from 0.5 to 1.5 percent, this rule generates greater profits than are earned if the stock is simply purchased at the beginning of the sample period and sold at the end—but *only* if the transactions costs (commissions, clearinghouse fees, and so on) incurred in pursuing the strategy are not taken into account. When these costs are included—and they are substantial due to the frequent trades produced by small filters—the trader always does better under the buy-and-hold alternative.[18]

Numerous runs, correlation, and trading rule tests have been conducted, none yielding results substantially different from those reviewed here. Because it is impossible to analyze every conceivable trading rule for every available stock, skeptics will always have reason to remain unconvinced; but the weight

[17] This trading strategy is very similar to the popular Dow Theory, a chartist scheme intended to identify price trends. Detailed analysis of the profitability of such trading rules may be found in Sidney S. Alexander, "Price Movements in Speculative Markets: Trends or Random Walks," *Industrial Management Review*, May 1961, pp. 7–26, and in Eugene F. Fama and Marshall Blume, "Filter Rules and Stock Market Trading Profits," *Journal of Business*, Special Supplement, January 1966, pp. 226–41.

[18] The fact that this chartist strategy can be used to earn "abnormal" returns in the absence of transactions costs is evidence against a strict random walk in stock prices, because it indicates a tendency for positive correlation in successive price changes. On the other hand, the departure from randomness is too slight to be useful as a forecasting device, because the excess profits available as a result of the observed correlation do not cover the costs involved in trying to exploit it. Indeed, although the Random Walk Model appears to hold only as a very close approximation to actual price behavior, the stock market is evidently extremely efficient in incorporating the information contained in past price changes into current price. Patterns in a price series are smoothed until any remaining patterns are not worth exploiting because of transactions costs. If transactions costs were zero, one would therefore expect stock prices to follow a random walk precisely.

of the evidence clearly favors acceptance of the Random Walk Model and the presence of market efficiency with respect to the information contained in the history of stock prices.[19]

The Semistrong Form

Basic Characteristics

Investigations of the semistrong form of the Efficient Market Hypothesis are concerned with the extent to which future prices can be predicted with the help of fundamental analysis. Like supporters of the weak form, proponents of the semistrong form assert that the current price of the stock contains all available information possessed by investors and that, because new information becomes available only randomly, there should be no reason to expect any systematic movement in stock returns. However, semistrong form supporters also argue that the current stock price fully reflects the information which only sophisticated analysis of fundamental factors can uncover. This argument implies that there is little point in engaging in fundamental analysis, because the market is so efficient that it reflects all publicly known fundamental factors.

> *The assertion that a market is efficient is vastly stronger than the assertion that successive changes in stock prices are independent of each other. The latter assertion—the weak form of the efficient market hypothesis—merely says that the current prices of stocks fully reflect all that is implied by the historical sequence of prices so that a knowledge of that sequence is of no value in forming expectations about future prices. The assertion that a market is efficient implies that current prices reflect and impound not only all of the implications of the historical sequence of prices but also all that is knowable about the companies whose stocks are being traded. This stronger assertion has proved to be especially unacceptable to the financial community, since it suggests the fruitlessness of efforts to earn superior rates of returns by the analysis of all public information. Although some members of the financial community were willing to accept the implications of the weaker assertion about the randomness of price changes and thereby to give up technical analysis, almost no members of the community were willing to accept implications of the stronger form and thereby to give up fundamental analysis.*[20]

The preceding quotation suggests that the semistrong form represents a direct challenge to fundamental analysis on the evaluation of publicly available data.

---

[19] It is unlikely that anyone who has discovered a profitable trading rule will ever make it public, because by doing so the profitability of the system will be quickly eliminated.

[20] James H. Lorie and Mary T. Hamilton, *The Stock Market: Theories and Evidence* (Homewood, Ill.: Richard D. Irwin, 1973), pp. 80–81. © 1973 by Richard D. Irwin, Inc.

Survey of Evidence

Tests of the semistrong form of market efficiency must begin with the selection of an appropriate bit of information from the vast array of available data to which stock prices might react. One technique that is widely used for assessing price responses to new information is based on the "Market Model."[21] This model posits a stable relationship between the returns on a stock during a period of time and the returns on the market portfolio (generally represented by a broad-based index) during the same time period. The estimated coefficient between the returns on a stock and the returns on the market portfolio—the beta coefficient—is then a measure of the riskiness of that stock relative to movements in the market as a whole. For example, changes in the returns on a stock with a beta of one, on average, tend to be the same as the changes in the return on the market as a whole. Similarly, changes in the returns on another stock with a beta of 1.5, on average, tend to change more than proportionately to changes in the return on the overall market. Investment advisers have found estimated betas to be useful in the construction of stock portfolios tailored to the individual risk tolerance of their clients. Efficient market researchers, however, have used the model for another purpose. Given both the observed returns on the market portfolio during a particular time period and a set of betas for various stocks estimated from historical data, the Market Model can be used to estimate the *normal* returns expected to accrue to each stock on the basis of its relationship with the overall market during that period. Because returns on individual stocks are also influenced by many firm-specific factors not captured by returns on the market portfolio, deviations of actual returns from those predicted by the model are to be expected. These deviations from normal returns in the period surrounding the announcement of new information can be used to measure the extent and the timing of the price reaction required for testing market efficiency.

One famous application of this technique examined the deviations from normal returns for a large sample of firms that had announced a coming stock split.[22] Examination of the cumulative deviations from normal returns for each stock for a period beginning 30 months prior to the announcement of the coming split and ending 30 months after the announcement revealed the following consistent pattern: The cumulative deviations increased *prior* to the announcement of the intended split and became flat on the announcement date and thereafter. Three important conclusions follow from this observation.

[21] See William F. Sharpe, "Capital Asset Prices: A Theory of Market Equilibrium Under Conditions of Risk," *Journal of Finance*, September 1964, pp. 425–42; John Lintner, "Security Prices, Risk, and Maximal Gains from Diversification," *Journal of Finance*, December 1965, pp. 587–615; and John Lintner, "The Valuation of Risk Assets and the Selection of Risky Investments in Stock Portfolios and Capital Budgets," *Review of Economics and Statistics*, February 1965, pp. 13–37. The seminal contributions in the development of the risk–return framework of portfolio analysis are by James Tobin, "Liquidity Preference as Behavior Towards Risk," *Review of Economic Studies*, February 1958, pp. 65–85 and Harry Markowitz, *Portfolio Selection: Efficient Diversification of Investment* (New York: John Wiley and Sons, 1959).

[22] See Eugene F. Fama, et al., "The Adjustment of Stock Prices to New Information," *International Economic Review*, February 1969, pp. 1–21.

First, the market evidently *anticipates* the split announcement, because returns in excess of those expected from the relationship of each stock to the market are present before the information is made public. Second, the information is completely reflected in price by the time the split is announced, because deviations from normal behavior cease to accumulate on that date. Third, the adjustment of stock prices to the new information is unbiased, because the cumulative deviations neither increase nor decrease in the 30 months after the announcement. Therefore, once a coming split has been publicly announced, the stock's price fully reflects this information and no further abnormal returns can be expected.

Efficient market tests such as this have been conducted for many other kinds of publicly available information; the conclusion that published data cannot be used to earn abnormal returns has rarely been refuted.[23] However, after the announcement of new information, trends in the cumulative deviations from normal returns (sufficient to more than cover the transactions costs) have occasionally been detected. Consequently, as in the case of the Random Walk Model, insofar as published information is concerned, there are exceptions to the Efficient Market Hypothesis. Such potentially profitable situations cannot be expected to be repeated, however, because their discovery will inevitably lead to their exploitation and consequent disappearance.[24] In any event, the weight of current evidence strongly favors market efficiency with respect to published information.

The Strong Form

Basic Characteristics

The strong form of the EMH is based on the assumption that stock prices reflect not only all publicly available information, but the information possessed *only* by corporate insiders and super analysts. Tests of the strong form "are concerned with whether all available information is fully reflected in prices in the sense that no individual unit has higher expected trading profits than others because he has monopolistic access to some information."[25]

[23] These studies are too numerous to cite here in toto. The volumes edited by James Lorie and Richard Brealey, *Modern Developments in Investment Management* (New York: Praeger, 1972) contain many early examples. In addition, nearly every issue of *The Journal of Finance*, *The Journal of Business*, and *The Journal of Financial and Quantitative Analysis* contains a new study of market efficiency. Two recent studies that fail to support the efficient market hypothesis are Stewart L. Brown, "Earnings Changes, Stock Prices, and Market Efficiency," *Journal of Finance*, March 1978, pp. 17–28 and Peter Lloyd Davies and Michael Canes, "Stock Prices and the Publication of Second Hand Information," *Journal of Business*, January 1978, pp. 43–56.

[24] This is a testable proposition. Because tests of market efficiency must of necessity be based on historical data (so that price adjustments can be observed both before and after the announcement of new information), studies which uncover an apparent departure from efficiency can be performed again as more recent information becomes available to determine if the profitable situation still exists.

[25] E. F. Fama, "Efficient Capital Markets: A Review of the Theory and Empirical Work," *Journal of Finance*, May 1970, p. 409.

The strong form of the EMH is extremely rigid. Its supporters assert that they could consider this form valid even if the super analysts can demonstrate that they can outperform the market some of the time:

> *Even if half of the professional money managers outperform the market as a whole, the market conforms to the strong form of efficiency as long as they do not generate superior results* consistently. *That is, in a strong form market, up to half of the time money managers could outperform the market as a whole, if only during the remainder of the time their performance was inferior to the general market.*[26]

Consequently, the strong form of EMH constitutes a direct challenge to the most knowledgeable segment of the investment community—institutional investors and professional money managers.

Survey of Evidence

Tests on the Market Model show a strong trend in stock price movements prior to the announcement of new information. This suggests that abnormal returns are being earned by someone during this period. This, in turn, suggests that the market is probably not efficient with respect to information not generally available, because the transactions of those few investors with access to the knowledge, either directly or through forecasts, must be the source of this abnormal return behavior. Indeed, this group causes the market to be efficient with respect to *available* information by impounding it in stock prices before it is made public. Theoretically, because price adjustments in an efficient market should be essentially instantaneous, the observed long and gradual adjustment may be viewed as the combined result of the slow dissemination of "inside" information and the limited financial resources of those who possess it. Still, in the absence of a complete monopoly over inside information, it is unlikely that any individual or group can consistently reap these excess returns. Because reliable data on insider trading is naturally difficult to obtain, only indirect tests of this form of the Efficient Market Hypothesis have been attempted.

One study compared the returns on a sample of mutual fund portfolios with those on unmanaged but equally risky (that is, having the same beta) portfolios for the period 1955–64.[27] The idea was to determine if portfolios managed by professional investors (who as a group might reasonably be expected to have superior insight into the significance of publicly available information as well as access to information not widely known by the general public) could outperform portfolios "managed" under a naive buy-and-hold

[26] Dan Dorfman, "Why Can't Research Directors Hold Their Jobs?" *Institutional Investor*, October 1973, pp. 48–50ff. Italics supplied.

[27] See Michael C. Jensen, "The Performance of Mutual Funds in the Period 1945–64," *Journal of Finance*, May 1968, pp. 389–416.

strategy. Only 26 of the 115 funds examined earned returns averaged over the entire period in excess of those produced by the naive strategy; the average return for all sample funds was well below that earned by the corresponding unmanaged portfolios. Furthermore, none of the funds could consistently beat the market; those which did so in one part of the sample period were unable to do so in another part. This important group of traders therefore did not appear to have continued access to information not already reflected in market prices.[28]

A Summary View

Extensive empirical analysis of stock price data has shown fairly convincingly that price changes follow a random walk and that new information is reflected in prices by the time it is publicly announced.[29] Significant price adjustments that occur prior to the release of new data suggest that market participants formulate and act on forecasts of coming events, as required by the assumption underlying the EMH, although it is doubtful that any one group is consistently able to earn the extraordinary returns available during this anticipatory period of adjustment. The stock market is apparently efficient in the narrow sense that it removes exploitable patterns in price series themselves and in the broader sense that current prices fully reflect other publicly available information.[30]

---

[28] These results may be sensitive to the particular definition of returns and to the form of the model used in the test. For a discussion of these issues, see Norman E. Mains, "Risk, the Pricing of Capital Assets, and the Evaluation of Investment Portfolios: Comment," *Journal of Business*, July 1977, pp. 371–84.

[29] Some studies have shown the existence of a certain degree of inefficiency in the market. For example, one study which investigated the impact of public announcements on quarterly earnings by analyzing prices and earnings for 96 firms during the 1963–68 period, revealed evidence of substantially increased earnings. See O. Maurice Joy, Robert H. Litzenberger, and Richard W. McEnally, "The Adjustment of Stock Prices to Announcements of Unanticipated Changes in Quarterly Earnings," *Journal of Accounting Research*, Autumn 1977, pp. 207–25. However, the weight of current evidence is still in favor of market efficiency.

[30] Several arguments are frequently advanced by the mutual fund community against the strong form; three of these follow. First, some superior fund managers will outperform their colleagues, at least over the short term. One of the fallacies of academic research is that it is typically conducted over a long period of time, during which the portfolio manager who made a fund successful may have moved on to a better job. We know of one estimate showing that money managers move, on average, every three years. Management ability is what is being analyzed. Second, there are valid reasons why funds like Dreyfus were outstanding performers in their early years, but not now. In the case cited, the increased size alone changed the fund's character. With $1.4 billion and about 200 common stocks in its portfolio now, it is not surprising that Dreyfus has slowed down. Third, we don't expect the same funds to be on top *every* year because we know aggressive funds will be top-rated in bull market years and conservative funds top rated in bear market years. To be even more precise, funds that have a policy of holding quality stocks will do better in one segment of a bull market, whereas funds holding speculative issues will shine in a different segment of a bull market.

Still, even though there are some superior performers, the vast majority of money managers, over the long run, are not likely to significantly better the averages adjusted for risk. Of course, this in no way implies that the professionals who "run" money are unskilled and incompetent. Quite the contrary, this form of the EMH has validity precisely because the pros are skilled and adept at finding values in the market when they exist.

The current status of the market efficiency debate is articulated by Lorie and Brealey, two founding fathers of the EMH:

> *It is extremely unlikely, in principle, that the efficient market hypothesis is strictly true, particularly in its strongest form. For example, as long as information is not wholly free, one might expect investors to require some offsetting gain before they are willing to purchase it. Nor does the empirical evidence justify unqualified acceptance of the efficient-market hypothesis even in its weakest form. The important question, therefore, is not whether the theory is universally true, but whether it is sufficiently correct to provide useful insights into market behavior. There is now overwhelming evidence to suggest that the random walk hypothesis is such a close approximation to reality that technical analysis cannot provide any guidance to the investment manager. When one turns to the stronger forms of the hypothesis, the evidence becomes less voluminous and the correspondence between theory and reality less exact. Nevertheless, the overriding impression is that of a highly competitive and efficient marketplace in which the opportunities for superior performance are rare.*[31]

Implications of the EMH

Security Analysis and Portfolio Management

Successful portfolio management in an efficient market depends not only on the portfolio manager's skills, but on the quality of inputs he or she receives from security analysts. Security analysis and portfolio management are intimately related. *Security analysis* refers to the determination of the present value of a security or the determination of its expected return and its degree of risk. Techniques for analyzing bonds and stocks were presented in Parts 2 and 3, respectively, in which we noted that securities whose present values are higher than their respective market prices are undervalued and therefore provide investors with attractive investment opportunities. *Portfolio management* refers to the handling of a pool of investible funds so that it yields an appropriate return consistent with the risk associated with the portfolio. Naturally, portfolio management includes *portfolio construction*—the selection of stocks and bonds to be included in the initial portfolio. As previously mentioned, selection of securities is the prime responsibility of the security analyst who makes selections on the basis of security values determined by fundamental analysis. The manager then completes the process by selecting from the set those securities that, as a group, meet the portfolio's predetermined risk–return criterion.

[31] James H. Lorie and Richard Brealey, *Modern Developments in Investment Management* (New York: Praeger, 1972), p. 102.

Construction of the initial portfolio, of course, completes only the initial phase of the task. The manager must continuously *manage* the portfolio in order to maximize the return, given the level of the risk assumed. Portfolio management also involves changing the asset mix in the portfolio in response to (1) unsatisfactory performance, (2) a change in the investor's risk preference, (3) a change in market conditions, or (4) changes in the characteristics of the assets themselves.

Types of Management

Even if the strong form of the EMH is discarded as being too rigid and unrealistic, the validity of the other two forms suggests that it is extremely difficult to "beat the market." The critical questions therefore become: What should be the objective of portfolio management? How should the ideal role of a portfolio manager be defined? These two questions are not easy to answer, because not everyone agrees with the results of the tests of the weak and semistrong forms. Nevertheless, in response to the debate on market efficiency, two types of portfolio management have emerged—passive management and active management.

Passive Management

Passive management accepts all forms of the EMH. That is, the concept accepts the premise that the market is so efficient that it is nearly impossible to construct a portfolio superior to the market portfolio. Therefore, it is asserted, an investor can do no better than to hold the market portfolio, either in its entirety or some fraction of it, depending on the investor's available resources. Therefore, the primary task of a passive portfolio manager should be to decide whether to convert the market portfolio into a leveraged or a lending portfolio in order to achieve the level of portfolio risk desired by the investor. Furthermore, he or she should reevaluate or reorganize the portfolio only when there is a change in either the investor's utility function or the market portfolio.

Active Management

Not everyone accepts the weak form and the semistrong form of the EMH. Those who reject the semistrong form maintain that by applying professional analytical skills a manager can construct a portfolio superior to the market portfolio. More specifically, through fundamental analysis an active manager first identifies undervalued securities. By selecting a group of stocks from this set, the active manager constructs a portfolio with an asset mix *different* from that of the market portfolio. Because this portfolio consists of undervalued securities, it is argued, with active management it will consistently outperform the market portfolio.

Despite numerous studies supporting the weak form of the EMH, many security analysts and portfolio managers still reject this form, thereby ratcheting portfolio management up to a still higher level. These managers assert that one can outperform the market by "timing" the market as well—that is, by predicting when the market or a given security is overbought or oversold, and acting quickly to capitalize on that information. This type of management is based on technical analysis. Therefore, portfolio managers who totally reject the EMH use both the fundamental and technical analysis as the basis for developing their active investment strategies.

The Portfolio Management Issue

Proponents of the EMH prefer passive management, whereas those who reject the EMH are likely to prefer active portfolio management. The techniques of both passive and active managements will be presented in Section 2. Although active management may involve both fundamental and technical analysis, the presentation will center solely around the former, because most important portfolio management is related to the semistrong form of the EMH and fundamental analysis.

SECTION 2 PORTFOLIO CONSTRUCTION AND MANAGEMENT

Passive Investment Strategies

Its Nature

The passive investment strategy, or the passive portfolio management, is based on the *Separation Theorem*. As discussed in Chapter 13, the theorem suggests that the market portfolio contains the ideal mix of securities, and that investors can make no better *investment* decision than to buy and hold all the securities included in the market portfolio. They may, however, decide to hold leveraged or lending portfolios, if their individual risk preferences differ from the degree of risk associated with the market portfolio.

The passive strategy requires no security analysis. This strategy requires an investor to hold the market portfolio, levered up by borrowing or loaned up by mixing the market portfolio with riskless assets. Only when there is a change in either the individual risk preference or the risk–return composition of the market portfolio should the passive manager be induced to reorganize the individual portfolio. Simply stated, a passive investment strategy requires a portfolio manager (hereafter called the PM) to construct and maintain a portfolio that falls on the Capital Market Line at all times. Although this strategy will never enable the passive manager to beat the market, it will ensure that the performance of his or her portfolio will approximately equal that of the market. Furthermore, by holding the market portfolio, the manager will drastically reduce both transactions and research costs. This is the essence of the passive investment strategy.

The role of a passive PM may now be summarized:[32]

1. Determination of the appropriate level of risk for the portfolio under management.
2. Achievement of the desired level of risk by constructing a portfolio of well-diversified common stocks which is either dampened through inclusion of riskless assets or levered by purchasing on margin.
3. Periodic review of the appropriateness of the level of risk.
4. Maintenance of the desired level of risk through portfolio reorganization.
5. Management of additions to, and deletions from, the portfolio in order to minimize taxes and provide for either necessary additional investment or reduction of investment in order to make disbursements.
6. Minimization of transaction costs.

Passive Management in the Real World

The notion that one cannot beat the stock market averages, but that there is a way to beat the professional money managers, has now been tested for several years through the management of *index funds*. These funds are merely portfolios that duplicate broad stock market averages such as the S&P 500. Many banks, investment management organizations, and corporate pension funds regularly invest their money in index funds as a matter of policy.

To be sure, duplicating the performance of the S&P 500 is not as simple as it might seem. Once a fund is set up, it can easily get out of balance with the S&P 500, because the weights of the companies in the index change whenever one of them sells new shares or repurchases its outstanding shares. In addition, dividends must be reinvested, yet they come in quantities too small to be spread across all 500 stocks. These difficulties make it impossible to match the S&P 500 precisely; however, it is fairly easy to *approximate* its performance closely.

Of the many institutions that construct index funds, three institutions that popularized the idea in their formative years are the Wells Fargo Bank in San Francisco, the American National Bank and Trust Company of Chicago, and Batterymarch Financial Management Corporation of Boston. Each differs significantly in its approach to the construction of index funds, as will be clear from the following discussion.[33]

Wells Fargo matches the S&P 500 by buying all the stocks in the index except the 17 it feels obliged to screen out as imprudent. The annual total return of its fund is expected to be within 100 basis points (1 percentage point) of the S&P 500 95 percent of the time and within 50 basis points two-thirds of the time. Any deviations between the index fund and the S&P 500 will be random—that is, they are as likely to be on the plus side as on the minus side.

Batterymarch uses a distinctly different method. It buys approximately 250 of the largest stocks in the S&P 500. These make up more than 90 percent of the

[32] James Lorie and Mary Hamilton, *The Stock Market: Theories and Evidence* (Homewood, Ill.: Richard D. Irwin, 1973), p. 109. © 1973 by Richard D. Irwin, Inc.
[33] A. F. Ehrbar, "Index Funds—An Idea Whose Time is Coming," *Fortune*, June 1976, p. 152.

Table 14–1 **Quarterly Returns for Index Funds and S&P 500: 1974–77**

Qtr./yr.	American National Bank	Batterymarch Financial	Wells Fargo	S&P 500
1/74	−2.80		−2.92	−2.81
2/74	−7.43		−7.90	−7.54
3/74	−25.62		−25.11	−25.05
4/74	9.04		9.13	9.41
Year	−27.02		−26.93	−26.03
1/75	23.40	21.3	22.56	22.90
2/75	15.67	14.9	15.24	15.31
3/75	−11.12	−11.0	−10.95	−10.93
4/75	8.64	8.7	8.76	8.64
Year	37.65	34.8	36.36	36.92
1/76	14.89	14.8	14.82	14.96
2/76	2.67	2.8	2.53	2.44
3/76	2.06	1.8	1.71	1.89
4/76	2.11	2.2	3.24	3.18
Year	22.93	22.8	23.63	23.64
1/77	−8.16	−7.4	−7.50	−7.44
2/77	3.07	3.2	3.31	3.28
3/77	−2.88	2.8	−2.77	−2.80
4/77	−0.09	−0.3	−0.11	−0.13
Year	−8.15	−7.4	−7.19	−7.17

SOURCE: Standard & Poor's. Reprinted by permission.

index's weight and are expected to produce results nearly as good as Wells Fargo's. However, the deviations are not random; the Batterymarch index funds will probably be up slightly less than the S&P 500 in good years and down slightly less in bad years, because the 250 largest stocks are not as risky as the 250 smallest.

American National uses still another method. Like Batterymarch, it buys approximately 250 of the S&P 500 stocks, but they are not all the largest. American National uses what is known as a "stratified sampling" method to select its stocks. The companies in the S&P 500 are divided into ten groups on the basis of their weights and risk levels. A computer then selects from among the ten groups to build a portfolio with the overall risk characteristics and industry diversification of the S&P 500, in much the same way that pollsters find a representative cross section of people to interview.

The performance of the three funds for the period 1974–77 is presented in Table 14–1. The table clearly reveals that these funds succeeded in almost matching market performance, thereby lending substantial credence to the argument that passive management provides managers with a viable investment strategy.

It should be emphasized that the passive investment strategy has by no means been accepted as the only market strategy. Many investors—especially professional money managers and institutional investors—firmly believe that the rewards of active money management exceed its attendant limitations. For them, there is no alternative to the development of active investment strategies aimed at *beating the market.*

Active Investment Strategies

Active investment managers reject the idea that the market portfolio is the most desirable. They assert that by applying superior technical and analytical skills it is possible to construct a portfolio which, if properly managed, will consistently outperform the market. In this section, the method of constructing an active management portfolio will be presented. Later, the technique for managing such a portfolio will be discussed.

Portfolio Construction

In constructing an efficient portfolio, managers employ a wide variety of investment philosophies and procedures. Some managers particularly emphasize those industrial sectors which they believe to be attractive; others confine their efforts to individual stock selection techniques. Still others concentrate on securities of a specific investment grade, such as growth company or income stocks. In fact, there may be as many methods of constructing a portfolio as there are portfolio managers. The method of portfolio construction described here is consistent with the modern portfolio theory; a summary of the key elements of the theory follows.

In Chapter 13, we noted that the *Capital Market Line* (*CML*) is the straight line on which all efficient portfolios lie and that the market portfolio has the optimum mix of risky assets. The superimposition of an investor's risk preference *indifference curve* on the CML determines the ideal mix of risky and risk-free assets for that investor. We also indicated that it is the *Security Market Line* (*SML*)—not the CML—which is used as the basis for selecting undervalued securities and portfolios. The modern portfolio theory asserts that unsystematic risk can be diversified away by constructing an efficient portfolio; consequently, investors should only be concerned with systematic risk, of which beta is the appropriate measure. The SML relates beta to expected return, and is a straight line on which both individual securities and efficient portfolios can lie. It follows, therefore, that because the SML is the locus of all points generated by the expected returns associated with their respective betas, at equilibrium all returns *should* theoretically fall on the SML. When the market is at a disequilibrium, however, returns of undervalued securities or portfolios will lie above the SML, and the returns of overvalued securities or portfolios will appear below the SML. The task of the PM, then, is to construct a portfolio by including in it an appropriate mix of undervalued securities which will put the portfolio in the desired risk category. That is, such a portfolio will have the desired risk and will have the potential for outperforming the market.

Within this theoretical framework, an active management portfolio can be constructed by following seven specific steps. These steps represent in large degree the basic investment management approach developed by Detroit Bank and Trust Company, who provided much of the following data and analytical methodology.

Step 1: The Stock Universe

A *stock universe* is the group of securities that security analysts are directed to analyze as the first step toward the construction of an initial portfolio. Conceptually, *all* securities trading on the market constitute the stock universe. However, such a universe would be inoperational and unwieldy, even for large institutional managers. Consequently, a method must be found to reduce the universe to a manageable size.

Clearly, no single selection process is generally acceptable. Some portfolio managers may choose stocks from selected industries; others may prefer to mix relatively stable stocks with volatile securities. Still others may like to concentrate on stocks of small and medium-size companies with high growth potential. Of these seemingly diverse processes for stock universe selection, one approach has a special appeal for large institutional managers. Of necessity, these managers command huge financial resources and must trade in large volumes. They must, therefore, be concerned with influencing the market prices of given stocks when these high volume transactions are effected. Consequently, as a matter of practical efficiency, PMs of large institutions, trust and pension funds primarily choose to include stocks of large corporations in their stock universe.

Having defined the criteria for selecting securities for the stock universe, the PM must address the issue of the number of different securities to be included in the universe. Although the maxim "the bigger the better" generally applies in this case, the critical constraints relative to the availability of resources and skills for analyzing a large universe of stocks must not be overlooked. Before the security analyst makes any recommendations to the PM, he or she must undertake an in-depth analysis of every stock included in the stock universe. Specifically, the present value of every stock must be determined. This involves, among other things, a critical analysis of the financial statements, a projection of earnings and dividends, and a determination of the appropriate discount rate.[34] With this constraint in clear view, a set of, say, 150 to 200 stocks may constitute an acceptable universe. However, individual portfolio managers may deviate from that range, depending on their capabilities and individual resources.

[34] A review of the analysis of Stanley Works presented in Chapter 11 will further illustrate this point.

Step 2: Expected Return

In Chapter 9, we pointed out that, by definition, the present value of an undervalued stock is higher than its market price. The price of a stock is readily available; the present value is calculated:

$$PV = \sum_{n=1}^{N} \frac{D_n}{(1+r)^n} + \frac{P_N}{(1+r)^N} \quad \textbf{(9–3 restated)}$$

In this case, values of the future dividend stream, D_n, the holding period price, P_N, and the appropriate discount rate, r, are provided by the security analyst, and the present value is calculated by solving the equation.

Three important observations follow. First, the estimation of present values is the task of the security analyst rather than the PM. Second, fundamental analysis is essential to estimating D_n, P_N, and r. Chapters 10 and 11 were devoted to a detailed discussion of fundamental analysis in general and the techniques for estimating future earnings growth in particular: The future earnings growth of a company is primarily dependent on its performance and the future success of the industry of which it is a part. Furthermore, the prospects of an industry are closely tied to the outlook for general economic conditions. A security analyst initially analyzes the economy and makes a national economic forecast. He or she then makes an industry and company analysis for each of the selected companies in order to estimate its future earnings growth. Those estimates provide the data not only for the expected dividend payments during the holding period, D_n, but for the holding period price, P_N.[35] Given the estimates for the future dividend stream, the holding period price, and the appropriate discount rate, the security analyst then determines each stock's present value.

Third, any divergence between the present value and the current price of a stock is assumed to be temporary in nature. Given sufficient time, demand and supply conditions tend to move toward *equilibrium*; that is, the market price of a stock moves toward its present value. Because it is the price which moves towards equilibrium, this adjustment process is referred to as *price-driven.* (More will be said later about this important concept in portfolio management.)

An equivalent approach to common stock valuation is to (1) assume as given the current market price, P_0, (2) estimate the future dividend stream, D_n, and the holding period price, P_N, and (3) calculate the rate of return, i, or the holding period yield of a common stock, by solving for i:[36]

$$P_0 = \sum_{n=1}^{N} \frac{D_n}{(1+i)^n} + \frac{P_N}{(1+i)^N} \quad \textbf{(9–27 restated)}$$

[35] The technique for determining the holding period price was explained in Chapters 9 and 11.

[36] Because annual dividend payments are likely to be uneven over time, the use of a computer is necessary to calculate the holding period yield. Of course, the discount factor may be estimated through trial and error.

Because the future dividend stream and future selling price are expected and not guaranteed, the holding period yield, *i*, can be called the expected return of the stock. (This approach will be used in this discussion of portfolio construction and also for constructing a real world portfolio later in the chapter.)

Step 3: Stocks' Beta

Today, many services publish betas of most stocks trading on the market. Wilshire Associates, Inc., Rosenberg Beta Service, and Merrill Lynch, for example, publish stock betas on a regular basis. In addition, some advisory services, such as the Value Line, calculate the betas which they use in their own analysis. A security analyst can obtain betas of all stocks from published sources or personally calculate them, if so disposed.

Step 4A: SML: Basic Approach

The next step is to plot on a graph the expected return–beta points for the 200 selected stocks (see Figure 14–5A). These points provide the ingredients for generating the least squares line, known as the Security Market Line (SML).[37] Point M on the SML, shown in Figure 14–5B, is the market portfolio, and its beta is equal to 1. The Y-intercept of the SML, R_f, is the risk-free asset whose beta is zero. Note that all the points do not fall on the SML. This implies that stocks appearing above the SML are undervalued, whereas those below the line are overvalued. For example, stock Z has a beta of 1 and lies above the market portfolio, M. Because Z is in the same risk class as the market, its expected return should be identical to that of the market. However, according to the security analyst, stock Z has a much higher expected return than M, and is therefore undervalued.

Step 4B: SML: Alternative Approach

The SML line developed in Step 4A could have an upward bias if some of the securities included in the set are special situations with unusually high expected returns for their risk class. If this bias is not desired, the following alternative to the construction of the SML can be adopted. First, the stocks can be divided into, say, five beta quintiles, with each quintile containing approximately the same number of stocks. Starting with Quintile 1, the risk of each stock group will progressively increase. That is, the first quintile will consist of stocks with lowest risk, and the fifth quintile will consist of stocks with the highest risk. Next, the *median* expected return and beta for each quintile can be calculated. This will negate the disproportionate impact of the few unusually high expected return stocks that might have been included in the set. Finally, a modified SML can be calculated on the basis of the five median points, as shown in Figure 14–5C.

[37] The Y-axis of Figure 14–5A through 14–5D is labeled $E(R_s)$, which is defined as expected return. Expected return and yield are used here as synonymous terms.

Figure 14–5

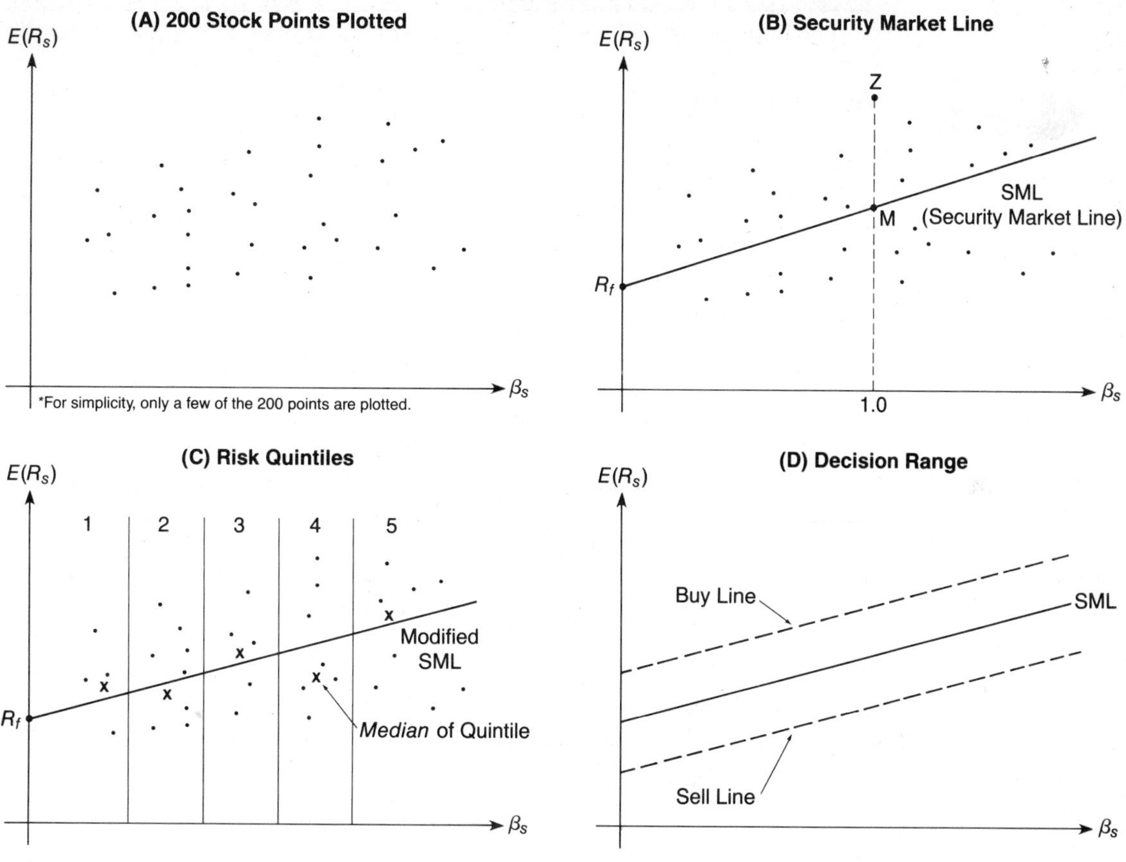

Step 5: The Decision Band

At equilibrium, all stocks should fall on the SML. Therefore, when the market is at a disequilibrium, stocks appearing above the SML are undervalued and those below the line are overvalued. It has already been stated that, in time, all stocks are assumed to gravitate toward the SML. These considerations form the basis for the development of a decision band.

Normally, because of its unique characteristics, the SML would be used as the decision line; that is, the PM could limit the selection set to the stocks lying above the SML and dispose of the stocks below the line. However, because the process by which stocks reach their equilibrium positions is neither consistent nor uniform, continuous upward and downward movements take place in the stock universe. Partly for this reason, and also due to the fact that expected returns of stocks vary purely due to short-term market fluctuations, it is advisable to replace the SML with a *decision range*, as demonstrated in Figure 14–5D. The limits of the decision range, called the *buy and sell lines*, may be fixed, respectively, at, for example, 1.0 percent above and below the SML.

The implications of the decision band should be spelled out. It is generally assumed that under- or overvalued stocks always have a tendency to move toward their present value; that is, stocks appearing above and below the SML eventually tend to move toward that line. This phenomenon provides an insight into an important portfolio construction strategy, as follows.

It was previously explained that the expected return, or yield, of a stock can be calculated by:

$$P_0 = \sum_{n=1}^{N} \frac{D_n}{(1+i)^n} + \frac{P_N}{(1+i)^N} \qquad \textbf{(9–27 restated)}$$

Assume that the values of P_0, D_n, P_N, and N of ABC stock are, respectively, \$38, \$2, \$60, and 5 years. The expected return of ABC is 14 percent:

$$\$38 = \sum_{n=1}^{5} \frac{\$2}{(1+i)^n} + \frac{\$60}{(1+i)^5}$$

From the present value tables, we see that at $i = 14$ percent:

$$\$38 = (\$2)(3.433) + (\$60)(.519)$$

Assume, further, that ABC is an undervalued stock and that appropriately priced stocks in the same risk class have an expected return of only 12 percent. If the expected return on ABC stock were to equal the 12 percent equilibrium return, the stock would have to sell at a higher price of \$41.23:

$$\$41.23 = (\$2)(3.605) + (\$60)(.567)$$

Therefore, all else being equal, the PM assumes that the price of ABC stock will eventually appreciate sufficiently to bring it to the price of appropriately valued stocks in the same risk class.[38] Similarly, the PM would expect the price of an overvalued stock, in time, to decline to the price of an appropriately priced stock in its risk class.

Therefore—and this is the essence of active portfolio management—the PM should include in the portfolio only undervalued stocks, which lie on or above the buy line. Stocks appearing on or below the sell line are overvalued and should be discarded in order to prevent their negative impact on the portfolio.

Step 6: Investor's Resources and Risk Preference

Before attempting to construct a portfolio, the PM should determine the risk preference of the investor. The risk an investor is willing to assume depends on wealth, income, psychological make-up, attitude toward security investment,

[38] The PM assumes that the stock price will reach an equilibrium before the end of the expected holding period.

Figure 14–6

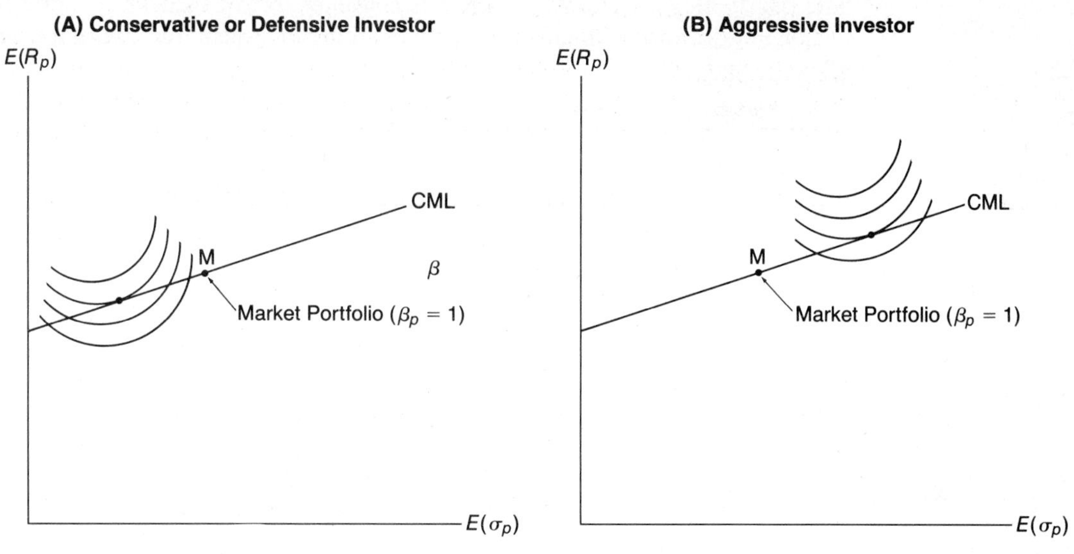

alternative investment holdings, and so on. Based on these and other related factors, the PM first classifies the investor according to his or her risk preference as either conservative (defensive) or aggressive. Then, largely by trial and error, the PM estimates the value of the portfolio beta that would be consistent with the investor's risk preference. In theory, this trial and error approach involves the determination of the point of tangency between the indifference curve and the Capital Market Line,[39] as shown in Figure 14–6. We will call a person who prefers that the portfolio beta be less than one (Figure 14–6A) a conservative or defensive investor, that is, one with low risk preference; conversely, a person who wants the beta of the portfolio to exceed one (Figure 14–6B) will be called an aggressive investor, that is, one with high risk preference.[40]

Determination of the ideal number of stocks to be included in a portfolio depends on the PM's ability to bring a set of competing factors into delicate balance. On the one hand, portfolio theory states that the more diversified the portfolio, the less will be its degree of unsystematic risk. On the other hand, resources and other real world cost factors impose severe constraints on the number of stocks that can be included in a manageable portfolio. Furthermore,

[39] Also see Chapter 13 for a discussion of this technique.

[40] Note that the terms "conservative" and "aggressive" are used here instead of "risk-averse" and "risk-taker." Technically, a risk-averse person wants larger and larger increases in expected returns as risk becomes greater, whereas a risk taker is one who is willing to accept smaller and smaller increases in expected returns as risk increases. Because the CAPM assumes a linear relationship between risk and returns, the amount of additional return for a unit of additional risk does not decrease as beta becomes greater than one. Consequently, in this context, we cannot use the terms risk-averse and risk taker.

it is desirable to include stocks in a number of industries in the portfolio: Effective diversification, not mere duplication, helps reduce the portfolio's unsystematic risk.[41] As a general rule, then, a *minimum* of 15 to 25 stocks covering the major industry or stock groups might constitute an acceptable size of a diversified portfolio.[42]

Step 7A: Portfolio Construction: Basic Approach

The PM may construct a portfolio in several ways, depending on personal preference as well as the resources at his or her command. One simple approach to portfolio construction follows. This is the simpliest way.

Assume that the PM determines that the investor wishes to include 25 stocks in the portfolio, and that he prefers a portfolio beta of .75. The manager *randomly* picks 25 stocks with relatively high expected returns from the five quintiles and determines that the portfolio beta works out to 1.5.

The PM recognizes that because the risk of the existing portfolio is higher than the investor's desired risk, risk-free assets must be included in the portfolio in order to achieve the desired results.[43] Mixing risk-free assets with the stock portfolio reduces the beta of the composite portfolio in the following manner. Suppose the total amount of investible funds is equally divided between risk-free assets and common stocks. By definition, the beta or volatility of risk-free assets relative to the market is zero, whereas the beta of the stock portfolio already constructed is 1.5. The beta of the composite portfolio would be .75 as follows:

Type of Security	Beta	Proportion Invested	Weighted Beta
Risk-free asset	0	.5	0
Common stock	1.50	.5	.75
		Portfolio Beta	.75

Note that the risk level or the beta of the composite portfolio can be easily altered by changing the relative weight of the portfolio components. For example, if the investor desires to hold a portfolio with a beta of, say, .975, the portfolio manager can achieve this objective by increasing the proportion of stocks to 65 percent:[44]

Type of Security	Beta	Proportion Invested	Weighted Beta
Risk-free asset	0	.35	0
Common stock	1.5	.65	.975
		Portfolio Beta	.975

[41] The topic of determining the relative weights among the stocks of selected industries will be discussed in a later section.

[42] In Chapter 13, it was demonstrated that a diversified portfolio consisting of about 20 stocks can eliminate most unsystematic risk.

[43] This will be achieved by reducing the weight of the stocks in the portfolio so that the total funds will be divided between risk-free assets and common stocks.

[44] The portfolio manager need not always combine stocks with risk-free assets. He or she can mix stocks with corporate bonds as well. However, because quantitative measures of bond risks are not readily available, the mixing of stocks and corporate bonds becomes more involved.

This portfolio is, of course, only one of many that can be constructed in this manner which will have the desired beta. For example, one could invest 95 percent of the funds in common stocks with a beta of 1.03 and the rest in treasury bills in order to obtain a portfolio beta of approximately .975.

Step 7B: Portfolio Construction: Sophisticated Approach

The method of portfolio construction described in Step 7A was simplistic. In the real world, most PMs do not use such a naive selection method. Managers of any reasonable size portfolio have access to computers that can be programmed to efficiently perform the task of stock selection. A quantitative technique that can be used for this purpose is called *linear programming*, and the problem of selection is solved by the method of optimization.[45] With few exceptions involving simple problems, computers are necessary to solve linear programming problems. Briefly, the technique enables the PM to maximize the expected return of the portfolio subject to a set of constraints. For example, the PM may specify that (1) the portfolio should have a given beta, (2) no more than a certain percentage of the total funds should be invested in any single stock or stocks of a single industry, and so on.[46] Although the technique is fairly involved, its implications are easily comprehensible, as can be seen from the following example.

The first constraint imposed on the portfolio is the beta, which is fixed at 1.2 in this example. The PM imposes two additional constraints on the portfolio. First, she specifies that no more than 7 percent of the total funds should be invested in any stock. This constraint will automatically lead to a selection of at least 15 stocks, thereby ensuring some diversification. Second, she indicates that no more than 10 percent of the total funds should be invested in the stocks of any one industry.[47] Note that these constraints, as well as others that could have been imposed, are largely determined by investor preference. It is important to recognize that while each constraint increases portfolio diversification—and therefore reduces its unsystematic risk—it also reduces the maximum return obtainable from that portfolio.

This, then, is a linear programming problem with specified constraints. From the set of undervalued stocks within the buy range above the SML, the linear programming solution will select an optimum portfolio which will not only maximize the expected return, but satisfy all the specified constraints.

---

[45] A lucid discussion of linear programming can be found in Bierman, Bonini, and Hausman, *Quantitative Analysis for Business Decisions* (Homewood, Ill.: Richard D. Irwin, 1977), pp. 247–323.

[46] Trust departments of most banks do not generally use linear programming because the tool is not sufficiently powerful to suit their purpose. The tool commonly used by professional portfolio managers is known as quadratic programming. An introduction to this tool is presented in the appendix to this chapter.

[47] These are by no means the only constraints that can be imposed on a portfolio. Depending on the capacity of the computer and the level of sophistication desired, other constraints can be added to the list. For example, if the investor is in a high income tax bracket, the computer may be instructed to concentrate on growth company stocks which have a low dividend yield.

Table 14–2

Stock Universe	Stock Group and Industry Weights	Stock Universe	Stock Group and Industry Weights
Consumer Goods & Services	**32.00**	**Capital Goods**	**18.00**
Automotive & Related	5.50	Aerospace & Electronics	2.00
Beverages	1.00	Electrical Equipment	2.50
Broadcasting & Publishing	3.00	Machinery & Machine Tools	1.50
Food & Related	4.00	Office & Business Equip.	8.00
Health Care	7.00	Oil Machinery & Services	4.00
Leisure & Recreation	1.00		
Photography	1.50	**Interest Sensitives**	**21.00**
Retail Goods & Retailing	6.50	Banking & Finance	4.00
Soaps & Cosmetics	2.50	Building & Related	3.00
		Insurance	4.00
Basic Goods & Services	**25.00**	Utilities—Electric	3.00
Chemicals	4.50	Utilities—Natural Gas	1.00
Metals & Mining	3.50	Utilities—Tels. Ex AT&T	1.00
Oils—Domestic	7.00	Utilities—AT&T	5.00
Oils—International	6.50		
Paper & Containers	1.50	**Multi-Industry & Misc**	**4.00**
Transportation	2.00	Multi-Industry & Misc	4.00

A Real World Portfolio

Now that the sophisticated technique for portfolio construction has been presented, this technique can be applied to the construction of a portfolio using real world data. This discussion will closely resemble the portfolio construction format just presented. The steps of portfolio management presented in this section represent in large degree the basic investment management approach developed by Detroit Bank and Trust Company, which provided much of the following data and analytical methodology. The beta values used in this analysis were generated by Wilshire Associates, Inc. Finally, throughout this discussion it will be assumed that the PM (1) possesses sufficient financial resources, and (2) has high analytical competence as well as easy access to a group of security analysts and large-scale computer facilities.

Step 1: The Stock Universe

First, the stock universe must be selected. Recognizing that he would frequently trade in thousands of shares of selected stocks involving large sums of money, the PM decides to include in the universe *primarily* stocks of large and medium-size companies. The PM creates a stock universe by making a two-pronged decision. First, as shown in Table 14–2, he selects 28 industries representing five major stock groups and covering a cross section of all industries. Second, from the entire set, the PM selects 168 companies which he believes to be an adequate

Table 14–3 **Stock Universe**

1. AT&T	43. CROWN ZELL	85. INGRS RAND	127. RALSTN PU
2. ABBOTT LAB	44. CRPNTR TEK	86. INLAND STL	128. RAYTHEON
3. ACF IND	45. DATAPOINT	87. INT TEL TL	129. REVCO D S
4. AIR PRDUCT	46. DAYTON CP	88. INTEL CORP	130. REVLON INC
5. ALEX&AL SV	47. DEERE CO	89. INTL FLV&F	131. ROADWAY EX
6. ALUM CO AM	48. DELTA AIRL	90. INTL PAPER	132. SCHLUMBRGR
7. AM BRDCST	49. DENNYS RES	91. JC PENNEY	133. SCOV MFG
8. AM GEN INS	50. DETROITBNK	92. JONSN–JNSN	134. SEARS ROE
9. AM GREETNG	51. DIGITL EQP	93. K MART CP	135. SHARED MED
10. AM HME PRD	52. DOVER CP	94. KELLOGG	136. SMITHKLINE
11. AM HOSP SU	53. DOW CHEM	95. KIM–CLARK	137. SO RAILWAY
12. AM INTL	54. DUN&BRADST	96. KRAFT INC	138. SOUTHL RTY
13. AM MED INT	55. DUPONT	97. LILLY ELI	139. SPERRY RAN
14. AM NAT RES	56. E KODAK	98. MARATH OIL	140. SQUARE D
15. AMP INC	57. EAGL PCHER	99. MARSH MCL	141. SQUIBB CP
16. ARA SERVIC	58. ECON LAB	100. MC DONALDS	142. ST OIL CAL
17. ARMST CORK	59. EMERSN ELC	101. MELLON NAT	143. ST OIL IND
18. ATL RCHFLD	60. EXXON CORP	102. MERCK&CO	144. STANLEY WK
19. AVON PRODT	61. FLA POW<	103. MESA PETE	145. STAUFER CM
20. BAKER INTL	62. FORD MOTOR	104. MILLER–WOH	146. STOR TECHN
21. BAXTER TRV	63. FOXBORO	105. MINN MININ	147. TEKTRONIX
22. BEATRCE FD	64. FT HOWARD	106. MOBIL CORP	148. TEXACO
23. BETZ LAB	65. GA PACIFIC	107. MONSANTO C	149. TEXAS INST
24. BIG THREE	66. GANNETT	108. MORGAN JP	150. TEXAS UTIL
25. BLAK&DECKR	67. GEN ELEC	109. MOTOROLA	151. TIMKEN CO
26. BRSTL–MYRS	68. GEN FOODS	110. NATL DETRO	152. TRANSAMERI
27. BUTLER MFG	69. GEN MOTORS	111. NEWENG G&E	153. UNION CAMP
28. BURROUGHS	70. GEN TEL&EL	112. NIELSEN A	154. UPJOHN
29. CAP CIT CM	71. GENU PARTS	113. NO STS P&M	155. US GYPSUM
30. CATERPILLR	72. GRAINGR WW	114. PAC G&E	156. UTD TELECM
31. CBS INC	73. GULF ST UT	115. PACCAR INC	157. W E HELLER
32. CHSBRO–PND	74. HALL FRANK	116. PACIFIC LU	158. W. DISNEY
33. CIT FINL	75. HALLIBURTN	117. PALL CORP	159. WACHOVIA
34. CITICORP	76. HAZELT LAB	118. PALM BEACH	160. WAL MART
35. CLARK EQUP	77. HERCULES	119. PAYLESS CA	161. WARN–LAMBT
36. COCA–COLA	78. HEWLETT–PK	120. PEPSICO	162. WATER ASSO
37. COLGATE PL	79. HILTON HTL	121. PETRIE STR	163. WEYERHSR
38. COMWLTH ED	80. HON IND	122. PFIZER	164. WHIRLPOOL
39. CONN GENL	81. HOSP OF AM	123. PHILLIPS P	165. WILLAMETTE
40. COOPER IND	82. HSEHOLD FN	124. PRCTR&GMBL	166. WISC EL PR
41. CORN GLASS	83. HUMANA INC	125. PUBSRV IND	167. XEROX
42. CPC INTL	84. IBM	126. R H MACYS	168. YELLOW FGT

number for the universe.[48] Each of the 168 selected stocks is assigned a number in Table 14–3.

[48] The portfolio manager believes that a set of 150 to 200 stocks, representing a cross section of all major industries, will be an adequate surrogate for the market and a reasonable stock universe. Although a larger universe such as the S&P 500 might be somewhat more representative of the market, the portfolio manager's staff is only large enough to analyze 150 to 200 stocks.

Step 2: Expected Returns

Next, the PM asks the security analysts to calculate the expected return for each of the 168 stocks. The method used for calculating these returns is the one explained in the previous section. Expected returns and current prices for all the stocks in the universe are provided in Table 14–4.

Table 14–4

Name	Current* Price	Beta β_s	Expected Return $E(R_s)$	Name	Current* Price	Beta β_s	Expected Return $E(R_s)$
1. AT&T	58.13	.51	14.7	40. COOPER IND	58.00	1.24	15.5
2. ABBOTT LAB	37.13	1.00	16.4	41. CORN GLASS	63.38	1.19	9.4
3. ACF IND	38.00	1.06	17.0	42. CPC INTL	54.50	.71	15.3
4. AIR PRDUCT	32.50	1.12	13.7	43. CROWN ZELL	37.88	1.06	16.2
5. ALEX&AL SV	31.75	1.22	15.7	44. CRPNTR TEK	30.75	.80	16.0
6. ALUM CO AM	55.25	1.05	16.6	45. DATAPOINT	86.00	1.88	23.4
7. AM BRDCST	46.68	1.41	17.0	46. DAYTON CP	44.25	1.28	15.9
8. AM GEN INS	37.63	1.68	16.4	47. DEERE CO	39.38	1.19	13.7
9. AM GREETNG	13.38	1.58	17.2	48. DELTA AIRL	45.25	1.48	14.8
10. AM HME PRD	28.38	.75	13.6	49. DENNYS RES	19.75	1.63	20.7
11. AM HOSP SU	32.63	1.16	12.5	50. DETROITBNK	28.25	.80	17.1
12. AM INTL	17.68	1.70	22.1	51. DIGITL EQP	63.25	1.35	17.0
13. AM MED INT	32.50	1.50	23.1	52. DOVER CP	60.75	1.03	16.1
14. AM NAT RES	43.50	.78	19.0	53. DOW CHEM	29.75	.97	15.4
15. AMP INC	39.25	1.19	13.8	54. DUN&BRADST	37.75	.99	14.4
16. ARA SERVIC	38.88	1.35	14.6	55. DUPONT	47.25	1.02	19.0
17. ARMST CORK	18.25	1.22	15.0	56. E KODAK	58.00	.95	15.3
18. ATL RCHFLD	70.38	.81	15.6	57. EAGL PCHER	23.00	1.08	16.0
19. AVON PRODT	52.00	1.11	15.4	58. ECON LAB	22.25	1.16	15.4
20. BAKER INTL	48.25	1.11	14.2	59. EMERSN ELC	35.75	1.00	13.9
21. BAXTER TRV	45.88	1.14	16.1	60. EXXON CORP	55.13	.74	15.5
22. BEATRCE FD	24.00	.88	15.3	61. FLA POW<	27.25	.92	15.8
23. BETZ LAB	35.50	1.13	15.9	62. FORD MOTOR	42.00	1.10	22.9
24. BIG THREE	40.25	1.14	16.7	63. FOXBORO	40.38	1.26	14.5
25. BLAK&DECKR	24.75	1.27	10.6	64. FT HOWARD	45.63	1.05	13.3
26. BRSTL–MYRS	36.00	.94	13.5	65. GA PACIFIC	28.75	1.09	15.2
27. BUTLER MFG	29.75	.84	18.8	66. GANNETT	45.75	.95	15.9
28. BURROUGHS	73.25	1.10	15.6	67. GEN ELEC	53.25	.97	14.8
29. CAP CIT CM	44.00	1.37	14.6	68. GEN FOODS	33.75	.85	16.4
30. CATERPILLR	56.25	.92	15.6	69. GEN MOTORS	59.13	.98	18.4
31. CBS INC	52.25	1.14	16.3	70. GEN TEL&EL	29.63	.61	15.5
32. CHSBRO–PND	25.25	.97	13.1	71. GENU PARTS	26.25	1.08	15.6
33. CIT FINL	56.38	1.22	10.8	72. GRAINGR WW	39.00	1.09	14.6
34. CITICORP	25.63	.96	17.0	73. GULF ST UT	13.00	.84	13.9
35. CLARK EQUP	42.75	1.23	14.7	74. HALL FRANK	27.00	1.35	15.5
36. COCA–COLA	40.25	.69	14.0	75. HALLIBURTN	77.38	.95	15.0
37. COLGATE PL	18.50	1.06	14.6	76. HAZELT LAB	13.75	1.64	17.4
38. COMWLTH ED	24.63	.69	14.3	77. HERCULES	20.50	1.23	20.5
39. CONN GENL	38.63	1.38	13.9	78. HEWLETT–PK	54.50	1.28	14.0

Table 14–4 (*continued*)

Name	Current* Price	Beta β_s	Expected Return $E(R_s)$	Name	Current* Price	Beta β_s	Expected Return $E(R_s)$
79. HILTON HTL	31.25	1.42	16.8	124. PRCTR&GMBL	79.00	.73	13.8
80. HON IND	16.75	1.88	18.8	125. PUBSRV IND	25.38	.84	14.2
81. HOSP OF AM	36.75	1.32	17.9	126. R H MACYS	42.00	1.36	16.5
82. HSEHOLD FN	21.75	1.37	16.7	127. RALSTN PU	11.88	.86	14.0
83. HUMANA INC	35.88	1.71	23.4	128. RAYTHEON	56.25	1.29	15.5
84. IBM	69.63	.89	16.2	129. REVCO D S	27.63	1.28	13.8
85. INGRS RAND	54.63	1.22	16.3	130. REVLON INC	53.50	.97	14.7
86. INLAND STL	36.63	.93	16.8	131. ROADWAY EX	28.25	1.48	17.1
87. INT TEL TL	30.25	1.10	18.7	132. SCHLUMBRGR	84.75	.90	15.5
88. INTEL CORP	56.00	1.85	13.1	133. SCOV MFG	19.63	1.21	19.0
89. INTL FLV&F	22.13	.97	14.3	134. SEARS ROE	19.75	1.13	18.1
90. INTL PAPER	44.50	1.07	16.2	135. SHARED MED	29.38	1.68	16.0
91. JC PENNEY	33.25	1.36	16.4	136. SMITHKLINE	47.63	1.04	17.5
92. JONSN–JNSN	77.00	.81	15.6	137. SO RAILWAY	56.00	1.00	16.9
93. K MART CP	27.13	1.24	14.1	138. SOUTHL RTY	39.25	1.47	14.6
94. KELLOGG	20.75	.80	13.5	139. SPERRY RAN	50.00	1.06	14.9
95. KIM–CLARK	44.38	1.00	17.0	140. SQUARE D	24.63	1.06	16.1
96. KRAFT INC	48.75	.74	15.6	141. SQUIBB CP	33.75	1.17	10.5
97. LILLY ELI	57.38	.86	12.7	142. ST OIL CAL	56.00	.79	13.5
98. MARATH OIL	39.25	.74	16.0	143. ST OIL IND	68.13	.72	15.2
99. MARSH MCL	66.75	.99	14.0	144. STANLEY WK	30.50	1.10	15.0
100. MC DONALDS	49.63	1.49	16.8	145. STAUFER CM	24.25	1.17	15.1
101. MELLON NAT	31.63	.88	15.6	146. STOR TECH	18.63	1.74	25.1
102. MERCK&CO	69.50	.86	12.0	147. TEKTRONIX	57.25	1.33	14.1
103. MESA PETE	64.25	1.75	14.0	148. TEXACO	28.63	.71	15.4
104. MILLER–WOH	22.75	1.75	21.9	149. TEXAS INST	95.75	1.24	13.3
105. MINN MININ	55.00	.92	14.6	150. TEXAS UTIL	19.38	.89	14.3
106. MOBIL CORP	42.63	.83	15.4	151. TIMKEN CO	60.63	1.02	16.3
107. MONSANTO C	56.50	1.15	16.0	152. TRANSAMERI	19.75	1.35	15.4
108. MORGAN JP	53.13	.88	15.4	153. UNION CAMP	17.00	1.01	14.9
109. MOTOROLA	48.88	1.44	13.5	154. UPJOHN	44.00	1.24	14.9
110. NATL DETRO	34.50	.81	15.9	155. US GYPSUM	13.75	1.09	16.7
111. NEWENG G&E	16.63	.61	15.8	156. UTD TELECM	20.50	.71	13.3
112. NIELSEN A	23.63	1.39	15.3	157. W E HELLER	33.13	1.33	12.2
113. NO STS P&M	25.13	.75	13.5	158. W. DISNEY	39.50	1.31	15.7
114. PAC G&E	24.00	.70	14.5	159. WACHOVIA	20.25	1.06	16.0
115. PACCAR INC	59.00	1.35	17.3	160. WAL MART	32.38	1.44	14.4
116. PACIFIC LU	51.00	1.00	14.8	161. WARN–LAMBT	24.00	1.00	14.8
117. PALL CORP	36.00	1.50	14.4	162. WATER ASSO	25.75	1.40	23.5
118. PALM BEACH	18.88	1.12	20.5	163. WEYERHSR	33.63	1.04	15.4
119. PAYLESS CA	16.13	1.50	17.0	164. WHIRLPOOL	21.50	1.32	18.0
120. PEPSICO	27.00	.96	14.2	165. WILLAMETTE	36.25	1.19	15.5
121. PETRIE STR	37.50	.98	16.2	166. WISC EL PR	25.38	.64	14.3
122. PFIZER	35.00	.99	12.4	167. XEROX	66.63	1.07	14.3
123. PHILLIPS P	40.25	.80	16.9	168. YELLOW FGT	22.00	1.41	17.9

* As of 8/24/79

Step 3: Stock Beta

As previously mentioned, several services publish betas of individual stocks. The PM obtains the betas for his stocks from Wilshire Associates, Inc. The beta values for each of the 168 stocks are presented in Table 14–4. The PM believes that the expected returns are *price-driven*—that, in time, the market price of each of the undervalued stocks will rise sufficiently to bring its expected return in line with the expected return of the appropriately valued stock in its risk class. The expected return–beta points of the 168 selected stocks are plotted in Figure 14–7, with each stock appropriately numbered for easy reference.

Step 4B: SML: Alternative Approach

The PM recognizes that if the SML were constructed on the basis of all the data points, it would have an upward bias, because he has selected a group of special situation stocks which have high beta values and, according to the security analysts, have unusually high expected returns. These stocks can be found in the upper right-hand corner of the graph in Figure 14–7. Included are the securities of Waters Associates (162), American Medical International (13), Humana, Inc. (83), Datapoint (45) and Storage Technology (146). Because the PM wishes to avoid an upward bias on the SML, he adopts an alternative procedure.

First, the PM groups the whole set into five beta quintiles of approximately equal size. These quintiles are presented in Table 14–5 and Figure 14–8. The quintiles are clearly marked in the figure for easy reference. Next, he calculates the median for each beta quintile, as shown at the bottom of Table 14–5, and marks them on Figure 14–8. Finally, he derives the equation of the least squares line by using the five median points.[49] The line, called the SML, is expressed as:

$$\begin{aligned} E(R_s) &= R_f + \beta_s[E(R_m) - R_f] \\ &= 13.84\% + \beta_s(1.66\%) \end{aligned}$$

The SML is graphed in Figure 14–9. Several observations can be made concerning this line. First, the Y-intercept of the SML is the return on the risk-free asset. By definition, the beta of the risk-free asset is zero; therefore, it must lie on the Y axis. Second, the upward slope of the SML is consistent with the theory that risk and return are positively related. Third, because the least squares technique is used here, the SML cuts through the median points and acts as the best representative line of these points.

Step 5: The Decision Band

For reasons explained in the previous section, the PM prefers a decision band over the SML as the decision line. Therefore, as revealed in Figure 14–10, he determines the buy and sell lines by respectively adding and subtracting 1

[49] See note 49 on page 640.

Figure 14–7

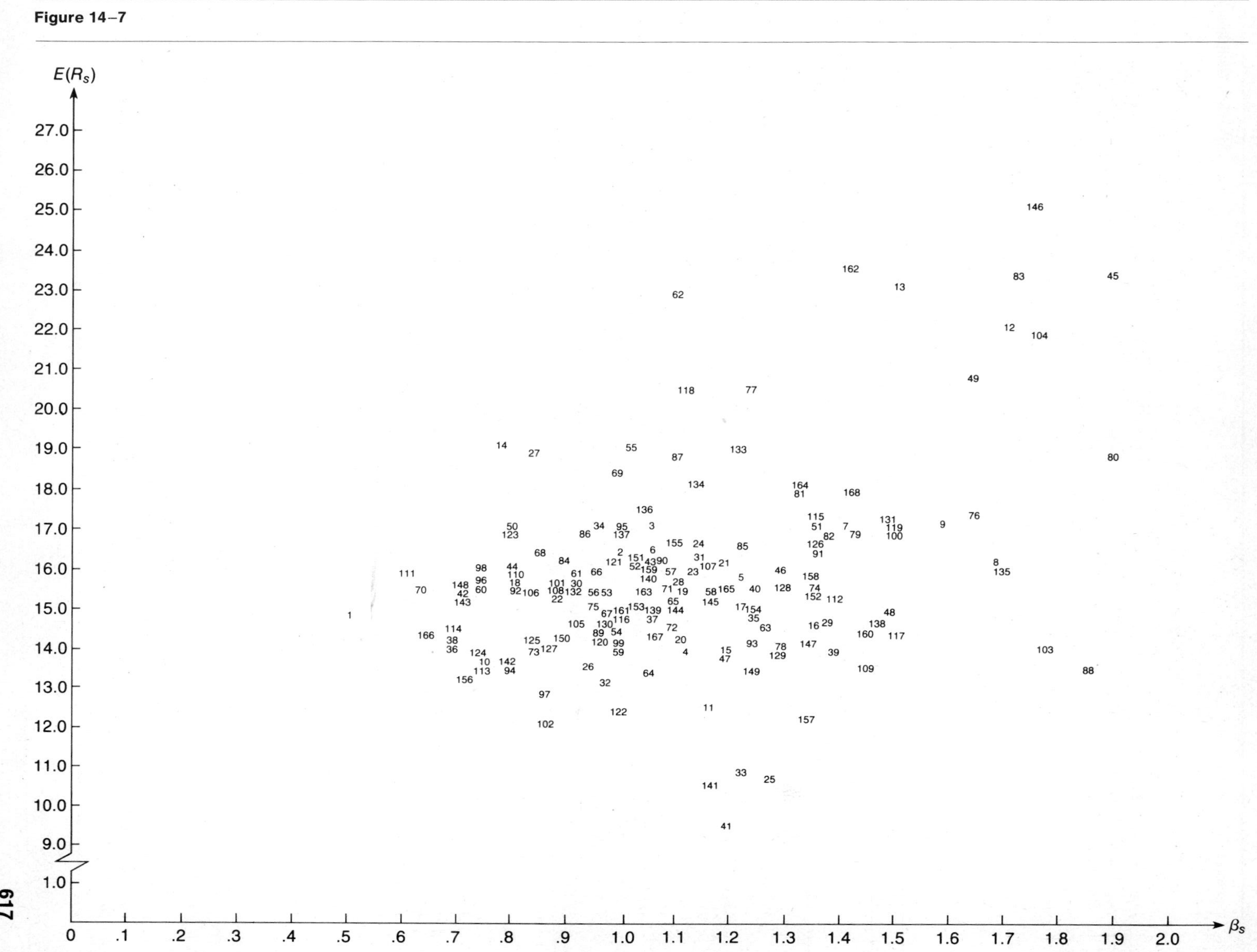

$E(R_s)$
27.0
26.0
25.0
24.0
23.0
22.0
21.0
20.0
19.0
18.0
17.0
16.0
15.0
14.0
13.0
12.0
11.0
10.0
9.0
1.0
0
.1
.2
.3
.4
.5
.6
.7
.8
.9
1.0
1.1
1.2
1.3
1.4
1.5
1.6
1.7
1.8
1.9
2.0
β_s

Table 14–5 **Risk Quintiles**

1	2	3	4	5
14. AM NAT RES	69. GEN MOTORS	62. FORD MOTOR	77. HERCULES	146. STOR TECHN
27. BUTLER MFG	34. CITICORP	118. PALM BEACH	133. SCOVILL MF	162. WATER ASSO
50. DETROITBNK	95. KIM–CLARK	55. DUPONT	164. WHIRLPOOL	83. HUMANA INC
123. PHILLIPS P	137. SO RAILWAY	87. INT TEL TL	81. HOSP OF AM	45. DATAPOINT
68. GEN FOODS	86. INLAND STL	134. SEARS ROE	85. INGRS RAND	13. AM MED INT
98. MARATH OIL	2. ABBOTT LAB	136. SMITHKLINE	21. BAXTER TRV	12. AM INTL
44. CRPNTR TEK	84. IBM	3. ACF IND	107. MONSANTO C	104. MILLER–WOH
110. NATL DETRO	121. PETRIE STR	155. U S GYPSUM	46. DAYTON CP	49. DENNYS RES
111. NEWENG G&E	66. GANNETT	24. BIG THREE	5. ALEX&AL SV	80. HON IND
96. KRAFT INC	61. FLA POW<	6. ALUM CO AM	158. W. DISNEY	168. YELLOW FGT
18. ATL RCHFLD	101. MELLON NAT	151. TIMKEN	165. WILLAMETTE	76. HAZELT LAB
92. JONSN–JNSN	30. CATERPILLR	31. CBS INC	40. COOPER IND	115. PACCAR INC
70. GEN TEL&EL	132. SCHLUMBRGR	43. CROWN ZELL	128. RAYTHEON	9. AM GREETNG
60. EXXON CORP	108. MORGAN JP	90. INTL PAPER	58. ECOM LAB	131. ROADWAY EX
148. TEXACO	53. DOW CHEM	52. DOVER CP	145. STAUF CHEM	51. DIGITL EQP
106. MOBIL CORP	22. BEATRCE FD	140. SQUARE D	17. ARMST CORK	7. AM BRDCST
42. CPC INTL	56. E KODAK	159. WACHOVIA	154. UPJOHN	119. PAYLESS CA
143. ST OIL IND	75. HALLIBURTN	57. EAGL PCHER	35. CLARK EQUP	79. HILTON HT
1. AT&T	67. GEN ELEC	23. BETZ LAB	16. ARA SERVIC	100. MC DONALDS
114. PAC G&E	116. PACIFIC LU	71. GENU PARTS	63. FOXBORO	82. HSEHOLD FN
166. WISC EL PR	161. WARN–LAMBT	28. BURROUGHS	93. K MART CP	126. R H MACYS
38. COMWLTH ED	130. REVLON INC	163. WEYERHSR	147. TEKTRONIX	91. JC PENNEY
125. PUBSRV IND	105. MINN MININ	19. AVON PRODT	78. HEWLETT–PK	8. AM GEN INS
36. COCA–COLA	54. DUN&BRADST	65. GA PACIFIC	15. AMP INC	135. SHARED MED
73. GULF ST UT	150. TEXAS UTIL	144. STANLEY WK	129. REVCO D S	74. HALL FRANK
124. PRCTR&GMBL	89. INTL FLV&F	153. UNION CAMP	47. DEERE CO	152. TRANSAMERI
10. AM HME PRD	120. PEPSICO	139. SPERRY RAN	149. TEXAS INST	112. NIELSEN A
113. NO STS P&M	127. RALSTN PUR	37. COLGATE PL	11. AM HOSP SU	48. DELTA AIRL
142. ST OIL CAL	99. MARSH MCL	72. GRAINGR WW	157. W E HELLER	29. CAP CIT CM
94. KELLOGG	59. EMERSN ELC	167. XEROX	33. CIT FINL	138. SOUTHL RTY
156. UTD TELECM	26. BRSTL–MYRS	20. BAKER INTL	25. BLAK&DECKR	160. WAL MART
97. LILLY ELI	32. CHSBRO–PND	4. AIR PRDUCT	141. SQUIBB CP	117. PALL CORP
102. MERCK&CO	122. PFIZER	64. FT HOWARD	41. CORN GLASS	103. MESA PETE
				39. CONN GENL
				109. MOTOROLA
				88. INTEL CORP

	Beta (β_s) Range	Mean β_s	Median β_s	Expected Return [$E(R_s)$] Range	Mean $E(R_s)$	Median $E(R_s)$
Beta Quintile 1	0.86–0.51	0.75	0.75	19.0–12.0	15.05	15.3
Beta Quintile 2	1.00–0.86	0.95	0.96	18.4–12.4	15.20	15.3
Beta Quintile 3	1.14–1.01	1.08	1.08	22.9–13.3	16.23	16.0
Beta Quintile 4	1.35–1.15	1.24	1.23	20.5– 9.4	14.68	14.9
Beta Quintile 5	1.88–1.35	1.53	1.48	25.1–13.1	17.47	16.8

Figure 14–8 **Risk Quintiles**

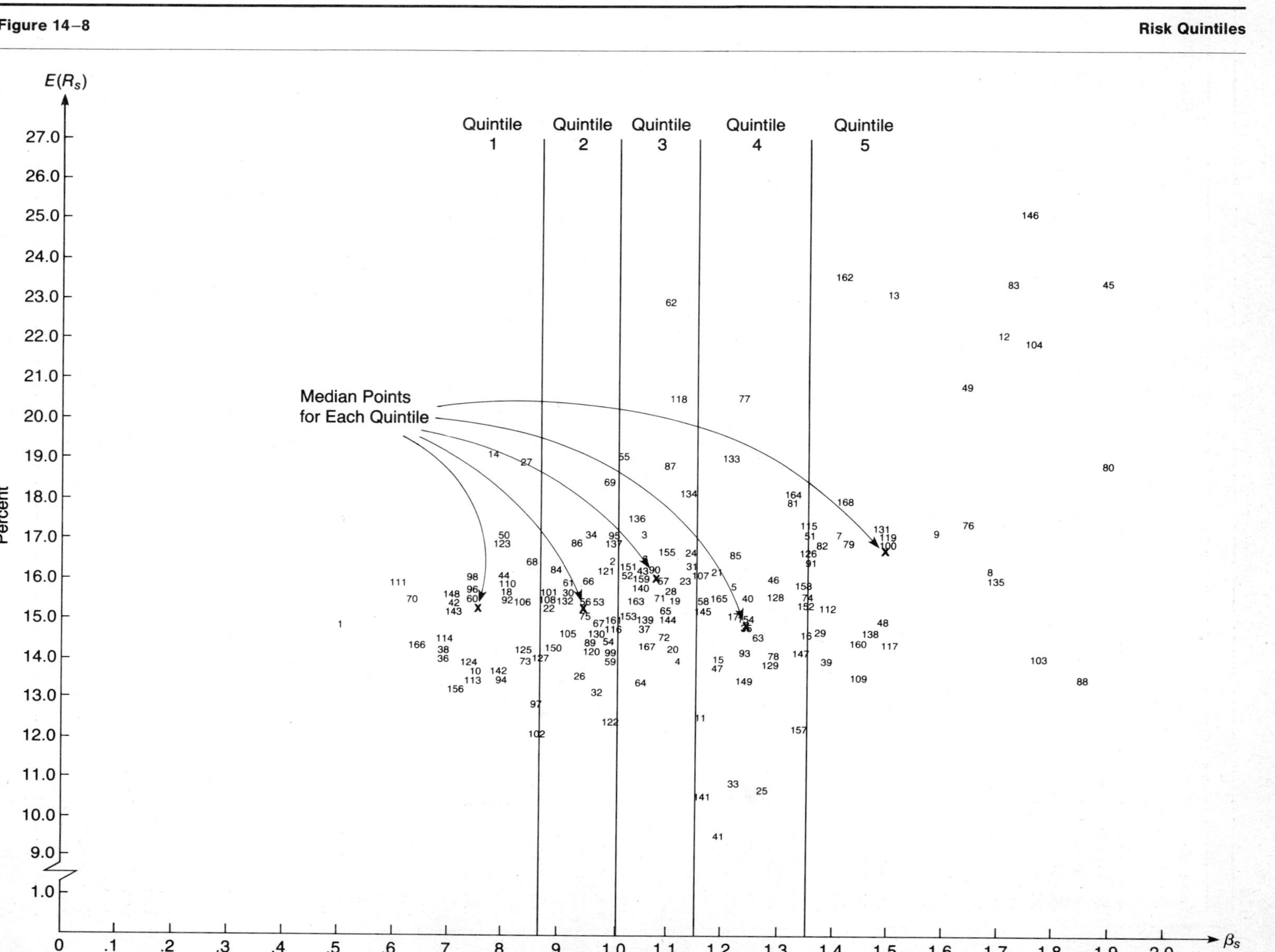

Figure 14–9 Security Market Line (SML)

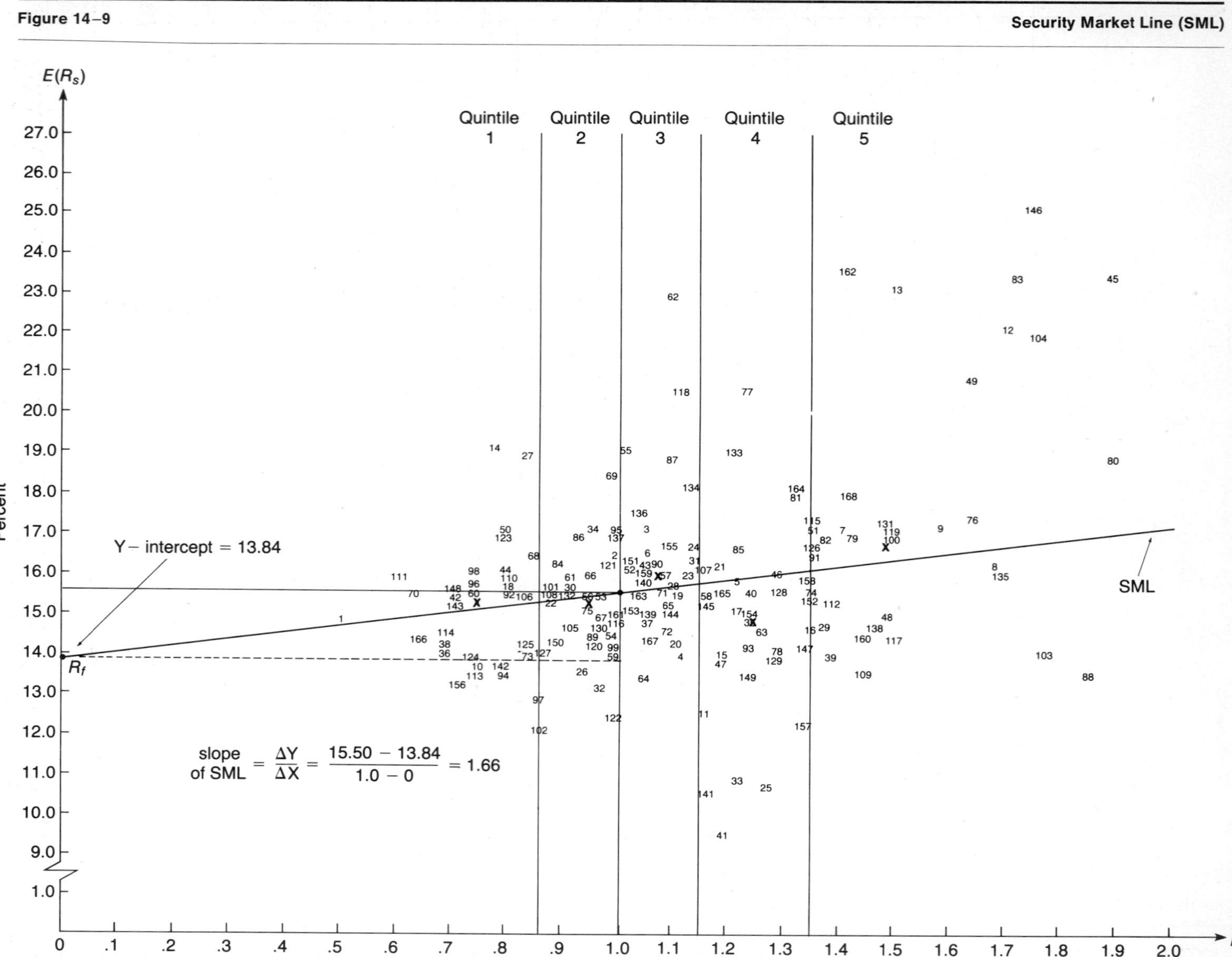

Figure 14–10

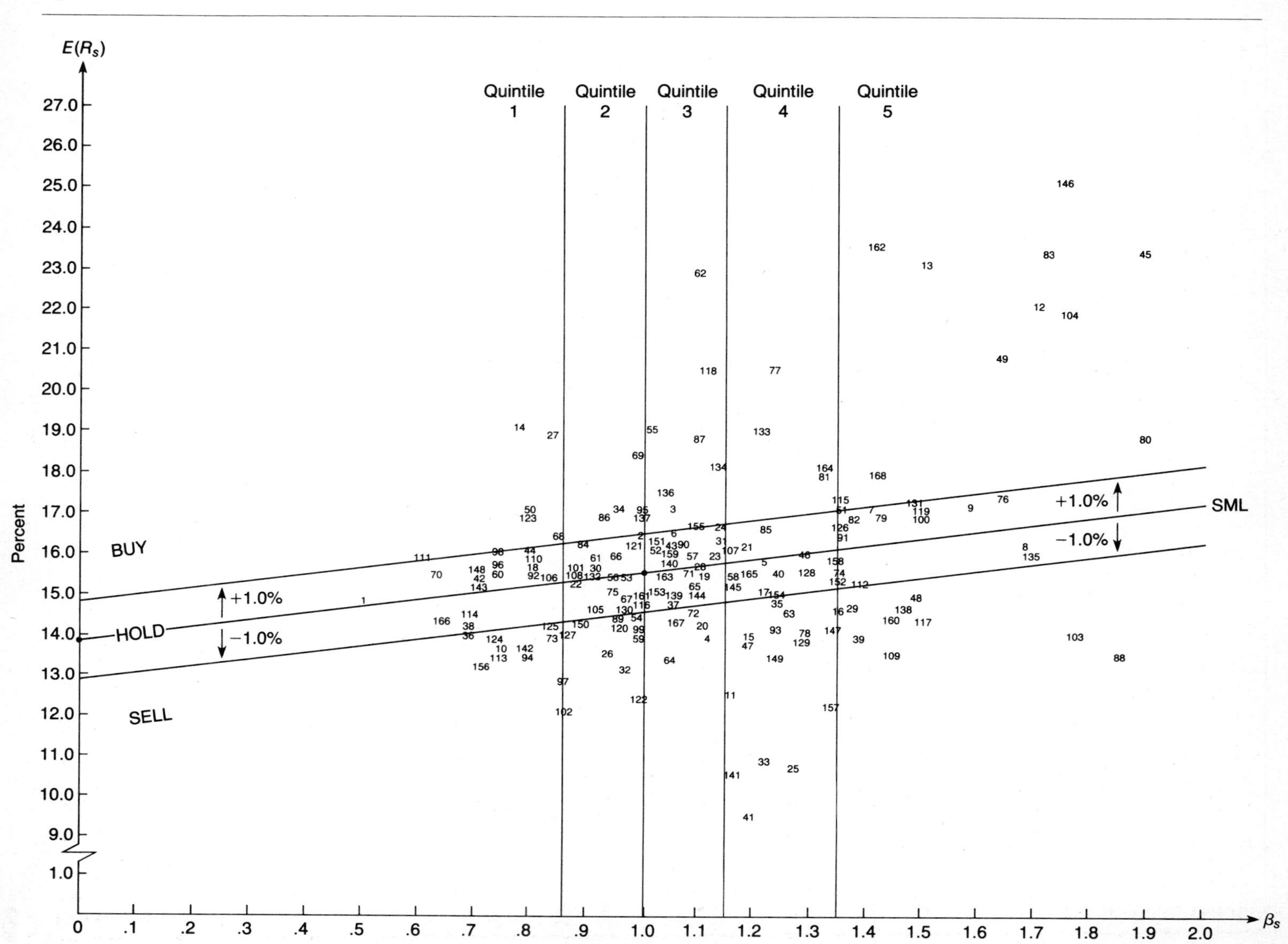

$E(R_s)$
Percent
Quintile 1
Quintile 2
Quintile 3
Quintile 4
Quintile 5
BUY
HOLD
SELL
+1.0%
−1.0%
SML
β_s
27.0
26.0
25.0
24.0
23.0
22.0
21.0
20.0
19.0
18.0
17.0
16.0
15.0
14.0
13.0
12.0
11.0
10.0
9.0
1.0
0
.1
.2
.3
.4
.5
.6
.7
.8
.9
1.0
1.1
1.2
1.3
1.4
1.5
1.6
1.7
1.8
1.9
2.0

Table 14–6 **"Buy" List from Stock Universe**

Stock	β_s	$E(R_s)$	Major Stock Group (Industry)	
Quintile 1				
14. AM NAT RES	.78	19.0	Interest Sensitives	(utilities—nat. gas)
27. BUTLER MFG	.84	18.8	Interest Sensitives	(building)
50. DETROITBNK	.80	17.1	Interest Sensitives	(banking and finance)
123. PHILLIPS P	.80	16.9	Basic Goods	(oil—domestic)
68. GEN FOODS	.85	16.4	Consumer Goods	(food and related)
98. MARATH OIL	.74	16.0	Basic Goods	(oil—domestic)
111. NEW ENG G&E	.61	15.8	Interest Sensitives	(utilities—electric)
Quintile 2				
69. GEN MOTORS	.98	18.4	Consumer Goods	(auto and related)
34. CITICORP	.96	17.0	Interest Sensitives	(banking and finance)
95. KIM–CLARK	1.00	17.0	Basic Goods	(paper and containers)
137. SO RAILWAY	1.00	16.9	Basic Goods	(transportation)
86. INLAND STL	.93	16.8	Basic Goods	(metals and mining)
Quintile 3				
62. FORD MOTOR	1.10	22.9	Consumer Goods	(auto and related)
118. PALM BEACH	1.12	20.5	Consumer Goods	(retail goods)
55. DUPONT	1.02	19.0	Basic Goods	(chemicals)
87. INT TEL TL	1.10	18.7	Multi-Industry	(multi-industry)
134. SEARS ROE	1.13	18.1	Consumer Goods	(retailing)
136. SMITHKLINE	1.04	17.5	Consumer Goods	(health care)
3. ACF IND	1.06	17.0	Capital Goods	(machinery)
155. U S GYPSUM	1.09	16.7	Interest Sensitives	(building)
Quintile 4				
77. HERCULES	1.23	20.5	Basic Goods	(chemicals)
133. SCOV MFG	1.21	19.0	Multi-Industry	(multi-industry)
164. WHIRLPOOL	1.32	18.0	Consumer Goods	(retail goods)
81. HOSP OF AM	1.32	17.9	Consumer Goods	(health care)
Quintile 5				
146. STOR TECHN	1.74	25.1	Capital Goods	(office and bus. equip.)
162. WATER ASSO	1.40	23.5	Capital Goods	(aerospace and electronics)
83. HUMANA INC	1.71	23.4	Consumer Goods	(health care)
45. DATAPOINT	1.88	23.4	Capital Goods	(office and bus. equip.)
13. AM MED INT	1.50	23.1	Consumer Goods	(health care)
12. AM INTL	1.70	22.1	Capital Goods	(office and bus. equip.)
104. MILLER–WOH	1.75	21.9	Consumer Goods	(retailing)
49. DENNYS RES	1.63	20.7	Consumer Goods	(leisure and recreation)
80. HON IND	1.88	18.8	Consumer Goods	(retail goods)
168. YELLOW FGT	1.41	17.9	Basic Goods	(transportation)
115. PACCAR INC	1.35	17.3	Consumer Goods	(auto and related)

percent to and from the SML. All stocks on or above the buy line then become candidates for inclusion in the portfolio; stocks on or below the sell line are included on the rejection list.[50]

Table 14–6 is the buy list of stocks from the stock universe, their individual reference numbers, their expected returns and betas, and their stock group and industry classification. For example, Storage Technology has a reference number of 146 and belongs to Quintile 5. It has a beta of 1.74 and an expected return of 25.1 percent. The company belongs to the office and business equipment industry, which is a part of the capital goods group.[51]

The theory behind the use of the decision band as a portfolio construction tool may be reiterated here. Inclusion of only the stocks above the buy line in the initial portfolio automatically ensures that the portfolio will have an expected return at least 1 percent higher than the expected market return for *any* given beta or risk class. Furthermore, it can be assumed that, although the stocks are currently at a disequilibrium, in time they will move toward an equilibrium position. Put differently, in time prices of these undervalued stocks will rise sufficiently, thereby moving them toward the SML. An important implication of this theory is that, because stocks are price-driven, every portfolio must be periodically reviewed and updated so the PM may actively consider the inclusion and exclusion, respectively, of stocks which have moved above and below the buy and sell lines.

Step 6: Investor's Resources and Risk Preference

The PM has now arrived at a crucial point in the task of portfolio construction. Before proceeding further, he must determine a beta for the investor's portfolio. After a careful consideration of all the important factors that influence an investor's risk preference, the PM determines that the investor prefers to take a risk slightly higher than that inherent in the market portfolio, and would prefer a portfolio beta of around 1.1.

Step 7A: Portfolio Construction: Basic Approach

Now that the buy line and the portfolio beta have been firmly established, a portfolio can be constructed. Table 14–7 presents a set of ten stocks randomly selected from the group of stocks appearing on or above the buy line. Remembering that the portfolio beta should be around 1.1, the PM selects both high

[50] Once the portfolio has been constructed, stocks included in the portfolio that subsequently fall below the sell line should be sold.

[51] For simplicity, the buy list presented here was calculated by selecting stocks from the group lying above the buy line drawn in Figure 14–10. Because drawing a line on a graph cannot always be considered a dependable procedure, a more accurate procedure would be to plug the beta value of each stock into the SML equation to determine whether or not the resultant expected return is at least 1 percent lower than the analyst's expected return.

Table 14–7

Stock	Quintile	Beta β_s	Expected Return $E(R_s)$	% of Portfolio	Portfolio β_p	Portfolio $E(R_p)$
14. AM NAT RES	1	.78	19.0	10%	.078	1.90
50. DETROITBNK	1	.80	17.1	10	.080	1.71
111. NEW ENG G&E	1	.61	15.8	10	.061	1.58
34. CITICORP	2	.96	17.0	10	.096	1.70
137. SO RAILWAY	2	1.00	16.9	10	.100	1.69
87. INT TEL TL	3	1.10	18.7	10	.110	1.87
136. SMITHKLINE	3	1.04	17.5	10	.104	1.75
77. HERCULES	4	1.23	20.5	10	.123	2.05
146. STOR TECHN	5	1.74	25.1	10	.174	2.51
49. DENNYS RES	5	1.63	20.7	10	.163	2.07
				100%	1.089	18.83%

and low beta stocks. The table shows that this ten-stock portfolio has a beta of 1.089 and an expected return of 18.83 percent.[52]

Two important caveats should be noted here. First, the stocks included in this portfolio were randomly selected from the buy list to satisfy the portfolio beta requirement. Note that the expected return of the portfolio is greater than the expected market return for this risk class by over 1 percent.[53] Second, the PM always has the choice of building a portfolio by mixing risk-free assets with risky securities. However, he must recognize that a portfolio containing only those stocks that lie *on or above* the buy line will always have an expected return higher than the one which mixes stocks on or above the buy line with risk-free assets which lie on the SML. Of course, this discussion may become purely academic if it becomes impossible to achieve a specified portfolio beta by including in it securities from the buy list. For example, if the investor specifies a beta too low to be achieved by investing in the buy list securities, then the PM would be forced to mix risk-free assets with risky securities to attain the desired portfolio beta.

Step 7B: Portfolio Construction: Sophisticated Approach

Although the simple technique has produced a portfolio in the appropriate risk category, the PM feels that it may not provide the highest possible expected

[52] As demonstrated in Chapter 13 and in Table 14–7, the expected return and beta of a portfolio equal the weighted average of the expected returns and betas of the individual securities in the portfolio, the weights being the proportions invested in the individual securities.

[53] The expected return of the portfolio is 18.83 percent. The expected return of the portfolio lying on the SML and in the same risk class as this portfolio has an expected return of only 15.65 percent:

$$\begin{aligned} E(R_p) &= R_f + \beta_p(E(R_m) - R_f) \\ &= 13.84 + (1.089)(1.66) \\ &= 13.84 + 1.81 \\ &= 15.65\% \end{aligned}$$

Table 14–8

Portfolio A

Maximize: Expected Return $[E(R_p)]$
Subject to: Beta $(\beta_p) = 1.089$

Stock	Quintile	Beta β_s	Expected Return $E(R_s)$	% of Portfolio	Portfolio β_p	Portfolio $E(R_p)$
14. AM NAT RES	1	.78	19.0	3.4%	.0265	.646%
62. FORD MOTOR	2	1.10	22.9	96.6	1.0626	22.120
				100.0%	1.0891	22.766%

Portfolio B

Maximize: Expected Return $[E(R_p)]$
Subject to: Beta $(\beta_p) = 1.089$

No more than 7.5% of portfolio can be invested in any single stock.

Stock	Quintile	Beta β_s	Expected Return $E(R_s)$	% of Portfolio	Portfolio β_p	Portfolio $E(R_p)$
14. AM NAT RES	1	.78	19.0	7.5%	.0585	1.4250
27. BUTLER MFG	1	.84	18.8	7.5	.0630	1.4100
50. DETROITBNK	1	.80	17.1	7.5	.0600	1.2825
123. PHILLIPS P	1	.80	16.9	7.25	.0580	1.2253
111. NEW ENG G&E	1	.61	15.8	7.5	.0458	1.1850
69. GEN MOTORS	2	.98	18.4	7.5	.0735	1.3800
62. FORD MOTOR	3	1.10	22.9	7.5	.0825	1.7175
118. PALM BEACH	3	1.12	20.5	7.5	.0840	1.5375
55. DUPONT	3	1.02	19.0	7.5	.0765	1.4250
77. HERCULES	4	1.23	20.5	7.5	.0923	1.5375
146. STOR TECHN	5	1.74	25.1	7.5	.1305	1.8825
162. WATER ASSO	5	1.40	23.5	7.5	.1050	1.7625
83. HUMANA	5	1.71	23.4	2.75	.0470	.6435
13. AM MED INT	5	1.50	23.1	7.5	.1125	1.7325
				100.0%	1.0891	20.1463%

return. He therefore decides to resort to the technique of linear programming to discover whether the expected return of the portfolio could be improved further.

Single Constraint

By using linear programming, the PM chooses stocks from the acceptable set to construct a portfolio that will maximize the expected return. The single constraint is that the portfolio beta should be 1.089—the same as that of the previous portfolio. The portfolio produced by the computer as the optimum portfolio is shown as Portfolio A in Table 14–8. Note that the portfolio

Table 14–9

Maximize: Expected Return [$E(R_p)$]
Subject to: Beta (β_p) = 1.089

No more than 7.5% of portfolio can be invested in any single stock.

Stock	Quintile	Beta β_s	Expected Return $E(R_s)$	% of Portfolio	Portfolio β_p	Portfolio $E(R_p)$
14. AM NAT RES	1	.78	19.0	5.0%	.0390	.950
27. BUTLER MFG	1	.84	18.8	5.0	.0420	.940
50. DETROITBNK	1	.80	17.1	5.0	.0400	.855
123. PHILLIPS P	1	.80	16.9	5.0	.0400	.845
68. GEN FOODS	1	.85	16.4	5.0	.0425	.820
98. MARATHN OIL	1	.74	16.0	5.0	.0370	.800
111. NEW ENG G&E	1	.61	15.8	5.0	.0305	.790
69. GEN MOTORS	2	.98	18.4	5.0	.0490	.920
34. CITICORP	2	.96	17.0	3.044	.0292	.517
86. INLAND STL	2	.93	16.8	5.0	.0465	.840
62. FORD MOTOR	3	1.10	22.9	5.0	.0550	1.145
118. PALM BEACH	3	1.12	20.5	5.0	.0560	1.025
55. DUPONT	3	1.02	19.0	5.0	.0510	.950
87. INT TEL TL	3	1.10	18.7	5.0	.0550	.935
77. HERCULES	4	1.23	20.5	5.0	.0615	1.025
133. SCOV MFG	4	1.21	19.0	5.0	.0605	.950
146. STOR TECHN	5	1.74	25.1	5.0	.0870	1.255
162. WATER ASSO	5	1.40	23.5	5.0	.0700	1.175
83. HUMANA	5	1.71	23.4	5.0	.0855	1.170
45. DATAPOINT	5	1.88	23.4	1.956	.0367	.458
13. AM MED INT	5	1.50	23.1	5.0	.0750	1.155
				100.0%	1.0889	19.520%

consists of only two stocks; of this, over 96 percent of the fund is invested in Ford Motor stock. The beta of the portfolio is 1.0891 and the expected return is 22.77 percent—almost 4 percent higher than the portfolio constructed without the use of linear programming.

Multiple Constraints

The PM recognizes that the two-stock portfolio violates the basic diversification principle and is therefore unacceptable. Consequently, he constructs a second portfolio subject to the following limitations: (1) The portfolio beta should be 1.089, and (2) no more than 7.5 percent of the total funds should be invested in any one stock (which guarantees that at least 14 securities will be included in the portfolio).

The portfolio constructed by the computer to meet these specifications is presented as Portfolio B in Table 14–8. Note that this portfolio has the same beta as the previous portfolio but has an expected return of 20.15 percent,

Table 14–10

Maximize: Expected Return $[E(R_p)]$
Subject to: Beta $(\beta_p) = 1.089$

No more than 7.5% of portfolio can be invested in any single stock, *and* not more than 25% in any major stock group.

Stock	Quintile	Stock Group	Beta β_s	Expected Return $E(R_s)$	% in Portfolio	Portfolio β_p	Portfolio $E(R_p)$
14. AM NAT RES	1	Int. Sensitive	.78	19.0	7.5%	.0585	1.4250
27. BUTLER MFG	1	Int. Sensitive	.84	18.8	7.5	.0630	1.4100
50. DETROITBNK	1	Int. Sensitive	.80	17.1	2.5	.0200	.4275
123. PHILLIPS P	1	Basic Goods	.80	16.9	7.5	.0600	1.2675
98. MARATHN OIL	1	Basic Goods	.74	16.0	2.5	.0185	.4000
111. NEW ENG G&E	1	Int. Sensitive	.61	15.8	7.5	.0458	1.1850
69. GEN MOTORS	2	Consumer Goods	.98	18.4	2.12	.0208	.3900
62. FORD MOTOR	3	Consumer Goods	1.10	22.9	7.5	.0825	1.7175
118. PALM BEACH	3	Consumer Goods	1.12	20.5	7.5	.0840	1.5375
55. DUPONT	3	Basic Goods	1.02	19.0	7.5	.0765	1.4250
87. INT TEL TL	3	Multi-Industry	1.10	18.7	7.5	.0825	1.4025
77. HERCULES	4	Basic Goods	1.23	20.5	7.5	.0923	1.5375
133. SCOV MFG	4	Multi-Industry	1.21	19.0	2.5	.0303	.4750
146. STOR TECHN	5	Capital Goods	1.74	25.1	7.5	.1305	1.8825
162. WATER ASSO	5	Capital Goods	1.40	23.5	7.5	.1050	1.7625
83. HUMANA	5	Consumer Goods	1.71	23.4	0.38	.0065	.0889
13. AM MED INT	5	Consumer Goods	1.50	23.1	7.5	.1125	1.7325
					100.0%	1.0892	20.0664%

Stock Group	% in Portfolio
Interest Sensitive	25.0%
Consumer Goods	25.0
Basic Goods	25.0
Capital Goods	15.0
Multi-Industry	10.0
Total	100.0%

which is lower than the return of Portfolio A. This demonstrates several important portfolio principles.

First, the two-stock portfolio presented as Portfolio A had an expected return of 22.77 percent and a beta of 1.0891. Because this is the optimum portfolio for that risk class, it is impossible to increase the expected return without increasing the portfolio beta.

Second, when an additional constraint was added, the expected return of Portfolio B dropped to 20.15 percent. That an imposition of additional or more restrictive constraints further lowers the expected return is clearly demonstrated in Table 14–9. In this example, the proportion of total funds that could be invested in any single stock was lowered from the previous level of 7.5 percent to 5 percent. This more restrictive constraint caused the expected return to decline to 19.52 percent. In a second example, to the original constraints of a beta of 1.089 and a 7.5 percent limit on any single stock another constraint is imposed: The percentage allowed in any major stock group is limited to 25 percent.[54] As demonstrated in Table 14–10, this additional constraint reduced the expected return from 20.15 to 20.07 percent.

These examples clearly demonstrate that the imposition of multiple constraints, which generally leads to greater diversification, involves a sacrifice of expected returns. However, the portfolio theory holds that such a sacrifice has its rewards; diversification is the basis for reduction—and eventual elimination—of unsystematic risk in a portfolio.

[54] The constraint values which limit individual stock and major stock group concentrations were selected arbitrarily for illustrative purposes only. Also, additional constraints could easily be added to ensure limited concentration in any single industry.

Further Consideration of SML*

Because the risk-free rate and expected risk premium for investing in stocks are likely to change over time, the position and the slope of the SML are likely to change as well. This phenomenon, coupled with the fact that rates on AAA bonds† change under varying market conditions, provides the development of a unique investment strategy.

Figure 14–A presents the changing positions of the SML in relation to the AAA bond rate. Two important observations can be made on the basis of this figure. First, the higher the SML in relation to the AAA bond rate, the more attractive the stocks become relative to bonds, because the expected rate of return on stocks progressively exceeds that on safe bonds. Second, the greater the slope of the SML, the more attractive the high beta stocks become relative to the low beta issues. Therefore, in June 1972, when the gap between the SML and the bond rate was narrow, and the SML was relatively flat, an investor would have done well to switch from stocks to bonds. The reverse strategy would have worked well in November of 1974 when conditions were opposite to those prevailing in June 1972. Furthermore, because the 1974 slope of the SML was steep, the aggressive investors would have benefited from investing in high beta securities.

* Adapted from Paul Blustein, "What's the Big Fuss About Modern Portfolio Theory?" *Forbes*, June 12, 1978, pp. 42–43.

† Remember that AAA bonds are of the highest quality.

Third, a greater degree
the expected return only v
things being equal, an inc
pected return. For examp
stocks for Portfolio B in
is allowed to increase fro
20.146 percent to 21.65 p
.90, the expected return o

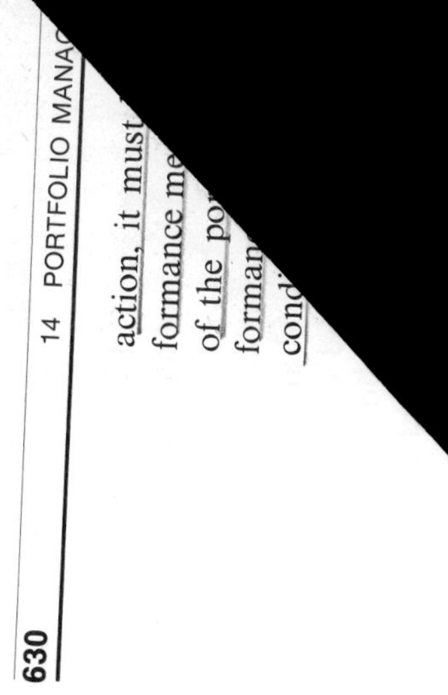
14 PORTFOLIO MANA
630
action, it must
formance me
of the po
forman
cond

Portfolio Management

Portfolio management i
identification of a portfo
risk preference. After the

Figure 14–A

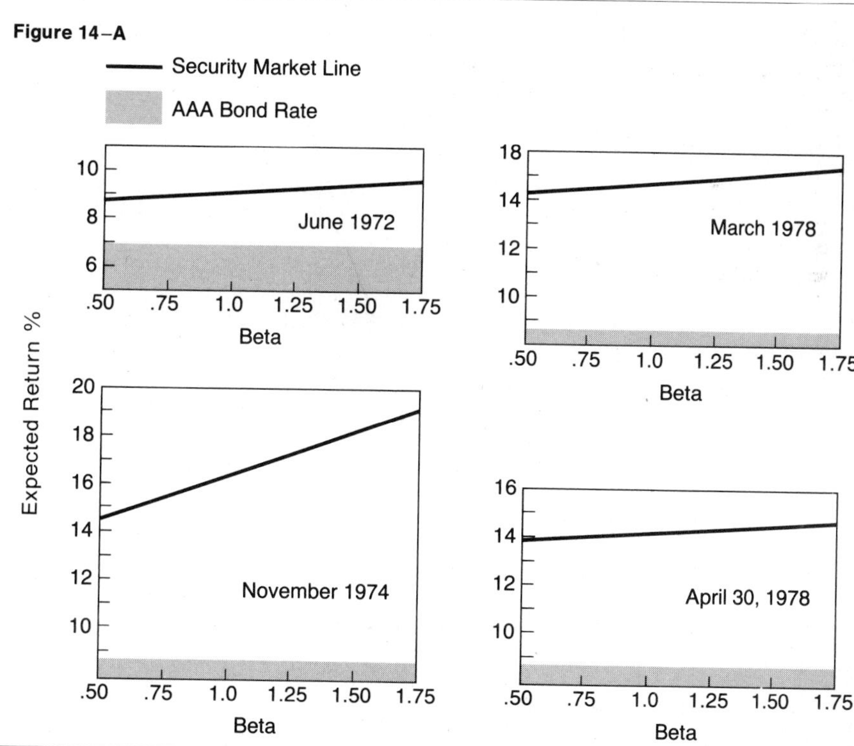

…be periodically evaluated according to some acceptable per…asure. The final step in portfolio management is a reorganization …tfolio because of the following conditions: (1) unsatisfactory per…ce, (2) a change in the investor's risk preference, (3) a change in market …itions, or (4) changes in the characteristics of the assets themselves.

Change in Key Variables

The previous discussion on portfolio construction has underscored an important point: A portfolio constructed for an investor can be considered ideal only if it is developed against the backdrop of the prevailing outlook for national economic, industry, and company conditions and if it is consistent with the risk preference of that investor. It follows, therefore, that any change in one or more of these factors would call for a reorganization of the portfolio.

More specifically, suppose an investor who originally had a low risk preference grows more aggressive. The PM will then identify a new indifference curve and construct the higher portfolio beta desired by the investor. A higher beta would invariably change the composition of the portfolio, because the manager would substitute more high return-high beta stocks for the low risk stocks. In a different situation where the investor wishes to commit more funds to his portfolio, the PM may alter the constraint to change, for instance, the percentage of total funds that can be invested in a single stock. Such examples could be easily multiplied.

A change in the forecast of national economic, industry and company conditions is another compelling reason for reorganizing a portfolio. If, for example, a severe recession has just been predicted for the next couple of years, it would be reasonable to assume that the expected returns of stocks would decline. Consequently, such a development would call for a reorganization of the existing portfolio. It should be emphasized, however, that both portfolio construction and portfolio reorganization require the PM to follow each of the seven steps presented earlier.

Unsatisfactory Performance

A portfolio may also be reorganized if its past performance has been unsatisfactory. Performance measures can range from calculating a simple rate of return on the original investment to more complex indicators. The rate of return measure is simple and needs no explanation. Discussions of several other sophisticated measures follow.

Reward-to-Variability Ratio William F. Sharpe used the Capital Market Line (CML) to measure the performance of a well-diversified portfolio. His measure, called the *Reward-to-Variability Ratio* (*RVR*), is a ratio of the excess return from a portfolio to the portfolio risk. Symbolically,

$$\text{RVR} = \frac{R_p - R_f}{\sigma_p} \tag{14-1}$$

where

$R_p - R_f$ = Return on portfolio over the risk-free rate
σ_p = Standard deviation, or risk of the portfolio

The RVR specifies the return over the risk-free rate earned by a portfolio per unit of risk assumed. Consequently, the higher the ratio, the better is the performance of the portfolio.

The Sharpe measure can be viewed from another angle. If the market was in equilibrium for the period under study, the rate of return that a portfolio *should have* earned, R'_p, equals:[55]

$$R'_p = R_f + \sigma_p\left(\frac{R_m - R_f}{\sigma_m}\right) \tag{14-2}$$

where

R'_p = Return the portfolio should have earned (if the market had been in equilibrium)
R_f = Rate of return on risk-free asset
R_m = Return on market
σ_m = Standard deviation or risk of the market
σ_p = Standard deviation or risk of the portfolio

If the actual return of a portfolio is greater than the return which should have been earned—that is, $R_p > R'_p$—then the portfolio has outperformed the market, given its level of risk. Similarly, if the actual return equals the return that should have been obtained, the portfolio did as well as the market.

[55] This equation is derived in the following manner: At equilibrium,

$$\frac{R'_p - R_f}{\sigma_p} = \frac{R_m - R_f}{\sigma_m}$$

$$R'_p - R_f = \sigma_p\left[\frac{R_m - R_f}{\sigma_m}\right]$$

$$R'_p = R_f + \sigma_p\left[\frac{R_m - R_f}{\sigma_m}\right]$$

For example, assume the following data for a given time period:

$$R_f = 8\%$$
$$R_m = 13\%$$
$$\sigma_m = .30$$
$$\sigma_p = .12$$

The portfolio should have returned 10 percent if the market was in equilibrium:

$$R'_p = .08 + .12\left(\frac{.13 - .08}{.30}\right)$$
$$= .08 + .02$$
$$= .10 \text{ (or } 10\%)$$

If the portfolio returned, say, 12 percent, then $R_p > R'_p$, and the performance of the portfolio was satisfactory.

Reward-to-Volatility Ratio Sharpe used the CML on which only efficient portfolios can lie. The *Reward-to-Volatility Ratio* (*RVLR*), developed by Jack Treynor, expresses the relationship of the excess return one achieves on any asset holding to the amount of *systematic risk* assumed. Symbolically,

$$\text{RVLR} = \frac{R_p - R_f}{\beta_p} \tag{14-3}$$

Treynor used the SML to develop his ratio. Remember that the SML is a straight line which relates expected return to only systematic risk and on which both individual securities and portfolios can lie. Here again, it is easy to see that the larger the RVLR, the better is the excess return per unit of risk, and the better the performance of the portfolio.

The Jensen Performance Index The *Jensen Performance Index* (*JPI*) is a variant of the RVLR measure.

If the market were in equilibrium for the period under study, the return that a portfolio *should have* earned, R'_p, would equal:

$$R'_p = R_f + \beta_p[R_m - R_f] \tag{14-4}$$

Note that this is simply the SML equation in historical terms.

However, if there were a temporary disequilibrium in the market which the portfolio manager was able to exploit, the actual return on the portfolio, R_p, would be greater than the return the portfolio should have earned, or $R_p > R'_p$. In this case, the actual return would equal:

$$R_p = \alpha_p^* + R_f + \beta_p[R_m - R_f]$$

where the portfolio manager would have achieved a *positive* risk-adjusted excess return ($\alpha_p^* > 0$), thereby making $R_p > R'_p$ and beating the market. However, if the risk-adjusted excess return were equal to zero ($\alpha_p^* = 0$), then R_p would equal R'_p and the manager would have performed as well as the market. Likewise, a portfolio with a negative risk-adjusted excess return ($\alpha_p^* < 0$) would have underperformed the market, because R_p would be less than R'_p.

In summary, the Jensen Performance Index can be expressed in the following form:

$$\text{JPI} = R_p - R'_p \tag{14–5}$$

Clearly, a positive JPI indicates that the portfolio manager is superior in market timing or stock selection. The reverse would be true for a negative JPI.

Regardless of which performance measure is used, an unsatisfactory performance calls for some action on the part of the PM. However, before acting on the results, an important limitation of these measures should be recognized. Because of the nature of performance measures, the success or failure of a portfolio should be judged over a relatively long period.

The Reorganization Process

Regardless of the causes that trigger the portfolio reorganization process, active portfolio management involves at least the steps already specified. The PM begins by reevaluating the risk preference or the utility function of the investor. An investor's risk preference is based on a host of factors which may change over time. A critical evaluation of these factors helps the PM to identify the appropriate indifference curve which, in turn, leads to a determination of the portfolio beta.

Next, the PM analyzes the portfolio constraints. In the previous example, he had decided to invest no more than 7.5 percent of the total funds in any one stock. The question must now be asked: How should these constraints be modified?

Constraints, of course, are an investor's indirect expressions of investment goals which may change over time. Consequently, the PM attempts to find out what goals have changed since the portfolio was first constructed or last reorganized. If the investor is now in a high income tax bracket, the emphasis might be shifted from income to growth company stocks in order to minimize the tax burden.[56] If more diversification is desired and the resources now permit it, the 7.5 percent constraint may be suitably modified. In short, the PM carefully evaluates the current situation and selects a set of constraints that will best achieve the investor's goals.

[56] The tax issue will be discussed in Chapter 16.

The third major step in active management revolves around the security analyst. He or she must recalculate the expected returns of all the securities in the universe by carefully analyzing the national economic, industry, and company conditions. The analyst must also generate the beta for each stock, either through personal calculations or by obtaining it from a beta service.

Once the expected return and the beta for each security in the stock universe have been obtained from the security analyst, the PM can proceed to repeat the entire process by performing several mechanical chores. First, the data points are plotted on a graph. Second, the set is divided into five beta quintiles. Third, the median for each quintile is calculated. Fourth, the SML is generated on the basis of the five median points. Fifth, the decision band is constructed by drawing a buy and sell line around the SML.

The fourth and final major step in active management requires that the PM sell the securities that have dropped below the sell line. However, stocks that have moved from their previous positions but are still within the decision band should be retained. Furthermore, stocks which are currently on or above the buy line but not in the portfolio should be analyzed for possible inclusion in the portfolio. It should be added here that because it may take a long time for stocks to move into an equilibrium position, and because it is assumed that the investor's risk preference remains fairly stable, it might be expected that the portfolio will be updated no more frequently than, say, twice a year.

A Final Note

In this section an attempt has been made to present in an analytical fashion the technique of active portfolio construction and management. This presentation was made with a two-fold objective in mind. The first objective was to demonstrate the theoretical underpinnings of portfolio management. The capital market theory asserts that every investor should strive to construct and maintain a well-diversified portfolio which carries no unsystematic risk. The second objective was to emphasize that, with active portfolio management, it is difficult to construct a portfolio that will diversify away all or most of the unsystematic risk while simultaneously maximizing an investor's expected return for a given value of beta.

It is necessary to add one final note. The actual process of portfolio construction and management is infinitely more complicated than it appears on the surface. Starting with an in-depth analysis of some 200 stocks in order to determine their expected returns and risks and ending with an optimal portfolio requires the skills, dedication, and total commitment of dozens of analysts, computer programmers, and a highly sophisticated portfolio manager capable of putting it all together. Needless to say, all of this is beyond the resources of all but the most resourceful investors. Nevertheless, these comprehensive and fairly sophisticated management procedures have been presented not only for pedagogical reasons, but to demonstrate the complexity and the involved nature of the task of portfolio management.

Summary

In the late 1950s and the early 1960s, the process by which common stock prices are determined became a controversial issue. This controversy later resulted in the establishment of the *Efficient Market Hypothesis* (*EMH*).

The *weak form* of the EMH implies that knowledge of trading volumes and past fluctuations in stock prices does not help investors in improving their performance. Results of tests of the weak form clearly favor its acceptance.

Supporters of the *semistrong form* argue that the current stock price fully reflects the information which only sophisticated analysis of fundamental factors can uncover. This argument implies that there is little point in engaging in fundamental analysis, because the market is so efficient that it reflects all publicly known fundamental factors. The weight of current evidence strongly favors the semistrong form of the EMH, although studies have shown some degree of inefficiency in the market.

The *strong form* is based on the assumption that the prices of stocks reflect all publicly available information as well as the information possessed only by super analysts. The evidence thus far does not fully support this form of the EMH.

Investors who accept all forms of the EMH prefer *passive portfolio management*. Those who reject at least the semistrong form attempt *active portfolio management*.

The passive portfolio management strategy, which is based on the Separation Theorem, requires no investment decision. Instead, it recommends that an investor hold the market portfolio, levered up by borrowing or loaned up by mixing the market portfolio with riskless assets. Only when there is a change in either the individual risk preference or the risk–return composition of the market portfolio should the passive manager be induced to reorganize the individual portfolio.

Active investment managers reject the idea that the market portfolio is the most desired portfolio. Instead, they assert that by applying superior technical and analytical skills it is possible to construct a portfolio which, if properly managed, will consistently outperform the market.

Under the active management strategy, an optimum portfolio can be constructed by undertaking a seven-step operation. These steps include, among other things, establishing a stock universe, developing the SML, determining the decision band, and specifying a set of constraints. The *linear programming technique* can then be used to determine an optimum portfolio.

Portfolio management involves a reorganization of the existing portfolio. The need for reorganization may arise because of a change in the investor's risk preference or in market conditions. A portfolio may also be changed if the past performance of the portfolio has been unsatisfactory. In reorganizing a portfolio, the manager must follow the same seven steps used for constructing a portfolio.

A Look Ahead

In this chapter, investors have been presented with a choice between passive and active portfolio management. Their choices are, however, not limited to these two types. Another choice—investing in the shares of investment companies—will be explored in Chapter 15.

Concepts for Review

Efficient Market Hypothesis (EMH)
- The weak form
- The semistrong form
- The strong form

Tests of market efficiency
Random Walk Hypothesis
Implications of the EMH
Passive investment strategy
Passive portfolio management
Index funds
Active investment strategy
Active portfolio management
Portfolio construction
Optimum portfolio
Capital Market Line (CML)
Security Market Line (SML)
Indifference curve
Stock universe
Portfolio size
Expected return–beta points
Market equilibrium
Price-driven
Decision range
Buy and sell Lines
Linear programming technique
Reward-to-Variability Ratio (RVR)
Reward-to-Volatility Ratio (RVLR)
Jensen Performance Index (JPI)

Questions for Review

1. What are the implications of rejecting the weak form of the EMH? What are the implications of accepting only the strong form of the EMH?
2. Compare passive with active portfolio management. Under what conditions would you subscribe to each approach?
3. How do the roles of the securities analyst and portfolio manager differ? How are they interrelated?
4. Is good portfolio management a substitute for good security analysis? Explain.
5. Investor W states that portfolio management is useless because the market is efficient. How would you respond?
6. Explain the advantages and disadvantages of diversification in active management.

7. Describe the seven steps an active portfolio manager should follow in order to construct a portfolio.
8. Describe the construction of the decision band. Why is it used?
9. What role do risk-free assets play in the construction of a portfolio?
10. Comment on the following statement: "Portfolio managers try to find an optimum portfolio, because it has the highest expected return."
11. How would you interpret a steeper slope of the SML? How would you interpret a lower SML relative to high quality bond yields?
12. Why does an active portfolio manager limit the size of the stock universe?
13. Portfolio Manager G constructs a portfolio comprised only of stocks which lie *above* the SML. However, after a year the return on the portfolio is below its expected return, and even below the expected market return for the same risk class. Is this possible?
14. Is there a difference between portfolio construction and portfolio management? Explain.
15. Compare the three portfolio performance measures. Are there any substantive differences between them?

Problems

1. You are a portfolio manager currently constructing a portfolio. Working with a stock universe of about 200 issues, security analysts have just given you the expected return and beta values for each stock. You promptly arrange the stocks into five risk quintiles; the risk of each group progressively increases, with the fifth quintile consisting of stocks with the highest beta values. The median beta and median expected return for each quintile are as follows:

Quintile	Median β_s	Median $E(R_s)$
1	.80	15.7
2	1.00	16.2
3	1.10	16.3
4	1.33	16.4
5	1.50	17.0

Using this data, derive the SML equation. Under what circumstances would you use median beta and expected return values to derive the equation? What is the alternative method?

2. Referring to the previous problem, you ask your assistant to analyze the security analysts' data on the stock universe and prepare a list of undervalued stocks from which you can select when building your portfolio. You specify that the previously derived SML and a 1 percent decision band should be used. He gives you the following list of stocks as shown in Table 14-A. Evaluate it and make modifications, if necessary.
3. You have been asked by a client to construct a "well-diversified" portfolio of common stocks with a beta of approximately 1.25. You give the job to your assistant, who proposes the following portfolio. The stocks were selected from the list finalized in the previous problem.

Table 14–A **Assistant's List of "Buy" Stocks**

Stock	β_s	$E(R_s)$	Major Stock Group
Quintile 1			
Cullen Frost Bankers	.80	18.1	Interest Sensitives
Armco, Inc.	.78	17.4	Basic Goods
Witco Chemical	.89	17.3	Basic Goods
Royal Dutch Petroleum	.65	16.7	Basic Goods
Alcan Aluminum	.88	17.0	Basic Goods
Florida Power & Light	.85	15.4	Interest Sensitives
Baltimore Gas & Electric	.75	14.8	Interest Sensitives
Foremost-McKesson	.90	18.1	Multi-Industry
Celanese	.91	18.1	Basic Goods
Texas Commerce Bankshares	.80	17.1	Interest Sensitives
Quintile 2			
Transway International	1.00	21.4	Basic Goods
Wells Fargo	1.00	17.8	Interest Sensitives
Koppers Co.	1.05	17.5	Basic Goods
Supermarkets General	1.04	16.6	Consumer Goods
Dayco Corp.	.95	16.5	Consumer Goods
Block (H&R) Inc.	1.05	17.7	Consumer Goods
Thomas & Betts, Inc.	.96		Capital Goods
Cities Service	.97	15.7	Basic Goods
Coors (Adolph)	.95	17.9	Consumer Goods
Lone Star Industries	1.04	17.8	Interest Sensitives
Quintile 3			
Zurn Industries	1.20	19.3	Capital Goods
Fox Stanley Photo	1.12	19.4	Consumer Goods
Shoneys, Inc.	1.10	17.6	Consumer Goods
Bandag, Inc.	1.21	17.9	Consumer Goods
Knight-Ridder Newspapers	1.08	17.0	Consumer Goods

Stock	β_s	$E(R_s)$	% of Portfolio
Cullen Frost Bankers	.80	18.1%	5
Texas Commerce Bankshares	.80	17.1	15
Wells Fargo	1.00	17.8	15
Kaufman & Broad	1.65	18.9	40
Lone Star Industries	1.04	17.8	25
			100

Your assistant notes that this portfolio has an expected return which exceeds the expected market return for the same risk class by over 1 percent.

a. In evaluating this portfolio, can you find any problems?
b. Can this portfolio be improved? If so, demonstrate how this can be accomplished.
c. Mention any assumptions or other factors that should be considered before the portfolio is finalized.

Table 14–A (*continued*) **Assistant's List of "Buy" Stocks**

Stock	β_s	$E(R_s)$	Major Stock Group
Quintile 3			
Bethlehem Steel	1.15	19.4	Basic Goods
Litton Industries	1.15	17.9	Multi-Industry
Hewlett-Packard	1.13	14.6	Capital Goods
Seaboard Coast Line	1.09	17.7	Basic Goods
ARA Services, Inc.	1.10	16.4	Consumer Goods
Quintile 4			
Payless Cashways	1.25	18.4	Consumer Goods
Metromedia	1.30	17.7	Consumer Goods
Data General, Inc.	1.30	19.7	Capital Goods
Avnet, Inc.	1.35	18.0	Capital Goods
Wang Laboratories	1.38	16.6	Capital Goods
Phelps Dodge Corp.	1.29	18.3	Basic Goods
Motorola, Inc.	1.25	15.3	Capital Goods
Marriot Corp.	1.39	14.3	Consumer Goods
Tesoro Petroleum	1.26	19.1	Basic Goods
City Investing	1.29	18.6	Multi-Industry
Quintile 5			
Saga Corp.	1.49	22.2	Consumer Goods
Wendy's International	1.45	23.6	Consumer Goods
Kaufman & Broad, Inc.	1.65	18.9	Interest Sensitives
Jerrico, Inc.	1.87	18.2	Consumer Goods
Resorts International	1.51	20.5	Consumer Goods
Itel Corp.	1.75	22.6	Capital Goods
Advanced Micro Devices	1.69	16.3	Capital Goods
MCA Inc.	1.48	14.8	Consumer Goods
Prime Computer	1.55	18.0	Capital Goods
Sante Fe International	1.50	26.1	Basic Goods

4. Consider the following data:

	Return	Beta	Standard Deviation
Market Portfolio	13.2%	1.00	.20
Risk-free Security	10.1	0	0
Portfolio N	11.9	.82	.13
Portfolio P	14.0	1.39	.27

a. Calculate the Reward-to-Volatility Ratio for portfolios N and P. Interpret your findings.

b. Recalculate the Reward-to-Volatility Ratio for each portfolio using an 8.7 percent risk-free rate. Interpret your findings.

c. Use the Reward-to-Volatility Ratio to evaluate each portfolio. What are your findings?

d. Use the Jensen Performance Index to evaluate each portfolio. What are your findings?

Footnotes

49. The least squares line is fitted through the median points as follows:

Calculation

X (β_s)	Y [$E(R_s)$]	XY	X^2
.75	15.3	11.475	.5625
.96	15.3	14.688	.9216
1.08	16.0	17.280	1.1664
1.23	14.9	18.327	1.5129
1.48	16.8	24.864	2.1904
$\sum$ = 5.50	78.3	86.634	6.3538

$$\text{Slope} = \frac{(5)(86.634) - (5.5)(78.3)}{(5)(6.3538) - (5.5)^2} = \frac{2.520}{1.519} = 1.66$$

$$\text{Y-intercept} = \left[\frac{78.3}{5}\right] - (1.66)\left[\frac{5.5}{5}\right]$$

$$= 13.84$$

SML Equation:

$$E(R_s) = 13.84\% + \beta_s(1.66\%)$$

Selected Readings

Alexander, Sidney S. "Price Movements in Speculative Markets: Trends or Random Walks." *Industrial Management Review*, May 1961.

Ambachtsheer, Keith P. and James L. Farrell, Jr. "Can Active Management Add Value?" *Financial Analysts Journal*, November–December 1979.

Arbit, Harold L. and James E. Rhodes. "Performance Goals in a Generally Efficient Market." *Journal of Portfolio Management*, Fall 1976.

Basu, S. "Investment Performance of Common Stocks in Relation to Their Price–Earnings Ratios: A Test of the Efficient Market Hypothesis." *Journal of Finance*, June 1977.

Bauman, W. Scott. "Performance Objectives of Investors." Occasional Paper No. 2. Charlottesville, Va.: Financial Analysts Research Foundation, 1975.

Bauman, W. Scott. "Evaluation of the Portfolio Management System." Occasional Paper No. 3. Charlottesville, Va.: Financial Analysts Research Foundation, 1975.

Bierman, Bonini, and D. Hausman. *Quantitative Analysis for Business Decisions*. Homewood, Ill.: Richard D. Irwin, 1977.

Bear, Robert M. and Adam K. Gehr. "Association of Returns to Alternative Investment Media: The Government Bond–Common Stock Case." *Journal of Economics and Business*, Fall 1975.

Beckerman, Neil G. "A Primer on Random Walks in the Stock Market." *New England Economic Review*, Federal Reserve Bank of Boston, September–October 1978.

Black, Fischer, Michael C. Jensen, and Myron Scholes. "The Capital Asset Pricing Model: Some Empirical Tests." In *Studies in the Theory of Capital Markets*. Ed. Michael C. Jensen. New York: Praeger Publishers, 1972.

Blume, Marshall E. "The Assessment of Portfolio Performance—An Application to Portfolio Theory." Unpublished Ph.D. dissertation, University of Chicago, 1968.

Blume, Marshall E. "Portfolio Theory: A Step Toward Its Practical Application." *Journal of Business*, April 1970.

Bower, Richard and Donald Wippern. "Risk–Return Measurement in Portfolio Selection and Performance Appraisal Models: Progress Report." *Journal of Financial and Quantitative Analysis*, December 1969.

Brown, Stewart L. "Earnings Changes, Stock Prices, and Market Efficiency." *Journal of Finance*, March 1978.

Chen, Andrew, Frank Jen and Stanley Zionts. "The Optimal Portfolio Revision Policy." *Journal of Business*, January 1971.

Cohen, Kalman J. and Jerry A. Pogue. "An Empirical Evaluation of Alternative Portfolio Selection Models." *Journal of Business*, April 1967.

Colker, S.S. "An Analysis of Security Recommendations by Brokerage Houses." *Quarterly Review of Economics and Business*, Summer 1963.

Cranshaw, T. E. "The Evaluation of Investment Performance." *Journal of Business*, October 1977.

Davies, Peter Lloyd and Michael Canes. "Stock Prices and the Publication of Second-Hand Information." *Journal of Business*, January 1978.

Dorfman, Dan. "Why Can't Research Directors Hold Their Jobs?" *Institutional Investor*, October 1973.

Ehrbar, A. F. "Index-Funds—An Idea Whose Time Is Coming." *Fortune*, June 1976.

Elton, Edwin J., Martin J. Gruber, and Manfred W. Padberg. "Optimal Portfolios from Simple Ranking Devices." *Journal of Portfolio Management*, Spring 1978.

Elton, Edwin J., Martin J. Gruber, and Manfred W. Padberg. "Simple Criteria for Optimal Portfolio Selection." *Journal of Finance*, December 1976.

Evaluation and Measurement of Investment Performance. Seminars on Portfolio Management. Charlottesville, Va.: Financial Analysts Research Foundation, 1977.

Evans, John L. "Diversification and the Reduction of Dispersion: An Empirical Analysis." *Journal of Finance*, December 1968.

Fama, Eugene F. "Components of Investment Performance." *Journal of Finance*, June 1972.

Fama, Eugene F. "Efficient Capital Markets: A Review of the Theory and Empirical Work." *Journal of Finance*, May 1970.

Fama, Eugene F., and Marshall Blume. "Filter Rules and Stock Market Trading Profits." *Journal of Business*, January 1966, Supplement.

Fama, Eugene F., et al. "The Adjustment of Stock Prices to New Information." *International Economic Review*, February 1969.

Farrar, Donald Eugene. *The Investment Decision under Uncertainty*. Englewood Cliffs, N.J.: Prentice-Hall, 1962.

Farrell, James, Jr. "The Multi-Index Model and Practical Portfolio Analysis." Occasional Paper No. 4. Charlottesville, Va.: Financial Analysts Research Foundation, 1976.

Farrell, James, Jr., and Keith Ambachtsheer. "Can Active Management Add Value?" Unpublished paper, 1979.

Ferguson, Robert. "Active Portfolio Management." *Financial Analysts Journal*, May–June 1975.

Ferguson, Robert. "Performance Measurement Doesn't Make Sense." *Financial Analysts Journal*, May–June 1980.

Fisher, Lawrence. "Using Modern Portfolio Theory to Maintain an Efficiently Diversified Portfolio." *Financial Analysts Journal*, May–June 1975.

Fisher, Lawrence, and J. Lorie. "Rates of Return on Investments in Common Stocks: The Year-to-Year Period, 1926–1965." *Journal of Business*, July 1968.

Friend, Irwin, and Marshall Blume. "Measurement of Portfolio Performance Under Uncertainty." *American Economic Review*, September 1970.

Friend, Irwin, and Douglas Vickers. "Portfolio Selection and Investment Performance." *Journal of Finance*, September 1965.

Gaumnitz, Jack E. "Investment Diversification under Uncertainty: An Examination of the Number of Securities in a Diversified Portfolio." Unpublished Ph.D. dissertation, Stanford University, 1967.

Goodzwaard, Maurice B., and Keith V. Smith. "How Trustmen View Their Objectives." *Institutional Investor*, February 1972.

Grubel, Herbert G. "The Peter Principle and the Efficient Market Hypothesis." *Financial Analysts Journal*, November–December 1979.

Hakansson, Nils H. "Capital Growth and the Mean-Variance Approach to Portfolio Selection." *Journal of Financial and Quantitative Analysis*, January 1971.

Hodges, Stewert D., and Richard A. Brealey. "Portfolio Selection in a Dynamic and Uncertain World." *Financial Analysts Journal*, March–April 1975.

Jacob, Nancy L. "A Limited-Diversification Portfolio Selection Model for the Small Investor." *Journal of Finance*, June 1974.

James, F. E. "Moving Monthly Averages—An Effective Investment Tool?" *Journal of Financial and Quantitative Analysis*, September 1968.

Jensen, Michael C. "The Performance of Mutual Funds in the Period 1945–64." *Journal of Finance*, May 1968.

Jensen, Michael C. "Risk, the Pricing of Capital Assets, and the Evaluation of Investment Portfolios." *Journal of Business*, April 1969.

Joy, O. Maurice, Robert H. Litzenberger, and Richard W. McEnally, "The Adjustment of Stock Prices to Announcements of Unanticipated Changes in Quarterly Earnings." *Journal of Accounting Research*, Autumn 1977.

Klemkosky, Robert C. "The Bias in Composite Performance Measures." *Journal of Financial and Quantitative Analysis*, June 1973.

Klemkosky, Robert C. "How Consistently Do Managers Manage?" *Journal of Portfolio Management*, Winter 1977.

Klemkosky, Robert C., and John D. Martin. "The Effect of Market Risk on Portfolio Diversification." *Journal of Finance*, March 1975.

Kuehner, Charles D. "Efficient Markets and Random Walk." In *Financial Analyst's Handbook*. Ed. Sumner N. Levine. Homewood, Ill.: Richard D. Irwin, 1975.

Levy, Haim. "Equilibrium in an Imperfect Market: A Constraint on the Number of Securities in the Portfolio." *American Economic Review*, September 1978.

Lintner, John. "Security Prices, Risk, and Maximal Gains from Diversification." *Journal of Finance*, December 1965.

Lintner, John. "The Valuation of Risk Assets and the Selection of Risky Investments in Stock Portfolios and Capital Budgets." *Review of Economics and Statistics*, February 1965.

Lorie, James, and Richard Brealey. *Modern Developments in Investment Management*. New York: Praeger, 1972.

Lorie, James, and Mary T. Hamilton. *The Stock Market: Theories and Evidence*. Homewood, Ill.: Richard D. Irwin, 1973.

Mains, Norman E. "Risk, the Pricing of Capital Assets, and the Evaluation of Investment Portfolios: Comment." *Journal of Business*, July 1977.

Mao, James C. T. "Essentials of Portfolio Diversification Strategy." *Journal of Finance*, December 1970.

Markowitz, Harry M. "Investment for the Long Run: New Evidence for an Old Rule," *Journal of Finance*, December 1976.

Markowitz, Harry M. *Portfolio Selection: Efficient Diversification of Investment*. New York: John Wiley and Sons, 1959.

Matulich, Serge. "Portfolio Performance with Lending and Borrowing." *Journal of Business Finance and Accounting*, Autumn 1975.

Miller, M. and M. Scholes. "Rates of Return in Relation to Risk: A Reexamination of Some Recent Findings." In *Studies in the Theory of Capital Markets*. Ed. M. Jensen. New York: Praeger, 1972.

Measuring the Performance of Pension Funds. Park Ridge, Ill.: Bank Administration Institute, 1968.

Osborne, F. M. "Brownian Motion in the Stock Market." *Operations Research*, March–April 1959.

Pearson, Karl, and the Right Honorable Lord Rayleigh. "The Problem of the Random Walk." *Nature*, 1904.

Phillips, Herbert E., and John P. Seagle. "Data: A Mixed Blessing in Portfolio Selection?" *Financial Management*, Autumn 1975.

Pogue, Gerald A. "An Intertemporal Model for Investment Management." *Journal of Bank Research*, Spring 1970.

Robbins, Sidney. *The Securities Markets*. New York: The Free Press, 1966.

Roberts, Harry V. "Stock Market 'Patterns' and Financial Analysis: Methodological Suggestions." *Journal of Finance*, March 1959.

Robichek, Alexander A., Richard A. Cohn and John S. Pringle. "Returns on Alternative Investment Media and Implications for Portfolio Construction." *Journal of Business*, July 1972.

Ruff, R. T. "The Effect of Selection and Recommendation of a Stock of the Month." *Financial Analysts Journal*, March–April 1965.

Schwartz, Robert A., and David K. Whitcomb. "Evidence on the Presence and Causes of Serial Correlation in Market Model Residuals." *Journal of Financial and Quantitative Analysis*, June 1977.

Sharpe, William F. "Capital Asset Prices: A Theory of Market Equilibrium Under Conditions of Risk." *Journal of Finance*, September 1964.

Stoffels, J. D. "Stock Recommendations by Investment Advisory Services: Immediate Effects on Market Pricing." *Financial Analysts Journal*, March 1966.

Tobin, James. "Liquidity Preference as Behavior Towards Risk." *Review of Economic Studies*, February 1958.

Treynor, Jack L. "The Coming Revolution in Investment Management." In *Methodology in Finance-Investments*. Ed. James L. Becksler. Lexington, Mass.: Lexington Books-Heath, 1972.

Treynor, Jack L. "How to Rate Management of Investment Funds." *Harvard Business Review*, January–February 1965.

Treynor, Jack L., and Fischer Black. "How to Use Security Analysis to Improve Portfolio Selection." *Journal of Business*, January 1974.

Wu, Hsiu-Kwang. "Corporate Insider Trading, Profitability and Stock Price Movement." Unpublished Ph.D. diss. University of Pennsylvania, 1963.

Appendix 14-A: Quadratic Programming*

In the body of the chapter, a method of portfolio optimization, referred to as linear programming, was introduced. This method allowed the investor to specify various boundaries for the values of any number of security characteristics such as beta, size of holdings, yield and so on. It also allowed the investor to constrain the *average value* of these characteristics when the portfolio was viewed as a whole entity. Finally, subject to satisfying these boundaries and constraints, the linear programming method of optimization isolated the portfolio(s) offering the highest possible expected return.

In general, the linear programming method has many virtues, not the least of which are simplicity and low cost. There is, however, a more sophisticated optimization technique which is referred to as *quadratic programming*. It is superior to linear programming in that it not only allows the investor to satisfy the boundaries and constraints (referred to above) that he wishes to place on the individual securities or the portfolio and to maximize expected portfolio return, but also to minimize portfolio risk defined as variance of portfolio return. This latter feature is unavailable when linear programming is used.

The portfolio optimization problem, in the context of quadratic programming, may be defined as follows:

* This appendix was written by George C. Eshelman, Trust Officer, Detroit Bank and Trust Company.

Minimize the value of

$$Z = -\lambda\left[\left(\sum_{i=1}^{n} X_i E(R_i)\right) - \left(\sum_{i=1}^{n}\sum_{j=1}^{n} X_i X_j \sigma_{ij}\right)\right]$$

subject to

$$\sum_{i=1}^{n} X_i = 1$$

where

X_i = The proportion of the portfolio invested in the ith security
X_j = The proportion of the portfolio invested in the jth security
$E(R_i)$ = The expected return on the ith security
σ_{ij} = The covariance of return between the ith and the jth securities
λ = The investor's degree of risk aversion (a Lagrangian multiplier).

For a fuller discussion of quadratic portfolio optimization, see Eugene Fama, *Foundations of Finance* (New York: Basic Books, 1976).

Investment Companies

Introduction

In Chapter 14, techniques of passive investment strategy were compared and contrasted with those of active investment strategy. Passive strategy constitutes the holding of the market portfolio, whereas active strategy requires the construction of a well-diversified portfolio of individual stocks designed to beat the market. Both strategies, however, require substantial financial resources. Moreover, active investment strategy requires intensive analysis of many securities as well as the use of mathematical programming to construct an optimal portfolio. Obviously, for many investors, these are elusive goals. Generally only institutional and sophisticated investors engage in sophisticated active management strategies.

An important fact that was omitted from the discussion in Chapter 14 was that investors—especially small investors—who are either unable or unwilling to engage in portfolio construction and management can still hope to reap the benefits of either passive or active management by investing in investment companies.

This chapter presents a critical review of investment companies as an alternative to individual portfolio management. Of necessity, our discussion will be directed toward the small investor, although many institutions also find investment companies to be a viable alternative to direct investment and portfolio management. In Section 1, the essentials of investing in investment companies is presented. Section 2 is devoted to a detailed discussion of techniques for selecting investment companies.

SECTION 1 ESSENTIALS OF INVESTMENT IN INVESTMENT COMPANIES

The Concept

Investment companies are based on a simple idea: Set a clearly defined investment objective; combine the funds of a large number of investors; invest judiciously to seek that common objective; and let the investors share all income and expenses, as well as profits and losses.

The only business of investment companies is the investment of shareholders' money in common stocks, preferred stocks, bonds, or other investment media. They purchase a large number of securities and attempt to maximize the expected return on the portfolio subject to a specified investment objective. They also supervise the management and administration of investments, for which they receive a percentage of the net asset value as a management fee.[1] In effect, an investment company is a single, large investment account owned by many investors who share its income, expenses, profits, and losses in proportion to their individual shares in the account. By owning a share in a portfolio with institutional size and management, small investors receive benefits they cannot usually get on their own. These benefits include broad diversification, competent portfolio construction and management, and a smaller impact from transaction and research costs.

Of these advantages of investment companies, competent portfolio management is particularly important. In Chapter 14, we noted that active portfolio construction and management involves several important steps. Extensive security analysis is required to determine the expected return and risk characteristics of a large number of stocks. The portfolio manager must select a group of securities which will maximize the expected return of the portfolio for a given level of risk. Great skill is needed to perform these tasks successfully. By pooling the resources of many investors, an investment company can afford the type of security analysis and portfolio management which could not be undertaken by an individual.

An important characteristic of investment companies is that—unlike banks, insurance companies, and pension trusts—they have no liabilities to speak of and therefore cannot become insolvent. It is, of course, true that the shares of an investment company are redeemable on demand. However, because they are redeemable at the current net asset value, the risk of insolvency is virtually eliminated.

[1] Net asset value is a measure of total assets minus the liabilities of the company.

The Historical Growth

An Overview

The first mutual funds were formed in 1924. By 1948, about 100 such companies with combined assets of about $1.5 billion had been created. Before 1929, mutual funds were completely overshadowed by the closed-end investment companies;[2] at that time, most such companies managed heavily margined speculative accounts. In the severe bear market which followed the stock market crash, heavy losses were inevitable in this type of security. Because of their dismal showing in the 1930s and also due to many abuses on the part of fund managers, investors grew apathetic toward mutual funds. However, the situation changed as a result of the passage of the Investment Company Act of 1940. Many of the provisions of this legislation codified practices followed by most investment companies from the start.

Toward the end of the 1950s, the foundations had been laid for the most important element in the advances of the 1960s: performance. This emphasis on securing rapid market appreciation in the net asset value contributed to the rapid growth of investment companies during the 60s and early 70s.

The Present

Approximately 700 mutual funds are now registered for sale in the United States. Shares of more than 60 closed-end investment companies are publicly available. Among them, these companies cover a complete spectrum of objectives, policies, possible risks and possible rewards. They also vary in size, age and the nature of their sponsorship.

The historical record asset growth in investment companies is presented in Figure 15–1. At the end of 1978, the total assets for the industry were approximately $64 billion, of which $58 billion were in open-end companies, and $6 billion in closed-end companies.

Table 15–1 is a classification of open-end companies, or mutual funds, by size and type. The table shows that 19.1 percent of the total assets were in funds larger than $1 billion, and 25.5 percent of the total assets were in funds with sizes ranging between $100–$300 million. When classified by investment objective, the growth and growth–income funds were the most popular, representing 44.5 percent of all mutual fund assets. Investment objectives of mutual funds will be discussed later in the chapter.

[2] An open-end investment company—popularly known as a mutual fund—continuously offers new shares. In contrast, after the initial public offering, the capitalization of a closed-end company remains unchanged. These two types of companies will be discussed in detail in the following section.

Figure 15–1

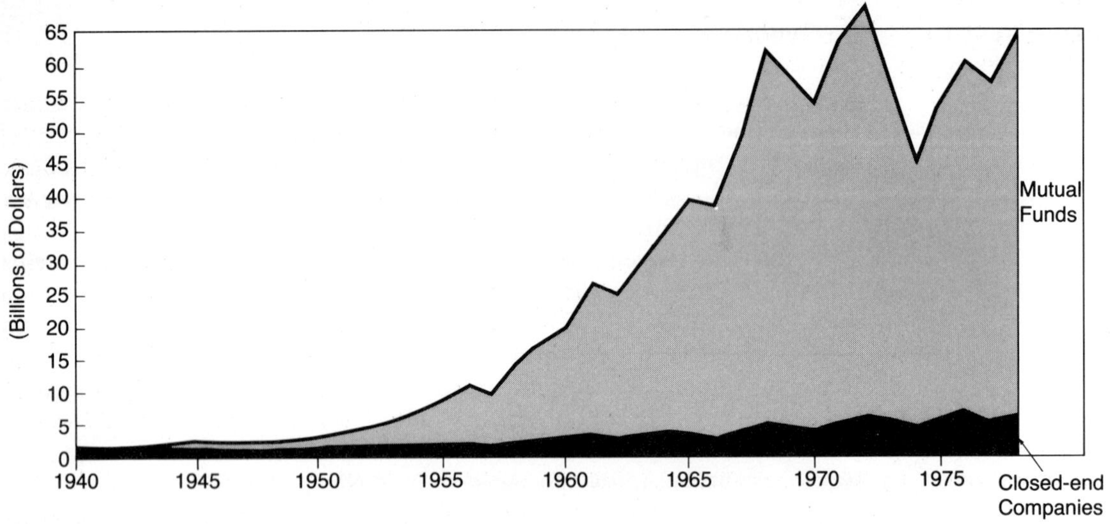

SOURCE: *Investment Companies* (New York: Wiesenberger Financial Services, 1979), p. 12.

Table 15–1

Classification of Mutual Funds By Size and Type (As of Dec. 31, 1978)

Size of Fund	No. of Funds	Combined Assets ($000)	% of Total	Type of Fund	No. of Funds	Combined Assets ($000)	% of Total
Over $1 billion	8	$11,139,700	19.1%	Common Stock:			
$500 million–$1 billion	17	11,536,000	19.8	Maximum Capital Gain	103	$ 4,619,300	7.9%
$300 million–$500 million	21	8,333,100	14.3	Growth	143	12,649,500	21.8
$100 million–$300 million	87	14,824,600	25.5	Growth and Income	80	13,209,800	22.7
$50 million–$100 million	79	5,747,300	9.9	Specialized	23	732,800	1.2
$10 million–$50 million	234	5,916,600	10.2	Balanced	25	3,811,400	6.6
$1 million–$10 million	128	636,500	1.1	Income	119	8,904,400	15.3
Under $1 million	26	10,600	0.1	Bond & pfd stock	11	1,119,600	2.0
Total	600	$58,144,400	100.0%	Money market	59	10,462,700	18.0
				Tax-exempt municipal bonds	37	2,634,900	4.5
				Total	600	$58,144,400	100.0%

SOURCE: *Investment Companies*, (New York: Wiesenberger Financial Services, 1979) p. 43.

Establishment and Management of Investment Companies

The Incorporation Process

Investment companies are the most closely regulated sector of the entire securities business. Among the laws affecting them are the Federal Securities Act of 1933, the Federal Securities Exchange Act of 1934, the Federal Investment Company Act of 1940, and the Federal Investment Company Amendments Act of 1970.

These various acts require that (1) there must be at least a minimum number of "outsiders" on the board of directors; (2) limitations must be placed on the amount of indebtedness which may be incurred by investment companies; (3) all companies must comply with the SEC's rules concerning the solicitation of proxies for voting on company matters; (4) managers obtain SEC approval before transacting business with the companies' managements; and (5) all investment companies must approve any change in fundamental investment policy by a vote of shareholders.

To become established, an investment company must observe various provisions of the law. These include appointment of a board of directors and the publication of an approved prospectus. The prospectus should specify details regarding the company's investment goals, management fees to be paid for performing the fiduciary duties, the sales commission, and ancillary factors.

The Management

The investment company is a unique corporation whose principal assets are the portfolio of marketable securities. The primary responsibility for the smooth functioning of a company rests on the board of directors. The board, in turn, generally hires a separate management company for the management of the company's portfolio.

Types of Investment Companies

Figure 15–2 is a detailed classification of investment companies. It reveals that investment companies can be broadly classified between unit investment trusts and management companies. The management group is further subdivided between open-end companies—popularly known as mutual funds—and closed-end companies.

Figure 15–2

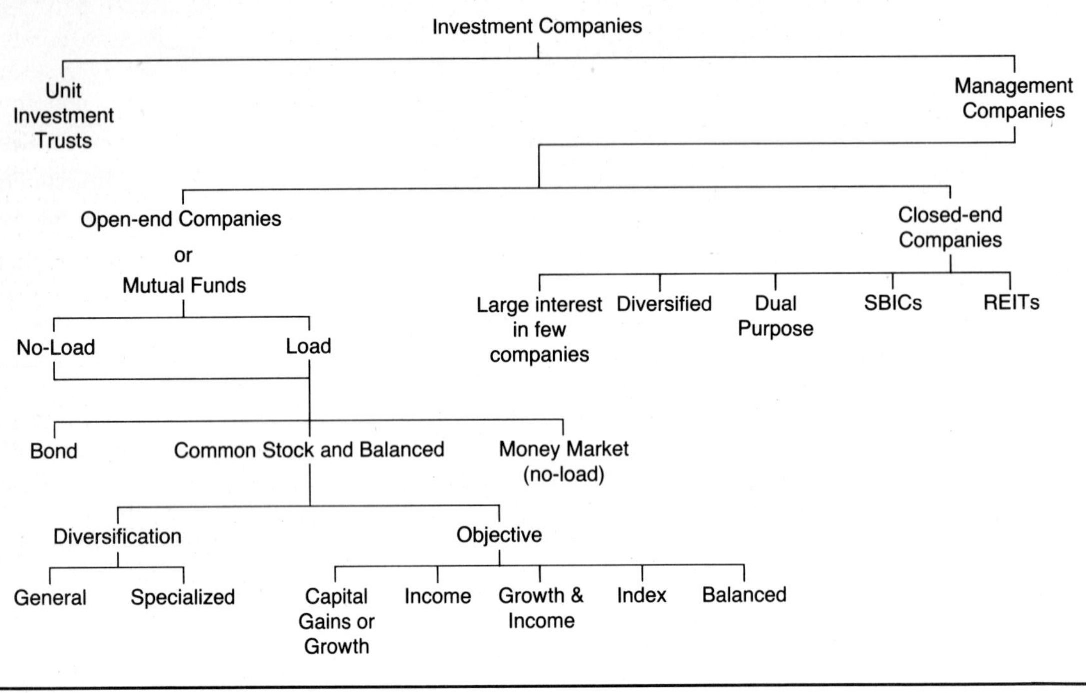

Unit Investment Trusts

Unit Investment Trusts (*UITs*) are composed of a fixed portfolio of long-term bonds with units sold at net asset value plus various charges. To form a UIT, the interested institution buys a group of fixed-income securities, deposits them with a trustee, and receives a number of shares representing the personal interest in those securities. These shares, known as redeemable trust certificates, are then sold to investors. All interest income received from the bond portfolio is paid by the trustee to shareholders.

UITs are unmanaged, fixed portfolios assembled and sold by investment bankers. They have a sales charge of 3.5 to 4 percent, but no annual management fee. Once a trust invests all its funds in bonds, normally it neither sells its holdings nor purchases new ones, although exceptions are made under unusual circumstances.

UITs are essentially for small investors seeking long-term investment. They enable the small investor to buy bonds with the safety of diversification.

The first UIT was established in 1961 by Ira Haupt & Company and John Nuveen & Company. A decade later, the unit trust movement got a big boost when Merrill Lynch took over a unit trust operation along with the rest of the bankrupt Goodbody firm. The movement was subsequently joined by Bache

Halsey Stuart Shields, Inc., Reynolds & Company, and other large investment firms. By 1979, annual sales of UITs totaled over $2 billion.

In addition to providing safety through diversity, because of their emphasis on long-term bonds, UITs provide higher returns than shorter term bonds.[3] However, like all fixed income securities, these trusts are subject to interest rate risk. Consequently, the values of UITs fluctuate widely with the fluctuations in the market interest rates. "At the bottom, with the widest swings, are the high-yield issues—long-term and low quality. With each 1 percent rise in long-term interest rates, their principal value can drop by 10 percent."[4] In addition to interest rate risk considerations, the understandable lack of liquidity of UITs can create problems for those investors who might be forced to liquidate their investment in the short run. In most cases, investors who must liquidate their units before the maturity date suffer large losses. Also, a secondary market for UITs is nonexistent. Primarily for this reason, UITs are "redeemed at the value of the bid prices of the bonds in the portfolio, which may be $2\frac{1}{2}$ points or more under the offering prices of the bond on which sales prices of the trusts are based. Since the trustees tend to sell the most easily liquidated bonds in the portfolio to pay off the withdrawing unit holders, regardless of current market conditions, the remaining unit holders are frequently left with a less liquid portfolio. . . ."[5]

In addition to these drawbacks, there are other disadvantages of investing in UITs. For example, as a matter of policy, UITs do not permit the compounding of returns through reinvestment in the trust. Also, as previously mentioned, sales charges of unit trusts as high as 4.0 percent may be prohibitive for short-term investors. Finally, in redeeming units tendered by shareholders, UITs frequently rely on bid rather than asked prices.[6] This method of unit valuation might cost investors as much as 3 percent and wipe out a substantial portion of their returns.

UITs are probably more suitable as a long-term rather than a short-term investment vehicle. For investors who prefer short-term investments, management companies are more appropriate. These companies can be either *open-end* or *closed-end companies.*

Open-end Companies

An open-end investment company—popularly known as a *mutual fund*—continuously offers new shares. It guarantees to redeem its shares at the net asset value at any time. This value is calculated at least daily (and typically more often) by adding the current market values of all securities in the fund's portfolio,

[3] Of course, this is true when market interest rates are higher for longer term securities, or when there is a normal yield curve.

[4] "Forbes Asks Stoever Glass About Unit Trusts Funds," *Newsletter*, Stoever Glass & Co., September 2, 1977, p.2.

[5] "Unit Trusts: Things Your Broker Doesn't Always Tell You," *Forbes*, August 1, 1977, p. 37.

[6] A bid price is the price the dealer will pay to *buy* the units from the investors. An asked price is the price at which he will *sell* the units to the investors. The bid price is lower than the asked price.

Table 15–2*

Mutual Funds

Tuesday, February 5, 1980

Price ranges for investment companies, as quoted by the National Association of Securities Dealers. NAV stands for net asset value per share; the offering includes net asset value plus maximum sales charge, if any.

Fund	NAV	Offer Price	NAV Chg.
Acorn Fnd	24.26	N.L.	−.07
ADV Fund	13.16	N.L.	+.05
Afuture Fd	18.03	N.L.	+.13
AGE Fund	3.78	4.08	−.01
AIM Funds.			
Conv Yld	12.37	13.23	+.03
Edsn Gld	12.78	N.L.	+.02
HiYld Sc	9.74	10.42	−.02
Alpha Fnd	14.39	N.L.	−.01
Am Birthrt	12.18	13.31	...
American Funds Group:			
Am Bal	8.36	9.14	−.02
Amcap F	12.09	13.21	...
Am Mutl	11.55	12.62	+.03
An Gwth	8.35	9.13	+.03
Bnd FdA	12.38	13.53	−.09
Cash Mt	1.00	N.L.	...
Fund Inv	7.80	8.52	+.02
Gth FdA	10.67	11.66	−.02
Inc FdA	7.66	8.37	...
I C A	8.86	9.68	+.02
Nw Prsp	7.79	8.51	+.01
Wash Mt	7.27	7.95	+.01
American General Group:			
A GnCBd	7.03	7.68	−.04
AG Entp	9.57	10.46	+.04
High Yld	10.19	10.93	...
A G Mun	20.56	21.59	...
A G Res	1.00	N.L.	...
A GnVen	18.33	20.03	+.03
Comstk	11.04	12.07	+.13
Eqty Gth	(z)	(z)	...
Fd Amer	9.43	10.31	+.01
Harbor	10.67	11.66	−.06
Pace Fd	21.92	23.96	+.03
Prov Inc	3.68	3.97	−.01
Am Grwth	10.05	10.84	+.25
Am Herito	2.98	N.L.	+.02
Am Ins Ind	5.15	5.63	−.01
Am Invest	9.59	N.L.	+.11
AmInv Inc	12.39	N.L.	+.13
AmNat Gw	3.88	4.24	...
Amway Mt	8.14	8.70	−.01
Am Opt Eq	(z)	(z)	...
Axe-Houghton:			
Fund B	7.83	8.51	+.01
Income	4.08	4.43	−.05
Stock Fd	7.64	8.35	+.04
BLC Gwth	15.59	17.04	+.03
Babsn Inc	1.50	N.L.	−.01
Babsn Inv	11.36	N.L.	+.05
Beacon Gr	10.54	N.L.	+.04
Beacon Hll	10.47	N.L.	+.05
Berger Group Funds:			
100 Fund	11.36	N.L.	...
101 Fund	9.77	N.L.	...
Bondsk Cp	(z)	(z)	...
Bos Found	9.67	10.57	−.02
Bull & Bear Group:			
Capam	9.65	N.L.	+.01
Capitl Sh	10.74	N.L.	+.05
Golcnd	14.32	N.L.	+.33
Calvin Bullock Funds:			
Bullock	14.70	16.07	+.02
Canadn	9.16	10.01	−.04
Div Shrs	2.79	3.04	+.01
Income	10.90	11.99	−.24
Ntwide	9.15	10.00	−.02
Cash Rsrv	1.00	N.L.	...
Cap Presv	1.00	N.L.	...
Cent Capitl	1.00	N.L.	...
Century Sh	11.40	12.29	−.01
Chan HiYd	10.41	11.16	−.03
Charter Fd	18.76	20.50	+.05
Chase Group of Boston:			
Fnd Bost	7.95	8.69	−.01
Front Cp	6.26	6.84	−.03
ShTr Bos	8.01	8.75	−.01
Special	9.13	9.98	...
Chem Fnd	8.66	9.46	+.04
Chepsd Dol	16.71	N.L.	+.05
Colonial Funds:			
Fund	10.33	11.29	+.03
Growth	6.65	7.27	+.01
Income	6.93	7.57	−.08
Optn Inc	11.10	12.13	−.01
Tax Mge	13.42	14.67	−.01
Senior Sc	7.61	8.32	−.07
Col Grwth	20.00	N.L.	+.10
Commonwealth Trust:			
A & B	1.09	1.18	...
C	1.52	1.64	...
Comp BdSt	9.12	9.81	+.04
Composit	8.91	9.58	+.03
Concord F	18.08	N.L.	−.02
Connecticut General:			
CG Fund	12.77	13.81	...
CG Incm	6.60	7.14	−.05
CG MBd	8.49	9.18	...
Consol Inv	11.12	11.62	−.13
Constlatn	14.57	N.L.	+.06
Cont Mtlv	7.45	N.L.	−.05
Coutry Cap	13.50	14.59	+.04
Daily Cash	1.00	N.L.	...
Daily Incm	1.00	N.L.	...
Delaware Group:			
Cash Res	10.00	N.L.	...
Decatr	13.73	15.01	+.01
Delchs F	7.62	8.33	−.08
TxFr Pa	8.04	8.42	...
Delw Fd	12.76	13.95	−.01
Delta Td	6.62	7.23	...
Direct Cap	3.14	N.L.	+.02
DodgC Bal	23.12	N.L.	−.03
DodgC Stk	19.04	N.L.	−.03
Drx Burnh	13.06	N.L.	+.05
Dreyfus Group:			
Dreyf Fd	13.89	15.18	−.01
Dreyf Lv	21.14	23.10	+.07
Dryf LAs	1.00	N.L.	...
Mny M S	1.00	N.L.	...
Numbr 9	10.02	N.L.	−.03
Spl Incm	7.34	N.L.	...
Tax ExB	13.06	N.L.	−.01
Third Cn	23.28	N.L.	+.08
Eagle Gth	9.83	10.74	...
Eaton & Howard:			
Balncd F	7.95	8.57	−.01
Cash Mg	1.00	N.L.	...
Foursq	8.98	N.L.	−.01
Growth	14.50	15.63	+.05
Income	4.73	5.10	−.02
Spec Fnd	10.71	11.55	+.02
Stock Fd	10.47	11.29	...
Elfun TIF	(z)	(z)	...
Elfun Trst	(z)	(z)	...
Evrgrn Fd	28.64	N.L.	−.02
Fairfld Fd	13.19	14.42	−.02
Farm B Gr	12.68	13.86	+.01
Federated Group:			
Am Lead	8.33	8.91	...
Hi Incm	12.31	13.17	−.04
M M M	1.00	N.L.	...
Mon Mkt	1.00	N.L.	...
Optn Inc	13.27	14.19	+.01
Tax Free	10.56	N.L.	−.01
US Gvt S	7.72	N.L.	−.03
Fidelity Group Funds:			
Aggr Inc	8.53	N.L.	−.01
Bd Corp	7.07	N.L.	−.04
Capital	(z)	(z)	...
Cash Res	1.00	N.L.	...
Contra	11.23	N.L.	...
Daily Inc	1.00	N.L.	...
Destiny	10.20	(z)	+.04
Eq Incm	21.13	N.L.	−.02
Fidel Fd	17.20	N.L.	...
Govt Sec	9.72	N.L.	...
High Yld	12.91	N.L.	...
Ltd Muni	8.68	N.L.	−.01
Mageln	53.57	N.L.	+.29
Muncpl	8.49	N.L.	−.01
Puritan	10.53	N.L.	−.01
Salem	6.71	N.L.	...
Thrift Tr	9.45	N.L.	−.02
Trend	27.03	N.L.	−.03
Financial Programs:			
Dynam	7.64	N.L.	+.01
Industl	5.40	N.L.	+.01
Income	8.84	N.L.	+.01
First Investors Fund:			
Bond Ap	(z)	(z)	...
Cash Mg	1.00	(z)	...
Discovr	8.38	9.16	+.16
Growth	9.91	10.83	+.01
Income	7.11	7.77	−.01
Stock Fd	7.51	8.21	−.01
Tx Exmt	9.60	10.35	...
Fst VRate	1.00	N.L.	...
44 Wall St	18.72	N.L.	+.06
Fnd Grwth	4.77	5.21	−.03
Founders Group Funds:			
Growth	6.67	N.L.	+.02
Income	13.99	N.L.	...
Mutual	8.89	9.72	+.02
Special	16.78	N.L.	+.06
Franklin Group:			
Brwn Fd	4.64	5.00	+.01
D N T C	11.66	12.57	...
Growth	6.89	7.43	+.01
Income	2.02	2.18	+.02
Liqd Ast	1.00	N.L.	...
US GvSc	7.80	8.41	−.09
Utilities	4.08	4.40	−.03
Res Capt	8.86	9.55	+.33
Res Eqty	5.08	5.48	...
Fundpack	(z)	(z)	...
Funds Incp Group:			
Cm IncS	8.56	N.L.	...
Currt Int	1.00	N.L.	...
Indus Tr	11.24	11.53	+.04
Pilot Fd	9.31	N.L.	+.03
GT Pac Fd	11.77	N.L.	−.07
Gatewy Op	15.40	N.L.	+.01
GE S&S Pr	(z)	(z)	...
Genl Secur	11.90	N.L.	+.07
Grad CRsv	1.00	N.L.	...
Grth IndSh	26.99	N.L.	+.04
Hamilton Group:			
Fund	4.76	5.20	+.01
Growth	9.59	10.48	+.03
Income	7.35	N.L.	+.02
Hartwll Gt	24.32	N.L.	+.05
Hartwll Lv	16.25	N.L.	+.04
Holding Tr	1.00	N.L.	...
Horace Mn	18.71	20.23	+.09
INA HiYld	9.88	10.60	−.03
IndsFd Am	6.59	N.L.	+.02
Intcap HiY	13.88	14.69	−.08
Intercap	1.00	N.L.	...
Int Investr	30.74	33.60	+1.23
Inv Guidan	12.53	N.L.	+.03
Inv Indicat	1.41	(z)	+.01
Inv Tr Bos	11.60	12.51	+.08
Investors Group Funds:			
IDS Bnd	4.73	4.91	−.01
IDS Cash	1.00	N.L.	...
IDS Gth	8.79	9.56	...
IDS HYd	4.43	4.62	...
IDS nwD	7.25	7.88	...
IDS Prog	3.93	4.27	...
IDS Tax	4.08	4.25	...
Mutual	9.11	9.90	+.01
Stock Fd	20.47	22.25	+.03
Selectv	7.55	8.11	...
Var Pay	8.10	8.81	+.01
Inv Resrch	6.30	6.89	+.04
I S I Group:			
Growth	6.89	7.53	+.12
Income	3.85	4.21	...
TrPa Shr	3.30	(z)	+.01
Trust shr	12.19	13.32	+.02
Istel Fund	29.22	30.12	+.19
Ivy Fund	8.31	N.L.	−.01
JP Growth	11.89	12.92	+.05
Janus Fnd	24.94	N.L.	+.09
Johnst Cap	23.98	N.L.	+.03
Jhnst Cash	1.00	N.L.	...
John Hancock Funds:			
Balanc	8.18	8.89	−.03
Bond Fd	(z)	(z)	...
Cash Mg	1.00	N.L.	...
Growth	8.84	9.61	+.06
Tax Ex	11.72	12.74	−.01
Kemper Funds:			
Income	x8.52	9.06	−.28
Growth	10.94	11.96	+.05
High Yld	9.73	10.43	−.08
Mon Mkt	1.00	N.L.	...
Muni Bd	9.14	9.60	−.01
Optn Inc	13.28	14.51	+.04
Summit	16.08	17.57	+.03
Technol	x11.20	12.24	+.03
Total R	x11.16	12.20	−.11
Keystone Custodian Funds:			
A Liq Tr	1.00	N.L.	...
Cust B 1	15.12	15.79	−.07
Cust B 2	17.15	18.74	−.01
Disct B 4	7.30	7.98	−.01
Cust K 1	7.18	7.85	−.01
Cust K 2	5.98	6.54	+.06
Cust S 1	19.10	20.87	+.02
Cust S 3	9.92	10.84	+.01
Cust S 4	7.59	8.30	+.05
Intl Fnd	4.05	4.43	+.06
Lexington Group:			
Cp Ledrs	12.56	13.84	−.08
Growth	11.17	12.21	−.02
Income	8.43	N.L.	−.04
Mon Mkt	1.00	N.L.	...
Resrch	17.73	19.38	−.03
Lifeins Inv	11.50	12.57	...
LiqCap Inc	10.00	N.L.	...
Loomis Sayles Funds:			
Cap Dev	15.81	N.L.	+.02
Mutual	13.85	N.L.	−.05
Lord Abbett:			
Affiliatd	8.71	9.40	+.02
Bnd Deb	9.45	10.33	−.04
Cash Res	1.00	N.L.	...
Devl Gro	14.97	16.36	+.11
Income	2.84	3.06	...
Lutheran Brotherhood:			
Broth Fd	11.18	12.22	−.01
Bro Inc	8.02	8.77	−.03
Br MMkt	1.00	N.L.	...
Bro MBd	8.20	8.96	...
Broth US	8.33	9.10	−.08
Massachusetts Co:			
Freedm	8.93	9.76	...
Indep Fd	11.74	12.83	+.01
Mass Fd	11.81	12.91	+.01
Income	12.00	13.11	−.03
Mass Financial Services:			
MIT	11.89	12.82	+.05
MIG	11.14	12.01	+.05
MID	13.84	14.92	−.05
MCD	14.24	15.35	+.03
MFD	19.59	21.12	+.06
MFB	12.33	13.29	−.11
MMB	8.49	8.91	
Special	17.06	18.64	+.07
Tax FrB	8.23	N.L.	−.03
Time Fd	12.17	13.30	+.03
OTC SecFd	24.39	26.51	...
Paramnt	10.33	11.29	−.01
Penn Mutl	6.25	N.L.	+.01
Penn Squ	7.90	N.L.	+.03
Phila Fund	9.91	10.83	...
Phonx Cap	10.40	11.37	−.09
Phoenx Fd	9.25	10.11	−.07
Pilgrim Group:			
Mag Cap	4.24	4.57	+.01
Mag Inc	8.00	8.63	+.02
Pilgr Fd	14.87	16.03	+.01
Pioneer Funds:			
Pionr Fd	18.07	19.75	...
Pionr II	10.99	12.01	−.02
Planned In	15.57	N.L.	+.06
PLIGRO	13.65	14.92	−.03
PLITRN	12.72	13.90	−.10
Price Rowe:			
Growth	12.10	N.L.	+.06
Income	9.13	N.L.	−.01
New Era	18.48	N.L.	+.09
Nw Horz	13.07	N.L.	+.02
Prime R	10.00	N.L.	...
Tax Free	9.06	N.L.	−.03
Pro Fund	8.50	N.L.	+.02
Pro Incom	8.57	N.L.	−.05
Pru SIP	12.77	13.96	+.08
Putnam Funds:			
Convert	x13.65	14.92	−.37
DDiv Tr	1.00	N.L.	...
George	13.58	14.84	−.05
Growth	12.63	13.80	−.01
High Yld	15.42	16.54	−.16
Income	6.13	6.57	−.04
Intl Equi	15.02	16.42	−.01
Investr	8.51	9.30	+.02
Option	13.34	14.58	+.01
Tax Ex	20.13	21.13	−.01
Vista Fd	15.53	16.97	−.02
Voyage	13.54	14.80	−.01
Rainbw Fd	3.27	N.L.	+.02
Reserv Fd	1.00	N.L.	...
Revere Fd	7.20	N.L.	...
Safeco Equ	11.06	12.09	...
Safeco Gth	15.05	16.45	+.01
StPaul Cap	11.78	12.53	+.02
StPaul Gro	13.71	14.59	+.04
Scudder Funds:			
Cash Inv	1.00	N.L.	...
Commn	12.85	N.L.	+.02
Income	11.60	N.L.	−.06
Intl Fnd	17.21	N.L.	−.02
Man Res	9.97	N.L.	...
Muni Bd	8.91	N.L.	−.01
Specl Fd	40.75	N.L.	−.03
Security Funds:			
Bond Fd	8.27	8.50	−.01
Equity	6.08	6.65	+.06
Invest	8.86	9.68	+.05
Ultra Fd	14.86	16.24	+.04
Selected Funds:			
Selct Am	7.00	N.L.	...
Selct Spl	15.67	N.L.	+.03
Sentinel Group Funds:			
Apex Fd	3.62	3.96	−.01
Bal Fund	7.45	8.14	−.04
Com Stk	12.77	13.96	+.01
Growth	10.82	11.83	+.02
Sentry Fd	18.39	19.99	+.02
Sequoia	24.88	N.L.	−.03
Shearson Funds:			
Apprec	31.62	34.56	+.11
Daily Dv	1.00	N.L.	...
Income	17.08	18.67	−.03
Invest	13.71	14.98	+.03
Shrm Dean	42.68	N.L.	+1.86
Sierra Gro	13.33	N.L.	...
Sigma Funds:			
Capitl Sh.	12.94	14.14	−.06
Invest Sh	10.97	11.99	+.01
Trust Sh	8.85	9.67	−.01
Venture	10.84	11.85	...
Sm Barney	13.55	14.26	+.02
Sm BrIncG	14.41	15.17	−.02
So GenFnd	14.88	15.88	+.04
Sowest Inv	9.12	9.86	+.08
SowInv Inc	4.66	5.04	−.04
Sovern Inv	13.49	14.20	+.03
State Bond Group:			
CmSt Fd	5.25	5.74	+.02
Diversf	5.24	5.73	+.01
Progrss	6.11	6.68	+.01
StateF Bal	11.83	N.L.	+.02
State FrGr	9.00	N.L.	+.03
StateSt (a)	58.44	58.80	+.18
Steadman Funds:			
Am Ind	3.18	N.L.	+.01
Assoc Fd	.97	N.L.	...
Inves Fd	1.47	N.L.	...
Oceang	8.74	N.L.	+.06
Stein Roe Funds:			
Balanc	19.86	N.L.	−.01
Cash Res	1.00	N.L.	...
Capit Op	16.35	N.L.	−.05
Stock Fd	16.31	N.L.	+.04
Strattn Gth	20.12	N.L.	+.04
Survey Fd	13.19	14.42	+.02
Tax Mg Ut	16.94	18.51	−.05

z-Quote not available. NL-No load. x-Ex-dividend. r-Ex-rights. d Ex-distribution. a-funds redemption price.

*Note: Some quotations are deleted.

SOURCE: *The Wall Street Journal*, February 6, 1980, p. 31.

subtracting the liabilities, and dividing the resulting figure by the number of outstanding shares of the fund's stock. Open-end or mutual funds are either no-load or load companies.

No-load Versus Load Funds

All mutual funds charge a management fee, which in most cases ranges from .75 to 1.00 percent of the total assets managed. In addition, *load funds* impose a sales charge, or load, of 7.5 to 8.5 percent at the time of purchase. Therefore, assuming a load charge of 7.5 percent, an investor purchasing $1,000 worth of shares of a load fund will receive only $925 worth of shares. In contrast, no sales charge, or load, is involved in the purchase of shares in a *no-load fund.*

At the end of 1978, 254 no-load funds were publicly available. The combined assets of these funds were $22 billion—38 percent of all mutual fund assets.

From the investor's point of view, the primary difference between a no-load and a load fund is that investing in a no-load fund requires that the investor take the initiative. Because brokers and dealers usually have little incentive for promoting investment in no-load funds, the investor must complete the selection process and determine which fund best suits his or her needs. Of course, the obvious advantage of the no-load fund is that no sales charge is involved. In itself, however, neither the presence nor the absence of a sales charge is a guarantee of superior or even average results.

Table 15–2, which presents the price quotations of several load and no-load funds dated February 5, 1980, reveals several interesting facts. First, no-load funds have an offer, or sale, price equal to the net asset value, because there is no load charge. For example, because Loomis Sayles Funds are no-load funds, their net asset value and offer price are identical. Second, the offer price of a load fund is higher than its net asset value per share, the difference representing its load charge. For example, the offer price of AGE Fund is $4.08, whereas its net asset value per share is only $3.78. The difference of $0.30 (7.94 percent) is the load charge. Finally, several investment companies manage more than one fund. Some of these are load funds; others are no-load funds. For example, of the 12 funds managed by the American Funds Group, one is a no-load fund. In contrast, two of the five managed by the Lexington group are of the no-load type. This feature of investment companies provides an added flexibility to those investors who wish to switch from one type of fund to another without changing the management.

No-load funds, as well as load funds, can be either bond funds, common stock funds and balanced funds, or money market funds. It is, therefore, appropriate to discuss these subgroups without further reference to their load features.

Bond Funds

There are two types of *bond funds*: Unit trusts, first offered in 1961, represent shares consisting of "units" or interests in an existing portfolio of bonds and has already been discussed; the newer type, initially offered in 1976, is structured like the conventional open-end investment company.

Following the passage of the Tax Reform Act of 1976, the open-end type of municipal bond funds—with features of tax-free, pass-through of income to the shareholders—came into existence. The first of these, Kemper Municipal Bond Fund, was organized in 1976. By the end of 1978, some 37 such funds had offered their shares to the public and total net assets had reached $2.6 billion.

Bond funds vary widely with respect to the investment philosophies which determine the types of bonds purchased. Some funds invest in high-grade corporate or tax-exempt municipal bonds; others specialize in government bonds or convertible bonds.

Many bond funds have relatively conservative investment policies, although bond funds that are speculative in nature are not uncommon. Most funds charge the shareholders a yearly management fee equal to $\frac{1}{2}$ percent of assets; in addition, other costs total $\frac{3}{4}$ to 1 percent of net asset value. This means that if a bond fund is to pay a dividend of 10 percent, its portfolio must earn an interest return of approximately 11.5 percent.

Bond funds may offer several advantages. First, municipal bond funds make it possible for small investors to take advantage of tax-free investment. The minimum initial investment can be as little as $100, and additional shares can be purchased in increments of $25. Second, bond funds permit the reinvestment of funds at a compound rate. Third, bond funds offer a great deal of liquidity. Investors in many bond funds are allowed to write checks against these funds. Without charge, they are also permitted to switch into other current funds, and even arrange for automatic transfer of money into these funds from checking accounts. Fourth, the portfolios of bond funds are actively managed. To the extent that fund managers can accurately forecast interest rates, they can take advantage of changes in interest rates. When interest rates are expected to rise and bond prices to fall, fund managers can, for example, shift out of long-term bonds and into shorter maturities. When interest rates are expected to fall, they can follow the opposite strategy.

Common Stock Funds and Balanced Funds

Common stock funds can be classified according to diversification or objective. On the basis of diversification, common stock funds may be either general common stock funds or specialized funds. When classified by objective, common stock funds can be capital gains or growth funds, income funds, index funds, or growth and income funds. *Balanced funds* hold a substantial portion of fixed income securities in addition to common stocks.

Diversification *General common stock funds*, by definition, hold a broadly diversified portfolio of common stocks. Stocks are generally selected from a large universe of securities and concentration is limited to any single industry or stock group. Also, because of tax and legal considerations, a regulated investment company cannot invest more than a small percentage of its total investible funds in any single stock. General common stock funds therefore tend to diversify away more unsystematic risk than mutual funds which specialize in certain industries or stock groups. Table 15–3 shows a sample portfolio. Note the large

Table 15–3

Fidelity Fund, Inc.
Investments—December 31, 1978
(showing Percent of Total Value of Investments)
Common Stocks—88.7%

Shares		Cost	Current Value (Note 1)
AEROSPACE—0.4%			
110,000	Lear Siegler, Inc.	$ 2,009,584	$ 1,980,000
AIRLINES—1.4%			
200,000	Eastern Air Lines, Inc.†	2,821,814	1,700,000
60,400	Northwest Airlines, Inc.	1,550,672	1,721,400
200,000	Trans World Airlines, Inc.†	3,718,377	3,525,000
		8,090,863	6,946,400
AUTO PARTS AND ACCESSORIES—0.7%			
220,000	Goodyear Tire & Rubber Co.	3,947,750	3,575,000
BANKS AND FINANCE—3.8%			
100,000	Chase Manhattan Corp.	3,224,735	2,937,500
200,000	First Chicago Corp.	4,140,785	3,800,000
174,000	Household Finance Corp.	3,504,813	3,045,000
150,000	MGIC Investment Corp.	3,504,109	2,756,250
100,000	Manufacturers Hanover Corp.	3,737,500	3,200,000
100,000	Wells Fargo & Co.	2,585,612	2,712,500
		20,697,554	18,451,250
BEVERAGES—0.6%			
120,000	PepsiCo, Inc.	3,032,937	3,075,000
BUILDING MATERIALS—1.2%			
132,500	Ideal Basic Industries, Inc.	3,023,317	2,898,438
137,900	Lone Star Industries, Inc.	2,963,033	2,913,137
		5,986,350	5,811,575
CHEMICALS—3.8%			
84,000	Celanese Corp.	3,514,449	3,402,000
15,000	duPont (E.I.) deNemours & Co.	1,812,762	1,905,000
175,000	Ethyl Corp.	3,774,113	3,762,500
134,000	Grace (W.R.) Co.	3,844,667	3,467,250
222,000	Hercules Inc.	3,717,338	3,635,250
48,500	Stauffer Chemical Co.	1,879,735	1,885,437
		18,543,064	18,057,437

Shares		Cost	Current Value (Note 1)
COMMUNICATIONS—2.8%			
150,000	American Telephone & Telegraph Co.	7,889,090	9,093,750
150,000	Northern Telecom Ltd.	4,909,006	4,593,750
		12,798,096	13,687,500
CONGLOMERATES—5.0%			
124,700	A-T-O Inc.	1,567,358	1,293,763
200,000	FMC Corp.	5,513,935	4,850,000
200,000	Gulf & Western Industries, Inc.	3,509,908	2,825,000
150,000	Loew's Corp.	5,114,181	6,225,000
300,000	Tenneco, Inc.	6,024,297	9,075,000
		21,729,679	24,268,763
CONSUMER NONDURABLES—0.2%			
94,800	Clorox Co.	979,018	1,019,100
DRUGS AND HOSPITAL SUPPLIES—8.5%			
125,000	American Home Products Corp.	3,574,290	3,515,625
130,000	American Hospital Supply Corp.	3,443,200	3,412,500
130,000	Bristol-Myers Co.	4,594,739	4,647,500
100,000	Merck & Co., Inc.	5,684,405	6,762,500
105,400	Revlon, Inc.	4,522,952	5,414,925
135,100	Richardson-Merrell, Inc.	3,234,925	3,242,400
128,200	Squibb Corp.	4,146,691	3,589,600
350,000	Sterling Drug Inc.	5,338,946	5,468,750
100,000	Upjohn Co.	4,500,199	4,887,500
		39,040,347	40,941,300
ELECTRICAL EQUIPMENT—3.7%			
300,000	Gould Inc.	5,974,486	7,837,500
150,000	RCA Corp.	4,169,294	3,956,250
350,000	Westinghouse Electric Corp.	6,094,811	5,818,750
		16,238,591	17,612,500
ENERGY, INTEGRATED DOMESTIC—4.3%			
100,000	Atlantic Richfield Co.	4,546,255	5,687,500
110,000	Mountain Fuel Supply Co.	4,145,226	3,286,250
105,200	Natomas Co.	4,338,972	4,378,950
130,000	Standard Oil Co. (Indiana)	5,348,776	7,361,250
		18,379,229	20,713,950

Table continued on following page

Table 15–3 (*continued*)

Shares		Cost	Current Value (Note 1)
ENERGY, INTEGRATED INTERNATIONAL—4.5%			
100,000	Exxon Corp.	3,548,261	4,912,500
120,000	Mobil Corp.	7,536,251	8,340,000
115,000	Standard Oil Co. of California	4,888,792	5,390,625
125,000	Texaco Inc.	2,982,700	2,984,375
		18,956,004	21,627,500
FOODS, PACKAGING, PROCESSING AND DISTRIBUTING—5.1%			
90,700	General Foods Corp.	2,954,982	2,913,738
105,300	Kroger Co.	3,230,758	3,751,312
500,000	Norton Simon, Inc.	13,209,035	8,250,000
150,000	Pillsbury Co.	5,993,840	5,550,000
103,000	Safeway Stores, Inc.	4,287,387	4,174,775
		29,676,002	24,639,825
INSURANCE—4.0%			
105,000	CNA Financial Corp.[†]	1,043,884	1,063,125
150,000	Combined Insurance Co. of America	2,733,125	2,681,250
240,000	Jefferson-Pilot Corp.	5,553,573	7,260,000
135,000	Liberty National Life Insurance Co.	3,835,658	2,970,000
150,000	Reliance Group, Inc.	4,875,317	5,381,250
		18,041,557	19,355,625
LEISURE TIME—2.0%			
140,000	Holiday Inns, Inc.	2,181,392	2,327,500
300,000	Mattel, Inc.	3,099,460	2,212,500
68,700	Time Inc.	2,573,680	2,936,925
69,900	Twentieth Century-Fox Film Corp.	2,076,987	2,158,162
		9,931,519	9,635,087
MACHINERY—1.8%			
65,800	Combustion Engineering, Inc.	2,819,282	2,130,275
100,000	International Harvester Co.	3,401,587	3,625,000
125,200	Parker Hannifin Corp.	3,102,202	3,067,400
		9,323,071	8,822,675
METALS, ALUMINUM AND COPPER—3.4%			
253,700	Alcan Aluminum Ltd.	6,986,312	8,594,088
200,000	Kaiser Aluminum & Chemical Corp.	3,323,391	3,500,000
132,300	Reynolds Metals Co.	3,533,090	4,316,287
		13,842,793	16,410,375
METALS, STEEL—2.2%			
200,000	Bethlehem Steel Corp.	5,993,730	3,925,000
130,000	Inland Steel Co.	4,172,166	4,550,000
100,000	Republic Steel Corp.	2,595,864	2,262,500
		12,761,760	10,737,500
OFFICE AND BUSINESS EQUIPMENT—13.8%			
160,000	Dataproducts Corp.	3,765,491	2,500,000
120,000	Honeywell, Inc.	5,808,420	8,340,000
120,000	International Business Machine Corp.	5,213,887	35,775,000
100,000	NCR Corp.	3,532,910	6,050,000
250,000	Pitney Bowes, Inc.	4,242,605	5,843,750
150,000	Xerox Corp.	8,496,322	7,893,750
		31,059,635	66,402,500
PAPER AND RELATED—1.6%			
105,000	Crown Zellerbach Corp.	3,836,596	3,255,000
150,000	St. Regis Paper Co.	5,093,348	4,237,500
		8,929,944	7,492,500
RESTAURANTS—1.2%			
120,000	McDonald's Corp.	2,389,913	5,580,000
RETAIL SALES—2.3%			
360,000	Allied Stores Corp.	5,077,251	7,830,000
200,000	Carter Hawley Hale Stores, Inc.	3,605,326	3,125,000
		8,682,577	10,955,000
TOBACCO—1.2%			
79,300	Philip Morris, Inc.	4,278,764	5,590,650
TRANSPORTATION—2.4%			
29,400	Burlington Northern, Inc.	1,173,668	1,043,700
157,000	IC Industries, Inc.	3,877,105	3,807,250
130,000	Union Pacific Corp.	3,218,488	6,695,000
		8,269,261	11,545,950

[†] Nonincome producing.

Table 15–3 (*continued*)

Shares		Cost	Current Value (Note 1)
UTILITIES, ELECTRIC—3.8%			
100,000	Commonwealth Edison Co.	2,524,665	2,587,500
177,000	Consolidated Edison Co. of New York, Inc.	4,392,990	4,093,125
120,000	Public Services Electric & Gas Co.	2,769,975	2,430,000
100,000	Southern California Edison Co.	2,425,571	2,575,000
100,000	Texas Utilities Co.	1,944,168	1,900,000
125,000	Tucson Gas & Electric Co.	2,006,523	1,953,125
200,000	Virginia Electric & Power Co.	2,927,000	2,800,000
		18,990,892	18,338,750
MISCELLANEOUS—3.0%			
160,000	Burlington Industries, Inc.	4,319,186	2,720,000
85,000	Minnesota Mining & Manufacturing Co.	4,305,558	5,344,375
	Other Common Stocks	6,510,997	6,329,988
		15,135,741	14,394,363
	Total Common Stocks	381,742,495	427,668,075
CONVERTIBLE PREFERRED STOCKS—0.7%			
100,000	Allegheny Airlines, Inc. $1.875 Series A	2,500,000	2,075,000
	Other Convertible Preferred Stock	1,319,440	1,372,525
	Total Convertible Preferred Stocks	3,819,440	3,447,525

BONDS—4.7%

Principal Amount		Cost	Current Value
$ 4,000,000	City Investing Co. s.f. deb. 9%, 1966	$ 3,532,500	$ 3,120,000
3,000,000	Digital Equipment Corp. cv. sub. deb. 4½%, 2002	3,000,000	3,300,000
1,350,000	Gulf & Western Industries, Inc. cv. sub. deb. 5½%, 1993	1,058,000	1,053,000
3,300,000	Reliance Financial Services s.f. deb. 8½% 1992	3,029,900	2,805,000
4,000,000	Sperry Rand Co. cv. sub. deb. 6%, 2000	4,443,750	4,540,000
4,000,000	U.S. Treasury notes 7⅛%, 1979	3,882,500	3,872,500
3,000,000	UAL Inc. cv. sub. deb. 8%, 2003	3,979,039	3,900,000
	Total Bonds	22,925,689	22,590,500
SHORT-TERM OBLIGATIONS—5.9%			
2,000,000	American Brands Inc. 10.35%, 2/9/79	1,977,000	1,977,000
3,000,000	Manufacturers Hanover Trust Co., certificate of deposit, 10.43%, 2/9/79	3,013,132	3,013,132
5,000,000	Western Electric Co. 10.30%, 2/8/79	4,944,208	4,944,208
18,390,000	Short-term investment under repurchase agreement with Bank of America at 9.70% due 1/2/79, collateralized by Federal National Mortgage Association 8.40%, 9/10/82	18,399,910	18,399,910
	Total Short-Term Obligations	28,334,250	28,334,250
	Total Investments (Note 1)	$436,821,874	$482,040,350
	Total Cost for Federal Income Tax Purposes	$441,483,499	

SOURCE: Fidelity Fund, Inc. Prospectus—May 1, 1979, Revised July 16, 1979, Boston, Mass., pp. 13–15.

number of securities included and the diversification across many industries; the highest concentration is in office and business equipment with 13.8 percent of the investible funds.

Specialized funds make stock selections from a universe which covers only a small or select group of industries or securities. For example, the Third Century Fund, which is managed by the Dreyfus Corporation, strives for growth, with income as a secondary objective. It aims to accomplish this by investing only in companies that contribute to the quality of life in America. In contrast, some funds concentrate on a particular industry or type of security. For example, some funds seek out companies that will benefit from scientific discoveries and technical advances. Others concentrate on such factors as energy, oceanographic research, utilities, and life insurance. Some search for "special situations"—that is, stocks which provide unusual but potentially high expected returns. The Over-the-Counter Securities Funds, as its name implies, primarily invests in unlisted stocks. Clearly, specialized funds tend to carry more unsystematic risk than common stock funds which select from a broader universe of stocks.

The list of specialized funds is indeed long and appears almost inexhaustible. Table 15–4 presents examples of types of specialization. A sample of specialized funds follows.

Several funds hold diversified portfolios of gold mining company stocks, largely in South Africa, the world's principal gold producer. One of the funds—Golconda Investors—has been keeping part of its investment in gold bullion. Shareholders of Research Capital Fund can have their dividends automatically reinvested in gold coins.

Vanguard's Explorer Fund was organized in 1967 with the objective of seeking long-term capital growth by investing primarily in equity securities of relatively small unseasoned or embryonic companies. In 1954, Energy Fund,

Table 15–4

Areas of Specialization	Particulars
Gold	Diversified portfolios of gold mining company stocks
Utilities	Specialize in securities of public utilities, generally with the objective of maintaining high current income through high dividend yields
Convertibles	Specialize in convertible bonds and convertible preferred stocks
Insurance	Invest in insurance company securities
Energy	Invest in stocks of companies in energy-related industries
Foreign stocks	Specialize in stocks of foreign companies whose shares are purchased either in the form of ADRs (see Chapter 3) or on foreign stock exchanges

Inc. was the first mutual fund created specifically to invest in the broad field of energy. Under its specialized investment policy, the fund concentrates assets in equity securities of companies operating in various segments of the field of energy and its sources. Utility shares make up almost the complete holdings of Drexel Utility Shares. Utility company shares are particularly attractive for investors seeking high dividend income.

Other lesser-known specialized funds include Hartwell and Oceanographic Funds. Hartwell Leverage Fund pursues a capital gains objective. Its investment techniques include leveraging, short selling, hedging, and option contracts. The objective of Oceanographic and Growth Fund is long-term growth; income is not a factor. Investments must come from a list prepared by management from companies that have some business in ocean-related activities.

Some funds invest in foreign companies. This group includes, among others, the Canadian Fund, Scudder International Fund, and Templeton World Fund. Some of the funds limit themselves to companies in one country; others range all over the world in search of profitable opportunities.

Among the lesser known specialized funds are the option and commodity funds. The Colonial, Kemper, Putnam and Franklin Research funds sell call options on stocks they own. This conservative use of options (rights to buy a stock at a certain price within a given period of time) aims at high returns by adding to the normal dividend the premiums received for writing options.[7] Commodity funds—such as Antares Futures Fund and Harvest Futures Fund—are organized as limited partnerships (the minimum investment is usually $5,000). These funds spread their risks across a dozen or more commodities.

Objective In Chapters 5 and 13, we pointed out that two kinds of risk—systematic and unsystematic—are associated with investment in common stock. Systematic risk is inherent in the market and generally cannot be reduced by diversification. Unsystematic risk, however, can be reduced, and even eliminated, by diversifying a portfolio. The success of the risk reduction process clearly depends on the *nature* of the diversification.

Few mutual funds have the stated objective of reducing or eliminating unsystematic risk. Most funds define their goals in terms of their income objectives. For example, some funds have an objective of maximizing capital gains income; others invest for current dividend income. In following a particular investment objective, a mutual fund might concentrate its investments in a certain group of securities with similar risk–return characteristics, most noticeably when the fund is specialized, as previously suggested. As a result, mutual funds can assume various degrees of unsystematic risk. This fact must always be remembered when investing in a mutual fund.

Another important point is that many mutual fund managers do not follow the portfolio management techniques explained in Chapter 14. First, although all mutual funds attempt to include only "undervalued" stocks in their portfolios, they do not necessarily compute the expected returns and betas of individual

[7] Stock options will be discussed in detail in Chapter 18.

securities, construct a security market line, and select stocks lying above a decision band. Instead, they may use other analytical techniques to pick stocks they expect will outperform the market. Second, mutual funds do not necessarily try to maximize the expected return subject to a *target beta*. However, the investment objective of a fund will dictate the risk–return characteristics of the securities selected and the degree of unsystematic risk associated with the portfolio.

Mutual funds can be classified according to their objectives.

1. *Capital gains or growth funds* cater to the needs of investors who prefer future long-term capital gains over immediate dividend income. Their investments are largely made in established companies that have demonstrated their ability to expand faster than the nation's economy as a whole.

2. *Income funds* basically favor securities with above-average current-income potential, although growth possibilities are not ruled out. Because the objective is to select stocks with high and stable dividend payments, income funds offer greater price stability than capital gains and growth funds.

3. *Growth and income funds* invest for a combination of capital gains and current income. For example, the primary objective of the portfolio in Table 15–3 is long-term capital gains; but to some extent the potential for growth is limited by seeking current income as a secondary objective. Therefore, a small portion of the portfolio is invested in utility stocks and fixed income securities. Of course, some funds seek income as the primary objective and growth as a secondary aim; still others seek an even balance between the two. Funds seeking both growth *and* income generally invest in a more broadly diversified group of securities than funds whose principal objective is current income; therefore the former tend to carry lower unsystematic risk than the latter.

4. *Index funds* are designed to match the performance of the aggregate market. They derive their justification from the premises of the Efficient Market Hypothesis. If a stock always sells at its value, nothing could be gained by trying to figure out which stocks are underpriced or overpriced. If the equilibrium assumption is true, then conventional managers who try to beat the market will actually underperform the averages, not because they are inept, but because buying and selling generate transaction costs. Index funds operate under the notion that matching the market averages will produce better long-run performance than the efforts of money managers who try to beat the market.

At this point a legitimate question is: Why is it not possible for a small investor to match the market's performance without going the mutual fund route? The answer, given in Chapter 14, needs to be repeated here.

To begin with, investing in a broad market average or index such as the S&P 500 requires financial resources well beyond the command of most investors. Moreover, duplicating the performance of the S&P 500 is not as simple as it might seem. Once a portfolio is set up, it can easily get out of balance with the S&P 500 because a sale of new shares or a repurchase of outstanding shares automatically results in a change in the index. In addition, dividends must be reinvested, yet they come in quantities too small to be spread across all 500 stocks. These problems make it difficult for individuals to duplicate the market's performance on their own.[8] Consequently, index funds are a useful investment vehicle for many investors.

5. *Balanced funds* hold bonds and preferred stocks in addition to common stocks in order to minimize market risk. For example, Composite Bonds and Stocks Fund invests approximately 35 percent of its resources in bonds, whereas Nationwide Securities Company carries about 25 percent in bonds and 6 percent in preferred stocks.

Money Market Funds

A *money market fund* (*MMF*) is an open-end investment company that invests only in short-term money market instruments.[9] Many MMFs were established around 1974 when money market rates reached their peak; by the end of 1979, these funds had over 1,000,000 shareholders with assets of approximately $25 billion.

The general operating characteristics of MMFs are fairly standard. Investors purchase and redeem MMFs without paying a sales charge. Fund expenses are deducted daily from gross income. Minimum initial investments for most funds vary from $500 to $5,000 (a very small number of funds require no minimum); others, designed for institutional investors only, require minimums of $50,000 or more. Most funds have a checking option that enables shareholders to write checks of $500 or more. Shares can also be redeemed at most MMFs by telephone or wire request, in which case the MMF either mails the payment to the investor or remits it by wire to the investor's bank account.

Three major types of investors use the MMFs—individuals, bank trust departments, and nonfinancial corporations. Without MMFs, the small individual investor would be unable to earn high market yields because the minimum investment required for money market instruments is generally very large and because regulations limit the rate that can be paid on time and savings deposits at depository institutions. MMFs are attractive to small savers because they provide a means to circumvent these obstacles. Many bank trust departments and nonfinancial corporations also use MMFs as a convenient way of managing large sums of cash for the short term.

Closed-end Companies

Although after the initial public offering closed-end companies may offer a new security issue to the public, because they do not usually do so, their capitalization generally remains unchanged. These security issues are bought and sold on the NYSE and in the OTC market.

Just as individual stock prices reflect changing market conditions, the net asset value of a closed-end company share reflects the ups and downs of the

[8] Of course, if well diversified, a portfolio of 20 or 25 stocks can follow the market very closely.

[9] For details, see Timothy Q. Cook and Jeremy G. Duffield, "Money Market Mutual Funds," *Economic Review*, Federal Reserve Bank of Richmond, July–August 1979, pp. 15–31.

Table 15–5 **Publicly Traded Funds**

Friday, November 9, 1979

Following is a weekly listing of unaudited net asset values of publicly traded investment fund shares, reported by the companies as of Friday's close. Also shown is the closing listed market price or a dealer-to-dealer asked price of each fund's shares, with the percentage of difference.

	N.A. Value	Stk Price	% Diff
Diversified Common Stocks Funds			
AdmExp	14.91	$11\frac{3}{4}$	−21.2
aBakerFn	71.52	50	−30.1
GenAlnv	16.59	$12\frac{1}{2}$	−24.7
Lehman	14.80	11	−25.7
Madison	20.59	$15\frac{3}{4}$	−23.5
NiagaraSh	16.49	13	−21.2
OseasSec	5.07	$3\frac{7}{8}$	−23.6
Source	22.22	$17\frac{3}{4}$	−20.1
Tri-Contl	23.72	18	−24.1
US&For	23.13	17	−26.5
Specialized Equity and Convertible Funds			
AmGnCv	24.93	$19\frac{1}{4}$	−22.8
bASA	41.85	$29\frac{1}{4}$	−30.1
aBncrftCv	24.27	$18\frac{3}{4}$	−22.7
Castle	22.85	$19\frac{3}{8}$	−15.2
CentSec	9.13	$6\frac{1}{8}$	−32.9
ChaseCvB	11.51	$9\frac{3}{4}$	−15.3
Claremont	17.21	$11\frac{1}{4}$	−34.6
CLAS	(−6.98)	$\frac{3}{8}$	—
CLAS Pfd	17.11	—	—
Cyprus	1.24	$2\frac{5}{8}$	+112.0
DrexelUt	18.09	18	− 0.5
Engex	6.49	$4\frac{1}{4}$	−34.5
Japan	10.45	9	−13.9
Nautilus	14.13	11	−22.2
NewAmFd	23.85	$18\frac{1}{4}$	−23.5
Pete&Res	32.15	$26\frac{1}{8}$	−18.7
RETIncC	3.10	$3\frac{1}{8}$	− 0.8
ValueLn	4.09	$2\frac{7}{8}$	−30.0

a-Ex-Dividend. b-As of Thursday's close.

SOURCE: *The Wall Street Journal*, November 12, 1979, p. 31.

securities it represents. The net asset value of the share of a closed-end company is determined by the relative forces of the demand for and supply of the stocks the company holds. The market value of a fund's portfolio fluctuates from day to day. Table 15–5 is a list of closed-end funds known as *publicly traded funds.* Note, however, that the shares of a closed-end fund *can* sell at a premium or a discount relative to the market value of the securities it holds. In other words, on any given day, the prevailing price can be higher or lower than the net asset value. For example, the table reveals that on November 9, 1979, AdmExp (Adams Express) sold at 21.2 percent discount, whereas Cyprus traded at a 112.0 percent premium. Most closed-end funds, however, sell at a discount from net asset value. Some of the reasons which have been offered to explain the existence of these discounts are (1) a lack of sales effort on the part of brokers, because they earn less commissions for trading closed-end fund shares than for shares of open-end load funds;[10] (2) a perceived marketability risk of closed-end fund shares due to the small number of shares outstanding; (3) the existence

[10] No-load fund shares are sold directly by the fund through a combination of advertising and direct solicitation.

of unrealized capital gains in the closed-end funds' portfolios, which can influence the timing of an individual's income tax liabilities; (4) the investors' attitudes concerning the abilities of closed-end fund managers; and (5) in some cases, management of portfolios holding significant amounts of highly illiquid securities.[11]

Closed-end companies may be classified into five groups: (1) large interest in a few companies, (2) diversified, (3) dual-purpose, (4) small business investment companies, and (5) real estate investment trusts. Of these, the first two differ mainly in the extent of diversification and require no further consideration. Differences in the last three groups, however, are more striking.

Dual-purpose Funds

Dual-purpose funds generally invest in a diversified group of securities. The funds are distinguished by the way they allocate investment returns to their shareholders through two classes of shares: income and capital. Investors who hold income shares receive all the current income payable on both the income and the capital shares. For example, if the fund is divided between 1 million income shares and 1 million capital shares, the income share owners are entitled to receive all the dividends earned by the entire 2 million shares. Any capital gains made on the 2 million shares are credited to those who hold the capital shares.

Dual-purpose funds do not distribute realized capital gains; instead, realized capital gains are retained in the funds. The funds will eventually redeem the income shares at their fixed redemption prices. Theoretically, the funds will also redeem the capital shares at their net asset values; in practice, however, the capital share owners will vote either to terminate their part of the fund or to continue it in some form.

Small Business Investment Companies

The Small Business Investment Companies Act of 1958 authorized the creation of Small Business Investment Companies (SBICs) to help supply the equity financing needs of small, growing businesses. The SBICs have limited borrowing ability from the Small Business Administration (SBA). Generally, the SBICs make long-term, convertible loans and equity investments in small businesses as defined by the SBA. A small fraction of SBICs trade in the OTC market, often at discount prices below their share liquidation values. Many SBICs are subsidiaries of banks, savings and loan associations, or wholesale firms.

After two decades of experience, the record of most SBICs has been disappointing. Many funds have remained undercapitalized and most have suffered from a variety of managerial problems.

---

[11] For a comprehensive discussion of closed-end investment company discounts, see Eugene J. Pratt, "Myths Associated with Closed-End Investment Company Discounts," *Financial Analysts Journal*, July–August 1966, pp. 79–82.

Real Estate Investment Trusts

A Real Estate Investment Trust (REIT) is essentially an investment company that invests in two groups, (1) commercial real estate (such as shopping centers, apartment houses, and office buildings) and (2) mortgages. Those that invest in real estate are known as equity REITs; those that invest in mortgages are called mortgage trusts. Very popular during the late 1960s and early 1970s, the REITs got into trouble during the 1973–74 collapse in commercial real estate. However, many of them have since recovered; at the end of 1979, over 200 REITs remained in business.

SECTION 2 TECHNIQUES OF FUND SELECTION

Investment Companies: Techniques of Selection

The preceding discussion of the various types of investment companies suggests that a decision to invest in an open-end or closed-end fund instead of in individual securities does not solve all of an investor's problems. In fact, investors electing to buy investment company shares must still make two major decisions: (1) which investment company to select and (2) when to buy and sell the shares.

The Selection Process

Competent selection of investment companies involves three major steps: (1) determination of investor's needs and desires; (2) identification of the investment companies most likely to meet investor's needs; and (3) evaluation of relative management abilities, as demonstrated by past results.

The Payment Plans

Mutual funds have developed at least three purchasing plans. Under the Direct Outright Purchase (DOP) plan, for each purchase investors receive certificates indicating their shareholding interests in the fund's securities, and they agree to accept in cash all dividends and capital gains distributions.

If the DOP plan seems unattractive or beyond reach, an investor may prefer the pay-as-you-go systematic plan, called the Voluntary Account (VA): A small initial investment of, say, $200 buys shares at the prevailing offering price per share on the day the order is received. When an investor joins a fund, the manager is told the amount of money the investor wishes to remit at regular (monthly or quarterly) intervals. The fund agrees to invest the money as soon as it is received so that it will not lie idle. As a general rule, the fund does not charge for holding shares in trust or for providing the opportunity for continuous and systematic investment.

An investor may also remit more than the stipulated amount. Failure to make a regular payment is not penalized. Also, the investor may withdraw shares at any time

Formulation of Investment Criteria

An individual interested in investing in an investment company should first formulate his or her investment objectives or criteria. For example, some investors might desire current income, whereas for tax reasons others might prefer long-term capital gains. Some like the objectives of various types of specialized funds, and others prefer the liquidity and high interest rates offered by money market funds. Enough kinds of funds are available to accommodate virtually any investment objective. Only the investor can make the final choice.

Selection of Investment Companies: Basic Issues[12]

Identifying Fund Objectives Once investors have established their objectives, they can select funds that appear to meet those objectives. There are several possible approaches; the most satisfactory may be a combination of several of them.

Investment companies set forth their objectives in prospectuses, shareholder reports, or supplementary sales literature. These publications either describe the goals of management, or those objectives for which particular securities appear appropriate. The investment objectives of a typical mutual fund are presented in Table 15–6.

In addition to studying the prospectus, an investor should examine the past record of dividend payments and price fluctuations of a fund to learn how close the company has come to fulfilling its stated purpose. For example, if long-term

[12] This section borrows heavily from "How to Select Investment Companies," in *Investment Companies* (New York: Wiesenberger Financial Services, 1979), pp. 47–48.

without penalty. Finally, provision is made for automatic reinvestment of dividends or gains distributions.

The DOP and VA plans give an investor varying degrees of freedom in setting up an individual investment pace. However, if an investor is afraid of failing to meet his or her investment objectives unless forced to save and invest, then the Contractual Plan (CP) might be preferable. This plan requires the investor to agree to make periodic payments of $25, $50, $100 or more over a period of years toward the goal of a specific sum. However, the agreement can be terminated at any time—it is essentially a promise to oneself. In the CP, up to 50 percent of the total amount of the first 12 payments is applied to sales charges rather than to the working principal. This feature, sometimes called the "front-end load," makes the plan a long-term program, because short-term selling would result in a loss of all the money paid for sales charges.

Table 15–6

Fidelity Fund, Inc.
82 Devonshire Street, Boston, Mass. 02109
Telephone nationwide 800-225-6190;
in Massachusetts (collect) 617-726-0650

SUMMARY INFORMATION

Investment Objective:	—The Fund is a diversified, open-end investment company which seeks long term capital growth. In order to provide a reasonable current return to shareholders on their capital, however, the Fund to some extent limits the emphasis on the growth objective by investing a portion of its portfolio in securities selected for their current income characteristics. There can, of course, be no assurance that this objective will be achieved.
Minimum Investments:	—There is no sales charge. The minimum initial purchase is $500. Subsequent purchases must amount to at least $25.
Investment Adviser:	—Fidelity Management & Research Company ("FMR" or the "Adviser") is the investment adviser to the Fund and is paid a monthly advisory and service fee composed of two elements: A Group fee based on the assets of all the Funds in the Fidelity Group and an individual Fund fee. At the level of Group assets for the month of June, 1979, the annual fee rate was approximately .5674% of the Fund's average net assets. See page 7. FMR is one of the largest private investment advisory organizations in the United States, serving as adviser to Funds with assets of more than $5.0 billion.
Exchange Privilege:	—Shares of the Fund may be exchanged for shares of any other eligible Fidelity Group Fund on the basis of the respective net asset values of the shares involved. See page 5.
Redemptions:	—Shares of the Fund are redeemable at any time at net asset value. See page 9.

Please retain this prospectus for future reference.

THESE SECURITIES HAVE NOT BEEN APPROVED OR DISAPPROVED BY THE SECURITIES AND EXCHANGE COMMISSION NOR HAS THE COMMISSION PASSED UPON THE ACCURACY OR ADEQUACY OF THIS PROSPECTUS. ANY REPRESENTATION TO THE CONTRARY IS A CRIMINAL OFFENSE.

Prospectus—May 1, 1979
Revised July 16, 1979

SOURCE: Fidelity Fund, Inc. Prospectus—May 1, 1979, Revised July 16, 1979, Boston, Mass., p. 1.

capital growth is the prime objective, the investor should find out how the current price compares with that prevailing, say, 10 years ago (or at the time the fund was started).

Income and Stability If current income is the investor's objective, he or she should first analyze the yield based on current price and the latest full-year dividends paid solely from investment income. Stability of capital is most clearly recognized in periods when the general level of security prices is dropping.

Mutual Funds and Closed-end Companies There is no reason to believe that either group is superior to the other in good management. Of course, a wider choice of objectives and policies is available among the far greater number of mutual funds.

One aspect of these two types of funds deserves special mention. The price of mutual fund shares always fluctuates directly with the market value of the company's portfolio holdings, because the price is based on the net asset value. There is no such direct relationship between the market price of a closed-end share and the value of the company's holdings.

Cost Comparisons A comparison of the transaction costs associated with investing in the different types of investment companies can be an important consideration when selecting a fund. The sales charge on open-end load funds is about 7.5 to 8.5 percent; the brokerage commissions charged for buying and selling closed-end company shares might be about a third less, depending on the price of the closed-end shares and the amount of money invested.[13] There is, as previously mentioned, no sales charge on no-load funds. If an investor, for example, is considering a load and no-load fund with similar risk characteristics, he or she should expect a higher return from the load fund to compensate for the transaction costs. Assuming there is an 8 percent sales charge on the load fund, its annual return would have to be about 2 percent greater than the no-load fund for investors in each fund to be even at the end of a five-year holding period. Of course, the impact of transaction costs becomes less significant for longer holding periods.

Selection of Investment Companies: Risk Category

Investor's Risk Preference The selection process cannot proceed further without the determination of the investor's risk preference. This topic was discussed in Chapter 14 and need only be summarized here. The risk or beta of the market portfolio, as measured by, say, the S&P 500, is assigned the value of one; the beta of risk-free assets is zero. An investor may express his or her risk preference in terms of beta.[14] The investor who is willing to assume no risk (except inflation risk) will select risk-free assets. A person who is willing to accept risk equal to that of the aggregate market may expect to receive a higher return, on the average, by investing in an index fund or some other well-diversified portfolio of securities.

[13] Because closed-end shares are traded on the NYSE as are other stocks, an investor would pay brokerage commissions to buy and sell.

[14] It is assumed that the investor can express his or her risk preference in terms of an approximate beta range.

Table 15–7

Mutual Fund Group	Monthly Standard Deviation*	Beta	Return†
Bond-preferred stock	1.78%	.23	48.3%
Income	2.71	.53	71.0
Balanced	2.78	.63	51.2
Growth–income	3.95	.89	64.7
Growth	4.40	.98	50.5
Aggressive growth	4.66	.97	71.9
Venture capital–special situations	6.77	1.29	150.0
S&P 500	4.18	1.00	57.2

* The dispersion of the funds' monthly total returns around their average returns.
† Net gain over three years (1975–77), counting price changes and reinvested dividends.

SOURCE: Reprinted with permission from *CHANGING TIMES* Magazine, © Kiplinger Washington Editors, Inc. "How to Figure the Risk When You Invest," *Changing Times*, August 1978, p. 9.

Selection of Funds, vis-a-vis Preferred Risk Short-term U.S. treasury bills, insured savings accounts, CDs,[15] and other highly liquid securities guaranteed by the U.S. government are considered risk-free assets. Consequently, investors who do not wish to assume any risk may invest directly in risk-free assets or select money market funds. Those who wish to hold the market portfolio may simply buy the shares of an index fund. Other investors must select their funds through a more involved process.

For illustrative purposes, Table 15–7 presents a list of different types of mutual funds and their respective returns and betas covering the period 1975–77. The S&P 500, of course, has a beta of one. Note that the positive relationship between risk and reward is evident at the two extremes. The risk of venture capital–special situation funds[16] was 3.8 times higher than the bond-preferred stock funds, as measured by their monthly standard deviation, and paid a return 3.1 times higher. The positive relationship between risk and return was not quite so evident in the case of other funds; however, it is not surprising to find a lack of correlation between beta and actual return over a relatively short period of time.

Selection of funds based on their betas has a practical value only if data on risks associated with individual funds are readily available. Unfortunately, the marketing labels such as "growth," "specialized," and so on used by the funds are of little value in determining their respective beta values. Fortunately, a book—*Investment Companies*—and a pamphlet—*Wiesenberger Performance Monthly*—published by Wiesenberger Services, Inc., contain *volatility* or risk rating for most mutual funds. A sample of this data, presented in Table 15–8,

[15] If the CD exceeds the FDIC insurance coverage, risk is involved.
[16] Venture capital is capital invested in new businesses, where the chances of success are often highly uncertain. These investments carry considerable risk.

Table 15–8 **Price Volatility of Mutual Fund Shares**

Because of varying investment objectives and portfolio policies, it is normal for the prices of some mutual fund shares to reflect rises and declines in the general stock market to a greater degree than do others. The relationship between percentage changes in a fund's asset value per share and the corresponding fluctuations in a broad index of common stock prices provides a measure of a fund's relative "volatility."

In the table below, price changes of leading funds—adjusted for capital gains distributed—are related to changes in the New York Stock Exchange Index of all common stocks listed on the Exchange, to provide a rough indication of volatility. The results are expressed as "factors." A volatility factor of 1.00 would mean that the adjusted asset value of a fund experienced a percentage change equal to that of the NYSE Common Stock Index between the same dates; a lower factor indicates a smaller rise or decline; a factor above 1.00 shows an advance or decline in excess of the Index.

The percentage changes in the NYSE Common Stock Index (composite) during the eight periods shown below were as follows:

April 28, 1971, to November 23, 1971	−14.1%
November 23, 1971, to January 11, 1973	+32.0%
January 11, 1973, to August 24, 1973	−17.3%
August 24, 1973, to October 26, 1973	+10.6%
October 26, 1973, to October 3, 1974	−45.1%
October 3, 1974, to July 15, 1975	+55.8%
July 15, 1975, to October 1, 1975	−14.2%
October 1, 1975, to March 24, 1976	+25.5%

Volatility is not a measure of management performance. It can be useful chiefly in estimating the relative extent of risk in declining periods and of gain potentials in shorter-term rising markets. Management performance, in contrast, is a long-term concept. Chapter 12 discusses this aspect of investment company selection. Performance data for most of the companies shown are included in "Management Results."

FUND	PRICE VOLATILITY							
Fund Name	Off Mkt 4/28/71 to 11/23/71	Up Mkt 11/23/71 to 1/11/73	Off Mkt 1/11/73 to 8/24/73	Up Mkt 8/24/73 to 10/26/73	Off Mkt 10/26/73 to 10/3/74	Off Mkt 7/15/75 to 10/1/75	Up Mkt 10/3/74 to 7/15/75	Up Mkt 10/1/75 to 3/24/76
Growth Funds (Objective: Maximum Capital Gains)								
Scudder Special Fund	0.98	0.87	1.52	0.91	1.15	0.87	1.28	1.23
Seaboard Leverage Fund	0.31	0.01	1.40	0.76	0.60	0.70	0.80	0.42
Security Equity Fund	1.08	0.98	1.43	1.83	0.94	1.07	1.25	1.08
Security Ultra Fund	0.50	1.35	1.99	1.58	1.06	1.71	1.62	1.60
Selected Opportunity	0.87	0.63	1.77	1.85	1.15	1.58	1.57	1.00
Selected Specl Shares	1.37	0.39	1.35	1.35	0.86	1.03	1.07	0.62
Sequoia Fund	0.71	0.62	1.24	1.20	0.75	1.14	0.85	1.39
Sherman, Dean Fund	2.54	0.20	0.60	0.49	0.64	1.59	1.34	0.46
Sigma Capital Shares	1.42	1.12	1.82	1.47	1.12	1.46	1.29	1.43
Smith Barney Equity Fd	0.66	1.19	1.42	1.71	0.94	0.82	0.87	0.74
Spectra Fund Inc	1.51	0.89	2.29	1.33	1.18	1.18	1.08	1.08
Steadman Amer Industry	1.12	0.43	1.64	1.70	0.89	0.54	1.04	0.51
Supervised Inv Summit	1.08	0.86	1.57	1.66	1.10	1.34	0.89	1.17
Tudor Hedge Fund	1.14	1.65	1.91	1.71	0.79	0.92	1.31	1.47
20th Century Inv-Gro	0.88	2.60	1.68	3.22	1.17	1.53	1.41	2.18

Table 15–8 (*continued*)

FUND	PRICE VOLATILITY							
Fund Name	Off Mkt 4/28/71 to 11/23/71	Up Mkt 11/23/71 to 1/11/73	Off Mkt 1/11/73 to 8/24/73	Up Mkt 8/24/73 to 10/26/73	Off Mkt 10/26/73 to 10/3/74	Off Mkt 7/15/75 to 10/1/75	Up Mkt 10/3/74 to 7/15/75	Up Mkt 10/1/75 to 3/24/76
Union Capital Fund	0.72	1.55	2.03	1.58	0.99	1.25	1.01	1.23
United Vanguard Fund	0.93	0.50	1.38	0.93	1.28	1.30	1.50	1.16
Value Line Specl Situa	2.25	0.36	2.07	1.46	1.04	1.42	1.49	1.66
Vance Sanders Spec Fd	0.84	1.02	1.60	1.82	1.14	1.23	1.20	1.10
Weingarten Equity Fund	0.43	1.26	1.46	1.66	1.15	1.51	1.20	0.90
Averages	1.12	1.01	1.54	1.38	1.01	1.12	1.15	1.04
Objective: Growth & Current Income								
First Investors Fund	1.33	0.73	1.42	1.28	0.89	0.73	0.84	0.94
Fletcher Fund	1.30	0.52	1.91	1.80	0.86	1.26	1.23	1.65
Founders Mutual Fund	1.20	0.98	0.87	0.99	0.88	0.97	0.87	1.06
Fundamental Investors	0.87	0.55	1.08	0.86	0.91	0.81	0.85	0.91
General Elec S&S Prog	0.59	1.46	0.76	0.52	1.17	1.06	1.18	0.90
General Securities	1.87	0.20	1.44	1.33	0.80	1.08	0.54	1.18
Guardian Mutual Fund	1.05	0.82	1.00	1.45	0.75	0.90	0.76	1.06
Hamilton Series H-DA	1.01	0.50	1.14	1.18	0.92	0.99	0.83	1.03
Imperial Capital Fund	0.81	0.98	1.03	0.90	0.82	0.53	1.03	0.87
Investment Co of Amer	0.88	0.91	1.05	1.53	0.88	0.91	0.91	0.95
Investment Trust Bostn	1.07	0.78	0.70	0.63	0.79	0.81	0.94	1.00
Investors Stock Fund	0.95	0.89	0.91	0.88	0.98	0.94	0.92	0.98
Isi Trust Fund	0.62	0.49	0.27	0.37	CT	0.22	0.69	CT
Istel Fund	0.93	0.79	0.68	0.75	0.66	0.66	0.07	0.01
Keystone S-1	0.56	1.12	0.70	0.68	1.04	1.08	1.17	0.87
Legal List Investmnts	0.29	0.87	1.04	1.40	0.82	0.96	1.01	0.59
Lutheran Brotherhod Fd	1.09	0.78	0.92	1.07	0.86	0.73	0.64	0.70
Mann (Horace) Fund	0.57	1.06	0.65	0.74	0.94	0.93	1.05	0.70
Mass Fincl Dev Fund	—	0.67	1.10	1.09	1.08	1.18	1.29	0.82
Mass Investors Trust	1.11	0.76	0.99	1.21	0.93	0.86	0.89	0.97
Averages	0.99	0.83	1.11	1.10	0.90	0.88	0.89	0.89
Objective: Income (Common Stock Policy)								
Babson (D L) Income Tr	0.18	0.16	0.59	0.41	0.28	0.06	0.16	0.14
BLC Income Fund	1.06	0.90	1.12	1.13	0.69	0.90	0.81	1.19
Corporate Leaders Tr B	0.72	0.89	1.05	1.12	0.95	0.83	0.63	0.93
Freedom Fund	0.79	0.55	1.06	1.35	0.77	0.52	0.77	0.61
Income Fund of America	0.44	0.33	0.86	0.74	0.51	0.58	0.69	0.94
Isi Income Fund	0.99	0.25	0.28	0.19	0.24	0.14	0.51	0.04
John Hancock Signature	0.93	0.73	1.02	1.07	0.83	0.72	0.67	0.93
Keystone S-2	0.86	0.92	0.70	1.01	1.09	0.98	1.17	1.06
Lincoln Natl Income	0.74	0.17	0.52	0.36	0.56	0.22	0.34	0.37
Mutual Inv Found-MIF	1.19	0.67	0.96	1.08	0.70	0.77	0.78	1.19
Nel Equity Fund	0.95	0.64	0.84	1.35	0.90	0.83	0.95	1.02
Phoenix Fund	0.37	0.19	0.84	0.55	0.53	0.27	0.30	0.48
Sentinel Income Fund	0.34	0.28	0.71	0.92	0.78	0.47	0.72	0.45

Table 15–8 (*continued*)

FUND	PRICE VOLATILITY							
Fund Name	Off Mkt 4/28/71 to 11/23/71	Up Mkt 11/23/71 to 1/11/73	Off Mkt 1/11/73 to 8/24/73	Off Mkt 1/11/73 to 10/26/73	Off Mkt 10/26/73 to 10/3/74	Up Mkt 10/3/74 to 7/15/75	Off Mkt 7/15/75 to 10/1/75	Up Mkt 10/1/75 to 3/24/76*
Sentinel Trustees Fund	0.49	0.98	0.59	2.04	0.87	0.69	1.23	0.86
Smith Barney Inc & Gro	—	—	1.32	1.06	0.80	0.58	0.60	0.98
United Contl Income Fd	0.76	0.36	1.01	0.51	0.78	0.48	0.64	0.72
United Income Fund	1.05	0.97	0.82	0.55	0.95	0.87	0.97	0.69
Washington Mutual Inv	1.01	0.64	1.14	1.41	0.72	0.90	0.65	1.11
Averages	0.76	0.57	0.86	0.94	0.72	0.60	0.70	0.76
Balanced Funds								
American Balanced Fund	0.69	0.46	0.83	0.61	0.72	0.51	0.58	0.73
Axe-Houghton Fund B	0.69	0.53	0.87	0.75	0.45	0.34	0.38	0.70
Boston Foundation Fund	1.01	0.63	1.09	0.96	0.83	0.68	0.70	0.55
Composite Bd & Stk Fd	0.64	0.45	0.81	0.92	0.62	0.53	0.57	0.61
Dodge & Cox Balanced	1.60	0.59	2.24	1.59	0.33	0.66	0.69	0.81
Eaton & Howard Balancd	0.62	0.67	0.58	0.78	0.81	0.59	0.54	0.62
Investors Mutual	0.63	0.60	0.78	0.49	0.80	0.60	0.72	0.76
Loomis-Sayles Mutual	0.71	0.70	0.68	0.79	0.89	0.76	0.80	0.72
Massachusetts Fund	0.57	0.75	0.76	0.84	0.79	0.55	0.59	0.55
Natl Balanced Fund	0.79	0.25	1.20	0.74	0.81	0.71	0.74	1.00
Nation-Wide Securities	0.57	0.47	0.72	0.67	0.73	0.66	0.62	0.81
Putnam (G) Fd Boston	0.57	0.91	0.64	0.58	0.90	0.69	0.90	1.01
Scudr Stvns & Clrk Bal	0.69	0.84	0.87	0.85	0.90	0.56	0.51	0.73
Shareholders Tr Boston	0.98	0.32	1.42	1.37	0.86	0.68	0.66	0.90
Sigma Trust Shares	0.75	0.63	1.21	0.75	0.56	0.40	0.49	0.73
State Farm Balanced Fd	0.79	0.40	0.99	0.64	0.71	0.58	0.50	0.64
Stein Roe & Farnham Bal	0.63	1.09	0.99	0.92	0.96	0.89	0.93	0.73
Uslife Balanced Fd	0.55	0.39	0.76	0.82	0.49	0.34	0.48	0.48
Vance Sanders Investr	0.71	0.54	0.97	0.95	0.76	0.63	0.68	0.64
Wellington Fund	0.86	0.58	0.88	0.77	0.80	0.54	0.70	0.78
Averages	0.75	0.59	0.96	0.84	0.74	0.60	0.64	0.73

NOTE: The averages shown for the *Maximum Capital Gains* and *Growth & Current Income* Groups include funds not listed in this exhibit.

SOURCE: *Investment Companies* (New York: Wiesenberger Services, Inc., 1976), pp. B-48–B-50.

can be used to develop the investment strategy outlined above. In this table, price changes of various funds are related to changes in the NYSE Index for several periods when the Index moved either up or down. A price volatility rating, interpreted the same as a beta coefficient, is assigned to the various funds for each period. The investor can identify the volatility of a fund on both the up

Table 15–9

Fund Group	Beta	Percent of Fund Invested	Weighted Beta
Bond-preferred stock	.23	50%	.115
Aggressive growth stock	.97	50	.485
Total Portfolio		100%	.600

The same objective could have been accomplished in a different manner, as shown below:

Fund Group	Beta	Percent of Fund Invested	Weighted Beta
Bond-preferred stock	.23	56%	.129
Growth	.98	30	.294
Special situations	1.29	14	.181
Total Portfolio		100%	.604

and the down sides. Note that of the four types of funds sampled here, the funds with the objective of maximizing capital gains had the highest average ratings—above 1.0 for every period. Growth and current income funds had the next highest average ratings, followed by income funds and balanced funds.

Reformulation of Investment Beta Investors need not confine themselves to a single type of fund. They can simultaneously invest in two or more types of funds in order to bring the value of the beta of their total investment to the desired level.

The mechanics of the process of reformulating beta are straightforward. Suppose an investor has determined that her risk preference is best expressed by a beta of approximately .60. Using the data presented in Table 15–9, she can accomplish her objectives by constructing either of the two portfolios in the manner demonstrated in the table.

An alternative to this technique involves the spreading of risk by buying two or more funds with the same objectives, assuming that there is a significant risk spread between various funds falling within the same group. For example, if an investor has decided to invest in growth stock funds, he might use the volatility ratings to balance a highly volatile fund against a lower one in the same group. Similarly, with income funds, the investor could pair a fund that invests largely in high-yield stocks with one that concentrates on bonds.

Examination of Track Record

Before making the final decision, an investor should examine the record of each selected fund and the records of other funds with similar objectives. This will indicate the type of periods in which the fund has performed well or poorly in

Table 15–10

Stock Group	S&P 500	Affiliated Funds	T. Rowe Price
Growth	39.8%	10.5%	80.2%
Cyclical	24.0	57.5	8.7
Stable	20.0	18.0	4.1
Oil	16.2	14.0	7.0
Total	100.0%	100.0%	100.0%
Portfolio Beta	1.00	1.09	1.11
Fund Performance	−29%	−16%	−42%

SOURCE: James L. Farrell, Jr., "Homogeneous Stock Groupings," *Financial Analysts Journal,* May–June 1975, p. 58.

Table 15–11 **Funds and Their Ratings**

Year	Keystone S-4	Chemical Fund	International Resources
1	29	1	10
2	1	39	37
3	38	14	39
4	5	27	22
5	3 (tied)	3 (tied)	35
6	8	33	1
7	35	1	37
8	1	27	39
9	1 (tied)	4	1 (tied)
10	36	23	11

SOURCE: Taken from Burton G. Malkiel, *A Random Walk Down Wall Street* (New York: W. W. Norton, 1975), p. 156.

the past. Mutual fund records can be analyzed by using the portfolio evaluation measures discussed in Chapter 14 (pp. 630–33). Also, if possible, the credentials of the portfolio managers should be carefully checked.

A word of caution should be added here. The selection of a mutual fund is rendered difficult because of the inconsistency of performance of individual mutual funds over time. For example, Table 15–10 shows the results of the Affiliated Funds versus T. Rowe Price during the 1973 to 1974 bear market. Given their respective betas, both funds should have performed worse than the market. However, the table shows that the Affiliated Funds performed much better than expected; it lost only 16 percent while the market declined 29 percent.

Even more revealing is a ten-year study by Eugene Fama, presented in Table 15–11, which demonstrates the inconsistent performance of three individual mutual funds. These three funds have gone back and forth from the top of the ranking (1) to the bottom (39).

Identification of Special Services

Other things equal, funds that provide a variety of special services and conveniences are preferable to those that do not. Several types of special services are offered by different funds.

First, many mutual fund shares can be redeemed quickly through a variety of convenient means. Second, most funds permit, without charge, the exchange of shares of one fund for another in the same management group. Third, many funds provide an annual summary of their investors' transactions in a convenient form. Finally, mutual funds provide other services, including the acceptance of investments for IRA and Keogh accounts (discussed in Chapter 16) and regular withdrawals from investors' accounts.

Switching Funds

Buying into a fund, of course, is just the beginning of an investment process. A change in the stock or bond market or in the investor's risk preference might necessitate switching, or liquidating investment in investment company shares. Each fund is committed to a particular investment philosophy which dictates the type of securities it will hold. Although its managers may alter the holdings fairly frequently, they cannot completely change direction to capitalize on basic changes in investment conditions. In fact, by the terms of their prospectuses, many funds are required to invest only in certain types or grades of securities. For example, an income fund may replace certain stocks with others, but even the new stocks will primarily be income stocks. Consequently, an income fund investor who is unwilling to hold income stocks has little choice but to move his or her money to another type of fund with a different goal or method of operation.

An important tax dimension of switching deserves special mention. Federal law states that a switch from one fund to another—even though the funds are in the same *management* organization—is counted as a sale of one security and the purchase of another. For some investors, especially those in a high income bracket, this tax aspect may act as a deterrent to switching from one fund to another.

Sources of Information

The availability of valuable sources of information is a prerequisite to an informed decision on the initial selection and subsequent switching of funds. Fortunately, there is no dearth of good information on investment companies.

One of the best sources of information is provided by *Investment Companies*, published annually by the Wiesenberger Investment Companies Service. In addition to containing valuable data on individual funds, the publication discusses such topics as appraisal of management, techniques for selecting management companies, and the regulation of mutual funds.

Regular, up-to-date statistics are also readily available. The *Wall Street Journal* publishes daily quotations on a large number of open-end funds. *Barron's* publishes a weekly list of quotations and the dividend income and capital gains for the past 12 months. Investors might also consult the quarterly survey of mutual funds in *Barron's* and the *Forbes* Annual Mutual Fund Survey and performance ratings of mutual funds.

Investment Companies: Active Versus Passive Management

At the beginning of this chapter, we noted that funds which employ passive management are known as index funds, whereas actively managed funds are known by a variety of names.

Historical Record of Active Management

Index funds employ passive management, attempt to duplicate the market's performance, and generally succeed in doing so. Because the market's performance is well documented and easily available, no further discussion of the historical performance of index funds is necessary. The rest of the section, therefore, is devoted to an examination of the performance record of active management of mutual funds.

The Jensen Study[17]

Of the numerous studies conducted concerning mutual funds' performance, most have shown results in general agreement with Michael Jensen's study of 115 mutual funds over the period 1945 to 1964.[18] Figure 15–3 presents the results of the Jensen study. In this figure, the Capital Market Line (CML) has been drawn between an assumed riskless rate of 3 percent and the market portfolio risk/return point. On average, after operating costs, net compounded profit rates were 1.1 percent below the CML, with only 39 of the 115 funds appearing above the line. After subtracting all management fees and transaction costs, and adding back a yield on idle cash, the funds closely approximated the market's return.

[17] Reprinted with permission from *Analyzing the Stock Market*, Second Edition, by H. Russell Fogler. Grid, Inc., Columbus, Ohio, 1978. Pages 133–36.

[18] Michael C. Jensen, "Risk, the Pricing of Capital Assets, and the Evaluation of Investment Portfolios," *Journal of Business*, April 1969, pp. 167–247; Michael C. Jensen, "The Performance of Mutual Funds in the Period 1945–1964," *Journal of Finance*, May 1968, pp. 389–416; K. K. Mazuy and J.L. Treynor, "Can Mutual Funds Outguess the Market?" *Harvard Business Review*, July–August 1966, pp. 131–36; Robert C. Klemkosky, "How Consistently Do Managers Manage?" *Journal of Portfolio Management*, Winter 1977, pp. 11–15.

Figure 15–3

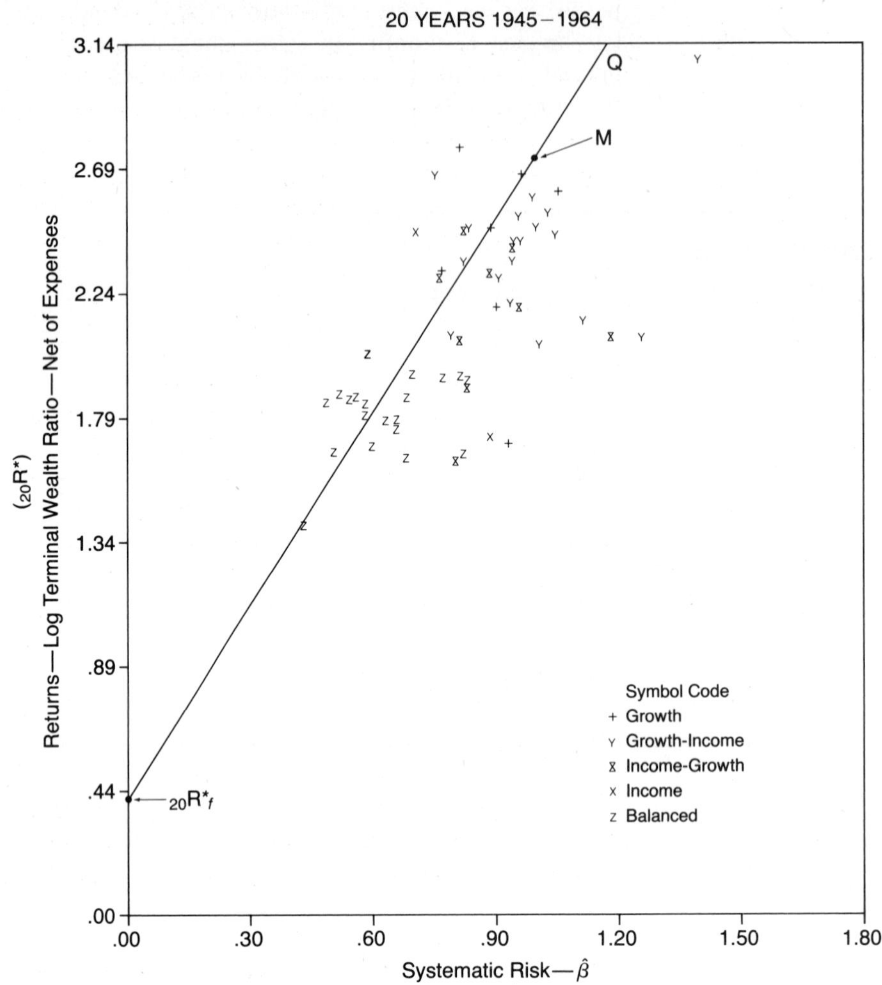

SOURCE: Michael C. Jensen, "Risk, the Pricing of Capital Assets, and the Evaluation of Investment Portfolios," *Journal of Business*, Volume 42 (April 1969), p. 233.

Jensen also analyzed the group of above-average performers in greater detail. He split his study into ten-year segments using returns to fund owners. He discovered that the winners in one period were not the outstanding winners next period, at least not by more than a random chance would suggest. However, the losers were somewhat consistent, presumably because they generated large transaction costs.

The FBC Study[19]

Professors Irwin Friend, Marshall Blume, and Jean Crockett (FBC) went beyond the Jensen study. They randomly selected 160 funds covering the period 1960–68, and split them into three beta categories of .5–.7, .7–.9, and .9–1.1. When the randomly selected portfolios were constructed so that equal dollar amounts were invested in each selected security, the mutual funds did not perform as well as the market. However, when randomly selected portfolios were constructed by including in them randomly selected stocks on the basis of their percentage aggregate market value compared to the total NYSE value, the mutual funds in the two higher beta categories significantly outperformed the random portfolios. As H. Russell Fogler has noted,

> *This result would seem to validate some of Friend and Blume's earlier criticism that high-beta portfolios are discriminated against by* theoretical *CML comparisons because empirical CML studies show that high-risk portfolios earn less excess return than in theory. Of course, 1960 to 1968 was a period of high rates of return in growth stocks, especially in the institutional favorites, thereby raising a cause-and-effect relation from the huge institutional buying of the 'top tier' stocks. Thus, the evidence on mutual fund performance* compared *to 'buying and holding' a market portfolio is mixed.*[20]

The Sharpe Study

William Sharpe evaluated the performance of 34 mutual funds during the period 1944–63.[21] The net rate of return was equal to price change, dividend, and capital distribution minus the cost of administration and management. As explained in Chapter 14, Sharpe used the Reward-to-Variability Ratio (RVR) to measure the performance of these funds. The RVR varied from .43 to .78 (compared to the DJIA's performance of .667).

The Sharpe study showed that, for the entire period, only 11 of the 34 funds performed better than the market. When the data was divided between the first (1944–53) and the second (1954–63) periods, and the performance of funds during the first period was used to predict the performance during the second period, Sharpe discovered that the RVR was not the best predictor of the future performance. Sharpe therefore concluded that

> *the average mutual fund manager selects a portfolio at least as good as the Dow-Jones Industrials, but that the results actually obtained by the holder*

---

[19] Irwin Friend, Marshall Blume, and Jean Crockett, *Mutual Funds and Other Institutional Investors: A New Perspective* (New York: McGraw-Hill, 1970).

[20] H. Russell Fogler, *Analyzing the Stock Market*, pp. 134–35.

[21] William Sharpe, "Mutual Fund Performance," *Journal of Business*, January 1966, pp. 119–38.

Table 15–12

Groups	Total Return 1979 Jan.–Aug.	Five Years Aug. '74–Aug. '79	Ten Years Aug. '69–Aug. '79	Total Assets (Billions)
370 Mutual funds	20.0%	116.3%	83.5%	$44.5
461 Bank pooled funds	13.0	76.9	77.8	20.6
53 Insurance companies*	17.2	91.2	54.2	12.2
S&P 500	17.8	90.9	70.4	N.M.

* Includes separate and variable accounts.
N.M.: Not meaningful.

SOURCE: Richard Phalon, "Friends in Need," *Forbes*, October 29, 1979, p. 79.

of mutual fund shares (after the cost associated with the operations of the fund have been deducted) fall somewhat short of those from the Dow-Jones Industrials.[22]

The McDonald Study[23]

The McDonald study, which analyzed 123 mutual funds covering the period 1960–69, divided the funds into five groups: (1) maximum capital gains, (2) growth, (3) income-growth, (4) balanced, and (5) income. The study calculated the following RVR for the 123 funds:

Average value for 123 funds: .112
Average value for all NYSE stocks: .113

These figures indicated that the funds performed worse than the market. The study also calculated the following average excess return relative to their respective betas:

Average value for 123 funds: .518
Average value for all NYSE stocks: .510

These data justified the conclusion that the funds outperformed the market. However, the gains posted by the mutual funds were marginal as compared to the nonmarket risk carried by them.[24]

[22] Reprinted from "Mutual Fund Performance," *Journal of Business*, p. 137, by William Sharpe by permission of the University of Chicago Press. © 1966 by the University of Chicago.
[23] For details see John G. McDonald, "Objectives and Performance of Mutual Funds, 1960–1969," *Journal of Financial and Quantitative Analysis*, June 1974, pp. 331–33.
[24] A rational explanation for this phenomenon is that mutual funds carry significant nonmarket risks despite the fact that they carry a large number of securities in their portfolios.

The Historical Returns

Table 15–12 presents the average one-, five-, and ten-year rates of return of 370 mutual funds relative to two other groups of actively managed funds and the S&P 500. Although this table is not based on any detailed risk-adjusted performance analysis, and the terminal date of August 1979 is selected arbitrarily, it indicates that, as a group, over the selected periods, several mutual funds have earned higher returns than the S&P 500 and the other managed funds.

Summary

Passive and active portfolio construction and management require substantial financial resources and skillful analysis and management. Small investors who are unable or unwilling to engage in portfolio management can still reap most of the benefits by investing in investment companies.

Investment companies are based on a simple idea: Set a clearly defined investment objective; combine the funds of a large number of investors; and invest them judiciously to seek that common objective. Then, the investors share all income and expenses, as well as the capital gains and losses.

Investment companies may be classified broadly into *unit investment trusts* and *management companies.* Management companies may be further subdivided into *open-end companies*—known as *mutual funds*—and *closed-end companies.*

Mutual funds can be either *load* or *no-load funds.* With load funds, the investor pays a sales charge of usually 7.5 to 8.0 percent at the time of purchase.

Classified by type of investment, mutual funds are either *bond funds, common stock funds* and *balanced funds*, or *money market funds.* Common stock funds may be classified further according to their investment *objectives* and *diversification.*

An investor should exercise care in selecting an investment company that will best serve his objectives.

The track record of mutual funds has been generally inconsistent. Some studies have shown that a few funds have gone back and forth from the top of the ranking to the bottom.

A Look Ahead

In all of the discussions on stocks, bonds, and portfolio construction and management, the topics of taxes and transaction costs were carefully omitted. These costs of investing, of course, are an important variable in the development of an investment strategy and will be explored in the next chapter.

Concepts for Review

Investment company
Unit Investment Trusts
Open-end companies
Mutual funds
Closed-end companies
No-load funds
Load funds
Bond funds
Common stock funds
General common stock funds
Specialized funds
Growth funds
Income funds
Growth and income funds
Balanced funds
Index funds
Money market funds
Dual-purpose funds
Techniques of fund selection
Switching funds
Investment companies: active vs. passive management

Questions for Review

1. What are investment companies and how do they differ from other types of companies? Why do investors buy investment company shares?
2. What are some of the important differences between closed-end funds and mutual funds?
3. What is the difference between a load and a no-load fund?
4. Describe how common stock funds and balanced funds can differ according to diversification and objective. How can an investor determine these characteristics in an investment company?
5. Do you think the policies of mutual funds differ from those of other institutional investors (such as life insurance companies, trust departments of banks and pension funds)? Explain.
6. What advantages do bond funds offer to investors?
7. Why would anyone buy a money market fund?
8. The Eaton & Howard Balanced Fund has a net asset value of \$7.28 per share and an offer price of \$7.85 per share. What does this tell you?
9. If a well-diversified portfolio of 15 to 25 common stocks can virtually eliminate unsystematic risk, why would an investment company purchase as many as 150 stocks?
10. What is an index fund? Why would an investor purchase shares of one?
11. Comment on the following statement: "Once you have decided to purchase shares of an investment company, no further decisions need be made."
12. What is the difference between a balanced fund and a common stock fund? Could either type of fund be defensive? Aggressive?

13. Should an investment company have outperforming the stock market as an investment objective?

14. What are specialized funds? Under what conditions would you advise an investor not to invest in one?

15. The investment objective of ABC Trend Fund reads as follows: "The Fund is a diversified, open-end investment company seeking capital gains through the interpretation of all factors believed to influence security prices, including technical factors. Of course, there can be no assurance that this objective will be achieved." What does this tell you about ABC Trend Fund? Would you consider investing in it? Explain.

16. Assume you have just decided to invest in an investment company. Outline the selection process you will undertake.

17. Summarize the historical record of mutual funds. How would you rate their performance record?

18. Many investors employ a strategy of switching mutual funds. Doesn't this defeat one of the main purposes of investing in mutual funds—eliminating the need to make investment decisions?

19. Why would an investor wish to purchase shares in more than one investment company?

20. Investor Q has decided to purchase XYZ Fund because its net asset value has risen by a larger percentage over the past two years than any other fund. Comment on this decision.

Selected Readings

Arditti, F. D. "Another Look at Mutual Fund Performance." *Journal of Financial and Quantitative Analysis*, June 1971.

Beman, Lewis. "The Year the Funds Beat the Averages." *Fortune*, April 10, 1978.

Bleakley, Fred. "Can Mutual Funds Come Back?" *The Institutional Investor*. June 1972.

Bogle, John C. "Mutual Fund Performance Evaluation." *Financial Analysts Journal*, November–December 1970.

Bogle, John C., and Jan M. Twardowski. "Institutional Investment Performance Compared: Banks, Investment Counselors, Insurance Companies and Mutual Funds." *Financial Analysts Journal*, January–February 1980.

Boudreaux, Kenneth J. "Discounts and Premiums on Closed-End Mutual Funds: A Study in Valuation." *Journal of Finance*, May 1973.

Calderwood, Stanford. "The Truth About Index Funds." *Financial Analysts Journal*, July–August 1977.

Carlson, Robert S. "Aggregate Performance of Mutual Funds, 1948–1967." *Journal of Financial and Quantitative Analysis*, March 1970.

Cohen, Kalman J., and Jerry A. Pogue. "Some Comments Concerning Mutual Fund Versus Random Portfolio Performance." *Journal of Business*, April 1968.

Cook, Timothy Q., and Jeremy G. Duffield. "Money Market Mutual Funds." *Economic Review*, Federal Reserve Bank of Richmond, July–August 1979.

"Dealing with Your Mutual Fund." *Changing Times*, November 1977.

Fama, Eugene F. "Components of Investment Performance." *Journal of Finance*, June 1972.

Ferguson, Robert. "Active Portfolio Management: How to Beat the Index Funds." *Financial Analysts Journal*, May–June 1975.

Fogler, H. Russell. *Analyzing the Stock Market*. Columbus, Ohio: Grid, 1978.

"Forbes Asks Stoever Glass About Unit Trust Funds." *Newsletter*, Stoever Glass & Co., September 2, 1977.

Friend, Irwin, Marshall Blume, and Jean Crockett. *Mutual Funds and Other Institutional Investors*. New York: McGraw-Hill, 1970.

Friend, Irwin, et al. *A Study of Mutual Funds*. Report of the Committee on Interstate and Foreign Commerce, 87th Congress, 2nd Session, August 28, 1962.

Gaumnitz, Jack E. "Appraising Performance of Investment Portfolios." *Journal of Finance*, June 1970.

Gentry, James A., and John R. Pike. "Dual Funds Revisited." *Financial Analysts Journal*, March–April 1968.

Glenn, Armon. "Banks Versus Funds: Investment Decisions of the Two Groups Differed Sharply." *Barron's*, October 3, 1977.

Glenn, Armon. "Switch to No-Load: More Mutual Funds are Dropping the Sales Charge." *Barron's*, June 6, 1977.

Glenn, Armon. "Yield-Conscious Investors Bid Eagerly for Tax-Exempt Bond Funds." *Barron's*, September 26, 1977.

Good, Walter, Robert Ferguson, and Jack Treynor. "An Investor's Guide to the Index Fund Controversy." *Financial Analysts Journal*, November–December 1975.

Greeley, Robert E. "Mutual Fund Management Companies." *Financial Analysts Journal*, September–October 1967.

Horowitz, Ira. "A Model for Mutual Fund Evaluation." *Industrial Management Review*, Spring 1965.

Horowitz, Ira. "The Reward-to-Variability Ratio and Mutual Fund Performance." *Journal of Business*, October 1966.

Horowitz, Ira, and Harold B. Higgins. "Some Factors Affecting Investment Fund Performance." *Quarterly Review of Economics and Business*, Spring 1963.

"How to Select Investment Companies." In *Investment Companies*. New York: Wiesenberger Financial Services, 1979.

Jensen, Michael C. "The Performance of Mutual Funds in the Period 1945–1964." *Journal of Finance*, May 1968.

Jensen, Michael C. "Risk, the Pricing of Capital Assets, and the Evaluation of Investment Portfolios." *Journal of Business*, April 1969.

Klemkosky, Robert C. "How Consistent Do Managers Manage?" *Journal of Portfolio Management*, Winter 1977.

Kraus, Alan, and Hans R. Stoll. "Parallel Trading by Institutional Investors." *Journal of Financial and Quantitative Analysis*, December 1972.

Levitz, Gerald D. "Market Risk and the Management of Institutional Equity Portfolios." *Financial Analysts Journal*, January–February 1974.

Levy, Haim, and Marshall Sarnat. "The Case for Mutual Funds." *Financial Analysts Journal*, March–April 1972.

Litzenberger, Robert H., and Howard B. Sosin. "The Performance and Potential of Dual Purpose Funds." *Journal of Portfolio Management*, Spring 1978.

Litzenberger, Robert H., and Howard B. Sosin. "The Structure and Management of Dual Purpose Funds." *Journal of Financial Economics*, May 1977.

Malkiel, Burton G. "Valuation of Closed-End Investment Company Shares." *Journal of Finance*, June 1977.

Mazuy, K. K., and J. L. Treynor. "Can Mutual Funds Outguess the Market?" *Harvard Business Review*, July–August 1966.

McDonald, John C. "Objectives and Performance of Mutual Funds, 1960–1969." *Journal of Financial and Quantitative Analysis*, June 1974.

Mills, Harlan D. "On the Management of Fund Performance." *Journal of Finance*, December 1970.

Murray, Roger F. "Indirect Investment in the Securities Market and the Individual Investor." *Journal of Contemporary Business*, Winter 1974.

"Mutual Funds Make a Comeback." *Dun's Review*, February 1978.

O'Brien, John W. "How Market Theory Can Help Investors Set Goals, Select Investment Managers and Appraise Investment Performance." *Financial Analysts Journal*, July–August 1970.

Phalon, Richard. "Closed-End Funds Seek a New Identity." *The New York Times*, June 11, 1977.

Pratt, Eugene J. "Myths Associated with Closed-End Investment Company Discounts." *Financial Analysts Journal*, July–August 1966.

Reilly, Frank K. "Institutions on Trial: Not Guilty." *Journal of Portfolio Management*, Winter 1977.

Rolo, Charles J. "Switching Mutual Funds to Beat the Market." *Money*, August 1978.

Rosenberg, Barr. "Institutional Investment with Multiple Portfolio Managers." *Proceedings of the Seminar on the Analysis of Security Prices*, University of Chicago, November 1977.

Rosenberg, Barr. "Performance Measurement and Performance Attribution." *Proceedings of the Seminar on the Analysis of Security Prices*, University of Chicago, May 1978.

Rosenberg, Barr. "Security Appraisal and Unsystematic Risk in Institutional Investment." *Proceedings of the Seminar on the Analysis of Security Prices*, University of Chicago, November 1976.

Sharpe, William F. "Linear Programming Algorithms for Mutual Fund Portfolio Selection." *Management Science*, March 1967.

Sharpe, William F. "Mutual Fund Performance." *Journal of Business*, January 1966.

Shelton, John P., Eugene F. Brigham and Alfred Hofflander. "An Evaluation and Appraisal of Dual Funds." *Financial Analysts Journal*, May–June 1967.

Simonson, Donald G. "The Speculative Behavior of Mutual Funds." *Journal of Finance*, May 1972.

Treynor, Jack L. "How to Rate Management of Investment Funds." *Harvard Business Review*, January–February 1965.

Treynor, J. L., and K. K. Mazuy. "Can Mutual Funds Outguess the Market?" *Harvard Business Review*, July–August 1966.

"Unit Trusts: Things Your Broker Doesn't Always Tell You." *Forbes*, August 1, 1977.

Weberman, B. "How to Pick a Municipal Bond Fund." *Forbes*, September 1, 1977.

West, Richard R. "Mutual Fund Performance and the Theory of Capital Asset Pricing: Some Comments." *Journal of Business*, April 1968.

Williamson, Peter J. "Measuring Mutual Fund Performance." *Financial Analysts Journal*, November–December 1972.

Tax Strategy and the Cost of Investing

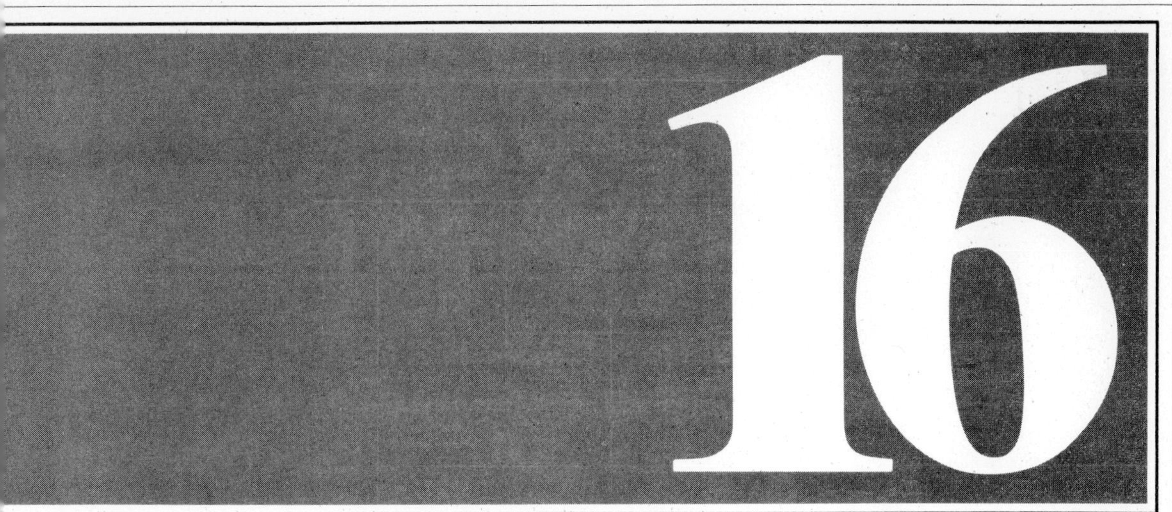

Introduction

Chapter 14 was devoted to a discussion of portfolio management in an efficient market. For simplicity, in that discussion, it was assumed that transaction costs and taxes were negligible, so the outcomes did not materially differ from the outcomes resulting from decisions made in a world with no investment costs. Unfortunately, investment decisions cannot be made without an active consideration of these costs, which can have a significant negative impact on a portfolio's return.

Investment costs can take many forms. They include information costs, interest cost on funds borrowed to purchase securities, transaction costs, and the payment of taxes on investment gains. Although all of these are important, this chapter concentrates on two major direct costs: Section 1 deals with the impact of taxes on the investment process; Section 2 deals with transaction costs.

SECTION 1 THE TAX STRATEGY

Income taxes have a substantial impact on the profitability of investments. However, to some extent, investors can control the amount of their tax liability. This section discusses important tax laws and concepts and provides a foundation on which an investor can plan his tax strategy.

Basic Tax Laws and Concepts

Computation of Federal Tax

Taxable Income

Federal taxes for individual taxpayers are computed by multiplying a person's *taxable income* by the appropriate *tax rate*. Taxable income is derived through a somewhat complicated procedure of calculating gross income and then sub-

Table 16–1 **Deriving Taxable Income**

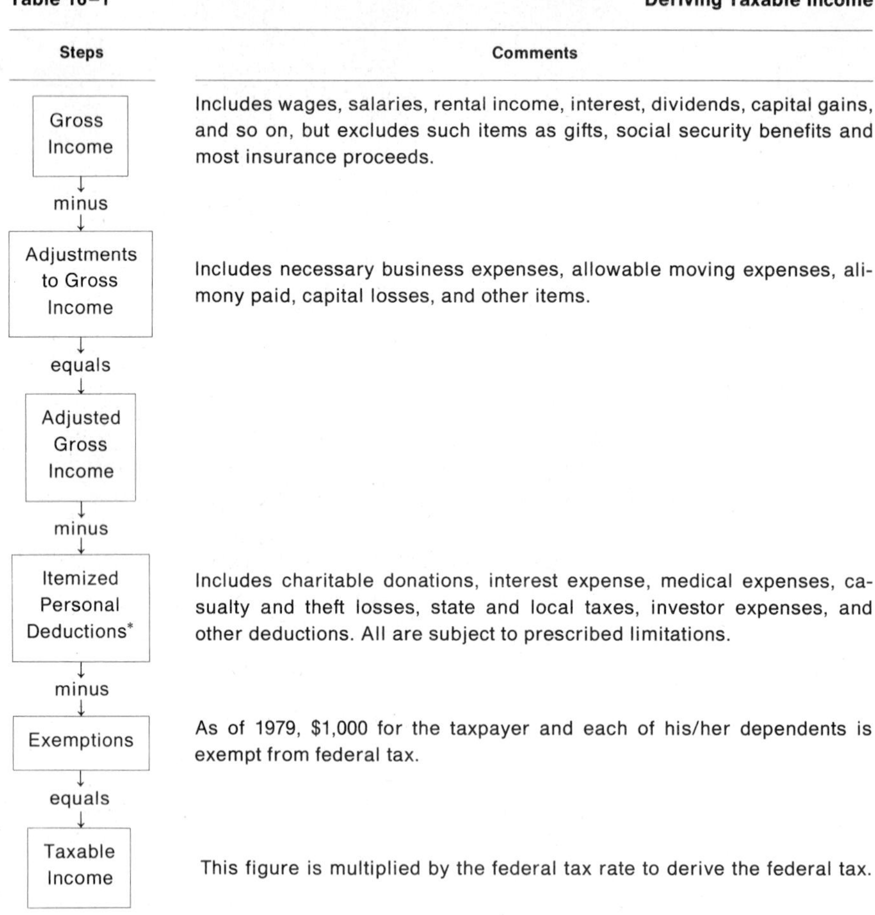

Steps	Comments
Gross Income	Includes wages, salaries, rental income, interest, dividends, capital gains, and so on, but excludes such items as gifts, social security benefits and most insurance proceeds.
minus	
Adjustments to Gross Income	Includes necessary business expenses, allowable moving expenses, alimony paid, capital losses, and other items.
equals	
Adjusted Gross Income	
minus	
Itemized Personal Deductions*	Includes charitable donations, interest expense, medical expenses, casualty and theft losses, state and local taxes, investor expenses, and other deductions. All are subject to prescribed limitations.
minus	
Exemptions	As of 1979, $1,000 for the taxpayer and each of his/her dependents is exempt from federal tax.
equals	
Taxable Income	This figure is multiplied by the federal tax rate to derive the federal tax.

* All taxpayers are given a standard deduction, called the zero bracket amount, from adjusted gross income. Only itemized deductions *in excess of* the standard deduction can be subtracted from adjusted gross income.

tracting various allowable deductions and exemptions. Table 16–1 illustrates and explains the process in its simplest form. It shows that taxable income can be minimized in any given year by minimizing *gross income* and maximizing *adjustments to gross income* and *itemized personal deductions*. The ultimate objective of a tax strategy, of course, is to control the amount of taxable income.

The Tax Rate

The federal tax rate applied to an individual's taxable income is determined by his or her filing status. Four sets of rates can be applied to various individuals: (1) married individuals filing joint returns or surviving spouses, (2) married individuals filing separate returns, (3) unmarried individuals, and (4) heads of households. The various tax rate schedules are presented in Table 16–2.

An unmarried taxpayer with taxable income of \$25,000 would pay taxes of \$5,952, as determined from the tax rate schedule C in Table 16–2.[1] The boxed tax bracket shows that the tax equals \$5,367 plus 39 percent of taxable income in excess of \$23,500, which amounts to \$5,952:

$$\begin{aligned}\text{Tax} &= \$5{,}367 + .39 \times (\$25{,}000 - \$23{,}500)\\ &= \$5{,}367 + .39 \times (\$1{,}500)\\ &= \$5{,}952\end{aligned}$$

Progressive Tax Structure

A glance at the federal tax rate structure reveals the *progressive* nature of federal taxes in this country; that is, tax rates increase with the amount of taxable income. For example, in the previous example, if a single taxpayer's taxable income increases from \$25,000 to \$27,500, an increase of 10 percent, the tax payable increases from \$5,952 to \$6,927, an increase of 16 percent.[2] Other examples using different taxable incomes or another filing status would produce similar results.

Marginal Versus Average Tax Rates

An understanding of the difference between *marginal and average tax rates* is crucial to the tax planning process. The average, or effective, tax rate is merely the total tax payable divided by the taxable income. In the previous example,

[1] For illustrative purposes, the tax is calculated from the tax rate schedules. In certain cases taxpayers may choose, or be required, to use *tax tables* instead of tax rate schedules. Using tax tables requires the computation of *tax table income* instead of taxable income. See the IRS Publication 17, *Your Federal Income Tax*, for details.

[2] The tax for a single taxpayer with \$27,500 taxable income would be:

$$\text{Tax} = 5{,}367 + .39 \times (\$27{,}500 - \$23{,}500) = \$5{,}367 + .39 \times (\$4{,}000) = \$6{,}927$$

Table 16–2

A. Married Individuals Filing Joint Return or Surviving Spouses

Taxable Income	Tax	% on Excess
$0—$ 3,400	$ —	—
Over 3,400	—	14
5,500	294	16
7,600	630	18
11,900	1,404	21
16,000	2,265	24
20,200	3,273	28
24,600	4,505	32
29,900	6,201	37
35,200	8,162	43
45,800	12,720	49
60,000	19,678	54
85,600	33,502	59
109,400	47,544	64
162,400	81,464	68
215,400	117,504	70

B. Married Individuals Filing Separate Returns

Taxable Income	Tax	% on Excess
$0—$ 1,700	$ —	—
Over 1,700	—	14
2,750	147	16
3,800	315	18
5,950	702	21
8,000	1,133	24
10,100	1,637	28
12,300	2,253	32
14,950	3,101	37
17,600	4,081	43
22,900	6,360	49
30,000	9,839	54
42,800	16,751	59
54,700	23,772	64
81,200	40,732	68
107,700	58,752	70

C. Unmarried Individuals

Taxable Income	Tax	% on Excess
$0—$ 2,300	$ —	—
Over 2,300	—	14
3,400	154	16
4,400	314	18
6,500	692	19
8,500	1,072	21
10,800	1,555	24
12,900	2,059	26
15,000	2,605	30
18,200	3,565	34
23,500	5,367	39
28,800	7,434	44
34,100	9,766	49
41,500	13,392	55
55,300	20,982	63
81,800	37,677	68
108,300	55,697	70

D. Heads of Households

Taxable Income	Tax	% on Excess
$0—$ 2,300	$ —	—
Over 2,300	—	14
4,400	294	16
6,500	630	18
8,700	1,026	22
11,800	1,708	24
15,000	2,476	26
18,200	3,308	31
23,500	4,951	36
28,800	6,859	42
34,100	9,085	46
44,700	13,961	54
60,600	22,547	59
81,800	35,055	63
108,300	51,750	68
161,300	87,790	70

NOTE: These rates were applicable to the income generated in 1979.

the average tax rate for a \$25,000 taxable income for a single taxpayer is 23.8 percent:

$$\frac{\text{Tax Payable}}{\text{Taxable Income}} = \frac{\$5{,}952}{\$25{,}000}$$

$$= 23.8\%$$

In contrast, the marginal tax rate is the rate imposed on the taxpayer's last dollar of income. Because the taxpayer earned \$25,000, the tax rate applicable to him reads as follows:

Taxable Income	Tax	% on Excess	
Over \$23,500	\$5,367	39%	←
\$28,800	\$7,434	44%	

In this case, the marginal tax rate is 39 percent. It should be noted that under the progressive tax structure, the marginal tax rate is always higher than the corresponding average tax rate.

Minimum and Maximum Taxes

Under the current tax law, marginal tax rates can be as high as 70 percent; however, the maximum tax rate on *earned income* is limited to 50 percent. "Earned income" covers salaries, bonuses, and other currently paid forms of compensation. Because investment income is not classified as earned income, it can still be taxed at the highest marginal rates.

In addition to the regular income tax, individuals also pay a 15 percent add-on *minimum tax* on certain *tax preference items*. These items include depletion, accelerated depreciation on real property, and stock options.* The tax applies only to the total of preference items exceeding \$10,000 or half of the regular tax liability, whichever is greater.†

A new alternative minimum tax now applies to the 60 percent portion of long-term capital gains not included in taxable gross income for the year. This alternative tax, however, is payable only if it exceeds an individual's regular tax liability *plus* the 15 percent add-on minimum tax described above. It is computed by adding the excluded portion of capital gains and excess adjusted itemized deductions to taxable income and subtracting a \$20,000 exemption. The first \$40,000 of the balance is taxed at a 10 percent rate, the next \$40,000 at 20 percent, and anything over that at 25 percent.

---

* The list includes other items as well. The exact amount of each preference item subject to the minimum tax must be calculated according to specific IRS guidelines. Corporations also pay a minimum tax, although in this case the method of tax calculation is different.

† Preference items also offset earned income eligible for the 50 percent maximum tax.

Why is the marginal tax rate so important for investors? The answer is clear. Income earned from investments is generally considered to be marginal; that is, it is usually additional income that an investor generates over and above his or her ordinary income from wages and salaries. Consequently, in considering the purchase of a particular security, the investor must consider the marginal tax rate that will apply to the *additional* income expected from that investment. Another interesting fact is that the maximum marginal tax rate (on unearned income) is 70 percent. Although this is quite high, a taxpayer's additional tax will never exceed any additional taxable income.

State Taxes

In addition to federal tax, investors are also subject to state taxes, which can vary substantially from state to state. For example, in New York the top tax rate can be as high as 15 percent, whereas in Delaware the maximum state tax rate is 19.8 percent. Many states levy a flat tax on all taxable income levels, while some states do not have any income tax.

Investors confronted with high state taxes might consider investing in U.S. government securities or municipal bonds issued by their resident state. Both types of securities provide interest income that is exempt from state taxes. Because state laws can vary substantially from state to state, this topic will not be discussed in detail.

Taxes and Securities

Stocks and fixed income securities generate gross income in the form of dividends, interest, and capital gains. There are several implications to these forms of income.

Interest and Dividend Income

Except for interest received on tax-exempt municipal bonds, interest received on fixed-income securities is treated as ordinary income, along with wages and salaries. Dividends are usually paid from current or retained earnings and are taxed as ordinary income to the shareholders. However, in some cases, dividends constitute a return of capital, and in other cases they are taxed as capital gains.

Dividend income is given a slight tax preference over interest income in that a small amount is excludable from ordinary income if received from a domestic corporation. The *dividend exclusion* is a maximum of $100 for a single person, or up to $200 for a married couple filing a joint return if each has at least $100 of dividend income.

Capital Gains and Losses

Capital gains are profits from selling or exchanging an asset, with the exception of assets used or held in the taxpayer's trade or business. Capital assets can be conveniently categorized into two groups: income producing and nonincome producing. Stocks and bonds purchased as investments are, naturally, income producing.

When a capital asset is sold for a profit, a tax must be paid on the *capital gain.* If the capital asset is held for less than a year, a *short-term capital gain* is realized and the *entire profit* is included in gross income. However, if a capital asset is held for more than 12 months, the profit from the sale is treated as a *long-term capital gain,* only 40 percent of which is included in the taxpayer's gross income. Because of this preferential tax treatment, even a taxpayer in the highest marginal tax bracket would pay a long-term capital gains tax of no more than 28 percent—that is, 70 percent of 40 percent. For example, for individuals in the 32 percent marginal tax bracket, the capital gains tax would only be 12.80 percent or 32 percent of 40 percent, as shown in Figure 16–1.

Figure 16–1

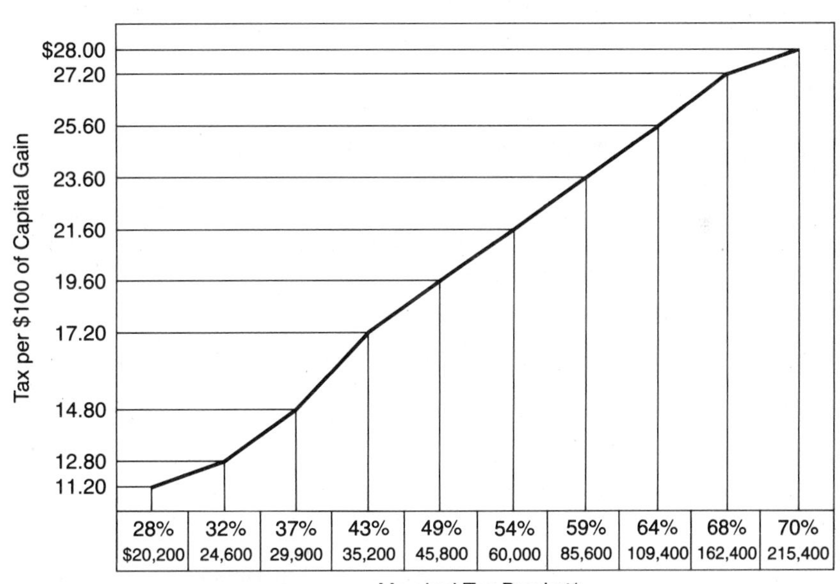

SOURCE: Reprinted from the December 31, 1979 issue of *Business Week* by special permission. © 1979 by McGraw-Hill, Inc.

Figure 16–2

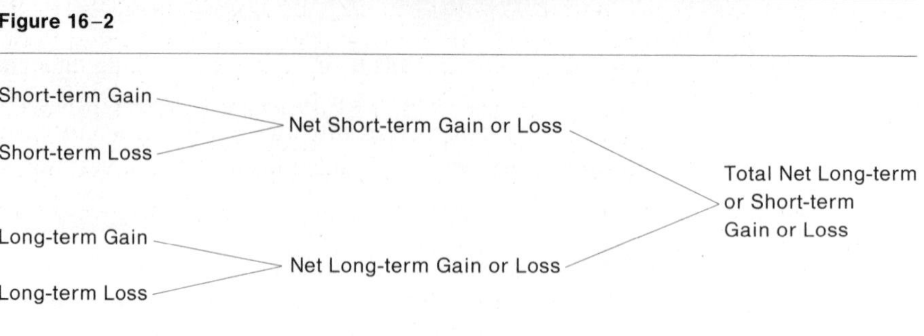

Losses on the sale of capital assets, such as stocks and bonds, are capital losses. If the asset was held for one year or less, the loss would be short term. If held for more than one year, the loss would be long term. If total capital losses during the year exceed capital gains, the excess may be used to affect up to $3,000 of ordinary income. Short-term capital losses offset ordinary income dollar for dollar, whereas it takes two dollars of long-term losses to offset one dollar of ordinary income. Any capital losses in excess of the amount needed to affect capital gains and $3,000 of ordinary income can be carried forward indefinitely. When carried forward, losses retain their original status as either short-term or long-term and must be used to affect capital gains in future years before they can be used to affect ordinary income.

For tax purposes, capital gains and losses are realized at the time of sale. When capital gains and losses are realized in the same tax year, a *net* long-term or short-term gain or loss must be calculated. Figure 16–2 illustrates the technique for such a calculation. First, short-term gains and losses are netted against each other, as are long-term gains and losses. Thereafter, these two net figures are netted against each other to determine the total *net long-term or short-term gain or loss* for the year.

Regulated Investment Companies

Income from investing in shares of regulated investment companies is taxed in essentially the same manner as income earned from the direct purchase of securities. If an investment company, such as a mutual fund, pays out at least 90 percent of its dividend and interest income and meets certain diversification requirements, it does not pay corporate taxes on the earnings.[3] Therefore, following the distribution of income by a fund, each shareholder pays taxes as though he had directly held all the securities in the investment company's portfolio.

[3] A unit trust, open-end or closed-end fund can qualify as a regulated investment company and receive this special tax treatment.

Within 45 days following the close of its taxable year, a regulated investment company is required to notify its shareholders which portions of its distributions represented capital gains and which represented ordinary income. Each shareholder then pays taxes on the capital gains distribution at the *long-term* capital gains rate and on ordinary income at the regular tax rate. Of course, any gain or loss realized when the mutual fund shares are sold is a short-term or long-term capital gain or loss, depending on the period for which they were held.

The Tax Impact

In this section, the bond and stock valuation formulas presented in earlier chapters will be modified to include the effect of tax on investment returns.

Bonds and Taxes

The following basic bond valuation formula was presented in Chapter 6:

$$P_0 = \sum_{n=1}^{N} \frac{C}{(1+i)^n} + \frac{P_N}{(1+i)^N} \qquad \textbf{(6–2 restated)}$$

This formula was later modified to introduce taxes into the valuation model:

$$P_0 = \sum_{n=1}^{N} \frac{C(1-t_n)}{(1+i_t)^n} + \frac{P_N - (P_N - P_0)cg}{(1+i_t)^N} \qquad \textbf{(6–5 restated)}$$

where

P_0 = Market price of the bond
C = Annual interest payments
t_n = Marginal income tax bracket of the investor
P_N = Par value of the bond
cg = Tax rate on long-term capital gains
N = Maturity of the bond
i_t = After-tax yield to maturity

Notice that the value of the first term, $C(1 - t_n)$, equals the amount of interest income the taxpayer retains after paying taxes of t_n percent.

The second term in Equation 6–5 introduces the capital gains tax. This tax equals the amount of the capital gains, $P_N - P_0$, multiplied by the marginal long-term capital gains tax rate,[4] cg, in the year, N, when the security matures.

[4] The marginal long-term capital gains tax rate will simply equal 40 percent of the regular marginal tax rate. Of course, if the bond is held for less than one year, the regular marginal tax rate for short-term capital gains would be used in solving Equation 6–5.

Therefore, the value, $P_N - (P_N - P_0)cg$, equals the maturity price, P_N, net of the capital gains tax.[5]

The concept embodied in Equation 6–5 was illustrated in Table 6–12 (p. 196). In this illustration, the pretax return on a bond selling at \$900 with five years to maturity, and a 7 percent coupon rate, is 9.62 percent. For an investor paying 30 percent tax on interest income and 12 percent (.30 × 40 percent) on long-term capital gains, the after-tax yield drops to 7.14 percent. Likewise, when the marginal tax rate increases to 60 percent and the capital gains tax rate increases to 24 percent (.60 × 40 percent), the after-tax yield declines to 4.66 percent.

Stocks and Taxes

The equation for calculating the after-tax yield of a stock, i_t, is similar to that used for a bond, because the effect of the tax laws on income from stocks and bonds is almost identical. In Chapter 9, it was demonstrated that the holding period yield or expected return on a stock can be found by solving for i in the following equation:

$$P_0 = \sum_{n=1}^{N} \frac{D_n}{(1+i)^n} + \frac{P_N}{(1+i)^N} \qquad \textbf{(9–26 restated)}$$

In this equation, i represents the yield before taxes. In order to measure the impact of tax on yield, Equation 9–26 is modified as shown below:

$$P_0 = \sum_{n=1}^{N} \frac{D_n(1-t_n)}{(1+i_t)^n} + \frac{P_N - (P_N - P_0)cg}{(1+i_t)^N} \qquad \textbf{(Eq. 16–1)}$$

where

P_0 = Current market price of the stock
D_n = Annual dividend payments
t_n = Marginal income tax bracket of the investor
P_N = Price at which stock is expected to be sold at the end of Period N
cg = Tax rate on long-term capital gains
N = Number of years the stock is expected to be held
i_t = After-tax holding period yield

For simplicity, this equation ignores the tax implications of the \$200 dividend exclusion that was explained earlier.

An illustration of the total impact of taxes on investment return follows. In Chapter 11, a projection was made of the dividends and future selling price for

[5] Of course, a capital gain can be realized on a bond if it is sold in the secondary market before it matures. Equation 6–5 uses the bond's par value or maturity price to determine the amount of any capital gain in order to derive an after-tax yield to maturity. Also, if a security is redeemed at a loss—that is, when $P_N - P_0$ is negative—a capital loss can be declared that will reduce taxable income and produce a tax savings. The savings are then added to the selling price of the security to derive the after-tax yield to maturity.

the common stock of Stanley Works for a five-year holding period (pp. 452–54). When discounted by the appropriate discount rate of 14.5 percent, the present value of the stock was calculated to be \$30.00:

$$PV = \frac{\$1.23}{(1.145)^1} + \frac{\$1.24}{(1.145)^2} + \frac{\$1.27}{(1.145)^3} + \frac{\$1.64}{(1.145)^4} + \frac{\$1.93}{(1.145)^5} + \frac{\$49.59}{(1.145)^5}$$
$$= \$30.00$$

Because the present value of \$30.00 was very close to the selling price, P_0, of \$29.50, if purchased at that price, the pretax expected return would be very close to the 14.5 percent required rate of return. However, if dividends and the future selling price are adjusted for taxes, the yield is reduced significantly. The following illustration measures the impact of tax on the yield by assuming that the marginal tax rate on dividends is 70 percent, and the long-term capital gains tax rate is 28 percent. For simplicity, the tax effects of dividend exclusion are ignored in this illustration. Solving Equation 16–1 by using the given data, we obtain:

$$\$29.50 = \frac{\$1.23(1-.70)}{(1+i_t)^1} + \frac{\$1.24(1-.70)}{(1+i_t)^2} + \frac{\$1.27(1-.70)}{(1+i_t)^3} + \frac{\$1.64(1-.70)}{(1+i_t)^4} + \frac{\$1.93(1-.70)}{(1+i_t)^5} + \frac{\$49.59 - (\$49.59 - \$29.50).28}{(1+i_t)^5}$$

$$\$29.50 = \frac{\$0.37}{(1+i_t)^1} + \frac{\$0.37}{(1+i_t)^2} + \frac{\$0.38}{(1+i_t)^3} + \frac{\$0.49}{(1+i_t)^4} + \frac{\$0.58}{(1+i_t)^5} + \frac{\$49.59 - \$5.63}{(1+i_t)^5}$$

Note that the expected price appreciation is \$20.09 (\$49.59 – \$29.50) and the capital gains tax is \$5.63. Solving for i_t in this equation, the expected *after-tax* return is approximately 9 percent, a substantial drop from the 14.5 percent *pretax* expected return.

Taxes and Investment Strategies

Most tax strategies applicable to securities investment are variations of two central themes. First, an important strategy deals with the *selection of securities* which are expected to provide tax-exempt investment income or long-term capital gains in lieu of taxable interest or dividends. A second strategy emphasizes tax savings through proper *timing* of stock and bond trades.

Securities for Tax-exempt Income

Municipal bonds provide the common investment vehicle for earning tax-exempt investment income. The tax advantages of municipal bonds were described extensively in Chapter 7 and are summarized here. These securities, which generally provide lower pretax yields than do taxable bonds, become attractive when the investor's marginal tax bracket is high enough to make their after-tax yields competitive with the after-tax yields on other fixed income securities. Table 7–8 (p. 243) and Equation 7–2 in Chapter 7 can be used to find the equivalent fully taxable yield on a tax-exempt bond selling at or near par value.

Tax Exempt Distributions*

Frequently, dividends declared by public utilities are partially or totally exempt from taxation. A list of utilities, and the percentage of their 1978 dividend payments which were nontaxable, are given in Table 16–A. In reality, these tax-exempt distributions are not dividends as defined by tax law, because the exempt portion is considered a return of invested capital to the shareholders.

This situation can be explained by referring to the differences in accounting methods. As a general rule, companies declare dividends out of profits measured by generally accepted accounting principles. However, for tax purposes, different accounting rules are applicable. To encourage construction and expansion of plant and equipment, utilities are allowed to depreciate these items at an accelerated rate. During the early years of construction, this results in depreciation charges greater than those used for financial accounting purposes. Also, utilities tie up large amounts of money in the construction of generating plants and facilities (which may take several years to build) before these plants can produce any revenue. Utilities are therefore allowed to credit earnings by a fictional sum as a "return" on this invested money. Because this income is not taxed, financial accounting income is higher than the taxable income. Eventually, the fictional income and excess depreciation charges create extra financial accounting income from which dividends may be declared. But because this extra income is not considered taxable income, it is classified by the IRS as a return of capital and is not taxed as income to the shareholders.

Whenever stockholders receive a "return of capital" dividend, they must reduce the purchase price, or basis, of the stock by this amount. For example, if an investor purchases XYZ Power Company at $20 and receives a $2 dividend, 50 percent of which is nontaxable, the new basis of the stock will be $19 [$20 – (.50)($2)]. This will increase the investor's taxable capital gain or decrease his capital loss when the stock is eventually sold.

---

* This piece is based on "Tax-Sheltered Dividends," *Forbes*, March 15, 1976, p. 112.

Although interest income from a municipal bond is tax exempt, any *capital gain* realized from its sale or redemption is subject to the standard capital gains tax. Therefore, if a municipal bond is purchased at a discount and redeemed at par value, for instance, a capital gains tax becomes payable.[6] Moreover, investors cannot borrow money to purchase municipal bonds, collect the tax-free interest income, and at the same time claim the interest expense on the borrowed money as an itemized personal deduction.[7]

[6] A capital *loss* can be declared on a municipal bond; however, under the present tax laws, this is only possible if the bond is *sold* at a loss in the secondary market prior to maturity.

[7] In addition, a taxpayer who purchases or holds tax-exempt securities with his own funds, and has other debt outstanding (a mortgage on a house, for example), may even run the risk of having the deduction for the interest expense partly or wholly disallowed on the assumption that the tax-exempt securities could have been sold to liquidate the debt.

Table 16–A

	1978 Payments ($)		
	Total Paid	Income	Nontaxable
American Electric Power	2.135	27%	73%
Cleveland Elec. Illum.	1.84	53	47
Columbus & So. Ohio Elec.	2.32		100
Dayton Power & Light	1.66	53.7	46.3
Interstate Pwr. (Del.)	1.4625	95.25	4.75
Long Island Lighting	1.6825	30	70
New York State Elec. & Gas	1.68	78	22
Niagara Mohawk Power	1.365	90	10
Ohio Edison	1.76		100
Philadelphia Electric	1.80	59	41
Portland General Electric	1.70		1.70
Pub. Svce. Elec. & Gas	2.08	*	*
Pennsylvania Pwr. & Lt.	1.92	†	†
San Diego Gas & Elec.	1.38		100
Southern Conn. Gas	2.30	35	65
Toledo Edison	2.12	85.3	14.7

* Mar. divd. 100% taxable; June divd. 96.8% nontaxable; Sept. & Dec. divds. 100% nontaxable.
† Jan., Apr. & July divds. fully taxable. Oct. divd. 28.69% nontaxable.

SOURCE: Adapted from Standard & Poor's *The Outlook*, March 19, 1979, p. 869.

Securities for Long-term Capital Gains

Discount Bonds

A bond sells at a discount when its coupon rate is lower than the prevailing market interest rate for bonds of similar quality and maturity. Investors purchasing discount bonds receive lower annual interest income, compared to newly issued bonds, but can earn an equivalent yield to maturity resulting from a capital gain expected to be realized when the bond is redeemed at par value. The lower the coupon rate is, the deeper a bond's discount, the lower the annual interest income received, and the higher the capital gain realized at maturity. The attractiveness of discount bonds from a tax viewpoint should therefore be clear: A significant portion of the bond's return is taxed as a long-term capital gain instead of ordinary income, assuming the bond is held for more than a year.[8]

An example of the tax benefits from discount bonds was illustrated in Table 8–9 (p. 280), which compared two similar bonds yielding 10 percent to maturity in ten years. However, one bond had a 10 percent coupon and sold at par; the other was a deep discount bond which had a 5 percent coupon and sold for \$693. For an investor in the 50 percent marginal tax bracket who pays a 20 percent capital gains tax, the after-tax yield, i_t, for the deep discount bond was 6.28 percent.[9] This was higher than the 5 percent after-tax return for the bond selling at par. Obviously, the investor should prefer the discount bond over the bond selling at par.

---

[8] This discount bond strategy described works only when bonds are purchased at a discount in the *secondary market.* If a bond is *issued* at a discount by a corporation in the primary market, the investor is required to include the discount in his or her gross income on a ratable basis over the life of the bond. More specifically, the bond-holder includes in his or her gross income a ratable monthly portion of the original issue discount multiplied by the number of full months the bond was held during the tax year. At the same time, however, the taxpayer also increases the cost, or basis, of the bond by the discount that is included in gross income.

Also, when taxable bonds are purchased at a *premium,* the investor may elect to realize a long-term capital loss when the securities are redeemed at maturity, assuming they are held more than 12 months, or may elect to amortize the premium over the life of the bond and *deduct the amortization each year* from gross income.

[9]

$$P_0 = \left[\sum_{n=1}^{N} \frac{C(1 - t_n)}{(1 + i_t)^N} \right] + \left[\frac{P_N - (P_N - P_0)(cg)}{(1 + i_t)^N} \right]$$

$$\$693 = \left[\sum_{n=1}^{10} \frac{\$50(1 - 5)}{(1 + i_i)^n} \right] + \left[\frac{\$1{,}000 - (\$1{,}000 - \$693)(.20)}{(1 + i_t)^{10}} \right]$$

$$\$693 = \sum_{n=1}^{10} \frac{\$25}{(1 + i_t)^n} + \frac{\$939}{(1 + i_t)^{10}}$$

Solving for i_t, $i_t = 6.28\%$.

Common Stocks

As with bonds, the tax impact on a stock's total return depends on the proportions of the return in the form of income and capital appreciation. By purchasing the common stock of growth companies which retain a large portion of earnings for expansion and pay out a small percentage in dividends, an investor can substitute long-term capital gains for current dividend income and take advantage of the more favorable long-term capital gains tax rate.

We noted earlier that the projected dividend stream and future selling price of Stanley Works' common stock, selling at $29.50, produced a pretax expected return of approximately 14.5 percent. The after-tax return on the stock was about 9 percent.

Clearly, because the capital gains tax is lower than the tax on dividend income, a stock expected to return a large proportion of its total return in the form of price appreciation is preferable to one that emphasizes dividends if the total pretax returns are the same. On the top half of Table 16–3, the pretax return of the ABC stock is calculated. The ABC stock is similar to Stanley Works, which sells for $29.50 and provides a 14.5 percent expected return over

Table 16–3

	Pretax Return	After-Tax Return
	$P_0 = \sum_{n=1}^{N} \frac{D_n}{(1+i)^n} + \frac{P_N}{(1+i)^N}$	$P_0 = \sum_{n=1}^{N} \frac{D_n(1-t_n)}{(1+i_t)^n} + \frac{P_N - (P_N - P_0)cg}{(1+i_t)^N}$
STOCK ABC Current Price: $P_0 = \$29.50$ Dividends: $D_1 = \$3.00$; $D_2 = \$3.25$; $D_3 = \$3.50$; $D_4 = \$3.75$; $D_5 = \$4.00$ Selling Price: $P_5 = \$35.00$ Tax Data: $t_n = 70\%$ $cg = (70\% \times 40\%) = 28\%$	$\$29.50 = \frac{\$3.00}{(1+i)^1} + \frac{\$3.25}{(1+i)^2} + \frac{\$3.50}{(1+i)^3} + \frac{\$3.75}{(1+i)^4} + \frac{\$4.00}{(1+i)^5} + \frac{\$35.00}{(1+i)^5}$ $i \approx 14.5\%$	$\$29.50 = \frac{\$3.00(1-.70)}{(1+i_t)^1} + \frac{\$3.25(1-.70)}{(1+i_t)^2} + \frac{\$3.50(1-.70)}{(1+i_t)^3} + \frac{\$3.75(1-.70)}{(1+i_t)^4} + \frac{\$4.00(1-.70)}{(1+i_t)^5} + \frac{\$35.00-(\$35.00-\$29.50)(.28)}{(1+i_t)^5}$ $i_t \approx 6\%$
STOCK XYZ Current Price: $P_0 = \$29.50$ Dividends: $D_1 = 0$; $D_2 = 0$; $D_3 = 0$; $D_4 = 0$; $D_5 = 0$ Selling Price: $P_5 = \$58.00$ Tax Data: $t_n = 70\%$ $cg = (70\% \times 40\%) = 28\%$	$\$29.50 = \frac{0}{(1+i)^1} + \frac{0}{(1+i)^2} + \frac{0}{(1+i)^3} + \frac{0}{(1+i)^4} + \frac{0}{(1+i)^5} + \frac{\$58.00}{(1+i)^5}$ $i \approx 14.5\%$	$\$29.50 = \frac{0(1-.70)}{(1+i_t)^1} + \frac{0(1-.70)}{(1+i_t)^2} + \frac{0(1-.70)}{(1+i_t)^3} + \frac{0(1-.70)}{(1+i_t)^4} + \frac{0(1-.70)}{(1+i_t)^5} + \frac{\$58.00-(\$58.00-\$29.50)(.28)}{(1+i_t)^5}$ $i_t \approx 11.15\%$

a five-year holding period. Notice that a larger portion of the return is received in the form of dividends than in the form of price appreciation. The dividend from the ABC stock is higher than that of Stanley Works for each year of the holding period; however, the selling price of the ABC stock is only expected to rise to \$35 per share, as compared to \$49.59 for Stanley Works. The after-tax return i_t, of ABC is computed in the top half of the table. Because ABC emphasizes dividend income more heavily than Stanley Works, the after-tax yield for ABC is only about 6 percent, compared to Stanley's yield of 9 percent. Clearly, taxes would constitute a significant factor in an investment decision between these two securities.

The lower half of Table 16–3 shows another interesting tax situation. The XYZ stock also has a current selling price, P_0, of \$29.50 and a 14.5 percent expected pretax return, but this company is expected to pay out no dividends over the five-year holding period. Instead, XYZ company will retain all of its earnings, thereby providing the shareholders with a potential for significant price appreciation. The expected selling price for XYZ of \$58.00 is higher than that of either Stanley Works or ABC. As expected, the tax impact on XYZ's return is minimized because the return on XYZ is taxed at the favorable 28 percent capital gains tax rate. As computed in the lower half of Table 16–3, the after-tax return on XYZ is about 11.15 percent, which is higher than the after-tax returns of Stanley Works and ABC.

Based on the foregoing illustration, the XYZ stock is the best investment, assuming that it is no riskier than the other two securities. However, in making such a choice an investor must not lose sight of risk considerations. Given an income stock and a growth company stock with equal expected pretax returns and equal risk, an investor would normally choose the growth company stock because of its preferential tax treatment. However, the risk usually varies directly with the expected returns; stocks with higher expected returns have higher betas. Therefore, if stock XYZ has a higher beta[10] than Stanley Works and ABC, the investor should select it over the two alternatives only if he is satisfied that the tax savings will adequately compensate for the additional risk.[11]

Additional factors should be considered before investing in securities primarily for realizing long-term capital gains. First, the investor should closely

[10] In this connection, note that riskier stocks have higher beta values. See Chapters 5 and 13 for details.

[11] Research has generally presumed that individual investors in high marginal tax brackets prefer and bid up the price of growth company stocks because of the differing tax rates on dividends and capital gains. This behavior is known as the "clientele effect." Black and Scholes determined that the clientele effect is negligible by testing the hypothesis that high growth, low dividend yield stocks, which generally have high beta values, should also have *risk-adjusted* returns that are historically lower than the pretax returns on higher dividend yield, lower beta stocks. However, studies using adjusted betas conclude that the impact is statistically significant. See F. Black and M. Scholes, "The Effects of Dividend Yield and Dividend Policy on Common Stock Prices and Returns," *Journal of Financial Economics*, No. 1, 1974, pp. 1–22. Also, see M.J. Brennan, "Taxes, Market Valuation and Corporate Financial Policy," *National Tax Journal*, No. 23, 1970, pp. 417–27.

examine the expected holding period of the stocks intended for purchase and attempt to estimate the *direction* of his or her marginal tax bracket.[12] If the estimated tax bracket at the expected time of the stock sale is considerably higher than the marginal tax rate applied to the dividend stream, much of the tax advantage of a long-term capital gain over dividend income would be negated. Second, for small investors, there is a tax advantage to buying higher dividend yielding stocks when the dividend income remains below the $200 tax exclusion level.

Convertible Bonds

Convertible bonds can be exchanged for common stocks at a predetermined conversion ratio. Because of the conversion privilege, convertible bonds generally carry a lower coupon rate than similar quality straight bonds. Investors in convertible bonds, therefore, accept lower current interest income; however, if the price of the common stock appreciates, the convertible bond should also increase in value. The investor can then sell the bond at a profit and pay the long-term capital gains tax. Convertible securities will be discussed in Chapter 17 in detail.

Timing Stock and Bond Sales

Because of tax-related considerations, the timing of the sale of a security is of critical importance for two reasons. First, the time of sale determines whether the gain or loss will be treated as long-term or short-term. Second, the time of sale determines the year in which the gain or loss is realized. This can be important, because an investor's marginal tax rate frequently varies from year to year. In addition, an investor can gain greater tax benefits by taking capital losses in years when he or she has not realized any long-term capital gains. If the investor has long-term capital gains, any capital losses must first be offset against such gains. This section discusses some strategies for timing sales with the objective of minimizing the capital gains tax and maximizing tax deductions from capital losses. (Although these strategies are discussed primarily with reference to stocks, they are also applicable to bonds.)

Basic Strategies

As previously mentioned, a capital gain or loss on a stock is realized in the year in which the security is sold. Long-term gains and losses are realized on stocks held for more than 12 months; short-term gains are realized and losses are

[12] For simplicity, the marginal tax rate, t_n, in the Stanley Works, ABC, and XYZ stock examples is assumed to remain *constant* for the entire holding period, with the long-term capital gains tax rate, *cg*, based on the current year marginal tax rate. In reality, these rates can change considerably as an individual's taxable income changes and as the tax laws are changed. It is possible, therefore, that the long-term capital gains tax at the end of a holding period would be greater than the current year tax on dividends.

incurred when stocks are held for less than one year. A long-term gain is preferred to a short-term gain for tax purposes, because only a portion of the long-term gain is subject to tax. In contrast, short-term capital losses are preferred to long-term losses, because short-term losses can be offset against ordinary income, dollar for dollar, whereas it takes two dollars of long-term capital losses to affect one dollar of ordinary income. As previously noted, the total amount of ordinary income that can be offset by capital losses in any one year is limited to $3,000.

First, capital gains are most effectively realized during years in which the investor's marginal tax rate is low. For example, if during a given year an investor's marginal tax bracket is low, during this year it would be beneficial for her to sell stocks and realize a capital gain. Likewise, capital losses result in the greatest tax savings during years in which the marginal tax rate is high and there are no long-term capital gains against which they must be offset.

Second, all else being equal, it is more advantageous to hold stocks until short-term gains become long-term gains. Depending on the investor's marginal tax rate and the amount of the gain, the tax savings can be substantial. Of course, when an investor defers a sale of stock to save taxes, he or she risks the possibility that the price of the stock being held may decline substantially, causing after-tax proceeds to be less than if the stock had been sold when the gain was still short-term.

Netting of Capital Gains and Losses

Timing the sale of securities in order to minimize the tax impact of capital gains and maximize the tax benefits of capital losses becomes more complicated when capital gains and losses are realized during the same year. Remember that when capital gains and losses are realized in the same year, *net* short-term capital losses must be offset against any long-term capital gains. Consequently, it is beneficial to realize *long-term* capital gains and *short-term* capital losses *in different years* so as not to net the two in a single year.

The idea just presented is demonstrated in Table 16–4. In Example 1, a long-term gain of $5,000 and a short-term loss of $5,000 are realized in the *same* year. When the gain and the loss are netted, the taxable income is unaffected by these transactions. In Example 2, the same gain and loss are realized in different years. In the first year, 40 percent of the $5,000 long-term gain, or $2,000, is included as taxable income. In the second year, $3,000—the maximum allowable amount of short-term loss—is deducted from taxable income. Finally, the remaining $2,000 loss is deducted in the third year. For the three-year period, an extra $3,000 can be deducted from taxable income by realizing the long-term gain in one year and the short-term loss in the subsequent year.

The advantage of timing capital gains and losses is not limited to the illustration just presented. It is also beneficial to net long-term losses against short-term gains in any given tax year rather than realize them in separate years. This allows capital losses that would only reduce taxable income by 50 percent

Table 16–4

	Year 1	Year 2	Year 3	Total Net Gain (Loss) for Years 1, 2 & 3
EXAMPLE 1				
Long-term gain and short-term loss realized in the *same* year:				
Long-term gain	$5,000	0		
Short-term loss	($5,000)	0		
Net gain (loss) for taxable income	0	0		0
EXAMPLE 2				
Long-term gain and short-term loss realized in *different* years:				
Long-term gain	$5,000	0	0	
Short-term loss	0	($5,000)	0	
Net gain (loss) for taxable income	$2,000*	($3,000)†	($2,000)	($3,000)

* Only 40% of the $5,000 long-term gain is included in taxable income.

† Only $3,000 of the $5,000 short-term loss may be deducted from taxable income in Year 2—the maximum allowable amount for a single year. The remaining $2,000 is carried forward and deducted in Year 3.

of the loss to cancel out short-term gains that would increase net income by 100 percent of the gain. This point is illustrated in Table 16–5. In Example 1, a $5,000 short-term gain and a $5,000 long-term loss cancel each other out in the first year, leaving the taxable income unaffected. However, when the same $5,000 short-term gain and the long-term loss are realized in different years, as shown in Example 2, the result is totally different. In the first year, the entire $5,000 short-term gain is included in taxable income, whereas in the second year only 50 percent of the $5,000 long-term loss is deducted. Therefore, for the two-year period, the investor includes an extra $2,500 in the taxable income when the long-term loss and the short-term gain are realized in different years.

Although the timing strategies described in this section can reduce an investor's tax liability, it is not advisable to time the realization of gains or losses for the sole purpose of achieving tax savings without giving consideration to the investment potential of the related securities; that is, the tax tail should not be allowed to wag the investment dog.

The Capital Gain Lock-in

Before selling a security and paying the tax on the gain, an investor should determine if a higher *after-tax return* can be realized by postponing the sale of a security and delaying the tax payment. Investors should be willing to realize a capital gain and pay the tax only if alternative investments can be expected

Table 16–5

	Year 1	Year 2	Total Net Gain (Loss) for Years 1 & 2
EXAMPLE 1			
Long-term loss and short-term gain realized in the *same* year:			
Long-term loss	($5,000)	0	
Short-term gain	$5,000	0	
Net gain (loss) for taxable income	0	0	0
EXAMPLE 2			
Long-term loss and short-term gain realized in *different* years:			
Long-term loss	0	($5,000)	
Short-term gain	$5,000	0	
Net gain (loss) for taxable income	$5,000	($2,500)*	$2,500

* Only 50% of the $5,000 long-term loss may be deducted for tax purposes.

to provide a greater after-tax return than the securities they hold.[13] This point is elaborated in the following example.

Consider the illustration presented in the top portion of Figure 16–3. Assume an investor is in the 50 percent marginal tax bracket, which puts him in a 20 percent long-term capital gains tax bracket. In Year 1, the investor purchases $100 worth of ABC stock, which appreciates to $200 by the end of Year 3. Expecting the stock's price to increase by an additional 50 percent in the next three years, the investor decides to hold the stock until the end of Year 6. The illustration shows that by the end of Year 6 the stock's price does in fact appreciate by 50 percent to $300. By selling the stock for $300, the investor realizes a long-term capital gain of $200, and his net return, after a capital gains tax of $40, is $160.

Let us compare the foregoing transaction with that of another investor who is in the same tax bracket. The second investor purchases $100 worth of ABC stock in Year 1 and watches it rise to $200 by the end of Year 3. However, rather than holding the ABC stock until Year 6 for an expected 50 percent additional appreciation, she decides to sell it and purchase stock XYZ, which has the same perceived risk as stock ABC but is expected to appreciate a little over 55 percent by the end of Year 6.

The bottom half of Figure 16–3 shows the results of this investment decision.[14] The ABC stock is sold for $200 in Year 3 and a $20 capital gains tax is

[13] This would not include sales of securities in liquidity-motivated transactions.

[14] For simplicity, in this example dividends are ignored.

Figure 16–3

Marginal tax bracket: 50%
Marginal capital gains tax (50% × 40%): 20%

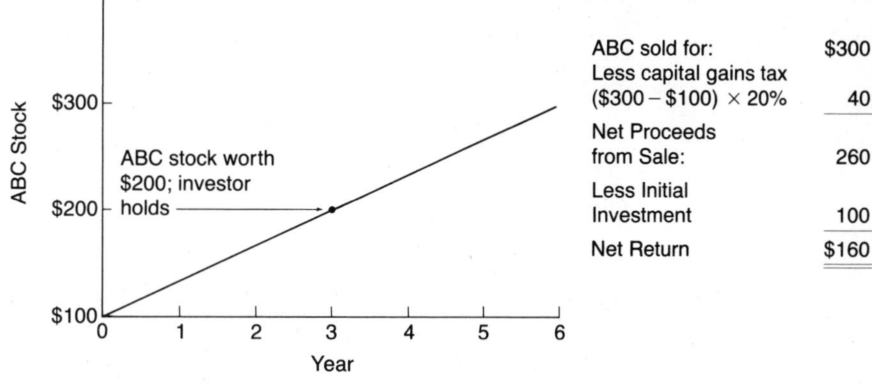

ABC sold for:	$300
Less capital gains tax ($300 – $100) × 20%	40
Net Proceeds from Sale:	260
Less Initial Investment	100
Net Return	$160

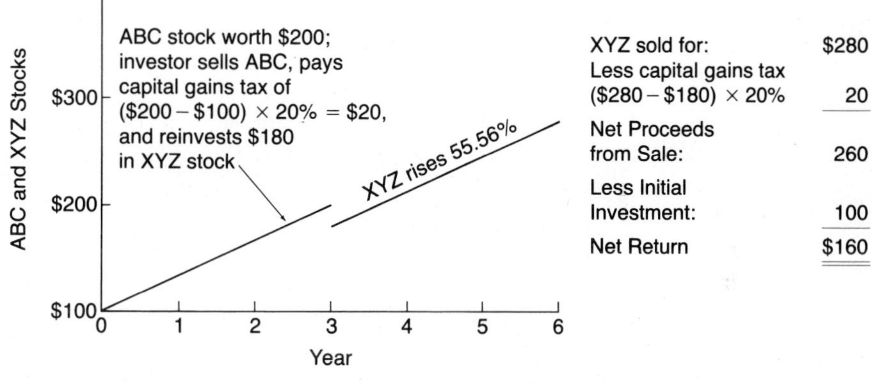

XYZ sold for:	$280
Less capital gains tax ($280 – $180) × 20%	20
Net Proceeds from Sale:	260
Less Initial Investment:	100
Net Return	$160

paid on the $100 long-term gain. The $180 net proceeds from the sale are then used to purchase the XYZ stock. Over the following three years the stock price rises to $280, an increase of 55.56 percent. The investor sells the stock for $280 and realizes a net return of $160 on her two investments—the same as the first investor realized in the previous example—after paying a capital gains tax of $20 on the sale of each.

Note that even though the second investor sells the original stock and purchases another that appreciates by a greater percentage, her total after-tax gain turns out to be the same as that of the first investor. In this example, if the investor could not replace the ABC stock at the end of Year 3 with another security that could be expected to appreciate more than 55 percent over the following three years, she should retain the ABC stock. The reason is obvious. After selling the ABC stock and paying the capital gains tax, there is less money to reinvest in another security; therefore, in order to make this switch profitable an alternative security would have to provide a higher expected percentage appreciation in value.

Wash Sale Alternatives

A popular tax strategy is to establish a tax-deductible loss by selling a security at a loss and soon repurchasing it. However, if the security is repurchased within 30 days, the transaction is known as a *wash sale* and the loss is not deductible for tax purposes. For a loss to be tax-deductible, an investor must wait for more than 30 days before repurchasing the same security. If investors wish to establish a tax loss while maintaining their investment position in a security, they can purchase an equivalent number of shares, hold all the shares for 31 days, and then sell the original holdings to accomplish their objective. However, if they are reluctant to double up on a holding, they can still avoid a wash sale by making a two-way exchange. This is done by selling the original stock at a loss and simultaneously buying another security with similar investment characteristics.

Bond Swapping

Investors can capitalize on declines in bond prices by swapping one bond for another and realizing a capital loss for tax purposes, while still realizing the same effective yield to maturity.

Assume an investor purchases a $1,000, 25-year bond at par with an 8 percent coupon. Assume further that five years later market interest rates rise to 10 percent, and the bond falls in price to $830, so that its yield to maturity will be 10 percent. If this happens to be a high taxable year for the investor, he can sell the bond for a capital loss of $170 and realize a substantial tax benefit. He can then purchase a bond of another company with the same maturity date, quality rating, and yield to replace the bond he sold.

Implications for Portfolio Management

In Chapter 14, we mentioned that active portfolio management involves selecting a group of securities which, if properly managed, consistently outperforms the market. For example, Table 14–8 presents a sample portfolio that maximizes the investor's expected *pretax* return while also achieving a specified portfolio beta and the desired level of diversification. However, the investor might improve his after-tax return, for example, by substituting lower-yielding municipal bonds for taxable securities with higher pretax expected returns.

Similarly, he might substitute growth company stocks for income stocks to achieve higher after-tax returns. Of course, in making these moves the investor should not lose sight of the constraints of diversification.

Tax Sheltered Investment Plans[15]

Tax Sheltered Intermediaries

In recent years, many individual investors have succeeded in reducing their tax burdens by investing in *tax-sheltered intermediaries*, such as employee pension plans, life insurance reserves, certain types of trusts, and profit sharing and stock bonus plans. In these plans, contributions by individuals are entrusted to a fiduciary—such as a bank or an insurance company—who acts as a portfolio manager.

The tax implications of investing in these plans are significant. Individual participants in the plans are taxed only as they receive benefits (payments) from the plans. By delaying the receipt of income until retirement, when an individual's marginal tax rate is likely to be considerably lower, individuals can reduce their tax liability substantially. The fiduciary pays no tax on the income as it is accumulated.

Keogh Plans

Keogh plans, which are available only to the self-employed, provide a valuable opportunity for postponing tax payments on investment income and capital gains. Allowable contributions to a Keogh plan are deductible for tax purposes in the year in which they are made. More importantly, when such a plan matures at an individual's retirement, taxes on the interest, dividends and capital gains are drastically reduced because of the individual's postretirement lower marginal tax bracket.

IRA Plans

A taxpayer who is not self-employed and does not participate in a pension plan is allowed to contribute 15 percent of his or her annual income into an *Individual Retirement Account* (*IRA*), subject to a maximum of $1,750.[16] Like the Keogh plan, the annual contributions are tax deductible and the accumulated dividends, interest, and capital gains go untaxed until the investor retires or withdraws the savings.

[15] A large number of other tax-sheltered investments and strategies are not covered here.

[16] The $1,750 maximum is valid if the taxpayer has a spouse who is currently unemployed. As an alternative, the taxpayer can contribute up to $875 a year into separate IRAs for himself and his spouse.

A spinoff of the usual IRA account is the "Rollover" IRA, established through a provision of the Pension Plan Reform Act of 1974. If an individual decides to take early retirement or change jobs and is subsequently paid a lump sum distribution from a pension or profit sharing plan, those funds might be taxable in the year they are received. However, the individual can avoid paying any current income tax by "rolling over" the lump sum distribution into an IRA account. Taxes on the accumulated capital gains, dividends, and income are thereby deferred until a later retirement year.

Miscellaneous Tax Strategies

Income Averaging

An investor experiencing a jump in taxable income in a given year can get a substantial tax break through income averaging. Under the income averaging provisions of the Internal Revenue Code, a taxpayer with unusually high income in a given year, relative to his or her average income of the previous four years, is permitted, in effect, to pay tax at a lower rate on some income than if income averaging were not used. The tax liability is based on the current year's rate, but a portion of the individual's income is placed in a lower tax bracket through the averaging process. The Internal Revenue Code specifies a set of conditions which must be met before this tax relief provision can be employed.

Investment Cost Deductions

Certain costs incurred in the process of making investment decisions, such as advisory service fees and subscriptions to periodicals, are deductible from taxable income. Interest on funds borrowed for purchasing securities are also treated as a deductible item. However, brokerage commissions on the purchase of securities are added to the cost of these securities.

SECTION 2 TRANSACTION COSTS

Types of Transaction Costs

Brokerage Commissions

Prior to 1975, the minimum commission rates charged by brokerage firms were set by the New York Stock Exchange. Before 1968, a fixed commission schedule specified a minimum charge per share that did not decrease with larger orders. Institutions were therefore charged the same commission per share as smaller investors, even though the per share cost of trading large blocks of stocks was lower. Because the institutions were not allowed volume discounts, they began to trade in the third and fourth markets. In December 1968, volume discounts and negotiated commissions were allowed on large trades in order to encourage institutional investors to trade on the NYSE. By April 1972, brokers and customers could negotiate the commission rates on portions of trades exceeding $300,000. Subsequently, rates on trading above this level dropped by more than 50 percent from the previous fixed rate. Finally, on May 1, 1975, the fixed commission schedule was lifted for *all* investors. Since then, every brokerage firm has been permitted by the SEC to set its own commission rates.

Table 16–6 presents a sample of commission rates on stocks and bonds which might be charged by a typical large, full-service brokerage house which

Table 16–6

A. Commission Charges on Stocks

Principal Value	Number of Shares: Below 100	Number of Shares: 100–1,000 Shares
$1,000–$2,500	1.6% of principal value plus $.03 per share plus $16	1.6% of principal value plus $.085 per share plus $18
$2,500–$5,000	1.18% of principal value plus $.03 per share plus $28	1.18% of principal value plus $.08 per share plus $30
$5,000–$20,000	1.18% of principal value plus $.03 per share plus $30	1.18% of principal value plus $.09 per share plus $32
$20,000–$30,000	$90	.8% of principal value plus $.09 per share plus $110
$30,000–$300,000	$88	.5% of principal value plus $.09 per share plus $190

B. Commission Charges on Bonds

Face Value of Bonds per Order		Rate per Face Value Amount
First 5M	$1,000–$5,000	$10.00 per $1,000
Next 20M	$6,000–$25,000	$ 7.50 per $1,000
Over 25M	$26,000 and over	$ 5.00 per $1,000

NOTE: These rates do *not* represent charges of any brokerage firm. This table is presented purely for illustrative purposes.

Figure 16–4 **Effective Commission Rates Since April 1975**
NYSE Member Firms—Overall

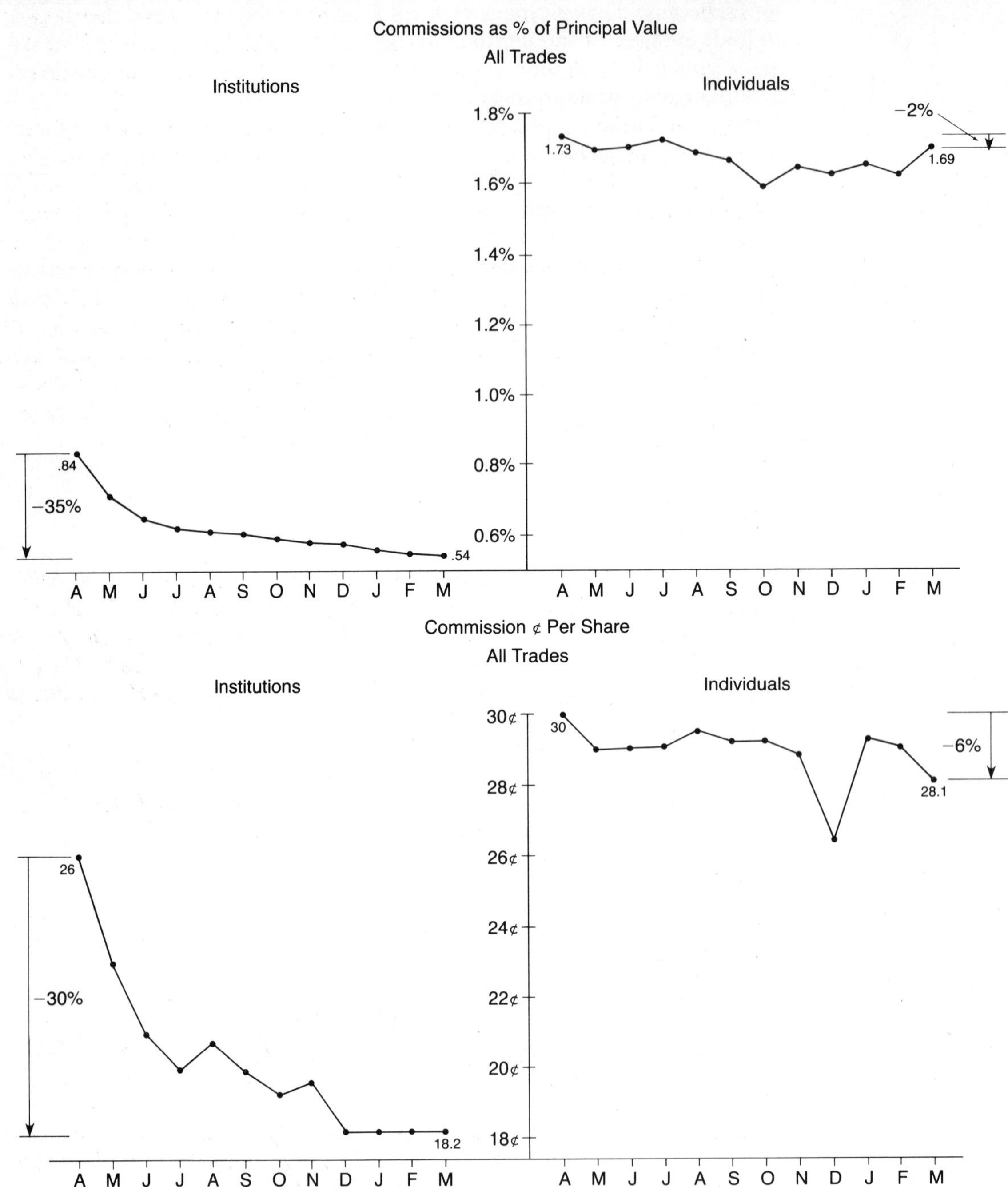

SOURCE: SEC, "The Effect of the Absence of Fixed Rates of Commissions," August 10, 1976

not only executes orders placed by customers, but provides other services, such as research advice or information. In general, the commission charge as a percentage of the principal value traded declines as the principal value of the trade increases. This rate structure tends to reflect the relatively lower per share cost of executing large trades.

The new flexible rate structure implemented in May 1975 had a significant impact on commission rates. Figure 16–4 summarizes the findings of an SEC study which evaluated this impact over the period April 1975 through March 1976. The figure indicates that over this period the average institutional commission declined substantially: The average commission as a ratio of the principal value traded dropped by 35 percent; the average commission charge per share dropped by 30 percent. Average commission rates for individual investors also declined during this period; however, this decline was much smaller than that for the institutions. Subsequently, discount brokerage houses for individual traders began offering rates that were significantly below those offered by the large, full-service brokerage houses. This point will be discussed in a later section.

Bid–Ask Spread

The *bid–ask spread* is the difference between the price a dealer in the OTC market is bidding for a stock and the price he or she is asking for it. The bid price is, of course, lower than the asking price. As mentioned in Chapter 3, the spreads for various stocks vary considerably. This is indicated by the following list of representative bid and asked prices for several OTC stocks as of November 16, 1979.

Stock	Bid	Asked	Spread
American Greetings	$11\frac{5}{8}$	12	$\frac{3}{8}$
Charming Shoppes	$8\frac{7}{8}$	$9\frac{3}{8}$	$\frac{1}{2}$
Detroitbank Corp.	$24\frac{1}{2}$	25	$\frac{1}{2}$
Floating Point Systems	10	$10\frac{3}{4}$	$\frac{3}{4}$
U.S. Surgical	26	$26\frac{3}{4}$	$\frac{3}{4}$
Cedar Point	$26\frac{1}{4}$	$27\frac{1}{4}$	1
Bird & Son	18	$19\frac{1}{2}$	$1\frac{1}{2}$
Gray Communications	29	31	2
Kansas City Life	$53\frac{1}{2}$	$55\frac{1}{2}$	2
National Valve & Mfg.	44	46	2

The spread generally widens for inactively traded securities; it also tends to increase with the amount of effort and risk involved in either finding buyers and sellers or maintaining an inventory of stock.[17]

[17] The bid–ask spread for bonds was discussed in Chapters 6, 7, and 8.

Brokers' Markups and Markdowns

An investor is not charged a commission when a broker acts as a principal in an OTC transaction; instead the investor is charged a *markup or markdown*. Acting as a principal, a broker sells the requested shares from inventory at a retail or "net price." The *net* price, however, is higher than the wholesale price which would be charged to other dealers. The difference is a *markup*, representing a profit for the brokerage firm for executing the order.[18] Similarly, a markdown is generated by a customer's sell order.

Odd-Lot Differential

An odd-lot refers to a trade involving fewer than 100 shares. Acting as a dealer, a specialist on the stock exchange charges an *odd-lot differential* equivalent to $\frac{1}{8}$ to $\frac{1}{4}$ point, or $12\frac{1}{2}$ to 25 cents per share. Incidentally, some brokerage firms, such as Merrill Lynch, have eliminated the differential for their customers by filling odd-lot orders through their own internal dealer market.

Implications for Portfolio Management

In Section 1, we noted that taxes both reduce portfolio returns and complicate portfolio management. Transaction costs also have an impact on portfolio management and portfolio returns.

In the case of passive portfolio management, transaction costs are incurred only when the initial portfolio is constructed and when additional trades are made to minimize taxes, make disbursements, or update the portfolio.

With active portfolio management, the transaction costs are considerably higher because the securities are traded more frequently in an attempt to beat the market. An active manager must therefore earn a higher return before transaction costs, if he is to match the performance of a passive manager.[19]

Reduction in Transaction Costs

The business of buying and selling securities cannot be conducted without incurring transaction costs. These costs can, nevertheless, be reduced by following a set of simple strategies.

[18] Sometimes, acting as a principal, a brokerage house will buy stock from another dealer at the dealer's "ask" price and *immediately* resell it to the customer at the retail or "net" price. In such cases, the broker is undertaking a riskless transaction, because the stock is never really held in its inventory. In this type of transaction, the SEC now requires that brokers disclose to their customers the amount of the markup or markdown they receive on the trade.

[19] Because above average analysis is needed to select undervalued stocks, active management will also generally lead to higher information costs.

Trading Frequency

Transaction costs can be reduced by trading less frequently. When a security is held longer, transaction costs on the purchase and sale of the security can be spread over a longer period of time. However, this strategy is more compatible with passive than active management.

Bid–Ask Spread

The impact of the bid–ask spread can be frequently reduced by trading in higher-quality issues in active markets. Transaction costs in the OTC market can also be reduced by trading in higher-priced securities, because a dealer's bid–ask spread does not generally change with movements in the stock price. For example, suppose ABC and XYZ stocks are identical in all respects but one: The XYZ is priced higher than ABC. The ABC stock is quoted at $9\frac{1}{4}$ bid and 10 ask, while the XYZ stock is quoted at $19\frac{1}{4}$ bid and 20 ask. The spread for ABC is 7.5 percent of the ask price, whereas for XYZ it is only 3.75 percent. Therefore, investors in ABC will pay twice as much in dealer fees as they would by investing in XYZ.

New Issues

Payment of transaction costs can be totally avoided by operating in the primary market for securities. As a general rule, new issues are distributed to the public through an underwriter. Because the underwriting costs are paid by the issuing firm, investors can purchase newly issued securities without paying any commission charges.

Commission Discounts

In recent years, many *discount brokerage houses* have been established to serve the needs of those investors and traders who make their own trading decisions. These houses primarily execute the orders placed by their customers and do not offer many of the other services offered by the large brokerage firms. The following chart lists the commission charges of one discount brokerage

Trade	Commission: Full Service Broker	Commission: Discount Broker
100 shares @ $20	$ 58	$ 30
200 shares @ $20	93	50
500 shares @ $20	195	95
1,000 shares @ $20	360	165
2,000 shares @ $20	570	250

Note: These representative rates, based on a 1979 survey, may have subsequently changed.

house and a large, full-service firm for a sample of stock trades. (See the bottom of page 715.) (The commissions charged may vary considerably between firms.)[20]

Miscellaneous Strategies

Transaction costs can also be reduced by purchasing stocks through dividend reinvestment plans. Such plans call for the pooling of individual shareholder dividends for the purpose of acquiring additional shares in the company. Each shareholder is then credited with the number of shares to which he or she is entitled. In most cases, a bank acts as the company's agent and makes purchases in the open market. Although bank charges and brokerage commissions are passed along to shareholders, these charges are much lower than shareholders would pay if they individually acquired these shares.

In addition to dividend reinvestment plans, some companies offer stockholder purchase plans. These plans allow investors to purchase additional shares at the time their dividends are reinvested, thereby providing them with the opportunity to save on commission charges.

Finally, small investors can reduce transaction costs by purchasing shares of no-load mutual funds, because these funds do not have any sales charges. In addition, investors also reap the benefits of low commission costs enjoyed by mutual funds on their large-scale transactions. However, there are some drawbacks to investing in mutual funds: All mutual funds charge a management fee which could negate the savings in transaction costs. Also, transaction costs of a fund that trades frequently could be higher than those generated by a long-term investor.

Summary

Individual investors pay taxes on interest, dividends, and *short-term capital gains* at ordinary income tax rates. *Long-term capital gains*, however, receive preferential tax treatment.

An understanding of the *marginal tax rate* is crucial to the development of an effective investment strategy because additional income generated by new investment is taxed at the marginal tax rate.

In considering stock and bond investment, an investor should be concerned with *after-tax returns*.

In developing investment strategies with taxes in mind, an investor should consider investing in securities which are expected to provide tax-exempt

[20] In addition to comparing the commission rates of discount brokers, the investor should also look at other factors. For example, some discounters might not pay a return on free credit balances, offer margin trading, or provide safekeeping for securities. Moreover, all brokers will not provide the same execution of orders. The floor brokers of some firms may be able to get better market prices on stock trades than others.

investment income or long-term capital gains in lieu of taxable interest or dividends.

Another tax strategy emphasizes tax savings through proper timing of stock and bond sales. This is important for two reasons. First, the time of sale determines whether the gain or loss will be treated as long-term or short-term. Second, the time of sale determines the year in which the gain or loss is realized.

Several tax sheltered investment plans are available to investors, including *Keogh* and *IRA plans* and investment in tax-sheltered intermediaries. These plans offer important tax advantages by allowing investors to defer tax payments until retirement, when an individual's marginal tax rate will probably be considerably lower.

Transaction costs include the *bid–ask spread*, *brokerage commissions*, *brokers' markup and markdown*, and the *odd-lot differential*. Like taxes, transaction costs have an impact on portfolio management and portfolio returns. The impact is considerably greater with active portfolio management than with passive management, because the active manager trades securities more frequently in an attempt to beat the market.

Several strategies are available to investors for reducing transaction costs. They include purchasing of new issues, trading in higher quality OTC securities, and dealing with discount brokerage houses.

A Look Ahead

This chapter has described the impact of taxes and transaction costs on the development of an overall investment strategy. This completes a discussion on the essentials of basic investment. More esoteric forms of investment will be discussed in the remaining chapters.

Concepts for Review

Taxable income
Tax rate
Adjustments to gross income
Itemized personal deductions
Progressive tax structure
Marginal and average tax rates
Dividend exclusion
Short-term capital gain
Long-term capital gain
Net capital gain or loss
Capital gain lock-in
After-tax return
Wash sale
Tax-sheltered intermediary
IRA and Keogh plans
Transaction costs
Bid–ask spread
Brokers' markup and markdown
Odd-lot differential
Discount brokers

Questions for Review

1. Explain the difference between gross income and taxable income.
2. Explain the difference between marginal and average tax rates. Why is the marginal tax rate important in investment decision-making?
3. Should an investor try to avoid moving into a higher marginal tax bracket? Explain.
4. What types of securities would you recommend to an investor in a high marginal tax bracket? Why?
5. Explain the advantage of receiving income in the form of a long-term capital gain instead of as interest or dividends. Does the advantage hold for all securities?
6. Investor Y is interested in purchasing securities for capital gains rather than current income because of the tax advantages. What factors should he consider?
7. Investor J's investment strategy is to incur the least possible tax liability. Comment on this approach.
8. What determines the tax rate an investor pays on investment income?
9. Timing is an important consideration in tax planning. Give examples of situations where properly timing stock or bond trades can reduce an investor's tax liability.
10. You are the portfolio manager of an employee pension fund. How will the tax laws influence your decision-making?
11. A broker calls and advises you to sell your shares of DEF stock, realize a profit, and reinvest in QUE stock. She emphasizes that QUE stock currently offers a greater expected return. What factors would you consider at this point?
12. What transaction costs may be incurred besides brokerage commissions?
13. Why do transaction costs make it difficult for the active portfolio manager to outperform the passive portfolio manager?
14. Comment on the following statement: "There is no transaction cost when buying or selling an OTC stock, because brokerage houses do not charge a commission for this type of trade."
15. Investor K is interested in purchasing mutual fund shares to reduce transaction costs. What factors should she consider?

Problems

1. Investor P and Q are married individuals filing a joint return in 1979, with a taxable income for the year of $94,382.
   a. Determine their marginal and average tax rates.
   b. If they earn an additional $8,415 in taxable investment income, how much additional tax will be due?
2. Investor Q is a single taxpayer with a 1979 taxable income of $30,000 *before* dividends, interest income, or capital gains and losses. Determine Investor Q's 1979 tax due in each of the following cases (a through m).

1979 Investment Results

		Interest Income		Capital Gains		Capital Losses	
	Dividends*	Corporate Bonds	Municipal Bonds	Short-term	Long-term	Short-term	Long-term
a.	$ 500	$ 500	$ 0	$ 0	$ 0	$ 0	$ 0
b.	3,500	0	0	0	2,500	0	0
c.	0	100	0	0	2,500	2,500	0
d.	100	0	900	0	2,500	0	3,000
e.	0	0	0	2,500	2,500	0	2,500
f.	0	0	0	4,500	0	4,500	0
g.	2,000	4,500	0	1,000	0	4,000	3,000
h.	4,000	0	750	0	0	0	4,000
i.	5,260	7,100	0	4,400	200	200	4,250
j.	0	300	200	900	1,900	1,900	900
k.	100	0	900	1,900	900	1,900	900
l.	200	0	200	0	0	2,000	2,000
m.	1,500	400	400	200	100	0	0

* Dividends paid from current or retained earnings by domestic corporations.

3. Investor M is in the 60 percent marginal tax bracket and interested in purchasing one of the bonds shown below. Which bond promises the highest after-tax yield to maturity? Assume Investor M's marginal tax bracket will not change.

	Price	Coupon	Years to Maturity
LMN City Sewer Bonds	$1,000	8%	10
QRS County, Montana	850	$5\frac{3}{4}$	10
ABC Corporation	1,000	12	10
XYZ Corporation	850	$9\frac{1}{2}$	10

4. In December 1979, Investor T is reviewing his tax situation for the year. The following capital gains and losses have already been realized in 1979:

Stock	Date Sold	Date Purchased	Gain (Loss)
Charter Co.	5/79	6/74	$12,800
Superscope	9/79	3/76	(3,000)
Federal Signal	8/79	9/74	5,000
Amdahl	7/79	8/78	(5,000)
K-Mart	2/79	2/77	(3,000)
Integon	8/79	1/78	4,200
Memorex	11/79	5/79	(2,700)
General Motors	3/79	10/76	(2,400)
Coors (Adolph)	1/79	9/75	(3,600)
Rolm Corp.	4/79	11/78	3,700

In addition, Investor T purchased 400 shares of Playboy Enterprises at $20\frac{1}{2}$ in April 1979. The stock is currently trading at 14 in December 1979. Investor T cannot decide if he should sell his Playboy shares this month and realize a short-term capital loss in 1979. Based on this information, what would you recommend? What other important factors should you consider in making your recommendation?

5. Investor Q purchased Computer Sciences common stock three years ago at $11.75 per share. The current price is $21.00. Based on your projection of the company's earnings and the stock's EM ratio, you expect the price to rise to $22.75 in two years. However, you also expect the price of Mohawk Data Sciences common stock, which has similar risk characteristics, to appreciate 50 percent over the same two-year period. Neither company pays a dividend.
   a. Would you advise Investor Q to switch stocks at this time? She is in the 50 percent marginal federal tax bracket and would hold either stock for two years. Show calculations to support your decision and clearly state any necessary assumptions.
   b. Suppose Investor Q originally purchased the Computer Sciences stock in the current year. Would your decision change? Explain.

Selected Readings

Black, F., and M. Scholes. "The Effects of Dividend Yield and Dividend Policy on Common Stock Prices and Returns." *Journal of Financial Economics*, 1972.

Brenna, M. J. "Taxes, Market Valuation and Corporate Financial Policy." *National Tax Journal*, 1970.

Elton, Edwin J., and Martin J. Gruber. "Marginal Stockbroker Tax Rates and the Clientele Effect." *Review of Economics and Statistics*, February 1970.

Federal Tax Course. Englewood Cliffs, N.J.: Prentice-Hall, 1980.

Jenkins, James W. "Taxes, Margining and Bond Selection." *Financial Analysts Journal*, May–June 1980.

U.S. Treasury Department, Internal Revenue Service. *Your Federal Income Tax*, Publication 17. Washington, D.C.: GPO.

5 Specialized Investment

Our main emphasis in this book has been on equity and fixed income securities. However, other specialized investment instruments frequently provide attractive investment opportunities.

Chapter 17 is an analysis of convertible securities, including convertible bonds, warrants, and stock rights. Each has special investment characteristics, an understanding of which is a prerequisite to investing successfully in these instruments.

Chapter 18 deals with stock options, one of the most popular, and most complicated, forms of specialized investment. Stock options are closely related to the stocks with which they are associated. However, because of leverage and other characteristics, options provide unique opportunities to sophisticated investors. Finally, Chapter 19 is devoted to a brief review of several esoteric investment instruments, including commodity futures, gold, and antiques.

Convertible Securities: Bonds, Warrants, Stock Rights

17

Introduction

Parts 2 and 3 contain detailed discussions of bonds and common stocks. In these discussions, the basic characteristics and investment features of these two types of instruments are spelled out. This chapter deals with a less familiar group of investment instruments: convertible bonds, warrants, and stock rights. Although each is a distinct security, they have one thing in common: Under prespecified terms all are convertible into common stock.

This chapter is divided into three sections. Section 1 is a detailed discussion of the theory and analysis of convertible bonds; a similar discussion on warrants is undertaken in Section 2. Finally, in Section 3, the valuation of stock rights and their place in the investment world are discussed.

SECTION 1 CONVERTIBLE BONDS

Introduction

An Overview

Convertible bonds[1] give the bondholder the right to convert bonds into common stock. Usually, the number of shares for which a convertible bond can be exchanged is fixed, and the conversion privilege lasts for the life of the bond.[2]

[1] Usually, a convertible security is either a bond or preferred stock that can be exchanged for common stock. However, this discussion concentrates on bonds, and the Convertible Valuation Model presented later is based primarily on convertible bonds.

[2] Sometimes the number of shares for which a convertible bond can be exchanged decreases as the bond's life approaches maturity. Also, in some cases, the conversion privilege ends before the bond matures.

Convertible bonds are considered a hybrid-type security because they combine the basic attributes of common stock *and* corporate bonds in a single security. Because these bonds can be exchanged for common stock at the initiative of the security holder, they can participate in the appreciation potential of the associated equities. In addition, convertible bonds can provide the investor with downside protection in the event of a significant decline in equity prices. Equally important, convertible bonds represent an obligation on the part of the corporation to make regular interest payments.

Convertible bonds are usually protected against stock splits and stock dividends. The terms of conversion are flexible so that the security holder will not be shortchanged as a result of changes in the price of common stock due to stock splits and stock dividends.[3] For example, if a bond is convertible into 20 shares—that is, the conversion ratio is 20—the conversion ratio would be increased to 40, after a 2-for-1 stock split.

Convertible bonds generally contain a *call provision*, which specifies the price at which the bond can be called away and retired at the option of the issuer. Generally, callable bonds are callable from the day they are issued; therefore, they do not enjoy a call protection. When a convertible bond is called, the holder has two options: Accept the call price or elect to convert the bond into common stock. Obviously, the bondholder will elect to convert if the conversion value of the bond—that is, the market value of the stock for which it can be exchanged—is greater than the call price.

Uses of Convertible Bonds

Corporations issue convertible bonds to accomplish a variety of objectives. First, convertible bonds can be issued to raise capital at an interest rate lower than would be possible through the issue of straight or nonconvertible bonds. Convertible bonds offer investors the opportunity to share in the potential capital gains of the common stock. Consequently, the prospective convertible bondholders generally are willing to accept a lower interest rate for the conversion privilege.

Second, if a company needs to sell a bond issue, frequently it will attach a convertible feature to the bond in order to enhance its marketability. Naturally, companies with low bond ratings are most likely to resort to this strategy, because these firms quite often have difficulty in selling straight bonds on the open market.

Third, convertible bonds are issued by companies that wish to sell common stock at prices higher than those currently prevailing. For example, suppose the earnings and stock price of ABC Corporation are currently depressed. However, management feels that in the foreseeable future the earnings will improve, resulting in a significant advance in the stock price. If the company currently needs to raise new capital and decides to issue new shares of common stock at

[3] Stock splits and stock dividends were discussed in Chapter 2.

this time when the stock price is depressed, it would have to issue more shares than would be necessary if new shares could be issued after the market price of the stock had appreciated. The firm can resolve this dilemma by issuing a convertible bond with a conversion price set at 15 to 25 percent above the current market price of the stock. When these bonds are converted to common stock, ABC will be required to give up 15 to 25 percent fewer shares than would be necessary if new capital had been raised through the issuance of common stock. The use of convertible bonds for this purpose is referred to as *deferred common stock financing.*

Finally, convertible bonds are popular instruments for facilitating mergers or buyouts. When two companies merge, frequently the shareholders of the acquired firm are offered convertible bonds in exchange for their common shares.

Features of Convertible Bonds

Table 17–1 summarizes the essential features of convertible bonds. The *conversion ratio* and *conversion price,* which refer to the terms of conversion of the bond into common stock, are virtually two aspects of the same relationship. In the example presented in Table 17–1, a \$1,000 bond is convertible into 12.5 shares of ABC stock. The conversion ratio is 12.5, and the conversion price is \$80 (\$1,000/12.5). If the bond were purchased for \$900 and subsequently converted, the purchaser would be paying, in effect, \$72 per share for the stock (\$900/12.5). This is the *conversion parity price.*

As mentioned earlier, the *conversion value* is the current value of the bond if it were immediately converted into common stock. If ABC stock is currently selling for \$46 per share and the conversion ratio is 12.5 shares per bond, the conversion value of ABC bond is \$575 (\$46 × 12.5).

The last two features of a convertible bond described in Table 17–1 are *conversion premium* and *premium over investment value.* The conversion premium measures the amount of the bond's market price in excess of its current value in common stock. Reasons for the existence of this premium are as follows:[4]

1. *Transaction costs.* Because the commission cost on bonds is generally less than on stocks of equivalent cost, it may be cheaper to buy bonds and convert them into stocks rather than purchase stocks directly.
2. *Income differences.* Interest payments on the bonds are generally higher than expected dividends on equivalent stocks.

[4] See R. Weil, J. Segall, and D. Green, "Premium on Convertible Bonds," *Journal of Finance,* June 1968, pp. 445–64.

Table 17–1 **Convertible Bond Features**

Term	Definition	Example
1. Conversion Ratio (CR)	The number of shares of stock for which each bond can be exchanged.	ABC Bond can be converted at the holder's option into 12.5 shares of ABC common stock. *Conversion Ratio* = 12.5
2. Conversion Price	The price at which the stock can be acquired in exchange for the convertible bond. Equals the *par value* divided by the conversion ratio.	Par value ABC bond = \$1,000 Conversion Ratio = 12.5 *Conversion Price* = \$1,000/12.5 = \$80
3. Conversion Parity Price	The actual price a convertible bondholder pays for common stock when bond is converted. Equals the bond's *purchase price* divided by the conversion ratio.	Purchase price of ABC bond (bought at discount) = \$900 Conversion Ratio = 12.5 *Conversion Parity Price* = \$900/12.5 = \$72
4. Conversion Value (CV)	Current value of bond if it were immediately converted into common stock. Equals the current price of stock times the conversion ratio.	Current price of ABC stock = \$46 Conversion Ratio = 12.5 *Conversion Value* = (\$46)(12.5) = \$575
5. Conversion Premium	The difference between the bond's current market price and its conversion value.	Current market price of ABC bond = \$730 Conversion Value = \$575 *Conversion Premium* = \$730 – \$575 = \$155
6. Investment Value	The theoretical price at which the bond's yield to maturity would equal the yield offered by a straight bond of similar quality and maturity.	Current market price of ABC bond = \$730 Investment value = \$670
7. Premium over Investment Value	The difference between the bond's market price and its investment value. Investment value is a theoretical price at which the bond's yield to maturity would be equal to the yield offered by straight bonds of similar quality and maturity.	Current market price of ABC bond = \$730 Investment Value = \$670 *Premium Over Investment Value* = \$730 – \$670 = \$60

3. *Financing costs.* It may be possible to borrow a larger percentage of the purchase price of the bond than an equivalent amount of stock.
4. *Antidilution clause.* The bond's indenture generally has provisions that offer protection against dilution through the sale of stock or distribution of assets.
5. *Price floor.* Because a convertible bond has a value as a bond as well as a stock, the bondholder has some protection against a decline in the price of the stock.

The premium over investment value measures the bond's market price in excess of its *investment value.* Investment value is equal to a theoretical price at which the bond's yield to maturity would equal the yield offered by a straight (nonconvertible) bond of similar quality and maturity. In the example in Table 17–1, the ABC bond has a conversion value of $575 and an investment value of $670. With the market price at $730, the conversion premium is $155 and the premium over investment value is $60.[5] Premiums are often expressed as percentages. Here, the conversion premium is 26.96 percent [($730 – $575)/$575]; the premium over investment value is 8.96 percent [($730 – $670)/$670].

Like any corporate bond, a convertible bond has a credit rating. More notable, however, is the fact that many convertible bonds have a rating of BBB or less. There are two reasons for this. First, many companies issuing convertible bonds are low rated and therefore have difficulty selling bonds without a convertible feature. Second, convertible bonds are subordinated debentures and are therefore considered riskier than their senior partners like secured bonds.

Theory of Convertible Bond Valuation

Investment Value Floor

The price of a convertible bond can never fall below its investment value—its estimated value as a bond without conversion privileges—because if the price of a convertible bond were to drop below this level, its yield to maturity would be higher than that of a straight bond of comparable quality and maturity, thereby making it undervalued relative to the straight bond. In such an event, investors would start purchasing the convertible bond, quickly driving up its price.

An important aspect of bond valuation which was discussed in Chapter 6 should be reiterated here. The present value of a straight or nonconvertible bond is calculated by:

$$PV = \sum_{n=1}^{N} \frac{C}{(1+r)^n} + \frac{P_N}{(1+r)^N} \qquad \text{(6–1 restated)}$$

where

PV = Present value of the bond

C = Annual interest payments

P_N = Par value of the bond

N = Maturity of the bond

r = The appropriate discount rate, or the investor's minimum required rate of return

[5] The market price and investment value of the ABC bond were selected for illustrative purposes only. No underlying assumptions were made about the bond's coupon rate or the market interest rate.

Table 17–2

	Convertible Bond Investment Value	Market Value of Straight Bond of Comparable Quality and Maturity
Par Value:	\$1,000	\$1,000
Coupon:	6%	8%
Maturity:	25 years	25 years
Appropriate discount rate:	8% (Yield of straight bond of comparable quality and maturity)*	8%
	$PV = \sum_{n=1}^{N} \frac{\$60}{(1+.08)^n} + \frac{\$1{,}000}{(1+.08)^N}$	$P_0 = \sum_{n=1}^{N} \frac{\$80}{(1+.08)^n} + \frac{\$1{,}000}{(1+.08)^N}$
EXAMPLE 1 Bond is issued—25 years until maturity	$N = 25$ $PV = \$60(10.675) + \$1{,}000(.146)$ $= \$786.50$	$N = 25$ $P_0 = \$80(10.675) + \$1{,}000(.146)$ $= \$1{,}000$
EXAMPLE 2 After 10 years—15 until maturity	$N = 15$ $PV = \$60(8.559) + \$1{,}000(.315)$ $= \$828.50$	$N = 15$ $P_0 = \$80(8.559) + \$1{,}000(.315)$ $= \$1{,}000$
EXAMPLE 3 After 15 years—10 until maturity	$N = 10$ $PV = \$60(6.710) + \$1{,}000(.463)$ $= \$865.60$	$N = 10$ $P_0 = \$80(6.710) + \$1{,}000(.463)$ $= \$1{,}000$
EXAMPLE 4 After 25 years—bond reaches maturity	$N = 0$ $PV = \$60(0) + \$1{,}000(1)$ $= \$1{,}000$	$N = 0$ $P_0 = \$80(0) + \$1{,}000(1)$ $= \$1{,}000$

* Market interest rate is assumed constant.

Table 17–2 presents the investment value of a convertible bond at different time intervals, beginning with its date of issue (Example 1) and ending with its maturity date (Example 4). The appropriate discount rate of the convertible bond is assumed to equal the yield of a comparable straight bond. These examples reveal that if the market interest rate remains unchanged during the life of the straight bond, the investment value of the convertible bond will (1) be at the lowest point on the date of issue, (2) progressively rise over time, and (3) equal, on maturity, its par value of \$1,000.

Table 17–2 reveals another important fact: Because the convertible bond has the conversion advantage over a straight bond, its coupon rate is lower than the coupon rate on a straight bond of comparable quality and maturity. As mentioned earlier, the reason for this is simply that the convertible bondholder sacrifices coupon payment in exchange for conversion privileges. The effect of such a differential coupon rate can be appreciated by comparing a convertible bond's investment value over time with the market value of a similar straight bond. Figure 17–1 reveals that a convertible bond has an *investment*

Figure 17–1

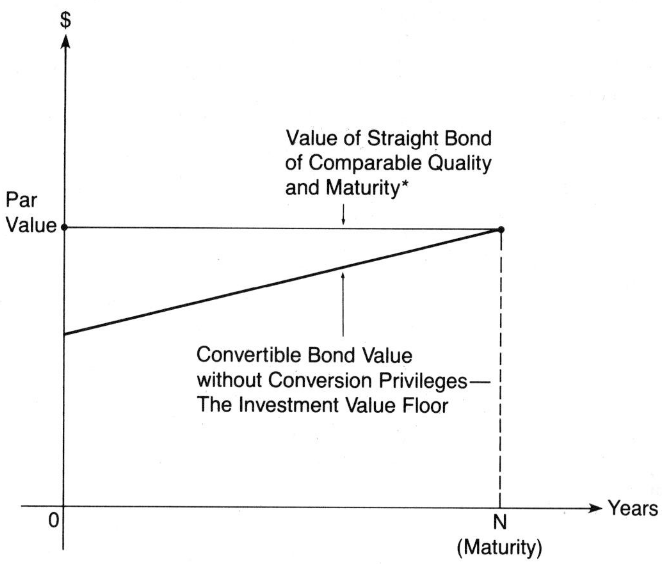

* Assumed to have been issued at par value. Convertible bond also issued at par value but with a lower coupon rate.
NOTE: Market interest rate assumed constant.

value floor below which *its* price will not fall,[6] and that the price differential between a convertible bond's investment value and that of a comparable straight bond diminishes as the date of maturity approaches. In this connection, it is important to point out that the investment value floor is very unstable because it moves up and down with changes in market interest rates. For example, when the market interest rate goes up, the investment value floor goes down.

Conversion Value Floor

The price of a convertible bond is subject to an additional lower boundary; it cannot fall below its conversion value. Again, the reason should be clear. As soon as the price of a convertible bond drops below its conversion value, bondholders find it more attractive to convert their bonds into common stock, thereby depleting the supply of these bonds and pushing up their prices.

[6] The investment value floor is often below the price at which the bond would sell if it were not convertible. However, when the conversion value is very low relative to the investment value, the convertible bond will be selling essentially as a straight bond and its price will be approximately the same as it would be if the bond were not convertible.

Figure 17–2

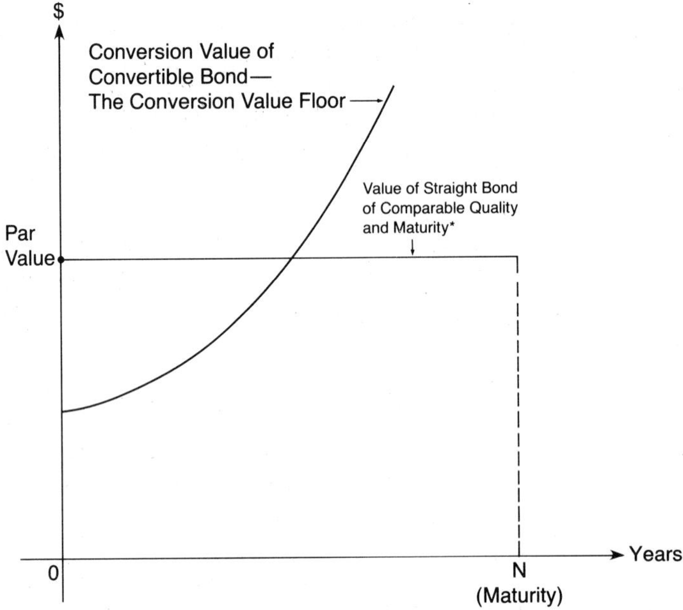

* Assumed to have been issued at par value. Convertible bond also issued at par value but with a lower coupon rate.
NOTE: Market interest rate assumed constant.

The time path of the *conversion value floor* of a convertible bond is shown in Figure 17–2. The illustrated time path of the conversion floor is based on the assumption that the stock price is growing at a constant rate. Note that although on the date of issue the conversion value is below its par value, over time the conversion value rises above par value. It may be recalled that the conversion value is simply the market price of the stock multiplied by the conversion ratio. Because the conversion ratio remains fixed, the conversion value can rise only as a result of an increase in the stock price. Although the future increases in the stock price cannot be accurately predicted, for the sake of a simple demonstration of the principle of the conversion value floor, it can be assumed that the stock will grow at a constant rate. Symbolically,

$$P_n = P_0(1 + g)^n \tag{17–1}$$

where

P_n = Price of stock at the end of year n
P_0 = Current market price of common stock
g = Growth rate of stock price

Assume a convertible bond has just been issued at par. The stock price is $40 and the conversion ratio is 20. The initial conversion value of the convertible bond, CV_0, is $800. Assuming that the stock's constant growth rate, g, is 10 percent, one year later the conversion value will be $880 [($40)(1.10)(20)]; after two years it will rise to $968 [($40)$(1.10)^2$(20)]. At this rate, in three years the conversion value would be $1,064.80 [($40)$(1.10)^3$(20)], which is *above* its par value (and also the assumed value of a comparable straight bond). Therefore, the shape of the conversion value curve is influenced by the expected growth in the price of the stock. In this example, at a growth rate of 2 percent it would take about 12 years for the conversion value to rise above its par value.

Market Value Floor

The lower boundary set by a combination of the investment value floor *and* the conversion value floor is known as the *market value floor*. This floor is graphically presented in Figure 17–3. In Figure 17–3A, it is shown that the convertible bond has an investment value floor or boundary designated by the labeled line beginning at point X. The conversion value floor of the bond, graphed in Figure 17–3B, is marked by the curve starting at point Y. The two floors are combined to generate the market value floor, which is represented by the solid line XPQ in Figure 17–3C.[7]

A complete model of a convertible bond is presented in Figure 17–4.[8] Note the downward sloping call price line which eventually reaches a point equal to the convertible bond's par value. Remember that from the day of issue most convertible bonds can be called away at a premium over par value. The call premium, which is highest when a bond is issued, progressively declines over time, finally disappearing at maturity.

The curve sloping upward from par value in Figure 17–4 represents the convertible bond's market value.[9] The shaded portion represents the bond's premium over the market value floor. Note that this premium declines the more the market price of the bond rises above the investment value and the call price. Eventually the premium disappears. The reason for this is simple. Bondholders realize that, if at any time the convertible bond is called by the issuer, they must either convert their bonds into common stock or have the bond redeemed at the call price. Because both of these values are lower than the convertible bond's market value, in either event the bondholder would lose the premium and suffer a loss. As the conversion value rises, other things being

[7] Because the investment value of a convertible bond is theoretical, it could be higher or lower than the conversion value at the date of issue. Thus, the market value floor could be the same as the conversion value floor.

[8] This figure represents only theoretical values of a convertible bond over time. Naturally, the investment value of the security can rise above the call price if market interest rates fall. The investment value can also be consistently above the conversion value.

[9] This assumes, of course, that the stock price continues to rise at a constant rate and the market interest rate remains constant.

Figure 17–3

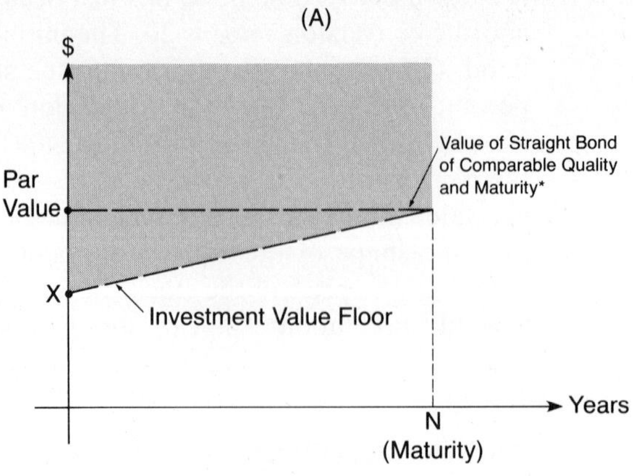

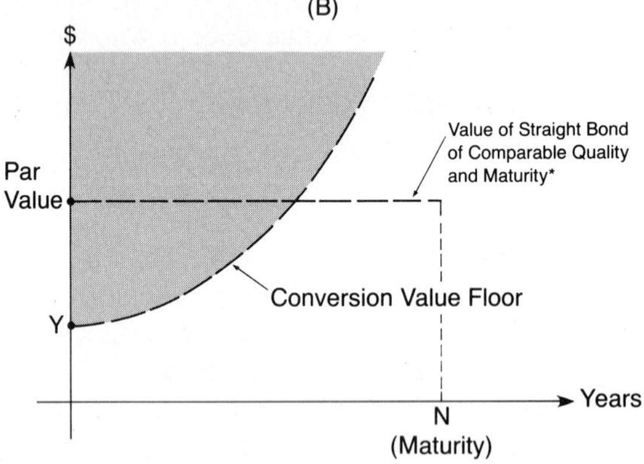

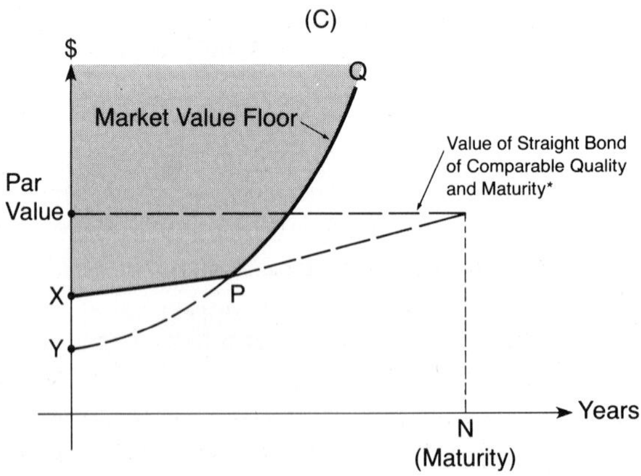

* Assumed to have been issued at par value. Convertible bond also issued at par value but with a lower coupon rate.

NOTE: Market interest rate is assumed constant.

Figure 17–4

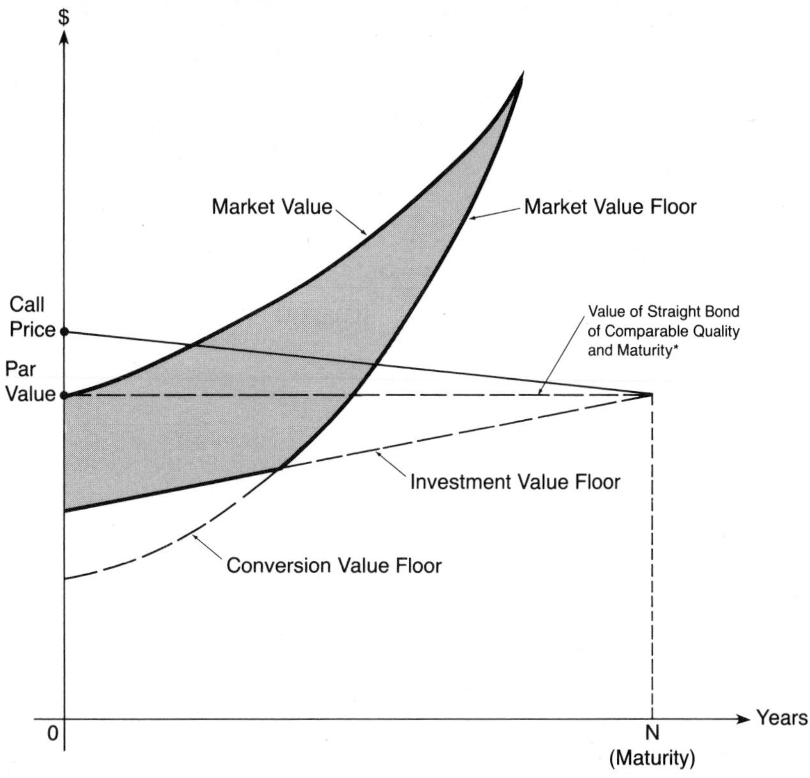

* Assumed to have been issued at par value. Convertible bond also issued at par value, but with a lower coupon rate.
NOTE: Market interest rate assumed constant.

SOURCE: Adapted from E. Brigham, "An Analysis of Convertible Debentures: Theory and Some Empirical Evidence," *Journal of Finance*, March 1966, p. 37.

equal,[10] the possibility of the bond being called away increases, and with it the loss potential also increases. Consequently, assuming that the market value of the stock is constantly rising, as time passes the potential bond buyer is willing to pay a progressively lower premium on the bond. Another reason for the shrinkage of the premium is that, with time, the investment value floor moves farther and farther away from the conversion value, thereby exposing the investor to a larger potential loss resulting from a decline in the price of the common stock.

[10] The possibility of the bond being called also depends on the level of market interest rates relative to the coupon rate on the bonds and on the need of the corporation to convert debt into equity capital.

The Real World

In the context of Figure 17–4, in the real world convertible bonds can move in step either with the common stocks into which they are convertible or with the bond market. In other words, convertible bonds sometimes sell essentially at their investment values (when the conversion value is far below the investment value) and at other times at their conversion values (when the conversion value is far above the investment value).

This point can be illustrated with two real world examples.[11] Aluminum Company of America, $5\frac{1}{4}\%$, 1991, is an example of a convertible bond that fluctuated with the common stock rather than with the straight bonds. On January 21, 1980, it was convertible into 17.86 shares of common stock, which was then selling at about $61, so it had a common-equivalent value of $1,090. Quoted at $109, or $1,090 per bond, the bond was selling at a price equal to its conversion value. But its current yield was 4.8 percent and its yield to maturity was 4.2 percent, 7.7 percentage points below the 11.9 percent yield of the S&P index of BBB-rated bonds. The convertible bond, therefore, would not be influenced by shifts in the general level of interest rates or other factors that affected the bond market.

An example of a convertible moving with the bond market rather than with the common stock can be found in the U.S. Steel, $5\frac{3}{4}\%$, 2001 convertible bond. On January 21, 1980 it was convertible into 15.94 shares of a stock selling at about $21, giving it a conversion value of $334.74, insignificant in relation to the bond's market price of 57, or $570. But its current yield was 10 percent and its yield to maturity was 10.9 percent, which on that date was competitive with yields available on straight bonds with A-ratings.[12]

The important feature of convertible bonds described above leads to the conclusion that if investors are interested in realizing *both* price protection and capital gains, they might prefer to buy convertibles that are not selling only as straight bonds or only as common stock.

Convertible Bond Valuation Model

Convertible bonds are a hybrid-type security. Consequently, both the bond and stock valuation models developed earlier should be used to construct a *Convertible Bond Valuation Model.* In this section, the technique for constructing such a model is presented in five steps.

[11] "Attractive Convertible Bonds," *The Outlook*, Standard & Poor's, January 21, 1980, p. 970.
[12] It should be noted, however, that the character of a convertible can be reversed by a substantial change in either the stock or bond market.

Step 1

Given the current market price of a bond, its yield to maturity can be calculated

$$P_0 = \sum_{n=1}^{N} \frac{C}{(1+i)^n} + \frac{P_N}{(1+i)^N} \qquad \textbf{(6–2 restated)}$$

where

P_0 = Market price of a bond
C = Annual interest payments
P_N = Par value of the bond
N = Maturity of the bond
i = The yield to maturity

This equation states that, given the market price of a bond, if the bond is held until maturity, the rate at which the series of interest payments and the par value are discounted is its yield to maturity.

Equation 6–2 must be suitably modified in order to make it applicable to convertible bonds, which differ from straight bonds in two important respects. First, the holding period of a convertible bond frequently is shorter than that of a comparable straight bond, because under appropriate conditions a convertible bond is likely to be converted into common stock before maturity. Consequently, the yield of the convertible bond should be calculated to the time when the bond is likely to be converted. Second, because a convertible bond is likely to be held until the company calls the bond and forces conversion, the conversion value of the bond at the end of the holding period is the relevant value; that is, the conversion value, rather than the par value, is the amount the investor will receive at the end of the holding period. This conversion value would probably differ from the maturity price of a straight bond. Incorporating these changes, Equation 6–2 becomes:

$$PC_0 = \sum_{n=1}^{H} \frac{C}{(1+i_{cv})^n} + \frac{CV_H}{(1+i_{cv})^H} \qquad \textbf{(17–2)}$$

where

PC_0 = Market price of the convertible bond
C = Annual interest payments
CV_H = Conversion value of the convertible bond at the end of period H
H = Expected holding period of the convertible bond
i_{cv} = Yield on the convertible bond

Equation 17–2 suggests that, given the current market price of a convertible bond, its yield, i_{cv}, can be calculated by determining the expected holding period, H, and its conversion value at the end of the holding period, CV_H. These two values can be determined by using parts of the Common Stock Valuation Model developed in Chapter 9.[13]

Step 2

In Chapter 9 it was mentioned that, assuming that an infinite stream of dividends can be projected,[14] the present value of a common stock can be determined by:

$$PV = \frac{D_1}{r - g} \qquad \textbf{(9–15 restated)}$$

Here, the expected dividend in the first year, D_1, is projected to grow at a constant rate, g. The dividend stream is discounted by a constant appropriate discount rate, r.

Substituting the current market price, P_0, for the present value, PV, and the yield, i, for the appropriate discount rate, r, Equation 9–15 becomes

$$P_0 = \frac{D_1}{i - g} \qquad \textbf{(17–3)}$$

If the yield remains constant, the stock price will increase each year at the growth rate, g. Equation 17–3, therefore, can be expressed in the following form:

$$P_n = P_0(1 + g)^n \qquad \textbf{(17–4)}$$

where

P_n = Price of stock at the end of year n

P_0 = Current market price of common stock

g = Growth rate of dividend and stock price

Therefore, if the current market price of stock is \$50, and the annual growth rate of dividend and stock price is 10 percent, the price of stock after, say, eight years will be \$107.20:

$$\begin{aligned} P_n &= P_0(1 + g)^n \\ &= \$50(1 + .10)^8 \\ &= \$107.20 \end{aligned}$$

[13] This discussion is based upon Eugene F. Brigham, "An Analysis of Convertible Debentures: Theory and Some Empirical Evidence," *Journal of Finance*, March 1966, pp. 35–54.

[14] In Chapter 9, the future selling price of a stock was expressed as a function of the earnings multiple and earnings. This was done primarily to enhance the real world implication of the Common Stock Valuation Model. Theoretically, the assumption that the stock price is a function of dividend growth is equally valid.

Step 3

Note that Equation 17–4 can be applied to the valuation of a convertible bond by incorporating in it the conversion ratio that measures the number of stocks that can be obtained for each bond. The conversion value of a convertible bond is determined by:

$$\text{Conversion value} = \text{Current price of stock} \times \text{Conversion ratio}$$
$$CV = P_0 \times CR$$

Because Equation 17–4 determines the market price of common stock during any given period, it can be stated that

$$CV_H = P_0(1+g)^H \times CR \tag{17–5}$$

where

CV_H = Conversion value of the convertible bond at the end of period H
P_0 = Current market price of common stock
g = Growth rate of dividend and stock price
CR = Conversion ratio
H = Expected holding period of the convertible bond

Step 4

Equation 17–5 can be incorporated into Equation 6–2 and 17–2, thereby producing the basic Convertible Bond Valuation Model:

$$PC_0 = \sum_{n=1}^{H} \frac{C}{(1+i_{cv})^n} + \frac{P_0(1+g)^H \times CR}{(1+i_{cv})^H} \tag{17–6}$$

where

PC_0 = Market price of the convertible bond
C = Annual interest payments
P_0 = Current market price of common stock
g = Growth rate of dividend and stock price
CR = Conversion ratio
H = Expected holding period of the convertible bond
i_{cv} = Yield on the convertible bond

The example in Table 17–3 demonstrates the use of the above model in the calculation of a convertible bond's yield. The assumption of an 8 percent growth

Table 17–3

Pertinent Data

Par value of convertible bond = \$1,000

Market price of convertible bond (PC_0) = \$ 950

Annual interest payments (C) = \$ 70

Current market price of common stock (P_0) = \$ 40

Growth rate of dividend and stock price (g) = 8%

Conversion ratio (CR) = 20

Expected holding period of the convertible bond (H) = 5 years

Bond Yield

$$PC_0 = \sum_{n=1}^{H} \frac{C}{(1+i_{cv})^n} + \frac{P_0(1+g)^H \times CR}{(1+i_{cv})^H}$$

$$\$950 = \sum_{n=1}^{5} \frac{\$70}{(1+i_{cv})^n} + \frac{\$40(1+.08)^5 \times 20}{(1+i_{cv})^5}$$

Solving for the convertible bond yield,* $i_{cv} \approx 11\%$

* At $i_{cv} = 11\%$

$$PC_0 = (\$70)(3.696) + [(\$40)(1.08)\ (20)](.593)$$
$$\approx \$950$$

rate of the common stock price leads to the estimation of the convertible bond's conversion value after a five-year holding period. The assumptions used for the estimation of the holding period are discussed in Step 5.

Step 5

It was previously mentioned that the holding period of a convertible bond frequently is shorter than that of a comparable straight bond, because it is likely to be converted into common stock. Steps 2 and 3 covered the determination of the conversion value for any given year. This step describes the estimation of the holding period.

Convertible bonds are frequently issued as a means of deferring common stock financing. This is done by fixing the conversion price 15 to 25 percent higher than the current stock price. When the bonds are converted, the corporation is obliged to issue fewer shares than would have been the case had the firm initially issued common stock to raise additional capital. Of course, this line of thought logically assumes that the firm expects the bonds to be converted at some point; if that were not the case, the firm would carry the debt instead of the desired form of financing, common equity.[15] Consequently, when the market price of the common stock rises sufficiently above its conversion price, the company frequently *calls the bond.* If the conversion value of the bond is *higher* than the call price, the bondholder will obviously convert it into common stock. It can therefore be safely assumed that a convertible bond is vulnerable to a forced conversion when the stock price rises above the conversion price.[16]

The task of estimating the holding period can now be put into proper perspective. Consider again the example given in Table 17–3. A $1,000 par value bond is convertible into 20 shares of stock, implying that the conversion price is $50 ($1,000/20). The current stock price is $40, and the projected growth rate of the stock price is 8 percent. An investor estimates that the bond will be called away at $60—a price level 20 percent higher than the $50 conversion price. If it is assumed that the holding period, H, of the bond equals the time it will take for the current stock price to reach $60, then the holding period can be estimated in the following manner:

$$P_H = P_0(1 + g)^H$$
$$\$60 = \$40(1 + .08)^H$$

Using the compound value table, the value of H is approximately 5, and the holding period is estimated to be five years. This was, of course, the value of the holding period used in the example given in Table 17–3.

Convertible Bond Strategies

Now that the Convertible Bond Valuation Model has been presented, a framework for determining the conditions under which convertible bonds might be preferable to straight bonds and to common stock can be developed.

Convertible Versus Straight Bonds

The yield on a convertible bond is calculated by solving for i_{cv} in the following equation:

$$PC_0 = \sum_{n=1}^{H} \frac{C}{(1 + i_{cv})^n} + \frac{P_0(1 + g)^H \times CR}{(1 + i_{cv})^H} \qquad \textbf{(17–6 restated)}$$

[15] Companies will not always wish to retire debt through conversion. This could be true of corporations that issue convertible bonds because they require smaller interest payments than comparable straight bonds. Also, a company's financial condition could change after the bonds are issued, making it more advantageous for it to carry the debt.

[16] A convertible bond can also be vulnerable to conversion, even if the stock price is below the conversion price. During periods of declining market interest rates, the bond's market price could rise above the call price based solely on its investment value.

Given the current price and the growth rate of the related common stock, the conversion ratio, and the holding period, the yield on the convertible bond can be determined. Similarly, the yield on a straight bond is calculated by solving for i:

$$P_0 = \sum_{n=1}^{N} \frac{C}{(1+i)^n} + \frac{P_N}{(1+i)^N} \qquad \text{(6–2 restated)}$$

Assuming that an investor must choose between a convertible bond and a straight bond which are identical in all other respects, the decision can be made in the following manner:[17]

Relationship of i to i_{cv}	Action Recommended
$i > i_{cv}$	Buy the straight bond.
$i = i_{cv}$	Buy either of the two bonds.
$i < i_{cv}$	Buy the convertible bond.

NOTE: i_{cv} = Yield on convertible bond; i = Yield on straight bond.

Convertible Bonds Versus Common Stock

Convertible bonds have one major advantage over common stocks: Their prices are less likely to drop during stock market declines than the prices of the stock for which they can be exchanged. Figure 17–5 shows the fluctuations in the price of Newhall Land and Farming Company's common stock and 6 percent convertible bond, maturing in 1995 and convertible into 24.39 Newhall shares. The conversion value line represents the stock price multiplied by the conversion ratio of 24.39. The bond prices are expressed as a percentage of the face amount. For example, 89 would be equivalent to $890. The common stock prices are in dollars. Note that during the 1971–74 period, buoyed by its investment value, the percentage decline in the bond price was considerably lower than the stock's price. Therefore, had an investor originally bought the bond instead of the stock, the loss would have been less.

However, it should be noted that the price of a convertible bond will sometimes drop more (that is, the percentage drop will be more) than the price of

[17] In order to better use this decision model, one should consider the same time periods for both investments. Note, however, that the yield on the straight bond is calculated through maturity, N, whereas the yield on the convertible bond is calculated only through the year of conversion, H, which is shorter than the year of maturity. The Convertible Bond Valuation Model might thus be extended to include the investment return from the date the bond is converted until maturity. The model would become complicated if the stock acquired through the conversion is not immediately sold. If that were the case, the return on the stock for this period would have to be estimated.

Figure 17–5

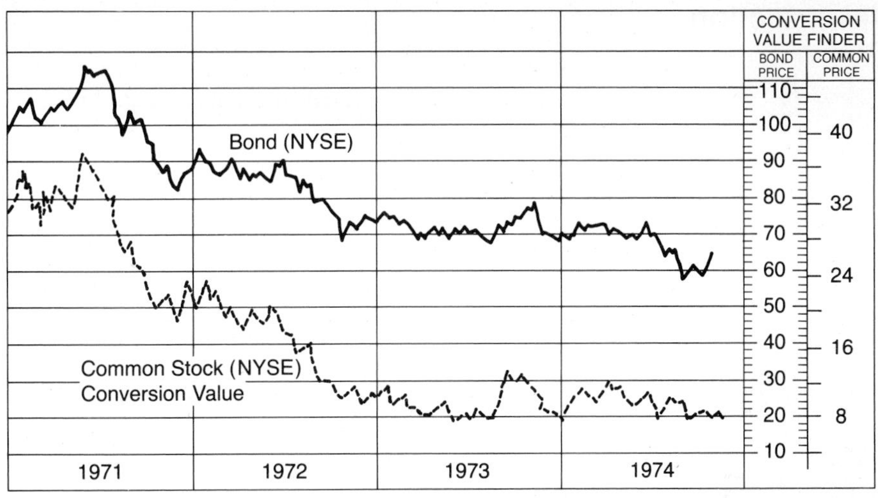

SOURCE: "Convertible Bonds: Stocks & Bonds in One Bundle," *Changing Times*, April 1975, p. 37.

the stock. If interest rates are rising and the bond is selling largely as a straight bond, this can happen because the conversion value is far below the investment value of the bond.

In conclusion, it can be stated that a convertible bond will almost invariably sell at a premium over its investment value when the conversion value exceeds the investment value; and it will usually sell at a premium (sometimes very small) over its conversion value whether or not the conversion value is higher or lower than the investment value. Furthermore, even with a substantial drop in the stock price, the market value of the bond will not fall below its investment value. Finally, if the market interest rate falls and the stock price rises after the issue of a convertible bond, the increase in the value of the bond could be substantially higher than the gain in the stock's value.[18]

However, during periods when market interest rates rise and common stocks register a decline, convertible bonds lose much of their attractiveness. Their value as bonds is adversely affected and the right to purchase stock is of dubious worth. Consequently, care should be exercised in purchasing convertible bonds.

[18] There are of course exceptions to this case. If, for example, the convertible bond is selling at a that case, if interest rates were to fall and the price of stock were to rise, the price of the bond might that case, if interest rates were to fall and the price of stock were to rise, the price of the bond might move up no more than the price of the stock, because the increase in the investment value (if it were still far below the conversion value) would have no impact on the bond price.

SECTION 2 WARRANTS

Introduction

A *warrant* is an option issued by a company to buy a stated number of shares of its common stock at a specified price. If the privilege to buy the stock with the warrant is not exercised, the warrant becomes worthless on the expiration date.

Warrants are generally used as a way of *sweetening up* a company's new issue of either preferred stock or bonds. They are issued on a long-term basis and a few have perpetual lives. Most warrants are not exercised until shortly before they expire. During their lifetime, warrants are favored as trading vehicles by investors who seek to realize substantial capital gains.

The Price Pattern

Theoretical Value and the Premium

The theoretical value of a warrant is calculated as

$$V_W = (P_0 - EP) \times Q \quad \text{and} \quad V_W \geq 0 \tag{17-7}$$

where

V_W = Theoretical value of one warrant
P_0 = Current market price of common stock
EP = Exercise price of warrant
Q = Number of shares each warrant entitles owner to purchase

Therefore, if warrants entitle their holder to purchase one share of ABC stock at \$50 and the ABC stock is selling at \$60, the theoretical value of a warrant is \$10:

$$V_W = (\$60 - \$50) \times 1 = \$10$$

If the market price of the warrant were \$12, it would be selling at a premium of \$2 over its theoretical value.

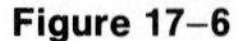

Figure 17–6 **Typical Price Pattern of Hypothetical Warrant**

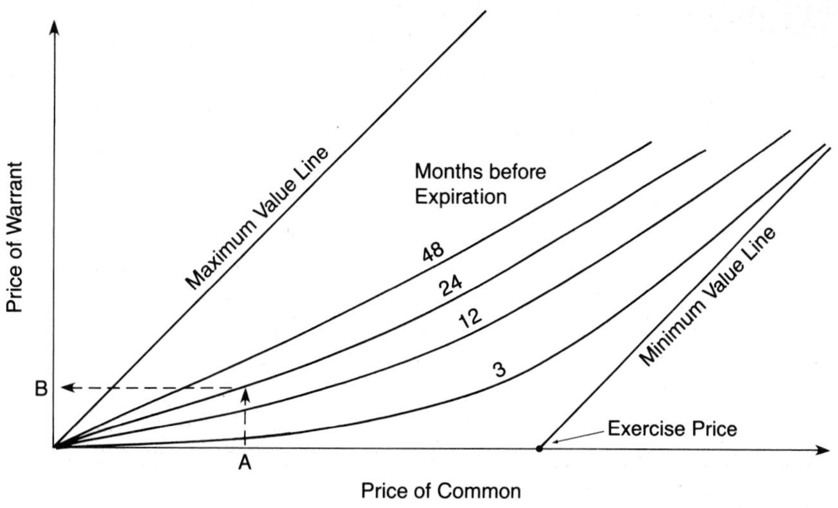

NOTE: As expiration approaches, the curves drop toward the minimum value line. If X common is at A 24 months before expiration, then X warrant will be near B.

SOURCE: From *Beat the Market: A Scientific Stock Market System,* by Edward O. Thorp and S. T. Kassouf (New York: Random House, 1967), p. 31. Copyright © 1967 by Edward O. Thorp and S. T. Kassouf. Reprinted by permission.

Price Boundaries

The market price of a warrant equals its theoretical value plus a premium. The premium is a function of the outlook for the future price of the stock, the amount of leverage available, and the length of time remaining until the warrant expires. Based on this relationship, a conceptual framework can be developed for analyzing the investment characteristics of warrants.

Because a warrant holder does not receive dividends, and because a warrant is an option to buy only one share of stock, the market price of a warrant will always be less than the market price of the stock. Therefore, if ABC common is selling for \$30, the related warrant price should not exceed that amount.

The minimum value of a warrant is set by its theoretical value—that is, the excess of the market price of the stock over the exercise price.[19] For example, if the exercise price is \$20 and the common stock is selling for \$30, the minimum value of the warrant is \$10 (\$30 – \$20). The upper and lower price boundaries of a hypothetical warrant are presented in Figure 17–6. As expected, the price of a warrant always fluctuates between the upper and lower price boundaries.

[19] Of course, if the market price of the stock is less than the exercise price, the warrant's theoretical value would be zero.

Theory of Warrant Valuation

The value of a warrant depends on three key variables: the outlook for the stock price, the leverage effect, and the time remaining until expiration.

Outlook for Stock Price

Basic to the understanding of a warrant's value is the fact that it is influenced by the outlook for the future price of the stock. Assume ABC warrants are trading on the AMEX at 6. Each warrant represents an option to buy one share of common stock at the price of $40 plus one warrant until the year 2000. At the present warrant price, the cost of one share of stock would be $46 if purchased with a warrant. But suppose the ABC common stock is trading on the NYSE at $20. The theoretical value of the warrant would be zero. The price of the stock would have to advance $26 a share, or 130 percent, before the theoretical value would equal the present warrant market price of $6. So the pertinent question is: Why are the warrants selling for $6 at this time? The answer is that a warrant with no theoretical value can command a price because it provides a long-term option on the stock. Investors are willing to pay a price for this option because the price of the stock—and the theoretical value of the warrant—might increase in the future.

The price investors are willing to pay for a warrant, therefore, is influenced by their expectations of how the price of the underlying stock will perform in the future. The higher investors expect the stock price to rise above the exercise price (during the life of the warrant), the more valuable will be the related warrant. The value of a warrant will also be influenced by the *volatility* of the underlying stock's price. With greater volatility, there is a greater potential for the stock price to rise above the exercise price. Consequently, there is a *positive* relationship between a warrant's value and the volatility of the related stock.

Leverage Effect

Another important dimension of a warrant's value is the *leverage effect*, which is elucidated in the following illustration. Assume an investor can purchase a common stock for $100 plus one warrant. If the common stock is currently selling for $110, the *theoretical value of the warrant* would be $10 ($110–$100). If the price of the common stock subsequently advances by 81.8 percent, from $110 to $200, the theoretical value of the warrant would increase to $100 ($200 – $100), an increase of 1,000 percent. Anyone who had invested in the warrant at its theoretical value of $10 would make a profit of 900 percent [($100 – $10)/$10] if the warrant were sold at its new theoretical value of $100. This idea is graphically presented in Figure 17–7. On the top half is graphed

Figure 17–7

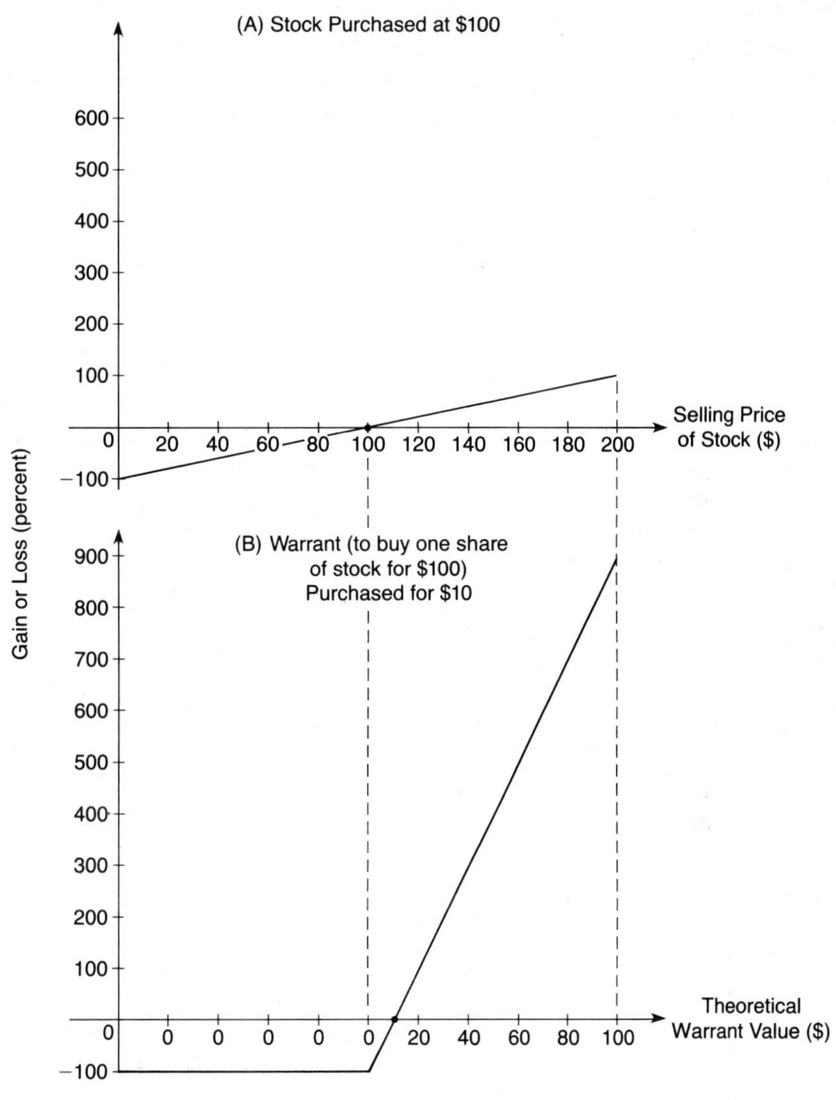

the percentage gain or loss on various selling prices of a stock purchased at $100. The bottom half shows the corresponding percentage gain or loss on a warrant to purchase the stock at the exercise price of $100. Note that, in this example, if the stock price fails to rise above $100, the warrant will not be exercised and 100 percent of the $10 investment will be lost. Only after the stock price rises above the $110 mark can the warrant be exercised for a gain.

Figure 17–8

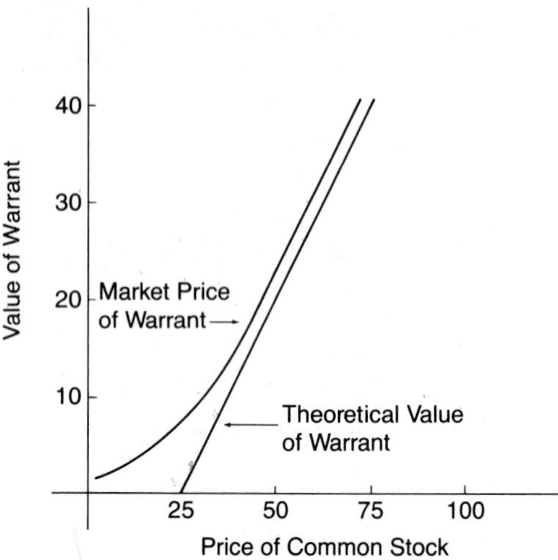

This leverage effect is a major reason as to why the market price of a warrant may exceed its theoretical value, or why it may sell at a *premium*. However, as revealed in Figure 17–8, the market price of a warrant approaches its theoretical value (or the premium decreases) as the price of the underlying stock progressively increases. An important reason for the narrowing spread between the market price of the warrant and its theoretical value is that the warrant investor's leverage *decreases* as the theoretical value of the warrant increases.

Table 17–4

Pertinent Data

Exercise price (EP) = \$20

Number of shares exchangeable per warrant (Q) = 1

Theoretical value (V_w) = $(P_0 - EP) \times Q$

Price of Common Stock	Percentage Increase	Theoretical Value of Warrant	Percentage Increase
\$30.00	—	\$10.00	—
36.00	20%	16.00	60.00%
43.20	20	23.20	45.00
51.84	20	31.84	37.24
62.21	20	42.21	32.57

This last point is demonstrated in Table 17–4. In this example the warrant gives the holder the option to purchase one share of stock for $20. Note that when the common stock price rises from $30 to $36—an increase of 20 percent—the gain in the warrant's theoretical value is 60 percent. However, as the stock price continues to rise by 20 percent, the percentage gain in the theoretical value of the warrant progressively declines. As revealed by Table 17–4, the leverage effect clearly diminishes as the warrant's theoretical value increases.

Time Remaining to Expiration

Warrants differ greatly in their expiration dates. Most warrants run 3-to-5 years, although some run 10-to-20 years and a few like Tri-Continental and Allegheny warrants are perpetual. A sample of expiration dates of warrants traded on the NYSE in 1979 follows:

Years of Life	Number of Warrants	Percentage of Warrants
0–1	27	23
1–2	25	21
2–3	24	21
3–4	13	11
4–5	6	5
5–10	12	10
10–30	6	5
Perpetual	4	4
	117	100

Figure 17–6 (p. 743) reveals an important fact. The price of a warrant gradually *declines* with a reduction in the number of months remaining before its expiration, because the opportunity to make a profit by trading a warrant declines as it approaches its expiration date. Of course, if not exercised, the warrant is rendered worthless on the expiration date.

The Real World

The popularity of warrants stems from the fact that they provide investors with a potential for large returns, as demonstrated earlier. However, they also have several drawbacks. Warrants pay no dividends, include no voting rights, and become worthless at expiration if the common stock is below or equal to the exercise price.

Generally, warrants are considered esoteric instruments in which mostly speculators are interested. Speculators often talk about the warrants of Tri-Continental, a firm providing investment advice, which hit the bottom at $1/32 in 1942. By 1946, they had rebounded to $\$5\frac{5}{8}$, and in 1969 they reached $\$75\frac{3}{4}$. A \$1,000 investment in this warrant eventually transformed itself into \$2.5 million. Between 1962 and 1966, United Air Lines warrants also rose from $\$4\frac{1}{2}$ to \$126. However, investors also remember the TWA warrants which plummetted from \$25 to zero in approximately six months as a result of a catastrophic drop in the price of TWA's common stock. Similarly, between 1968 and 1970, Ling–Temco–Vought warrants fell from \$83 to $\$2\frac{1}{4}$. Also, between 1966 and their expiration date the following September, Mack Trucks warrants fell from $\$33\frac{1}{2}$ to zero. Clearly, for every success story in warrants, there are numerous failures.

SECTION 3 STOCK RIGHTS

Introduction

One of the methods that a publicly held company may use to raise additional funds is to offer stock to its own shareholders, so the existing shareholders' interest in the company can be protected. For example, suppose a shareholder owns 10 percent, or 100,000 shares of XYZ, which has 1 million shares outstanding. If the company issues an additional 1 million shares and this shareholder does not purchase any new shares, the relative interest of this shareholder would drop to 5 percent (100,000/2 million). For this reason, many companies offer the present shareholders the privilege of purchasing the new stock in proportion to their existing holdings, so they can maintain the same percentage equity in the firm. This privilege is called a *preemptive right. Stock rights* are issued because of the stockholders' preemptive rights. The existing shareholders are not required to pay any commission or odd-lot charges when they receive stock rights. Rights are issued for a short period of time, usually two to ten weeks, and they become worthless after the expiration date.

Figure 17–9 presents the complete life story of a stock right. Assume that on February 5, the XYZ company announces it will issue one right for each of the million shares outstanding and specifies that five rights will entitle the holder to purchase one share of stock for \$50. The five-to-one ratio is called the *rights exchange ratio*, and the \$50 price is known as the *subscription price*. To ensure the sale of the new stock, the subscription price is usually set *below* reasonable expectations of its market value. Stockholders not interested in purchasing additional shares at the reduced price are permitted to sell their rights on the open market, much like common stocks.[20]

[20] Trading in rights often begins prior to their actual availability, with the rights sold for delivery on a *when-issued* basis.

Figure 17–9

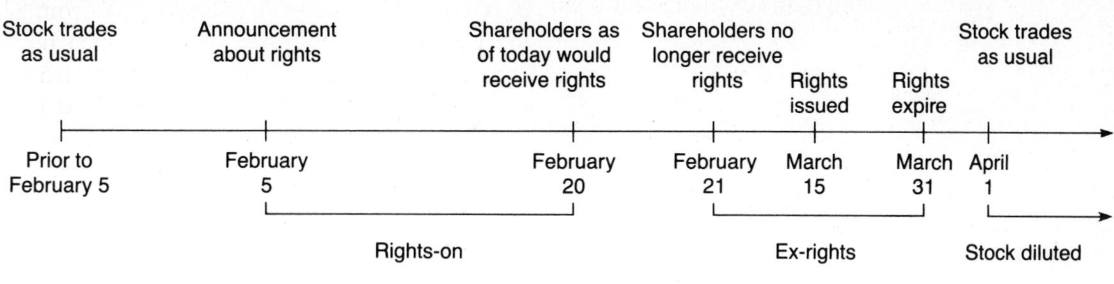

After the terms of the new equity financing have been established, the company announces that on March 15 these rights will be issued to stockholders on record at the close of business on February 20. The period of February 5 to February 20 is called the *rights-on* period. Beginning with February 21 until the rights expire on March 31, investors purchasing the XYZ stock will not receive rights; hence, the stock will trade *ex-rights.* By March 31, all rights that have not been exercised will expire and, beginning April 1, the new shares along with the old ones will begin to trade on the market.

Rights Exchange Ratio

The *rights exchange ratio,* or the number of rights needed to purchase one share of the new stock, is determined on the basis of the amount of funds the company wishes to raise and the subscription price at which the new stock is to be sold. Symbolically,

$$R = \frac{NSO}{NE/P_S} \tag{17–8}$$

where

R = Number of rights needed to buy one share of stock, or the rights exchange ratio

NSO = Number of shares outstanding

NE = New equity funds to be raised

P_S = The subscription price

Therefore, if XYZ has 1 million shares outstanding, and it wishes to raise $10 million by selling 200,000 new shares at a subscription price of $50 per share, the rights exchange ratio will be 5-to-1:

$$R = \frac{1{,}000{,}000}{\$10{,}000{,}000/\$50}$$
$$= 5$$

This implies that an investor must surrender five rights plus $50 to receive one share of the newly issued stock. It should be emphasized here that every existing shareholder receives one right for every share of stock he or she owns. For example, if a shareholder owns 100 shares of the XYZ stock, she will receive 100 rights. At the rights exchange ratio of 5-to-1 and the subscription price of $50, she would be entitled to purchase 20 shares (100/5) of the new stock by tendering 100 rights plus $1,000.

Theory of Rights Valuation

Rights-On

The Conceptual Framework

Table 17–5 presents the pertinent details relating to the proposed sale of 200,000 new shares by XYZ corporation. The current market price of XYZ stock is $70 per share. The company issues 200,000 rights to the present shareholders and the subscription price is fixed at $50 per share. Assuming that the market value of XYZ Corporation increases by the amount of new funds raised, after the financing is completed, the market value of XYZ will increase by $10 million to $80 million. In addition, because the total amount of shares will simultaneously increase to 1.2 million, the market value per share will drop to $66.67 ($80 million/1.2 million).

As previously mentioned, during the rights-on period, each shareholder is issued rights equal to the number of shares he or she owns. According to the terms of new financing, any XYZ investor holding five rights can now purchase one new share for only $50, instead of the new market price of $66.67, thereby realizing a gain of $16.67 per share. Consequently, the theoretical value of each right is $3.33 ($16.67/5).

After the new equity financing is completed, the market value of the stock should drop from $70 to $66.67 per share. However, because the value of each right is $3.33, the price of stock during the rights-on period—the rights-on stock

Table 17–5

Pertinent Data

Number of XYZ shares outstanding	= 1 million
Market price per share	= \$70
Market value of XYZ Corporation	= 1 million × \$70 = \$70 million
New shares to be issued	= 200,000
Subscription price	= \$50
Rights exchange ratio	= 5-to-1

After the completion of new equity financing:

Market value of XYZ Corporation	= \$80 million
New market value per share (\$80 million/1.2 million)	= \$66.67
Excess of new market price over the subscription price	= \$16.67
Rights exchange ratio	= 5-to-1
Value of each right: \$16.67/5	= \$3.33

price—will be \$70 (\$66.67 + \$3.33). Of course, after the termination of the rights-on period, the new shareholders will not receive any rights. Consequently, all other factors remaining constant, the ex-rights price of the stock will revert to \$66.67 per share.

The Basic Formula

The theoretical value of a right during the rights-on period can be directly calculated as

$$V_R = \frac{P_{RO} - P_S}{Q + 1} \tag{17–9}$$

where

V_R = Theoretical value of one right
P_{RO} = Rights-on stock price
P_S = Subscription price
Q = Number of rights needed to purchase one share

In the previous example, the value of rights was \$3.33. This is confirmed by using Equation 17–9:

$$V_R = \frac{\$70 - \$50}{5 + 1}$$
$$= \$3.33$$

Ex-Rights

Investors purchasing the XYZ stock during the ex-rights period will not receive free rights. For them the value of the stock or the ex-rights stock price will simply be \$66.67 per share. The theoretical value of the rights already issued and trading on the market can be determined by:

$$V_R = \frac{P_{ER} - P_S}{Q} \tag{17–10}$$

where

V_R = Value of one right
P_{ER} = Ex-rights stock price
P_S = Subscription price
Q = Number of rights needed to purchase one share

Thus,

$$V_R = \frac{\$66.67 - \$50}{5}$$
$$= \$3.33$$

The Profit Potential

Rights offer a speculator excellent opportunities for realizing a large return on investment if the related stock price advances during the life of the rights. Of course, if the stock price declines, the speculator can lose the entire investment.

Because of their short life, stock rights usually sell at a price close to their theoretical value. However, if investors expect the price of the stock to rise substantially before the expiration date of the rights, they will be willing to pay a premium for the rights, because, compared to stocks, rights offer leverage and a potential for realizing significantly higher returns.

Table 17–6

Pertinent Data

Ex-rights stock price (P_{ER}) = \$66.67

Subscription price (P_S) = \$50

Number of rights needed to purchase one share (Q) = 5

Theoretical value of rights (ex-rights) given by:

$$V_R = \frac{P_{ER} - P_S}{Q}$$

$$= \frac{\$66.67 - \$50}{5}$$

$$= \$3.33$$

Example	Ex-rights stock price advances from \$66.67 to:	Percentage Increase	Theoretical rights value advances from \$3.33 to:	Percentage Increase
1	\$70	5.0%	\$4.00	20.12%
2	75	12.5	5.00	50.15
3	80	20.0	6.00	80.18
4	85	27.5	7.00	110.21

Table 17–6 demonstrates how the theoretical value of a right is likely to fluctuate with an advance in the stock price. When the stock sells at \$66.67, the value of the right is \$3.33. If the stock price advances by 5.0 percent to \$70, the right's theoretical value would increase by 20.12 percent to \$4.00.[21] In another case, a 12.50 percent increase in the stock price would produce a 50.15 percent increase in the value of the right. Of course, the stock price would have to rise within a short period for the right holders to capitalize on this favorable price situation. Because most stocks do not significantly appreciate in price in a few weeks, rights generally do not sell at a premium. However, if investors foresee a special situation which could lead to a substantial price appreciation of a given

[21] Of course, the degree of leverage will vary with different situations. For example, assume the following:

Ex-rights stock price, P_{ER} = \$75

Subscription price, P_S = \$70

Number of rights needed to purchase one share, $Q = 5$

$$V_R = \frac{\$75 - \$70}{5} = \$1.00$$

If the stock price advances 5.0 percent, from \$75 to \$78.75, the theoretical value of the right will rise to \$1.75, a gain of 75 percent. A 12.5 percent rise in the stock price to \$84.37 would cause the right's value to rise to \$2.87, a 187.5 percent gain. The leverage here is clearly greater than that presented in the example given in Table 17–6.

stock in the near future, they would be willing to pay a premium for the related rights, and these rights would sell above their theoretical value.

To summarize, the value of a right is determined by the same factors that determine the value of a warrant. These factors are, it may be recalled, the outlook for the future stock price, the leverage effect, and the time remaining until expiration. In addition, another important variable is the excess of the market price of the stock over the subscription price.

Summary

Convertible bonds, warrants, and stock rights have one thing in common: Under prespecified terms all are convertible into common stock.

Convertible bonds issued by corporations give their holders the right to convert into common stock. The number of shares a convertible bond can be exchanged for is usually fixed and the conversion privilege typically exists for the life of the bond. Convertible bonds are a hybrid-type security in that they combine the basic attributes of common stock and corporate bonds in a single security.

A convertible bond's *investment value* is a theoretical price at which the bond's yield to maturity would be equal to the yield offered by straight bonds of similar quality and maturity.

Conversion value refers to a convertible bond's value if exchanged for stock at the stock's current market price. The price of a convertible bond should not fall below either its conversion value or investment value. The combination of these price floors is called the *market value floor*. These floors move up and down with the price of the stock and market interest rates.

The determination of the yield of a convertible bond is complicated by the fact that, under appropriate conditions, it is likely to be exchanged for stock before maturity. A special valuation model should therefore be used to estimate the return on this type of security.

A *warrant* is a long-term option issued by a company on its common stock. Warrants are generally used as a way of enhancing a company's proposed new issue of either preferred stock or bonds. If the privilege to buy the stock with the warrant is not exercised, on the expiration date the warrant becomes worthless.

The *theoretical value of a warrant* equals the difference between the market price of the stock and the exercise price, multiplied by the number of shares that can be purchased with one warrant. A warrant with no theoretical value can command a price because it provides an option on the stock for a period of time and because it possesses the power of *leverage*.

The *market price of a warrant* is its theoretical value plus a *premium* which is a function of several variables, including the outlook for the price of the stock, the amount of leverage and the time to expiration.

Many companies offer their stockholders the privilege of purchasing newly issued stock in proportion to their existing holdings, so they can maintain their original percentage equity in the firm. This privilege is called a *preemptive right*. Rights, like warrants, offer speculators opportunities for realizing a large return on investment through leverage. However, the profit potential is limited because rights expire in a relatively short time.

A Look Ahead

This chapter has dealt with convertible securities. Another investment instrument available which deserves a careful analysis is known as options—the subject for discussion in the next chapter.

Concepts for Review

Convertible bonds
Call provision
Uses of convertible bonds
Conversion ratio
Conversion price
Conversion value
Conversion premium
Premium over investment value
Investment value floor
Conversion value floor
Market value floor
Convertible Bond Valuation Model
Convertible versus straight bonds
Convertible bonds versus stocks
Warrants
Leverage effect
Theoretical value of warrant
Premium on warrant
Stock rights
Rights exchange ratio
Subscription price
Rights-on
Ex-rights

Questions for Review

1. Comment on the following statement: "Convertible bonds, warrants, and stock rights are basically the same because they are all convertible into common stock."
2. Why would a company issue convertible bonds instead of straight bonds or common stock?

3. Investor M wants to purchase a convertible bond because she feels this investment instrument has all the advantages, but none of the risks of common stock and straight bonds. What is your response?
4. Explain the following terms: conversion ratio, conversion price, conversion value, and conversion parity.
5. What are the critical variables in determining the yield on a convertible bond? How can values for these variables be estimated?
6. It is possible to calculate a yield to maturity for a convertible bond; however, it is often argued that the yield to maturity is not an appropriate yield concept to apply to a convertible bond. Do you agree?
7. What is meant by the "floor" for a convertible bond?
8. For convertible bonds, what is meant by the premium over the market value floor? In theory, this premium should progressively decline and finally disappear over time. Why?
9. An investor can voluntarily convert a convertible bond into common stock at any time during the life of the convertible provision. Under what circumstances would conversion take place?
10. It is asserted that an investor can lose a greater percentage of his investment in a convertible bond than in the common stock into which the bond is convertible. Is this possible? Explain.
11. Outline the differences in potential risk and rewards from investing in common shares versus warrants.
12. What are the maximum and minimum price levels of warrants? Why do these levels exist?
13. Should an investor consider purchasing a warrant with no theoretical value? Explain.
14. Would you expect the premium on a warrant to increase or decrease as the underlying stock price increases?
15. What is the major difference between warrants and stock rights? How does this difference affect the potential risk and rewards of each?

Problems

1. Investor X just paid $1,200 for an ABC Bond that has a 6 percent coupon and a 15-year maturity. The bond is convertible into 20 shares of ABC common stock, currently priced at $55 per share. Similar quality bonds due in 15 years, but without a conversion feature, are yielding 6 percent to maturity.
   a. Find the conversion ratio, conversion price, conversion parity price, and conversion value of the bond.
   b. Find the conversion premium and premium over investment value.
   c. What is the lowest price at which you would expect the ABC Bond to sell at this time?

d. Investor X is considering converting the bond. What would you advise?
e. Suppose ABC Company calls the bond at 104. At what price would the bond sell after the call announcement is made? What should Investor X do?

2. BCF Company recently issued a 20-year bond at par with a 6 percent coupon that is convertible into 35 shares of BCF common stock. The stock is now selling for $20.50 per share; a similar straight-debt bond now yields 8.0 percent to maturity.
a. What is the bond's conversion value and investment value?
b. What premium are investors paying above the greater of the conversion or investment value?
c. Suppose you expect the BCF bond to be called when the market price of the stock exceeds the conversion price by 15 percent. Assuming the stock price rises by an average annual rate of 8 percent and market interest rates do not fall, what is the expected holding period of the bond?
d. Using the information in part (c) of this problem, determine the yield on this bond through the expected holding period. (Note: The call price of the bond is 106 at the issue date, and will decline each year thereafter.)
e. Under the assumptions stated in part (c) of this problem, would it be possible to earn a higher return on the BCF bond than that estimated in part (d)? Explain.

3. Warrants issued by BTU Corporation allow the holder to buy one share of BTU common stock for each warrant held. The stock is selling for $30 and the exercise price is $26.
a. What is the theoretical value of a BTU warrant?
b. What happens to the theoretical value if the common stock price advances 15 percent—from $30 to $34.50?
c. What happens to the theoretical value if the common stock price advances from $34.50 by another 15 percent?
d. If the common stock is selling for $30 and the warrant is selling for $7, what premium are investors paying for the warrant?
e. What is the highest price at which the warrant could sell when the stock is selling for $30?
f. If a warrant is purchased for $7, at what price would BTU stock have to sell in order to *exercise* the warrant for a profit? Could a profit ever be made if the stock price does not reach this level?

4. CMG Company has just announced a rights offering that will allow shareholders to purchase one new share of common stock for each 10 now held. CMG stock is currently selling for $116 per share. The subscription price will be $105 per share.
a. What is the theoretical value of each right?
b. Suppose the price of CMG stock rises to $123 per share. Find the new theoretical value of each right. Also compute the percentage price change of CMG stock and the percentage change in the theoretical value of each right.
c. Repeat the exercise in part (b) of this problem, but assume the price of CMG stock falls to $110 per share.
d. When CMG stock goes ex-rights, what should its price be?
e. Suppose CMG stock has gone ex-rights and is selling for $119 per share. Find the theoretical value of each right.
f. Suppose CMG stock has gone ex-rights and is selling for $120 per share. Is it possible for the rights to sell for $1.75 at this time? Explain.

Selected Readings

"Attractive Convertible Bonds." *The Outlook*. Standard & Poor's, January 21, 1980.

Ayres, Herbert F. "Risk Aversion in the Warrant Market." *Industrial Management Review*, Fall 1963.

Baumol, William J., Burton G. Malkiel, and R. E. Quandt. "The Valuation of Convertible Securities." *Quarterly Journal of Economics*, February 1966.

Bierman, Harold J., Jr. "The Cost of Warrants." *Journal of Financial and Quantitative Analysis*, June 1973.

Brennan, M. J., and E. S. Schwartz. "Convertible Bonds: Valuation and Optimal Strategies for Call and Conversion." *Journal of Finance*, December 1977.

Brigham, Eugene F. "An Analysis of Convertible Debentures: Theory and Some Empirical Evidence." *Journal of Finance*, March 1966.

Frank, Werner G., and Jerry J. Weygandt. "A Prediction Model for Convertible Debentures." *Journal of Accounting Research*, Spring 1971.

Hayes, Samuel L., III, and Henry B. Reiling. "Sophisticated Financing Tool: The Warrant." *Harvard Business Review*, January–February 1969.

Ingersoll, Jonathan. "An Examination of Corporate Call Policies on Convertible Securities." *Journal of Finance*, May 1977.

Jennings, Edward H. "An Estimate of Convertible Bond Premiums." *Journal of Financial and Quantitative Analysis*, January 1974.

Kassouf, Sheen T. "Warrant Price Behavior 1945–1964." *Financial Analysts Journal*, January–February 1968.

Liebowitz, Martin L. "Convertible Securities." *Financial Analysts Journal*, November–December 1974.

Miller, Alexander B. "How to Call Your Convertibles." *Harvard Business Review*, May–June 1971.

Parkinson, Michael. "Empirical Warrant–Stock Relationships," *Journal of Business*, October 1972.

Pease, Fred. "The Warrant—Its Powers and Its Hazards." *Financial Analysts Journal*, January–February 1963.

Poensgen, Otto H. "The Valuation of Convertible Bonds." *Industrial Management Review*, Fall 1965 and Spring 1966.

Rush, David F., and Ronald W. Melicher. "An Empirical Examination of Factors Which Influence Warrant Prices." *Journal of Finance*, December 1974.

Samuelson, Paul A. "Rational Theory of Warrant Pricing." *Industrial Management Review*, Spring 1965.

Shelton, John P. "The Relation of the Price of a Warrant to the Price of Its Associated Stock." *Financial Analysts Journal*, May–June 1967, and July–August 1967.

Soldofsky, Robert M. "Yield–Risk Performance of Convertible Securities." *Financial Analysts Journal*, March–April 1971.

Sprenkel, Case M. "Warrant Prices as Indicators of Expectations and Preferences." *Yale Economic Essays*, Fall 1961.

Stone, Bernell K. "Warrant Financing." *Journal of Financial and Quantitative Analysis*, March 1976.

Turov, Daniel. "Dividend Paying Stocks and Their Warrants," *Financial Analysts Journal*, March–April 1973.

Van Horne, James C. "Warrant Valuation in Relation to Volatility and Opportunity Costs," *Industrial Management Review*, Spring 1969.

Vinson, Charles E. "Pricing Practices in the Primary Convertible Bond Market." *Quarterly Review of Economics and Business*, Summer 1970.

Walter, James E., and Agustin V. Que. "The Valuation of Convertible Bonds." *Journal of Finance*, June 1973.

Weil, Roman L., Jr., Joel E. Segall, and David Green, Jr. "Premiums on Convertible Bonds." *Journal of Finance*, June 1968; also, "Premiums on Convertible Bonds: Reply." *Journal of Finance*, December 1972.

Stock Options

18

Introduction

In Chapter 17, we examined in detail three investment instruments—convertible bonds, rights, and warrants—which provide the holder with an option on the issuer's stock. In this chapter, we will consider options created by parties other than the company on whose stock the option is written. Such options have been bought and sold through dealers over-the-counter for many years. Only recently have they been listed on exchanges. This development has had a profound impact on the amount of option trading.

This chapter essentially covers three areas: (1) the working of the options market and the recent changes which have helped popularize options trading, (2) the determination of the value of options, and (3) various options trading methods and related considerations.

The Background

A *stock option* is a contract which gives the holder the right to buy (in the case of a *call option*) or to sell (in the case of a *put option*) 100 shares of stock at a specified price within a set period of time. For example, in December 1981, Investor A might purchase one GM March 60 Call, giving him the right to purchase 100 shares of GM stock at $60 a share before the expiration of the option in March 1982. The GM stock is known as the *underlying security*, and the $60 figure is referred to as the *striking price*. The writer of the option receives the price (called the *premium*) and is required to deliver 100 shares of GM stock at $60 per share if the holder of the option decides to exercise it.

An option carrying the right to sell stock to the option granter, or writer, is termed a *put* because it allows the buyer to put the stock to the writer. If Investor A purchased a GM March 60 put in December 1981, he would have an option to sell 100 shares of GM stock at the $60 striking price before the March 1982 *expiration date*. The writer of the put would, of course, be obliged to purchase the stock at $60 if the put option were exercised.

Stock options are now traded on a number of organized exchanges, including the Chicago Board Options Exchange, which is still the volume leader. Daily trading activity and prices are summarized in the financial pages of major newspapers. Table 18–1 shows a portion of the quotations for the Chicago Board Options Exchange from the December 5, 1979 issue of the *Wall Street Journal*.

Using the General Motors options as an example, we see that a number of GM options are being traded. These include put options as well as call options, with striking prices of $50, $60, and $70 a share, and with expiration dates in December 1979, March 1980, and June 1980. Looking specifically at the March 60 Call, we see that 225 contracts were traded that day, and the last price was 11/16, or $68.75 for an option on 100 shares. The closing price for General Motors stock was $51, which was $9 less than the striking price for this option.

Option trading on organized exchanges first began in 1973. Prior to the establishment of the *Chicago Board Options Exchange* (*CBOE*) in April of that year, buying and selling of stock options were done through over-the-counter dealers belonging to the Brokers and Dealers Put and Call Association. The market was quite fragmented and disorganized. If, for example, Investor A wanted to buy an option which was not being advertised by one of the dealers, he would call an investment firm to indicate the stock and expiration date in which he was interested. The firm would then look for an investor willing to write such an option. This was often a difficult and sometimes impossible task. Once a buyer and seller were matched, they would negotiate the option premium. If the option buyer decided later that he no longer wanted the contract, it could be very difficult to sell it in the secondary market. It was for these and related reasons that the old put-and-call market never became very large.

The CBOE[1]

Establishment of the CBOE led to dramatic changes in option trading. Most obviously, it created a central marketplace. This facilitated trading, the dissemination of information, and surveillance of the market. Other important

[1] For details on the operation of the CBOE, see *Option Trading on the Chicago Board Options Exchange* (Chicago: Chicago Board Options Exchange, 1973).

Table 18–1

Chicago Board

Option &	price	Dec Vol.	Dec Last	Mar Vol.	Mar Last	Jun Vol.	Jun Last	N.Y. Close
Bruns	..10	11	1⅝	74	2	75	2 5-16	11½
Bruns	..15	120	1-16	184	¼	98	9-16	11½
Dow Ch	25	28	7¼	11	7½	a	a	32
Dow Ch	30	414	2 5-16	203	3½	64	4⅜	32
Dow Ch	35	240	⅛	214	1 3-16	187	2	32
Dow Ch	40	a	a	20	¼	46	⅞	32
Ford	30	b	b	131	2¾	77	3¾	31⅛
Ford	...35	145	1-16	200	13-16	83	1¾	31⅛
Ford	40	a	a	29	¼	122	⅝	31⅛
Ford	...45	a	a	20	1-16	a	a	31⅛
Gen El	45	479	1⅝	29	3¼	1	4⅝	46
Gen El	50	182	1-16	114	1	56	2	46
Gen El	.55	a	a	12	¼	52	13-16	46
G M	50	953	1 13-16	272	4	174	5⅛	51
G M p	...50	1994	9-16	764	2⅜	136	3¼	51
G M	60	28	1-16	225	11-16	198	1½	51
G M p	...60	672	9	536	9	72	9⅜	51
G M	70	5	1-16	51	⅛	157	⅜	51
G M p	70	20	18¾	a	a	1	19¼	51
Glf Wn	.10	1692	8⅞	116	9⅛	b	b	19⅜
Glf Wn	15	5279	4⅜	2215	4¾	398	5⅛	19⅜
Glf Wn	20	5220	⅜	3666	1⅞	757	2½	19⅜
I T T	...25	252	1 5-16	43	2⅜	145	2 15-16	26⅛
I T T	...30	20	1-16	175	7-16	208	⅞	26⅛
K mart	20	27	5	b	b	b	b	24⅝
K mart	.25	108	½	93	1½	37	2 1-16	24⅝
K mart	.30	20	1-16	16	7-16	21	¾	24⅝
Kenn C	20	17	7¼	6	7½	b	b	26⅞
Kenn C	.25	524	2¼	201	3½	76	4½	26⅞
Kenn C	.30	348	3-16	476	1 5-16	176	2 3-16	26⅞
Mc Don	40	5	2⅝	65	4⅜	1	5¼	42½
Mc Don	45	110	5-16	78	1 13-16	a	a	42½
Mc Don	50	a	a	48	⅝	4	1½	42½
N C R	..60	129	4⅝	9	7⅝	a	a	64⅛
N C R	..70	45	⅜	93	2 13-16	a	a	64⅛
N C R	..80	a	a	14	15-16	5	1¾	64⅛
R C A	..20	a	a	9	3¾	a	a	23⅜
R C A	..25	107	3-16	62	1	68	1¾	23⅜
R C A	..30	a	a	20	3-16	b	b	23⅜
Sears	..15	a	a	15	3⅞	404	4⅜	18⅜
Sears	...20	121	1-16	164	⅞	70	1⅜	18⅜
Sears	..25	a	a	2	⅛	2	¼	18⅜
Syntex	..30	71	8⅞	88	10	5	9¾	38⅞
Syntex	..35	466	4¼	299	6⅛	105	6⅝	38⅞
Syntex	..40	1999	1 3-16	864	3⅜	68	4⅝	38⅞
Syntex	..45	529	⅛	667	1⅜	20	2½	38⅞
		– Jan –		– Apr –		– Jul –		
Alcoa	..50	23	3¾	a	a	3	6⅝	51⅝
Alcoa	...60	12	3-16	10	1¼	13	2	51⅝
Am Exp	30	a	a	10	2¾	a	a	31¾
Am Tel	.50	1	4	a	a	4	5⅝	53⅜
Am Tel	.55	191	11-16	260	1¾	32	2¾	53⅜
Am Tel	.60	4	1-16	4	¼	b	b	53⅜
Atl R	..60	45	21½	a	a	b	b	80½
Atl R	...70	100	11⅝	30	13½	4	14¼	80½
Atl R	...80	427	3⅞	124	6¼	9	8	80½
Avon	...35	b	b	8	5⅜	2	6	38½
Avon p	...35	b	b	130	13-16	18	1¼	38½
Avon	...40	478	1 3-16	71	2⅜	34	3⅜	38½
Avon p	..40	866	2	139	2 11-16	56	3¼	38½
Avon	...45	106	¼	154	1	106	1 9-16	38½
Avon p	..45	214	6⅜	136	6⅜	103	6¾	38½
Avon	...50	a	a	29	⅜	62	⅞	38½
Avon p	...50	38	11¼	11	11⅞	a	a	38½
BankAm	25	a	a	49	3	5	4⅛	26¾
BankAm	30	25	¼	44	⅞	16	1⅞	26¾
Beth S	.20	44	1⅛	76	1⅞	7	2⅝	20
Beth S	.25	22	⅛	25	7-16	31	⅞	20
Burl N	..50	1	9⅜	a	a	a	a	57¾
Burl N	.60	38	1⅞	26	4⅝	23	5⅞	57¾
Burl N	.70	33	¼	53	1⅝	b	b	57¾
Burrgh	..70	4	11½	a	a	a	a	80
Burrgh	.80	18	3¾	5	6⅛	a	a	80

The Exchange where the options are traded.

The Underlying Security

The "p" indicates the option is a put. Puts are currently traded on only a limited number of issues.

The Striking Price. Note that GM call and put options are available at striking prices of 50, 60, and 70.

The Premium, or market price of the option.

Expiration Date of the option is the Saturday following the third Friday of the month. Note that GM options are available with expiration dates in December 1979, March 1980, and June 1980.

The Volume, or number of contracts traded.

The Closing Price of the underlying stock on the New York Stock Exchange.

NOTE: The symbol "b" means that no options are offered for the given expiration date and strike price. The symbol "a" means that options are available but were not traded that day.

SOURCE: Quotations from *The Wall Street Journal*, December 5, 1979, p. 32. Reprinted by permission of *The Wall Street Journal*,

changes included the creation of the Options Clearing Corporation, the standardization of expiration dates and striking prices, and the resulting improvement of the secondary market.

The Clearing Corporation

One of the most significant outgrowths of the CBOE is the *Options Clearing Corporation* (*OCC*). The importance of the OCC's role can best be seen by tracing the steps of an option trade.

Suppose Investor A wants to sell a single GM March 60 call option and that Investor B (speculator) wishes to buy the same option. Each will place an order with a broker, and those orders will be transmitted to the floor of an exchange where that option is traded. There the broker representing the buyer will attempt to negotiate the premium with the broker for the option writer. However, as we shall see, the deal will *not* be closed by the writing of a call option and its direct delivery by the seller to the buyer.

A stock option transaction generates a set of contractual relationships. After the two brokers have negotiated the premium, the broker for the seller delivers a call option contract to the OCC, promising to deliver 100 shares of GM upon payment of $60 a share before the March 1980 expiration date, which is the first Saturday following the third Friday of the month, or, in this case, March 22. The OCC executes an identical call option contract for Investor B. With this, Investor B acquires the right to purchase 100 shares of GM from the OCC for the period of the option upon payment of the striking, or exercise, price of $60, and Investor A assumes a conditional obligation to deliver the same number of shares to the OCC. The OCC is a contractual intermediary in all exchange-traded stock options.[2]

The functions performed by the OCC are vital to the existence of a healthy secondary market for options. Option buyers want a good secondary market so they can sell their options before expiration. Option sellers (writers) want a good secondary market so they can, in effect, cancel out their positions by purchasing the same options they have sold.[3] For example, if the prices of both the option and the underlying stock are beginning to rise sharply and the writer of a call option expects this to continue, he can buy the same kind of

[2] When an option holder decides to exercise a call option, he calls his brokerage firm which, in turn, informs the OCC that it is exercising an option which it holds on that stock. To complete the exercise, the OCC proceeds to select, at random, a broker on whom it holds an identical option. That broker then selects one of its customers who has written call options to deliver the stock according to the terms of the option contract. The broker's selection can be made randomly or by any other reasonable method. Put options are exercised in a similar way.

[3] When a call option writer wishes to terminate an obligation to deliver stock prior to the expiration date of the option, he makes a "closing purchase transaction," also called "buying in." In this transaction, the writer buys an option with an identical striking price and expiration date. The outstanding option is then offset at the OCC with the option purchased in the closing purchase. A call option purchaser can terminate his position by writing an identical option in what is known as a "closing sale transaction." In any case, when an investor terminates a position as a writer or a buyer, no other investor holding an opposite position is affected.

option he previously sold. If a buyer wishes to exercise his option at any time, then the OCC is obligated to deliver the underlying stock to the exercising buyer.

Standardization of Exercise Dates and Striking Prices

To encourage option trading, the CBOE requires standardization of option contracts. In any year, there are only four potential expiration dates for options on the stock of any one company. Only the three nearest dates are open for trading at any one time. All options expire on the Saturday following the third Friday of the specified month. The option quotations in Table 18–1, for example, show that on December 5, 1979, only the GM options expiring in December 1979, March 1980, and June 1980 were available for trading.[4]

Standardized striking prices are established at 5-point intervals for stocks trading below 50, at 10-point intervals for stocks trading between 50 and 100, and at 20-point intervals for those above 100. When an option contract is initiated, the CBOE sets the striking price approximately equal to the price of the underlying stock. For example, if the market price of GM stock is 63 when trading is initiated for September options, the striking price will be set at 60. New striking prices are used for new options when the price of the underlying stock advances or declines sufficiently to warrant new prices. Referring to Table 18–1, if the price of GM were to decline below $50, options with a new striking price of $45 would be introduced.

The standardization of the terms of stock options concentrates trading in a small number of contracts for the stock of any one company, rather than spreading it out over hundreds of different contracts, as was the situation in the older over-the-counter market. As a result, the secondary markets are now considerably more active, and stock options are considerably more liquid than they were previously.

Growth in Options Trading

In 1973, when the CBOE was established, it sponsored trading in call options on 16 common stock issues, including the stocks of AT&T, ITT, Xerox, Ford Motor Company, Exxon, Sears, GM, and IBM. By 1979, the CBOE was joined by four other exchanges—the American Stock Exchange, the Philadelphia Stock Exchange, the Midwest Stock Exchange, and the Pacific Stock Exchange. By year-end, these five exchanges were sponsoring trading in call options of about 220 stock issues and put options on 25 of these issues.

The tremendous growth in option trading on the CBOE and other exchanges points to a bright future for the exchanges. In fact, the trading volume has grown consistently, from under 6 million call option contracts in 1974 to approximately 50 million in 1979.

---

[4] Other options expire in the months of January, April, July, and October, or the months of February, May, August, and November. These are called expiration cycles.

Table 18–2

A. **Closing Prices of IBM Call Options on September 1, 1978***
In dollars; per share optioned

Striking Price	Expiration Date Oct. 21 1978	Jan. 20 1979	April 21 1979
240	56.00	58.75	62.00
260	38.00	41.00	45.75
280	20.63	26.75	32.38
300	8.63	15.13	20.00

B. **Closing Prices of IBM Put Options on September 1, 1978***
In dollars; per share optioned

Striking Price	Expiration Date Oct. 21 1978	Jan. 20 1979	April 21 1979
240	.07	1.19	2.88
260	.56	3.75	6.50
280	3.63	9.00	11.63
300	11.63	17.00	20.25

* International Business Machines stock closed at $293.50 per share on the New York Stock Exchange on September 1, 1978.

SOURCE: Kenneth Garbade and Monica Kaicher, "Exchange-Traded Options on Common Stock," Federal Reserve Bank of New York, *Quarterly Review*, Winter 1978–79, p. 31.

The Value of an Option[5]

The Basic Concept

An option has value if its holder could profit by exercising it immediately, or if investors believe that a holder will be able to profit by exercising it before the expiration date.[6] If IBM stock is trading at, say, $293.50 per share,[7] an option to purchase the stock at a price of $240 per share is clearly a valuable right. An option to purchase the stock at $300 a share is also valuable to any investors who believe that the price of IBM stock will rise above $300 before the expiration date of the option.

Table 18–2 shows the closing prices for 12 different IBM call options and a similar number of put options on the CBOE on September 1, 1978. Table 18–2A shows that the price of a call option decreases as the striking

[5] This section is based upon Kenneth Garbade and Monica Kaicher, "Exchange-Traded Options on Common Stock," Federal Reserve Bank of New York, *Quarterly Review*, Winter 1978–79, pp. 27, 30–33.

[6] It is noted in Appendix 18–A of this chapter that, under one theory of option pricing, the price of an option is equal to the present value of the projected price of the option on its expiration date.

[7] On December 19, 1978, IBM announced a four-for-one stock split, to take effect on or after May 10, 1979. Following the effective date of the split, each outstanding exchange-traded option contract for 100 shares of IBM became four contracts for 100 shares each, with the striking prices equal to one quarter of the original striking prices. For example, the holder of one call option contract for 100 shares at $260 per share became the holder of four call option contracts for 100 shares each at $65 per share. The stock split had no impact on the economic position of either the writers or holders of IBM options. In the example in the body of the chapter, all IBM options expire *on or before* April 21, 1979; therefore, they are not affected by the stock split.

price of the option increases. An option to purchase IBM at a price of $260, for example, is more valuable than a call option with the same expiration date and a striking price of $280. The table also shows that the price of an option increases with the time to maturity of the option. An option to purchase IBM stock on or before April 21, 1979 provides more opportunity for capital gain than an option which expires on January 20, 1979. Table 18–2B shows that, because it is an option to sell, the value of a put option increases with the striking price as well as with the time to maturity.

Call Options—Intrinsic Value[8]

In Table 18–2, consider the IBM October 280 call option. Because IBM was trading at $293.50 at the close on September 1, 1978, the option had an *intrinsic value* of $13.50 a share. The intrinsic value of a call option is its value, before transaction costs, to an investor who would buy the option and exercise it immediately. If the market price of the stock, P_0, is greater than the striking or exercise price, P_s, a call option has positive intrinsic value, $P_0 > P_s$, and is said to be *in-the-money*. If the stock's current market price is less than the striking price, $P_0 < P_s$, the option has zero intrinsic value and is *out-of-the-money*. The IBM October 300 call option shown in Table 18–2 was out-of-the-money and had zero intrinsic value on September 1, 1978.

The market price, or the premium, of an unexpired option will nearly always be equal to or greater than its intrinsic value. If the option price falls below the intrinsic value, net of transaction costs, arbitrageurs will buy the options, exercise them, and immediately sell the stock.[9] Such riskless arbitrage prevents the option price from falling substantially below the intrinsic value of the option. Table 18–3 shows the intrinsic values of the 12 call option contracts shown in Table 18–2. All of the option prices exceed the corresponding intrinsic values.

Call Options—Time Value

Market participants are usually willing to pay more than the intrinsic value for an option, because they expect the market price of the stock (and the intrinsic value of the option) to increase before the option expires. The amount by which the market price (premium) of an option exceeds its intrinsic value is its *time value*.

[8] During the three years ending in 1979, put options were available on only 25 stocks—five at each of the five options exchanges. In early 1980, however, the SEC announced its plans to allow put trading on all the stocks for which call options were traded. However, because trading in call options remained more popular than trading in put options, this section on option valuation and the following sections on options trading discuss only call options.

[9] *Arbitrage* is the simultaneous purchase and sale of identical securities at different prices in different markets or the simultaneous purchase and sale of securities which are thought to be substitutes for one another in the same market. In an intrinsic value arbitrage, the purchase of the option and simultaneous sale of the stock will yield a profit at no risk and is, therefore, called *riskless arbitrage*. Other arbitrage activities may involve risk, but are nevertheless undertaken if their anticipated profits far outweigh their risks.

Table 18–3

Intrinsic Values of IBM Call Options on September 1, 1978*
In dollars; per share optioned

Striking Price	Oct. 21 1978	Expiration Date Jan. 20 1979	April 21 1979
240	53.50	53.50	53.50
260	33.50	33.50	33.50
280	13.50	13.50	13.50
300	0	0	0

* Computed as the greater of (a) zero and (b) the difference between the closing stock price of $293.50 and the strike price of the option.

SOURCE: Kenneth Garbade and Monica Kaicher, "Exchange-Traded Options on Common Stock," Federal Reserve Bank of New York, *Quarterly Review*, Winter 1978–79, p. 31.

That options should have a positive time value can be easily understood by considering out-of-the-money options with zero intrinsic value, $P_0 < P_s$. Most out-of-the-money options are clearly not worthless; some investors believe there is a chance that the market price of the stock will move above the striking price before the expiration date. As revealed in Tables 18–2 and 18–3, the premium for an IBM October 300 call option was $8.63 per share on September 1, 1978, even though the underlying stock was trading at less than $300 per share and had a zero intrinsic value. Investors believed it was possible for the stock price to rise above $300 during the fifty days remaining until the expiration date.

Table 18–4

Time Values of IBM Call Options on September 1, 1978*
In dollars; per share optioned

Striking Price	Oct. 21 1978	Expiration Date Jan. 20 1979	April 21 1979
240	2.50	5.25	8.50
260	4.50	7.50	12.25
280	7.13	13.25	18.88
300	8.63	15.13	20.00

* Computed as the difference between the closing option price in Table 18–2A and the intrinsic value of the option in Table 18–3.

SOURCE: Kenneth Garbade and Monica Kaicher, "Exchange-Traded Options on Common Stock," Federal Reserve Bank of New York, *Quarterly Review*, Winter 1978–79, p. 31.

Table 18–4 shows the time values of the twelve IBM call option contracts. Observe that the time values of options with a common striking price increase with the length of time to expiration. This shows that "time" really is a valuable aspect of an option.

The Total Value

Figure 18–1 shows the relation between call option prices and stock prices, both expressed as a percentage of the option striking price, for IBM options with three different expiration dates. On its expiration date, the price of an option will lie on the intrinsic value line. Prior to that date, the value of an option varies with the price of the underlying stock, approximately as shown in the figure. The option price/stock price curve shifts closer to the intrinsic value line as the expiration date approaches. This downward shifting shows

Figure 18–1 **Estimated Values of IBM Call Options as a Function of the Stock Price on September 1, 1978***

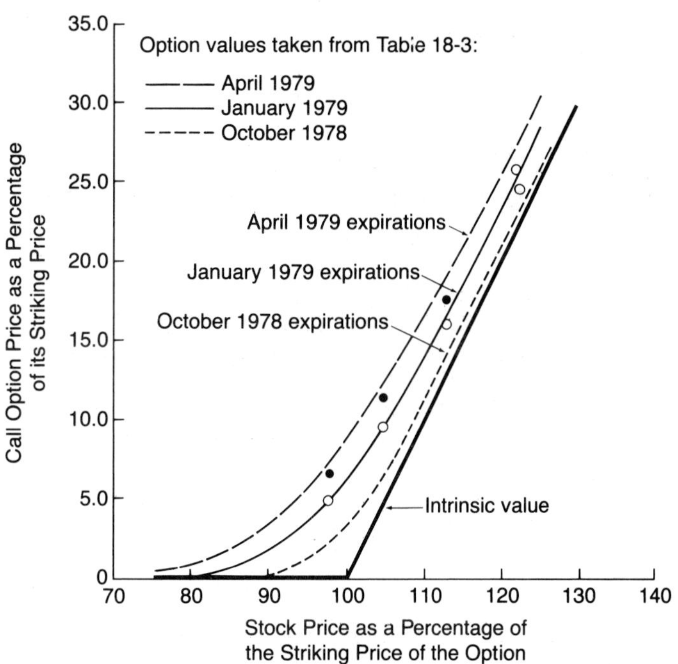

* See Appendix 18–A for method of estimation.

SOURCE: Kenneth Garbade and Monica Kaicher, "Exchange-Traded Options on Common Stock," Federal Reserve Bank of New York, *Quarterly Review*, Winter 1978–79, p. 33.

why market participants sometimes refer to an option as a *wasting asset.* If the price of the stock does not rise, the value of an option declines as it approaches the expiration date.

The option price/stock price curves shown in Figure 18–1 were computed from a theoretical model of option pricing derived from the Fischer Black and Myron Scholes model, now in general use by participants in the options markets. Interestingly, only a hand calculator is necessary to estimate the value of an option using the Black–Scholes model. In fact, several programmable hand calculators now have magnetic strips precoded with the formula. As soon as the key values are supplied to it, such a calculator can automatically estimate the value of a given option. For those who wish to use the Black–Scholes model on a large scale, several more sophisticated electronic information systems are available.

Briefly, the Black–Scholes model is based on the assumption that if taxes and transaction costs are ignored, an investor could adjust hedge positions almost constantly. The model derives the value of a call option from (1) the price of the underlying stock, (2) the striking price of the option, (3) the time remaining to the expiration of the option, (4) the level of interest rates, and (5) the volatility of the price of the underlying stock. The model is widely used to search for situations in which the prevailing option prices are different from their respective theoretical values. The Black–Scholes model is described in Appendix 18–A.

Option Price/Stock Price Relationships

Figure 18–1 also plots the values of the 12 IBM call options shown in Table 18–2. Although the option price/stock price curves in Figure 18–1 are based on a theoretical model, the proximity of the actual IBM option prices to their predicted values suggests the model is reasonably accurate.

Suppose, for example, that the price of IBM common stock increases on the NYSE, but the IBM option prices remain unchanged on the CBOE. The option price/stock price curves imply that the options have become "undervalued"—that is, below their theoretical values derived from the now higher price of the underlying stock. This may lead some market participants to buy the options and, if they want to hedge their risk, sell the stock short. Their transactions drive up the price of the options relative to the stock price. Such arbitrage activity will continue until the predicted option price/stock price relationships are reestablished.[10]

In conclusion, it may be stated that the option price/stock price curves in Figure 18–1 illustrate a price level equilibrium between the stock and options markets. The curves do not give any hint, however, as to whether price changes will first appear in the stock market or in the options market.

[10] Because clearing charges and other transactions costs are incurred in trading both stock and options, an option price/stock price discrepancy must be large enough to permit an arbitrageur to make a profit net of those costs. Therefore, there is a region around the "equilibrium" option value within which the actual option price can fluctuate freely without inducing arbitrage activity.

Options Trading: Basic Methods

The options market provides opportunities for many kinds of investment strategies, especially since the introduction of puts in the trading market. This section deals with the basic methods of buying and selling call options. An understanding of these methods is essential for pursuing more advanced trading techniques.

Purchasing Call Options

The Concept of Leverage

The lure of purchasing either call or put options is *leverage*. If the price of a stock rises substantially during the term of an option, an investment in the option may yield a much higher return than an investment in the underlying stock. On the other hand, an option purchase exposes an investor's capital to greater risk.

Consider the following example. In December 1980, the stock of XYZ Company is selling at $40. Investor A feels that the stock price will increase substantially in the near future; however, instead of buying 100 shares of the XYZ stock for $4,000, she purchases ten March 40 calls at 4, which means $400 for each option on 100 shares. The $4,000 investment in options gives Investor A the right to buy 1,000 shares of XYZ stock at $40 per share any time before the options expire in March. By investing $4,000 in options instead of in the stock, Investor A has, in effect, acquired an interest in ten times as many shares of the stock of XYZ. However, this interest may end up being worth nothing if the price of the stock does not rise and the options are never exercised.[11]

Call Options at Expiration

Continuing with the above example, the risks and potential rewards of purchasing calls can be illustrated by assuming that the options are held until expiration. At expiration, the market value of the option will be no greater than its intrinsic value, because the time value will have disappeared.

Table 18–5 compares the potential profits and losses from investing in XYZ options with the results from investing in XYZ stock.[12] Part 1 shows a range of possible stock prices at the expiration date of the options. When the stock price is above the striking price, the options are exercised. Part 2 shows the

---

[11] All call options will not provide this same leverage. Given a stock price, the leverage will increase as the premium declines, because more options can be purchased for a given amount.

[12] For simplicity, taxes and transaction costs are omitted from the discussion.

Table 18–5

Part 1			Part 2 100 Share Stock Purchase $40 per Share		Part 3 Options to Purchase 1,000 Shares (10 XYZ 40 Calls Purchased for $400 Each)			
(1) XYZ Stock Price at Expiration	(2) Striking Price of Call Options	(3) Options Exercised?	(4) Profit or (Loss) on Stock	(5) Return (Loss) on $4,000 Investment	(6) Profit from Exercising Options	(7) Options Cost	(8) Profit Less Options Cost	(9) Return (Loss) on $4,000 Investment
0	$40	No	($4,000)	(100)%	0	($4,000)	($4,000)	(100)%
$ 20	40	No	(2,000)	(50)	0	(4,000)	(4,000)	(100)
30	40	No	(1,000)	(25)	0	(4,000)	(4,000)	(100)
40	40	No*	0	0	0	(4,000)	(4,000)	(100)
41	40	Yes	100	2.5	$ 1,000	(4,000)	(3,000)	(75)
42	40	Yes	200	5	2,000	(4,000)	(2,000)	(50)
43	40	Yes	300	7.5	3,000	(4,000)	(1,000)	(25)
44	40	Yes	400	10	4,000	(4,000)	0	0
45	40	Yes	500	12.5	5,000	(4,000)	1,000	25
50	40	Yes	1,000	25	10,000	(4,000)	6,000	150
60	40	Yes	2,000	50	20,000	(4,000)	16,000	400
70	40	Yes	3,000	75	30,000	(4,000)	26,000	650
80	40	Yes	4,000	100	40,000	(4,000)	36,000	900
100	40	Yes	6,000	150	60,000	(4,000)	56,000	1,400

* Assume that options will only be exercised if the stock price *exceeds* the striking price.
Note: Taxes and transaction costs are ignored.

profit or loss that would be realized from the purchase of 100 shares of stock at $40 a share, and the positive or negative percentage return on the $4,000 investment. Part 3 shows the profit and loss picture for the call options. Note that although the options can be exercised at a profit when the stock price is over $40 per share, the investor will not break even until the profit covers the $4,000 cost of the options. In this case, the price of XYZ stock must exceed $44 for a profit to be made (Column 8). If the price of XYZ stock is at or below $40 at the time of expiration, the options will not be exercised and the *entire* investment will be lost.

Table 18–5 also demonstrates that if an investor seeks higher returns by investing in options rather than stock, he must be prepared to assume greater risks.[13] This can be clearly seen by comparing Columns 5 and 9. For example, if the stock reaches $45 before the expiration date, the sale of the stock will yield a profit of only 12.5 percent as compared to a profit of 25 percent when the options are exercised. However, if the stock price declines to, say, $30 when the options expire, the entire investment in options will be lost, whereas by selling the stock the investor will incur a loss of only 25 percent.

[13] The option purchaser can limit losses by purchasing fewer options. However, the percentage gain or loss on investment will remain the same. In this sense, an option purchase will always be riskier than the stock purchase.

Trading Before Expiration

Option holders frequently terminate their contracts in the secondary market prior to the expiration date in order to realize a gain or limit a loss. Before the date of expiration, options command a *time value.*[14] Consider again the example of the XYZ stock and the March 40 calls. Assume that by the end of February, XYZ stock rises from $40 to $46 per share, an increase of 15 percent, while the call options advance from 4 to 7, a gain of 75 percent. Each call option now has an intrinsic value of 6 ($46 – $40) and a time value of 1 ($7 – $6). At this time, Investor A could close out her contracts in the secondary market for $7,000 and capitalize on the increase in the premium. She also has the choice of holding on to the options in the hope that the premium will increase further as a result of an increase in the stock's price. However, she must recognize that, if the stock price remains unchanged at $46 until the option expires, the time value will disappear, thereby resulting in a decrease of $1,000 ($7,000 – $6,000) in the value of her options. Furthermore, if the stock price were to drop below $40 by the expiration date, the entire intrinsic value would be lost.

Let us continue with the previous example. Suppose Investor A inaccurately predicts the performance of the XYZ stock during the December–March period. By February, if the stock price declines by 5 percent to $38, the call options with only about a month remaining until expiration, would probably sell under 1—a decline of over 75 percent. Investor A could then continue to hold her options in the hope that the stock price would rise by the third Friday in March. However, she should recognize that the value of the call would now be only the time value, and this would decline as the expiration date draws near. The option would eventually become worthless if the XYZ stock stayed at or below the $40 striking price. If Investor A saw little chance for the price of the stock to rise above $40 soon, she might be wise to terminate the contract, thereby limiting her losses.

Writing Call Options

Remember that the option writer *collects* an option premium for contracting to deliver 100 shares of a specified stock at a predetermined striking price during some specified time interval. Therefore, whereas the purchaser of a call option speculates that the underlying stock price will rise substantially prior to the expiration date, the writer speculates that the stock price *will not* record a significant increase. Incidentally, investors can write either uncovered (naked) or covered calls; writing uncovered calls is a speculative trading strategy, writing covered calls constitutes a conservative approach to option writing.

Uncovered Calls

An investor writing an *uncovered call does not* own the underlying stock he or she is contracting to deliver at the striking price. As a result, the potential for losses can be large if the stock price advances.

---

[14] However, when an option trades deep in-the-money, it may sell at, or slightly higher than its intrinsic value.

Table 18–6

Part 1			Part 2: Options to Deliver 1,000 Shares (10 XYZ Calls Written—$400 Premium Collected on Each Option)		
(1) XYZ Stock Price at Expiration	(2) Striking Price of Call Options	(3) Options Exercised by Holder?	(4) Loss on Stock Delivered to Option Holder	(5) Premium Received	(6) Premium Less Loss on Stock
0	$40	No	0	$4,000	$ 4,000
$ 20	40	No	0	4,000	4,000
30	40	No	0	4,000	4,000
40	40	No*	0	4,000	4,000
41	40	Yes	($ 1,000)	4,000	3,000
42	40	Yes	(2,000)	4,000	2,000
43	40	Yes	(3,000)	4,000	1,000
44	40	Yes	(4,000)	4,000	0
45	40	Yes	(5,000)	4,000	(1,000)
50	40	Yes	(10,000)	4,000	(6,000)
60	40	Yes	(20,000)	4,000	(16,000)
70	40	Yes	(30,000)	4,000	(26,000)
80	40	Yes	(40,000)	4,000	(36,000)
100	40	Yes	(60,000)	4,000	(56,000)

* Assume that options will only be exercised if the stock price *exceeds* the striking price.
Note: Taxes and transaction costs are ignored.

Consider the XYZ March 40 calls selling in December for a premium of 4, with the price of the XYZ stock at $40. Investor B writes 10 call options on the stock and collects $4,000 ($400 × 10). In selling these options, he promises to deliver 1,000 shares of XYZ stock at $40 per share any time before the March expiration date.[15]

Table 18–6 shows the potential profits and losses for the option writer over a range of stock prices at the date of expiration. As shown in Part 1, the holder of the call options will only exercise them if the stock price exceeds the striking price (Column 3). Should the stock price decline *below $40* and remain there until expiration, Investor B will not have to deliver the stock and, as revealed in Part 2, he will make a $4,000 profit from the option premium (Column 6).

Let us now consider a different situation in which the price of the XYZ stock advances to, say, $60 before the expiration date. When the option is exercised, Investor B will have to buy 1,000 shares of XYZ at $60 per share and deliver them to the option purchaser for $40 per share. The resulting loss will be $20,000 on the shares delivered minus the $4,000 premium initially received, or a net loss of $16,000 (Column 6). In this example, the XYZ stock price can rise to $44 per share before Investor B sustains a loss. Note that although the maximum profit the investor can make is only the $4,000 premium he collects (Column 5),

[15] Selling uncovered calls, as demonstrated in this example, is essentially a form of leveraged short selling.

there is no limit to the potential loss he may suffer (Column 6). For this reason, writing uncovered calls is considered a speculative strategy.

In the above example, it was assumed that the writer of the uncovered calls had no other alternative than to wait for the options to expire. That, of course, is not the case. Uncovered option writers can realize a profit or limit a loss by later purchasing the same option on the exchange, thereby offsetting or cancelling out the original option. For example, suppose that in late February, the XYZ stock rises to $46 and the call option premium reaches 7. If Investor B feels that the XYZ stock will continue to advance, he can purchase 10 XYZ March 40 calls for $7,000 ($700 × 10). The originally written and newly purchased calls will cancel each other, thus relieving Investor B of his obligation to deliver the XYZ stock. In this case, his loss would be $3,000—that is, the $7,000 purchase price minus the $4,000 collected as premium.

Covered Calls

Investors write *covered calls* when they own the shares of the underlying stock that they are contracting to deliver before the expiration date. Covered call writing is a *conservative* strategy, because it is primarily a means of earning additional income from a stock investment. This additional income provides a downside protection from price movements in the underlying stock.

Assume Investor B has purchased 1,000 shares of XYZ stock at a cost of $40 per share. Hoping to earn additional income on this investment, he writes 10 XYZ March 40 calls for a premium of 4, thereby receiving premium income of $4,000 ($400 × 10). If the stock price remains unchanged at $40 and the option expires worthless, Investor B can consider the entire $4,000 premium as additional income which supplements any dividends received during this period. However, by writing this option, Investor B gives up the potential gain from an appreciation in the stock price above the striking price, because an exercise of the call forces him to deliver the stock at the striking price of $40 a share. Of course, Investor B does have the choice of writing a call with a *higher* striking price. However, in that case, he would collect a smaller premium, because the higher striking price would make the option worth less to an option buyer.

In this example, the $4,000 premium income can be considered a form of downside protection against a decline in the XYZ stock price. Should XYZ stock fall to $36 per share, for example, the call options will expire worthless and the $4,000 premium received will make up for the $4,000 decline in the market value of the stock. Covered call writing can thus be used to reduce the risk of stock ownership. Put differently, in this strategy, the price appreciation is limited by the striking price of the call option, and any loss is reduced by the amount of the premium received. This concept is illustrated in Figure 18–2. The figure shows a comparison of the potential per share profit or loss at expiration for an investment in XYZ stock and the covered call sale described in the foregoing example. Note that for the covered call, the profit ceiling is $4 per share and the breakeven stock price is $36, which is $4 *below* the current market price. The covered call strategy is preferable to the strategy of investing only in the stock if the stock price is not expected to rise above the $44 level.

Figure 18–2

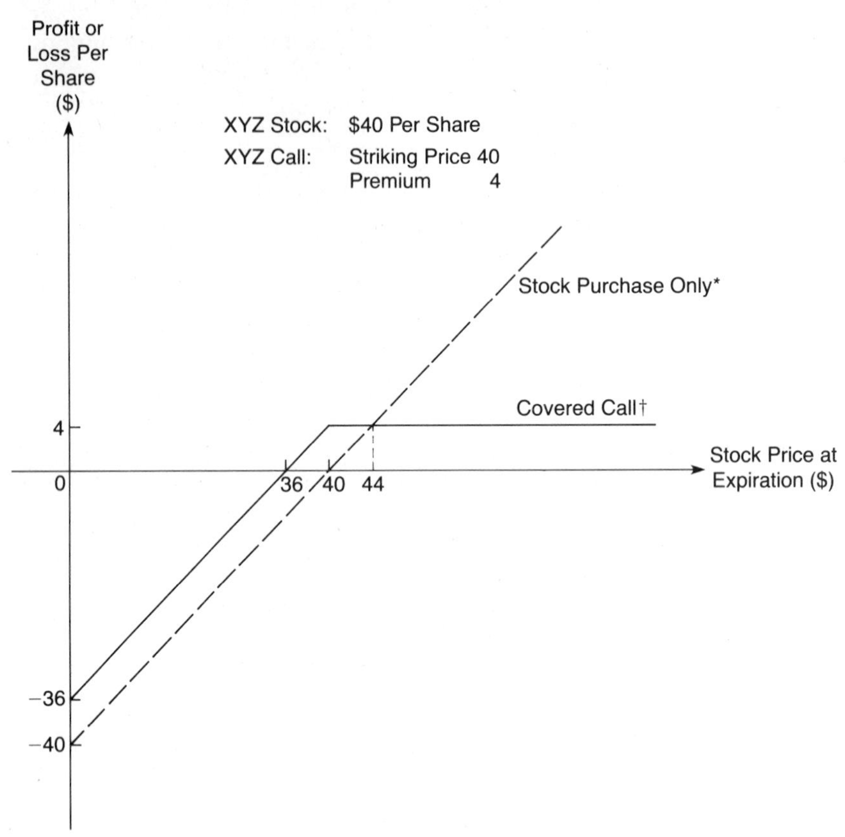

* Assume no dividends paid on stock.
† One XYZ call is written for every 100 shares of XYZ stock owned.

Additional Considerations

Selection of Striking Price

In the previous examples, the options were purchased or written with a striking price equal to the current market price of the stock, or *at the money*. However, that need not necessarily be the case. An investor can also purchase or write other types of options, known as out-of-the-money and in-the-money. The relationship between the striking price of an option and the market price of the related stock is a major determinant of the riskiness of an option.

Of the three types of options previously mentioned out-of-the-money options are the riskiest *to purchase*, because they will become worthless if the stock price does not exceed the striking price when the options expire. An option is less risky to purchase when it trades in-the-money, because it may maintain some intrinsic value even with a decline in the stock price. The premiums for out-of-the-money options are, of course, smaller and the potential rate of return greater than with in-the-money options.

An example will illustrate this point. Assume that XYZ stock is trading at $43\frac{1}{2}$, and an investor has the choice of purchasing one of the following four calls: XYZ 40 at $5\frac{1}{4}$; XYZ 45 at $2\frac{3}{8}$; XYZ 50 at $\frac{7}{8}$; and XYZ 60 at $\frac{1}{8}$. All are assumed to have the same expiration date. Table 18–7 shows the intrinsic value of each call option at various stock prices. For each option, the table also specifies the percentage return or loss on the premium paid. Note that the option that is the deepest out-of-the-money, XYZ 60, provides the largest possible return of 3,900 percent (Column 9). However, in order for this option to become profitable, the stock price must move from $\$43\frac{1}{2}$ to over \$60; otherwise, the entire investment in the option would be lost. The lower the striking price, the smaller will be the possibility of sustaining a loss, but also the smaller the potential percentage return on the investment. The in-the-money call option, XYZ 40, clearly has the least leverage and is the least risky of the four options under review (Column 3).

For the covered call writer, a lower striking price lowers the risk associated with a decline in the price of the stock, but increases the probability that the option will be exercised, depriving the writer of any gain from an increase in the price of the stock.

An *uncovered* call writer's risk and reward combination is the reverse of the risk–reward combination of a call buyer. The more an option is in-the-money when it is written, the greater its risk and reward. Conversely, the deeper the option is out-of-the-money, the smaller is its risk and reward. When the option

Table 18–7 **XYZ Call Options (Stock Price at $43\frac{1}{2}$)**

Stock Price Moves to:	Option: XYZ 40		XYZ 45		XYZ 50		XYZ 60	
	Premium: $5\frac{1}{4}$		$2\frac{3}{8}$		$\frac{7}{8}$		$\frac{1}{8}$	
	Description: In-the-Money		Close-to-the-Money		Out-of-the-Money		Out-of-the-Money	
(1)	(2) Intrinsic Value	(3) Return (Loss) on Investment*	(4) Intrinsic Value	(5) Return (Loss) on Investment*	(6) Intrinsic Value	(7) Return (Loss) on Investment*	(8) Intrinsic Value	(9) Return (Loss) on Investment*
\$35	0	(100)%	0	(100)%	0	(100)%	0	(100)%
40	0	(100)	0	(100)	0	(100)	0	(100)
45	\$ 5	(5)	0	(100)	0	(100)	0	(100)
50	10	90	\$ 5	111	0	(100)	0	(100)
55	15	186	10	321	\$ 5	471	0	(100)
60	20	281	15	532	10	1,043	0	(100)
65	25	376	20	742	15	1,614	\$5	3,900

* Return (Loss) on Investment = [(Intrinsic Value − Option Premium)/Option Premium].
Note: Taxes and transaction costs are ignored.

is out-of-the-money, the option writer receives only a small premium for the call, but the stock price must have a significant upward move before the writer will have to deliver the required shares and suffer a loss. When the option is in-the-money, the writer collects a larger premium. However, the more the option is in-the-money, the greater the probability that the option will be exercised, requiring the writer to buy the stock in the market and sell it to the option holder at a loss.

Referring to the previous example, an uncovered call writer's risk associated with the XYZ 60—the deepest out-of-the-money option—is lowest. Note that the stock price must increase from $43\frac{1}{2}$ to over $60\frac{1}{8}$ before the writer will suffer a net loss on his options investment. Because he received a $\frac{1}{8}$ premium for writing the call, the stock price must rise by more than $\frac{1}{8}$ above the \$60 striking price before a loss is incurred. In contrast, the option writer's risk in the XYZ 40 is the highest, even though he collects a larger premium of $5\frac{1}{4}$ for writing the call. The stock price need only increase from $43\frac{1}{2}$ to over $45\frac{1}{4}$ (or $5\frac{1}{4}$ points above the \$40 striking price) before he would incur a loss from writing the option.[16]

Selection of Expiration Date

Investors also have alternatives in terms of the expiration date of an option, which is yet another important determinant of an option's risk. For an investor purchasing a call option, all else being equal, the closer the expiration date of an option, the greater is its risk and reward. If a call is trading out-of-the-money, for example, an imminent expiration date allows little time for the stock price to rise high enough (above the striking price) to give the call a positive intrinsic value. Consequently, in this case, the risk of losing the entire investment is greater than it would be in a comparable situation where the expiration date was further away. It should be noted, however, that because call options with close expiration dates command small premiums, these options provide the investors a potential for earning higher percentage returns than those with longer expiration dates.

Covered call writers also find options with shorter expiration dates to be risky. The smaller premium from these options provides less downside protection from a decline in the price of the stock related to the option. Of course, in such cases, the writers are exposed for a shorter period of time; that is, in writing options with short expiration dates, these writers limit their appreciation potential for a shorter period of time. In contrast, the uncovered call writer faces higher risk when selling calls with *longer* expiration dates. The reason is obvious: Longer expiration dates allow more time for the stock price to increase, which increases the loss potential for the writer.

[16] Note that the option would be exercised at any price above 40 before expiration; however, if the writer must deliver the stock at a price below $45\frac{1}{4}$, the loss from purchasing the stock and selling it to the option holder would be less than the premium he received. Thus he would still have a net gain from writing the option.

Options Trading: Advanced Methods

Spreading

The options market lends itself to many sophisticated investment strategies. One such strategy is known as spreading. *Spreading*, or the simultaneous purchase and sale of different option contracts, is an arbitrage of relative values between two options rather than between an option and the underlying stock. It is usually undertaken by floor traders on an options exchange, because their access to trading in options is quicker than the access of off-floor arbitrageurs. The speed with which transactions can be completed is an important consideration in spreading, because spread positions are subject to a variety of risks. Specifically, in addition to the risks associated with option purchase and writing, spread positions are subject to certain special risks. These include (1) difficulty of execution, (2) risk of exercises, and (3) higher risks due to the closing out of one side of a spread transaction. A brief description of the special risks follows.

First, spread orders require the simultaneous execution of both a purchase and a writing transaction. Consequently, within the time limits designated by the investor, these orders might become more difficult to execute than those for regular options. Second, an option writer who is forced to purchase or deliver the underlying stock is no longer in a spread position, but continues to hold the option on the other side of the spread and is therefore subject to the risks of that position.[17] Third, certain of the advantages of maintaining a spread position may be lost if the investor liquidates either side of the spread in a closing purchase or sale transaction. For example, if as a result of the closing out of one side of the spread an investor becomes an uncovered writer of an option, he may receive a margin call, because he will no longer have the privilege of using special margin requirements applicable to certain spread positions.

The technique of spreading can be explained with an example. Assume XYZ stock is selling at $50 per share and two XYZ call options are trading on the market: An XYZ March 50 call is offered at 4 and a March 55 call at $1\frac{1}{2}$. An investor *purchases* one March 50 call for $400 and simultaneously *sells* one March 55 call for $150. His net cost is the *spread* between the two options—$2\frac{1}{2}$ or $250 ($400 – $150). Subsequently, the price of XYZ stock rises to $58, and the premiums on the March 50 and March 55 options increase to 10 and 4, respectively. The spread having widened from $2\frac{1}{2}$ to 6 (10 – 4), the investor decides to realize a profit by *selling* the March 50 call and *buying back* the March 55 option in the secondary market. Technically, the investor bought a $2\frac{1}{2}$ point

[17] Unless, of course, the investor exercises the option held either to obtain the underlying security for delivery in the case of a call spread, or to dispose of the underlying security in the case of a put spread. If the market value of the option held in the spread reflected significant time value, exercise of the option would result in loss of that value. The investor could completely eliminate his risk by buying back or selling the remaining portion of the spread.

spread and sold it for 6, with a resulting profit of $350:

March 50 Call		March 55 Call	
Purchased	($400)	Sold	$150
Sold	$1,000	Purchased	($400)
Profit	$600	Loss	($250)
Net Profit: $600 − $250 = $350			

This operation is known as a *bull price spread*, because the investor anticipates a rise in the price of the underlying stock and a widening in the gap between the two options. The reason for a widening of the gap due to an increase in the stock's price can be explained by means of the following illustration:

	March 50 Option			March 55 Option		
Stock Price	**Original Price**	**Price After Stock Price Increase**	**Percentage Change**	**Original Price**	**Price After Stock Price Increase**	**Percentage Change**
$50	4			$1\frac{1}{2}$		
$58		10	150%		4	166.67%

Even though the percentage increase in both options is approximately equal, because the March 50 option has a higher premium base than the March 55 option, any increase in the price of the underlying stock results in a widening of the gap between the *premiums* of the two options. Note that the investor could have purchased only the March 50 call and realized a $600 profit in this situation; however, by engaging in a bull price spread the maximum loss was limited to the $250 net cost of the options. By only purchasing a March 50 call at 4, the potential loss would have been $400.

The investor could have reversed the original buy–sell cycle; that is, had he *bought* the March 55 call at $1\frac{1}{2}$ and sold the March 50 call at 4, he would have collected a $250 net premium. This is called a *bear price spread*; it is created when the investor does not expect the underlying stock to increase in price. If the stock price remains at $50 or below, the spread between the options will narrow and eventually disappear on the expiration date. If the options expire worthless in this example, the investor will make a $250 profit on the net premium collected. If, on the other hand, the stock price rises, a loss will be incurred; however, this loss will not be as great as would be the case if only the March 50 call is sold.

A variant of the price spread, known as the *calendar spread*, refers to the simultaneous purchase and sale of options with the same exercise price, but with different expiration dates. As it is for the price spread, the idea here is to initiate a calendar spread when the spread is narrow and close it down as soon as the spread sufficiently widens, thereby making a profit. Note that a calendar spread is like a bull price spread in that the spread is expected to widen.

Spreads can also be created in several other different ways in order to satisfy investors with a taste for almost any risk–return combination. Many of these spreads are quite complex. The spreads described in this section, however, illustrate the basic framework for developing more sophisticated spread strategies.

Hedging[18]

Premiums earned by an option seller from writing options provide a hedge against price declines, because a decline in the market price of the underlying stock is offset to the extent of the premium. The technique of reducing the loss potential resulting from a price decline is known as *hedging*.

It was previously demonstrated that an investor can provide *limited* downside protection against stock price declines by writing covered calls on as many shares as he or she actually owns. An investor wishing to hedge *fully* a long stock position against small price changes, however, must write options on more stock than he or she owns.

Figure 18–1 demonstrated that call option prices and stock prices are positively related. However, they do not always move in lockstep with each other. Unless an option is deep in-the-money, a $1 change in the price of the underlying stock will produce a less than $1 change in the option value.[19] Expressed another way, on one share, the ratio of the *change* in the dollar price of an option per $1 *change* in the stock price will be less than 1.0. This ratio is known as the *hedge ratio*,[20] and is the key to the development of a strategy to protect against the risk of small changes in the stock price.

To better understand how writing call options can reduce the risk on a stock position, consider writing January 280 calls against a position in IBM stock. As shown in Table 18–8, on September 1, 1978 a $1 increase or decrease in the price of IBM stock would have been accompanied by approximately a $0.77 increase or decrease in the price of the January 280 call option.[21] Suppose an investor owned 10,000 shares of IBM stock and wrote calls on 13,000 shares of the stock. If her stock decreased in value by $1 per share, the options would decrease in value by $0.77 per share optioned. The investor could then repurchase the options which she previously wrote, at a cost $10,000 less than the

[18] This section borrows heavily from, and in part reproduces, Kenneth Garbade and Monica Kaicher, "Exchange-Traded Options on Common Stock," Federal Reserve Bank of New York, *Quarterly Review*, Winter 1978–79, pp. 33–36.

[19] Although a $1 change in the price of the underlying stock may produce a less than $1 change in the option premium, the percentage change in the option value will be greater. Therefore, this discussion is still consistent with the earlier statements that options are leveraged investments.

[20] Hedge ratios range from zero to one. Although options deep in-the-money move lockstep with the stock price and have a hedge ratio equal to 1.0, options for out-of-the-money have ratios at or close to zero.

[21] The figure of $0.77 is an estimate generated by the Black–Scholes model.

Table 18–8 **Estimated Hedge Ratios for IBM Call Options on September 1, 1978***

Change in dollar price of an option on one share per $1.00 change in the stock price

Striking Price	Oct. 21 1978	Expiration Date Jan. 20 1979	April 20 1979
240	1.00	.98	.96
260	.97	.91	.88
280	.81	.77	.77
300	.46	.56	.61

* See Appendix 18–A for method of estimation.

SOURCE: Kenneth Garbade and Monica Kaicher, "Exchange-Traded Options on Common Stock," Federal Reserve Bank of New York, *Quarterly Review*, Winter 1978–79, p. 31.

revenues she received when she wrote them ($10,000 = 13,000 shares optioned × $0.77 per share optioned). This gain just balances the decline in the value of her stock. Conversely, had the price of IBM stock increased by $1 a share, the investor would have gained $10,000 on her stock position and lost $10,000 on her option position. Note that the short position in options is a hedge against the risk of small changes in the price of the underlying stock. The decision to write calls on 13,000 shares, rather than on 14,000 shares or 12,000 shares, is based on this balancing or hedging—that is, 13,000 = 10,000/0.77.

Although investors can protect their stock position against small stock price changes, they can still sustain losses if there is a large stock price change, because hedge ratios tend to decrease as the price of the stock increases. Therefore, the only way to *completely* avoid the risk of unanticipated price change is to sell the stock. Also, when hedging in the manner described here, investors must closely watch the price of the stock, because hedge ratios are likely to change with fluctuations in the price of the related stock.

Tax Considerations

The Buyer

From the point of view of the buyer, the option represents a capital asset, and the premium is treated as a nondeductible capital expenditure. Any gain or loss in a closing sale transaction, such as a resale in the secondary option market, is treated as a short-term capital gain or loss. If a buyer exercises the option and acquires the stock, the option cost and the commission are added to the exercise price to arrive at the cost of the stock. The law states that the holding period of the stock begins the day the option is exercised, not the day the option is purchased.

The Writer

The tax liability of an option writer depends primarily on the way in which the option is terminated. If the option is allowed to expire, the premium constitutes ordinary income, which is assumed to have been earned on the expiration date. If the option is exercised by the buyer, the premium received by the writer is treated as part of the proceeds from the sale of the underlying stock and is taken into account in calculating the writer's capital gain or loss on the stock. In order for a premium to qualify as a long-term gain, the underlying stock must be held for over one year. Finally, if the writer closes out his or her position by buying back the option, the differences between the premium originally received and the amount paid in closing out the transaction is treated as ordinary income or loss and is assumed to have been earned or lost on the day the transaction is closed.

Summary

A *stock option* is a contract allowing a trader to buy or sell 100 shares of stock at a specified price during a specified period of time, regardless of the market price of that stock. There are two basic types of option contracts: calls and puts.

A *call option* gives the holder the right to purchase from the writer of the option 100 shares of a specified stock—called the *underlying stock*—at a designated *striking price* on or before an expiration date.

A *put option* involves the right to sell a stock. The put option holder can sell 100 shares of some underlying stock to the writer of the put option, before the expiration date, at a designated striking price.

Call options have a positive value because investors believe that sometime before the option expires the price of the underlying stock will be higher than the price at which it can be purchased by exercising the option. The value of an option depends on its *striking price* and *expiration date.*

The excess of the current stock price over the striking price is called the *intrinsic value* of the option. If an option has a positive intrinsic value, it is said to be *in-the-money*. If the stock price is less than the striking price, it has zero intrinsic value and is said to be *out-of-the-money*.

An option commands a premium over its intrinsic value if investors believe that the market price of the stock (and the intrinsic value of the option) will sufficiently increase before the expiration date to enable the holder to realize a profit. When the market price of an option exceeds its intrinsic value, the option is said to have a positive *time value.*

Investors *purchasing* calls make a *leveraged* investment in the underlying security; that is, a purchase of call options controls more shares than an equal investment in the stock. Although there are exceptions, when the price of an underlying stock goes up, frequently the call option shows a greater percentage increase. However, if the price of the stock declines or remains stable, call options increase exposure to losses.

Investors can *write* (sell) uncovered or covered call options. Writing an *uncovered call* is a speculative strategy used when the writer expects a decline in the price of the underlying stock. *Covered call writing* is a conservative strategy which reduces the risk of stock ownership.

Options on a stock are available with various strike prices and expiration dates. The choice of a strike price and expiration date can reduce or increase the risk of an option purchase or sale.

More advanced option trading strategies include spreading and hedging. *Spreading* involves the simultaneous trading of different option contracts. *Hedging* is a technique involving the sale of call options to avoid the risk of small price changes of a stock.

A Look Ahead

This chapter was basically an analysis of stock options. A number of diversified investment instruments will be discussed in Chapter 19.

Concepts for Review

Stock option
Call option
Put option
Underlying stock
Striking price
Option premium
Expiration date
CBOE
Options Clearing Corporation
Intrinsic value
In-the-money
Out-of-the-money
Time value
Total value
Options and leverage
Option writing
Covered call
Uncovered call
Bull price spread
Bear price spread
Hedging
Hedge ratio

Questions for Review

1. How is the CBOE different from the original over-the-counter option market? What major factors differentiate them?
2. What is the Options Clearing Corporation? Why is it called a contractual intermediary?
3. Explain why an option has value.
4. How does the price of a call option vary with the striking price? The time to maturity? How does the price of a put option vary with the striking price? The time to maturity?
5. What is the intrinsic value of an option? Would anyone ever purchase an option with zero intrinsic value? Explain.
6. Why is an option called a wasting asset?
7. Explain the concept of leverage as it relates to call options.
8. A broker explains the attractiveness of purchasing call options as follows: "Purchasing call options is the perfect investment. You can earn a much higher return than an investment in the underlying stock, but there is much less risk. Losses are limited to only the price you pay for the option." What is your response?
9. Investor Z states that an option cannot sell at a price above its intrinsic value on the expiration date. What is your reply?
10. Investor C says, "Stock options are for speculators." Comment on this statement.
11. Why would the volatility of an underlying stock be an important consideration when purchasing or writing an option? When purchasing a call option, would a more volatile underlying stock make the option riskier?
12. Investor K purchases a call option on Amerada Hess stock in June 1981. The shares are currently trading at $55 per share. Which of the following options would be the riskiest to buy: A November 40, November 50, or a November 60? If she writes an uncovered call on this stock, which of the following options would be least risky: A July 50, November 50, or a February 50? Explain your answers.
13. Explain the difference between writing covered and uncovered call options.
14. What is a bull price spread? Why would an investor engage in such a spread instead of simply buying a call option?
15. Investor M wishes to hedge his long position in Mesa Petroleum stock. Would you recommend that he write call options to accomplish this? Under what circumstances?

Problems

1. A Boeing November 30 call option is selling for $7\frac{1}{4}$ ($725). The stock is selling for $35\frac{7}{8}$.
   a. What is the intrinsic value of the option?
   b. What is the time value?
   c. What will happen to the value of the option if the price of Boeing stock remains stable until the expiration date?

d. Assume Investor Q purchases a call option and will hold it until expiration. Compare his potential percentage return from the call option with his potential percentage return from Boeing stock over the same period. Consider the following possible stock prices at the expiration date in your computations: \$20, \$30, \$35, \$40, \$50, and \$60.

e. Repeat part (d) of this problem, assuming that Investor Q purchases a Boeing November 40 call option at $1\frac{3}{4}$ (\$175).

2. Referring to the previous problem, assume that Investor Q writes a Boeing November 30 covered call.
   a. Compare his potential profits and losses, at expiration, from writing the covered call and simply holding 100 shares of Boeing stock. Use the same stock prices at expiration as in part (d) of the previous problem.
   b. What is Investor Q's maximum possible profit and loss?
   c. Repeat parts (a) and (b) of this problem, but assume that Investor Q writes a November 40 covered call.
   d. Would it be more conservative to write a November 30 or a November 40 covered call?

3. Referring to Problem 1, calculate the potential profits and losses from writing a Boeing November 30 and November 40 uncovered call option. Use the same stock prices at the expiration date as in part (d) of that problem. Which of these options is riskier to write?

4. Investor H holds a Revlon September 45 call option which she purchased at $4\frac{3}{4}$ (\$475). It is the last day of the option's life and Revlon stock is trading at $47\frac{3}{8}$.
   a. Should she exercise the option?
   b. For what range of stock price on Revlon should Investor M exercise the call?
   c. For what range of stock price on Revlon would Investor M realize a net loss (including the premium paid for the option)?

Selected Readings

Black, Fischer. "Fact and Fantasy in the Use of Options." *Financial Analysts Journal*, July–August 1975.

Black, Fischer, and Myron Scholes. "The Pricing of Options and Corporate Liabilities." *Journal of Political Economy*, May 1972.

Black, Fischer, and Myron Scholes. "The Valuation of Option Contracts and a Test of Market Efficiency." *Journal of Finance*, May 1972.

Boness, A. J. "Elements of a Theory of Stock Option Value." *Journal of Political Economy*, April 1964.

Brody, Eugene D. "Options and the Mathematics of Defense." *Journal of Portfolio Management*, Winter 1975.

Connelly, Julie. "How Institutions Are Playing the Options Game." *Institutional Investor*, February 1972.

Cox, John C., and Stephen A. Ross. "The Valuation of Options for Alternative Stochastic Processes." *Journal of Financial Economics*, January–March 1976.

Dimson, Elroy. "Instant Option Valuation." *Financial Analysts Journal*, May–June 1977.

Ederington, Louis H. "Living With Inflation: A Proposal for New Futures and Options Markets." *Financial Analysts Journal*, January–February 1980.

Galai, Dan. "Pricing of Options and the Efficiency of the Chicago Board Options Exchange." Unpublished Ph.D. dissertation, University of Chicago, March 1975.

Galai, Dan. "Tests of Market Efficiency and the Chicago Board Options Exchange." *Journal of Business*, April 1977.

Garbade, Kenneth, and Monica Kaicher. "Exchange-Traded Options on Common Stock." Federal Reserve Bank of New York, *Quarterly Review*, Winter 1978–79.

Gastineau, Gary L., and Albert Madansky. "Why Simulations are an Unreliable Test of Option Strategies." *Financial Analysts Journal*, September–October 1979.

Gould, J. P., and D. Galai. "Transaction Costs and the Relationship Between Put and Call Prices." *Journal of Financial Economics*, July 1974.

Gross, LeRoy. *The Stockbroker's Guide to Put and Call Option Strategies.* New York: Institute of Finance, 1974.

Hausman, W. H. "Theory of Option Strategy Under Risk Aversion." *Journal of Financial and Quantitative Analysis*, September 1968.

Hettenhouse, George W., and Donald Puglisi. "Investor Experience With Put and Call Options." *Financial Analysts Journal*, July–August 1975.

Katz, Richard C. "The Profitability of Put and Call Option Writing." *Industrial Management Review*, Fall 1963.

Kruizenga, Richard J. "Profit Returns from Purchasing Puts and Calls." In *Random Character of Stock Market Prices.* Ed. Paul Cootner. Cambridge, Mass.: MIT Press, 1964.

Malkiel, Burton G., and Richard E. Quandt. *Strategies and Rational Decisions in the Securities Options Market.* Cambridge, Mass.: MIT Press, 1969.

Merton, Robert E. "The Relationship Between Put and Call Option Prices: Comment." *Journal of Finance*, March 1973.

Merton, Robert E. "The Theory of Rational Option Pricing." *The Bell Journal of Economics and Management Science*, Spring 1973.

Merton, Robert E., Myron S. Scholes, and Matthew L. Gladstein. "The Returns and Risk of Alternative Call Option Portfolio Investment Strategies." *Journal of Business*, April 1978.

Merton, Robert E., Myron S. Scholes, and Matthew L. Gladstein. "A Simulation of Returns and Risk of Alternative Option Portfolio Investment Strategies." *Journal of Business*, April 1978.

Miller, Jarrot T. *Options Trading.* Chicago: Henry Regnery Co., 1975.

Noddings, Thomas C. *CBOE Call Options: Your Daily Guide to Portfolio Strategy.* Homewood, Ill.: Dow Jones-Irwin, 1975.

Option Trading on the Chicago Board Options Exchange. Chicago: Chicago Board Options Exchange, 1973.

Platnick, Kenneth. *The Option Game: Puts and Calls and How to Play Them.* New York: Communi-Concepts, 1975.

Puglisi, Donald J. "Rationale for Option Buying Behavior: Theory and Evidence." *Quarterly Review of Economics and Business*, Spring 1974.

Reback, Robert. "Risk and Return in CBOE and AMEX Option Trading." *Financial Analysts Journal*, July–August 1975.

Rosen, Lawrence R. *How to Trade Put and Call Options.* Homewood, Ill.: Dow Jones-Irwin, 1974.

Smith, Clifford W., Jr. "Option Pricing: A Review." *Journal of Financial Economics*, January–March 1976.

Smith, Keith V. "Option Writing and Portfolio Management." *Financial Analysts Journal*, May–June 1968.

"Some New Approaches to Playing the Options Game." *Institutional Investor*, May 1975.

Stoll, Hans R. "The Relationship Between Put and Call Option Prices." *Journal of Finance*, December 1969.

Wellemeyer, Marilyn. "The Values in Options." *Fortune*, November 1973.

Zieg, Kermit C., Jr. *The Profitability of Stock Options*. Larchmont, N.Y.: Investors Intelligence, 1970.

Appendix 18-A: The Black-Scholes Option Pricing Model*

In 1973, Fischer Black and Myron Scholes advanced a model for valuing call options on securities such as common stock.[1] Their model has since become widely accepted and used by financial market participants. The authors showed that the value of a call option depends on five parameters: (1) the price of the underlying stock, denoted S; (2) the striking price of the option, denoted E; (3) the time remaining to the expiration of the option, denoted t; (4) the level of interest rates, denoted r; and (5) the volatility of the price of the underlying stock, denoted v. The stock price, S, and the option striking price, E, are measured in dollars per share and the time, t, remaining to expiration is measured in years or fractions thereof. The interest rate, r, is usually taken as the rate on high-quality commercial paper having a maturity comparable to the expiration date of the option. The stock price volatility, v, is measured as the variance per year of the natural logarithm of the stock price.

The Black–Scholes model for the dollar value, C, of a call option is:

$$C = S \cdot N[d_1] - E \cdot N[d_2] \cdot e^{-rt}$$

*Reproduced from Kenneth Garbade and Monica Kaicher, "Exchange-Traded Options on Common Stock," Federal Reserve Bank of New York, *Quarterly Review*, 1978–79, p. 40.

[1] Fischer Black and Myron Scholes, "The Pricing of Options and Corporate Liabilities," *Journal of Political Economy*, 81 (May–June 1973), pp. 637–54.

where

$$d_1 = \{\ln[S/E] + (r + v/2)t\}/\{vt\}^{\frac{1}{2}}$$
$$d_2 = d_1 - \{vt\}^{\frac{1}{2}}$$
$$N[x] = (2^{\text{II}})^{-\frac{1}{2}} \int_{-\infty}^{x} e^{-u^2}\, du$$

Figure 18–1 (p. 769) shows the predicted values of call options on IBM stock computed from the Black–Scholes model for three different values of t. In that figure, option values are expressed as a percentage of the striking price of the option—that is, as the ratio C/E. The stock price is also expressed as a percentage of the striking price, or as the ratio S/E. The interest rate was set at 8.5 percent per annum, or $r = 0.085$. This is approximately the rate on high-quality commercial paper that prevailed at the beginning of September 1978.

The only unobservable variable in the Black–Scholes model is the stock price volatility, v. This variable can be estimated by computing the value of v, which leads to a predicted option price equal to the actual market price of the option.[2] When this was done for the 12 call options on IBM on September 1, 1978, the average v was .0372. This implies that there was approximately a 66 percent chance that the price of IBM stock would vary in one day by less than 1 percent of its previous closing price.[3] The value of $v = .0372$ was used to compute the option values shown in Figure 18–1. The volatility parameter can also be estimated from the historical price volatility of a stock if one is willing to assume that the future price volatility will resemble the historical volatility.

Clifford Smith has pointed out that the Black–Scholes option pricing model may be interpreted as the *expected intrinsic* value of an option, on its expiration date, multiplied by a discount factor which converts that future value to a present value.[4] The expected future intrinsic value depends on the probability that the option will expire in-the-money, and therefore depends on the volatility of the underlying stock. Other things being equal, options on more volatile stocks have a higher probability of expiring with a greater in-the-money value than options on more stable stocks. Therefore, the value of an option increases with stock volatility.

[2] This method of obtaining the volatility parameter is discussed by Richard Schmalensee and Robert Trippi, "Common Stock Volatility Expectations Implied by Option Premia," *Journal of Finance*, 33 (March 1978), pp. 129–47.

[3] The variance of the log of the price of IBM stock is 0.0372 per year, or .000102 per day (.000102 = 0.0372/365). The standard deviation of the change in the log of the stock price over a one-day interval is therefore .0101 [$.0101 = (.000102)^{\frac{1}{2}}$], or about 1 percent. Because the probability that a normally distributed variable will be less than one standard deviation from its mean is about 66 percent, the probability that the price of IBM will change by less than 1 percent in value in one day is about 66 percent.

[4] Clifford Smith, Jr., "Option Pricing: A Review," *Journal of Financial Economics*, 3 (January–March 1976), pp. 3–51, footnote 22.

The Black–Scholes pricing model is frequently used by market participants to estimate the hedge ratio and the elasticity of an option. The hedge ratio is defined as the ratio of simultaneous *dollar* changes in option and stock prices. It can be shown that the hedge ratio of an option is $N[d_1]$. This result was used to compute the entries of Table 18–8 (p. 782). The elasticity of an option is defined as the ratio of simultaneous *percentage* changes in option and stock values. From the Black–Scholes model, this ratio is $S \cdot N[d_1]/C$. The values of the hedge ratio and elasticity of an option both depend on the volatility parameter. Because that parameter cannot be estimated without error and because a particular estimate depends on the method of estimation, the computed hedge ratio and elasticity can only be viewed as imperfect estimates of the true values.

Appendix 18-B: Instant Option Valuation*

A nomogram based on the Black and Scholes model is presented in Figure 18–A. Let us closely examine the essentials of this nomogram.

Suppose an investor is valuing an eight-month call option and that the stock has an annual standard deviation of 60 percent, the risk-free rate of interest is 10 percent, the share price is $52, and the exercise price is $40. First, in Figure 18–A the investor draws a vertical line through the maturity of the option, which is eight months in this case. This line will intersect the curves representing an annual standard deviation of 60 percent and the risk-free rate of interest of 10 percent.

Second, the investor draws a horizontal line from the point of intersection between the line and the curve representing the interest rate of 10 percent through to the right-hand side of the nomogram. This line will pass through the curves representing share price as a percentage of exercise price. The example defines a ratio of 130 percent (100 × $52/$40). So, for the third step, the investor draws a vertical line from the point of intersection with the 130 percent curve up to the top of the nomogram.

For step four, the investor must go back to the original line drawn through the maturity of the option. From the intersection of that line with the curve representing the appropriate standard deviation (in this case, 60 percent), she

* This discussion is based on Elroy Dimson, "Instant Option Valuation," *Financial Analysts Journal*, May–June 1977, p. 62–69.

Figure 18–A

Valuing a Call Option

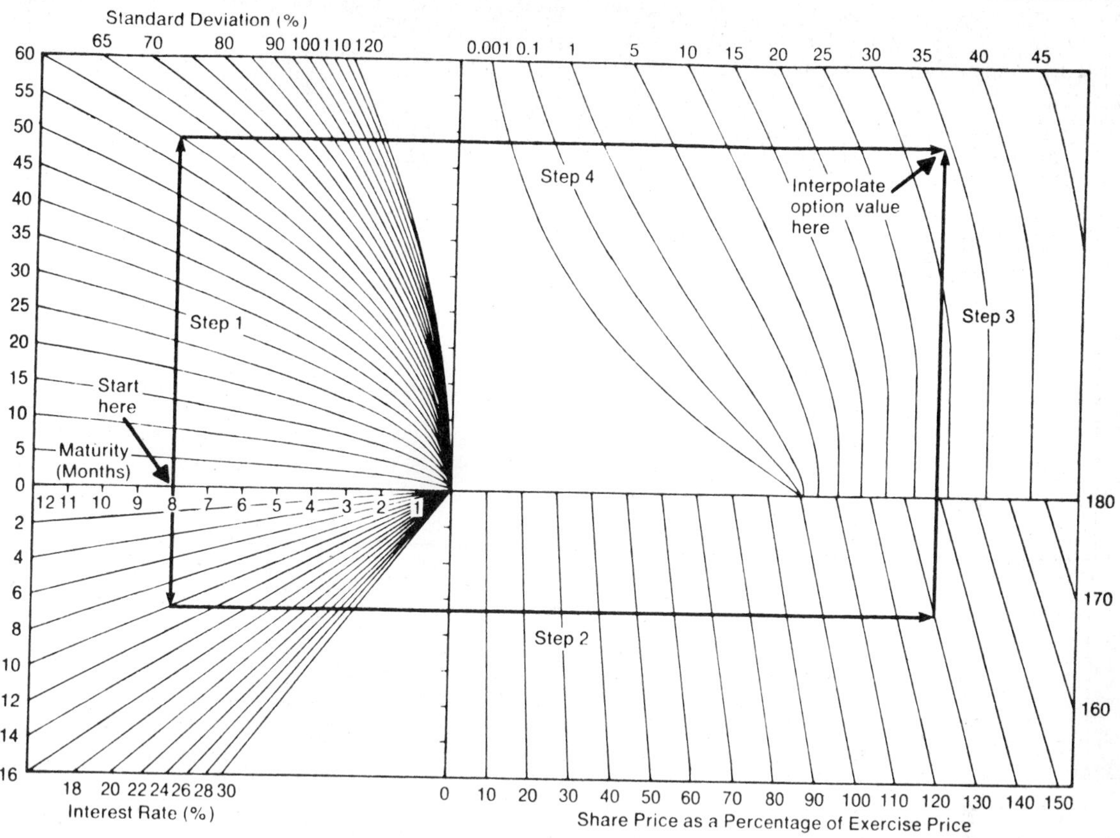

SOURCE: Elroy Dimson, "Instant Option Valuation," *Financial Analysts Journal*, May–June 1977, p. 64

draws a line that extends into the upper right-hand quadrant. This line will intersect the vertical line drawn through that quadrant, and the point of intersection of the two lines represents the value of the call option. In this example, the value is 34 percent of the share price; the option is therefore worth \$17.68 (\$52 × .34).

Although the current share price, exercise price, and interest rate can be known with certainty, the investor can only estimate standard deviation. The nomogram, however, enables her to examine the impact of changes in the estimated standard deviation on the option value. She can do this simply by drawing alternative horizontal lines through plausible alternative values of the standard deviation. Using this example, standard deviations of 55 percent and 65 percent would result in option values of about 33 and 35.1 percent of the share price, or \$17.16 and \$18.25, respectively.

The illustration just presented assumes that the standard deviation of the stock as given. In the real world, however, a stock's future standard deviation is never known; therefore, a nomogram can be used *in reverse* to estimate the standard deviation of an underlying stock.

Assume the following data are given:

Time remaining until expiration:	9 months
Current market price of stock:	\$24
Exercise price:	\$20
Option price:	\$6
Market interest rate:	8 percent

The volatility or standard deviation can be estimated by using Figure 18–B, as follows.

Figure 18–B **Estimating the Standard Deviation Implied by a Call Option**

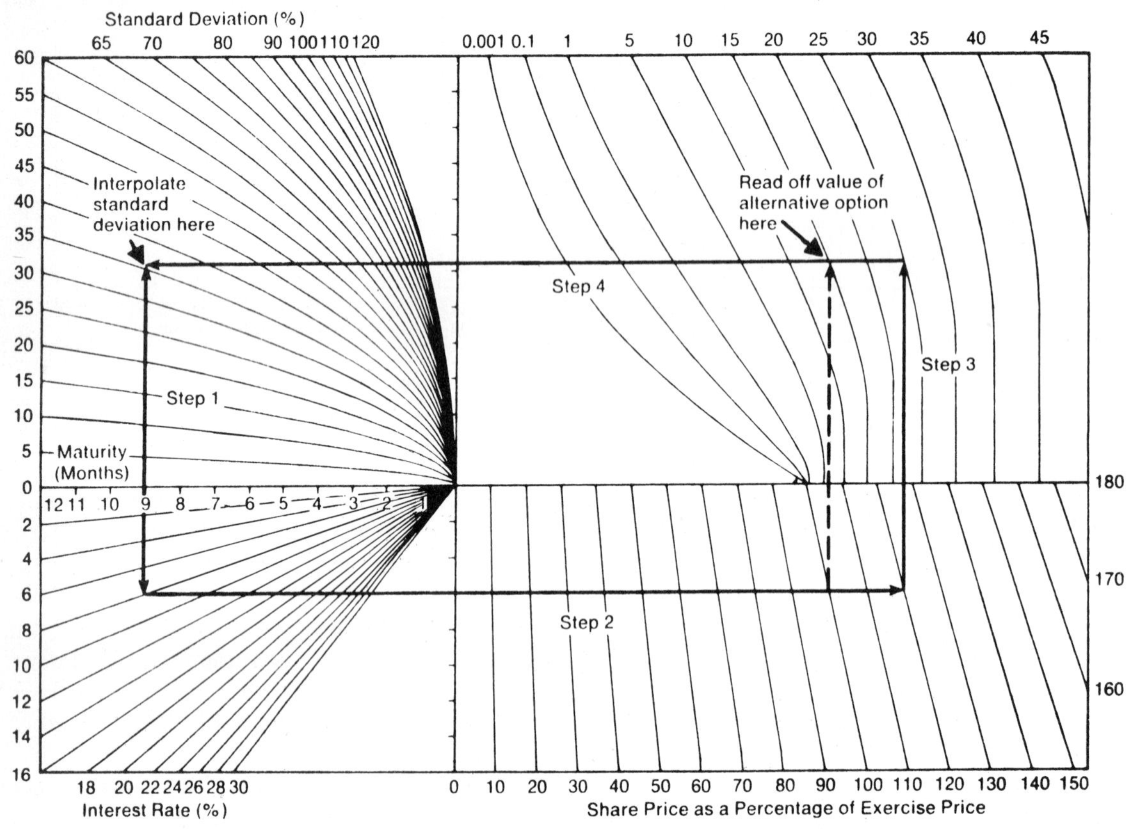

SOURCE: Elroy Dimson, "Instant Option Valuation," *Financial Analysts Journal*, May–June 1977, p. 64.

In Figure 18–B, first a vertical line is drawn through the nine-month maturity, a horizontal line is drawn through the intersection of the latter with the 8 percent interest rate, and a vertical line is drawn through its intersection with the curve corresponding to share price as a percentage of exercise price (in this case, 120 percent). Because the option price is known to be 25 percent of the share price, a horizontal line can be drawn through the intersection of the 25 percent curve with the vertical line. The final step is to interpolate the standard deviation (36.8 percent) from the upper left quadrant of the nomogram.

With Figure 18–B, the investor can value any option on the stock, provided it is of the same maturity. The dotted line in Figure 18–B illustrates the valuation of an option for which exercise price is equal to the current share price; it is worth 15.3 percent of the share price, or $3.67.

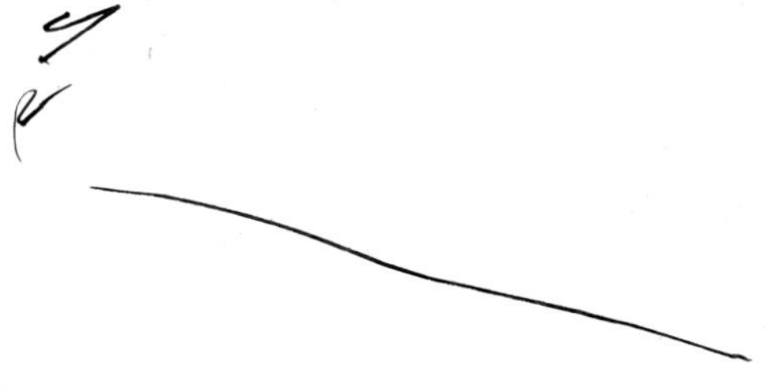

Diversified Investments

Introduction

Chapters 17 and 18 were devoted to a discussion of two specialized forms of investment—convertible securities and stock options. This chapter covers a group of diversified investments, each with its unique investment characteristics.

The discussion in previous chapters has proceeded along the following lines. A valuation model has first been presented. Thereafter, a given investment instrument has been analyzed within the framework established by the valuation model. Because of the nature of the investment instruments being discussed here, in this chapter our method of presentation will be significantly different. More specifically, this chapter is divided into three sections concerning real estate; commodities futures; and precious metals, art and antiques. Each section begins with an overview of the investment instrument, followed by a set of guidelines for investing in that instrument. The discussion concludes with a few investment caveats.

SECTION 1 REAL ESTATE

An Overview

Following the 1974–75 recession, the real estate industry experienced an uninterrupted boom that lasted through the end of the decade. As revealed in Figure 19–1, the growth was enjoyed by all types of real estate investment,

Figure 19–1

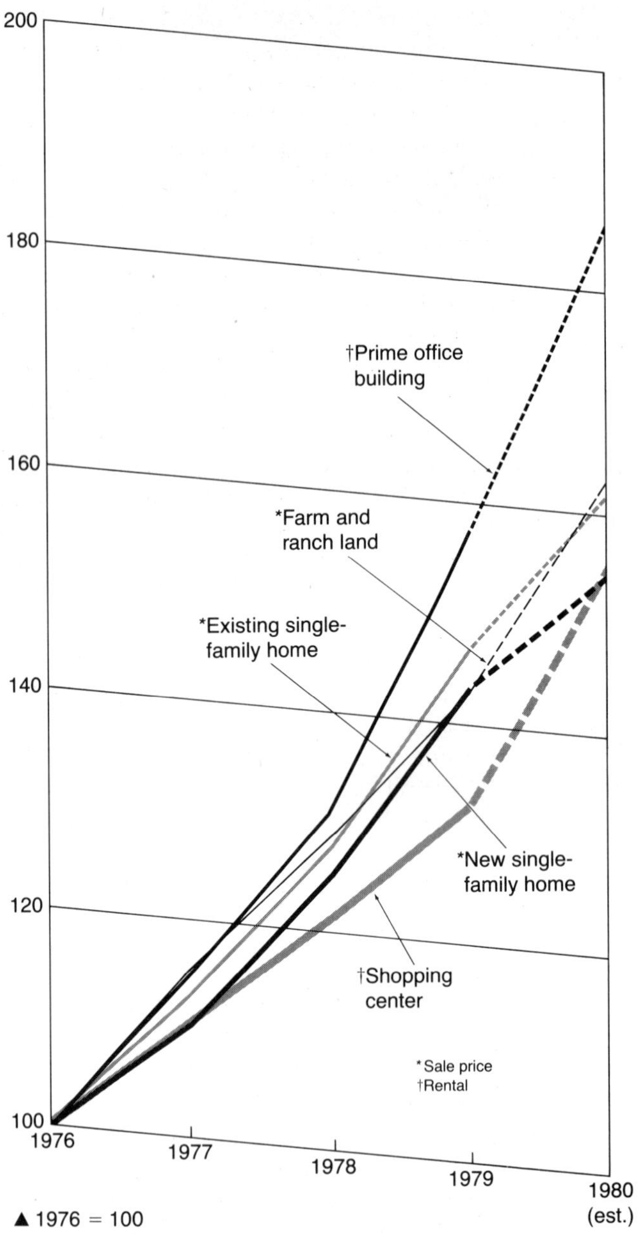

SOURCE: *Business Week*, December 31, 1979, p. 138.

although the surge in the prime office building category was the most impressive.

Many factors contributed to the spectacular growth of the real estate industry. Investors, wary of world-wide inflation, a continued weakening in the value of the dollar, and a dismal showing in the equity market, turned to real estate for investment. Also, as continued rise in personal income pushed investors into higher tax brackets, many became interested in real estate as a tax-sheltered investment. Some investors purchased apartments built under various federal programs. These investments were tailored almost entirely toward sheltering income from other sources and therefore were purchased mostly by syndicates for resale to investors in high tax brackets. Others invested in officially designated landmark structures that were converted for new use in the hope of generating income that was sheltered from federal income tax. Still others invested in office buildings and other real estate projects for sheltering their income.

In the beginning of 1980, the torrid real estate boom of 1976–79 appeared to be slowing down. High interest rates kept growth in commercial development considerably lower than in past years. As the economy slowed, leasing of commercial space and the big rent increases of past years also moderated, and prices and yields on commercial properties diminished. However, real estate continued to provide a good investment outlet for those investors who had the financial ability and the skill to spot unusual investment opportunities.

Types of Real Estate Investment

Residential Property

One of the most popular and most important forms of real estate investment is residential property. The natural real estate investment for most people is the single-family home or condominium. Owning a home has several tax advantages. First, interest payments on the mortgage and property taxes are fully deductible. Second, if owned for more than a year, any realized gains in the value of the house are taxed at favorable capital-gains rates. Third, a homeowner can defer realizing a capital gain by buying another, more expensive, home. Fourth, if a homeowner is over fifty-five when the home is sold, $100,000 of the gains are tax exempt.

There are risks in investing in residential property as well. In an inflation-stricken economy, adoption of a tight money policy dries up the supply of funds to housing. High and increasingly volatile long-term rates cause a massive shift of funds from the long-term, fixed-rate market to other markets. A continuous increase in the prices of homes (156 percent between 1969–1979) makes it progressively more difficult for most people to own homes. Another risk is the potential for a significant drop in real estate prices after a sharp rise in real estate prices, such as occurred in the late 1970s. Other specific risks include lack of liquidity and diversity in residential investment, ever-increasing taxes on residential property, and a possible change in the size and type of homes in which people might invest in the future. Despite these risks, reasonably priced residential property in a good location continues to provide an attractive form of investment for many people.

REITs

The passage of an act of Congress in 1960 revived interest in the type of group real estate investment known as *real estate investment trusts*, or *REITs*. These institutions are exempt from taxation if they (1) have 75 percent of their assets in real estate, mortgages, cash, or government securities at the end of each quarter; (2) derive 75 percent of their gross income from real estate; (3) distribute 90 percent of their income to shareholders (officially known as beneficiaries); and (4) have at least 100 shareholders, no five of whom can control more than half of the shares. In exempting the REITs from taxation, the lawmakers intended that these institutions be publicly held and that they be instrumental in diverting public funds primarily into the real estate industry.

Shares of REITs are generally readily marketable, especially those listed on national or regional stock exchanges. Because a REIT is, in effect, a closed-end investment company, its price is determined in the open market. The price of REIT shares may be above or below the actual book value of the real estate holdings. There are many types of REITs on the market. Some emphasize equity investment; others specialize in investment in mortgages.

Syndicates and Limited Partnerships

Syndicates facilitate the raising of capital and the sharing of investment risks. A syndicate is usually formed by a real estate manager who raises capital from individual investors. A syndicate offers the inexperienced real estate investor an opportunity to participate in a large real estate venture.

Syndicates are frequently organized as limited partnerships in which the risks of limited partners are limited to their investment in these partnerships. If the partnership qualifies as such, there is no double taxation on real estate limited partnerships; moreover, accounting losses may affect taxes due on any income distributions and may also offset income from other sources. However, limited partnership interests often are not readily marketable. The three main objectives of real estate limited partnerships are to offer tax shelter, provide tax-free cash flow, and convert ordinary income into long-term capital gains which receive favorable tax treatment.[1]

[1] For details, see William C. Drollinger, *Tax Shelters and Tax-free Income for Everyone*, 3rd ed. (Orchard Lake, Mich.: Epic, 1977), pp. 19–78.

Real Estate Investment: A Conceptual Framework

The limited supply of land relative to the ever-increasing demand for it, rapid inflation, and the dismal showing of the stock market in the 1970s are the key factors that have contributed to a booming real estate market. However, a conceptual framework is still a prerequisite for a successful investment in real estate.

Leverage

A key element in real estate investment is financial leverage. It refers to the use of borrowed money to finance a portion of the cost of an asset, such as stocks, bonds, or real estate. The rules which generate benefits for the investor applying leverage to real estate buying are especially attractive, as will become evident from the following illustration. To keep the arithmetic simple, in our illustrations we shall ignore commission costs and legal expenses associated with the purchase and sale of property.

Assume that last year Investor W made a cash purchase of a piece of land for $10,000 and that he has just sold it for double that price, making a 100 percent ($10,000) profit on his original investment. Had he wanted to take advantage of leverage in this case, he would have bought the property with, say, $1,000 of his own money, borrowing the rest ($9,000) from a mortgage company. In that case, ignoring the interest cost of the loan, the investor would have made a 1,000 percent profit—that is, a $10,000 profit on an investment of only $1,000. The transactions are summarized in the following table:

	No Leverage		Leverage	
	At Purchase	After Sale	At Purchase	After Sale
Value of property	$10,000		$10,000	
Debt	0		9,000	
Equity	10,000		1,000	
Sales price		$20,000		$20,000
Profit		10,000		10,000
Return on investment		100%		1,000%

If Investor W had borrowed $9,000 at, say, 10 percent interest, he would still get a return of 910 percent—far greater than his 100 percent return without leverage.

An important dimension of using leverage in financing real estate property is that if investors can determine how much they will make on the borrowed money, then they can calculate the net return on the investment.[2] If, for example, the investor borrows an amount equal to his equity (a 1-to-1 ratio), then, if the investment earns 8 percent and he pays 7 percent for borrowed money, he makes 9 percent:

Borrow	$100,000	Earn on	$200,000
at 7%	0.07	at 8%	0.08
	$ 7,000		$ 16,000

Effect of leverage:

Earnings on $200,000	$ 16,000
Interest on $100,000	$ 7,000
Earnings on $100,000 equity	$ 9,000

Ratio of earnings to equity $\frac{\$\ 9{,}000}{\$100{,}000} = 0.09 \text{ (or } 9\%)$

If the investor borrows at a 2-to-1 ratio, he makes 10 percent:

Borrow	$200,000	Earn on	$300,000
at 7%	0.07	at 8%	0.08
	$ 14,000		$ 24,000

Effect of leverage:

Earnings on $300,000	$ 24,000
Interest on $200,000	$ 14,000
Earnings on $100,000 equity	$ 10,000

Ratio of earnings to equity $\frac{\$\ 10{,}000}{\$100{,}000} = 0.10 \text{ (or } 10\%)$

A 3-to-1 ratio brings the investor 11 percent—he makes 8 percent on $100,000 plus 1 percent on $300,000.

A word of caution: In the examples just given, it was assumed that, as expected, the investor's business ventures were profitable. But what if they were not? Leverage works in reverse, too. If an investor borrows at 7 percent and earns only 6 percent, then at a 1-to-1 ratio of borrowing to equity he will earn

[2] Reprinted by permission, from *Real Estate Investment Strategy*, Second Edition, by Maury Seldin and Richard H. Swesnik, Copyright © 1979 by Johy Wiley & Sons, Inc.

only 5 percent:

Borrow	$100,000	Earn on	$200,000
at 7%	0.07	at 6%	0.06
	$ 7,000		$ 12,000

Effect of leverage:

Earnings on $200,000	$ 12,000
Interest on $100,000	$ 7,000
Earnings on $100,000 equity	$ 5,000

Ratio of earnings to equity $\dfrac{\$\ 5{,}000}{\$100{,}000} = 0.05$ (or 5%)

Let us repeat here our first example, but now assuming that the investor was forced to sell his $10,000 property for only $6,000. The situation in that case would be as follows:

	No Leverage		Leverage	
	At Purchase	After Sale	At Purchase	After Sale
Value of property	$10,000		$10,000	
Debt	0		9,000	
Equity	10,000		1,000	
Sales price		$6,000		$6,000
Loss		(4,000)		(4,000)
Loss as percent of original investment		(40%)		(400%)

The technique of using leverage as a means of stretching investment dollars should now be clear: The greater the leverage, the greater the percentage gain to the investor if the property appreciates in value, but the greater the percentage loss if the property depreciates in value.

Depreciation

Tax law allows investors to deduct each year from their incomes a certain amount representing depreciation to income-producing property.[3] The reason for the existence of this law is that in time any income-producing property—an

[3] Note that the IRS only allows depreciation on income-producing real estate property as a deductible item. No depreciation is allowed on land.

apartment complex, an office building, or a shopping plaza—will become so dilapidated and run down that it will no longer produce any income for the owner. Permitting property owners to depreciate their property is an effective method by which capital can ultimately be returned to them.

Depreciation Methods

There are several ways to calculate depreciation. Although a number of methods of figuring depreciation are recognized by the IRS, the following two methods are most frequently used.

Straight-line Method Under the straight-line method, the property, less its estimated salvage value, if any, is depreciated in equal annual installments over its estimated useful life. For example, assume in January 1980, Investor P buys a building for $100,000. Its useful life is 20 years. Its expected salvage value is zero. In 1980, Investor P claims a depreciation deduction of $5,000 [$100,000/20]. If she continues to own the building, she will deduct $5,000 in depreciation per year from her income in each of the following nineteen years.

Declining Balance Method The accelerated depreciation method that provides for greater deductions in the earlier years of ownership and smaller deductions in later years is known as the declining balance method. Such a method simply permits the depreciation allowance to be taken earlier. But no matter which technique of depreciation allowance is employed, it is not possible to deduct an amount that would exceed the cost of the property, less the salvage value.

Declining balance rates are 200, 150, and 125 percent. The 200 percent rate (double-declining rate) allows the greatest deductions in the early years; however, this method cannot be used to depreciate certain types of property.

The following example contrasts the 200 percent method with the straight-line method. Suppose Investor W purchases and rents apartments in a new multifamily building for $250,000. The estimated useful life of the building is 50 years. Under the straight-line method, Investor W gets a depreciation deduction of 2 percent each year, or $5,000.[4] Under the double declining balance method, he uses 4 percent of the *remaining balance* each year. The comparative depreciation data under the 200 percent method for a three-year period are given below:

First year: 4 percent of $250,000 or $10,000
Second year: 4 percent of $240,000 ($250,000 – $10,000), or $9,600
Third year: 4 percent of $230,400 ($240,000 – $9,600), or $9,216.

[4] Under the straight-line method, the depreciation would be 2 percent per year, but not necessarily $5,000. If there is salvage value, the annual deduction would be less.

Using the straight-line method, Investor W would have deducted $5,000 in each year. It should be obvious that in later years, although Investor W would deduct depreciation of $5,000 per year under the straight-line method, he would deduct less under the declining balance method.[5]

Profitable Sales of Depreciable Property

Profit may be realized on the sale of real estate property due to an appreciation in the market value of that property and/or because depreciation has reduced the cost carrying basis of the asset to an amount below its current selling price. Assume a real estate property cost $50,000; depreciation claimed was $48,000. It was sold for $50,000. The profit on this transaction was $48,000:

Sale proceeds		$50,000
Original cost	$50,000	
Less: Depreciation	48,000	
Cost carrying basis	2,000	2,000
Profit		$48,000

In this case, as a general rule, the $48,000 profit resulting from the sale of property at a price higher than the cost carrying basis (which was reduced by depreciation) would be taxed as a capital gain. An exception to this general rule, which is brought about by the method used for depreciating the property, is discussed in the following section.

Recapture of Depreciation

The term *recapture of depreciation* refers to the manner in which the excess depreciation (that is, excess of accelerated depreciation over straight-line depreciation) would be recaptured and taxed as ordinary income when the real property is sold. The amount of recapture depends on the rate of depreciation claimed. The following table (covering a four-year period relating to a real property with a life of 20 years) presents the concept of recapture:

Year	Accelerated Depreciation	Straight-line Depreciation	Recapture
1	$21,000	$10,000	$11,000
2	16,800	10,000	6,800
3	13,440	10,000	3,440
4	10,750	10,000	750

[5] Another well-known method is the sum-of-the years'-digits method. Under this method, the investor adds the digits of the number of years in the useful life of the asset. For example, if the useful life is five years, the digits 1 through 5 total 15 (1 + 2 + 3 + 4 + 5). Each year, the depreciation deduction is equal to that portion of the depreciable cost that the remaining useful life of the asset bears to the total sum of the digits.

Amounts specified in the "Recapture" column are taxable as ordinary income. For example, if the real estate property is sold at the end of Year 3, the total amount to be recaptured would be $21,240 ($11,000 + $6,800 + $3,440). It should be added here that complex recapture rules apply to realty. Depending on the type of realty held, the method of depreciation and the period held, all, part, or none of the depreciation may be subject to recapture.

Tax Considerations

Several tax-related advantages are associated with real estate investment. The objective of most investments in real estate—often called real estate tax shelters—is to reduce the tax liability by claiming depreciation and interest deductions and realizing profits as long-term capital gains (as opposed to short-term capital gains and ordinary income) which receive preferential treatment under the tax law.

The tax benefits generated by a real estate investment can be substantial. If an investor purchases a piece of income producing property and borrows a substantial portion of the purchase cost, he or she can receive tax write-offs for interest expense and depreciation charges which might *exceed* the initial investment. The largest part of the write-offs typically occurs within the first four or five years. Of course, any gain on the sale of the property will be taxed at favorable long-term capital gains rate, if the realty is held for more than one year.

Investors may enjoy additional tax breaks. If an investor makes a profitable sale of depreciable property and elects to report it on an installment basis, ordinary income must be reported before any of the capital gain is reported. However, if the investor receives less than 30 percent down payment on the sale price, then he or she is permitted to allocate the profit element of each installment payment between ordinary income and capital gain.

The Caveats

Technical Knowledge

Success in land investment is assured only when the investor knows how to buy and sell a piece of land at the right price and at the right time. This is by no means easy, and it is virtually impossible for a neophyte to operate in this field with any degree of consistency.

To be sure, there are several dimensions of technical knowledge that one must acquire in order to become a successful real estate investor. First, an investor must be able to critically evaluate both undeveloped and developed lands. It is, of course, true that undeveloped land often has a much greater potential for price appreciation than its developed counterpart, but an investor may be wiped out if the undeveloped land is never developed. Also, the development of raw land can be a lengthy process. The land must be divided into lots, utilities must be brought to it, and the roads and streets must be paved—all of which requires large amounts of money.

Selling land—even undeveloped land—is much more difficult than buying it. Some land may have to be held for a generation or more before an investor can sell it and make a profit. In some cases, the wait may not be worthwhile if the potentials for price increase appear to have disappeared. A buyer may not be readily available in some cases; in others, the owners may not be willing to sell their property at a loss even though the prospects for profit appear dim. In short, even for knowledgeable investors, selling real estate property at a desirable price and at an opportune time may not always be possible.

Large Financial Investment

An important feature of land investment is that the more money an investor has, the better the deal he or she can get. Investors with less than $10,000 have a slim chance of owning a valuable piece of property. Some land brokers in the fast-growing areas of the country advise their prospective clients to invest at least $50,000 each, and many in the booming states would not even entertain a request for land costing less than $100,000. Few people can invest such large sums of money in real estate property except in the form of group ownership.

Lack of Liquidity

Once money is invested in land, investors should not expect to recoup their principal for a long time. Most properties have a gestation period of at least several years, and some need considerably more time to appreciate in value.

Investors may also experience considerable delays in liquidating their real estate property. The right type of buyer must come along at the right time. Sometimes a number of offers and counteroffers must be exchanged between buyer and seller before the price can be settled. Finally, even under the best circumstances, legal matters are likely to take several months to complete. During this period, money is tied up and can be freed only if the investor is willing to sell the property at a price substantially lower than its appraised value.

High Property Taxes

In recent years, local property taxes in most places have skyrocketed, and these taxes can lower considerably the profit margin of a piece of land. For example, if the annual local property tax on a $100,000 property is levied at $5,000 and the assessment remains unchanged for five years, at the end of this five-year period the breakeven point on this piece of property (not counting sales expenses and tax benefits) would be $125,000. In addition, the complex ways in which these taxes are determined by the government frequently create frustrations for property owners. These frustrations can be further aggravated if one attempts to have property reassessed, because court action in such matters is notoriously slow.

Burdens of a Landlord

For many individuals, an undesirable aspect of owning real estate property—whether it is a piece of land or a large apartment complex—lies in becoming a landlord. Landlords must successfully perform numerous diversified chores. They must handle complicated legal matters and deal with paper work. If they own apartment buildings or commercial property, they must collect rent, handle delinquents, stop violations of the lease, maintain the property, and generally keep peace and order. A landlord must cope with the laws that heavily favor tenants and must bear the cost of vacancies when they occur. Of course, a landlord may ease his or her burdens by hiring a competent lawyer, an accountant, a maintenance expert, and a general manager; however, by so doing he or she will undoubtedly reduce—perhaps even lose—the net income from real estate property. Also, the fact a real estate property (excluding land) is a wasting asset should not be overlooked.

Caveat Emptor

Fraudulent methods of selling real estate properties are not uncommon. Many sales of undeveloped land, even unusable fragments of desert, are made at free dinners organized by land promoters. Many developers also use the lure of a "free vacation" to get prospective buyers into their offices.

The expression *caveat emptor*—let the buyer beware—is particularly applicable to the purchase of real estate properties. Investors in real estate should observe at least the following rules before buying real estate property: First, real estate properties should not be purchased by mail. Second, the credentials of the developer should be thoroughly investigated. Third, every contract should be carefully examined. Finally, the law should be studied to ensure that the investor gets its full protection.

SECTION 2 THE COMMODITY FUTURES MARKET

An Overview

There are five principal commodity exchanges in the United States. The 132-year-old *Chicago Board of Trade* is by far the largest, accounting for more than one-half of total trading. It trades in the futures of corn, wheat, oats, soybeans, soybean oil, soybean meal, plywood, and silver. The *Chicago Mercantile Exchange* is the second largest exchange. Handling contracts in live cattle, live hogs, frozen pork bellies, lumber, grain, sorghum, and Idaho potatoes, this exchange accounts for about 25 percent of total trading.

The Mercantile Exchange also has a subsidiary exchange known as the International Monetary Market, which trades futures in eight different foreign currencies. Both exchanges also offer interest-rate futures contracts, which have become increasingly popular since their inception in the mid-1970s.

The Commodity Exchange Inc. of New York offers futures contracts in gold, silver and copper, and is the third-largest U.S. commodity futures exchange. Other important New York exchanges include the New York Coffee and Sugar Exchange, the New York Cocoa Exchange, the New York Cotton Exchange, and the New York Mercantile Exchange. The Kansas City Board of Trade and the Minneapolis Grain Exchange offer futures contracts in types of wheat different from the Chicago Board. The Mid-America Commodity Exchange in Chicago offers contracts in several major commodities.

All these futures markets operate in much the same fashion. Like stock exchanges, commodity exchanges are membership organizations. Most members are either engaged in producing, marketing, or processing of commodities, or are brokers for others. Nonmembers trade through brokerage firms, which hold memberships through partners or offices. The exchanges are supported by dues and assessments on members.

The main commodities traded on exchanges are wheat, corn, and soybeans. Other commodities include cattle, pork bellies, eggs, and potatoes. The major U.S. exchanges and their most active commodity futures are presented in Table 19–1.

Table 19–1 **Major U.S. Exchanges and Their Most Active Commodity Futures* July 1970–June 1971**

Exchange	Major Commodities	Contract Size	Annual Volume of Trading (Contracts)	Number of Futures	Price Quoted In	Minimum Price Change
Chicago Board of Trade	Wheat (soft)	5,000 bu	582	5	¢/bu	1/8¢/bu = $12.50/contract
	Corn	5,000 bu	2,734	5	¢/bu	1/8¢/bu = $12.50/contract
	Soybeans	5,000 bu	2,653	7	¢/bu	1/8¢/bu = $12.50/contract
	Soybean oil	60,000 lb	1,470	8	¢/lb	1/100¢/lb = $ 6.00/contract
	Soybean meal	100 tons	634	8	$/ton	$.05/ton = $ 5.00/contract
Chicago Mercantile Exchange	Cattle (live)	40,000 lb	606	6	$/cwt	$.025/cwt = $10.00/contract
	Pork bellies	36,000 lb	1,526	7	$/cwt	$.025/cwt = $ 9.00/contract
	Eggs (shell)	21,000 dz	524	12	¢/dz	$ .05/dz = $10.50/contract
New York Mercantile Exchange	Potatoes	50,000 lb	206	4	$/cwt	$.01/cwt = $ 5.00/contract
Kansas City Board of Trade	Wheat (hard)	5,000 bu	201	5	¢/bu	1/8¢/bu = $12.50/contract

* Commodities regulated under the Commodity Exchange Act.

SOURCE: *Annual Summary of Commodity Futures Statistics*, 1970–71, USDA, Commodity Exchange Authority.

Figure 19–2

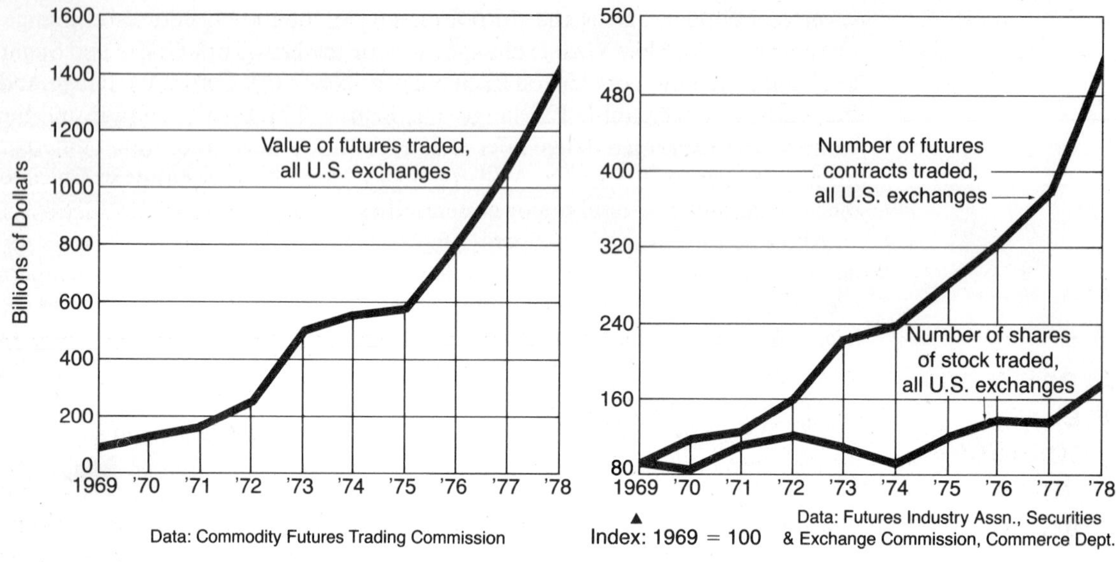

SOURCE: *Business Week*, June 11, 1979, p. 63.

Figure 19–3

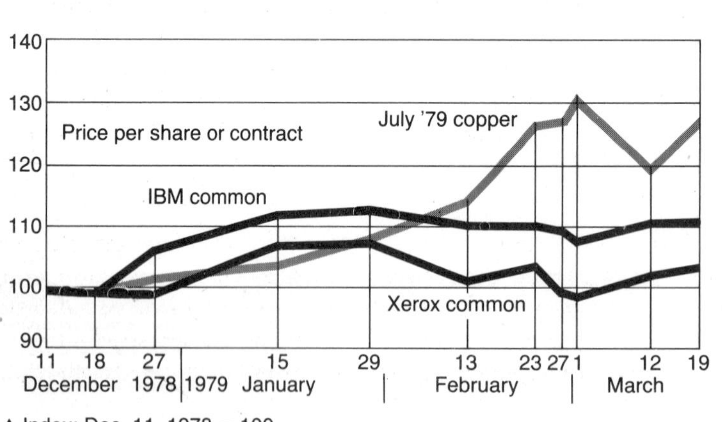

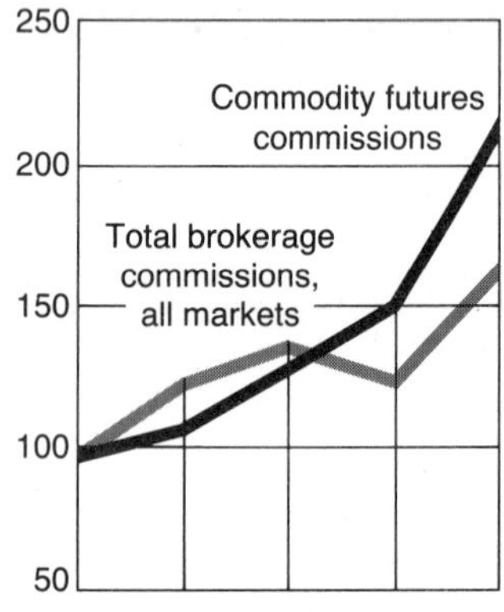

SOURCE: *Business Week*, June 11, 1979, p. 64.

Commodities prices tend to follow the business cycle—falling in recessions and rising in booms. Sometimes, however, a spectacular increase captures the imagination of investors. Average prices for commodities tripled in the 1940s, eased off for the next 20 years, then tripled again in the 1970s.

Figure 19–2 charts a decade of growth in commodity futures. The figure reveals that commodity futures constitute a $1.4 trillion market and outrace the action in stock. In 1979 alone, the contract volume was 32 percent ahead of the level reached in 1978, while the volume in interest rate futures surged about 250 percent. Also, as revealed by Figure 19–3, commodity futures generate large brokerage business as well as generous profits for successful investors.

Trading on the Commodity Futures Market

Its Nature

The word *commodity* refers to both broad and narrow classes of objects. Commodities are the bulk products of farms, processors, and mines traded on organized markets where contracts are authorized for maturity or delivery in future months. Grains, livestock, metals, currencies, citrus products, cotton, eggs, and lumber are examples of commodities.

The function of a *futures market* is to

> *improve the quantity and quality of available market information, permit a reduction in transaction costs; provide for the transference of risk to those willing to carry it, hence reducing the total costs of marketing; and facilitate the response to changes in existing or anticipated market conditions. Futures markets, by providing an opportunity to hedge and to forward price, and by serving as a temporary alternative market, offer firms, both farm and agribusiness, profit opportunities that would otherwise not be available to them.*[6]

The *hedger* is the farmer or processor who uses the futures market to ensure a unit price by selling contracts if he or she is now the owner of the commodity being grown or processed. In contrast, a *speculator* attempts to benefit from the fluctuations in the price of the commodity. If prices rise, the speculator can make money by buying low and selling high, or if they fall, he or she can make money by selling high and buying back low.

[6] Quoted in Michael Weinberg, "Who Are Those Commodity Speculators and What Are They Doing to Us?" in *Before You Speculate*, Chicago Mercantile Exchange, 1973, p. 32.

The Risk Factor[7]

Before the Civil War, each individual who owned wheat bore the full risk while it was in his hands. Because the farmer was the original holder, he carried the risk up to the minute he sold his grain. Because farmers brought their wheat to market within a very short period, the market was glutted during the harvest season and prices took a beating. When the year's crop was almost used up, supplies often became short and prices high. Millers either had more wheat offered to them at harvest time than they could use, or they had to pay premium prices to stay in business toward the end of the crop year. To protect themselves from these violent seasonal swings, they introduced the practice of buying and selling for "forward delivery." This simply meant that a miller would, for example, agree on May 1 to buy 5,000 bushels of wheat for 90 cents per bushel to be delivered on August 1. In other words, the buyer and seller both agreed on a price *today* for a sale that would not be completed for three months.

Although this was far from an ideal solution of the price problem, it made it possible for the miller to plan ahead with reasonable assurance that skyrocketing prices would not wreck his business. The seller, however, was still faced with the possibility that prices would rise and that he would be forced to deliver wheat worth a lot more than he had agreed to sell it for. For example, if he sold 5,000 bushels forward at 90 cents per bushel and then had to deliver three months later when wheat was worth, say, $1.10 per bushel, he would have lost a possible profit of $1,000.

The seller did not appreciate being placed in this situation. Consequently, the practice developed for buying and selling these forward contracts so that the holder of a contract who did not wish to assume the risk could transfer it to someone who was willing to carry it.

The Two Markets

In the 1860s, the practice of buying and selling for forward delivery became so common in Chicago that the brokers found it advantageous to adopt formal rules and regulations for governing the trade and, finally, to adopt standard "futures" contracts. Today there are two markets in wheat and two markets for some score of other staple commodities. One market is the "actual," "spot," or "cash" market. This is the market in which a speculator or a hedger might actually buy one bag of corn to feed chickens or 100,000 bushels of wheat to grind into a few dozen carloads of flour. When the farmer goes into the county elevator with a truckload of grain and sells it, he is selling *cash* wheat.

[7] With slight modifications, this section and the two that follow are reproduced from the in-house booklet, *How to Buy and Sell Commodities* (New York: Merrill Lynch Pierce Fenner & Smith, Inc.), p. 6.

The other market for wheat is the futures market. When a trader deals in futures, he is making a contract to deliver or to receive wheat at some stated time in the future. If he buys a future, he is in fact *making a contract to buy and pay in full* for a given amount of wheat, at a set price, to be delivered to him in a specified month. If the trader sells a future, he is in fact making a contract to deliver a given amount of wheat under the same conditions.

When a trader buys a future, he is actually *making* a brand new contract. When he sells a future that he had bought earlier, he is making an offsetting contract, with the result that he will neither receive nor deliver wheat. However, when buying or going long on a commodity contract, a new contract is not always created. If one buys a contract from an already existing "long," no new contract is made, but the ownership of a new contract is changed.

Each new purchase and sale represents the creation of a new, legally binding contract to transfer a given amount of actual commodity, say, wheat. Each sale of a contract previously bought and each purchase of a contract previously sold offsets the first transaction. Any difference between the price at the time the original contract is made and the price at the time the reverse contract is made is settled in cash. If the contract is not liquidated by a reverse operation, then it must be fulfilled by delivery of the grain.

But we are getting a little afield. We began with a discussion of *price*. Now we have two markets in which wheat is bought and sold. In one market actual wheat is bought and sold on a negotiated basis. This is the *cash market*. Buyers and sellers quite often meet face to face. In all cases, the agreement between them calls for the transfer of a specific lot of a specific grade of grain. It calls for either immediate or forward delivery. The contract can be canceled only by an agreement between the two contracting parties. In other words, a sale of cash wheat is like any ordinary commercial transaction with which investors are familiar.

The other wheat market is the *futures market*. In it traders buy and sell on an exchange under terms of a *standard* contract that calls for delivery of a set amount of a basic grade of wheat, with other specified grades also deliverable but at stated price differentials. A trader never sees the party on the other side of the contract. In most cases, the *commodity is not actually delivered; instead, the original contract is offset by a reverse contract before delivery time.*

With two markets, of course, there are two sets of prices. The cash price of wheat varies from year to year and from month to month. However, most of the headlines referring to the price of wheat or other staple commodities relate not to the cash price, but to prices quoted for futures—for the commodity to be delivered under a contract made on a futures exchange. The exchange itself does not set prices, but merely facilitates trading and records the prices at which trades are made each day between openly bidding buyers and sellers.

Figure 19–4 illustrates how futures and cash prices look during a normal year when plotted together. Notice that at the beginning the line representing futures is above the line representing the cash price, but that the two lines meet and cross each other. Throughout the period covered, the two lines fluctuate more or less together. It is this price relationship and this constant coming

Figure 19–4

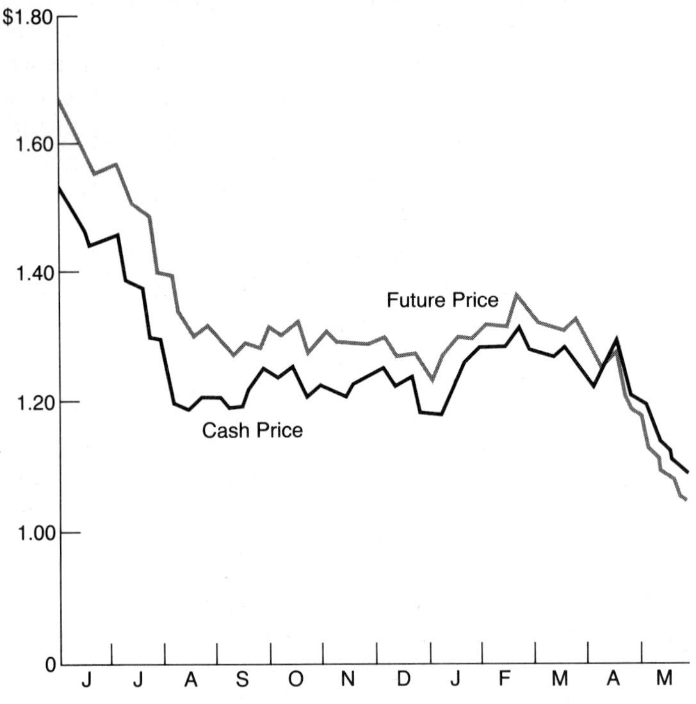

SOURCE: *How to Buy and Sell Commodities* (New York: Merrill Lynch Pierce Fenner & Smith), p. 8.

together of cash and futures prices that gives the futures markets their economic reason for existence. Understanding this relationship is the first requirement for intelligent operation. This relationship is also the key that makes it possible for the farmer, the merchant, and the manufacturer to transfer the risk of price fluctuation from themselves to someone else.

Determination of Futures Prices

A futures contract provides in effect that Seller Q will deliver to Buyer Z 5,000 bushels of wheat in an approved warehouse sometime during the month of September, the day to be determined by Seller Q. The wheat will be one of several specified grades. Prices are quoted in terms of a basic grade, but a number of other grades may be delivered at the option of Seller Q. If it is a higher grade, Buyer Z will pay a little more for it (a premium); if it is of a little lower grade, Buyer Z will pay less for it.

When a price is quoted for September wheat, it means wheat for delivery in September. When the current month is quoted, it means the price for wheat to be delivered later in the present month.

Each month has its own price, so that in effect there are a whole series of prices beginning with the price of wheat today (the cash price) and then prices extending month by month into the future. Actually, for wheat the only actively traded future months are those calling for delivery in March, May, July, September, and December, and no contracts are made for longer than 12 months. In other commodities, other months are "active." The months that are active are determined by the customs of the trade.

Why is wheat for delivery in September cheaper (or dearer) than wheat for delivery immediately? What is the relationship among the prices of the various months? Why does the price of a future always approximate the price of cash grain when the future becomes current?

It is easiest to get a clear picture of the relationship of this series of prices if we consider an example. Assume that the cash price of wheat on July 1 is $3.50 a bushel, that the crop has all been harvested, and that consumption will remain at a constant rate—that is, that the supply-and-demand situation can be accurately predicted for the next two months. The pertinent question is: What will wheat be worth two months from now if all factors affecting the market remain constant?

If a trader were to buy 5,000 bushels of wheat on July 1, it would cost him $17,500 (5,000 × $3.50). Furthermore, storage on the wheat for the next two months would probably be about $1\frac{3}{4}$ cents per bushel a month, or $175. Any prudent trader would insure his $17,500 investment against fire, and that would cost another $3 or so. He would also either have to borrow the money to buy the wheat and pay interest on his loan or, if he used his own money, he would have to consider the opportunity cost of losing the interest he would earn if it were not tied up in wheat. Let us assume that the trader borrowed $17,675 ($17,500 + $175) at 12 percent; for a two-month period, this would add another $354 to the cost of the wheat.

The carrying charges the trader would have to pay on the wheat if he held it for two months—interest, storage, and insurance—would then total $532. Add this to the cost of 5,000 bushels of wheat ($17,500), and the trader would have $18,032 as the total cost of his wheat two months hence. This comes out to approximately $3.60 a bushel. This is what wheat would cost him two months from now. Of this figure, 10 cents represents the approximate carrying charges that would have to be paid by whoever held the wheat—a new buyer, the farmer, the wholesaler, the miller.

If cash wheat is selling at $3.50 a bushel on July 1 and September wheat is selling at $3.60, the difference between the two markets would be considered normal, and it could be stated that September wheat was selling at a premium of 10 cents.

If the price on July 1 for cash wheat is $3.50 a bushel and the price for September futures is $3.60, what will be the price of December futures? In other words, what is the price relationship among various future deliveries? Because the carrying charges are 5 cents a month and December is five months away, the

Figure 19–5 **Daily Closing Prices, Three Futures Contracts for Wheat on Chicago Board of Trade, May 1 to November 30, 1967**

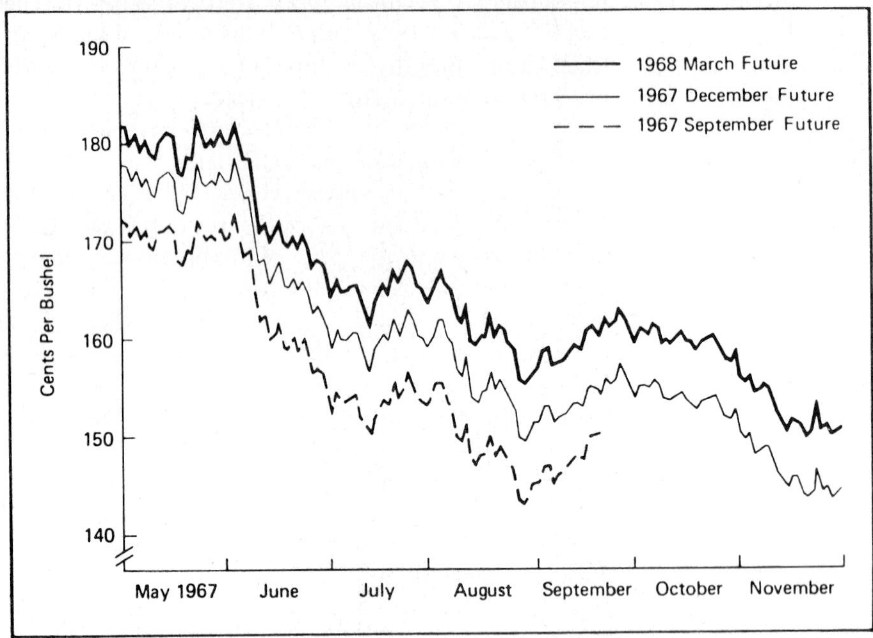

SOURCE: U.S. Department of Agriculture, Commodity Exchange Authority, *Trading in Wheat Futures, May–November 1967* (March 1968).

price would be \$3.75. The premium on a December contract is therefore 25 cents.

It should be clear from this discussion that future prices of a commodity are related to each other. Figure 19–5 charts the daily closing prices of three future contracts for wheat on the Chicago Board of Trade. The close relationship among the three is quite revealing.

Under *normal* circumstances the price of wheat for future delivery is the current price *plus* the carrying charges from today until the time of delivery. The only problem is that circumstances in this uncertain world are rarely normal. Premiums are usually less than carrying charges. In fact, futures often sell for less than cash wheat; that is, they sell at a discount. When more distant futures are selling below the nearer months in this manner, the market is said to be inverted.

The price at which a commodity for future delivery sells reflects the appraisal of supply and demand *today* for the commodity at the selected *future* date. If buyers and sellers generally think that the price will be lower in the future, the price of the commodity for future delivery would most likely be less than the cash price for immediate delivery, despite the cost of carrying the commodity.

Why do the cash price and the futures price always approach one another as the month of delivery nears? The answer, of course, is implicit in the reasons given for the difference in price. As the time for which storage, interest, and insurance are required gets shorter, the cost of holding wheat until delivery gets progressively smaller until it finally disappears. In other words, if the future is to be delivered immediately, then as far as price is concerned, it might as well be cash wheat for immediate delivery.[8]

Hedging Arithmetic[9]

Clearly, the futures market provides a means whereby the investor can transfer the risks to speculators by hedging. A *hedge* is established by taking a position in futures equal to, and opposite to, an existing or anticipated cash position. The arithmetic of hedging is simple and can be explained with the help of a set of "T" accounts.

Suppose that on December 1 a grain elevator operator has in storage 5,000 bushels of soybeans valued at $6.60 per bushel. To protect against a price decline he sells a May futures contract for $6.80 per bushel. In February, he will simultaneously *sell* soybeans and *buy* a May futures contract. Assume that by February, when he sells the cash soybeans and buys the futures contract, both cash and futures prices have declined 10 cents per bushel. As presented below, the elevator operator will have lost 10 cents per bushel when he sold the cash

Cash Market	Futures Market
December 1 Cash price of $6.60 per bushel	December 1 Sell 5,000 bushels of May futures at $6.80 per bushel
February 1 Sell 5,000 bushels of soybeans at $6.50 per bushel Loss on cash grain = 10 cents per bushel	February 1 Buy 5,000 bushels of May futures at $6.70 per bushel Gain on futures = 10 cents per bushel

Net gain or loss = 0

[8] The cash price and the futures price are, of course, seldom identical at delivery time because among other things, the sellers usually have the option of selecting the type of wheat to be delivered.

[9] See Thomas E. Snider, "Using the Futures Market to Hedge," Federal Reserve Bank of Richmond, *Monthly Review*, 59(August 1973), pp. 4–7.

soybeans and gained 10 cents per bushel when he bought back the futures contract.

The loss on the cash price was exactly offset by the gain on the futures price. Although the hedge protects against a loss, it also precludes a gain from a price increase. For example, assume that in the previous example the price of soybeans had risen. In this example, had he not hedged, the elevator operator would have gained an extra 10 cents per bushel.

In the previous example, the hedge worked perfectly; that is, the loss in the cash market was exactly offset by the loss in the futures market. However, this situation rarely occurs in practice. Cash and futures prices usually vary together in response to fluctuating market conditions, but they generally do not move in lock-step fashion.

The difference between the futures price on any exchange and the local cash price is called the *basis*. The basis varies among geographic locations and changes from month to month in each location, normally narrowing as the delivery month approaches.

In the case of grains, cash prices at most locations around the country are usually below the Chicago futures price. The basis primarily reflects the cost of transportation and storage. At any specific time, for example, the basis in a local area will approximately equal the cost of delivering the grain to the city in which the exchange is located plus the cost of storing it until the delivery month. The basis is normally highest at harvest time, when cash prices are depressed relative to futures. Because the basis reflects storage costs, it usually narrows as the month of delivery approaches. Even though the basis varies from month to month, it usually follows a fairly consistent and distinct pattern.

A Speculator's Transaction

To many traders willing to assume a high degree of risk, speculation in the futures markets is quite attractive. Because futures can be purchased with as little as 5 percent margin, a large percentage return on investment can be realized.

The margin in futures trading is significantly different from the margin in stock and bond trading (discussed in Appendix 2 to Part 3: Margin Trading, pp. 512–19). Strictly speaking, the purchase (or sale) of a commodity futures contract is not an investment but a viable *instrument of intent*. The buyer of November soybeans, for example, does not own the soybeans. He or she only *agrees to purchase* in November a specified number of bushels of this commodity for a specified amount of money. To legalize the agreement, and to provide some assurance that the buyers and sellers will fulfill their obligations, the commodity exchanges set a performance bond—commonly called the margin. Whereas a margin trader in stocks must put up 50 percent of the total purchase amount and borrow the balance from a broker, the purchaser of a futures contract is required to put up a security deposit of only 5 to 10 percent of the total contract value. Unlike the margin trader in stocks, the futures contract purchaser pays no interest on the balance, because no money has been borrowed.

Margins in commodity markets have enabled speculators to enjoy substantial leverage. Assume a speculator purchases a contract on November soybeans (5,000 bushels) at $6.60 per bushel. Although the soybeans she contracted for are valued at $33,000 (5,000 × $6.60), she might put up as margin only 10 percent or $3,300 of the contract price. A 10 percent increase in the price of November soybeans will produce a profit of $3,300 (excluding a small transaction commission), which is a 100 percent return on the speculator's initial investment. Of course, if the price of soybeans were to decline by only 10 percent, the speculator's initial investment would be lost.

In practice, a commodity trader's account with the broker is credited or debited at the end of each business day, depending on whether the commodity contract increased or decreased in value from the previous day's close. If the contract value were to increase, the trader's account would be credited with additional equity and he or she would be permitted to withdraw the profit. If, however, the contract value were to decrease, the account would be debited and he or she would most likely be given a *margin call* in the form of a request for additional funds in order to maintain the required margin balance. If the trader does not put up the additional money, the broker would have the right to liquidate the contract.

The Caveats

First, a commodity trader or speculator should not only be aware of the attendant risks of trading in commodity futures, but should also be financially willing and able to sustain frequent losses without being wiped out.

Second, if the trader intends to speculate with a relatively large part of his total investible funds, he should then commit himself to acquiring an intimate knowledge of the commodities in which he intends to trade and of the impact that weather, crop reports, economic conditions, and political developments can have on their prices. In addition, he should educate himself in regard to the new market variables: currency fluctuations, East-West trade, export problems, and the energy crisis.

Third, trading in commodity futures is especially difficult for small investors because they must inevitably compete against giant grain merchants with huge financial and technical resources at their command.

The commodity futures markets have much to offer the serious trader or the speculator: The possibility of substantial profits in a short period of time, with a risk factor commensurate with the profit potential involved. But futures trading can be a bewildering and costly experience if one tries it without a thorough understanding of the functioning of the market. Great care should therefore be exercised in indulging in commodity futures investment.

SECTION 3 PRECIOUS METALS, ART, AND ANTIQUES

Gold

An Overview

Until 1933, the gold window at the U.S. treasury was always open to both individual citizens and foreign governments. In 1933, President Roosevelt devalued the dollar against gold and ended the practice by which individual citizens could freely buy and sell gold. Nearly four decades later, in August 1971, the United States closed its gold window even to foreign official dollar holders, thereby ending the last functional link between the dollar and monetary gold. Finally, on December 31, 1974, the United States government revoked a 41-year ban on U.S. citizens' ownership of gold; a week later, on January 6, 1975, it started auctioning a portion of its gold stock on the open market. The auction was conducted by the General Services Administration, a housekeeping arm of the U.S. government, indicating that henceforth the U.S. government will handle gold as though it was just another article owned by it.

The historical decision presaging an end to the monetary role of gold has made the value of gold one of the most controversial topics in the world of finance. At the one extreme are the "gold bugs" who consider that gold has been the panacea for all financial ills through 6,000 years of human development. At the other extreme are those who concur with John Maynard Keynes' view that gold is the "barbaric relic" of the past.

A more balanced view of gold is that it is a commodity, and as such, its price can fluctuate like the price of any industrial commodity. But gold is a "special" commodity because of its monetary connotation, its beauty, and durability.

Gold Price Determinants

In order to understand how the value of gold is determined, we need to consider the related supply and demand factors. In the past, because gold was the basis for most international currencies, its value was determined by monetary considerations. Now, like any other commodity, its price is determined by the relative supply and demand forces.

The Supply

The supply of gold is dependent on the free-world output, of which 90 percent is accounted for by South Africa, and the output of the communist block, of which the USSR is the single largest producer. World supply is dependent on the production problems experienced in South Africa and the USSR, as well as the gold strategies and foreign-exchange needs of these two countries. Russian sales depend largely on the market price and on the size of liabilities incurred by the

USSR in its transactions with the West. In South Africa, the central bank performs the role of a price leader by withholding gold from the market in the face of sluggish demand or an unusual increase in supply, such as the treasury sales from the U.S. gold stock.

It is noteworthy that the production of the noncommunist countries—the largest source of gold—is steady and only moderately sensitive to changes in real price. Although average free-world production tends to increase when the gold price rises faster than the general price level, the price elasticity of the gold supply is not high. In other words, a 10 percent increase in the price of gold leads to much less than a 10 percent increase in output—and then only with a lag, because the output of the mines cannot be instantaneously adjusted to changing price expectations.

Because of its relative stability—and therefore predictability—free-world gold production tends to be a relatively unimportant factor in price determination. Far more volatile—and therefore more potent as a determinant of short-run market prices—are official sales. In other words, the market supply is dominated by the amount of monetary gold held by central banks and by the amount in private gold holdings, which together are many times larger than annual world production. Consequently, at any given time, the total supply of gold could be highly influenced by the decisions of both the central banks to sell gold and private citizens to hold the precious metal.

The Demand

Efforts to isolate the key element on the demand side of the gold-price equation are beset by great difficulties. The approach followed by virtually all analysts is to distinguish between the "industrial" and "other" sources of demand for gold. Industrial demand reflects the requirements of those who provide saleable goods and services—jewelers, dentists, electronics manufacturers, and so on. The demand by "others" satisfies the desires of investors, inflation hedgers, arbitrageurs, coin collectors, hoarders and speculators.

What makes gold different from other metals is that private demand often exceeds industrial usage. Furthermore, besides its tendency to change abruptly, private demand is almost impossible to measure. In fact, history suggests that the private demand for gold varies directly with the extent to which people feel economically insecure at any given moment. In general, and in recent years especially, when the stability of government or the economy has been threatened, the demand for gold has usually sharply increased. In times of potential crisis, many people turn to gold for protection against uncertainty. These so-called "gold bugs" believe that in time paper money will lose most or all of its value and that the government will not redeem currency for anything like its original worth. Furthermore, these people fear that paper money will not be accepted as a reliable pricing mechanism or means of exchange, because people will not trust its value. Consequently, they purchase gold, thereby increasing the demand for this metal.

The Record

The price of gold, which was $35 an ounce for decades, and below $40 until 1972, approached $800 early in 1980, before declining to a lower level. The rising price trend has been neither smooth nor consistent. In fact, gold prices have been extremely volatile and the future of gold remains uncertain.

Figure 19–6

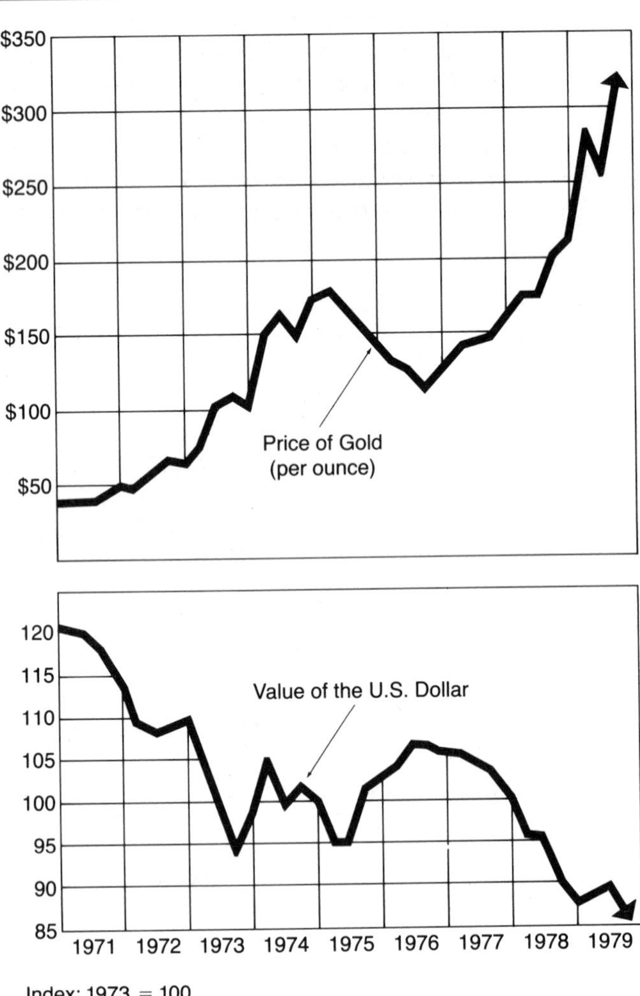

SOURCE: Martin Mayer, "The Message from the Gold Markets," *Fortune*, November 5, 1979, p. 60.

A closer analysis of gold price movements reveals some interesting facts. As shown in Figure 19–6, the spectacular price increases of the 1970s reflected the dramatic decline in the dollar's buying power. Faced with the prospect of progressively higher prices, consumers simply altered their expenditure patterns, spending dollars at a rapid rate and frequently investing their savings in gold.

The relationship between the stock market and gold mining company stocks, revealed in Figure 19–7, is equally dramatic. When the economic situation worsens, investors turn to precious metals, especially gold. Its price is moved by the inflation rate: When the inflation rate declines, investors turn their attention mainly to stocks and bonds. But when inflation reasserts itself, interest rates rise, stock and bond prices fall, and investors' money flows into gold.

The monetary explanation of the fluctuation in gold prices is evident in Figure 19–8. The lagged correlation between the rise and fall of the Federal Reserve's credit and the rise and fall of gold is not perfect, but there is a clear, positive relationship between the two. In fact, after a varying but short lag, almost every reacceleration of the Federal Reserve credit in the three-year period ending in January 1980 was accompanied by an acceleration in the price of gold.

Figure 19–7

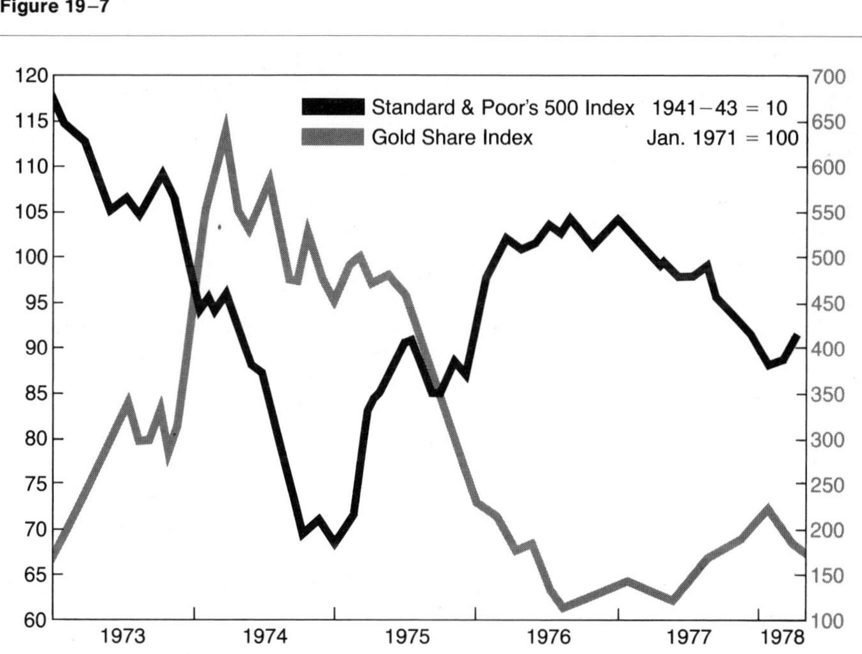

SOURCE: Jane B. Quinn, "Playing the Gold Game." *Newsweek*, June 12, 1978, p. 19E. Chart by Fenga & Freyer, Inc.

Figure 19–8 **Gold and the Federal Reserve Bank Monthly Close, 1977–1980**

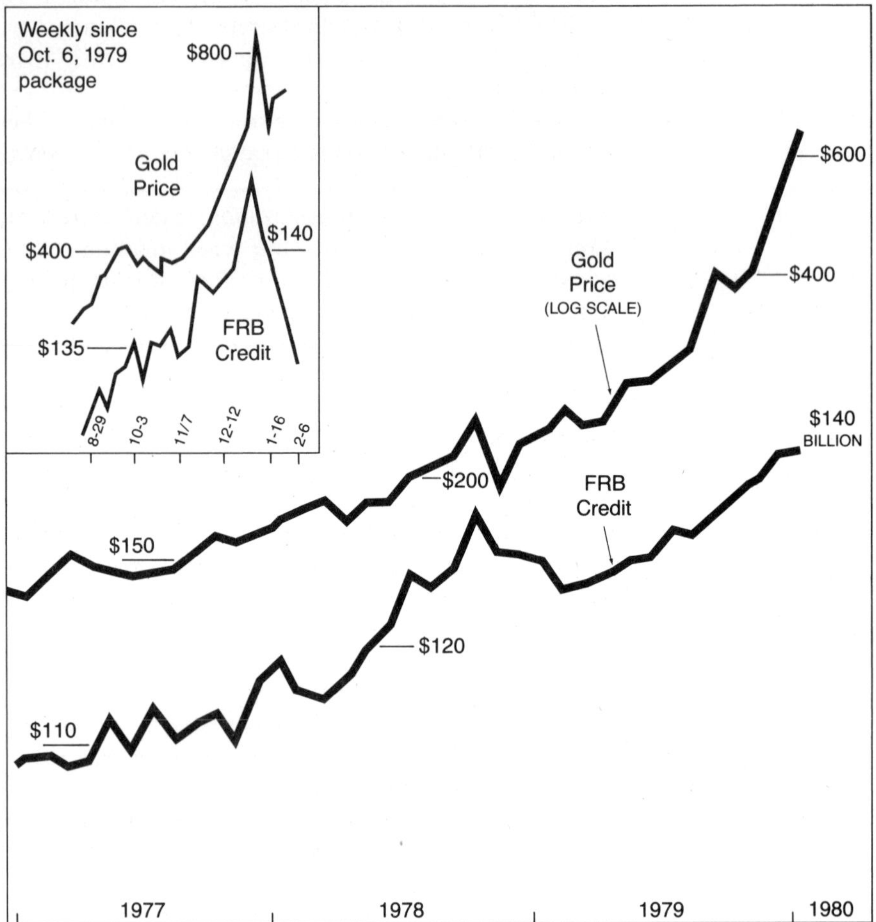

The price of gold in dollars and total Federal Reserve Bank credit in billions.

SOURCE: C. F. Management, reprinted in Lewis E. Lehrman, "Gold is not a Side Show," *Wall Street Journal*, February 20, 1980, p. 22.

It has always been difficult to make a prediction of the price of gold. Although the method of determining the price of gold as a commodity is still valid, the psychological dimension of gold as a perfect hedge against inflation and as a protector of wealth have influenced the price of gold in unpredictable ways. Whether the price of gold will rise in the future to new record high levels is anybody's guess.

Forms of Investment

There are several methods of investing in gold. Table 19–2 outlines the six key methods: Krugerrands, bullion, futures, stocks, jewelry, and certificates.

Krugerrands[10]

The most widely used method of investing in gold in the United States is putting cash into gold coins. Many people like coins with numismatic value. The Krugerrand is a one-ounce gold coin issued by the Republic of South Africa. The key feature of the Krugerrand is its liquidity and divisibility. The price is related to the wholesale London gold price with the coins trading at a 5–8 percent premium over the London price. Also, it is divisible in the sense that an investor can purchase ten Krugerrands and then sell off portions of the gold holdings.

Bullion

Gold bullion bars come in 100- and 400-ounce sizes. At early 1980 market prices, 2,000 ounces of bars, the minimum investment, would cost $1 million and are therefore practical only for wealthy investors. The bars can be purchased at a small commission in the commodity market by paying the full price. Investors may either leave the bars in a bonded commodity warehouse or take physical possession.

Futures

A "future" is a contract for 100 ounces of gold to be delivered on a specified future date. The purchase of gold futures can be highly leveraged; that is, investors can buy gold futures on margin account with small downpayments. As they do for other commodities, investors buying gold on margin tend to realize substantial gains if the appropriate future gold price advances; but they also stand to lose a large portion of their initial investment if the future price declines.

Stocks

Gold stocks are a highly leveraged means of investing in gold, because a small movement in the price of gold can result in a much greater change in the earnings of a mine and the price of its stock. Most of the gold mining stocks are related to South African companies. The major American gold producer is Homestake Mining, but gold represents only a small portion of its earnings. There are several Canadian mines which derive most of their earnings from gold. Among them are Campbell Red Lake, Dome Mines, Ltd. and Giant Yellowknife.

[10] Other gold coins besides Krugerrands are now readily available. For example, Canadian gold coins are regularly advertised in the *Wall Street Journal*.

Table 19–2

Type of investment	Minimum investment	Additional costs: Storage	Additional costs: Commission	Pros and cons
Krugerrands	1-oz. coin at London price	Cost of a bank safe deposit box	5%–8%	Liquidity and ease of resale are the keys. Coins can be bought through currency dealers or jewelers and stored at home or in a bank safe deposit box. There are no assay charges, but no income either. Some states levy sales taxes. Leverage is possible through purchases on a 20% to 33% margin.
Bullion	2,000 oz. of bars at London price	½% per year at warehouse	3%	This is the cheapest way to buy gold, since purchasing in bulk cuts the commission. But bullion must be stored and insured, and it cannot be divided up for sales of smaller quantities. There are often assay charges on resale and no income. Again, some states levy sales taxes. Some leverage is possible through purchases on a 20% to 33% margin.
Futures	$1,000 minimum margin per 100-oz. contract	—	$45 to $55	This provides the greatest leverage in trading gold. There is tremendous liquidity because the U.S. has the most active futures markets in the world. The margin is typically 5%. Because delivery is hardly ever taken, there are no storage or insurance costs. But leverage works both ways, and the losses can be substantial.

SOURCE: *Business Week*, February 5, 1979, p. 98.

A wide variety of gold mutual funds offer an alternative to investing directly in gold or gold stocks. Some have combination portfolios of bullion and stocks; others hold only stocks. Dreyfus Gold Deposits buys nothing but bullion for participants.

Jewelry

Jewelry has a unique attribute of providing psychological pleasure while acting as an investment for many gold investors. But the quality of jewelry varies widely from 14 karats to 24 karats and an investor must have knowledge of the quality of jewelry in which he or she invests.

Certificates

Gold certificates are nontransferable statements of ownership of gold in warehouses generally located in states or countries that do not levy sales taxes.[11]

[11] Gold certificates are now being issued by some banks.

Table 19–2 (*continued*)

Type of investment	Minimum investment	Additional costs: Storage	Additional costs: Commission	Pros and cons
Stocks	Varies according to market conditions	—	\$20 to \$30	These involve either U.S. or Canadian gold mining shares or American depositary receipts of South African mines. Dividend returns are exceptionally high, with yields of 20% common. But stock prices fluctuate with the price of gold. Many mining companies make money only when gold is above \$200 per oz. There may be political risks in owning South African paper.
Jewelry	\$25	—	—	This has the unique attribute of feeling sensuously good on the human body while providing a hedge against inflation and a declining dollar. But the quality of gold in jewelry varies widely from 14 karats, or only 58.5% fine gold, to 24 karats, or 100% fine gold. You need knowledge to buy wisely, and you usually pay a high premium over the intrinsic value of the gold.
Certificates	\$2,500	$\frac{1}{2}$% per year for gold at warehouse	3%	The certificates are nontransferable statements of gold ownership in warehouses generally located in states or countries that do not levy sales taxes. They permit the purchase of gold in modest quantities without taking physical possession. The initial order is for \$2,500, but additions of only \$100 are permitted afterward. Storage and insurance costs must be paid. There is no leverage.

Data: BW estimates

Minimum investment is \$2,500; commissions are 3 percent on purchase and 1 percent on the sale. The major drawback of gold certificates is their limited marketability.

The Caveats

As with most investments, the value of gold at any given time depends on factors beyond the investor's control. In addition, there are several drawbacks to investing in gold.

First, although it may appreciate in value, gold does not earn interest. Second, as noted, gold is expensive. Third, gold is expensive to protect. Fourth, gold is expensive to sell. Unless the investor keeps gold with the dealer, he will have to pay to have it assayed before it can be sold. Frequently the investor must also pay a premium to sell gold through a respected dealer. Finally, for an investor in gold, fraud is a real danger. For example, gold bars may contain less gold than they should and coins can be counterfeited.

Diamonds

An Overview

Gold has been called the Number 1 inflation hedge over the years. This is only a partial truth. For example, in 1979 gold bullion more than doubled in value. However, during the same year silver increased by 300 percent.

An interesting fact revealed by Figure 19–9: During 1979, the price of a one-carat diamond increased less than the increase in the price of gold. However, a long view of diamonds, given in Figure 19–10 paints a different picture. The figure demonstrates the "staircase" formation that diamonds have carved out over the past decade. This constant series of higher plateaus in diamond prices results from the rigidly controlled market that DeBeers, the international diamond consortium based in London, maintains with its dealer network. The figure also reveals that, over the years, diamonds have performed far better than either gold or silver. Over the ten-year period ending in 1978, diamonds

Figure 19–9

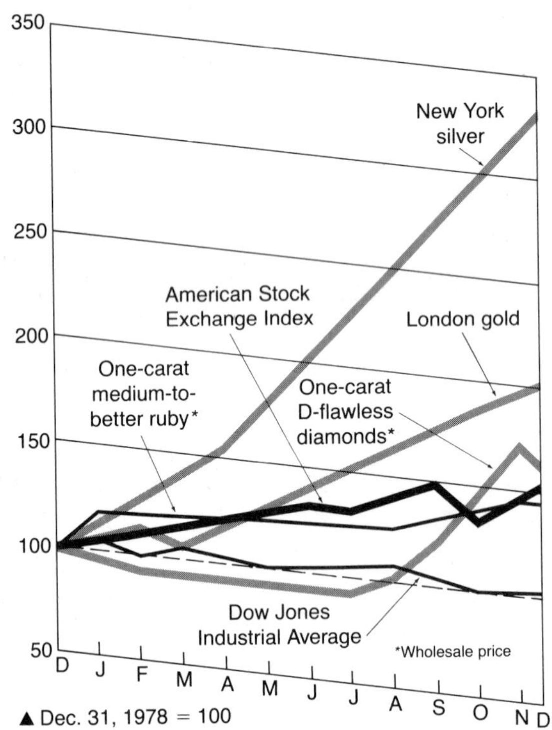

SOURCE: *Business Week*, December 31, 1979, p. 142.

Figure 19–10

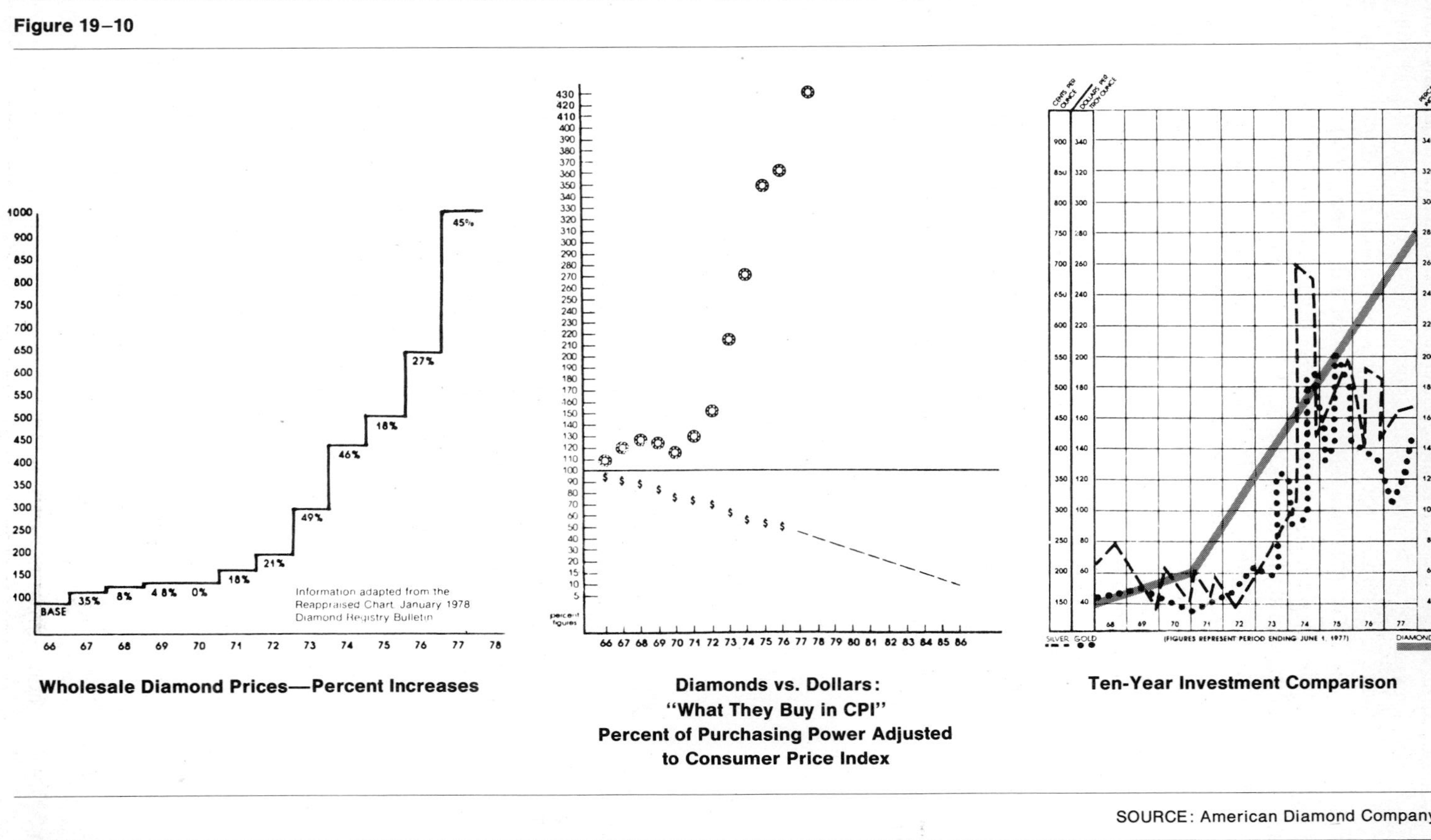

Wholesale Diamond Prices—Percent Increases

Diamonds vs. Dollars: "What They Buy in CPI" Percent of Purchasing Power Adjusted to Consumer Price Index

Ten-Year Investment Comparison

SOURCE: American Diamond Company.

appreciated 12.6 percent per year. Meanwhile, the consumer price index increased at an approximate annual rate of 6.5 percent, and the value of the average common stock increased at an annual rate of just 2.8 percent.

By 1980 the rising trend in diamond prices appeared to be continuing. Although the market for diamonds does not have the breadth or the liquidity of the market for stocks and bonds, they continue to provide an attractive form of investment for many investors. Much of the demand for diamonds still comes from individuals, but institutions that once invested only in stocks and bonds have progressively become buyers of diamonds. This trend, of course, was the result of a shift from financial to tangible assets as the world economic situation continued to worsen.

The Drawbacks

Despite the venerable history of diamonds, any investment in diamonds should not be made without due consideration of the fact that although there is a great demand for fine diamonds, they are highly illiquid. Furthermore, because a diamond retailing for $7,500 to $10,000 costs only $5,000 in the primary market, a sharp price gain must be realized before the investment becomes profitable. Also, there always exists the possibility of fraud. The New York Attorney General's office recently accused a prominent diamond dealer of fraudulent practices: Some of his diamonds were actually zirconium; he fraudulently described low-quality stones as being of investment grade; he gave out false diamond-grading certificates; he falsely said his stones were priced just above wholesale; and he held out hopeless promises for profit.

The Caveats

Although there is no substitute for a careful analysis of the product and its market, some broad trading guidelines may nevertheless be followed by diamond investors.

First, investors should invest only in diamonds that have at least one carat. Smaller stones do not significantly appreciate in price. In 1979, the price of diamonds under .5 carat actually declined by 25 percent; by contrast, top-grade stones of a carat or more jumped 20 percent just over the summer.

Second, investors should invest only in colorless—or nearly colorless—diamonds with few flaws. Unfortunately, there is no reliable index of diamond prices. Some average price quotations are of course available, but actual prices vary greatly, depending on the different opinions of dealers and graders.

Third, diamonds should be purchased only for the long-term. After discounts and commissions, it usually takes several years before an investor can sell diamonds and break even. Moreover, because diamonds are highly illiquid, it may take several months to liquidate these investments.

Finally, investors should protect themselves against fraud by insisting on certification by the Gemological Institute of America (GIA). They should also demand an iron-clad money-back guarantee if the gem turns out to be something other than promised.

Silver, Platinum, Copper

As revealed by Figure 19–11, 1979 was a "golden year" for silver. However, the rise in silver prices has not always been this spectacular. In fact, the price of silver has been quite volatile, as was partly evidenced by the fact that on March 27, 1980, silver prices plummeted to around $10 from a high of around $50 reached just a few months earlier. Also, quite frequently dealer mark-ups are so high that the market must perform extremely well before investors can profit from their investment in silver. For these reasons, investors should use extreme caution when investing in silver.

Figure 19–11 **Explosion in Metal Prices**

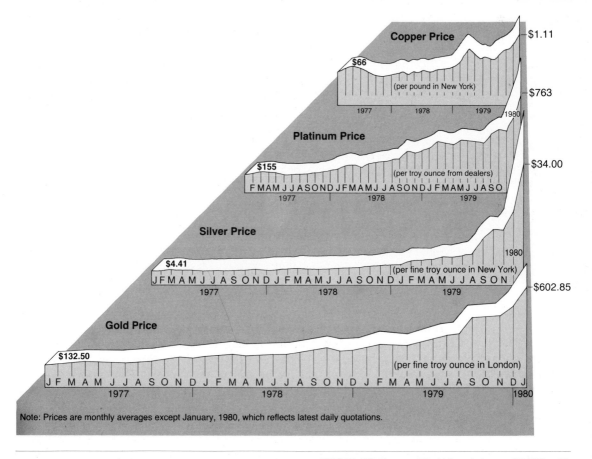

SOURCE: *U.S. News and World Report*, January 21, 1980, p. 75.

Caution should also be exercised in investing in other metals like platinum and copper. Prices of these metals have also exploded in recent years. However, because of their price volatility, trading in these metals has resulted in a long list of winners and losers.

Art and Antiques

An Overview

The attractiveness of art and antiques as an investment vehicle is underscored by the following passage:

> *In this thirty-third year of worldwide inflation, "investing" became very difficult since, with debasement of currency running to 18 percent to 20 percent unofficially during 1973, all yields in the classic meaning of the term simply ceased to exist. Loss of purchasing power generally exceeded the profits realized in Minidollars, Minifrancs or Minimarks—not to speak of Microsterling. The debacles in stock markets, and the tragedies of bond holders and of owners of savings bank accounts, along with the unstable political conditions which prevailed throughout the year, underscored once more the merits of objects of art and culture as vehicles for the protection of capital.*[12]

Recent increases in the price of antiques and art objects testify to the widespread investor interest in them. Recently, Matisse paintings sold for more than $1 million, a Tiffany lamp for $350,000, and an elegant paper weight for $96,000. But although these high-priced items always make the headlines, quality art and antiques can be far more affordable than many investors realize. At Sotheby Parke Bernet, Inc., New York, the nation's largest auction house, 84 percent of all objects sold in 1979 traded for less than $1,000.

The Caveats

Art, antiques, etchings, and other exotic objects constitute a specialized form of investment. However, knowledgeable investors may benefit from observing the following guidelines.

First, the investor should learn to recognize the factors that can make the price of an investment object go up or down so that he or she can take advantage of such fluctuations. In the case of art objects, for example, value is determined by a combination of several factors: artistic quality, rarity, condition, authenticity, historic appeal, provenance, and fashion. Etchings, drawings, and pastels

[12] Franz Pick, "Care to See My Etchings?" *Barron's*, December 31, 1973, p. 11. Reprinted by permission of *Barron's* © Dow Jones & Company, Inc., 1973. All Rights Reserved.

increase in price when they are authentic, have been produced by internationally famed artists, and are in demand as collectors' items. Such examples can be multiplied.

Second, it helps to get reliable information from some reputable dealer or expert, and also from authentic publications such as *International Art Market*, which deals with art, antiques, etchings and other objects.

Third, an investor should try to be selective. In 1979, speculators purchased anything that bore the name of Picasso, anything Victorian, Oriental, or that was classified as Americana. Specialists suspect that many of these speculators have invested their money in objects that have little lasting value. An investor should always believe the adage, "All that glitters is not gold," because he or she is not buying for pleasure but for profit.

Finally—and this is important—if an investor wishes to invest in an object, he or she should attempt to acquire it at an auction rather than from a dealer. As the *International Art Market* newsletter points out, "You are better off competing with a dealer when he's trying to buy at wholesale, than later on, paying *his* retail price."

Summary

Although it may possibly be a rewarding investment, real estate can be a risky proposition. Real estate investment takes special attributes not required for other investments.

Besides undeveloped land, other means of investing in real estate include residential property, office buildings, shopping centers, condominiums, and co-operative apartments. Individuals can invest in real estate through individual ownership, syndicates or partnerships, or shares of *REITs*.

Leverage is an important concept in real estate investment. It refers to the investing of borrowed money in earning assets. Although leverage allows investors to magnify profits earned on an asset, it also compels them to accept magnified losses when they make bad investments.

The tax law allows investors to deduct each year from their income the amount representing *depreciation* to their income-producing property. Two depreciation methods are *straight-line* and *declining balance methods.* The law states that the profit on a real estate transaction is the difference between the sale price and the depreciated value (cost basis) of the property. The excess of accelerated depreciation over straight-line depreciation is recaptured and taxed as ordinary income.

The objective of most investments in real estate is to reduce the tax liability by claiming depreciation and interest deductions, and realizing long-term capital gains which receive preferential treatment under the tax law.

Commodity futures are claims on a certain amount of goods with the promise that the commodities will be delivered by a certain date. The *futures market* serves essentially as a *hedge* for the farmer or processor; it transfers risk and the possibility of large profits to speculators.

The future price of a commodity represents the current price of the good plus carrying charges under normal conditions. But the futures price may be higher or lower than the cash price, depending on the buyers' and sellers' views of the futures market for the commodity.

Gold is a commodity, and as such, its price can fluctuate like the price of any industrial commodity. But gold is a unique vehicle, because it has a monetary connotation as well as a private appeal. It can be held in the form of *coins, bullion, futures, stocks, jewelry*, and *certificates*. Each has advantages and limitations.

In the past, diamonds have consistently appreciated in price. However, they are a highly illiquid investment; moreover, because of large mark-ups, a substantial price gain must normally be realized before the investment becomes profitable.

Art and antiques are for investors with special knowledge of these objects. Because prices of art and antiques vary considerably and their value is determined by several factors which can be difficult to assess, care should be exercised when investing in them.

Concepts for Review

REITs
Syndicates
Limited Partnerships
Leverage
Depreciation
Straight-line depreciation
Declining balance depreciation
Recapture of depreciation
Chicago Board of Trade
Chicago Mercantile Exchange
Commodity
Futures market
Futures contract
Hedger
Speculator
Cash market
Basis
Krugerrands
Gold bullion
Gold futures
Gold certificates

Questions for Review

1. What are the various types of real estate in which one can invest? Which of these do you think would be difficult for individuals to own? Explain.
2. Discuss the advantages and risks of investing in residential property. How does such an investment differ from investing in REITs, syndicates, and limited partnerships?

3. Comment on the following statement: "Over the long-term, the price of land must rise substantially. The world's population continues to increase, but the supply of land is fixed."
4. What depreciation methods are available to the owner of income-producing property? Why is the selection of a depreciation method an important consideration?
5. How can a real estate investment be used to reduce an investor's tax liability?
6. Describe the liquidity of the real estate market. Is liquidity an important consideration in real estate investing? Explain.
7. Comment on the following statement: "In general, the function of the commodity futures market is to provide an arena where investors can profit from commodity price changes."
8. What is the cash price of a commodity? What is the future price? How are they related?
9. What is *hedging*? What is the objective of this strategy?
10. Why is there a large profit potential for speculators in the commodity futures market?
11. What is the difference between purchasing stocks and commodity futures on margin?
12. Why is it difficult to predict the price of gold?
13. What are the drawbacks to investing in gold?
14. Investor K states that he would consider investing in diamonds only for the long-term. What is your response?
15. Would you consider the market for art and antiques to be efficient? Explain.

Appendix 19-A: Economic Analysis of Gold Price Movements†

To begin, it is useful to distinguish between gold stocks and flows. The stock of gold is the quantity held at a given time, whereas the net flow of gold is the change in that stock during a particular interval of time. Production flows add to stocks as newly mined and refined gold becomes available to the market; consumption flows deplete stocks as gold is put to uses that render it irrecoverable. Gold's use in electronics, for example, depletes stocks of gold, since recycling gold is frequently uneconomical in these applications. The metal's use in art also depletes stocks because once incorporated in a work of art, gold is no longer available to the market. Presumably, if such a work of art is deemed "priceless," no price of gold would cause the work to be scrapped and the gold to be melted down, regardless of how high the price might be. In view of these distinctions, gold stocks should be understood to mean readily marketable stocks at a particular time.

Owners of gold stocks have the choice of selling gold today or storing it for future sale. This decision depends on current and anticipated future prices. The storage of gold yields no return other than the prospect of an appreciation in price. The assumption about rational behavior implies that participants in the

†With suitable modification this appendix reproduces Peter A. Abken, "The Economics of Gold Price Movements," Federal Reserve Bank of Richmond, *Economic Review*, March–April 1980, pp. 3–5.

gold market act to maximize anticipated net revenue from the storage of gold. They store a quantity of gold such that the anticipated appreciation in the price of gold equals the net marginal costs of storing gold.

Net marginal costs of storage are implicit storage costs that consist of the following components: (1) marginal outlay for storage, (2) marginal interest cost, and (3) marginal convenience yield. Marginal outlay costs comprise the charges for warehousing (in vaults) and insuring additional stocks of gold. The marginal interest cost reflects the opportunity cost of owning additional stocks of noninterest-bearing gold rather than alternative interest-bearing assets. Finally, the marginal convenience yield is the monetary value imputed to holding gold stocks for commercial uses which require gold for fabricating goods. The convenience yield accrues from avoiding costly changes in the production schedule and the associated frequent spot purchases of gold. Additionally, stocks of gold prevent loss of sales because of temporary shortages of gold on hand for fabrication.[1]

Marginal storage costs are defined above as net of the marginal convenience yield, which has the opposite sign from the other marginal components. The marginal convenience yield is a decreasing function of stocks held, diminishing to zero for some sufficiently large level of stocks. As long as the marginal convenience yield is positive, it offsets the other marginal costs of storage to some degree. Equation 1 expresses the definition of net marginal storage costs mathematically:

$$(1)\quad \text{NMSC} = \text{mo} + \text{mi} - \text{mc}$$

The net marginal storage costs, NMSC, are the sum of the marginal outlay, mo, and the marginal interest cost, mi, minus the marginal convenience yield, mc.

The equilibrium relationship between anticipated gold price appreciation and net marginal storage costs is summarized in the following relationship:

$$(2)\quad E(P_{t+1}) - P_t = \text{NMSC}$$

Equation 2 indicates that equilibrium in the gold market requires the difference or spread between the market's anticipated price of gold next period, $E(P_{t+1})$, and the current price, P_t, to equal net marginal storage costs, NMSC.

The aggregate effect of individual market participants seeking profits assures that the equilibrium condition in the gold market holds. A geometric model of price movements will help illustrate the relationship between the price spread and net marginal storage costs. For this exposition, marginal outlay and convenience yield are assumed to be negligible compared to the marginal interest cost. Under these conditions, if the interest rate is r percent, then the full equilibrium rate of gold price appreciation over the period will be r percent. Such an equilibrium is shown in Figure 19–A for a gold price of P_0 at the beginning

[1] This discussion of storage applies to any storable commodity.

Figure 19–A

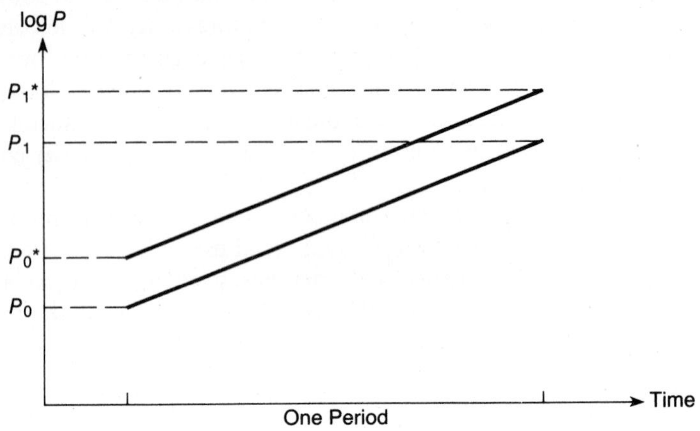

of the period, and a price of P_1 at the end of the period, where the percentage price appreciation $\log P_1 - \log P_0$ is r percent.[2]

Now suppose some economic or political disturbance occurs that causes market participants to revise their anticipations of price appreciation so that an incipient excess demand (positive or negative) develops at the initial price. Market participants will try to profit from the change in anticipations and in so doing will bring the anticipated price spread over the period back into equality with the interest rate. Specifically, suppose the anticipated end of period gold price rises from P_1 to P_1^* so that the anticipated capital gain on gold over the period momentarily exceeds r percent. Market participants will attempt to realize profits by storing gold; but since the stock of gold is essentially fixed, they will only succeed in bidding up the spot price. Equilibrium will be restored at a new spot price of P_0^*, where the anticipated capital gain has been brought back to r percent.

It should be emphasized that the anticipated future price does not completely determine the spot price. A change in current supply conditions could affect the spot price which in turn would cause anticipated future prices to be revised via the storage adjustment process. In this connection it is important to note that individuals may choose to hold more wealth in gold than in other assets in times

[2] The reader may wonder how this theory of gold price movements would account for secularly stable gold prices. In this situation, the anticipated price of gold would equal the current price. Individuals would be willing to hold gold, a noninterest-bearing asset, only if net marginal storage costs for gold were zero. This implies that the marginal convenience yield would offset the positive marginal interest cost, which would occur for sufficiently small stocks of gold.

Figure 19–B **Percentage Spread Between the October 1980 Futures Price and the December 1979 Futures Price During 1979** (End of Week Data)

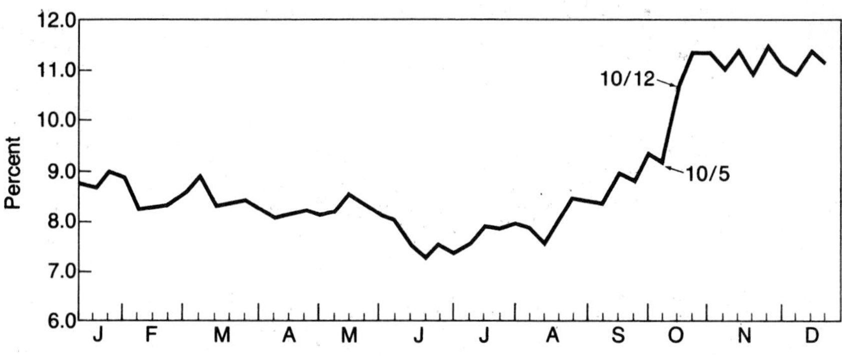

of political and economic uncertainty because of the greater security and anonymity of gold. Such a shift in the composition of wealth might be made without regard for the metal's future rate of price appreciation. The spot price of gold would be bid upward, drawing gold out of storage for sale on the spot market. The anticipated future price of gold would also rise, since the interest rate would otherwise exceed the price spread.

The preceding theory of gold price movements is readily applied to gold futures markets.[3] An individual's decision to store gold for future sale requires a prediction of the gold price. Futures trading facilitates this process by making market price anticipations explicit in futures prices. According to the theory of gold price movements, net marginal storage costs should influence the spread between futures prices.

Figure 19–B shows the percentage spread between the prices of the October 1980 and the December 1979 futures contracts during 1979.[4] From January through September 1979, the spread fluctuated around 8 percent. After September, the spread widened rapidly and varied around 11 percent. The greatest increase of 1.53 percentage points occurred between the observations on October 5, 1979 and October 12, 1979. This was the week the Federal Reserve

[3] A futures market is a market for the deferred (future) delivery of a commodity. The gold futures market broadens the time frame for buying and selling gold. Gold may be bought and sold for immediate delivery in the spot market, or it may be bought and sold today for deferred delivery via the purchase and sale of gold futures contracts. A futures contract is a legally binding agreement to buy or sell a standardized amount of a commodity in a specified future period at a specified price. The price of this financial instrument is determined in an open, competitive auction on the trading floor of a futures exchange.

[4] These contracts were traded on the Commodity Exchange in New York.

announced a more restrictive monetary policy. The associated rise in short-term interest rates sharply increased the opportunity cost of storing gold.

In the particular case of the futures contracts in Figure 19–B, the relevant opportunity cost is not a directly observable interest rate. Rather, it is a forward interest rate over a 10-month period beginning in December 1979 given implicitly in the term structure of interest rates. The forward rate implicit in the futures price spread for these contracts was in the neighborhood of 10 percent at an annual rate in the months before the October 6th policy change. The implicit forward rate increased to roughly 13 percent following the policy change. This observation is consistent with the view that the market anticipated persistently higher interest rates associated with tighter monetary policy. Consequently, the spread between gold futures prices increased because of the higher anticipated net marginal storage costs for holding gold.

Appendix: Mathematical Tables

Table A–1 **Compound Value: Fixed Sum Factor (CVFF)**
Fixed amount = $1

Period	1%	2%	3%	4%	5%	6%	7%
1	1.010	1.020	1.030	1.040	1.050	1.060	1.070
2	1.020	1.040	1.061	1.082	1.102	1.124	1.145
3	1.030	1.061	1.093	1.125	1.158	1.191	1.225
4	1.041	1.082	1.126	1.170	1.216	1.262	1.311
5	1.051	1.104	1.159	1.217	1.276	1.338	1.403
6	1.062	1.126	1.194	1.265	1.340	1.419	1.501
7	1.072	1.149	1.230	1.316	1.407	1.504	1.606
8	1.083	1.172	1.267	1.369	1.477	1.594	1.718
9	1.094	1.195	1.305	1.423	1.551	1.689	1.838
10	1.105	1.219	1.344	1.480	1.629	1.791	1.967
11	1.116	1.243	1.384	1.539	1.710	1.898	2.105
12	1.127	1.268	1.426	1.601	1.796	2.012	2.252
13	1.138	1.294	1.469	1.665	1.886	2.133	2.410
14	1.149	1.319	1.513	1.732	1.980	2.261	2.579
15	1.161	1.346	1.558	1.801	2.079	2.397	2.759
16	1.173	1.373	1.605	1.873	2.183	2.540	2.952
17	1.184	1.400	1.653	1.948	2.292	2.693	3.159
18	1.196	1.428	1.702	2.026	2.407	2.854	3.380
19	1.208	1.457	1.754	2.107	2.527	3.026	3.617
20	1.220	1.486	1.806	2.191	2.653	3.207	3.870
25	1.282	1.641	2.094	2.666	3.386	4.292	5.427
30	1.348	1.811	2.427	3.243	4.322	5.743	7.612

Table A–1 (*continued*)

Period	8%	9%	10%	12%	14%	15%	16%
1	1.080	1.090	1.100	1.120	1.140	1.150	1.160
2	1.166	1.186	1.210	1.254	1.300	1.322	1.346
3	1.260	1.295	1.331	1.405	1.482	1.521	1.561
4	1.360	1.412	1.464	1.574	1.689	1.749	1.811
5	1.469	1.539	1.611	1.762	1.925	2.011	2.100
6	1.587	1.677	1.772	1.974	2.195	2.313	2.436
7	1.714	1.828	1.949	2.211	2.502	2.660	2.826
8	1.851	1.993	2.144	2.476	2.853	3.059	3.278
9	1.999	2.172	2.358	2.773	3.252	3.518	3.803
10	2.159	2.367	2.594	3.106	3.707	4.046	4.411
11	2.332	2.580	2.853	3.479	4.226	4.652	5.117
12	2.518	2.813	3.138	3.896	4.818	5.350	5.926
13	2.720	3.066	3.452	4.363	5.492	6.153	6.886
14	2.937	3.342	3.797	4.887	6.261	7.076	7.988
15	3.172	3.642	4.177	5.474	7.138	8.137	9.266
16	3.426	3.970	4.595	6.130	8.137	9.358	10.748
17	3.700	4.328	5.054	6.866	9.276	10.761	12.468
18	3.996	4.717	5.560	7.690	10.575	12.375	14.463
19	4.316	5.142	6.116	8.613	12.056	14.232	16.777
20	4.661	5.604	6.728	9.646	13.743	16.367	19.461
25	6.848	8.623	10.835	17.000	26.462	32.919	40.874
30	10.063	13.268	17.449	29.960	50.950	66.212	85.850

Period	18%	20%	24%	28%	32%	36%
1	1.180	1.200	1.240	1.280	1.320	1.360
2	1.392	1.440	1.538	1.638	1.742	1.850
3	1.643	1.728	1.907	2.067	2.300	2.515
4	1.939	2.074	2.364	2.684	3.036	3.421
5	2.288	2.488	2.932	3.436	4.007	4.653
6	2.700	2.986	3.635	4.398	5.290	6.328
7	3.185	3.583	4.508	5.629	6.983	8.605
8	3.759	4.300	5.590	7.206	9.217	11.703
9	4.435	5.160	6.931	9.223	12.166	15.917
10	5.234	6.192	8.594	11.806	16.060	21.647
11	6.176	7.430	10.657	15.112	21.199	29.439
12	7.288	8.916	13.215	19.343	27.983	40.037
13	8.599	10.699	16.386	24.759	36.937	54.451
14	10.147	12.839	20.319	31.961	48.757	74.053
15	11.974	15.407	25.196	40.565	64.359	100.712
16	14.129	18.488	31.243	51.923	84.954	136.97
17	16.672	22.186	38.741	66.461	112.14	186.28
18	19.673	26.623	48.039	85.071	148.02	253.34
19	23.214	31.948	59.568	108.89	195.39	344.54
20	27.393	38.338	73.864	139.38	257.92	468.57
25	62.669	95.396	216.542	478.90	1033.6	2180.1
30	143.371	237.376	634.820	1645.5	4142.1	10143.

Table A–1 (*continued*)

Period	40%	50%	60%	70%	80%	90%
1	1.400	1.500	1.600	1.700	1.800	1.900
2	1.960	2.250	2.560	2.890	3.240	3.610
3	2.744	3.375	4.096	4.913	5.832	6.859
4	3.842	5.062	6.544	8.352	10.498	13.032
5	5.378	7.594	10.486	14.199	18.896	24.761
6	7.530	11.391	16.777	24.138	34.012	47.046
7	10.541	17.086	26.844	41.034	61.222	89.387
8	14.758	25.629	42.950	69.758	110.200	169.836
9	20.661	38.443	68.720	118.588	198.359	322.688
10	28.925	57.665	109.951	201.599	357.047	613.107
11	40.496	86.498	175.922	342.719	642.684	1164.902
12	56.694	129.746	281.475	582.622	1156.831	2213.314
13	79.372	194.619	450.360	990.457	2082.295	4205.297
14	111.120	291.929	720.576	1683.777	3748.131	7990.065
15	155.568	437.894	1152.921	2862.421	6746.636	15181.122
16	217.795	656.84	1844.7	4866.1	12144.	28844.0
17	304.914	985.26	2951.5	8272.4	21859.	54804.0
18	426.879	1477.9	4722.4	14063.0	39346.	104130.0
19	597.630	2216.8	7555.8	23907.0	70824.	197840.0
20	836.683	3325.3	12089.0	40642.0	127480.	375900.0
25	4499.880	25251.	126760.0	577060.0	2408900.	9307600.0
30	24201.432	191750.	1329200.	8193500.0	45517000.	230470000.0

Table A–2 **Present Value: Fixed Sum Factor (PVFF)**
Fixed amount = $1

Period	1%	2%	3%	4%	5%	6%	7%	8%	9%	10%	12%	14%	15%
1	.990	.980	.971	.962	.952	.943	.935	.926	.917	.909	.893	.877	.870
2	.980	.961	.943	.925	.907	.890	.873	.857	.842	.826	.797	.769	.756
3	.971	.942	.915	.889	.864	.840	.816	.794	.772	.751	.712	.675	.658
4	.961	.924	.889	.855	.823	.792	.763	.735	.708	.683	.636	.592	.572
5	.951	.906	.863	.822	.784	.747	.713	.681	.650	.621	.567	.519	.497
6	.942	.888	.838	.790	.746	.705	.666	.630	.596	.564	.507	.456	.432
7	.933	.871	.813	.760	.711	.665	.623	.583	.547	.513	.452	.400	.376
8	.923	.853	.789	.731	.677	.627	.582	.540	.502	.467	.404	.351	.327
9	.914	.837	.766	.703	.645	.592	.544	.500	.460	.424	.361	.308	.284
10	.905	.820	.744	.676	.614	.558	.508	.463	.422	.386	.322	.270	.247
11	.896	.804	.722	.650	.585	.527	.475	.429	.388	.350	.287	.237	.215
12	.887	.788	.701	.625	.557	.497	.444	.397	.356	.319	.257	.208	.187
13	.879	.773	.681	.601	.530	.469	.415	.368	.326	.290	.229	.182	.163
14	.870	.758	.661	.577	.505	.442	.388	.340	.299	.263	.205	.160	.141
15	.861	.743	.642	.555	.481	.417	.362	.315	.275	.239	.183	.140	.123
16	.853	.728	.623	.534	.458	.394	.339	.292	.252	.218	.163	.123	.107
17	.844	.714	.605	.513	.436	.371	.317	.270	.231	.198	.146	.108	.093
18	.836	.700	.587	.494	.416	.350	.296	.250	.212	.180	.130	.095	.081
19	.828	.686	.570	.475	.396	.331	.276	.232	.194	.164	.116	.083	.070
20	.820	.673	.554	.456	.377	.312	.258	.215	.178	.149	.104	.073	.061
25	.780	.610	.478	.375	.295	.233	.184	.146	.116	.092	.059	.038	.030
30	.742	.552	.412	.308	.231	.174	.131	.099	.075	.057	.033	.020	.015

Period	16%	18%	20%	24%	28%	32%	36%	40%	50%	60%	70%	80%	90%
1	.862	.847	.833	.806	.781	.758	.735	.714	.667	.625	.588	.556	.526
2	.743	.718	.694	.650	.610	.574	.541	.510	.444	.391	.346	.309	.277
3	.641	.609	.579	.524	.477	.435	.398	.364	.296	.244	.204	.171	.146
4	.552	.516	.482	.423	.373	.329	.292	.260	.198	.153	.120	.095	.077
5	.476	.437	.402	.341	.291	.250	.215	.186	.132	.095	.070	.053	.040
6	.410	.370	.335	.275	.227	.189	.158	.133	.088	.060	.041	.029	.021
7	.354	.314	.279	.222	.178	.143	.116	.095	.059	.037	.024	.016	.011
8	.305	.266	.233	.179	.139	.108	.085	.068	.039	.023	.014	.009	.006
9	.263	.226	.194	.144	.108	.082	.063	.048	.026	.015	.008	.005	.003
10	.227	.191	.162	.116	.085	.062	.046	.035	.017	.009	.005	.003	.002
11	.195	.162	.135	.094	.066	.047	.034	.025	.012	.006	.003	.002	.001
12	.168	.137	.112	.076	.052	.036	.025	.018	.008	.004	.002	.001	.001
13	.145	.116	.093	.061	.040	.027	.018	.013	.005	.002	.001	.001	.000
14	.125	.099	.078	.049	.032	.021	.014	.009	.003	.001	.001	.000	.000
15	.108	.084	.065	.040	.025	.016	.010	.006	.002	.001	.000	.000	.000
16	.093	.071	.054	.032	.019	.012	.007	.005	.002	.001	.000	.000	
17	.080	.060	.045	.026	.015	.009	.005	.003	.001	.000	.000		
18	.089	.051	.038	.021	.012	.007	.004	.002	.001	.000	.000		
19	.060	.043	.031	.017	.009	.005	.003	.002	.000	.000			
20	.051	.037	.026	.014	.007	.004	.002	.001	.000	.000			
25	.024	.016	.110	.005	.002	.001	.000	.000					
30	.012	.007	.004	.002	.001	.000	.000						

Table A–3 **Compound Value: Annuity Factor (CVAF)**
Amount of annuity = $1

Period	1%	2%	3%	4%	5%	6%
1	1.000	1.000	1.000	1.000	1.000	1.000
2	2.010	2.020	2.030	2.040	2.050	2.060
3	3.030	3.060	3.091	3.122	3.152	3.184
4	4.060	4.122	4.184	4.246	4.310	4.375
5	5.101	5.204	5.309	5.416	5.526	5.637
6	6.152	6.308	6.468	6.633	6.802	6.975
7	7.214	7.434	7.662	7.898	8.142	8.394
8	8.286	8.583	8.892	9.214	9.549	9.897
9	9.369	9.755	10.159	10.583	11.027	11.491
10	10.462	10.950	11.464	12.006	12.578	13.181
11	11.567	12.169	12.808	13.486	14.207	14.972
12	12.683	13.412	14.192	15.026	15.917	16.870
13	13.809	14.680	15.618	16.627	17.713	18.882
14	14.947	15.974	17.086	18.292	19.599	21.051
15	16.097	17.293	18.599	20.024	21.579	23.276
16	17.258	18.639	20.157	21.825	23.657	25.673
17	18.430	20.012	21.762	23.698	25.840	28.213
18	19.615	21.412	23.414	25.645	28.132	30.906
19	20.811	22.841	25.117	27.671	30.539	33.760
20	22.019	24.297	26.870	29.778	33.066	36.786
25	28.243	32.030	36.459	41.646	47.727	54.865
30	34.785	40.568	47.575	56.805	66.439	79.058

Period	7%	8%	9%	10%	12%	14%
1	1.000	1.000	1.000	1.000	1.000	1.000
2	2.070	2.080	2.090	2.100	2.120	2.140
3	3.215	3.246	3.278	3.310	3.374	3.440
4	4.440	4.506	4.573	4.641	4.770	4.921
5	5.751	5.867	5.985	6.105	6.353	6.610
6	7.153	7.336	7.523	7.716	8.115	8.536
7	8.654	8.923	9.200	9.487	10.089	10.730
8	10.260	10.637	11.028	11.436	12.300	13.233
9	11.978	12.488	13.021	13.579	14.776	16.085
10	13.816	14.487	15.193	15.937	17.549	19.337
11	15.784	16.645	17.560	18.531	20.655	23.044
12	17.888	18.977	20.141	21.384	24.133	27.271
13	20.141	21.495	22.953	24.523	28.029	32.089
14	22.550	24.215	26.019	27.975	32.393	37.581
15	25.129	27.152	29.361	31.772	37.280	43.842
16	27.888	30.324	33.003	35.950	42.753	50.980
17	30.840	33.750	36.974	40.545	48.884	59.118
18	33.999	37.450	41.301	45.599	55.750	68.394
19	37.379	41.446	46.018	51.159	63.440	78.969
20	40.995	45.762	51.160	57.275	72.052	91.025
25	63.249	73.106	84.701	98.347	133.334	181.871
30	94.461	113.283	136.308	164.494	241.333	356.787

Table A–3 (*continued*)

Period	16%	18%	20%	24%	28%	32%
1	1.000	1.000	1.000	1.000	1.000	1.000
2	2.160	2.180	2.200	2.240	2.280	2.320
3	3.506	3.572	3.640	3.778	3.918	4.062
4	5.066	5.215	5.368	5.684	6.016	6.362
5	6.877	7.154	7.442	8.048	8.700	9.398
6	8.977	9.442	9.930	10.980	12.136	13.406
7	11.414	12.142	12.916	14.615	16.534	18.696
8	14.240	15.327	16.499	19.123	22.163	25.678
9	17.518	19.086	20.799	24.712	29.369	34.895
10	21.321	23.521	25.959	31.643	38.592	47.062
11	25.733	28.755	32.150	40.238	50.399	63.122
12	30.850	34.931	39.580	50.985	65.510	84.320
13	36.786	42.219	48.497	64.110	84.853	112.303
14	43.672	50.818	59.196	80.496	109.612	149.240
15	51.660	60.965	72.035	100.815	141.303	197.997
16	60.925	72.939	87.442	126.011	181.87	262.36
17	71.673	87.068	105.931	157.253	233.79	347.31
18	84.141	103.740	128.117	195.994	300.25	459.45
19	98.603	123.414	154.740	244.033	385.32	607.47
20	115.380	146.628	186.688	303.601	494.21	802.86
25	249.214	342.603	471.981	898.092	1706.8	3226.8
30	530.312	790.948	1181.882	2640.916	5873.2	12941.0

Period	36%	40%	50%	60%	70%	80%
1	1.000	1.000	1.000	1.000	1.000	1.000
2	2.360	2.400	2.500	2.600	2.700	2.800
3	4.210	4.360	4.750	5.160	5.590	6.040
4	6.725	7.104	8.125	9.256	10.503	11.872
5	10.146	10.846	13.188	15.810	18.855	22.370
6	14.799	16.324	20.781	26.295	33.054	41.265
7	21.126	23.853	32.172	43.073	57.191	75.278
8	29.732	34.395	49.258	69.916	98.225	136.500
9	41.435	49.153	74.887	112.866	167.983	246.699
10	57.352	69.814	113.330	181.585	286.570	445.058
11	78.998	98.739	170.995	291.536	488.170	802.105
12	108.437	139.235	257.493	467.458	830.888	1444.788
13	148.475	195.929	387.239	748.933	1413.510	2601.619
14	202.926	275.300	581.859	1199.293	2403.968	4683.914
15	276.979	386.420	873.788	1919.869	4087.745	8432.045
16	377.69	541.99	1311.7	3072.8	6950.2	15179.0
17	514.66	759.78	1968.5	4917.5	11816.0	27323.0
18	700.94	1064.7	2953.8	7868.9	20089.0	49182.0
19	954.28	1491.6	4431.7	12591.0	34152.0	88528.0
20	1298.8	2089.2	6648.5	20147.0	58059.0	159350.0
25	6053.0	11247.0	50500.0	211270.0	824370.0	3011100.0
30	28172.0	60501.0	383500.0	2215400.0	11705000.0	56896000.0

Table A–4 **Present Value: Annuity Factor (PVAF)**
Amount of annuity = $1

Period	1%	2%	3%	4%	5%	6%	7%	8%	9%	10%
1	0.990	0.980	0.971	0.962	0.952	0.943	0.935	0.926	0.917	0.909
2	1.970	1.942	1.913	1.886	1.859	1.833	1.808	1.783	1.759	1.736
3	2.941	2.884	2.829	2.775	2.723	2.673	2.624	2.577	2.531	2.487
4	3.902	3.808	3.717	3.630	3.546	3.465	3.387	3.312	3.240	3.170
5	4.853	4.713	4.580	4.452	4.329	4.212	4.100	3.993	3.890	3.791
6	5.795	5.601	5.417	5.242	5.076	4.917	4.766	4.623	4.486	4.355
7	6.728	6.472	6.230	6.002	5.786	5.582	5.389	5.206	5.033	4.868
8	7.652	7.325	7.020	6.733	6.463	6.210	5.971	5.747	5.535	5.335
9	8.566	8.162	7.786	7.435	7.108	6.802	6.515	6.247	5.995	5.759
10	9.471	8.983	8.530	8.111	7.722	7.360	7.024	6.710	6.418	6.145
11	10.368	9.787	9.253	8.760	8.306	7.887	7.499	7.139	6.805	6.495
12	11.255	10.575	9.954	9.385	8.863	8.384	7.943	7.536	7.161	6.814
13	12.134	11.348	10.635	9.986	9.394	8.853	8.358	7.904	7.487	7.103
14	13.004	12.106	11.296	10.563	9.899	9.295	8.745	8.244	7.786	7.367
15	13.865	12.849	11.938	11.118	10.380	9.712	9.108	8.559	8.060	7.606
16	14.718	13.578	12.561	11.652	10.838	10.106	9.447	8.851	8.312	7.824
17	15.562	14.292	13.166	12.166	11.274	10.477	9.763	9.122	8.544	8.022
18	16.398	14.992	13.754	12.659	11.690	10.828	10.059	9.372	8.756	8.201
19	17.226	15.678	14.324	13.134	12.085	11.158	10.336	9.604	8.950	8.365
20	18.046	16.351	14.877	13.590	12.462	11.470	10.594	9.818	9.128	8.514
25	22.023	19.523	17.413	15.622	14.094	12.783	11.654	10.675	9.823	9.077
30	25.808	22.397	19.600	17.292	15.373	13.765	12.409	11.258	10.274	9.427

Period	12%	14%	16%	18%	20%	24%	28%	32%	36%
1	0.893	0.877	0.862	0.847	0.833	0.806	0.781	0.758	0.735
2	1.690	1.647	1.605	1.566	1.528	1.457	1.392	1.332	1.276
3	2.402	2.322	2.246	2.174	2.106	1.981	1.868	1.766	1.674
4	3.037	2.914	2.798	2.690	2.589	2.404	2.241	2.096	1.966
5	3.605	3.433	3.274	3.127	2.991	2.745	2.532	2.345	2.181
6	4.111	3.889	3.685	3.498	3.326	3.020	2.759	2.534	2.339
7	4.564	4.288	4.039	3.812	3.605	3.242	2.937	2.678	2.455
8	4.968	4.639	4.344	4.078	3.837	3.421	3.076	2.786	2.540
9	5.328	4.946	4.607	4.303	4.031	3.566	3.184	2.868	2.603
10	5.650	5.216	4.833	4.494	4.193	3.682	3.269	2.930	2.650
11	5.938	5.453	5.029	4.656	4.327	3.776	3.335	2.978	2.683
12	6.194	5.660	5.197	4.793	4.439	3.851	3.387	3.013	2.708
13	6.424	5.842	5.342	4.910	4.533	3.912	3.427	3.040	2.727
14	6.628	6.002	5.468	5.008	4.611	3.962	3.459	3.061	2.740
15	6.811	6.142	5.575	5.092	4.675	4.001	3.483	3.076	2.750
16	6.974	6.265	5.669	5.162	4.730	4.033	3.503	3.088	2.758
17	7.120	5.373	5.749	4.222	4.775	4.059	3.518	3.097	2.763
18	7.250	6.467	5.818	5.273	4.812	4.080	3.529	3.104	2.767
19	7.366	6.550	5.877	5.316	4.844	4.097	3.539	3.109	2.770
20	7.469	6.623	5.929	5.353	4.870	4.110	3.546	3.113	2.772
25	7.843	6.873	6.097	5.467	4.948	4.147	3.564	3.122	2.776
30	8.055	7.003	6.177	5.517	4.979	4.160	3.569	3.124	2.778

Table A–5 **Common Logarithms**

N	0	1	2	3	4	5	6	7	8	9
10	0000	0043	0086	0128	0170	0212	0253	0294	0334	0374
11	0414	0453	0492	0531	0569	0607	0645	0682	0719	0755
12	0792	0828	0864	0899	0934	0969	1004	1038	1072	1106
13	1139	1173	1206	1239	1271	1303	1335	1367	1399	1430
14	1461	1492	1523	1553	1584	1614	1644	1673	1703	1732
15	1761	1790	1818	1847	1875	1903	1931	1959	1987	2014
16	2041	2068	2095	2122	2148	2175	2201	2227	2253	2279
17	2304	2330	2355	2380	2405	2430	2455	2480	2504	2529
18	2553	2577	2601	2625	2648	2672	2695	2718	2742	2765
19	2788	2810	2833	2856	2878	2900	2923	2945	2967	2989
20	3010	3032	3054	3075	3096	3118	3139	3160	3181	3201
21	3222	3243	3263	3284	3304	3324	3345	3365	3385	3404
22	3424	3444	3464	3483	3502	3522	3541	3560	3579	3598
23	3617	3636	3655	3674	3692	3711	3729	3747	3766	3784
24	3802	3820	3838	3856	3874	3892	3909	3927	3945	3962
25	3979	3997	4014	4031	4048	4065	4082	4099	4116	4133
26	4150	4166	4183	4200	4216	4232	4249	4265	4281	4298
27	4314	4330	4346	4362	4378	4393	4409	4425	4440	4456
28	4472	4487	4502	4518	4533	4548	4564	4579	4594	4609
29	4624	4639	4654	4669	4683	4698	4713	4728	4742	4757
30	4771	4786	4800	4814	4829	4843	4857	4871	4886	4900
31	4914	4928	4942	4955	4969	4983	4997	5011	5024	5038
32	5051	5065	5079	5092	5105	5119	5132	5145	5159	5172
33	5185	5198	5211	5224	5237	5250	5263	5276	5289	5302
34	5315	5328	5340	5353	5366	5378	5391	5403	5416	5428
35	5441	5453	5465	5478	5490	5502	5514	5527	5539	5551
36	5563	5575	5587	5599	5611	5623	5635	5647	5658	5670
37	5682	5694	5705	5717	5729	5740	5752	5763	5775	5786
38	5798	5809	5821	5832	5843	5855	5866	5877	5888	5899
39	5911	5922	5933	5944	5955	5966	5977	5988	5999	6010
40	6021	6031	6042	6053	6064	6075	6085	6096	6107	6117
41	6128	6138	6149	6160	6170	6180	6191	6201	6212	6222
42	6232	6243	6253	6263	6274	6284	6294	6304	6314	6325
43	6335	6345	6355	6365	6375	6385	6395	6405	6415	6425
44	6435	6444	6454	6464	6474	6484	6493	6503	6513	6522
45	6532	6542	6551	6561	6571	6580	6590	6599	6609	6618
46	6628	6637	6646	6656	6665	6675	6684	6693	6702	6712
47	6721	6730	6739	6749	6758	6767	6776	6785	6794	6803
48	6812	6821	6830	6839	6848	6857	6866	6875	6884	6893
49	6902	6911	6920	6928	6937	6946	6955	6964	6972	6981
50	6990	6998	7007	7016	7024	7033	7042	7050	7059	7067
51	7076	7084	7093	7101	7110	7118	7126	7135	7143	7152
52	7160	7168	7177	7185	7193	7202	7210	7218	7226	7235
53	7243	7251	7259	7267	7275	7284	7292	7300	7308	7316
54	7324	7332	7340	7348	7356	7364	7372	7380	7388	7396
55	7404	7412	7419	7427	7435	7443	7451	7459	7466	7474
56	7482	7490	7497	7505	7513	7520	7528	7536	7543	7551
57	7559	7566	7574	7582	7589	7597	7604	7612	7619	7627
58	7634	7642	7649	7657	7664	7672	7679	7686	7694	7701
59	7709	7716	7723	7731	7738	7745	7752	7760	7767	7774
60	7782	7789	7796	7803	7810	7818	7825	7832	7839	7846

Table A–5 (*continued*)

N	0	1	2	3	4	5	6	7	8	9
61	7853	7860	7868	7875	7882	7889	7896	7903	7910	7917
62	7924	7931	7938	7945	7952	7959	7966	7973	7980	7987
63	7993	8000	8007	8014	8021	8028	8035	8041	8048	8055
64	8062	8069	8075	8082	8089	8096	8102	8109	8116	8122
65	8129	8136	8142	8149	8156	8162	8169	8176	8182	8189
66	8195	8202	8209	8215	8222	8228	8235	8241	8248	8254
67	8261	8267	8274	8280	8287	8293	8299	8306	8312	8319
68	8325	8331	8338	8344	8351	8357	8363	8370	8376	8382
69	8388	8395	8401	8407	8414	8420	8426	8432	8439	8445
70	8451	8457	8463	8470	8476	8482	8488	8494	8500	8506
71	8513	8519	8525	8531	8537	8543	8549	8555	8561	8567
72	8573	8579	8585	8591	8597	8603	8609	8615	8621	8627
73	8633	8639	8645	8651	8657	8663	8669	8675	8681	8686
74	8692	8698	8704	8710	8716	8722	8727	8733	8739	8745
75	8751	8756	8762	8768	8774	8779	8785	8791	8797	8802
76	8808	8814	8820	8825	8831	8837	8842	8848	8854	8859
77	8865	8871	8876	8882	8887	8893	8899	8904	8910	8915
78	8921	8927	8932	8938	8943	8949	8954	8960	8965	8971
79	8976	8982	8987	8993	8998	9004	9009	9015	9020	9025
80	9031	9036	9042	9047	9053	9058	9063	9069	9074	9079
81	9085	9090	9096	9101	9106	9112	9117	9122	9128	9133
82	9138	9143	9149	9154	9159	9165	9170	9175	9180	9186
83	9191	9196	9201	9206	9212	9217	9222	9227	9232	9238
84	9243	9248	9253	9258	9263	9269	9274	9279	9284	9289
85	9294	9299	9304	9309	9315	9320	9325	9330	9335	9340
86	9345	9350	9355	9360	9365	9370	9375	9380	9385	9390
87	9395	9400	9405	9410	9415	9420	9425	9430	9435	9440
88	9445	9450	9455	9460	9465	9469	9474	9479	9484	9489
89	9494	9499	9504	9509	9513	9518	9523	9528	9533	9538
90	9542	9547	9552	9557	9562	9566	9571	9576	9581	9586
91	9590	9595	9600	9605	9609	9614	9619	9624	9628	9633
92	9638	9643	9647	9652	9657	9661	9666	9671	9675	9680
93	9685	9689	9694	9699	9703	9708	9713	9717	9722	9727
94	9731	9736	9741	9745	9750	9754	9759	9763	9768	9773
95	9777	9782	9786	9791	9795	9800	9805	9809	9814	9818
96	9823	9827	9832	9836	9841	9845	9850	9854	9859	9863
97	9868	9872	9877	9881	9886	9890	9894	9899	9903	9908
98	9912	9917	9921	9926	9930	9934	9939	9943	9948	9952
99	9956	9961	9965	9969	9974	9978	9983	9987	9991	9996

Index

V

W

Y

Z

A 1
B 2
C 3
D 4
E 5
F 6
G 7
H 8
I 9
J 0